KODANSHA
ENCYCLOPEDIA OF
JAPAN

Distributors
JAPAN: KODANSHA LTD., Tokyo.
OVERSEAS: KODANSHA INTERNATIONAL LTD., Tokyo.
   U.S.A., Mexico, Central America, and South America: KODANSHA INTERNATIONAL/USA LTD.
      through HARPER & ROW, PUBLISHERS, INC., New York.
   Canada: FITZHENRY & WHITESIDE LTD., Ontario.
   U.K., Europe, the Middle East, and Africa: INTERNATIONAL BOOK DISTRIBUTORS LTD.,
      Hemel Hempstead, Herts., England.
   Australia and New Zealand: HARPER & ROW (AUSTRALASIA) PTY. LTD., Artarmon, N.S.W.
   Asia: TOPPAN COMPANY (S) PTE. LTD., Singapore.

Published by Kodansha Ltd., 12-21, Otowa 2-chome, Bunkyo-ku, Tokyo 112 and Kodansha
International/USA Ltd., 10 East 53rd Street, New York, New York 10022.
Copyright © 1983 by Kodansha Ltd.
All rights reserved.
Printed in Japan.
First edition, 1983.

LCC 83-80778
ISBN 0-87011-628-2 (Volume 8)
ISBN 0-87011-620-7 (Set)
ISBN 4-06-144538-3 (0) (in Japan)

Library of Congress Cataloging in Publication Data
Main entry under title:

Kodansha encyclopedia of Japan.

   Includes index.
   1. Japan—Dictionaries and encyclopedias. I. Title:
Encyclopedia of Japan.
DS805.K633 1983   952'.003'21   83-80778
ISBN 0-87011-620-7 (U.S.)

KODANSHA
ENCYCLOPEDIA OF
JAPAN

8

KODANSHA

T

temples

The word temple (*tera* or *jiin*) in this encyclopedia refers to a Buddhist establishment in which Buddhist images are enshrined, priests or nuns usually reside, and ceremonies and religious practices take place. Today there exist over 77,000 temples of various sects in Japan.

The first temple in Japan is said to be the Mukuharadera, founded in 552, when Soga no Iname, leader of a faction favoring the introduction of BUDDHISM to Japan, converted his residence at Mukuhara into a temple (see SOGA FAMILY). He enshrined a Buddhist image that had been presented to Emperor Kimmei (r 531 or 539 to 571) by King Song of the Korean kingdom of Paekche. An epidemic, attributed by the anti-Buddhist faction at court to the native gods' anger over the importation of Buddhism, struck the country, however, and the temple was burnt and the image cast into a canal. In 587 SOGA NO UMAKO, Iname's son, defeated the anti-Buddhist Mononobe family in battle. He then built the Hōkōji at Asuka in 596. Considered the first true temple built in Japan, the Hōkōji consisted of a main hall, enshrining a bronze image of Śākyamuni Buddha, two other main halls to the east and west, as well as three pagodas. During the 6th to 7th centuries Buddhism grew under state patronage. It was during this time that Prince SHŌTOKU is said to have built the so-called Seven Great Temples of Nara, including SHITENNŌJI, HŌRYŪJI, and DAIANJI. *Ujidera*, temples built by the chiefs of lineage groups (UJI) to pray for the groups' prosperity, were constructed in various parts of Japan. During the reign of Emperor Temmu (r 672–686), it is recorded that Buddhist chapels were set up in each provincial capital and staffed with monks called *kokushi* (national teachers).

In the year 742, Emperor SHŌMU (r 724–749), in imitation of Tang (T'ang) China, ordered the construction of a KOKUBUNJI (provincial temple) and *kokubunniji* (provincial nunnery) in each province. In the *kokubunji* prayers were offered for the protection of the state, and in the *kokubunniji*, to expiate sins. By 780 most of these temples had been completed. TŌDAIJI was built in the capital, Heijōkyō (now the city of Nara), as the head *kokubunji*, and the unveiling of its main image, a 16-meter high statue of the Buddha Vairocana, was held with great pageantry in 752. By the Nara period (710–794), there were some 360 temples in Japan, and as monastic precepts became formalized, a distinction between private and government temples was made. During this period, which was marked by the creation of a system of state-regulated Buddhism, the prosperity of temples was considered a direct reflection of the power of the state and much of its revenue and manpower was expended to construct Buddhist temples.

During the Heian period (794–1185), the TENDAI SECT and SHINGON SECT, which eventually replaced NARA BUDDHISM as the central force in Japanese Buddhism, were established. The Tendai temples ENRYAKUJI and MIIDERA and the Shingon temples KŌYASAN and Kyōō Gokokuji (also known as TŌJI) gained adherents from among the imperial family and the nobility. Temples in the outlying provinces began to commend their lands to powerful temples in the capital, Kyōto, in order to protect their holdings; these lands (SHŌEN) in time became the economic mainstay of the major temples. Enryakuji and KŌFUKUJI in particular came to possess vast landholdings and maintained a contingent of WARRIOR-MONKS. They also became centers of commerce and handicrafts. In the latter half of the Heian period, the idea of *mappō*—that the world was approaching a degenerate age marked by the destruction of Buddhist teachings—took hold (see ESCHATOLOGY). As a result, worship of the Pure Land, centered on the belief that one could be reborn in the Amida's Pure Land, became widespread (see PURE LAND BUDDHISM). The nobility constructed many Buddhist halls enshrining Amida, including the Hōōdō at the temple BYŌDŌIN.

In the late 12th century, the KAMAKURA SHOGUNATE extended its patronage to the Zen RINZAI SECT, then newly transmitted from China, to counter the established Tendai and Shingon sects. Zen temples were built with shogunate assistance in Kamakura, Kyōto, and other parts of the country. Later, in imitation of Song (Sung) China, KENCHŌJI, TENRYŪJI, and other prominent Zen temples were organized into the GOZAN system. The older sects, such as Tendai and Shingon, also continued to flourish during this period, establishing such institutions as *monzeki* (temples headed by members of the imperial family) and *inge* (subtemples of *monzeki* in which monks of noble origins monopolized the highest offices).

Soon after the establishment of the MUROMACHI SHOGUNATE in 1338, the shōgun ASHIKAGA TAKAUJI ordered the construction of Rinzai sect temples called Ankokuji (or Ankokuzenji) in each province. These temples flourished as the *bodaiji* (burial temples) of the SHUGO DAIMYŌ (military lords) of the respective provinces. The Muromachi period (1333–1568) saw the rapid spread among the common people of various Pure Land, Zen, and Nichiren sects. These sects organized a network of DANKA (parishioners) and established intimate connections with the faithful by performing funeral rites and memorial services. In particular, the JŌDO SHIN SECT, with its head temple, the HONGANJI, at its apex, developed into a large and conservative religious force by systematically organizing adherents who gathered at its branch temples and preaching centers (*dōjō*). In the late 1400s Honganji adherents came into armed conflict with local rulers and succeeded in occupying parts of the Hokuriku, Tōkai, and Kinki districts (see IKKŌ IKKI). Nichiren sectarians, who were entrenched in Kyōto, also came into conflict with the warrior-monks of Enryakuji in 1536 (see TEMMON HOKKE REBELLION).

In the latter half of the 16th century, many warriors vied with one another to unify the country. One of them, ODA NOBUNAGA, reduced to ashes Enryakuji, Kongōbuji, Negoroji, and Honganji in order to destroy their military power. The hegemon TOYOTOMI HIDEYOSHI, who succeeded him, placed the temples under his control by conducting a survey of their lands and reassessing the tax base.

In 1603 the TOKUGAWA SHOGUNATE (1603–1867) was inaugurated. While recognizing and supporting Buddhism as the state religion, it moved to establish complete control over the various Buddhist sects. It issued a series of regulations, institutionalized the relationship between head and local temples, ordered strict observation of the priestly and temple hierarchy, and outlawed the building of private temples. With the adoption of the NATIONAL SECLUSION policy in 1639 and the strict proscription of Christianity, it decreed that all Japanese register with a local temple (see TERAUKE; SHŪMON ARATAME). The temple-*danka* relationship was thus formalized, and the temples became, in effect, the shogunate's agents for the administration of the census. Together with guarantees of their ownership of land and the establishment of a strict hierarchical relationship between the head and local temples, the temples found their position firmly established. But as a result of these privileges, institutional Buddhism as a whole became worldly and degraded, far removed from the religious aspirations of the common people. In the latter part of the Edo period (1600–1868), as the shogunate and *daimyō* domains (*han*) found themselves in fiscal difficulties, the financial support accorded to the temples came under criticism, and, coupled with the common people's resentment of the temples as agents of feudal control, the move to suppress Buddhism gained widespread support. Various domains carried out policies aimed at the amalgamation of Buddhist temples or their suppression.

After the Meiji Restoration in 1868, the new government, intent on establishing Shintō as the national religion, ordered the separation of Buddhism from Shintō. All Buddhist images and implements were removed from Shintō shrines, and shrines for the local gods (*jinushi no kami*) and for guardian gods (*garanjin*) in Buddhist temple grounds were dismantled (see SHINTŌ AND BUDDHISM, SEPARA-

TION OF). Concurrent with the enforcement of the separation of Buddhism from Shintō, an often violent anti-Buddhist movement erupted in parts of Japan; temples were demolished or closed and Buddhist statues and implements were destroyed (see HAIBUTSU KISHAKU). The temple registration system was abolished. In 1871 many temple lands were confiscated by the government, resulting in a grave economic crisis for the temples (the damage to the Shin and Nichiren sects, which did not rely on their landholdings for economic support, was less drastic). Buddhism, now subordinated to STATE SHINTŌ, was placed under stringent state control, and the building of new temples was strictly regulated. The temple-*danka* relation, as well as the hierarchical structure linking local and head temples continued. Religious activities stagnated and declined, however, and funeral services and memorial rites became the sole link between the temple and the people.

Under the 1947 constitution, FREEDOM OF RELIGIOUS FAITH was guaranteed. Although the temples suffered from war damage and the postwar land reform, they gradually recovered beginning in the mid-1950s. Some temples tried to attract followers by preaching worldly benefits; others supplemented their income by opening their grounds to the public. The vast majority of small temples, however, are experiencing financial difficulties, and priests sometimes hold concurrent jobs outside the temple. Despite these difficulties, Buddhist temples, pressed by the increasing influence of the NEW RELIGIONS, are trying to come to grips with the need to modernize.

Murakami Shigeyoshi

temple town → monzen machi

Tempō Famine

(Tempō no Kikin). Nationwide famine between 1833 and 1836 (Tempō 4–7). Because of cold weather, flooding, and high winds, the harvest in 1833 was only 30 to 70 percent of the normal yield, and rice prices rose steeply. There followed poor harvests in 1834 and 1835 and a disastrously low yield of about one-third the normal amount in 1836. The resulting scarcity sent prices even higher, and destitute peasants flocked to the cities. Many died of starvation and disease, particularly in northeastern Japan, and there were even reports of cannibalism. The shogunate tried to meet the crisis by distributing rice, setting up shelters, regulating prices, prohibiting hoarding, and restricting *sake* production. Various domains also instituted assistance measures, but they were largely ineffective. It was to seek relief that ŌSHIO HEIHACHIRŌ rose in rebellion in Ōsaka, and peasant uprisings broke out in many other areas as well. See also KYŌHŌ FAMINE; TEMMEI FAMINE; TEMPŌ REFORMS.

Tempō Reforms

(Tempō no Kaikaku). Reforms undertaken during the Tempō era (1830–44). Narrowly defined, the term refers to those reforms initiated by the shogunate leader MIZUNO TADAKUNI during the years 1841–43 (Tempō 12–14); more broadly it embraces the several contemporary reforms undertaken by *daimyō* as well as the Tokugawa shogunate.

The Tempō reform program has been seen by historians in several ways: for example, as the last of the three great conservative reforms of the Edo period (1600–1868; the other two being the KYŌHŌ REFORMS and the KANSEI REFORMS), or, for example, as marking the emergence of new "absolutist" forces that eventually led to the MEIJI RESTORATION of 1868.

Shogunate Reforms——During the 1830s Japan experienced widespread crop failures and consequent hardship and unrest (see TEMPŌ FAMINE). During those years foreign ships appeared offshore in unprecedented numbers, and the MORRISON INCIDENT of 1837 together with knowledge of the accelerating imperialist activity of Western powers in China suggested the imminence of a major foreign crisis.

Mizuno Tadakuni, chief among senior councillors (RŌJŪ), as well as others both within and without the shogunate were alarmed by the situation, and the death of the powerful retired shōgun TOKUGAWA IENARI in early 1841 enabled them to initiate a vigorous policy of reform. In the summer of 1841 Tadakuni had the new shōgun, Tokugawa Ieyoshi (1793–1853), announce his intention to restore the spirit of the Kyōhō and Kansei reform eras. There were several facets to the ensuing reform, but the basic objectives were to increase food production, improve the morals and morale of both *samurai* and the general public, strengthen the government fisc, and enhance governmental military capability.

To increase food production, Tadakuni initially forbade peasants to divert their energies from agriculture and later ordered those living in Edo (now Tōkyō) to return to their home villages (see HITOGAESHI). He also ordered the stockpiling of rice and undertook a major land reclamation project in the Imbanuma swamps northeast of Edo.

To improve the morals and morale of samurai and the general public, Tadakuni ousted a number of men from office, punished others on charges of corruption, and ordered daimyō and lesser samurai to practice greater frugality and self-discipline. He reissued a number of sumptuary regulations and outlawed gambling, unregulated prostitution, and related professions. He attempted to lessen urban hardship by ordering merchants to reduce the prices of specified commodities and by prohibiting the production of such items as luxury ceramics.

Tadakuni regarded the growth of commercial activity as harmful to government, samurai, and the general public, and he wished to halt it. To that end he abolished long-standing merchant monopoly associations (KABUNAKAMA) and ordered daimyō to discontinue or restrict to their own domains various commercial and monetary arrangements carried on for domainal benefit.

To meet shogunate fiscal needs, Tadakuni ordered economies of operation, instructed merchants to make monetary contributions to the shogunate, and tried to increase the effectiveness of tax collection. As longer-range projects he developed plans to improve the currency by reminting depreciated coins, many of which had been issued during the 1830s, and initiated a program designed to bring under direct shogunate control all the easily accessible arable lands directly surrounding the great cities of Edo and Ōsaka (see AGECHIREI).

To strengthen military capabilities, he ordered samurai to practice military arts and instructed EGAWA TARŌZAEMON to cast firearms. He authorized TAKASHIMA SHŪHAN, who had been testing Western-style firearms and cannon for some time, to train soldiers in their use. And he opened a new artillery training area and ordered daimyō to modernize and strengthen their domainal artillery.

To avoid a foreign crisis, Tadakuni had the shogunate modify its policy of forbidding foreign ships to approach the coastline (see GAIKOKUSEN UCHIHARAI REI) by reviving an earlier regulation of 1806 that permitted such ships to obtain necessary stocks of food and drinking water. Then, to pacify domestic critics who protested that concession, he took steps to strengthen coastal defenses, control unauthorized foreign trade, and strengthen shogunate control of the port towns of Uraga and Niigata.

Whether one views Tadakuni's reform as one of the three conservative reforms or as a historic watershed, it is clear that he failed to achieve his goals. Some of his policies worked at cross-purposes, and every one of them angered somebody. By early 1843 he was facing stiff criticism, and the order that transferred fiefholders away from Edo and Ōsaka proved to be the last straw. The reaction was abrupt, and a month later the order was retracted and Tadakuni resigned from office.

Domainal Reforms——The Tempō Reforms were not limited to the shogunate, because the issues they addressed, most notably the problem of governmental debt, were shared by most domains. These problems had worsened during the early 19th century because many domains had adhered to policy lines shaped by the shogunate. They did so largely because the early decades of the century (the BUNKA AND BUNSEI ERAS) were relatively benign ones, during which the shōgun Ienari's marriage, adoption, and consort arrangements had woven such an extensive web of kinship bonds and obligations among powerful figures in domains throughout the land that critics of the status quo were unable to secure power and undertake reforms. Only during the 1830s, as widespread difficulties engulfed the country, did it become possible for domain reformers to thrust aside the old guard and initiate new policies.

The purposes and character of these reforms anticipated and paralleled those of the shogunate. This was not only because the shogunate and the domains faced similar problems but also because their institutional systems and political values were similar. One notable variation was in the handling of commercial monopoly opportunities. In some domains reformers tried to strengthen control of certain profitable businesses as a way to increase domainal revenue (see HAN'EI SEMBAI). In others reformers attacked monopolies as the shogunate did. The latter policy seems nowhere to have worked, whereas the former failed in some domains and benefited the exchequers of others.

One of the first domains to initiate a Tempō reform was the Tokugawa domain at Mito (now part of Ibaraki Prefecture). There the faction supported by Ienari's allies was defeated in a bitter internal contest, and the reform-oriented TOKUGAWA NARIAKI became daimyō in 1829. Nariaki undertook a program of reform designed to revitalize samurai morale, strengthen Mito's military capability, and ease its fiscal difficulties.

In the Saga domain in Kyūshū (now Saga Prefecture) a new daimyō, NABESHIMA KANSŌ, took office in 1830 and initiated a vigorous program designed to strengthen Saga's finances, reinvigorate its retainers, and assure rice production. Like Nariaki, Kansō made particular efforts to strengthen his military forces because of the evidence of an increasing foreign presence in East Asia. On the other hand, whereas Mito had moved to strengthen domainal control of certain business activities, Saga reformers tried to eliminate commercial monopolies.

A year later leaders of the Satsuma domain (now Kagoshima Prefecture) initiated reforms designed to revitalize that domain's finances. Like Mito, Satsuma tried to turn commerce to government advantage. Reformers there took firm control of a lucrative sugar trade with the Ryūkyū Islands that proved to be one of the most successful ventures of the whole Tempō reform era.

As the decade passed and natural disasters created widespread unrest, other domains too undertook reform. The future shogunate reformer, Mizuno Tadakuni, initiated reforms in his domain at Hamamatsu, and after special difficulties in 1836 he launched a vigorous policy of retrenchment, public relief, autarky, and anticommercialism.

Far to the west, Chōshū (now Yamaguchi Prefecture) had also experienced severe unrest in the early 1830s, and a change of daimyō in 1836 permitted new leaders to emerge. When the new daimyō, Mōri Takachika (1819–71), returned to his domain in 1838, he appointed MURATA SEIFŪ to head a reform program. Like those of Tadakuni and other domainal leaders, the reforms in Chōshū were designed to solve fiscal problems, restore samurai vigor, ease popular hardship, and increase rice production. And like Mizuno and the leaders in Saga, reformers in Chōshū sought to abolish monopolies, not turn them to government advantage.

With the death of Ienari and the shogunate's launching of a reform, leaders in many other domains were also encouraged: in Tosa a daimyō change in 1843 permitted the initiation of reform, but it soon aborted. Elsewhere, too, reforms were started and then foundered; the collapse of the shogunate's efforts and the subsequent harsh punishment of Tadakuni doubtless undermined the positions of many reformers in the domains.

Despite considerable effort, nowhere did the Tempō Reforms achieve all that the leaders intended. Many achieved next to nothing; others had a modest and temporary ameliorative effect. In some places portions of reform were successful, notably Satsuma's strengthening of its sugar monopoly. But of the three great reforms the Tempō Reform was the least successful.

■ ——— W. G. Beasley, *The Meiji Restoration* (1972). Albert M. Craig, *Chōshū in the Meiji Restoration* (1961). Kitajima Masamoto, *Mizuno Tadakuni* (1969). Tsuda Hideo, *Tempō kaikaku* (1975).

Conrad TOTMAN

tempura

A well-known Japanese food in which fresh fish, shellfish, or vegetables are dipped into a batter *(koromo)* of flour mixed with egg and water and then deep-fried. The essence of *tempura* is the harmonious blend of the golden crisp crust and the lightly cooked fish or vegetable; the key to this is the correct temperature of the oil and the light mixing of the batter. *Tempura* is at its best eaten right after frying, dipped into a side dish of special *tempura* sauce with grated radish. The sauce is a mixture of one part light soy sauce, one part *mirin* (a sweet *sake*), and four to six parts *dashi* (soup stock) that has been simmered and cooled.

A wide variety of foods can be used as ingredients for *tempura*. In a *tempura* restaurant, low-fat fish such as smelt *(kisu)*, sweetfish *(ayu)*, a kind of whitebait *(shirauo)*, conger eel *(anago)*, cuttlefish *(ika)*, and shellfish such as shrimp and scallop are used. Vegetables include lotus root, mushrooms, ginkgo nuts, beefsteak plant *(shiso)*, and green peppers.

Many theories exist about the derivation of the word *tempura*, but it is generally thought to be a corruption of the Portuguese word *tempero*, "cooking," or the Spanish word *templo*, "temple." The latter derivation may be explained by the abstinence from meat observed by Christians on Fridays—hence the association with "temple." In the mid-16th century many items from Portuguese and Spanish civilization were brought to Japan, including methods of frying game. In an earlier period, cooking with oil had entered Japan from China as part of a vegetarian diet, and *tempura* was the final result of the merger of these two elements and of the further adaptation to the tastes and customs of the Japanese. At the beginning of the 19th century in particular, open-air *tempura* stalls serving small fish that had been caught nearby became popular in Edo (now Tōkyō). Eventually these stalls developed into *tempura* restaurants. Today *tempura* is an indispensable part of the diet of every Japanese whether in restaurants, where it is often cooked in front of the customer, at dinner parties and banquets, or at home. *Tsuji Shizuo*

Tempyō culture

The culture of the Tempyō era (729–749), a subperiod of the Nara period (710–794); it roughly coincides with the reign (724–749) of the emperor SHŌMU. In this period the Chinese-inspired *ritsuryō* system of government was further developed, and through missions to China (see SUI AND TANG [T'ANG] CHINA, EMBASSIES TO) Japan received direct influence from the cosmopolitan culture of T'ang China.

Under the patronage of the devout Shōmu, Buddhism was adopted as the national religion and provincial temples (KOKUBUNJI) were built throughout Japan, with TŌDAIJI in Nara as the head temple. Many outstanding temple buildings (the Octagonal Hall or Yumedono at HŌRYŪJI; the main hall at SHIN YAKUSHIJI), Buddhist statues (the Jū Dai Deshi or Ten Great Disciples of the Buddha at KŌFUKUJI), Buddhist paintings (the Kichijōten, or goddess of good fortune at YAKUSHIJI), and other Buddhist works were produced. In addition to wood and gilt bronze, new materials, clay and dry lacquer *(kanshitsu)*, were used in sculpture, making possible a wide range of expressive techniques. Several thousand articles from this period have been preserved at the SHŌSŌIN repository at Tōdaiji. See also HISTORY OF JAPAN: Nara history; BUDDHIST SCULPTURE; PAINTING; BUDDHIST ART.

ten → heaven

tenant farmer disputes

(kosaku sōgi). Between 1917 and 1941 there occurred 72,696 tenant disputes with landlords, usually at the subadministrative village or hamlet *(buraku)* level. These disputes, unlike the peasant uprisings (HYAKUSHŌ IKKI) of the Edo (1600–1868) and early part of the Meiji (1868–1912) periods, were aimed not at external authority but at landlords with local holdings and reflected greater class consciousness among the rural poor. The most common tenant demands were rent reductions to compensate for harvest losses caused by natural disasters (especially in the 1920s) and continued tenancy when landlords attempted to change tenants or cultivate the land themselves (especially in the 1930s). The usual tenant tactics were the formation of hamlet tenant unions, refusal to pay all or part of the rent, collective cultivation of tenanted fields to provide economic support and solidarity for their union, nonviolent harassment of landlords, and negotiations. Landlords reacted by forming their own organizations. They exerted economic pressure, made use of kinship, pseudokinship, and patron-client ties, turned to negotiations, and, when all else failed, demanded court hearings to deprive tenants of their tenancy. Over 90 percent of the disputes ended in compromise, frequently mediated through the government's tenancy conciliation system established in 1924. The rest were mostly resolved in the tenant's favor.

These disputes are interpreted variously, but primarily according to the views of two schools of Japanese economic historians. One, the KŌZAHA, emphasizes the deleterious impact of long-standing feudal landownership patterns on modern landlord-tenant relations, while the other, the RŌNŌHA, stresses the invidious effects of the replacement of these feudal remnants by a capitalistic market economy. Both schools agree that the spread of rural poverty, as reflected in the growth of tenanted land from 27 to 45 percent of the arable total between 1868 and 1908, was the major cause of tenant farmer unrest.

Other causes have been suggested as well, especially the impact of modernization on both landlords and tenant farmers. Modern landlords became more capitalistic, sought nonagricultural areas for investment, began to abandon their traditional paternalistic practices, and even to withdraw themselves and their benefactions from the hamlets, to the regret of their tenants. Tenant farmers became increasingly entrepreneurial between 1900 and 1930 because stable and then falling rents, the use of new tools, seeds, and fertilizers, and greater crop diversification encouraged by the spread of a market economy increased the tenants' income and heightened their expectations. These economic changes, together with increased peasant literacy and awareness of urban labor and socialist activities in Japan and abroad, induced tenant farmers to seek additional profits by challenging their landlords.   *Richard* SMETHURST

Tenchi, Emperor → Tenji, Emperor

Tenchūgumi Rebellion

An uprising in 1863 by antishogunate, proimperial loyalists who called themselves the Tenchūgumi (Heavenly Retribution Band) in Yamato Province (now Nara Prefecture), a territory under direct shogunate control. Like the IKUNO DISTURBANCE, it is considered important today because some of its participants were peasants.

The SONNŌ JŌI (Revere the Emperor, Expel the Barbarians) movement reached a peak in 1863 when imperial loyalists from Chōshū (now Yamaguchi Prefecture) dominated Kyōto. Planning to have the emperor personally lead an army against the foreigners, activists from several domains first organized an imperial visit to Yamato shrines to pray for success. The visit was announced on 25 September. The next day the Tenchūgumi, consisting of some 75 activists, set out for Yamato to raise an imperial army, destroy shogunate authority in the region, and welcome the emperor when he arrived. Yoshimura Toratarō (1837–63), a village headman (*shōya*) from the Tosa domain (now Kōchi Prefecture) acted as the principal commander, while a young court noble, NAKAYAMA TADAMITSU, was the nominal leader. A number of masterless *samurai* (RŌNIN or rōshi) as well as local samurai (GŌSHI) also joined. On 29 September the group attacked the office of the shogunal intendant (DAIKAN) at Gojō, killing him and his deputies. Local peasants joined the cause, attracted by promises of tax relief. However, in the COUP D'ETAT OF 30 SEPTEMBER 1863 the extremist forces were expelled from Kyōto by those of more moderate domains, and the shogunate dispatched troops to quell the Tenchūgumi rebellion. Yoshimura was wounded in the fighting and committed suicide, but Nakayama and a few others escaped to Chōshū.

Tendai sect

Buddhist sect, the Japanese counterpart of the Chinese Tiantai (T'ien-t'ai) sect, founded in Japan in 806 by SAICHŌ (767–822). Together with SHINGON, it was the dominant sect of the Heian period (794–1185). Although the popular Buddhist movements of the Kamakura period (1185–1333) such as the JŌDO SECT (Pure Land sect) and NICHIREN SECT evolved from it, Tendai itself was closely identified with the court nobility through its history. In 1571 its temple headquarters of ENRYAKUJI on Mt. Hiei (HIEIZAN) was almost completely destroyed by the warlord ODA NOBUNAGA, and the sect never fully recovered from this crushing blow.
Chinese Tiantai —— The Tiantai sect in China was founded by Zhiyi (Chih-i; 538–597) and along with the Huayan (Hua-yen; J: Kegon) sect was considered to be one of the two great philosophical sects of Chinese Buddhism. Doctrinally, Tiantai synthesizes the diverse teachings of the Buddha as found in the Hīnayāna and Mahāyāna scriptures, utilizing the message of the LOTUS SUTRA as its unifying framework. Classifying the sutras according to the time and manner in which the Buddha purportedly preached them and according to their content, Tiantai sees the Buddha's supreme teaching manifested in pure form in the Lotus Sutra, which taught the oneness of Buddhism and expounded a strongly affirmative attitude toward the phenomenal world.

Tiantai philosophy was based on the fundamental Mahāyāna teaching of emptiness—that all things, being impermanent, are devoid of self-entity. The main points of Tiantai's interpretation of this teaching are as follows: (1) To say that all things have no self-entity is to say that nothing exists of itself. (2) This is not to say that nothing at all exists, but rather that the state of ultimate reality is beyond all conceptualization in such terms as existence or nonexist-

ence. (3) Whatever that state of ultimate reality may be, it never occurs in the abstract but is identical with this impermanent phenomenal world. (4) Hence "everything is real," "each thing is identical with all things," and "one's ignorant, unenlightened state is identical with the state of Buddhahood."

Tiantai equally emphasized the need to practice meditation to aid in the realization of these teachings, and to this end established a set of meditational practices. These practices almost all involved meditation on a specific Buddha or bodhisattva, such as Amitābha (J: Amida) or Avalokiteśvara (J: Kannon). Tiantai practices were highly eclectic, synthesizing various types of meditational practices expounded in many sutras.

Saichō. Although copies of Tiantai writings were available in Japan by the mid-8th century, they had no far-reaching influence until Saichō discovered them in the 790s. As a young man, Saichō had become dissatisfied with the increasing worldliness of the Buddhism of his day (called NARA BUDDHISM, since it was centered at the great temples of Nara) and in 785 had secluded himself in a thatched hut on Mt. Hiei to live in meditation and prayer. Gradually he began to attract disciples and lay patrons including the reigning emperor KAMMU, and to create a small monastic community.

After discovering Tiantai and seeing in it an alternative to Nara Buddhism, Saichō went to China in 804 to receive accreditation from a Chinese Tiantai master. During his nine-month stay, he fulfilled this goal at the headquarters of the Chinese sect, Mt. Tiantai. At the very end of his stay, he also learned some rituals from a master of ESOTERIC BUDDHISM.
Founding of Japanese Tendai —— Upon returning to Japan, Saichō received from Emperor Kammu official recognition of the Tendai sect on Mt. Hiei. Kammu, however, stipulated that esoteric Buddhism be part of the Tendai sect. From its very founding Tendai was unique in two ways. (1) Unlike the schools of Nara Buddhism, several of which could be found coexisting in the Nara temples, Tendai transmitted only its own teachings on Mt. Hiei. (2) Esoteric rituals were incorporated into the Tendai sect from its inception, and for this reason Japanese Tendai diverged from its Chinese counterpart, which transmitted only the Tiantai doctrines.

Kūkai's esoteric Buddhism. The first challenge to the Tendai sect came from KŪKAI (774–835), the founder in Japan of the Shingon sect, who had acquired a mastery of esoteric Buddhism in China. Saichō's Tendai sect had the official mandate from the court for performing esoteric Buddhism, but Kūkai's knowledge of esoteric Buddhism was far superior to that of Saichō. At first, between 809 and 816, Saichō regarded Kūkai as a teacher and colleague. But their friendship ended when Kūkai made it increasingly clear that he considered esoteric Buddhism to be superior to all other forms of Buddhism, and, finally, refused to return one of Saichō's disciples who had defected to him.

The bodhisattva precepts. An even graver challenge came from Nara. Under the existing system, all novice monks in central Japan were required to be tested and to receive final ordination at Nara. Many novices from Mt. Hiei who went to Nara chose to remain there. In 818 Saichō asked the court for permission under which the Tendai sect would utilize the Mahāyāna bodhisattva precepts as the basis for final ordination in place of the traditional Hīnayāna precepts. (The bodhisattva precepts were simpler and did not distinguish between monks and laymen. Although they were widely accepted in China, they had never been used as the basis for ordination as had the traditional Hīnayāna precepts.) Saichō was in effect petitioning for a separate ordination system for Tendai, which was tantamount to a request for Tendai institutional independence. He also proposed that Tendai monks serve the nation as teachers of Buddhism after having first stayed on Mt. Hiei for 12 years of study.

Opposition from the Nara monks to Saichō's proposal was so strong that the court withheld its reply. Finally seven days after Saichō's death in the sixth month of 822, the court gave its approval. The following year, the court gave official recognition to the Tendai center on Mt. Hiei by naming it ENRYAKUJI after the name of the year period in which it was founded.
Saichō's Successors —— After Saichō's death, Kūkai grew in prominence and was much honored as a master of esoteric Buddhism. His center was on Mt. Kōya (KŌYASAN) in what is now Wakayama Prefecture. Not only did Kūkai have a better mastery of esoteric Buddhism than any Tendai monk, but he declared esoteric Buddhism to be superior to all other sects, including Tendai. Saichō's successors were unable to refute Kūkai, nor could they compete with him in the performance of esoteric rituals. At last, in 835, just before his death, the court officially recognized Kūkai's sect of

Tengu

Contemporary bronze image of a *tengu* wearing the cap of a mountain ascetic *(yamabushi)*. Yakuōin, Hachiōji, Tōkyō Prefecture.

esoteric Buddhism. This Shingon sect became Tendai's great rival.

Ennin and Enchin. Tendai's fortunes were revived by ENNIN (794–864), who went to China in 839 and stayed for nine years, thoroughly studying, among other things, esoteric Buddhism. Upon his return to Japan, Ennin revived the Tendai sect's position at court through his mastery of esoteric Buddhist rituals and received honor after honor from the emperor. It is to Ennin that credit for firmly establishing esoteric Buddhism in Tendai must be given.

ENCHIN (814–891) repeated Ennin's accomplishment. He left for China in 853, also to study esoteric Buddhism, and returned in 858. Like Ennin, he was much honored by the court. In the 10th century, a bitter rivalry developed between monks of Ennin's line and those of Enchin's line, until finally in 993, the latter moved out of Enryakuji as a body and established themselves at Onjōji (see MIIDERA) at the foot of Mt. Hiei. Subsequently there were occasional armed clashes between the monks of Enryakuji and Onjōji.

Annen. Annen (b 841) in a sense completed the work of Ennin and Enchin. Whereas his predecessors had tried to synthesize the philosophies of Tendai and esoteric Buddhism, Annen took this to an extreme by interpreting Tendai completely from the viewpoint of esoteric Buddhism, declaring it to be superior to Tendai and even claiming the name Shingon for his sect.

Hongaku. From the 9th century on, Tendai monks showed little interest in esoteric philosophy. Nevertheless, esoteric philosophy did have a significant impact on Tendai. The 11th and 12th centuries saw the proliferation of secret Tendai writings from master to disciple, expounding an extreme form of Tendai philosophy. Called HONGAKU, it affirmed the reality of the world as-it-is and sentient beings as-they-are as identical to enlightened beings *(hotoke)* and went so far as to deny any moral distinctions. This Hongaku philosophy was the result of esoteric influence on traditional Tendai philosophy. Hongaku philosophy greatly influenced the sects that later grew out of Tendai.

Pure Land Buddhism. The most significant development in Tendai after the 9th century was the growth of Pure Land Buddhist teachings. KŪYA (903–972), RYŌGEN (912–985), GENSHIN (942–1017), and RYŌNIN (1073–1132) all contributed to the Tendai Pure Land movement, which culminated in the Kamakura period with the establishment of independent Pure Land sects, such as the Jōdo sect of HŌNEN (1133–1212) and the JŌDO SHIN SECT of SHINRAN (1173–1263).

At its zenith, during the 10th and 11th centuries, Tendai received the generous patronage of emperors and of powerful families such as the FUJIWARA FAMILY. The Lotus Sutra was very popular among the Heian aristocracy, as were esoteric rituals. Aristocratic families built many private Tendai temples whose abbacies were restricted to family members. Like Shingon, Tendai eventually created a system whereby Shintō gods (KAMI) were incorporated as objects of worship. However, unlike Shingon, it made little effort to attract the masses. Rather, all its potentially popular elements broke away during the Kamakura period. The Pure Land Buddhism of Hōnen and Shinran, the Lotus Sutra faith of Nichiren (1222–82), and even Zen all had their roots in Tendai, but eventually asserted their independence. Thus, as the fortunes of the court aristocracy declined, so did those of Tendai.

Destruction of Enryakuji. Moreover, from the 11th century onward, as Enryakuji grew into a wealthy and powerful center, there appeared a class of monks known as WARRIOR-MONKS, who did not hesitate to use violence to defend the temple's interests. They frequently put pressure on the court and often took sides in military and political disputes. Finally, in 1571, Oda Nobunaga ended their military and political influence by destroying almost all of the vast temple complex of Enryakuji. This act signaled the end of Tendai's influence. During the Edo period (1600–1868), Tendai recovered somewhat, reviving its tradition of orthodox philosophical studies, but it never regained its former prominence.

As of 1980, there were 4,245 Tendai temples, 17,115 clergymen and religious personnel, and 5,297,055 lay members.

📖——Fukuda Gyōei, *Tendaigaku gairon* (1954). Sasaki Kentoku, *Tendai kyōgaku* (1951). Ui Hakuju, "A Study of Japanese Tendai Buddhism," *Philosophical Studies of Japan* 1 (1959).

Zenryū SHIRAKAWA

Tendō

City in central Yamagata Prefecture, northern Honshū. It developed as a castle town of the Tendō family during the 14th century and later as a market town. In 1831 it became the castle town of the Oda family. Tendō makes about 95 percent of all *shōgi* (Japanese chess) pieces in the country. Agricultural tools and furniture are also produced. Farm products include cherries, apples, and grapes. The Tendō Highland is suited for camping and skiing. The Tendō Hot Spring is located here. Pop: 52,599.

tengu

An uncanny and ambivalent creature with long beak and wings, glittering eyes, and a man's body, arms, and legs. A variant form, sometimes credited with higher rank, has a long nose, white hair, and red face and carries a feather fan.

Various interpretations have been given to this enigmatic figure. He is principally seen as a *keshin* (AVATAR) or transformation of a YAMA NO KAMI, the guardian of certain mountains with a particular affinity for huge trees. Numerous references to him in medieval literature reveal him as a subtle enemy of Buddhism, kidnapping Buddhist priests and tying them to the tops of trees, implanting thoughts of greed and pride in their minds, or feasting them on dung magically disguised as delicious food. He is also feared as an abductor of children, and for his powers of illusion and demoniacal possession. The particular arrogance of the fallen priest, he who has achieved extra power through religious disciplines, but has used it merely to inflate his own egotism, is also attributed to the *tengu*. The *tengudō* is a particular transmigratory realm reserved for such persons.

Conversely the *tengu* is often represented in legend and in the traditional performing arts as a benign protector and transmitter of supernatural skills. He is closely associated with the YAMABUSHI, being often depicted as wearing items of the *yamabushi*'s distinctive costume.

Various inexplicable phenomena in mountains are often credited to the *tengu*. Loud and terrifying laughter in a quiet forest, for example, is known as *tenguwarai*. See also BAKEMONO.

📖——Carmen Blacker, *The Catalpa Bow* (1975). Hirata Atsutane, *Kokon yōmi kō* (1828). *Konjaku monogatari* (book 20), ed Yamada Tadao, in *Nihon koten bungaku taikei*, vol 4 (Iwanami Shoten, 1958). M. W. de Visser, "The Tengu," *Transactions of the Asiatic Society of Japan* 36.2 (1908). Carmen BLACKER

Tengutō no Ran → Mito Civil War

Tenji, Emperor (626–672)

(also called Tenchi). The 38th sovereign *(tennō)* in the traditional count (which includes several nonhistorical emperors); he reigned from 661 to 672, although his formal enthronement did not take place until 668. He was the son of the 34th sovereign, Emperor Jomei (593–641; r 629–641), and was known as Prince Naka no Ōe. Because he was only 15 at his father's death, his mother, Jomei's consort (kōgō), ascended the throne as Empress Kōgyoku (see SAIMEI, EMPRESS). The SOGA FAMILY was then at the peak of its power, virtually eclipsing the imperial house. Naka no Ōe learned of Chinese political institutions from his teacher, MINABUCHI NO SHŌAN, and he plotted with his fellow student FUJIWARA NO KAMATARI (then called Nakatomi no Kamatari) to overthrow the Soga. They carried out a coup in 645 and reorganized the government on the Chinese model (see TAIKA REFORM).

As regent for his uncle Emperor KŌTOKU, who had succeeded Kōgyoku at the time of the coup, Naka no Ōe's power exceeded that of the emperor himself. While directing the various reform measures, he removed himself from the capital at Naniwa (now Ōsaka; see NANIWAKYŌ) to Asuka. After Kōtoku's death and the reaccession of his mother as Empress Saimei—an unprecedented event for which he was responsible—Naka no Ōe devoted himself to foreign relations and military affairs.

Saimei died in 661, but for seven years Naka no Ōe, unwilling to relinquish the regency—the real locus of power—to his brother Prince Ōama (later Emperor TEMMU), refused to be enthroned, although he continued to rule and to reshape the government. In 663 he raised an army to aid the Korean kingdom of PAEKCHE, but the Japanese were defeated by the combined forces of SILLA and Tang (T'ang; 618–907) China in the Battle of HAKUSUKINOE. In 667 he moved the capital to ŌTSU NO MIYA (near Lake Biwa in present Shiga Prefecture) and in the following year formally ascended the throne as Emperor Tenji. As emperor, he established a standardized system of household registration (KŌGONEN-JAKU), drew up the ŌMI CODE of laws, and implemented other policies that further consolidated the power of the centralized state. KITAMURA Bunji

tenjōbito

General term for court officials of the Heian period (794–1185) who enjoyed the privilege of imperial audience (shōden) in the Seiryōden, the emperor's living quarters. They included all officials of the third rank or higher as well as those of the fourth and fifth ranks who were specially favored. The chamberlains (or archivists, kurōdo; see KURŌDO-DOKORO), though they held only the sixth rank, were also permitted audience. Tenjōbito were also known as kumonoue-bito, or those above the clouds, although this term could refer to any member of the court nobility. By contrast, those who were not allowed audience were termed jigenin, those at ground level. The number of tenjōbito was originally set at 30 but later increased to about 100. This system of restricting the right of audience was practiced also by retired emperors, retired imperial consorts, and crown princes. G. Cameron HURST III

tenjōgawa

(river with a raised bed). A river whose bed has become higher than the adjacent land. Because of the large difference in altitude between the upper and lower reaches of Japanese rivers and streams, most rivers in Japan have swiftly flowing currents and carry large quantities of silt and sand. As a result, tenjōgawa can occur naturally where embankments have been built to prevent river flooding, since silt and sand deposits carried along by streams build up along these embankments and thus cause riverbeds to become higher. The danger of flooding thereby increases, and the embankments are made still higher. The Jōganjigawa, a river in Toyama Prefecture, and the Kusatsugawa, a river in Shiga Prefecture, are two examples of tenjōgawa.

tenkan nōryoku

(capacity for change). The capacity of Japanese enterprises to innovate and adapt to technological change is considered a key factor in the rapid growth of the nation's postwar economy. This flexibility originates from a number of features of the Japanese economy, among them the high level of education of the work force, well-motivated employees, and the system of career-long employment practiced by major corporations. Career-long employment allows corporate management to make substantial investments in employee training, through both in-house programs and specialized education

overseas. In addition, employees work their way up the corporate structure before assuming management-level positions. This provides them with a well-rounded knowledge of the firm's business and enhances their ability to learn and adopt new technology. Employees displaced by new processes can easily be absorbed into other sections of the company, since they are familiar with all facets of the enterprise. See also EMPLOYMENT SYSTEM, MODERN.

This capacity for change is also evident in the Japanese economy as a whole. The transition to a modern, industrialized economy took place gradually, a situation which minimized the social friction often associated with rapid change. The government smoothed the path for change through efforts to maintain price levels for agricultural products, subsidies to the textile industry, and import controls to protect corporations that were poor competitors internationally. As a result, Japan has avoided many of the side effects of sudden industrial change, such as high unemployment and social instability. See also TECHNOLOGY TRANSFER. TOMISAWA Konomi

tenkō

(literally, "change of direction"). A term used figuratively to refer to an individual's formal rejection of an ideological commitment, usually under some pressure. Originally used of persons who recanted their affiliations with the JAPAN COMMUNIST PARTY (JCP) and belief in communist ideology and subsequently used of other ideological shifts. Tenkō is sometimes translated as "ideological conversion," but its emphasis is on the rejection of a previously held ideological belief rather than the acceptance of a new one. Some degree of coercion is usually implied, and the process of tenkō may be understood as a type of thought reform.

The term was coined in 1933 by SANO MANABU and Nabeyama Sadachika (1901–79), two high officials of the JCP. They were arrested in 1929 for violating the PEACE PRESERVATION LAW OF 1925, tried with over 250 others in 1931–32, found guilty, and sentenced to life imprisonment. As Peace Preservation Law violators, they were considered "thought criminals" (shisōhan). Their crime had been to lead an organization (the JCP) that advocated overthrow of the KOKUTAI (the national polity that was thought to be unique to Japan) and the capitalist economic system.

On 10 June 1933, eight months after their sentencing, Sano and Nabeyama announced from prison that they had made a political "change of direction" and were breaking their ties with the Communist Party. They published a statement that listed their reasons for leaving the party and set forth their new beliefs, which acknowledged the special role of the emperor and their acceptance of the kokutai.

Tenkō as Government Policy —— Sano and Nabeyama made their ideological change voluntarily but with the cooperation and encouragement of prison authorities, who allowed them to meet together over a period of months to discuss their ideas and write a joint statement. The authorities publicized the statement and used it to pressure others. Within a month, 548 others had made similar recantations, and the movement continued to spread. Some of these retractions were voluntary, with some individuals using the opportunity to express their doubts and frustrations. Soon, however, it became government policy to resolve thought crimes by inducing the thought criminal to recant.

Beginning in December 1933, all thought criminals were classified according to their degree of recantation. There were three categories of complete tenkō for persons who renounced all revolutionary thought but took various positions regarding future activity in legal social movements. Two categories of semi-tenkō (juntenkō) covered persons who were wavering in their ideological beliefs or who had agreed to give up all activity in social movements without changing their beliefs. A final category was for persons who remained recalcitrant. Within a decade, out of a total of 2,440 communists prosecuted under the Peace Preservation Law, 51.1 percent were classified as having undergone a complete tenkō, 47.4 percent a semi-tenkō, and only 1.5 percent (37 persons) were completely unreformed (hitenkō).

Forms of Coercion —— Various forms of coercion, both physical and psychological, were used to achieve tenkō. For minor offenders, a potent inducement was the promise of release from custody. Manipulation of trial dates and access to medical care, visitors, and items sent to prisoners from the outside were also common. There was some beating and torture, but such techniques were more often used to extract confessions and evidence than to obtain tenkō statements. The most powerful tactic was to instill a sense of guilt and obligation toward other family members, and toward the emperor and the nation.

Types of Tenkō——Regardless of the degree of coercion, *tenkō* usually involved some genuine internal change. Only a small number of cases can properly be called *gisō tenkō* (false recanting), in which the person deliberately lied about his beliefs in order to be released from prison and continue in the movement. Many more gave up their beliefs only under great pressure.

Tenkōsha (persons who underwent *tenkō*) usually followed one of four patterns. Some remained highly political in outlook and made a carefully reasoned shift from one set of political beliefs to another set which they claimed was more appropriate to contemporary conditions in Japan. The emotional impetus for such a shift generally came from feelings of nationalism at variance with the internationalist stance of the JCP. A second group was motivated by political loyalties to individuals and recanted in order to follow a faction leader who had already announced his *tenkō*. Still another group of *tenkōsha* experienced spiritual conversions. They abandoned communist ideology when they realized, often after a personal confrontation with death, that it was no longer emotionally satisfying and subsequently embarked on a spiritual quest for a new belief. Many of them turned to religion; others sought personal meaning in Japanese cultural tradition. This category included many writers, who later recorded their personal ideological and spiritual struggles in a literary movement known as *tenkō bungaku* (ideological transformation literature). A fourth group of *tenkōsha*, the most numerous but least visible, gave up all political participation and withdrew into family and work.

Administration of Tenkō——In the initial wave of recanting following Sano and Nabeyama's joint *tenkō*, any expression of *tenkō*, written or oral, was accepted at face value. Later, as *tenkō* became a matter of policy, systematic procedures evolved. Persons arrested for Peace Preservation Law violations were routinely asked to report in writing their ideological beliefs and state of repentance. Throughout the judicial process, from interrogation through indictment, trial, and sentence-serving, the defendant was actively encouraged to recant. The decision to do so had an immediate impact upon the proceedings.

A *tenkō* made at the time of arrest or during the lengthy interrogation period usually resulted in the person's release under the informal supervision of the official handling the case. *Tenkō* at a later point in the judicial process required both a written statement (*tenkōsho*) and, if release from custody was involved, an appearance before a judge. Over half of those indicted made a *tenkō* before they came to trial, and half of those prosecuted subsequently made a complete *tenkō*.

After 1936 a new "THOUGHT CRIMINAL" PROBATION LAW provided supervised probation and rehabilitation services for *tenkōsha* who were released from custody. The pervasiveness of *tenkō*, especially at early stages of the judicial process, is demonstrated by the fact that over 13,000 persons were handled under the new law during its first two years of operation, although fewer than 3,000 persons were ever convicted of thought crimes during the 20-year life of the Peace Preservation Law.

Extension of Tenkō——By 1936 the combination of intensive application of the Peace Preservation Law and *tenkō* had completely destroyed the communist movement, and with it the last vestige of political opposition to Japan's military expansion. The standard of loyalty required for an acceptable *tenkō* rose steadily during the late 1930s as the whole nation shifted to the right. Following the outbreak of the SINO-JAPANESE WAR OF 1937–1945 *tenkō* began to be used as an expression of loyalty, even by those whose loyalty had never been seriously in question. Legal political organizations, such as the SHAKAI TAISHŪTŌ (Socialist Masses Party), published *tenkō* statements to reiterate their willingness to remain within the narrowing limits of permitted political expression, and liberal intellectuals made *tenkō* statements prior to accepting government positions. The demand for *tenkō* was so all encompassing that a modification of the Peace Preservation Law permitting preventive detention was passed in 1941, so that the handful of *hitenkōsha* whose sentences were completed would not have to be released while still unconverted. They remained in prison until they were freed by American OCCUPATION forces in October 1945.

Postwar Legacy——In the postwar era, *tenkō* became a troublesome and highly emotional issue for the Left. The dozen *hitenkōsha* released from prison became the nucleus of a new Japan Communist Party and a moral standard against which the others would be judged. Only a fraction of those who had recanted rejoined the Communist Party after the war, but the number was still substantial. Hundreds more participated in other organizations in the burgeoning Left. Some claimed to have made *gisō tenkō* (to have submitted under extreme physical duress), and others simply announced another *tenkō* back into the party.

Significance of Tenkō——At a broader level, *tenkō* epitomized the failures of personal responsibility and principled opposition that liberal intellectuals have struggled to comprehend in both personal and national terms since the war. *Tenkō* played an important part in integrating even the most divisive elements in prewar Japanese society into the war effort. The phenomenon of ideological recantation is certainly not unique to Japan, but seldom has it been so formally elaborated, nor has it had such far-reaching implications for a nation.

■——George M. Beckmann and Okubo Genji, *The Japanese Communist Party, 1922–1945* (1969). Richard Mitchell, *Thought Control in Prewar Japan* (1976). Patricia G. Steinhoff, "Tenkō Ideology and Societal Integration in Prewar Japan," PhD dissertation, Harvard University (1969). Kazuko Tsurumi, *Social Change and the Individual* (1970). Shunsuke Tsurumi, "Cooperative Research on Ideological Transformation," *Journal of Social and Political Ideas in Japan* 2 (April 1964). Shisō no Kagaku Kenkyūkai, ed, *Tenkō*, 3 vols (1978).   *Patricia G.* STEINHOFF

Tenninkyō

Gorge on the upper reaches of the river Chūbetsugawa (a tributary of the ISHIKARIGAWA), central Hokkaidō. Towering cliffs formed by columnar joints rise from the gorge, and many huge rocks dot the area. Site of Hagoromo Falls, the largest in Hokkaidō, and of Tenninkyō Hot Spring. Part of Daisetsuzan National Park. Length: approximately 8 km (5.0 mi).

tennis

Tennis was played in Japan by foreign missionaries in the early part of the Meiji period (1868–1912); however, the American surgeon Dr George A. Lealand is credited with formally introducing the game to the Japanese (1878). A standard tennis ball was used at first, but because of the difficulty of obtaining standard balls, Japanese-style tennis, using a softer ball, was invented around 1890 and thereafter spread throughout the country, particularly among students. When Keiō University, a major private university in Tōkyō, began to use the standard ball in 1913, many other colleges followed this change. From that time up until the present, two types of tennis have been played in Japan: one using the standard ball and following international rules (*kōkyū*) and one using a softer unpressurized rubber ball and following a slightly different set of rules (*nankyū*). The basic differences between standard tennis and the type using a softer ball are that, in the latter, only doubles are played and the height of the net is 106 centimeters (42 in) at both poles and the center of the net (as compared to standard tennis, in which it is 107 cm or 42 in at the poles and 91 cm or 36 in at the center of the net). From the early 1920s, national tennis championships have been held for each of the two different styles of tennis, and tennis associations for each style also exist. Tennis using the softer ball has spread from Japan to other countries, and since 1976 international championships have been held, involving teams from eight nations: Japan, South Korea, Taiwan, Venezuela, Brazil, Hong Kong, Zaire, and the United States.   *WATANABE Tōru*

tennō → emperor

Tennōki and Kokki

(Record of the Emperors and Record of the Nation). Japan's earliest known written histories. The chronicle *Nihon shoki* (720) states that they were compiled by Prince SHŌTOKU and SOGA NO UMAKO in 620 and that they were destroyed by the fire in which Umako's son Emishi perished during the TAIKA REFORM of 645. Since the works are no longer extant, we can only guess at their contents, but they are thought to have been, like the TEIKI, organized around the genealogy of the imperial house.   *G. Cameron* HURST III

tennō kikan setsu

The theory that the emperor is an organ of the state, the state being a legal person in which sovereignty is vested. It achieved considerable influence in academic and bureaucratic circles in the period 1920–35, when it enjoyed quasi-official sanction as the basis of a "liberal" interpretation of the 1889 CONSTITUTION of the Empire of Japan.

The phrase gained currency when it became identified with "liberal constitutional heresy," a principal target of right-wing criticism in the great academic and official purge of 1935–37. A dramatic episode in that season of political reaction was the so-called Affair of the Emperor-as-Organ-of-the-State Theory. Gaining front-page coverage in 1935 and early 1936, it brought a previously obscure academic theory to public notice and culminated in the forced withdrawal from official and academic positions and honors of its most noted advocate, MINOBE TATSUKICHI, emeritus head of the law faculty of Tōkyō University and member of the House of Peers.

The gravamen of the charges against Minobe was his long-standing advocacy, as a teacher and writer in constitutional studies, of the state-sovereignty theory and of its patently offensive (to conservatives) corollary that the emperor was merely an organ of the state and did not possess sovereignty in his own right.

Minobe was not the first to propound the state-sovereignty theory in Japan. He had heard it as a student at Tōkyō University even before the customary postgraduate study in Germany that preceded his own academic career at the university. In Germany Minobe was confirmed in his understanding and appreciation of the state-sovereignty and monarch-as-state-organ doctrines and accepted them as concepts useful for liberalizing an absolutist constitutional order. The animus behind his critics' allegations of lese majesty was the realization that such theories could serve as the basis of an interpretation of the constitution that elevated the authority of the Diet at the expense of the military and the bureaucracy.

The state-sovereignty theory, as it came to the Japanese, was a product of late 19th-century German theories of state and constitution. It was a positivistic conceptual refinement of the idea of the state as the locus of historical and ethical value and as an organic entity, a legal person, to which rights and limitations were attributable. Such ideas were part of the constitutional theory to which ITŌ HIROBUMI (chief architect of the 1889 constitution) and others had been introduced in the lectures of Rudolf von GNEIST and Lorenz von STEIN. By the time the Tōkyō University law faculty cadets began arriving in Germany in the 1890s, the state-as-person theory was being strongly and explicitly asserted by Georg Jellinek (1851–1911) and taught by leading positivist interpreters of the German imperial constitution, notably by Paul Laband (1838–1918). Minobe acknowledged a heavy debt to the ideas of Jellinek and Laband.

An important corollary of the idea of the state as a legal person was the notion that the monarch was but one organ of the state, albeit a centrally important one as the "bearer in his own person of the state's sovereignty." Although it totally lacked a democratic impulse, this theory did give latitude to the aspirations of those who hoped for the emergence of responsible constitutional government. No doubt a vision of a tamed monarchy, operating in the context of political, legal, and economic liberalism, lay behind the promotion of the theory in Japan. There, as in Germany, it was part of a general theory of constitutional interpretation that reflected middle class and popular urban interests. Interestingly enough, its brief ascendency at Tōkyō University coincided with its demise in Germany with the beginning of the Weimar era, a demise that foreshadowed its disappearance in Japan with the constitutional revolution of 1946–47.

Although virtually all Japanese constitutional theorists who had studied in Germany absorbed the idea of the state as sovereign, some rejected its application to Japan, seeing it as incompatible with the official orthodoxy of the Meiji state. According to the official definition of "national polity" (KOKUTAI) and the plain language of the 1889 constitution and its attendant rescripts, the emperor was, as lineal descendant of a transcendent being, possessor in his own right of absolute authority. To those who affirmed this position, the theory of the emperor as an organ of the state was blasphemous, and the liberal constitutional inferences drawn from it were seditious. But the times were against such conservatives.

The consonance of the emperor-organ theory with the march of historical events is reflected in Minobe's career. He had first asserted the theory in 1903; he elaborated on it in successive editions of his books from 1908 to 1928. His position was indeed vigorously attacked by a colleague, UESUGI SHINKICHI, in a great debate in 1912–13; but he was appointed nonetheless to the chair of constitutional science at Tōkyō University, then to the headship of its law faculty (1924–34), and eventually to serve on the higher civil service

examination board. To be sure, the philosophy of state sovereignty was not universally endorsed even by those who shared a liberal interpretation of the constitution. It was subject to attack stemming not from strictly Japanese ideological concerns but from conceptual and epistemological objections raised by advocates of Hans Kelsen's (1881–1973) positivistic theory of "pure law" among others. These academic attacks, however, had little to do with the demise of Minobe's liberal constitutional school after 1935.

Its demise was due rather to the rise in Japan of militarism, which had as little use for the constitutional order served by the emperor-organ theory as TAISHŌ DEMOCRACY had had for the "national polity" loyalists. The 1934–35 attack on Minobe was merely a minor incident in the general collapse of "normal constitutional government" and the drift toward military-bureaucratic dictatorship. It came not from the academy but from various small superpatriotic groups, linked with veterans' organizations, who were incited by fascistic ideologues and abetted by some high bureaucratic figures. The attack was conducted in public in an effort to arouse widespread alarm that such an outlandish blasphemy should enjoy favor at the peak of the imperial university system. Minobe became the first and most famous victim of a general academic purge carried out under the banner of "national polity clarification" (see KOKUTAI DEBATE).

After World War II, few if any Japanese academics and intellectuals espoused this now obsolete theory. Nonetheless, there has been considerable interest in the theory's role in the evolution of Meiji and Taishō government. Marxist writers have been particularly interested in its instrumentality in the cause of capitalism. Much attention has also been directed to the Affair of the Emperor-as-Organ-of-the-State Theory as a cause célèbre in the history of academic freedom and academic politics in Japan.

■ ——— Ienaga Saburō, *Minobe Tatsukichi no shisōshiteki kenkyū* (1964). Ienaga Saburō, *Nihon kindai kempō shisōshi kenkyū* (1967). Frank O. Miller, *Minobe Tatsukichi: Interpreter of Constitutionalism in Japan* (1965). Richard H. Minear, *Japanese Tradition and Western Law: Emperor, State, and Law in the Thought of Hozumi Yatsuka* (1970). Minobe Tatsukichi, *Kempō kōwa* (1908). Minobe Tatsukichi, *Kempō satsuyō* (1923). Miyazawa Toshiyoshi, *Tennō kikan setsu*, 2 vols (1970). Richard J. Smethurst, "The Military Reserve Association and the Minobe Crisis of 1935," in George M. Wilson, ed, *Crisis Politics in Prewar Japan* (1970). David A. Titus, *Palace and Politics in Prewar Japan* (1974). Frank O. MILLER

tennō no ningen sengen → emperor, renunciation of divinity by

Tennōzan

Hill in southern Kyōto Prefecture, central Honshū. The Yamazaki district at the foot of the hill was the site of a decisive battle where TOYOTOMI HIDEYOSHI defeated the forces of AKECHI MITSUHIDE, the murderer of ODA NOBUNAGA in 1582 (see YAMAZAKI, BATTLE OF). In 1963 a tunnel for the Meishin Expressway was bored through the hill. Height: 270 m (886 ft).

Tenri

City in northern Nara Prefecture, central Honshū. Originally a market town which grew up in the vicinity of Isonokami Shrine, it is now known primarily as the headquarters of TENRIKYŌ, a modern Shintō sect. There are numerous buildings connected with Tenrikyō, including those of the TENRI CENTRAL LIBRARY, TENRI UNIVERSITY, and Tenri Sankōkan Museum. Pop: 64,899

Tenri Central Library

(Tenri Chūō Toshokan). Library in the city of Tenri in Nara Prefecture; it serves a multiple role in its support of the activities of the TENRIKYŌ sect of Shintō. Opened in 1926 with 26,000 volumes, the library has grown to become an important repository of Japanese and Western collections. The holdings approach 1.5 million items, including books, manuscripts, reports, and documents, about three-fourths of which are in East Asian languages. Among the outstanding collections are the Wataya Bunko, some 17,000 volumes of *renga* and *haikai* assembled from various private libraries, including that of the Nakayama family, descendants of the founder of Tenrikyō; the Kogidō Bunko, some 7,000 items including both printed and manuscript Chinese and Japanese books, letters, and calligraphic pieces from the Kogidō school founded by ITŌ JINSAI; and the Yorozuyo Bunko, an outstanding collection of Christian missionary materials, particularly from 16th- and 17th-century China and Japan. The Lafcadio Hearn Bunko is a collection of holographs, early drafts, many editions, and other memorabilia connected with that author. The Tenri collection boasts some 50 titles designated as National Treasures or Important Cultural Properties by the Ministry of Education. *Theodore F. WELCH*

Tenrikyō

(literally, "religion of divine wisdom"). One of the largest of Japan's contemporary religious groups. Tenrikyō was founded by NAKAYAMA MIKI (1798–1887), a resident of the village of Shōyashiki (now Mishima in the city of Tenri in Nara Prefecture), who claimed she had received a revelation from God on 9 December 1838. According to Tenrikyō tradition, three days later, on 12 December (Tempō 9.10.26), the Nakayama family accepted God's request that Miki become the shrine of God and thus establish the Tenrikyō teaching. This event occurred toward the end of the Edo period (1600–1868), when the common people were caught in the midst of social turmoil and confusion.

Historical Development —— Miki wanted to deliver people from both individual suffering and social evils and to bring about the *kanrodai sekai*, the ideal, perfect world where mankind establishes a blissful life *(yōkigurashi)* in union with God the parent *(oyagami)*. To outsiders the religion seemed a social reform movement which aimed to create a new order at the expense of established vested interests. Thus, the growth of Tenrikyō led to many years of persecution for both founder and followers. Although Miki, as the shrine of God, remained aloof from the laws and orders of the government, her disciples made many attempts to obtain government sanction during the formative period of the religion, hoping to ease the persecution against themselves.

Amid intensified persecution, Miki wrote the main scriptures of Tenrikyō and taught her disciples the hand movements for the *kagura-zutome* (salvation dance service), the most important rite in Tenrikyō. She also determined the precise location of the *jiba* (a sacred spot in the main temple) in 1875. On 18 February 1887 (Meiji 20.1.26), as her disciples performed the prohibited service around the *kanrodai*, the symbolic monument erected at the *jiba*, Miki allegedly passed from a corporal to a purely spiritual state. The faithful of Tenrikyō believe that since then the soul of the founder has remained in the sanctuary of the *jiba* and is constantly helping followers to work toward realization of the ideal world. Miki's passage into this new state became the doctrinal core of the Tenrikyō faith.

After Miki's death God was believed to speak through Iburi Izō (1833–1907), Miki's most trusted disciple. Under his leadership Tenrikyō entered a new era of organizational development and was finally granted some measure of government recognition as a religious organization. The religion was nevertheless subject to governmental regulation and classified as belonging to SECT SHINTŌ (as opposed to STATE SHINTŌ). Furthermore, Tenrikyō was forced to adjust its religious activities to conform to the nationalist policies of the government. Privately, the church struggled to keep Miki's teachings intact, spreading throughout Japan by 1895 and beginning activities in the United States in 1896, Taiwan in 1897, Korea in 1898, and China in 1901.

Soon after the Japanese were guaranteed religious freedom in the new 1947 constitution, Tenrikyō entered a third phase of development, characterized by the *fukugen* (restoration of the original teachings) movement. This movement was a significant step toward the independence of the Tenrikyō faith from other Shintō sects. In 1980 Tenrikyō had approximately 2.5 million followers in Japan and more than 16,000 churches scattered throughout Japan and the world, including the United States, Canada, Mexico, Brazil, Korea, Taiwan, and Zaire. The sect also operates TENRI UNIVERSITY, a museum, a hospital, a radio station, and TENRI CENTRAL LIBRARY.

Doctrine —— God, as revealed through Miki, is called Tenri Ō no Mikoto (literally, "Lord of Divine Wisdom"). As the creator of man, God is defined as *moto no kami* (original God) and *jitsu no kami* (true God). The attributes of God are explained symbolically in terms of the *tohashira no kami* (10 deities), each representing a specific function of God in relation to human life. God is further defined as *tsukihi* (moon and sun) in a conceptual rather than a phenomenal sense, illustrating his pantheistic and immanent nature, and finally as *oyagami* (God the parent), to express both his transcendent and personal aspects.

According to Tenrikyō, God the parent created human beings in order to delight in their life of joy and harmony. But because of man's selfishness, the world's condition became contrary to his expectation, hence the need for a revelation in order to save mankind. This revelation took place through the three preordinations—soul, place, and time—which historically represented by the soul of Miki, the *jiba* or holy place of the original creation, and the time of the revelation, respectively. The three preordinations form the point where man can come into direct contact with God's *tasuke* (salvation). To participate in *tasuke,* one must purify one's heart and mind, reflecting therein the will of God through *makoto shinjitsu* (sincerity). The purification process involves removing the *yattsu no hokori* (eight dusts), which accumulate in the mind from selfish motivations and from the improper use of human freedom; these are not evils as such but rather pollutions that can be cleansed from the mind. Human sufferings stem from a "dusty" heart and mind, and thus the removal of dust is stressed in order to uncover one's true, pure nature. Only with a pure heart and mind can one recognize the world as a manifestation of God's work. To distinguish the true and eternal self from one's phenomenal existence, one must realize that one's body is *kashimono-karimono*, "something lent, something borrowed," from God. Thus death is defined as *denaoshi* (fresh start), or a new opportunity to purify one's soul.

Three actions are encouraged in order to attain salvation. Of these, receiving *osazuke* (holy grant) is considered most essential, enabling one to be reborn as a new being at the *jiba*. Once *osazuke* is received, a person can perform works for others as an agent of God. The practice of *hi no kishin* (daily service) is another way to achieve personal perfection; one offers selfless devotion to God through *hi no kishin* within one's given role and position in society. Finally, repeated pilgrimages to the *jiba* are urged for renewal of faith. These actions culminate in a blissful and harmonious life leading to the *kanrodai sekai.*

Scripture —— Three scriptures comprise the basic canon of Tenrikyō: the *Mikagura uta* (Songs for the Sacred Dance), the *Ofudesaki* (Tip of the Divine Writing Brush), and the *Osashizu* (Divine Directions). Written from 1866 to 1875, the *Mikagura uta* contains the songs to accompany the dance services in Tenrikyō devotional rites. It consists of five parts, the first three being the songs for the *kagura-zutome,* and the fourth and fifth, the songs for the holy dance. The *Ofudesaki,* composed from 1869 to 1882, consists of 17 chapters of 1,711 verses written in *waka* (5-7-5-7-7-syllable) form. This scripture sets forth the basic tenets of Tenrikyō doctrine, such as the creation of human beings, the concept of God, the meaning of the *jiba* and *kanrodai,* and the importance of the *kagura-zutome* service. The first two scriptures were personally written by Miki. The *Osashizu* is a collection for the directions revealed to Iburi Izō from 1887 to 1907. These directions fall into two categories: *kokugen* (incidental directions) and *sashizu* (directions given in response to the inquiries of followers). The *Osashizu* contains more elaborate doctrinal structures than the other two scriptures.

📖 —— Henry van Straelen, *The Religion of Divine Wisdom: Japan's Most Powerful Religious Movement* (1954). Tenri Daigaku Oyasato Kenkyūjo, *Tenrikyō jiten* (1977). Tenrikyō Church Headquarters, *Tenrikyō, Its History* and *Teachings* (1966). Tenrikyō Church Headquarters, *Ofudesaki: The Tip of the Divine Writing Brush* (1971). Tenrikyō Church Headquarters, *The Doctrine of Tenrikyō* (1972). Tenrikyō Church Headquarters, *Mikagura uta: The Songs for the Tsutome* (1972). *Toyoaki UEHARA*

Tenri University

(Tenri Daigaku). A private, coeducational university located in the city of Tenri, Nara Prefecture. Its predecessor is Tenri Gaikokugo Gakkō (Tenri School of Foreign Languages) founded in 1925 by the religious organization, TENRIKYŌ. Japan's first private coeducational institute of foreign languages, its aim was to educate Tenrikyō missionaries to work abroad. In 1944 it was recognized as a college. It adopted its present name in 1948. It maintains faculties of humanities, foreign languages, and physical education. Eight languages are taught, including Indonesian and Korean. The Oyasato Research Institute is well known. Enrollment was 2,357 in 1980.

tenryō

The personal domain of the Tokugawa shōguns, administered by the shogunate *(bakufu)* and others on its behalf during the Edo period (1600–1868). On occasion, the term has been used loosely to denote all Tokugawa land. Such use is unwarrantable, for a third of the land, having been awarded in fief to HATAMOTO ("bannermen"; senior shogunal vassals), was not *tenryō* but *hatamoto ryō*, and as such was administered by, and its taxes paid to, individual *hatamoto*, not to the shōgun or his agents.

At the beginning of the 17th century TOKUGAWA IEYASU, the first Tokugawa shōgun, had direct control of land with an assessed productivity of 2.5 million *koku* (see KOKUDAKA). The tax from this land, roughly 40 percent of each crop, sustained most of his *samurai*, who held no fiefs, and also the TOKUGAWA SHOGUNATE, his newly formed national government. By the end of that century, energetic successors had doubled that inheritance; where the *daimyō* domains (HAN) accounted for land producing 18 million *koku*, and *hatamoto* fiefs for another 2.5 million, the Tokugawa *tenryō*, at a little over 4 million, represented some 17 percent of Japan's agricultural production.

One casualty of this otherwise gratifying development was the geographical unity of the Tokugawa domain. Whether as an embattled chieftain, or as Japan's military overlord, Tokugawa Ieyasu had always contrived to keep his own fief fairly unified. The dividends, both literal, in the form of taxation, or figurative, in the forms of administrative efficiency and military security, were obvious. Such a dramatic increase in Tokugawa *tenryō*, however, made these forfeit. By the early 19th century the *tenryō* was scattered over the face of the Japanese islands, in 47 of its 68 provinces. As the table makes clear, slightly more than half may have been concentrated in the area of greatest Tokugawa authority—the eastern seaboard, from the Kantō Plain down to Ōsaka—but a very substantial portion was located in areas where Tokugawa influence was at best intermittent. The likelihood, therefore, of effective or coherent administration was proportionately reduced. Much of the *tenryō* was too fragmented to make an efficient tax base and was so difficult to police and administer as to preclude Tokugawa participation in monopoly activities of the sort engaged in by many domains.

It was symptomatic of this diminished control that the Tokugawa government was so ready to thrust its administrative responsibilities—and therefore much of its authority—onto others. In some cases where *tenryō* was dispersed, the shogunate found it easier to place responsibility for the gathering of its taxes and the well-being of its inhabitants upon a neighboring daimyō. Such land, known as mandated territory *(azukari-dokoro)*, was still *tenryō* but, nevertheless, tended to become part of the domain entrusted with it. By 1804 more than 15 percent of *tenryō* had been assigned in this way. Even under the best conditions, however, the Tokugawa encountered problems with the administration of their *tenryō*. Management was largely in the hands of civil servants called intendants (DAIKAN or GUNDAI), who, under the general supervision of the commissioners of finance, were responsible for their particular areas. To control such men—often employed, in the first place, because of their local knowledge or local prestige—proved extremely difficult. Despite occasional dramatic purges, the intendants probably controlled their areas as much in their own interests as in those of the Tokugawa, reserving tax rice for their own use and passing their official positions on to their sons.

Like so many other aspects of the political structure of the BAKU-HAN SYSTEM (shogunate and domain system), the *tenryō* never entirely fulfilled its founders' expectations. It reached its maximum relatively early, at the beginning of the 18th century, and thereafter was allowed to decline, dipping to less than 4.25 million *koku* in 1838. What remained was notably undersurveyed, since no full-scale survey was carried out after 1694–95, and the shogunate was therefore denied access to much increased production. Unkinder still, the shogunate rarely received its proper share of *tenryō* taxation; the intendants or, in the case of *azukari-dokoro*, daimyō and their agents were to see to that. The *tenryō*, since it never provided less than 40 percent of the shogunate's revenue, and often accounted for more, was the major single source of government income. It was a Tokugawa tragedy that even this should have been inadequate.

■■ ——Kitajima Masamoto, *Edo bakufu no kenryoku kōzō* (1964).
Harold BOLITHO

Tenryū

City in western Shizuoka Prefecture, central Honshū. On the river Tenryūgawa. Its lumber industry draws on the cedar and cypress forests nearby. Tea and *shiitake* (a species of mushroom) are also cultivated. Attractions include excursions down the river and the ruins of Futamata Castle. Pop: 25,126.

Tenryō

Tenryō Distribution, 1804 (in koku [1])			
Region	Mandated territory	Intendant control	Total tenryō
Kantō	—	1,022,000	1,022,000
Kinai	115,000	572,000	687,000
Tōkaidō	70,000	618,000	688,000
Hokkoku	387,000	966,000	1,353,000
Chūgoku	51,000	361,000	412,000
Saigoku	40,000	136,000	176,000
Total	663,000	3,675,000	4,338,000

[1] 1 *koku* = about 180 liters or 5 US bushels.

NOTE: Kantō: approximately the same area denoted by the same term today (i.e., Tōkyō, Chiba, Saitama, Kanagawa, Ibaraki, and Tochigi prefectures); Kinai: Kyōto-Ōsaka-Nara area; Tōkaidō: Pacific Ocean side of central Honshū; Hokkoku: Sea of Japan side of central Japan, and northern Honshū (the *tenryō* did not extend into Hokkaidō at that time); Chūgoku: Inland Sea side of Honshū; Saigoku: Kyūshū and Shikoku regions.

SOURCE: Kitajima Masamoto, *Edo bakufu no kenryoku kōzō* (1964).

Tenryūgawa

River in Nagano and Shizuoka prefectures, central Honshū; originating in Lake Suwa and flowing south into the Enshū Sea in western Shizuoka Prefecture. The Ina Basin, on the upper reaches, is a rich farming area, and the plain area on the lower reaches produces fruit and vegetables. In its middle reaches, past the city of Iida, the river forms rapids near TENRYŪKYŌ, a scenic gorge. With five dams along its reaches, the Tenryūgawa is an important power source for central Japan. The city of Hamamatsu is located on the lowlands, and its development has resulted in an increased number of industrial plants and residences in the area. Length: 250 km (155 mi); area of drainage basin: 5,090 sq km (1,965 sq mi).

Tenryūji

Head temple of the Tenryūji branch of the RINZAI SECT of Zen Buddhism; located in Ukyō Ward, Kyōto. ASHIKAGA TAKAUJI (1305–58), the founder of the Muromachi shogunate (1338–1573), decided to establish Tenryūji in 1339 in memory of Emperor Go-Daigo (r 1318–39), who had been an early benefactor of Takauji but died opposing him (see KEMMU RESTORATION). The temple was also to commemorate the many warriors who had fallen in the civil war that preceded establishment of the new shogunate. To raise money for the construction of the temple, Takauji's brother, Tadayoshi, commissioned a special ship known as the TENRYŪJI-BUNE (Tenryūji ship) to engage in trade relations with China, provided that the sponsors of the ship would contribute 5,000 *kan* of copper cash to the Tenryūji. Actual construction began in 1340 on the site of the residence of Emperor Go-Saga (r 1242–46) and was completed in 1344. The distinguished Zen master and confidant of Takauji, MUSŌ SOSEKI (1275–1351), was appointed its first abbot. In 1386 Tenryūji, which with its 120-odd subtemples, halls, and chapels constituted the largest Zen monastery in the western half of Kyōto, was formally ranked first among the major Zen temples (GOZAN) in that city. Tenryūji suffered extensive damage from fires no less than eight times, the last being in 1864 when the rebel Chōshū army encamped in the temple precincts during the HAMAGURI GOMON INCIDENT. Reconstruction began shortly thereafter and was completed in 1900. Tenryūji became an independent branch of the Rinzai sect in 1876.
Stanley WEINSTEIN

Tenryūji-bune

(Tenryūji temple ship). Japanese trading vessel that made a government-authorized voyage to and from China in the mid-14th century.

Its trip to Yuan (Yüan) dynasty (1279–1368) China was commissioned in 1341 by order of ASHIKAGA TADAYOSHI, the powerful younger brother of the first Muromachi shōgun, ASHIKAGA TAKAUJI. The shogunate hoped to raise funds to build the temple TENRYŪJI to honor and appease the spirit of GO-DAIGO, the emperor it had recently deposed. MUSŌ SOSEKI, founding father of the Tenryūji, was put in charge of the project, and he secured the appointment of the Hakata trader Shihon as captain. Shihon guaranteed a profit of 5,000 *kan* (see MONEY, PREMODERN) of copper cash for the temple in return for shogunate protection from pirates. The *Tenryūji-bune* appears to have left Japan in 1342 and to have returned the following year; it was the first Japanese ship authorized to sail to China after the MONGOL INVASIONS OF JAPAN in 1274 and 1281.

Tenryūkyō

Transverse valley in the city of Iida, Nagano Prefecture, central Honshū. Located where the river TENRYŪGAWA cuts its way through the Akaishi Mountains, it is a gorge formed by the erosion of gneiss and granite. Sheer cliffs tower on both sides and the flow of the river is rapid. It is the terminus for boating trips on the Tenryūgawa.

Tenshō Ken'ō Shisetsu → mission to Europe of 1582

tenugui

Rectangular cotton gauze cloth primarily used as a towel or headcovering. A *tenugui* is approximately 37 centimeters (13 in) wide; its length varies, as it is cut according to design from a dyed bolt of fabric. *Tenugui* were originally made of undyed linen, but from the Edo period (1600–1868) cotton was used. Red or indigo dyeing, tie-dyeing, and other techniques for adorning *tenugui* were gradually developed. With the increasing popularity of *kabuki,* the practice arose of printing *tenugui* with the crests of famous actors. Soon schools of traditional dance and music began designing their own *tenugui,* and even today these are sold or given as souvenirs. Often shops and business firms distribute *tenugui* at their openings, and almost all localities print souvenir *tenugui* for tourists. *Tenugui* have been used as towels and as headbands for tying up the hair or for absorbing perspiration. As head coverings, *tenugui* were draped and tied in numerous styles which often indicated the wearer's status, or, in the theater, the character type being portrayed. Although they have all but been replaced by terry cloth for use as towels, *tenugui* are still used as head-coverings, rags, souvenirs, and advertisements. See also HEADGEAR. ENDŌ Takeshi

Terada Torahiko (1878–1935)

Physicist; essayist. Born in Tōkyō. Also known as Yoshimura Fuyuhiko. He attended the Fifth Higher School in Kumamoto, where he was inspired by NATSUME SŌSEKI, who was teaching there, to write HAIKU. Even after he began teaching physics at Tōkyō University, from which he graduated, he continued his literary activities under the tutelage of Sōseki. He received a doctorate in 1908 and went to Europe in 1909 in order to further his study of geophysics and seismology. In 1916 he became a professor at Tōkyō University. Although a physicist by profession, his fame is based largely on his skill as an essayist. Some of his literary essays can be found in the collections *Fuyuhikoshū* and *Yabukōjishū,* both published in 1923. His complete works, which cover a wide range of topics, have been collected in the *Terada Torahiko zenshū* (Iwanami Shoten, 1950). James R. MORITA

Terada Tōru (1915–)

Literary critic; scholar of French literature. Born in Kanagawa Prefecture. Graduate of Tōkyō University. Terada gained recognition as a literary critic with his first collection of critical essays, *Sakka shiron* (1949), in which he dealt with MASAOKA SHIKI, MORI ŌGAI, and other Japanese writers. He also wrote on modern French literature, producing essays on such writers as Balzac, Valéry, and Camus. Free of allegiance to any school of criticism or political ideology, he fashioned these essays from his close, sensitive readings of literary works. His works include *Bungaku: Sono naimen to gaikai* (1959) and *Baruzakku: Ningen kigeki no kenkyū* (1953).

Teradaya Incident

(Teradaya Jiken). Incident of 21 May 1862 (Bunkyū 2.4.23) at the Teradaya, an inn on the outskirts of Kyōto, in which antiforeign imperial loyalists, many of them from the Satsuma domain (now Kagoshima Prefecture), were killed. In the spring of 1862 SHIMAZU HISAMITSU, the de facto leader of Satsuma, went to Kyōto, leading 1,000 Satsuma troops, to suppress radical loyalists. ARIMA SHINSHICHI and other Satsuma activists in Kyōto mistakenly assumed that Hisamitsu had come to assist the court in expelling foreigners who had been permitted under the terms of the ANSEI COMMERCIAL TREATIES to live in Japan. They also planned a general uprising against the Tokugawa shogunate but, receiving no encouragement from Hisamitsu, decided to assassinate various shogunate officials. Hearing of this, Hisamitsu sent a party of nine *samurai* to the loyalists' Teradaya lodgings to instruct them to abandon their plan. When Arima and his men refused, violence broke out, and seven of the conspirators, including Arima, were killed. This incident considerably weakened the loyalist movement in Satsuma.

Terakado Seiken (1796–1868)

Writer of the late Edo period. Born in Hitachi Province (now Ibaraki Prefecture), he studied Confucianism and the Chinese classics before going to Edo (now Tōkyō), where he opened a school. In 1832 he began writing *Edo hanjō ki* (1832–36), a series of humorous and gently satiric essays describing various aspects of life in Edo, such as the red-light district and entertainments like *sumō* wrestling and RAKUGO. The first of several such works, it immediately became popular but was banned for its criticism of the Tokugawa shogunate. Terakado was forced to leave Edo during the TEMPŌ REFORMS; he traveled throughout northern Japan, calling himself an "unnecessary man" (*muyō no hito*). His *Niigata hanjō ki* (1859) is a description of life in the Niigata area.

terakoya

Generic term used today for the popular schools of the Edo period (1600–1868). The word is first recorded in 1716. *Terako* (which appears in the title of a book published some 20 years earlier) means "schoolchild," literally, "temple child," an etymology which presumably reflects an earlier state of affairs when priests provided such formal instruction as was available. *Terakoya* simply means a shop or house which takes in pupils for a living. The word originated in western Japan; its use later spread, but still, at the end of the Edo period, *tenaraisho* (writing school) remained the more common word in Edo (now Tōkyō).

There is no certain evidence on which to base an estimate of the growth and extent of *terakoya* education during the period. It does seem, though, that school attendance and literacy increased rapidly in the 19th century. By the end of the period, at a very rough estimate, something like 40 percent of the boys and 10 percent of the girls of each age group were attending one of these schools for at least a part of their childhood. The average conceals wide regional disparities, however. Towns naturally had higher attendance rates than the country; the northeast and Kyūshū were particularly low—and had a particularly low ratio of boys to girls—5 boys to every girl in the northeast, compared with 40 in Edo.

Town schools were mostly family affairs of a single teacher or married couple (one-third, in Edo, were run by women) and 50 or 60 pupils. Some, often run by *samurai,* catered primarily or exclusively to samurai children, some to commoners. In the villages, older retired men, usually of the rich farmer or headman class, often taught reading and writing as a benevolent paternalistic exercise of their community responsibilities—and often, as memorial-stone lists of pupils show, taught children of the poorest as well as of the better-off farmers. Most town teachers probably relied on their teaching for a living, but although a daily "expenses" charge was levied by some teachers—for charcoal heating in winter or for re-covering the *tatami* mats—there was a general reluctance on the part of teachers to so lower their dignity as to sell their services and treat the sacred matter of learning as a commodity transaction. Hence, parents' payments were made in the form of thank-you gifts, money—doubtless in standard conventional amounts—offered duly wrapped in gift wrappings on appropriate festive occasions.

The staple activity of these schools was writing practice. (Some of the teachers had pretentions not just to a neat hand but to calligraphic artistry and might take adult calligraphy pupils too.) Teaching was individual. Teachers would provide each child in turn with a model—or show him the finer points of a model in his copybook—and send him back to his desk to practice. The morning might end with reading practice in unison. Many schools, especially those for merchants' children, also taught arithmetic on the ABACUS, and some taught more gracious accomplishments—in western Japan, for instance, *utai*, the dramatic poetry recited at weddings and festivals, and for girls there might be sewing and flower arrangement.

If the *terakoya* gave anything of a broader education it was thanks to the copybooks which were published in great profusion. (At least 7,000 separate publications are known.) The basic form, the ŌRAIMONO, was a collection of letters for all seasons arranged, thesauruslike, to bring in as many words as possible. The pattern was set by the TEIKIN ŌRAI, a famous text of the 14th century which went on being reprinted despite its irrelevance to the very different society of the 18th and 19th centuries. More contemporary texts often concentrated on the vocabulary of specific occupations but were often intermixed with a wide range of worldly wisdom: mixtures of half-believed superstitions, calendrical law, elementary botany, folk medicine, hints on etiquette, and so on. Another staple was moral exhortation (of a generally authoritarian, obedience-stressing kind, but intermixed with more collateral emphases on neighborliness, friendship, and responsibility) and, of course, the whole business of learning to write—the emphasis on posture and on calmness of spirit, on correctly oriented hearts being reflected in correctly oriented scripts—was imbued with a great deal of character-building morality. Children had a good chance of coming out of such an education not only with useful skills of literacy and numeracy, but with their minds quickened and still undulled by the more solemn and mechanically repetitive learning which characterized the more advanced Confucian schools of the samurai.

Ronald P. DORE

Terashima Munenori (1832–1893)

Diplomat. Born of *samurai* stock in the Satsuma domain (now Kagoshima Prefecture); student of Western medicine. In 1862 he went to Europe as a member of a mission from the Tokugawa shogunate (see SHOGUNATE MISSIONS TO THE WEST). He returned to Japan in 1863 and was personally involved in the hostilities that broke out between Britain and Satsuma that year (see KAGOSHIMA BOMBARDMENT). He later taught at the Kaiseijo, the shogunate school for Western studies in Edo (now Tōkyō). In 1865 he went to England as a member of the Satsuma domain's mission to that country, which returned to Japan the following year. After the Meiji Restoration of 1868 Terashima became a junior councillor (*san'yo*) in the new government. In 1873 he was named foreign minister; in that capacity he negotiated the Treaty of ST. PETERSBURG (1875) with Russia and in 1878 planned the Yoshida–Evarts Convention, in which the United States recognized tariff autonomy for Japan (it was never put into effect because of British opposition). Terashima was also responsible for the negotiations concerning the MARIA LUZ INCIDENT, involving a Peruvian ship transporting Chinese coolies that stopped in Japan. In 1891 he became vice-president of the Privy Council.

Terauchi Hisaichi (1879–1946)

Field marshal and commanding general of the Imperial Japanese Army who served as commander in the South Pacific throughout World War II. Born in Yamaguchi Prefecture, the oldest son of General and Prime Minister TERAUCHI MASATAKE, he graduated from the Army Academy in 1899 and the Army War College in 1909. He served as army minister after the aborted coup d'etat by army officers in the FEBRUARY 26TH INCIDENT of 1936 and further intensified the confrontation between the military and political parties by engaging in a heated debate in the Diet with Hamada Kunimatsu (1868–1939) of the RIKKEN SEIYŪKAI in 1937. He also served as commander of the army in North China immediately after the outbreak of the SINO-JAPANESE WAR OF 1937–1945 in July. There are two conflicting assessments of Terauchi: one holds that he was a mediocre general who never rose to the stature of his father, but was pushed forward by members of the military brain trust to become the figurehead of the military clique; the other maintains that he was a magnanimous leader who was even greater than his father.

KONDŌ Shinji

Terauchi Masatake (1852–1919)

General and prime minister. Born in the Chōshū domain (now Yamaguchi Prefecture), he was educated at the Ōsaka Heigakuryō military school. Although he lost the use of his right hand while fighting for the Meiji government during the SATSUMA REBELLION, he rose rapidly in the army. As the first inspector-general of military education (1898) he worked to systematize military training. Terauchi served as army minister in the first KATSURA TARŌ cabinet during the Russo-Japanese War (1904–05) and remained in the post through several cabinets until 1910, when he was appointed the first governor-general of Korea, having directed its annexation by Japan. During his tenure he systematically crushed all anti-Japanese activity. In 1916, after the fall of the ŌKUMA SHIGENOBU cabinet, he was named prime minister. Convinced that the government should not be left to political parties, he chose only civil bureaucrats as cabinet ministers. In foreign policy the main events of Terauchi's premiership were the so-called NISHIHARA LOANS to shore up the government of Duan Qirui (Tuan Ch'i-jui) in China, the LANSING-ISHII AGREEMENT recognizing Japan's special interests in China, and Japanese participation in the SIBERIAN INTERVENTION by Allied forces during World War I. On the home front, Terauchi was unpopular with the public, which identified him with the Chōshū clique in the government (see HAMBATSU), and he was forced to step down with the outbreak of the nationwide RICE RIOTS OF 1918 resulting from wartime inflation. TERAUCHI HISAICHI was his son.

terauke

(temple guarantee). A method of social control used in the Edo period (1600–1868) by the Tokugawa shogunate and the *daimyō* domains, ostensibly for the purpose of searching out adherents of the proscribed Christian faith but actually with the wider effect of the surveillance of the entire population. The system developed as part of the period's religious inquisition (SHŪMON ARATAME) from the 1630s, when the certificate of affiliation with a Buddhist temple came to be required as proof that a suspect was not in fact a Christian; by 1639, neighborhood associations in cities such as Ōsaka were being ordered to conduct a yearly search of Christians and obtain a Buddhist temple's assurance of any newcomers who bought or rented houses; in 1665, the shogunate ordered a detailed scrutiny of the population, "listing the name of the temple that stood as guarantor of each person's religion"; by the 1670s, a temple's guarantee (*tera-shōmon*) was required of anyone entering service.

The system matured at the beginning of the 18th century, when the family rather than the individual became the unit of affiliation with a Buddhist parish temple (*dannadera*); in the great Kanazawa domain of the Maeda family (comprising most of what are now Toyama and Ishikawa prefectures), for example, laws to that effect (*ikka ichiji hōrei*) were enacted between 1696 and 1713. The result was that every person was upon birth enrolled as a parishioner of his family's temple and listed as such in the so-called religious inquiry registers (*shūmon aratame chō*), which were compiled and attested by the temple and forwarded through local officials to the domainal lord; in addition, the temple's attestation was required prior to marriage, travel, change of residence, or entry into service. In exchange for undertaking to guarantee the religious conformity of the populace and thereby becoming an arm of the regime, the Buddhist church of the Edo period was guaranteed a mass of affiliates and a stable base of economic support. In the long run, however, this privileged position was not beneficial to Japanese Buddhism, since the predetermined enrollment of people in specific, approved temples fostered not a committed faith but the perfunctory observance of religious forms.

The *terauke* system was directed not only against Christians but also against other proscribed religious groups, such as the uncompromising FUJU FUSE SECT of Nichiren Buddhism, which was in 1669 excluded from the temple guarantee. The system collapsed along with the Tokugawa regime in the Meiji Restoration (1868). Its most notable achievement undoubtedly was the compilation of accurate population registers; but the *shūmon aratamechō* were replaced by a new type of household register (*koseki*) in 1871, when a national census law was promulgated (see HOUSEHOLD REGISTERS).

George ELISON

Terayama Shūji (1936–1983)

Primarily known as an avant-garde playwright; also a critic, scriptwriter, novelist, filmmaker, essayist, and poet. He was born in rural

Aomori Prefecture and lost his father in World War II. Reared by one of his maternal relatives who managed a movie theater, he literally lived behind the movie screen. At age 19, Terayama won a major national prize for TANKA poetry and dropped out of Waseda University. After publication of a collection of his miscellaneous poems, *Den'en ni shisu* (1965, To Die in the Country), he began to write and produce plays. In 1967, he founded his personal troupe, the Tenjō Sajiki (Upper Balcony).

Among Terayama's chief plays are *Jashūmon* (Heathen Gate), *Aomori ken no semushi otoko* (The Hunchback of Aomori), and *Sho o suteyo machi e deyō* (1969, Throw Away the Books, Take to the Streets). He made the latter into a feature film in 1971. His other motion pictures include several short works along with the features *Tomato Kechappu Kōtei* (Emperor Tomato Ketchup) and *Den'en ni shisu* (1974).

Terayama wrote feature film scripts for SHINODA MASAHIRO, HANI SUSUMU, and other mainstream film directors as well as radio and television plays. His 1969 reportage of the trans-Pacific underground appeared in *Amerika jigoku meguri* (Touring the American Hell).

In most of his plays, Terayama's main characters are children in revolt. Their target for total destruction—through rape, murder, or any violent means—is the family. His theater, in its quintessential form, is a claustrophobic place of encounter where the cruelty is literal and can include physical assault on the harassed audience. Performance for him is not a show to create illusion or to display talent but the "means to generate and experience chaos."

J. L. ANDERSON

Terazaki Kōgyō (1866–1919)

Japanese-style painter. Born to an impoverished *samurai* family in what is now Akita Prefecture, he studied first with a KANŌ SCHOOL painter, later with the MARUYAMA–SHIJŌ SCHOOL artist Hirafuku Suian (1844–90) and the painter Sugawara Hakuryū (1833–98). In 1888 he went to Tōkyō, and in 1891 he was active in the formation of the progressive Japan Youth Painting Society (after 1897 the Japanese-style Painting Society, Nihonga Kai). He taught at the Tōkyō Bijutsu Gakkō (now Tōkyō University of Fine Arts and Music) until 1898, when he followed OKAKURA KAKUZŌ, who left that year to found the JAPAN FINE ARTS ACADEMY (Nihon Bijutsuin). Kōgyō taught there but also resumed teaching at the Tōkyō Bijutsu Gakkō in 1901. He successfully competed in many exhibitions. He was a judge at the BUNTEN government-sponsored art exhibitions and was named an artist for the imperial household (*teishitsu gigeiin*). He made a number of prints while working as a correspondent during the Russo-Japanese War (1904–05). In 1910 Kōgyō toured China with YOKOYAMA TAIKAN, a trip that inspired new versions of the classical subject *Eight Views of the Xiao (Hsiao) and Xiang (Hsiang)* from both artists. Kōgyō's best-known work is his set of four paintings, *Valleys: Four Themes* (1909), from sketches done in Nagano Prefecture. His realistic style fused Maruyama–Shijō and literati-painting (BUNJINGA) approaches with Western perspective, modeling, and shading. See also NIHONGA.

Frederick BAEKELAND

Terebi Asahi → Asahi National Broadcasting Co, Ltd

Terebi Tōkyō → Television Tōkyō Channel 12, Ltd

teriyaki

Method of cooking pieces of fish or meat by broiling over an open fire and repeatedly basting with a sauce made of strong soy sauce and *sake* or a sweetened wine called *mirin* until the surface is glazed and slightly burnt. *Teri* means "glaze" and *yaki* means "to broil or grill." It is a popular method of cooking large fish with a relatively high fat content, such as yellowtail, salmon, and trout, or more delicate fish and shellfish such as harvest fish *(Pampus argenteus)*, Spanish mackerel, pike conger *(Muraenesox cinereus)*, and shrimp. Beef, pork, chicken, and duck may also be prepared this way. The *teriyaki* method is also used for *yakitori*, or bite-sized pieces of chicken meat or giblets threaded on a skewer, and *kabayaki*, slices of eel or conger *(Astroconger myriaster)* split and grilled.

Tsuji Shizuo

territorial waters

(ryōkai). The delimitation of territorial waters, a concept which had been totally alien to Japan, became a necessity for Japan as a modern state in the middle of the 19th century. Japan's first official declaration concerning territorial waters came in 1870, when the Franco-Prussian War broke out in Europe and the Japanese government issued a Proclamation of Neutrality (Proclamation No. 546 of 1870) stipulating that "the contending parties are not permitted to engage in hostilities in Japanese harbors or inland waters, or within a distance of three nautical miles (1 nautical mile = 1.85 km or 1.15 mi) from land at any place, such being the distance to which a cannonball can be fired." This was regarded as Japan's first proclamation of a three-nautical-mile limit for territorial waters. This proclamation embodied what was regarded as an established precept of international law of the time.

Since then, Japan has continued to adhere to the three-mile limit not only for its own territorial waters but also as a rule of international law which should be applied throughout the world. It upheld this position at the Hague Conference for the Codification of International Law in 1930 and again in 1958 at the United Nations Conference on the Law of the Sea (UNCLOS I). In 1960, at the Second United Nations Conference on the Law of the Sea (UNCLOS II) a compromise proposal for a six-nautical-mile limit and a further six-nautical-mile exclusive fishery zone was put forward. Japan was prepared to accept this arrangement, but when it failed to win acceptance, Japan reverted to the traditional three-mile rule.

It was only in 1977 that the Japanese government decided to modify its position in view of changing international trends. The Law on Territorial Waters enacted in that year (Law No. 30 of 2 May 1977), provides for a limit of 12 nautical miles, except for the Sōya Strait, the Tsugaru Strait, the eastern channel of the Tsushima Strait, the western channel of the Tsushima Strait, and the Ōsumi Strait, for which the three-mile limit remains in effect pending the outcome of the Third United Nations Conference on the Law of the Sea (UNCLOS III). It is expected that this conference will fix the breadth of territorial waters at 12 miles but that international straits will be subject to provisions guaranteeing the right of transit passage. See also FISHERY AGREEMENTS.

Owada Hisashi

territory of Japan

The territory of a state in international law comprises the land, the TERRITORIAL WATERS, and the territorial airspace to which the sovereignty of the state extends. It was incumbent upon Japan, when it was introduced into the international community by the opening of the country in the middle of the 19th century, to delimit and define the extent of its territory as a new member of the international legal community.

The land territory of Japan at the time of its admission into the international community consisted of four main islands, Honshū, Kyūshū, Shikoku, and Hokkaidō, together with a number of small islands appertaining thereto. There were a few peripheral areas, however, where the exact territorial limit of the sovereignty of Japan was less clear.

1. One was the area bordering with Russia, including both the Kuril Islands and Sakhalin. A series of negotiations were held between Japan and Russia with a view to determining the boundary, starting with the visit of Admiral Evfimii Vasil'evich PUTIATIN, who came to Nagasaki in August 1853, but without much success. At the establishment of normal relations between the two countries, agreement was reached in the Treaty of Commerce, Navigation, and Delimitation signed on 7 February 1855, that the boundary between Japan and Russia passed between the islands of ETOROFU and URUPPU and that Sakhalin remained, as in the past, in the joint possession of Japan and Russia. Further negotiations ensued, however, and on 7 May 1875, the Treaty of Exchange of Sakhalin for the Kuril Islands was signed. By this treaty, Japan ceded to Russia its rights on Sakhalin, while Russia ceded to Japan the Kuril Islands, comprising 18 islands from Shumushu in the north to Uruppu in the south. See ST. PETERSBURG, TREATY OF.

2. The RYŪKYŪ ISLANDS presented another case. The ruler of the Ryūkyū Islands, whose people belong to the same race as the mainland Japanese, started to pay tribute to the Ming dynasty of

China in 1372 upon the latter's demand. The ruler was given in return the title of king of Chūzan. He continued to send tribute to the succeeding Qing (Ch'ing) dynasty, while at the same time sending envoys with tribute to the shogunal government of Japan. In 1609 the lord of the Satsuma domain in Kyūshū, with the authorization of the shogunate, dispatched troops to Okinawa and forced the ruler of the Ryūkyūs to swear allegiance. When the Meiji government abolished the feudal system and introduced a new system of administration based on prefectures, the ruler of the Ryūkyūs was appointed king of the Ryūkyū Han (domain) in 1872, but in 1879 the Ryūkyū Han was abolished and replaced by Okinawa Prefecture, as an integral part of the new system of administration of modern Japan. See OKINAWA.

3. The OGASAWARA ISLANDS (or Bonin Islands), an archipelago extending from the middle of Honshū southeast into the Pacific, were first discovered by Ogasawara Sadayori in 1593 but later became the subject of claims by foreign powers toward the end of the Tokugawa shogunate. After the Meiji Restoration (1868), the government decided in October 1875 to clarify the situation and established an Ogasawara Islands Office in the Home Ministry, which enacted various regulations concerning the islands. It formally declared the incorporation of these islands under the administration of Japan. This action met with little resistance from the foreign powers involved.

4. In addition, a number of small islands in waters in the vicinity of Japan became subject to claims of title by Japanese nationals in the late 19th century, and the government took measures to incorporate them into the territory of Japan. Some of the important islands are as follows. MINAMI TORISHIMA (Marcus Island), an island lying to the east of the Ogasawara Islands, was incorporated into the administration of Tōkyō Prefecture by a cabinet decision in 1898. The Volcano Islands (Kazan Rettō; see IŌ ISLANDS), lying to the southwest of the Ogasawara Islands, were incorporated into the administration of Okinawa Prefecture by a cabinet decision in 1896. (These islands, together with the Ogasawara Islands, are now under the administration of Tōkyō Prefecture.) The SENKAKU ISLANDS, lying near the Ryūkyū Islands, were incorporated into the administration of Okinawa Prefecture by a cabinet decision also in 1896. The Daitō Islands, lying to the east of the Ryūkyū Islands, were incorporated into the administration of Okinawa Prefecture by cabinet decisions in 1885 and 1900. Naka no Torishima, an island lying northeast of the Ogasawara Islands, was incorporated into the administration of Tōkyō Prefecture by a cabinet decision in 1908. TAKESHIMA, an island lying in the Sea of Japan between Japan and Korea, was incorporated into the administration of Shimane Prefecture in 1905.

A major modification of the territorial limits of Japan came with the SINO-JAPANESE WAR OF 1894–1895. By the Treaty of Shimonoseki, concluded at the end of the war, China ceded to Japan Formosa (TAIWAN) and the Pescadores (Penghu). See SHIMONOSEKI, TREATY OF.

The RUSSO-JAPANESE WAR of 1904–05 brought about another major modification. By the Treaty of Portsmouth, Russia ceded to Japan the southern half of Sakhalin south of the 50° parallel, thus modifying the territorial arrangement established by the treaty of 1875 (see PORTSMOUTH, TREATY OF). In addition, Japan acquired the right of lease that Russia had been exercising over the GUANDONG (KWANTUNG) TERRITORY in Manchuria, though this was not a territorial acquisition by Japan in the strict sense of the word.

In 1910 Korea, which had been placed under the protectorate of Japan by the KOREAN-JAPANESE CONVENTION OF 1905, was incorporated into the territory of Japan. By the conclusion of the Treaty regarding the Annexation of Korea to the Empire of Japan, the emperor of Korea made complete and permanent cession to the emperor of Japan of all rights of sovereignty over the whole of Korea, thus expanding the territory of Japan to include the entire Korean peninsula (see KOREA AND JAPAN: early modern relations).

World War I, in which Japan participated on the side of the Allied powers against Germany, did not bring to Japan any territorial addition in the strict sense. The Treaty of Versailles, through its Covenant of the League of Nations, established the mandate system under which Japan became entrusted with the administration of some former German colonies in the Pacific, consisting of 623 islands which included the Caroline Islands, the Mariana Islands, and the Marshall Islands (see VERSAILLES, TREATY OF).

As a result of World War II, however, Japan lost most of the territories it had acquired through the period covered above and was reduced to something less than what it had been when it started as a modern state with the Meiji Restoration. By article 2 of the SAN FRANCISCO PEACE TREATY of 1951, Japan renounced all rights, title,

and claim to: (a) Korea, including the islands of Quelpart (Chejudo), Port Hamilton (Komundo), and Dagelet (Ullungdo); (b) Formosa and the Pescadores; (c) the Kuril Islands and that portion of Sakhalin and the islands adjacent to it over which Japan acquired sovereignty as a consequence of the Treaty of Portsmouth; (d) areas administered in connection with the League of Nations mandate system; (e) any right or title to or interest in connection with any part of the Antarctic area; and (f) the Spratly Islands and the Paracel Islands (both in the South China Sea).

Thus the San Francisco Peace Treaty of 1951 clearly defined the scope of the territory of Japan as of the present, subject to the following comments concerning three peripheral areas of Japan:

1. The Northern Territories, which comprise the islands of KUNASHIRI, Etorofu, SHIKOTAN, and the HABOMAI ISLANDS, have been under Soviet occupation since the end of World War II. Japan's claim to them is based on the position that they are not part of the Kuril Islands that Japan renounced in the San Francisco Peace Treaty and that they have never been under foreign possession, always constituting an integral part of Japan. The Soviet Union takes the position that there exists a series of international agreements under which these islands have legitimately become part of its own territory. The dispute still continues with no concrete prospect of settlement in sight.

2. TAKESHIMA (Tokto) has been under occupation by the Republic of Korea. The Korean side contests the legality of the incorporation of this island into the administration of Shimane Prefecture in 1905, based on the position that Koreans had a prior knowledge of it and effected occupation and that the act of incorporation was carried out at a time when Korea, under the protectorate of Japan, could not effectively lodge a protest. The dispute continues and no settlement is in sight.

3. The SENKAKU ISLANDS, placed under the administration of the United States under article 3 of the Treaty of Peace with Japan, were returned to the administration of Japan (Okinawa Prefecture) by the Okinawa Reversion Agreement of June 1971. Since the late 1960s, the government of the People's Republic of China and authorities in Taiwan have been claiming that these islands (Diaoyutai or Tiao-yü-t'ai Islands) are Chinese. See also the section on territory and administrative divisions in JAPAN. *Owada Hisashi*

tertiary industries

Industries that produce an intangible product, including wholesale and retail sales, banking, insurance, real estate, transportation, communication, public utilities, medical care, and public service.

Employment in tertiary industries has grown dramatically in the past century. Some 82 percent of the Japanese population was employed in PRIMARY INDUSTRIES (agriculture, fishing, and forestry) in 1878; by 1970, this figure had fallen below 20 percent. Employment in SECONDARY INDUSTRIES (manufacturing) and tertiary industries was 6 percent and 12 percent, respectively, in 1878; by 1970, these sectors accounted for 35 percent and 47 percent of employment. Until 1973, employment in the secondary and tertiary industries increased in parallel, but since then manufacturing employment has stagnated (see table at PRIMARY INDUSTRIES). Prior to the early 1970s, secondary industries had been spurred by the strong demand for manufactured goods as living standards rose; subsequently, there was a change in purchasing habits as consumers strove to improve the quality of their daily lives, and such tertiary industries as transportation and medical care grew as a result.

Tertiary industries accounted for 48.9 percent of the national product in 1960 and 54.3 percent in 1970; this share is expected to continue to increase in the future; in actuality, demand for services will grow in parallel with increases in disposable income. From 1965 to 1975 the increase in labor productivity in tertiary industries was a low 2.9 percent, compared with an average annual increase of 8.2 percent for primary industries and 3.9 percent for secondary industries. The productivity gap has led to a rise in the price of services. Low productivity in the tertiary sector has also led to increasing employment, since more employees were required to meet increases in demand.

Employment in tertiary industries in Japan stood at 251 per 1,000 population in the late 1970s, a level comparable to that in the United States in 1948. Judging from employment trends in the United States since then, the employment absorption power of Japanese tertiary industries still has room for long-term expansion. However, some 52 percent of service employment in Japan is concentrated in small-scale wholesale, retail, and transport enterprises, compared with 40 percent in the United States. It can be concluded, therefore, that excess employment exists among small service enterprises in Japan, and that the potential for expansion lies in such public service areas as medical care, insurance, education, and social welfare. In welfare services, special and comparatively high levels of technology and skills are required in many cases. It is also conceivable that some activities associated with secondary industries will expand into independent tertiary operations, providing new outlets for employment. *KATŌ Hiroshi*

Teshigahara Hiroshi (1927–)

The Japanese film director best known for the 1964 picture *Suna no onna* (Woman in the Dunes). Teshigahara was born in Tōkyō, the son of the well-known *ikebana* master, Teshigahara Sōfū, founder of the Sōgetsu school of flower arrangement. After having made a number of short films, mostly on the traditional arts of Japan, Teshigahara completed his first feature film in 1962. This was *Otoshiana* (Pitfall), scripted by the novelist and dramatist, ABE KŌBŌ. This began a collaboration that extended through the director's career. Following *Suna no onna*, Teshigahara directed *Tanin no kao* (1966, The Face of Another) and *Moetsukita chizu* (1968, The Ruined Map), both based on novels by Abe. These were followed by *Natsu no heitai* (1972, Summer Soldiers), scripted by John Nathan.

A meticulous craftsman, Teshigahara interests himself particularly in the visual aspects of filmmaking, including the photography and the decor, and takes endless pains over the physical appearance of his picture. Conversely, he does not to this extent interest himself in his actors. Since many of the actors he uses are from the stage, the result is a wide variation in the acting level of his films. Similarly, he does not interest himself in script problems. Consequently, when the script is good, as in *Suna no onna*, the resultant film is good; when it is weak or confused, or when an actor exerts especial influence (as did Katsu Shintarō in *Moetsukita chizu*), the results are uneven.

After the failure of *Natsu no heitai*, Teshigahara retired from film work and became a potter, working mainly in Fukui Prefecture. At the same time he separated from his second wife, the actress Kobayashi Toshiko, and has since made no films, though he has achieved a new reputation with his ceramics.

At the same time, he continues an earlier interest in experimental cinema. It was he who encouraged showings and contests of such pictures at the old Sōgetsu Kaikan in Tōkyō. Upon completion of the new headquarters in 1978, he headed a committee to show experimental films—made by Japanese and foreigners alike—to inaugurate contests and to maintain a collection and provide a showplace for the films. *Donald RICHIE*

Teshikaga

Town in eastern Hokkaidō. On the upper reaches of the river Kushirogawa. Principal farm products are potatoes and sugar beets. Dairy farming and forestry are also active. The greater part of the town is located in the Akan National Park. Attractions include two caldera lakes, Kutcharo and Mashū, and Teshikaga and Kawayu hot springs. Pop: 12,205.

Teshima Toan (1718–1786)

Religious and moral teacher. A disciple of ISHIDA BAIGAN, he laid the basic institutional foundations for the SHINGAKU movement. His work in this area helped Shingaku to become a major source of ethical guidance for the merchants and townsmen (CHŌNIN) of the Edo period (1600–1868).

Toan was born into a well-to-do merchant family in Kyōto. His parents encouraged his scholarly interests, and at the age of 18 he was allowed to enter Baigan's school. Toan underwent an enlightenment experience at the school and studied for almost a decade with Baigan until the latter's death in 1744.

Toan was himself an eloquent speaker and drew large crowds to his lectures. He set about editing Ishida's writings and also elaborated and clarified some of his mentor's basic ideas. At the same time, Toan created the institutional framework which enabled Shingaku to become a national movement. In 1765 he moved his family to a larger residence, part of which served as a lecture hall. This hall, called the Gorakusha, became the prototype for others. By 1782 three additional halls had been set up by Teshima's followers in Kyōto: the Shūseisha, the Jishūsha, and the Meirinsha. Each of these had a resident master, or *shashu*, and a number of students in

residence. These three halls later came to be regarded as the organizational and spiritual core of the national movement.

By Toan's death in 1786, 22 more halls had been established in the provinces, and this number eventually grew to over 180. Thus the organizational pattern and popular doctrinal formulations of the national Shingaku movement may both be attributed in large measure to the work of Teshima Toan.

Among Toan's students were NAKAZAWA DŌNI, Uekawa Kisui (1748–1817), and Fuse Shōō (1725–85). His most influential writings were the *Zadan zuihitsu* (1771), *Chishin bengi* (1773), and *Kaiyū taishi* (1773).

■——Robert N. Bellah, *Tokugawa Religion* (1957). Shibata Minoru, ed, *Teshima Toan zenshū* (Seibundō, 1973).

Thomas M. HUBER

Teshiogawa

River in northern Hokkaidō, originating on the slope of Teshiodake, the highest peak of the Kitami Mountains, flowing north through Shibetsu, Nayoro, and Bifuka basins, to enter the Sea of Japan near the town of Teshio. The lower reaches meander through the Sarobetsu Plain, which is composed of peat bogs. Length: 256 km (159 mi); area of drainage basin: 5,590 sq km (2,158 sq mi).

Teshio Mountains

(Teshio Sanchi). Mountain range running north to south along the Sea of Japan coast, northwestern Hokkaidō. The highest peak is Pisshirizan (1,032 m; 3,385 ft), noted for its dense primeval forests and deep snow. Extensive lumbering is done throughout the entire range. There are coal mines in the Rumoi and Tempoku districts.

Teshio Plain

(Teshio Heiya). Extends along the lower reaches of the river Teshiogawa, northwestern Hokkaidō. Comprises Kamisarobetsu, Shimosarobetsu, and Ubushi Plains. A low and swampy plain that developed from a lagoon bordered by sand dunes along the Sea of Japan. It is composed of numerous peat bogs, pasture land, and wild, uncultivated land. Area: approximately 500 sq km (193 sq mi).

Tessai → Tomioka Tessai

Tessai Art Museum

(Tessai Bijutsukan). Located at Takarazuka, Hyōgo Prefecture. The museum, opened in 1975, houses the collection of about one thousand paintings and examples of the calligraphy of TOMIOKA TESSAI, the last great BUNJINGA painter. *Laurance ROBERTS*

Tesshū Tokusai (?–1366)

Early *suibokuga* (INK PAINTING) artist of the Muromachi period (1333–1568). A Zen monk, he was a disciple of MUSŌ SOSEKI, the founder of the Kyōto temple Tenryūji. Tesshū went to China and studied calligraphy, poetry, and painting and visited various Zen institutions. In 1342 a farewell poem was presented to him by Nanchu Shishuo (Nan-ch'u Shih-shuo; fl 1338–44), the abbot of the monastery Zhengtiansi (Cheng-t'ien-ssu) in Suzhou (Soochow). Tesshū probably returned to Japan the following year. For a time he went back to Kyōto as the primate *(shuso)* of Tenryūji; in 1347 he became the abbot of the Hodaji temple in Awa Province (now Tokushima Prefecture) and shortly thereafter Zuikōji temple in Harima Province (now part of Hyōgo Prefecture). In 1362 he was appointed abbot of Manjuji, one of the five major Zen monasteries in Kyōto (see GOZAN). He retired to Ryūkōin, a subtemple of Tenryūji, where he died in 1366.

Tesshū was in China at approximately the same time as the Zen monk-painter MOKUAN REIEN, whose works are almost exclusively based on themes inspired by Zen teachings and executed in the style then current among Chinese Zen clerics. By contrast, Tesshū's works reflect the aesthetic taste and learning of the literati. His calligraphic works take subjects not from the Zen literary repertoire, but from Chinese classical poetry, and he was particularly appreciated for his *sōsho* (grass-style) writing. Unlike that of many contemporary Zen priests, Tesshū's calligraphy reflects mastery of the orthodox Chinese calligraphic style that was revived during the

Yuan (Yüan) dynasty (1279–1368). He was also a skillful poet, as seen in his poetry anthology *Embushū*. Some paintings traditionally attributed to Tesshū were inspired by Zen allegorical themes such as monkeys and reeds and geese, but it is his ink paintings of orchids, bamboos, and grapes—subjects favored by the literati and literati monk-painters—for which he is best known.

■——Shimada Shūjirō, ed, *Zaigai Nihon no shihō*, vol 2 (1979). Yoshiaki Shimizu and Carolyn Wheelwright, ed, *Japanese Ink Painting* (1976). *Yoshiaki* SHIMIZU

tetsudō basha → horsecars

Tetsugen (1630–82)

Tetsugen Dōkō. Zen monk of the ŌBAKU SECT. Born in Higo Province (now Kumamoto Prefecture). Upon the arrival in Japan of the Chinese monk Yinyuan Longqi (Yin-yüan Lung-ch'i; J: INGEN Ryūki), he became a disciple of the master and later of his student Muan (J: Mokuan; 1611–84). Learning that the Buddhist canon *(Daizōkyō)* had not yet been printed in its entirety in Japan, he collected funds and labored for more than 10 years, completing this task in 1678. This printing is known as the Tetsugen or Ōbaku edition and even today is considered an important legacy. The printing blocks are still at the temple MAMPUKUJI. Tetsugen propagated Ōbaku teachings widely and was long remembered for his charitable works during the great famine which beset the Kyōto–Ōsaka area in 1682. *MATSUNAMI Yoshihiro*

teuchi

The custom of clapping hands to confirm a negotiation concluded between two parties; also known as *tejime*. Believed to have been derived from the Shintō custom of clapping one's hands *(kashiwade)* in front of the shrine. It is customary to clap three times in unison. Among gamblers, actors, and other members of the demimonde, a special *teuchi* ceremony is held to mark an agreement or the resolution of a feud. Even today, among merchants, it is not unusual to close special meetings and commemorative events with clapping of the hands. *TSUCHIDA Mitsufumi*

Textbook Scandal of 1902–1903

(Kyōkasho Gigoku). The discovery in 1902–03 of nationwide bribery in the selection of elementary- and middle-school textbooks. Textbooks had been published by private companies, which, following approval by the Ministry of Education, submitted them for selection by prefectural committees. Competition for selection was fierce, and rumors of wide-scale bribery circulated; one company was said to have distributed ¥360,000 in less than two years. In December 1902 the Ministry of Justice initiated secret investigations. As a result, by March 1903 over 200 people, including school inspectors, former prefectural governors, and textbook company presidents had been arrested; 116 were found guilty. Minister of Education Kikuchi Dairoku (1855–1917) took responsibility for the incident and resigned. The scandal convinced the government of the need to centralize the selection of textbooks in the Ministry of Education. In 1903 the first *kokutei kyōkasho* (national textbooks) were issued.

textile industry

The textile industry was the first modern industry established in Japan and the largest industry in the country prior to World War II. In 1937, 38.6 percent of all industrial workers were employed in the industry, with textile production constituting 27.7 percent of the total industrial product and textile exports accounting for 56 percent of all Japanese exports in money terms. As a peacetime industry, textiles witnessed dark days during World War II, because much of the industry's equipment and facilities was either scrapped to be turned into weapons and shells or damaged during air raids. As a result, production capacity at the end of the war was only 30 percent of the prewar level. The cotton spinning industry, in particular, because it did little business with the military, was reduced to 16 percent of its former scale. Overseas assets were all lost to the industry as a result of Japan's defeat in the war. Early in the postwar period, measures were taken to rehabilitate the industry, since textile exports were an important source of foreign exchange. By 1956, production had ex-

ceeded its prewar peak. However, the emergence of the cotton spinning industry in developing countries, especially in Southeast Asia, and the fact that China, a principal export market for Japanese textiles before the war, had become communist and thus difficult for Japan to trade with, led to a decline in the status of the textile industry and in its proportion of total exports.

The chemical fiber industry developed rapidly in the first decade after the war, followed by the synthetic fiber industry in the second postwar decade; the two new branches of the industry exported increasing amounts in the 1960s. Today, however, chemical and synthetic fiber goods manufactured by countries in Southeast Asia dominate the export market. In addition, since the sharp rise in oil prices in 1973, Japanese textile products have become more expensive than American ones, since manufacturers in the United States have been able to rely on comparatively cheap domestic oil and natural gas. This has led to a further decline in the international competitiveness of Japanese textiles. As a result, Japanese textile imports exceeded exports after 1973. Japanese synthetic textile enterprises are currently entering the Southeast Asian textile field as multinational companies, while domestically they are shifting their emphasis to the growing fashion products market, where color, pattern, and design are more important than price. *SUZUKI Hiroaki*

textiles

From its beginnings in the simple twisted cords of prehistoric man, the history of Japanese textiles has been punctuated by the same waves of outside influence that mark other facets of the history of this island country. Throughout the ages, Japan has imported textiles and technical knowledge both from the continent, especially from Korea and China, and from Southeast Asia, especially from India and the Ryūkyū Islands. As in other areas of East Asia, artisans worked primarily with bast fibers (ASA) and SILK until the important introduction of cotton from India via China and Korea in the 16th century. Since the Meiji Restoration (1868), European and American influence has been strong, and other fibers have come into common use, notably wool and, more recently, the various manmade synthetic fibers.

In the periods of assimilation that generally followed each wave of outside contact, Japanese adapted the new designs and techniques to meet their own needs and tastes. Although these varied considerably from period to period, we can discern a general preference for composite constructions and for designs and colors derived from the nature, scenery, and everyday life of the islands rather than from abstract or mythological creations. An enjoyment of the new and exotic has been coupled with a respect for the old that has led to careful preservation of many old textiles. Although the Japanese have always been justifiably proud of their woven textiles, many of their finest textiles have been dyed and their most innovative and important contributions to textile techniques have been in dyeing. High points are the pure color and color combinations of the Heian period (794–1185); the stitch-resist, ink brush-painted *(tsujigahana)* costumes *(kosode)* of the latter part of the Muromachi period (1338–1568) and the early part of the Azuchi-Momoyama period (1568–1600); the composite, figured silks, including NŌ theater costumes, of the Azuchi-Momoyama period and the early part of the Edo period (1600–1868); and the woven strips, *katazome*, and *kasuri* hemps and cottons of the late Edo period. The 20th-century folkcraft *(mingei)* movement and government legislation to preserve and promote hand-weaving and dyeing also deserve special note.

Jōmon Period (ca 10,000 BC–ca 300 BC)——Archaeological evidence indicates that the early inhabitants of Japan pulled fibers from the inner bark of certain trees, shrubs (wisteria, mulberry), and grasses (hemp) and twisted them simply by hand to form cords and later to make straw mats and probably other coarse textiles in various preweaving techniques such as netting, plaiting, and probably twining. They were also skilled basket makers. It is unclear whether the people of the Jōmon period developed weaving themselves or whether this important advance was brought from the Asiatic mainland by a new migration of peoples that started at the end of the 3rd century BC.

Yayoi Period (ca 300 BC–ca AD 300)——The people of the Yayoi period cultivated fiber-bearing plants, including the lustrous longstaple ramie that they had brought with them from the continent. They spun and dyed thread and wove it into cloth, which they pounded smooth and pliant with wooden mallets. Sporadic contact with the continent continued. Around AD 200, the Chinese court sent a gift of silkworms to the rulers in Japan, as well as gifts of red and blue silks, silk brocades, and probably small-pointed tie-dye. The queen HIMIKO is reported to have returned the gift in 243 with well-woven vegetal fiber cloth and rough silk. Although some of these textiles were referred to by the same word *(nishiki)* that was used for Chinese brocades, they were probably of the simplest plain weave construction. Design seems to have been effected by skillful manipulation of color—by vertical strips of red (madder), blue (indigo), and yellow (various wild grasses and barks), and by the use of different colors in the warp and weft to create an iridescent effect in the finished cloth.

Yamato Period (ca 300–710) —— As the strength of the Japanese court grew and intercourse with the continent increased, textiles became a major item of tribute. Although some rough silk was produced, the finest cloth was generally woven of well-spun plant fibers. This reflected in part the replacement of the heavy stone and iron spindles of the early Yayoi period by lighter ones generally made of bone or wood. Color manipulation continued to be the primary means of decoration, although solid red and the extensive use of lustrous pure white were also characteristic of the period.

In an effort to improve and disseminate the production and weaving of silk, the Yamato rulers, especially the emperors ŌJIN (late 4th to early 5th century) and Yūryaku (latter half of the 5th century), actively recruited continental weavers, mostly from the kingdoms of Paekche (southern Korea) and Wu (southern China). These weavers were treated with respect, given clan status, and granted tracts of land throughout Japan. Many of their names, or portions thereof, became incorporated into the language of weaving. By the early 5th century, members of the HATA FAMILY (*hata* is the word for "loom") were weaving tribute silk so soft and warm that the delighted emperor NINTOKU (early 5th century) declared it fit even for imperial clothing—some indication of the quality of silk weaving that had preceded this. Although continental weavers are thought to have introduced NISHIKI (in the form of a warp brocade in the style of the Han dynasty; 206 BC–AD 220) and *aya* (twill) techniques in the late 5th century, archaeological evidence suggests that throughout most of the period, at least, domestic silk was still comparatively rough, of plain weave structure, and generally either monochrome or patterned with simple vertical stripes.

Asuka and Nara Textiles —— The Asuka period (latter part of the 6th century to 710) saw a wave of continental influence that crested in the Nara period (710–794) and brought with it the introduction of Buddhism and a radical reorganization of the central government and indeed of the whole society. In material culture, Chinese influence was particularly great, extending from the architecture of the greatest temples to the smallest articles of apparel and household furnishings and triggering an explosion of arts and crafts. Textiles were a highly valued and very important part of this material culture. They were a major form of tribute payment and could be substituted for corvée service (see SO, YŌ, AND CHŌ). Distinctively colored garments were used to distinguish court ranks. Embroidered Buddhist images and startlingly beautiful dyed and woven ceremonial banners adorned the major temples. Richly patterned woven textiles were used for ceremonial costume by the aristocracy and head priests, and wax-stamped dyed patterns decorated the fine costumes of court and temple dancers. Interior spaces of palaces and temples were divided by screens with finely dyed landscape panels. Richly patterned silks, often used in combination, covered pads, cushions, and armrests were used in conjunction with numerous other articles for daily, ceremonial, and religious use.

Two great collections of textiles from this period remain, one from the early Asuka period and one from the mid-Nara period. The earliest collection is that of the temple HŌRYŪJI (currently housed within the TŌKYŌ NATIONAL MUSEUM), which dates from the late 6th and early 7th centuries. Although the Hōryūji collection is the smaller, it contains many excellent pieces and, with the addition of some fine Buddhist textiles preserved in other temples in and around the ancient capital area, provides a solid base for a study of changes in style and technical developments from the mid-6th through the 8th centuries. Many, if not most, of the finest of these textiles were imported from the mainland, and a significant percentage of the rest was produced by or under the direct supervision of continental artisans.

The second collection is that of the SHŌSŌIN repository in Nara, which contains well over 100,000 textiles donated to or used in the temple Tōdaiji or in the imperial palace in the mid-8th century. Many of the palace textiles date from the consecration service of the image of the Great Buddha in 752, an impressive ceremony attended by priests from as far away as India. Many of these were personal effects of Emperor SHŌMU, dedicated by his widow after his death in 756. The collection also includes provincial tribute textiles, workmen's uniforms, and other textiles designed for everyday use.

The Shōsōin textiles show a very high level of technical expertise and represent most major areas of the textile arts—plain and figured weaving, resist dyeing, embroidery, braiding, and a little printing, painting, patchwork, and felt making. The dyed and woven textiles have similar motifs. Landscapes, mythical and real animals, birds, abstracted flowers, arabesques, and a variety of geometric motifs are among the most common. Certain elements can be traced as far as Egypt, Assyria, Persia, and eastern Rome. Color was strong and clear, and the pure rendition of dyed color reached a very high level that was to be fully maintained in the Heian period. Simple dyeing was done in the provinces, but the most complex, imported, and difficult colors were apparently rendered in the Palace Dyeing Office.

Textiles in the Shōsōin —— The major categories in the Shōsōin collection are woven textiles, resist-dyed textiles (SANKECHI), embroidered textiles *(shishū)*, and braided and plaited textiles *(kumihimo)*. The woven textiles can be classified as follows.

Plain weave silks and ramies. These consist mostly of tribute cloth from the provinces, undyed or monochrome (red, blue, or yellow). The fineness of the silk varies considerably, depending on its source.

Nishiki (brocades). These include a wide variety of multicolored, figured silk fabrics executed in a number of different techniques (including tapestry and double weave), but most often brocade weaving. The oldest examples (like those in the Hōryūji) are of a Han-dynasty type of warp-patterned brocade; the most numerous are of a popular Tang (T'ang) dynasty (618–907) weft-patterned technique that permitted the use of a greater number of colors and comparative ease and freedom in pattern execution.

Aya (figured twills). Second only to *nishiki* in popularity, these are also complex figured silks, though generally monochrome and usually, but not always, with the pattern and/or background effected in a straight twill weave. Patterns range from small background motifs on ground cloth for pattern dyeing to complex landscapes.

Ra and sha (gauzes). These delicate patterned silk fabrics with a netlike structure were formed by the twisting and interlocking of warp threads held in place by weft. The gauzes were used as clothing and as ground cloth for many block-resist (*kyōkechi*) dyed pendants and ceremonial banners.

The *sankechi* include stamp-applied, wax-resisted (*rōkechi*), tie-dyed (*kōkechi*), and block-resisted (*kyōkechi*) textiles. The latter comprise a fascinating and very beautiful group of textiles with multicolored landscape designs of animals and trees. Often executed on fine-patterned gauze, they were used as the body and/or pendants of banners for Buddhist rituals. The cloth was apparently folded in four and pressed between two blocks with patterns engraved on them. The desired dye was allowed to penetrate the appropriate grooved areas, possibly through a series of capped openings in the blocks. See TIE-DYEING; WAX-RESIST DYEING.

Shishū textiles were used for articles as divergent as the imperial shoes and the headings of the most magnificent banners and Buddhist images. Yamato embroidery tended to employ a type of chain stitch while a long, plain stitch in almost untwisted silk was favored for the full, rich embroidery of the early part of the Nara period. Most examples for both periods are in double-face embroidery, often done, apparently, by women in the court rather than by professional embroiderers. See EMBROIDERY.

Government efforts to import and disseminate textile techniques were particularly prominent in the early 8th century, when common artisans as well as master craftsmen were enthusiastically welcomed from the continent. The TAIKA REFORM of 645 had called for central supervision of textile production, and finally in 701 an Office of the Guild of Needleworkers, an Office of the Guild of Weavers, a Palace Dyeing Office, and a Bureau of the Palace Wardrobe were established. The two latter were responsible for sewing and dyeing for the court, and the two former directed the textile craft in general. The Office of the Guild of Weavers was initially quite small and seems to have put most of its energies into designing, teaching, and supervision. Much of the actual production was done elsewhere in the capital and later in the provinces as well. In 711, this office sent weavers to several outlying districts to teach patterned silk weaving. Apparently these provincial weavers had already attained a fairly high level of the basic skill in the production and weaving of plain silk, for they were able to send *nishiki* and *aya* tribute cloth to the capital in the following year.

Heian Period and Kamakura Period (1185–1333) —— In 794 the capital was moved from Nara to Heiankyō (Kyōto). The Office of the Guild of Weavers and other textile workshops were reestablished within the palace compound, and a weaving district was built to the south of the palace. Provincial weaving steadily improved in quality, and by the end of the 8th century figured silks (nishiki, aya) and complex silk gauze (ra) comprised an important part of tribute payments. Even the distant Tōhoku region (northern Honshū) contributed silk thread.

Intercourse with the continent continued until the end of the 9th century, but the move to Heiankyō coincided with the beginning of a period of national isolation. The world of the Heian court, also, was geographically circumscribed and small in scale. Increasingly disinterested in affairs of state, the Heian aristocrats turned their attention to aesthetic pursuits. The poignant elegance with which they expressed their feelings in poetry and music is also evident in the clothing they wore—in the sculptured, multilayered robes of the women and the wide, loose trousers and full aya (figured twill) or ra (gauze) patterned overgarments worn by men.

Pure color and its combinations were more important in these garments than woven or dyed designs. The multilayered woman's costume (later often referred to as jūnihitoe) consisted of as many as 20 layers, most of which were solid-color, fine, soft silk kimono-like undergarments worn one over the other and showing only in narrow bands at the neck and sleeve openings. Colors were arranged in gradated and contrasting combinations to echo the season, occasion of the day, the mood of the wearer, or a feeling she wanted to convey. Most of the dyeing was done in the palace, tribute textiles being dyed in the cloth after they reached the capital. See DYES AND DYE COLORS.

The art of the pure rendition of color and the sensitivity with which colors were blended and contrasted have probably never been higher. On the whole, however, Heian artisans used fewer and simpler dyeing techniques than their Nara forbears. Only shading, tie-dye (sometimes used to create cloudlike shaded effects), delicate ink brushwork (used, perhaps in combination with embroidery, on the long loose skirt, mo, women might wear over the jūnihitoe), and a simple medallion-patterned stamp, ban-e (generally with Chinese motifs of lions and bears and often used on dancers' and guardsmen's costumes), seem actually to have been used. The major categories of Nara weaves, ra (gauze), aya (figured twill), and nishiki (brocade), continued, but in simplified form. The more subdued monochromatic aya was preferred to the rich ornate potential of nishiki. A typical woven overgarment might have scattered medallion motifs executed in a simple weft-float brocade (futae-ori) in a variety of soft colors over a clear green ground of small-patterned aya. Gradually, smaller and simpler designs emerged that, in time, came to be used to indicate the rank or status of the wearer.

Court culture limped on in the Kamakura period and saw the final standardization of both color combinations, which were organized under clearly defined, though poetic, names, and standardization of woven patterns related to rank (yūsokumon). With the gradual impoverishment of the court, the Office of the Guild of Weavers declined and, in the early 13th century, collapsed. Its place was taken by guildlike groups of private weavers in the capital and in a few provincial areas.

The most interesting group of extant textiles from the turbulent Kamakura period is, appropriately, the armor (see ARMS AND ARMOR). This was typically made of small metal plates laced together by rows of silk braids (KUMIHIMO) executed in a carefully conceived variety of techniques and color combinations designed to astound the enemy. Leather edges and breast plate were decorated with small stencil-dyed patterns made by stamping a stencil (originally probably metal, later tanned paper) into softened deerskin with the feet until it was securely imbedded and then rubbing the color (often safflower crimson and indigo blue) through the stencil opening. Sometimes the leather was simply smoked. This is the earliest definite example of the use of the stencils in Japanese textile history.

Contemporary picture scrolls (EMAKIMONO) tantalizingly suggest the existence of another group of interesting late-Heian and Kamakura period textiles. These scrolls depict commoners dressed in short, narrow-sleeved kimono-type garments with strong designs of woven stripes and checks and, most notably, bold graphic dyed motifs of everyday objects. Some of the designs were probably simply drawn or painted on the cloth, others seem to have employed a well-developed form of stitch-resist, and the underarmor clothing of warriors, in particular, shows motifs that appear to have been executed with some sort of a paste-resist, the first suggestion we have of this important development.

Muromachi Period and Azuchi-Momoyama Period —— From the late Heian period, private trade ships, often sponsored by a wealthy military lord or powerful temple, had brought back small quantities of cloth from Song (Sung) and later Yuan (Yüan) China (11th–14th centuries). Trade increased after official relations were established with Ming (1368–1644) China. In the 16th century significant numbers of textiles began to enter the country from Southeast Asia and India as well, as Portuguese traders and missionaries found their way to Japan and as Japanese trade and pirate ships ventured further afield. From China came new types of patterned silk weaving, damasks (donsu), simple and figured satins (shusu, rinzu), woven stripes (kantō), rich, heavy brocades woven of gold and silver threads (KINRAN AND GINRAN), embroidery (shishū), gold leaf imprint (inkin), new patterned gauzes (RO AND SHA, monsha, kinsha) and, at the very end of the 16th century, light, crinkly silk crepe (CHIRIMEN). From India came cotton calico (SARASA) and handsome stripes (tōzan). A few really exotic textiles found their way into the country, such as the shōgun ASHIKAGA YOSHIMITSU's beloved Chinese ceremonial costume (a gift from the Ming emperor in the early 15th century) and, in the latter half of the 16th century, ODA NOBUNAGA's bird-feathered tabard (jimbaori), TOYOTOMI HIDEYOSHI's tabard with European tapestry designs, as well as hats, trousers, velvet capes, and other articles of European dress. These proved to be a passing fad. It was the new Chinese figured silks, southern stripes, and Indian resist-dyed cottons that were to have a significant and lasting effect on the subsequent development of Japanese textiles.

These imported textiles were coveted by military lords and higher-ranking members of their retinues, aristocrats, Buddhist and Shintō priests, and well-to-do merchants alike, enriching dealers in port towns and in the capital and stimulating domestic attempts to imitate them. The finest were so valuable that they were used only in tiny bits, as edgings of scrolls and for various appurtenances of the TEA CEREMONY, or sewn together as in the fine patchwork coat (dōbuku) that was a valued gift from Oda Nobunaga to UESUGI KENSHIN. Chinese fabrics and imitations and adaptations were also used in the Nō drama as it became fashioned into a symbol of the culture and wealth of its military patrons. See THEATRICAL COSTUMES.

The influx of highly prized textiles from the continent naturally stimulated domestic attempts to imitate them, but this was not easily accomplished, as Ming weaving differed in several important respects from the basically Tang-derived weaving of Muromachi-period Japan. Specifically, it depended for many of its effects on (1) an extensive use of glossed silk (silk with the natural gum or sericin removed), which has a lower tensile strength than unglossed silk, made possible by well-developed techniques of twisting and plying, techniques that also permitted the development of silk crepe; (2) an extensive use of satin weave (an irregular twill with long floats and single interlacements of warp and weft), a weave that shows to advantage the lustrous quality of glossed silk; and (3) the use of improved looms and specifically devices for raising the required pattern threads accurately and quickly. Despite study trips to China and some importation of technical knowledge and improved looms, it was not until the end of the 16th and beginning of the 17th centuries that Japanese weavers fully mastered the major techniques of Ming weaving and were able to imitate the coveted Chinese silks.

During the devastating ŌNIN WAR (1467–77), most of the weavers fled Kyōto, some to the port city of Sakai (near Ōsaka), others to Nara. Much of the capital was burned and the old weaving district was completely destroyed. It was this period that saw the full emergence of the kosode (an early form of KIMONO) as one simple robe of soft white silk with free-style designs executed in a variety of well-known nonloom techniques that required few tools beyond needle, thread, brush, ink, and a dyepot.

The importance of the mid-15th century adoption of the kosode, formerly an undergarment, as dress appropriate even for the most elegant occasions can hardly be overestimated. On its single surface were to be concentrated all the arts of weaver and dyer, and its distinctive form was to foster the development of free-style graphic designs that used the whole robe almost as a canvas. Although the general level of textiles produced during most of the Muromachi period remained low, a general increased prosperity, examples afforded by much-admired imported textiles, and the widespread use of a simple single-layered garment combined to prepare the way for a stunning outburst of new dyed, woven, and embroidered textiles in the 16th and early 17th centuries.

One of the loveliest textiles of the period, and one that represents a milestone in the development of the kosode was known as TSUJI-GAHANA, "flowers-at-the-crossing." In its earliest form it was characterized by stitch-resist graphic designs of birds and flowers enhanced with delicate ink brushwork over a diagonal lattice. The late 15th and the 16th centuries saw the development of *surihaku* (from Chinese *inkin*), stenciled designs of gold or silver foil impressed over paste (contiguous triangles were very popular). Embroidery was sometimes worked to imitate woven brocade. It was sometimes used in conjunction with *tsujigahana*. It was also often employed with *surihaku* (a combination called *nuihaku*) to add a sense of depth and textural richness to the dull, flat sheen of the foil. A paste-resist and stencils were used together to produce tiny-patterned designs (see KOMON) sometimes used by warriors for everyday attire and, in the Edo period (1600–1868), for the stiff *kamishimo*, men's upper garments worn on formal occasions by *daimyō* and higher-class *samurai*.

The weavers returned to the capital in the latter part of the 15th century and settled in what had been the western camp *(nishijin)* during the Ōnin War, an area still known today as Nishijin (see NISHIJIN-ORI). By the beginning of the 16th century they had rebuilt their looms, many of which were used to produce the large quantities of simple, soft white silks and satins needed for ground fabric for the fashionable *tsujigahana*, and embroidered and foil-impressed *kosode*. Powerful guilds vied for control of the market and, after 1571, for the coveted distinction of being designated official weavers to the court. Aided by warlord Toyotomi Hideyoshi's encouragement of the textile industry in general and of Nishijin in particular, weavers from the capital went to Sakai and even to China to study. By the end of the century they were able to start production of luxurious Ming-style gold and silver brocades, damasks and figured satins, silk crepes, and patterned gauzes. They also began to combine and adapt these techniques with older ones to suit the needs and tastes of their luxury-loving, *kosode*-wearing patrons. See KARA-ORI.

Edo Period —— When TOKUGAWA IEYASU set up his new government in Edo (now Tōkyō), Kyōto workshops were firmly reestablished at the hub of a thriving textile industry. New developments in weaving, dyeing, and embroidery appeared in rapid succession to meet the demands of a widening samurai and merchant clientele heady with peace and a growing prosperity. After 1615, these developments took place in relative seclusion from the outside world. They were also shaped by a long series of sumptuary edicts designed not only to encourage frugality on all levels of society, but to make visible the distinctions between the samurai estate and the lower orders of farmer, artisan, and merchant.

The Tokugawa family themselves appreciated fine textiles and patronized the best weavers and dyers, using their products for their own clothing and for the sumptuous costumes of the Nō stages they supported. They also recognized the economic potential of the textile industry and established cartels to control the importation and distribution of highly prized Chinese raw and glossed silk thread (ITOWAPPU).

The continued growth of an urban-centered economy increased the economic power of merchants, who developed a distinctive urban culture, which exercised a very strong influence on the development of the textiles arts. Forbidden to wear the rich brocades beloved by the upper classes, 17th-century merchants and their wives turned to the dyers. Exploiting their techniques to the fullest, the dyers were soon producing textiles to rival the finest products of the Nishijin looms in style, variety, skill, and even sheer expense. *Sōkanoko* is a good example of the spirited interplay between style-conscious merchants and the shogunate edict makers. This was a tie-dyed textile in which a whole *kosode* was covered with minute, hand-tied dots of resisted white, placed with such exquisite care on a simple monochrome ground that a large overall pattern could be suggested merely by leaving the appropriate small sections of the costume untied. The result was unostentatious, except to a practiced eye able to calculate the time and skill required to produce it and thus understand the display of wealth that it represented. The late 17th century also saw the development of paste-resist dyeing to produce freely executed painterly designs. See YŪZEN.

The government issued edict after edict to curb the excesses of samurai and merchant alike, but these were either simply ignored or, more frequently, cleverly circumnavigated, and the 17th century witnessed a wave of increasingly sumptuous and extravagant textiles that peaked in the GENROKU ERA (1688–1704). Genroku was an important watershed in textile history, the final high point in the development of the Kyōto-based woven, embroidered, and dyed silks of the late Momoyama and early Edo periods. Its end marked the beginning of a decline of Kyōto as the most important center of textile production, a general dispersal of the industry to Edo and the

provinces, and an enforced abandonment by the merchants of silks and satins, even if dyed, for the handsome striped, checked, stencil-dyed, and hazy-patterned (KASURI) hemps and cottons that were to be their trademark in the 18th and 19th centuries.

The 18th century opened with a severe inflation that seriously affected the Nishijin district, which was set back further by two serious fires (1730, 1788) and by the defection of weavers with important trade secrets to rival weaving communities. In 1720 some of the best weavers went to Edo to work as official weavers to the Tokugawa, and in 1738 others moved to Kiryū, in what is now Tochigi Prefecture, where the high quality of the work they supervised and the efficient production soon transformed that weaving community into a formidable rival to a faltering Nishijin. The silk industry in general thrived in the late Edo period with early 18th-century improvements in the production of raw silk thread and the development of almost virtuosic weaving and dyeing skills. Like many other arts supported primarily by the later Tokugawa shōguns and their retainers, however, these 18th- and early-19th-century silks seem stultified and repetitious.

The 18th-century commmercialization of all segments of the economy, including agriculture, led to a significant increase in local industry. Cloth used in the cities was increasingly woven in the countryside by peasant weavers who, at least by the end of the century, were often working in well-organized groups. Styles were set by city merchants, especially those in Edo and Ōsaka. Typical of their *asa* and cotton garments were KATAZOME (rice-paste-resist, stencil-dyed cloth), *shima* (woven stripes), and *kasuri* (ikat textiles).

A discussion of the late Edo period would be incomplete without mentioning some of the textiles produced by farmers and fishermen for their own use. A deep INDIGO blue from the vats of the local indigo dyer was the predominant color, and rural textiles include blue and white versions of the *kasuri,* stripes, and *katazome* of the city merchants. Typical also are large pictorial designs reserved with a freely applied paste, such as a felicitous tortoise, crane, and pine-tree motif on a fisherman's festival coat. Although not indigent, these people were frugal, and stitching for added strength and warmth (SASHIKO), patching, and rag weaving *(saki-ori)* were common. Stitching was generally worked into geometric designs, some very complex. Rag weaving was done with equal care. Narrow strips were torn from old cloth, sorted by color (shades of blue), stitched end to end, and woven (as weft) into heavy, warm work jackets. The AINU in northern Japan had their own distinctive clothes. Notable among them is a brown elm-bark fiber coat with geometric appliqué work, often of blue cotton.

Bold but seldom self-consciously ostentatious, with function always a primary consideration, these textiles displayed a rugged vitality and a certain quiet strength later to be so much admired by YANAGI MUNEYOSHI, whose thinking molded the aesthetic for the folkcraft movement of the 20th century. See FOLK CRAFTS.

Another group of textiles much admired by Yanagi and his followers was from the Ryūkyū Islands. OKINAWAN TEXTILES have been highly prized in Japan since they were first introduced through the Satsuma domain (now Kagoshima Prefecture) at the beginning of the Edo period. They are distinguished by a sophisticated yet simple abstract patterning, exquisite craftsmanship, and fine coloration. Beautiful in their own right, they also had a significant influence on the development of certain well-known Japanese textiles, such as *kasuri.*

Meiji Period (1868–1912) to Present —— The Meiji Restoration of 1868 opened floodgates to the West and started Japan on a rapid course of modernization and industrialization. The textile industry, already quite well organized, absorbed simple modernization easily, and the export of raw silk (especially to a Europe suffering from a severe silkworm blight) produced a significant portion of Japan's foreign currency in the 19th century.

The 20th century has seen not only the development of a highly modernized TEXTILE INDUSTRY but also a modest resurgence of public interest in traditional textiles fostered, in part, by the folkcraft movement of the late 1920s. Government legislation (1955, 1975) now attempts to preserve the finest of the old hand-techniques of weaving and dyeing throughout the country. See also TEXTILES, CARE AND PRESERVATION OF.

■ —— Barbara Adachi, *The Living Treasures of Japan* (1973). Endō Motoo, *Orimono no nihonshi* (1971). Japan Textile Color Design Center, *Textile Designs of Japan* (1959), a comprehensive catalog of designs. Tomiyama Hiroki and Ōno Tsutomu, *Nihon no dentō orimono* (1967). Nishimura Hyōbu, *Orimono*, no. 12 of *Nihon no bijutsu* (April 1967), this series includes several other issues on specific textiles or textile techniques. Seiroku Noma, *Japanese*

Costume and Textile Arts, tr Armins Nikouskis (1975). Shōsōin Jimusho, *Shōsōin no hōmotsu: Senshoku: Textiles in the Shōsōin* (1963, 1964), in Japanese and English. Tsunoyama Yukihiro, *Nihon senshoku hattatsu shi* (1968). Yamanobe Tomoyuki, *Some,* no. 6 of *Nihon no bijutsu* (November 1966).   Mary DUSENBURY

textiles, care and preservation of

There are various methods for the daily care and storage of KIMONO and the restoration and conservation of ancient textiles, such as those stored in the 8th-century SHŌSŌIN art repository. The principal object is to preserve the fabric from light, heat, and dust.

A kimono is still an important part of the Japanese wardrobe and many are treasured heirlooms handed down from mother to daughter. After being worn, a kimono is aired before it is put away. The type of kimono, the fiber of which it is woven, and the manner in which it is dyed will determine how it should be folded. There are three major methods of folding a kimono: *hondatami, yagudatami,* and *ishōdatami. Hondatami* causes the fewest creases because the kimono is folded along the seams, but it has the most folds. *Yagudatami* has fewer folds but creates a larger bulk, while *ishōdatami* decreases the chances of fading because the garment is folded inside out. It is advisable to change periodically the method of folding to prevent the development of permanent creases.

After a kimono is folded it is encased in a paper wrapper and stored in a chest with wide, shallow drawers. Mothballs are in common usage today, but it was customary in the past to place in each drawer small pouches of camphor, cloves, sandalwood, aloeswood, and spikenard. Once a year, usually in the summer, kimonos and their accessories are brought out to air in a cool room away from direct sunlight.

A good kimono, usually made of silk, is taken completely apart before it is washed, thoroughly rinsed, and stretched out on a frame to dry. The pieces are then sewn back together by hand. The life span of an old kimono is often extended by bleaching and redyeing.

The conservation of ancient textiles is an even more delicate and time-consuming process. The Shōsōin is rich in textiles brought to China from India and Persia (now Iran) over the famous SILK ROAD and from there to Japan. Conservation work on these textiles has been going on for the past 50 years and continues to this day. Fragments that can be handled are placed on a damp sheet of paper and smoothed with a wet brush. Tweezers are used to align the threads of each piece before it is left to dry. Particularly fragile pieces are reinforced with WASHI, Japanese handmade paper, pasted on with a rice-starch solution (today, insecticide is usually added to this solution); the fragment is then sandwiched between glass or bound and mounted on a folding screen or hanging scroll.   Susan BARBERI

Thai-Japanese Alliance

(Nittai Dōmei). A military alliance between Thailand and Japan during World War II, established under a pact signed in Bangkok on 21 December 1941. Under the terms of the agreement, which went into effect immediately, Thailand and Japan agreed to respect each other's suzerainty, provide mutual aid against military attack from any third power, and refrain from making any separate peace with enemy countries. The pact is also said to have included a secret protocol whereby Japan agreed to help Thailand regain the four states of northern Malaya lost to Britain, and Thailand, to assist Japan in its war against the United States and Great Britain. Thailand did, in fact, declare war against the United States and Britain in January 1942. The alliance was terminated with Japan's defeat in 1945.   ICHIKAWA Kenjirō

Thailand and Japan

Thailand and Japan began trading in the 17th century, and as early as the 1620s, a settlement of Japanese in Thailand was presided over by YAMADA NAGAMASA. The two countries have a natural affinity, sharing a heritage of a rice-based economy, Buddhist religion and culture, and a history of independence from colonial domination. Thailand was allied with Japan during World War II, and although postwar relations have at times been strained by controversies over war reparations and continuing Thai fears of Japanese economic domination, relations between the two countries have increased in scale and importance, especially since the 1970s.

Early Relations —— Early in the 17th century, a settlement of Japanese merchant-adventurers led by Yamada was established in Ayuthaya, then the capital of Siam (Thailand). This NIHOMMACHI, or Japanese town, was burned down by the Siamese in 1630 shortly after the death of Yamada. During the period of Japan's NATIONAL SECLUSION (1639–1858), Siamese goods were brought into Japan by Chinese merchants.

From the mid-19th century, both Siam and Japan engaged in treaty negotiations with Western powers. In fact, Townsend HARRIS, the first American consul general to Japan, negotiated a commercial treaty with Siam before arriving in Japan in 1856 to negotiate a similar treaty. Siam and Japan issued a declaration of friendship in 1887 and signed a trade and navigation treaty in 1898. Siam, however, lagged behind Japan in its efforts to modernize, and at the turn of the century, it invited Japanese advisers to help update its legislation, medical science, railway technology, silkworm cultivation, and arts and crafts. After a constitutional revolution in 1932, Siam followed Japan's lead in demanding the renegotiation of unequal commercial treaties with Western countries. In 1937 Siam regained complete control of trade tariffs with Japan in return for its support in 1933 of Japan's withdrawal from the League of Nations, after the League had placed sanctions on Japan because of its involvement in China. Siam's name became Thailand in 1939.

Relations during World War II —— Japan and Thailand signed a friendship treaty in June 1940, and Thailand joined the Japanese attack on French Indochina in November of that year. Through Japanese mediation, Thailand recovered four border states in Laos and Cambodia from the French in July 1941 (this territory was relinquished after the end of the war). Under the terms of the friendship treaty, immediately after the outbreak of World War II, the Thai government gave permission to Japanese troops to use Thailand as a base for mounting an invasion into British Malay and Burma. Thai Premier Marshal PHIBUL SONGKHRAM concluded an alliance pact with Japan on 21 December 1941 and declared war on the United States and Great Britain in January 1942. Phibul also signed an economic pact in 1942, promising to supply the Japanese army with munitions, and a cultural pact promoting intellectual and student exchange programs. At the same time, PRIDI PHANOMYONG, regent of the king of Thailand, organized the anti-Japanese FREE THAI MOVEMENT (FTM) with the aim of cooperating with similar movements in the United States and Britain.

In July 1943 Japanese Prime Minister TŌJŌ HIDEKI visited Thailand and reached an agreement with Phibul ceding territory under Japanese occupation in British Malay and Burma to Thailand. In return for control over this territory, Phibul was expected to participate in the Greater East Asia Conference held in Tōkyō in November 1943, but he sent Prince Wan Waitayakorn instead and hoped to disassociate himself with the Japanese since defeat seemed inevitable. At the end of 1943, the FTM launched an underground movement against the Japanese army and sent secret information to the British air force for use in air raids on Thailand. In July 1944 Phibul resigned from the premiership and was succeeded by Kuang Aphaiong and a cabinet of FTM ministers.

When the Japanese army in French Indochina suddenly arrested Vichy French officials and imposed a military government, the FTM in Thailand began preparing a military coup against the Japanese army, a plan that did not materialize until 15 August 1945, the date of the Japanese surrender. On 16 August, Pridi, regent of the king, renounced the 1942 declaration of war. Although the United States accepted this move, Britain did not, and occupied Thailand in September to disarm both the Japanese and Thai armies. The Japanese population of 115,000 soldiers and 3,500 civilians in Thailand was held until the summer of 1946, when all of them, apart from 126 Japanese with permanent visas, were repatriated.

The Postwar Period —— Within two years of the end of the war, the civilian government in Thailand concluded peace treaties with Great Britain and China. It joined the United Nations in December 1946. In 1947, however, the military overthrew the civilian government and in 1948 Marshal Phibul was reinstated as premier. He adopted anticommunist and pro-American policies in the cold war period. Meanwhile, occupied Japan began to import Thai rice again early in 1948, and a Japanese government liaison office was set up in Bangkok in March 1951. After the signing of the SAN FRANCISCO PEACE TREATY in September of the same year, diplomatic relations were reestablished and an embassy was opened in Bangkok in 1952.

Remaining unresolved between the two countries was the problem of the wartime special yen account debt that had been accumulated by the Japanese military in Thailand. In April 1955 Phibul, as prime minister, visited Japan, accepted partial payment of ¥5.4 billion (US $15 million), and agreed to the postponement of the remaining ¥9.6 billion (US $26.7 million) payment until 1961. Phibul withdrew from politics after being overthrown in a coup in 1957 and was exiled in Japan from 1958 to 1964. Thai survey groups visited Japan in 1959 and 1961, and joint ventures were begun under a Thai industrial promotion act issued in 1960. In November 1961 Japanese Prime Minister IKEDA HAYATO visited Thailand and announced the payment of the balance of the special yen account debt. Since 1962 Japan has provided factory facilities, machines, and technicians to Thailand, the cost of which has been borne by the Japanese government.

Trade between the two countries had increased steadily. By the end of the 1960s annual imports from Japan reached $470 million (36 percent of Thailand's total imports), while exports to Japan reached $160 million (21 percent of total exports). The imbalance of trade led to governmental and civilian conferences beginning in 1968, through which Thailand promoted the development of new commodities for export to Japan. In the educational field, Japan has assisted in the development of teaching materials and Japanese studies classes for universities since 1965; it has also provided technical assistance for dam, road, and bridge construction, telecommunications, and electric power since 1968.

The 1970s ——— As Japanese firms began to expand their interests in Thailand, anti-Japanese sentiments emerged. In January 1971 university students in Bangkok held demonstrations against what they called Japanese economic imperialism and asked Japan to remedy the trade imbalance. The movement paved the way for the antimilitary coup in October 1973. Under the new civilian government, the student and labor movements flourished. Foreign companies, including Japanese joint ventures, hesitated to increase investment in Thailand during this period. In January 1974 Japanese Prime Minister TANAKA KAKUEI's visit to Thailand was met by vigorous anti-Japanese protest. The issue of foreign investment in Thailand was debated by Thai and foreign economists. After the coups in 1976 and 1977, the military regained power, and the investment climate stabilized. In January 1979, when Thai Premier Kriansak Chamanan visited Japan, the Japanese government promised to provide increased aid for the economic and social development of Thailand.

🔖 ———Nishino Junjirō, *Nittai yonhyakunen shi* (rev ed, 1978).
ICHIKAWA Kenjirō

thalidomide children

Children born between 1958 and 1963 with extreme deformities of arms and legs (phocomelia) and other external and internal body parts. Their mothers had used sedatives or nausea-controlling drugs that contained the chemical thalidomide during their first seven weeks of pregnancy. West Germany, where thalidomide was developed, has 2,000 to 3,000 victims; Japan is second, with more than 1,000, about 200 of whom have reportedly survived into the 1970s.

In late 1957, Dai Nippon Pharmaceuticals applied to Japan's Ministry of Health and Welfare for permission to manufacture thalidomide. The ministry summarily approved the application, although the company provided no data on side or long-term effects. In January 1958, Dai Nippon began selling the drug, and within three years 14 other companies were marketing thalidomide under various names throughout Japan.

The first warning came in November 1961 from the German physician Widuking Lenz, who demonstrated with epidemiological methods a relationship between a sudden rise in the characteristic arm-and-leg deformities of phocomelia and the use of thalidomide by pregnant women. Six days after his announcement, the German pharmaceutical firm ceased production and initiated a recall. By the end of 1961, most Western European nations had followed the German lead of prohibiting thalidomide use.

In Japan, however, officials of the Ministry of Health and Welfare considered the German actions motivated by newspaper sensationalism and not based on scientific proof. Only in May 1962 did Dai Nippon Pharmaceuticals voluntarily stop distributing medicines with thalidomide, and not until September of that year did it begin to recall the drug from store shelves. According to one scientific estimate, this one-year delay after the Lenz warning led to the birth of nearly one-half of the thalidomide children in Japan.

The first civil damage suit for a thalidomide child in Japan was filed in June 1963. By 1972, 63 families had filed suits against both Dai Nippon Pharmaceuticals and the central government. Until 1973, the defendants denied both that thalidomide had caused the birth defects and that the government and industry were legally responsible. As a result, Japan's thalidomide children remained without a program to care for them for 15 years. Only in December 1973, after testimony for the case had concluded at the Tōkyō District Court, did the government and the company admit a cause-and-effect relationship between drug and defects and accept responsibility for the tragedy. They then requested an out-of-court settlement, which was signed in October 1974. In addition to a monetary damage compensation, the government and the company agreed to provide for health management, nursing assistance, rehabilitation programs, education, and employment for the thalidomide children.
🔖 ———Bernard A. Becker, "Teratogens," in Louis J. Casarett and John Doull, ed, *Toxicology: The Basic Science of Poisons* (1975). "Tokushū: Saridomaido jiken no wakai," *Jurisuto* (15 December 1974).
Michael R. REICH

theater, traditional

There are five major genres of Japanese traditional theater: *bugaku* (see GAGAKU), NŌ, KYŌGEN, BUNRAKU, and KABUKI, all of which are still being performed. Though different in content and style, they are linked by strong aesthetic relationships behind which lie centuries of assimilation and modification derived from a confluence of sources, both inside and outside Japan. Cultural interpenetration has provided a common pattern throughout Asia, where the evolution of the performing arts has been governed by concepts that assume an integral relationship between dance, music, and lyrical narrative. These three have always been treated as an extension of the poetic art and their organic synthesis as a cardinal principle of dramatic expression. It is a concept that was given articulate statement in the classical Sanskrit treatises on dance and drama compiled between the 2nd and 8th centuries AD. As texts on the aesthetics of performance, their influence has been far-reaching in Asia, where traditional stage practices owe much to early Hindu sources. In the "Sadoshima nikki" ("Sadoshima's Diary") chapter of *Yakusha rongo* (1776; tr *The Actors' Analects*, 1969), for example, the kabuki actor Sadoshima Chōgorō (1700–57) defines an aesthetic of dance that reads like a paraphrase from the Sanskrit text of Nandikeśvara's *Abhinayadarpanam* (tr *The Mirror of Gesture*, 1936), suggesting deep processes of historical transmission.

Asian theatrical tradition has naturally evolved many distinct styles and modes while exploring various methods of expression which have become characteristic of particular regions over the course of time, but whatever the innovations, the organic synthesis of the disparate elements of speech, music, and dance, remained a basic recipe for performance. It led to the emergence of highly developed presentational styles of which the five Japanese genres named above represent supreme examples. Each of them constitutes a culminating point in a phase of artistic synthesis brought to maturity through succeeding periods of Japanese cultural history.

Among the five genres, *bugaku* stands apart as a ceremonial dance style associated only with court ritual, in which the theatrical element is minimal and music predominates. It incorporates aesthetic and structural principles which were current in the 8th century when Japan was undergoing a period of cultural absorption under the dominant influence of China. *Bugaku* itself as the accessory of *gagaku* is impregnated with admixtures of Central Asian, Indian, and Korean elements assimilated by China from where the fundamental choreographic style of *bugaku* was transmitted to Japan. Ceremonial dancing was common in ancient Chinese ritual, and as far back as the Zhou (Chou) dynasty (1027 BC–256 BC) dance was officially divided into civil and military styles performed for propitiatory purposes. In the treatises of Zhu Zaiyu (Chu Tsai-yü; 1536–1611), who recorded in scientific detail the rules and theories of ancient Chinese dance and music, it is possible to trace the affinities of the symmetrical, rigidly patterned choreography, frequency of paired dancers, and strictly compartmented dance forms of *bugaku* with its ancient Chinese sources. In its final manifestation, however, *bugaku* is an entirely Japanese form that has undergone considerable aesthetic transmutation. It remains as a still-extant style of performance embodying forms and principles long obsolete in continental Asia. In contributing to the pattern of cultural penetration, *bugaku* also signalizes a transitory stage as Japan moved out of the sphere of external cultural influences and traveled an independent path.

Nō, *kyōgen, bunraku,* and *kabuki,* by contrast, are indigenous forms of theatrical expression representative of successive periods of political and social change in Japan. Nō and *kyōgen* both belong to an age when the ferment from Chinese influences was still potent beneath the surface of Japanese cultural exploration; *bunraku* and *kabuki* belong to a period when Japan became politically isolated from the outside world.

Nevertheless, the continuum of traditional Japanese theater reflected adherence to established Asian dramatic principles emphasizing symbolism and allusive imagery, as opposed to the Aristotelian concept of mimesis, the imitation of reality, which has dominated occidental dramatic theory. The high purpose of Japanese theater has been to induce a mood, an immediate aesthetic experience drawing an instantaneous response in the mind of the spectator beyond the constraints of empirical time and space. This is achieved at different levels of provocation commensurate with the nature of the particular theatrical genre, but the principle beneath is constant whatever the level of approach.

The Nō drama, for example, profoundly influenced in aesthetic content and dramatic structure by medieval Buddhist thought, which rejects factual reality as illusory, seeks to reveal the momentariness of a higher reality through stage techniques which stress imagery, metaphor, and symbolism. In Buddhist theory it is only at the moment of instant perception that anything exists, and this points to the fleeting character of all existence, and by inference to the relevance of dramatic expression as evinced in the rhythms of Nō performance and its changing outlines. Nō performance is based on a theory of psychological perception called YŪGEN, just as classical Sanskrit drama was similarly ruled by the theory of *rasa*. Both terms are untranslatable as logical English, and both have separate connotations as the expression of two individual cultures, but both are concerned with the affinity between performer and spectator, defined as an existent mutual aesthetic comprehension released through the transcendental immediacy of the theatric process. Both the Nō and Sanskrit theaters attained maturity as highly refined styles, nonrealistic and nondemocratic in their emphasis on personal communication, as distinct from the civic function of Aristotelian theory. Though Sanskrit drama is now obsolete as a live art, Nō continues as an active embodiment of principles germinal to the classic dramatic theories of an Asian past.

Kyōgen, the comic interludes that are an integral part of Nō performance, poke fun at human frailties long the butt of the professional storyteller, that pillar of the great Asian oral tradition from which the spirit of kyōgen is derived. In its treatment of social pretensions, this entertainment reflects a universal propensity for playing on connubial discord, deflating the self-esteem of authority, mocking at quackery, and highlighting the trials and tribulations of the servant class, which are common themes for jest the world over. Through its use of stylized vocal forms, pantomime, and spatial control, kyōgen preserves some of the formal elegance of Nō with which it is so closely linked. There is a great deal in its artless humor and oral techniques that is reminiscent of the clowning on the traditional Chinese stage and the way the latent reactions of the audience are stimulated. The Chinese comic actor is also descended from a long storytelling tradition and the servants, stupid officials, shrews, and bumpkins he portrays come from the same gallery of characters familiar to the kyōgen actor, with whom the Chinese actor is again united in degrading the priest. In each case the nature of the comic action is physical and situational, inciting revelation of what people would be and what they really are. In both kyōgen and Chinese performance, the comic actor becomes a catalyzing agent through arrangement of his appearance within the main action of the plays. In kyōgen the interval between the principal acts of a Nō performance is given over to the comic actor, and in the Chinese theater the script is devised to yield the stage to him, in both cases as a relief from the tensions of the straight performance.

Bunraku has a unique place in the theater world of Japan, where puppet performance has been accepted on equal terms with orthodox theater. Indeed, it is impossible to speak of bunraku without mention of *kabuki*, because the story of their development has been one of complementary relationships and influences. A sizable part of the kabuki repertoire consists of plays originally devised for the puppet drama, which has also been a seminal influence in shaping kabuki styles of acting. Bunraku in turn has taken much from the sophisticated technical presentation of kabuki and has incorporated some of its popular dance dramas in the puppet repertoire. In their size, the technical construction of their heads, and the general principles of manipulation, bunraku puppets bear a family resemblance to those once common in the Guangdong (Kwantung) area of southern China. However, though there are elemental similarities

suggestive of a common genesis, bunraku puppets are more technically complex and characterized by a degree of formal realism not found in any other Asian puppet forms. The unique bunraku practice of using three puppeteers to manipulate a single character on stage, together with the precise craftsmanship involved in the coordination of narrative and SHAMISEN music, produces a theatric coalescence of considerable emotional intensity. Through such means the audience is able to perceive the fusion of the separate structural elements while experiencing the confluence of their sensory appeal in the dramas acted out before them.

This absolute deployment of speech, sound, movement, and space as equal contributory forces is carried to a supreme point in kabuki. There, theatrical synthesis reaches a powerful degree of instantaneous communication by using visual and aural techniques in cumulative assailment of the playgoer's senses and emotions. A germinative factor in these methods has been the perfecting of narrative musical forms elaborated from earlier styles of ballad recitative to music, and these have profoundly affected the direction of kabuki as a popular entertainment.

There is much in the background and methods of kabuki that is reminiscent of the Beijing (Peking) theater, at least as the latter existed in the past. Both catered to an ordinary public who went to the theater as habitués for whom virtuoso acting was the main attraction. The female impersonator was, and in kabuki still is, central to the nature of performance in China and Japan. The great Chinese female impersonator Mei Lanfang, when invited to perform in Japan in the years 1919, 1924, and 1956, was enthusiastically received by kabuki audiences, a measure of the mutual artistic understanding implicit between the two traditional theater styles. In both of them actresses were proscribed in the interests of ethical codes and preserving public order. It was not until after the Meiji Restoration of 1868 that the restriction was lifted in Japan, whereas Chinese prejudice against women on the stage persisted long after the rise of the Republic in 1911. Paradoxically, female impersonation continues as an accepted feature of kabuki acting, whereas in China it became vitiated and finally relegated to the status of theatrical convention after 1949.

Stylization conditions every level of performance on the kabuki and Beijing stages, where speech makes common cause with pure sound patterns, rhyming, and the play of words made possible through the homonymic nature of Chinese and the syllabism of Japanese linguistic forms. Song is used constantly in both theaters to convey mood, emphasize emotional tensions, and provide an exposition of stage events. In the Chinese theater, however, the actors do all the singing, performing solo and duet to instrumental accompaniment. By contrast, in kabuki it is the members of the narrative music ensembles seated on stage who sing, and in a predominantly choral style. Where a Chinese actor stresses a dramatic climax in a round of song, the actor in kabuki achieves the same purpose with dance and pantomime, accompanied by the vocal artistry of the musical ensemble. The use of stereotyped modal patterns to create mood, tempo, and rhythm, is typical of both Chinese and Japanese traditional music and serves an essential dramatic purpose in complementing the progression of the stage events. The musicians in the two theaters were formerly seated on stage; they no longer are in China, but there was a marked visual contrast between the ritualistic formality of the Japanese musicians and the casual behavior of their Chinese counterparts, although they served a similar theatrical purpose.

Archetypal characterization is the basis for both Chinese and Japanese traditional acting styles and this has led to highly systematized vocal and gestural techniques, dance forms, and combat styles, and these together with costume and makeup are used to identify the specific character roles for the audience. Symbolic use of color, decoration, and historical motifs are essential features of stage costumes, which lay stress on theatrical function and spectacle rather than historical accuracy. It would be true to say, however, that in many kabuki plays, especially those dealing with the merchants and townspeople of the 18th and 19th centuries, there is greater attention to historical accuracy than in the Chinese theater, and this would be true of so many of the elaborate wigs used by the actors, which are a distinctive feature of kabuki stage costuming. The fantastic *kumadori*, painted facial makeup used in kabuki bravura roles to symbolize, good, evil, and the sheer bombast of power, through their color and patterns, have an equivalent in the Chinese *lianpu (lien-p'u)*, the painted makeup of the Beijing stage which is used for similar symbolic functions and styles of acting. They have a long history of usage in China dating from Ming times (1368–1644) and in the past were used in greater elaboration and variety than those of the kabuki.

A significant difference between kabuki and the Chinese theater lies in the former's use of elaborate stage settings and properties, together with the *hanamichi*, or runway, devised to carry the action offstage into the auditorium itself. These settings have been a powerful factor in developing the synthesis of theatric form already discussed and have inspired a method of acting that is unique to the kabuki. The stark, bare, platform of the Chinese stage with its rudimentary properties presents the antithesis of Japanese staging practices, although it is a question of approach rather than intent; the different stage structures serve a single functional purpose in furthering the development of form within space which is so vital within the contexts of the two individual styles of acting.

The kabuki and the Beijing theater represent a culmination of development in two traditional styles of popular theater with collateral relationships. Though different and apart, they have evolved within comparable historical circumstances and have been nourished from the roots of a greater Asian tradition. In this, an aesthetic of dramatic performance has given credence to the provocation of the spectator's total sensory receptivity, in preference to verbal rationalization based on literary and visual logic. Japanese traditional theater has endowed this aesthetic with a unique appeal.

A. C. Scott

theatrical costumes

The particular styles of dress or sets of garments worn in the various traditional performing arts of Japan. Theatrical costumes reflect the period of history in which the stage arts of Japan developed and the social class that patronized the performances. In ancient *bugaku* (see GAGAKU) court dances one sees the flowing trousers and broad sleeves of Heian-period (794–1185) court apparel. In NŌ and KYŌGEN plays one sees robes that were in style in the 15th and 16th centuries and fabrics reflecting the development of complex weaving techniques. On the BUNRAKU and KABUKI stage, the ordinary cotton dress of the Edo-period (1600–1868) merchant class appears alongside silks with stenciled and painted designs. These costumes suggest social status and character, often with little historical accuracy in recreating fashions of the period supposedly represented. But in their style, design, and patterns they have the bold contrast necessary for theatrical effect.

All the stage arts of Japan are tradition oriented, and the types of costumes worn for performances have been prescribed for centuries; costumes have been preserved and collected, and some that are worn today date from the 18th and 19th centuries. In the beginning no clear rules controlled the choice of costume. The actor selected the combination of robes he felt was most appropriate from what was available. Experimentation led to accepted standards. In *bugaku* and Nō this progression from freedom to prescribed tradition was accomplished along with an overall process of regulation, which took place in the 9th and 17th centuries respectively. In bunraku and kabuki, each costume for each role went through a period of experimentation until one actor hit on the perfect assembly.

Bugaku Costumes —— The oldest of Japan's stage arts still performed is the choreographed court dance, or *bugaku*. In the 9th century various dances brought from the Asian continent came together and were integrated to suit Japanese tastes. These slow dances generally use free-flowing, layered costumes which trail behind the performer. Over several layers of silk KIMONO, wide trousers, and figured vest, is worn a broad-sleeved cloak of silk gauze called a *hō*. The color of this garment indicates the style of the dance: orange for dances of the left, often originating in China, and green or blue for dances of the right, which found their way to Japan through Korea. The idea of wearing layers of clothing with edges of each layer showing through at the collar and sleeves was integral to Heian court dress, and though never again as elaborately worked out, continued to influence Japanese apparel through successive periods.

Costumes for more active dances, such as the solo running or military dances, allow for greater freedom of movement by binding the trousers and full-sleeved cloak at the ankles and wrists with drawstrings. Over these a fringed apron of heavy brocade hangs down to the knees and is held in place with a metal belt.

Headgear includes a variety of stiffened black hats or cloth hoods and sometimes a mask. All dancers wear silk shoes *(shigai)*, which swish against the stage floor and emphasize the pulse of the music with a flash of white.

Nō and Kyōgen Costumes —— Nō costumes are the only theatrical costumes that have been recognized as works of art. They are treasured for their sophisticated weaves and designs and are collected and displayed by museums.

The patronage of the shōgun ASHIKAGA YOSHIMITSU, who brought early Nō players into close contact with the 14th-century military aristocracy, prepared the way for the development of sumptuous Nō costumes. Pleased with a day's performance, a lord would reward an actor with a cloak or gown, which would then be worn for performances. Records show that although in the 14th century most of these garments were of plain silk, in the 15th century brocade (NISHIKI), satin, and complex weaves reserved for the privileged class saw increased use on the Nō stage. Many of these were imports from China. Only in the latter part of the 16th century, with the rise of the *kosode* (an early form of kimono) and advances in weaving technology, did Nō costumes develop into stylized garments distinct from everyday wear. By the 17th century, the weavers of the Nishijin district of Kyōto were producing costumes designed especially for the Nō with imaginative, complex designs; the aesthetic of YŪGEN, or refined elegance, which lies at the core of the Nō performance, became the goal in costume production as well. Additional incentive for superior quality in costuming was provided by powerful *daimyō* such as those of the TOKUGAWA FAMILY and HOSOKAWA FAMILY, who vied with each other in building up wardrobes for private performances. By the late 18th century, the large designs and brilliance of the earlier costumes gave way to more subdued, standard-pattern repetition, reflecting the taste of the time. Today, although occasional new patterns are created, most of the Nō costumes produced are imitations of older ones.

Nō costumes are worn in layers—generally a soft underkimono covered by a stiff brocade *kosode* kimono (ATSUITA for male roles and KARA-ORI for female roles). In addition, divided skirts (*ōguchi* or *hangiri*) and cloaks of brocade or gauze (*happi, kariginu, chōken*), often with double-width sleeves, may be worn. Parts of the costume may be donned or discarded during performance, the variety of ways of draping garments greatly increasing their flexibility.

The stiffness of the fabric, aided by liberal padding around the body, gives the costumed figure a well-defined outline and larger-than-life appearance. The restrained movements of the actor-dancer—centered on an erect posture with steps accented by white *tabi* socks and restricted gesture—accentuate the effect. The MASKS, wigs, and headgear complete the sublimation of the actors' individuality.

The choice of costume bespeaks the role and the actor's interpretation. The types of garments worn are prescribed by tradition and dictated by the exact nature of the role, but the particular designs and colors reflect the actor's own vision. In selecting a pattern, the actor will take into account season, density of design, color, correlation with other costumes, and *kurai* or dignity. The same assemblage hardly ever appears twice, even over a period of decades. Each school of Nō has its wardrobe, and the finest costumes are reserved for the sole use of the school's greatest actors.

Costumes for the comic *kyōgen*, which are performed during the intervals between Nō plays, typify the clothing and manners of lower-class *samurai* and servants. The stencil dyes on the cotton *kataginu* (a type of vest) show imaginative use of common objects to create striking designs.

Bunraku Costumes —— The puppet theater developed in the early 17th century. It was a source of romantic escape for the rising merchant class and low-ranking samurai who made up the viewing audience. Stylized realism through lifelike gestures of carefully crafted, large wooden puppets was the goal of the puppeteers. Costumes were devised to suggest body contour, and also to allow for three men to operate each puppet. The style of kimono worn during the Edo period, bound with a broad OBI (sash), provides a ready camouflage for a hole in the back to allow a puppeteer's left hand to hold up the puppet while operating the head from within the body. At the same time, the open sleeves allow another operator to stand away from the puppet and manipulate its arms from behind.

Only when the action requires it is the puppet dressed in layers of clothing. The several layers that make up the real outfit are indicated for the audience by strips of extra material sewn at the collar and sleeve, and by padding the garments. The *obi* is stitched to the kimono. Costume changes involve momentarily ducking out of sight and transferring the head to a new body. Extra-long garments are used to create an impression of joints and limbs by means of diagonal balance and angular movements. Feet for the female puppets are indicated by the operator by plumping the hem of the kimono with his fists.

A costumer creates, cares for, and coordinates the costumes, relying heavily on tradition. Patterns and colors suggest character traits such as wickedness or submissiveness as well as social status and role. Though the costumes are not unlike those used in kabuki, they have generally been free from restrictive regulations. Since the material used was not woven specially for the puppets, the designs are disproportionately large, an effective stage device copied by kabuki actors.

Kabuki Costumes —— Kabuki also prospered in the Edo period. While many kabuki stories are based on historical episodes, for which clever reconstructions of samurai dress and armor were devised, others present romances among the merchant class. For these, the costumes reflect the everyday clothing of the merchant, wife, GEISHA, and dandy. Actors competed to introduce new fashions and colors, many of which were adopted by fashion-conscious people in the audience. Kabuki helped popularize the use of family CRESTS (mon) as decoration on the sleeves, front, and back of the kimono; fashions in designs and ways of tying obi were also influenced by kabuki.

By the Genroku era (1688–1704), when kabuki was in full flower, costuming had become extravagant and flamboyant. But in the 18th century government sumptuary laws barred commoners (including actors) from wearing certain colors and complex weaves, and actors were forced to find ways to bypass the regulations; this they did by substituting embroidery for brocade and by inventing new uses of stencil dyes. The need for unencumbered movement led to such theatrical innovations as stiffening the oversized sleeve of the suō (a broad-sleeved jacket) with bamboo splints to convert it into the semblance of a shield, and false collars to suggest the many layers of a Heian woman's costume without its weight. Emphasis on splashy effect gave rise to the art of onstage quick costume changes (hikinuki). By removing a few key threads, a costume is unsewn in seconds, and the actor appears in new array. In the Meiji period (1868–1912), the lifting of government restrictions on apparel led to a vogue of realism aimed at historical accuracy, destroying the unique inventiveness characteristic of kabuki costume.

Until theater costume departments were established in the Meiji period, each actor was responsible for his own wardrobe. The unbalance this created was offset by the advantages of competition, which permitted an actor to advance his fame through elaborate costuming that he could pass on as tradition to successive actors.

Often the patterns used in costumes contained implicit messages in their color or design. Bandō Hikosaburō IV (1800–1873) had the characters of his name worked into a repeat design on cloth that now goes by his name. By slipping off one sleeve, actors playing the Soga brothers (see SOGA MONOGATARI) in Kongen kusazuri biki reveal their personalities by means of pictures reading "I care" and "I don't care" on their under kimonos. Such explicit use of costume as an extra-verbal supplement of the action corresponds to the complex punning and double meanings found in kabuki dialogue. See also CLOTHING; TEXTILES.

📖 —— Fujishiro Tsugio, Shashin de miru Nō no shōzoku (1972). Kitamura Tetsurō, Nōshōzoku, in Nihon no bijutsu, vol 42 (1970). Noma Seiroku, Japanese Costumes and Textile Arts, tr Armins Nikovskis (1974). Ruth H. Shaver, Kabuki Costume (1966). Tokugawa Yoshinobu, Tokugawa Collection: Nō Robes and Masks (1977). Carl Wolz, Bugaku: Japanese Court Dance (1971). Monica BETHE

theocracy

(shinsei). The ancient Japanese state was, at least in theory, a theocracy in that religious ceremonies (matsuri) and the act of governing (matsurigoto) were regarded as one, the emperor (tennō) being the central figure in both the government and the indigenous Japanese Shintō religion. The emperor was held to be "a god in the form of a man" (arahitogami), not merely a representative of the gods, whose sovereign function it was as chief-of-state and high priest to perform those ceremonies upon which the welfare of the nation was believed to rest. The imperial system was an actualization of these two ideas of the unity of religion and government and of emperor-as-god. Although actual government power was almost always held by secular figures, this system remained a basic principle until the 1947 CONSTITUTION established the separation of religion and state and ensured freedom of religion. FUJITA Tomio

thistles

(azami). Perennial herbs of the family Compositae. The species most commonly found in Japan is the noazami (Cirsium japonicum), which is widely distributed throughout the country except for Hokkaidō. It reaches a height of 60–90 centimeters (24–35 in). The spiny stem branches at the head and bears reddish purple tubulous flowers in May and June. The noazami is distinguished from other thistle plants by the sticky substance on its involucre. Many varieties are found in Japan, with flowers ranging from white to pale red and dark purple. The hanaazami and doitsuazami, used in flower arrangements, are varieties of the noazami.

Other Japanese thistle species include the noharaazami (C. tanakae), which closely resembles the noazami but has no sticky substance on its involucre; the taiazami (C. fauriei), with spiny leaves, which grows to over 1 meter (3.3 ft) in height; the moriazami (C. dipsacolepis), with thick edible roots; the hamaazami (C. maritimum), found on beaches; and the largest of all, fujiazami (C. purpuratum). MATSUDA Osamu

this-worldliness

(gensei shugi). Generally speaking, Japanese religions emphasize not death and the afterlife but the procurement of blessings in the present life and for this reason are often described as "this-worldly." Among Japanese there is a strong tendency to see this world as continuous with the next or other world. As a result of this attitude, the solution to the problems of sin and suffering is sought in the present world, and acquisition of material benefits through the agency of gods and Buddhas in the other world holds an important role in religious activities. Prayers are often said for rain or sun, eradication of disease, greater fortune, and so forth. Consequently, self-denial and rejection of the things of this world do not in general have the importance given them by other religions.

This tendency is found not only in the indigenous SHINTŌ faith but in BUDDHISM as well. Buddhism was first introduced to Japan in the 6th century as a means of gaining worldly benefits, especially to enhance the power of the fledgling state. With the introduction of ESOTERIC BUDDHISM, esoteric Buddhist rituals for this-worldly benefits came to play an important role in Japanese religious life. Today, the so-called NEW RELIGIONS appeal most strongly to those looking for the realization of an ideal life here and now. FUJITA Tomio

thought and culture

The fundamental changes in Japanese history have arisen from the introduction of wet-rice agriculture from South China and machine industry from the West, producing first an agricultural revolution and then an industrial revolution. The effects have been so deep and extensive that the history of Japan can be divided into a stone-tool age, an agricultural age, and an industrial age. The first, a long period characterized by the use of stone tools made by hand, was a time when life was sustained, and culture formed, by the hunting of wild animals and the gathering of food from trees and other plants that could survive in the climate of the Japanese islands. This was a period thousands of years long that came to a close around the end of the Jōmon period (ca 10,000 BC–ca 300 BC). The second age, running from the beginning of the Yayoi period (ca 300 BC–ca AD 300) to the end of the Edo period in 1868, was a time when society and culture were formed by a life in which productivity was increased by the use of metal tools for rice production and handicraft industry, and when a maximum use was made of Japan's special climatic conditions. But no sharp break occurred between the food-gathering and agricultural ages for, as archaeological investigations show, a centuries-long transition ensued in which food gathering and rice agriculture coexisted. Another long transition will probably occur between Japan's agricultural age and its industrial age, for only 100 years have elapsed since machine production became prominent. It can therefore be assumed that only after another long period of transition will production be entirely by machines, leading to a time when life and culture will be disassociated from climatic conditions.

If one accepts this periodization, an entirely different view of Japanese history emerges. Japanese scholars would have to realize, first of all, that what has been viewed as the special character of Japanese thought and culture is no more than the special character of life in Japan during the 2,000 years or so of wet-rice agriculture, which is now being rapidly changed by the concerns and interests of souls of loyal retainers and righteous warriors who had lost their lives in a civil or foreign war. Moreover, a *kami* worshiped at a particular shrine was frequently replaced by another *kami,* sometimes without the worshipers realizing that a change had been made. Such lack of interest in the identity of a *kami* led the poet SAIGYŌ (1118–90) to state that "It does not matter who or what is enshrined."

That the forms of *kami* worship, as well as the nature and identity of *kami,* were constantly changing is closely related with another fact: the absence of any original or basic doctrine of belief, leaving Japan's religion without sacred scriptures like the Judeo-Christian Bible or the Islamic Koran. And yet throughout Shintō history there was always an urge for the religion to express itself doctrinally. This apparent contradiction of having no basic scripture and at the same time wanting to express itself doctrinally has given the history of Shintō an intellectual fragmentation and historical discontinuity not found in other living religions. Shintō does, however, have three basic qualities that have been obstinately retained until the present day.

Functionalism. The first quality is what might be called "the logic of disguise and transformation," a quality that is not prominent in other religions but is a function of Shintō's lack of articulated thought. The logic of disguise and transformation is similar to the linking by association that often takes place in the linked verse genre called *renga* (see RENGA AND HAIKAI), a popular poetic form of the Muromachi period. In this poetry each verse was composed by a different poet. Any given verse took on various meanings from the verses that followed it. For example, when a given verse "the flickering flames seen/are but the firefly" *(hi ka to miyuru wa/hotaru narikeri)* is followed by "Amidst the reeds/enfolding the fisher's boat/in the dark night" *(isaribune/tomaru ashima no/kuraki yo ni),* the "flames" in the first verse then by association take on the meaning of a fishing fire. If another verse "How quickly spring has gone/among the darkly scorched pampas/growing dense in fields" *(haru wa haya/suguro no susuki/shigeru no ni)* is then affixed, the "flames" become a lingering field fire. Such connections between a given verse and affixed verses are not unlike the connections between various forms of *kami* worship at different times and places, connections made by the "logic of disguise and transformation." This kind of loose linkage, which can be referred to as functionalism, is the best explanation for the rather nebulous way widely different forms of Shintō thought and practice have been tied together. It is appropriate to use this term to express a logic of thought formation marked by a free change of form involving a continuous return to a new starting point, not to a single point in history but to a series of starting points—a logic that is a kind of dialectic between rapid change and restorative strength, compromise and preservation, change and continuity.

Life centeredness. While functionalism refers to the quality that lies behind the changeableness of Shintō beliefs and practices (to the change of the doll's clothing), the doll itself has had two additional qualities. The first is found in the worship—throughout the entire span of Shintō history—of the creative or procreative power *(musubi)* of *kami.* *Kami* have always been thought of as having an unseen mysterious power (a procreative spirit) to propagate and enrich all forms of life. *Kami*-honoring festivals *(matsuri)* are made up of rituals for the renewal or strengthening of the procreative power. Rites performed at a *matsuri* are thus a form of magic. All prayers offered up to *kami* are essentially requests that life be generated or enriched—for greater physical comfort or greater prosperity. Muraoka Tsunetsugu has pointed out that the ethic of ancient Shintō assumed that anything in harmony with the exercise of the mysterious power of a life-giving *kami* was "good" and that anything obstructing it was "bad." Only to the extent that Shintō was fused with future-oriented religions like Buddhism or Christianity was it ever concerned with the question of death. No evidence can be found in the *Kojiki, Nihon shoki,* FUDOKI, MAN'YŌSHŪ, or KOGO SHŪI that a *kami* worshiped at a shrine was ever buried in a grave, or that a person buried in a grave was ever worshiped at a shrine. This does not mean that the Japanese people had no conception of what followed life but rather that concerns about death lay outside the sphere of *kami* worship. Therefore when Buddhism was introduced to Japan in the 6th century, death and rites honoring the dead were thought of as Buddhist concerns. Thus we have a phenomenon unlike anything seen elsewhere in the religions of the civilized world: a dividing-up of religious functions by which *kami* worship was focused on life and Buddhist worship on death.

Community-ism. The third quality of *kami* worship is seen in a common, deep, and pervasive assumption that the procreative power

he
r-
e.
as
ng
at
00
he
at
ef
ve
ri-
es
ke
ke
pa-
ve
ns,
lar
of
m,
en
nor
en-
pre

f a
nd
s a
out
sic
ali-
ms
iod
yth
co-
rial
untry.
Kamakura
and the Shintō

doll was given a new set of clothes: *kami* were now thought of as manifestations of Buddha with the modification of the concept of HONJI SUIJAKU (prime noumenon and its manifestations) and the syncretic religion known as RYŌBU SHINTŌ (Dual Shintō). Then in the Muromachi period (1333–1568), when ZEN Buddhism provided stimulation for new intellectual and cultural developments and the syncretistic Three Teachings (Confucianism, Buddhism, and Taoism) were popular, the old clothes of the previous period were discarded in favor of a new garb: YOSHIDA SHINTŌ. After the beginning of the Edo period (1600–1868) and the support of Confucianism by the Tokugawa shogunate, the Shintō doll appeared as Confucian Shintō (Juka Shintō), for example, Ritō-shinchi Shintō or SUIKA SHINTŌ. But in the middle of that same period, when native thought known as National Learning (KOKUGAKU) began to spread, the old Confucian clothes were replaced with Ancient Learning Shintō (Kogaku Shintō). Then the addition of Christian influences to National Learning thought produced Ancient Way Shintō (Kodō Shintō) and *kami*-Christ Shintō (Shinki Shūgō Shintō). At the beginning of the Meiji period in 1868 and the establishment of what has been described as the "family-state ideology," Shintō took the form of STATE SHINTŌ or SHRINE SHINTŌ. And after World War II all imperialistic thoughts and practices were eliminated and new democratic ones embraced.

Looking back over the history of Shintō, we find that, along with changes in its external features of *kami* worship, ideas about the nature of *kami* also changed. Most *kami* discussed in the 8th-century *Kojiki* were thought of as ancestral *kami* of prominent families, especially the imperial family. But during the later period of Shintō fusion with Buddhism, a *kami* was seen as a manifestation of a particular Buddha or bodhisattva, and at later times of Confucian influence—especially after 1600—as a manifestation of the Supreme Ultimate (Taikyoku). The rise of National Learning caused people to think of their deities as ancestral *kami* of Japan's imperial house and of the people themselves, and under the influence of Christianity as creators, sustainers, or supreme judges—something like a *deus.* And with the post-1868 preoccupation with state Shintō, a *kami* was no longer simply an ancestral *kami* of the IMPERIAL HOUSEHOLD and the Japanese people but was identified with the of a *kami* is effective only within a clearly defined geographical area, benefiting only the community residing in that area. In other words, a *kami* exercises its mysterious life-giving power in only one particular area, whether big or small, and is never a universalistic deity that exercises its power everywhere. (The old word used for such particularistic exercise of *kami* power was *shiru*, which also denoted the marking off of boundaries, such as stretching a rope [*shimenawa*] around a particular area. The area marked off for *kami* occupation was then called a *shiro*—the noun form of *shiru*; this area might be an entire island or province. The place for *kami* worship [*yashiro*] also contained the noun *shiro*.) From such thinking emerged the idea that a sacred land or province (*shinkoku*) was a taboo area that had been occupied by a particular *kami*. Here too are the origins of the political and intellectual logic which led people to use *shiru* when referring to the administration of political affairs and also to the acquisition of knowledge.

A *kami*-honoring festival carried out by a community residing in a clearly defined geographical area was held for the purpose of renewing and increasing the strength of the community, thereby strengthening its solidarity. For individual members, the ethical ideal was harmony (*wa*). All actions that obstructed harmony were bad (*ashi*), and those that advanced it were good (*yoshi*). The ancient Shintō insistence upon rightness (MAKOTO) and correct feelings (*naoki kokoro*) arose from a persistent and deep desire to harmonize an individual's actions with the community's collective will.

A *kami* could and did extend its occupied area whenever its power, and the power of the worshiping community, expanded. Areas occupied by other *kami* were incorporated therein. The Shintō view of space as developed mythologically and historically is thought to have provided the prototype of a world outlook expressed in such terms as *bampō o shite sono tokoro o eshimu* (let ten thousand countries occupy the proper territories) and HAKKŌ ICHIU (let the whole world be under one roof). The idea that a *kami*-occupied area, while closed and self-contained, could be indefinitely expanded stands in sharp contrast to the Chinese idea of the Four Areas and the Five Directions and of the Five Generalships and the Nine Provinces.

So while Shintō has been adapting itself to the changing conditions of Japanese history—taking on different forms of thought and ritual—it has had three special qualities: functionalism; life-centeredness; and community-ism. Its life-centeredness is rooted in reverence for life and is marked by a practical life-will in which prayers are offered up for the procreation of life, for the regeneration of life, and for the prosperity of life. The place where this life-centeredness (the basic life principle) is actualized is the community. And the logic by which life-centeredness, and community-ism are realized is here called funtionalism. Thus *kami* worship of Japan has had three mutually interdependent dimensions. A *kami* may be said to be a deification of the community life-will that is subjected to change according to the conditions of time and place. A *kami* does not transcend human society or the historical changes of society, nor is it universal or eternal, as in such religions as Christianity and Islam.

Development——Foreign as well as indigenous principles of cultural formation were influential throughout Japan's agricultural age. As early as the Nara period, Tang (T'ang) China cultural imports had qualities that did not exist in, and were in conflict with, the basic qualities of Japanese culture discussed above, pitting China's classicism against Japan's functionalism, the idealism of China against the realism (life-centeredness) of Japan, and Chinese universalism against Japanese community-ism. Thus the development of Japanese thought and culture in the agricultural age can be traced by analyzing the continuous interaction between foreign and native cultural characteristics.

Stages of Chinese cultural influence. The interaction between Chinese and Japanese principles of cultural formation is most clearly seen in the history of Japanese law, contrasting the aristocratic (Chinese) laws of the pre-Kamakura periods with the military (Japanese) laws of the Kamakura period and after.

The years of the Nara and early Heian periods, roughly 700 to 900, are commonly referred to as the time of government by law, a form of government based on penal and administrative laws (*ritsuryō*; see RITSURYŌ SYSTEM) introduced from China. These imported laws had been codified in China for the purpose of realizing Confucian political ideals that were universal and eternal—transcending time, place, and man. It was assumed that by following such laws, Confucian ideals could be realized anywhere and at anytime. But the military laws that emerged in Japan after the beginning of the

Kamakura period were for a military government and had been developed by military leaders who had emerged victorious from the JŌKYŪ DISTURBANCE of 1221. The Jōei Shikimoku (see GOSEIBAI SHIKIMOKU), a classical military code compiled by HŌJŌ YASUTOKI (1183–1242) in 1232, did not therefore take the form of a Chinese penal and criminal code but was compiled with stress upon the military Way of Reason (*dōri*). Articles of frugality and respect for *kami* would seem to be appropriate for any age, but 13th-century military officials felt that these articles, as well as others, were particularly required by the conditions of the day. Nevertheless, the Jōei Shikimoku was to become a classical code for later military governments as well, down to the end of the Edo period in 1868. Of course later military officials did not consider 13th-century laws suitable for their own times but honored the Jōei Shikimoku as a classic, not because it helped them to resolve current problems but because it revealed the military-government ideal: the Way of Reason. It was felt that by reading the Jōei Shikimoku carefully a person would come to comprehend the theory (functionalism) of military administration. So this first classical military code was not at all like the Chinese classical codes that had provided pre-1200 Japanese aristocrats with eternal and universal foundations of government.

When dealing with later administrative and judicial affairs, military officials of the Muromachi period tried to apply the Way of Reason to the conditions of their day by making their own *shikimoku* and additions (*shikimoku tsuika*) to them; and military officials of the Edo period frequently issued prohibitions called *hatto* (see, for example, BUKE SHOHATTO). Although collections of such laws were made in order to establish basic standards for administration and justice, no attempts were made to theorize principles of military government, or to codify premises for the actualization of those principles. The spirit of the Jōei Shikimoku was thus inherited and developed. As to the meaning of the Way of Reason (the basic principle of military government after the codification of the Jōei Shikimoku), it can be concluded that it was not merely military custom but, in the final analysis, expressed a military community's desire for a life of peace and prosperity at each point in time.

In sum, classicism can be seen as a theory of cultural formation that arose from Chinese attempts to faithfully honor and actualize—anywhere and at any time—classical models formed by the symbolization and conceptualization of what were considered eternally and universally valid ideas. Functionalism, on the other hand, is seen as a theory of cultural formation manifested in concrete forms that have been constantly changing in response to the special conditions of particular times and places.

In studying the interaction between two types of Chinese culture (that rooted in the agricultural life of South China, and that of North China), and the culture of Japan, we detect three distinct periods. During the first period Japan was subjected to the influence of the system of thought based upon the Chinese cosmological theory of the five elements, along with Confucianism and Taoism introduced from North China, but in those early times not many art forms or institutional arrangements were introduced, and, consequently, Japan's wet-rice culture was not yet deeply affected by Chinese civilization. The second period, beginning in about 600, was marked by massive and rapid importation of a wide range of cultural forms from North China, creating a Chinese cultural layer above the indigenous Japanese one. After about 900, these imports were gradually Japanized by a process that strengthened and stimulated Japan's unique culture. The third period, beginning after about 1200, was a time when continental influence was largely from South China. By then Japanese culture had been strengthened by importations from North China and now, after a period of Japanization, southern Chinese imports were used for creating greater Japanese cultural independence. So in considering the interaction between Chinese and Japanese culture, we should give careful consideration to the Japanese response to different types of Chinese influence in different periods of history. We should also consider the way the Japanese qualities discussed above interacted with opposing Chinese ones.

Life-centeredness versus transcendence. The effect of life-centeredness on the transcendent teachings of imported Buddhism is most clearly revealed in the fact that Japanese Buddhists of the Nara period taught that the worship of Buddha could benefit this life. Priests prayed for the protection of the state according to the teachings of the Golden Light Sutra (J: *Konkōmyō kyō*; Skt: *Suvarṇaprabhāsottama-sūtra*) and the Kegon Sutra (J: *Kegonkyō*; Skt: *Avataṃsaka-sūtra*), and during the Heian period, according to the LOTUS SUTRA (J: *Myōhō renge kyō*; Skt: *Saddharmapuṇḍarīka-sūtra*). After about the middle of the Heian period esoteric Buddhism of the TENDAI SECT and SHINGON SECT—in which practitioners sought worldly benefits—became popular. It was then that the Buddhist doctrine of expedience (hōben setsu), associated with an emphasis upon worldly benefits, affected Shintō thought, resulting in the development of what has been called a Shintō-Buddhist fusion (shimbutsu shūgō).

The mainstream of aristocratic Buddhism, generally referred to as Holy Path Buddhism (shōdō bukkyō), held that "everything has a Buddha nature" and included two doctrinal tendencies drawing men's minds from the particular to the universal and transcendent: the "realizing Buddhahood" (shikaku) tenet that a person (the particular) could achieve Buddhahood (the universal) by Buddha's power; and the "innate Buddhahood" (HONGAKU) tenet that an individual has the power to fuse Buddha with himself or is himself the Buddha.

Both tenets are found in the writings of SAICHŌ (767–822), the founder of the Tendai sect of Japan. "Realizing Buddhahood" is seen in his argument that the Lotus Sutra (Buddha's last and highest teaching) contains an easy way of salvation (igyō) that was imparted by Buddha in order to show sentient beings how they might be saved through expedient means. "Innate Buddhahood" is found in such statements as the one which declares that Buddha-nature is inherent in each individual, even before he experiences enlightenment. From the former emerged PURE LAND BUDDHISM; and from the latter came the school of oral transmission (kudenhōmon).

The religious movement that emerged from the "realizing Buddhahood" tenet, Pure Land Buddhism, began to develop on Mt. Hiei (Hieizan; see ENRYAKUJI) with the work of the monk GENSHIN (942–1017), who taught that the individual would be welcomed by the Buddha AMIDA (Skt: Amitābha) into the Pure Land paradise after death if that person followed the "easy way" of constantly reflecting on the beautiful features of Amida (kansō). Next, HŌNEN (1133–1212) maintained that if a person followed the "easy way" of repeating the sacred name of Amida (see NEMBUTSU), he would receive the blessings of Amida while alive and be welcomed into the Pure Land by Amida immediately after death. SHINRAN (1173–1263) went further and taught that if an individual simply had faith in the power of Amida's original vow (hongan), the power of that "original vow" would reside in his defiled heart, making it possible for him to be reborn in the Pure Land paradise after death. In short, Amida would live in this world with every individual; a believer would be promised rebirth in paradise while continuing to be engaged in such secular activities as fishing, farming, hunting, trading, and gratifying his personal desires. During the latter part of the Muromachi period, "original vow temples" (honganji) of the Pure Land sect were built in towns or villages where the economic activities of townspeople were honored and encouraged as "sacred service" to Amida. It should be borne in mind, however, that after death, and after birth in Pure Land paradise, the individual was thought of as having, by his own power and Buddha's help, discarded his particular passions (bonnō) and having been elevated to the universal state of Buddhahood.

"Innate Buddhahood" ideas can also be detected in the writings of Genshin. In his classic treatise, ŌJŌYŌSHŪ (The Essentials of Pure Land Rebirth), he exalts Pure Land thought but makes the following point about the lostness (mayoi) of human beings: since all sentient beings are emanations of the full awareness (engaku) of Buddha, both life and death are nirvana and all passions are Buddhahood. For him both are the same thing, with nothing standing between man and full awareness. Genshin lamented the fact that human beings, having been blinded by impure desires, had forgotten the road of innate Buddhahood. So while Genshin was later thought of as the founder of the Pure Land movement, he was also thought of as the founder of innate Tendai Buddhism or the school of oral transmission. But after him, Pure Land and innate Buddhism were sharply differentiated. According to a recent author, the oral tradition and doctrines written down on strips of paper (kirigami) of the latter Buddhism began to be collected after about the 12th century. Some time toward the close of the 13th century they were compiled into what was called the Sanjūyonka no kotogaki (The Thirty-Four Articles). By this development, the particular is accepted as the universal and enlightenment is thought not to exist outside the passions of sentient human beings.

Toward the end of the Kamakura period the two Buddhist currents ran parallel—and stood in intellectual opposition—to each other; they then merged in the higher synthesis of Zen Buddhism. This merger is reflected in the Zen concept of "my heart is Buddha" (zeshin zebutsu) in which the mundane is elevated to the divine and the divine is brought down to the mundane. Now particularity itself is universality. By taking the position that there is no universal outside the particular, Zen teachings have placed Buddha completely within the individual. Finally Giyō Hōshū (1363–1424) of the RINZAI SECT of Zen proclaimed a unity of Zen and Confucianism. He further maintained that, since there was a relationship of form and function between the two, a person who had achieved Zen enlightenment would be able to realize it in human society according to Confucian principles. Later on, FUJIWARA SEIKA (1561–1619) and HAYASHI RAZAN (1583–1657) advocated a Confucianism that was independent of Zen. These Edo-period Confucianists gave greater emphasis than did others to the sovereignty and creativity of the Great Ultimate, not as a celestial entity but rather as a principle existing within human society as the will of community life, for the community ethic or, as they called it, the will of heaven (temmei) was not realizable outside the life of the community. Probably we can say that by making use of Confucianism organizationally, and on a grand scale, they were deifying the will of community life in a Shintō manner.

Community-ism versus universalism. When the Japanese imperial court introduced the ritsuryō system during the reign of Emperor Temmu (r 672–686), it tended to destroy the power of the families (uji) that were the foundation stones of the old UJI-KABANE SYSTEM. Sub-families, however, were recognized as families with their own chieftains (uji no kami) who were then given titles (kabane). After assessing the power and titles of clans and the personal abilities of their chieftains, these leaders were given appropriate offices and ranks in the new administrative structure. Thus the new sinified system, and its rationale, were placed above the old clan system and its rationale, creating a two-layered state structure and supporting ideology. The Kojiki and Nihon shoki were compiled in response to this two-layered situation.

Ideologically, the old Shintō view of a great sacred ruler (ōgimi)—handed down from the family or clan age and centered on the idea that a ruler should be descended from the sun goddess (AMATERASU ŌMIKAMI)—now stood below the imported Confucian idea that a virtuous ruler was the son of heaven (tenshi) who receives the heavenly commands and the Buddhist idea that he was a state head (kokuō) who receives Buddha's protection. From these two thought layers emerged the idea of Japan's sovereign as an EMPEROR (tennō) descended from the sun goddess and protected both by heaven and Buddha.

Placing a Chinese-like bureaucracy above family chieftains also produced a two-tiered court aristocracy that was symbolized—around the 10th century—by the phrase "Japanese spirit and Chinese knowledge" (WAKON KANSAI). As time passed, the two layers began to combine to such an extent that emperors had to issue regulations that were in clear conflict with the sinified civil and penal codes compiled more than two centuries earlier. Attempts were made to incorporate offending regulations into the old legal codes and, in that way, to revitalize them, but after Japan discontinued the practice of sending official missions to China at the end of the 9th century, deterioration of the sinified upper layer advanced rapidly. This process is clearly seen in the early years of REGENCY GOVERNMENT when FUJIWARA FAMILY heads, always close relatives of a young emperor's mother, conducted affairs of state as the emperor's regent; but it is even clearer toward the end of the Heian period when a retired sovereign assumed control of administrative affairs as head of the imperial house (see INSEI).

In the military government of the Kamakura period, community-ism, rooted in the life of wet-rice agriculture, became directly and openly manifested in the structure and ideas of Japanese politics. Since, however, relationships of control characteristic of a military house were then merely introduced into those of an aristocratic house, the feudal age had, strictly speaking, not yet arrived; and as the period of the Hōjō regency was ushered in, at the end of the 13th and the beginning of the 14th centuries, the two types of house still existed side by side. But with the Muromachi period, forms of military politics were firmly established; and at that time the political structures of aristocratic houses were embraced by, and fused with, those of military houses, giving rise to a military system focused on military governors (SHUGO) and absorbing the provincial governors (KOKUSHI) of the old legal codes into its system.

The ideology of this militarized order was found in the Zen thought of the Rinzai sect which propounded such ideas as "my heart is Buddha," the "pliable heart" (jūnanshin), and "harmony" (wa) as making it possible for a community (kyōdōtai) to be established anywhere at any time. Eventually, with the advocacy of a Zen and Confucian unity, the Zen idea of a flexible heart was identified with the Zhu Xi (Chu Hsi) Confucian idea of "the middle not yet developed" (mihatsu no chū), the objective base upon which a morally ordered community could be realized. This Zen-Confucian ideology supported the establishment of feudal communities by daimyō (warlords) during Japan's civil war period (roughly between 1467 and 1568).

It was not, however, until the Edo period that the Shintō conception of space and other Shintō assumptions were fully realized in the structure and thought of the state. This came at the time of building a domain (HAN) system in which han (headed by a warlord whose house had emerged during the period of civil wars) was now subordinated to the SHOGUNATE, the centralized military government headed by a shōgun. It was then that the Zhu Xi school of Confucianism (see SHUSHIGAKU) supplied feudal communities with an ideology which proclaimed that the sovereign will of heaven was immanent in, and realized by, the centralized control of the shogunate and the local control of a han. The townspeople (CHŌNIN) of the period accepted this ideology and ISHIDA BAIGAN (1685–1744) transformed it into one for the governed. But the person who, from a position among the townspeople, transformed this ideology into a new kind of Shintōism was MOTOORI NORINAGA (1730–1801). By making use of the universalism of Zhu Xi philosophy, he tried to give an international character to Japan's particularistic Shintō principles, making them potentially realizable all over the world. Here is a notable case of the Shintō conception of space being broadened and reproduced.

Functionalism and classicism. In the Nara period when the sinified ritsuryō system was being established, the logic of Chinese classicism was introduced, along with cultural artifacts and institutional forms, to Japan from North China. This logic was gradually weakened by Japan's unique logic of functionalism which emerged from the life of wet-rice agriculture. The interaction between the two led to the development of a hybrid "logic of accommodation to the requirements of time, place, and human ability" (jishoki sōō no ronri), one which argued that ideal models should be adapted to the current situation. This logic was propounded by Saichō, who claimed that his particular form of Buddhism was appropriate to the age of transition from imitation law (zōhō) to the end of law (mappō) to the peripheral area in which Japan was located (hendo), and to the current state of deterioration in human ability (rekki). Such thought was expressed in religious movements that picked up strength as political control shifted from the Fujiwara family to retired emperors after about 1100, encompassing the rise of Pure Land Buddhism and the spread of the Shintō doctrine that a kami was a manifestation of a certain Buddha (honji suijaku). But the logic of adaptation to the conditions of time and place, and to the state of human ability, received its clearest expression early in the Kamakura period—as "the logic of selecting [the particular form of Buddhism for the particular time, place, and state of human ability]" (senchaku no ronri). In 1198 Hōnen wrote in his *Senchaku hongan nembutsu shū* (The Selection of the *Nembutsu* of the Original Vow; see SENCHAKUSHŪ) that people in Japan should select and practice only one form of Buddhism: the original vow of Amida, the form appropriate for the final age of the Buddhist Law (which Japanese Buddhists thought to have begun in 1052), and for the deteriorated state of human ability in the peripheral land of Japan. Hōnen's view on this point was further developed by Shinran, who went so far as to say, in his *Kyōgyōshinshō* (True Doctrines, Practice, Faith, and Attainment), that bad people could achieve rebirth in the Pure Land paradise. DŌGEN (1200–1253) in the SHŌBŌ GENZŌ (Treasury of the True Dharma Eye), as well as NICHIREN (1222–82) in the RISSHŌ ANKOKU RON (A Treatise on Pacifying the State by Establishing Orthodoxy), applied this logic of selection.

At the time of the Hōjō regency in the 13th and early 14th centuries, there was a shift from classicism to functionalism as the dominant logic of cultural formation—a shift first noted in the Jōei Shikimoku of 1232. Later on, in the period of conflict between the NORTHERN AND SOUTHERN COURTS between 1336 and 1392, an entirely different "logic of all-inclusiveness" appeared in the thought of the Rinzai sect of Zen, notably in the *Muchū mondōshū* (Collection of Questions and Answers [Exchanged] in a Dream) written by MUSŌ SOSEKI (1275–1351). This logic, recognizing the reality of multiplicity, was manifested in such expressions as "nonselection" (mu shusha) and "no distinction between right and wrong" (mu zehi). Then in the years of the Muromachi shōguns came "a logic of time, place, and position" (jishoi ron) that was just the opposite of the Heian "logic of adaptation to time, place, and human ability"

(jishoki ron), for the former saw the universal and the ideal only in particular responses to the conditions of time, place, and position. This logic was further developed in the Edo period, especially by NAKAE TŌJU (1608–48), who maintained that there was a fundamental difference between the heart (kokoro) and the imprint (ato) of law, that what is written in Chinese classics is the imprint of law, and that living law (kappō) emerges when one becomes aware of the heart (intent) of law by examining its recorded forms (imprints). Nakae therefore saw current laws as reflecting intent and, without slavish attachment to recorded texts, attempted to adjust his thinking to what the sages had intended. KUMAZAWA BANZAN (1619–91) took a similar stance in his *Shūgi gaisho:* "Since the ancient way was followed by deciding what was best for the time, place, and position, one should consider the heart (kokoro) and not the imprint (koto) of a matter." Functionalism continued to spread with the passage of time. OGYŪ SORAI (1666–1728) wrote in his *Kinroku gaisho:* "Military principle (gunri) has been developed in the military strategies of the past, and we can devise a proper military strategy for today if we grasp the military principles through the strategies of the past." Similarly, KAIHŌ SEIRYŌ (1755–1817) said, "Don't follow the words of Mencius and Confucius, but be instructed by their intentions." In a book entitled *Yōshindan,* he rejected classical thought and called for a living intelligence (katchi) that would change according to circumstances. In the first three decades of the 19th century the logic of functionalism reached its highest point of development, taking, when popularized, the form of an opportunism and situationalism in which it was a rule to have no rules. MATSUDAIRA SADANOBU (1758–1829) wrote that the "true principle is non-principle". There is no need to detail further evidence of functional thought, of which there are multiple examples.

Throughout the history of Japanese thought and culture we see continuous interaction with, but an increasing independence from, the imported cultural thought of China. That is, the unique cultural will of Japan, emerging from and matured by the life of rice production, was at first the agency by which the imported culture of North China was Japanized. Toward the end of the Heian period (the last part of Japan's aristocratic age) and during the Kamakura period (the first part of Japan's military age) the culture of South China came to be accepted and utilized in Japanese thought and culture. Then a truly Japanese culture began to emerge, placing the Muromachi period at the beginning of Japan's modern age and showing why the Kamakura and Muromachi periods have been identified with the flowering of Japanese culture and the Edo period, especially the early decades of the 19th century, with the ripening of its fruit.

After the Meiji Restoration of 1868, the old military-political communities called han were abolished; but community units that had supported the han—the village (mura) and blood-related houses (IE)—continued on into the new industrial age. The Meiji CONSTITUTION of 1889, and the civil codes of 1896 and 1898, placed such feudal organizations as the ie at the base of its new state structure, but above that stood the imported economic forms of Western capitalism and the political forms of democracy. Consequently, the house-based constitutional state of Japan still had a two-layered structure. And in the interpretations and revisions of the IMPERIAL RESCRIPT ON EDUCATION of 1890, we also see two layers of thought. At the bottom was an old feudal ethic that stressed loyalty to the ruler and filial piety (chūkun kōshin), but at the top was a contradictory, modern Western ethic stressing patriotism and individualism (jishu aikoku). Interaction between the two was expressed in such slogans as "loyalty to the ruler and love of country" (chūkun aikoku), an ethic for Japan's new community-ism. The Meiji government found the origins of its community ethic in ancient Japanese myths, but it tried to create a new state myth (through interpretations and revisions of the ancient myth), which it used to support new popular beliefs, adding a new set of clothes to the Shintō doll that was then called Shrine Shintō.

With Japan's defeat in World War II, the Meiji government's state system and ideology were destroyed. Nevertheless, such cultural traditions as the following remain: the Japanized North China cultural tradition of the Nara–Heian period; the militarized cultural tradition which had benefited, in the Muromachi and Edo periods, from South China cultural importations; and the old Shintō culture of primitive times supporting those two traditions. After Japan's defeat in World War II, however, democratic politics and capitalist economics together constituted a layer that stood above the old traditions and which became increasingly stronger. Because of the interaction of the two layers, democratic politics has been deeply affected by community-oriented localism and factionalism, while capitalist economics has been influenced by a community-oriented "my company" ideology that is reflected in the practices of lifelong employment and promotion by seniority. Such interaction helps to explain why the Japanese have been able to adjust themselves easily and quickly to changes at both the local and international levels, and why Japan has enjoyed political stability as well as economic prosperity. Traditional roots remain strong, and under the banner of "build up the hometown," people are trying to restore old geographical communities and to create new residential ones. Under the influence of such slogans as "Discover Japan," hordes of tourists are visiting old centers of traditional culture, particularly Nara, Kyōto, and Ise but also local castle towns. In Tōkyō many are seeking out vestiges of Japan's feudal past: young people are flocking to Zen temples or to places where they can study such traditional arts as the tea ceremony and flower arranging, and the number of visitors to shrines is said to be the largest in history. It would appear, then, that we need not worry about the preservation of Japan's cultural traditions, yet Japan has been changing very rapidly since its defeat in World War II. The high rate of economic growth, and the rapid development of science and technology, are causing Japan's villages—the ultimate base of Japan's traditional thought and culture—to disappear, a process associated with the disappearance of rice growing, central to Japan's productivity for about 2,000 years and to the rice-growing culture. Today's world is absorbed in problems of energy and food. The former is intertwined with the current shift to the life of machine production, and the latter with the preservation of traditional culture—with the maintenance of cultural identity. As we move from the agricultural age to the machine age, and as individual states become more deeply involved in international affairs, we will continue to ask how the cultural forms of the two ages affect each other, and what traditions should be discarded or preserved.

ISHIDA Ichirō

"Thought Criminal" Probation Law

(Shisōhan Hogo Kansatsu Hō). A law, passed by the Diet in May 1936, which provided for a probationary period *hogo kansatsu* (literally, "protective supervision") for so-called thought criminals *(shisōhan)* arrested under the PEACE PRESERVATION LAW OF 1925 (Chian Iji Hō), whether indicted or not. (Probation usually was for two years but could be shortened or extended.) Passage of the law was a logical result of the Justice Ministry's program for suppressing thought criminals and thought crimes. Earlier, in the MARCH 15TH INCIDENT of 1928, the state had used the Peace Preservation Law to arrest thousands of thought criminals and to break the back of the JAPAN COMMUNIST PARTY; however, the government's control over the numerous thought offenders who had been either released without prosecution or paroled from prison was lax. Therefore, justice officials felt it necessary to prevent unreformed offenders from repeating their antistate crimes and to aid them in their mental and economic rehabilitation. To this end they had to create a method of formally reintegrating those individuals who had legally been cast out of society. The 1936 law filled this need and solidly established the category of thought crime *(shisō hanzai)* in the legal system. The new law was designed to keep thought criminals under indirect surveillance, reform their thinking and keep them from backsliding into another thought crime, and help them find employment. A key concept in this law was TENKŌ (conversion): a change in ideological position on the part of former antistate radicals who had undergone self-criticism and who had returned to the ideological position supported by the state.

◼——Hasebe Kingo, "Shisōhan no hogo ni tsuite," *Shihō kenkyū* 21.10 (1937). Richard H. Mitchell, *Thought Control in Prewar Japan* (1976).   Richard H. MITCHELL

Three Monkeys

(San'en, Sanzaru, or Sambikizaru). Figures of three monkeys *(saru)* who clasp both hands over eyes, ears, or mouth, thus not seeing *(mizaru),* not hearing *(kikazaru),* or not speaking *(iwazaru).* Beginning in the latter years of the Muromachi period (1333–1568), it became customary to carve these figures on *kōshintō,* stone pillars used during the observances of KŌSHIN. The Three Monkeys may also be related to the Sannō belief complex, wherein monkeys play the role of divine messengers. According to the KIYŪ SHŌRAN, an early-19th-century reference work, the Three Monkeys represent the Santai (Three Truths) advocated by the TENDAI SECT of Buddhism. The Tendai founder, SAICHŌ, is said to have carved a repre-

sentation of this ideal in the form of monkeys. There exist both statues with three monkeys performing the separate actions as well as images with one monkey performing all three.   INOKUCHI Shōji

thrushes

Birds of the family Muscicapidae, subfamily Turdidae, of which the best-known in Japan is the *tsugumi* (dusky thrush: *Turdus naumanni*), 24 centimeters (9 in) long, with spotted breast, white streak of feather above the eye ("eyebrows"), and chestnut-colored wings. Breeding in Siberia, it migrates to Japan in the fall, preferring mountain woodlands where it subsists on berries and seeds. With the onset of colder weather it flies southward and spends the winter on river banks and in open fields, eating earthworms, insects, berries, and seeds. It is a legally protected species.

Besides the *Turdus naumanni,* other species of the subfamily Turdidae found in Japan are the resident birds *toratsugumi* (White's ground thrush; *T. dauma*), *akahara* (brown thrush; *T. chrysolaus*), and *akakokko* (Izu island thrush; *T. celaenops*). The *kurotsugumi* (gray thrush; *T. cardis*) and *mamijiro* (Siberian thrush; *T. sibiricus*) summer in Japan; the *shirohara* (pale thrush; *T. pallidus*) and *mamichajinai* (gray-headed thrush; *T. obscurus*) winter there.

TAKANO Shinji

Thunberg, Carl Peter (1743–1828)

Swedish physician and botanist who visited Japan in 1775. After studying medicine and botany with Carolus Linnaeus (1707–78) at the University of Uppsala, he joined the Dutch East India Company as a ship's doctor. Sailing around the Cape of Good Hope, he arrived in 1775 at Nagasaki, the only Japanese port then open to foreign (Dutch and Chinese) trade under the Tokugawa shogunate's NATIONAL SECLUSION policy. During his year-long stay, Thunberg collected more than 800 specimens of flora and lectured to such scholars as KATSURAGAWA HOSHŪ and NAKAGAWA JUN'AN on Western medicine, botany, zoology, and astronomy. After returning to Sweden he taught at Uppsala. He wrote several books on Japan, including the *Flora Japonica* (1784).

Tianjin (Tientsin) Convention

Agreement that resolved Sino-Japanese misunderstandings growing out of the Korean-led KAPSIN POLITICAL COUP of 1884; also known as the Li-Itō Convention. The Chinese representative, LI HONGZHANG (Li Hung-chang), and ITŌ HIROBUMI of Japan met at China's northern port of Tianjin in April 1885 and agreed that both nations would withdraw troops from Korea within four months of the treaty's conclusion; King KOJONG would be advised to hire instructors from a third nation to train the Korean army; and, most important, neither nation would send troops to Korea without prior written notice to the other. Designed to prevent unilateral action on the Korean peninsula by either nation, the last provision nevertheless proved to be no deterrent when the next serious confrontation in Korea escalated into the SINO-JAPANESE WAR OF 1894–1895. See also KOREA AND JAPAN: early modern relations.

C. Kenneth QUINONES

tie-dyeing

(shiborizome; shibori). A method of resist dyeing in which the required design is securely tied or stitched onto the fabric before it is dyed. Early surviving fragments of Japanese tie-dye (known as *kōkechi;* see SANKECHI) are preserved in the 8th-century SHŌSŌIN art repository in Nara. In these, the fabric was pulled up at irregular intervals and tied at the base with thread, leaving small grain-like points. The only evidence of tie-dyeing from the Heian period (794–1185) comes from picture scrolls (EMAKIMONO) and documents. Illustrations of *mitsume* and *yotsume* (indigo tie-dye) and *kanoko shibori* (mini-dot tie-dye) can be seen in the 13th-century scroll *Ippen Shōnin eden* (Pictorial Biography of the Monk Ippen). In the Kamakura period (1185–1333) *nuishime* (stitch-resist tie-dye) developed together with the first examples of stencil-printed tie-dye imitations. By the middle of the Muromachi period (1333–1568), tie-dyeing became a popular textile art form. A new technique called TSUJIGAHANA was developed at this time: a combination of stitch-resist tie-dye and hand-drawn motifs often depicting figurative elements. Later, embroidery was added for enrichment. During the Edo period (1600–1868) an exotic type of *kanoko shibori* emerged in which the wrinkles left after tie-dyeing were preserved, giving the fabric an undulating, textural depth. *Sōkanoko,* or tie-dyeing of the entire surface of a garment into mini-resist dots on a uniform background color, also became fashionable, and tie-dyed hair ornaments were used to adorn the elaborate HAIRSTYLES then in vogue.

Tie-dye methods are traditionally used for KIMONO, *haori* (kimono jacket), and OBI (sash) fabrics as well as for accessories and *futon* (bed) and *zabuton* (cushion) covers. *Kanoko shibori* or *kyōkanoko,* tiny dye-resist circles on fine silk, is a special product of Kyōto; *miura shibori,* tie-dyed bird or chick-like designs on cotton, is produced in Arimatsu and Narumi in the city of Nagoya.

In present-day tie-dye production, dot stencils with the desired design are used to mark the design onto the fabric. With different color zones indicated, the material is tied by hand or with a hook and shuttle device according to the stencil design. The fabric is then either hand painted with dye or vat-dyed before being steamed and untied.

📖 ——Itō Toshiko, *Tsujigahana* (1972). Japan Textile Color Center, *Textiles of Japan,* vols 1, 2, and 3 (1959). Kitamura Tetsuo, *Shibori* (1970). Kyōto Shibori Kōgyō Kyōdō Kumiai, *Kyōkanoko* (1975).   Frances ERGEN

Ting Ju-ch'ang → Ding Ruchang (Ting Ju-ch'ang)

Titsingh, Izaak (1744?–1812)

Dutch trade commissioner in Nagasaki; diplomat. Born in Amsterdam. After training as a medical doctor he joined the Dutch East India Company and went in 1768 to its Asian headquarters at Batavia in Java. He was sent to Japan three times (1779–80, 1781–83, and 1784) to head the Dutch trading post at DEJIMA in Nagasaki. During his stay he made the acquaintance of Japanese scholars of WESTERN LEARNING and also made two official visits to the shogunate in Edo (now Tōkyō). In 1784 Titsingh returned to Batavia, and after serving as a trade commissioner in Bengal and as Dutch ambassador to the Chinese court in 1794, he returned to Holland in 1809. His books about Japan, *Mémoires et anecdotes sur la dynastie régnante des djogouns, souverains du Japon* (1820) and *Cérémonies usitées au Japon pour les mariages et les funérailles* (1819), are valuable for their accounts of the people and customs during the latter half of the 18th century.

Tōa Dōbunkai

(East Asia Common Culture Society). Organization founded in 1898 by the pan-Asianist politician KONOE ATSUMARO to promote mutual understanding between Japan and China in the wake of the SINO-JAPANESE WAR OF 1894–1895. The society, which carried on mainly educational activities, stressed that the two nations shared a "common culture" because they both used the written characters *(kanji)* that had developed in ancient China. In 1899 the society opened a school, the Dōbun Shoin, in Nanjing (Nanking). In 1901 the school was moved to Shanghai and renamed the Tōa Dōbun Shoin; it recruited students from all parts of Japan to study Chinese language and culture. Attached to this institution, which was accredited as a college in 1939, was a high school for Chinese students. The society also sponsored a school in Tōkyō that offered preparatory courses to Chinese students who had come to Japan for higher education. The Tōa Dōbunkai published several journals and magazines, including *Shina* (China), as well as research publications on China and Manchuria. Graduates of the college in Shanghai eventually numbered nearly 5,000, and many of them played an important part in promoting Japan's expansionist interests on the Asian continent. Both the college and the society were abolished at the end of World War II. See also PAN-ASIANISM.

Tōa Domestic Airlines Co, Ltd

(Tōa Kokunai Kōkū). Air transport company. Aside from air transport, it is also engaged in the leasing of helicopters. It is the third largest airline in Japan, after the JAPAN AIR LINES CO, LTD, and the ALL NIPPON AIRWAYS CO, LTD. Established in 1964 as the Japan Domestic Airlines Co (Nihon Kōkū), it took its current name in 1971 when it merged with the Tōa Airways Co (Tōa Kokunai Kōkū). In 1982 it served a network of 39 cities and operated about 330 flights a day, covering 72 routes. Aircraft in its fleet included 17 DC-9-41s, 40 YS-11s, and 16 helicopters. Sales for the fiscal year ending March 1982 totaled ¥109.5 billion (US $454.9 million), and the company was capitalized at ¥9.5 billion (US $39.5 million). Corporate headquarters are located in Tōkyō.

Tōagōsei Chemical Industry Co, Ltd

(Tōa Gōsei Kagaku Kōgyō). Company engaged in the manufacture and sale of caustic soda, chlorine products, fertilizer, synthetic resins, and other chemicals. The firm was established in 1933 and is a member of the MITSUI group. It has developed its own technology for producing acrylic esters and a quick-setting adhesive, Aron Alpha, and operates joint venture companies with the Rohm & Haas Co of the United States and Ato Chimie S.A. of France. Future plans call for the expansion of its fine chemicals department. Total sales in 1981 were ¥80.8 billion (US $369.1 million), and the company was capitalized at ¥7 billion (US $32 million). Corporate headquarters are located in Tōkyō.

Tōa Nenryō Kōgyō

Refining company producing various types of oil and petrochemical products. Tōa Nenryō Kōgyō was established in 1939 with capital provided by 10 companies dealing in oil. Its refineries in Wakayama, Shimizu (Shizuoka Prefecture), and Kawasaki started operating in 1941, 1943, and 1962, respectively. The company's daily crude oil refining capacity is 430,500 barrels. In 1949 Tōa Nenryō concluded an agreement with the Standard Vacuum Oil Co, Ltd (now the Esso Eastern Co and Mobil Petroleum Co) covering capital, technology, oil supply, and sale of oil products. Since then, it has come to engage solely in refining; its products are sold through ESSO STANDARD OIL CO, LTD, and MOBIL SEKIYU, while its materials for petrochemical products are processed by Tōnen Sekiyu Kagaku. Tōa Nenryō has advanced into a wide range of business areas through the creation of subsidiaries and joint ventures. In 1959 it established Tōnen Tanker, which is engaged in crude oil transport, and in 1972 Tōa Nenryō and Nichimō Co, Ltd, established a sales company, Kygnus Sekiyu Co, Ltd. The company is the principal member of the Tōnen group. Annual sales totaled ¥1.2 trillion (US $5.5 billion) in 1981 and were composed of benzine (38 percent), heavy oil (28 percent), light oil (23 percent), and lubricating oil and other products (11 percent). Some 25 percent of the company's capital of ¥22.3 billion (US $101.9 million) was provided by Esso Eastern and another 25 percent by Mobil Petroleum. Corporate headquarters are located in Tōkyō.

Tōa Remmei

(East Asian League). An ultranationalist organization formed in October 1939 by the pan-Asianist military man ISHIWARA KANJI and others to support Prime Minister KONOE FUMIMARO's "New Order in East Asia" (TŌA SHINCHITSUJO). The league numbered about 15,000 members and published the magazine *Tōa remmei.* It called for the pooling of the economic resources of Japan, MANCHUKUO (Japan's puppet state in Manchuria), and China, the establishment of an integrated defense effort, and political autonomy for the participating nations as a way of opposing Western imperialism in East Asia and preparing for the "final war" with the United States. A branch was established in Nanjing (Nanking), with WANG JINGWEI (Wang Ching-wei) as its head. Ishiwara retired from active duty in 1941, and the following year the organization dissolved under strong pressure from Army Minister TŌJŌ HIDEKI, who had always been critical of Ishiwara's unorthodox views. It was reorganized as the Tōa Remmei Dōshikai and concentrated on domestic problems such as agricultural reform. The group was disbanded by order of the OCCUPATION authorities after World War II. Revived in 1952, it now advocates rearmament and political neutrality.

Tōa Shinchitsujo

("New Order in East Asia"). Slogan proclaiming the objective of Japan's China policy; first used in a statement by Prime Minister KONOE FUMIMARO on 3 November 1938, in which he announced that the purpose of Japan's military presence in China was to help build a new order in East Asia that was based on political, economic, and cultural ties and cooperation among China, MANCHUKUO (the Japanese puppet state in Manchuria), and Japan. The war in China, which had begun in July 1937, threatened to become a protracted one, despite efforts by the Konoe government to convince CHIANG KAI-SHEK to enter negotiations, and on 16 January 1938 Konoe had declared (in what is known as the first Konoe statement) that Japan would no longer deal with the Nationalist Chinese government. This meant that Japan would continue to use arms to settle disputes with China. Chinese resistance was more persistent than expected, however, and Konoe was forced to try a different approach, hence his 3 November 1938 statement proposing the creation of a "New Order" in East Asia (the second Konoe statement). To this end he hoped to find a prominent Chinese official who would cooperate with Japan's new policy. Seeing indications that WANG JINGWEI (Wang Ching-wei), a former associate of Sun Yat-sen and an important member of the Nationalist Chinese government, might be willing to work with Japan, Konoe issued a third statement in December 1938, in which he reaffirmed Japan's intention to establish a new order in East Asia based on the three principles of "mutual friendship, anticommunism, and economic cooperation." Wang Jingwei deserted the Nationalist government in 1939 and became the head of a puppet government set up in Nanjing (Nanking) in March 1940. The slogan, which was no more than a rationalization of Japan's invasion of China, prefigured another phrase, Dai Tōa Kyōei Ken (GREATER EAST ASIA COPROSPERITY SPHERE), that was used later during World War II.

Tōa Washinkai

(East Asia Friendship Society; Ch: Dongya Heqin Hui or Tung-ya Ho-ch'in Hui). Group formed in Tōkyō in 1907 by the Chinese anarchistic revolutionaries Zhang Ji (Chang Chi; 1882–1947) and Liu Shipei (Liu Shih-p'ei; 1884–1919). They envisioned an alliance of the peoples of Asia to establish their national independence and oppose the colonization of Asia by the West. In addition to Chinese participants, membership included Indians, Filipinos, and Japanese. Before the group was firmly established, however, Zhang was forced to leave Japan, and the group's activities came to a halt in 1908.

Harada Katsumasa

Toba

City in eastern Mie Prefecture, central Honshū. Toba developed as a landing point for pilgrims to ISE SHRINE and as a castle town of the Kuki family during the Edo period (1600–1868). Still a transportation center, it also has an active fishing industry. It is a base for tourists to Ise-Shima National Park. Pop: 28,812.

tobacco

(tabako). Tobacco is thought to have been introduced into Japan toward the end of the 16th century, probably brought from the Philippines or Macao by Spanish or Portuguese merchants. Records show that tobacco was first cultivated in Nagasaki in 1605. Only four years later, fights broke out in Kyōto between two gangs who used long, heavy iron tobacco pipes as weapons; this resulted in an ordinance prohibiting the use of tobacco.

The Tokugawa shogunate (1603–1867) had a house rule against smoking and repeatedly issued ordinances against using tobacco, but these injunctions were rarely heeded. Wealthy merchants of Edo (now Tōkyō) became so fond of such extravagances as gold and silver tobacco pipes and cases that the shogunate issued statutes prohibiting excessively ornate smoking paraphernalia.

The traditional Western-style pipe made of clay or briar was not adopted in Japan; instead, the Japanese used a long, slender tobacco pipe *(kiseru)* with a small metal bowl big enough for only two or three puffs at a time.

During the Meiji period (1868–1912) the cigarette (also referred to as *tabako*) came into fashion in Japan. In 1875 the Japanese government began issuing licenses for tobacco dealers. In 1904, in order to raise revenue for the Russo-Japanese War (1904–05), the government made the sale of tobacco a government monopoly, which it remains to this day (see JAPAN TOBACCO AND SALT PUBLIC CORPORATION).

Although most Japanese cigarettes are made from domestically grown tobacco, some tobacco from the United States, Canada, Mexico, and Brazil is added for improved taste and aroma. Smoking in Japan could qualify as a national habit. Approximately 43 percent of the adult population smokes: 73 percent of adult men and 15 percent of adult women. The total domestic export and import sales of cigarettes for 1979 was 300 billion cigarettes, or roughly ¥2 trillion (US $10 billion).

Ishizaki Jūrō

Toba, Emperor (1103–1156)

The 74th sovereign *(tennō)* in the traditional count (which includes several nonhistorical emperors); reigned 1107–1123. The eldest son of Emperor Horikawa (1079–1107; r 1087–1107). Toba's rule was overshadowed by his grandfather, the retired emperor SHIRAKAWA, who controlled the government from his cloistered quarters; after Toba retired, he himself exercised power for 27 years during the reigns of his sons SUTOKU, Konoe (1139–55; r 1142–55), and GO-SHIRAKAWA (see INSEI). In 1142 he forced Sutoku to abdicate, replacing him with Konoe, his two-year-old son by Bifuku Mon'in, his empress. Konoe died when only 16—it was rumored that the resentful Sutoku had cast a spell—and Toba, instead of enthroning Sutoku's son, saw to it that another of Sutoku's younger brothers was installed as Emperor Go-Shirakawa. The bitterness between Toba and Sutoku was to be one of the major causes of the HŌGEN DISTURBANCE of 1156. Toba also succeeded in acquiring a vast number of landed estates (SHŌEN) through commendation, a practice generally discouraged by retired emperors, and bequeathed them to his wife and Go-Shirakawa the year before his death. For all his worldly machinations, he was a devout Buddhist, making more than 22 pilgrimages to Kumano Shrine and establishing the Saishōji temple in Kyōto.

Toba–Fushimi, Battle of

The first of a series of military conflicts (see BOSHIN CIVIL WAR) that accompanied the Meiji Restoration of 1868; fought on 27 January 1868 (Keiō 4.1.3). Hoping to dislodge the forces of the Satsuma (now Kagoshima Prefecture) and Chōshū (now Yamaguchi Prefecture) domains, which had seized the Kyōto palace and proclaimed an "imperial restoration" (ŌSEI FUKKO) on 3 January, Tokugawa shogunate troops stationed at Ōsaka Castle set out for Kyōto on 25 January. On the 27th they were intercepted at Toba and Fushimi, south of Kyōto. Despite their numerical superiority, they were defeated by the better-armed and better-organized Satsuma–Chōshū forces.

tōbaku no mitchoku

(secret imperial orders to overthrow the shogunate). Imperial orders to depose the shōgun TOKUGAWA YOSHINOBU, believed to have been secretly transmitted in 1867 to the political leaders of the Satsuma (now Kagoshima Prefecture) and Chōshū (now Yamaguchi Prefecture) domains, the two centers of the movement to overthrow the Tokugawa shogunate. By arrangement of ŌKUBO TOSHIMICHI of Satsuma and the influential court noble IWAKURA TOMOMI, a court official named Ōgimachi Sanjō Sanenaru (1820–1909) is said to have delivered a letter addressed to the *daimyō* of Satsuma to Ōkubo himself and a similar one addressed to the daimyō of Chōshū to Hirosawa Saneomi (1833–71). The orders were nullified the very day they were issued, 9 November, when the shōgun formally "returned" his mandate to the emperor (see TAISEI HŌKAN). The letters survive, but since they contain neither the emperor's handwriting nor the seals of any court officials in charge of imperial rescripts, some scholars believe them to be forgeries.

Toba Sōjō (1053–1140)

Painter and priest of the TENDAI SECT who held many official posts, including that of *sōjō* (high priest); his popular name combines this title with Toba, the place of his residence as *bettō* (intendant) of the Shōkongōin in Kyōto. The son of the courtier Minamoto no Takakuni (known as Uji Dainagon; 1004–77), his Buddhist name was Kakuyū. Reared in a literary atmosphere, he entered the Buddhist priesthood as a young man, achieving the rank of *hokkyō* in 1079. His career as a Buddhist official began with his appointment to the post of *bettō* of the temple Shitennōji in 1081. He subsequently served as *bettō* of several other Tendai temples and rose to the rank of *hōgen* in 1113 and *hōin* in 1121. In 1132 he became *sōjō*, in 1134 he became *daisōjō* (senior high priest), and in 1135 or 1138 he was appointed briefly to the post of Tendai *zasu* (chief priest of Enryakuji, the head temple of the Tendai sect). In his late years, Kakuyū resided at the Hōrin'in of the Onjōji (Miidera), becoming its *chōri* (head priest) in 1135. He is also sometimes referred to as Hōrin'in no Sōjō.

Kakuyū's long and distinguished career as a high-ranking Tendai priest and official is substantially documented. Less securely veri-

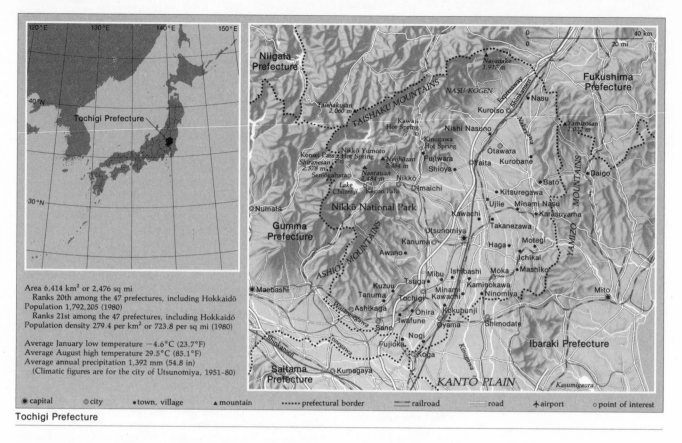

Area 6,414 km² or 2,476 sq mi
Ranks 20th among the 47 prefectures, including Hokkaidō
Population 1,792,205 (1980)
Ranks 21st among the 47 prefectures, including Hokkaidō
Population density 279.4 per km² or 723.8 per sq mi (1980)

Average January low temperature −4.6°C (23.7°F)
Average August high temperature 29.5°C (85.1°F)
Average annual precipitation 1,392 mm (54.8 in)
(Climatic figures are for the city of Utsunomiya, 1951-80)

◉ capital　　◎ city　　• town, village　　▲ mountain　　••••• prefectural border　　▭▭ railroad　　▭ road　　✦ airport　　○ point of interest

Tochigi Prefecture

fied, but of equal importance in terms of his later reputation, is his work as a painter, principally of Buddhist images. His name is recorded in various literary sources as a painter of Buddhist icons, including the *tobira-e* (door paintings) in NINNAJI in 1135. His familiarity with Buddhist iconography is likely to have been enhanced by his work as annotator of the *Hōrin'in zuzō*, a compendium of iconographic drawings produced at the temple where he long resided. He is somewhat unusual among Buddhist artists of the latter part of the Heian period (794–1185) in that he also attained very high rank as a priest.

Literary records indicate that his activity as a painter was probably not limited to Buddhist iconographic paintings. His name has long been associated with lively and even humorous paintings. Toba Sōjō was formerly considered to have painted the SHIGISAN ENGI EMAKI and the CHŌJŪ GIGA. The *Shigisan engi,* however, is now known to be a work of the late 12th century and is no longer attributed to this artist. Similarly, the third and fourth scrolls of the *Chōjū giga* belong stylistically to a substantially later period. In the absence of any documentary proof, various opinions are held concerning his possible authorship of the first two scrolls (or portions thereof) of the *Chōjū giga;* his association with paintings of unusual and humorous subjects was established so early by the account of his work in the 13th-century anthology KOKON CHOMONJŪ that it is difficult to discount entirely his traditional association with the type of subject matter contained in the *Chōjū giga*. At present, no known painting is acceptably documented as the work of Toba Sōjō.
🐾——Tani Shin'ichi, "Kakuyū to Chōjū giga kan," in *Nihon emakimono zenshū,* vol 3 (Kadokawa Shoten, 1959). *Ann* YONEMURA

Tobe

Town in central Ehime Prefecture, Shikoku. Borders the city of Matsuyama on the north. Its Tobe ware, mainly vases, chinaware, utensils for the tea ceremony, and, more recently, porcelain insulators, dates from 1597. Mandarin oranges are grown, and there is some dairy farming. Pop: 16,458.

tobera

(tobira or Japanese pittosporum). *Pittosporum tobira*. An evergreen shrub of the family Pittosporaceae that grows wild in the coastal areas of central and western Honshū, Shikoku, and Kyūshū as well as China and southern Korea. It is also cultivated in gardens as an ornamental. The plant reaches a height of 2–3 meters (7–10 ft). The leaves are alternate and grow densely on the upper part of the branch; they are obovate oblong in shape and have a slightly glossy surface. The stem and leaves have a peculiar smell which is particularly strong in the skin of the roots. The fragrant flowers are dioecious and bloom about June, changing from white to yellow. Fruits are capsules which split into three sections and reveal sticky red seeds when ripe. The name *tobera* or *tobira* (door) comes from the custom of inserting branches of this tree in the doorway of one's house on the day of SETSUBUN to keep demons out. (In some localities the *hiiragi* or holly osmanthus is used instead.) Also, infusions of *tobera* leaves are used as a folk remedy for skin diseases.
MATSUDA Osamu

Tobishima

Island in the Sea of Japan, 39 km (24 mi) northwest of the city of Sakata, northwestern Yamagata Prefecture, northern Honshū. It is a breeding ground for sea gulls. Fishing is the principal industry. Area: 2.3 sq km (0.89 sq mi).

Tobishima Corporation

(Tobishima Kensetsu). A company engaged in public works, construction, and real estate operations, Tobishima Corporation was founded in 1883. Its specialties are the construction of hydroelectric plants and railroad projects; before World War II, it constructed 40 percent of Japan's hydroelectric plants. It is active in the procurement of overseas contracts, particularly in Southeast Asia. Future plans call for the strengthening of its management department and an increase in systems work, utilizing its engineering department to the fullest. Sales for the fiscal year ending March 1982 totaled ¥300.3 billion (US $1.2 billion), and the company was capitalized at ¥7.1 billion (US $29.5 million). Corporate headquarters are located in Tōkyō.

Tōbu Railway Co, Ltd

(Tōbu Tetsudō). A major railway company engaged in bus and rail transport services and in real estate, Tōbu Railway was established in 1897. With its base in the northern KANTŌ REGION, the company

Tōdaiji —— Daibutsuden (Great Buddha Hall)

Known as the largest wooden building in the world, the present *daibutsuden* dates from 1709 but was extensively renovated from 1974 to 1980. 57.0 × 50.4 m; height 47.3 m. Nara. National Treasure.

operates a total of 483 kilometers (300 mi) of railway lines and ranks third among Japan's private railways. It is also the leading member of the Tōbu group of approximately 80 affiliated firms, including the Tōbu department stores. The Tōkyō–Nikkō Line operated by the company transports approximately 150,000 foreign tourists annually. Sales for the fiscal year ending March 1982 totaled ¥137 billion (US $569.1 million), and the firm was capitalized at ¥20.3 billion (US $84.3 million) in the same year. Corporate headquarters are located in Tōkyō.

Tochigi

City in southern Tochigi Prefecture, central Honshū. Tochigi developed as a POST-STATION TOWN on the highway to NIKKŌ. Since the beginning of the Meiji period (1868–1912) lime, *sake* brewing, and *geta* (wooden clogs) industries have flourished. There are also machinery and plastics industries. Pop: 85,592.

Tochigi Prefecture

(Tochigi Ken). Located in central Honshū and bordered by Gumma, Fukushima, Ibaraki, and Saitama prefectures. The YAMIZO MOUNTAINS on the east and Taishaku and Ashio mountains on the west are separated by a central plain watered by the Nakagawa and several other rivers. The climate is distinguished by moist, hot summers and dry, cool winters.

Known after the TAIKA REFORM of 645 as Shimotsuke Province, the area came under the control of the ASHIKAGA FAMILY in the latter part of the Kamakura period (1185–1333). It was divided into numerous *daimyō* domains in the Edo period (1600–1868) and given its present name and boundaries in 1873.

Rice is the principal crop, and other grains and vegetables are produced in the central plains area. Forestry and woodworking industries are active. Copper mining was formerly a major industry, but since World War II the machine, metal, and textile industries have become more prominent.

NIKKŌ NATIONAL PARK, which includes the TŌSHŌGŪ mausoleum built by the Tokugawa shogunate, Lake Chūzenji, Kegon Falls, the mountain known as Shiranesan, the river Kinugawa, and the Nasu Highland, draw visitors from far and wide. The town of Mashiko in southeastern Tochigi is famed for its handmade pottery (see MASHIKO WARE). Area: 6,414 sq km (2,476 sq mi); pop: 1,792,205; capital: Utsunomiya. Other major cities include Ashikaga, Tochigi, Sano, Kanuma, and Oyama.

tochinoki → horse chestnut, Japanese

Tochio

City in central Niigata Prefecture, central Honshū, on the upper Kariyatagawa, a tributary of the river Shinanogawa. Noted for its

heavy snowfall. Tochio was traditionally known for its Tochio *tsumugi* (a silk cloth); since World War II, it has developed as a manufacturing center for synthetic fibers. Pop: 30,694.

Toda

City in southeastern Saitama Prefecture, central Honshū; separated by the river Arakawa from Tōkyō. Toda developed as a river crossing point on the highway Nakasendō during the Edo period (1600–1868). Today, it is a transportation center located on National Route No. 17. A boat course located here was used during the Tōkyō Olympic Games (1964). Pop: 78,343.

Toda Construction Co, Ltd

(Toda Kensetsu). General construction company established in 1881. The company was a pioneer in the construction of Western-style buildings when Western architecture was first introduced to Japan. It advanced into the public works sector in 1956 and into the individual housing field, as well as the real estate business, in 1969. Through its subsidiary firms it is engaged in paving roads and consulting on public works projects. It also has subsidiary firms in the United States and Brazil. Sales for the fiscal year ending September 1981 totaled ¥325 billion (US $1.4 billion), and the firm was capitalized at ¥8.6 billion (US $37.4 million) in the same year. Corporate headquarters are located in Tōkyō.

Tōdaiji

A major monastery-temple belonging to the KEGON SECT of Buddhism. It was erected by order of the emperor SHŌMU (r 724–749) in the eastern sector of Nara, the capital of Japan between the years 710–784, to become the most important religious institution within the network of provincial monasteries and convents (KOKUBUNJI) throughout Japan. Immense in scale, Tōdaiji represented the culmination of Buddhist architecture accomplished under imperial sponsorship. The principal image of the temple, a colossal bronze statue popularly called the Nara Daibutsu (Great Buddha of Nara), was installed in its main hall of worship, the *daibutsuden* (great Buddha hall). When the icon was completed in 752, it was the largest and most splendid ever produced in Japan. The image embodied the Buddha Birushana (Skt: Vairocana), who was regarded by the Kegon sect to be the cosmic, central Buddha, presiding over myriads of worlds, each in turn ruled by a lesser Buddha, as described in the Flower Wreath Sutra (J: *Kegonkyō*). The great image compared so favorably in both size and magnificence with contemporary Buddhist statues produced in cosmopolitan centers of Tang (T'ang) China (618–907) that it stood as the symbol of Japan's rise from a backward country to a highly developed one. Over the centuries the icon was severely damaged several times and finally restored to its present form in 1692. Most of the Tōdaiji buildings extant today are restorations of earlier structures. They contain masterpieces of Buddhist sculpture made through the ages.

The origin of Tōdaiji goes back to the Kinshōji, a temple that had existed in the eastern sector of the present-day Tōdaiji compound. Here, Rōben (689–773), a scholar-monk of the Kegon sect who was to become the first abbot of Tōdaiji, had been active in 733. Rōben is commemorated by a portrait-statue made around 1019 and kept in the *kaizandō* (founder's hall). The *kondō* (main hall) of Kinshōji, where Rōben had worshiped, was referred to in a record of 749 as the Kenjakudō after its chief cult image, the Fukūkenjaku Kannon (Skt: Amoghapāśa). This building probably is the extant inner sanctuary of the *hokkedō* (lotus hall), popularly known as the Sangatsudō (Third Month Hall), where the Lotus Sutra *(Hokekyō)* is chanted yearly during the third month *(sangatsu)*. The main icon of the *hokkedō* is the Fukūkenjaku Kannon, a splendid, dry-lacquer statue over 6.5 meters (21.3 ft) high, made around 746, which could have been the Kinshōji image mentioned above. On the same dais, to the left and right of the great Kannon, are preserved some of the finest lacquer and clay sculptures made during the Tempyō era (727–748). Behind the Fukūkenjaku Kannon facing north is enshrined a clay statue of the guardian deity Shikkongōshin (or Shūkongōjin; Skt: Vajradhāra). Made around 733, it had been worshiped by Rōben in Kinshōji.

In 741 the Kinshōji became the provincial monastery-temple for Yamato Province (now Nara Prefecture). At that time the temple was renovated and renamed Konkōmyōji after the Sutra of the Golden Light (J: *Konkōmyō kyō*). Construction of a colossal Buddha had originally begun in Shigaraki, which served as the temporary capital in 743, but two years later, when Nara was redesignated the capital, the project was moved to Konkōmyōji.

The temple was first referred to as Tōdaiji in 747, when construction of its major buildings was begun. An immense area extending over seven city blocks of Nara was allocated for the Tōdaiji compound. The ground was bounded by walls to the south, the west, and partially to the north. The eastern sector stretched into the Kasuga hills. There was a gate facing north and three leading into the city through the western wall, but the main entrance was through the *nandaimon* (great south gate), which was on an axis with the *daibutsuden*. Now reduced in size, this edifice originally had an 11-bay facade and 7-bay sides. It was 48.5 meters (159.1 ft) high and occupied an area of 88 by 51.5 meters (288.7 by 169 ft). Between the *nandaimon* and the *chūmon* (inner gate) that led to the precinct of the *daibutsuden* were two seven-storied pagodas, one to the east and the other to the west, each 100 meters (328.1 ft) high. On an axis to the north of the *daibutsuden*, flanked by a belfry and a sutra repository, was the *kōdō* (lecture hall), enclosed on three sides by monks' quarters that were connected to a refectory on the east by a corridor. So monumental were the major buildings of Tōdaiji that they were supplied with individual enclosures.

The *daibutsuden*, with its gigantic statue cast in gilded bronze, was completed in 752, when the most magnificent consecration ceremony ever held in Japan took place in the courtyard in the presence of the by-then retired emperor Shōmu, his consort the empress Kōmyō, and the reigning empress Kōken. In attendance were 10,000 monks and dignitaries from abroad, who witnessed this solemn ceremony symbolizing the unity of Buddhism with the state. Splendid objects used during the ceremony were placed in the SHŌSŌIN, a storehouse located on the grounds of Tōdaiji, northwest of the *daibutsuden*.

In 754 a hall for the ordination of monks, the *kaidan'in*, was established by GANJIN (Ch: Jianzhen or Chien-chen), a noted Chinese monk who had been invited to Japan to introduce the orthodox ordination procedures of China. The *kaidan'in* burned down three times, the present one dating from 1731. On its altar are placed images of the Shitennō (Four Heavenly Kings), which are outstanding examples of Tempyō-era clay modeling. By 798 the vast compound of Tōdaiji and its buildings were completed. According to Tōdaiji records, 50,000 carpenters, 370,000 metal workers, and 2,180,000 laborers worked on its construction and furnishings. The enormous expenses virtually brought the nation to the brink of bankruptcy.

Little remains of the 8th-century buildings of Tōdaiji except the Tegai Gate of the western wall and the inner sanctuary of the *hokkedō*. The *daibutsuden*, the towering pagodas, and most of the other buildings were deliberately destroyed by the army of Taira no Shigehira in 1180 as punishment for the help armed Tōdaiji monks had extended to the rival Minamoto family during the TAIRA-MINAMOTO WAR. The following year the Taira were defeated, and reconstruction of Tōdaiji began under the direction of the abbot Shunjōbō Chōgen (1121–1206), who devoted the last 25 years of his life to the project. He is commemorated by a portrait-statue, made shortly after his death, that is enshrined in the Shunjōdō, a hall built in 1704. The *daibutsuden* and other buildings were repaired or replaced in a bold style that Chōgen had observed during a visit to Southern Song (Sung) China in 1167–68. It is characterized by deep, overhanging eaves supported by tiers of bracket arms with increasing outward projection. This new architectural style, known as the "great Buddha style" (*daibutsuyō*) or the "Indian style" (*tenjikuyō*) is well preserved in the *nandaimon*, for which in 1203 the famed sculptors UNKEI and KAIKEI made the powerful guardian statues of the Niō (Benevolent Kings). The "Indian style" was modified shortly after Chōgen's death, as may be observed in the sturdy bell tower, the *kaizandō*, and other buildings.

Disaster struck again in 1567, when, in the course of a battle, General Matsunaga Hisahide set fire to the *daibutsuden* and various other buildings. The Daibutsu, now headless, was not fully restored until 1692, when the rebuilding of Tōdaiji was sponsored by the Tokugawa shogunate. The *daibutsuden* visible today dates for the most part from 1709. With its prominent "Indian style" bracketing and a facade only two-thirds its former length, the *daibutsuden* lacks the stylistic uniformity and refinement of its 8th-century predecessor. However, it remains to this day the most prominent edifice in Nara and is generally regarded as the largest wooden structure in the world. A magnificent view of the *daibutsuden* is afforded from the Nigatsudō (literally, "Second Month Hall"), built in 1669 into a

hill in the northeastern sector of Tōdaiji, where a popular ceremony known as Omizutori, involving a water offering to the Eleven Headed Kannon, is celebrated in the second month each year.

📖 —— Takeshi Kobayashi, *Nara Buddhist Art: Tōdaiji* (1975).

Lucie R. WEINSTEIN

Toda Jōsei (1900–1958)

Religious leader and second president of the SŌKA GAKKAI, a lay organization of the Nichiren Shōshū sect of Buddhism. Born in the city of Kaga, Ishikawa Prefecture, he became an elementary school teacher in Tōkyō in 1920. The principal at that school was MAKIGUCHI TSUNESABURŌ, who founded the forerunner of the Sōka Gakkai in 1930. Toda later became Makiguchi's close friend and chief disciple.

During the 1930s Toda became increasingly involved in Sōka Gakkai activities. On 6 July 1943 he, Makiguchi, and 19 other Sōka Gakkai officials were arrested on charges of violating the 1941 revision of the PEACE PRESERVATION LAW OF 1925 because of their opposition to the state religion, Shintō, and the government's war policies. Makiguchi died in prison in 1944, but Toda was released on 3 July 1945. He immediately began to rebuild the Sōka Gakkai and was inaugurated as its second president in May 1951. By the time of his death on 2 April 1958, he had built it into one of the largest of Japan's NEW RELIGIONS and had laid the groundwork for its further expansion in the 1960s. A prolific writer, Toda also published many books and articles about the Sōka Gakkai.

Toda Mosui (1629–1706)

WAKA poet and theoretician of the early part of the Edo period (1600–1868). Real name Toda Yasumitsu; born in Suruga Province (now Shizuoka Prefecture). One of the earlier and more trenchant critics of the ossified traditions and archaic compositional strictures of the secretly transmitted poetics of the KOKIN DENJU, his activity in Edo (now Tōkyō) paralleled the efforts of KEICHŪ and SHIMOKŌBE CHŌRYŪ in Ōsaka. The main statement of his views is contained in his *Nashimotoshū* (1698), a treatise on poetics. Also of note is his *Murasaki no hitomoto* (1682), whimsical descriptions of famous places in Edo, where he lived as an eccentric recluse.

Toda Teizō (1887–1955)

Sociologist. Born in Hyōgo Prefecture. A graduate of and later professor at Tōkyō University. He introduced American methods of sociological research to Japan. Toda was particularly interested in the Japanese family, and where previous scholars had specialized in abstract analyses of the family system, he used actual case studies and statistics from Japan's first population census (1920) to formulate his theories. He published his findings in *Kazoku kōsei* (1937). In 1923 he founded the Japan Sociological Society. Other works include: *Kazoku no kenkyū* (1926) and *Shakaigaku gairon* (1952).

HASUMI Otohiko

Todoroki Falls

(Todoroki no Taki). Located on the upper reaches of the river Kaifugawa, the town of Kainan, southern Tokushima Prefecture, Shikoku. Also called Todoroki Kujūku Taki (99 Falls of Todoroki) because there are dozens of falls within a distance of 5 km (3 mi), with Todoroki Falls the principal one. During Todoroki Shrine's autumn festival, a portable shrine (*mikoshi*) is carried into the basin of the falls.

Tōdō Takatora (1556–1630)

Warrior and *daimyō* of the Azuchi–Momoyama (1568–1600) and early Edo (1600–1868) periods. Born in Ōmi Province (now Shiga Prefecture), Takatora entered the service of ASAI NAGAMASA. He later became a vassal of Hashiba Hidenaga (1541–91), half-brother of the national unifier TOYOTOMI HIDEYOSHI, and fought in Hideyoshi's campaigns in Kyūshū and the INVASIONS OF KOREA IN 1592 AND 1597. With the deaths of Hidenaga and Hidenaga's son, Hidetoshi, Takatora took holy orders, but he was persuaded by Hideyoshi to resume secular life and become castellan (*jōdai*) of Uwajima Castle in Shikoku. After Hideyoshi's death, Takatora allied himself with TOKUGAWA IEYASU; in recognition of his services in the Battle of SEKIGAHARA (1600), which established the hegemony of the Tokugawa family, he was awarded half of Iyo Province (now Ehime

Prefecture). His holdings were gradually increased, and by the end of his career they were assessed at more than 300,000 *koku* (see KOKUDAKA). Apart from his military valor and strategic brilliance, Takatora was also noted as an able administrator of his domain.

Tōei Co, Ltd

One of Japan's major motion picture production and distribution companies. It was established in 1949 as Tōkyō Eiga Haikyū for the purpose of distributing films produced by the Tōyoko Eiga studio of Kyōto and the Ōizumi Eiga studio of Tōkyō. The three merged in 1951 to form the present Tōei Co, which grew through the mass production of popular historical dramas to enjoy a golden era in its early years. As Japan's film industry fell into decline, Tōei produced amusement films, including various *yakuza* (gangster) series, creating a boom and ushering in such stars as Nakamura Kinnosuke, Ōkawa Hashizō, Tsuruta Kōji, TAKAKURA KEN, and Sugawara Bunta. The company has produced films by such well-known directors as UCHIDA TOMU, IMAI TADASHI, FUKASAKU KINJI, and Kudō Eiichi.   SHIRAI Yoshio

tōfu

(bean curd). As an inexpensive and plentiful source of protein, *tōfu* has long been a mainstay of the Chinese and Japanese diet. It is said to have been first made by the Chinese 2,000 years ago and introduced to Japan in the 7th century. *Tōfu* is made from soybeans that are soaked in water, mashed to a paste-like consistency, heated, and then sieved through a cloth. The liquid, called *tōnyū*, is then coagulated with magnesium chloride or calcium sulfate and put aside. When the liquid is relatively thick and left to coagulate as it is, it is called *kinugoshi*. It is soft and finely textured. *Momengoshi* is made by pouring the liquid into a perforated mold lined with a piece of cloth. *Tōfu* is usually sold in squares.

Tōfu may be processed in various ways. *Aburaage* and *namaage* are made by frying *tōfu* from which excess water has been pressed. *Gammodoki* is made the same way, with bits of carrot and sesame seeds added. *Kōridōfu* is made by freezing and drying *tōfu*. *Okara*, the substance left after extracting the liquid, has a unique texture and flavor. *Yakidōfu* is made by toasting squares of bean curd made firm by extracting excess water.

Tōfu is eaten in a number of ways, as evidenced by the Edo-period (1600–1868) cookbook *Tōfu hyakuchin*, which lists a hundred methods of cooking *tōfu*. It can be used as an ingredient in soup or SUKIYAKI. As *yudōfu*, it is kept warm in a pot of hot water and dipped into a mixture of soy sauce, minced scallion, and spices; as *hiyayakko*, it is eaten the same way, but chilled; as *dengaku tōfu*, it is covered with a *miso* mixture and broiled.   ŌTSUKA Shigeru

Tōfukuji

Head temple of the Tōfukuji branch of the RINZAI SECT of ZEN Buddhism. Located in Higashiyama Ward, Kyōto. Tōfukuji was founded in 1236 with the support of the powerful courtier and imperial regent Fujiwara no Michiie (1193–1252) on the site of the remains of the temple Hosshōji, which had been the main temple of the FUJIWARA FAMILY for over 300 years. Actual construction began in 1239, and in 1243 the priest ENNI, the nominal founder, who had studied in China for six years, took up residence there. Michiie died before completion of the temple in 1255; his role was continued by ICHIJŌ SANETSUNE.

The name Tōfukuji was created by borrowing from the names of the temples TŌDAIJI in Nara and KŌFUKUJI in Kyōto. As one of the five GOZAN temples, Tōfukuji enjoyed an early period of prosperity. However, fires in 1319 and 1334 destroyed much of the temple complex. In 1347 the *butsuden* (Buddha hall) was reconstructed and in later years other buildings were rehabilitated by the Fujiwara family, the HŌJŌ FAMILY, the ASHIKAGA FAMILY, TOYOTOMI HIDEYOSHI, and TOKUGAWA IEYASU, successively. In 1881 much of the temple was again burned down; in the following decades the temple was gradually rebuilt and was completed with the reconstruction and dedication of a new *butsuden* in 1934.

At present the main buildings of Tōfukuji are a *zendō* (meditation hall), a *butsuden*, a *hōjō* (abbot's living quarters), a *kaizandō* (founder's hall), a *yokushitsu* (bath house), a *tōsu* (lavatory), a *sammon* (main gate), and various other gates. There were at one time 53 *tatchū* (subsidiary temples) within the Tōfukuji complex, but after the Meiji Restoration (1868) the number declined and today there are only 25.

The *sammon* is thought to have been built sometime between 1384 and 1428; it is the oldest of its kind in Japan and has been designated a National Treasure. Hanging inside the gate is a large work of calligraphy by Ashikaga Yoshimochi (1387–1428); there are also paintings ascribed to MINCHŌ and his disciples, as well as images of Śākyamuni Buddha and 16 RAKAN (Skt: *arhat*, "worthy ones"), among others.

The *hōjō* was destroyed by fire in 1881 and rebuilt in 1890. It boasts several magnificent gardens in the style of the Kamakura period (1185–1333), landscaped by Shigemori Mirei (1896–1975), a modern expert on garden design. The south garden, a dry landscape garden in the Zen style, is especially well known.

The *tōsu* and the *yokushitsu*, both of which have been designated Important Cultural Properties, are renowned structures of the Tōfukuji. The *tōsu* is one of the oldest and largest structures of its kind in Japan. The *yokushitsu* is the oldest standing bath house in Kyōto; along with the *tōsu*, it is an indication of the importance of daily hygiene in the practice of Zen.

Other Important Cultural Properties include the *niōmon* (two guardians gate), the *aizendō* (a hall dedicated to Aizen Myōō [Skt: Rāgarāja]), and the bell tower, all of which were transported from Manjuji, a nearby temple that is now a subordinate temple of Tōfukuji.

Tōfukuji preserves many other important cultural works of art, documents, and manuscripts. At Manjuji there is an image of the Buddha AMIDA believed to have been sculpted in 1007 and ascribed to GENSHIN, a Tendai monk. At Ryūgin'an there is a statue of the priest Mukan Fumon (1212–91), probably executed between 1291 and 1303. In the *butsuden* there is a statue of Fudō Myōō (see MYŌŌ) ascribed to Kōshō, a sculptor of Buddhist images of the middle part of the Heian period (794–1185), and a large scroll painting of the Buddha's experience of nirvana by Minchō. On the ceiling of the same building is a painting of a dragon done by the modern painter DŌMOTO INSHŌ. Among other paintings are a portrait of the Chinese priest Wuzhun Shifan (Wu-chun Shih-fan; 1177–1249) as well as portraits of Enni Ben'en by Minchō.   Hoyu ISHIDA

Tōfutsu, Lake

(Tōfutsuko). Lagoon on the coast of the Sea of Okhotsk, northeastern Hokkaidō. Located east of the city of Abashiri, it is famous for its white swans and wild flowers, which grow on the coastal sand dunes. Formerly used as a training ground by members of Japan's antarctic expedition team. Area: 9.3 sq km (3.6 sq mi); circumference: 30 km (19 mi); depth: 2.5 m (8.2 ft).

Togakushi Kōgen

Highland between the mountains Iizunayama and Togakushiyama, northern Nagano Prefecture, central Honshū. Famous for its large bird nesting area and alpine flora. Popular for camping in summer and skiing in winter. A special product is buckwheat. Part of Jōshin'etsu Kōgen National Park. Elevation: 1,200 m (3,936 ft).

Togakushiyama

Mountain in northern Nagano Prefecture, central Honshū. It is composed of agglomerate and has sharp cliffs. The mountain is a noted training place for mountain ascetics (see SHUGENDŌ), and women were once forbidden to climb it. The entire mountain is covered with beech forests and is part of Jōshin'etsu Kōgen National Park. Height: 1,911 m (6,268 ft).

Tōgane

City in central Chiba Prefecture, central Honshū. During the Edo period (1600–1868) Tōgane was the distribution center for marine products from the Kujūkurihama coastal area and agricultural products from the Kujūkurihama Plain. Chief industries are commerce and agriculture (rice, tomatoes, and cucumbers). Industrialization is proceeding with the construction of chemical and machinery plants. Pop: 35,611.

Togariishi site

Archaeological site of the Middle Jōmon period (ca 3500 BC–ca 2000 BC); located in Nagano Prefecture near the foot of the group of volcanoes known as Yatsugatake, at an altitude of 1,050 meters (3,444 ft); named for the jagged rocks *(togariishi)* found in the area. The site was discovered in 1893; excavations in 1940–42 and in 1954 uncovered the remains of 33 PIT HOUSES and a large number of stone implements such as scrapers, both chipped and polished types of axes, adzes, and stone querns, as well as beads (see BEADS, ANCIENT), JŌMON FIGURINES, and clay earplugs (see EAR ORNAMENTS, ANCIENT). Large Middle Jōmon settlement sites like Togariishi are found in abundance in the mountainous region around Yatsugatake (see IDOJIRI ARCHAEOLOGICAL HALL). Because of the size, number, and close proximity of these sites, several scholars believe that some sort of cultivation sufficient to sustain a large community was practiced in addition to hunting and gathering. See also JŌMON CULTURE.

📖 ——Chino Machi Kyōiku Iinkai, ed, *Togariishi* (1957).

ABE Gihei

Togashi family

Warlords of the Togashi district of Kaga Province (now part of Ishikawa Prefecture) during the early part of the Muromachi period (1333–1568). Since the late Kamakura period (1185–1333) the Togashi had held the post of military governor *(shugo)* of Kaga for several generations. Late in the 14th century they were for a time subordinated to the SHIBA FAMILY but soon regained their position. Following a succession dispute, in 1447 the family split into two branches, with the head of each branch governing half of Kaga. Although the family was reunited 30 years later under Togashi Masachika (1455?–88), the latter was killed in 1488 in an uprising of the Jōdo Shin sect (see IKKŌ IKKI) and the Togashi fell into obscurity. A member of the family served as a model for the character Togashi (the official in charge of guards at the barrier or checkpoint) in several well-known literary works, including the military chronicle GIKEIKI, the Nō play *Ataka,* and the *kabuki* play *Kanjinchō.*

Tōgatta Hot Spring

(Tōgatta Onsen). Located on an eastern foothill of the Zaōzan Mountains, southwestern Miyagi Prefecture, northern Honshū. A radioactive spring; water temperature 60–70°C (140–158°F). This famous spa sits on the left bank of the river Matsukawa, a tributary of the Abukumagawa, and has been known since ancient days for its medicinal waters. It is a popular tourist attraction throughout the year. Tōgatta *kokeshi* (wooden dolls) are a famous product of this area.

Tōgō Heihachirō (1848–1934)

Fleet admiral in the IMPERIAL JAPANESE NAVY. Born in the Satsuma domain (now Kagoshima Prefecture). As a youth Tōgō participated in the conflict between his domain and Great Britain (see KAGOSHIMA BOMBARDMENT) in 1863. He served on the domainal warship *Kasuga* during the BOSHIN CIVIL WAR that accompanied the restoration of imperial rule in 1868. He studied naval science in Great Britain from 1871 to 1878 and was commissioned a lieutenant, first class, upon his return to Japan.

A captain at the time of the SINO-JAPANESE WAR OF 1894–1895, he was a commanding officer of the *Naniwa* when it sank a British merchant ship carrying Chinese soldiers off the Korean peninsula. At the time the incident caused considerable controversy at home and abroad, but the final verdict determined that Tōgō had acted within the bounds of international law.

Following the war he served successively as head of the Naval War College, commander of Sasebo Naval Station, commander in chief of the standing fleet during the BOXER REBELLION in China (1900), and commander of the Maizuru Naval Station. Tōgō was appointed commander in chief of the Combined Fleet in December 1903. Becoming an admiral in 1904, he led naval operations during the RUSSO-JAPANESE WAR. Under his command, the Combined Fleet intercepted and destroyed the Russian Baltic fleet at the Battle of TSUSHIMA on 27–28 May 1905.

After the war he was named chief of the NAVAL GENERAL STAFF OFFICE, war councillor to the emperor, and was promoted to the rank of fleet admiral in 1913. He was in charge of the education of Prince Hirohito, the present emperor, from 1914 to 1924. Although he did not fill any official post during this period, he continued to exert a strong influence as a senior member of the navy.

A man of unquestioning loyalty to the emperor and to his country, known for his sincerity, taciturnity, and humility, Tōgō was re-

spected as the model naval officer. He was honored with a state funeral. Tōgō Shrine, located in Harajuku, Tōkyō, was founded in his memory.

ICHIKI Toshio

Tōgō Shigenori (1882–1950)

Diplomat. Born in Kagoshima Prefecture. Having graduated from Tōkyō University, he joined the Ministry of Foreign Affairs and served in numerous diplomatic posts in Asia, Europe, and the United States, becoming ambassador to Germany in 1937 and ambassador to the Soviet Union in 1939. He played an important role in settling Japanese fishing and territorial disputes with the Soviet Union. He was opposed to the formation of the Axis alliance. Joining the TŌJŌ HIDEKI cabinet as minister of foreign affairs in 1941, he participated in the unsuccessful prewar negotiations with the United States. He resigned the following year in protest against the formation of the Greater East Asia Ministry. Favoring an early peace, Tōgō joined the SUZUKI KANTARŌ cabinet as minister of foreign affairs in 1945 and led the effort to negotiate Japan's surrender. He was sentenced to a 20-year prison term as a class A war criminal by the International Tribunal for the Far East in 1946 (see WAR CRIMES TRIALS). His stepson, Tōgō Fumihiko, was Japanese ambassador to the United States in the late 1970s.

tōgyū → bullfighting

Tōhaku → Hasegawa Tōhaku

Tōhata Seiichi (1899–1983)

Agricultural economist. Tōbata is the correct pronunciation of his name, but he is widely known as Tōhata. Born in Mie Prefecture. Graduate of and later professor at Tōkyō University. He studied under J. A. Schumpeter (1883–1950) in Germany, and because of his liberal, fresh approach became a leading authority in his field. After World War II he served concurrently as director of the National Research Institute of Agricultural Economics, the Ministry of Agriculture and Forestry, and the Institute of Developing Economies. He continued to serve in a number of important public posts, such as president of the Agricultural Administration Council and of the Tax System Council. He wrote *Nihon nōgyō no tenkai katei* (1936, The Development of Japanese Agriculture) and translated Schumpeter's *History of Economic Analysis* (1955–62).

KATŌ Shunjirō

Tōhō Co, Ltd

(Tōhō Kabushiki-Gaisha). One of Japan's major motion picture producers and distributors as well as a general entertainment company. It was established in 1937 as Tōhō Eiga Co through the merger of the Shashin Kagaku Kenkyūjo Co with the J. O. Film Studio and two other companies. In 1943 this merged with the Tōkyō Takarazuka Gekijō to form the present Tōhō Co, Ltd. Although it was hard hit by the TŌHŌ STRIKE of 1948 and the creation of the SHIN TŌHŌ CO, LTD, it recovered through the adoption of a producer system and the consequent production of large-budget films. It was renowned for its comedies depicting the lives of common people. KUROSAWA AKIRA's first film, *Sugata Sanshirō* (1943), was produced by this company, as well as his recent *Kagemusha* (1980). MIFUNE TOSHIRŌ also made his debut with this company. With the decline of the film industry, it is currently placing more emphasis on the production of television programs and the promotion of live shows.

SHIRAI Yoshio

Tōhō Gakuen School of Music

(Tōhō Gakuen Daigaku). A private, coeducational music college, located in Chōfu, Tōkyō Prefecture. It began as the Sansui Girls' High School in 1941, and became a women's junior college in 1955. In 1961 it was established as a four-year college. The faculty of music offers two majors: composition and performance. Saitō Hideo (1902–74) contributed to the development of the college and educated many outstanding musicians, including OZAWA SEIJI. Enrollment was 775 in 1980.

Tōhōkai

(Far East Society). Rightist political group founded by NAKANO SEIGŌ in May 1936. Four years earlier, Nakano and ADACHI KENZŌ had formed the political organization KOKUMIN DŌMEI; disagreeing with Adachi over policy, Nakano left to form the Tōhōkai. Inspired by the writings of the ultranationalist ideologue KITA IKKI, the Tōhōkai called for national reform but insisted that it be done by parliamentary means. Absorbed by the IMPERIAL RULE ASSISTANCE ASSOCIATION in 1940, it broke away a year later and fared poorly in the 1942 wartime election. It became sharply critical of the TŌJŌ HIDEKI cabinet, and in October 1943 Nakano was arrested on charges of conspiring to overthrow the cabinet. On the day of his release he committed suicide, and the Tōhōkai, deprived of its leader, in effect ceased to exist.

Tōhō Kaigi

(Far Eastern Conference). 1. Conference called by Prime Minister HARA TAKASHI in May 1921 to discuss the withdrawal of Japanese forces that had been stationed in Shandong (Shantung) Province, China, and in Siberia since World War I as well as Japanese interests in Manchuria and Mongolia. The meeting included ministerial officials, Japanese officials of Japanese colonies, and military officials with responsibility for policy on the Asian continent. They resolved to protect Japanese interests in Manchuria, more specifically to support the Manchurian warlord ZHANG ZUOLIN (Chang Tso-lin) in defense of Manchuria and Korea against Soviet infiltration.

2. Conference called by Prime Minister TANAKA GIICHI in the summer of 1927 to formulate a China policy in the aftermath of the military expedition to Shandong, then engulfed in civil war, to protect the lives of Japanese residents (see SHANDONG [SHANTUNG] QUESTION). Participants included foreign ministry bureaucrats, general staff and members of the war ministries, and Japanese colonial officials. The meeting endorsed a "positive" China policy, i.e., maintaining Japan's position in China even at the risk of using arms and expanding Japan's special interests in Manchuria by encouraging native separatist movements. Soon after the conference, the Nationalist government in China made public the so-called TANAKA MEMORANDUM, a memorial supposedly presented by Tanaka to the emperor containing detailed plans for the annexation of China. Doubts continue to exist as to its authenticity, but at the time it provoked violent anti-Japanese feelings in China.

Tōhoku Electric Power Co, Inc

(Tōhoku Denryoku). Company providing electricity to the six prefectures of the TŌHOKU REGION and Niigata Prefecture in northern Honshū. Established in 1951, its supply capacity totals 7.7 million kilowatts, consisting of 1.8 million kilowatts of hydroelectricity and 5.9 million kilowatts of thermoelectricity. In 1981 it operated a total of 212 hydroelectric plants and 12 thermoelectric plants with an annual supply of 37.6 billion kilowatt-hours. Tōhoku Electric operates Japan's largest geothermal electric plant, the Kakkonda generator in Iwate Prefecture, and in 1982 was constructing a nuclear plant in Onagawa, Miyagi Prefecture, scheduled to open in mid-1984. In the fiscal year ending in March 1982 annual sales totaled ¥984.2 billion (US $4.1 billion), distributed as follows: electric power 63 percent, electric lighting 30 percent, and others 7 percent. In the same year the company was capitalized at ¥240 billion (US $997 million). Its head office is in Sendai, Miyagi Prefecture.

Tōhoku region

(Tōhoku chihō). Also called Ōu Chihō. Region encompassing the entire northern end of the island of Honshū and consisting of Aomori, Iwate, Akita, Yamagata, Miyagi, and Fukushima prefectures. This region comprises the ancient provinces of Mutsu and Dewa.

The Tōhoku region is largely mountainous, with numerous basins, mountain valleys, and small coastal plains. Most towns and cities are concentrated along the Pacific and Sea of Japan coasts and in the centers of several basins. The Ōu Mountains run north to south dividing the region through the center. To the west the Dewa Mountains and the Echigo Mountains run parallel to the coast. To the northeast the Kitakami Mountains front the Pacific Ocean and are separated from the Ōu Mountains by the broad Kitakamigawa valley. In the southeast the river Abukumagawa flows inland from the Abukuma Mountains along the coast. The region includes the Nasu and Chōkai volcanic zones. The climate is highly seasonal with short summers and long winters, and the Sea of Japan side is an area of heavy snowfall.

In ancient times the area was inhabited by the aboriginal people known as EZO (also pronounced Ebisu or Emishi), and it was only in the Kamakura period (1185–1333) that it came fully under the control of the central government. Still economically backward, it is primarily an agricultural area, with rice as the primary crop (20 percent of the national yield). Potatoes and apples are also grown, and dairy farming is increasing. Forestry is important. The area off the Sanriku Coast (Aomori, Iwate, and Miyagi) is a rich fishing ground. Coal production in the Jōban mining area has declined, but petroleum and natural gas are still tapped in Akita and Yamagata. The iron, steel, cement, chemical, pulp, and petroleum refining industries have been developing since the 1960s in the areas surrounding the cities of Hachinohe, Akita, and Iwaki, and around Sendai.

Four national parks, Towada–Hachimantai, Rikuchū Coast, Bandai–Asahi, and Nikkō are in the region, as well as six quasi-national parks. The number of tourists is expected to increase with the opening of the Japanese National Railways Tōhoku Shinkansen Line. The principal city is Sendai. Area: 66,900 sq km (25,823 sq mi); pop: 9,572,231.

Tōhoku University

(Tōhoku Daigaku). A national, coeducational university located in the city of Sendai, Miyagi Prefecture. Founded as Tōhoku Imperial University in 1907, it now maintains faculties of letters, education, law, economics, science, medicine, dentistry, pharmacology, engineering, and agriculture. It is known for the following institutes: Research Institute for Iron, Steel, and Other Metals; Institute for Agricultural Research; Research Institute of Mineral Dressing and Metallurgy; Research Institute for Tuberculosis and Cancer; Research Institute for Scientific Measurements; Institute of High Speed Mechanics; Research Institute of Electrical Communication; and Chemical Research Institute of Non-Aqueous Solutions. Enrollment was 9,539 in 1980.

Tōhō Rayon Co, Ltd

(Tōhō Rēyon). Spinning company engaged in the production of acrylic fibers, rayon, cotton, and other yarns. It is affiliated with the NISSHIN SPINNING CO, LTD. Founded in 1934 to produce staple fibers, it adopted its present name in 1950. In 1961 it developed Beslon, an acrylic fiber which is currently its leading product. Sales for the fiscal year ending March 1982 totaled ¥78.4 billion (US $325.7 million), distributed as follows: Beslon 45 percent, rayon 22 percent, cotton yarn 18 percent, and others 15 percent. In the same year the company was capitalized at ¥3 billion (US $12.5 million). Corporate headquarters are located in Tōkyō.

Tōhō Strike

(Tōhō Sōgi). One of the major labor disputes of the post–World War II period; it involved the management and the employees' union of the TŌHŌ CO, LTD, the motion picture company. The dispute arose in early April 1948 when the company, then in financial trouble, announced the dismissal of 270 employees, all members of the company union. The union launched a strike on 17 April and occupied the company's studio in Kinuta, Tōkyō, while the management countered by obtaining a court injunction forbidding the union members to enter the studio grounds. The dispute escalated until 19 August, when the injunction was implemented by about 2,000 armed policemen, with the support of Occupation forces (50 soldiers with seven tanks and three airplanes). The union members left the studio but continued the strike. The dispute ended on 19 October 1948, when the management agreed to reduce sharply the number of dismissals.

Tōhō Zinc Co, Ltd

(Tōhō Aen). Maker and smelter of nonferrous metals, mainly zinc and lead. Established in 1937, it has concentrated on smelting imported ores because of their scarcity in Japan. It imports ore from mines it has developed in Peru, and is currently exploring lead mines in Iran and Guatemala. It is known for its innovative techniques in electrolytic ironmaking and in recovering valuable metals from ore wastes. Sales for the fiscal year ending March 1982 totaled ¥59.1 billion (US $245.8 million) and the company was capitalized at ¥5 billion (US $20.7 million). Its head office is in Tōkyō.

Toi

Korean term for the Jürchen, a Tungusic people of Manchuria who were subjects of the Khitan Liao dynasty (907–1125) and the Korean state of KORYŎ during the 11th century but went on to found their own Jin (Chin) dynasty (1125–1234). Whereas in Japan this Korean term was used to refer specifically to the Jürchen, in Korea it was also used to refer to various other peoples in the area north of Korea. In 1019 some 50 Toi ships sailed from the Korean coast and suddenly attacked Tsushima, Iki, and northwestern Kyūshū, burning, looting, and seizing Japanese prisoners. The attack was repulsed by officials attached to the government headquarters at DAZAIFU, but many of the prisoners were carried off to Korea. Ultimately, some 270 Japanese, rescued from the Jürchen by Koryŏ, were returned to Japan with an official escort.　　　　*G. Cameron HURST III*

toimaru

Shipping agents of the Kamakura (1185–1333) and Muromachi (1333–1568) periods who lived in port towns and major trading centers and engaged in the handling and shipping of commercial goods. In the latter part of the Heian period (794–1185) such men, called *toi,* had been employed at a limited number of ports as salaried shipping agents for the proprietors of landed estates (SHŌEN). By the Kamakura period they were becoming independent of the *shōen* proprietors and were found in most of the major ports, such as Hyōgo (now part of Kōbe) and Tsuruga (now in Fukui Prefecture), as middlemen who arranged for the storage, handling, and shipping of tax rice and other commodities from the hinterland. They also provided lodging and transportation for estate owners and other travelers. By the late Muromachi period many of these agents had become wholesale dealers, called TOIYA, in trade centers like Kyōto and Nara, specializing in the large-scale distribution of such staples as rice, *sake,* salt, fish, and oil. They came to play an important role in commerce during the Edo period (1600–1868).

Toimisaki

Cape in southern Miyazaki Prefecture, Kyūshū. Extends south into the Pacific Ocean embracing Shibushi Bay. It is a mountainous region that ends abruptly in a series of cliffs along the coast. Noted for a large herd of wild horses which graze there and for the many sago palms which grow in the vicinity of Misaki Shrine. Part of Nichinan Coast Quasi-National Park.

toiya

Also pronounced *ton'ya.* A type of middleman-merchant who played a key role in Edo-period (1600–1868) commerce. Called TOIMARU in the Kamakura (1185–1333) and Muromachi (1333–1568) periods. These merchants included both the *shiire-doiya,* who sold goods on commission to the *nakagai* (distributor or retailer), and the *niuke-doiya,* who bought and sold goods on speculation. From the middle of the Edo period most *toiya* were of the latter kind. Some specialized in certain kinds of products and others concentrated on goods from specific regions of the country. These *toiya* formed guildlike associations (KABUNAKAMA) that maintained a thriving monopoly on commerce throughout the Edo period, despite a temporary ban on their activities in the middle of the 19th century. After the Meiji Restoration of 1868 the distinction between the *toiya* and the *nakagai* became blurred, and the modern wholesaler came into existence. See also NIJŪSHIKUMI-DOIYA; TOKUMI-DOIYA.

tōji

(also pronounced *toji*). Japanese SAKE (rice wine) brewer. Specifically, the occupational title for the head overseer of the crew that carries out *sake*-brewing operations. It is thought that the word *tōji* originally stood for the wife of the household *(toji)* whose job it was to make *sake* in ancient times. Because *sake* was brewed during approximately 100 days from December through March, the off-season for farming, *tōji* were also known as "100-day men" *(hyakunichi otoko).* The term is particularly associated with *sake* brewers of the Tamba region of Kyōto Prefecture, the Tajima district of Hyōgo Prefecture, and the Mihara region of Hiroshima Prefecture.　　　　*NOGUCHI Takenori*

Tōji

A monastery-temple, officially called the Kyōō Gokokuji, located in Minami Ward, Kyōto. Tōji, founded in 796 by imperial order, is today the head temple of the Tōji branch of the SHINGON SECT of Buddhism. The original buildings of the temple have not survived but were replaced with later reconstructions. The existing *kondō* (main hall), sponsored in 1599 by TOYOTOMI HIDEYORI, is one of the largest Buddhist buildings erected during the Azuchi-Momoyama period (1568–1600). The five-storied pagoda rebuilt in 1644, with support from the shōgun TOKUGAWA IEMITSU, is the tallest in Japan and a Kyōto landmark. In addition to its impressive array of buildings, Tōji possesses an extraordinary collection of Buddhist art. Sculpture, paintings, mandalas, implements used in esoteric rituals, outstanding works of calligraphy, and many manuscripts furnish material proof that Tōji was the center of Shingon practice in Kyōto.

In 794, when the capital was transferred to Kyōto, two temples were founded for the protection of the city: Tōji (East Temple) and the short-lived Saiji (West Temple). They were situated on either side of the Rajōmon (commonly called Rashōmon), the gate which marked the south entrance to the central avenue leading to the imperial palace. When the emperor SAGA appointed KŪKAI abbot of Tōji in 823 the temple was effectively transformed into a Shingon monastery. The following year it was designated the Kyōō Gokokuji combining the title of two sutras invoked in Shingon services for the protection of the state: the *Kongōchō daikyō kyō* (Skt: *Vajraśekhara-sūtra*) and the *Ninnō gokoku kyō* (Skt: *Prajñāpāramitā-sūtra*). Kūkai enlarged Tōji by adding other buildings to suit the needs of esoteric rituals and established it as Kyōto's main Shingon monastery where the study and practice of esoteric Buddhism flourished.

Kūkai, posthumously called Kōbō Daishi (the Great Master Kōbō), was one of Japan's foremost Buddhist leaders. He was distinguished as a scholar and was well versed in Chinese classics, literature, and history. He wrote extensively on Buddhist texts and was accomplished as an artist and calligrapher. After spending two years in China, Kūkai returned in 806 to establish the Shingon sect in Japan. In 816 the court gave him title to Mt. Kōya (KŌYASAN), where he built the Kongōbuji, the first exclusively Shingon temple in Japan; it later became the head temple of the Kōyasan Shingon sect.

When the emperor ordered Kūkai to settle in Kyōto in 823, Tōji was already 27 years old. It was a traditional temple not unlike those of the Nara period (710–794), in which the main buildings, *nandaimon* (great south gate), *kondō, kōdō* (lecture hall), and *jikidō* (refectory) are ranged, one behind the other, on a north-south axis. Instead of two pagodas, Kūkai built only one pagoda in the southeast corner of the Tōji compound in 826. It was to function not as a monument for a relic in the traditional manner but as a place for the mandalas of the two realms, the Womb Realm (TAIZŌKAI) and the Diamond Realm (KONGŌKAI), which showed in diagrammatic form the relationships among the esoteric divinities used for contemplation and rituals.

The *kondō,* built in 798, was retained by Kūkai in its original form. The esoteric transformation of the temple was manifested primarily in the lecture hall, where traditionally monks assembled to study and discuss Buddhist scripture. Here Kūkai designed an interior in 826 suitable for the most important esoteric rituals. On a long, rectangular altar-platform he placed sculptures of 21 deities arranged in mandala form. The central position is occupied by the seated image of the Buddha DAINICHI (Mahāvairocana), who represents all creation as well as ultimate reality. From Dainichi radiate the Buddhas of the Four Directions whose four images surround him. To the east of this group are the personifications of "perfect and indestructible wisdom" in the form of the Five Great Bodhisattvas (Go Dai Bosatsu), who, in turn, are balanced to the west by the Five Wisdom Kings (Go Dai Myōō), with Fudō MYŌŌ, "the Immovable One," at the center. The Wisdom Kings, ferocious in expression, personify the wrath of Dainichi Nyorai directed against evil. On either side of the altar are esoteric transformations of the guardian figures of Bonten (Brahmā) and Taishakuten (Indra). The Shitennō (the Four Heavenly Kings) stand guard at the corners of the altar.

The *kōdō* was completed in 839 when the "eye-opening" or consecration ceremony was held. Although some of the deities had been known in Nara during the 8th century, never before had they been produced with such awe-inspiring power. Devotion to the Five Wisdom Kings was unknown until they appeared as a group for the first time at Tōji. They soon became popular as divine intermediaries with Dainichi Nyorai. Among them, Fudō Myōō was considered to be especially efficacious.

Tōjimbō

A section of the geological formation known as Tōjimbō, in which jagged pillars of rock have been formed by the Sea of Japan through erosion.

A second statue of Fudō Myōō carved in wood shortly after Kūkai's death is enshrined in the *mieidō* (portrait chapel). Rarely on view, the image is in excellent condition. A temple tradition has it that this Fudō had been worshiped by Kūkai, whose residence stood on the site of the present *mieidō*.

After Kūkai's death a cult began to develop around him; it gained momentum during the Kamakura period (1185–1333), when portraits of him were circulated throughout Japan. A statue of Kūkai carved in 1233 by Kōshō, a son of the famous sculptor UNKEI, was placed in a separate sanctuary in the *mieidō*, which from that time on was also known as Taishidō (The Hall of the Great Master). To this day, on the 21st of every month, a service is held at Tōji to commemorate the death of Kūkai; thousands of devotees stream into the temple to worship before the image of the illustrious founder of the Shingon sect.

■——Takaaki Sawa, *Art in Japanese Esoteric Buddhism* (1972).
Lucie R. WEINSTEIN

Tōjimbō

Scenic spot on the Sea of Japan coast, Fukui Prefecture, central Honshū. Pillarlike joints of pyrozene andesite thrust up 25 m (82 ft) high from the sea, presenting a spectacular sight. Pleasure boats are available. Part of Echizen-Kaga Quasi-National Park.

Tōjin Okichi (1841?–1890)

("Foreigner's Okichi"). Young girl sent to serve Townsend HARRIS, the first American consul in Japan, in response to his request for "female attendants"; real name, Saitō Kichi. Born in Izu Province (now part of Shizuoka Prefecture), Okichi lived with her widowed mother in the port of Shimoda. She entered Harris' service in May 1857 (another attendant was provided for Harris' interpreter, Henry C. J. HEUSKEN) but was returned home after three days by Harris, who complained that her skin was infected. Though she had been handsomely paid, the double stigma of having been sent to the American and then rejected made Okichi an object of ridicule, hence her nickname. She moved to Yokohama, where she lived with a carpenter, and later returned to Shimoda to work as a hairdresser. In 1882 she opened a small restaurant. By this time she had become a heavy drinker, and, faced with bankruptcy, she drowned herself. Okichi's tragic life has been the subject of many works, including *Tōjin Okichi* (1928–31), a fictionalized account of her life by Jūichiya Gisaburō (1897–1937).

Tōji Treasure House

(Tōji Hōmotsuden). Located at TŌJI, a SHINGON SECT temple in Kyōto. This treasure house, opened in 1965, holds many of the famous Buddhist statues, paintings, sutras, and other objects owned by the temple. The paintings include the famous large portraits of seven patriarchs of the Shingon sect. Of these, five are by the Chinese artist Li Zhen (Li Chen) and were brought back from China in 806 by KŪKAI, the founder of the Shingon sect in Japan. There is also a set of the Jūniten (12 Devas Who Protect Buddhism) painted by TAKUMA SHŌGA. The manuscripts include a letter in Kūkai's

hand and his *Shōrai mokuroku* (Memorandum on the Presentation of the List of Newly Imported Sutras). The *kōdō* (lecture hall) contains statues arranged according to the precepts of the *Ninnōgyō* (one of the *Prajñāpāramitā* sutras) mandala. *Laurance* ROBERTS

Tōjō Gimon (1786–1843)

Japanese-language scholar. Born in Wakasa Province (now part of Fukui Prefecture), he later succeeded his father as the head of a Buddhist temple. Tōjō's research focused chiefly on Japanese conjugated words (verbs and adjectives), and it was he who devised the names for conjugational forms still in use today in the traditional grammar (see JAPANESE LANGUAGE STUDIES, HISTORY OF). He also did research on the phonology of Chinese loanwords. His writings include *Katsugo shinan* (2 vols, 1844). *SHIMADA Masahiko*

Tōjō Hideki (1884–1948)

Army general and prime minister (1941–44). Born in Tōkyō, the son of an army officer, Tōjō graduated from the Military Academy and in 1914 from the Army Staff College at the top of his class. He was a military attaché in Switzerland and Germany from 1919 to 1922, and on his return to Japan he taught at the Army Staff College and worked in the Army Ministry before being appointed commander of the First Infantry Regiment in 1929. At the time of the MANCHURIAN INCIDENT in 1931 he was a section head in the Imperial Army General Staff Office. During this period, when many young officers were clamoring for an imperial government supported by the military, Tōjō joined the Issekikai, a group formed by NAGATA TETSUZAN, and the so-called Control faction (TŌSEIHA), which called for technological innovation within the military.

In 1933 he was promoted to major general, but because of the dominance of the more ideological Imperial Way faction (KŌDŌHA) he was assigned to relatively obscure posts. Tōjō was transferred to the military police headquarters of the GUANDONG (KWANTUNG) ARMY in Manchuria in 1935, and after the attempted coup d'etat by Kōdōha officers in the FEBRUARY 26TH INCIDENT (1936), he was responsible for the arrest of all Kōdōha sympathizers in the Guandong Army. He was next assigned to the staff headquarters of the Guandong Army. Joining forces with KISHI NOBUSUKE, then an adviser to the puppet government of Manchuria (MANCHUKUO), and AIKAWA YOSHISUKE, head of the Manchuria Heavy Industries Company, Tōjō built up a new power group, the so-called Manchuria faction. A month after the outbreak of the Sino-Japanese War in July 1937, Tōjō, as chief of staff of the Guandong Army, assumed direct control of the regiments and oversaw the removal of Chinese Nationalist troops from Chahar. Friction developed between Tōjō, who advocated a full-scale war in China, and ISHIWARA KANJI, chief of the Operations Section of the General Staff, who opposed escalation of the war; but Tōjō succeeded in having Ishiwara transferred to Tōkyō.

In May 1938 Tōjō returned to the center of power in Tōkyō. As army vice-minister in the KONOE FUMIMARO cabinet he demonstrated the abilities that earned him the sobriquet "razor-sharp Tōjō." In opposition to Tada Shun, the vice-chief of the Army General Staff, who favored peace negotiations with Chiang Kai-shek, Tōjō continued to support the expansion of the war.

After the fall of the YONAI MITSUMASA cabinet in July 1940, Tōjō was appointed to the posts of army minister and chief of the Manchuria Bureau in Konoe's second cabinet. Encouraged by the successful German blitzkrieg on the European front, he pushed for the conclusion of the TRIPARTITE PACT with Germany and Italy and the invasion of French Indochina. He also pushed toward the absorption of all political parties into the IMPERIAL RULE ASSISTANCE ASSOCIATION. He remained as army minister in Konoe's third cabinet (July 1941).

In view of Japan's steadily deteriorating relations with the United States, it was decided to hold an imperial conference (GOZEN KAIGI) on 6 September 1941; an "outline for implementing the national policy of the empire" was proposed, according to which Japan would go to war if the two countries could not reach some sort of accommodation by early October. Tōjō opposed Konoe's desire for rapprochement with the United States, and the entire cabinet resigned.

At the recommendation of KIDO KŌICHI, the lord keeper of the privy seal (NAIDAIJIN), Tōjō was named prime minister in October 1941. He formed a cabinet with members of his faction from the Manchuria period, taking for himself the post of army minister. The government continued to negotiate with the United States but at the same time prepared for war. The succession of victories after the attack on Pearl Harbor (7 December 1941; 8 December, Japanese time) strengthened Tōjō's position. He managed to suppress all opposition in the April 1942 general election and to make the Imperial Rule Assistance Association a mere subsidiary organ of the government.

In 1943 Tōjō took on the additional post of chief of the newly created Military Procurement Ministry (Gunjushō), and in February 1944 he became chief of the General Staff. But criticism of Tōjō mounted with Japan's deteriorating fortunes in the war, and in July 1944, soon after the fall of Saipan, he was removed from office by a group led by Konoe and Admiral OKADA KEISUKE. After Japan's defeat (August 1945), Tōjō attempted to kill himself on learning of his imminent arrest by the American Army. He was indicted by the International Military Tribunal (see WAR CRIMES TRIALS) as a class A war criminal and was hanged on 23 December 1948. Tōjō was a typical military bureaucrat—hardworking, efficient, and decisive. Loyal to his emperor to the end, he did everything he could to exonerate Hirohito from any blame for his role in the war.

Awaya Kentarō

Tōjō Misao (1884–1966)

Linguist. Born in Tōkyō, he graduated from Tōkyō University and was a professor at Gakushūin University. He was the founder of dialectology in Japan, his most important work being the classification of Japanese dialects. His major publications are: *Dai Nihon hōgen chizu: Kokugo no hōgen kukaku* (1927), a dialect atlas of Japan; *Hōgen to hōgengaku* (1938), a study of dialects and dialectology; *Zenkoku hōgen jiten* (1951), a dictionary of Japanese dialects; and *Bunrui hōgen jiten* (1954), a classificatory dictionary of dialects.

Uwano Zendō

Tokachidake

Active stratovolcano, in Chishima Volcanic Zone, central Hokkaidō. Two great eruptions occurred in 1926 and 1962, causing loss of life and crop damage. The volcano still emits smoke. Numerous hot springs on the slopes serve as bases for climbing and skiing. It is part of Daisetsuzan National Park. Height: 2,077 m (6,813 ft).

Tokachigawa

River in central Hokkaidō, originating on Tokachidake, one of the major peaks that are part of Daisetsuzan National Park, and flowing southeast through Tokachi Plain to the Pacific Ocean. Riverbank terraces and swampland form much of the area along the middle and lower reaches. The water is utilized for irrigation, industry, and electric power. Salmon fishing and sand and gravel exploitation are the principal industries. Length: 178 km (110 mi); area of drainage basin: 8,400 sq km (3,242 sq mi).

Tokachi Plain

(Tokachi Heiya). Located in southeastern Hokkaidō. Most of the plain consists of diluvial upland covered with volcanic ash, but there are also alluvial lowlands on the river Tokachigawa and a coastal plain along the Pacific Ocean. This plain is Japan's greatest producer of beans, sugar beets, potatoes, and hay. Dairy farming also flourishes. The land area worked by one farming household, averaging about 10 hectares (25 acres), is one of the largest in the country. The major city is Obihiro. Area: approximately 3,600 sq km (1,390 sq mi).

tokage

Eumeces latiscutatus. The *tokage* is a small lizard native to Japan with a blackish brown body, fine yellow or green longitudinal stripes, and a bright green tail. It reaches a length of 16–21 centimeters (6–8 in). Commonly found in flatlands and low mountains of Hokkaidō, Honshū, Shikoku, and Kyūshū, it is especially numerous in western Japan, often inhabiting gardens. It likes dry ground, lives in small holes or embankments, and preys in the daytime on small animals such as earthworms and insects. The female lays six to twelve eggs in May or June. Another lizard seen in various places in Japan, the *kana hebi (Takydromus tachydromoides)*, resembles this species in shape and size but is brown all over.

Imaizumi Yoshiharu

Tōkai

City in Aichi Prefecture, central Honshū, on the Chita Peninsula, Ise Bay, some 16 km (10 mi) south of Nagoya. Formerly known for its *nori* (seaweed), it now has many chemical and heavy industrial complexes and is rapidly becoming a dormitory suburb of Nagoya. Pop: 96,049.

Tōkai

(Tōkai Mura). Village in eastern Ibaraki Prefecture, central Honshū, on the Pacific Ocean. With the construction of the ATOMIC ENERGY RESEARCH INSTITUTE here in 1956, Tōkai has developed as the atomic power center of Japan. Numerous atomic power plants and related installations are located here. Pop: 29,197.

Tōkai Bank, Ltd

(Tōkai Ginkō). One of Japan's major city banks, with its main center of business in the Nagoya area. Tōkai Bank traces its roots back to the 1870s, when modern banking was first introduced to Japan; one of its earliest predecessors, the Eleventh National Bank (later the Aichi Bank), was established in 1877. It took its present form in 1941 as a result of the merger of the Aichi Bank, Itō Bank, and Nagoya Bank. It now holds a leading position in retail banking, with a broad base in the corporate and industrial sectors, and a rapidly expanding international network in key financial and business centers in Europe and the United States, as well as Southeast Asia. Tōkai Bank has over 230 domestic branches and 26 overseas offices and affiliates. At the end of March 1982 deposits totaled ¥10.6 trillion (US $44 billion), with time deposits accounting for 64 percent, ordinary deposits 11 percent, current deposits 9 percent, call deposits 8 percent, and others 8 percent. It was capitalized at ¥75 billion (US $311.6 million) in the same year. The bank's headquarters are located in Nagoya.

Tōkaidō

(Eastern Sea Road). The highway that ran from Edo (now Tōkyō) to Kyōto, a route of approximately 488 kilometers (303 mi) generally following the Pacific coast; an extension continued to Ōsaka. Along the road were 53 POST-STATION TOWNS offering a variety of goods and services for the convenience of travelers. These became famous in art and literature (especially the woodblock prints of HIROSHIGE) as the Fifty-Three Stages of the Tōkaidō (Tōkaidō Gojūsantsugi).
History—— The Tōkaidō is an ancient highway, a natural route determined by Japan's mountainous geography. From the time that a central government first crystallized in the Yamato area (around present-day Nara; see YAMATO COURT), the Tōkaidō was the most important route to the east. It was used by military expeditions as the state sought to extend its hegemony and then, as some measure of control became an actuality in the 7th and 8th centuries, by civil administrators, Buddhist priests establishing state-supported temples like the KOKUBUNJI, and others representing the developing central bureaucracy. It was then that the outlying provinces were grouped into seven regions (see GOKI SHICHIDŌ), each traversed by a major highway (the regions bore the same names as the highways; thus Tōkaidō could mean either Eastern Sea Road or Region of the Eastern Sea, i.e., the Pacific side of central Honshū). Thereafter such roads were truly national when there was a strong central government but lapsed into local links when provincial powers, asserting their autonomy, erected barriers and toll gates at their frontiers.

Of the main highways, the San'yōdō, which ran from the capital, Kyōto, west to Dazaifu in northern Kyūshū, was long the most important. But in the late 12th century the headquarters of shōgun MINAMOTO NO YORITOMO was established at Kamakura, and the Tōkaidō became the main artery between the imperial capital at Kyōto and the military capital at Kamakura.

Development—— The golden age of the Tōkaidō was the Edo period (1600–1868). In its early years the Tokugawa shogunate systematically directed a policy of road improvement. Throughout the country, highways were constructed and reconstructed, with emphasis on such roads as the Five Highways (GOKAIDŌ) radiating from Edo, where the shogunate established its capital. Between the late 17th century and the late 18th century, Edo grew from a village to one of the largest cities in the world; ancient Kyōto and the commercial city of Ōsaka were the country's other major cities. The Tōkaidō, linking them, became in a very real sense Japan's "Main Street." It was one of the world's busiest highways.

The few Westerners to travel in Japan during the Edo period—notably the physicians attached to the Dutch factory at DEJIMA—marveled at how smooth and clean the road was, at the conveniences offered, and at the volume of traffic. The roadbed averaged about 5.5 meters (18 ft) wide, although it was officially claimed to be somewhat broader. It consisted of a deep layer of crushed gravel covered with sand, but on mountainous slopes that were subject to erosion it was paved with stone. There were gutters for drainage, and sometimes a mountain stream was diverted alongside so that people and horses could take refreshment. Embankments were planted with pines or cedars to provide shade. Each ri (3.93 km; 2.44 mi) was marked by a mound (ICHIRIZUKA) planted with a nettle tree, and stone guideposts pointed the way at crossroads. In many places Buddhist images stood as protective icons.

Travel—— There was almost no wheeled traffic on the road; heavy, bulky cargo moved by sea. There were pack horses, shod, like men, with straw and led by hostlers (BASHAKU); occasionally a man might ride on the pack. The standard vehicle on the Tōkaidō was the palanquin (KAGO). These ranged in size and style from a daimyō's norimono, a relatively roomy, highly decorated box with sliding doors, to a simple, open seat light enough to be carried by two bearers. Even commoners were permitted to ride if the latter were available.

Most rivers were bridged, had ferries, or could be forded. But large rivers like the Abekawa (which runs through the present-day city of Shizuoka) and the Ōigawa (a few kilometers west of Shizuoka) were sometimes impassable torrents for as long as a month at flood time. At such times travelers might use the alternate road, the NAKASENDŌ (Central Mountain Road), also called the Kiso Kaidō (Kiso Road), over the inland mountains, a longer and more difficult but very scenic route. Even when these rivers were at their normal, low level, a traveler had to be carried across in a palanquin or on the shoulders of a porter. Fees for this service were determined by the depth of the water, but at midstream a passenger might be stalled for hard bargaining. Long ferries were authorized to carry passengers across the huge inlet called Lake Hamana and across the northern end of Ise Bay in order to avoid the formidable rivers in the area of present-day Nagoya.

In addition to the natural hazards of rivers and mountains, there were governmental barriers (SEKISHO) where travelers were inspected for proof of identity and travel permits. The strictest was in the Hakone mountains, considered the gateway to the Kantō Plain and Edo. There officials were on the watch for guns being smuggled into the city or women escaping from it; either could signal rebellion against the shogunate (wives and daughters of the daimyō who were away in the provinces were required to reside in Edo as hostages under the system of alternate attendance; see SANKIN KŌTAI).

Stages—— The shogunate supervised the entire highway to keep it safe and convenient and ordered the establishment of the 53 post stations, keeping most of them under its direct control; the rest were managed by daimyō related to the Tokugawa (SHIMPAN) or direct vassals to the Tokugawa (FUDAI). Most stages maintained a force of 100 pack horses and 100 porters; mountainous terrain or a difficult river crossing might mean that one or the other figure would be larger. In addition, when heavy official travel warranted it, each stage had the authority to levy more men and horses from a designated surrounding area; these levies (SUKEGŌ) often worked hardship on farmers, and many a farmer's son, having tasted the excitement of the Tōkaidō, descended to the ranks of the hard-drinking, gambling, whoring porters, the rough, tough roustabouts of the road (see KUMOSUKE).

Every stage had from about 50 to 200 inns, headed by one or more HONJIN (officially appointed inns for daimyō), that had fine rooms and gardens. There were lesser inns (waki honjin, "side" or subsidiary honjin) for officials and samurai, inns for ordinary travelers, and flophouses for porters. If a stage became crowded, every house in the village took in guests. A few of the large stages had licensed quarters, but almost every inn had complaisant maids if not prostitutes; as the day waned these women would stand in front touting the inn and hustling travelers off the road.

Lining the street at each stage were shops offering simple necessities like tobacco and straw sandals, tea and refreshment, souvenirs, and local products; the last became so well known that a knowledgeable traveler could recite his way from one end of the highway to the other, naming local specialties instead of the towns and villages.

Distinctive features of the stages were dogleg crooks in the road at both ends and a shady detour to a Shintō shrine or Buddhist temple. The detour offered a daimyō an excuse to avoid meeting a daimyō of higher rank, before whom he would have to make some form of obeisance, and the doglegs screened the approach of that other daimyō, since it would be unseemly to scuttle off the road after a superior was in view.

Between the 53 official stages were numerous clusters of inns, teahouses, and shops called "halfway stages" (ai no shuku). Indeed, practically every house along the road catered to wayfarers in one way or another.

Travelers—— Travelers of every status used the road. Of the country's approximately 250 daimyō, about 150 used the Tōkaidō to and from Edo on the journeys required by the system of alternate attendance at the shōgun's court; a great daimyō moved with mettlesome pomp and an entourage that might stretch for miles (see DAIMYŌ PROCESSIONS). Courtiers proceeded on ceremonial visits between shōgun and emperor. The best of the new crop of tea was carried annually to the shōgun from Uji, near Nara; on the road it took precedence over even the greatest daimyō.

Swift couriers (HIKYAKU) carried official tidings, and associations of merchants set up their own courier services to link operations and to carry private messages (a relay of couriers could get a message from Edo to Kyōto in 2 or 3 days, while normal, uninterrupted travel took 12). Peddlers sold patent medicines, fabrics, and notions. Mendicant priests offered talismans, exorcism, and cures; itinerant nuns (bikuni), despite their religious garb, offered themselves. Storytellers and entertainers vied for coins.

Commoners thronged the road on business, pleasure, or pilgrimages to some great Buddhist or Shintō mecca; travel was the greatest adventure available to ordinary people, and pilgrimages afforded an acceptable excuse; the most popular goal, the ISE SHRINE, drew multitudes. Guidebooks proliferated, charting the route, listing points of interest, accommodations, and prices, with counsel on how to avoid illness, confidence men, and sneak thieves.

Today—— The Tōkaidō Road still exists as a highway that in part overlays the old road. Roughly parallel to it are a limited access toll highway and the Tōkaidō Lines of the conventional railway and of the modern "bullet" trains (SHINKANSEN). A few short stretches of the old road still exist to stir the imagination.

——Robert B. Hall, "Tokaido: Road and Region," The Geographical Review (July 1937). Jippensha Ikku, Tōkaidōchū hizakurige (1802–22), tr Thomas Satchell as Shank's Mare (1929); contemporary fiction about the adventures of two happy-go-lucky Tōkaidō travelers. Engelbert Kaempfer, The History of Japan (1906), contains a vivid account of his two journeys to Edo in 1691 and 1692. Mitsui Takaharu, Nihon kōtsū bunka shi (1942), contains a bibliography. Philip Franz von Siebold, Manners and Customs of the Japanese (1841), contains an account of his journey to Edo in 1826. Charles Nelson Spinks, "The Tōkaidō in Popular Literature and Art," Transactions of the Asiatic Society of Japan, 3rd ser, 3 (1954). Oliver Statler, Japanese Inn (1961).　　　Oliver STATLER

Tōkaidō bunken ezu

A series of woodblock prints by the artist Hishikawa MORONOBU (d 1694) depicting the 53 post-stations of the TŌKAIDŌ, the highway linking Edo (now Tōkyō) and Kyōto, with descriptions of famous places along the way; published in 1690 as a set of five folding books. Considered the prototype of Japanese guidebooks, the set is a valuable source for local geography and history.

Tōkaidōchū hizakurige → Jippensha Ikku

Tōkaidō megalopolis

General term for the region along the Pacific coast of Honshū extending west from Tōkyō to Ōsaka and Kōbe. It is the political, economic, and cultural center of Japan with approximately 40 percent of its population and 70 percent of its industrial output in a stretch of land that accounts for only 17 percent of the nation's area. It encompasses most of the big cities in Japan such as Tōkyō, Yokohama, Kawasaki, Nagoya, Kyōto, Ōsaka, and Kōbe along with their numerous satellite cities and suburbs.

Tōkaidō Yotsuya kaidan

(The Ghost Story of Tōkaidō Yotsuya). KABUKI play by TSURUYA NAMBOKU. Often called Yotsuya kaidan. His masterpiece and the most famous ghost play of the classical Japanese theater. The story is about a *rōnin* or masterless *samurai*, Tamiya Iemon, who is persuaded by his rich neighbors to abandon his wife, Oiwa, to achieve social status and wealth. The play shows with wonderful skill the horrible way in which the heroine, Oiwa, is disfigured by poison, the sadistic way in which her husband treats her despite her having just given birth to their son, and then how she is transformed into a revengeful ghost. This ghost play has an interesting relationship with *Kanadehon chūshingura*, the celebrated play about the revenge of the 47 *rōnin* (see FORTY-SEVEN RŌNIN INCIDENT). The characters in both plays are from the same camps of loyal and disloyal retainers and the two plays were originally performed over two days in alternating parts. Whereas *Kanadehon chūshingura* depicts a revenge of honor and loyalty, *Tōkaidō Yotsuya kaidan* portrays those who have failed to be loyal, therefore, incurring the revenge of frightful ghosts. Tsuruya Namboku, a commoner, did not write about loyal people. On the contrary, he dealt at length with the fallen ones: the corrupted, sadistic, and criminal. This play appears to criticize the role of the samurai class who served the shogunal court which fell in the Meiji Restoration (1868) only 44 years after the play's first performance. *Tōkaidō Yotsuya kaidan* can, in this regard, be seen as a premonitory work.

■——Tsuruya Namboku, *Tōkaidō Yotsuya kaidan* (1825), tr Jeanne Sigée as *Les Spectres de Yotsuya* (1979).   *Jeanne* SIGÉE

Tōkai Sanshi (1852–1922)

Novelist; politician. Real name Shiba Shirō. Born in Kazusa Province (now part of Chiba Prefecture). As a youth, he fought for the losing Tokugawa side against the imperial forces in the BOSHIN CIVIL WAR. Afterwards he worked his way through school, then went to the United States in 1879 to study at Harvard University and at the University of Pennsylvania. Back in Japan after six years, he wrote his epic-length political novel (SEIJI SHŌSETSU) *Kajin no kigū* (1885–97, Chance Meetings with Beautiful Women), based partly on his experiences in America. In this work, a Japanese expatriate meets two women revolutionaries, one Irish and one Spanish, at Independence Hall in Philadelphia, and the three proceed to expound at great length on their national histories and to express patriotic concern for their countries' future destinies. Despite its awesome length and absence of real plot, the novel became a bestseller and exerted great influence on the younger generation. Withdrawing from the literary world, he became involved in politics, serving several terms in the lower house of the Diet after 1892. His principal works are *Tōyō no kajin* (1888, A Beauty of the Orient), a novel, and *Ejiputo kinsei shi* (1889, Modern History of Egypt).

Tōkai Shizen Hodō

Nature trail along the foothills of mountains on the old highway TŌKAIDŌ, including the Tanzawa Mountains, the highland Asagiri Kōgen, HŌRAIJISAN, Sekigahara, the Yōrō Mountains, the SUZUKA MOUNTAINS, Mt. Hiei (HIEIZAN), and ARASHIYAMA. It links important points in national, quasi-national, and prefectural parks in the area. Length: 1,376 km (854 mi).

Tōkai University

(Tōkai Daigaku). A private, coeducational university whose central administrative offices are located in Shibuya Ward, Tōkyō. The School of Aeronautics in the city of Shimizu, Shizuoka Prefecture, and the School of Radio Science in Tōkyō, both founded by Matsumae Shigeyoshi (b 1901) in 1943 and 1944, respectively, were combined in 1945 to form Tōkai University. In 1950, the university was reorganized into four faculties, one two-year junior college, and attached facilities including the Tōkai FM broadcasting station. The university has been expanding throughout Japan, and now has eight campuses. It maintains faculties of liberal arts, letters, politics and economics, physical education, engineering, oceanography, science, and medicine. The school is known for the following institutes: Institute of Oceanic Research, Research and Development Institute, Research Institute of Civilization, Research Institute of Visual Arts, Research Institute of Industrial Science, Institute of Student's Studies, Institute of Social and Behaviorial Science, and Research Institute of Educational Technology. Enrollment was 31,952 in 1980.

Tōkamachi

City in southern Niigata Prefecture, central Honshū. Tōkamachi has long been known for its fine silk. It is also known for its very heavy snowfall. The Torioi Festival in January and the Snow Festival in February are famous. Several hot springs are located nearby. Pop: 49,555.

Tōkan kikō

Travel diary of the Kamakura period (1185–1333). Authorship unknown, although it is often attributed to the scholar Minamoto Chikayuki (dates unknown). It is a record of a journey from Kyōto to Kamakura, taken in the autumn of 1242. Imbued with Buddhist feelings, its sensitive observations of people and places during some two weeks on the road and a two-month residence in Kamakura are especially memorable for the elegant *wakan konkō* prose style (classical Japanese with a heavy use of words and phrases from classical Chinese literature). As an important piece of travel literature from the Kamakura period, along with the KAIDŌKI, its prose style has influenced such later works as the HEIJI MONOGATARI. See also TRAVEL DIARIES.

Tokara Islands

(Tokara Rettō). Group of islands extending from southern Kagoshima Prefecture, Kyūshū, to AMAMI ŌSHIMA. It is part of the SATSUNAN ISLANDS. The climate is subtropical; farming and fishing are the principal activities.

Tōka zuiyō

(Leaves from the Peach Blossom [Manse]). A book of records and traditions of the Ichijō family (see GOSEKKE), written in 1480 by ICHIJŌ KANEYOSHI as a guide for his son Fuyuyoshi (also pronounced Fuyura; 1464–1514), who had succeeded him as family head. *Tōka zuiyō* (the title refers to the author's personal library) contains rules of deportment, descriptions of traditional family customs, records of inheritance, and an inventory of family estates and possessions.

Tōkeiji

Also known as Matsugaoka Gosho. Convent in the city of Kamakura, Kanagawa Prefecture, belonging to the Engakuji branch of the RINZAI SECT of Zen Buddhism. Tōkeiji was founded in 1285 by the widow of HŌJŌ TOKIMUNE, regent of the Kamakura shogunate, to serve as a refuge for women who wanted to escape from unhappy marriages. According to the regulations of the convent, which received imperial sanction, any woman who spent three years (in actuality two years) in the convent devoting herself to the religious life could have her marriage terminated. (Hence the temple was popularly known as Enkiridera, or Temple for Divorce; see KAKEKOMIDERA.) It was specifically forbidden for a husband to enter Tōkeiji in pursuit of a wife who was seeking a divorce. Among the famous abbesses of the convent were the daughters of Emperor Go-Daigo (r 1318–39) and of the warrior leader TOYOTOMI HIDEYORI (1593–1615). With the establishment of the Meiji government in 1868, the convent lost its special privileges. After becoming almost defunct, Tōkeiji was reestablished as a monastery by Shaku Sōen (1859–1919), the famous abbot of ENGAKUJI. The temple's library, MATSUGAOKA BUNKO, was built in memory of the Zen scholar D. T. SUZUKI.   *Stanley* WEINSTEIN

Toki

City in southeastern Gifu Prefecture, central Honshū, on the river Tokigawa. Toki is known primarily for its ceramics; many of its wares are exported. Pop: 65,038.

Tokieda Motoki (1900–1967)

Linguist and Japanese grammarian. Born in Tōkyō; graduated from Tōkyō University, majoring in Japanese, in 1926. He served as professor of Japanese at Seoul University from 1927 until 1943, when he succeeded HASHIMOTO SHINKICHI (1882–1945) as professor of Japanese at Tōkyō University.

Tokieda worked in the grammar of both classical and modern Japanese. He is noted for his *gengo katei setsu* (process theory of language), which he placed in opposition to European structural linguistics, particularly the work of Ferdinand de Saussure (1857–1913). His approach was based both on introspective psychology and on earlier studies of Japanese, particularly those of SUZUKI AKIRA (1764-1837).

Tokieda's grammatical system is based on the distinction between *shi* (those words which express the mind's experience) and *ji* (those words which express the mind's activity), that is, between conceptualized and affective elements, or perhaps between semantic and pragmatic elements. It thus follows the tradition of YAMADA YOSHIO (1873-1958) or MATSUSHITA DAIZABURŌ (1878-1935) as against that of Hashimoto Shinkichi. Another key idea is the *ireko-gata kōzō* (nested box structure), which Tokieda adopted in contrast to the linear *bunsetsu* (phrase) structure used by Hashimoto.

Tokieda's ideas have been much criticized, and his work has not achieved the definitive status accorded at an earlier period to Hashimoto's. But it is probably the most influential approach to Japanese grammar of the post-World War II period, and many of Tokieda's former students remain active in developing it. See also JAPANESE LANGUAGE STUDIES, HISTORY OF. *George* BEDELL

Toki family

Provincial leaders in Mino (now part of Gifu Prefecture) from the 12th to the mid-16th century. Claiming descent from MINAMOTO NO YORIMITSU, the Toki were prominent vassals *(gokenin)* of the Kamakura shogunate (1192-1333). For his support of ASHIKAGA TAKAUJI in the founding of the Muromachi shogunate (1338-1573), Toki Yoriyasu (1318-87) was appointed military governor (SHUGO) not only of the family base in Mino but also of Owari (now Aichi Prefecture) and Ise (now Mie Prefecture). Thus the Toki family was ranked with the ŌUCHI FAMILY and the AKAMATSU FAMILY as one of the most powerful provincial leaders up to the end of the 14th century. Toki power began to erode during the ŌNIN WAR (1467-77), when the family was gradually displaced by the Saitō, who were deputy military governors *(shugodai)*. In 1542 Toki Yorinari was defeated by SAITŌ DŌSAN, and the family lost its domain in Mino. The Toki later became direct vassals *(hatamoto)* of the Tokugawa shogunate (1603-1867).

Tokio Marine & Fire Insurance Co, Ltd

(Tōkyō Kaijō Kasai Hoken). Japan's largest property insurance company, established in 1879 by SHIBUSAWA EIICHI. It was the first such company founded in Japan, and is a major member of the MITSUBISHI group. Of the 22 property insurance companies in Japan, it boasts the largest total sales and leads also in the fields of marine, fire, automobile, and new types of insurance. At the time it was established, it was engaged in marine insurance only. It began overseas operations from an early period, opening offices in Paris, London, and New York in 1890 under the name Tokio Marine. In 1944 the original Tokio Marine & Fire Insurance Co, the Mitsubishi Marine & Fire Insurance Co, and the Meiji Fire & Marine Insurance Co merged to form the present company. After World War II, when marine insurance entered a long period of stagnation, the firm concentrated its efforts on fire and automobile insurance.

Aside from its main office in Tōkyō, the company has a total of 27 major offices, 284 branches, 121 service centers, and about 30,500 agents in Japan. It also has 35 offices in 23 countries overseas. It is currently emphasizing the internationalization of its operations and the development of homeowner's insurance, and has invested heavily to expand both its sales network and the organization of its local service systems.

The company's total assets of ¥1.4 trillion (US $5.8 billion) at the end of March 1982 ranked first in Japan, accounting for some 17.3 percent of the total assets of all the nation's property insurance companies. In the same year the company's net income from premiums totaled ¥533.7 billion (US $2.2 billion), broken down as follows: automobile insurance, ¥186.2 billion (US $773.5 million), constituting 34.9 percent; fire insurance, ¥90.6 billion (US $376.4 million), constituting 17 percent; marine insurance, ¥94.7 billion (US $393.4 million), constituting 17.7 percent; and others, ¥162.2 billion (US $673.8 million), constituting 30.4 percent. The firm was capitalized at ¥68 billion (US $282.5 million) in 1982.

Tokitsugu Kyō ki

Thirty-seven volume diary by Yamashina Tokitsugu (1507-79), a court noble, covering the years 1527 to 1576. As head of the office responsible for imperial household finances (Uchikuraryō), a hereditary position held by his family, Tokitsugu was able to observe closely the indigence of the imperial family during a period of continual civil strife. He describes having to save funds for imperial trips and borrow ceremonial robes and accoutrements. The diary is useful for its account of conditions in the capital and in Yamashiro, where Tokitsugu owned an estate, as well as for its references to literature, court rituals, and music, subjects in which the author was well versed.

tokiwazu-bushi

Type of music for KABUKI, accompanied by SHAMISEN and other instruments. In 1730 Miyakoji Bungonojō (1660-1740) and his follower Mojidayū (1709-81) brought from Kyōto to Edo (now Tōkyō) a new style of kabuki chant which rapidly became popular there but was banned by the government in 1739, perhaps because of intrigue by rival singers. Bungonojō returned to Kyōto, and the old Miyakoji style eventually disappeared; but under the name Tokiwazu, Mojidayū obtained permission to continue in Edo and, from 1747 onward, performed a series of new pieces, together with the *shamisen* player and composer Sasaki Ichizō I (d 1768). These included the well-known *Seki no to*, *Yamamba* (or *Yamauba*), and *Modorikago*. Meanwhile in 1748 Mojidayū's son established a branch line, performing another new style, *tomimoto-bushi*. After Mojidayū's death *tokiwazu-bushi* continued, and it gave rise to further subschools of both chant and *shamisen*. The most distinguished chanters of modern times are Tokiwazu Mojibei III (1888-1960), Chitose Dayū (b 1916), and Tokiwazu Kikusaburō (b 1930). The main *shamisen* school of *tokiwazu-bushi* was founded by Kishizawa Shikisa I (1730-83), Ichizō I's successor.

As music, *tokiwazu-bushi* drew on the traditions of GIDAYŪ-BUSHI, which it adapted for the kabuki theater, particularly to accompany dance episodes. It has a more dignified character than KIYOMOTO-BUSHI: the singing is purer and less nasal, and the accompanying ensemble is less bright in sound. However, it uses the same medium-sized *shamisen*, and some of the same melodic patterns, such as *otoshi*. The present repertoire contains over 70 pieces of various types, including *Noriaibune*, *Kumo no ito*, *Kuruwa hakkei*, *Yama-meguri*, and *Omiwa*.

📖 ——Gunji Masakatsu, ed, *Tokiwazu*, vol 7 of *Hōgaku taikei* (1971). *David B.* WATERHOUSE

Toki Zemmaro (1885-1980)

WAKA poet and scholar of Japanese literature. Pen name Toki Aika. Born in Tōkyō. Graduate of Waseda University. He began writing *waka* while still a middle-school student. His *waka* were original in that they were written and printed in roman letters and in three lines (independent of their syllable count) instead of the traditional two. They were often compared with the *waka* of ISHIKAWA TAKUBOKU, with whom Toki established a lifelong friendship. His poetry is notable for its focus on daily life rather than on nature and the seasons. An editorial staff member of the influential newspaper *Asahi shimbun*, he was also active in the postwar national language reform program. In 1947 he received the Japan Academy Award for *Tayasu Munetake* (1942-46), a study of the poet TAYASU MUNETAKE. Toki's principal poetry collection is *Naki warai* (1910).

Tokkō → Special Higher Police

Tokkōtai → Kamikaze Special Attack Force

Tokoname

City in Aichi Prefecture, central Honshū; some 34 km (21 mi) south of Nagoya. High-quality clay from nearby mountains is used for making TOKONAME WARE. There is a ceramics museum featuring both old and contemporary products. Fishing, manufacture of cotton cloth, and *nori* (a kind of seaweed) culture are also carried out. Pop: 54,346.

Tokoname ware

(tokoname-yaki). A strong, heavy, reddish brown ware made from the early 12th century to the first half of the 16th century, with some production continuing to the present. The kilns are distributed throughout the Chita Peninsula, a narrow strip of land jutting into

Mikawa Bay south of the present-day city of Nagoya, Aichi Prefecture.

The earliest datable Tokoname piece is a jar with three lines incised horizontally around the body. It was excavated at the Imamiya Shrine in Kyōto and has an epitaph bearing a date equivalent to 1125. Similar jars were made at a slightly earlier date at the SANAGE kilns, east of Nagoya and about 25 kilometers (15.5 mi) north of the present-day city of Tokoname. This, together with the fact that the most numerous product of the Tokoname kilns, a small unglazed bowl (YAMACHAWAN), was also transmitted from Sanage, leads scholars to believe that potters actually immigrated to Tokoname from Sanage and established kilns there sometime in the late 11th or early 12th century.

Because the Chita Peninsula was a farming area, the kilns prospered only by producing durable, functional products needed by the farmers in their daily lives. Over 520 kilns have been excavated thus far. Their limited variety of products, in addition to the abovementioned types, included large jars with wide mouths, large jars, grinding bowls, and water vases. Many of these jars were used for cinerary urns or sutra burials, in addition to their usual uses. The jars were made by the coiling technique with the walls left rather thick for strength. They were then fired in a through-draft or tunnel kiln (anagama), usually to stoneware hardness (above 1,250°C or 2,282°F). The body, because of its high iron content, usually became a reddish brown. A dark olive, natural ash glaze typically formed on the shoulder, running irregularly down over the body.

Although a rather large scale of production has continued to the present, the most typical and best jars were made from the second half of the 13th to the first half of the 15th century.

Richard L. MELLOTT

Tokonami Takejirō (1867–1935)

Politician. Born in Satsuma Province (now Kagoshima Prefecture). Tokonami entered government service upon his graduation from Tōkyō University. After serving in various prefectural posts, he was elected to the Diet in 1914 as a member of the RIKKEN SEIYŪKAI party. He became home minister in the HARA TAKASHI (1918) and TAKAHASHI KOREKIYO (1921) cabinets. Politically ambitious, he led a group of Seiyūkai members who supported the nonparty cabinet of KIYOURA KEIGO to form the SEIYŪ HONTŌ party (1924). The party was unable to attract a sufficient following, and in 1927 it merged with the KENSEIKAI to form the RIKKEN MINSEITŌ. Two years later Tokonami rejoined the Seiyūkai but was expelled when he joined the OKADA KEISUKE cabinet (1934) as communications minister without party consent. Tokonami was connected with several bribery scandals. He helped to found the nationalistic DAI NIPPON KOKUSUIKAI (Great Japan National Essence Society) in 1919.

Tokorogawa

River in northeastern Hokkaidō, originating in the Ishikari Mountains and flowing through Kitami Basin into the Sea of Okhotsk. Areas along the upper reaches are covered with forests and a lumber industry has developed. The middle and lower reaches form an agricultural district. Length: 144 km (89 mi); area of drainage basin: 1,930 sq km (745 sq mi).

Tokorozawa

City in southern Saitama Prefecture, central Honshū; some 30 km (19 mi) from Tōkyō. Tokorozawa developed as one of the POST-STATION TOWNS on the highway Edo Kaidō in the Edo period (1600–1868). It was also known as a production and distribution center for silk. Japan's first airport was built here by the Imperial Japanese Army; it became an American air base after World War II but was returned to Japan in 1971. Local products are tea, cotton sheets, and bamboo wares. Today it is one of the principal dormitory suburbs of Tōkyō. Attractions include Lake Sayama and UNESCO Village. Pop: 236,477.

Tokoyo

(the "eternal land"). An imaginary realm in Japanese mythology. Of uncertain location, Tokoyo is generally conceived as a world beyond the sea, an oceanic paradise vaguely connected with immortality and fertility. Legends concerning Tokoyo appear in the KOJIKI (712, Record of Ancient Matters) and NIHON SHOKI (720, Chronicles of Japan), the two oldest extant histories of Japan, and in several of the FUDOKI (regional gazetteers). According to the *Kojiki* and *Nihon shoki,* the dwarf deity Sukunahikona no Kami came mysteriously riding over the waves in a miniature boat fashioned from the pod of the *kagami* plant. Sukunahikona assisted the god ŌKUNINUSHI NO MIKOTO in creating and solidifying the land, whereupon he departed for Tokoyo. (According to one version, Sukunahikona went to the isle of Awa and climbed a stalk of millet, from which he was flipped off and propelled to Tokoyo.) The *Nihon shoki* also credits Sukunahikona and Ōkuninushi with the establishment of medicine and the control of animals and identifies Sukunahikona as patron deity of alcoholic beverages. The stories surrounding Sukunahikona exemplify the belief in MAREBITO, mysterious visitors from the other world who confer material and cultural benefits upon mankind.

Human culture heroes may also visit Tokoyo, but their return to the earthly realm is fraught with grief because of the time differential between this world and the eternal land. Urashima no Ko, whose story appears in the *Tango fudoki* and the MAN'YŌSHŪ, an 8th-century collection of Japanese classical poetry, is said to have fallen asleep beside a multicolored tortoise which turned into a beautiful woman and transported him to Tokoyo. After three years he returned to his native village, but all had changed and neither his home nor anyone he knew was to be found. Upon inquiry he learned that over 300 years had elapsed during his absence. In loneliness and despair he sought reunion with his wife in Tokoyo, but, in breaking his promise not to open the jeweled box she had given him, he was rendered unable to return. Similarly, the *Kojiki* and *Nihon shoki* relate that Tajimamori was sent to Tokoyo by Emperor Suinin to retrieve the fruit of the "seasonless, ever-fragrant tree" but that he died of grief when he returned from his arduous mission 10 years later only to learn that the emperor had already passed away. The *Nihon shoki* version of this episode reveals the influence of the Chinese beliefs surrounding the realm of the Taoist immortals (SENNIN), with which the notion of Tokoyo later became amalgamated in the popular consciousness.

Kyōko Motomochi NAKAMURA

Tokto → Takeshima

Tokubetsu Kōtō Keisatsu → Special Higher Police

Tokuda Kyūichi (1894–1953)

Politician and leading communist figure. Born in Okinawa, Tokuda attended night school at Nihon University and graduated in 1920. Even as a high school student he was interested in socialism, and in 1920 he joined the Shakai Shugi Dōmei, a socialist study group. He attended the Far Eastern People's Conference (January–February 1922) held under Comintern auspices in Moscow and helped to form the JAPAN COMMUNIST PARTY (JCP) in 1922. In February 1928 he ran unsuccessfully for the Diet as a candidate of the RŌDŌ NŌMINTŌ (Labor–Farmer Party). Soon after, he was arrested in the government roundup of leftists known as the MARCH 15TH INCIDENT; he remained in prison until October 1945, refusing to recant. He became secretary-general of the postwar JCP in 1945 and was elected the following year to the House of Representatives for the first of three terms. With the so-called RED PURGE by OCCUPATION authorities in 1950, Tokuda persuaded the party to resort to violent tactics, and he himself went underground. He died in Beijing (Peking). Tokuda's impassioned speeches were said to have contributed to the JCP's popularity in the immediate postwar years, but he was also criticized for his authoritarian manner. Together with SHIGA YOSHIO he wrote an account of their imprisonment, *Gokuchū jūhachinen* (1947, Eighteen Years in Jail).

Tokuda Shūsei (1871–1943)

Author. Real name Tokuda Sueo. Born in Kanazawa. Much of Shūsei's fiction is autobiographical, often centering upon his wife or women friends; his name is usually associated with Japanese NATURALISM (shizen shugi), a literary movement that flourished in Japan from about 1907 through 1911. Unlike some Japanese naturalists, Shūsei was relatively unconcerned with the intellectual bases and philosophical implications of literary naturalism. The realistic style and frank autobiography of Japanese naturalism suited him perfectly. Philosophically, his work is marked more by a familiar Japanese fatalism than by Western determinism.

Tokugawa family——Chart 1

Tokugawa Shogunal Line		
1. Ieyasu	(1543–1616) (r 1603–05)	
2. Hidetada	(1579–1632) (r 1605–23)	
3. Iemitsu	(1604–51) (r 1623–51)	
4. Ietsuna	(1641–80) (r 1651–80)	
5. Tsunayoshi	(1646–1709) (r 1680–1709)	son of Iemitsu
6. Ienobu	(1662–1712) (r 1709–12)	son of Tsunashige of Kōfu collateral line; grandson of Iemitsu
7. Ietsugu	(1709–16) (r 1713–16)	
8. Yoshimune	(1684–1751) (r 1716–45)	son of Mitsusada of Kii collateral line; grandson of Yorinobu; great-grandson of Ieyasu
9. Ieshige	(1711–61) (r 1745–60)	
10. Ieharu	(1737–86) (r 1760–86)	
11. Ienari	(1773–1841) (r 1787–1837)	son of Harusada of Hitotsubashi collateral line; grandson of Munetada; great-grandson of Yoshimune
12. Ieyoshi	(1793–1853) (r 1837–53)	
13. Iesada	(1824–58) (r 1853–58)	
14. Iemochi	(1846–66) (r 1858–66)	son of Nariyuki of Kii; grandson of Ienari
15. Yoshinobu	(1837–1913) (r 1867)	son of Nariaki of Mito collateral line; son by adoption of Masamaru of Hitotsubashi collateral line

⚡ Adoption.

NOTE: The numbers 1 through 15 indicate the order of shogunal succession.

A frail youth, raised in poverty, with a somewhat drunken father unable to accept the *samurai* Tokuda family's fall in status after the social changes of the Meiji Restoration (1868), Shūsei kept company with his mother and sisters rather than with male playmates. Although he wrote many autobiographical stories, Shūsei could never bring himself to write of his childhood. He began his writing career around the turn of the century as one of the principal followers of the well-known author OZAKI KŌYŌ, but after Kōyō's death in 1903, he moved from the romantic style associated with Kōyō to the blend of realism and confession known as *shizen shugi*. This move is reflected in *Arajotai* (1908, The New Household), which treats the frustrations of a young working-class couple Shūsei had observed. Thereafter, however, Shūsei wrote mostly autobiographical fiction. *Kabi* (1911, Mold), for example, covers a period of about five years in his life, beginning with his marriage in 1902 to his housekeeper's daughter. *Kabi* is a classic example of the Japanese genre known as the I-NOVEL *(watakushi shōsetsu)*.

In *Tadare* (1913, Festering), Shūsei put aside autobiography to deal with a favorite subject: a woman of the demimonde. *Tadare* is more subjective and less factual than *Kabi*. When his wife died in 1926, Shūsei began a series of affairs with younger women—aspiring novelists, *geisha*, and others. They provided the inspiration for a long string of stories, including his best-known works, *Kasō jimbutsu* (1935–38, Masquerading Characters) and *Shukuzu* (1941, Miniature). *Kasō jimbutsu* recounts the most passionate and notorious of Shūsei's affairs. Although told primarily from the man's (Shūsei's) point of view, its chief success is in the characterization of his mistress, a beautiful, brazenly nonconformist novelist and divorcee with several children. *Shukuzu,* like many of his works, first appeared in newspaper serialization and is highly episodic. However, the young geisha heroine is treated in depth and with sympathy. The serialization of *Shukuzu* was halted by wartime authorities and never completed.

■——Tokuda Shūsei, *Shūsei zenshū* (Rinsen Shoten, 1974). Tokuda Shūsei, "Kunshō" (1935), tr Ivan Morris as "The Order of the White Paulownia" (1961). Noguchi Fujio, *Tokuda Shūsei den* (1965). Noguchi Fujio, *Tokuda Shūsei nōto* (1972). Robert Rolf, "Shūsei, Hakuchō and the Age of Literary Naturalism, 1907–1911," PhD dissertation, University of Hawaii (1975).   Robert ROLF

Tokugawa Akitake (1853–1910)

Daimyō of the Mito domain (now part of Ibaraki Prefecture); son of TOKUGAWA NARIAKI. In 1867, a year before the Meiji Restoration, he attended the Paris International Exposition as shogunal representative. Receiving word of the imminent demise of the shogunate, he hastened back to Japan. He joined the imperial side in the BOSHIN CIVIL WAR, and upon the establishment of the PREFECTURAL SYSTEM by the new government, he was appointed governor of Mito. He also participated in the government-sponsored development of Hokkaidō.

Tokugawa bakufu → Tokugawa shogunate

Tokugawa family

One of the major warrior lineages in Japanese history, the Tokugawa dominated politics from 1600 to 1868. Their period of rule is known as the Tokugawa period or, more commonly, as the EDO PERIOD, after their seat of government at Edo (now Tōkyō). The family's fortunes were established by TOKUGAWA IEYASU, who founded the TOKUGAWA SHOGUNATE. His was the last and most powerful of the three shogunates that ruled Japan from 1192 until the MEIJI RESTORATION of 1868.

Origins——Ieyasu's ancestral family emerged from historical obscurity during the 15th century. At that time it was a local warrior family established in the foothills of Mikawa Province (now part of Aichi Prefecture) east of Nagoya. Resident in the vicinity of the village of Matsudaira, it was known as the Matsudaira family. The first reliably identifiable Tokugawa ancestor was Matsudaira Chikauji, who lived sometime around 1400. Chikauji's descendants slowly extended their influence southward from the Matsudaira vicinity to the coastal section of Mikawa. About six generations later Matsudaira Kiyoyasu (1511–35) established control over most of the province. In 1535, however, he was killed and was succeeded by his young son Hirotada (1526–49).

Hirotada was able to preserve his family's position only by commending himself to his powerful neighbor, the *daimyō* IMAGAWA YOSHIMOTO. Twelve years later, military reverses compelled Hirotada to send his four-year-old son Takechiyo (later known as Ieyasu) to Yoshimoto as a hostage. In 1560 Yoshimoto died in battle and Takechiyo, now 17 years old, returned home and took charge of his remaining vassals and family members. The following spring he commended his family to his other powerful neighbor and erstwhile enemy ODA NOBUNAGA.

By 1567 the Matsudaira family controlled most of Mikawa Province (now part of Aichi Prefecture) and that winter Takechiyo changed his name to Tokugawa Ieyasu. Records of uncertain veracity indicate that his ancestor Chikauji had been given as an adoptive heir to the childless Matsudaira family by a Tokugawa lineage that had subsequently disappeared. Ieyasu evidently took the name Tokugawa because he wished to be designated governor of Mikawa (Mikawa no kami) and court genealogists said his Matsudaira ancestry lacked hereditary qualification for the title. The Tokugawa name, by contrast, was held to meet the requirement of prior rank. Scholars have also suggested that Ieyasu changed his name in order to place social distance between himself and the heads of other Matsudaira lineages, some of whom had shown a strong interest in seizing Ieyasu's position as chief of the main lineage. Whatever his motive, the name change proved useful a few years later when genealogists were to claim that the shadowy Tokugawa family traced its ancestry back to the illustrious MINAMOTO FAMILY and that in consequence Ieyasu could legitimately claim the hereditary title of SHŌGUN bestowed on the founder of the KAMAKURA SHOGUNATE (1192–1333).

Tokugawa family——Chart 2

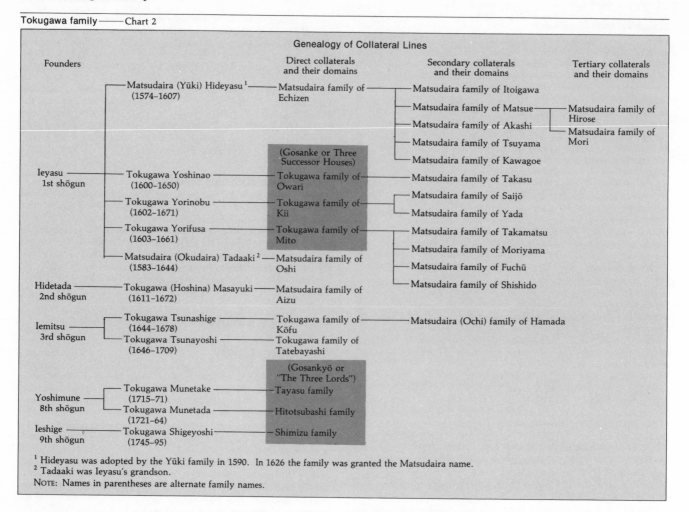

Genealogy of Collateral Lines

[1] Hideyasu was adopted by the Yūki family in 1590. In 1626 the family was granted the Matsudaira name.
[2] Tadaaki was Ieyasu's grandson.
NOTE: Names in parentheses are alternate family names.

Ieyasu's rapid rise to national power culminated in his victory in the Battle of SEKIGAHARA in 1600. In 1603 the court formally recognized his preeminent political position by designating him shōgun, signifying that he ruled the land at the behest of the emperor in the legitimate tradition of the earlier shogunates.

The Names Matsudaira and Tokugawa —— The Tokugawa family was thus a direct outgrowth of the Matsudaira family. However, since the name Matsudaira was later used by many families, the relationship of the two became complicated.

Matsudaira families fell into four general categories. The first consisted of the true Matsudaira lineages. Well before Ieyasu's day the Matsudaira had established several branches besides his, and each traced its ancestry to one of the family heads between Chikauji and Hirotada. Some of those lines died out, but others survived into the 20th century. Most continued to be called Matsudaira, but some used names such as Ogyū, Hisamatsu, Ōkōchi, Sakurai, and Fujii.

The second category of Matsudaira were branches of the Tokugawa shogunal line. The single largest bloc of those later Matsudaira was the direct collateral line based at Fukui and its several branches.

The third category of Matsudaira lineages consisted of a number of Tokugawa vassal (FUDAI) families that acquired the name Matsudaira through special service or association with the early shōguns. They used Matsudaira sometimes as a secondary name and sometimes as a primary name. The category included families named Okudaira, Honjō, Toda, Matsui, Yanagisawa, and certain Ogyū and Hisamatsu. For the most part they behaved and were treated as fudai families, but a few, notably Okudaira of Oshi (now part of Saitama Prefecture), Hoshina of Aizu (now part of Fukushima Prefecture), and Ochi of Hamada (now part of Shimane Prefecture), managed to maintain a familial identification successfully.

The fourth category consisted of powerful unrelated, nonvassal TOZAMA ("outside") families for whom Matsudaira became an honorary name. The name was awarded liberally by Ieyasu and later shōguns as a means of cultivating good will. By the late Edo period, most of the greatest tozama families, including the main lines of the MAEDA, DATE, Kuroda, SHIMAZU, and MŌRI families, were honorary Matsudaira.

After taking the name Tokugawa, Ieyasu chose to treat the early Matsudaira kinsmen as fudai rather than as related families. In consequence they tended to behave and to be treated as fudai lineages throughout the Edo period, and their status became very similar to that of fudai daimyō who later bore the name Matsudaira as a mark of special distinction. The great tozama daimyō with the honorary Matsudaira name continued to be regarded in the main as tozama daimyō. Thus three of the four Matsudaira categories were not really regarded or treated as relatives of the Tokugawa shogunal line. When historians speak of the Tokugawa family as a lineage or kinship group, therefore, they properly include the shogunal line itself, those of its branches called Tokugawa, and those called Matsudaira (see Charts 1 and 2). They do not include the original Matsudaira kinsmen, the later fudai Matsudaira, or the unrelated honorary tozama Matsudaira.

The Tokugawa Kinship Group —— In basic character the Tokugawa family was an ordinary Japanese familial unit or "house" (ie or ke) consisting of the main lineage (honke) and its collaterals (bunke). The main lineage was that of the shogunal succession headquartered in the city of Edo. The collateral lines were the related or SHIMPAN daimyō. The greatest of the Tokugawa shimpan houses in time produced branches of their own, secondary and tertiary collaterals, and the whole Tokugawa family, including these later collaterals, eventually came to number about 20 lineages in all.

Of these several shimpan lineages, three were of exceptional stature. These were the GOSANKE or Three Successor Houses, headquartered in the cities of Mito, Nagoya, and Wakayama and usually known as the houses of Mito, Owari, and Kii. The three respective domains of Mito (now part of Ibaraki Prefecture), Owari (now part of Aichi Prefecture), and Kii (now Wakayama Prefecture), were established as the domains of the younger sons of Ieyasu. They and their descendants kept the family name Tokugawa. Three other less prestigious branch lines were established in the 18th century by the shōguns Yoshimune and Ieshige, and they were known collectively as the GOSANKYŌ or Three Lords. They also retained the name Tokugawa. The other *shimpan* used the name Matsudaira and were known collectively as *kamon* (related houses).

Altogether the Tokugawa kinship group controlled much of Japan. Its very size made it fragile, however, because the interests of its many constituent parts did not always coincide. Nonetheless some cohesion was retained through intrafamilial marriage and adoption arrangements that periodically strengthened the bonds of kinship. These patterns persisted because in the Tokugawa family, as in others, collaterals were expected to provide successors for the parent line should the latter fail to produce an heir. The Gosanke and later the Gosankyō furnished shogunal heirs from time to time, and certain secondary collaterals in turn provided heirs to major *shimpan* as the need arose. Conversely, when a parent line had a surfeit of progeny, branch lines often adopted them as heirs. In all these arrangements, the branches benefited through their strengthened ties to the greater, wealthier main line.

The Shogunal Line ——— There were 15 shōguns during the Edo period. Eight succeeded their fathers and 6 were adoptive heirs. A few were gifted rulers, some were ordinary, and several were unfit for the position.

Ieyasu held the shogunal title for only two years before transferring it to his son TOKUGAWA HIDETADA in 1605 to establish a precedent for shogunal succession. After Ieyasu's death in 1616, the capable Hidetada kept the Tokugawa position intact. He in turn retired in 1623 and supervised his son TOKUGAWA IEMITSU until his own death in 1632.

Iemitsu's rule was distinguished by diplomatic shrewdness and the use of restrictive administrative procedures, notably SANKIN KŌTAI, the system of alternate attendance at Edo. Upon his death in 1651 he was succeeded by his eldest son, TOKUGAWA IETSUNA, a child who allowed his advisers to manage state affairs.

For four shogunal generations thereafter, a combination of political problems and personal limitations served both to weaken shogunal power within the government at Edo and to weaken Edo's position vis-à-vis the country as a whole. Until his death in 1680 the childless Ietsuna remained a passive ruler, guided by HOSHINA MASAYUKI and later by SAKAI TADAKIYO. He was succeeded by his younger brother TOKUGAWA TSUNAYOSHI, the daimyō of a large domain headquartered at Tatebayashi (in what is now Gumma Prefecture). Tsunayoshi was a more forceful leader, but he inherited a regime with fiscal problems, and he was only moderately successful in solving them. He was a scholarly and erudite man, but his practice of lavishly rewarding loyal supporters such as YANAGISAWA YOSHIYASU, together with rather unorthodox religious attitudes and unseemly private habits, provoked widespread disapproval. By the time he died in 1709 agitation for reform was strong.

His only son having predeceased him, Tsunayoshi was succeeded by TOKUGAWA IENOBU, the grown son of his brother Tsunashige (1644–78) and the daimyō of a large domain headquartered at Kōfu (in what is now Yamanashi Prefecture). On the advice of the scholar ARAI HAKUSEKI, Ienobu undertook to restore Tokugawa prestige. After only three years of conservatively reformist rule, however, he died and was succeeded by his son Ietsugu, who in turn died in 1716 at the age of seven.

By 1716 the Tokugawa shogunate had evolved from the dynamic regime of the early shōguns into a rather listless regime beset by day-to-day problems and sagging morale, and the agitation that had accompanied Ienobu's succession revived; but the forceful leadership of Ietsugu's successor, TOKUGAWA YOSHIMUNE of Kii (Wakayama), strengthened the shogunate's control over the daimyō. In the KYŌHŌ REFORMS Yoshimune implemented vigorous programs of fiscal reorganization, encouraged scholarship, and reinforced discipline both within and without the shogunate. In 1745 he retired and for six years supervised his eldest son, TOKUGAWA IESHIGE, who was physically unable to govern.

From the time of Yoshimune's death in 1751 until the accession of the last shōgun, TOKUGAWA YOSHINOBU (also known as Keiki), in 1866, six successive shōguns allowed their principal advisers to handle most affairs of state. Ieshige left most matters in the hands of Ōoka Tadamitsu. His son and successor, Ieharu (1737–86), similarly entrusted affairs to TANUMA OKITSUGU. When Ieharu's only son died prematurely, he adopted as his heir TOKUGAWA IENARI, a son of his cousin Harusada (1727–89) of Hitotsubashi. By the time of Ieharu's death and Ienari's succession in 1787 a combination of natural disasters (see TEMMEI FAMINE), fiscal problems, and official abuse had generated reformist demands even greater than those that had accompanied Tsunayoshi's death.

Ienari held office for 50 years, longer than any other shōgun, and supervised his son Ieyoshi even after retirement. During his first years as shōgun, his regent MATSUDAIRA SADANOBU carried out a program known as the KANSEI REFORMS. After Sadanobu's fall from power in 1793, Ienari left most matters in the hands of successive advisers, notably Mizuno Tadaakira (1762–1834). In one way, however, Ienari was effective in preserving Tokugawa rule: he sired as many as 55 children, and by judicious adoption and marriage arrangements he was able to construct a web of familial ties that bound a large number of powerful daimyō and other important people to himself, thereby offsetting the general discontent of the age.

Toward the end of his long rule, accumulated difficulties and new national hardships (see TEMPŌ FAMINE) generated a groundswell of reformism. It was led by the dynamic daimyō of Mito, TOKUGAWA NARIAKI, and supported by the senior shogunate official MIZUNO TADAKUNI. Reformist sentiments resulted in the TEMPŌ REFORMS. Tokugawa Ieyoshi (1793–1853), who succeeded Ienari in 1837, accepted Tadakuni's reformist leadership, but when Tadakuni proved overzealous, he replaced him with the more moderate ABE MASAHIRO.

Ieyoshi and Abe were at the helm of the shogunate when Commodore Matthew C. PERRY's fleet reached Japan in 1853. In subsequent years, as Japan was buffeted by the demands of Western imperialists, the Edo regime was headed by two weak shōguns in succession. On Ieyoshi's death in July 1853, his sickly son Iesada succeeded but died five years later, shortly after the senior councillor II NAOSUKE had gained control of the faltering regime. Iesada was succeeded in turn by his young cousin TOKUGAWA IEMOCHI, who was a grandson of Ienari and the daimyō of Wakayama. By the time Iemochi died in 1866 and was succeeded by Yoshinobu, the energetic son of Nariaki of Mito, the process of political decay had advanced so far that despite a year of frenetic but intelligent reform, the regime collapsed in the face of the movement to restore direct imperial rule.

In the settlement that followed the Meiji Restoration, the former shogunal family received a large domain in the area around Sumpu (now the city of Shizuoka), where Ieyasu had originally risen to power. Three years later, when the daimyō domains were abolished by imperial decree (see PREFECTURAL SYSTEM, ESTABLISHMENT OF), the Tokugawa received a substantial financial settlement and various honors. The principal branches of the Tokugawa family survived, and a few of their members, such as TOKUGAWA IESATO and Tokugawa Muneyoshi (b 1897), had distinguished careers in public service. However, the family never regained any of the political influence it had once enjoyed.

📖 ———Kitajima Masamoto, *Tokugawa shōgun retsuden* (1974). Nakamura Kōya, *Tokugawake* (1966). George Sansom, *A History of Japan, 1615–1867* (1963). Conrad Totman, *Politics in the Tokugawa Bakufu, 1600–1843* (1967). Conrad TOTMAN

Tokugawa Hidetada (1579–1632)

Second shōgun of the Tokugawa shogunate; third son of the first shōgun, TOKUGAWA IEYASU. He served as the general of one of his father's armies in the campaign that led to the Battle of SEKIGAHARA (1600) and the sieges of Ōsaka Castle (1614–15). Although he officially became shōgun when Ieyasu retired in 1605, father and son ruled jointly as Ōgosho Sama ("His Retired Majesty") and Gosho Sama ("His Majesty") until 1616, with Ieyasu and his staff retaining the preponderance of power, especially in foreign affairs. Although this arrangement created tensions between Ieyasu's court at Sumpu (now the city of Shizuoka) and Hidetada's in the shogunal capital of Edo (now Tōkyō), it proved a useful mechanism for guaranteeing shogunal succession in the Tokugawa house at a time when its dynastic claims had not yet been fully recognized. Hidetada repeated his father's action, retiring in 1623 and installing his son TOKUGAWA IEMITSU as the third shōgun. These two ruled jointly as Ōgosho and Gosho until Hidetada's death in 1632. Hidetada's reign was a period of institutional consolidation in the new shogunate: strengthening control over the *daimyō*, the Tokugawa collaterals, and the imperial court, reorganizing the executive organs of the shogunate, and regulating Christianity and foreign trade more closely.

Ronald P. TOBY

Tokugawa Iemitsu (1604–1651)

Third shōgun of the Tokugawa shogunate (1603–1867); ruled 1623–51. Eldest legitimate son of the second shōgun, TOKUGAWA HIDETADA; his mother was a younger sister of Lady YODOGIMI. For a time it appeared that Iemitsu would be denied the succession in favor of his younger brother Tadanaga (1606–33), but thanks to the intercession of his wet nurse, KASUGA NO TSUBONE, he was confirmed as shōgun in 1623 when his father abdicated. After his father's death in 1632, in anticipation of further trouble, Iemitsu forced his brother to commit suicide. Drawing on the advice of such men as DOI TOSHIKATSU, ABE TADAAKI, and MATSUDAIRA NOBUTSUNA, Iemitsu carried out important administrative reforms to consolidate shogunal rule. He stiffened the discipline of the military houses by augmenting the BUKE SHOHATTO promulgated by his grandfather Ieyasu, the founder of the shogunate. He tightened his control over the *daimyō* by compelling them to reside at the shogunal capital in alternate years (see SANKIN KŌTAI) and strengthened the internal organization of villages (see GŌSON SYSTEM) by enacting such measures as the TAHATA EITAI BAIBAI KINSHI REI, which forbade the sale of rice land. He intensified the persecution of Christians and, after suppressing the SHIMABARA UPRISING (1637–38) in southern Kyūshū, enforced a strict NATIONAL SECLUSION policy that closed Japan to all but a handful of Chinese and Dutch merchants. The shogunate reached the height of its power during Iemitsu's rule and assumed the form that it was to retain until its collapse in the 1860s. Iemitsu was succeeded by his eldest son, TOKUGAWA IETSUNA.

TAKAGI Shōsaku

Tokugawa Iemochi (1846–1866)

The 14th shōgun of the Tokugawa shogunate; reigned 1858–66. His name before he became shōgun was Tokugawa Yoshitomi. Born to the Kii branch of the Tokugawa family in the Wakayama domain (now Wakayama Prefecture and part of Mie Prefecture; see GO-SANKE), he was a grandson of the 11th shōgun, TOKUGAWA IENARI. When the question of choosing a successor to the childless and ailing shōgun Iesada (1824–58) arose in 1858, reform-minded forces in the shogunate led by MATSUDAIRA YOSHINAGA supported TOKUGAWA YOSHINOBU of the Hitotsubashi branch, while conservative forces led by II NAOSUKE supported Yoshitomi. Ii's forces won out, and Yoshitomi, still a child of 12, became shōgun and was renamed Iemochi. Following the assassination of Ii Naosuke in 1860 (see SAKURADAMONGAI INCIDENT), his successors, hoping to bolster the authority of the shogunate, put into action his plan for a MOVEMENT FOR UNION OF COURT AND SHOGUNATE. To effect this reconciliation between Kyōto and the shogunate, Iemochi in 1862 married Princess KAZU, the sister of Emperor KŌMEI. In a further attempt to check the antishogunate movement incited by the signing of the ANSEI COMMERCIAL TREATIES with the United States and other Western powers, Iemochi broke with a 200-year tradition and made three trips to the imperial court in Kyōto. On the last of these, taken in 1866 to command a punitive expedition against Chōshū (see CHŌSHŪ EXPEDITIONS), the most extreme antishogunate domain, Iemochi fell ill and died in Ōsaka Castle. He was succeeded by Yoshinobu, who became the 15th and last Tokugawa shōgun.

TANAKA Akira

Tokugawa Ienari (1773–1841)

The 11th shōgun of the Tokugawa shogunate, he held his title longer than any other in his line, from 1787 to 1837, and dominated the politics of Japan from the 1790s until his death. His historical importance has been underestimated, however, probably because neither his techniques of governance nor his policy lines have won subsequent approbation and consequent scholarly attention.

Ienari was the son of Harusada (1727–89), *daimyō* of the branch family of Hitotsubashi (see GOSANKYŌ) and was designated heir to the childless shōgun Ieharu (1737–86; r 1760–86) in 1781; he became shōgun six years later at the age of 13. At first the KANSEI REFORMS of the senior councillor (*rōjū*) MATSUDAIRA SADANOBU dominated the scene, but with Sadanobu's retirement from office in 1793, Ienari came into his own; his rule, which embraced the BUNKA AND BUNSEI ERAS (1804–30), was characterized by the absence of political movement. These years were blessed with a succession of good harvests, and the government supplemented its land-tax income with a generally effective policy of monetary manipulation. At the heart of the stability, however, was Ienari's vigorous program of kinship politics. He sired some 55 children by 40 consorts and maintained hundreds of other ladies in his household (ŌOKU). With unequaled skill he forged a nationwide network of kinship links through marriages, adoptions, and the exchange of consorts, gifts, and favors. Ienari's wife was the daughter of the powerful Satsuma (now Kagoshima Prefecture) daimyō Shimazu Shigehide (1745–1833). Ienari placed

his sons and daughters in many daimyō houses, and in other domains his government bought friendship through political bargains.

By their nature these links were fragile and could not stand up to severe strain, but for three relatively benign decades Ienari's arrangements—also describable as nepotism, corruption, and fiscal abuse—served to perpetuate stability. During the 1830s, however, crop failures gave rise to widespread distress (see TEMPŌ FAMINE) and declines in shogunate revenues. To meet the situation the shogunate resorted to massive recoinages that weakened the currency and fostered more inflation. In the outcome the broader picture of Ienari's political success was obscured by the great stress and political crisis of his final years.

■ ——Conrad Totman, *Politics in the Tokugawa Bakufu, 1600–1843* (1967). Tsuda Hideo, "Tokugawa Ienari," in Kitajima Masamoto, ed, *Tokugawa shōgun retsuden* (1974).

Conrad TOTMAN

Tokugawa Ienobu (1662–1712)

The sixth shōgun of the TOKUGAWA SHOGUNATE; ruled 1709–12. The eldest son of the lord of the Kōfu domain (now part of Yamanashi Prefecture), Tokugawa Tsunashige (1644–78), who was a brother of the fourth and fifth shōguns, TOKUGAWA IETSUNA and TOKUGAWA TSUNAYOSHI, Ienobu succeeded his father as lord of Kōfu in 1678 at the age of 16. He was adopted in 1704 as the heir to his uncle, the childless Tsunayoshi, whom he succeeded as shōgun on the latter's death in 1709. Ienobu's short rule was marked by a series of Confucian-inspired reforms (SHŌTOKU NO CHI) urged by his tutor and political adviser ARAI HAKUSEKI. Another prominent figure in the shogunate under Ienobu was his chamberlain (*sobayō-nin*) MANABE AKIFUSA, a former Nō actor who managed shogunate affairs as Ienobu's favorite. On his death Ienobu was succeeded by his four-year-old son, Ietsugu (1709–16; r 1713–16). Manabe and Arai remained leading figures in the shogunal government, developing further the reforms begun under Ienobu until Ietsugu's death three years later. That event brought to an end the main line of the Tokugawa house descended from the second and third shōguns, TOKUGAWA HIDETADA and TOKUGAWA IEMITSU. A new shogunal line was inaugurated by the head of the Kii branch of the Tokugawa family (see GOSANKE), TOKUGAWA YOSHIMUNE, who succeeded Ietsugu as the eighth shōgun.

Yoshiyuki NAKAI

Tokugawa Iesato (1863–1940)

The first head of the Tokugawa family after the Tokugawa shogunate was overthrown in the MEIJI RESTORATION of 1868. After the 15th shōgun, TOKUGAWA YOSHINOBU, retired, Iesato became head of the family and under the new Meiji government was appointed governor of Shizuoka Prefecture. In 1877 he went to England, where he studied for five years; when he returned to Japan in 1882 he was given the title of prince. He became a member of the House of Peers at its inception in 1890 and became president of the House in 1903, remaining in that position until his retirement in 1933. Following World War I, he was appointed a delegate to the WASHINGTON CONFERENCE on naval disarmament. He also served as president of the Japan Red Cross, the Nichibei Kyōkai (Japan-America Society), and various other organizations.

Tokugawa Ieshige (1711–1761)

The ninth shōgun of the TOKUGAWA SHOGUNATE; ruled 1745–60; the eldest son of the eighth shōgun, TOKUGAWA YOSHIMUNE. Unlike his father, one of the most competent and robust of the Tokugawa rulers, Ieshige suffered chronic ill health and had a speech defect. His succession to the office of shōgun at the age of 34 created a controversy among shogunate leaders, because his younger brothers Munetake (1715–71) and Munenobu (1721–64) were obviously better qualified. Nevertheless, he was elevated by his aging father, who, during the first two years of Ieshige's rule, continued to direct state affairs as retired shōgun (ŌGOSHO). Uninterested in government, Ieshige left shogunate affairs in the hands of his chamberlain Ōoka Tadamitsu (1709–60), who claimed to be the only person who could understand Ieshige's barely intelligible speech. Ieshige retired in 1760 and assumed the position of *ōgosho* but died the following year. His eldest son, Ieharu (1737–86), succeeded to the shogunal office. His second son, Shigeyoshi (1745–95), founded the house of Shimizu, and his two younger brothers Munetake and Munenobu established the other two of the three senior collateral houses (GO-

Tokugawa Ieyasu

Detail of a votive portrait of Ieyasu deified as Tōshō Daigongen ("Great Incarnation Who Illuminates the East"). One of eight such portraits painted by Kanō Tan'yu at the behest of Ieyasu's grandson, Iemitsu, and housed at the temple Rinnōji in Nikkō, Tochigi Prefecture. Ink and colors on paper. 195 × 59 cm. 1642.

SANKYŌ), the Tayasu and Hitotsubashi. Ieshige was an excellent player of Japanese chess (shōgi) and wrote a book on the subject.

Yoshiyuki NAKAI

Tokugawa Ietsuna (1641–1680)

The fourth shōgun of the TOKUGAWA SHOGUNATE; ruled 1651–80; eldest son of the third shōgun, TOKUGAWA IEMITSU. Unlike his father, Ietsuna was a mediocre ruler. He took office at the age of 10 as the first child shōgun of his line and was assisted by the leading members of his father's entourage, including HOSHINA MASAYUKI, MATSUDAIRA NOBUTSUNA, and SAKAI TADAKIYO. Even after reaching adulthood, Ietsuna, who suffered from ill health, continued to rely on advisers, remaining a figurehead shōgun. Shogunate affairs were managed by the senior councillor (rōjū) Sakai Tadakiyo, who was nicknamed Geba Shōgun because of the location of his house in front of the main gate of Edo Castle, where the sign geba (dismount!) was posted. Ietsuna died without issue at the age of 39 and was succeeded as shōgun by his younger brother TOKUGAWA TSUNAYOSHI.

The three decades under Ietsuna may be regarded as a transitional period between the martial formative years of the shogunate and the peaceful, settled, middle years. The last, fruitless attempt to overthrow the Tokugawa, the KEIAN INCIDENT, took place at the very beginning of Ietsuna's rule. The custom of committing suicide after one's master's death (JUNSHI) was prohibited in 1663. Under Ietsuna the shogunate extended its sponsorship of Confucian learning; one of the chief scholarly achievements of his rule was the compilation of the history Honchō tsugan (1670, Speculum of Japan) by HAYASHI RAZAN and his son. *Yoshiyuki NAKAI*

Tokugawa Ieyasu (1543–1616)

The warrior chieftain who, outwitting many of his major contemporaries and outliving and outprocreating the rest, survived Japan's late 16th century wars of unification to set up the TOKUGAWA SHOGUNATE (Tokugawa bakufu).

Background—— Born Matsudaira Takechiyo in the small castle of Okazaki in Mikawa Province (now part of Aichi Prefecture), Ieyasu had a decidedly military background. His father, Matsudaira Hirotada (1526–49), whose first son he was, was a petty chieftain allegedly descended from the Minamoto house, the founders of the Kamakura shogunate, through the Nitta line. His mother, known to posterity as Odai no Kata (1528–1602), was the daughter of a neighboring warrior leader, Mizuno Tadamasa of Kariya in Mikawa.

At the time of Ieyasu's birth, his father was engaged in a desperate effort to fight off incursions from his predatory neighbors to the west, the Oda of Owari Province (now part of Aichi Prefecture). To help himself in his efforts, Ieyasu's father decided to make an alliance with powerful neighbors to the east, the Imagawa of Suruga Province (now part of Shizuoka Prefecture), with whom the Matsudaira were on marginally better terms. It was to cement this alliance that Matsudaira Hirotada in 1547 dispatched the four-year-old Ieyasu to the Imagawa as a hostage. Ieyasu never saw his father again. On his way to the Imagawa headquarters at Sumpu (now the city of Shizuoka), Ieyasu was captured by a party of enemy troops and taken to the Oda Castle at Nagoya. There he stayed for two years until 1549, in which year, after his father's premature death, the Matsudaira and Oda houses agreed to a truce. This, however, meant only a brief return to Okazaki for Ieyasu. The alliance with the Imagawa still required a security, so the seven-year-old Ieyasu went almost directly to the Imagawa domain, exchanging, in effect, one form of captivity for another.

Twelve years later, at the end of this second period of captivity, Ieyasu, now in his 18th year, had changed his name from Matsudaira Takechiyo to Matsudaira Motoyasu, taken his first wife, fathered his first son, and fought his first battle. No doubt he would have continued as a professional hostage, for it was a role which suited his Imagawa hosts (who had the use of Matsudaira land and vassals) very well, had it not been for the intervention of the Oda family, now capably led by a young tactician named ODA NOBUNAGA. In 1560 Nobunaga dealt the Imagawa house the first of a series of shattering blows by killing its leader, IMAGAWA YOSHIMOTO, and routing its forces at Okehazama. The ensuing uncertainty gave Ieyasu the chance he needed to return to his ancestral castle and there assume command of his father's old vassals, leaderless for the past 12 years.

Early Career—— It was not long before Ieyasu, newly independent, made the first of many decisions which were finally to put him at the pinnacle of Japanese military society. In 1561 he abandoned his alliance with the Imagawa, allying himself instead with the much more promising Oda Nobunaga. He never regretted it, for, having thus secured his western flank, he began enlarging his domain at Imagawa expense. Little by little he encroached on Imagawa holdings in Mikawa, and by 1568 his eastward expansion had made him master of the provinces of Mikawa and Tōtōmi (now part of Shizuoka Prefecture). He had also in the intervening years changed his personal name from Motoyasu to Ieyasu, symbolizing his liberation from the Imagawa, and had been permitted by imperial order to substitute for Matsudaira the more ancient family name of Tokugawa.

In 1570 Tokugawa Ieyasu moved his headquarters eastward from Okazaki to Hamamatsu, formerly part of the Imagawa domain. Having done so, his alliance with Oda Nobunaga, until that time purely defensive in character, entered a much more active stage. In that same year at Anegawa near Lake Biwa, the Oda and Tokugawa forces combined to destroy the power of two local warrior houses, the Asai and Asakura, in a decisive battle (see ANEGAWA, BATTLE OF) in which firearms—still something of a novelty—played a significant part.

From 1572 to 1582, still allied with Oda Nobunaga, Ieyasu gradually expanded his territorial grasp and also the size of his armed forces, fighting for much of the time against the TAKEDA FAMILY, with whom he shared a common frontier on the river Ōigawa. The contest began badly in 1572, when the redoubtable TAKEDA SHINGEN led an army into the Tokugawa domain in a battle at Mikatagahara, and gave Ieyasu the worst drubbing of his career. Fortunately for Ieyasu, however, Shingen was soon to die and was succeeded by his son Katsuyori (1546–82), an altogether more manageable opponent. Successive battles—at Nagashino in 1575 and Takatenjin in 1581—drove the Takeda back, leaving Tokugawa Ieyasu master not only of Mikawa and Tōtōmi, but of Suruga as well.

During this period, Ieyasu stood very much in Nobunaga's shadow. The situation had its disadvantages, most notably in 1579, when Ieyasu was obliged to put his wife (who was from an Imagawa vassal family) to death, and force his first-born son to commit suicide to reassure his ally and overlord, Nobunaga, of his own loyalty. (Both wife and son were suspected by Nobunaga of having colluded with the Takeda.) Yet on the whole the association was a fruitful one for Ieyasu. He profited during Nobunaga's lifetime and was to profit still more at Nobunaga's death in 1582, for with his customary pragmatism Ieyasu reacted to the turmoil after Nobunaga's assassination at the hands of AKECHI MITSUHIDE by making himself master of the Takeda heartland—the provinces of Kai and Shinano (now Yamanashi and Nagano prefectures). By 1583, therefore, Tokugawa Ieyasu, holding five provinces, was very much a man to be reckoned with among the contending factions of central Japan.

Certainly Nobunaga's successor, TOYOTOMI HIDEYOSHI was obliged to reckon with him. Relations between the two men began inauspiciously in 1583, when Ieyasu resisted several overtures from Hideyoshi. In 1584 Hideyoshi retaliated with an attack upon a Tokugawa fortress on Mt. Komaki in a battle which spilled over to the nearby Nagakute area (see KOMAKI NAGAKUTE CAMPAIGN). These two engagements, although inconclusive, were enough to persuade both men that a truce, and a rough alliance, were to be preferred—for the moment, at least—to further fighting. Therefore, in 1584, much as his father had once sent him away as a hostage, so did Ieyasu send a son to Hideyoshi for adoption, philosophically receiving in return two years later Hideyoshi's 43-year-old sister, specially divorced so that she might marry him.

In the years that followed, any tensions persisting between the two men were kept hidden. Hideyoshi was busy in Shikoku and Kyūshū, while Ieyasu was preoccupied with the administration of his five provinces. In 1590, however, the two men joined forces to attack the great Kantō chieftain, Hōjō Ujimasa (1538–90), in his castle at Odawara. To Ieyasu, who committed 30,000 troops to the battle, this was a logical development in a process which had already brought him to the very borders of the Hōjō domain. Victory would certainly increase his empire still further. To Hideyoshi, with a larger enterprise in mind, it was an opportunity to rid himself of one of the last remaining obstacles in the way of national unification.

Move to Edo ——— Both men were to see their ambitions realized, after a five-month siege, at Odawara in 1590 (see ODAWARA CAMPAIGN). By overthrowing the Hōjō, Hideyoshi won a degree of control in eastern Japan unrivaled since the Kamakura period (1185–1333). Ieyasu, too, received more land, but not at all in the form he had anticipated. When the siege was over, it was announced that his domain would be increased, but in return he would be required to surrender the five provinces he had won, including Mikawa, his native province, and move together with his vassals, their wives, and their children, to a completely new and unfamiliar area. His new domain was to embrace the provinces of Musashi, Izu, Sagami, Kazusa, and Shimōsa, together with parts of Hitachi, Awa, Kōzuke, and Shimotsuke—effectively, the KANTŌ PLAIN and its surrounding hills.

The new domain had certain advantages. It was larger, considerably more productive (since it was held to have an annual productive capacity of nearly 2.5 million *koku*; 1 *koku* = about 180 liters or 5 US bushels), and geographically much more unified than his former possessions. On the other hand, neither he nor any of his generals knew the new area, a fact which left him at a strategic, administrative—and probably fiscal—disadvantage.

Awkward though it was, Ieyasu had no way of refusing the offer. Less than a month later, at the head of a large number of men, he moved into his new domain. His first years there were to be very busy: first, like any good warrior he had to see to his security, and he did this by distributing the most distant and strategically important parts of his new domain as fiefs to his more capable officers. Then he had to set up the machinery of local government and tax collection. Finally he needed headquarters of a size and splendor appropriate to his responsibilities. This, particularly, was not easy. He could, perhaps, have taken over the old Hōjō stronghold at Odawara, but he preferred not to, choosing instead a location much closer to the center of his new domain. This was Edo, a little fishing town on the edge of the swamp fringing what is now Tōkyō Bay. Its only previous military significance had been as the site of a small fortress built over a century earlier by a local warrior. For the next 15 years, although he was usually absent from Edo and busy with matters of greater moment, Ieyasu laid the foundations for Edo's future eminence, ordering the construction of a great fortress, a network of canals, a system of water supply, and ordering, too, the drainage of the swamp which lay between the town and the sea.

It was perhaps as well for Ieyasu that his former rival was also busy. In 1592 Hideyoshi began his invasion of Korea, an enterprise which consumed what was left of his life, just as it consumed the energies and resources of those warrior-leaders forced to take part. Ieyasu, however, maintained a comfortable distance from it, for the

sum total of his involvement was a period of 18 months spent at campaign headquarters in Kyūshū. Otherwise his resources were substantially untouched.

His success in organizing his new domain and in escaping Hideyoshi's more burdensome impositions left Ieyasu well placed to take advantage of the next opportunity to come his way. This was the death of Hideyoshi in 1598. Shortly before he died, Hideyoshi made his senior generals, Ieyasu among them, swear to serve his five-year-old son, TOYOTOMI HIDEYORI, as faithfully as they had served him. Within two years of Hideyoshi's death, however, Ieyasu had broken that promise, using a son, an adopted daughter, and two granddaughters to form alliances with four powerful warrior families, and encouraging others to send hostages to him in Edo. Naturally he did not go unopposed, particularly in western Japan. In 1600, ISHIDA MITSUNARI, one of Hideyoshi's vassals, armed with promises of support from the Konishi, Ankokuji, Ukita, Chōsokabe, Mōri, and Shimazu families, declared war against him. Ieyasu was only too ready to respond. On 21 October 1600 (Keichō 5.9.15), Ieyasu led an army of 104,000 men into battle at Sekigahara, and by the end of the same day had won an easy victory.

It is undeniably tempting to regard this battle as decisive both for the unification of Japan and for the establishment of a lasting Tokugawa government. Certainly, while not all Japanese military leaders may have taken part in it, not one was indifferent to its outcome. It is also true that as a result of the Battle of Sekigahara Tokugawa Ieyasu came to assume a great many of Hideyoshi's powers, establishing his control over the city of Kyōto (and hence over the emperor, who lived there) and claiming authority over all Japanese daimyō by the simple expedient of punishing those who had sided against him, depriving them of their fiefs, or else removing them to a safe distance.

Shōgun ——— Undoubtedly Tokugawa Ieyasu was the most powerful warrior-leader in Japan after 1600. His assumption in 1603 of the ancient title of *seii tai shōgun* ("barbarian-subduing generalissimo") at the hands of Emperor Go-Yōzei (1571–1617) did no more than confirm what was already unmistakable. Thenceforth he and his descendants were, like their predecessors of the Minamoto and Ashikaga families, held to be entitled to speak for the emperor on national affairs and held also to be personally responsible for the safety of the realm. As commander-in-chief of the entire samurai class, too, it was expected that the SHŌGUN would be obeyed by all military overlords and their vassals.

Ieyasu did not hold his new position for long. In 1605, then in his 63rd year, he resigned from office in favor of his third son, TOKUGAWA HIDETADA, and two years later retired to Sumpu, where as a child he had spent 12 years as hostage to the Imagawa family.

It must be realized, however, that although retired, Ieyasu had by no means reliquished his authority. All he had done was set Hidetada to work under proper supervision on the straightforward and tedious business of shogunal administration, reserving for himself matters of more importance, as for example, foreign affairs. Ieyasu was keenly interested in both foreign trade and foreign technology, as his earlier patronage of William ADAMS and Lodenstijn JAN JOOSTEN and his correspondence with the monarchs of Spain, the Netherlands, and Britain attest. At Sumpu he had the time to engage in such correspondence and also to question foreign visitors brought there for that purpose.

Above all, however, Ieyasu was concerned about Japan's internal strategic balance. Despite the victory at Sekigahara, the situation for the Tokugawa was far from comfortable, for they were dependent upon other warriors who could withdraw their support at any time. Any discontent with the Tokugawa shogunate, therefore, would weaken its position; any discontent, too, would inevitably gather around Hideyoshi's son, Toyotomi Hideyori. From Sumpu therefore Ieyasu began to prepare for the second stage of his move to power. In the winter of 1614 and again in the following spring, he launched two attacks on Ōsaka Castle, Hideyori's fortress, finally taking it and destroying its outer fortifications. Hideyori, knowing full well what Ieyasu had in store for him, chose to commit suicide; his seven-year-old son, Kunimatsu, (less prescient) was beheaded (see also ŌSAKA CASTLE, SIEGES OF).

With the fall of Ōsaka Castle, and the total destruction of the Toyotomi house, little more remained of Ieyasu's life. In 1613–14 he had advisers draw up what were to become the two basic documents of early Tokugawa legislation—the BUKE SHOHATTO (Laws for Military Houses) and the KINCHŪ NARABI NI KUGE SHOHATTO (Laws Governing the Imperial Court and Nobility), both of which were issued in 1615. At the beginning of 1616 he took ill. Whether his illness was due to a chill, caught during a winter hawking expedition, or brought on by acute indigestion after a surfeit of *tempura* is still a matter for dispute. What is certain is that he was immediately brought to bed, dying on 1 June 1616 (Genna 2.4.17). In accordance with his last wishes, his remains were taken to Kunōzan, a few miles away. A year later, perhaps not quite so much in accordance with his last wishes, they were removed to NIKKŌ, where, by imperial decree, he was canonized under the title of Tōshō Daigongen, a manifestation of the Buddha as healer. It was thus that later generations were to know him as Gongen Sama—the protector of his people and of the regime he had founded.

Achievements——In assessing the contribution of Tokugawa Ieyasu to Japanese history, the historian encounters a number of problems. After all, Ieyasu founded a dynasty spanning more than two-and-a-half centuries, and since such achievements are unusual, it is always tempting to assign unusual qualities to men of this kind. Scholars have praised Ieyasu's righteousness and benevolence, although the evidence suggests that if indeed he did possess these qualities, he exercised them in moderation. Others have paid tribute to his passion for scholarship, noting his patronage of teachers like HAYASHI RAZAN, and indeed it does seem true that he was as interested in learning as any busy man of affairs can be; yet, in his own reading, as in his patronage, his concerns were always selective, and always eminently practical. Many historians, too, have been beguiled into crediting him with the achievements of his subordinates or successors, and some have praised him for social and economic developments of which in fact he may well have been unaware, or in which he played no part.

Despite the uncritical admiration so often turned in his direction, it seems unlikely that in his preoccupations and his attitudes to government and administration Tokugawa Ieyasu was anything other than a man of his times. His entire life was spent in war. He saw his first battle at the age of 16 and his last at 73, just a few months before he died. By training and by temperament, therefore, he was an autocrat, recognizing only the constraints of strategic necessity. It is doubtful that this old soldier could ever have come to terms with the bureaucratic system in which his successors came to be so tightly enfolded.

What marks Ieyasu off from his great contemporaries, Oda Nobunaga and Toyotomi Hideyoshi, is not his ability, for all three were capable men. Nor is it his flexibility in the face of changing economic and social realities, since none could be said to be, by whatever definition, more "modern" than the others. It was, effectively, a matter of luck that Japan came to be ruled by a Tokugawa, rather than an Oda or Toyotomi government. The success of the Tokugawa lay in two pieces of good fortune. First, Nobunaga died in 1582 and Hideyoshi in 1598, while Ieyasu, although born within 10 years of each of them, lived on until 1616. Second, Nobunaga was survived by three sons, of whom two were soon to die, and Hideyoshi by only one, but Ieyasu left five of his nine sons behind him. One of them, his eldest surviving son, Hidetada, had already been shōgun for more than a decade, and three others were firmly settled as daimyō of Owari, Kii (now Wakayama Prefecture), and Mito (now part of Ibaraki Prefecture).

Ultimately, the achievement of Tokugawa Ieyasu was that by the time of his death he had brought peace and an unprecedented degree of unity to Japan and had provided a succession stable enough to withstand his passing. Others of his contemporaries could perhaps have achieved as much, but none could have done more.

■——Kitajima Masamoto, *Tokugawa Ieyasu* (1963). Nakamura Kōya, *Tokugawa Ieyasu Kō den* (1965). Nakamura Kōya, *Ieyasu no seiji keizai shinryō* (1968). Nakamura Kōya, *Tokugawa Ieyasu monjo no kenkyū*, 5 vols (1957–71).   *Harold* BOLITHO

Tokugawa jikki

(True Chronicle of the Tokugawa). Historical work compiled by the TOKUGAWA SHOGUNATE; in 516 chapters it records the political achievements of the first 10 shōguns, from TOKUGAWA IEYASU to Tokugawa Ieharu (1737–86; r 1760–86). Some 20 historians, under the direction of HAYASHI JUSSAI, were engaged in the project, which was begun in 1809 and completed in 1849. The information is accurate, and the sources are carefully documented. A sequel, *Zoku Tokugawa jikki*, intended to cover the rule of the 11th shōgun, TOKUGAWA IENARI, and his successors, was interrupted by the MEIJI RESTORATION of 1868 and never completed.

Tokugawa Kazuko (1607–1678)

Also known as Tōfuku Mon'in. Daughter of the shōgun TOKUGAWA HIDETADA and consort of Emperor GO-MIZUNOO. Her marriage to the emperor in 1620 was part of the Tokugawa shogunate's strategy to bolster its claims to legitimacy by strengthening ties with the imperial court. Kazuko bore the emperor two sons and five daughters, but both sons died young. Go-Mizunoo, upset over the SHIE INCIDENT and other shogunate interference in court affairs, abdicated in favor of Kazuko's eldest daughter, Okiko, who became Empress Meishō (1623–96; r 1629–43). Kazuko continued until her death to exert influence in the court as stepmother of the emperors Go-Kōmyō (r 1643–54), Gosai (r 1655–63), and Reigen (r 1663–87), all sons of Go-Mizunoo by other women. Her large income from the shogunate allowed her to be a generous patroness of the arts and Buddhist temples.

Tokugawa Keiki → Tokugawa Yoshinobu

Tokugawa kinrei kō

A 102-volume collection of the laws and regulations of the Edo period (1600–1868); compiled by the Ministry of Justice between 1878 and 1890. It is divided into two sections, the first containing regulations for the imperial court, *daimyō*, shrines and temples, and transactions with foreign countries, and the second containing penal codes and cases. It is an invaluable source of information on the government, economics, legal system, and social conditions of the period.

Tokugawa Mitsukuni (1628–1700)

The second lord (*daimyō*; from 1661 to 1690) of the Mito domain (now part of Ibaraki Prefecture), a grandson of the national unifier TOKUGAWA IEYASU, and the driving force behind the compilation of the classic DAI NIHON SHI (History of Great Japan). Popularly known as Mito Kōmon.

The compilation of the *Dai Nihon shi*, a comprehensive account of Japanese history from its origins to the 14th century that had grown to 397 volumes by its completion in 1906, engaged Mitsukuni's attention from 1657 until his death. Its structure and moralistic aims he derived from the Chinese dynastic histories, while the inspiration for its grand scope he attributed to a reading of the monumental Chinese historical classic *Shi ji* (*Shih chi*; Records of the Historian) during his youth.

At Mitsukuni's invitation, 130 Japanese and Chinese scholars participated in this editorial project at his domain's residences (see SHŌKŌKAN) in Edo (now Tōkyō) during his lifetime; the most famous participants were Sassa Sōjun (1640–98), KURIYAMA SEMPŌ, MIYAKE KANRAN, and ASAKA TAMPAKU. In 1698, a year after the chronicles of the first 100 emperors had been completed, the editorial work was shifted to Mito, where it came to serve as the scholarly basis for the MITO SCHOOL of learning.

Mitsukuni also gained fame for his effective and benevolent rule of Mito. He successfully stabilized his administration by reinforcing his band of retainers and consolidating his hold over the castle town. He actively promoted paper production, gold mining, horse breeding, and shipbuilding and even sent an expedition to open trade with the Ezo district (now Hokkaidō). His agricultural policies closely accorded with the practices of the Chinese Confucian rulers he emulated. He reduced the annual rice tax (NENGU), set up famine-relief granaries, and encouraged peasants to study herbal medicine, turn from their unorthodox religions, and practice the virtues of filial piety and chastity. By the time he retired in 1690, however, the domain was experiencing financial difficulties, and concentration of land in the hands of rich merchants and powerful farmers had led to the growing impoverishment of the peasantry. Alarmed at what he saw as the corruption of *samurai* morals, Mitsukuni killed the domain's senior councillor with his own sword as a warning to others to reform.

His reputation as a wise ruler was somewhat tarnished by this incident, but respect for his generally enlightened rule persisted among the people. When the residents of Edo heard of his death, they expressed their sorrow with the refrain, "The world has lost two treasures, the gold mines of Sado and Mito Kōmon (Tokugawa Mitsukuni)." The popular image of Mitsukuni as the ideal feudal ruler was later reinforced by a mid-19th-century account of his fictional travels around the country and by a subsequent version of these tales, probably created by an Ōsaka storyteller in the 1890s.

▰ ——Tokugawa Kuniyuki, ed, *Mito Gikō zenshū*, 3 vols (Kadokawa Shoten, 1970). *Suzuki Eiichi*

Tokugawa Musei (1894–1971)

Entertainer and writer. Real name Fukuhara Toshio. Born in Masuda, Shimane Prefecture. He started out as a narrator for silent movies and became chief narrator for the Shinjuku Musashinokan Theater in Tōkyō. He was popular, particularly among intellectuals, for his witty and eloquent style. After the introduction of talkies he became a comedian, helping to organize the troupe Warai no Ōkoku in 1933. In 1937, together with Iwata Toyoo (also known as SHISHI BUNROKU) and Tamura Akiko, he founded the theater group Bungakuza and appeared in stage plays and films. He also appeared regularly in the Nihon Hōsō Kyōkai (NHK; Japan Broadcasting Corporation) radio game show "Hanashi no izumi" (1946–64). He was given the Hōsō Bunka Shō, an award for radio performers (1950), the Kikuchi Kan Shō (1955), a literary prize, for his art of conversation, and several imperial awards for his contributions to the entertainment industry. He was made an honorary citizen of Tōkyō in 1965. *Itasaka Tsuyoshi*

Tokugawa Nariaki (1800–1860)

Daimyō of the Mito domain (now part of Ibaraki Prefecture) and father of the 15th and last Tokugawa shōgun, TOKUGAWA YOSHINOBU. An active reformer in domainal government and a leader in the SONNŌ JŌI (Revere the Emperor, Expel the Barbarians) movement of the last years of the Tokugawa shogunate, he was a vocal opponent of II NAOSUKE in the 1857–58 dispute over shogunal succession and the signing of the HARRIS TREATY. He is also known by his posthumous name, Rekkō.

Nariaki became lord of the powerful senior collateral (GOSANKE) domain of Mito in 1829 after a succession dispute in which he was backed by the reform-minded faction within the domain. As daimyō he embarked on a program of administrative reforms, giving prominent posts to such capable men of the reform faction as FUJITA TŌKO and AIZAWA SEISHISAI. In 1841 he established a school named the Kōdōkan to foster the so-called WESTERN LEARNING as well as the *sonnō jōi* cause. As foreign warships appeared increasingly in Japanese waters, he carried out military reforms and had bells forcibly collected from temples throughout his domain and melted down to make cannon for coastal defenses. Nariaki's *sonnō jōi* activities aroused the enmity of the shogunate, and in 1844 he was removed as daimyō and ordered into domiciliary confinement. He relinquished the headship of the family to his eldest son, Yoshiatsu. The confinement order was lifted in 1849.

During the national turmoil following the visit of Matthew C. PERRY in 1853, Nariaki was invited by the senior councillor (*rōjū*) ABE MASAHIRO to serve the shogunate as an adviser on maritime defenses. Abe hoped to use Nariaki, who was popular among anti-shogunate daimyō, to effect a conciliation among shogunate, imperial court, and daimyō and thus shore up the shogunate's faltering position. However, the conciliation plan broke down when Abe died in 1857.

In the succession dispute of 1857–58 following the death of the 13th shōgun, Iesada, Nariaki was at the center of the Hitotsubashi faction, the group backing his seventh son, Yoshinobu, who had been adopted as head of the Hitotsubashi house (see GOSANKYŌ). Nariaki was thus in opposition to Ii Naosuke, a strong backer of TOKUGAWA IEMOCHI. After Ii had become great elder (*tairō*) and installed Iemochi as the 14th shōgun in 1858, Nariaki again came into conflict with Ii over the Harris Treaty, signed that same year. He criticized Ii for signing it without obtaining imperial approval. The shogunate retaliated (see ANSEI PURGE) by condemning Nariaki to lifetime confinement in Mito, where he died on 29 September 1860. *Tanaka Akira*

Tokugawa period → Edo period

Tokugawa political system → bakuhan system

Tokugawa shogunate

(Tokugawa *bakufu*). The last, and longest-lived, of Japan's three warrior governments, the first two being the KAMAKURA SHOGUNATE (1192–1333) and the MUROMACHI SHOGUNATE (1338–1573). It was founded in 1603, when TOKUGAWA IEYASU, having proved himself more powerful than any of his warrior contemporaries, was commissioned to form a government by the Emperor Go-Yōzei (r 1586–1611). The title he took, *seii tai shōgun* ("barbarian-subduing generalissimo"; see SHŌGUN), was in origin a military one, and therefore his government, like all such governments since 1192, carried the appropriately military designation of *bakufu*, or general headquarters, referred to in this encyclopedia as shogunate. Thereafter the office of shōgun, and with it nominal leadership of the shogunate, was invested in 15 successive heads of the TOKUGAWA FAMILY in a progression which came to an end with the resignation of TOKUGAWA YOSHINOBU, the last shōgun, late in 1867 (see MEIJI RESTORATION).

Responsibilities —— In the context of 1603, the granting of any imperial title—even one as venerable as *seii tai shōgun*—was largely without meaning. The imperial authority had been in eclipse for too long for matters to have been otherwise. Such titles, indeed, had come to belong to anyone with the military force to claim them, and, moreover, had come to depend on that military force for whatever degree of effectiveness they had. The title itself carried no authority, as several shōguns of the ASHIKAGA FAMILY had discovered; neither had any emperor the power to buttress it. Ieyasu assumed it, therefore, and his successors kept it, on precisely those terms, knowing that their tenure was conditional, not upon imperial approval, but upon their ability to resist any other challenger.

Nevertheless, although the title of shōgun—like the other sonorous titles accompanying it—minister of the right, chieftain of the Minamoto house, rector of the defunct Junna and Shōgaku academies—was an empty one, those who chose to assume it also assumed certain responsibilities. A shōgun, by intent, if not in fact, was preeminent among Japanese warriors, and this position, far more than his title, meant that certain things were expected of him, and of his government. It was expected, more than anything else, that he would take responsibility for the performance of certain imperial functions—functions which, while still vested, by divine right, in the emperor, had long since been appropriated by others.

One such function, for which he had the clearest possible mandate, was the pacification of barbarians, and in Tokugawa hands this was to become a pretext for the strictest control of foreign trade and diplomacy, both of which, manifestly, involved "barbarians." By this mandate the Tokugawa restricted all foreign contact, under the Sakoku (NATIONAL SECLUSION) edicts of 1633–39, and monopolized what was left. Naturally, too, the mandate was held to cover national defense, and the shōgun could therefore reserve the right to levy contributions of men and money—sometimes for matters only remotely concerned with defense—from provincial rivals.

Similarly, the obligation to pacify barbarians came, by extension, to cover also the pacification of Japanese, since it was generally assumed that internal unrest would attract foreign predators. The Tokugawa shōguns were to use this to justify the elimination of threats to their regime, since, like all rulers, they equated peace with submission to themselves. Therefore they claimed the right to keep regional independence—military and fiscal—within reasonable bounds, to avoid challenges of the kind which had overturned the Kamakura and Muromachi shogunates. In another sense, a still broader interpretation of the mandate was possible. Any unrest whatsoever, even that without discernable political object, together with such conditions as might provoke it, was of legitimate concern to the shōgun in his role as keeper of the peace. This produced the Tokugawa commitment to the famous Confucian four-class system of *samurai*, farmer, artisan and merchant (SHI-NŌ-KŌ-SHŌ), in which it was hoped that every respectable man would know his place and his obligations, and consequently escape the corrosive and disruptive forces of greed, ambition, and self-indulgence. It also produced a readiness to interfere in a wide range of matters, from debt repudiation to prohibition of the sale of agricultural land, related to the well-being of the samurai and the farmers, the two social classes to which the government was most committed.

The responsibilities of the Tokugawa and their government by no means ended there; it was also expected that, like previous shogunates, the Tokugawa shogunate would assume responsibility for two other important imperial functions, that of law giver, and, closely linked to it, that of moral arbiter.

Ieyasu had recognized this obligation—first, modestly enough, with his efforts to unify the currency and standardize national weights and measures, and then, rather more conspicuously, with the BUKE SHOHATTO (Laws for Military Houses) and the KINCHŪ NARABI NI KUGE SHOHATTO (Laws Governing the Imperial Court and Nobility). His grandson, the third shōgun, TOKUGAWA IEMITSU, was to continue it, issuing a set of laws, the Shoshi Hatto (Regulations for the Vassals), to his own vassals in 1632, and then, three years later, instructing all *daimyō* to follow shogunate legal precedents when drawing up laws for their own domains. Still more important, however, was his decision, again in 1635, to revive the HYŌJŌSHO (Judicial Council), the national tribunal of both the Kamakura and Muromachi shogunates. This tribunal, which heard all those disputes too complex to be settled by customary legal processes, confirmed the shogunate as the center of Japanese law. TOKUGAWA YOSHIMUNE, the eighth shōgun, was to consolidate this position with the compilation, in 1742, of the KUJIKATA OSADAME-GAKI, a legal code of far greater scope than the GOSEIBAI SHIKIMOKU of 1232, its Kamakura predecessor.

From its position of eminence the Tokugawa shogunate was to issue a never-ending succession of instructions to the Japanese people. Undoubtedly many of these were prompted by its legal responsibilities, and were meant to be interpreted literally. Others, however, while forbiddingly legal in appearance, were to be enforced only intermittently, being designed above all as instruments of guidance and encouragement. These, with their detailed prohibitions of overeating, overdressing, overelaborate coiffures, gambling, and whoring in unlicensed areas, as with their encouragement of filial piety, and kindness to animals, sprang out of the shogunate's other area of responsibility, that of moral arbiter. So, too, the willingness with which the shogunate censored books, plays, and prints; several pornographers were to discover too late that the shogunate's censorship was not inspired exclusively by political considerations.

Above all, as moral arbiter, the Tokugawa shogunate was to find itself committed on the philosophical level. This was expressed negatively, in the first instance, with prohibitions not only of CHRISTIANITY, but also of certain forms of Buddhism, like the FUJU FUSE SECT, and ultimately in the discouraging of some varieties of Confucianism. It found its positive expression in the encouragement the shogunate was prepared to offer Neo-Confucianism (SHUSHIGAKU) and those who professed it. Such encouragement, while often exaggerated as far as the early 17th century is concerned, was nevertheless real and came to be reflected throughout the entire education system. Its influence on individual behavior in the Edo period (1600–1868) may be debatable, but there is no doubting its impact on the moral and political vocabulary of the time, which was profound.

Powers——The effective discharge of these responsibilities, particularly when they were defined so broadly, required a degree of coercive power unusual in the context of Japan's recent history. In its formative period the shogunate had that power—not, it must be emphasized, because of the imperial commission granted to Ieyasu in 1603, which simply imposed a patina of legitimacy, but for two very much more tangible reasons. One was the massive Tokugawa victory at the Battle of SEKIGAHARA (1600), which had won Ieyasu pledges of allegiance from all surviving warrior-leaders. This was enough to establish him, for the time being, as Japan's most powerful military figure. The other was the destruction, in 1615, of TOYOTOMI HIDEYORI (1593–1615), who had offered the only possible alternative to Tokugawa rule. Dissenters, therefore, had no cause around which to assemble.

The main outlines of this shogunal power were to be revealed in 1615, within two months of the fall of ŌSAKA CASTLE and the death of Toyotomi Hideyori. They took the form of two sets of instructions, one directed at the emperor's court in Kyōto, and the other at the daimyō, or provincial military leaders; in each the shogunate affirmed a degree of authority previously unknown.

A reading of the 17-clause Kinchū Narabi ni Kuge Shohatto, for example, leaves no doubt of the shogunate's readiness to abandon its pose as imperial servant in favor of the greater security offered by the role of imperial master. Under its terms, the emperor and those about him were encouraged to devote themselves to academic and artistic matters and, by implication, to stay clear of politics. To make certain of this, the shogunate reserved the power of veto in the appointment of senior court officials, enabling it to surround the emperor with none but those on whose discretion it could rely.

The 13-clause Buke Shohatto, announced 10 days earlier, was equally ambitious. As with the regulations for the imperial court, many of its provisions were of a generally noncontroversial nature, enjoining amongst other things, devotion to the skills of war and peace, and the adoption of a sober and frugal life style. It also contained, however, half a dozen articles of an altogether more serious kind, in which daimyō were forbidden to harbor fugitives, or to allow into their domains people from elsewhere, or to begin new fortifications, or to contract marriages without shogunate approval, or to provide themselves with large escorts except upon official business. They were also instructed to inform the shogunate of suspicious developments in other domains. Taken together, these articles represent an intrusion by the shogunate into areas where previously no central government had been able to penetrate. Later versions, particularly that of 1635, were to take the shogunate still further, with prohibitions both against the private imposition of tolls and the construction of large ships.

Clearly in its relations with the imperial court and with the daimyō, the shogunate's aim was to control them, and by controlling them, to perpetuate its own authority. In the case of the court, which had no military or economic power of its own, and which was, moreover, situated within a restricted area, such control offered no difficulty. The shogunate simply took charge of the city of Kyōto, and with it, of the emperor and his attendants, who vanished from national political life until revitalized by the crisis of the mid-19th century.

Control of the daimyō, scattered through the length and breadth of the Japanese islands, posed rather more difficulties. The key lay in the HAN, or daimyō domain, from which each daimyō derived economic and military strength, and without which he could not function. It was of the utmost importance to the Tokugawa government, therefore, that the shōgun establish his ultimate right to all domains. This was, of course, accomplished in principle after the Battle of Sekigahara, when each daimyō was obliged to swear loyalty to the head of the Tokugawa house. Thereafter the same principle was to be asserted again and again, at the accession of every new daimyō and every new shōgun, with an exchange of documents in which in return for a pledge of allegiance the daimyō received a deed certifying his right to the income of his domain.

It was, nevertheless, far too important a matter to be left at the level of ceremonial symbolism, as the early shogunate took care to establish. In the years between 1600 and 1650, the Tokugawa government was conspicuously active in domain allocation, as if to warn daimyō that, no matter how they had originally acquired their domains, continued tenure depended upon their good behavior. During that period, for example, the shogunate was to create 172 new daimyō, as a reward for notable service, and to grant fief increases to a further 206 for the same reason. Another such device, employed on 281 occasions over the same 50 years, was the transfer of daimyō from one domain to another, with the quality of the new fief corresponding to the degree of service rendered. This had the additional effect of breaking residual bonds between daimyō families and particular areas, thereby reinforcing the shogunate's central position. Most devastating of all was the shogunate's readiness to withdraw domains altogether. During the first half of the 17th century some 213 daimyō were to lose all or part of their domain in punishment for some offense, whether real or fictitious. There could have been no better method of displaying to the daimyō just how conditional their positions were.

The ultimate right to give and take domains was the shogunate's major weapon against daimyō independence, and therefore of the utmost importance to the government's continued effectiveness and, indeed, its continued existence. Without strong central control of the provincial warriors, Japan under the Tokugawa shogunate would have remained rent by civil wars. But the daimyō also needed to be kept under surveillance if they were not to pose a threat to the central government, just as they needed to be kept from dangerous degrees of affluence, so the shogunate paid attention to these matters as well. In surveillance, the shogunate maintained a group of officials, headed by the ŌMETSUKE (inspectors general), whose prime duty it was to initiate confidential enquiries about daimyō behavior. To this were added the *junkenshi*, parties of inspectors sent around the country from time to time to make enquiries of a more formal kind. Most ambitious of all, however, was the SANKIN KŌTAI system, formally initiated in 1635, under which each Japanese daimyō was obliged to spend every alternate year in residence in Edo (now Tōkyō), where his activities could be subjected to regular scrutiny.

It was no less important that daimyō be made to shoulder as much expense as possible, to make sure that, even should they nour-

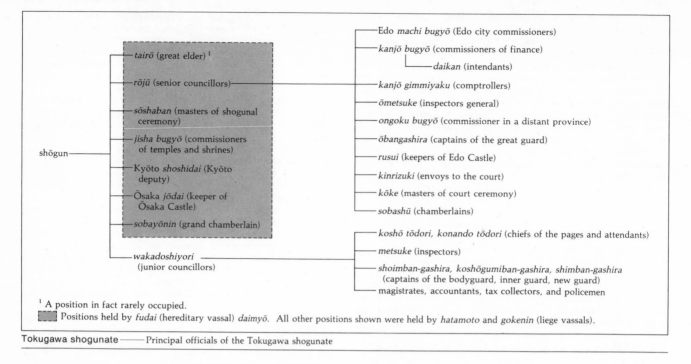

```
                                           ┌── Edo machi bugyō (Edo city commissioners)
                                           ├── kanjō bugyō (commissioners of finance)
                    ┌── tairō (great elder)¹       └── daikan (intendants)
                    │
                    ├── rōjū (senior councillors) ──┼── kanjō gimmiyaku (comptrollers)
                    │                         ├── ōmetsuke (inspectors general)
                    ├── sōshaban (masters of shogunal    ├── ongoku bugyō (commissioner in a distant province)
                    │   ceremony)              ├── ōbangashira (captains of the great guard)
                    ├── jisha bugyō (commissioners   ├── rusui (keepers of Edo Castle)
                    │   of temples and shrines)     ├── kinrizuki (envoys to the court)
  shōgun ───────────┤                         ├── kōke (masters of court ceremony)
                    ├── Kyōto shoshidai (Kyōto       ├── sobashū (chamberlains)
                    │   deputy)
                    ├── Ōsaka jōdai (keeper of
                    │   Ōsaka Castle)
                    ├── sobayōnin (grand chamberlain)
                    │
                    └── wakadoshiyori ─────────┬── koshō tōdori, konando tōdori (chiefs of the pages and attendants)
                        (junior councillors)    ├── metsuke (inspectors)
                                           ├── shoimban-gashira, koshōgumiban-gashira, shimban-gashira
                                           │   (captains of the bodyguard, inner guard, new guard)
                                           └── magistrates, accountants, tax collectors, and policemen
```

¹ A position in fact rarely occupied.

▨ Positions held by *fudai* (hereditary vassal) *daimyō*. All other positions shown were held by *hatamoto* and *gokenin* (liege vassals).

Tokugawa shogunate —— Principal officials of the Tokugawa shogunate

ish any undetected ambitions, sheer lack of funds would discourage open rebellion. The shogunate, accordingly, spent its early years building, at daimyō expense, a series of castles at strategic points in the provinces, both strengthening itself and weakening those it feared. EDO CASTLE, too, the center of shogunal government, became, through daimyō contributions, the largest and most opulent of all Japanese castles. Then, when the shogunate saw no further need for defensive military installations, it was able to set daimyō to work on undertakings of a humbler, if more useful sort, having them provide men, money, and materials for flood control and drainage projects.

These were all costly enough, but they were not to be compared with the inroads made upon daimyō budgets by their *sankin kōtai* obligations. Not only did these keep the daimyō available in Edo each alternate year, and thereby inhibit the development of antigovernment conspiracies; they also kept them poor, as much with the need to maintain and staff two or three permanent official residences (and rebuild them whenever they burned down), as with the constant expense of moving large numbers of attendants either to or from Edo once a year.

Military Position —— Despite the legitimacy conferred by the emperor on Tokugawa rule in 1603, and despite the frequent reiteration of daimyō oaths of allegiance, the Tokugawa shogunate owed its commanding position to its military capacity, which far outstripped that of any individual daimyō. Without that capacity there would have been little imperial recognition, and even less daimyō deference.

At the core of the shogunate's military machine stood the Tokugawa vassals. These were men who, for the most part with no domains of their own to govern, lived permanently in Edo, either staffing the civil service and the regular army, or else, if not employed in either sphere, remaining in reserve. At the highest level were the HATAMOTO ("bannermen"), those who, retaining the right of direct audience with the shōgun, were held to be closest to him, and had incomes and responsibilities to match. In 1722 they numbered a little over 5,000. Below them were the Tokugawa GOKENIN ("housemen"), of whom, in 1722, there were more than 17,000, a number which may have swelled slightly during the remainder of the shogunate's life, and below them again were the retainers of both *hatamoto* and *gokenin*. The numbers of the latter group are uncertain, but it has been estimated that, in combination, all three varieties of Tokugawa vassals might have numbered as many as 60,000 at any given time.

A vassal band of 60,000 may seem formidable enough, but the figures are deceptive, for two reasons. In the first place, only a small percentage of these men could have been held, even by the most elastic definition, to constitute a standing army at any given time. Many of them, indeed, were servants, whether civil or domestic,

others had no official employment of any sort, and almost all were more accustomed to drawing salaries than swords. In terms of an effective, readily-mobilized military force, the shogunate was restricted to the small number of men on active duty in the various brigades of guards.

In the second place, although the shogunate could draw on military reserves several times greater than those available to any single daimyō, even such a figure as 60,000 is dwarfed beside the more than 200,000 other samurai who, through their daimyō employers, were Tokugawa vassals only at second hand. In theory the shogunate could call on them for assistance at any time. Actually, however, their prime loyalties went to their daimyō, and, in the event of any conflict between daimyō and shogunate, there was no doubt that their support would go to the former. The shogunate, therefore, at no stage enjoyed absolute military supremacy. Its continued existence was predicated first of all upon the unquestioning support of two groups of daimyō—the SHIMPAN, themselves cadet members of the Tokugawa house, and the FUDAI ("hereditary" vassals), daimyō who had been Tokugawa vassals before the Battle of Sekigahara and who had been raised to daimyō rank by them following Sekigahara or later. It also required the neutrality of at least some of a third group, the TOZAMA ("outside lords"), territorial magnates whose families had risen to eminence independent of the Tokugawa.

Financial Position —— Just as the Tokugawa shogunate's military position fell far short of total superiority, so too did the financial base upon which it rested, although here, too, its resources were many times larger than those of even the greatest daimyō. Effectively, the shogunate held 25 percent of Japan's registered arable land, of which a minimal portion was distributed in fief to senior *hatamoto*. Of what remained, land assessed at a massive four million *koku* (see KOKUDAKA) was TENRYŌ—the personal domain of the shōgun—taxes from which went directly to the shogunal treasury. No single daimyō could have hoped to compete with this; even the largest of them, the MAEDA FAMILY of the Kaga domain (now Ishikawa and Toyama prefectures) could draw directly on an area only one-tenth as productive.

Nor did the shogunate's advantages end there. Tokugawa Ieyasu had seized Japan's major gold and silver mines, at Izu, Iwami, Sado, and elsewhere, and they, together with whatever came from them, were to remain Tokugawa property thereafter. Similarly, he had also appropriated what were then Japan's three wealthiest cities—Kyōto, Sakai, and Nagasaki; added to Edo, already part of the Tokugawa domain, and Ōsaka, to be acquired in 1619, this secured command of the main centers of Japanese commercial life for the next 200 years. From Nagasaki, where a vestigial foreign trade continued (see NAGASAKI TRADE), it was to derive a steady, if small, income. Elsewhere it used its position of authority first to grant extensive patents of monopoly, in return for which merchants were required to pay an annual tax known as MYŌGAKIN and also, later, to levy forced contributions (GOYŌKIN) from members of the merchant community. Currency debasement, too, begun in 1695 and carried out thereafter on three separate occasions, was another important source of income inaccessible to daimyō.

Administrative System —— The Tokugawa shogunate functioned on two different levels. It was, in one sense, a national government, with responsibilities far transcending those of any daimyō. In another sense, however, the shogunate was itself a daimyō government, if on a rather larger scale. Not surprisingly, therefore, much of its administrative system reflected this duality.

At the very top was the shōgun, perhaps the only person capable of straddling both levels, for he was, at one and the same time, the man entrusted by the emperor with the cares of national administration, and also the head of the Tokugawa house. Whenever circumstances warranted it—as, for example, when the shōgun was young, or ill, he could be assisted in both areas of responsibility by a member of one of the leading *fudai* daimyō houses, acting as TAIRŌ or great elder. This latter position, however, was far from regular, being occupied only occasionally, and, curiously enough, as often under mature and healthy shōguns as under those who were for any reason incapacitated.

Below the unifying figure of the shōgun, the shogunate's administration split abruptly into separate areas of national and local responsibility. National affairs, which included foreign relations, coastal defense, the allocation of daimyō domains, and relations between the shogunate and the daimyō in general, were concentrated in the hands of a small group of men, seldom more than five or six in number, known as RŌJŪ or senior councillors. They were themselves daimyō, although of that variety, the *fudai*, who, formerly Tokugawa vassals, owed their rise to Tokugawa favor, and from whom, therefore, one might expect unswerving loyalty. The *rōjū* met as a formal council to debate issues of particular importance, but otherwise rotated responsibility among themselves, with each member taking charge of general administration for a month at a time.

Beneath the *rōjū*, and under their direct charge, were other officials also concerned with national matters, among them the KYŌTO SHOSHIDAI or Kyōto deputy, and the Ōsaka *jōdai* or the keeper of Ōsaka Castle. Both were important positions, the former acting as shogunal ambassador to the imperial court, and the latter assuming responsibility for the peace of western Japan, where shogunate authority was more uncertain. *Fudai* daimyō monopolized these positions, too, together with another office of national importance, that of JISHA BUGYŌ or commissioners of temples and shrines. Despite the restriction implicit in their title, those who held this position (perhaps four or five at any one time) maintained a watching brief over developments in the daimyō domains, sharing this function also with the *ōmetsuke*, the four or five samurai of *hatamoto* rank who constituted the shogunate's censorate.

In contrast to the level of government dealing with national affairs, in which all positions of influence were reserved for *fudai* daimyō, the lower level was staffed exclusively by *hatamoto* and *gokenin*. Here four or five WAKADOSHIYORI, or junior councillors, presided over the organization and welfare of Tokugawa vassals. As with their senior colleagues, the *wakadoshiyori* rotated routine administration among themselves. Like them, too, they were supported by a number of lesser officials—guard captains, inspectors (METSUKE), magistrates, accountants, tax collectors, and policemen.

The shogunate's administration, described thus, appears to have been at least as coherent as any other system of government, but here, too, no less than with shogunate military capacity, appearances are deceptive. It was, in fact, despite the precise definition of roles, the neat division of responsibilities, and the regular rotation of office, a system which functioned only on paper. The shōgun, for example, the man ultimately accountable for all shogunate actions, was held to have absolute authority. Few were to exercise it, and those who did had to fight for it, often by-passing the formal machinery of government in the process; those who did so successfully—notably TOKUGAWA TSUNAYOSHI (1646–1709) and TOKUGAWA IENARI (1773–1841)—were never to be forgiven for it. All too frequently, the shōgun was overshadowed by others. On occasion, as with the early years of TOKUGAWA HIDETADA (1579–1632), Tokugawa Iemitsu and TOKUGAWA IESHIGE (1711–61), the incumbent shōgun was directed by his father. At other times, the formal chain of command notwithstanding, the *rōjū* determined policy without reference to the shōgun.

The rotation of office at senior levels, too, was more formidable in theory than it ever was in practice. The commonly accepted rationalization was that it would prevent any one *rōjū* from seizing powers properly residing with the shōgun. In this it failed, as the occasional appearance of political bosses like TANUMA OKITSUGU (1719–88), MATSUDAIRA SADANOBU (1758–1829), and MIZUNO TADAKUNI (1794–1851) makes clear. Each of these men dominated the policy making of his day, and did so largely through control of a *rōjū* council stacked with his nominees. Had this not been done, any decisive response to critical situations would have been virtually impossible.

The machinery of the Tokugawa shogunate has been criticized on other grounds as well. It has been said, for example, that a system restricting senior positions (and therefore political power) to *fudai* daimyō ran the risk of alienating all those many daimyō—*shimpan* and *tozama*—who, while no less concerned with the fate of the country, were denied a voice in its affairs. There is little evidence, however, to suggest that political office was eagerly sought, even by those eligible for it, nor that those without it were necessarily also without influence. The shogunate seemed impressively self-contained, but in fact it could never afford to ignore the daimyō opinions which reached it through a variety of channels, formal and otherwise. There is even less evidence to suggest that the distinction between *fudai* daimyō and others was of any significance, nor that the reactions of *fudai* daimyō in any given situation would have been markedly different from those of their *shimpan* or *tozama* fellows.

In another sense, however, the Tokugawa shogunate was unnecessarily restricted in its recruitment for official positions, to such an extent that its efficiency can only have been seriously impaired. Its very highest office, that of shōgun was inherited, and therefore the qualities of its incumbents were a matter of genetic chance. Accordingly, while some shōgun were capable and energetic enough, others were too sickly, or not sufficiently interested, or, occasionally, just not smart enough, to fill the office adequately. The situation was perhaps less severe in subordinate posts, but there was never any question of selecting the best-qualified people in Japan for administrative position. The most responsible offices were limited either to daimyō—and by no means all of them—or to *hatamoto* and *gokenin* who, as we have seen, represented only a tiny minority of the samurai class. Even then, most official positions were reserved for men of particular ranks. Despite the lip service given to the selection of talented men, and despite the introduction in 1723 of a TASHIDAKA (supplementary stipend) system designed to widen eligibility for government posts, there was never any consistent attempt to find the right man for the right job. If occasionally people of such stature as ARAI HAKUSEKI (1657–1725) and Tanuma Okitsugu could break into the charmed circle from outside, they were usually chased out again.

Achievement —— It is perhaps cause for wonder that so haphazard a government should have achieved anything of note, the more so when it is considered that, in almost every respect, the elements of Tokugawa control assembled so laboriously in the first half of the 17th century were thereafter allowed to crumble away so quickly. Inspection of daimyō domains soon became a formality, with daimyō being notified of *junkenshi* tours well in advance, to spare them embarrassment. The shōgun's right to allocate daimyō domains, too, barely survived the 17th century; confiscation of domains was to be virtually unknown in the 18th and early 19th centuries, and few daimyō were ever moved. When occasional transfer attempts were made in the 19th century, they encountered so much general resistance as to oblige the shogunate to abandon them. This was not entirely unexpected in a political organization in which, it will be remembered, the central government—itself often entirely in the hands of daimyō administrators—remained dependent upon general daimyō goodwill for its survival.

More remarkable, perhaps, was the progressive impairment of the Tokugawa financial position, which, originally, had seemed so impregnable. Like all governments of the BAKUHAN SYSTEM (shogunate and domain system), however, the shogunate was overtaken by the general fiscal malaise. At the end of the 17th century, for example, production in its gold and silver mines had virtually ceased. Much more seriously, the land tax, the major source of shogunate revenue, had begun to decline, too. An attempt to restore it along orthodox lines, in the KYŌHŌ REFORMS of the early 18th century, was successful for a time, but land-tax revenue nevertheless reached its peak in 1744, and steadily declined thereafter. Neither the KANSEI REFORMS, toward the end of that century, nor the TEMPŌ REFORMS, launched in 1841, could retrieve the situation. Accordingly, Japan was to enter one of the most dangerous periods of its entire history with only the remnants of a strong central government, and when contact with the outside world was resumed, these, too, were soon to disappear. All that was left was the carapace of a government, and, with it, the problem of how far, and by whom, that carapace was to be disjointed.

The two and a half centuries of Tokugawa rule had been a time of unparalleled peace for the Japanese people. Apart from the sizable insurrection at Shimabara in 1637–38 (see SHIMABARA UPRISING), and an abortive conspiracy in the KEIAN INCIDENT of 1651, only occasional agrarian protests (HYAKUSHŌ IKKI) were to disturb the public order until well into the 19th century. The shogunate has been awarded much of the credit for this, for sealing the country off from foreign interference, and, at roughly the same time, in 1635, ordering the daimyō not to pursue private quarrels among themselves. To many critics, however, this period of peace is seen as the product of iron repression, reinforced by a national network of spies, and perpetuated by violence. This is not true. The shogunate, although responsible for much legislation of a repressive kind, at no stage had the power to carry it out. It was never strong enough to be totalitarian, although on occasion, particularly under Tsunayoshi in the 17th century, Tanuma Okitsugu in the 18th, and Mizuno Tadakuni in the 19th, it tried, without success, to move in that direction. Such powers as it had were conditional upon daimyō goodwill or neutrality, and it could never, therefore, risk outright confrontation with them.

To some extent, the Tokugawa Peace was produced by a variety of factors completely unrelated to shogunate policy. It is far more likely that the even tenor of life in the towns and villages of the *bakuhan* system was due less to government interference, than to the lack of it, in combination with the readiness of such communities to regulate themselves. Japan's freedom from war, too, had little to do with the shogunate. Its National Seclusion policy was initiated in the most favorable circumstances, when all it encountered was perfunctory protests. It was perpetuated not by shogunate authority, but by foreign indifference. Equally, it was daimyō passivity and suspicious unwillingness to cooperate with each other, together with, it must be added, shogunate reluctance to provoke them, which assured so long a period of internal peace. When, from the 1840s onward, both foreign indifference and the passivity of some daimyō came to an end, so too did the government which had relied on them. See also HISTORY OF JAPAN: Edo history.

▰———Harold Bolitho, *Treasures among Men: The Fudai Daimyō in Tokugawa Japan* (1974). Fujino Tamotsu, *Shintei bakuhan taisei shi no kenkyū* (1975). John W. Hall, *Tanuma Okitsugu* (1955). Kitajima Masamoto, *Edo bakufu no kenryoku kōzō* (1964). Herman Ooms, *Charismatic Bureaucrat: A Political Biography of Matsudaira Sadanobu* (1975). Conrad Totman, *Politics in the Tokugawa Bakufu, 1600–1843* (1967). Harold BOLITHO

Tokugawa Tsunayoshi (1646–1709)

Fifth shōgun of the Tokugawa shogunate; ruled from 1680 to 1709. The fourth son of TOKUGAWA IEMITSU, the third shōgun, Tsunayoshi served as *daimyō* of the Tatebayashi domain in Kōzuke Province (now part of Gumma Prefecture) before succeeding his elder brother TOKUGAWA IETSUNA as shōgun in 1680. In the early part of his rule Tsunayoshi had the assistance of the great elder (*tairō*) HOTTA MASATOSHI, and together they governed firmly and fairly. After Masatoshi's death in 1684, however, Tsunayoshi began to rely heavily on his grand chamberlain (*sobayōnin*) YANAGISAWA YOSHIYASU, while he himself retired more and more from directive duties. As a result, the government began to deteriorate steadily. Moreover, in order to check the depletion of shogunate funds, Tsunayoshi instituted a policy of debasement of the gold and silver coinage; this, together with an increase in the annual land tax (*nengu*), caused great confusion in prices.

Tsunayoshi's rule largely coincided with the GENROKU ERA, which was characterized by lavish spending and spiraling prices resulting from misguided fiscal legislation. The shogunate's outlays grew steadily, leading to the continued worsening of its finances. Many scholars point to these economic trends as the source of later troubles for the shogunate.

Tsunayoshi was fond of learning and made the teachings of the Chinese philosopher Zhu Xi (Chu Hsi; see SHUSHIGAKU) the official regimen for government bureaucrats. At the same time, he courted political disaster and drew the criticism of all by promulgating from 1685 onward the highly unpopular "Edicts on Compassion for Living

Things" (SHŌRUI AWAREMI NO REI), which ordained the death sentence for killing a dog, among other oppressive measures. Society rewarded him with the nickname "the dog shōgun" (*inu kubō*).

TAKAGI Shōsaku

Tokugawa Yoshimune (1684–1751)

Eighth shōgun of the Tokugawa shogunate and initiator of the KYŌHO REFORMS; ruled from 1716 to 1745. Born the third son of Tokugawa Mitsusada (1625–1705), head of the Kii branch of the Tokugawa family, Yoshimune was made *daimyō* of the minor domain of Sabae (now part of Fukui Prefecture) in 1697. In 1705, following the deaths of his two elder brothers, he became daimyō of the Kii domain (now Wakayama Prefecture). When the death in 1716 of the child shōgun Ietsugu (b 1709) brought the main line of the Tokugawa family to extinction, the 32-year-old Yoshimune was chosen by the heads of the Three Successor Houses (GOSANKE) of the Tokugawa family and the senior council (*rōjū*) of the shogunate to continue the shogunal succession. To secure the continuation of his bloodline, Yoshimune, following the example of the dynastic founder, TOKUGAWA IEYASU, founded two branch families, the Tayasu and Hitotsubashi houses. Together with a third house, the Shimizu house, founded by Yoshimune's son TOKUGAWA IESHIGE, these branch houses descended from Yoshimune were known as the Three Lords (GOSANKYŌ) in contrast to the original three cadet branches of the Tokugawa founded by Ieyasu, the Three Successor Houses (Gosanke). The main and branch houses descended from Yoshimune supplied the remaining seven shōguns of the Edo period (1600–1868).

One of the most forceful and capable of the 15 Tokugawa shōguns, Yoshimune succeeded during his reign in further extending the autocratic powers of the shōgun within the ruling structure. Benefiting from his previous practical experience as daimyō, he developed a variety of means of maximizing his direct knowledge of shogunate affairs and administration. The most novel of these means was the MEYASUBAKO, a box posted at one of the gates of Edo Castle from 1721 in which townspeople could deposit complaints and suggestions for the shōgun's personal consideration, bypassing the normal channels of jurisdictional hierarchy. Yoshimune also often ignored such channels in his dealings with the shogunate bureaucracy, directly interviewing middle-level officials on points of administration and policy rather than going through senior officials. He further organized a personal surveillance group of 20 retainers who had come with him from Kii, whom he sent out to investigate conditions in various daimyō domains. The information gained in these ways he put to use in making bureaucratic appointments, seeking out and promoting competent and reliable officials, and exerting his authority over the bureaucratic apparatus.

Such enhancement of the shōgun's personal authority was not a new departure; it was rather the culmination of trends dating from the beginning of the reign of the fifth shōgun, TOKUGAWA TSUNAYOSHI, 40 years earlier. However, by adopting a political style sharply different from that of his predecessors, Yoshimune managed to surmount some of the problems that had marked those trends in their earlier stages. Although the extension of his authority and realization of his policies depended on his forging alliances with officials who were not necessarily a part of the established order, Yoshimune's active involvement with various areas of government enabled him to remain far less dependent than his predecessors on personal attendants appointed to high rank and position. Such independence helped preserve his own freedom of initiative and was a critical factor in his success in reducing the confrontation between newcomers personally associated with the shōgun (*shinsan*) and the established hereditary vassals (FUDAI) of the shogunate that had led to a stalemate in policy matters during the preceding reign. Upon becoming shōgun Yoshimune immediately took action to repair relations with the *fudai*. He paid ceremonious respect to leading representatives of the *fudai* and aligned himself with the hostility against the most notable newcomers of the previous reign, the chamberlain MANABE AKIFUSA and the political adviser ARAI HAKUSEKI, by abolishing the ideological reforms through which the latter had sought to bolster the authority of the shōgun, such as use of the title "king" (*kokuō*) for the shōgun in relations with foreign countries and the importation of ritual from the imperial court at Kyōto.

However, beneath the surface of revocation of the innovations of the previous reign and restoration of the ways of the founders of the shogunate, in the critical areas of shogunate structure and financial affairs, Yoshimune continued many of the policies initiated by his immediate predecessors. His cultivation of the *fudai* smoothed the way for an overhaul of administration that in effect further reduced the traditional role of the high-ranking *fudai* in shogunate affairs. This overhaul was part of a series of reforms known from the name of the era as the Kyōhō Reforms and is often considered synonymous with Yoshimune's reign.

The staging of the reform reflected graphically Yoshimune's skill at political maneuvering. In the early years of his rule Yoshimune was constrained by the presence of particular senior councillors who, as leading representatives of the *fudai*, had sponsored his designation as shōgun. Gradually, however, these inherited senior councillors retired or died, and when, in the spring of 1722, the last active figure among them lay on his deathbed, Yoshimune moved decisively. He designated his own appointee "senior councillor responsible for financial affairs" (*kattegakari rōjū*), and rapidly developed a core of officials from the finance and judicial commission (KANJŌ BUGYŌ) under the direct jurisdiction of this senior councillor as the central policy formulation group of the shogunate in place of the traditional collegial meetings of the senior councillors. It was this core of officials that was largely responsible for initiating and carrying out the Kyōhō Reforms.

The reforms, intended to restore the shogunate and the *samurai* class to financial solvency, bore Yoshimune's personal imprint in many ways. Calling for a general retrenchment, he personally led the way in rejecting the luxurious lifestyle of his predecessors for one of spartan frugality. He had the living quarters of the previous shōgun torn down, choosing to make do with the former shōgun's antechamber for his own quarters, wore plain clothes, and ate vegetarian dishes and brown rice for his daily meals. He sought to counter the seductive lure of urban life and to improve samurai morale and physical fitness by sponsoring a revival of martial activities and sports. He himself frequently went out hunting, wearing cotton clothes and straw sandals and stopping in casually at the houses of farmers to rest or eat lunch. Intellectually pragmatic, he gave support to the compilation of legal precedents and statutes and to scientific experimentation of various sorts, using part of the gardens within Edo Castle for crop experimentation. His interest in science led in 1720 to partial relaxation of the ban on Western books.

——Tsuji Tatsuya, *Tokugawa Yoshimune* (1958).

Kate NAKAI

Tokugawa Yoshinobu (1837–1913)

The 15th and last shōgun of the Tokugawa shogunate, who ruled during most of 1867. Also known as Tokugawa Keiki. Yoshinobu was born in Edo (now Tōkyō), the seventh son of TOKUGAWA NARIAKI, lord of the Mito domain (now part of Ibaraki Prefecture) and head of one of the three senior branches (GOSANKE) of the Tokugawa family. Taken back to Mito by his father, he was educated by AIZAWA SEISHISAI and other Mito scholars and acquired a reputation as an unusually intelligent and promising lad. At the age of 10 he returned to Edo, where he was designated heir and later head of the Hitotsubashi house, one of the three junior collateral houses (GOSANKYŌ) of the Tokugawa family that supplied heirs to the shogunate. This appointment made him a likely candidate for the shogunal succession, should a shōgun fail to produce an heir.

In 1857, even as the American consul-general Townsend HARRIS was pressing the shogunate for a commercial treaty, the shōgun Iesada (1824–58) fell ill. He had no heir, and the deteriorating political situation prompted serious discussion of the succession. A number of powerful *daimyō*, notably MATSUDAIRA YOSHINAGA of the Echizen or Fukui domain (now part of Fukui Prefecture) and SHIMAZU NARIAKIRA of the Satsuma domain (now Kagoshima Prefecture), championed Yoshinobu's candidacy on the grounds that the times required an able shōgun. II NAOSUKE of the Hikone domain (now part of Shiga Prefecture) and a number of men close to Iesada supported a rival candidate, TOKUGAWA IEMOCHI of the house of Kii, who, as a descendant in the main line, had a better genealogical claim to the title. In mid-1858, Ii became great elder (*tairō*) and gained control of the shogunate; shortly afterward he arranged both Iemochi's succession and the signing of the HARRIS TREATY.

Yoshinobu's supporters protested Ii's actions, and Ii responded by punishing them under house arrest. He stripped some daimyō of their titles and punished even more harshly lesser critics of his rule (see ANSEI PURGE). Yoshinobu, who had aligned himself with those opposing Ii, was deprived of his headship of the Hitotsubashi house

and ordered into domiciliary confinement; he remained politically inactive until 1862.

By then, Ii was dead at the hands of assassins, and the great daimyō had resumed their political maneuvering. They were supported by several nobles at the imperial court and by radical proimperial *samurai*. Their combined pressure led the shogunate to repudiate Ii's policies; Yoshinobu was reinstated as head of the Hitotsubashi house and shortly after designated regent (*kōkenshoku*) to the shōgun. His attempts to heal the breach between the shogunate and the great daimyō were unsuccessful, however, and in 1863 he resigned his regency. Nonetheless, he continued to be embroiled in the politics of the day, and early in 1864 he was named protector of the court (*kinri shuei sōtoku*) with primary responsibility for keeping order in the vicinity of Kyōto. As the proimperial movement gathered momentum, Yoshinobu spoke out frequently in support of Tokugawa interests. In 1866, owing in part to Yoshinobu's insistence, the shogunate sent a punitive expedition against the Chōshū domain (now Yamaguchi Prefecture), the stronghold of proimperial sentiment, in an attempt to reassert Edo's control over the country (see CHŌSHŪ EXPEDITIONS). The war went badly for the shogunate from the start, and within a few weeks the shōgun Iemochi sickened and died. After persistent urging, most especially by the shogunate's senior official, ITAKURA KATSUKIYO, Yoshinobu agreed to succeed Iemochi as head of the Tokugawa family. In January 1867 he accepted the title of shōgun.

Yoshinobu thus took charge of the Tokugawa regime just as it was suffering the worst military defeat in its history. He was concerned to secure the honor and well-being of his family, but at the same time he strongly suspected that the Tokugawa political order was an anachronism. This perception predisposed him to political experimentation, and, following the defeat by Chōshū, he, Itakura, OGURI TADAMASA, and several other officials set to work to reform the government. During a year of frenetic activity, they overhauled the military system, reorganized the civil administration, promoted industrial development, and expanded foreign intercourse, with the aim of creating a unified state. Yoshinobu himself spent most of his time in Kyōto, maneuvering with the great daimyō, the court, and foreign envoys.

Proimperial leaders in Satsuma and Chōshū were alarmed by Yoshinobu's reforms and redoubled their own efforts. By late 1867 they felt sufficiently strong to carry out a coup d'etat in Kyōto; they proclaimed an "imperial restoration" and ordered Yoshinobu to surrender his domains. Attempts at year's end to reverse the coup precipitated the BOSHIN CIVIL WAR, in which the shogunal armies were quickly defeated. Thoroughly disheartened by the abrupt military collapse, Yoshinobu decided to capitulate. One of his chief officials, KATSU KAISHŪ, conducted the delicate negotiations, and within three months Edo was in the hands of the imperial army.

Yoshinobu retired to Mito, where he lived in seclusion while the imperial armies pacified central Japan. Late in the summer of 1868 he went to Sumpu (now the city of Shizuoka) where TOKUGAWA IEYASU, the founder of the dynasty, had lived in retirement 250 years earlier. For the rest of his life he lived quietly, receiving honors and titles from the new Meiji government, reminiscing about the 1860s, and leaving politics to the victors. (See also MEIJI RESTORATION.)

——Shibusawa Eiichi, *Tokugawa Yoshinobu Kō den*, 8 vols (1918–31).

Conrad TOTMAN

tokuju

(special procurements). Foreign procurements of goods and services which helped Japan's economy to recover and expand after World War II. The first surge of such procurements occurred during the KOREAN WAR, when Japanese firms received a huge quantity of special orders for goods and services from overseas because of their geographical proximity to Korea and their supply capabilities. In a narrow sense the term *tokuju* referred to goods and services supplied to the United Nations Forces in Korea, and in a wider sense it also included goods and services supplied to the United Nations troops, primarily American, stationed in Japan. Special procurements were initially made for military blankets, trucks, shells, and barbed wire, but later there was an increased demand for materials to be used in the reconstruction of Korea. Services demanded included repairs on trucks and tanks, transportation, and communications.

During 1950–53, special procurement expenditures in the narrower sense amounted to US $1 billion (US $0.7 billion for goods,

US $0.3 billion for services), while procurements in the wider sense reached between US $2.4 billion and US $3.6 billion. The procurement orders initially came from the Headquarters of the US Eighth Army, but after 1951 they were issued by the US Army Procurement Office in Japan. Coming just in the period when the United States was reducing its aid to Japan, special procurement expenditures raised domestic production, improved business profits, and helped the balance of international payments, thereby contributing toward Japan's economic independence. Later, orders for goods and services by the American military during the Vietnam War provided further stimulus for the Japanese economy.   Katō Masashi

Tokumi-doiya

(Ten Groups of Wholesalers; also pronounced Tokumi-don'ya). A merchant association of the Edo period (1600–1868) consisting of wholesale dealers in Edo (now Tōkyō) who bought commercial goods from a similar group of suppliers in Ōsaka known as the NIJŪSHIKUMI-DOIYA; the association had a virtual monopoly on important commodities sent from Ōsaka. The name comes from the fact that the association was originally made up of ten *(tō)* groups *(kumi)* of wholesale dealers (TOIYA), each of which handled a different set of commodities, such as cotton and textiles, herbs and sugar, matting, oil, *sake,* lacquer ware, wax, and paper. The organization was formed in 1694 to deal collectively with disputes among shipowners, wholesalers, and merchants over damaged and lost cargo. Together with its Ōsaka counterpart, the association controlled the *higaki* KAISEN, cargo ships that specialized in the transport of goods between Ōsaka and Edo. In 1730 the *sake* wholesalers seceded from the group and used another kind of ship, known as *taru kaisen,* leading to competition between the two shipping lines. The Tokumi-doiya gradually expanded to include nearly 100 groups. It was temporarily abolished under the TEMPŌ REFORMS (1830–43) but was revived in 1851 and then permanently disbanded at the time of the Meiji Restoration in 1868.

Tokunaga Sunao (1899–1958)

Novelist. Born in Kumamoto Prefecture. A member of a working-class family, he completed middle school while working for a living. Beginning in 1922 he worked as a typesetter in Tōkyō, where he participated in labor activities and the so-called PROLETARIAN LITERATURE MOVEMENT. He gained recognition as a writer for his novel *Taiyō no nai machi* (1929) about the 1926 KYŌDŌ PRINTING COMPANY STRIKE, in which he had participated. After writing mainly autobiographical novels during the war years because of government suppression of proletarian literature, he reemerged as a major left-wing author with such works as *Tsuma yo nemure* (1946–48) and *Shizuka naru yamayama* (1949–54).

tokunō

(model farmer). Also called *tokunōka.* A slogan used by government agricultural officials from the 1920s through World War II as part of a campaign to spur agricultural production. Experienced farmers who could serve as models for others in the agricultural community were recognized as *tokunō* for this purpose, especially during the economically depressed years following World War I. *Tokunō* were analogous to the RŌNŌ of earlier eras. During the food shortages of World War II, the populations of whole villages were exhorted to become *tokunō.*

Tokunoshima

Island 50 km (31 mi) southwest of the island of AMAMI ŌSHIMA of Kagoshima Prefecture, Kyūshū. One of the Amami Islands, it is surrounded by coral reefs. The northern part of the island is hilly, and the southern part is a wide plateau. The climate is subtropical, and the island is the habitat of the poisonous snake called *habu.* Principal activities are cattle raising and the growing of sugarcane, bananas, and pineapples. The island also has a well-developed tourist industry; one well-known local event is fighting between black bulls. Area: 248 sq km (95.7 sq mi).

tokura → dosō

tokusei

(literally, "virtuous acts of government"). Decrees issued by the government during the medieval period (13th–16th centuries) to give relief—usually in the form of an amnesty or remission of taxes or debts—to certain groups. They arose from the ancient Chinese Confucian belief that natural and human disasters occur when a ruler is not "virtuous." As early as the 8th century, Japanese sovereigns granted *tokusei* in order to increase their apparent virtue and bring about the cure of an ailing member of the imperial house, the end of a particularly serious famine or epidemic, or the elimination of some disturbance that was threatening the state. *Tokusei* were also issued, quite early, to ward off calamities at the time of an important state event, such as an enthronement or a change of capital. Twenty are recorded for the Nara period (710–794) and slightly fewer for the Heian period (794–1185).

In 1297, under the Kamakura shogunate (1192–1333), a different kind of *tokusei* was proclaimed by the military government for the purpose of strengthening the position of its retainers. A succession of droughts, extended military operations in distant regions of Japan, and high-interest-bearing loans made by wealthy merchants were causing an increasingly large number of retainers to sell or mortgage the land that had been entrusted to them by military superiors. In attempting to check the impoverishment of its retainers, the Kamakura government devised a *tokusei* that not only forbade the sale and foreclosure of retainer land but allowed a retainer to repossess lost land unless it had been held by some other retainer for more than 20 years or unless transfer to another retainer had been officially approved. Moreover, if a retainer had lost his land to a nonretainer, he could regain possession no matter how many years had elapsed since sale or foreclosure. Finally, this *tokusei* stipulated that charges against a retainer for defaulting on his loan would not be heard in military courts. Although loans made by pawnshops were not canceled, the rights and interests of moneylenders were so seriously affected by the 1297 *tokusei* that retainers began to suffer from the loss of credit, causing the authorities later to revise, and then to rescind, the order.

Toward the middle of the Muromachi period (1333–1568), a time of unusual political turbulence and rapid development in monetary exchange, *tokusei* were proclaimed frequently in order to quell peasant rebellions *(tokusei ikki).* After the historic uprising of 1441, when *tokusei*-demanding farmers and landholders gained the backing of many soldiers and nobles, peasant mobs declared their own *tokusei.* Forcing their way into one pawnshop after another, angry peasants would seize all pawned articles and burn all loan documents. The Ashikaga military government also took to collecting a certain percentage of every loan canceled by a *tokusei,* thus acquiring a needed source of income and further stimulating the spread of debt cancellations. Thirteen *tokusei* were issued during the rule (1443–74) of ASHIKAGA YOSHIMASA alone.

During the later years of the Muromachi period, when local lords were strengthening their hold over their domains, peasant uprisings were more easily quashed. Nevertheless, many lords issued *tokusei* in times of economic stress. This practice, also followed by the great 16th-century hegemons ODA NOBUNAGA and TOYOTOMI HIDEYOSHI, continued on into the Edo period (1600–1868), but by then the remissions were designated KIENREI (debt cancellations).

Delmer M. Brown

Tokushima

Capital of Tokushima Prefecture, Shikoku, on the river Yoshinogawa. The city developed as a castle town after the construction of Tokushima Castle in 1586 by the Hachisuka family. It prospered as a shipping port for indigo during the Edo period (1600–1868). Designated as one of the NEW INDUSTRIAL CITIES in 1963, Tokushima is the location of lumber, furniture, foodstuff, chemical, and textile industries. Attractions are the ruins of Tokushima Castle, Bizan Park, and the AWA DANCE festival held every August. Pop: 249,343.

Tokushima Plain

(Tokushima Heiya). Located in northern Tokushima Prefecture, Shikoku. Bordered by both the Pacific Ocean and the Kii Channel, and situated along the Median Tectonic Line (see JAPAN: geological

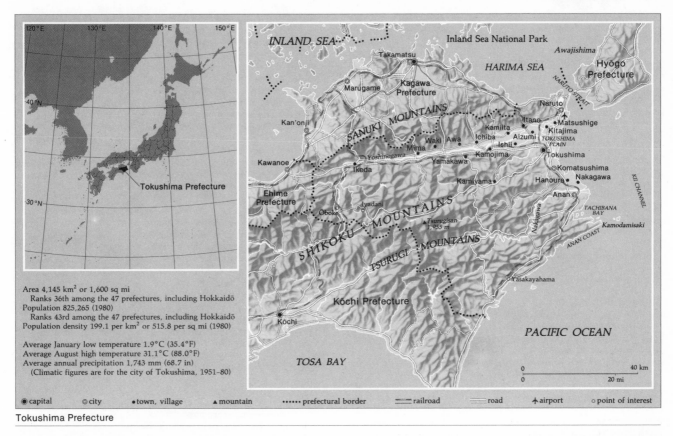

Area 4,145 km² or 1,600 sq mi
  Ranks 36th among the 47 prefectures, including Hokkaidō
Population 825,265 (1980)
  Ranks 43rd among the 47 prefectures, including Hokkaidō
Population density 199.1 per km² or 515.8 per sq mi (1980)

Average January low temperature 1.9°C (35.4°F)
Average August high temperature 31.1°C (88.0°F)
Average annual precipitation 1,743 mm (68.7 in)
  (Climatic figures are for the city of Tokushima, 1951–80)

◉ capital   ⊙ city   ● town, village   ▲ mountain   ····· prefectural border   ══ railroad   ══ road   ✈ airport   ○ point of interest

Tokushima Prefecture

structure), this flood plain of the river Yoshinogawa consists of extensive alluvial fans below the scarps, some river terraces, and the delta. In the Edo period (1600–1868) the indigo plant was cultivated on the uplands, but today rice, mulberry trees, tobacco, and vegetables are grown. The major city is Tokushima. Length: 15 km (9 mi); width: 80 km (50 mi).

Tokushima Prefecture

(Tokushima Ken). Located on eastern Shikoku and bordered by Kagawa Prefecture and the Inland Sea to the north, the Kii Channel and the Pacific Ocean to the east, Kōchi Prefecture to the south, and Kōchi and Ehime prefectures to the west. The terrain is predominantly mountainous, and the largest plains are found around the YOSHINOGAWA, Shikoku's longest river, and the river NAKAGAWA. The climate is generally mild.

Known as Awa Province after the TAIKA REFORM of 645, the area was dominated successively by the Hosokawa, Chōsokabe, and Hachisuka families during the feudal period, and was a center of salt, tobacco, and indigo production. The prefecture took its present boundaries and name in 1880.

It is a predominantly rural prefecture. Rice, fruits, and vegetables are grown mainly in the north. Forestry and fishing are important in the south. Paper and chemical production is gradually being added to traditional industries such as textiles, woodworking, and food processing.

Tourist attractions are the whirlpools off NARUTO, part of the INLAND SEA NATIONAL PARK, and the mountain TSURUGISAN. The Awa *odori* (Awa dance) festival in August attracts visitors to TOKUSHIMA, the capital of the prefecture. Area: 4,145 sq km (1,600 sq mi); pop: 825,265. Other major cities include Naruto and ANAN.

tokusō

The patrimonial head of the main branch of the powerful HŌJŌ FAMILY, which monopolized the position of SHIKKEN (shogunal regent) during the Kamakura period (1185–1333). The term was originally the Buddhist name of HŌJŌ YOSHITOKI, who became the second *shikken* and consolidated the political power of his family. Later, the term *tokusō* came to be used for all successors to the main Hōjō line. At first the titles of *shikken* and *tokusō* were held by the same man; the positions came to be held separately in 1256, when

HŌJŌ TOKIYORI took holy orders and relinquished the *shikken* post to his father's cousin Hōjō Nagatoki (1229–64), since his own son and heir, HŌJŌ TOKIMUNE, was only five years old. Tokiyori continued to control the shogunate, however. He also chose to operate outside the HYŌJŌSHŪ (Council of State) and other formal structures of the shogunate, holding secret meetings *(yoriai)* at his private residence with retainers who had a personal allegiance to him. This practice was continued by Tokimune, who became RENSHO (cosigner to the *shikken*), and in time the *tokusō* came to dominate the *shikken*. The *tokusō's* tenure as military governor (SHUGO) of more than a half-dozen provinces, as well as his possession of lands *(tokusō ryō)* throughout Japan, further bolstered his political ascendance.

Tokutomi Iichirō → Tokutomi Sohō

Tokutomi Roka (1868–1927)

Real name Tokutomi Kenjirō. Born in Higo Province (now Kumamoto Prefecture); studied at what is now Dōshisha University. One of the most colorful figures of the first half of the modern period, and the author of two of its most popular novels. Part of his fame is due to his resistance to the traditional authority of the family (which few in his day were willing to question so openly), a resistance that culminated in 1902 in a dramatic "parting message" addressed to the head of the family, his elder brother Iichirō (pen name TOKUTOMI SOHŌ). *Hototogisu* (1898–99; tr *Namiko*, 1904), the novel which established his reputation, reflects this impulse to question the harshness with which the supremacy of the family often bore on individuals. Crude and melodramatic by modern standards, but still moving because of the intensity of feeling behind it (it was based on an actual case, involving the daughter of an army general), it tells of a young bride who is divorced at her mother-in-law's insistence when she is found to be suffering from tuberculosis. It was followed by *Omoide no ki* (1901; tr *Footprints in the Snow*, 1970), which was reprinted 145 times in the 25 years after its appearance and is now an accepted classic of the period. In this novel of a young man's development in the 1880s and 1890s, inspired in part by a reading of *David Copperfield*, Tokutomi conveys admirably the excitement of a period of dramatic change and the impact on Japanese youth of notions of political freedom, Christianity, and romantic love. Some of the descriptions of provincial ways and of characteristic features of Japanese life of the period—such as the small private boarding schools, physically spartan but with a fanatical dedication to learning and a powerful bond uniting teacher and student—are among the most appealing in the literature. Towards the end, there is a hint of disillusion with the new competitive, materialist society. But Tokutomi lacked the intellectual equipment to go beyond attractive popular fiction to a deeper probing of the problems of his time, and the rest of his work does not live up to its early promise.

His life, however, continued to express a powerful if eccentric individuality. A visit to Tolstoy at his estate, Yasnaya Polyana (he later tried to follow Tolstoy's advice to live like the peasants, and became known as the "Saint of Kasuya," a village that has now been swallowed up in Tōkyō, though his house is still lovingly preserved), a stormy marriage, the vicissitudes of which he chronicled unashamedly in his writing, a "conversion" experience on the summit of Mt. Fuji (Fujisan), a naive but courageous personal appeal (in English) for racial equality and disarmament addressed to the statesmen gathered at Versailles after World War I, are some of its highlights.

Continuing Japanese interest in Tokutomi's outspokenness and "sincerity" is demonstrated by the recent publication of a massively detailed, three-volume biography (Roka Tokutomi Kenjirō, 1972–74) by Nakano Yoshio. That Tokutomi should have been chosen as the subject of such a study is all the more remarkable, as biography "in depth" is rare in Japan, and some consider Roka Tokutomi Kenjirō to be the first genuine example of this genre.

📖 ——Tokutomi Roka, Tokutomi Roka zenshū, 20 vols (Shinchōsha, 1928–30). Tokutomi Roka, Hototogisu (1898–99), tr Sakae Shioya and E. F. Edyett as Namiko (1904). Tokutomi Roka, Omoide no ki (1901), tr Kenneth Strong with biographical introduction as Footprints in the Snow (1970). Nakano Yoshio, Roka Tokutomi Kenjirō, 3 vols (1972–74).   Kenneth STRONG

Tokutomi Sohō (1863–1957)

Real name Tokutomi Iichirō. Journalist and historian; older brother of the author TOKUTOMI ROKA. Active as a social commentator and spokesman for popular and national ideals for modern Japan from the 1880s to the end of World War II, Sohō was one of Japan's most prolific writers and publishers. In 1887 Sohō founded a publishing house, the Min'yūsha (Society of the People's Friends), which from 1887 to 1898 put out KOKUMIN NO TOMO (The Nation's Friend), a political, economic, social, and literary review. This review was Japan's first general magazine and the most influential of the 19th century. The Min'yūsha published two other journals during this period, Katei zasshi (Home Journal; 1892–98) and an English-language version of Kokumin no tomo called The Far East (1896-98). It also published and edited, from 1890 to 1929, the Kokumin shimbun, one of the most important Japanese newspapers of the period. In addition to his publishing activities, Sohō wrote more than 350 works on such subjects as domestic and international affairs, history, biography, and literature. His 100-volume work Kinsei Nihon kokumin shi (A History of Early Modern Japan), an exhaustive study of Japan from the late 16th to the 19th century that he wrote between 1918 and 1952, won him many honors and prizes.

Sohō was born in Minamata, Higo Province (now Kumamoto Prefecture). He was the first son in a respected family of local officials. He was educated first in the Chinese and Japanese classics and then, from 1875, in Western subjects at such schools as the KUMAMOTO YŌGAKKŌ and the missionary-supported Dōshisha (now DŌSHISHA UNIVERSITY) in Kyōto. During this time he converted to Christianity but quit the church after leaving Dōshisha in 1879. In the early 1880s, Sohō was in Kumamoto, where he was active in the local FREEDOM AND PEOPLE'S RIGHTS MOVEMENT and ran a private school, Ōe Gijuku, which taught mainly Western subjects. In 1886 he left Kumamoto for Tōkyō.

While teaching, studying, and writing in preparation for a career in journalism, Sohō developed a powerfully articulated conception, derived from his studies of Western liberal-democratic social thinkers, of how Japan should proceed to become modern, "wealthy and strong," and equal to the great Western nations. He called his view heimin shugi. It represented the general notion of a free and open and democratic political, economic, and social order. His advocacy of Western-oriented democratic reforms in politics and society captivated large segments of the population; young people in particular were attracted to Sohō and his reformist ideals as presented in the books Shōrai no Nihon (1886, The Future Japan), Shin Nihon no

seinen (1887, Youth of New Japan), and the magazine Kokumin no tomo.

Heimin shugi was grounded on a romantic, idealized view of Western industrial democracies, of how they had evolved and were currently developing. From the early 1890s Sohō began to realize that his reformist ideals were unrealistic and also unrepresentative of conditions in the modern West. Consequently he began to alter his views of how modern Japan should progress and developed new collectivist and statist-oriented principles for the nation. The humiliating experience of the TRIPARTITE INTERVENTION of Russia, Germany, and France in 1895, which took away concessions gained in the SINO-JAPANESE WAR OF 1894–1895, nurtured in him a passion for revenge against Russia; it led to an intense commitment to promoting the national purpose of making Japan a strong imperialist power, capable of militarily securing and defending the national interests.

This change in principles from heimin shugi to statism and militant imperialism, coupled with his becoming, after 1895, a friend, confidant, and adviser to the nation's leaders—the Meiji oligarchy—caused Sohō to be scorned as an "apostate" by many of his liberal, democratic-oriented followers and successors. On two occasions, in 1905 and 1913, Sohō and his newspaper were targets of attack in fierce riots against the government of KATSURA TARŌ, the political leader with whom Sohō worked most closely.

Sohō nonetheless adhered to his conservative and militant nationalistic principles; in the 1920s and 1930s, when Japan faced severe difficulties in foreign affairs, Sohō's advocacy of national cooperation, unity, and harmony in time of crisis had wide popular appeal; he became, indeed, one of the nation's most popular spokesmen for the ideals of imperial Japan.

Because of his prominence as a nationalist, Sohō was arrested as a class A war criminal suspect by the Allied OCCUPATION authorities in December 1945. He was held under house arrest until August 1947 and was barred from public office until the end of the Occupation in April, 1952 (see OCCUPATION PURGE).

Sohō was also a noted connoisseur of old Japanese, Chinese, and Korean books, and his library, known as the Seikidō Bunko, was one of the finest collections of its kind in modern Japan.

📖 ——John D. Pierson, Tokutomi Sohō, 1863–1957: A Journalist for Modern Japan (1980). Kenneth B. Pyle, The New Generation in Meiji Japan (1969). Sugii Mutsurō, Tokutomi Sohō no kenkyū (1978). Tokutomi Iichirō, Sohō jiden (1935).   John D. PIERSON

Tokuyama

City in southeastern Yamaguchi Prefecture, western Honshū. Tokuyama earlier flourished as a castle town. Industrialization began with the construction of giant soda and metal plants during the 1920s. A huge petrochemical industrial complex is located here. Pop: 111,468.

Tokuyama Soda Co, Ltd

Company engaged in manufacture of cement, plastics, and other chemical and synthetic products. It was established in 1918 for the domestic production of soda by Iwai Katsujirō, founder also of a predecessor of the NISSHŌ IWAI CORPORATION. The company grew with the development of the rayon industry in the 1930s. In 1937 it started to use wastes from the manufacture of soda to produce cement. After World War II it adopted electrolytic techniques for soda production, moved into the petrochemical field, and began making ion exchange membranes for salt production. Sales for the fiscal year ending March 1982 totaled ¥170.8 billion (US $709.5 million). In the same year the export ratio was 10 percent and the company was capitalized at ¥6.6 billion (US $27.4 million). Its head office is in Tokuyama, Yamaguchi Prefecture.

Tōkyō

Capital of Japan. Located on the Kantō Plain, on the Pacific side of central Honshū. Bordered by Chiba Prefecture on the east, Saitama Prefecture on the north, Yamanashi Prefecture on the west, Kanagawa Prefecture on the southwest, and Tōkyō Bay on the southeast. Under its administration are islands scattered in the western Pacific, among them the IZU ISLANDS and the OGASAWARA ISLANDS.

Strained by a rapidly increasing population, Tōkyō was administratively enlarged in 1943 through the amalgamation of surrounding districts and suburbs to form Tōkyō To (Tōkyō Prefecture or Tōkyō

Tōkyō

Recently built skyscrapers in the Shinjuku district form the backdrop to a portion of the centuries-old Imperial Palace grounds.

Metropolitan Prefecture; officially Tōkyō Metropolis). At present, Tōkyō Prefecture comprises 23 wards *(ku)*, 26 cities *(shi)*, 1 county *(gun)*, 4 island administrative units *(shichō)* and 15 towns and villages *(chō, son)*. The Metropolitan Government Office is located in Marunouchi, Chiyoda Ward.

Area: 2,145.38 sq km (828.32 sq mi); population: 11,615,069; population density: 5,414.0 persons per sq km; number of households: 4,309,394.

Natural Features —— Tōkyō was known by the name Edo (literally, "estuary") before the Meiji Restoration (1868), and the principal rivers of the Kantō region—the EDOGAWA, ARAKAWA, and SUMIDAGAWA—still flow to the sea through eastern Tōkyō. Along the alluvial plains of the old river TAMAGAWA, volcanic ash emitted from the Fuji–Hakone Volcanic Range accumulated to form the MUSASHINO PLATEAU where the western wards (commonly known as the YAMANOTE district) and outlying districts are located. Some areas in the eastern wards (the SHITAMACHI district) lie 2–3 meters (6.5–10 ft) below sea level; the highest point in Tōkyō Prefecture is Mt. Kumotori (Kumotoriyama) to the west (2,018 m; 6,619 ft).

The four seasons of the year are sharply delineated and the climate is generally mild, with the highest average monthly temperature in August (30.8°C; 87.4°F) and the lowest in January (0.5°; 32.9°F); in summer te temperature occasionally soars above 30°C (86°F), and in winter it may dip below the freezing point. Summers are hot and humid, with a rainy season from early June to mid-July; winters are dry, with cold winds blowing in from the northwest and the humidity dropping below 50 percent. Typhoons spawned in the central Pacific are frequent in the months of September and October. The annual precipitation is 1,460 mm (57.5 in).

Fauna and Flora —— Pollution and unchecked land development ravaged the animal and plant population in Tōkyō Prefecture during the 1960s, but, with stricter pollution controls, 370 out of the approximately 570 bird species found throughout Japan have been sighted within Tōkyō. Common birds in Tōkyō include the hooded gull, the official bird of Tōkyō; waterfowl such as the seagull and wild duck; winter migratory birds such as the thrush and the redstart; summer migratory birds such as the swallow, brown hawk owl, stonechat, cuckoo, and blue-and-white flycatcher; birds which migrate only within Japan such as the bush warbler, black-faced bunting, Japanese great tit, and Japanese jay; and nonmigratory birds such as the sparrow, crow, and pigeon. The last three in particular have increased tremendously in number in recent years and become something of a nuisance.

Other wildlife found in the mountainous areas within the bounds of Tōkyō Prefecture include the Japanese antelope, raccoon dog *(tanuki)*, fox, flying squirrel, rabbit, squirrel, and, rarely, wild boar, and bear.

The official tree of Tōkyō is the ginkgo, which is utilized as a shade tree throughout the city. Other representative trees in Tōkyō include the cherry, zelkova, Japanese oak, and *kunugi (Quercus acutissima,* a kind of oak). In the outlying mountainous districts are found cryptomeria and Japanese cypress *(hinoki),* used for building, and Japanese oak and *kunugi,* used for making charcoal; the box tree and camellia are found on the Pacific islands under the administration of Tōkyō.

History —— Numerous Jōmon-period (ca 10,000 BC–ca 300 BC) sites have been found on the Musashino Plateau in the west, and the *shitamachi* lowlands have revealed relics from the Yayoi period (ca 300 BC–ca AD 300) and Kofun period (ca 300–710). These latter give evidence of the transition from a hunting and food-gathering economy to a farming economy and the accompanying change from a primitive communal society to a class society. Under the KOKUGUN SYSTEM adopted at the time of the TAIKA REFORM of 645, Japan was divided into some 50-odd provinces and MUSASHI PROVINCE was established in what is today Tōkyō, Saitama, and eastern Kanagawa prefectures. Its administrative center was located in what is now the city of FUCHŪ, which served as the political center of the province for nearly 900 years until the collapse of the centralized government system and the emergence of the *samurai* class at the end of the 12th century. Edo then became the focal point of the Kantō region, and during the civil wars of the 15th century, the warrior ŌTA DŌKAN constructed the predecessor of EDO CASTLE at the present site of the Imperial Palace.

After nearly a century of warfare, TOYOTOMI HIDEYOSHI partially unified the country and dispatched TOKUGAWA IEYASU to Kantō in 1590, making him lord of Edo Castle. After Hideyoshi's death, Ieyasu completed the unification of Japan and established the TOKUGAWA SHOGUNATE in Edo in 1603. He constructed a castle town there with a samurai residential district on the castle's western side. To the east, marshland was reclaimed, and a commercial and industrial area taking advantage of river and canal transportation came into being. As the city flourished, merchants and artisans flocked to Edo; the population reached 1 million in 1695, making it the largest city in the world at that time. The arts, long the domain of the aristocracy and the samurai, came to be enjoyed by the rising merchant class (CHŌNIN), who gave fresh impetus to HAIKU, NŌ, KABUKI, and UKIYO-E.

In 1867 the Tokugawa shogunate came to an end, and with the MEIJI RESTORATION the following year, Edo, renamed Tōkyō ("capital of the east"), became the national capital. The imperial family took up residence at Edo Castle in 1869, and the former strict segregation of samurai and merchant quarters ended. In 1871 Tōkyō became an urban prefecture *(fu)* under the new administrative system (see PREFECTURAL SYSTEM, ESTABLISHMENT OF) and in 1878 was organized into 15 wards. It grew steadily in importance as the political, commercial, and financial center of Japan. Although almost completely destroyed in the TŌKYŌ EARTHQUAKE OF 1923, it was largely rebuilt by 1930. In 1932, 20 more wards were added to the initial 15, bringing the population to 5.2 million. Then in 1943 Tōkyō Fu and Tōkyō Shi were merged and the name changed to Tōkyō To, or Tōkyō Metropolitan Prefecture (officially Tōkyō Metropolis). The present system of 23 wards plus various other municipal units was also created at that time.

Much of Tōkyō was destroyed during World War II by American bombing, especially in the spring of 1945. After Japan's defeat, Tōkyō remained the seat of government, with the General Headquarters of the Supreme Commander of the Allied Powers (GHQ–SCAP) located there until the end of the Occupation in 1952. During the period of economic recovery starting in the 1950s, large enterprises increasingly concentrated their managerial operations in Tōkyō. This resulted in an increase in population from 6.3 million in 1950 to 9.7 million in 1960.

The city undertook a feverish building program in preparation for the 1964 Tōkyō Olympic Games, and by 1965 the population had reached 10.9 million, resulting in serious housing problems and the skyrocketing of land prices. Although a program of building satellite city centers has been successfully carried out to alleviate the concentration of main offices of large enterprises in the central part of the city, many serious housing, transportation, and environmental problems remain.

Local and Traditional Industry —— Local industries were long centered in the three *shitamachi* wards of Taitō, Sumida, and Arakawa, but in recent years, the surrounding wards, particularly Adachi and Katsushika, have witnessed an influx of plants and factories. Products include clothing, knitted goods, precious metals, cigarette cases and lighters, toys, umbrellas, watches, leather goods, pencils, and binoculars.

Among traditional industries, fabric making has been prominent. Cities within Tōkyō Metropolitan Prefecture such as HACHIŌJI, ŌME, and MUSASHI MURAYAMA have been noted for the production of fabrics since the Edo period (1600–1868), and the island of HACHIJŌJIMA is noted for its *kihachijō* dyed fabric. Traditional products include dyed fabrics such as *tōkyō-zome komon*, Tōkyō *tegaki yūzen*, and Tōkyō *honzome yukata*, braided cord, silverware, Buddhist altars, lacquer ware, *bekkō* (tortoise shell) goods, ornamental hairpins, *kimekomi* dolls, and *zōri* (traditional footwear).

Other traditional products are *nishiki-e* (colored woodblock prints), kites, *chiyogami* (traditional paper with colored patterns), and combs. Many craftsmen are located in the *shitamachi* section, particularly in Asakusa, Taitō Ward; they face the problem of small demand for their products and the difficulty of finding successors. Many doll wholesalers with a history dating back to the Edo period are also located in Nihombashi and Asakusabashi, but the actual production is being carried out in Saitama Prefecture.

Modern Industry —— A consumer city in the Edo period, Tōkyō developed into a center of secondary industries from the Meiji period (1868–1912) until the end of World War II. However, after 1965, tertiary industries—such as commerce, finance, transportation, communication, and service industries—began to surpass secondary industries, and as of 1979 primary industries constituted only 0.4 percent of the total industries in Tōkyō; secondary industries, 31 percent (compared to 50 percent in the 1960s); and tertiary industries, 68.6 percent. The most numerous of the tertiary industries are wholesale and retail stores, which number approximately 224,000 (over 400,000 if restaurants and other eating and drinking establishments are included); the sales of retail and wholesale stores exceed ¥10.1 trillion annually.

Tōkyō boasts a total of approximately 740,000 enterprises; these employ some 7,160,000 workers, of whom 5,430,000 live in the city. With a volume of production totaling ¥28 trillion, the enterprises in Tōkyō constitute 12.5 percent of the national total in number, 13–14 percent in number of employees, and 18–19 percent in production value. Many large Japanese corporations have their head offices in Tōkyō; these are particularly concentrated in Chiyoda, Chūō, and Minato wards, where the number of enterprises comes to 110,000 and that of employees, 2,300,000. Other main offices of large corporations are located in Shinjuku, Bunkyō, Shibuya, and Toshima wards, where approximately 100,000 enterprises employ 1,050,000 workers. However, the average number of employees in an enterprise in Tōkyō is 9.6 persons, and enterprises employing more than 100 persons number only 3,000 or 0.4 percent of the total number of enterprises in Tōkyō, with a total of 1,060,000 employees or 14.9 percent of the total employees in Tōkyō (1978 figures).

As new business buildings take over the central part of the city, small shops and permanent residents have been forced out, creating the so-called doughnut phenomenon. The pollution problem of the 1970s also forced large manufacturing plants (metals, textile, foodstuffs, lumber) and related factories from the *shitamachi* lowlands to the outlying districts or to reclaimed land in Tōkyō Bay, and industrial plants formerly located on littoral districts have moved out of the city to adjacent prefectures. Large printing plants are also being forced out of the wards, leaving only the smaller plants to do work for publishing firms, of which Tōkyō possesses 80 percent of the nation's total.

Another recent development has been the growth of the Shinjuku, Shibuya, and Ikebukuro districts. Now known as satellite city centers, they have become flourishing business and recreation districts, and large-size business buildings have been constructed in these three districts in recent years. The doughnut phenomenon, originally in the central part of the city, has spread to these satellite centers, and in 1980 the population of Tōkyō witnessed a decline for the first time in its history.

Finance —— Tōkyō is also a major financial center. Although the number of bank branches (approximately 1,000) composes only 14.3 percent of the nation's total, their combined deposits were 45 percent (¥4.8 trillion) and their loans—in the main to large enterprises—43 percent (¥5.3 trillion) at the end of 1979. In addition, some 1,300 offices of mutual banks, credit banks, industrial and commercial union banks, credit unions, labor banks and other financial institutions are located in Tōkyō, and post offices are also engaged in banking activities. The number of credit loan companies

Tōkyō

Two hours by train from Shinjuku, Lake Oku Tama in northwestern Tōkyō Prefecture is one of the sources of drinking water for the city.

Tōkyō

An aerial view of the Kasumigaseki district. The home of numerous government agencies, this district forms the political center of Japan.

has increased sharply in recent years, reflecting their importance as financial institutions.

Transportation —— Tōkyō is served by two airports: Tōkyō International Airport (commonly called Haneda Airport), the main terminal for domestic flights located in the southern end of the city, and NEW TŌKYŌ INTERNATIONAL AIRPORT (commonly called Narita Airport), located 66 kilometers (41 mi) east of Tōkyō and linked to the city by rail and bus lines.

The nation's main trunk lines are concentrated in Tōkyō, with terminals at Tōkyō, Ueno, and Shinjuku stations. Trains for the west (Nagoya, Ōsaka, Kyōto) leave from Tōkyō Station (Tōkaidō and SHINKANSEN lines); trains for Tōhoku, Hokkaidō, and the Sea of Japan area originate from Ueno Station (Tōhoku, Takasaki, Jōban, and Jōetsu lines). From Shinjuku Station, trains connect the city with the mountainous regions of central Japan (Chūō line). Trains on the Tōhoku Shinkansen and Jōetsu Shinkansen lines leave from Ōmiya Station in Saitama Prefecture.

The three principal commuter lines are the Yamanote line, a loop around the heart of the city; the Keihin Tōhoku line running through Tōkyō and Saitama and Kanagawa prefectures, and the Sōbu line connecting Tōkyō and Chiba. A network of private railway lines radiates outward from the principal stations on the Yamanote line, and 11 private and metropolitan subway lines have replaced the old network of streetcars in the heart of the city. Tōkyō is also well served by buses, with mainly city-operated buses running within the bounds of the Yamanote line and mainly privately operated ones outside it.

Expressways connect the city to various regions. Among these toll roads are the Shuto expressway, approximately 130 kilometers (80 mi) long with a daily traffic of 600,000 vehicles (1979), the Tōmei expressway (to Nagoya), the Tōhoku expressway (to Aomori), the Kan'etsu expressway (to Niigata), and the Chūō expressway (to Nagoya).

Tōkyō

The main Ginza intersection, of Harumi-Dōri from the left and Chūō-Dōri (popularly called Ginza-Dōri).

Tōkyō

The Kaminarimon ("thunder gate") of Asakusa Kannon (Sensōji), a popular temple in the heart of the Asakusa district in eastern Tōkyō.

It is estimated that a total of 1,500,000 commuters are on the move daily, and the average time spent commuting one way to or from Tōkyō had reached over 90 minutes in 1979.

Public Institutions and Services —— Government buildings are concentrated in the Kasumigaseki area in Chiyoda Ward. The Diet, the National Diet Library, and the Supreme Court building are in neighboring Nagatachō. The Tōkyō Metropolitan Government has jurisdiction over city services and in matters concerning corporations; ward, city, and town offices handle matters directly concerning their citizens. Alien registration and taxation are two of the matters handled by the latter.

Health services. Public hygiene and health are the responsibility of the local municipal offices. As of 1980 there were 742 hospitals in the Tōkyō Metropolitan Area, with some 120,000 beds, and about 11,000 smaller clinics (with fewer than 20 beds), with 18,000 beds. Physicians number some 20,000, and there are roughly 6,500 dental clinics.

Police and fire departments. The Metropolitan Police Department in 1981 had 96 police stations within the metropolitan area, with 9 riot and armored car forces. The Metropolitan Fire Board in 1981 had 8 district headquarters, 75 main fire stations, and numerous branch stations. These fire-fighting units also carry out rescue and ambulance operations. There are also citizen-manned fire brigades in the various autonomous municipalities within the greater Tōkyō Metropolitan Area.

Utilities. The Water Bureau of the Tōkyō Metropolitan Government is in charge of the city water supply system, with separate water departments present in the cities within the metropolitan area. TŌKYŌ ELECTRIC POWER CO, INC, is in charge of generating, transmitting, and supplying electricity to the entire Kantō region; servicing is carried out by the company's branch offices. TŌKYŌ GAS CO, LTD, produces the city's gas and distributes it to each household through pipes. Bottled propane gas is used in outlying areas.

Educational services. Tōkyō is a major educational center. In 1980 approximately 1,026,804 students were enrolled in 1,370 primary schools, 424,448 in 613 junior high (middle) schools, and 226,067 in 316 high schools. In addition, some 664,000 college students, or 40 percent of the total number in Japan, attended the 85 junior colleges and 103 universities located in Tōkyō. In recent years there has been a trend for colleges and universities to move from the crowded central city to surrounding areas.

The city is also the location of numerous academic societies, including the JAPAN ACADEMY, the SCIENCE COUNCIL OF JAPAN, and the JAPAN ART ACADEMY.

Library services in Tōkyō in 1980 included 6 metropolitan government-operated LIBRARIES, 123 library branches established and run by the wards, and 18 operated by cities and towns in the metropolitan area. Some 200 special libraries are also located in Tōkyō, but only about 30 of these are open to the general public.

Cultural and Recreational Facilities —— *The arts.* Western culture was introduced into Japan through the gateway of Yokohama and Tōkyō after the Meiji Restoration, and Tōkyō today offers a blend of traditional and modern arts. *Kabuki,* popular since the Edo period, is still being performed today, as are other traditional performing arts such as NAGAUTA (singing) and *buyō* (dance). RAKUGO, a form of comic storytelling, has long been a favorite among *shitamachi* residents. There are eight large-scale theaters in Tōkyō, including the Kabukiza and the National Theater, and numerous smaller ones. There are also 15 concert halls with a seating capacity of over 1,000 in central Tōkyō; Nippon Budōkan Hall with a seating capacity of 20,000 is also often used for concerts.

There are about a dozen large national and municipal MUSEUMS and art museums in Tōkyō and over 60 smaller private collections. The latter include such specialized collections as those devoted to transportation, broadcasting, sports, kites, swords, and the like. There are over 400 art galleries in the city; department stores also hold many exhibitions.

The media. Tōkyō is also a major information center. Eight general NEWSPAPERS are published in Tōkyō (including four English-language newspapers), as well as three economic and industrial newspapers and six sports newspapers; more than 6,500,000 newspaper copies are printed each day (1980). Two daily newspapers are published by political parties and two news service companies are headquartered in Tōkyō. In addition, it is estimated that roughly 250 monthly and 300 weekly magazines were being published in the early 1980s in Tōkyō. It is difficult to obtain exact figures because of the great fluctuations in magazine publishing: 170 new magazines were published in 1981, and 150 ceased publication.

A large proportion of television programming in Japan also originates in Tōkyō from the two noncommercial Japan Broadcasting Corporation (NHK) channels and the five commercial channels located there. There are also four local UHF channels and numerous radio stations, including the Far East Network of the American military forces in Japan.

Parks and sports facilities. Although small by Western standards, numerous parks are scattered throughout Tōkyō. Major parks in central Tōkyō include the Imperial Palace grounds, HIBIYA PARK, UENO PARK, and the MEIJI SHRINE Outer Garden. There are also some 15 zoological and botanical gardens in the metropolitan area.

Public sports grounds are found in Yoyogi Park, Meiji Shrine Outer Garden, Komazawa Olympic Park, National Nishigaoka Stadium, Kōtō Ward-operated Yumenoshima, and the Meguro Ward-operated Kinuta; if privately run facilities are included, sports facilities in Tōkyō total some 14,000. Baseball has long been popular and many baseball stadiums are located in Tōkyō; those at Kōrakuen and the Meiji Shrine Outer Garden are used for professional games.

Daily Life —— The more than 11,000,000 residents of Tōkyō (1978) live in a total of 4,240,000 dwellings, most of them wooden structures with an average floor space of 30–50 square meters. The average household consists of a husband, his wife, and 1.5 children. The husband is usually a salaried worker earning about ¥3,307,000 a year and spending an average of 3 hours a day commuting (1978). Most families return to their hometown twice a year, during the midsummer BON FESTIVAL and the NEW YEAR holidays; they also go on short one-day trips on the average of once every three months.

Points of Interest —— Situated in the center of Tōkyō and surrounded by a moat and high stone walls is the Imperial Palace, still retaining vestiges of its former glory as the residence of the Tokugawa family.

To the east lies Ginza, an area measuring 1.5 kilometers (0.9 mi) north to south and 1 kilometer (0.6 mi) east to west and known for

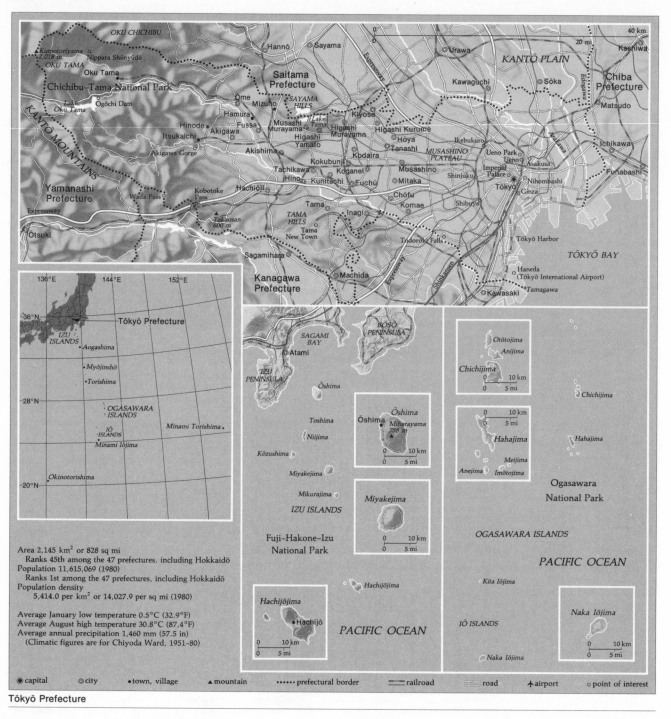

Tōkyō Prefecture

Area 2,145 km² or 828 sq mi
  Ranks 45th among the 47 prefectures, including Hokkaidō
Population 11,615,069 (1980)
  Ranks 1st among the 47 prefectures, including Hokkaidō
Population density
  5,414.0 per km² or 14,027.9 per sq mi (1980)

Average January low temperature 0.5°C (32.9°F)
Average August high temperature 30.8°C (87.4°F)
Average annual precipitation 1,460 mm (57.5 in)
  (Climatic figures are for Chiyoda Ward, 1951–80)

◉ capital   ◎ city   ● town, village   ▲ mountain   ····· prefectural border   ══ railroad   ═══ road   ✈ airport   ○ point of interest

its fine shops, department stores, and numerous restaurants, bars, and cabarets. Further south lies the HAMA DETACHED PALACE GARDEN, a fine example of a feudal lord's residence. It was originally owned by the Tokugawa family, and the family's guardian temple, ZŌJŌJI, is located nearby.

North of the Ginza is Nihombashi, the commercial hub of the city, from which all distances from Tōkyō to places throughout Japan are measured. Nearby are the districts of Kanda, renowned for its bookshops and universities, and Akihabara, famous for its discount stores selling all kinds of electrical appliances. Further to the north lie Ueno and the 84-hectare (about 207 acres) Ueno Park, a former shogunal estate which today houses the TŌKYŌ NATIONAL MUSEUM (opened in 1938), the NATIONAL SCIENCE MUSEUM, the NATIONAL MUSEUM OF WESTERN ART, the UENO ZOOLOGICAL GARDEN, and the temple KAN'EIJI.

To the east of Ueno is the oldest temple in Tōkyō, the Asakusa Kannon, in the heart of the *shitamachi* district, with its many shops still selling traditional handicrafts.

Another point of interest in the capital is the Diet building, an imposing three-story structure completed in 1936. Nearby Roppongi, situated close to Tōkyō Tower (built in 1958 for television transmission), houses over 30 foreign embassies. Neighboring Akasaka is known for its luxurious nightlife.

Near Shibuya Station lies Meiji Shrine, dedicated to Emperor Meiji (1852–1912) and his consort; designed in classic Shintō style, it was completed in 1920. Yoyogi Sports Center adjoins the shrine and was the site of the Olympic village during the 1964 Tōkyō Olympics. The National Stadium and NHK Broadcasting Station are also located in the vicinity, as is Harajuku, a fashionable district popular with young people.

The area around Shinjuku Station—which has the highest rate of passenger turnover in the country—is rapidly being developed, with game centers, restaurants, and theaters in the Kabukichō area on the eastern side of the station. The western side now has numerous high-rise buildings, hotels, shops, and offices, including the 47-story Keiō Plaza Hotel, the 52-story Sumitomo building, and the 55-story

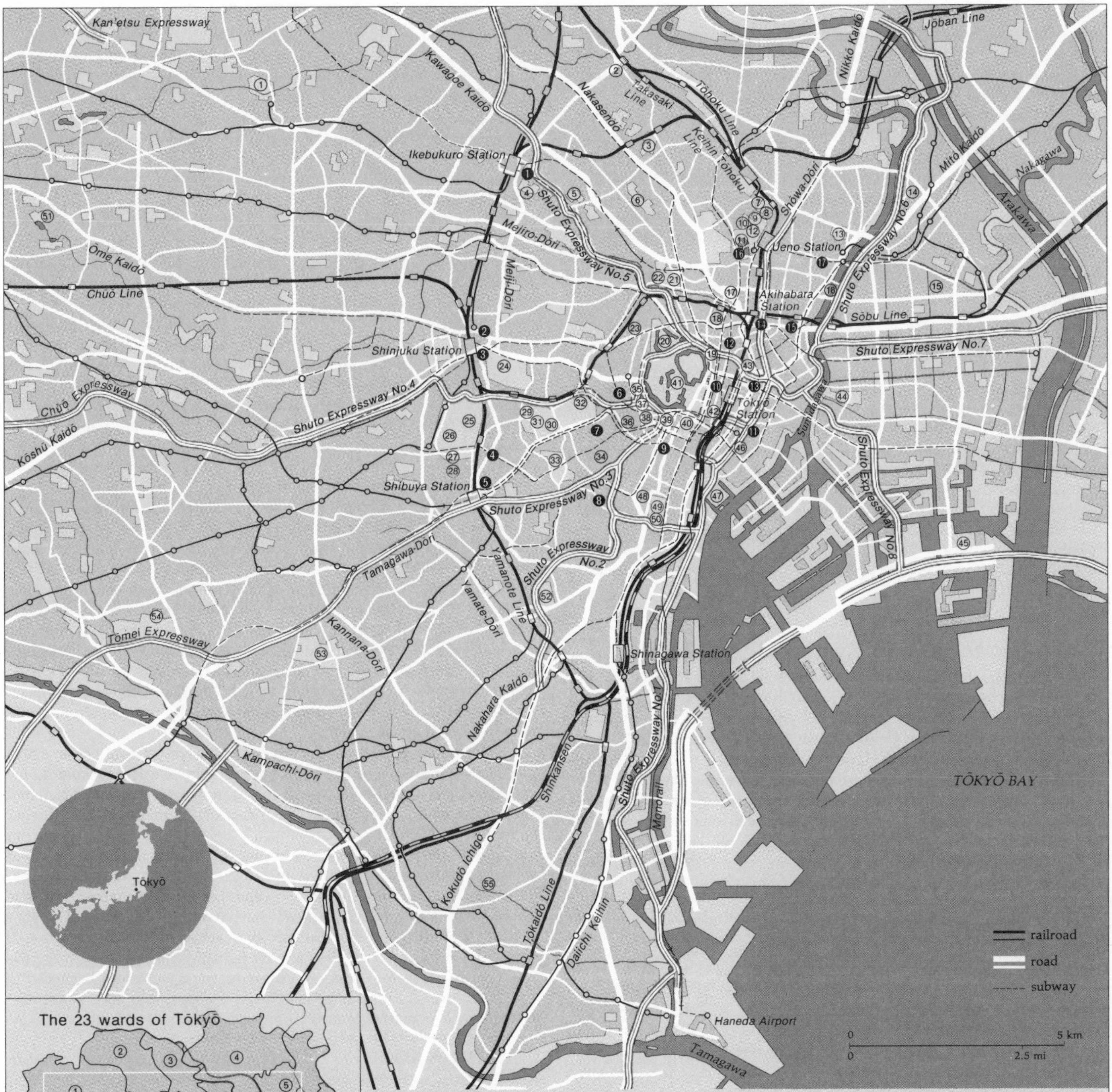
Kan'etsu Expressway
Kawagoe Kaidō
Nakasendō
Takasaki Line
Tōhoku Line
Keihin Tōhoku Line
Nikkō Kaidō
Jōban Line
Ikebukuro Station
Shuto Expressway No.5
Meijio-Dōri
Meiji-Dōri
Shōwa-Dōri
Mito Kaidō
Nakagawa
Arakawa
Shuto Expressway No.6
Ueno Station
Ōme Kaidō
Chūō Line
Akihabara Station
Sōbu Line
Shuto Expressway No.7
Shinjuku Station
Chūō Expressway
Shuto Expressway No.4
Kōshū Kaidō
Tōkyō Station
Sumidagawa
Shuto Expressway No.9
Shibuya Station
Shuto Expressway No.3
Shuto Expressway No.2
Tamagawa-Dōri
Yamanote Line
Yamate-Dōri
Kannana-Dōri
Shuto Expressway No.8
Tōmei Expressway
Shinagawa Station
Nakahara Kaidō
Kampachi-Dōri
Shuto Expressway No.1
Shinkansen
Monorail
TŌKYŌ BAY
Tōkyō
Kokudō Ichigō
Tōkaidō Line
Daiichi Keihin
railroad
road
subway
Haneda Airport
Tamagawa
0 5 km
0 2.5 mi

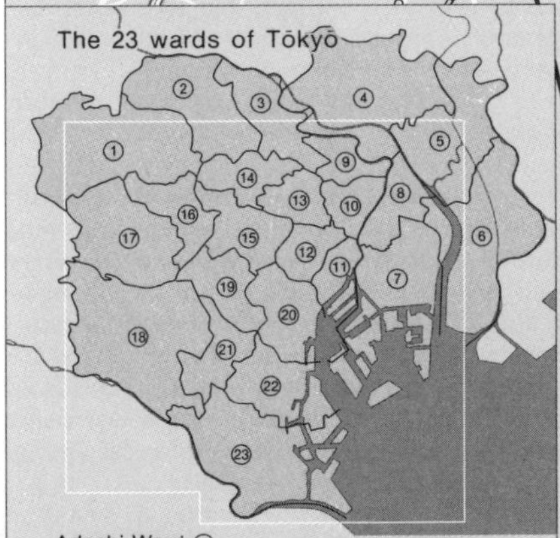
The 23 wards of Tōkyō

Adachi Ward ④
Arakawa Ward ⑨
Bunkyō Ward ⑬
Chiyoda Ward ⑫
Chūō Ward ⑪
Edogawa Ward ⑥
Itabashi Ward ②
Katsushika Ward ⑤
Kita Ward ③
Kōtō Ward ⑦
Meguro Ward ㉑
Minato Ward ⑳
Nakano Ward ⑯
Nerima Ward ①
Ōta Ward ㉓
Setagaya Ward ⑱
Shibuya Ward ⑲
Shinagawa Ward ㉒
Shinjuku Ward ⑮
Suginami Ward ⑰
Sumida Ward ⑧
Taitō Ward ⑩
Toshima Ward ⑭

Districts
Akasaka ❼
Akihabara ⓮
Asakusa ⓱
Asakusabashi ⓯
Ginza ⓫
Harajuku ❹
Ikebukuro ❶
Kabukichō ❷
Kanda ⓬
Kasumigaseki ❾
Marunouchi ❿
Nagatachō ❻
Nihombashi ⓭
Roppongi ❽
Shibuya ❺
Shinjuku ❸
Ueno ⓰

Points of interest
Akasaka Detached Palace ㉜
Aoyama Cemetery ㉝
Asakusa Kannon (Sensōji) ⑬
Asukayama Park ②
Bank of Japan ㊸
Diet ㊳
Gokokuji ⑤
Hama Detached Palace Garden ㊼
Hibiya Park ㊵
Hie Shrine ㊱
Hikawa Shrine ㉞
Hommonji (55)
Hyakkaen Garden ⑭
Imperial Palace ㊶
Jingū Stadium ㉚
Kabukiza ㊻
Kameido Temmangū ⑮
Kanda Shrine ⑰
Kan'eiji ⑦
Kinuta Sports Ground (54)
Kishimojin ④
Kiyosumi Garden ㊹
Koishikawa Botanical Garden ⑥
Kokugikan ⑯
Komazawa Olympic Park (53)
Kōrakuen Garden ㉒
Kōrakuen Stadium ㉑
Meiji Shrine ㉕
Meiji Shrine Outer Garden ㉛
Metropolitan Fire Board ⑲
Metropolitan Government Office ㊷
Metropolitan Police Department ㊴
National Diet Library ㊲
National Museum of Western Art ⑫
National Park for Nature Study (52)
National Science Museum ⑨
National Stadium ㉙
National Theater ㉟
NHK Broadcasting Station ㉘
Nicolai Cathedral ⑱
Nippon Budōkan Hall ⑳
Rikugien Garden ③
Shiba Park (50)
Shinjuku Gyoen National Garden ㉔
Tōkyō National Museum ⑧
Tōkyō Tower ㊽
Toshimaen Amusement Park ①
Ueno Park ⑪
Ueno Zoological Garden ⑩
Yasukuni Shrine ㉓
Yoyogi Park ㉖
Yoyogi Sports Center ㉗
Yumenoshima Sports Ground ㊺
Zempukuji Park (51)
Zōjōji ㊾

Mitsui building. Another fast-growing commercial center is Ikebukuro, where the 60-story Sunshine building was completed in 1980.

Among the national parks within Tōkyō Metropolis are CHICHI-BU–TAMA NATIONAL PARK in the northwest and OGASAWARA NATIONAL PARK and part of FUJI–HAKONE–IZU NATIONAL PARK.

◼︎ ——International Geographical Union, *Geography of Tōkyō and Its Planning* (1957). Kiuchi Shinzō, ed, *Tōkyō* (1968). Kodama Kōta, *Tōkyō To no rekishi* (1969). Maurice Moreau, *Tokyo* (1976). Nihon Chiri Gakkai, *Geography of Japan* (1980). Nihon Chishi Kenkyūjo, *Tōkyō To* (1967). Tōkyō To Gikai Gikaikyoku, *Tosei yōran* (1980). Tōkyō To Chō, *Tōkyō Shi shi kō* (1911–). Tōkyō To Kōbunsho Kan, *Toshi kiyō* (1953–). SUZUKI Masao

Tōkyō Bay

(Tōkyō Wan). Inlet of the Pacific Ocean on the coast of Tōkyō, Kanagawa, and Chiba prefectures, central Honshū. Extends between the Miura and Bōsō peninsulas. Connected with the Pacific Ocean by the Uraga Channel. Fishing and fish culture were active here until the beginning of the Shōwa period (1926–) but ceased almost completely with the development of the Keihin Industrial Zone. A large number of industrial plants and port facilities are located on reclaimed land along the bay, and air and water pollution currently presents a serious problem. Some of Japan's largest ports are located on this important bay, including Tōkyō, Yokohama, Kawasaki, Yokosuka, and Chiba. The trade volume handled by the port of Yokohama is the largest in Japan. The bay is rather shallow, averaging from 12 to 13 meters (39–43 ft), with the deepest point around 50 meters (164 ft).

Tōkyō Broadcasting System, Inc (TBS)

(Tōkyō Hōsō). A Tōkyō-based commercial radio and television broadcasting company serving the Kantō (eastern Honshū) area. Established in 1951 as the first greater Tōkyō commercial radio station, it followed with television broadcasts in 1955. The company, which is presently allied with the large national newspaper MAINICHI SHIMBUN, operates with major funding from a group of banks and life insurance firms. It is affiliated nationally with some 25 other commercial radio and television stations which together comprise the Japan News Network (JNN). It is also a key affiliate of the Japan Radio Network (JRN). NAKASA Hideo

Tōkyō Daigaku Tōyō Bunka Kenkyūjo → Institute of Oriental Culture, Tōkyō University

Tōkyō Earthquake of 1923

Also called Kantō Earthquake. Earthquake in Tōkyō and surrounding prefectures on 1 September 1923; the Japanese term, Kantō Daishinsai (Kantō Great Disaster) also refers to the damage that ensued in the next few days. The earthquake struck at 11:58 AM with a violent uplift of the land mainly in seven prefectures: Tōkyō, Kanagawa, Chiba, Ibaraki, Saitama, Yamanashi, and Shizuoka (damage was also reported in Nagano, Gumma, and Tochigi prefectures). The quake, which has since been assigned a magnitude of 7.8 on the Meteorological Agency of Japan scale (see EARTHQUAKES), was followed by another severe tremor 24 hours later and by several hundred minor tremors that caused little or no damage but kept the population in a state of agitation. The earthquake damaged many buildings and killed or injured a large number of people outright. Fire, however, did more damage than the tremor itself. Many people had begun charcoal or wood fires for their noon meal; the initial shock scattered burning embers, which started numerous fires that could not be extinguished. In the cities of Tōkyō and Yokohama, the latter the nation's largest port, these fires spread rapidly and consumed extensive areas of the downtown sections.

Official statistics, although not verifiable or entirely reliable, reveal the extent of the disaster. A total of 104,619 people were reported dead or missing and 52,074 were injured. Of the dead and missing, 91,995 were from urban Yokohama and Tōkyō, and only 12,624 were from rural areas, where fire was not a serious problem. The statistics estimate that the total population of the area was about 11,758,000 and that 3,248,205 people had their homes damaged or destroyed. In metropolitan Tōkyō the population was 2,265,000, of

whom 1,604,321 (70.85 percent) lost their homes, while the figures for Yokohama were 442,600 and 378,704 (85.56 percent), respectively. The statistics also show that 30.37 percent of all homes in the Kantō region were at least heavily damaged and that 20.39 percent of the total were completely destroyed. In Tōkyō 73.39 percent of the homes were damaged and 63.18 percent destroyed (only 0.88 percent by the tremor and the rest by fire), and in Yokohama, which was closer to the epicenter, 95.03 percent were damaged and 72.53 percent destroyed (9.82 percent knocked down). Fire did the most damage, destroying 16.66 percent of all the houses in the seven-prefecture region, but 62.30 percent of the houses in Tōkyō, and 62.71 percent in Yokohama. Estimates of property damage incurred in the disaster range from ¥0.5 billion to ¥10 billion; the official statistics accept the figure of ¥5,506,386,034. Insurance policies generally excluded earthquake damage, but in 1924 provision was made by the government for sympathy payments through insurance companies. Only about ¥100 million was ever paid, however, leaving both public bodies and private individuals to cope on their own.

Urban building techniques were responsible for the enormous damage by fire. Most homes and businesses and many public buildings were constructed of wood and other highly flammable materials. In addition, there were few open spaces that might have functioned as firebreaks, and buildings and streets were too congested to slow, much less stop, the flames.

The fires, fanned by steady breezes, spread rapidly and developed into firestorms. Intensely heated air rose to a high altitude, creating a partial vacuum that drew fresh air into the fires at ground level. The winds thus created were estimated to be in excess of 70–80 kilometers (45–50 mi) per hour. Associated with these firestorms were cyclones or tornadoes, exceedingly rare in Japan. Several cyclones were sighted in downtown Tōkyō. The cyclones were especially deadly because they consisted primarily of superheated air from which most of the oxygen had been burnt. One cyclone passed over the vacant grounds of the Military Clothing Depot in Honjo, where many had found refuge from the flames; some 40,000 people suffocated to death.

The disaster destroyed city services and functions. Water mains and fire hydrants were ruptured by the tremor and unavailable for fire fighting; telephone and telegraph systems were knocked out, and even radio communication with the rest of the country was difficult, forcing the government to rely partly on military fliers and carrier pigeons. The government itself was in disarray: Prime Minister KATŌ TOMOSABURŌ had died on 25 August, and on 2 September politicians hastily formed a new cabinet led by YAMAMOTO GONNO-HYŌE. The new cabinet declared martial law as one of its first acts. Within the urban disaster areas, however, order was further disrupted by rumors that Koreans were lighting fires and poisoning the few remaining water sources. Police services were too disrupted to counteract the rumors or control the populace, and as a result citizens formed vigilante groups to protect themselves and their neighborhoods. Before the authorities were able to reestablish control, these groups had killed many Koreans and some Japanese mistaken for Koreans; estimates range from a few hundred to as many as 6,000.

A number of radicals and workers were also murdered by military policemen *(kempeitai)* after martial law was declared and some 35,000 troops entered the disaster area. On 4 September military police arrested and killed several radical unionists and four members of vigilante groups at the Kameido police station (see KAMEIDO INCIDENT). On 16 September military police arrested and killed the anarchist ŌSUGI SAKAE, his wife, ITŌ NOE, and his 6-year-old nephew. While high-level involvement in either crime was never proved, the two incidents exemplify the breakdown of order among even the authorities in the devastated capital region.

Thomas A. STANLEY

Tōkyō Electric Power Co, Inc

(Tōkyō Denryoku). Company supplying electricity to Tōkyō Prefecture and the eight surrounding prefectures of Tochigi, Gumma, Ibaraki, Saitama, Chiba, Kanagawa, Yamanashi, and Shizuoka (east of the river Fujikawa). Of the nine electric power companies in Japan, each of which has a monopoly on the supply of electricity in its own region, Tōkyō Electric Power is the largest. It is also the biggest private electric power company in the world in capital, equipment, and facilities, as well as the volume of electricity supplied. The firm's forerunner was Tōkyō Electric Lighting, established in 1883 as Japan's first electric company. It took its present name in 1951. In the fiscal year ending March 1982 electric power sales totaled 136.1 billion kilowatt-hours and accounted for 31 percent of the national total; the areas serviced by the company produced some 35 percent of Japan's entire industrial output. In 1981 it had a capacity of 32.9 million kilowatts, of which 72 percent came from 28 thermoelectric plants, 14 percent from 1 atomic power plant (in Fukushima Prefecture), and 14 percent from 162 hydroelectric plants. It has 10 thermoelectric plants capable of producing more than 1 million kilowatts each, and imports approximately 12 million kiloliters (3 billion gal) of crude oil per year. It also imports liquefied natural gas (LNG) and nuclear fuel on long-term contracts. Current plans call for increasing by 1985 the output of hydroelectric power generation by 13 percent, thermoelectric power generation by 63 percent, and atomic power generation by 24 percent. Plans also call for a diversification of energy sources centering on coal, LNG, and nuclear power as substitutes for oil in order to reduce the company's dependence on oil imports. The company's annual sales totaled ¥3.3 trillion (US $13.7 billion) in the fiscal year ending March 1982, of which electric light power accounted for 31 percent, other electric power 66 percent, and other sales 3 percent. It was capitalized at ¥650 billion (US $2.7 billion) in the same year. Corporate headquarters are located in Tōkyō. See also MATSUNAGA YASUZAEMON; KIKAWADA KAZUTAKA.

Tōkyō Gas Co, Ltd

(Tōkyō Gasu). Company supplying city gas to approximately 6.1 million customers in Tōkyō and the eight nearby prefectures of Saitama, Kanagawa, Chiba, Gumma, Tochigi, Ibaraki, Yamanashi, and Nagano. It is also engaged in the sale of various types of gas appliances as well as gas facility contracting projects. It is the world's largest private gas company. It was established in 1885 when Tōkyō Prefecture divested its gas enterprise. SHIBUSAWA EIICHI became the company's first president. Gas was first used in Japan for lighting purposes, but during World War I it began to be used for heating and gradually became popular among households as an energy source. The company proceeded to develop gas actively as a fuel source and grew rapidly through expanding its production facilities, strengthening its management structure, and absorbing other gas companies. In 1952 it became the first in Japan to use heavy oil for the production of gas in place of the conventional coal. In 1969 the company, jointly with TŌKYŌ ELECTRIC POWER CO, INC, was the first jointly to import LNG (liquefied natural gas) from Alaska in an effort to convert to that fuel. The company's technology for the construction of underground tanks to store LNG is highly respected overseas. Technical exchanges with the United States, Britain, West Germany, China, and other countries have become frequent in recent years. Annual revenue totaled ¥669.7 billion (US $2.8 billion) at the end of March 1982, of which gas accounted for 78 percent, sales of gas appliances 10 percent, orders received for gas projects 6 percent, coke 4 percent, and other sources 2 percent; capitalization stood at ¥129.8 billion (US $539.2 million) in the same year. Corporate headquarters are located in Tōkyō.

Tōkyō Geographical Society

(Tōkyō Chigaku Kyōkai). An academic society founded in 1879 for the purpose of introducing modern European scientific thought and furthering the spread of geographical research in Japan. It has some 600 members who specialize in geography, geology, or geophysics. It promotes the exchange of ideas and information among specialists both at home and abroad, sponsors lectures and research programs, and publishes a journal, Chigaku zasshi (Journal of Geography; first issued in 1889). *SHIKI Masahide*

Tōkyō Hōsō → Tōkyō Broadcasting System, Inc (TBS)

Tōkyō Institute of Technology

(Tōkyō Kōgyō Daigaku). A national, coeducational college located in Meguro Ward, Tōkyō. Established in 1881 as the Tōkyō School of Technology (Tōkyō Shokkō Gakkō), it became a national college in 1929. It maintains a faculty of science and engineering, and the research laboratories of Resources Utilization; Precision Machinery and Electronics; Engineering Materials; and Nuclear Reactor Research. Enrollment was 3,269 in 1980.

Tōkyō Kokuritsu Bunkazai Kenkyūjo → Tōkyō National Research Institute of Cultural Properties

Tōkyō Kokuritsu Hakubutsukan → Tōkyō National Museum

Tōkyō Metropolitan Archives and Records Institute

(Tōkyō To Kōbunsho Kan). Library specializing in the collection, preservation, editing, and reprinting of documents and historical materials relating to metropolitan Tōkyō; located in Minato Ward, Tōkyō. The institute was formed in 1968, when some of the functions of the Documents Examination Section of the Metropolitan Tōkyō Bureau of General Affairs were taken over by the Tosei Shiryōkan (founded in 1943), which was then given its present name. Its collection of some 85,000 documents date from the Meiji period (1868–1912). Its publications include Tōkyō hyakunenshi, vols 1–6 (1972–73; supplement 1979); Tosei jūnen shi (1954); Tosei nijūnen shi (1965); and the continuing series Tōkyō Shi shikō (110 vols since 1911); and Toshi kiyō (28 vols since 1953). *Theodore F. WELCH*

Tōkyō Metropolitan Area

(Shutoken). Also known as the National Capital Region. Consists of Tōkyō, Saitama, Chiba, Kanagawa, Ibaraki, Tochigi, Gumma, and Yamanashi prefectures, although for all practical purposes the Shutoken encompasses the area within a 100-km (62-mi) radius of central Tōkyō. It is the economic, political, and cultural center of the nation, with Japan's greatest concentration of population.

Tōkyō has expanded well beyond its administrative limits since the end of World War II and has developed close industrial, economic, and transportation relationships with its seven neighboring prefectures. Therefore, the region has come to be viewed as a single entity in the formulation of comprehensive urban plans for Tōkyō. The National Capital Region Development Law (Shutoken Seibi Hō) was implemented by the national government in 1956 and partially amended in 1966. Its aims were to stop the overconcentration of population and enterprise in central Tōkyō, to control the disorderly sprawl into the suburbs, and to define several regions for urban development in outlying areas. Plans to reverse the flow of people into the metropolitan region are still in progress. Long-term government plans call for a gradual redistribution and decentralization of the functions of the capital city of Tōkyō.

Tōkyō Metropolitan Hibiya Library

(Tōkyō Toritsu Hibiya Toshokan). One of six prefectural libraries maintained by the Tōkyō metropolitan government, and the most important prefectural library in Japan. Since its establishment in 1908 it has remained at its present site in Hibiya Park in central Tōkyō, although it was totally destroyed by bombing in 1945. In 1949 service was restored in a triangular-shaped, reinforced concrete building. Although the capacity of the library is 500,000 volumes, many of its books and some of its previous functions have been transferred to a new facility, the Tōkyō Metropolitan Central Library, in Azabu, Minato Ward. The Hibiya Library remains strong in the areas of literature and the humanities and the social and natural sciences. Of special value is the Tōkyō Shiryō Collection, comprising some 44,000 items relating to the city's history, including prints, records, manuscripts, city maps, and plans. Major collections purchased after the war total 130,000 volumes, with special strength in premodern literature, especially the 20,000-volume Kaga Bunko Collection. The library also publishes a journal, Hibiya, which contains articles of general professional interest. *Theodore F. WELCH*

Tōkyō Metropolitan Police Department

(Keishichō). The police force of Tōkyō Prefecture, with over 40,000 police officers. It is commanded by a superintendent general who is appointed by the NATIONAL PUBLIC SAFETY COMMISSION with approval from the prime minister and the five-member Tōkyō Metropolitan Public Safety Commission (To Kōan Iinkai). The 828-square-mile (2,145 sq km) area of Tōkyō Prefecture, with a population over 11 million, is divided into eight police districts, within which 94 police stations (keisatsusho) are located.

Like the police in all prefectures, police officers of Tōkyō are divided into administrative, personnel and training, traffic, guard, patrol, public security, criminal investigation, and crime prevention specializations. Because of Tōkyō's role as capital, and political and economic hub of the nation, guard and public security duties are particularly crucial and are performed by the RIOT POLICE (Kidōtai) of the Metropolitan Police Department (MPD).

The MPD was established in 1874. Immediately after the Meiji Restoration (1868), warriors of the respective *han* (feudal domains) were stationed in Tōkyō to maintain public safety, and in 1871, *rasotsu* (later called *junsa,* policemen) policed the city. With the establishment of the HOME MINISTRY in 1873, responsibility for the city's public safety was placed directly under its jurisdiction. The Metropolitan Police Department as a separate entity was established in 1874 with Kawaji Toshiyoshi as its first superintendent general. In 1877 the MPD was temporarily absorbed by the Police Bureau of the Home Ministry, but in 1881 it was again separately reestablished. The superintendent general of the Metropolitan Police Department was under the direct supervision of the home minister but had broad authority—control and jurisdiction over all police stations, fire stations, and prisons in Tōkyō, and in some cases, supervision of the heads of wards, cities, towns, and villages within Tōkyō Prefecture.

In 1947 the MPD became an autonomous police department under the Tōkyō Metropolitan Public Safety Commission and had jurisdiction over only the 23 urban wards of Tōkyō. With the revision of the Police Law in 1954, it again became the police agency of the entire Tōkyō Prefecture. *Walter AMES*

Tōkyō National Museum

(Tōkyō Kokuritsu Hakubutsukan). Located in Ueno Park in Tōkyō. The museum has the finest and most extensive collection of Japanese art and archaeology in the world. It also has excellent collections of Chinese and Korean art and archaeology, sculpture from Gandhara and nearby regions, and ethnographical items from Hokkaidō, Taiwan, Korea, and Southeast Asia. Japanese art is housed in the main building; Japanese archaeology in a second building, the Hyōkeikan; objects, largely of the 6th and 7th centuries, presented by the authorities of the temple Hōryūji (see HŌRYŪJI, TREASURES OF) to the Imperial Household in 1876 and now on loan to the museum, in a third building. The latest addition to the complex is the Tōyōkan (1968), which contains Chinese, Korean, and other Asian (except Japanese) art. Among the Japanese paintings owned by the museum is one of the bodhisattva Fugen Bosatsu (Skt: Samantabhadra; Heian period: 794–1185); Kamakura (1185–1333) narrative scrolls; Muromachi (1333–1568) *suibokuga* (INK PAINTING); KAKEMONO (hanging scrolls) and screens from every school of the Edo period (1600–1868). The large print collection includes every famous name in the field, from MORONOBU and the KAIGETSUDŌ SCHOOL to HIROSHIGE and HOKUSAI. There is also a good selection of Western-style painting of the Meiji period (1868–1912). Much of the outstanding Buddhist sculpture is on long-term loan from various temples. The whole range of Japanese pottery, from the Nara period (710–794) to the present, and of Japanese porcelain of the Edo period is amply shown by examples from every well-known kiln. The large lacquer collection includes such pieces as a famous writing box by KŌRIN. The museum engages in an active program that covers temporary exhibitions of great distinction, publications, research, and conservation. See also MUSEUMS. *Laurance ROBERTS*

Tōkyō National Research Institute of Cultural Properties

(Tōkyō Kokuritsu Bunkazai Kenkyūjo). One of two national research institutes maintained by the Agency for Cultural Affairs under the Ministry of Education; located in Ueno Park, Tōkyō. Founded in 1930 as the Institute of Art Research with a bequest from the artist KURODA SEIKI, it became a government organization in 1952. The institute currently employs a research staff of 46, divided among an archive and four other departments with independent facilities for the study of Japanese art and art history, traditional performing arts, scientific problems in the conservation of cultural objects, and the restoration and preservation of cultural properties. Journals published include *Bijutsu kenkyū* (The Journal of Art Studies), *Nihon bijutsu nenkan* (The Yearbook of Japanese Art), *Omban mokuroku* (Catalog of Phonograph Records), *Hyōjun Nihon buyō fu* (Standard Japanese Choreographic Notation for Traditional Dances), *Geinō no kagaku* (Science of Performing Arts), and *Hozon kagaku* (Conservation Science). Library resources amount to 30,000 volumes. See also NARA NATIONAL RESEARCH INSTITUTE OF CULTURAL PROPERTIES. *Gina Lee BARNES*

Tōkyō Olympic Games

Held 10–24 October 1964. The 18th Summer Olympic Games and the first to be held in Asia. There were more than 5,500 participants from 94 nations. Forty-seven world records and 111 Olympic records were set. The efficiency of operation, the fairness of the judges, and the splendor of the grounds were uniformly praised and considered to have more than justified the budget of ¥1.08 trillion (US $3 billion). Tōkyō was to have been the site for the 12th Olympic Games (1940), but the plan was canceled because of Japan's war with China.

Tōkyō ordinance decision

A Supreme Court decision of 20 July 1960 concerning the constitutionality of a Tōkyō ordinance regulating such public demonstrations as parades and open-air meetings. The Supreme Court reversed a Tōkyō District Court decision of 13 October 1959 which had declared the ordinance invalid. The ordinance in question was a KŌAN JŌREI (prefectural public safety ordinance) of the sort enacted by various local governments. Most *kōan jōrei* set up a permit system under which anyone who sponsors an open-air assembly or a demonstration is required to apply for permission to the police or the public safety commission concerned a stipulated number of days before the day of the proposed event. The police have more or less discretionary power in dealing with the application. Thus, it may be argued that *kōan jōrei* constitute an invalid previous restraint on the people's freedom of assembly guaranteed by article 21 of the 1947 constitution, a controversial issue in constitutional law. Many lower courts declared *kōan jōrei* invalid in the early 1950s. In 1954 the Supreme Court examined the constitutionality of *kōan jōrei*. The court upheld a Niigata ordinance, arguing that under this particular ordinance the police had practically no discretionary power in regulating the people's FREEDOM OF ASSEMBLY. However, the court's argument was rather vague and not very persuasive. Thus, despite the court decision, *kōan jōrei* remained a controversial issue. In 1959 the Tōkyō District Court, citing the grounds of the Niigata decision of the Supreme Court, invalidated the Tōkyō ordinance. Tōkyō's *kōan jōrei* was considered crucial to the government in their efforts to subdue the massive protest demonstrations in the nation's capital against the 1960 revision of the United States–Japan Mutual Security Treaty. Agreeing to review the district court decision without further litigation at intermediary courts, the Supreme Court vacated the lower court's judgment, stating that although the ordinance granted some discretionary power to the police, participants in the protest demonstrations might become riotous and harmful to the public peace. Thus, according to this ruling, granting the police discretionary power to deal with "potential riots" was permissible in this instance. *OKUDAIRA Yasuhiro*

Tōkyō Rose

The nickname given by American military men in the Pacific theater during World War II to a number of female announcers broadcasting entertainment and propaganda programs from Radio Tōkyō, the overseas bureau of the Japan Broadcasting Corporation (NHK). One such announcer was Iva Toguri D'Aquino, born in California in 1916 and a graduate of the University of California at Los Angeles, who was caught in Japan on a visit to relatives when the war broke out in 1941. While working as a part-time typist at NHK, she had been recruited for "Zero Hour," a program organized by three Allied prisoners of war. Her job was to introduce popular music with humorous light banter. In September 1945 D'Aquino was identified by two American newspapermen, Clark Lee and Harry T. Brundidge, as the "one and only Tōkyō Rose." Arrested and imprisoned by American military authorities in October 1945, she was released in 1946 after a thorough investigation of her wartime activities. In 1948 the Department of Justice, under heavy domestic political pressure, decided to prosecute her for treason. A San Francisco jury found her guilty in September 1949, and she was imprisoned for over six years. In 1976 former prosecution witnesses revealed they had given false testimony against her under government pressure. In January 1977 D'Aquino was pardoned by President Gerald Ford.

Masayo Umezawa Duus

Tōkyō San'yō Electric Co, Ltd

(Tōkyō San'yō Denki). Manufacturer of household electrical products, electronic equipment, office equipment, and semiconductors. A subsidiary of the SAN'YŌ ELECTRIC CO, LTD, it is in charge of the parent company's production division. It was established in 1959 in Gumma Prefecture. Its television sets, refrigerators, refrigerated showcases, air conditioners, acoustic equipment, and semiconductors are sold under the brand name Sanyo. The company began production of glass vacuum-tube solar collectors in 1978. It is active in the development of new fields and conducts extensive sales and production activities overseas. Sales for the fiscal year ending November 1981 totaled ¥268.3 billion (US $1.2 billion); the export ratio was 31 percent. The company was capitalized at ¥16.6 billion (US $74.2 million) in the same year. The head office is in Gumma Prefecture.

Tōkyō shimbun

A large, influential local daily newspaper serving readers of the greater metropolitan Tōkyō area. The *Tōkyō shimbun* began publishing in 1942 as a result of the enforced wartime merger of two older established Tōkyō dailies, the MIYAKO SHIMBUN and KOKUMIN SHIMBUN. Under restrictions imposed on the use of paper by the government during the last years of World War II, it dropped its morning edition and became an evening paper in 1944. It continued to be Tōkyō's only evening paper for some years after the end of the war, during which time it experienced considerable growth in readership. This was due in part to the serial publication of a long line of popular newspaper novels (see SHIMBUN SHŌSETSU), beginning with volume five (earlier volumes were serialized in the *Miyako shimbun*) of OZAKI SHIRŌ's mammoth novel *Jinsei gekijō* (1933–60). The morning edition was revived in 1956. The *Tōkyō shimbun* is highly regarded for its comprehensive coverage of the arts and cultural events. The company has four main offices in Japan, located in Tōkyō, Hamamatsu, Nagoya and Kanazawa, and a branch office in Ōsaka. There are 13 overseas bureaus. The *Tōkyō shimbun* carries the Associated Press (AP), United Press International (UPI), Radio Press, China News Service, and Korean Press Service. In 1979 it had a circulation of 845,000 for its morning edition and 641,000 for its evening edition.

Tōkyō Steel Mfg Co, Ltd

(Tōkyō Seitetsu). Steel company manufacturing steel bars and angles for construction use. It was established in 1934. Originally it produced shapes, bars, and other products through the open-hearth method, but switched to electric furnaces and expanded its operations to the production of rolled products in the 1970s. It absorbed Tosa Steel Works, Ltd, in 1975 to become a major electric furnace steelmaker. It has been managed since its inception by the Iketani family and has remained independent of several depression cartels formed by the steel industry, following instead a management practice of large investments in equipment during slumps and expansion during booms. It has remained on a firm financial footing. It has a joint venture in the United States producing steel plates. Sales totaled ¥157.3 billion (US $713.5 million) in the fiscal year ending November 1981; the export ratio was 24 percent. It was capitalized at ¥4 billion (US $18.5 million) in the same year. The head office is in Tōkyō.

Tōkyō Tower

(Tōkyō Tawā). Tower built in 1958 in the center of the Tōkyō metropolitan area for the purpose of telecasting throughout the Kantō region. It rises 333 meters (1,093 ft) from the base; it has a nine-channel broadcast antenna at the top and two observation decks.

Tōkyō University

(Tōkyō Daigaku). Usually referred to in English as the University of Tōkyō. A national, coeducational university located in Bunkyō Ward and with a liberal arts campus in Meguro Ward, Tōkyō. It was established as the first Japanese university (see UNIVERSITIES AND COLLEGES: history of Japanese universities) in 1877 by the unification of the Kaisei Gakkō and Tōkyō Igakkō, which had been founded in the Edo period (1600–1868) as the shogunate-sponsored centers of Western learning Kaiseijo (see BANSHO SHIRABESHO) and IGAKUJO. Renamed Tōkyō Imperial University in 1886, it was the only such university until the establishment of Kyōto Imperial University in 1897. In 1947 its name was changed back to Tōkyō University and in 1949 it was reorganized to incorporate the First Higher School and Tōkyō Higher School. The university has maintained a graduate school since 1886 and at present comprises 10 faculties: letters, education, law, economics, science, medicine, pharmacology, engineering, agriculture, and a college of general education. It has long been considered the most influential of all Japanese universities. The following research institutes are located at the university: Cosmic Ray Laboratory, Institute for Nuclear Study, Institute for Solid State Physics, Ocean Research Institute, Institute of Medical Science, Tōkyō Astronomical Observatory, Earthquake Research Institute, Institute of Oriental Culture, Institute of Social Science, Institute of Journalism, Institute of Industrial Science, Historiographical Institute, and Institute of Applied Microbiology. Enrollment in 1980 was 14,167.

Tōkyō University of Education

(Tōkyō Kyōiku Daigaku). A national coeducational university located in Bunkyō Ward, Tōkyō. Established in 1949, uniting Tōkyō University of Literature and Science, Tōkyō Higher Normal School, Tōkyō School of Agricultural Education, and Tōkyō School of Physical Education. In 1978 it was incorporated into the newly formed TSUKUBA UNIVERSITY.

Tōkyō University of Fine Arts and Music

(Tōkyō Geijutsu Daigaku). A national, coeducational university located in Taitō Ward, Tōkyō. Formed in 1949 by uniting the Tōkyō School of Fine Arts and the Tōkyō School of Music, both founded in 1887 (the former opened in 1889, the latter in 1890). It maintains faculties of fine arts and music. The most famous art and music school in Japan, it has graduated many outstanding artists and musicians. Enrollment was 1,876 in 1980.

Tōkyō University of Foreign Studies

(Tōkyō Gaikokugo Daigaku). A national, coeducational university located in Kita Ward, Tōkyō. Originally the Tōkyō Academy of Foreign Languages, established in 1897, it attained university status in 1949. It maintains a faculty of foreign languages and the Institute for the Study of Languages and Cultures of Asia and Africa, as well as a special program in Japanese language and culture for foreign students. Enrollment was 2,420 in 1980.

Tōkyō War Crimes Trial → war crimes trials

Tōkyō Women's Christian University

(Tōkyō Joshi Daigaku). A private liberal arts university for women located in Suginami Ward, Tōkyō. Founded in 1917 by the Presbyterian missionary August Karl REISCHAUER, (1865–1936) and his colleagues. In the following year NITOBE INAZŌ was elected its first president. He was succeeded in 1924 by Japan's first woman university president, YASUI TETSU. In 1949 the institution was recognized as a four-year university. Its Institute for Comparative Studies of Culture is well known. There is also an affiliated two-year college. Enrollment was 2,470 in 1980.

Tōkyū Car Corporation

(Tōkyū Sharyō Seizō). A manufacturer of rolling stock, containers, and vehicles such as dump trucks and trailers, Tōkyū Car Corporation was established in 1948. A member of the Tōkyū group, it is one of the producers of SHINKANSEN carriages and the largest producer of electric trains for public use in Japan. Its production capacity for containers is the greatest in the world. It exports more than 90 percent of its containers for sea transport. Sales for the fiscal year ending March 1982 totaled ¥87.1 billion (US $361.8 million), of which exports comprised 42 percent, and it was capitalized at ¥4.5 billion (US $18.7 million) in the same year. The head office is in Yokohama. See TŌKYŪ CORPORATION.

Tōkyū Construction Co, Ltd

(Tōkyū Kensetsu). General contractor. Established in 1959, the company is a major member of the Tōkyū group, one of the largest real estate developers in Japan. Efforts are being made to engage in huge dam and tunnel projects, urban redevelopment, and the Tōkyū group's overseas projects. Sales totaled ¥246 billion (US $1.07 billion) in the fiscal year ending in September 1981; the company was capitalized at ¥6.3 billion (US $27.4 million) in the same year. The head office is in Tōkyō. See TŌKYŪ CORPORATION.

Tōkyū Corporation

(Tōkyō Kyūkō Dentetsu). Company engaged in commuter transportation (railway and bus) throughout the southwest region of the Tōkyō metropolis. Tōkyū is also the largest real estate developer in Japan and the leader of a business group consisting of 250 companies. Established in 1922 as a local railway company in southwest Tōkyō, the company now operates 100 kilometers (62 mi) of railway lines and 521 kilometers (324 mi) of bus lines. It has diversified into real estate development, with projects throughout Japan and in Asia, Australia, mainland United States, Hawaii, and the Pacific islands. The development of the city of Tama-Den'en, a new suburban community in the southwestern part of Tōkyō with a projected population of 400,000, began in the mid-1950s; this will be the largest private-sector urban development in the world.

The Tōkyū group is engaged in four major areas: transportation, development, distribution and retailing, and recreation and leisure. Tōkyū Corporation acts as the information center and manages financial and human resources. The major companies in the group are TŌA DOMESTIC AIRLINES CO, LTD; TŌKYŪ LAND CORPORATION; the Tōkyū hotel chain (the largest in Japan); Tōkyū Advertising Agency, Inc, (the fourth largest); and TŌKYŪ DEPARTMENT STORE CO, LTD. Tōkyū Corporation became active in overseas business in the early 1970s when it launched regional development projects in Hawaii and Seattle. The first international project of the group was the opening of a department store in Hawaii in 1959. Tōkyū Hotels International operates six hotels abroad with a total of 2,800 rooms. TŌKYŪ CAR CORPORATION has the largest share of the world market in marine steel containers.

Gross sales of the Tōkyū group at the end of March 1982 were ¥2 trillion (US $8.3 billion), of which distribution and retailing accounted for 41 percent, development 25 percent, transportation 20 percent, and recreation and leisure 14 percent. Group employment was 75,600. Total sales for Tōkyū Corporation in the fiscal year ending March 1982 totaled ¥161.5 billion (US $671 million), which broke down as follows: railway and tramcar 33 percent, real estate 34 percent, bus 13 percent, and others 20 percent. It was capitalized at ¥29.1 billion (US $120.9 million) in the same year. The head office is in Tōkyō.

Tōkyū Department Store Co, Ltd

(Tōkyū Hyakkaten). Company chiefly engaged in the department store business. Established in 1919, Tōkyū Department Store Co also operates restaurants and amusement centers, as well as engaging in the import-export business. A major member of the Tōkyū group's marketing department, the company took its present name in 1958 with the merger of the Shirokiya Department Store and the Tōyoko Department Store. In 1959 the company opened the Shirokiya, Inc, department store in Hawaii and in 1974 the Tokyu Feedlot Co in Australia. In 1977 the company established the Saint Germain, America, bakery in Hawaii; it is planning to establish businesses in Los Angeles and Paris. Sales for the fiscal year ending January 1982 totaled ¥248.9 billion (US $1.1 billion) in 1981; the company was capitalized at ¥5.5 billion (US $24.5 million) in the same year. The head office is in Tōkyō. See TŌKYŪ CORPORATION.

Tōkyū Land Corporation

(Tōkyū Fudōsan). Company engaged in real estate, particularly development for housing projects and construction of houses. Tōkyū Land Corporation was founded in 1953 when it became independent of the TŌKYŪ CORPORATION. A member of the Tōkyū group, the company grew rapidly by developing land along the railway lines of the Tōkyū Corporation. It has a joint venture company in Bandung, Indonesia, which is involved in construction of houses. Future plans call for the diversification of its businesses to such projects as

amusement areas. Sales totaled ¥146 billion (US $555.8 million) in the fiscal year ending September 1982; the company was capitalized at ¥12 billion (US $45.6 million) in the same year. The head office is in Tōkyō.

tolerance in Japanese religion

BUDDHISM and SHINTŌ, the two most important Japanese religions, can be said to be fundamentally tolerant religions as compared to such monotheistic religions as Christianity, Judaism, and Islam. (The suppression of Christianity for almost 300 years, not long after its introduction in the 16th century, was based on political rather than religious motives. See CHRISTIANITY; ANTI-CHRISTIAN EDICTS; PERSECUTIONS AT URAKAMI.) Buddhism holds that any of the different philosophies and beliefs that humanity possesses can become the occasion by which the desire for enlightenment is awakened. It affirms the existence of all personal gods as various manifestations of the ultimate being. For this reason, Buddhism, rather than rejecting other religions, tends to integrate them into its own religious system. Esoteric Buddhism in particular aggressively appropriated Indian gods into its fold and developed into a polytheistic religion.

Japanese Buddhism inherited without drastic change the fundamentally mystical orientation and polytheistic tendency of Chinese Buddhism. Early in Japanese history an amalgamation of Buddhism and Shintō took place, and the theory of HONJI SUIJAKU, in which indigenous gods were considered Japanese manifestations of Buddhas and bodhisattvas, became widely accepted. The fundamental unity of Buddhism, Confucianism, and Shintō, or these three and Taoism, was even maintained by some.

From the Kamakura period (1185–1333) on, certain Japanese Buddhist sects such as the Pure Land sects (see PURE LAND BUDDHISM) and the NICHIREN sect became increasingly exclusive and intolerant. The JŌDO SHIN SECT, believing exclusively in the practice of reciting the name of the Buddha Amida (the NEMBUTSU), rejected the worship of all other gods and spirits as well as other forms of religious practice. The Nichiren sect, believing in the practice of reciting the title of the Lotus Sutra, strictly rejected all other religions and philosophies. In their proselytizing, the members of this sect employed an aggressive approach called shakubuku (or hashaku) in which conversion was accomplished by intimidation or even force.

Shintō began as an ethnocentric religion with communal rites (matsuri) as its central element. On the whole it was accommodating toward other religions. With the arrival of Buddhism, Shintō accepted the Buddhas and bodhisattvas as "gods of neighboring countries." As the amalgamation of Buddhism and Shintō took place, syncretic deities that reflected this process began to appear. Through its amalgamation, not only with Buddhism but also with Taoism, Confucianism, and other beliefs from China, Shintō systematized its doctrines, rituals, and practices, thus molding what became its own characteristic religious system. YOSHIDA SHINTŌ, which considered Daigen Sonshin as the absolute God, and RESTORATION SHINTŌ, which considered Amenominakanushi no Kami as the god of creation and ruler of the universe, rejected other religions; nevertheless, in general, Shintō was unwavering in its tolerance for other religions. From the Meiji Restoration of 1868 until the end of World War II, however, Shintō was given a special status by the government as the religion of the Japanese nation, which was asserted to be a religious community (see STATE SHINTŌ); all other religions, Buddhism, Christianity, and the so-called NEW RELIGIONS, suffered suppression and interference. — MURAKAMI Shigeyoshi

Tomakomai

City in southwestern Hokkaidō, on the Pacific Ocean. Tomakomai was settled by colonist militia (TONDENHEI) from the mainland in the late 19th century. It is the leading producer of paper in the country. Oil refineries and aluminum and lumber plants are located here. Completion of a man-made port in 1976 has led to further industrialization. Pop: 151,969.

Tomb period → Kofun period

tomeyama

(literally, "mountain preserves"). Regulations issued during the Edo period (1600–1868) prohibiting entry into or use of certain forest

Tomioka Silk-Reeling Mill

The interior of the mill soon after it began operating as portrayed in a contemporary three-panel woodblock print. Detail. Entire print 73 × 37 cm. Ca 1872. Yokohama Silk Museum.

lands for hunting or lumbering; the term referred also to the restricted areas themselves. Although the issuing authorities claimed that these regulations were for the sake of preserving the beauty of the forests, in many cases they were intended to protect the private interests of the *daimyō*. *Tomeyama* regulations were occasionally invoked on a temporary basis when disputes arose over IRIAI (commonage rights).

Tomii Masaaki (1858–1935)

Legal scholar and codifier of the prewar Civil Code. Born in Kyōto. After graduating from the Tōkyō School of Foreign Languages in 1877, he studied at the University of Lyons and was awarded a doctoral degree in law. Returning to Japan in 1883, he was appointed professor at Tōkyō University, where he lectured on civil law until 1918. Although he had been trained in France, he objected to the immediate enactment of the 1890 civil code for its exclusive reliance on the Napoleonic Code and suggested that elements from English and German civil law also be incorporated (see CIVIL CODE CONTROVERSY). Accordingly, in 1893 he was named, together with HOZUMI NOBUSHIGE and UME KENJIRŌ, to the commission to amend the code; the Civil Code, as finally enacted in July 1898, was almost entirely German in inspiration. In 1919 he was appointed to a committee to revise the parts relating to family law (Shinzoku Hō) and inheritance law (Sōzoku Hō). His principal work is *Mimpō genron* (3 vols, 1903–29, Principles of Civil Law). He is also remembered as one of several academics who advocated war on the eve of the Russo-Japanese War (1904–05). See SHICHIHAKASE JIKEN.

Katō Ichirō

tomikuji

(fortune lot). Type of lottery that flourished in cities during the Edo period (1600–1868). Derived from MUJIN, mutual aid financial associations, which originated in the Muromachi period (1333–1568). Sponsors sold numbered wooden lots and held drawings at temples or shrines to decide winners. It was also called *tomitsuki* (fortune stab), because the winning lot was selected by plunging a stick with a drill bit on its end into a large box and twisting it until a single lot was pierced. Since *tomikuji* were conducted in order to raise funds for the repair of temple or shrine buildings, they received shogunal sanction. However, fraudulent practices were common, and in 1842 *tomikuji* were outlawed.

Inagaki Shisei

Tomimoto Kenkichi (1886–1963)

Potter. The greatest of the modern Japanese potters to specialize in porcelain, although he worked in earthenware and stoneware as well. He was also an influential teacher and leading member of various organizations of artists and craftsmen. His complex, vigorous patterns of stylized blossoms in overglaze enamel, gold, and silver on white porcelain have never been surpassed. He was also a master of bold yet naturalistic plant motifs in underglaze cobalt blue. Unlike many earlier artist-potters, he insisted on throwing his own pots as well as applying the decoration.

Tomimoto was born in Ando, Nara Prefecture, near the famous temple HŌRYŪJI. He studied architectural design at the Tōkyō Bijutsu Gakkō (now Tōkyō University of Fine Arts and Music) in 1908 and went to England for further design study. In 1911 he returned to Japan. In 1912 he began the study of ceramics under Kenzan VI; his fellow student was the English potter Bernard H. LEACH (1887–1979).

In 1915 Tomimoto built a kiln of his own in Ando, his birthplace, and worked there until 1926. His earliest pieces were low-fired RAKU WARE, a type he soon abandoned as too breakable. He turned to stoneware, taking inspiration from Korean ceramics of the early Yi dynasty (1392–1910), whose brushed-slip and slip-inlaid decoration had long been admired by Japanese connoisseurs. Tomimoto used a gray stoneware clay from the bottom of a pond near his home.

From 1926 to 1946 Tomimoto lived in Tōkyō, where he made mainly porcelain: blue and white, overglaze enameled, and plain white, the latter inspired by 18th- and 19th-century Korean porcelain. Tomimoto was courageous in producing plain white pieces at a time when both Japanese and Western taste preferred elaborate decoration. His enameled porcelain was influenced by his study of the KUTANI WARE of Ishikawa Prefecture. In 1944 he began teaching ceramics at the Tōkyō Bijutsu Gakkō.

At the age of 60, Tomimoto moved to Kyōto, where he remained until his death. He continued to produce porcelain, but also made enamel-decorated earthenware, a Kyōto technique perfected by NONOMURA NINSEI and KENZAN. Beginning in 1949, Tomimoto taught ceramics at the Kyōto City University of Fine Arts (now Kyōto City University of Arts). In 1955 the Japanese government designated him one of the first LIVING NATIONAL TREASURES. *Robert Moes*

Tominaga Nakamoto (1715–1746)

Scholar of the Edo period (1600–1868) who was known for his critical views on Buddhism, Confucianism, and Shintō; also known as Tominaga Kensai. His father Norimichi was one of several well-to-do Ōsaka merchants who helped to found the KAITOKUDŌ, a school for local townsmen; it is not certain, however, whether his son studied at this school. From youth Tominaga showed signs of intellectual precocity; sometime in his twenties he left his family and began teaching at his own home in Ōsaka. He died when only 31.

Tominaga's studies centered on the historical development of Buddhism, Confucianism, and Shintō. In his work *Shutsujō kōgo* (also read *Shutsujō gogo;* Buddha's Comments after His Meditation) of 1745, he asserted that the existing body of Buddhist teachings contained later accretions and did not represent original Buddhism. Furthermore, he maintained, those teachings claiming to be older were in fact newer. He did not deny the verity of Mahāyāna Buddhism but he did object to its attribution of various sermons and texts to Buddha himself. Again, in his *Setsuhei* (no longer extant, but described by Tominaga in another work, *Okina no fumi*), he criticized Confucianism from the same perspective.

Perhaps his short critique *Okina no fumi* (1746, Writings of an Old Man) spells out most clearly his views on Buddhism, Shintō, and Confucianism. Writing that both Buddhism and Confucianism had evolved under particular historical and geographical circumstances, he argues that it is both impossible and meaningless for the Japanese to try to adopt them. As for the native cult of Shintō, which developed in the ancient past, he says that it is equally impossible to practice. He concludes that those ethical and religious tenets which cannot be observed are invalid, that is to say, cannot be considered the true moral way *(makoto no michi),* and only those initial teachings which follow common sense and are easy to put into practice can be called true and valid. In more everyday terms, Tominaga called on his readers to concentrate on the work at hand, to be upright and circumspect in word and deed, to defer to one's parents, and to be loyal to one's lord.

■——Mizuta Norihisa and Arisaka Takamichi, *Tominaga Nakamoto; Yamagata Bantō,* in *Nihon shisō taikei,* vol 43 (Iwanami Shoten, 1973).

Tomioka

City in southwestern Gumma Prefecture, central Honshū, on the river Kaburagawa. The TOMIOKA SILK-REELING MILL, the country's first Western-style thread-reeling factory, was established here by the government in 1872. The building, as well as the enterprise, is now maintained by Katakura Industries, Ltd. There are also electrical appliance, automobile parts, and rubber industries. Sericulture and dairy farming are active. Pop: 48,046

Tomioka Silk-Reeling Mill

(Tomioka Seishisho). A model filature established by the Meiji government in Tomioka, Gumma Prefecture, in 1872 (see GOVERNMENT-OPERATED FACTORIES, MEIJI PERIOD). The government hired a French engineer, P. Brunat, to supervise the construction and operation of the plant, imported machinery from France, and recruited workers primarily from among the daughters of former *samurai (shizoku)*. The factory played an important role in the diffusion of mechanized reeling in Japan. Having experienced managerial difficulties from the beginning, the plant was sold to MITSUI in 1893 (see KAN'EI JIGYŌ HARAISAGE) and then transferred to the Hara Gōmei Company in 1902. In 1938 its management was entrusted to the Katakura Silk-Reeling and Spinning Company, which formally absorbed the operation in the following year. It is now known as the Katakura Industries Tomioka Silk-Reeling Mill. See photo on preceding page. *TANAKA Akira*

Tomioka Tessai (1837–1924)

Last major artist in the BUNJINGA (literati painting) tradition in Japan; one of the great modern masters of Japanese art. Real name Tomioka Yūsuke; later changed to Tomioka Hyakuren. Born in Kyōto into a family that supplied clothing and accessories to Buddhist temples, Tessai first studied ancient Japanese classics under the KOKUGAKU scholar ŌKUNI TAKAMASA with the aim of becoming a Shintō priest. At the age of about 20 he became a protégé of the Buddhist nun ŌTAGAKI RENGETSU, who taught him poetic composition and encouraged his study of painting. He also studied prose composition in both Japanese and Chinese style, history, and Neo-Confucian philosophy (YŌMEIGAKU) along with SHINGAKU, an ethicoreligious movement of the Edo period (1600–1868). During the late years of the Edo period he was associated with the proimperialist movement dedicated to overthrowing the Tokugawa shogunate and restoring the emperor to power (see SONNŌ JŌI). By the time this movement finally succeeded, in 1868, many of his associates and teachers had lost their lives.

During the Meiji period (1868–1912), Tessai traveled throughout Japan visiting famous and scenic places that became the subjects of many of his paintings. A visit to Hokkaidō led to several paintings of Ainu life and customs, including a pair of screens dated 1896 now in the Tōkyō National Museum. He served as a Shintō functionary in several shrines, but gradually turned to painting as his chief occupation and means of livelihood, while, in theory, keeping always his amateur status by insisting on the primacy of his scholarship. During the period of Japan's rapid modernization he championed old traditions against the new Westernized styles.

In 1882 Tessai settled in Kyōto, where he spent the rest of his life painting and reading the thousands of books he had collected. In 1907 he was commissioned to paint for the Meiji emperor. He was appointed as an artist to the imperial household *(teishitsu gigeiin)* in 1917 and named to the Imperial Fine Arts Academy (Teikoku Bijutsuin) in 1919, but he did not take these honors seriously, believing they had come too late to be significant. His most prolific and creative period was the decade of his 80s. Demand for his works greatly increased during these late years, and he worked constantly. His total life's output has been estimated at over 20,000 paintings, and on one occasion he produced 70 in a single day. The works of his last few months he signed "at the age of 90," but he died just before reaching that age, on 31 December 1924.

Tessai's earliest paintings follow the *bunjinga* styles of the early 19th century, showing the influence of such artists as TANOMURA CHIKUDEN, NUKINA KAIOKU, OKADA HANKŌ, and others. He also worked on occasion in virtually all the styles and traditions associated with Kyōto: the YAMATO-E style based on the courtly art of the Heian (794–1185) and later periods, the RIMPA style of SŌTATSU and KŌRIN, the semifolk art of ŌTSU-E, and the style (or form) of *haiga*, sketchy pictures done to accompany HAIKU poems. Elements of all these appear from time to time in his later works.

Tessai's best works, however, belong to the current within *bunjinga* that was based on the paintings of late Ming dynasty (1368–1644) artists of Suzhou (Soochow) in Jiangsu (Kiangsu) Province in China and introduced to Japan by SAKAKI HYAKUSEN. This

Tomioka Tessai

Detail of a painting of Eishū, one of the Taoist Isles of Immortals. Painted in the last year of Tessai's life, the work shows the concern with themes of longevity characteristic of his later years. Hanging scroll. Ink and colors on paper. 142.6 × 40.2 cm. 1924. Kiyoshikōjin Seichōji, Hyōgo Prefecture.

kind of painting (in contrast to the drier, more intellectualized *bunjinga* type) tended to use rich colors, to portray evocative scenes of people enjoying nature, to include lively figures in the landscapes, and to illustrate literary themes or episodes from history and legend. Tessai wrote long inscriptions on many of his works, identifying and explicating the subjects but also displaying his sinological knowledge. He depicted many incidents from the life of Su Shi (Su Shih, pen name Su Dongpo or Su Tung-p'o; 1036–1101), the Song (Sung; 960–1279) scholar-official poet who was also the founder of the literati movement in painting. Having the same birthday as Su, Tessai felt a mysterious affinity with him. He also painted a number of illustrations to Su's famous "Red Cliff Ode" (Ch: Chibi fu or Ch'ih-pi-fu). He often portrayed the bodhisattva KANNON and other Buddhist subjects, as well as Taoist and Confucian figures; moreover, he sometimes combined these into subjects of his own devising to symbolize the unity of East Asian religious and philosophical traditions by showing their founders riding in a single boat. In his late years he frequently executed pictures symbolic of longevity—pine trees, the god of longevity (Jurōjin), and the Taoist Isles of Immortals.

His late works, on which his present fame chiefly rests, are powerful, original compositions. Some are painted in brilliant colors which, together with the semifacetious grotesqueries and distortions of form, justify his reputation as a kind of East Asian fauve. Others are in ink monochrome, or ink with touches of light color, and often feature areas of heavy black ink laid on in bold brushstrokes. Tessai's distinctive brushwork is seen also in his calligraphy, which has established him as one of the major modern masters of that art.

In their combination of popular themes and styles with scholarly content, Tessai's paintings have achieved a unique place in modern Japanese art, appealing to both traditionalist and modernist tastes. Similarly, his success in reconciling an air of freedom and spontaneity with technical discipline embodies an ideal long established in East Asia but seldom so well achieved in modern times. These qualities, along with others—his humor, his narrative skill—have made him one of the most popular of recent Japanese artists. Exhibitions of his paintings and calligraphy are held frequently in Japan, and many books on him have been published. The largest and finest collection of his works is that of the Kiyoshi Kōjin Seichōji, a Buddhist temple near Takarazuka, Hyōgo Prefecture. A Tessai Museum there has several changing exhibitions each year and a Tessai Institute conducts research on his life and works.

🕮——Kyōto National Museum, *Tessai* (1973). Tarō Odakane, *Tessai: Master of the Literati Style*, tr Money Hickman (1965). Tomioka Masutarō et al, *Tessai taisei*, 4 vols (1976). *James* CAHILL

Tomita Keisen (1879–1936)

Japanese-style (NIHONGA) painter. Real name Tomita Shizugorō. Born in Hakata (now the city of Fukuoka), he first studied painting at the local KANŌ SCHOOL atelier. In 1896 he moved to Kyōto and became a pupil of the MARUYAMA-SHIJŌ SCHOOL painter Tsuji Kakō (1870–1931). On his own he studied the Buddhist painting of the Nara (710–794) and Heian (794–1185) periods. Fascinated with the life and art of SENGAI GIBON (1750–1837), he took up the practice of the Zen-related arts, but it was the paintings of his contemporary, TOMIOKA TESSAI (1837–1924), that excited his interest in literati painting (BUNJINGA). When Tomita exhibited his masterpiece *Ubune* (1912, Cormorant Fishing), he attracted the attention of YOKOYAMA TAIKAN and soon after joined the reorganized Nihon Bijutsuin (JAPAN FINE ARTS ACADEMY). Tomita drew on a wide variety of sources to develop his own approach to Japanese-style painting; his work shows great charm and warmth.

Tomita Tsuneo (1904–1967)

Novelist. Born in Tōkyō as the son of Tomita Tsunejirō, a famous judoist. Graduate of Meiji University. He started writing poems and plays while still a student. He was essentially a writer of popular novels, most of them in the early years of the Meiji period (1868–1912). He was the first recipient of the Naoki Prize after World War II for *Irezumi* (1947) and *Men* (1948). Tomita is best known, however, for his earlier novel *Sugata Sanshirō* (1942), in which he portrays a young man who dedicates his life to *jūdō*. It was made into a film in 1943 by KUROSAWA AKIRA. Other works include *Benkei* (1951–55) and *Yawara* (1964–65).

Tomoe Gozen (fl late 12th century)

Legendary female warrior; concubine of MINAMOTO NO YOSHINAKA, commander of Minamoto forces in the earlier phases of the TAIRA-MINAMOTO WAR (1180–85). According to the 13th-century military romance HEIKE MONOGATARI, Tomoe Gozen accompanied Yoshinaka when he fled Kyōto in 1184, pursued by his erstwhile Minamoto allies, who were intent on punishing him for his treachery and abuse of power while in command. Tomoe, one of Yoshinaka's last surviving companions, was urged to flee lest he be embarrassed by the enemy's discovery that a woman was with him; but she refused to go until she had taken the head of an enemy warrior to prove that her prowess was equal to any man's. She then escaped, and is said to have either remarried or lived out her life as a nun. Her exploits are recounted in a Nō play, *Tomoe*, attributed to the great playwright ZEAMI. *Barbara L.* ARNN

Tomonaga Shin'ichirō (1906–1979)

Theoretical physicist and corecipient of the 1965 Nobel Prize in physics. Known for his numerous pioneering contributions in fundamental physics, including a theory that reconciled the theory of quantum electrodynamics with the special theory of relativity. Born in Tōkyō, he graduated from Kyōto University in 1929. He went to Germany in 1937 to study atomic theory under Werner Heisenberg. Returning to Japan two years later, he was inspired by the works of YUKAWA HIDEKI and SAKATA SHŌICHI and developed a new insight that led to his Nobel Prize–winning theory. In 1953, along with Yukawa and Sakata, he became one of the key administrators of the newly established Research Institute for Fundamental Physics at Kyōto University. He served as president of Tōkyō University of Education from 1956 to 1962, and he was also an active participant in the worldwide crusade for peaceful use of atomic energy. He received the Order of Culture in 1952. His publications include *Ryōshi rikigaku* (1952–53; tr *Quantum Mechanics*, 1962), an important textbook in modern physics, and *Supin wa meguru* (1974), a highly readable account of quantum physics written for the layman.

Tomo no Kowamine → Jōwa Conspiracy

tomo no miyatsuko

Leader of a hereditary service corporation (*tomo* or BE) of workers who furnished labor, goods, and other economic services to the YAMATO COURT during the 5th and 6th centuries. Many *tomo no miyatsuko* held the honorary cognomen (KABANE) *miyatsuko*, indicating a lower status than the cognomen *atai*, commonly conferred on the administrative and provincial elite (KUNI NO MIYATSUKO). Some of the more prominent *tomo no miyatsuko* were the Ōtomo and the Mononobe, who performed military services, and the Imbe and Nakatomi, who performed religious functions. After the TAIKA REFORM of 645 some *tomo no miyatsuko* were granted the more prestigious cognomen of *muraji*, gaining thereby the position of court nobles. Others were made low-ranking officials (*tomobe*) under the RITSURYŌ SYSTEM and charged with supervising artisans (*shinabe*, *zakko*). See also UJI-KABANE SYSTEM. *KITAMURA* Bunji

Tomo no Yoshio → Ōtemmon Conspiracy

Ton'a (1289–1372)

Classical (WAKA) poet, critic, apologist of the conservative poetic school, and Buddhist priest. His lay name was Nikaidō Sadamune. Born into a military family, he developed an interest in poetry from an early age and became a disciple of NIJŌ TAMEYO, head of the dominant conservative Nijō poetic house, and in 1312 joined the priesthood of the Tendai sect. Thenceforth he was a frequent participant in poetic gatherings, contests, and parties in the Kyōto capital. He developed friendly relations with the major literary figures of the age and came to be known with the priests Keiun (d ca 1369), Jōben (d ca 1356), and YOSHIDA KENKŌ as one of the Four Guardian Kings of Classical Poetry (Waka Shitennō) of his age. More talented than his Nijō teachers and patrons, he became indispensable as a defender and spokesman for the conservative cause, and in 1365 he was called upon to complete the compilation of the 19th imperial anthology (*chokusenshū*) of classical poetry, the *Shin shūishū* (New Collection of Gleanings) when the official compiler, Nijō Tameaki, died suddenly.

Ton'a passed on the traditions of the faltering Nijō line to a new generation of classical and *renga* (linked verse) poets outside the court aristocracy. At the same time, he numbered among his students the great Fujiwara noble, statesman, and *renga* poet NIJŌ YOSHIMOTO and the shōgun ASHIKAGA TAKAUJI. Some 45 of his poems are included in various imperial anthologies beginning with the 15th, the *Shoku senzaishū* (1320, Collection of a Thousand Years Continued). His personal collection, *Sōanshū* (Collection of the Hermit's Cottage), including much of the best work he wrote from his youth until his early 70s, contains more than 2,000 poems. He was also the author of important writings, including *Seiashō* (Notes of a Frog at the Bottom of a Well), a poetic treatise and collection of lore completed circa 1360–64; and *Gumon kenchū* (Wise Answers to Foolish Questions), a set of replies to questions on classical poetry completed in 1363. He also left a fragmentary diary, *Jūrakuan ki* (Record of the Hermitage of the Ten Pleasures), dated 1364, describing his life and conversations on Buddhism and poetry.

🕮——Robert H. Brower and Earl Miner, *Japanese Court Poetry* (1961). *Robert H.* BROWER

Tonami

City in western Toyama Prefecture, central Honshū. Tonami developed as a market town in the 17th century. Principal products are rice and tulip bulbs, the latter being mainly for export to the United States and Canada. Pop: 35,831.

Tonami Plain

(Tonami Heiya). Located in western Toyama Prefecture, central Honshū. Bordering the Sea of Japan, it consists of alluvial fans of the river Shōgawa and graben valleys to the east and west. Peculiar to the rice-producing area are isolated farmhouses surrounded by trees planted as windbreaks. It is also noted for tulip bulbs. The major city is Tonami. Area: approximately 400 sq km (154 sq mi).

tonarigumi

(neighbor groups). The smallest unit of general mobilization during World War II. Units of 10 to 15 households had been established in large cities in 1938 for fire-fighting and civil defense. On 11 September 1940, by order of the Home Ministry, these were officially organized into a nationwide network of neighborhood groups (*rimpohan*, commonly called *tonarigumi*). Participation was compulsory. Besides circulating notices from the central and local governments, each unit was collectively responsible for allocating government bonds, civil defense, public health, and fire-fighting activities, rationing consumer goods, and so forth. Like the similar GONINGUMI system of the Edo period (1600–1868), the system proved to be an effective means of social control. It was abolished in 1947. See also CHŌNAIKAI; NATIONAL SPIRITUAL MOBILIZATION MOVEMENT.

HARADA Katsumasa

Tondabayashi

City in southeastern Ōsaka Prefecture, central Honshū; some 22 km (14 mi) southeast of Ōsaka. Its principal industries are spinning and the manufacturing of bamboo products and glass bowls. Agricultural products include eggplants, cucumbers, mandarin oranges, and strawberries. At the center of the city is a JINAICHŌ, constructed in 1560 as a temple town of the JŌDO SHIN SECT temple Kōshōji. The headquarters of the PL KYŌDAN, a religious organization, was built here in 1954. Also of interest are the tomb of the 7th-century political figure Prince SHŌTOKU at the temple Eifukuji and the remains of Chihayajō, a fortress associated with the 14th-century warrior KUSUNOKI MASASHIGE.

tondenhei

(colonist militia). A term of ancient Chinese origin, applied in Japan to soldiers recruited to open up new farmland in Hokkaidō and to defend it in case of need. In 1869 the Meiji government established the Hokkaidō Colonization Office (KAITAKUSHI) in Sapporo in recognition of Hokkaidō's increasing importance both as Japan's northern defense perimeter and as a potential contributor to its food production. Because few people were eager to settle in the harsh northern climate, the government in 1874 adopted a plan, suggested by KURODA KIYOTAKA, whereby former *samurai* in the northern prefectures, many of whom had been unemployed since the Meiji Restoration of 1868, were enlisted and given various forms of assistance to establish themselves in Hokkaidō. By 1882, when the Colonization Office was abolished and authority over the *tondenhei* transferred to the Army Ministry, more than 2,400 people had been settled in the northern island. As Russia's interest in the Far East became more visible around 1890, Japan intensified efforts to increase its presence and strengthen its defenses in Hokkaidō by recruiting some 40,000 people—commoners as well as former samurai—from all parts of the country. With the growth of the civilian population and the establishment of the Seventh Army Division in the area, the *tondenhei* system was abandoned in 1903.

Tonegawa

River in the Kantō region, central Honshū, originating in Tangoyama, a mountain between Gumma and Niigata prefectures, entering the Kantō Plain at the city of Maebashi, and flowing southeast into the Pacific Ocean at the city of Chōshi, Chiba Prefecture. It is the third longest river in Japan; the area of its drainage basin is the largest. Until 1622 it joined the ARAKAWA and emptied into Tōkyō Bay. Its course was artificially changed early in the Edo period (1600–1868) in order to prevent floods in the city of Edo (now Tōkyō), as well as to secure water for irrigation of the farmland along what became its lower reaches. The river has long been utilized for irrigation, and with the development of the Tōkyō Metropolitan Area, numerous dams have been constructed to meet the increasing demand for drinking and industrial water. The area where the river originates is part of Jōshin'etsu Kōgen National Park, and the lower reaches are part of Suigō–Tsukuba Quasi-National Park. Length: 322 km (200 mi); area of drainage basin: 16,840 sq km (6,500 sq mi).

Tonegawa zushi

Gazetteer compiled by Akamatsu Sōtan, a native of Fukawa, Shimōsa Province (now Ibaraki Prefecture), consisting of six fascicles and printed in 1855. The book covers historical and scenic sites as well as noteworthy temples and shrines along the river TONEGAWA from its middle reaches to the town of Chōshi, where the river flows into the Pacific. The gazetteer is especially detailed in its information about the area near Chōshi.

In writing the book, Akamatsu drew on many written sources. A map of the entire river, as well as illustrations—many of them by leading artists—of temples, shrines, festivals, castle ruins, local products, vegetation, and so forth, are provided. The book, written in a lively style, is also invaluable for the study of local history. A new edition, with an introduction by the noted folklorist YANAGITA KUNIO, was published in 1938 as part of the Iwanami Bunko series.

ŌTō Tokihiko

toneri

Attendants who served the sovereign and other members of the imperial family in ancient Japan. Recruited mainly from the sons of local chieftains, *toneri* remained loyal to their masters in times of crisis. One such instance was the JINSHIN DISTURBANCE of 672, in which attendants of Prince Ōama (later Emperor TEMMU) played a significant role in gaining victory for their master. Later, under the TAIHŌ CODE (701), *toneri* became a segment of the lower bureaucracy, serving high-ranking nobles as well as members of the imperial family. The position was sought by many young men, since it was regarded as ensuring future success. *Michiko Y. AOKI*

Toneri, Prince (676–735)

Court official of the Nara period (710–794). The third son of Emperor TEMMU, his mother was Princess Niitabe, a daughter of Emperor TENJI. After the establishment of the RITSURYŌ SYSTEM of government, a power struggle developed between members of the imperial family and the aristocratic faction that controlled the Grand Council of State (Dajōkan), the central organ of the government. As a leader of the imperial party, Prince Toneri became increasingly influential, especially after the death of his brothers, Princes Osakabe and Hozumi. In 718 he was given the rank of *ippon*, the highest granted to members of the imperial family, and in the following year became an adviser to Crown Prince Obito, the future Emperor SHŌMU. With the death of the powerful statesman FUJIWARA NO FUHITO in 720, Toneri became administrator (*chidajōkanji*) of the Dajōkan, at the time the highest post in the government. Following the rebellion and forced suicide of Prince Nagaya no Ō in 729 (see NAGAYA NO Ō, REBELLION OF), he helped to arrange the elevation of the imperial consort KŌMYŌ to the rank of nonreigning empress (*kōgō*). Toneri is best remembered as the chief compiler of the NIHON SHOKI, Japan's first official history (see also RIKKOKUSHI). His seventh son, Prince Ōi (733–765), became Emperor Junnin (r 758–764). *YAGI Atsuru*

Tonghak Rebellion

(J: Tōgaku no Ran). A Korean peasant uprising that was the immediate cause of the SINO-JAPANESE WAR OF 1894–1895. Leaders of the Tonghak (J: Tōgaku; Eastern Learning) religious cult rallied peasants suffering from famine and official corruption in southwestern Korea and marched on the capital in 1893 to petition King KOJONG for reforms. The religious movement, formed as a counter to Sōhak (J: Seigaku; Western Learning, i.e., Catholicism) in the mid-19th century, had been suppressed by Kojong's father, the TAEWŎN'GUN, during the 1860s as a heterodoxy and a threat to the state. The uprising developed into a massive rebellion in the spring of 1884. When limited reform failed to satisfy the Tonghak, the Korean army was ordered to disband the rebels. Kojong turned to China for military aid after Korean troops proved unable to quell the revolt. Chinese forces arrived in June 1894. Japanese troops also landed in June and a month later attacked Chinese troops, igniting the Sino-Japanese War.

When the Tonghak rose again after the fall harvest, the Japanese army dispatched a force from the fighting front and, by January 1895, had ruthlessly and totally suppressed them. In the end the Tonghak Rebellion brought only misery to the Korean people and provided Japan with a pretext to further its aggressive designs against the Korean nation. See also KOREA AND JAPAN: early modern relations. *C. Kenneth QUINONES*

Tōno

City in southeasten Iwate Prefecture, northern Honshū. It developed as a castle town of the Nambu domain and as a distribution center for regional products. The chief occupation is rice farming. Apples, tobacco, and hops are also grown. Dairy farming has replaced the traditional horse breeding. Tōno is known among students of folklore as the setting for TŌNO MONOGATARI, a collection of local legends put together by YANAGITA KUNIO. Pop: 31,059.

Tōnomine

Hill in the city of Sakurai, Nara Prefecture, central Honshū. The summit is known as Haretsuyama. On the southern slopes is the Danzan Shrine, known for its ornate architecture and dedicated to FUJIWARA NO KAMATARI. Height: 619 m (2,030 ft).

Tōno monogatari

(The Legends of Tōno). Book by the folklorist YANAGITA KUNIO (1875–1962). Published in 1910, it is considered a modern Japanese literary and folklore classic. Set in the mountain village of Tōno in remote Iwate Prefecture, this volume represents Yanagita's most dramatic attempt to recreate in literary form the psychic landscape of the Japanese peasantry. Influenced by Turgenev's *A Sportsman's Sketches* and challenging what he saw as the urban bias of Japan's naturalist-school writers, Yanagita hoped *Tōno monogatari* would bring the oral tradition of the countryside to the attention of other writers.

Tōno monogatari taps the most vigorous stream of Japanese oral narrative tradition, the legends *(densetsu),* which were more intimately bound up with daily village life and thought than the generally stereotyped FOLKTALES. The book is rich in the familiar Japanese imagery of festivals, animals, and mountain people. It offers a vision of a typical villager growing up in a world full of dangers from invisible forces and malevolent creatures shuttling between the human and animal kingdoms.

▬——Yanagita Kunio, *Tōno monogatari,* tr Ronald A. Morse as *The Legends of Tōno* (1975).   *Ronald A.* MORSE

Tonomura Shigeru (1902–1961)

Novelist. Born in Shiga Prefecture. Graduate of Tōkyō University. He succeeded his father as a cotton merchant and struggled with the family's depression-stricken business for several years. Driven by a long-cherished desire to become a writer—he started a literary magazine with several classmates while at the university—he transferred the family business to his younger brother and turned his attention to professional writing. He gained recognition with a trilogy composed of *Kusaikada* (1934–38), *Ikada* (1954–56), winner of the Noma Prize, and *Hanaikada* (1957–58). These three works trace the saga of his family as well-established merchants since the mid-18th century. His later works are written in an autobiographical style. Other works include "Rakujitsu no kōkei" (1960), a short story, and *Miotsukushi* (1960), a novel which won the Yomiuri Literary Prize.

Tonoshō

Town in the western part of the island of SHŌDOSHIMA; administratively a part of Kagawa Prefecture, Shikoku. A base for ferry boats connecting Honshū and Shikoku, the town has numerous inns and shops catering to tourists. There are also spinning and stone quarrying industries. Olive trees are cultivated on nearby hills. Pop: 21,398.

Tō no Tsuneyori (1401–1484)

Classical (WAKA) poet; warrior. A key figure in the history of the esoteric ritual of "transmitting the secrets of the KOKINSHŪ" (Kokin Denju). Also known as Tōyashū.

Tsuneyori was born into a military family which had for more than 10 generations been known as a poetic house, its successive heads having been honored by inclusion of their poems in imperial anthologies. Tsuneyori's father Masuyuki was on intimate terms with the important poet and teacher SHŌTETSU (1381–1459) and is recorded as having appeared at poetry gatherings with his eldest son Ujikazu during the 1430s. Tsuneyori also studied under Shōtetsu

and more particularly under the priest Gyōkō (1391–1455), an important conservative poet and representative of the hereditary Nijō school. Tsuneyori's *Tōyashū kikigaki* records the teachings of Gyōkō and Shōtetsu as well as other poetic lore and events of importance of the early 1450s. At the same time Tsuneyori was caught up in the constant warfare of the age, spending a good deal of his time in battle for a decade before and during the protracted ŌNIN WAR of 1467–77. A famous story tells how one of his poems softened the heart of the warrior Saitō Myōshun, moving him to give back some territory he had gained in a siege of the stronghold of Tsuneyori's brother Ujikazu.

Rightly or wrongly, Tsuneyori is best known to posterity for having consolidated one of the two lines of the ritual of imparting the secrets of the *Kokinshū,* which he administered to the great *renga* (linked verse) poet SŌGI (1421–1502) in 1471. For this he was scorned by the famous 17th-century scholar MOTOORI NORINAGA, who wrote that "of all the scoundrels who have led posterity into error, this Tsuneyori is the worst." In fact, the "secrets" were trivial, and the whole ritual was intended to convey to its recipient a kind of legal status as a "legitimate" poet and authority on classical poetic tradition. The blame lies more with the age than with any one individual, classical poetry for many years before the time of Tsuneyori having come to be regarded as a kind of hereditary property. However that may be, it was a sign of the changed times that the aged warrior Tsuneyori went to Kyōto in 1480 to teach classical poetry to a court noble, the regent Fujiwara no Masaie, and to the shōgun Ashikaga Yoshihisa (1465–89)—a striking example of how a knowledge of the traditional arts and courtly accomplishments had passed from the hands of the Kyōto aristocrats to a member of the warrior class. In fact, Tsuneyori was virtually the only one during the turbulent times of the Ōnin War who had a knowledge of the "true tradition" of the Nijō poetic school. His transmission of such knowledge to the foremost *renga* poet Sōgi greatly enhanced his importance in the eyes of succeeding generations of literati.

Two collections of Tsuneyori's poems exist—one containing 400 poems, the other 165. In addition, he is noted for his commentaries on older poetry, particularly that of Fujiwara no Teika (FUJIWARA NO SADAIE; 1162–1241), and for other handbooks and treatises.   *Robert H.* BROWER

ton'ya → toiya

tō on

(the Tang [T'ang] pronunciation). One of the several varieties of *on* readings of Chinese characters (KANJI) as used in Japan. *On* readings are Japanese approximations of the way the characters were pronounced in Chinese, and for any one character there may be two or three possible *on* readings (reflecting the Chinese pronunciations of different periods and different regions). *Tō on* is a broad category that includes pronunciations introduced to Japan over several centuries after the Tang dynasty (618–907), and the *tō* (Tang) of the name is an epithet for China as a whole rather than a reference to the dynasty. These pronunciations are much closer to the pronunciation of modern Chinese than the earlier *kan on* (pronunciations introduced during the Tang dynasty) or the still older *go on.*

The earliest *tō on* are pronunciations introduced in relations with the Song (Sung) dynasty (960–1279) through the activities of Zen scholar monks; these are often distinguished as *sō on* (the Song pronunciation). The larger category of *tō on* includes the pronunciation (largely introduced by Zen monks) of Nanjing (Nanking) and the area south of the Yangzi (Yangtze) River during not only the Song but also the Yuan (1279–1368) and Ming (1368–1644) dynasties; it also includes pronunciations from Hangchou (Hangchow) and the surrounding Zhejiang (Chekiang) region that were introduced through official contact with China at the port of Nagasaki during the Edo period (1600–1868). Thus *tō on* represents a varied range of pronunciations, none of which, however, are from the north of China. *Tō on* pronunciations are found mostly in Zen technical terms and in a few names of Chinese customs, artifacts, etc of the above-mentioned periods. See ON READINGS.   YAMADA Toshio

Topaz Relocation Center

A wartime relocation facility for Japanese Americans, located near Delta, Millard County, Utah, in operation from 11 September 1942 until 31 October 1945. It held a maximum of 8,130 inmates at any one time; a total of 11,212 persons were confined there. Internees came from the San Francisco Bay area of California. See also JAPANESE AMERICANS, WARTIME RELOCATION OF; WAR RELOCATION AUTHORITY.

■ ——Leonard Arrington, *The Price of Prejudice: The Japanese-American Relocation Center in Utah during World War II* (2nd ed, 1979). Mine Okubo, *Citizen 13660* (2nd ed, 1979).

Roger DANIELS

Toppan Printing Co, Ltd

(Toppan Insatsu). A comprehensive printing company, Toppan was established in 1900 as a relief printer. It has an integrated production system, stretching from the design of printing-related products to finished products. It is the second largest printing company in Japan, after DAI NIPPON PRINTING CO, LTD. At its inception the company's business was limited to the printing of securities, books for publishers, and business forms; it then began the manufacture of paper containers, office equipment, wrapping material, and precision electronic components, expanding into a comprehensive printing company. It is known for its receptiveness to the development of new technology, products, and fields. It provides consulting assistance to client enterprises through the Toppan Idea Center. The company currently exports its technologies for relief printing, new gravure plate-making processes, the Toppan Multibottle for volatile resins, an automatic color correcting device known as the Toppan Image Conductor, and sterile medical wrapping material. Sales for the fiscal year ending May 1982 totaled ¥448 billion (US $1.9 billion), of which general printing work constituted 62 percent, publications 20 percent, paper containers 14 percent, and securities printing 4 percent. The company was capitalized at ¥20.6 billion (US $87 million) in the same year. The head office is in Tōkyō.

tops

(*koma*). For centuries the top has been a popular toy in Japan. Japanese tops, like their counterparts in other cultures, are made of wood, bamboo, seashell, metal, and so forth, and come in a variety of shapes and sizes. They are spun either by hand or by string.

Tops were introduced to Japan in the 8th century from China via Koma, the Japanese name for the Korean kingdom of Koguryŏ, hence the term *koma*. Originally tops were used as a form of entertainment at court functions or as a means of diversion by the nobility. By the 17th century the top had become a form of amusement for the common people and developed thereafter as a children's toy.

The shape of the Japanese top depends on the material used and the locale in which it is made. Many have holes cut or bored in them to produce a humming sound when spun. In this way they resemble the Western humming top. Among Japanese tops, the Hakata *koma*, produced in the Hakata region of Kyūshū, has been especially popular.

Saitō Ryōsuke

Topy Industries, Ltd

(Topii Kōgyō). A manufacturer of structural shaped steel, affiliated with the NIPPON STEEL CORPORATION, Topy Industries was established in 1934. It produces a variety of processed steel products such as section steel, steel plates, aluminum wheels, and components of construction machinery. It possesses high-quality technology for the rolling and shaping of special profile steel products such as rims, ring bars, and bulldozer components. It has established an import and sales company in the United States. Sales for the fiscal year ending March 1982 totaled ¥145.3 billion (US $603.6 million), and the company was capitalized at ¥6 billion (US $24.9 million). The head office is in Tōkyō.

toraijin → kikajin

Toranomon Incident

Assassination attempt on the life of the then prince regent Hirohito. On the morning of 27 December 1923, Namba Daisuke (1899–1924) made an indelible mark on the minds of Japanese officials and future historians by attempting to assassinate Prince Regent Hirohito, who was on his way to open the new Diet session. The incident took place at the Toranomon intersection in Tōkyō. Namba's regicidal attempt was primarily motivated by leftist ideology and a strong

desire to avenge the execution of KŌTOKU SHŪSUI, who had been implicated in the HIGH TREASON INCIDENT OF 1910.

Namba, who came from a distinguished family in Yamaguchi Prefecture, was for most of his short lifetime a loyal supporter of the imperial system and had even thought of pursuing a career in the army. Beginning in 1919, however, his political position changed as he attended leftist political lectures, participated in demonstrations to support the suffrage movement, and read newspaper accounts of the High Treason Incident. While it is difficult to say exactly what event or which piece of writing triggered Namba's drastic action, it seems that in 1921 an article by KAWAKAMI HAJIME, in which the self-sacrificing role of young Russian revolutionaries was stirringly portrayed, convinced Namba that the revolution had succeeded because of sacrifices made by dedicated terrorists. Finally, angered by the brutal slaying of Koreans and Japanese socialists and anarchists in the aftermath of the Great TŌKYŌ EARTHQUAKE OF 1923, he decided that it was time for direct action.

Namba hid in the crowd pressing into the intersection at Toranomon and fired at the prince regent. Namba's single shot into the regent's automobile missed its target but exploded like a powerful bomb in the midst of an already severely stressed society and officialdom. The stunned survivors of the earthquake were still living in the shambles caused by that devastating event; police and justice authorities were in the midst of the preliminary examination of suspected communists arrested throughout Japan and Korea in June, and rumors were circulating that the police had in custody a Korean anarchist who had plotted to kill the emperor and prince regent. Namba's assassination attempt and subsequent trial must be evaluated with these developments in the background.

Justice officials carefully investigated Namba's motives and announced to the public that he was insane; nevertheless, after a closed trial, he was sentenced to death on 13 November 1924 and executed two days later. During his trial, Namba insisted that he was a communist and that he had acted to avenge the unjust execution of Kōtoku Shūsui. The trial record, together with the results of an examination by professors at Tōkyō University Medical School, supports Namba's contention that his was a rational act inspired by leftist ideology. Comments made later by justice officials in support of new legislation to control people like Namba show that officials secretly held the view that Namba was rational. It may never be known why the government chose to declare Namba insane, but perhaps it was an effort to calm the people in the wake of the earthquake. Most Japanese would have accepted this explanation, since they could not have conceived of a rational person attacking the emperor.

Namba's act had serious political consequences: the new government of YAMAMOTO GONNOHYŌE took responsibility for the incident and resigned; other officials followed its example. Former Justice Minister HIRANUMA KIICHIRŌ, who was promoting antiradical legislation, reacted by pulling conservatives and ultranationalists together in a new organization called the KOKUHONSHA (National Foundations Society) for the purpose of enlightening the nation about dangerous foreign ideologies. Finally, the Toranomon Incident was cited by officials in the Justice and Home ministries as a compelling reason for the passage of the PEACE PRESERVATION LAW OF 1925.

■ ——Richard H. Mitchell, *Thought Control in Prewar Japan* (1976). Tanaka Tokihiko, "Toranomon jiken: Kōtaishi o sogeki shita Namba Daisuke," in Wagatsuma Sakae, *Nihon seiji saiban shi roku: Taishō* (1969).

Richard H. MITCHELL

Tōray Industries, Inc

(Tōre). Largest manufacturer of synthetic fibers in Japan; also produces plastics and chemicals. Established in 1926 as Tōyō Rayon Co, Ltd, to manufacture rayon, it was a subsidiary of MITSUI & CO, LTD, a major Japanese trading firm. The company assumed its present name in 1970 and is a member of the Mitsui group. In 1951 the company started nylon production with technology from E. I. DuPont de Nemours & Co of the United States. In 1957 it imported jointly with TEIJIN, LTD, technology for polyester production from Imperial Chemical Industries, Ltd, of the United Kingdom. In 1964 it started producing Toraylon, an acrylic fiber, using its own technology, and thus attained the capacity to produce the three key synthetic fibers. Production of rayon yarn and rayon staple were discontinued in 1963 and 1975, respectively. In 1969 a plant was built in Kawasaki to produce cyclohexane and para-xylene. Ecsaine, a synthetic suede, was developed in 1970, and production of carbon fibers began in 1971.

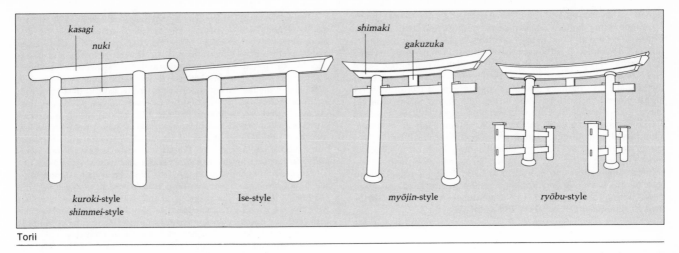

kasagi
nuki
shimaki
gakuzuka

kuroki-style
shimmei-style

Ise-style

myōjin-style

ryōbu-style

Torii

The company is a partner in 35 overseas ventures in 15 countries. Among its technology exports are polyester technology to the Soviet Union (1978), carbon fiber technology to Union Carbide Corporation of the United States (1978), plastic lens-coating technology to American Optical Co of the United States (1978), and ABS resin-manufacturing technology to Borg–Warner Corporation of the United States (1979). Future plans include expansion of plastics production and emphasis on specialty products. During the fiscal year which ended in March 1982 sales on an unconsolidated basis came to ¥556.8 billion (US $2.3 billion), of which synthetic fibers accounted for 73 percent, plastics for 17 percent, and others for 10 percent. In the same year export sales accounted for 28 percent of total sales. Tōray was capitalized at ¥57.4 billion (US $238.5 million) in 1982. The head office is in Tōkyō.

Toride

City in southern Ibaraki Prefecture, central Honshū. Situated on the river Tonegawa, Toride flourished from early times as a river port and POST-STATION TOWN. Industrial products include cameras, machinery, tools, and foodstuffs. Pop: 71,246.

torii

A gatelike structure placed at key points in a SHINTŌ shrine precinct or path leading to the shrine and functioning both as a gate marking the sacred space and as a symbol of the shrine. Since there is no established theory regarding its origin, the *torii* in its present form might best be considered indigenous to Japan. The *torii* at the secondary shrines of the ISE SHRINE, the *torii* in front of the main shrine at the Wakamiya of KASUGA SHRINE, and the tripartite *torii* (mitsudorii) at ŌMIWA SHRINE all have doors, and so it seems that the *torii* originally functioned as a gate indicating the place of worship.

Although the *torii* was originally made of wood, many have been made of stone since the Kamakura period (1185–1333). The basic structure of a *torii* is two columns, on top of which is placed a top rail (the *kasagi*); a little below the top rail is a second horizontal rail penetrating both columns (the *nuki*). When unbarked logs are used, it is called a *kuroki-* (black wood) style *torii*, which is considered to be the pristine, primitive form. Among *torii* built with barked logs, there is the *shimmei*-style *torii* with a log for the top rail and a second rail that penetrates but does not protrude beyond the columns. There is also the Ise-style *torii* with a pentagonal top rail and a second rail that also does not protrude beyond the columns. The above-mentioned *torii* use straight members with no curves.

Although there are variations, the style of *torii* most often seen today is the *myōjin*-style. Its columns lean somewhat inward from the bases, the top rail curves gently upward toward the ends, and below the top rail there is a secondary top rail called a *shimaki*. Between this and the second rail (*nuki*)—at the center of both—is placed a vertical strut (*gakuzuka*), on which is hung a tablet (*gaku*) with the name of the shrine.

The next most common style after the *myōjin* is the *ryōbu*-style. As its other name, *yotsuashi* (four-legged style), indicates, there are four posts located in the front and back of the columns, to which they are tied by penetrating horizontal ties. The *yotsuashi torii* at

the ITSUKUSHIMA SHRINE is the best known of this style.

Itō Nobuo

Torii Kiyohiro (fl 1751–1763)

Torii-school printmaker. Little is known of his life. His date of birth is unrecorded in contemporary records but he is believed to have died young. Guesses as to Kiyohiro's teachers include TORII KIYONOBU II, TORII KIYOMASU II, and TORII KIYOMITSU I. Since the *Torii ga keifu* (a Torii family record) reports Kiyohiro's presence in the Torii atelier in 1763, it seems certain that officially he was still a pupil of Kiyomasu II, who died in the same year. He seems to have been most strongly influenced by Kiyomitsu, the third titular head of the Torii school. Kiyohiro's art reveals a dependence on that of Kiyomitsu, and on that of his contemporary, ISHIKAWA TOYONOBU. His special genius was in the freshness of his compositions and the youthful character of his designs. He was also a master of *abuna-e* (risqué pictures) and illustrated several novelettes. He worked in either two-block or three-block color prints. A classic example of Kiyohiro's work, which dates to 1754, is a large two-color print showing the KABUKI actors Onoe Kikugorō I (see ONOE KIKUGORŌ) and Bandō Hikosaburō II painting the gentle figure of the actor Segawa Kikunojō I on a standing screen. *Howard A. LINK*

Torii Kiyomasu I (fl 1697–mid-1720s)

Torii-school printmaker who specialized in Edo KABUKI theatrical prints. Aside from the same surname, no firm genealogical connection has ever been proven between TORII KIYONOBU I, the founder of the Torii school, and Kiyomasu I. According to one theory these artists are one and the same person; according to other theories Kiyomasu is a brother or son of Kiyonobu. It is possible that Kiyomasu and his namesake, TORII KIYOMASU II, originally represented a branch of the Torii family in Edo (now Tōkyō), distinct from the Ōsaka–Kyōto branch headed by Kiyonobu and his father. This theory is given support by the recent discovery of the veteran Edo artist Torii Kiyotaka, who possibly headed the Edo Torii school.

The absence of either the Kiyotaka or Kiyomasu name in the earliest Torii genealogy devoted to the Kiyonobu lineage, as well as significant differences of regional character in Kiyonobu and Kiyomasu's primary art styles, offers additional support to the theory of the two branches of the Torii school. Moreover, two separate tombstones, one for Kiyonobu and his lineage, and one for Kiyomasu and his lineage, with different family crests on each, were recorded by the *ukiyo-e* scholar Inoue Kazuo in 1923; the tombstones were destroyed, a few months after Inoue had seen them, in the Great Tōkyō Earthquake of 1923. The dates on the tombstone reserved for Kiyomasu provide evidence that there must have been a second artist who used this name, a master of lesser talent who apparently married into the Kiyonobu branch in 1724. The identity of the first Kiyomasu, however, remains uncertain, though it is known that he occasionally signed his name "Torii *uji* [family] Kiyomasu," suggesting that he held a ranking position in the Edo branch of the Torii school.

No signed and dated illustrated books or SHUNGA (erotic picture) albums by Kiyomasu I are known to have survived. The earliest signed art by Kiyomasu I is a small group of single-sheet prints commemorating kabuki performances, dating from 1697 to 1704. These prints are all done in the bravura style reserved for the depiction of Edo actors. It is thought that Kiyomasu I may have invented this heroic form, which features the "wiggling-worm line" and "gourd-shaped legs" that were to become two of the hallmarks of the school's art. Perhaps the most important print from this early group, colored in swashbuckling orange-red, yellow, subdued olive-green, and pale blue, is a print showing the actors Ichikawa Danjūrō I and Yamanaka Heikurō in the act of ripping apart an elephant. This magnificent design, signed and sealed Kiyomasu, can be securely dated to 1701. In later years his style took on a softened, more elegant quality. His output was large, and along with hand-colored single sheets he is known to have designed playbills and EMA (votive pictures). In addition, a number of unsigned illustrated books dating from 1697 to 1710 contain illustrations recently attributed to Kiyomasu I in collaboration with Kiyonobu I.

Howard A. LINK

Torii Kiyomasu II (1706–1763)

Torii-school printmaker specializing in Edo KABUKI theatrical prints. Possibly the second titular head of the Torii school. Some critics believe that Kiyomasu II and TORII KIYONOBU II are the same person, but this theory does not conform with genealogical or artistic evidence. Art historian Inoue Kazuo suggests that Kiyomasu II was adopted as a *muko yōshi* (son-in-law legally adopted into his wife's family) by TORII KIYONOBU I upon marrying his eldest daughter in 1724. His association with his namesake, TORII KIYOMASU I, is uncertain, but he may have originally been part of the Edo branch of the Torii school prior to his marital adoption in 1724. He began work in the mid-1720s designing picture books, one in collaboration with Kiyonobu II. His large output also included hand-colored prints of actors and in later years, two-color block prints. His work is rather uneven, particularly in the hard lines of these later prints, but his earlier prints are very fine in a quiet, subdued way. He had many pupils working in the atelier at the time of his death, including his son TORII KIYOMITSU I, who was to become the third titular head of the school, Kiyohiro (fl 1751–63), Kiyoharu (fl 1700–1730), Kiyotsune (fl 1750s–70s), and Kiyohide (fl ca 1750).   *Howard A. LINK*

Torii Kiyomitsu I (1735–1785)

Torii-school painter and printmaker who specialized in Edo KABUKI actor prints. The third titular head of the Torii school. Born in Edo (now Tōkyō) at Naniwachō, he studied *ukiyo-e* under his father, TORII KIYOMASU II. Kiyomitsu produced actor pictures, kabuki placards, and kabuki posters for the Edo stage. In this work he followed the traditional style of the Torii school. He also designed a variety of illustrated books from the 1760s to the 1780s. Most of his single-sheet prints were done during the period 1740 to 1765. Toward the end of this period, he began to produce single sheets utilizing four or more colors printed from blocks, presaging the magnificent full-color prints of Suzuki HARUNOBU in 1765. Between these experiments, he is said to have been the originator of the so-called *tashokuzuri* (polychrome print), though this is not precisely correct since the color harmony of his art belongs to the traditional age of *ukiyo-e* rather than to the new, elaborate full-color palette of the 1760s. For example, the small portrait of the female impersonator Segawa Kikunojō I, from a play given in 1768, utilizes five printed colors, yet the color harmonies do not fully reflect the new polychrome tradition commercially introduced three years earlier. His artistic style is somewhat stiff and prosaic; Kiyomitsu's talent did not lie in invention. At his best, however, he produced some unexpectedly satisfying designs. His output was great and he had a number of pupils including young TORII KIYONAGA, Kiyochika, Kiyohisa, Kiyohiro, and Kiyotsune, who also studied under Kiyomasu II.   *Howard A. LINK*

Torii Kiyonaga (1752–1815)

Torii-school print designer and painter. Fourth titular head of the Torii school and last major Torii artist. His origin is uncertain but he may have been the son of a bookseller. In the early years of the Meiwa era (1764–72) he became a pupil of TORII KIYOMITSU I, the third titular head of the Torii school.

The earliest surviving works by Kiyonaga date from 1770 and are clearly signed Torii Kiyonaga. His period of activity extended over more than 40 years to 1815. More than one thousand works—color prints, picture-book illustrations, EMA (votive pictures), and paintings by this gifted master—survive and can be divided into three distinct periods. The first period, from approximately 1770 until 1780, is confined chiefly to actor prints of the KABUKI theater as well as illustrated books. He signed his full name, Torii Kiyonaga, during this period. From around 1775 to 1780 he turned out at least 25 illustrated books in 65 volumes. His style of actor prints during this formative period follows that of his mentor, Kiyomitsu. His illustrated books show traces of the style of Suzuki HARUNOBU, with added influence from KITAO SHIGEMASA and ISODA KORYŪSAI.

During his second period, 1781 to 1785, he usually signed himself Seki Kiyonaga. This was the period in which he developed the "Kiyonaga beauty"—the portraits of full, statuesque women, which were to be a strong influence on all artists of the last 15 years of the 18th century. Salient characteristics from this time can be seen in his diptych print *New Year's Scene at Nihombashi*, showing a procession of gaily clad townspeople crossing this famous bridge. Kiyonaga's impeccable space disposition, the subtly varied position of the figures, and the breadth of the background landscape produce an exceptionally satisfying design. At least 66 of his illustrated books, in 176 volumes, are known to survive from this period. Around 1787 Kiyonaga is said to have given up illustrating beautiful women in favor of actor pictures in order to fulfill his duty as fourth titular head of the Torii school. He also devoted his attention to the future of the fifth titular head of the school, the young Torii Kiyomine. Between 10 and 20 actor pictures survive from this last period as well as three *ehon banzuke* (illustrated souvenir booklets of kabuki performances) and a few illustrated books, some of humorous verse.

After 1800 his career seems to have faded. The art of Kiyonaga at its best reveals the perfect blending of the Torii vitality with the grace of such artists as Harunobu and NISHIKAWA SUKENOBU. The result is a kind of sheer perfection that is immediately disarming, if a shade remote. Kiyonaga's art was part of a trend toward realism: there is in his actor studies an interest in portraiture, and in his depictions of women he employed Western perspective in rendering background and landscape.

▬▬ Muneshige Narazaki, *Kiyonaga*, tr John Bester (1969).

Howard A. LINK

Torii Kiyonobu I (1664?–1729)

Ukiyo-e painter and printmaker who specialized in illustrations for the Edo KABUKI stage from 1697 to around 1727; traditional founder of the TORII SCHOOL. He was the son of Torii Kiyomoto (1645?–1702), a former actor who turned to sign painting for kabuki theaters. According to the *Torii ga keifu* (a Torii family record), he was born in Ōsaka in 1664, moved to Edo (now Tōkyō) with his father in 1687, and settled at Nambachō.

His earliest surviving woodblock works—two signed, illustrated books dated 1697—reveal the strong influence of Hishikawa MORONOBU and his decadent contemporary SUGIMURA JIHEI. The prints and illustrated books dated from 1698 onward and attributed to him consist largely of scenes from plays and of depictions of actors, probably stimulated by the Torii family tradition of painting kabuki posters (*kamban-e*). His theatrical depictions, for the most part decorative and curvilinear in style, no doubt derived from the more polished and elegant acting tradition of the Ōsaka–Kyōto region. His figures were round and full and drawn with a heavy curvilinear line, like that used in poster paintings. His work lacked the calligraphic virtuosity of his enigmatic contemporary, TORII KIYOMASU I, whose bravura style more closely suited the rough acting tradition of Edo. He is said to have also studied under Torii Kiyotaka, a veteran Torii artist of the Edo kabuki theater.

His signed masterpieces include two *orihon* (folding albums): *Fūryū yomo byōbu*, two volumes of illustrations of actors of the past and present, and *Keisei ehon*, a book of courtesan portraits, both published in 1700. Kiyonobu's depiction of kabuki actors is quiet and decorative. Two copies of the *Fūryū yomo byōbu* survive, one at the Museum of Fine Arts, Boston, and the other at the Riccar Art Museum, Tōkyō. The only surviving copy of *Keisei ehon* is owned by the Art Institute of Chicago. Also surviving are at least three SHUNGA (erotic picture) albums, in various states of completeness, published between 1700 and 1711, and 25 signed, single-sheet prints depicting leading actors of the day published between 1698 and 1727. As founder of the Torii school, he is said to have had a large following, which included TORII KIYONOBU II, TORII KIYOMASU II, Torii Kiyotada (active 1720s–40s), Torii Kiyoshige (active late 1720s–early 1760s), and Torii Kiyomoto (active 1720s–40s). A number of other artists were influenced by his persuasive style, including OKUMURA MASANOBU, Nishimura Shigenaga (ca 1697–1756), Kondō Kiyoharu (active 1704–20), and Hanekawa Chinchō (1679–1754). The KAIGETSUDŌ SCHOOL artists were directly influenced by his illustrated book *Keisei ehon*.   Howard A. LINK

Torii Kiyonobu II (fl 1725–ca 1760)

Torii-school printmaker who specialized in Edo KABUKI actor prints. According to one persistent theory, Kiyonobu II is the same artist as TORII KIYOMASU II. A more likely theory suggests that he was a son of TORII KIYONOBU I, who adopted the name upon his father's retirement in 1727 or death in 1729. The scholar Inoue Kazuo suggests that he died in 1752. If so, still a third artist utilizing the name Kiyonobu must be presumed, since prints dating from as late as 1760 and signed Kiyonobu survive. Kiyonobu II is known to have collaborated on a picture book with Kiyomasu II some time in the mid-1720s, proof that there were two independent artists. He produced a number of single-sheet prints of actors and theatrical scenes, hand-painted or printed from two blocks. Many of his compositions are banal and uninteresting, which perhaps accounts for the fact that he did not become the second titular head of the Torii school. One good surviving example of his work is a small, hand-colored print showing Ichikawa Danjūrō II as Soga no Jūrō Sukenari in a 1733 play. Although finely designed and executed, this work still lacks the strength of the first Kiyonobu's powerful compositions or the tour de force of the first Kiyomasu's bravura style.

Howard A. LINK

Torii Pass

(Torii Tōge). Located between the valley KISODANI and the Matsumoto Basin, western Nagano Prefecture, central Honshū. It forms a watershed for both the Sea of Japan side and the Pacific side. It was well traveled in ancient days as a pass on the highway NAKASENDŌ. Altitude: 1,197 m (3,902 ft).

Torii Ryūzō (1870–1953)

Archaeologist; anthropologist. Born in what is now Tokushima Prefecture. Interested in anthropology, archaeology, and history from an early age, Torii became a pupil of noted anthropologist TSUBOI SHŌGORŌ in 1892; he subsequently became a specimen classifier in the anthropology department of the College of Science at Tōkyō University. Though Torii did not receive a formal college education (he was a self-taught anthropologist), he went on to become head of the anthropology department at Tōkyō University. He was appointed assistant professor at the university in 1921 and later held professorships at Kokugakuin and Sophia universities. His approach to anthropological research emphasized not only the study of archaeological remains and artifacts but in-depth research into the lives of the various races inhabiting East Asia; his studies covered a wide range of fields including anthropology, folklore, and linguistics. Between 1895 and 1910, Torii led research expeditions to the Liaodong (Liaotung) Peninsula, the Yalu Basin, Taiwan, the Kuril Islands, Manchuria, Okinawa, Mongolia, Korea, and Sakhalin. He made more than 20 research trips to Korea and extensively surveyed ancient tumuli in the Nangnang district of P'yŏngyang. During his later years he engaged in studies of the culture of the Liao (916–1125) and Jin (Chin; 1125–1234) dynasties. He began delving into the cultures of the Jōmon (ca 10,000 BC–ca 300 BC) and Yayoi (ca 300 BC–ca AD 300) periods of Japan from around 1917 and wrote numerous treatises on these two periods, including *Suwashi* (1924, History of Suwa) and *Yūshi izen no Nippon* (1925, Prehistoric Japan). In 1939 Torii was invited by Yanjing (Yenching) University in Beiping (Peiping; now Beijing or Peking) to become a visiting professor. He returned to Japan in 1951 and died in Tōkyō in 1953.

Torii school

School of UKIYO-E print designers. The tradition of designing theatrical billboards, programs, illustrated books, and prints for the Edo (now Tōkyō) KABUKI stage was a monopoly of the Torii school for over half of the 18th century. Beginning in the latter part of the Genroku era (1688–1704), the Torii family of artists established a standard in the representation of kabuki subject matter that was to influence *ukiyo-e* for decades to come.

TORII KIYONOBU I (1664?–1729) has traditionally been regarded as the founder of the school, but research in recent years has shown that at least two artists using the Torii name preceded him. Torii Kiyomoto (1645?–1702), Kiyonobu's father, is designated in the *Torii ga keifu*, a family record written down in the Meiji period (1868–1912), as an Ōsaka actor-artist who moved to Edo with his family in 1687. He set up residence in Nambachō and in 1692 began to design *kamban-e* (theatrical posters) for the Ichimuraza, one of the three officially licensed kabuki theaters in Edo.

Recent research has also uncovered the artist Torii Kiyotaka. This recondite master, although not listed in the *Torii ga keifu*, is mentioned in another book, the *Fūryū kagami ga ike* (1709), as being a teacher of Kiyonobu I and the "veteran artist" of the Torii school. Recent speculation suggests that he may have been part of an independent branch of the Torii family at work in Edo before Torii Kiyomoto and his son Kiyonobu I came to Edo from Ōsaka.

TORII KIYOMASU I may have descended from this Edo branch of the family, for he was fully contemporary with the first Kiyonobu, yet there is no mention of his name in the family records.

Kiyonobu I is regarded as the first titular head of the Torii school. The second titular head of the school is a matter of dispute. Following Kiyonobu's death in 1729, a second artist of the school adopted the name Kiyonobu (see TORII KIYONOBU II), but he did not receive the titular mantle of the school. Other sources and a tombstone inscription suggest that TORII KIYOMASU II, Kiyonobu's son-in-law, received this honor.

The third titular head of the school was TORII KIYOMITSU I, the son of Kiyomasu II. Unfortunately, this third great master's own son, Kiyohide, who showed great artistic promise from an early age, died in 1772. In order to assure a successor in the Torii school, Kiyomitsu gave his son-in-law, an artist of little talent, the artistic name Kiyohide and devoted a great deal of energy to his artistic education.

Following Kiyomitsu's death in 1785, the members of the atelier, represented by Kiyotsugu, Kiyotoki, Kiyokatsu, and Kiyosaka, decided to take TORII KIYONAGA, one of Kiyomitsu's best students, as their teacher. The theater owners also asked Kiyonaga to take over the position of head of the school, despite the fact that Kiyomitsu's son-in-law had a stronger claim. It was not until 1788 that Kiyonaga officially became the fourth titular head of the school, when Kiyomitsu's daughter, Ei, gave birth to a long-awaited male heir, Shōnosuke, who was to become known as Kiyomine. This artist eventually became the fifth head of the Torii school when he assumed the name Kiyomitsu II. Kiyomitsu II died in 1868, the year of the Meiji Restoration. The Torii family of artists has continued down to the present day.

——Laurance Binyon and J. J. O'Brien Sexton, *Japanese Colour Prints* (rev ed, 1960). Margaret O. Gentles, *The Clarence Buckingham Collection of Japanese Prints* (1965). Chie Hirano, *Kiyonaga, A Study of His Life and Works* (1939). Inoue Kazuo, *Torii Kiyonobu to Torii Kiyomasu*, vol 5 of *Ukiyo-e no kenkyū* (1923). Donald Jenkins, *Ukiyo-e Prints and Paintings: The Primitive Period 1680–1745. An Exhibition in Memory of Margaret O. Gentles* (1971). Howard A. Link, "Speculations on the Genealogy of the Torii Masters," in *Ukiyo-e Art* (1972). Howard A. Link, *The Theatrical Prints of the Torii Masters* (1978). Muneshige Narazaki, *Kiyonaga*, tr John Bester (1969).   Howard A. LINK

Torii Shinjirō (1879–1962)

Industrialist. Founder of SUNTORY, LTD. Born in Ōsaka. After a period of apprenticeship, Torii established Torii Shōten, the forerunner of Suntory, in 1899. Based on his success in producing Akadama port wine in 1907, Torii devoted his efforts to the domestic production of whiskey; he started marketing whiskey under the Suntory brand in 1929. After World War II, with the appearance of Torys, an inexpensive whiskey developed by the firm, Torii's position as leader of the Japanese whiskey industry became indisputable. In the true spirit of an Ōsaka merchant, however, he never wavered from his "customers first" policy. He also devoted one-third of the company's profits to social projects.   KATSURA Yoshio

Torii Sosen (1867–1928)

Journalist. Born in Kumamoto Prefecture; real name Torii Teruo. Studied at the Doitsu Kyōkai Gakkō in Tōkyō. In 1889, after a study tour in China, he joined the staff of NIHON, a newspaper noted for its nationalistic outlook, and became known for his trenchant criticisms of government policy. In 1897 he changed to the newspaper *Ōsaka asahi shimbun*. His editorials were influential in promoting various democratic movements in the Taishō period (1912–26). For this he earned the opprobrium of the government, and in 1918 he was accused by the TERAUCHI MASATAKE cabinet of having violated the PRESS LAW OF 1909 and was forced to resign (see ŌSAKA ASAHI HIKKA INCIDENT). In 1918, along with other staff members who had also left, he started the newspaper *Taishō nichinichi shimbun*. In the face of obstruction by the *Asahi shimbun* and the *Mainichi shimbun*, another Ōsaka newspaper, it soon collapsed, and Torii withdrew from journalism.   *Kōuchi Saburō*

Torii Yōzō (1804–1874)

City commissioner (MACHI BUGYŌ) of the city of Edo (now Tōkyō) from 1841 to 1844. Major architect of the BANSHA NO GOKU, the shogunate crackdown on scholars of WESTERN LEARNING in 1839. The second son of the Confucian scholar HAYASHI JUSSAI, he was adopted into the Torii family. Yōzō was appointed to the shogunate post of METSUKE (inspector) in 1837, and in that year he dealt effectively but harshly with an uprising in Ōsaka caused by a rice shortage (see TEMPŌ FAMINE; ŌSHIO HEIHACHIRŌ). Two years later, in the BANSHA NO GOKU incident, he had 26 members of the SHŌSHIKAI, a study group of concerned scholars and intellectuals of Western learning, arrested on the charge of criticism of shogunate policy and conspiracy to go abroad. Before his fall from political power in 1844, Yōzō also played a major role in the TEMPŌ REFORMS, a drastic economic reform carried out by the shogunate government during the early 1840s.

Torikaebaya monogatari

A court narrative of the latter part of the Heian period (794–1185) whose extant texts are revisions from the early part of the Kamakura period (1185–1333). The author's identity is unknown, but the work is certain to have been written by a lady familiar with court life. Critical essays of the 13th century allude to the established reputation of both old and new versions.

The overlying theme of *Torikaebaya monogatari* (roughly, A Tale of Changing Roles) is misappropriation of the parental role in ensuring the education of one's children to acceptable social roles. Yet throughout this work runs a secondary theme of yearning for a communion in marriage based less on sexual roles than on companionship. As his two children reach maturity, a court minister decides to allow his strident and loquacious daughter to be initiated to court life with all the rank, role, and public responsibility of a man. This he considers a matter of destiny as well as retribution. Likewise, his son, who has evinced unmistakable affinities for the feminine sequestered role, is allowed to be taken into palace service as lady companion to the heir apparent (who is in this case a girl, there being no suitable male prince). Both children marry in their adopted social roles, which in the daughter's case creates inevitable difficulties. Misappropriation of the parental role is resolved when the children restore themselves to the social roles appropriate to their sex; after a brief interlude in seclusion at a temple, each finds greater happiness in the life begun by the other. The daughter's marriage is dwelt on at length. Dialogue in these portions stresses companionship rather than sexual pairing as a lost ideal of the marriage relationship. Following the final switch, large families accrue to each, and all ends in conviviality.   *Kenneth L. RICHARD*

tori no ichi

(festival of the rooster). A festival held on the days of the rooster (*tori*; see JIKKAN JŪNISHI) in November at various Shintō shrines of the type called Ōtori shrines. The festival is also called *otorisama* and *tori no machi*. The first "day of the rooster," in the month (the day recurs in 12-day cycles) is called *ichi no tori*, the second *ni no tori*, and the third, if there is one that year, *san no tori*. It is thought that there will be many fires in a year that has a *san no tori*. The headquarters of the various Ōtori shrines is in the city of Sakai in Ōsaka Prefecture. There are also many related branch shrines in the Tōkyō area, the one in the Asakusa district being especially popular.

The chief deity in these shrines was originally venerated by warriors as the god of success in war, but it later becomes the god of good luck in general (*tori* is a homophone for the verb "to fetch").

Tori no ichi

A stall selling *kumade*—rakes to "rake in" good fortune—during the annual *tori no ichi* at the Ōtori Shrine in Asakusa, Tōkyō. The actual shape of the large *kumade* held by the vendor is obscured by the many auspicious objects attached to it.

On the day of the festival, vendors line up on both sides of the street in front of the shrine, selling various charms such as *kumade* (rakes, to "rake in" fortune) decorated with imitation gold coins and the like.   *INOKUCHI Shōji*

Torishima

Volcanic island approximately 280 km (174 mi) south of Hachijōjima of the IZU ISLANDS. It is the southernmost island in the Izu Islands. It was settled in 1886, but the entire population was killed in a large volcanic eruption in 1902. A meteorological observatory was later established on the island; with the resumption of volcanic activity in 1965 the staff was evacuated and the island became uninhabited. It is known as the home of an albatross which is protected as an endangered species. Area: 4.5 sq km (1.7 sq mi).

Toro site

Archaeological site of the Late Yayoi period (ca AD 100–ca AD 300) located in marshland along the east bank of the river Abekawa in the Toro district of the city of Shizuoka, Shizuoka Prefecture; discovered in 1943. Excavations in 1947–50 yielded the remains of 12 surface dwellings surrounded by wooden stakes, two storehouses raised on poles, and more than 40 paddies demarcated by footpaths and extending over 10 hectares (24.7 acres). The dwellings were oval in floor plan, measured 7 to 12 meters (23 to 39 ft) in diameter, and had hearths in the center. An excavation in 1965 further revealed a primitive dam for irrigation. Recovered artifacts include YAYOI POTTERY; wooden household implements such as bowls, ladles, mallets, pestles *(kine)*, looms, and rice-paddy clogs (TAGETA); a bronze bracelet, glass beads, baskets, nets, and fishhooks made of bone. Rice and beans have also been found. These findings have enlarged our understanding of YAYOI CULTURE, and in particular the life of Japan's earliest agricultural people. See also KARAKO SITE.
■ ——Nihon Kōkogaku Kyōkai, ed, *Toro* (1954).   *ABE Gihei*

tortoises → turtles

tortoiseshell ware

(*bekkō-zaiku*). Handcrafted items made from the shells of tropical and subtropical tortoises. The best shells, found in the Celebes and New Guinea, tend to be light brown and semitransparent. Japanese tortoiseshell has, in the past, been harvested in the seas off Nagasaki and Kagoshima prefectures and Okinawa; today it is mostly imported.

Although *bekkō* is sometimes used without modification, it is often processed into uniform thickness and pieced together into the desired shape or design. The pieces are soaked in water for softening, layered, then shaped over wet wood and pressed between metal iron molds heated to between 100 and 150°C (212°-304°F). It can also be softened by heat before being molded into shape. These techniques are uniquely Japanese.

The 8th-century SHŌSŌIN art repository at Nara houses some examples of tortoiseshell ware, including a BIWA (a lutelike musical instrument) with transparent *bekkō* as a covering over MOTHER-OF-PEARL INLAY, a design popular in the Nara period (710–794). As a substitute for tortoiseshell, horses' hooves were apparently also used at this time.

Tortoiseshell ware was very popular in Japan during the 17th and 18th centuries, especially for hair ornaments (see KANZASHI). More recently, tortoiseshell has been used for eyeglass frames, barrettes, pipes, buckles, cufflinks, necklaces, and earrings. The chief production center for Japanese tortoiseshell ware is Nagasaki.

NAKASATO Toshikatsu

torts

(fuhō kōi). The body of private law defining the scope of a person's legal interests protected from unjustified interference by others and granting the injured person a right to compensation from the person responsible for the harm. Articles 709–725 of Japan's CIVIL CODE deal with torts and have remained unchanged since the code's promulgation in 1898. Judicial interpretation of their content, however, especially of articles 709 and 710, which provide the basis of tort doctrine, has undergone considerable development since the 1920s, development which accelerated in the 1970s because of the increase in environmental tort litigation.

Simply stated, there are three elements of tort liability in Japan today: substantial injury to a protected interest; proof of the defendant's intent or negligence; and legal causation. Although there has been a significant relaxation of the requirements for proof of negligence and of causation in recent environmental cases (see ENVIRONMENTAL LAW), the major doctrinal developments in torts have been in the definition of protected interests. Initially, damage to a right explicitly recognized in the Civil Code, such as ownership, was considered required by the language of article 709. Then in a landmark case in the 1920s, the scope of tort law protection was expanded to include implied legal "interests" as well as explicit rights. The definition of bodily integrity as mentioned in article 710 has also recently been expanded to include a wide range of psychological and emotional concerns that go well beyond the initial restriction to physical health. Similarly, the courts have fashioned a right to privacy out of the article 710 inclusion of reputation as a protected interest, thereby expanding defamation actions significantly.

These doctrinal developments have contributed to an expansion of the role which private tort litigation plays in Japanese society beyond the resolution of personal injury cases. Questions of privacy now must be considered in literary and journalistic decisions, and tort litigation based on psychological as well as physical environmental concerns often successfully challenge public and private development efforts.

——Lawrence W. Beer, "Defamation, Privacy, and Freedom of Expression in Japan," *Law in Japan* 5.192 (1972). Ichirō Katō, "The Concerns of Japanese Tort Law Today," *Law in Japan* 1.79 (1967). Frank K. Upham, "After Minamata: Current Prospects and Problems in Japanese Environmental Litigation," *Ecology Law Quarterly* 8.2 (1979).

Frank K. UPHAM

Tosa

City in central Kōchi Prefecture, Shikoku. Takaoka, its central district, has long been known for its handmade Japanese paper *(washi).* Local products are rice, vegetables, rushes *(igusa;* used to cover *tatami* mats), bonito, and *katsuobushi* (dried bonito used as a soup stock). The city is served by the Japanese National Railways Dosan line. Pop: 31,677.

Tosa Bay

(Tosa Wan). Inlet of the Pacific Ocean, in southern Kōchi Prefecture, southern Shikoku. Extends from MUROTOZAKI, a cape in the east, to ASHIZURIMISAKI, a cape in the west. A major fishing area; major marine products are bonito and tuna. Ports along the bay include Muroto, Kōchi, Susaki, and Shimizu.

Tosa dog

(Tosa *inu).* The Japanese fighting dog, developed in Kōchi Prefecture (formerly Tosa Province) after the Meiji period (1868–1912). The breed was formed through cross-breedings between the indig-

enous big game hunting dogs and imported large breeds. Throughout history, DOGFIGHTING has been very popular in the Tosa area, as in the Akita area, and in order to increase body size and fighting ability the "bloods" of larger foreign breeds (bulldog, mastiff, Great Dane, etc) were introduced. The Tosa dog is a very powerful, mastifflike dog. A large, stout body, with pendulous ears and a slender, stretched tail typifies the breed. Coat hair is short. Coloring is brown, although the muzzle is generally more darkly colored. Its fighting instinct is very strong. Dogfighting, as historically developed in the Kōchi area, has very complex sporting rules. Depending on the fighting ability and weight of the dogs, they are divided into a number of ranks in much the same way as *sumō* wrestlers.

——Nagakura Yoshio, ed, *Nihonken* (1975). Takahisa H. et al, *Nihonken no kenkyū* (1938). Aiken no Tomo, ed, *Tosa inu shashin taikan* (1955).

Hiroshi SAKAMOTO

Tosaka Jun (1900–1945)

Educator and philosopher. Born in Tōkyō, he graduated from Kyōto University, where he studied philosophy. Early in his career he came under the influence of MIKI KIYOSHI, but he later turned from Miki's Neo-Kantianism to dialectical materialism, emphasizing the social responsibility of scholarship. In 1931 he joined the faculty of Hōsei University in Tōkyō; the following year he established the Association for the Study of Materialism (Yuibutsuron Kenkyūkai) to promote the scientific examination of social phenomena. In 1934 Tosaka was dismissed from his position at Hōsei University for allegedly harboring unsafe ideas. In his book *Kagakuron* (1935, On Science), he attempted to formulate a unitary philosophy that embraced the world of the natural and social sciences. He was arrested in 1938 under the PEACE PRESERVATION LAW OF 1925 (Chian Iji Hō) and died in prison just before the end of World War II.

Tosa mizuki

(winter, or flowering, hazel). *Corylopsis spicata.* A deciduous tree of the witch-hazel family (Hamamelidaceae) which grows wild in the limestone coast regions of Kōchi Prefecture (the old Tosa Province) in Shikoku and elsewhere. It is also grown in gardens as an ornamental. Height is about 2–3 meters (about 7–10 ft) and the branches grow thickly. The leaves are alternate, broad and oval. In spring the nearly stalkless flowers bloom in drooping clusters (racemes) before the leaves come out. The flowers are bell-shaped and creamy yellow with five spatulate petals and five red stamens inside. The wild Tosa *mizuki* is known as a characteristic plant of limestone areas.

Similar to the Tosa *mizuki* is the Hyūga *mizuki (C. pauciflora),* a deciduous shrub which grows wild in mountainous regions of central Honshū and is also cultivated as an ornamental. The branches are thin, the leaves small, and the flowers grow in clusters of two or three. The flower has almost no stalk and is a vivid yellow. See also WITCH HAZEL.

MATSUDA Osamu

Tosa nikki → Ki no Tsurayuki

Tosa school

School of painting that specialized in the native Japanese YAMATO-E style from the beginning of the 15th century to the end of the 19th century. Tosa-school painters worked primarily for the imperial court and specialized in courtly themes such as scenes from classical literature, especially the TALE OF GENJI. The typical Tosa style was characterized by a fine, delicate line, great attention to detail, lavish use of colors, and somewhat flat, decorative composition.

The Tosa family genealogy that was established in the Edo period (1600–1868) traces the lineage of the school to the 11th-century painter Fujiwara no Motomitsu. Motomitsu and his successors were alleged to belong to the so-called Kasuga school of painting, which upheld the native style and resisted Chinese influence. The Tosa family also claimed as its forbears such 12th-century artists as Fujiwara no Takayoshi and Tokiwa Mitsunaga, to whom were attributed the illustrated handscrolls GENJI MONOGATARI EMAKI and BAN DAINAGON EKOTOBA, respectively. The use of Tosa as a family name supposedly began in the early 13th century, when the court painter Fujiwara no Tsunetaka was appointed vice-governor of Tosa Province (now Kōchi Prefecture).

Actually, reliable historical evidence of the use of the name by a painter begins only in 1406, the date of a document that refers to the painter Fujiwara no Yukihiro as Tosa Shōgen; Shōgen was one of his offical titles, and Tosa referred to his position as governor of that province. Furthermore, on the *Yūzū nembutsu engi,* an illustrated Buddhist handscroll (1414; in the temple Seiryōji in Kyōto) the name of Tosa Yukihiro appears together with the names of five other artists who were probably his pupils—Rokkaku Jakusai, Awataguchi Takamitsu, Tosa Mitsukuni, Tosa Eishun, and Kasuga Yukihide.

Yukihiro's father Fujiwara no Yukimitsu had held the position of *edokoro azukari* (superintendent of the imperial painting bureau). Thereafter the post became virtually hereditary in the Tosa family. The family's prestige reached its height under Tosa Mitsunobu (1434–1525), who is traditionally classed with the semilegendary Mitsunaga and the later revivalist Tosa Mitsuoki (1617–91) as one of the "Three Brushes" responsible for the fame of the Tosa school. Mitsunobu's works include EMAKIMONO (illustrated handscrolls), Buddhist paintings, and portraits. He is especially well known for his *emaki,* including the *Seisuiji engi* (also known as *Kiyomizudera engi*) and *Seikōji engi* (Tōkyō National Museum); indeed, he is often regarded as the last noteworthy exponent of the *emakimono* tradition.

In the 16th century extensive interactions developed with the rising KANŌ SCHOOL. The Kanō style was based on Chinese-style ink painting but incorporated a decorative quality, often enhanced by the use of brilliant colors and gold, that is assumed to have been derived from the tradition of *yamato-e* as represented by the Tosa school. A generally accepted legend maintains that Mitsunobu's daughter married KANŌ MOTONOBU, who thereby inherited some of the Tosa family business. Motonobu is also said to have collaborated on a screen project with Mitsunobu's son Mitsushige (1496–ca 1559). A number of Kanō artists produced paintings of the literary subjects which were the specialty of the Tosa school, and these works show a strong Tosa influence.

Mitsushige was less able than his illustrious father, and the status of the Tosa family began to decline. A drastic blow to the family fortunes occurred in 1569, when Mitsushige's heir Mitsumoto was killed in battle. The leadership of the family and the position of *edokoro azukari* were inherited by the younger son or pupil, Mitsuyoshi (1539–1613). Somewhat later Mitsuyoshi fled the turbulent capital for the neutral port city of Sakai, where he eked out a living painting a variety of minor works, turning to BIRD-AND-FLOWER PAINTINGS as the demand for courtly subjects declined. The post of *edokoro azukari* passed to the Kanō family.

Mitsuyoshi's son Mitsunori (1583–1638) spent most of his life in Sakai, returning in his last years to paint fans for the imperial court. The revival of the Tosa school was brought about by Mitsunori's son Mitsuoki (1617–91), who moved back to Kyōto in 1634 and was appointed *edokoro azukari* in 1654. He specialized in elegant paintings of flowers and birds, particularly quails, and was much influenced by his study of Chinese paintings of this type.

Mitsuoki's descendents maintained their prominence at court throughout the Edo period, producing flower-and-bird paintings as well as paintings of traditional literary subjects. In their hands the Tosa style hardened into a highly formalized set of conventions featuring precise outlines filled in with strong, flat colors. More vigorous works were produced by artists of the SUMIYOSHI SCHOOL, a 17th-century offshoot of the Tosa school, who included contemporary genre scenes in their repertoire.

As the official repository of the *yamato-e* tradition the Tosa school exerted a wide influence on other schools of painting, especially during the Edo period. Perhaps the most interesting of these connections was the influence of the Tosa style on book illustrations and hence on UKIYO-E. During the 16th and early 17th centuries crude versions of the Tosa style were used extensively for the brightly painted, illustrated editions of native literature known as Nara *ehon.* Near the beginning of the 17th century, the *sagabon* printed editions of ISE MONOGATARI included woodcut illustrations in a Tosa-like style. Printed books were illustrated almost exclusively in this manner until the last quarter of the century, when artists like Hishikawa MORONOBU (d 1694) transformed the style into true *ukiyo-e* woodblock prints. *Sarah* THOMPSON

Tosa Shimizu

City in southern Kōchi Prefecture, Shikoku, on the Pacific Ocean. Most of the city is forested, but rice, tea, and vegetables are grown in the coastal areas. Its port is a base for deep-sea fishing. Attractions include ASHIZURIMISAKI, a cape in the ASHIZURI-UWAKAI NATIONAL PARK, and the scenic coasts of Tatsukushi and Monokoshi.

Tosa Shimizu is the birthplace of NAKAHAMA MANJIRŌ, the first Japanese to go to the United States. Pop: 24,253.

Tōseiha

("Control" faction). Army officers united by their opposition to General ARAKI SADAO and his policies as war minister from 1931 to 1934. Consisting of the UGAKI KAZUSHIGE faction and other army groups blocked from promotions by Araki and his KŌDŌHA faction, the Tōseiha was a nonregional coalition that opposed Araki's reintroduction of regional politics into army appointment and policy decisions. Many army officers associated with the Tōseiha were very promising graduates of the Army War College who strongly opposed Kōdōha policies that threatened to impede the mechanization of the army and integration of Manchuria into the Japanese economy. Lacking leadership, this coalition lasted only until TŌJŌ HIDEKI, MUTŌ AKIRA, and other members rose to power upon Araki's resignation in 1934. The term Tōseiha was actually a pejorative expression coined and used only by Kōdōha sympathizers.

■ ───James B. Crowley, "Japanese Army Factionalism in the Early 1930's," *Journal of Asian Studies* 21.3 (1962).

Toshiba Corporation

(Tōkyō Shibaura Denki). Large manufacturer of heavy electric machinery, home electric appliances, and industrial electronic and telecommunications equipment. It has production and sales bases throughout the world and is second only to HITACHI, LTD, in scale and sales proceeds among electric companies in Japan. Its forerunner was Shibaura Engineering Works Co, Ltd, established in 1904 for the manufacture of electric communications equipment and generators. After a 1939 merger with Tōkyō Electric Co, Ltd, which was producing light bulbs and other electric light equipment, it took its present name and grew into a comprehensive electric products manufacturer. It has long had close ties to General Electric Co of the United States and is affiliated with the Mitsui group. During the 1950s it grew as a result of the development of electric power generation and the tremendous rise in demand for home electric appliances. It expanded into the fields of atomic power, energy-related equipment, semiconductors, office automation, and electronic equipment for medical purposes. Tōshiba's technology for electricity generation is among the most sophisticated in the world, and the company sells facilities for hydroelectric, thermoelectric, geothermal, and atomic power generation throughout the world. It has successfully marketed multipurpose process computers; automation systems for the steel, electric power, and chemical industries; and circulation systems for airports, harbors, and railways. It is also active in overseas production and has color television production plants in the United States and the United Kingdom as well as a semiconductor plant in the United States. Tōshiba has a total of 23 overseas subsidiaries, and its products are sold overseas through 22 additional sales subsidiaries. Sales for the fiscal year ending March 1982 totaled ¥1.7 trillion (US $7.1 billion), of which heavy electric machinery constituted 39 percent, home electric appliances 33 percent, and industrial electronic equipment 28 percent. In the same year the export ratio was 28 percent and capitalization stood at ¥123.8 billion (US $514.3 million). The head office is in Kawasaki, Kanagawa Prefecture.

Tōshiba Machine Co, Ltd

(Tōshiba Kikai). Manufacturer of machine tools, machinery for the production of synthetic resins, and other industrial machinery. It was established in 1938 when the Tsurumi plant (Yokohama) of the Shibaura Engineering Works Co, Ltd (now the TŌSHIBA CORPORATION) became independent of its parent firm. It took its present name in 1961. It specializes in large tooling machines, particularly roll grinding machines, of which 50 percent is exported. The company has exported its products to the United States, Southeast Asia, and Europe. In recent years it has emphasized more the production of machine tools for the aircraft industry. It has a joint manufacturing venture in Taiwan and sales subsidiaries in the United States, Singapore, and Brazil. Sales for the fiscal year ending March 1982 totaled ¥94.4 billion (US $392.2 million); the export ratio was 26 percent. In the same year the company was capitalized at ¥6.7 billion (US $27.8 million), with 51 percent of the shares held by Tōshiba Corporation. The head office is in Tōkyō.

Tōshōdaiji——Main hall (kondō)

The hall dates from the latter half of the 8th century but was remodeled, with an altered roofline, during the Edo period. National Treasure.

toshigami

("god of the NEW YEAR," also called *wakamatsusama* or *wakatoshi-sama*, "lord of the New Year"). A type of deity invoked and welcomed at each household at the turn of the year. According to 19th-century philologist MOTOORI NORINAGA, in archaic Japanese *toshi* means "rice" as well as "calendar year," and this observance was part of an annual cycle of AGRICULTURAL RITES.

On New Year's Day the *toshigami* pays an annual visit to bring blessings to each family, promising a good crop to farmers, good business to merchants, a big catch to fishermen, and so forth. On New Year's Eve a male member of the family, often the head of the household, prepares himself for the divine visit, cleaning the house and setting up a special altar, shelf, or alcove adorned with pine and other evergreen branches as a temporary seat of the divine. He keeps vigil and after midnight goes out to retrieve new water from the well or visit a temple or shrine, according to various local customs. Traditional dishes are prepared on New Year's Eve and offered to the visiting deity on New Year's Day with *sake* (rice wine) and *mochi* (rice cakes), an indispensable part of this ritual throughout Japan. In eastern Japan, men are or were generally in charge of cooking during the first three days of the year. Images of the *toshigami* vary from those of an aged man and wife to that of a goddess, but most depict aged men and may represent the collective ancestral spirit of each family.   Kyōko Motomochi NAKAMURA

Tōshi kaden

(Biographies of the Fujiwara Family, *tō* being the alternate pronunciation for the Chinese characters *fuji* and *shi* meaning family); also known as *Kaden*. A two-section biography of three early members of the FUJIWARA FAMILY; compiled sometime around 760. The first section, written by FUJIWARA NO NAKAMARO, is an account of the life of his great-grandfather FUJIWARA NO KAMATARI, the first to be granted the surname (this section alone is called the *Taishokukan den*, from a common name for Kamatari). The second, by the priest Enkei, is a life of Kamatari's grandson Fujiwara no Muchimaro (680–737); and a variant version also includes the biography of Kamatari's son Jōe.   G. Cameron HURST III

Toshima

Volcanic island approximately 20 km (12 mi) south of the island of ŌSHIMA off the Izu Peninsula, central Honshū. Like Ōshima, Toshima is one of the Izu Islands and is under the administration of the Tōkyō prefectural government. Steep basalt cliffs descend to the coasts. The island's climate is warm, with strong winds and little precipitation. It is known for camellias. Area: 4.2 sq km (1.6 sq mi); circumference: 7 km (4 mi).

Toshima Ward

(Toshima Ku). One of the 23 wards of Tōkyō. During the Edo period (1600–1868), Toshima developed as a village on the Nakasendō (a major highway). Since World War II, it has grown rapidly and is now a commercial and residential area centered on Ikebukuro Station. With numerous wholesale and retail stores, Ikebukuro has become one of Tōkyō's major shopping centers. It is also a major center of transportation, with many bus, rail, and subway lines. Pop: 288,553.

toshi no ichi → year-end fair

Tōshin Steel Co, Ltd

(Tōshin Seikō). A shaped-steel manufacturer specializing in angles, deformed bars, and channels, this firm was established in 1950 when the material plant of the TŌSHIBA CORPORATION, the Tōshiba Steel Co, Ltd, became independent of its parent firm. In 1955 it concluded a raw material, product sales, and capital tie-up with NIPPON KŌKAN. In 1970 it merged with Nisshin Seikō Co, Ltd, an affiliate of Nippon Kōkan, to acquire a nationwide market share. In 1973 it merged with Harima Tekkō Co, Ltd, to complete the unification of Nippon Kōkan–affiliated electric furnace steelmakers. It has a joint manufacturing venture in Indonesia. Sales for the fiscal year ending March 1982 totaled ¥112.1 billion (US $465 million). In the same year the export ratio was 29 percent and capitalization stood at ¥3.6 billion (US $15 million). The head office is in Tōkyō.

toshiyori

(elders). A generic term of ancient usage, *toshiyori* (literally, "grown old") referred to the acknowledged senior members of social groups. Occasionally a group would have a single elder, but usually there were several, who acted as a collegial group. During the Muromachi period (1333–1568) the term was applied to some government officials, and during the Edo period (1600–1868) the title *toshiyori*, or variants thereof (such as RŌJŪ, WAKADOSHIYORI, and KARŌ), came to signify several regularized positions of great political authority. Elsewhere the term was used widely. In the shogunal household a group of elderly supervisory women were called *otoshiyori*. Supervisors of shogunate silver-minting operations *(ginza)*, as well as heads of many business groups, were known as *toshiyori*. In Edo (now Tōkyō), Ōsaka, and other towns important town officials were known as *machi-doshiyori*, and in many villages local officials were known as *toshiyori* (see MURA YAKUNIN).   Conrad TOTMAN

Tōshōdaiji

Buddhist monastery founded in 759 in the western sector of the ancient capital Nara by the Chinese monk Jianzhen (Chien-chen), who is known to the Japanese as GANJIN. Tōshōdaiji became the head temple of the RITSU SECT, which was responsible for the ordination of the Buddhist clergy during the latter half of the 8th century. Whereas other temples were destroyed by fires and civil wars, Tōshōdaiji remained relatively untouched, so that the layout of its main buildings preserves the atmosphere of an 8th-century temple compound. The Tōshōdaiji *kondō* (main hall) is the only hall of its kind extant from the Nara period (710–794). The three main images housed within, the Buddha Rushana (Skt: Vairocana) flanked to the left by the Buddha Yakushi (Skt: Bhaiṣajyaguru; the Buddha of healing) and to the right by Senju Kannon (Thousand-armed KANNON), are masterpieces of gilded lacquer sculpture made shortly after the temple was founded. The *kōdō* (lecture hall) was once an assembly hall *(chōshūden)* of the Imperial Palace in Nara which was dismantled and rebuilt at Tōshōdaiji in 760. Although somewhat reduced in size and remodeled during the 13th century, the *kōdō* remains basically an 8th-century secular structure, the only extant specimen of Nara palace architecture. The statues housed in the *kōdō* are invaluable for the study of the evolution of sculpture of the late Nara period.

The anniversary of Ganjin's death is celebrated yearly on 6 June in the *kōdō* and the *mieidō* (hall of the founder's image), where a statue of Ganjin is kept. This celebrated statue, made of hollow dry lacquer, depicts Ganjin, seated in meditation as a dignified abbot whose inner strength and determination are mixed with a saintly gentleness in his features. The eyes are closed in a way that indicates his blindness. The portrait was allegedly made by a disciple shortly before Ganjin's death in 763.

Two Japanese monks who had gone to China in 733 met Ganjin in 742 and invited him to come to Japan to teach the *vinaya* (the code of monastic discipline) and to conduct proper ordination ceremonies.

Ganjin accepted their invitation and in the following year set out on the dangerous journey to Japan accompanied by disciples, artists, sculptors, decorators, and others. During the period 743–748 they made five attempts to cross the ocean, all unsuccessful because of weather conditions, pirates, or shipwrecks. Some of the disciples drowned, and Ganjin became blind during the fifth attempt. Finally he was granted passage on a ship returning with the Japanese ambassador to China. Ganjin arrived in Nara in the spring of 754. At TŌDAIJI he administered the *bosatsukai* (precepts for Mahāyāna bodhisattvas) to some 400 persons, including members of the imperial family, and reordained 80 monks. There he also founded the *kaidan'in*, the hall containing the platform required by the Ritsu sect for proper ordination. After residing at Tōdaiji for five years, Ganjin was presented by the imperial family with a valuable plot of land, not far from YAKUSHIJI, where the residence of Prince Niitabe (d 735), a son of the emperor TEMMU, had stood. It was on this land that Ganjin built Tōshōdaiji, a monastery dedicated to the training of Ritsu monks. He moved there in 759, devoting the rest of his life to the monastery and to lecturing on monastic discipline. He also conducted prayers for the repose of the soul of Emperor SHŌMU and erected a new ordination platform at Tōshōdaiji by order of Empress KŌKEN, who received the bodhisattva precepts here, as did some 100 other officials, including the highest ministers of state. The monastery continued to prosper under the leadership of Ganjin's disciples with the help of imperial patronage. By the beginning of the Heian period (794–1185) Tōshōdaiji was considered one of the finest temples in Nara. However, the widespread popularity of the esoteric Buddhism of the TENDAI SECT and SHINGON SECT led to a decline in the fortunes of the Tōshōdaiji during the Heian period. Toward the end of the 12th century eminent monks began to appear who devoted themselves to revitalizing the Nara sects. Among them was Jōkei, also known as Gedatsu Shōnin (1155–1213), a scholar of the Ritsu and Hossō schools who became the 19th abbot of Tōshōdaiji. He converted a part of the *higashimuro* (eastern monks' quarters) into the *raidō* (worship hall) where he revived ancient ceremonies. His work was continued by Kakujō (1194–1249), who became abbot in 1244 and actively promoted the Ritsu sect. With the patronage of the shogunate, Kakujō carried out extensive repairs on the monastery.

The *kondō*, begun while Ganjin was still alive, reflects the architectural style of the late Nara period. It is a majestic single-storied building with a massive hipped roof and boldly overhanging eaves. The slopes of the roof, originally less steep, are topped by *shibi* or "hawk tail" roof ornaments fastened to both sides of the main ridge. The facade is preceded by a colonnade which sets off a deep porch. The wooden pillars are carefully spaced with the widest opening in the center and gradually narrowing spaces between the columns on either side. This device imparts a sense of stability to the building, reminiscent of the Parthenon, whose columns are also unevenly spaced. Aside from the aesthetically satisfying aspect, the spaces between the columns were calculated so that, when the original large doors were opened during services, the worshiper could see the golden images in the *kondō* from the outside.

The interior is dominated by the three giant images of the Buddha Rushana (Skt: Vairocana) and his attendants Yakushi and Senju Kannon placed on a stone platform altar. Between them stand the much smaller wooden figures of Bonten (Brahmā) and Taishakuten (Indra). The four corners of the dais are guarded by the Shitennō (the Four Heavenly Kings; see TEMBU). The image of Rushana, the all-pervading, central Buddha of the universe, who manifests himself in countless worlds in the form of Śākyamuni Buddha, is based on the description in the *Bommōkyō* (Skt: *Brahmajāla-sūtra*), the main sutra of the Ritsu school. The colossal image is seated on an eight-tiered lotus pedestal made of hollow dry lacquer (*dakkatsu kanshitsu*) covered with gold leaf. On each of the lotus petals is depicted a Śākyamuni Buddha. Other transformations of Rushana as Śākyamuni, nearly 1,000 in all, are represented on the mandorla in back of the image.

The Senju Kannon (about 5.35 m or 18 ft high), is a lacquer image with a wooden core (*mokushin kanshitsu*). Over 900 of its 1,000 arms are still intact. They radiate outward in all directions, graphically displaying the merciful character of Kannon, who reaches out into every sphere of human experience. Most of the arms are small and symbolic, but 38 of them are larger, holding sacred emblems such as swords, bows, and arrows to defeat the enemies of sentient beings and ropes that never fail to catch anyone led astray by illusions. Others hold lotuses, waterflasks, and disks of the sun and the moon as well as images of the Buddha and the

Tōshōgū

The Yōmeimon, the main gate at the Tōshōgū shrine in Nikkō. Known as one of the most elaborately decorated gates in Japan, this ceremonial gate has hip gables at the left and right and cusped gables on all four sides. Painted wood decorated with black lacquer and gold leaf. 1636. National Treasure.

dharma wheel. Ganjin worshiped the Senju Kannon, possibly because the image was believed to cure blindness. The NIHON RYŌIKI, an anthology of Buddhist legends compiled early in the 9th century, relates the story of a blind man who meditated on the hand holding the sun disk, which emits light continuously, until his vision was restored. The people of Nara were so overawed by the Senju Kannon in Tōshōdaiji that they believed it was made by a divine spirit in human form.

To the left of Rushana is the monumental statue of Yakushi, made of gilded dry lacquer over a wooden core like the Senju Kannon. Yakushi's identity has at times been questioned because he is conceived of here without his usual attribute: the medicine vessel. Both wood-core lacquer images are stiffer in posture than the hollow lacquer sculpture of Rushana, but stylistic differences between the attendant images indicate that the Yakushi was made slightly later than the Senju Kannon. Whereas the Nara naturalism that permeates the portrait of Ganjin is still apparent in the drapery of the Kannon as it falls in loops across the legs, in the statue of Yakushi the pleats are carefully arranged in vertical folds between the legs and on both sides of them. This formalism, emphasizing the firm roundness of the legs, first appeared at Tōshōdaiji and is known as the Tōshōdaiji style. Further examples of it are to be found in the sculptures of the *kōdō*. See also BUDDHIST SCULPTURE.

Lucie R. WEINSTEIN

Tōshōgū

Shintō shrine in the city of Nikkō, Tochigi Prefecture, dedicated primarily to the founder of the Tokugawa shogunate, TOKUGAWA IEYASU, and since 1873, to two other military figures, TOYOTOMI HIDEYOSHI and MINAMOTO NO YORITOMO. After Ieyasu's death, his remains were interred at first on Mt. Kunō (KUNŌZAN) in Shizuoka Prefecture. The following year, Ieyasu was posthumously deified as Tōshō Daigongen (The Great Incarnation Who Illuminates the East) by the imperial court. He was declared by the court to be a divinity of the first rank, and his remains were moved to their present site at Nikkō, where a shrine was established to house them. The present highly ornate shrine buildings and gateways were erected by the third Tokugawa shōgun, Iemitsu, in 1636. As the cult of the deified Ieyasu spread, more than 100 Tōshōgū shrines were built in other parts of Japan. The annual festival, now celebrated on 17 May, features a parade of parishioners dressed as warriors. See also FUTARAYAMA SHRINE.

Stanley WEINSTEIN

Tōshoku, Ltd

A company selling agricultural and marine products, sugar, grain oil, and feedstuff, Tōshoku was established as a result of the dissolution of the MITSUI *zaibatsu* in 1946 and uses the brand name Top Food. The company grew at an annual rate of more than 10 percent in the late 1970s. The volume of food products handled by the company was the largest in Japan in 1979. It has branches and subsidiaries in 20 cities around the world, including New York, London, and Singapore. It is currently conducting triangular trade and engaged in economic cooperation projects. Sales for the fiscal year ending October 1981 totaled ¥833 billion (US $3.6 billion), and capitalization stood at ¥4.8 billion (US $20.7 million). The head office is in Tōkyō.

Tōshūsai Sharaku → Sharaku

Tosu

City in eastern Saga Prefecture, Kyūshū. A former POST-STATION TOWN, Tosu is still an important transportation center. Foodstuffs, flour, tobacco, bicycles, household medicines, and tires are produced here. The mounded tomb *(kofun)* at Tashiro is noted for the colored designs on its chamber walls. Pop: 54,259.

tōsuiken

(power of supreme command, i.e., of the military). The authority to command and use the armed forces. Article 11 of the Meiji CONSTITUTION of 1889 states that "the Emperor has the supreme command of the Army and Navy," and until the end of World War II the dominant interpretation was that this power was to be exercised without the participation of the IMPERIAL DIET. It was maintained that the ARMY GENERAL STAFF OFFICE (established in 1878) and the NAVAL GENERAL STAFF OFFICE (separated from the former in 1893) were empowered, as the highest institutions of the military command, to "assist" the emperor in exercising his power of command and that neither the cabinet nor the Imperial Diet had the right to interfere. This principle, which was referred to as the independence of the supreme command, meant in effect that the army and navy were independent of the civilian government.

This independence was reinforced by the interpretation given to article 12 of the Meiji Constitution, which provides that "the Emperor determines the organization and peace standing [forces to be maintained in times of peace] of the Army and Navy." Although the understanding had been that these determinations would actually be made, under the emperor, by the cabinet—or more precisely by the Minister of the Army and Minister of the Navy as cabinet members—there was a strong feeling, particularly among the military, that such matters too were part of the power of the supreme command and beyond the authority of the cabinet.

At the time of the ratification of the London Naval Limitations Treaty signed on 22 April 1930 (see LONDON NAVAL CONFERENCES) there was a confrontation between the civil government and the Naval General Staff Office over the interpretation of the power of supreme command. A great outcry arose from the Naval General Staff when the cabinet of HAMAGUCHI OSACHI accepted the provision of the treaty retaining the capital-ship ratio of 5:5:3 from the WASHINGTON NAVAL TREATY OF 1922 and setting the ratio of smaller ships at 10:10:7 for the United States, Great Britain, and Japan, respectively. The Naval General Staff Office opposed the ratification of the treaty, insisting that this determination of the peace standing of the navy solely by the cabinet and without the approval of the Naval General Staff Office was an infringement on the power of supreme command. The PRIVY COUNCIL and the RIKKEN SEIYŪKAI party, the latter for purely political reasons, sided with the navy. Hamaguchi, however, withstood the mounting pressure from the navy and right-wing organizations. After a bitter struggle, the treaty was ratified by the Privy Council. In November 1930 Hamaguchi was shot by a nationalist; he died in August of the following year. In a larger sense the crisis set the stage for terrorist acts of succeeding years in which ultranationalist soldiers and civilians, frustrated in their plans for expansion abroad and reform at home, decided to take political action into their own hands. See OCTOBER INCIDENT; LEAGUE OF BLOOD INCIDENT; MAY 15TH INCIDENT.

Totoki Baigai (1749–1804)

BUNJINGA painter, poet, and calligrapher. Real name Totoki Shi. Born in Naniwa (now Ōsaka), Baigai received a Confucian education, studying the Chinese classics with the philosopher Itō Tōsho. He also studied privately with Chō Tōsai, a well-known calligrapher from Nagasaki. In 1784 Baigai was invited to Nagashima in Ise (now Mie Prefecture) by the art-loving *daimyō* Masuyama Sessai to serve as a resident Confucian scholar. He founded a domainal school of Confucian studies and was named its head. In 1790 he was granted permission by his lord to visit Nagasaki, but he overstayed his leave and lost his position with the Masuyama family. He subsequently retired to Ōsaka, where most of his dated paintings were done after 1792. Baigai remained active in scholarly circles and counted among his friends such painters as URAGAMI GYOKUDŌ, OKADA BEISANJIN, and Kimura Kenkadō (1736–1802).

Baigai's themes were primarily landscapes, and secondarily, the "four gentlemen" (SHIKUNSHI: bamboo, plum, orchid, and chrysanthemum). Freedom of brushwork is characteristic of his style, and in general Baigai seems to have been more interested in spontaneity than in technical perfection. As a result, his works are rather uneven in quality. An interesting feature in many of his paintings is that although his brushwork is rough, blunt, and straightforward, the overall mood of his compositions is quiet and restrained.

Pat FISTER

Tōtō, Ltd

(Tōtō Kiki). A manufacturing enterprise that controls 60 percent of the market for sanitary ceramic ware and metal fittings, Tōtō also produces bathtubs, washstands, toilet fixtures, and other sanitary equipment. It was established in 1917 when the Kokura plant (Fukuoka Prefecture) of NORITAKE CO, LTD, became independent of its parent firm. The company grew rapidly after World War II to meet the great demand for sanitary ceramic ware caused by a boom in housing and by a Westernization of the Japanese lifestyle. The company later began production of bathtubs and washstands and became a comprehensive manufacturer of housing equipment. It has a joint manufacturing venture in Indonesia. Sales for the fiscal year ending November 1981 totaled ¥135 billion (US $603.4 million), and capitalization stood at ¥13 billion (US $58.1 million) in the same year. The head office is in Kita Kyūshū, Fukuoka Prefecture.

Totoya Hokkei (1780–1850)

UKIYO-E artist; a follower of *ukiyo-e* master Katsushika HOKUSAI. A native of Edo (now Tōkyō), his real name was Iwakubo Tatsuyuki. Originally a fishmonger (Totoya literally means "fish shop"), he studied painting under Kanō Yōsen'in (1735–1808). He later became a pupil of Hokusai and moved to the Akasaka district in Edo, where he became a professional artist, mastering Hokusai's style in both prints and *ukiyo-e* paintings. In prints he specialized in SURIMONO and illustrations of comic verse (KYŌKA).

Anne Nishimura MORSE

Totsukawa

Village in southern Nara Prefecture, central Honshū, on the river Totsukawa. Mentioned in medieval military chronicles such as the HŌGEN MONOGATARI and the TAIHEIKI, Totsukawa was the base of the Southern Court during the dynastic schism of the period of Northern and Southern Courts (1336–92). It is now a sparsely populated mountain village, many of its residents having gone to Hokkaidō after a flood in 1889. There is a large lumbering industry. Totsukawa Hot Spring draws tourists. Pop: 6,628.

Totsukawa

River in southern Nara Prefecture, central Honshū, flowing south along the Kii Mountains and joining the river Kitayamagawa to form the KUMANOGAWA. It has carved deep gorges along its course, and dams have been constructed for electric power. There are cedar forests along the river and a flourishing lumber industry. Length: 141 km (88 mi); area of drainage basin: 996 sq km (384 sq mi).

Tottori

Capital of Tottori Prefecture, western Honshū. It developed as a castle town of the Ikeda family from the 17th century. Seriously

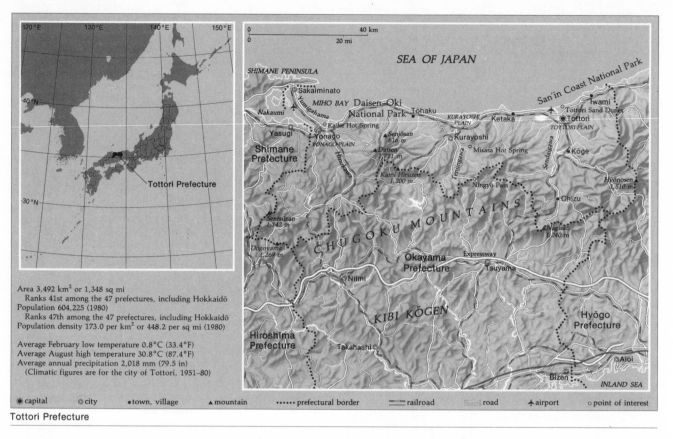

Area 3,492 km² or 1,348 sq mi
 Ranks 41st among the 47 prefectures, including Hokkaidō
Population 604,225 (1980)
 Ranks 47th among the 47 prefectures, including Hokkaidō
Population density 173.0 per km² or 448.2 per sq mi (1980)

Average February low temperature 0.8°C (33.4°F)
Average August high temperature 30.8°C (87.4°F)
Average annual precipitation 2,018 mm (79.5 in)
 (Climatic figures are for the city of Tottori, 1951–80)

⊙ capital   ◎ city   ● town, village   ▲ mountain   ••••• prefectural border   ≡≡≡≡ railroad   ≡≡≡≡ road   ✦ airport   ○ point of interest

Tottori Prefecture

damaged by an earthquake in 1943 and fire in 1952, the city has been completely rebuilt, with active electrical appliance, woodwork, food, and machinery industries. The city is served by the Japanese National Railways San'in line. Tottori University is located here. Local attractions include TOTTORI SAND DUNES and Tottori Hot Spring. Pop: 131,060.

Tottori Plain

(Tottori Heiya). Located in eastern Tottori Prefecture, western Honshū. This flood plain of the river Sendaigawa has large tracts of sand dunes on the coast. Rice is grown in the lowlands, and pears are cultivated on the surrounding foothills and along the coastal sand dunes. Numerous tomb mounds (KOFUN) dot the plain. The major city is Tottori. Area: 80 sq km (31 sq mi).

Tottori Prefecture

(Tottori Ken). Located in western Honshū and bounded by the Sea of Japan on the north, Hyōgo Prefecture on the east, Okayama and Hiroshima prefectures on the south, and Shimane Prefecture on the west. Much of the terrain is mountainous, with the CHŪGOKU MOUNTAINS running across the southern part of the prefecture. Level areas are concentrated along rivers and near the Sea of Japan coast. The climate is temperate and relatively dry.

Archaeological remains from the Jōmon (ca 10,000 BC–ca 300 BC) and Yayoi (ca 300 BC–ca AD 300) periods have been found in this area. Under the 7th-century system of provinces (KOKUGUN SYSTEM) the area was composed of the provinces of Inaba and Hōki. It was ruled by various feudal lords until the Meiji Restoration of 1868. The present boundaries were drawn up in 1881.

Because of its remoteness from major population and economic centers, Tottori has remained predominantly agricultural. Products include rice, livestock, fruits, vegetables, and tobacco. Its pears are especially prized. Other industries include fishing, forestry, and food processing. YONAGO and SAKAIMINATO have each been designated as a New Industrial City in the Nakaumi Zone (see NEW INDUSTRIAL CITIES) in line with the prefecture's plans to modernize its industries.

Attractions include the Sea of Japan coast, particularly the TOTTORI SAND DUNES in the SAN'IN COAST NATIONAL PARK, DAISEN, the training center for mountain ascetics in the DAISEN–OKI NA-

TIONAL PARK, and hot spring resorts like Misasa and Kaike. Area: 3,492 sq km (1,348 sq mi); pop: 604,225; capital: TOTTORI. Other major cities include KURAYOSHI and Yonago.

Tottori Sand Dunes

(Tottori Sakyū). On the east coast of Tottori Prefecture, western Honshū. The dunes have been a notable feature of the area since ancient times, but their features are gradually changing today with the planting of trees and irrigation to turn them into arable land. Vegetables and tobacco are now being cultivated. Designated as a natural monument, the dunes are part of San'in Coast National Park. Length: 16 km (10 mi); width: 2 km (1.2 mi); highest point: 92 m (302 ft).

Towada

City in southeastern Aomori Prefecture, northern Honshū. Towada was settled by a *samurai* from the Nambu domain in 1855. Principal products are rice and fruit; there is also cattle and hog raising. Pop: 58,896.

Towada–Hachimantai National Park

(Towada–Hachimantai Kokuritsu Kōen). Situated in northern Honshū, in Aomori, Akita, and Iwate prefectures. The park consists of two separate mountainous regions some 50 km (31 mi) apart. The northern Towada region has the volcanoes of HAKKŌDASAN in the north and Lake TOWADA in the south. From this large caldera lake, noted for its clarity and depth (326.8 m; 1,072 ft), the OIRASEGAWA flows toward the Pacific Ocean through deep ravines and valleys scattered with large boulders. The southern Hachimantai region consists of an extensive plateau with numerous volcanoes, including HACHIMANTAI (1,614 m; 5,294 ft) and Yakeyama (1,366 m; 4,480 ft) in the north, KOMAGATAKE (1,637 m; 5,369 ft) in the south, and IWATESAN (2,041 m; 6,694 ft) in the east. The park is celebrated for numerous hot spring resorts: Sukayu and Tsuta, west of Hakkōdasan; Hachimantai Hot Spring on Hachimantai; and Nyūtō, north of Komagatake. The forests in both regions are noted for the Maries fir (Aomori *todomatsu*). Area: 833.5 sq km (321.7 sq mi).

Tottori Sand Dunes

Towada–Hachimantai National Park

The upper reaches of the river Oirasegawa in the spring.

Book Four opens in 1289 with Lady Nijō, now a Buddhist nun, setting out on a series of journeys that take her throughout Japan and put her in contact with people from all levels of society. She never completely loses touch with the capital, however, and she concludes Book Five with an account of the services there marking the third anniversary of Go-Fukakusa's death.

Lady Nijō lived in a period of transition from an aristocratic culture to one dominated by the warrior class. What makes *Towazugatari* particularly important to students of Japanese culture is its descriptions of life in both worlds. Lady Nijō gives us an intimate portrait of aristocratic life in Kyōto and fascinating glimpses of the world outside: entertainers at way stations, former prostitutes turned nuns, a local warlord who mistreats his help and attempts to retain Lady Nijō against her will, military leaders in Kamakura attempting to ape aristocratic manners, and Shintō priests at the Ise Shrine. The book presents a clear contrast between the elaborate ceremonial of court religion and the simplicity of popular Buddhism.

Towazugatari is the culminating work in the long court tradition of autobiographical writing (NIKKI BUNGAKU). Lady Nijō's account is more novelistic than most; she makes good use of the techniques developed in earlier narrative fiction (MONOGATARI BUNGAKU), skillfully incorporating poems in her prose and drawing freely on earlier works, especially the TALE OF GENJI (*Genji monogatari)*, the poetry of SAIGYŌ, whom she much admired, and popular Buddhist tales (SETSUWA BUNGAKU). She lays bare her loves and fears, her indiscretions and devotions with a fine combination of self-pity (an acceptable emotion in her culture) and humor.

The text of this remarkable work was probably never widely circulated and was completely forgotten by the 18th century. A single manuscript survived to be discovered in 1940 by the literary scholar Yamagishi Tokuhei in the holdings of the Imperial Household Library in Tōkyō. Only in the mid-1960s, when annotated editions first became available in Japan, was the significance of the work finally recognized.

▬▬——*Towazugatari* (ca 1307), tr Karen Brazell as *The Confessions of Lady Nijō* (1973). Karen Brazell, "Towazugatari, Autobiography of a Kamakura Court Lady," *Harvard Journal of Asiatic Studies* 31 (1971). Matsumoto Yasuji, *Towazugatari no kenkyū* (1971). Tsugita Kasumi, ed, *Towazugatari*, in *Nihon koten zensho* (Asahi Shimbun Sha, 1966). *Karen* BRAZELL

towns and villages, consolidation of

(*chōson gappei*). Merger of two or more towns or villages adjacent to each other. The purpose is to create a local autonomous body with strong administrative and financial power as well as to make administration more effective. During the first consolidation carried out in 1889, a total of 71,314 towns and villages were merged to create 39 cities and 15,820 towns and villages. Under the Towns and Villages Consolidation Promotion Law (Chōson Gappei Sokushin Hō) of 1953, the approximately 10,000 towns and villages in the country were reduced to 3,975 by 1956. NISHIKAWA Osamu

Tōya, Lake

(Tōyako). Caldera lake near Uchiura Bay, southwestern Hokkaidō. Located within Shikotsu–Tōya National Park. This round-shaped lake is one of the northernmost ice-free lakes in Japan. Nakajima, a volcanic cone, is located in the center of the lake. Tōyako Hot Spring and two volcanoes, SHŌWA SHINZAN and USUZAN, are nearby. Famous for its lake festival held in early July every year. Area: 69.4 sq km (26.8 sq mi); circumference: 46 km (29 mi); depth: 179.7 m (589.4 ft); altitude: 84 m (276 ft).

Toyama

Capital of Toyama Prefecture, central Honshū. Situated on the river Jinzūgawa, Toyama developed as a castle town of the Maeda family during the Edo period (1600–1868) and was known for its itinerant medicine vendors. The city is served by the Japanese National Railways Takayama and Hokuriku lines. It is now the center of the so-called Hokuriku Industrial Zone, with aluminum refining, shipbuilding, and machinery industries. Pears, tea, and vegetables are grown here. Toyama University, the Toyama City Folk Art Museum, and a city science museum are located here. Pop: 305,054.

Towada, Lake

(Towadako). Square-shaped double caldera lake. Between Aomori and Akita prefectures, northern Honshū, south of the Hakkōda volcanic mountain group. The river Oirasegawa flows out from the eastern side of the lake. Fish breeding has flourished since the *himemasu* (*Oncorhynchus nerka* var. *adonis*) was released into the lake in 1903. Its water does not freeze in winter. The lake is the main attraction of Towada–Hachimantai National Park. This area is noted for its spring and autumn foliage. Area: 59.9 km (23.1 sq mi); circumference: 44 km (27 mi); depth: 326.8 m (1,072 ft); altitude: 400 m (1,312 ft).

Towazugatari

(An Uninvited Confession). An autobiographical narrative of 36 years (1271–1306) in the life of Lady Nijō (also known as Go-Fukakusa In no Nijō), a high-ranking Kyōto aristocrat. Completed ca 1307; translated as *The Confessions of Lady Nijō* (1973). Her tale begins with a description of how, at age 14, she became the concubine of a young retired emperor and ends, several love affairs later, with an account of her mature life as a wandering Buddhist nun.

Little is known about the author except through her autobiography; even her name, Lady Nijō (Nijō Dono), is merely a court title. Her family, the Koga or Nakanoin, had produced successful poets and courtiers for generations, but Lady Nijō had the misfortune of being left an orphan when she was only 15. She proved capable, however, of doing extremely well on her own. Not only did she have the affections of the retired emperor GO-FUKAKUSA, but she was loved by one of his close advisers, the powerful Saionji Sanekane (1249–1322) and by Go-Fukakusa's half-brother, a Buddhist high priest. The complications arising from these and other relationships form the major action of the first three books of *Towazugatari*. In 1283 Lady Nijō was expelled from Go-Fukakusa's palace because of his empress's jealousy and her own indiscretions with his brother and archrival, the retired emperor Kameyama.

Toyama Bay

(Toyama Wan). Inlet of the Sea of Japan in northern Toyama Prefecture, central Honshū. Known as the home of the firefly squid (*hotaruika*). Fishing is good along the continental shelf in the western part of the bay. Commercial and industrial ports, including Toyama and Shin Toyama, are located along the bay. Forms part of the Noto Peninsula Quasi-National Park.

Toyama Kametarō (1867–1918)

Geneticist. Noted for his pioneer studies and experiments dealing with applied eugenics. Born in what is now Kanagawa Prefecture and graduated from Tōkyō University, Toyama served as principal of a sericulture school and as a professor at Tōkyō University. While engaged in work to improve silkworm varieties, he discovered that Mendel's laws applied to insects. He argued for the application of Mendelism in eugenics, a field of study introduced to Japan at the end of the Meiji period (1868–1912).   *Suzuki Zenji*

Tōyama Kinshirō (?–1855)

City commissioner (MACHI BUGYŌ) of Edo (now Tōkyō) famed for his knowledge of Edo residents and his compassion for criminals; also known as Tōyama Kagemoto. Said to have been wild and dissolute in his youth, he subsequently reformed and held several official posts under the Tokugawa shogunate. In 1840 he became Kitamachi *bugyō*, or commissioner of the northern half of Edo. He earned the gratitude of the townsmen by preventing the demolition of playhouses, one item decreed by the TEMPŌ REFORMS. He fell afoul of TORII YŌZŌ, a strict reformist who served as commissioner of the southern half of Edo, and was demoted to the post of inspector general (ŌMETSUKE) in 1843. After Torii's downfall in 1844, Tōyama assumed his former foe's position. He retired seven years later and took Buddhist orders. Tōyama's feats of detection as a magistrate (one of his duties as a commissioner), his humanity, and his wise and impartial judgments are still celebrated in popular literature.

Toyama Masakazu (1848–1900)

Educator and poet. Also known as Toyama Shōichi. Born in Edo (now Tōkyō). After studying at the BANSHO SHIRABESHO, the shogunate school for Western studies, he traveled to England in 1866. In 1870 he went to the United States to study science and philosophy at the University of Michigan. Upon his return to Japan, he became the first Japanese professor of philosophy and sociology at Tōkyō University. He was appointed president of the university in 1897 and also served briefly as education minister in the third ITŌ HIRO-BUMI cabinet (1898). As an adherent of the Spencerian theory of cultural evolution, Toyama advocated replacing the Japanese writing system with the more "progressive" Roman alphabet and founded a society to promote this idea, the Rōmajikai. He was also interested in poetry and drama and, with INOUE TETSUJIRŌ and YATABE RYŌ-KICHI, produced *Shintaishi shō* (1882), a book of modern-style Japanese and translated poetry.

Tōyama Mitsuru (1855–1944)

Right-wing political leader; advocate of Japanese expansion on the Asian continent and a founder of such ultranationalist groups as the GEN'YŌSHA. The third son of Tsutsui Kamesaku, a *samurai* of the Fukuoka domain (now part of Fukuoka Prefecture), he was later adopted into his mother's family and assumed the surname Tōyama.

Tōyama attended a private school, where he became close friends with Hiraoka Kōtarō (1851–1906) and Hakoda Rokusuke (1850–85), two future collaborators, and began to interest himself in political trends. He joined the activities of the Kyōshisha, a group of former samurai who were dissatisfied with the new Meiji government, and as a result was arrested in 1876 and imprisoned. He was in prison when the SATSUMA REBELLION began and was thus frustrated in his wish to join SAIGŌ TAKAMORI's anti-government forces. After the rebellion was quelled, Tōyama was released. In 1879, together with Hiraoka and Hakoda he organized in Fukuoka the Kōyōsha, a group supporting the FREEDOM AND PEOPLE'S RIGHTS MOVEMENT calling for a popular assembly. Before long, however, Tōyama began to feel the movement's limitations. In 1881 the Kōyōsha changed its name to Gen'yōsha and, headed by Hiraoka, be-

gan to promote the cause of Japanese expansion on the continent. The Gen'yōsha favored a hard-line foreign policy, and Tōyama was always in the forefront of its attacks on what it considered to be weak-kneed government policy on the issue of revision of the Unequal Treaties (see UNEQUAL TREATIES, REVISION OF).

During this period Tōyama became strongly concerned with promoting Japanese interests in China, joining forces with Arao Sei (1859–96), who was sent to China by the Imperial Army Staff Office to gather intelligence. Tōyama also showed an active interest in Korean matters, providing assistance to the political exile KIM OK-KYUN. It is said that Tōyama built up funds for his activities by buying rights to the Chikuhō coalfield in northern Kyūshū and then reselling them at a high profit to MITSUBISHI and other *zaibatsu*.

When details of Foreign Minister ŌKUMA SHIGENOBU's proposals on treaty revision became known in 1889, Tōyama organized a protest movement. He was implicated in the throwing of a bomb at Ōkuma by a member of the Gen'yōsha and was arrested but soon released. During Japan's second general election in 1892 Tōyama gave secret support to the bribery and intimidations carried out by Home Minister SHINAGAWA YAJIRŌ.

Just before the SINO-JAPANESE WAR OF 1894–1895 Tōyama began to favor taking direct personal action on the continent. He helped organize the Ten'yūkyō, a paramilitary force whose activities in Korea were a prelude to those of the Japanese army (see KOREA AND JAPAN: early modern relations). He strongly felt that the establishment of control over Manchuria would be an important step in Japan's continental expansion; in this connection he became a member of the anti-Russian TAIRO DŌSHIKAI when it was formed in 1903 and argued for opening hostilities against Russia. In the course of the revolutionary movement in China he gave support to its leader, SUN YAT-SEN, and when the revolution of 1911 occurred, he went to China as an adviser to the new government. However, his real aim was to attempt to persuade Sun and other Chinese leaders to place Manchuria under Japanese domination in return for aid to the revolution.

Following the Chinese Revolution Tōyama tended not to engage openly in political agitation but rather to remain in the background, coordinating the activities of right-wing groups and working to maintain links between them and members of government and military circles. He thus came to have great influence as a behind-the-scenes manipulator, not only with respect to Japan's Asian policy but also with respect to domestic politics. Although Tōyama was in retirement during World War II, he maintained his standing as grand old man of Japanese nationalism, reigning over right-wing groups, such as the Gen'yōsha and the AMUR RIVER SOCIETY, that he had helped bring into existence. See also RIGHT WING.

📖 ───Marius B. Jansen, *The Japanese and Sun Yat-sen* (1954).

Harada Katsumasa

Toyama Plain

(Toyama Heiya). Located in northern Toyama Prefecture, central Honshū. Bordering the Sea of Japan, it consists of the piedmont alluvial fans of the rivers Kurobegawa, Jōganjigawa, and Jinzūgawa, all of which originate in the Hida Mountains. Rice is cultivated with the help of an irrigation network, and industries are being developed. The major cities are Toyama and Takaoka. Area: 990 sq km (382 sq mi).

Toyama Prefecture

(Toyama Ken). Located in central Honshū and bounded by Toyama Bay and the Sea of Japan on the north, Niigata and Nagano prefectures on the east, Gifu Prefecture on the south, and Ishikawa Prefecture on the west. The central part of the prefecture is a plains area surrounded by mountains to the east, south, and west, and watered by several rivers. The winters are marked by heavy snowfall and cloudy weather.

Known after the TAIKA REFORM of 645 as Etchū Province, the area came under the control of the MAEDA FAMILY in the Edo period (1600–1868). The present name of the prefecture dates from 1871, and its present boundaries from 1883.

Rice is the major agricultural crop. Tulip bulbs are exported. The availability of cheap hydroelectric power from Toyama's numerous rivers has spurred the development of the chemical, metal, machinery, lumber-processing, and textile industries. Fishing is also important.

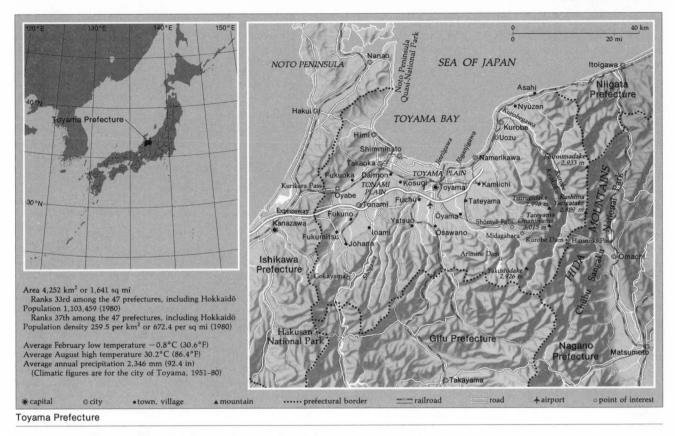

| ⊙ capital | ⊚ city | • town, village | ▲ mountain | ····· prefectural border | ══ railroad | ══ road | ✈ airport | ○ point of interest |

Toyama Prefecture

Major attractions include the Kurobe Gorge–Tateyama district, part of CHŪBU SANGAKU NATIONAL PARK, and the seacoast around the city of Himi, part of the Noto Peninsula Quasi-National Park. The Gokayama district in the southwestern part of the prefecture is noted for its farmhouses, which are in the style with steeply pitched roofs known as *gasshō-zukuri* (see MINKA), and the southwestern edge of the prefecture is a part of the HAKUSAN NATIONAL PARK. Area: 4,252 sq km (1,641 sq mi); pop: 1,103,459; capital: Toyama. Other major cities include Takaoka, Himi, Uozu, and Shimminato.

Tōya maru Disaster

The sinking on 26 September 1954 of the *Tōya maru,* a Japan National Railways passenger ferry, with a loss of 1,155 lives; one of the worst sea disasters in Japanese history. A typhoon originating in Kyūshū suddenly increased in velocity and force and hit northern Japan. Five ships were sunk and many others damaged, but the largest casualty was the *Tōya maru,* which capsized and sank after leaving the port of Hakodate on its run to Aomori. The incident brought into question regulations concerning navigation under emergency conditions and prompted improvements in hull structure. MINAKAMI TSUTOMU later wrote a detective novel, *Kiga kaikyō* (1962, The Straits of Starvation), in which the *Tōya maru* tragedy figures.

Tōyo

City in eastern Ehime Prefecture, Shikoku, on the Hiuchi Sea. It is primarily an industrial city, with numerous textile mills and aluminum, machinery, and chemical plants. There is a ferry service connecting Tōyo with Ōsaka. Pop: 33,838.

Toyoake

City in central Aichi Prefecture, central Honshū. Formerly a farming area, it now has metal and machinery industries and is fast becoming a suburb of Nagoya. The site of the Battle of OKEHAZAMA (1560) is within the city limits. Pop: 54,673.

Tōyō Aluminium

A top manufacturer of aluminum foils and aluminum paste, this firm was established in 1931 jointly by the Alcan Aluminium Co of Canada and Sumitomo Shindo Kokan (now SUMITOMO LIGHT METAL INDUSTRIES, LTD). It is a member of the Sumitomo group. Originally engaged in the manufacture of aluminum foils and plates, it commenced production of aluminum paste in 1957. It is also a major producer of aluminum cans. It has a joint manufacturing venture in South Korea. In 1981 sales totaled ¥39.2 billion (US $179 million), and the company was capitalized at ¥2.7 billion (US $12.3 million), of which 50 percent was invested by Alcan Aluminium. The head office is in Osaka.

Tōyōbō Co, Ltd

(Tōyō Bōseki). A spinning company engaged in the manufacture of synthetic fiber and cotton and woolen goods, Tōyōbō was established in 1914 through the merger of Ōsaka Spinning Co, established in 1882 by SHIBUSAWA EIICHI and others, and Mie Spinning Co, established in 1886. Sales of the company's cotton goods are the largest in the industry. In 1956 Tōyōbō added the manufacture of acrylic fiber to its cotton, woolen, and chemical fiber products. In 1961 it developed and commercialized polyester fiber, and in 1966, after merging with Kureha Spinning Co, the firm started producing nylon. Tōyōbō produces goods from every natural fiber, except silk and flax, and from the three major synthetic fibers. In 1955 the company established a wholly owned subsidiary in Brazil called Tōyōbō, Brazil. Since then, it has expanded overseas and currently has five companies in Brazil, five in Central America, two in the United States, one each in Canada and Australia, and six in Southeast Asia. There is also a total of 22 overseas affiliates. In response to the stagnation in textile sales, the company is planning to expand plastics production (film resin) and to enter the fields of environment control systems and medical equipment. Sales for the fiscal year ending April 1982 totaled ¥317 billion (US $1.3 billion), of which synthetic fiber textiles comprised 57 percent, cotton goods 18 percent, woolen goods 5 percent, and others 20 percent. The export ratio was 15 percent and capitalization stood at ¥30.4 billion (US $124.2 million) in the same year. The head office is in Ōsaka.

Tōyō Bunko

(Oriental Library). A world-famous research collection on Asian history and culture, the first of its kind privately established in modern Japan. In 1917 Iwasaki Hisaya (1865–1955), son of IWASAKI

YATARŌ, founder of the Mitsubishi *zaibatsu*, began this library with the purchase of the Asiatic library of George Ernest Morrison (1862–1920), a long-term China correspondent for the *Times* of London who had collected nearly every Western book ever published on China. The addition of more Western-language studies plus Chinese, Japanese, Indian, and other Asian-language works have made the library's holdings of over 500,000 volumes one of the largest and most comprehensive collections on Asia in the world. Known initially as the Morrison Bunko, it received its present name in 1924, when the Iwasaki family donated endowment funds and a building at its present site in Bunkyō Ward, Tōkyō. During World War II its books were kept for safety in northeastern Japan. Upon their return to Tōkyō in 1948 the library was made part of the NATIONAL DIET LIBRARY, a status it holds to this day. In 1967 an annex was added to house new materials on modern China.

The Tōyō Bunko is also well known as a research institute. It publishes a Japanese-language journal, a journal of Western-language translations of Japanese scholarship on Asia, and numerous scholarly books in addition to holding lectures and exhibits.

Theodore F. WELCH

Toyoda Automatic Loom Works, Ltd

(Toyoda Jidō Shokki Seisakusho). Manufacturer of textile machinery, small commercial cars, automobile engines, industrial rolling stock, compressors for automobile air conditioners, and casting machines. It is one of the world's leading producers of spinning and weaving machinery and of forklift trucks. Toyoda Automatic Loom Works was established in 1926 to manufacture the shuttle-changing automatic looms invented by TOYODA SAKICHI. In 1933 an automobile division and a steel-making division were added in order to begin production of automobiles. The auto division became independent in 1937 as TOYOTA MOTOR CO, LTD, while the steel-making division became independent in 1940 as AICHI STEEL WORKS, LTD; these companies are the primary companies of the Toyota group. After World War II the company diversified its operations in the following areas: automotive gasoline engines in 1952, gasoline engine forklifts in 1956, compressors for auto air conditioners in 1959, and small-business cars and battery-type forklifts in 1967. A technological tie-up with George Fisher, Ltd, of Switzerland in 1971 led Toyoda to the field of metal-casting plants. The company's textile machinery division grew rapidly as a result of the spread of textile manufacturing in developing countries and the structural reform of the industry in advanced industrial countries. Technical tie-ups and joint ventures have been conducted with European and American textile-machinery makers, including Rieter Machine Works, Ltd, and Sulzer Brothers, Ltd, both of Switzerland. The company has thus consolidated its position as one of the top textile-machinery manufacturers in the world. Sales for the fiscal year ending March 1982 totaled ¥226 billion (US $938.9 million). The company was capitalized at ¥10.7 billion (US $44.4 million) in the same year. The head office is in Kariya, Aichi Prefecture.

Toyoda Sakichi (1867–1930)

Inventor and industrialist. Born in Shizuoka Prefecture. His early fascination with looms developed into a lifetime of research and innovation that produced the first Japanese-designed power loom in 1897 and an automatic power loom in 1926, at the time the most advanced weaving machinery in the world. His inventions revolutionized the Japanese textile industry and enabled Japan to assume virtual control of the international silk trade in the 1920s. The industrial research complex he developed became the base from which evolved many other industries, including TOYOTA MOTOR CORPORATION, the giant automobile manufacturer.

Toyoda Shirō (1906–1977)

Film director; born in Kyōto. As a boy he was quite sickly, once even being told that he would probably not live to be 20. He developed an early and strong interest in literature and theater. His original ambition after graduating from high school was to write for the stage and it was with that in mind that he left Kyōto for Tōkyō in 1924. His elder brother introduced him to a friend who was a director for the Nikkatsu Mukōjima studios (see NIKKATSU CORPORATION). Toyoda was offered a job as a scriptwriter there and it was not long before his interest in the theater was transformed into an enthusiasm for films. A short time later he was persuaded by direc-

tor SHIMAZU YASUJIRŌ to join SHŌCHIKU CO, LTD, as an assistant director. In 1929, when he was only 23 years old, Toyoda was promoted to the job of director.

In his first feature *Irodorareru kuchibiru* (1929, Painted Lips) he did not follow the standard practice of opening sequences with a long shot meant to give the viewer a sense of place. Rather, Toyoda opened every sequence of the film with a close-up. Close-ups of real and plausible characters were more important to him than panoramic views of social themes, and this fact contributed to Toyoda's reputation as an actor's director.

Another facet of Toyoda's work was his involvement in the *jumbungaku* (pure literature) movement which flourished in the Japanese cinema in the late 1930s. The movement consisted of a loosely organized group of directors who shared an interest in bringing works of serious literature to the screen. Toyoda's *Wakai hito* (1937, Young People), based on a novel by ISHIZAKA YŌJIRŌ, stressed the cinematic, or pictorial, aspects of the book rather than straining for a literal rendering of the novel. Throughout his career, Toyoda maintained this interest in making literature cinematic. Examples best known to American audiences are *Gan* (1953, The Wild Geese; shown abroad as *The Mistress*), an adaptation of a MORI ŌGAI novel, noted for its magnificent recreation of Meiji-period atmosphere, and *Yukiguni* (1956, Snow Country), from the novel by KAWABATA YASUNARI.

Other notable films have been *Kojima no haru* (1940, Spring on Leper's Island), selected as the best film of 1940 in a poll conducted by *Kinema jumpō*, Japan's leading film magazine; *Meoto zenzai* (1955, Marital Relations); *Neko to Shōzō to futari no onna* (1956, A Cat, Shōzō, and Two Women), which gave prominence to the comic talents of actor MORISHIGE HISAYA; and *Amai ase* (1964, Sweet Sweat), for which KYŌ MACHIKO won several acting awards. Most of Toyoda's later films were made for the Tōhō Co, Ltd.

David OWENS

Toyoda Tsūshō Kaisha, Ltd

Trading firm handling the import and export business of the TOYOTA MOTOR CORPORATION, and of other members of the Toyota group. Established in 1948, the company initially engaged in the export and domestic sale of spinning and weaving machinery produced by TOYODA AUTOMATIC LOOM WORKS, LTD. Later it began to handle the various products and raw materials of the Toyota group companies. Some 70 percent of the firm's total sales are accounted for by these products. It is planning to become a comprehensive trading firm through expanding the operations of its 26 overseas business offices and 44 overseas subsidiaries. Sales for the fiscal year ending March 1982 totaled ¥1 trillion (US $4.2 billion), and the company was capitalized at ¥7.2 billion (US $29.9 million) in the same year. The head office is in Nagoya.

Toyogawa Canal

(Toyogawa Yōsui). Irrigation canal in southeastern Aichi Prefecture, central Honshū. Water sources are Lake Sakuma and the river Ōnyūgawa in the Tenryūgawa system. The canal branches at the city of Shinshiro. The eastern branch extends to the tip of the Atsumi Peninsula; the western branch extends to the city of Gamagōri. Completed in 1968, it irrigates approximately 20,000 hectares (49,400 acres) of farmland. It also provides drinking and industrial water to the cities of Toyohashi and Toyokawa. Length of eastern canal: 76 km (47 mi); length of western canal: 36 km (22 mi).

Toyohashi

City in southeastern Aichi Prefecture, central Honshū; on the river Toyogawa. In the Edo period (1600–1868) it was known as Yoshida and flourished as a castle town and POST-STATION TOWN. A silk-reeling center before World War II, it now produces textiles, lumber, machinery, and food. Water from the TOYOGAWA CANAL is used to irrigate vegetable fields. Eels are also raised. Urigō, a Yayoi-period (ca 300 BC–ca AD 300) archaeological site, is located here. Pop: 304,274.

Tōyō Ink Mfg Co, Ltd

(Tōyō Inki Seizō). A company engaged in the manufacture and sale of printing ink, chemicals, coloring agents for synthetic resins, and printing materials, Tōyō Ink was established in 1907; it is the largest producer of printing ink in Japan. With printing ink as its principal line of business, the company plans to become a comprehensive coloring-agent company in the future. It has subsidiaries in the United States and Belgium and affiliated companies and offices in Southeast Asia. It is currently engaged in research and development in electronics, educational projects, and energy-related fields. Sales totaled ¥132 billion (US $548.4 million) in the fiscal year ending in March 1982. The company was capitalized at ¥10 billion (US $41.5 million) in the same year. The head office is in Tōkyō.

Tōyō Jiyūtō

(Oriental Liberal Party). Populist political party formed in November 1892 by ŌI KENTARŌ and other defectors from the JIYŪTŌ (Liberal Party) with the support of TARUI TŌKICHI and other advocates of popular rights. The party organized associations advocating constitutional representative government and economic security for the poor and labor through government control of the general economy. It also published Japan's first labor magazine, Shin Tōyō (New Orient). The party held four seats in the fourth and fifth Diets. In October 1893 it joined with other nationalistic groups and organized the Greater Japan Association (Dai Nihon Kyōkai) to press the government to adopt a more aggressive foreign policy, particularly to prohibit the residence of foreigners outside the treaty ports (see NAICHI ZAKKYO). Two months later the party disbanded because of internal dissension. See also POLITICAL PARTIES.

tōyō kanji

(Chinese characters for daily use). The 1,850 Chinese characters (KANJI) that were officially selected for general use and issued by the Japanese cabinet and Ministry of Education under the title Tōyō kanji hyō (Table of Chinese Characters for Daily Use) on 16 November 1946. Superseded in October 1981 by the JŌYŌ KANJI. The institution of the Tōyō kanji hyō represented one of a number of major post–World War II reforms affecting the written language (see JAPANESE LANGUAGE REFORMS). From as early as the opening years of the Meiji period (1868–1912) formal proposals were made advocating the reduction and even the abolition of the Chinese characters used to write Japanese in favor of the increased use of the native phonetic syllabary (kana) or of romanization, but the institution of the 1,850 tōyō kanji in 1946 represented the first actual implementation of reform in the written language.

There were nationalistic, practical, and political reasons behind this particular reform. It was hoped that by reducing the total number of Chinese characters in general use, the increased reliance on the Japanese syllabary would boost the people's pride in, and respect for, the native word and bring out the intrinsic beauty of the language from behind its Chinese facade. It was also felt that restricting the use of Chinese characters in this way would make day-to-day living and business more efficient, expedite the printing process, and reduce the burden of language instruction in the schools. Finally, the creation of a simplified system of writing accessible to all people was seen as an instrument for promoting the cause of democracy and raising the level of popular culture.

The Tōyō kanji hyō was provisional in that it was originally anticipated that further reductions in the number of characters would be made, but the total number did in fact remain unchanged until 1981, despite a number of substitutions that were made after the original publication. According to the preface, the 1,850 characters were to be used in laws and official documents, as well as in magazines, newspapers, and other public writings. Private diaries, letters, technical and other special writings, and the text of the Constitution of 1947 were exempt from government adoption. As may be expected, the most consistent adherence to the tōyō kanji was seen in government laws, public notices, and newspapers, while other writings—scholarly, literary, and technical—all continued to use non-tōyō kanji to a varying extent.

The characters in the table are arranged according to the radical (the characteristic or identifying structural element) under which they belong. One hundred and thirty characters are given in an abbreviated or simplified orthography now regarded as the officially accepted form. (The shapes of the characters were standardized in a supplementary table in 1949, and more of the characters were simplified.) The Tōyō kanji onkun hyō (Table of ON READINGS [the Japanized Chinese pronunciation] and KUN READINGS [Japanese semantic gloss] for the Chinese Characters for Daily Use), published in 1948, prescribed the official readings for the 1,850 characters. The same year, 881 characters from the list were selected as Chinese

characters for education through grade six, and issued under a separate title (these are popularly known as KYŌIKU KANJI or "education characters"). The problem of what to do about characters used in proper names was temporarily deferred in 1946, but the following year the Family Registration Law (Koseki Hō) and Family Registration Law Enforcement Regulations (Koseki Hō Sekō Kisoku) specified that starting in 1948 characters for newly registered given names of babies be chosen from among the tōyō kanji. In 1951 the government decided to issue a supplementary list of 92 characters entitled Jimmeiyō kanji beppyō (A Supplementary Table of Chinese Characters for Use in Personal Names), and, in 1976, 28 more characters were added in the Jimmeiyō kanji tsuika hyō (Table of Additional Characters for Use in Personal Names). These lists, however, did not impose any restrictions on the readings for each character, and uncommon readings are legally possible.

After a government reevaluation of the Tōyō kanji hyō, 28 character-substitutions and 2 minor reading changes were made in 1954 and some substantial changes regarding readings in 1973, but these limited revisions by no means rectified the table's inherent shortcomings. For example, no provision was made for many important proper and place names which are in daily use in Japan. Neither of the characters in the very common surname Satō nor the second of the two characters used in the names of the large cities of Ōsaka and Sapporo were listed. There were many inconsistencies in the choice of characters generally. One wonders why, for example, we find the little-used character for the word maku (membrane) but not the character for the word hada (skin), and why the character for kujira (whale) is listed but not the one for maguro (tuna). As it stands, the list does not appear to provide an adequate basic written vocabulary for its users.

The Tōyō kanji hyō imposed serious restrictions on the language. In compound-character words, all unlisted characters had to be replaced with tōyō kanji even at the risk of obscuring the compound's original meaning. In some cases, whole words were superseded by one composed of tōyō kanji, and in others, words formerly written with characters had to be written in kana.

A number of objections to the tōyō kanji system were raised. Many persons found it awkward to read in kana a word they were accustomed to seeing in kanji and felt that the characters were too few in number and had been selected too arbitrarily. It was also argued that when kanji are not used, the meaning and aesthetic quality of a word are difficult to perceive and that it is hard to separate words. Finally, some feared that students who had learned only the 1,850 characters would inevitably lose contact with Japan's earlier written tradition.

On the positive side, the implementation of this reform was a major factor in Japan's achievement of a very high literacy rate in recent decades since the war. The fact remains, however, that the Tōyō kanji hyō saw only limited application on the whole, and a large volume of Japanese writing remained out of the reach of readers with only tōyō kanji training. The admissibility of this tōyō kanji double standard whereby the government guidelines for kanji use applied only to certain kinds of writing may be seen, perhaps, as tacit official recognition of the fact that the 1,850-character system could only go so far in meeting the language needs of a sophisticated public. See also JŌYŌ KANJI.

━━━━Kokugo Mondai Kenkyūkai, comp, Kokugo no atarashii kakikata (1947). Roy A. Miller, The Japanese Language (1967). Mori Shō, ed, Tōyō kanji jiten (1969). Satō Kiyoji, ed, Buntaishi, gengo seikatsushi, vol 6 of Kōza kokugoshi (Taishūkan, 1972). Tsukishima Hiroshi, Kokugogaku (1965). Joseph K. Yamagiwa, "Reforms in the Language and Orthography of Newspapers in Japan," Journal of the American Oriental Society 68.1 (1948).

Judith N. RABINOVITCH

Toyokawa

City in eastern Aichi Prefecture, central Honshū. From the end of the Edo period (1600–1868) it developed as a shrine town around the Toyokawa Inari Shrine. Metal, machinery, and lumber industries were set up after World War II. Vegetables are grown in the suburbs. Pop: 103,097.

Tōyō keizai shimpō

(Eastern Economic Review). Economic journal founded in 1895 by Machida Chūji (1863–1946), a journalist who later became a successful entrepreneur and politician, with financial support from SHIBUSAWA EIICHI and other influential businessmen. It began as a fortnightly, but in 1919 it became a weekly. Editors after Machida included the economist Amano Tameyuki (1860–1938), Miura Tetsutarō, and ISHIBASHI TANZAN. The general tenor of the magazine was liberal, democratic, and anti-imperialist; it was especially critical of Japan's expansionist policies on the Asian continent, making it unique for its time. Renamed *Shūkan tōyō keizai* (Weekly Eastern Economic Review) in 1945, it is still in publication.

TANAKA Akira

Tōyō Kōgyō Co, Ltd

Manufacturer of Mazda automobiles. It is the fourth largest auto manufacturer in Japan. The company is closely related to the Sumitomo group. Founded in 1920 as Tōyō Cork Kōgyō Co, Ltd, the firm assumed its present name in 1927. In 1931 Tōyō Kōgyō started production of three-wheeled light trucks and in the 1960s became a full-line automotive manufacturer. In 1979 accumulated total production passed 10 million units.

In 1967 Tōyō Kōgyō introduced the world's first twin-rotor rotary engine automobile (the Cosmo Sports/110S), becoming the only automotive manufacturer in the world to mass-produce vehicles powered by three different types of engine: the conventional piston engine, the rotary engine, and the diesel engine. Mazdas are exported to more than 100 countries through a network comprising some 120 distributors, nearly 5,000 dealers, and 16 knockdown assembly plants. Sales outlets throughout Japan number about 1,600. Factory production in the fiscal year ending October 1981 totaled 1,253,228 cars and trucks, an increase of 4.9 percent over 1980. To meet the need for small and efficient cars in the 1980s, Tōyō Kōgyō is concentrating its development efforts on fuel economy improvement, weight reduction, noise reduction, and advanced electronics applications. Total sales were ¥1.2 trillion (US $4.4 billion) in the fiscal year ending October 1982; the sales breakdown was passenger cars 57 percent, trucks 26 percent, and parts and others 17 percent. The company was capitalized at ¥42.6 billion (US $156.9 million) the same year. The head office is in Hiroshima.

Tōyō Kōhan Co, Ltd

Company engaged in the manufacture and sale of tin plates, tin-free steel (Hi-Top brand), vinyl-coated steel (Vinyltop brand), tin mill products, other chemically treated steel sheets, and cold-rolled steel sheet strips in coils. Tōyō Kōhan was established in 1934 to supply tin plates to TŌYŌ SEIKAN KAISHA, LTD. The company has the largest market share in vinyl-coated steel and the second largest market share in tin-free steel. It has exported technology for tin mill products and other chemically treated steel sheets to West German, British, and Canadian mills. Sales for the fiscal year ending March 1982 totaled ¥112.6 billion (US $407.8 million), of which exports comprised 16 percent, and the company was capitalized at ¥5 billion (US $20.8 million) in the same year. The head office is in Tōkyō.

Toyokuni → Utagawa Toyokuni

Tōyō Menka Kaisha, Ltd

(Tōmen). A *sōgō shōsha* (general trading company), Tōyō Menka Kaisha operated as the cotton division of MITSUI & CO, LTD, until becoming independent in 1920. It ranks seventh among the nine *sōgō shōsha* in Japan. After World War II the company, which originally handled only textile products, began to handle iron and steel products, machinery, chemical goods, fuel, and food. It has 28 branches and offices in Japan and 85 overseas branches, offices, and subsidiaries. At the end of March 1982, annual sales totaled ¥3.7 trillion (US $15.4 billion), of which domestic trade constituted 37.9 percent, exports 24.3 percent, imports 25.3 percent, and trade between foreign countries 12.5 percent. By product, the company's business was as follows: metals and metal ores 17.8 percent, machinery and construction 21.2 percent, chemicals and fuel 24.7 percent, food 16.2 percent, textiles 16.2 percent, and lumber 3.9 percent. Capitalization stood at ¥16 billion (US $66.5 million) the same year. The head office is in Ōsaka.

Toyonaka

City in northwestern Ōsaka Prefecture, central Honshū. It is a residential suburb of Ōsaka, with numerous small- to middle-scale metal, machinery, tool, and knitted goods industries. Toyonaka is the site of Ōsaka International Airport, Ōsaka University, and an open-air museum of old Japanese farmhouses. The Senri Hills have been developed as part of Senri New Town, a planned residential city. Pop: 403,185.

Toyooka

City in northern Hyōgo Prefecture, western Honshū; on the river Maruyamagawa. Toyooka flourished as a castle town of the Kyōgoku family during the Edo period (1600–1868). Local products include traditional wicker luggage (*yanagigōri*) and luggage made of vinyl and leather. Its coastal area is part of San'in Coast National Park, the main attraction of which is the cave called GEMBUDŌ. Nakajima Shrine is a fine example of Muromachi period (1333–1568) architecture. Pop: 47,457.

Toyosaka

City in northern Niigata Prefecture, central Honshū, on the lower reaches of the river Aganogawa. Toyosaka developed as a market and weaving town. Today, it is rapidly becoming a suburb of the nearby city of Niigata. It is known for the migratory birds that settle on the lagoon called Fukushimagata. Pop: 42,097.

Tōyō Seikan Kaisha, Ltd

Japan's largest manufacturer of containers for canned food. Tōyō Seikan Kaisha was established in 1917 by Takasaki Tatsunosuke to produce metal receptacles for canning salmon and sea trout caught in northern waters by Japanese fishing fleets. Tōyō Seikan Kaisha now dominates more than half of the domestic market. In 1941, with the merger of seven other can makers, Tōyō Seikan Kaisha monopolized the manufacture of cans in the country. After World War II the company was divided again into smaller companies under a law intended to eliminate excessive concentration. After 1954 the company started modernization of its production methods through a technological tie-up with Continental Can of the United States and from the 1970s onward, started to manufacture soft drink cans and plastic containers. Technologically, Tōyō Seikan Kaisha is one of the top can makers in the world and exports its technology to Thailand, South Korea, Indonesia, and the United Kingdom. The company also owns TŌYŌ KŌHAN CO, LTD, a tin plate manufacturer. Sales for the fiscal year ending March 1982 totaled ¥304 billion (US $1.2 billion), and the company was capitalized at ¥8.2 billion (US $34 million) in the same year. The head office is in Tōkyō.

Tōyō Shakaitō

(Oriental Socialist Party). Radical peasant political association organized by TARUI TŌKICHI and others on 25 May 1882. Claiming the support of more than 3,000 peasants in Shimabara, Nagasaki Prefecture, it called for political morality, economic equality, and the greatest welfare for the greatest number. It further advocated collective ownership of land and natural resources, abolition of all forms of hereditary wealth, and communal rearing of children. Although the association was quickly outlawed for being communistic or nihilistic and formally disbanded on 20 June, Tarui continued to agitate for its goals until his arrest and imprisonment in January 1883.

Toyoshima Yoshio (1890–1955)

Author. Born in Fukuoka Prefecture. Graduate of Tōkyō University. A member of the Tōkyō University students' literary coterie magazine, *Shinshichō* (third series), he won recognition for his short story "Kosui to karera" (1914). Toyoshima was a prolific writer, producing short stories, plays, and children's stories. He is known for his translations of Western literature, among them Romain Rolland's *Jean Christophe* (1910) and *The Thousand and One Nights*, from Burton's translation (1940–59). His principal work is a collection of short stories, *Yamabuki no hana* (1954).

Toyota

Industrial zone in the city of Toyota, showing one of the automobile assembly plants of Toyota Motor Corporation.

Tōyō Soda Mfg Co, Ltd

(Tōyō Sōda Kōgyō). Comprehensive chemical company. Manufacturer of organic and inorganic chemicals, petrochemicals, and electrochemicals. When it was founded in 1935, Tōyō Soda's initial activity was the manufacture of soda ash and caustic soda with its own ammonia soda process. Success in this field led to the establishment of various other chemical plants—for bromine in 1942, portland cement in 1953, vinyl chloride monomer and low-density polyethylene in 1966. A full 10 percent of its staff is involved in research and development. The company maintains joint ventures in Greece, Indonesia, the Netherlands, and Iran, as well as overseas subsidiaries in Amsterdam and Atlanta. Sales for the fiscal year ending March 1982 totaled ¥206.1 billion (US $856.2 million), with petrochemicals accounting for 35 percent, portland cement 17 percent, soda chemicals 20 percent, metal products 6 percent, fertilizers 5 percent, and other products 17 percent. The export ratio was 15.3 percent in that year. The company was capitalized at ¥17.5 billion (US $72.7 million) the same year. The head office is in Tōkyō.

Tōyō Suisan Kaisha, Ltd

A company producing and selling instant and frozen food, Tōyō Suisan was established in 1953. It is the largest manufacturer of instant food in the industry. It has an overseas subsidiary in Los Angeles called Maruchan, Inc. The company is affiliated with Campbell Soup Co of the United States, whose juices and soups it produces and sells in Japan as Campbell Toyo, Ltd. Future plans call for the expansion of its overseas markets. Sales totaled ¥87.2 billion (US $362.2 million) in the fiscal year ending in March 1982; the company was capitalized at ¥2.9 billion (US $12 million) in the same year. The head office is in Tōkyō.

Toyota

City in central Aichi Prefecture, central Honshū. Located on the river Yahagigawa, it is known primarily as the headquarters of the TOYOTA MOTOR CORPORATION; the first plant was built in 1938. Sanage Shrine is situated in the foothills of Sanageyama. Pop: 281,609.

Toyota Auto Body Co, Ltd

(Toyota Shatai). An automobile body manufacturer affiliated with the TOYOTA MOTOR CORPORATION, Toyota Auto Body was established in 1945 when the Kariya plant, birthplace of the Toyota car, became independent of the parent auto company. It manufactures the bodies of Toyota Motor's small-sized passenger cars, and is also developing special and multipurpose cars. Toyota Auto Body has grown with the development of the Toyota group. Sales for the fiscal year ending March 1982 totaled ¥223 billion (US $926.4 million), practically all of which was accounted for by the Toyota group. The company was capitalized at ¥3.8 billion (US $15.8 million) in the same year. The head office is in Kariya, Aichi Prefecture.

Toyotake Yamashiro no Shōjō (1878–1967)

Chanter (tayū) in the JŌRURI form of narrative chanting associated with the BUNRAKU puppet theater. Born in Tōkyō. Original name Kanasugi Yatarō. His theatrical career began on the KABUKI stage, where between the ages of 4 and 10 he played children's roles (koyaku). At the age of 7 he commenced training in the GIDAYŪ-BUSHI style of chanting. In 1889 he became a disciple of Takemoto Tsudayū II (1839–1912) of Ōsaka's Bunrakuza puppet theater, with which he was to remain affiliated throughout his career. In 1909 he succeeded to the professional name Toyotake Koutsubodayū. Koutsubodayū was noted for his formal analysis of the various recitation (katari) styles, and the majority of chanters today have been stylistically and technically affected by him. In 1947 he was granted the court title Yamashiro no Shōjō by Prince CHICHIBU in recognition of his importance to jōruri. MOTEGI Kiyoko

Tōyō Takushoku Kaisha

(Oriental Development Company). A Japanese government-supported company formed in 1908, soon after the establishment of Korea as a Japanese protectorate (see KOREAN-JAPANESE CONVENTION OF 1905), to develop agriculture in Korea. One-third of its capital and extensive landholdings were provided by the Korean government. The main office was in Seoul. Besides agricultural management and irrigation projects, the company helped Japanese immigrants settle in Korea by providing low-interest loans. Although ostensibly under joint Korean-Japanese management, it was in fact run by the Japanese, especially after their annexation of the country (1910). Through its control of numerous enterprises ranging from mining to rails and electricity, the Tōyō Takushoku Kaisha became a major economic force and the largest landholder in Korea. In 1917 it moved its main office to Tōkyō, increased its capital fivefold, and expanded its operations to Manchuria, North China, and the South Pacific. It was dissolved by the OCCUPATION authorities immediately after World War II.

■ ——Tōyō Takushoku Kaisha, Tōyō takushoku kabushiki kaisha sanjūnenshi (1938).

Toyota Motor Corporation

(Toyota Jidōsha). Manufacturer of passenger cars, trucks, buses, and prefabricated houses. Japan's largest automaker and the second largest in the world in 1981, the company is the nucleus of the Toyota group. The company began as the automobile division of TOYODA AUTOMATIC LOOM WORKS, LTD, in 1933 and became independent of the parent firm in 1937. The first A-1 prototype was completed in 1935, and by 1941 monthly production of passenger cars totaled 2,000 units. After World War II it rejected capital tie-ups with foreign companies and chose instead to follow its own course. The Toyopet Crown, placed on the market in 1955, played a significant role in the motorization of Japan. Models introduced since then include the Publica and the small-sized Corona, Corolla, and Celica. Toyota vehicles are known for their quality and efficiency. The sale of the products had been the responsibility of its sales company, Toyota Motor Sales Co, Ltd, from 1950 to June 1982. Effective July 1982, Toyota Motor Co, Ltd, and Toyota Motor Sales Co, Ltd, merged, forming Toyota Motor Corporation.

TOYOTA AUTO BODY CO, LTD; KANTŌ AUTO WORKS, LTD; and DAIHATSU MOTOR CO, LTD, are engaged in the assembly of Toyota Motor's cars, while more than 200 firms provide car components, including NIPPONDENSŌ CO, LTD, and AISIN SEIKI CO, LTD. By adopting a "just in time" delivery system for car parts, the company has succeeded in minimizing its inventory of unfinished products. It has 27 plants overseas, including operations in the United States and Australia. Its profit ratio and retained profit are high and its financial position sound. Sales for the fiscal year ending June 1982 totaled ¥3.8 trillion (US $15.2 billion), distributed as follows: passenger cars 58 percent, trucks and buses 22 percent, and others 20 percent. The export ratio was 43 percent and capitalization stood at ¥100 billion (US $398 million) the same year. The head office is in the city of Toyota, Aichi Prefecture.

Tōyō Tire & Rubber Industry Co, Ltd

(Tōyō Gomu Kōgyō). Rubber company manufacturing automobile tires, industrial and chemical products, and shoes. It is the fourth largest manufacturer of car tires in Japan, specializing in radial tires for trucks and buses and large-size special tires. It was established in 1943 when TŌYŌBŌ CO, LTD, purchased several rubber companies to increase its influence in the rubber field and merged them to create the present firm. The company has sales companies in the United States, Australia, and West Germany. Sales for the fiscal year ending March 1982 totaled ¥162.9 billion (US $676.7 million) and the export ratio was 29 percent. Capitalization stood at ¥6.7 billion (US $27.8 million) in the same year. The head office is in Ōsaka.

Toyotomi Hidetsugu (1568–1595)

Also known as Toyotomi Hidetsugi. Nephew and adopted son of TOYOTOMI HIDEYOSHI; participated in Hideyoshi's military campaigns between 1583 and his unification of Japan in 1591. On 1 February 1592 (Tenshō 19.12.18), after the death of his natural son Tsurumatsu (1589–91), Hideyoshi retired as imperial regent (kampaku) and, 10 days later, had this post transferred to Hidetsugu so as, in the words of a contemporary Jesuit, "to delyver the Japonian monarchie to the posteritie of his owne stock"; uncle and nephew were the only two men of military provenance ever to hold that office. Hideyoshi transferred the Juraku no Tei, his nonesuch "Palace of Assembled Pleasures" in Kyōto, to Hidetsugu along with the title of kampaku.

Hidetsugu proved unequal to the thankless task of holding this highest of all posts in the aristocratic hierarchy while yet having to subordinate himself to the wishes of Hideyoshi as TAIKŌ (a title applying to the father of the kampaku). Although contemporary sources, including the reports of Jesuit missionaries, praise Hidetsugu for various cultural accomplishments, in particular for his love of the Nō, the classics, and calligraphy, his personal excesses are even more notorious; he appears to have had an inordinate lust for blood. Moreover, he seems to have used the vestigial powers of his office to interfere with certain of Hideyoshi's decisions. When Hideyoshi's natural son Hiroi (TOYOTOMI HIDEYORI; 1593–1615) was born, Hidetsugu's position became perilous. In 1595 he was disgraced, exiled to the Shingon monastery on Mt. Kōya (Kōyasan), and ordered to commit suicide. His family, close retainers, and the women of his entourage were executed by the remorseless Hideyoshi; the Juraku no Tei was dismantled; and Hidetsugu's head was exposed to public view in Kyōto. *George ELISON*

Toyotomi Hideyori (1593–1615)

Son of the national unifier TOYOTOMI HIDEYOSHI and his concubine YODOGIMI. His father, whose only other natural child, Tsurumatsu, had died at the age of two in 1591, did everything in his power to ensure Hideyori's succession to his own supreme position in Japan. The disgrace and forced suicide of Hideyoshi's adopted son, TOYOTOMI HIDETSUGU, in 1595 may at least partly be attributed to that wish, as may Hideyoshi's institution of a council of "Five Great Elders" (Gotairō) that same year; Hideyoshi's deathbed plea in 1598 to the five (TOKUGAWA IEYASU, MAEDA TOSHIIE, Mōri Terumoto [1553–1625], UESUGI KAGEKATSU, and UKITA HIDEIE), "Again and again, I beg you to take care of Hideyori," is famous. Unfortunately for the Toyotomi, the most trusted of these protectors, Maeda Toshiie, died te year after Hideyoshi, and the most powerful, Tokugawa Ieyasu, had his own contrary ambitions. After Ieyasu's victory in the Battle of SEKIGAHARA in 1600, and especially after he founded the Tokugawa shogunate in 1603, Hideyori was in effect reduced to the position of one among many daimyō. He continued to be appointed to high court ranks, ascending to the post of udaijin (minister of the right) in 1605, but he was increasingly isolated in his stronghold at Ōsaka as Ieyasu worked to consolidate his regime. In 1614 Ieyasu used a specious casus belli (the so-called SHŌMEI INCIDENT) to provoke an armed conflict with this last challenger to the legitimacy of his rule; there followed the two Ōsaka Campaigns, in which the Tokugawa were victorious (see ŌSAKA CASTLE, SIEGES OF). As Ōsaka Castle was about to fall on 3 June 1615 (Keichō 20.5.7), Hideyori's wife (Ieyasu's granddaughter) SEN HIME was sent from the burning fortress to intercede for her husband. Her plea was fruitless. The next day, Hideyori and his mother Yodogimi committed suicide in a last, unsurrendered tower of their castle. Kunimatsu, his seven-year-old son by a concubine, was executed in Kyōto, and a six-year-old daughter was immured in a nunnery. *George ELISON*

Toyotomi Hideyoshi (1537–1598)

Warlord of humble origins who in 1590 completed the work of national reunification begun by ODA NOBUNAGA. A brilliant strategist

Toyotomi Hideyoshi

Detail of a votive portrait commissioned by Hideyoshi's vassal Tanaka Yoshimasa (1548–1609). This is the oldest known painting of Hideyoshi and bears an inscription by the Zen priest Nanka Genkō (d 1604) with the date Keichō 3 (1598), the year of Hideyoshi's death. Ink and colors on silk. Entire work 111 × 62 cm. Kōdaiji, Kyōto.

and shrewd politician, he usually showed a generosity toward his enemies untypical of his time. His social reforms, while having the fundamental aim of strengthening his hold on the country, nevertheless showed an awareness of the many socioeconomic problems of the age. Thus, despite his grandiose plans for conquest abroad and the megalomania of the last few years of his life, he is without doubt one of the great figures in Japanese history.

At his birth Hideyoshi was called Hiyoshimaru, later changed to Tōkichirō, the family name being Kinoshita. In 1558 on entering Nobunaga's service, he was called Kochiku; in 1562 he changed this to Hideyoshi, and in 1572 changed the family name Kinoshita to Hashiba. In 1585 he was appointed imperial regent (kampaku); in 1586 he was appointed grand minister of state (dajō daijin) and was given the family name Toyotomi. Hideyoshi is popularly known as TAIKŌ, the honorary title for a retired kampaku.

Early Years —— Hideyoshi was born in 1537 (some scholars give the date as 1536) at Nakamura in Owari Province (now part of Aichi Prefecture), the son of Kinoshita Yaemon, a foot soldier (ashigaru) in the service of Oda Nobuhide (1510–51), father of Nobunaga. He soon left home and went into service with Matsushita Kahyōe, lord of Kunō (in Tōtōmi Province, now part of Shizuoka Prefecture). The story that he then joined the robber band of Hachisuka Masakatsu (1526–88), with whom he was to remain associated in later years, is most probably apocryphal. In 1558 Hideyoshi presented himself to Nobunaga, a rising star who was already master of the Kiyosu region of Owari. Nobunaga quickly took a liking to Hideyoshi and nicknamed him Saru ("Monkey"). At the time, in the struggle for military hegemony, the army of IMAGAWA YOSHIMOTO, lord of Mikawa (now part of Aichi Prefecture), Tōtōmi, and Suruga (the latter two both now part of Shizuoka Prefecture) provinces, was advancing on Kyōto. But in his path lay the lands of Nobunaga, who defeated him in the Battle of OKEHAZAMA in 1560. It is interesting that the three most important shapers of premodern Japanese history, Nobunaga, Hideyoshi, and TOKUGAWA IEYASU (who fought for Imagawa), were all engaged in this battle. It was Hideyoshi who ensured the victory over Saitō Tatsuoki at Inabayama by constructing at night a fortress facing the enemy. By mid-1573 Nobunaga was firmly established in central Honshū, having destroyed his brother-in-law ASAI NAGAMASA (one of whose daughters, YODOGIMI, was to become Hideyoshi's favorite concubine) and his erstwhile ally ASAKURA YOSHIKAGE. The Asai lands in Ōmi Province (now Shiga Prefecture) were given to Hideyoshi, who established his headquarters there at Imahama (now Nagahama). He exempted the town from taxation to stimulate its growth and also encouraged the development of the province.

General under Nobunaga (1574–1582) —— In 1575 Nobunaga was defeated in a naval battle in the bay of Ōsaka by the combined forces of Mōri Terumoto (1553–1625) and the temple-fortress ISHIYAMA HONGANJI. Nobunaga retaliated by dispatching two armies—one led by AKECHI MITSUHIDE in the north and a second, led by Hideyoshi, in the south—in a pincer movement aimed at subduing the Mōri home base in western Honshū. Hideyoshi took the strategically situated castle of Himeyama (later Himeji, in Harima Province; now part of Hyōgo Prefecture) in 1577 by persuading the governor of the castle to open the gates to him. Siegecraft was to become his specialty: in 1581 he took the fortress of Tottori in Inaba Province (now part of Tottori Prefecture); a year later he took Takamatsu Castle in Bitchū Province (now part of Okayama Prefecture) by employing the novel tactic of flooding (*mizuzeme*; see SHIMIZU MUNEHARU).

Taking the Reins of Power (1582–1587) —— It was during the siege of Takamatsu Castle that Nobunaga was treacherously assassinated by Mitsuhide (see HONNŌJI INCIDENT). Informed of his master's death, Hideyoshi quickly made peace with the Mōri and defeated Mitsuhide in the Battle of YAMAZAKI on 2 July 1582 (Tenshō 10.6.13). At the great council held in the castle of the Oda (from which only Ieyasu was absent), Hideyoshi, who presented himself as the "Great Avenger," overrode the opposition led by SHIBATA KATSUIE and persuaded the participants to nominate Oda Hidenobu (1580–1605), the infant grandson of Nobunaga, as the heir. Thus, at 45, Hideyoshi was master of the provinces of Ōmi, Harima, Yamashiro, Tamba (the last two now part of Kyōto Prefecture), and Kawachi (now part of Ōsaka Prefecture). Then, by defeating Shibata Katsuie at SHIZUGATAKE, he annexed Echizen, Kaga, and Noto (now Fukui and part of Ishikawa prefectures), and Etchū (now Toyama Prefecture). He distributed these provinces as rewards to his most faithful supporters, including MAEDA TOSHIIE. In 1584, after the KOMAKI NAGAKUTE CAMPAIGN, he arrived at a settlement with Ieyasu, who, fearing Hideyoshi's ascendance, had supported Oda Nobukatsu (1558–1630), Nobunaga's son. He then subdued all of Kii Province (now Wakayama Prefecture), destroying the warrior-monks at the temple Negoroji, who had been supplying arms to his enemies, and destroyed the organization (IKKŌ IKKI) of the Jōdo Shin sect of Saiga in that province. He proceeded to conquer the CHŌSOKABE FAMILY of Shikoku. By the end of 1585, Hideyoshi, newly appointed *kampaku*, could lay claim to all civil and military powers by delegation of the emperor; there remained only Kyūshū and the area from the Kantō to the northeast to conquer. During these campaigns, he had begun to implement the policy of *kuniwake*, a redistribution of fiefs aimed at reducing the powers of the entrenched provincial *daimyō* and placing trustworthy leaders at strategic points. He continued the land survey (KENCHI) begun by Nobunaga, adopting a new method of land measurement. This program was not only one of the most effective instruments of political control that Hideyoshi devised but was also to lead to a better exploitation of land resources.

The Kyūshū Campaign (1587) —— Hideyoshi had received repeated requests from ŌTOMO SŌRIN of Bungo Province (now part of Ōita Prefecture) to intervene in Kyūshū and thwart the expansionist designs of the SHIMAZU FAMILY of Satsuma Province (now part of Kagoshima Prefecture). Hideyoshi would have preferred to negotiate, but the arrogant attitude of Shimazu Yoshihisa (1533–1611) forced him to go into battle. The campaign was not easy, but in the end Hideyoshi prevailed, by force and by ruse. Kyūshū was restructured: the Shimazu were confined to their lands in the south, and three of Hideyoshi's most loyal commanders—KATŌ KIYOMASA, KONISHI YUKINAGA, and KURODA NAGAMASA—were placed in the center. Ōtomo was reestablished in Bungo, the Mōri given a large part of the north, and Chikuzen Province (now part of Fukuoka Prefecture) given to Kobayakawa Takakage (1533–97).

At the end of the Kyūshū campaign occurred Hideyoshi's first skirmish with Christianity. Previously, if he had not fully shared Nobunaga's sympathy for the foreign religion, he had been more than simply tolerant. Now, on 23 July 1587 (Tenshō 15.6.18), he issued an 11-point edict prohibiting forced conversion and, more important, denouncing Christianity as even more subversive than the notorious Ikkō of the Jōdo Shin sect. The following day he presented to the Jesuit missionaries the Edict of Expulsion that began with the well-known statement "Japan is the land of the *kami*" (see ANTI-CHRISTIAN EDICTS). There has been much speculation about

the reason for Hideyoshi's *volte-face*. In any event, although the edict was not enforced for some years, Hideyoshi had made it clear that his only interest in Europeans was for purposes of trade.

After imposing his conditions on the Shimazu and putting the trading port of Nagasaki under his jurisdiction (taking it from the Jesuits, who had been given control by the Christian daimyō ŌMURA SUMITADA), Hideyoshi made a triumphal return to Kyōto. He celebrated his victory with the most famous party in Japanese history, the great outdoor tea ceremony at Kitano Shrine. In May 1588 Hideyoshi displayed his wealth before the emperor Go-Yōzei (r 1586–1611) in his new abode, the Juraku no Tei (or Jurakudai) at Kyōto, where all the daimyō pledged obedience to the emperor and his regent, Hideyoshi. In the same year he carried out his famous SWORD HUNT on a national scale. This had the double aim of reducing the likelihood of armed rebellion and of separating the peasantry from the warrior class. It was the prelude to the population census of 1590, which further bound the peasants to the land, and to the eventual establishment of distinct social classes: *samurai*, farmers, artisans, and merchants (SHI-NŌ-KŌ-SHŌ).

The Kantō Campaign (1590–1591) —— Hideyoshi's conquest of the northeast remained barred by the Later HŌJŌ FAMILY, who occupied the Kantō and were linked to Ieyasu by marriage. After several attempts to settle matters peacefully, Ieyasu sided with Hideyoshi. The Hōjō concentrated all their forces at Odawara (in Sagami Province, now Kanagawa Prefecture). This was a serious tactical error, and Hideyoshi was able with comparative ease to destroy the allies of the Hōjō and besiege Odawara Castle. During the long ODAWARA CAMPAIGN, he allowed his warriors to send for their women and he himself sent for his favorite Yodogimi, who in 1589 had presented him with a long-desired heir, Tsurumatsu. Odawara capitulated on 12 August 1590 (Tenshō 18.7.13), and the Kantō provinces were reorganized. In order to remove Ieyasu from central Japan, Hideyoshi gave him six Kantō provinces in exchange for his former holdings in Mikawa, Tōtōmi, and Suruga. He also placed GAMŌ UJISATO at Kurokawa in Mutsu Province (now the city of Aizu Wakamatsu in Fukushima Prefecture) to keep an eye on Ieyasu and the regions to the north. In the autumn of 1591 Hideyoshi crushed all resistance in the far north of Honshū. The military reunification of Japan was now complete; all territory belonged to Hideyoshi or to his enfeoffed vassals, and a new feudal hierarchy had been established.

The Invasions of Korea (1592, 1597) —— Once master of Japan, Hideyoshi began to look across the sea, returning to his long-contemplated project for a pan-Asian kingdom. In his mind, the invasion of Korea was to be but the first phase of the conquest of China. This was not to be, and the enterprise was marked by a series of mishaps largely because Hideyoshi never set foot in Korea and was content to direct operations from Nagoya (now the city of Karatsu, Saga Prefecture) and later from the capital. The first expedition, in 1592, ended in a draw after the Japanese encountered determined resistence from the Koreans. The second, in 1597, was abandoned with Hideyoshi's death in 1598. See INVASIONS OF KOREA IN 1592 AND 1597.

Final Years —— In his last years, especially after 1593, Hideyoshi seemed almost to have lost touch with the reality around him. Two years earlier his son Tsurumatsu had died, and Hideyoshi, despairing of having other sons, had nominated his nephew TOYOTOMI HIDETSUGU as his heir. He had passed on to him the title of *kampaku* and taken for himself that of *taikō* on 11 February 1592 (Tenshō 19.12.28). He had also begun the construction of a fortified residence at Fushimi, near Kyōto, having decided to leave Juraku no Tei for his nephew. Then, while he was at Nagoya, Yodogimi presented him with another son, TOYOTOMI HIDEYORI. The child appeared to become his only interest in life and was indirectly to cause Hidetsugu's fall from favor. Convinced that Hidetsugu, who was known for his viciousness, was plotting against his life, Hideyoshi forced him to commit suicide in August 1595, after first banishing him into exile on Kōyasan. Determined to destroy all possible rivals to Hideyori, he then turned on the members of Hidetsugu's family, including his three small children. He had become increasingly suspicious in his later years, having, for example, ordered SEN NO RIKYŪ, his trusted adviser and tea master to commit suicide as early as 1591. Anxious for the future of his successor, he created a council of Five Great Elders (Gotairō) and made them swear allegiance to Hideyori. He also became increasingly fearful of Western interference in the country's internal affairs, especially after the Spanish ship *San Felipe* was shipwrecked on the Japanese coast in 1596 (see SAN FELIPE INCIDENT). On that occasion the Spanish captain, Francisco de

Olandia, spread the rumor that his king was planning to conquer the world and that the Spanish friars were the advance guard. Further irritated by the continuous bickering between the Jesuits and the Franciscans, Hideyoshi sentenced 26 Christians to death—the TWENTY-SIX MARTYRS of Nagasaki.

Hideyoshi fell ill in the summer of 1598. He once more summoned the five elders to Fushimi to swear loyalty to Hideyori and support to the house of Toyotomi. His mind began to wander, and he died on 18 September 1598 (Keichō 3.8.18). His character is best understood through his private letters to his wife Nene (Kita no Mandokoro), his mother Ōmandokoro, his children, and his concubines. They show him to be open and affectionate, genial, and impatient with formality. It was unfortunate that his insatiable thirst for power came to cast a shadow of terror during the last years of his life.

■——Adriana Boscaro, *101 Letters of Toyotomi Hideyoshi* (1975). Walter Dening, *The Life of Toyotomi Hideyoshi* (1930, repr 1955). Kuwata Tadachika, *Toyotomi Hideyoshi kenkyū* (1975). George Sansom, *A History of Japan, 1334–1615* (1961). Suzuki Ryōichi, *Toyotomi Hideyoshi* (1969).   Adriana BOSCARO

Tōyō Trust & Banking Co, Ltd

(Tōyō Shintaku Ginkō). A representative Japanese trust bank, the Tōyō Trust & Banking Co was founded in 1959 through the merger of the trust business of the SANWA BANK, LTD, and the Kōbe Bank, Ltd (now TAIYŌ KŌBE BANK, LTD), as well as the securities agency business of the NOMURA SECURITIES CO, LTD. Tōyō Trust specializes in registered securities transactions, investment consultation, underwriting of securities investment trusts, investment management, and other securities-related business. The company is currently diversifying into individual annuity trusts and real estate. The company had ¥5.2 trillion (US $21.6 billion) in available funds at the end of March 1982. It was capitalized at ¥26 billion (US $108 million) in the same year. The head office is in Tōkyō.

toys, traditional

The earliest documentary evidence for the existence of toys in Japan dates from the Heian period (794–1185), but there can be little doubt that the origin of toys goes back even further. Among the treasures in the 8th-century SHŌSŌIN repository in Nara are boards used for playing GO; however, these were no doubt imported from China. It has been suggested that some of the smaller HANIWA grave figures may have been used as toys, and that playthings made of perishable materials such as straw, paper, wood, and cloth may have existed in prehistoric times. Many early toys were no doubt connected with sacred places and used in folk festivals, as is the case with some popular folk toys used today. Other toys, however, were used for children's games from the outset.

The greatest age for all kinds of toys was the Edo period (1600–1868), when Japan was at peace and the common people had enough leisure time to produce and enjoy folk toys. Until then, toys had been made largely for members of the court and the aristocracy. Their production continues today, but, unfortunately, competition from cheap, machine-made toys of plastic, celluloid, metal, and wood is threatening to destroy the traditional industry. While folk toys have become very popular and are eagerly collected by FOLK CRAFTS enthusiasts, their manufacture has declined and accounts for only a small percentage of total Japanese toy production.

Types of Toys —— There are almost one thousand different types of folk toys, which can be roughly divided into three main groups. First, there are the simple playthings intended for children; second, the more artistic toys that may be enjoyed by children but are also appreciated for their artistry by adults; and third, the charms and dolls that are connected with local legends and traditions. Typical of the first category are the clay and paper dolls, balls (TEMARI), TOPS, and simple games that are found all over Japan. Far more interesting and beautiful are the objects belonging to the second group. Outstanding among them are the often large and magnificently decorated KITES with pictures of KABUKI actors or popular deities, some of them masterpieces of folk art. Other fine objects are the battledores and shuttlecocks, which are still widely used, especially on New Year's Day, for a game known as HANETSUKI. The battledore or HAGOITA is usually decorated with brightly colored paintings of actors or beautiful ladies on one side and floral designs on the other. But most characteristic are the numerous toys belonging to the third

Traditional toys

A papier-mâché toy dog (*inu hariko* or *Azuma inu*) of the type popular in the Tōkyō area since the Edo period.

category, which were originally religious in character, although this is often lost on the contemporary user. For example, in Tōkyō newly born infants are often presented with toy dogs, believed to be protective charms. Made at Nihombashi in Tōkyō, these are called *inu hariko* or *Azuma inu* and are sold at local Shintō shrines. Other popular toys of this type are the toy horses that are found in many localities and are often connected with sacred places. Very popular also are the *daruma* dolls, stylized representations of Bodhidharma (J: Bodai Daruma or Daruma), the founder of Zen Buddhism, which are today looked upon as good luck emblems (see DARUMA FAIRS). The *shishi* or lion masks are also clearly of Buddhist origin but are now widely used for protection and good luck. There are many such objects that serve as talismans to prevent sickness, help one avoid bad luck, and ensure prosperity and good harvests.

Materials Used —— One of the most striking features of Japanese folk toys is the great variety of materials employed in their manufacture. The most common material is wood, used for example in KOKESHI dolls and *shishi* masks; but clay, found in the beckoning cats (MANEKINEKO) and other figurines, is equally popular. Paper is used for kites and small dolls and so are many other substances. Papier-mâché is employed in *daruma* dolls and *inu hariko;* straw is used for the sacred horses; bamboo for the TAKETOMBO, a spinning toy, and for the rods holding small cloth monkeys. Among the more unusual toys are the horned owls called *mimizuku* made of Zebra grass and sold at the Kishibojin Shrine in Zōshigaya in Tōkyō, and the blowfish lanterns made in Enoshima of blowfish skin. Other toys are made of a combination of materials, such as the battledores that combine wood and cloth, and the shuttlecocks made from a large seed or wooden ball and a feather. Interesting also are the beautiful toy balls (*temari*), found in many parts of Japan, that are made of a paper core wrapped in cloth and covered with colorful threads.

Regional Variations —— Japanese handcrafted toys are usually made in local workshops, often by farm families during their idle hours to supplement the family income, and they often have a strong regional or even local flavor. Folk toys were traditionally made in all parts of Japan with the exception of Hokkaidō (there, except for Ainu carvings, no such tradition existed). Today they are most common in Tōhoku in northern Honshū and the more rural sections of Kyūshū; however, some folk toys are still being made in such urban centers as Tōkyō, Ōsaka, and Kyōto. Altogether there are over 100 centers specializing in regional toys. These regional toys may be used for a specific local festival or sold only at one temple or shrine. The horned owl, for example, is only found in Tōkyō and the spouting whale is only seen in Nagasaki, where the whale was originally employed in floats used in festivals started by the Suwa Shrine as a counter-measure against Christianity. Wheeled wooden toys are characteristic of Kyūshū; the papier-mâché figures of the young priest Junshin and his ladylove Ouma are only found in Kōchi Prefecture in Shikoku; and *kokeshi* dolls are typical of the Tōhoku district. The Kyōdo Gangu Kan in Kurashiki, Okayama Prefecture houses several thousand examples of regional toys. See also DOLLS; GAMES.

■——Sakamoto Kazuya, *Japanese Toys,* with photography by Sonobe Kiyoshi, tr Charles Pomeroy (1965).   Hugo MÜNSTERBERG

Traditional toys

This papier-mâché toy whale from Nagasaki is fashioned after one of the floats paraded in the city's annual festival, Okunchi.

tozama

(literally, "outside" vassals). A term by which *samurai* lords, such as the Hōjō regents of the Kamakura period (1185–1333) and the Ashikaga shōguns of the Muromachi period (1333–1568) distinguished samurai lineages that were not subordinate to their own family through kinship or hereditary service from their hereditary vassals (FUDAI). During the Edo period (1600–1868) the Tokugawa shogunate identified as *tozama daimyō* those lords who had acquired their daimyō status under ODA NOBUNAGA or TOYOTOMI HIDEYOSHI and who had sworn fealty to the Tokugawa family before or after the decisive Battle of SEKIGAHARA (1600). Daimyō lineages descended from the dynastic founder, TOKUGAWA IEYASU, were called SHIMPAN, and hereditary vassal daimyō whose allegiance antedated Sekigahara were designated *fudai*. *Tozama*, such as those of the domains of Chōshū, Satsuma, and Tosa (now Yamaguchi, Kagoshima, and Kōchi prefectures, respectively), generally held higher rank and larger domains, tended to regard *fudai* daimyō as social inferiors, and strove to maintain their distinctive identity. *Fudai* daimyō, on the other hand, were more dependent on the shogunate for aid and protection, but they had a virtual monopoly on shogunate offices and were more secure in their status. The relatively precarious position of the *tozama* is reflected in the changing numbers of daimyō due to dispossession (KAIEKI). Whereas in 1602 there were 117 *tozama* as opposed to 78 *fudai* and shimpan, by 1795 there were only 98 *tozama* as opposed to 168 *fudai* and shimpan lords.

Conrad TOTMAN

track and field events

Track and field events were introduced to Japan in the 1870s from England and the United States. Japanese track and field competition developed as a student sport; the first meet was held in 1874 at the Tsukiji Naval Academy in Tōkyō. In 1883 an athletic meet was held at Tōkyō University under the direction of Fredrick W. Strange, a language instructor from England. The events at that meet were similar to those of today. Thereafter, track meets became popular at other schools and, from about 1890, outstanding athletes were invited to participate. Participation on the international level began with the 1912 Stockholm Olympics. In the 1924 Paris Olympics, ODA MIKIO placed sixth in the triple jump and subsequently Japan entered its "golden age," winning this event three times in a row at the Olympic Games in Amsterdam (1928), Los Angeles (1932), and Berlin (1936). Japanese athletes also did well in other Olympic

events and in other international meets during these years. In the post-World War II period, they have been most successful in the marathon (see MARATHONS). *Maeda Wakaki*

Trademark Law

(Shōhyō Hō). The Trademark Law of 1959 established a registration system under which trademarks are protected by granting the owner of a registered trademark the exclusive right to use his trademark for designated goods. A trademark *(shōhyō)* is defined as "characters, letters, figures, or signs, or any combination of these and colors, which a person who, as a business, produces, processes, certifies, or assigns goods uses on such goods." This definition does not include service marks or trade names.

In order to obtain registration, the trademark under application must be distinctive, but proof of use is not necessary. In order to prevent unused trademarks from remaining in the trademark registry, the burden of proving use is imposed upon the owner of a registered trademark when an interested party initiates a proceeding before the Patent Office to cancel the registration on the ground of nonuse for three consecutive years; the owner is also required to prove use for three years before he applies for a renewal of the registration.

The owner of a well-known trademark may obtain a defensive mark registration. This system, together with the system of allowing registration of associated trademarks, is modeled after British trademark law. The exclusive right of the owner of a registered trademark extends primarily to the designated goods unless the trademark has become well-known and is entitled to a broader protection under the Unfair Competition Prevention Law (Fusei Kyōsō Bōshi Hō).

The Trademark Law provides three types of civil remedies for trademark infringement: injunction, damages, and measures to restore the business reputation of the plaintiff. Trademarks are regarded as property distinct from the business or goodwill associated with them, and therefore trademarks can be assigned without involving the transfer of any business associated with the mark and can be subject to an exclusive or nonexclusive license. Trademarks can be coowned or pledged. *Doi Teruo*

trade name

(shōgō). In Japanese law, a name used for an article or a service by a trader or company in the conduct of its business, and distinguished from ordinary names and nonbusiness names such as pen names and professional names. It must be possible to write and pronounce a trade name; a figure or a symbol may not be a trade name. Individual traders may select and register only one trade name for each business. A trader is not required to choose a trade name, but a company must select and register a trade name. Even though a company engages in more than one business, it may have only one trade name. A company must indicate in its trade name whether it is a joint-stock company, limited liability company, unlimited partnership company, or limited partnership company (COMMERCIAL CODE, art. 17). Similarly, certain businesses, such as banks and insurance companies, must indicate the nature of their business in their trade names. A user of a trade name has the right to prohibit the use of the same or similar trade name by others; this right is scrupulously protected where the trade name has been duly registered.

Kitazawa Masahiro

"transcendental" cabinets

(chōzen naikaku). Cabinets intended to be above the partisan interests of political parties. The term was first used by Prime Minister KURODA KIYOTAKA in a speech he made to government officials on 12 February 1889, the day after the promulgation of the Meiji CONSTITUTION. It reflected the profound distrust of the government leaders toward political parties, which in turn assailed the idea of a nonparty cabinet as a mere pretext for continued dominance of the government by cliques (see HAMBATSU). The concept of a "transcendental" cabinet was revived several times, most notably in the early 1920s, with the KATŌ TOMOSABURŌ, YAMAMOTO GONNOHYŌE, and KIYOURA KEIGO cabinets, and in the 1930s with the formation of the so-called national unity cabinets *(kyokoku itchi naikaku)* by SAITŌ MAKOTO, OKADA KEISUKE, and their successors after the MAY 15TH INCIDENT of 1931.

translation rights

(hon'yakuken). The right to reproduce a book, article, or other original piece of writing in another language. Under the Japanese COPYRIGHT LAW (Chosakuken Hō) of 1970, the author of a work has the exclusive right to reproduce the work (art. 21) as well as the exclusive right to translate or adapt it into another language (art. 27). Thus, the author of a work may authorize others to translate it under terms and conditions stipulated in a contract. Since copyright consists of a set of rights, including translation rights, and since these are transferable in whole or in part (art. 61 [1]), the translation rights can be transferred. When a copyright is transferred without specifically mentioning the translation rights, it is presumed that the original holder of copyright retains translation rights (art. 61 [2]).

When a work is translated, the translation is a derivative work which is protected as an independent work of authorship. The translator's copyright protection for the translation lasts from the moment of its creation until 50 years after his or her death (art. 51).

When a derivative work is created from a particular work such as a translation, the author of the original work is entitled to exercise the same rights as those held by the author of the derivative work (art. 28). Thus, when a translation is used as the basis of a motion picture, authorization must be obtained not only from the translator but also from the author of the original work.

Since Japan is a member of the Universal Copyright Convention, Japanese publishers may avail themselves of the right to translate works from foreign languages under conditions described in article 5 (2) of the convention and also under the provisions of the 1959 Law concerning Exceptional Provisions to the Copyright Law, Required upon the Enforcement of the Universal Copyright Convention (Bankoku Chosakuken Jōyaku no Jisshi ni Tomonau Chosakuken Hō no Tokurei ni Kansuru Hōritsu). *Doi Teruo*

transportation

As an advanced industrial country, Japan has a highly developed domestic and international transportation network. The system as it now exists was developed in the century following the Meiji Restoration of 1868, but even earlier the transportation system was relatively sophisticated for a preindustrial society.

History of Transportation —— *Pre-Meiji.* During the early periods of Japanese history, and especially during the official contacts of the 7th to 9th centuries, goods and people traveled extensively in SHIPS between Japan and the Asian mainland (see SUI AND TANG [T'ANG] CHINA, EMBASSIES TO). Within Japan, the establishment of a rice tax system and legal system in the late 7th century brought with them the construction of the first major roads. Because Japan is a mountainous country, however, the Inland Sea had been a major transportation route among settlements in Japan from early times. Protected from the open ocean, its shores were a natural setting for the major centers of early Japanese civilization.

In the late 9th century, official contact with China was broken off. However, private trade and other contacts continued and by the early 14th century Japanese sailors had begun to venture into the China Sea in great numbers. At first, intercourse was limited to unorganized trade and piracy by WAKŌ, but in 1401, the Muromachi shogunate (1338–1573) started official trade with China (see TALLY TRADE). By the 16th century the Japanese had become major traders in the China Sea region.

After the establishment of the Tokugawa shogunate (1603–1867), international transportation activity was halted by the NATIONAL SECLUSION (Sakoku) policy, which was in force from 1639 to 1853. No Japanese were allowed to travel abroad, and only the Dutch and Chinese were permitted limited trading at Nagasaki. Prohibition of international travel led to limits on the maximum size of coastal vessels (to ensure against illegal use in overseas trade), and lack of foreign interaction caused Japanese shipbuilding technology to fall far behind the West.

Domestic transportation, on the other hand, grew and was improved greatly in the context of peace, stability, and economic growth of the Edo period (1600–1868). Coastal shipping routes were established and extended from the Inland Sea to Edo (now Tōkyō), and from Hokkaidō through the Sea of Japan to the Inland Sea (see KAISEN). Coastal shipping moved the great bulk of the expanding commodity trade, permitting Ōsaka's growth as a rice center and general commodity trading center. The road network was also improved during the Edo period, partly to meet the needs imposed by the SANKIN KŌTAI system, whereby each *daimyō* traveled between his domain and Edo with his retinue every other year.

Beyond a certain point, however, Tokugawa transportation progress was severely constrained. Fear of revolt led to a prohibition of bridges over major rivers, preventing development of overland wagon transportation. Goods moving overland were carried by horse or porter, limiting quantities and keeping transportation costs high. Rivers in Japan are shallow, rocky, and subject to great seasonal variations in flow, preventing development of inland water transportation systems except in a few limited areas (such as the Kantō Plain).

Meiji period to World War II. Modern transportation began in Japan following the Meiji Restoration when the Tokugawa prohibitions on travel were eliminated and Japan began to absorb Western technology. Changes occurred at a dizzying pace. The first RICKSHAWS (jinrikisha) were built in 1870, the first train ran between Tōkyō and Yokohama in 1872, the first electric trolley ran in Kyōto in 1895, the first automobile was imported in 1899, the first airplane produced domestically in 1911, and the first automobile produced in 1912. In shipping, Western sailing and steam vessels replaced most Japanese sailing vessels within 20 years of the Meiji Restoration. The government took an active role in subsidizing shipbuilding of oceangoing vessels and the government shipyards became an important training ground in Western techniques for Japanese workers. From the 1880s onward the rail network expanded rapidly and in 1906 major portions of it were nationalized. In 1927 the first subway in Tōkyō began operation. Buses began operating in 1910 and trucking companies in 1915, with rapid expansion taking place after the TŌKYŌ EARTHQUAKE OF 1923. During the 1930s taxis developed into an important means of urban transportation. Airplane construction was begun by a number of companies in the 1920s, but most production was directed toward military aircraft.

Statistics on pre-World War II transportation are extremely poor except for the railroads, but it is clear that by the 1940s the mainstays of the domestic passenger transportation system were the railroads (including extensive urban trolley lines), while domestic freight transportation was conducted mainly through coastal shipping and the railroads. Trucks were used largely to deliver freight from railroad stations. Roads were improved and bridges built by the government, but by the time of World War II, Japan's intercity road network remained unpaved. International transportation was provided by freight and passenger ships. During the war, the merchant marine fleet was virtually destroyed, but the rail network never became a primary bombing target. However, the railroads did suffer from bombing in urban target areas and from inadequate maintenance. As gasoline was reserved for the military, civilian cars were converted to run on gas generated from car-mounted charcoal burners.

Postwar transportation. At the conclusion of World War II, the transportation system was in ruins. The damaged rail network was burdened with meeting the major part of passenger and freight transportation needs: in 1950 the railroads provided 90 percent of total domestic passenger-kilometers, and 52 percent of domestic freight ton-kilometers (see Tables 1 and 2). Out of this devastated situation, tremendous growth and change took place in Japanese transportation.

Growth of total domestic passenger travel and freight transportation has been somewhat slower than growth in the gross national product (GNP), because economic activity has been concentrated in the Pacific Belt running from Tōkyō to Ōsaka. This concentration has cut transportation needs per unit of final output. Growth of transportation activity was rapid during the 1955–73 period, however, with passenger-kilometers increasing at an average annual rate of 8.1 percent and freight ton-kilometers at 9.1 percent. Certainly the transportation system has not been an obstacle to economic expansion. Many parts of the network are characterized by great efficiency.

Within this overall picture of expansion, there have been major shifts in relative shares of each mode of transportation. The postwar era has been characterized by an explosive growth in the number of automobiles, trucks, and airlines. By 1979 the rail share of total domestic passenger transportation had fallen to 40 percent, with automobiles increasing from less than 1 percent in 1950 to 41 percent in 1979. Scheduled airlines have grown rapidly but still occupy a small 3 percent share of total passenger output (but a much larger part of travel between distant locations such as Tōkyō and Sapporo). Buses compete with the railroads to some extent, but they mainly provide feeder service to train stations or operate in rural areas where there is no rail service.

In freight transportation the changes have been even more dramatic. The rail share of total domestic ton-kilometers fell to 9.8

percent by 1979, while trucks expanded from 8 percent in 1950 to 39 percent in 1979, and coastal shipping expanded from 39 percent to 51 percent. Air freight remains negligible and river freight no longer exists.

These changes in passenger and freight transportation, with the decline of the railroads in both markets, reflect what was an abnormally high rail share in the early postwar period, as well as the growth of a vigorous domestic automotive industry. Japanese geography is favorable to coastal shipping, and the generally short distances are suitable to trucking and automobiles.

Another major change in transportation was the dramatic slowing of activity following the OIL CRISIS OF 1973. Passenger travel growth declined from its 8.1 percent average of 1955–73 to only 1.7 percent during 1973–76, increasing to 4.1 percent in 1979. Freight transportation dropped from a 9.1 percent growth rate to an absolute decline at an annual rate of 3 percent and rose again to 7.5 percent in 1979. Within this slow growth framework, autos, trucks, and airlines continued to perform relatively better.

International transportation has also expanded. International air travel has grown at a tremendous pace: scheduled Japanese airlines carried only 112,000 passengers in 1955 but reached 3.2 million by 1976. During 1979 a total of 5.11 million international passengers arrived in Japan (by Japanese and foreign airlines and by ship), and another 5.12 million passengers departed from Japan. Scheduled passenger liners no longer cross the Pacific, but the Soviet Union still provides passenger service on the Hong Kong–Yokohama–Nahodka route, and cruise vessels call at major Japanese ports. With Japan dependent to such a large degree on imports in a number of vital raw materials, development of international freight transportation has been essential to Japan's economic growth.

The Postwar Transportation Network —— With the tremendous growth of autos, trucks, and airlines, Japan now has an advanced transportation network with many interacting and competing parts. Some forms of transportation are owned and operated wholly or partially by the government (the Japanese National Railways and Japan Airlines) with others completely private.

Transportation administration. Before World War II, the MINISTRY OF TRANSPORT directly administered the nationalized railway system, with additional departments added as other forms of transportation began to develop. During the OCCUPATION (1945–52), the present administrative structure of Japanese transportation evolved. Under pressure to reduce the size of the government, SCAP (the headquarters of the Allied Occupation of Japan) ordered the nationalized railway system to become a public enterprise, which was done in 1949 when the JAPANESE NATIONAL RAILWAYS (JNR) was created. At the same time, the Ministry of Transport was reorganized. Under the reorganization law, the ministry was given administrative functions dealing with water, land, and air passenger and freight transportation; ships, sailors, and marine safety; railway cars and other land transportation vehicles; warehousing; and weather forecasting. While this list includes a diverse set of administrative functions, some other important functions were not placed under the ministry. Highway construction (see JAPAN HIGHWAY PUBLIC CORPORATION) and the establishment of expressway tolls are under the control of the MINISTRY OF CONSTRUCTION, and the automotive industry has the cooperation of the MINISTRY OF INTERNATIONAL TRADE AND INDUSTRY. The Ministry of Transport officially oversees JNR management, but its power to influence JNR policy is extremely weak and in reality the most important control functions lie with the MINISTRY OF FINANCE and the DIET. In addition, the Ministry of Finance maintains budgeting approval authority for all Ministry of Transport and Ministry of Construction spending on transportation infrastructure projects funded by the Japanese government.

In addition to economic regulation functions a major portion of Ministry of Transport activities is directed to other areas: maritime safety, maritime accidents, maritime labor relations, weather forecasting, air traffic control, and a variety of training centers and research institutes. Ministry involvement is much stronger in maritime and aviation affairs than in other transportation areas because many activities related to other modes of transportation fall under the jurisdiction of other agencies of the government. The police are responsible for enforcing highway laws, the construction ministry for highway safety designing, and the JNR for railway technical research and railway training.

Railroads. The network of RAILWAYS is divided into two parts: the government-owned JNR and a number of smaller private railways. According to the law which nationalized part of the rail system in 1906, all major intercity trunk lines were to be nationalized,

leaving private railways in the role of feeder lines to urban areas and sightseeing areas. In the late 1970s the rail system comprised 26,700 operation-kilometers, of which JNR operated 21,200, or 80 percent of the total. JNR owns both intercity trunk lines and a large number of secondary, largely rural, lines. JNR provides both passenger and freight services, and private railways are almost entirely specialized in passenger service.

As a public enterprise, the JNR budget must be approved by the Diet, and until 1978 rate control was split between the Diet and the Ministry of Transport. Rates are divided into basic rates and express train surcharges. Basic rate changes required Diet approval, but express charge changes needed only ministry approval. In 1978 basic rate approval, within maximum annual limits, was shifted to the Ministry of Transport.

Passenger service on JNR includes both intercity trains and urban feeder service. In 1950, JNR alone generated 58.9 percent of all domestic passenger-kilometers, but this figure had fallen to 25 percent by 1979. Despite slower growth than other modes of passenger transportation, JNR has responded to changing passenger demand through a number of significant technological changes—of which the high-speed SHINKANSEN is the most striking.

Freight transportation on JNR has not fared as well as passenger service. With a low growth rate of only 1.7 percent annually during 1955–73, and falling traffic since then, the JNR share in total domestic ton-kilometers fell from 51 percent in 1950 to only 10 percent in 1979. Much of the loss of market share has been beyond the control of JNR management, since it has been due in large measure to a decline in domestic coal production, the rapid rise of manufactured freight with demand characteristics suited best to motor carriers, a tendency for industry to develop in clusters around major ports (enhancing access to coastal and international shipping), and the liability imposed by an awkward rail freight forwarding system. In 1950 virtually all nonbulky carload and less-than-carload shipments were loaded and unloaded at JNR freight stations with delivery performed only by licensed freight forwarders. Rising labor costs and relocation of industries farther away from JNR lines made the railroad more susceptible to motor carrier competition. Given the short distances involved in Japanese transportation, JNR cannot effectively compete for much of the merchandise freight with a high time value. Government regulation also contributed to freight problems; since all freight rates were subject to Diet approval until 1978, JNR freight rate levels and structures were very inflexible.

The major innovative move JNR has taken in freight service has been container service (called container on flat car—COFC), which began in 1959 and now generates 20 percent of JNR freight ton-kilometers. This system is unrelated to the marine container system which gained popularity in international shipping; JNR containers are smaller, and the railroad hauls very few of the larger marine containers. Through the operation of scheduled container-only trains (patterned after the British freightliner) beginning in 1969, JNR has successfully competed with trucks on some routes. Other freight innovations have included specialized freight cars, unit trains, automated freight yards, and consolidation of small freight stations.

Since 1964 JNR has produced a constantly increasing deficit, which has become a major problem. In 1979 this deficit was ¥821.8 billion, or US $3.7 billion. Efforts to eliminate deficits have been to no avail and the government has gradually come to consider subsidies for some parts of JNR service (such as rural branch lines). Attitudes and policies concerning JNR deficits continue to be in a state of change.

The private rail industry in Japan is quite distinct from JNR and is generally divided into two parts. Of these, the most important in terms of transportation output is a group of 14 large private railways. In addition, there are 59 much smaller railways which are too small to have any significant impact on total transportation activity. Unlike JNR, private railways are not restricted from operating nonrail businesses and have evolved into conglomerates of related activities, including sports stadiums, baseball teams, department stores, amusement parks, and real estate. Private railway profits from railroad activity are small (and often negative), but by operating other businesses along their own rail lines, they benefit from increased patronage not reflected in rail profits alone. Most private rail lines radiate out from urban areas, and in most locations do not compete directly with JNR for traffic.

Private railways have also instituted a number of technical changes, including extensive electrification, ticket vending machines, and improvements in rail passenger vehicles. Because private railways operate in high-density traffic areas, they have found electrifi-

Table 1

Domestic Passenger Transportation
(in billions of passenger-kilometers)

	Rail			Bus	Automobile	Ship	Scheduled airlines	Total
	JNR	Private	Total					
1950	69.0	36.5	105.5	8.3	0.7	2.6	—	117.1
1960	124.0	60.4	184.3	44.0	11.5	2.7	0.7	243.3
1970	189.7	99.1	288.8	102.9	181.3	4.8	9.3	587.2
1974[1]	215.6	108.5	324.0	115.8	228.4	7.8	17.6	693.6
1979	194.7	117.8	312.5	108.3	319.9	6.4	30.2	777.3

Average annual
growth rate (%)

1955–73	4.7	4.8	4.7	9.1	24.8	7.5	27.4	8.1
1973–76	0.4	1.3	0.7	−4.2	5.4	−4.4	7.2	1.7

[1] Note influence of the oil crisis of 1973 on figures.

Table 2

Domestic Freight Transportation
(in billions of metric ton-kilometers)

	JNR	Private railways	Motor carriers		Coastal shipping	Total
			Commercial	Noncommercial		
1950	33.3	0.5	2.4	3.1	25.5	64.8
1960	53.6	0.9	9.6	11.2	63.6	138.9
1970	62.4	1.0	67.3	68.6	151.2	351.0
1974	51.6	0.9	72.0	58.7	192.4	375.8
1979	42.3	0.8	98.2	74.7	225.8	442.0

NOTE: Figures in both tables may not add to totals due to rounding.
SOURCE (both tables): Un'yushō (Ministry of Transport),
Un'yu keizai tōkei yōran (annual): 1981.

Railways

—— Shinkansen
—— Other railways

Principal ports

⊙ Ports designated as especially
important for foreign trade
• Other major ports

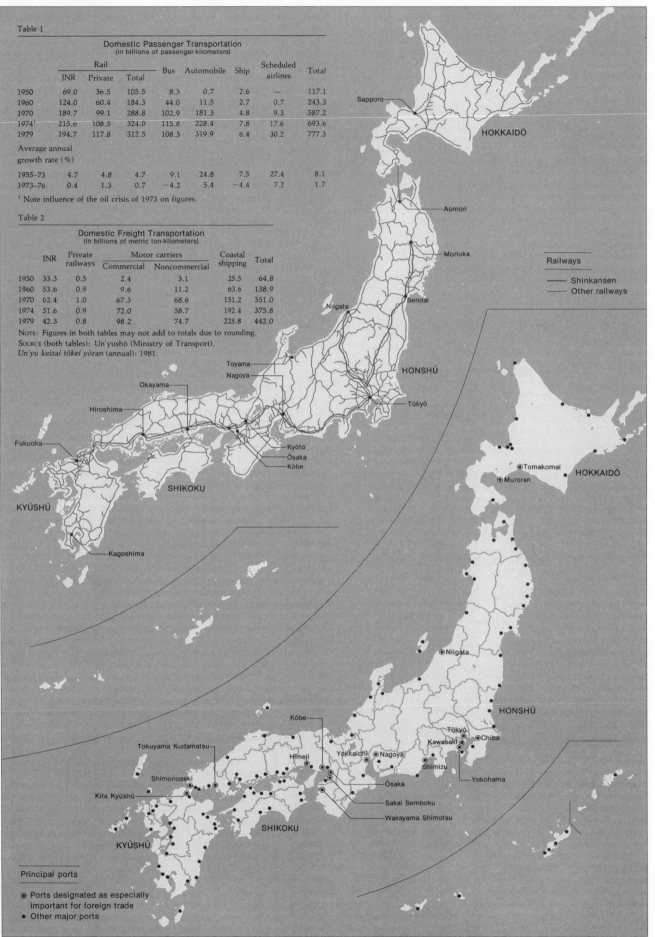

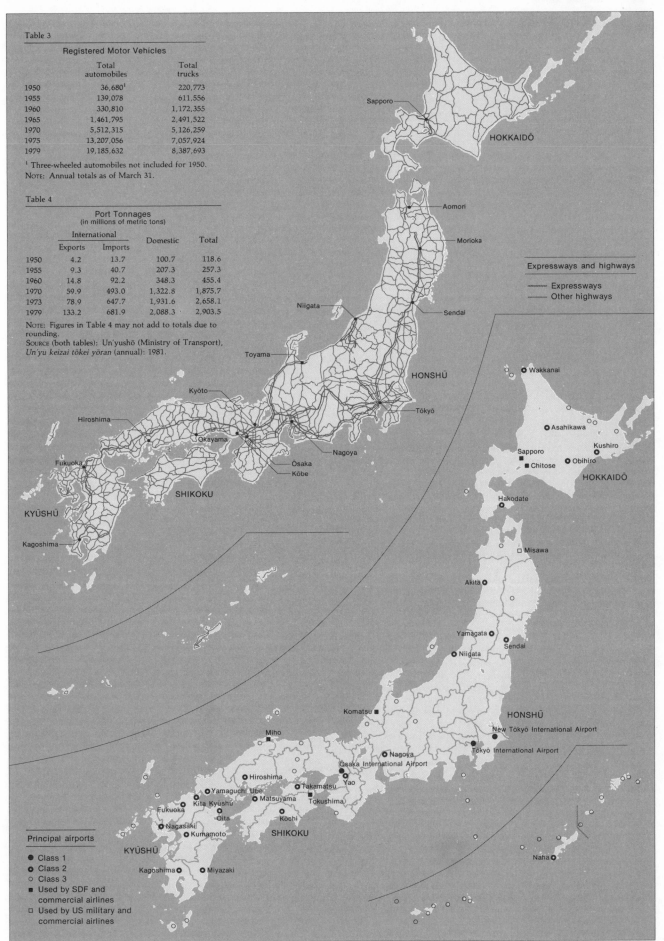

Table 3

Registered Motor Vehicles

	Total automobiles	Total trucks
1950	36,680[1]	220,773
1955	139,078	611,556
1960	330,810	1,172,355
1965	1,461,795	2,491,522
1970	5,512,315	5,126,259
1975	13,207,056	7,057,924
1979	19,185,632	8,387,693

[1] Three-wheeled automobiles not included for 1950.
NOTE: Annual totals as of March 31.

Table 4

Port Tonnages
(in millions of metric tons)

	International		Domestic	Total
	Exports	Imports		
1950	4.2	13.7	100.7	118.6
1955	9.3	40.7	207.3	257.3
1960	14.8	92.2	348.3	455.4
1970	59.9	493.0	1,322.8	1,875.7
1973	78.9	647.7	1,931.6	2,658.1
1979	133.2	681.9	2,088.3	2,903.5

NOTE: Figures in Table 4 may not add to totals due to rounding.
SOURCE (both tables): Un'yushō (Ministry of Transport), *Un'yu keizai tōkei yōran* (annual): 1981.

Expressways and highways

 Expressways
—— Other highways

Principal airports

● Class 1
◉ Class 2
○ Class 3
■ Used by SDF and commercial airlines
□ Used by US military and commercial airlines

cation to be profitable; fully 91 percent of all private railway operation-kilometers are electrified.

Motor vehicles. Private automobiles have been one of the fastest growing segments of domestic passenger transportation because of three factors which were especially important during the 1960s decade. These were rapid growth of income to a point where families could afford automobiles, the development of a domestic AUTOMOTIVE INDUSTRY geared to the specific needs of the domestic market (small-sized vehicles with right-hand drive), and the improvement of roads. Automobile ownership increased from only about 331,000 vehicles in 1960 to over 19 million in 1979 (Table 3). Paving on national highways was extended from 29 percent in 1960 to 93 percent in 1975. Japan also completed its first limited access expressway in 1965 and by 1978 had developed a total of 2,194 kilometers (1,362 miles) (see EXPRESSWAYS). The major expressway route in Japan is from Sendai down the Pacific Ocean side of Japan through Tōkyō as far as Kōbe. Even as late as 1960, 20 percent of all automobiles were business vehicles (taxis and chauffered company vehicles) and private automobiles generated only 45 percent of total automobile passenger-kilometers. During the 1960s, the growth of private, nonbusiness automobile ownership was explosive, at an annual rate of 35 percent. By 1975 private automobiles were 98 percent of total registrations and produced 93 percent of automobile passenger-kilometers.

During the 1970s automobile transportation growth slowed, marking the end of the transition phase represented by the 1960s. Total automobile passenger-kilometers grew at an annual rate of only 5.9 percent for the 1970-76 period and 5.7 percent for the 1977-79 period. Even after the oil crisis of 1973, however, automobile traffic has continued to increase faster than other forms of passenger traffic. Growth in the number of registered vehicles has not slowed as much as passenger-kilometer growth, indicating that people are driving their cars less. Automobile ownership will never reach US levels for a number of reasons, including urban traffic congestion, lack of parking (most firms do not provide employee parking), and the high cost of fuel in Japan.

Freight motor carriers have also benefited from the improvement of highways during the postwar period. As roads have improved, trucks have increased in size. Whereas most commercial trucks did not exceed a 5-ton capacity in the mid-1950s, 15-ton trucks are now common and the number of trailer trucks is also increasing rapidly (though they are only a small percentage of all trucks). There are three main categories of motor carriers: route carriers (operating over specified routes with scheduled services), regional carriers (operating unscheduled service within a specified region), and noncommercial carriers (firms operating for their own business and not for hire). The Ministry of Transport controls licenses for route and regional commercial carriers and also must approve rate levels, but neither entry nor rates are effectively controlled. Under conditions of easy entry and illegal rate flexibility, the Japanese motor carrier industry has grown in size tremendously, without showing signs of financial instability or high failure rates.

Noncommercial trucking produces 45 percent of motor carrier ton-kilometers, providing some additional competition for commercial carriers, but much of the noncommercial output is in retail store delivery services. Because car ownership is still far from universal (especially in the congested major metropolitan areas), retail stores provide extensive delivery services for their customers.

Marine transportation. Japan is an island country with a coastline marked by innumerable small and large harbors. Economic growth brought a great increase in both domestic and international seaborne freight. Because Japan is deficient in many raw materials, the rapid economic growth of the postwar period created a great need for raw material imports. To pay for those imports, exports also expanded, again largely seaborne.

Total tonnage handled by Japanese ports grew at an annual rate of 14 percent from 1955 to 1973. Export tonnages are lower than imports because exports are less bulky, high value-added manufactured goods. Almost three-quarters of the tonnage handled in ports during this period was domestic coastal shipping freight. The major international ports are the Tōkyō Bay area (Tōkyō, Yokohama, Kawasaki, and Chiba), Nagoya, the Ōsaka Bay area (Ōsaka and Kōbe), Kita Kyūshū, and Wakayama Shimozu (a major oil port).

As wages have risen, the Japanese shipping industry has been losing ground to foreign competition. In 1979 only 20.7 percent of export tonnage and 38.4 percent of import tonnage moved on Japanese vessels. Flags of convenience—Japanese-owned vessels registered in foreign countries—have been increasing to gain the advantage of lower-cost labor. Coastal shipping is provided entirely by Japanese vessels.

Supporting the rise in shipping volumes, the Japanese government has invested considerable money in improved harbor facilities, including the installation of extensive container-handling equipment as marine containers came to dominate merchandise transportation. The government has also provided aid of various kinds to the shipping industry, which has not been very profitable. In 1963 a special international shipping industry law was passed, tying access to low-cost loans for modernization to merger plans promoted by the Ministry of Transport to strengthen the financial viability of the companies. Coastal shipping companies, which tend to be very small, were given low-cost loans to promote modernization and were permitted to form cartels to improve their rate bargaining position with large shippers. The Ministry of Transport also has authority to regulate the growth of the coastal shipping fleet by setting annual guidelines and refusing to register new vessels beyond the established limits. Both coastal and international shipping firms were hurt by the oil crisis; in 1976, 40 international shipping companies had a combined profit of only ¥401 million (US $1.35 million) and 178 coastal shipping firms had a combined loss of ¥4.4 million (US $14,800).

Accompanying Japan's increased domestic and international maritime freight, the SHIPBUILDING INDUSTRY expanded to a point where Japan became the world's largest shipbuilder. Not only were Japanese shipyards building ships for domestic ownership, but also for export; construction of ships for foreign owners has always exceeded 50 percent of total construction. Japan pioneered the construction of supertankers, which were instrumental in supplying Japan's energy needs at substantially reduced transportation costs. By the early 1970s Japan produced 50 percent of the annual new ship tonnage worldwide—far ahead of any other single nation. This success brought Japan into conflict with European shipyards and protectionist attitudes of European governments.

The oil crisis and the ensuing severe recession brought an oversupply of ships worldwide and depression to Japanese shipbuilding. During the 12 months preceding March 1978, 28 small shipyards went bankrupt, and in the spring of 1978 a major shipyard (SASEBO HEAVY INDUSTRIES CO, LTD) received emergency government aid to prevent bankruptcy. Shipbuilding has been classed as a structurally depressed industry by the government, and plans call for elimination of 35 percent of shipbuilding capacity by 1985.

Air transportation. Passenger airlines were prohibited by SCAP until 1951. At that time the Ministry of Transport was given control over licensing airline routes and fares. Following the end of the Occupation, the Ministry of Transport Civil Aviation Agency recommended establishment of one international airline (also to operate domestic trunk lines) and two domestic local line airlines, separated geographically. JAPAN AIR LINES CO, LTD (JAL) was correspondingly established in 1953 as the international airline with 50 percent government capital participation, and approval given to two private regional firms.

Following this initial organization, the two regional carriers merged, forming ALL NIPPON AIRWAYS CO, LTD (ANA). Faced with financial problems, ANA was granted access to mainline domestic routes in 1959 and provided strong competition for JAL. These are now the two main scheduled airlines in Japan. In addition, there are two smaller scheduled airlines (Tōa Domestic and Nansei) as well as 36 small unscheduled airlines.

The opening of JNR's high-speed passenger train service between Tōkyō and Ōsaka in 1964 was a severe blow to the air industry, causing absolute declines in traffic and operating deficits for both JAL and ANA in 1965 and 1966. However, aside from this temporary decline, the airlines have generally operated at a profit and traffic has grown tremendously. As shown in Table 1, Japan's domestic airline passenger-kilometers grew at an annual rate of 27 percent over the period 1955-73. Growth slowed following the oil crisis but remained well above the growth of total passenger traffic. Overseas passenger traffic carried by JAL has likewise expanded at a rate of 25 percent for 1960-76.

To handle the increased air traffic, AIRPORTS have also expanded, and in the spring of 1978, the NEW TŌKYŌ INTERNATIONAL AIRPORT replaced the crowded Haneda airport as the main international airport for Tōkyō. The opening of this airport was delayed for six years by protests of local farmers and radical student supporters. Haneda became a domestic airport (except for Taiwan's China Airlines, which cannot land at the same airport as the airline of the People's Republic of China). The government is also considering plans to extend the runways of a number of smaller regional airports to expand their capacity and upgrade their capability to handle jet aircraft. See also AVIATION.

Commercial aircraft is the only form of transportation equipment which Japan has purchased almost entirely from abroad. While Japan did develop one military plane and produces other military planes for the Self Defense Forces under license from United States manufacturers, it does not produce any large commercial aircraft. Procurement of foreign commercial planes, in fact, led to the LOCK-HEED SCANDAL in 1976, in which Lockheed officials admitted to paying bribes which allegedly went to high government officials for purposes of influencing ANA to choose the Lockheed Tristar as its next plane.

Transportation and Society ——— *Urban transportation.* JNR, the private railways, automobiles, buses, and SUBWAYS comprise the urban transportation system in Japan. Dependence on private automobiles, however, is much lower than in the United States for commuting or general urban travel. Scheduled buses in Japan act largely as feeders to railway stations, with those serving private railway stations often operated by the private railway conglomerates. Subways in the two largest urban centers (Tōkyō and Ōsaka) are extensive, technically efficient, and expanding. Most subways are municipally owned.

One of the major problems in Japanese transportation is that all forms of urban transportation remain very crowded during the rush hour. Part of the crowding problem is due to inadequate allocation of investment by the government to urban transportation facilities. In addition, the rate of population growth in major urban and surrounding suburban areas (especially in the Tōkyō metropolitan area) has been very high, as people migrate from rural areas. This rapid rise has strained the capacity of transportation facilities.

Continued heavy reliance on public transportation, and especially rail, stems from high population density, highway congestion, relative operating costs, and considerations of energy conservation and pollution abatement. A slowing of population shifts toward large metropolitan areas combined with rising government expenditures on social infrastructure in the future should eventually alleviate problems of crowding. For example, in 1971 the government began to give private railways financial aid in constructing new feeder lines in metropolitan areas (such as to new areas of apartment complexes). Even if the overall size of investment has been limited, the Japanese have developed a highly efficient system in which trains (JNR, private, and subway) are frequent, fast, and safe. The main constraint on additional speed of service is the fact that rail lines were constructed at a time when automobiles and buses did not exist, and stations were thus built close together.

A major feature of Japanese urban transportation is the information which is offered at various spots. All bus stops indicate bus destinations and scheduling. All buses post route maps visible to the riders, and larger bus terminals have route maps printed next to the schedule information. Large maps showing fares to other stations are located by the ticket vending machines in all train stations. In major train stations, each train line is assigned permanent station platforms and clear signs indicate the location of each line. Complete train schedules are always prominently visible near the ticket sales areas and also on each station platform.

Coordination and control. Coordination among the different segments of the transportation system and control of transportation activities is an area in which Japan has had problems. Administration of each transportation mode is governed by a separate law and is represented by a separate bureau within the Ministry of Transport. The major result of this legal framework and resulting administrative structure is very weak coordination of the different ministry bureaus. Each pursues policies regarding the transportation mode under its jurisdiction without consideration for the overall effects of its policies. In addition, the separation of administrative functions regarding transportation among ministries has led to lack of coordination, especially concerning the important area of highway investment under Ministry of Construction control.

Ministry of Transport officials have been aware of their weak ability to coordinate policy. To improve coordination, four planning groups within the ministry were established (overall, urban, rates, and physical distribution), but without specific changes in legislation enabling the ministry to exercise real coordinating power, the role of these planning units remains limited.

An overall problem in transportation planning has been that the government in the past has been unwilling to invest sufficient sums in transportation infrastructure (or social infrastructure in general) in order to maintain a small government budget. This attitude may be now changing as Japanese economic growth slows and the government must play a larger role. Limited resources have led to special problems for the JNR because pressure from the Ministry of Finance and the Diet to operate without a deficit were combined with nonremunerative, Diet-imposed commuter discounts. With large, profitable surcharges for the Shinkansen, JNR tended to allocate investment funds toward the Shinkansen and away from commuter lines. Many groups in Japan have criticized JNR for this allocation, but the choice was a logical one, and the solution is a larger total investment budget and explicit subsidy or other support by the government for expanded commuter capacity.

Other areas of specific government control over transportation activity have been criticized in Japan. From 1948 to 1978 approval of basic fares and the size of the commuter discount on JNR by the Diet made Japan the only industrial nation in the world where the national legislative body controlled railroad fares. This put pressure on politicians to resist fare increases and exacerbated JNR deficits. Rate approval, within maximum annual limits, has now been transferred to the Ministry of Transport.

At the other extreme, the ministry has authority to set commercial trucking rates but lacks the ability to enforce these rates because of insufficient personnel and the large number of small trucking firms. Officials perceive this situation as a problem, while economists favor this unofficial state of free competition.

The association of Japan Air Lines with the government had led to a different sort of problem. The Ministry of Transport has refused requests by US airlines to expand discount fares and charter flights to Japan for fear of hurting JAL's profit position. This is a case where government control has led to government protection of a quasi-cartel situation to the detriment of passengers.

Safety. The major cause of passenger fatalities in Japan is highway accidents. Despite the continuing rapid increase in highway traffic, however, major safety campaigns have led to a steady decline in highway deaths since 1970. This absolute decline is accompanied by a decline in fatalities per registered motor vehicle, which have been decreasing throughout the postwar period. Injuries have also been dropping since 1970, and injuries per registered vehicle since 1960. These trends reflect added investment in sidewalks, guard rails, covered drain sewers, additional traffic signals, and pedestrian walk signals. The Ministry of Transport also has spent increasing amounts on improving car inspection techniques and expanding inspection facilities. Expenditures on this and other road safety programs by the ministry alone amounted to ¥19 billion in 1975 (US $64 million).

Railroad accidents have declined from a peak level in 1960, with an accompanying fall in fatalities. One of the principal causes for this decline has been the rehabilitation of both JNR and the private railways from poor physical conditions following World War II. Great improvements have been made in grade crossing safety—the installation of additional crossing signals and crossing gates and the elimination of some level crossings. Rail fatalities are somewhat misleading because almost 50 percent of these are suicides. For instance, only two passengers were killed in train crashes on JNR in 1974; the remainder of the 662 fatalities for that year was due to grade crossing accidents or suicides. Although Ministry of Transport reports consider transportation accidents still too frequent, the fact that the absolute number of accidents and fatalities of all types has been declining in the face of steadily increasing passenger travel and traffic congestion is remarkable.

New technology. During the postwar period, Japan has undergone a transportation revolution. Some of this has been directly imported; commercial aircraft is an example. Other areas have followed foreign developments, such as marine containers and automobile design. But in some areas Japan has developed its own approach, particularly in the field of rail transportation. The SHIN-KANSEN is the most impressive of the changes which have occurred. It represents a singular ability to adapt existing available domestic and foreign technology to create a new system superior in speed to any operation elsewhere in the world. It has remained one of the few profitable operations in the entire JNR system and has been successfully extended beyond its original Tōkyō–Ōsaka route to Fukuoka in Kyūshū. As many as ten 100 MPH (average speed terminal to terminal) trains depart Tōkyō Station each hour, and while minor problems have cropped up, no passenger fatalities have occurred since the line opened.

Other changes have been implemented on JNR and private railroads. These include elimination of the last steam locomotives in 1976, computerization of seat reservations, automatic vending machines for short distance passenger tickets, development and extensive use of concrete ties and concrete slab track structures, and automatic train control (ATC) to stop trains overriding trackside stop signals.

Safety has been a major concern in technology. Developments in rail signaling and train control have virtually eliminated train crashes and kept the Shinkansen safety record perfect. Japan's automobile pollution standards have been made the strictest in the world, and automobile manufacturers have complied with them without lengthy delays. Japanese automobiles sold abroad have earned a reputation for high quality engineering and design.

Looking toward the future, both JNR and Japan Air Lines are experimenting with magnetic linear motors. This is a system wherein vehicles are lifted a fraction of an inch off a special track by magnetic forces, eliminating the friction of wheels. Linear motor vehicles are capable of operation at speeds over 300 MPH, with an energy cost less than that for airplanes, and they are much quieter than either airplanes or conventional trains. JNR already has run prototype vehicles on a test track and hopes to use this concept for its next generation of Shinkansen. JAL hopes to build a system to transport passengers from Tōkyō to the new international airport in Narita, Chiba Prefecture.

▬▬▬▬Kōtsū Kyōryokukai, *Kōtsū nenkan* (annual). Nakanishi Ken'ichi and Hirooka Haruya, ed, *Nihon no kōtsū mondai* (1973). Ōshima Fujitarō and Kurazono Susumu, *Nihon kōtsū seisaku no kōzō* (1975). Ueji Tatsunori, *Un'yushō* (1974). Un'yushō, *Un'yu keizai yōran* (annual). Edward J. LINCOLN

Transportation Museum

(Kōtsū Hakubutsukan). Museum with a permanent collection and display of land, sea, and air transportation facilities, both originals and models. Opened in 1921 as a railroad museum, it is situated in Chiyoda Ward, Tōkyō. Models and actual examples of early steam locomotives, rickshaws, canoes, helicopters, and other vehicles are exhibited. For demonstration purposes many of these are equipped for actual operation. FUJIKAWA Kinji

travel

(tabi or ryokō). The archetype of Japanese travel is the pilgrimage (junrei; see PILGRIMAGES), popular since the Heian period (794–1185) among the aristocracy, who visited such holy places as ISE SHRINE, KUMANO SANZAN SHRINES, HASEDERA, and SHITENNŌJI. With peace and prosperity in the Edo period (1600–1868), pilgrimages were undertaken by all classes of people. Lodging houses and souvenir shops flourished, and several set circuits became established. Among these were the 88 Temples of Shikoku and the 33 Holy Places of the Western Provinces. More arduous journeys were made to holy mountains such as KŌYASAN and FUJISAN (Mt. Fuji). In addition, visits were often made on certain death anniversaries, and even today it is not infrequent to make pilgrimages to all the spots once visited by a famous personage. The celebrated HAIKU poet BASHŌ, for example, traveled to the sites the poet-monk SAIGYŌ had visited.

Pilgrims are still seen in Japan. Dressed in traditional white costumes and carrying walking-sticks, they usually travel in groups. Many travel itineraries include famous temples and shrines or perhaps less famous ones that have a personal significance or are known for their efficacy in bringing material goods, fortune, or health.

HOT SPRINGS have been considered beneficial to health since ancient times, although today they are visited more for relaxation than for medicinal value. The hot springs of Arima in Hyōgo Prefecture, Dōgo in Ehime Prefecture, and Atami in Shizuoka Prefecture are particularly popular. Many companies choose hot-spring resorts for their annual outing or convention.

During the Edo period the systemization of highways (KAIDŌ) by the Tokugawa shogunate and the development of facilities for travelers led to an increase in travel for recreation. According to the KIYŪ SHŌRAN, pilgrimages declined, while trips for pleasure increased. One such journey was fictionally portrayed by a popular writer of the day, JIPPENSHA IKKU, in *Tōkaidōchū hizakurige* (1802–22; tr *Shank's Mare*, 1929), sketches of the humorous mishaps that befall a pair of city travelers wandering through the countryside. The tradition of ascetic travel in Japan was upheld by priests and haiku poets who propagated their teachings and skill as they journeyed around the country. Bashō's famous travel diary, *Oku no hosomichi* (1694; tr *The Narrow Road to the Deep North,* 1966) stands as one of the most poetic records of such ascetic journeying.

The Japanese love of travel is well documented in TRAVEL DIARIES (kikō), some of which, like the *Izayoi nikki* (Diary of the Waning Moon) by ABUTSU NI and the *Tosa nikki* by KI NO TSURAYUKI, date back to the Heian period. In time certain places came to be associated with specific poems and aesthetic responses and trips were made especially to visit these sites (see UTA MAKURA). Beginning in the Edo period, more objective travel accounts with geographical and historical information came to be written.

Of the several highways that traversed Honshū, the most picturesque was the TŌKAIDŌ, which ran 565 kilometers (351 mi) between Edo and Kyōto. This was the highway celebrated by Jippensha Ikku in his comic tale; it was traveled by *daimyō* processions heading toward Edo (Tōkyō) for the required attendance at the shōgun's court (see SANKIN KŌTAI). Scenes of the Tōkaidō have been preserved in the wood-block prints of HIROSHIGE.

Japan's high economic growth since the late 1960s has spurred both domestic and international travel. Sports and recreation are emphasized today, with resorts providing golf courses and tennis courts, swimming pools, and ski lifts. Flocks of college students and other young adults go mountain-climbing. Camping is popular in the 27 national parks and elsewhere. Lodgings run the gamut from Western-style hotels, Japanese INNS (ryokan), and government-sponsored people's lodges (kokumin shukusha) to youth hostels and guesthouses (MINSHUKU). Domestic travel has been made comfortable and efficient by the extensive rail system (see RAILWAYS), supplemented by bus lines, which run to almost every small town throughout Japan. Airlines service several dozen cities. Travel by car has increased dramatically and resorts now have large parking areas.

Although the Japanese penchant for GROUP TRAVEL may be on the wane, even in 1978 the percentage of those traveling alone was a mere 4 percent, while family travel accounted for 39 percent of all travel. Family travel appears to be increasing and honeymoons are more popular than ever. Because of limited vacation time and the increasing cost of transportation, short trips have become popular, although Japanese travelers abroad numbered 3.5 million in 1978. NAITŌ Kinju

travel diaries

(kikō). In Japanese literary history the term kikō bungaku (travel diary literature) applies to a body of literature dealing exclusively with the theme of travel. *Kikō* are generally short prose accounts of journeys, often anonymous and often containing many poems. The theme of travel has a long tradition in Japanese literature, with its roots in the kiryoka (travel poems) of the 8th-century poetry anthology MAN'YŌSHŪ. These are poems with short prose accounts of officials' journeys between the capital in the Yamato region (now Nara Prefecture) and the seat of the government-general in Kyūshū. Approximately 70 travel diaries written between the Heian period (794–1185) and 1600 are extant, and many more were produced during the Edo (1600–1868) and Meiji (1868–1912) periods. The earliest Japanese literary work of note that could be called a true travel diary is the *Tosa nikki* (935, Tosa Diary) of KI NO TSURAYUKI, a description, including poems composed along the way, of a journey taken by the poet and his entourage from Tosa (now Kōchi Prefecture), where he had served as governor, to Kyōto, by then the capital. However, this is usually classified by Japanese literary historians as an example of the related genre of NIKKI BUNGAKU (diary literature) rather than as a *kikō* proper. The SARASHINA NIKKI (ca 1059), which is also usually assigned to the *nikki* genre, begins with an extended passage describing the author's journey as a young girl from Kazusa Province (now part of Chiba Prefecture) to the capital. Accounts were also written during the Heian period of imperial progresses to the countryside and to temples, but these were chiefly records of poems composed en route, and it was not until the Kamakura period (1185–1333) that travel diaries flourished as a distinct genre.

The location of the administrative offices of government in Kamakura after the founding of the Kamakura shogunate in 1192 led to an increase in travel along the highway TŌKAIDŌ to Kyōto and the proliferation of kikō such as the KAIDŌKI and TŌKAN KIKŌ. In the Muromachi period (1333–1568) many linked-verse (renga; see RENGA AND HAIKAI) poets, most notably SŌGI and SŌCHŌ, wrote diaries of their travels in the provinces where they were employed by local lords as preceptors in the literary classics. Matsuo BASHŌ, the peripatetic Edo-period haiku poet, wrote a number of *kikō* interspersed with verses describing his experiences. Certainly the most renowned travel diary of the period was his *Oku no hosomichi*

(1694), in which the journey becomes a metaphor for the passage of life itself.

A characteristic feature of *kikō* is their inclusion of poems dealing with places along the way concerning which a poetic tradition has evolved (see UTA MAKURA). The lyricism and often highly wrought style of the travel diary influenced other genres into which passages describing journeys *(michiyuki)* were introduced. There are noteworthy examples in war tales such as the HEIKE MONOGATARI and the TAIHEIKI, and the *michiyuki* or travel section became a standard element in the NŌ drama and was used to particular effect, often as the penultimate scene, in BUNRAKU (the puppet theater).

Distinction between Kikō and Similar Genres —— One obvious feature that helps to set *kikō* apart from *nikki* or other genres dealing with the theme of travel is the wording of their titles. Whereas *nikki* (diaries), for example, often include the word *nikki* in their titles, the titles of *kikō* often include the term *ki* (account; record), used in such phrases as *gokōki* (also *gyokōki* or *gyōkōki; account of an imperial journey), *michi no ki* (also *dōki; travelogue), and *mōde no ki* (also *sankeiki* or *junreiki; account of a pilgrimage). Although in many cases such titles were given to the texts by later compilers and copiers, they do indicate a consciousness of the *kikō* as a separate genre of autobiographical or chronicle literature. Consciousness of *kikō* as an independent genre is also indicated by the fact that many of the poems from *kikō* accounts included in poetic anthologies are identified as being from *michi no ki*. Although a number of diaries *(nikki)* include more or less lengthy travel sections, these sections may have constituted separate *kikō*, which were added to the diaries by later copiers and compilers. This may have been the case with IONUSHI (latter part of the 10th century), *Izayoi nikki* (see ABUTSU NI), and TOWAZUGATARI. The travel sections *(michiyuki)* found in poem tales *(uta monogatari;* see MONOGATARI BUNGAKU), war tales (GUNKI MONOGATARI), collections of anecdotal tales (SETSUWA BUNGAKU), and in Nō, puppet, and KABUKI plays, are often studied independently as such. *Kikō* are classified as a separate genre in the GUNSHO RUIJŪ and *Fusō shūyō shū* (1689), two anthologies of classical writing compiled during the Edo period.

Consciousness of *kikō*—the development of which runs parallel to and often overlaps that of *nikki*—is manifested in their formal content as well. Elements such as a lengthy sojourn at one place during a journey are often consciously omitted. From start to finish, *kikō* are chiefly concerned with the theme of travel as a realm complete in itself. *Kikō* are a literature of movement as opposed to rest, and descriptions of extended stops on a journey are treated as separate genres of literature, examples of which include the various *sōan no ki* (accounts of grass huts) and *taizai ki* (accounts of sojourns). Whereas the narrative unit in the similar genre of *nikki* is chronological, in the *kikō* it is geographical. The *nikki* rely upon a temporal order, the *kikō* more upon a spacial order. The *nikki*, if not a confessional memoir, to which category the *Sarashina nikki* may belong, is often limited to a singular experience and therefore to a central theme, such as specific court functions in the *Murasaki Shikibu nikki* (see MURASAKI SHIKIBU), a happy love affair in the *Izumi Shikibu nikki* (see IZUMI SHIKIBU), or a deteriorating love affair in the KAGERŌ NIKKI. The *kikō*, however, tend to be written by older persons and usually recount a solitary confrontation with nature, which often has religious overtones.

Kikō are often limited to one-way journeys, usually away from home or the capital. The "journey away" is a pattern already visible in the travel poems *(kiryoka)* of the *Man'yōshū*. In the Muromachi period, however, records of a larger number of two-way journeys were written. Yet, even in such cases, the focus is more on the going than the return. Also in the Muromachi period a number of pilgrimage diaries were written which describe journeys without a fixed destination, deriving from a type of Buddhist pilgrimage called *kaikoku* or *rokujūrokubu*, meaning a pilgrimage around the sixty-six provinces *(kuni* or *koku)* of Japan.

Language —— The *kikō* contain a combination of prose and poetry of varying ratios and a variety of styles. The dominant prose style is a mixture of Chinese (KAMBUN) and Japanese *(wabun)* called *wakan konkōtai*, a style adopted especially from the beginning of the Kamakura period in such *kikō* as the *Kaidōki* (1223) and the *Shinshō hōshi nikki* (1225). The mixture of these two styles made it possible to combine the subjective impressionism and lyrical natural description that was typical of *wabun* with the more objective descriptions and documentary listings that were associated with *kambun*.

A large number of *kikō* were entirely in *kambun* as documentary records intended for archives and without any artistic pretense.

Such *kikō* cannot be considered literature and are primarily of historical interest. Others such as FUJIWARA NO SADAIE's (Fujiwara no Teika's) *Go-Toba In Kumano gyokō ki* (1201), though written in *kambun*, possess literary quality heightened by the poems that are included.

There are also a number of *kikō* (or *kikō* sections) written in pure *wabun* by leading figures of certain schools of poetry who were commissioned to write official travel accounts. To this category also belong *kikō* in which lengthy prose sections are avoided in favor of simple indications of the geographical locations where the poems were composed; e.g., "at such and such a place" (. . . *ni te),* followed by a poem. The style and descriptive methods of a *kikō*, or its parts, bring it into close relationship with other genres of classical Japanese literature, for instance, collections of WAKA poetry *(wakashū),* poem tales *(uta monogatari),* or essays (ZUIHITSU), or with picture scrolls (EMAKIMONO).

Although various styles of poetry can be found in *kikō*, there are accounts that use only one form of poetry (e.g., *waka* or HAIKU). Also, there are many works that include a mixture of poetic forms: *waka* and *haiku* in *Tsukushi michi no ki* (1480); *waka* and Chinese verse *(kanshi)* in *Fujikawa no ki* (ca 1470); *tanka* and *chōka* (genres of *waka)* in *Izayoi nikki* and *Kyūshū no michi no ki* (1473); *waka, haiku,* and comic verse known as KYŌKA in *Jōha fujimi dōki* (1576). The form of poetry more or less determines, or at least influences, the style and mood of a *kikō*, as the nature of *kyōka* heightens the effect of the humorous Edo-period travel tale *Tōkaidōchū hizakurige* (1802–22; Shank's Mare) by JIPPENSHA IKKU.

The inclusion of poetry as a general feature of *kikō* indicates to some extent a consciousness of readership and makes the *kikō* a public record rather than a *journal intime*. In order to be understood by a wide audience, stereotypical descriptions of places and time-honored poetic allusions and quotations are used. Almost all place-names mentioned in *kikō* belong to the category of *uta makura*, names of places familiar to readers of classical Japanese poetry. Place-names other than *uta makura* are often deliberately omitted.

Types of Kikō —— *Kikō* were written by poets who traveled for official or quasi-official purposes or by hermits whose reasons for traveling were more or less of a private nature. Official travelers who wrote *kikō* were usually members or leading figures of established schools of poetry such as the Nijō, Kyōgoku, and Reizei. Their *kikō* tend to reflect the poetics of the schools and include only commonly accepted poetic imagery and allusions. Among such travel diaries are those by poets who were engaged to accompany *(zuikō)* imperial, shogunal, or military expeditions and to produce *kikō* as official records. Hermits often traveled to holy places such as the temples Kōyasan and Zenkōji and the shrines at Kumano, Ise, and Sumiyoshi. According to their accounts, they often traveled on such occasions as the anniversaries of the deaths of religious figures or teachers of poetry. The poet-monk Shōkō took such a trip 13 years after the death of his teacher SHŌTETSU and wrote the dairy *Shōkō nikki* (1473). In many cases hermits traveled in late autumn (early winter in the lunar calendar) for the purpose of ascetic privation, and their poetry is often marked by a melancholy tone (see WABI; SABI).

In the Nara (710–794) and Heian periods, travel other than official was rare, and *kikō* are mainly a phenomenon of the middle ages (about 1200–1600) and of the Edo period, when travel became increasingly common. Most Heian-period diary literature deals with court life or specific court functions, with the exception of the 10th-century *Tosa nikki* and the 9th-century *Nittō guhō junrei kōki* by the monk ENNIN, and autobiographical *kikō* were for the most part a phenomenon of later periods.

Among the travel diaries of the Edo period are some which were written by accomplished poets. KARASUMARU MITSUHIRO, who studied poetry under HOSOKAWA YŪSAI, wrote *Nikkōsan kikō* as a poetic account of the transfer of TOKUGAWA IEYASU's bones from Mikawa Province (now part of Aichi Prefecture) to the mausoleum at NIKKŌ. Among poetic *kikō* written by women of this period are the *Tōkai kikō* (1681) and *Kika nikki* (1689) by Inoue Tsūjo and the *Kōshi michi no ki* (1720) by Takejo. Poetic *kikō* were often written by well-known scholars such as HAYASHI RAZAN, KAMO NO MABUCHI, and MOTOORI NORINAGA. In their almost exclusive concentration upon the imperial and Shintō heritage of the nation, the records by the two latter authors reflect their intellectual convictions.

Travel writings by Matsuo Bashō such as *Kashima kikō, Oi no kobumi, Oku no hosomichi, Nozarashi kikō,* and *Sarashina kikō* preserve the medieval style of *kikō*. Bashō's disciples continued the tradition; MUKAI KYORAI's *Ise kikō* and HATTORI RANSETSU's *Sō-yūkō* describe a journey coinciding with the seventh anniversary of Bashō's death. The *Mita kyō monogatari* (1781) by Hakurikan Bōun and the *Sado nikki* (1775) of Tansui are further examples of *haikai kikō*, a genre in which *haikai* (*haiku*) poets continued to write throughout the Edo period.

Many of the accounts written during this period are distinguished by their objectivity. These were written mainly by government or domain officials on administrative errands; pilgrims and merchants; and amateur scholars of geography, botany, medicine, and art.

Tachibana Nankei (1753–1805) and SUGAE MASUMI are among the most noteworthy travel diarists of the Edo period. Their journeys were motivated by an interest in pharmacy and medicine, and their *kikō* were among the most widely read. Sugae Masumi's *Masumi yūranki* includes descriptions of farmers, fishermen, woodcutters, and other folk of the northeast and Hokkaidō as seen from the point of view of a pharmacist. Tachibana Nankei saw the world through the eyes of a medical doctor in his *Tōyūki* and *Seiyūki*. Both authors included climatic, geographical, historical, and cultural information in their *kikō*.

As a result of peace and the shogunate's NATIONAL SECLUSION policy, travel within the country reached an unprecedented popularity during the Edo period. Pilgrimages to the Ise Shrine and mountain climbing flourished, and there are records from this period of journeys to distant places, such as the Ryūkyū Islands in the south and Hokkaidō in the north. Accounts during this period differ from the medieval *kikō* not only in their realism but also in the motives of the authors, who sought adventure and scientific knowledge. However varied in quality, they reflect a search for the new and the alien.

The tradition of *kikō* was carried on in the Meiji period by poets and novelists like TAYAMA KATAI, Ōmachi Keigetsu (1869–1925), and Chizuka Reisui (1868–1942). *Kikō* continue to be written today, but compared with traditional models, they tend to resemble the genre known as ZUIHITSU, or the personal essay.

▬▬▬▬ Fukuda Hideichi and Herbert Plutschow, *Nihon kikō bungaku binran* (1975). Earl Miner, tr, *Japanese Poetic Diaries* (1969), contains a translation of *Tosa nikki*. Ivan Morris, tr, *As I Crossed a Bridge of Dreams* (1971), a translation of *Sarashina nikki*. Edwin O. Reischauer and Joseph K. Yamagiwa, tr, *Translations from Early Japanese* (1951), contains a translation of *Izayoi nikki*. Nobuyuki Yuasa, ed and tr, *Bashō: The Narrow Road to the Deep North and Other Travel Sketches* (1966).   *Herbert E.* PLUTSCHOW

treaties

(*jōyaku*). Written agreements establishing legal rights and duties between nations. In Japan treaties are concluded by the cabinet, which, however, must obtain the prior or, in certain circumstances, subsequent approval of the Diet. The attestation of the emperor is necessary as proof that the correct procedures were followed in concluding the treaty. A treaty is given the force of law upon its promulgation, which is effected by the emperor with the advice and consent of the cabinet. Promulgation makes the treaty and its provisions public and is accomplished through publication in the OFFICIAL GAZETTE (*Kampō*).

Article 98, section 2 of the constitution declares that "treaties concluded by Japan and established laws of nations shall be faithfully observed." This is interpreted as meaning that treaties become part of Japanese domestic law. It is generally recognized that treaties take precedence over other laws, but opinion is divided as to whether treaties take precedence over the constitution. Those who argue for the precedence of treaties over the constitution cite article 98, section 2, of the constitution and the internationalist spirit in which it was written. Proponents of constitutional precedence point out that a constitutional amendment requires a national referendum, whereas the approval of the Diet is sufficient to conclude a treaty. They also argue that granting precedence to treaties could contradict the constitution's fundamental principle of sovereignty of the people. In theory, it is possible for a treaty to be concluded and promulgated only to be later judged unconstitutional and invalid by courts using the power of judicial review. Since, however, in international law a ratified treaty cannot be declared invalid unilaterally, it would have to be abrogated through negotiations with the other nation or nations party to it.   HIGASHI Jutarō

Treaty of Peace with Japan → San Francisco Peace Treaty

Trio-Kenwood Corporation

(Torio). Company producing and selling audio and communications equipment and testing instruments. It is one of the largest audio equipment manufacturers in Japan. It was established in Nagano Prefecture in 1946 as a maker of radio components and communications equipment, and began mass-producing audio and communications equipment in 1955. It was the first to put transistorized amplifiers on the market in 1962 and in 1966 started selling solid-state audio products, an epoch-making event in the industry. Overseas activities started with the export of FM tuners to the United States in 1957. In 1958 it established a sales company, Kenwood Electronics, Inc, and in 1980 had a total of nine overseas subsidiaries. Its products, under the brand name Kenwood, are exported to approximately 100 countries. Sales for the fiscal year ending May 1982 totaled ¥64 billion (US $271 million), of which audio products constituted 70 percent, communications equipment 20 percent, testing instruments 6 percent, and others 4 percent. In the same year the export ratio was 64 percent and capitalization stood at ¥1.97 billion (US $8.3 million). The head office is in Tōkyō.

Tripartite Intervention

(Sangoku Kanshō). Diplomatic pressure, brought to bear by Russia, France, and Germany, that forced Japan to relinquish the Liaodong (Liaotung) Peninsula in southern Manchuria, the greatest prize it had won in the SINO-JAPANESE WAR OF 1894–1895. The Western powers had not intervened directly in the war, but they were concerned about the future of East Asia, a region considered ripe for development and political transformation. Realizing that instability in one part of the world would affect the subtle overall relationship between "developed" and "undeveloped" countries, and thus among the great powers themselves, they wished to prevent any radical change in international relations in Asia.

Even before the signing of the Treaty of SHIMONOSEKI between China and Japan on 17 April 1895, several European powers had expressed concern over its terms. They were particularly worried about the territorial disposition of China, viewing with alarm the possibility of the collapse of the Manchu dynasty. Such a development would intensify international rivalries in China and throw the country into hopeless political chaos. When, on 4 April, the Japanese government showed tentative peace terms to Western representatives in Tōkyō, the Russian minister intimated that Japanese acquisition of southern Manchuria might incur Western intervention.

The warning went unheeded, however, and the treaty was signed. Immediately the European governments joined forces to dislodge Japan from the Liaodong Peninsula. Germany was particularly eager to participate in order to assert itself as a world power. With no substantial commercial or strategic interests at stake in China, it sought to take advantage of the pervasive concern with stability in East Asia to ingratiate itself with the other powers and particularly to prevent the recently concluded Franco-Russian alliance from isolating it throughout the world. Thus, joint action with these two powers would serve to maintain a degree of flexibility in international politics. Russia and France reciprocated such thinking. They had no definite strategy in East Asia or toward Japan, although Russia had always hoped to obtain an ice-free port in Northeast Asia. Their basic concern was to minimize adverse repercussions that changes in China might have upon European politics. The other great power, Britain, was also invited to join in the action, but the Liberal government was leery of being drawn into continental politics.

On 23 April 1895 the governments of France, Germany, and Russia "advised" the Japanese to restore the Liaodong Peninsula to China in return for an increased indemnity payment. Known as the Tripartite Intervention, this action immediately caused a sensation in Japan. Despite intimations that such an intervention might ensue, Tōkyō had been confident that the European powers would be unable to act in concert. When the three powers presented their ultimatum, the Japanese realized at once that resistance was out of the question. They sought British and American intercession, but in vain. The only course left was to accept the "advice" in order to save the rest of the treaty. On 5 May the ITŌ HIROBUMI government notified the three powers that the Liaodong Peninsula would be restored to China in return for the latter's payment of an indemnity of 30 million taels (about ¥450 million). All Japanese forces were withdrawn from the peninsula by December. The peninsula did not long remain free of foreign control, however. In 1898 Russia was to demand, and obtain, from China a 25-year lease of Port Arthur (Ch: Lüshun) and Dalien (Ta-lien; J: Dairen), at the southern tip of the peninsula (both now part of Lüda or Lü-ta). This precipitated a crisis between Japan and Russia that resulted in the RUSSO-JAPANESE WAR of 1904–05.

The emotional and psychological impact of the Tripartite Intervention on Japan was enormous. The Japanese had for years thought of expansion as a national and natural right, a necessity for their development as a modern state. Expansion into Taiwan and Korea was still possible, thanks to the treaty provisions; but the hope of expansion on the Northeast Asian continent, into the frontier land of Manchuria, had been frustrated. Japan assumed that the Western powers wanted Manchuria for themselves, and their might was superior. Force, not justice or national rights, seemed to have triumphed. There was, of course, a great deal of self-deception and self-righteousness in such thinking. Manchuria was, after all, Chinese territory. But the prevailing view among Japanese of the time was that the Chinese were incapable of protecting and developing the land, and that Japan was destined to bring peace, progress, and prosperity to the Asian continent. That dream was now shattered, and the Japanese of that generation never forgot what they considered an unspeakable national humiliation. It would result in two basic changes of attitude. First, Japan would recognize international relations for what they were and play the game of power politics just as the Western nations did. Second, it would strive to avenge itself, so that ultimately the Europeans would have to accept it as an equal. The first objective was easy to achieve: Japan would soon be an imperialist power in East Asia. But the second goal remained elusive. The sense that, no matter how hard it tried, Japan might never be recognized as a great power equal to the Western nations was to remain a dominant theme in Japan's foreign relations.

📖 ——— William L. Langer, *The Diplomacy of Imperialism* (1956). Ian Nish, *The Anglo-Japanese Alliance* (1966). *Akira* IRIYE

Tripartite Pact

(Nichidokui Sangoku Dōmei). Military pact signed by Japan, Germany, and Italy in Berlin on 27 September 1940. After the MANCHURIAN INCIDENT of September 1931, Japan broke with the principles of the Washington Conference and established the puppet state of MANCHUKUO. Following the LYTTON COMMISSION report, in 1933 Japan withdrew from the League of Nations and became increasingly isolated internationally. From 1935 on, however, it became apparent that the aggressive military policies of Germany, Japan, and Italy were drawing them closer together, and in November 1936 the ANTI-COMINTERN PACT was signed between Japan and Germany. They were joined by Italy in November 1937. Japan had thus allied itself with the fascist countries, ostensibly in the anti-Soviet, anticommunist cause, in order to break out of its solitary position and to advance its imperialist designs on the Asian continent.

After initial victories, Japan found itself stalemated in the SINO-JAPANESE WAR OF 1937–1945. It hoped to break the deadlock by further strengthening the Axis tie and by aggressive political maneuvering. In January 1938, at about the same time Germany had decided to conquer Europe, it put out feelers to Japan about the signing of a military pact that would eliminate resistance and interference from England and France. The Japanese army actively favored it, and in July 1938 the KONOE FUMIMARO cabinet, after a ministerial conference, decided in favor of strengthening the Japanese-German-Italian alliance. The army and the so-called reform faction in the Ministry of Foreign Affairs hoped for a military pact directed not only against the Soviet Union but also against all other non-Axis nations. However, the majority of the navy and the Ministry of Foreign Affairs insisted on excluding England and France as potential enemies.

The conclusion of the German-Soviet nonaggression pact in August of 1939, then, came as a complete surprise. The HIRANUMA KIICHIRŌ cabinet resigned with the words, "a complicated and strange state of affairs has developed in Europe." The alliance issue subsided for a time, but with the success of Germany's blitzkrieg tactics in Europe, the question of a pact with Germany and Italy was once again brought up by the army and proponents of military ex-

pansion in Southeast Asia. The YONAI MITSUMASA cabinet debated the feasibility of a three-nation alliance, but in the face of criticism from the army for being too pro-American it was obliged to resign, and in July 1940 the second Konoe cabinet was formed.

Before forming his cabinet, Konoe had already decided on strengthening the Axis alliance in order to establish what he named the "New Order in East Asia" (TŌA SHINCHITSUJO). He instructed the foreign minister, MATSUOKA YŌSUKE, to initiate negotiations for the three-nation pact. Matsuoka had been the leading advocate of withdrawal from the League of Nations at the time of the Manchurian crisis and was known as a German sympathizer. The rise of Matsuoka signaled the end of the pro-British policy that had prevailed since the signing of the ANGLO-JAPANESE ALLIANCE in 1902. In August 1940 Heinrich Stahmer arrived in Tōkyō as a special envoy; the Matsuoka–Stahmer conference began in September. By allying with Japan, Germany hoped to discourage the United States from participation in the European war. Fearing that its continued objection, however passive, would deepen antagonism with the army and provoke a political crisis, the navy finally agreed to the signing of the pact.

The pact was signed on 27 September 1940 in Berlin. The main points were: the signatories would mutually recognize the establishment of the New Order in Europe and Greater East Asia and their respective positions of leadership; if any of the signatories were attacked by a nation not involved in the European war or Sino-Japanese conflict at the time of the signing, the others would aid with every political, economic, and military means; the pact did not affect each signatory's political relationship with the Soviet Union; the pact was to be in effect for a period of 10 years.

The Tripartite Pact was essentially an agreement on the redivision of the world by the three signatory countries and a military alliance primarily against the United States. It served to strengthen the anti-Axis alliance of the United States, England, France, and Holland. With the outbreak of the German-Soviet war in June 1941, the Allies were joined by the Soviet Union. The world was now divided into the two main camps of Axis and Allied powers, and World War II developed on a full scale. After Japan attacked Pearl Harbor in 1941, the Axis powers agreed not to negotiate for peace unilaterally, and Germany and Italy declared war against the United States. In January 1942 a military agreement designating the respective military operating areas of the Axis powers was signed. In contrast to the Allies, who succeeded in coordinating a unified global strategy, however, Japan, Germany, and Italy never organized an effective cooperative effort. With the surrender of Italy in September 1943 and the total collapse of Germany in May 1945, the Tripartite Pact was completely shattered. *Awaya* Kentarō

Truman, Harry S. (1884–1972)

The 33rd president of the United States (1945–53). Born in Missouri. Truman entered the United States Senate in 1934, became vice-president in 1944, and assumed the presidency in 1945 on the death of Franklin D. Roosevelt at a crucial time in history, the last year of WORLD WAR II. He met with Winston Churchill and Joseph Stalin at the Potsdam Conference in July 1945 to discuss surrender terms for Japan and plans for reorganizing the postwar world. While at the conference, he received word of the successful American testing of the ATOMIC BOMB and authorized its use against Japan in order to end the war quickly. After World War II, he carried out the Marshall Plan and implemented the Truman Doctrine to contain communist expansion. When the communist North Korean armies invaded South Korea in 1950, Truman sent American troops to Korea under the aegis of the United Nations. He recalled General Douglas MACARTHUR in 1951, when MacArthur insisted on carrying the war into Mainland China against presidential orders. This demonstration of the American concept of the preeminence of civil over military authority left a deep impression on the Japanese.

trust

(shintaku). A system in which one person places property (such as money, securities, immovable property) under the control and management of another. In Japanese law, the person requesting such management is referred to as the settlor (itakusha), and the person administering the assets is referred to as the trustee (jutakusha). The distinguishing characteristic of a trust is that certain specified property is transferred from the settlor to the trustee to be managed by the trustee.

At present there are seven trust and banking companies in Japan; one city bank also carries on trust activities in addition to its other business. In 1978 the total value of property received in trust arrangements by these banks reached ¥35 trillion (US $167 billion). Of this amount, the bulk of the property was in the form of cash. These funds held in trust constitute about 10 percent of the total funds held by all private financial institutions in Japan. Thus commercial trusts have compiled strong business records.

With the exception of such commercial trusts, however, trusts are not common among the general populace of Japan. One reason for this is that Japan, unlike the United States and Great Britain, has no historical tradition of trusts, so there is little familiarity with the general concept. Moreover, from a legal standpoint, the CIVIL CODE of 1896 provided various other legal devices for the management of assets, including the devices of agency, delegation, and deposits, so the need for trusts has not been great.

In Japan the Trust Law (Shintaku Hō) of 1922 constitutes the legal basis of trusts. This law was based on the English trust system, the product of a long historical development, but the law was written so as to conform with other legal concepts in the Civil Code, which itself is based on principles of French and German law.

Under the Trust Law, charitable trusts are recognized in addition to regular private trusts. Thus the Civil Code and the Trust Law provide, respectively, the similar legal devices of the nonprofit foundation and the charitable trust as methods to engage in charitable activities in such areas as social welfare, religion, and education. These similar devices constitute a framework that can be used in accordance with the wishes of the benefactor.

For charitable activities the device of nonprofit foundations was used almost exclusively until very recently. Since 1977, however, understanding of trusts has been expanding, and charitable trusts have come into greater use, chiefly for the purposes of student scholarship funds, funds for academic research, and aid to developing nations. There has been a steady trend toward use of charitable trusts by conservation movements, along the lines of the National Trust concept in Britain. TANAKA Minoru

Ts'ai O → Cai E (Ts'ai O)

Ts'ao Ju-lin → Cao Rulin (Ts'ao Ju-lin)

Tsingtao → Qingdao (Tsingtao)

Tsou T'ao-fen → Zou Taofen (Tsou T'ao-fen)

Tsu

Capital of Mie Prefecture, central Honshū. Situated on Ise Bay, it was formerly called ANOTSU and known as a prosperous port town. During the Edo period (1600–1868) it developed as a POST-STATION TOWN on the road leading to ISE SHRINE and as a castle town of the Tōdō family. Tsu is a center of textile, electrical machinery, and shipbuilding industries. Agriculture, fishing, and commerce also flourish. Mie University is located here. The coast at Akogiura, the remains of Tsu Castle, and the temple Senshūji draw visitors. Pop: 144,991.

tsuba

Japanese sword guard; the disc or plate that separates the blade from the handle of the sword. A typical *tsuba* is approximately 8 centimeters (3 to 3.5 in) wide and has a center hole *(nakagoana)* for the tang of the sword. Most commonly made of steel, but frequently of other metals or alloys; it ensures that the hand does not slip up onto the blade and it affords some protection from an opponent's blade. The weight of the guard also functions to bring the sword's center of gravity closer to the handle of the sword, adding "balance" and force to a blow, and reducing fatigue to the wrist. In most fully mounted Japanese swords, the weight of the guard is proportional to the length and weight of the blade so that the point of percussion is in the principal striking area of the blade *(monouchi)*, approximately 10 to 15 centimeters (4–6 in) below the tip of the blade. Thus the weight of the blade is distributed to maximize impact and minimize recoil. Since the sword was the most important possession of the *samurai* warrior, *tsuba* and other metal fittings were considered ap-

Tsuba

Top: A late-16th-century iron *tsuba* with an openwork depiction of a crab. 8.9 × 8.6 cm. Tōkyō National Musuem. Bottom: A late-17th-century bronze *tsuba* by Tsuchiya Yasuchika, whose signature is visible to the left of the center hole. The inlaid design of plovers is executed in differently colored metals. 8.1 × 7.9 cm. Private collection.

propriate objects for exquisite craftsmanship and beauty and were frequently decorated with the warrior's family crest or that of his clan chief, or with Buddhist symbols or other designs of spiritual or religious significance.

Tsuba were made in various shapes; the majority were round or oval but also common were squares, lozenges, and a shape peculiar to *tsuba* known as *mokkō*, a circle with elliptical indentations around the edge giving the disc a lobed shape, the number of lobes generally being four but often being as many as six or eight. Many fanciful shapes and irregular forms also were employed, the most important and common being the *aoitsuba*, a rounded square with a heart-shaped perforation at each corner, used especially on more formal sword mounts.

The surface finish of *tsuba* and other metal sword fittings *(kodōgu)* generally established the basic impression of the object's artistic structure. A type of finishing done with special chisels to produce an effect like that of rough stone, termed *ishime*, was popular, as was *nanako*, a surface with tiny, raised dots. Often a steel surface was decorated with the marks of the hammer *(tsuchime)*. Polished surfaces were also used, particularly as a background for inlays *(zōgan)*; the inlays were not infrequently the designs of a great painter or printmaker and were sometimes made in collaboration with the artist. *Hirazōgan* is a type of flat inlay in which various colored metals or their alloys are embedded in the surface of a metal of another color and then polished. Various types of engraving were also employed, such as *kebori*, or hairline engraving, and *katakiribori*, a type of engraving in which a V-shaped groove is made vertical on one side, oblique on the other. In the case of older steel guards, the design was often an openwork silhouette *(sukashibori)* of a shrub or tree, or sometimes of a geometric object, a family crest, animals, birds, or other objects drawn from nature.

The various ways in which the rim of a sword guard is finished indicate not only the period in which it was made but also the particular school where it was crafted. The rims were occasionally provided with a decorative cover *(fukurin)* of silver, bronze, or gold for preservation of the edge of the guard.

History —— The earliest extant sword guards date from the Nara period (710–794). Among these early sword guards are some in an oval shape made of iron and with simple decoration of perforations; others are made of bronze or copper or have traces of gold and are in various specialized shapes. Still preserved in shrines and in good condition are some swords carried by chieftains in the Heian period (794–1185); some of these have sword guards and other metal fittings worked in detail and with beautiful decorative work.

In the Kamakura period (1185–1333), a simplified but functional sword guard was used that consisted of iron discs alternating with hard leather and covered with lacquer. More elaborate guards, often of simple beauty of design, were made of steel hammered out either by armor makers or by the swordsmiths.

In the Muromachi period (1333–1568), increasingly elaborate designs began to appear, principally geometric patterns or designs drawn from nature, or simple designs of perforations or hammerwork on steel. In this period perforated steel guards with intricately worked design of extraordinary artistic beauty appeared. An alloy peculiar to Japan, called *shakudō*, a mixture of red copper bronze with a small percentage of gold, also began to be used. In the finished *tsuba* this was pickled to a dark blue-black color, the surface in many instances decorated by minute dots of extraordinary regularity of arrangement in the *nanako* ("fish roe") technique, each formed individually by a hollow-nosed punch. Other alloys also were used, notably one of gray color composed of varying mixtures of silver and copper called *shibuichi*. Of course in some instances pure gold or silver were used, as well as various colors of brass and bronze. Two important swordsmith artists, Kaneie and Nobuie, produced highly sophisticated work toward the end of the 16th century. Kaneie's abstract, three-dimensional designs, usually with mystic and somber content, were carved in relief on the steel of the *tsuba*.

The early 17th century saw a veritable explosion of artistic talent expended on these small, metal sword fittings. Intricately decorated sword guards of jewellike quality, engraved and inlayed with alloys of many colors, or with CLOISONNÉ, appeared. In fineness of construction, conception, and exposition, *tsuba* and other metal sword fittings reached a peak that was maintained until the end of the 19th century. This art finally expired with the regulations promulgated by the new Meiji government in 1870, when it was forbidden either to make or wear swords. Although metalworkers continued for some time to make small art objects in metal, the art of making *tsuba* and other sword fittings was substantially lost.

Sword Fittings —— In addition to sword guards, various other small metal fittings, or *kodōgu*, were employed in the mounting of the sword blade and these also came to be crafted by metal artists. The Gotō family, beginning in the 15th century, were the predominant artists of sword fittings; the 16 principal generations of the Gotō family, along with their many branch families, continued to work until near the end of the Edo period (1600–1868). Their early work was centered on the smaller metal fittings of the sword, notably the pair of *menuki*, or beautifully carved small metal ornaments of various alloys, often of gold, cast and chiseled and carved in the most intricate and refined degree of beauty and bound under the silk cord wrappings of the handle of the sword. Probably in their original function they served the purpose of giving a contoured shape to the handle so as to permit a more secure grip.

A little later, the Gotō family began to produce *kōgai* and *kozuka* as well, two articles that were inserted in pockets or slots on the side of the scabbard. The *kōgai* was a blunt, pointed awllike instrument that probably initially served as a simple tool for repairing the lacings of armor and so on. The *kozuka* was a small knife with an artistically worked handle, a companion piece to the *kōgai*, generally made of the alloy *shakudō*. Where *kōgai* and *kozuka* were to accompany a sword, oval perforations in the sword guard, on each side of the *seppadai*, or central raised oval area, were made to permit the upper end of these fittings to project slightly through the sword guard so that they could be withdrawn without drawing the sword. These articles were made to consort not only with each other in terms of design, but with two other metal articles, the *fuchi* and *kashira*, the first a ferrule on the handle of the sword where it butted against the *seppadai* of the sword guard, and the latter a pommel at the end of the handle. The *fuchi* and *kashira* were made as a pair with closely related designs and of identical composition. *Shakudō* was favored for this, but brass, silver, gold, or bronze were also used. *Nanako* was frequently used in finishing the surface of the *kozuka, kōgai, fuchi,* and *kashira* as well as the end cap *(kojiri)* at the bottom of the scabbard.

The fittings on the scabbard *(saya)* were equally refined: through a slotted knob called *kurigata* affixed to the side of the scabbard a braided cord *(sageo)* was passed to hold the scabbard firmly in the sash of the samurai warrior. The *kurigata* was commonly made of polished horn; when it was made of metal it was decorated to consort with the other fittings. Finally, a hook *(origane)* was affixed to the side of the scabbard to catch on the under edge of the warrior's sash, to keep the scabbard firmly in place while the sword was being drawn.

In the late Muromachi and throughout the Edo period the samurai commonly wore two swords, a longer one and a shorter one, termed *daishō*, or individually referred to as *katana* and *wakizashi*. Fittings for a pair of swords were generally made en suite of an identical pattern or design. The Gotō family came to be bound by tradition to very strict rules governing the metal, the pattern, and the various designs that were proper, eventually adapting themselves almost exclusively to the most formal type of sword fitting, worn principally at the courts of the various local rulers or of the shōgun or the emperor. See also SWORDS.

📖 H. C. Gunsaulus, *Japanese Sword-mounts* (1923). S. Hara, *Die Meister Der Japanischen Schwertzieraten*, 2 vols (1931, 1932). H. L. Joly, ed, *Catalogues of Collections: W. L. Behrens (1913); G. H. Naunton (1912); J. C. Hawkshaw et al (1910)*. Satō Kan'ichi, *Higo kinkō taikan* (1964). E. A. Seemann, ed, *The Mosle Collection*, 7 vols (1932). Torigoe Kazutarō, *Tsuba kanshōki* (1965). P. Vautier, ed, *Sammlung Oeder*.   Walter Ames COMPTON

tsubaki → camellias

Tsubaki Chinzan (1801–1854)

Painter in the BUNJINGA tradition. Real name Tsubaki Hitsu. Chinzan was a *samurai* official in the service of the shogunate in Edo (now Tōkyō), where he was born. He studied painting under Kaneko Kinryō and briefly under TANI BUNCHŌ. But his principal teacher was WATANABE KAZAN, whose confidant and close friend he became. Among Chinzan's pupils was Kazan's son, Watanabe Shōka. Chinzan is especially noted for his BIRD-AND-FLOWER PAINTING *(kachōga)* and for his use of color. He was learned in many areas, including the martial arts of the samurai class, music, and poetry. In his portraits, he shows his strong debt to his teacher Kazan and to the West, especially in matters of brush tone and shading.   C. H. MITCHELL

Tsubaki Hot Spring

(Tsubaki Onsen). Located in the southern part of the town of Shirahama, southwestern Wakayama Prefecture, central Honshū. A hydrogen sulfide spring; water temperature 34–40°C (93–104°F). Facing the Kumano Sea, this ancient spa is located in a coastal area that is popular with bathers and anglers. The number of villas and inns has increased greatly since World War II.

Tsubakurodake

Mountain in northwestern Nagano Prefecture, central Honshū, in the eastern part of the Hida Mountains. Pure white rock towers of weathered granite stand near the summit. The hiking trail from this mountain to YARIGATAKE is one of the most popular in the JAPANESE ALPS. Hot springs are in the southeastern foothills. Height: 2,763 m (9,063 ft).

Tsubame

City in central Niigata Prefecture, central Honshū. Situated on the river Shinanogawa, Tsubame developed as a river port. During the Edo period (1600–1868) it became known for its files, *kiseru* (traditional smoking pipes), and copper ware. It is the country's leading manufacturer of tableware for export, producing 98 percent of the total. Pop: 44,236.

Tsuboi Kumezō (1858–1936)

Historian. Born in Ōsaka. Tsuboi studied political economy and chemistry at Tōkyō University and, after teaching briefly in both faculties, went to Germany and Austria to study history. Returning to Japan, he taught once more at Tōkyō University. His book *Shi-*

gaku kenkyū hō (1903, Methods of Historical Research) introduced German techniques of historical analysis to Japan. A scholar of broad interests, he also wrote on diplomatic history and cultural anthropology.

Tsuboi Sakae (1900–1967)

Novelist; children's story writer. Maiden name Iwai. Born on the island of Shōdoshima, Kagawa Prefecture. After marrying the anarchist poet TSUBOI SHIGEJI in 1925, she became active in the PROLETARIAN LITERATURE MOVEMENT. Her works, mostly set on Shōdoshima, are rich in local color; while sometimes criticized as sentimental, they express her deep concern for social justice. Her novel *Nijūshi no hitomi* (1952; tr *Twenty-Four Eyes,* 1957), about the enduring friendship between a teacher and her 12 students, was made into a popular film in 1954, directed by KINOSHITA KEISUKE. Her other works include the children's story "Kaki no ki no aru ie" (1949; tr "Under the Persimmon Tree," 1965); and the novel *Uchikake* (1956, A Robe), about four generations of a village family.

Tsuboi Shigeji (1898–1975)

Poet. Born in Kagawa Prefecture. Studied at Waseda University. Tsuboi gained prominence as an anarchist poet in the early 1920s, publishing his work in the anarchist poetry magazine *Aka to kuro* (1923–24) that he helped to found. He gradually turned to Marxism and became active in the so-called PROLETARIAN LITERATURE MOVEMENT. In 1945 he helped to found the Shin Nihon Bungaku Kai, a Marxist literary group. His work is characterized by a bluntness of expression and ironic humor. He married the novelist TSUBOI SAKAE. Works include *Atama no naka no heishi* (1956), a collection of poems, and *Teikō no seishin* (1949), a collection of critical essays.

Tsuboi Shōgorō (1863–1913)

Physical anthropologist and archaeologist; born in Edo (now Tōkyō). In 1884, as an undergraduate in zoology at Tōkyō University, he excavated the MUKŌGAOKA SHELL MOUND together with Arisaka Shōzō, and discovered the first YAYOI POTTERY. In the same year, he also founded the Anthropological Association (now the Anthropological Society of Nippon). After completing graduate school in anthropology at Tōkyō University, he spent three years (1889–92) studying in Britain and France. Upon his return, he established the first courses in anthropology at Tōkyō University in 1893.

Tsuboi is known for his theories on the origin of the Japanese (i.e., that the Koropokguru, a people with small stature who appear in AINU legends, were the earliest occupants of the archipelago) and on the nature of KŌGOISHI sites—theories which are now defunct. He was a prolific writer, publishing many of his site reports on YOKOANA (tunnel tombs) and SHELL MOUNDS excavations in the *Jinrui gakkai hōkoku* (now *Jinruigaku zasshi*), the official organ of the Anthropological Association of Tōkyō.   J. Edward KIDDER, Jr.

Tsubota Jōji (1890–1982)

Novelist, writer of children's literature. Born in Okayama Prefecture. Graduate of Waseda University. He first gained recognition as a children's story writer with a collection of his early works *Shōta no uma* (1927). He found it difficult to publish during the late 1920s and early 1930s, when the literary scene was dominated by the so-called PROLETARIAN LITERATURE MOVEMENT, but he reemerged after the mid-1930s with his trilogy of children's stories, including the winner of the Shinchōsha Literary Prize, *Kodomo no shiki* (1938). His stories portray the pure and innocent world of childhood, often set against the uglier aspects of reality. In 1955 he received the Japan Art Academy (Nihon Geijutsuin) Award and from 1964 was a member of the academy. The two other books of his trilogy are *Obake no sekai* (1935) and *Kaze no naka no kodomo* (1936).

Tsubouchi Shōyō (1859–1935)

Critic, playwright, translator, and novelist. A major figure in the modernization of Japanese literature. Born Tsubouchi Yūzō in the village of Ōta (now Mino Kamo) near Nagoya. In 1876 he moved to Tōkyō and entered preparatory school. Graduating from Tōkyō University in 1883, he became a professor at what is now Waseda University and, in 1891, editor of its literary journal, *Waseda bungaku.*

Tsubouchi Shōyō

Photographed on the occasion of his last Shakespeare lecture at Waseda University in December 1927.

Shōyō's remarkable career bore its earliest fruit in translations. Having voraciously read Western authors in college, particularly the English Romantics, he began translating his favorites. He was a meticulous scholar who established a high standard for subsequent translators. His crowning achievement here was the complete translation of Shakespeare's works, accomplished between 1883 and 1928, and still admired today.

Shōyō's contributions in criticism and fiction closely followed his first translations. Reading Western works convinced Shōyō that the state of Japan's literature was deplorable. If in the West fiction and drama were respected and praised and authors and playwrights were admired and honored, the same should be true in Japan. Shōyō initiated this struggle with simultaneous campaigns on two fronts. In his criticism he attempted to define the major characteristics of Western literature, to explain its techniques, and to elucidate its principles. Realism, objectivity, characterization, unity, and seriousness of tone and purpose had to be inculcated. *Shōsetsu shinzui* (1885–86, The Essence of the Novel) was the most thorough, important, and effective aspect of Shōyō's critical offensive.

Reform, Shōyō held, must begin with establishing literature as an independent art for its own sake. The political novel (SEIJI SHŌSETSU) should be abandoned because it restricted art to utilitarian and political purposes and was too manifestly a foreign, imported form. This left the tradition of Edo period (1600–1868) popular literature (GESAKU) as the primary material from which to mold a new, modern fiction. Once divested of its frivolous aspects and Confucian ethics, it could be transformed and elevated by imbuing it with contemporary settings, modern manners and customs, objective description, philosophical depth, and psychological realism. Plenary realism was the keynote of Shōyō's program, and fictional focus was to be firmly upon the actual emotions, thoughts, and behavior of veritable individuals.

To demonstrate and promulgate his ideas, Shōyō produced nine important fictional works between 1885 and 1890. The best known are *Tōsei shosei katagi* (1885–86), *Imo to sekagami* (1886), *Matsu no uchi* (1888), and *Saikun* (1888). Though these showed a steady advance toward realism, none fully realized Shōyō's goals. Too often they suffered from obsolete content, didactic preachments, fractured plots, stereotyped characterization, or artificial endings, and failed to transcend their *gesaku* models. Nevertheless, they were bold experiments that would open the way for others and change the nation's literary course.

Leaving fiction to more capable hands, Shōyō turned to drama after 1888. With his plays and dramatic criticism, Shōyō attained his greatest successes. In such essays as "Wagakuni no shigeki" (1893–94) and "Shingakugeki ron" (1904), he again condemned moral and political utilitarianism, championed realism, and demanded that drama be a serious, independent art. Popular theater had to be rehabilitated from a vulgar entertainment for the uncultured; acting and dancing had to be improved and revitalized; texts had to resonate with artistry and beauty; plays had to reflect rational development, authentic circumstances, and genuine emotions. The essential means of creating a new drama lay in carefully combining selected elements and techniques of Western and traditional drama and music, and then transmuting these into a sophisticated dramatic form.

As before, Shōyō immediately attempted to illustrate and disseminate his concepts through concrete application. Between 1894 and 1920 he wrote dozens of plays marked by a startling variety of length, form, and innovation. Excepting his masterpiece "Shinkyoku Urashima" (1904), however, Shōyō once more failed to follow his own requirements rigorously or to surmount the models he wished to renovate. His plays were riddled with inferior characterization, episodic structure, unleavened content, and fabricated emotion. Even so, these courageous efforts pointed theater and drama in new directions.

As a theorist, critic, and translator, Shōyō deservedly ranks at the apex of modern Japanese literary history. He was unquestionably a powerful catalyst in modernizing Japan's literature. Much of the criticism of his deficiencies in practical application overlooks the magnitude of the forces Shōyō confronted, the impossibility of total brilliance in every area of his radical experiments, and the sincerity of his intentions and efforts. Shōyō always desired the best and was modest enough to pass the banners of artistic regeneration and refinement to more creative talents when they appeared. His supreme contribution was perhaps the absolute conviction that slavish adoption of alien forms was sterile; that the traditional literary arts could not be jettisoned wholesale but must be selectively refashioned and reanimated. Every great Japanese writer since Shōyō has rediscovered that profound insight.

■——Tsubouchi Shōyō, *Shōyō senshū*, 17 vols (Daiichi Shobō, 1977).   *Thomas E.* SWANN

Tsuboya ware

(tsuboya-yaki). Ceramics produced in the city of Naha, Okinawa Prefecture. Made from local clays with painted or incised floral, animal, or geometric patterns. Glazes are red and green, and are lightly applied; for slip decoration, a yellowish clay that fires a deep white is used. Since these pieces are fired at low temperatures, bonding is rather weak. Both climbing kilns *(noborigama)* and through-draft kilns *(anagama)* are used.

Among the types of Tsuboya ware, there are two main categories. *Arayaki* consists mostly of large vessels for *sake* or *miso* storage and is fired either unglazed or with manganese glaze. *Jōyaki*, which is the more common, is a feldspathic glazed ware consisting mostly of smaller items such as tableware. Tsuboya-ware products include burial urns with sculpting.

The history of Okinawan wares goes back approximately 500 years. Okinawa's oldest pottery products seem to have been tiles; in the 14th and 15th centuries, with the beginning of trade with China and the South Sea islands, many foreign ceramics, the so-called *namban-yaki*, were imported and their techniques were adopted locally. In 1682 the monarchical government moved all the kilns to Tsuboya in what is now the city of Naha. The industry supplied wares for use within the Ryūkyū kingdom and for use as tribute to the Satsuma domain (now Kagoshima Prefecture), the de facto ruler, as well as to other *daimyō* families. After Okinawa became one of the prefectures of Japan in 1879, Tsuboya-ware production became a civilian-run industry; since the end of World War II, Okinawans have protected, transmitted, and further cultivated ceramic production. Today, there are 12 functioning kilns in Tsuboya alone.

Ann B. CARY

Tsuburaya Eiji (1901–1970)

Special effects technician; known for his work on such monster pictures as *Gojira* (1954, Godzilla) and numerous war films. Real name Tsuburaya Eiichi. Born in Fukushima Prefecture. Typical of his work were his special effects for *Hawai-Marē oki kaisen* (1942, The War at Sea from Hawaii to Malaya), a film directed by YAMAMOTO KAJIRŌ which was aimed at elevating home-front morale during World War II. In this film Tsuburaya recreated the attack on Pearl Harbor by the use of impressive miniature sets. So impressive was the movie that when shown at factories and plants producing war

matériel, productivity is reported to have shot up. After the war Tsuburaya took charge of special effects in a number of other war pictures including *Taiheiyō no washi* (1953, Eagles of the Pacific), in which he constructed an actual-size replica of the aircraft carrier Hiryū and a 13-meter-long model of the battleship YAMATO that was capable of navigation.

Beginning with *Gojira* in 1954, directed by Honda Inoshirō, Tsuburaya also created various prehistoric-animal-like creatures which wreaked havoc on modern society in a series of science fiction and monster pictures that became a big line of hits for Daiei (DAIEI CO, LTD). In these movies Tsuburaya had more authority than the actual director. In 1963 he organized his own Tsuburaya Special Productions.   *ITASAKA Tsuyoshi*

Tsuchida Bakusen (1887–1936)

Japanese-style painter whose works combined Western and traditional Japanese painting techniques. Born on the island of Sado in Niigata Prefecture. Real name Tsuchida Kinji. He went to Kyōto in 1903 to become a Buddhist monk, a goal he soon abandoned in order to study painting. He studied first with TAKEUCHI SEIHŌ and later at the Kyōto Kaiga Semmon Gakkō (now Kyōto City University of Arts). In 1912 he studied painting in Europe. In 1918, with MURAKAMI KAGAKU, he founded the Kokuga Sōsaku Kyōkai (National Creative Painting Association); the works Bakusen exhibited with this group reveal a bold combination of Japanese and Western styles, which influenced the modernization of Japanese-style painting (see NIHONGA). In 1934 he was appointed to the Teikoku Bijutsuin (Imperial Fine Arts Academy).

Tsuchii Bansui → Doi Bansui

tsuchi ikki

Peasant uprisings of the Muromachi period (1333–1568), particularly during the 15th century; also known as *do ikki*. Most of them took place in the economically advanced provinces adjacent to Kyōto, where the early development of village self-rule (see SŌ) contributed to solidarity and political consciousness among the peasantry. The term *tsuchi ikki* embraces a wide spectrum of uprisings, ranging from petition and protest to violent rebellion against authority. In the second half of the 14th century, grievances were generally directed to estate (SHŌEN) proprietors, and the most common demands involved the reduction of tax burdens (NENGU) and corvée (BUYAKU) or the removal of unpopular estate officials.

In the 15th century, when uprisings were at their height, debt cancellation became the principal goal. Economic power during this period was concentrated in the hands of the *sakaya dosō* (literally, "brewer-brokers"; see SAKAYA and DOSŌ), local entrepreneurs, usually *sake* brewers, who used their profits to establish lucrative pawnbrokerages. The *sakaya dosō* were not only an important source of tax revenue for the Muromachi shogunate but were also the major suppliers of credit to villagers in the central provinces. The demonstrators attacked the warehouses of the *sakaya dosō*, whom they saw as the major exploiters, and "settled accounts" by destroying the records of their debts. In most cases, however, the object was to induce the shogunate to proclaim a cancellation of debts (TOKUSEI). Although it did so repeatedly, debt cancellations were no more than a temporary solution because they disrupted a credit relationship that the peasants could not do without.

While *tsuchi ikki* were in general motivated by local economic concerns, they sometimes involved large numbers of peasants and considerable geographic areas. For example, in a *tsuchi ikki* originating in Yamashiro Province (now part of Kyōto Prefecture) in 1441, tens of thousands of peasants, some of them from Izumi and Kawachi provinces (both now part of Ōsaka Prefecture), seized control of all the approaches to Kyōto and forced the shogunate to issue a *tokusei* edict. The fact that the largest uprisings occurred in times of turmoil within the shogunate—such as 1428, when the shōgun Ashikaga Yoshimochi died, or 1441, when the shōgun Ashikaga Yoshinori was assassinated, and the period of the Ōnin War (1467–77)—underlines their political significance. But by the latter part of the 15th century the *tsuchi ikki* had begun to lose their impetus. An important reason was that the *dogō* (the affluent upper stratum of the peasantry), who had provided the leadership for the *tsuchi ikki*, tended to become minor proprietors and to come to terms with the emerging local military leaders, the KOKUJIN. With the appearance soon after of the SENGOKU DAIMYŌ (territorial lords), the erstwhile leaders of the *tsuchi ikki* were used to control the peasantry on behalf of the daimyō. See also IKKI; HYAKUSHŌ IKKI.

——David L. Davis, "*Ikki* in Late Medieval Japan," in John W. Hall and Jeffrey P. Mass, ed, *Medieval Japan* (1974). Kurokawa Naonori, "Chūsei kōki no nōmin tōsō: Tsuchi ikki kuni ikki," in *Kōza nihonshi*, vol 3 (Tōkyō Daigaku Shuppankai, 1970). Minegishi Sumio, ed, *Doikki*, vol 9 of *Shimpojiumu Nihon rekishi* (Gakuseisha, 1974). Nakamura Kichiji, *Tokusei to doikki* (rev ed, 1966).

Michael SOLOMON

Tsuchimikado, Emperor (1195–1231)

The 83rd sovereign *(tennō)* in the traditional count (which includes several nonhistorical emperors); reigned 1198–1210. The eldest son of Emperor GO-TOBA, he ascended the throne at an early age, while his father retained control of court politics as retired emperor. In 1210 he was forced to abdicate in favor of his younger brother, the future emperor JUNTOKU, for refusing to support Go-Toba's intrigues against the Kamakura shogunate. Although he was held blameless after the JŌKYŪ DISTURBANCE (1221), when both Go-Toba and Juntoku were exiled for attempting to overthrow the shogunal regent HŌJŌ YOSHITOKI, Tsuchimikado chose exile in Tosa Province (now Kōchi Prefecture). He died in Awa Province (now Tokushima Prefecture).

G. Cameron HURST III

Tsuchiura

City in southern Ibaraki Prefecture, central Honshū; on Lake Kasumigaura. During the Edo period (1600–1868) Tsuchiura flourished as a castle and POST-STATION TOWN. The Kasumigaura Naval Air Force base that was located here has been converted into foodstuff and textile plants. Vegetables and fruit are grown. Pop: 112,517.

Tsuchiya Bummei (1890–   )

Tanka (31-syllable WAKA) poet. Born in Gumma Prefecture. Graduate of Tōkyō University. Tsuchiya studied poetry with ITŌ SACHIO, and in 1925 published his first collection, *Fuyukusa*. In 1930 he succeeded SAITŌ MOKICHI in the editorship of the *tanka* magazine ARARAGI. As a poet he wrote with verity about daily life and upheld the traditions of realist *tanka*. Among his published works are *Ōkanshū* (1930) and *Sankokushū* (1935), two volumes of *tanka* verse, and the *Man'yōshū shichū* (1949–56), a 20-volume commentary on the MAN'YŌSHŪ, the oldest extant anthology of classical Japanese poetry.

ASAI Kiyoshi

Tsuda College

(Tsuda Juku Daigaku). A private women's college located in the city of Kodaira, Tōkyō Prefecture. Its origin lies in the Joshi Eigaku Juku (English School for Women) founded in 1900 by TSUDA UMEKO in Kōjimachi (now a part of Chiyoda Ward), Tōkyō. The school was renamed Tsuda Eigo Juku (Tsuda English School) in 1930 and was moved to its present site. In 1943 a department of mathematics was established, and in 1949 the school adopted its present name. The college has always maintained excellence in the field of English literature. There are faculties of letters and science. The school's Research Institute of Language is well known. Enrollment was 2,357 in 1980. See also WOMEN'S EDUCATION.

Tsuda Mamichi (1829–1903)

Legal scholar and government official. Born in the Tsuyama domain (now part of Okayama Prefecture). As a youth Tsuda studied WESTERN LEARNING under MITSUKURI GEMPO and military science under SAKUMA SHŌZAN. He became an instructor at the BANSHO SHIRABESHO, the Tokugawa shogunate's bureau of Western Learning, and in 1862 he was sent by the shogunate to Holland to study at the University of Leiden. On his return in 1865, he became an instructor at the Kaiseijo, the successor to the Bansho Shirabesho. He also worked on his lecture notes from Simon Vissering's courses on law and economics at Leiden and published them as *Taisei kokuhō ron* (1866, On Western Law), the first Japanese book on the subject. After the Meiji Restoration of 1868, Tsuda joined the Ministry of Justice and helped with the codification of the SHINRITSU KŌRYŌ. He subsequently served in the Army Ministry, where he helped to draft the Army Penal Code, in the Genrōin (Chamber of Elders, a

protosenatorial body), and in the Diet. As a member of the MEIROKUSHA, the society organized to introduce Western ideas and culture, he wrote some 29 articles for its magazine, *Meiroku zasshi*.

Tsuda Sen (1837–1908)

Leading agricultural writer of the Meiji period (1868–1912). He studied Dutch and English at the end of the Edo period (1600–1868) and, along with FUKUZAWA YUKICHI, accompanied the government mission to the United States in 1867. In 1874 he won public attention with his work, *Nōgyō sanji*, a study of natural and artificial crop pollination based on observations he had made in Austria. He also founded Gakunōsha, a society for the study of agriculture, issued the popular agricultural magazine *Nōgyō zasshi*, and continued to write until late in his life. Since World War II he has gained posthumous recognition as a critic of bureaucratic policies in agriculture. His daughter, TSUDA UMEKO, founded Joshi Eigaku Juku, now known as Tsuda College.

KATŌ Shunjirō

Tsuda Sōgyū (?–1591)

Wealthy merchant and tea connoisseur of the Azuchi-Momoyama period (1568–1600). The oldest son of Tsuda Sōtatsu (1504–66), an influential merchant of the great port city of Sakai and also a devotee of the tea cult, Sōgyū served the hegemons ODA NOBUNAGA and TOYOTOMI HIDEYOSHI as master of the tea ceremony *(sadō)*. Together with SEN NO RIKYŪ, he was responsible for organizing Hideyoshi's famous extravaganza, the outdoor tea ceremony at Kitano Shrine in 1587, and is generally ranked with them as one of the three great tea masters of his age.

Tsuda Sōkichi (1873–1961)

Historian. An authority on ancient Japanese and Chinese history and thought. Born in Gifu Prefecture. Graduated from Tōkyō Semmon Gakkō (Waseda University). A student of SHIRATORI KURAKICHI, an authority on Oriental history, Tsuda entered the Research Section of the SOUTH MANCHURIA RAILWAY, of which Shiratori was section head, in 1908. He became professor at Waseda University in 1919 and contributed much to the study of ancient Chinese history and philosophy as well as criticism of the Japanese classics.

Tsuda made his greatest contribution to the world of scholarship in Japan by demonstrating textually that the KOJIKI and NIHON SHOKI, ancient chronicles of Japan dating from the 8th century, are not objective descriptions of historical facts but fabrications made by court compilers to justify imperial rule. For his work he came under attack from rightists, who accused Tsuda of desecrating the dignity of the imperial family. Four of his major books were banned in 1940, and Tsuda and his publisher Iwanami Shigeo were later indicted and sentenced to three months in jail with a two-year suspended sentence.

Tsuda's *Bungaku ni arawaretaru waga kokumin shisō no kenkyū* (Studies on the Thought of Our People as Expressed in Literature; 1916–21, repr 1951–54) is another contribution to the history of Japanese thought. In this work he discussed the life of the people from the time of the empress Suiko (r 593–628) to the end of the 19th century as expressed in Japanese literature. Tsuda is also known for his studies, based upon rigorous textural criticism, of the Chinese Confucian and Taoist classics.

Considered a progressive for his scholarly works, Tsuda surprised his admirers after World War II when he took a strong anticommunist stand and produced works advocating respect toward the emperor. He received the Cultural Medal in 1949.

The complete works of Tsuda have been published in 33 volumes by Iwanami Shoten (1963–65). Works concerning Japanese history, thought, and literature include *Kojiki oyobi Nihon shoki no shin kenkyū* (1919), *Nihon jōdaishi kenkyū* (1930), and *Jōdai Nihon no shakai oyobi shisō* (1933); those concerning Chinese culture include *Dōka no shisō to sono tenkai* (1927), *Saden no shisōshiteki kenkyū* (1935), and *Rongo to Kōshi no shisō* (1946).

Tsuda Umeko (1865–1929)

Educator; founder of TSUDA COLLEGE. Born in Edo (now Tōkyō); second daughter of TSUDA SEN, a *samurai* who later became an expert on Western agricultural techniques. One of the first Japanese women to study abroad, she (then only age 6) was the youngest of 5 girls among the 54 students sent with the IWAKURA MISSION to the

United States in 1871. She lived with an American couple in Washington, DC, studied at private girls' schools, and was baptized a Christian. In 1882 she returned to Japan, where she first became a tutor in the household of the oligarch ITŌ HIROBUMI and then taught in the new school for daughters of the nobility, the Kazoku Jogakkō. Encouraged by her friend Alice BACON, she went again to the United States from 1889 to 1892 to study biology and education at Bryn Mawr College in Pennsylvania. Back in Tōkyō, Tsuda continued teaching until in 1900 she was able to found her own Women's English School (Joshi Eigaku Juku; now Tsuda College). Although it began with only 10 students, the school grew and made a great contribution to the development of women's higher education by exposing its students to a relatively modern atmosphere and curriculum and by preparing them for economic independence as secondary-school English teachers, at that time one of the few socially acceptable occupations for women; it was officially recognized as a professional school in 1905. That same year Tsuda also served as a principal organizer of the Japanese branch of the Young Women's Christian Association (YWCA). In 1907 and again in 1913, she returned to the United States to help promote cultural and educational exchanges; and, despite a long battle against diabetes, she continued working on behalf of her school until her death.

Tsugaru Peninsula

(Tsugaru Hantō). Located in northwestern Aomori Prefecture, northern Honshū, and bounded to the east by Mutsu Bay, to the north by the Tsugaru Strait, and to the west by the Sea of Japan. The Tsugaru Plain, which covers the western half of the peninsula, is a rich agricultural region, with large annual yields of apples and rice. The eastern portion comprises the low-lying Tsugaru Mountains. TAPPIZAKI, a cape on the northernmost tip of this peninsula, is the site of the southern exit of the Seikan (Aomori–Hakodate) Tunnel, an undersea railway tunnel between Honshū and Hokkaidō, still under construction in 1982; completion expected in 1986. Area: 1,300 sq km (502 sq mi).

Tsugaru Plain

(Tsugaru Heiya). Located in western Aomori Prefecture, northern Honshū. Bordering the Sea of Japan, this flood plain of the river Iwakigawa, which empties into Lake Jūsan, has been formed by the filling of the extensive marshlands behind the coastal sand dunes. Rice is grown, and the output of apples, cultivated on the foothills of Iwakisan and on the levees, ranks first in Japan. The major city is Hirosaki. Area: approximately 1,000 sq km (386 sq mi); length: 60 km (37 mi); width: 20 km (12 mi).

Tsugaru Strait

(Tsugaru Kaikyō). Between southern Hokkaidō and northern Honshū, connecting the Sea of Japan and the Pacific Ocean. Ferries are in service across this strait and the Seikan Tunnel, an undersea railway tunnel, between the cape Tappizaki, Aomori Prefecture, northern Honshū, and Yoshioka near the cape Shirakamimisaki in Hokkaidō was under construction in 1982; completion expected in 1986. Length: 130 km (80.7 mi); width: 20–50 km (12–31 mi); deepest point: 449 m (1,473 ft).

Tsuga Teishō (1718–1794?)

Author and physician of the Edo period (1600–1868). Born in Ōsaka. He wrote pedantic adaptations of Chinese vernacular fiction, mostly ghost stories, which are considered the forerunners of the YOMIHON genre. He also published a collated edition of the Chinese dictionary Kangxi zidian (K'ang-hsi tzu-tien). His major works are Hanabusa sōshi (1749) and Shigeshige yawa (1766). UEDA AKINARI, a contemporary writer of yomihon romances, is said to have studied medicine under Teishō.

tsuge

(Japanese box). Buxus microphylla var. japonica. Also called asamatsuge. An evergreen tree of the box family (Buxaceae) which grows wild on hills in Kyūshū, Shikoku, and western and central Honshū and is also cultivated in various parts of Japan. Its straight trunk reaches a height of 1–3 meters (3–10 ft). The leaves are about 2 centimeters (0.7 in) long, elliptical in shape and leathery, their deep green upper surface smooth and shiny, and their lower surface pale green with prominent midribs on both sides. In the spring small pale yellow flowers bloom in the axils of the smaller branches.

Naturally hard, heavy, and yellow in color, boxwood is a favorite material for combs, engraving blocks, and seals. Another variety of tsuge, Hachijō tsuge (B. microphylla var. japonica f. major), grows in relatively warm areas such as the Izu Islands and is known for its larger and thicker leaves. A variety of cultivated tsuge, himetsuge (B. microphylla), usually planted in gardens, grows only 60 centimeters (2 ft) high, with foliage so thick that the entire tree resembles a large ball.　　　　　　　　　　　　　　　　　　MATSUDA Osamu

tsugumi → thrushes

tsuihō → banishment

tsujigahana

("flowers-at-the-crossing"). A decorative textile design method mainly using tie-dyeing (shiborizome); popular from the middle of the Muromachi period (1333–1568) to the early years of the Edo period (1600–1868) for kosode (an early form of KIMONO). The oldest extant piece of tsujigahana fabric is a temple banner that has sewn into it a piece of paper with the date Kyōroku 3 (1530); however, the date of origin of the fabric itself is uncertain.

In this method the fabric was most often a silk called nerinukiji, woven with raw silk thread as warp and glossed silk thread as weft, and dyed by soaking in vegetable dyes such as those made from safflower and indigo. The techniques of dyeing included stitching the design closely with a fine thread of asa (flax), winding the cloth onto a water-resistant core and immersing in dye; tying up undyed white areas of the cloth in bunches and dyeing those parts different colors from the rest of the cloth; and leaving the base white and dyeing the parts to be colored. Apart from these three methods, there were many additional variations, such as brush painting flowers or birds with sumi (India ink) or shu (cinnabar), embroidering, and pressing or rubbing gold or silver leaf (surihaku).

The origins of tsujigahana remain somewhat unclear for there is little documentation, but the beauty and refinement of this decorative technique are undisputed. See also TEXTILES.　　　HIROI Nobuko

tsujigiri

(literally, "cutting down at the crossroad"). Random, unprovoked killing by samurai. The victims were innocent passersby and were usually attacked at nighttime by samurai who wished to test their swords, to improve their martial skills, or simply to rob. Such killings occurred most frequently in the early years of the Edo period (1600–1868). The Tokugawa shogunate (1603–1867) strictly forbade tsujigiri and set up patrol groups (see JISHIMBAN AND TSUJIBAN) to prevent it. The KUJIKATA OSADAMEGAKI code prescribed public humiliation (hikimawashi) followed by beheading as punishment for the crime. During the peaceful and stable middle years of the Edo period, incidents of tsujigiri became extremely rare, but there was a resurgence in the years leading to the overthrow of the shogunate.

Tsuji Kunio (1914–)

Novelist; scholar of French literature. Born in Tōkyō. Graduate of Tōkyō University. He began writing while studying in France from 1957 to 1961. After his return to Japan, he gained recognition for his novel, Kairō ni te (1962–63), which was serialized in the magazine Kindai bungaku. He continued to write while teaching French at Rikkyō University in Tōkyō. Free of the somber realism that colors the mainstream of postwar literature, his style conveys an inner liberation of the spirit. Other novels include Azuchi ōkan ki (1968) and Sagano meigetsu ki (1971).

Tsuji Masanobu (1902–1961?)

Army officer and politician. Born in Ishikawa Prefecture. Graduated from the Army Academy in 1924. He was a staff officer of the GUANDONG (KWANTUNG) ARMY, the Japanese field army in Manchuria at the time of the NOMONHAN INCIDENT, a border dispute with the Soviet Union. During World War II he played a leading role in developing strategy as a staff officer at Imperial Headquarters

(DAIHON'EI). He was stationed in Thailand at the time of Japan's surrender, but he escaped British efforts to try him as a war criminal, and, returning to Japan, he published his first book, *Senkō sanzenri* (1950, Three Thousand Miles Underground). He was elected to the House of Representatives in 1952 and to the House of Councillors in 1959. While traveling in Laos during the civil war there in 1961, he disappeared. In 1968 he was declared legally dead.

HATA Ikuhiko

Tsujimura Jusaburō (1933–   )

Artist, puppeteer, and producer of puppet shows. Born in China. Tsujimura got his start at a theater workshop that specialized in making small articles for use on the puppet stage. Around 1960 he set his mind on becoming a puppet maker and devoted himself to this craft. Over the years Tsujimura has introduced his audience to many different puppet characters, each endowed with its own unique personality. More recently NHK, the public television network, has aired puppet shows produced and performed by Tsujimura. He has also done illustrations for novels serialized in newspapers.

YAMADA Tokubei

tsujiura

Divining the future (*uranai*) by stationing oneself at a crossroads (*tsuji*) at dusk and listening to the chance words of passersby; these words were then regarded as oracular. The practice is related to the folk belief in MAREBITO, gods who were thought on rare occasions to appear from afar bestowing blessings. In ancient times this practice, attested to in the 8th-century poetic anthology MAN'YŌSHŪ, was termed *yūke*, or "evening divination." Eventually the rite of *tsujiura* became connected with the worship of DŌSOJIN, or roadside deities. By the Edo period (1600–1868), *tsujiura* had degenerated into the roadside hawking of rice crackers containing printed fortunes. See also DIVINATION.

INOKUCHI Shōji

Tsuji Zennosuke (1877–1955)

Historian. Born in Hyōgo Prefecture. He studied history at Tōkyō University and joined the HISTORIOGRAPHICAL INSTITUTE affiliated with the university in 1902. From 1911 onward he taught concurrently at the university, becoming a full professor in 1923. Tsuji was the author of numerous studies of Buddhism, including his 10-volume *Nihon bukkyō shi no kenkyū* (1944–55, Studies on the History of Buddhism in Japan), for which he was awarded the Japan Academy Prize in 1921. He also received the Order of Culture (Bunka Kunshō) in 1952.

Tsukamoto Kunio (1930–   )

WAKA poet. Born in Shiga Prefecture. Graduate of Ōsaka University of Foreign Studies. While working for a trading company, he published two poetry collections, *Sōshoku gakku* (1956) and *Nihonjin reika* (1958), which established his name as a *waka* poet. His unconventional style—irregular line division, frequent use of uncommon Chinese characters and abstract terms—made him a leading avant-garde *waka* poet in the late 1950s and 1960s. After 1970 he also wrote novels. His principal works include the poetry collections *Suisō monogatari* (1952) and *Saredo yūsei* (1975), and a collection of *tanka* criticism, *Yūgure no kaichō* (1971).

Tsukigase

Village in northwestern Nara Prefecture, central Honshū. Green tea is grown. The village is noted for its plum trees, there are some 7,000, and the dye (*ubai*) made from the fruit. Lake Tsukigase, created by Takayama Dam, is located here. Pop: 2,111.

tsukimono

Discarnate entities which are believed to "possess" a human being, causing a variety of bodily and mental torments. The term applies primarily to certain animals credited with the power of assuming invisible form and entering the human body through one of its orifices. Such animals are of two broad types: a four-legged creature usually described as a fox (*kitsune*) and a snake known as *tōbyō*. The "fox" is found widely distributed over the island of Kyūshū, the Kantō and Kansai districts, and along the Sea of Japan coast. In Shikoku and the Chūgoku district it is known as a "dog," *inugami*, and in the north under the name of *izuna*. A peculiar feature of the belief is that none of these animals resembles its namesake. The "fox" is described as resembling a small weasel, and the snake as short and fat like a fish.

As regards their baleful activities toward man, the *tsukimono* can be usefully divided into two categories: those that molest human beings from their own volition, as from a desire to revenge themselves for insult or ill usage, or from a passion for certain food only obtainable through a human intermediary; and those that are directed to their evil deeds by another person, known as *kitsunetsukai* or "fox employer." Such persons, after getting the creature into their power by feeding it, use it as a servant or messenger to prosecute their private grudges. Along the coast of the Sea of Japan a peculiar form of this belief still survives. Certain families, known as *kitsune-mochi* or fox owners, are believed to keep such animals in their houses and to transmit their power over them in the female line. Until comparatively recently such families were strictly ostracized.

The torments caused by *tsukimono* range from bodily aches and pains, through hallucinations auditory and visual, to cases of true apparent possession, in which the "fox" speaks through the victim's mouth with a strange voice and vocabulary often larded with uncharacteristic rudeness and obscenity. The approved method of cure is through the services of a Buddhist priest or ascetic who has acquired power through austerities.

In addition to these animals, under the heading of *tsukimono* may also be classed: (1) dead ancestral spirits, discontented through neglect on the part of their descendants, who possess one of the culprits in order to call attention to their plight; (2) *kami* enraged by profanation of their shrines. Examples of each may be found in profusion in medieval literature and in certain districts even today.
——Carmen Blacker, *The Catalpa Bow* (1975). B. H. Chamberlain, *Things Japanese* (1890).

Carmen BLACKER

Tsukuba Academic New Town

(Tsukuba Kenkyū Gakuen Toshi). Town in Ibaraki Prefecture, central Honshū; on the southern slope of Tsukubasan. This planned academic community, which comprises six towns and villages, was completed in 1979. Forty-five state and private educational and research institutions, including Tsukuba University, formerly Tōkyō University of Education, are located here.

Tsukubasan

Mountain in central Ibaraki Prefecture, central Honshū. It is the main peak of the Tsukuba Mountains. The summit consists of two peaks, Nantaisan and Nyotaisan. It is mentioned in the MAN'YŌSHŪ (an 8th-century collection of poems) and is now a recreation site serving the Tōkyō metropolitan area. On the summit are Tsukuba Shrine and a meteorological observatory. The summit commands a view of the Kantō Plain. The TSUKUBA ACADEMIC NEW TOWN is at its foot. Tsukubasan is a part of Suigō Tsukuba Quasi-National Park. Height: 876 m (2,873 ft).

Tsukubashū

Renga (linked verse) anthology (see RENGA AND HAIKAI). Compiled in 1356 by NIJŌ YOSHIMOTO with the assistance of his teacher GUSAI. The title alludes to a passage in the 8th-century chronicle NIHON SHOKI in which the legendary hero Prince YAMATOTAKERU and an old man link verses to form what is said to be the first *renga*. Mount Tsukuba (Tsukubasan), which was nearby, is mentioned in the poem, and its name subsequently became almost synonymous with *renga*. The 20 chapters of the *Tsukubashū* contain over 2,000 individual verses (in the form of linked pairs, not entire *renga* sequences). These are arranged in categories such as the seasons, religion, love, and travel, on the pattern of the 10th-century *waka* anthology, KOKINSHŪ. Over 400 poets are represented, from ancient times down to the compilers and their contemporaries, including emperors as well as commoners. This anthology, which established *renga* as a respected literary form, offers a panoramic view of its development. In 1357 the collection was designated the first imperially recognized anthology of *renga*.

Tsukuba University

(Tsukuba Daigaku). A national, coeducational university located in the TSUKUBA ACADEMIC NEW TOWN in Ibaraki Prefecture. Founded in 1973, it absorbed TŌKYŌ UNIVERSITY OF EDUCATION in 1978. The university is an attempt at reform within the Japanese university system, based upon a new system of cluster colleges designed to encourage interdisciplinary education. The first cluster comprises faculties of letters, law and politics, economics, and general science; the second cluster, faculties of agriculture and forestry, biological sciences, comparative culture, and human sciences; and the third cluster, faculties of technological and information sciences, and socioeconomic planning. In addition there are schools of medicine, physical education, and art and design. Graduate programs are offered in most disciplines. Enrollment was 6,570 in 1980.

tsukuda

Rice land under the direct administration of the proprietor of an estate (SHŌEN). *Tsukuda* were cultivated by peasants and semi-serfs (GENIN) as a form of corvée labor (BUYAKU). The proprietor furnished seed, tools, fertilizer, and sometimes food to the cultivators, who in return were obliged to surrender their entire crop. Until the 11th century *tsukuda* normally accounted for the largest and most fertile portion of an estate. This portion declined from the 12th century onward, when *tsukuda* fell into the contrasting category of *myōden,* estate lands to which independent farmers (MYŌSHU) held hereditary rights of cultivation and were obliged to pay annual rice taxes (NENGU). Estate managers (SHŌKAN) and later, during the Kamakura period (1185–1333), shogunate-appointed military land stewards (JITŌ) were assigned *tsukuda* with the right to requisition labor. Thus began the process whereby estate proprietors, largely court nobles and religious institutions, lost control of their *shōen* in the 14th and 15th centuries.

Tsukumi

City in southeastern Ōita Prefecture, Kyūshū. Rich deposits of lime have made it a center of the cement industry. Mandarin oranges are grown in the surrounding hills. Pop: 30,453.

Tsukushi Mountains

(Tsukushi Sanchi). Also called Chikushi Mountains. A series of mountain ranges covering the greater part of Saga and Fukuoka prefectures, northern Kyūshū. The main range is the SEFURI MOUNTAINS to the west. The Tsukushi Mountains consist of many small- or medium-sized peaks, the highest being Sefurisan (1,055 m; 3,460 ft). The Chikuhō and Saga coalfields are located here.

Tsukushi Plain

(Tsukushi Heiya). Also known as Chikushi Plain. Located in Fukuoka and Saga prefectures, Kyūshū. Bounded by fault scarps to the south and northeast, this plain borders the Ariake Sea. It consists of the floodplain and delta of the river Chikugogawa and has extensive alluvial fans. It is marshy land with numerous creeks. Along the seacoast is a vast area of reclaimed land. In this rich rice-producing area dairy farming also flourishes. The major cities are Kurume and Saga. Area: approximately 1,200 sq km (463 sq mi).

Tsumago

District in southwestern Nagano Prefecture, central Honshū. Part of the town of Nagiso, at the southern edge of the valley of KISODANI. In the Edo period (1600–1868), Tsumago was a post-station town on the highway Nakasendō. It retains many of the features of the ancient post-station towns.

tsumi

In modern Japanese the word *tsumi* is the equivalent of such English words as sin, offense, or crime. However, in ancient times, it was a broad term applied to actions or conditions which cause the degeneration of, or hinder, the proper growth and development of the lifeforce; the concept of *tsumi* was closely related to the notion of KEGARE, or ritual impurity. The oldest extant enumeration of *tsumi* is

that of the "Ōharae no Kotoba" found in the ENGI SHIKI, an imperially ordered collection of government regulations, including Shintō-related religious regulations, compiled in the 10th century, where *tsumi* are divided into heavenly *tsumi (amatsu tsumi)* and earthly *tsumi (kunitsu tsumi).* Among the heavenly *tsumi* are: *ahanachi* (destroying ridges between fields), *mizoume* (burying irrigation ditches), *hihanachi* (destroying aqueducts), *shikimaki* (double planting of seeds), *kushizashi* (driving stakes in mud to cause harm), *ikihagi* (skinning animals alive), *sakahagi* (skinning animals backwards), and *kusohe* (polluting a pure place with excrement). Earthly *tsumi* are listed as: *ikihada tachi* (injuring the skin and causing blood to run), *shinihada tachi* (desecrating a corpse), *shirahito* (irregularities in skin pigment such as vitiligo or albinism), *kokumi* (skin eruptions such as warts or tumors), *onoga haha okaseru tsumi* (incest between mother and son), *onoga ko okaseru tsumi* (incest between father and daughter), *haha to ko okaseru tsumi* and *ko to haha okaseru tsumi* (having intercourse with a mother and her daughter), *kemono okaseru tsumi* (bestiality), *hau mushi no wazawai* (calamities brought on by noxious insects, reptiles, and so forth), *takatsukami no wazawai* (celestial calamities such as lightning or eclipses), *takatsutori no wazawai* (calamities caused by birds), *kemono taoshi* (harming draft animals with curses) and *majimono suru tsumi* (placing curses on people).

The heavenly *tsumi* derive from the KOJIKI (712, Records of Ancient Matters) and the NIHON SHOKI (720, Chronicle of Japan), where they are enumerated as those offenses committed by SUSANOO NO MIKOTO in defiance of his sister, the imperial ancestress, AMATERASU ŌMIKAMI, who ruled the heavenly sphere of TAKAMAGAHARA, and for which Susanoo was punished by banishment from that realm (hence the designation heavenly *tsumi*). In addition to the crimes of Susanoo listed in the "Ōharae no Kotoba," the *Nihon shoki* records that Susanoo also set loose *ame no fuchigoma* (heavenly colts) in the fields at harvest time. When we consider the fact that agriculture was the life-sustaining occupation of the age, it is natural that these actions, all of which obstruct farming activities, should be considered the most serious crimes.

Among the earthly *tsumi,* the *Kōtaijingū gishiki chō* of 804 includes *kawairi hoyake no tsumi* (death due to drowning or fire), not mentioned in the "Ōharae no Kotoba."

While ethical crimes were gradually systematized in the criminal codes, the ancient notion of *tsumi* was transmitted in Shintō ritual. It is significant that not only evil actions, but also uncontrollable natural calamities, were termed *tsumi.* The belief that *tsumi* may be brought on by powers outside the realm of individual responsibility underlies the importance of purification rites in Shintō ceremony. The "Ōharae no Kotoba" states that after the purification (HARAE), "each and every *tsumi* has ceased to exist." According to the well-known philologist and KOKUGAKU (National Learning) scholar MOTOORI NORINAGA, Shintō posits the belief that not only the misfortunes that afflict man in his lifetime, but also the evils which a man himself commits, are the acts of Magatsuhi no Kami, the god of calamities, although there are conflicting opinions (notably that of HIRATA ATSUTANE) on this score. Moreover, it is possible for the same deity to appear as a good god who enhances a man's life, or as an evil god with negative influences harmful to men. The myth says that for his crimes in Takamagahara, Susanoo had to present varied offerings *(chikura no okido)* to the gods. His facial hair and the nails of both hands and feet were extracted as punishment, and he was banished from the heavens. Upon his descent to Izumo he subdued the *yamata no orochi* (eight-headed serpent), which was causing harm to the gods of that country.

Hence the term *tsumi* does not imply a fixed essence or substance of a thing or action, but refers to a temporary state of existence—that is, a state which limits life and obstructs its growth and development through the loss of purity or exhaustion of the lifeforce. Hence religious responsibility includes (1) maintaining one's purity and participating in the gods' activities aimed at regenerating and creating this world by worshiping them, and (2) atoning for crimes or impurities. Because ritual purity is considered essential, taboos against coming into contact with pollution are strictly observed in Shintō shrines and festivals. Among them, the greatest taboo is that of coming into contact with the pollution of death or blood. (The Engi Shiki required that persons whose relatives had died spend up to 30 days of retreat at home *[bukki]* for extraordinary penance). At some shrines, abstinence from eating meat and fish is also observed. The custom of abstainers' using a special fire *(bekka)* is intended to guard against the transmission of pollution through fire. See also EVIL. *Ueda Kenji*

tsumugi

(pongee). Hand-woven fabric made from yarns of uneven thickness, manually spun from floss silk. Resembling cotton in texture, it has the luster unique to silk. Woven patterns of KASURI (ikat) and stripes are common. It is mainly used for traditional Japanese clothing. The best-known varieties are: Ōshima *tsumugi*, Yūki *tsumugi*, Murayama-Ōshima *tsumugi*, and Oitama *tsumugi*. See also TEXTILES. *HOSODA Kazuo*

Tsunashima Ryōsen (1873–1907)

Religious philosopher and literary critic. Real name Tsunashima Eiichirō. Born in Okayama Prefecture; graduate of Tōkyō Semmon Gakkō (now Waseda University). Ryōsen was converted to Christianity in his youth. Ryōsen published literary criticism during his university days, contributing to the journal *Waseda bungaku*. During a bout of illness he came under the influence of EBINA DANJŌ, then a pastor at a church in Kōbe, and in 1902 published his first work on comparative religion, *Hiai no kōchō* (1902). In 1905 he wrote about his own religious experiences in *Yo ga kenshin no jikken* (1905). His writings have been collected in 11 volumes in *Ryōsen zenshū* (Shunjūsha, 1921). *ASAI Kiyoshi*

Tsunetō Kyō (1888–1967)

Legal scholar specializing in jurisprudence. Born in Shimane Prefecture. Tsunetō studied at the First Higher School (Daiichi Kōtō Gakkō) in Tōkyō, where he became a close friend of AKUTAGAWA RYŪNOSUKE and KIKUCHI KAN, both celebrated writers of the 1920s. After graduation from Kyōto University in 1916, he became a professor first at Dōshisha and then at Kyōto University. Resigning in 1933 in connection with the KYŌTO UNIVERSITY INCIDENT, he became a professor (1940) and later president of Ōsaka Commercial College (now Ōsaka Municipal University). Originally a student of neo-Kantian philosophy, Tsunetō ranged widely over the social sciences and the humanities. In addition to legal philosophy, his research and teaching activities included international law, history of political thought, and economic philosophy. After World War II, with SUEKAWA HIROSHI, he was active in the movement for constitutional government as a central figure in the Kansai Constitutional Study Group. In 1949 he was named to the JAPAN ACADEMY and in 1957 was cited for distinguished cultural service. His writings include *Hihanteki hōritsu tetsugaku no kenkyū* (1921, Critical Studies in the Philosophy of Law), *Hōritsu no seimei* (1927, The Life of the Law), *Hō no kihon mondai* (1936, Fundamental Problems of Law), *Hō no honshitsu* (1968, The Essence of the Law), *Tetsugaku to hōgaku* (1969, Philosophy and Law), and *Hō to dōtoku* (1969, Law and Morality). *TANAKA Shigeaki*

Tsunoda Ryūsaku (1877–1964)

Scholar of Japanese history and thought who taught at Columbia University and founded its Japanese collection. Tsunoda was born in Gumma Prefecture in 1877. After graduating in 1896 from Tōkyō Semmon Gakkō (now Waseda University), he taught English in Kyōto, Fukushima, and Sendai. From 1909 to 1917 he served as principal of the Hawaii Chūgakkō in Honolulu. After his arrival at Columbia in 1917, to study under John Dewey, he conceived the plan of establishing in New York a library which would make possible the serious study of Japanese culture. He returned to Japan to solicit gifts for what became in 1931 the Japanese Collection of Columbia University. He taught at Columbia from 1928 until he retired in 1955, and even afterward he frequently came back to teach. Although his lectures inspired American scholars in many branches of Japanese studies, his publications were few. *Ihara Saikaku* (1897) was the first study of that author. His chief works in English were *Japan in the Chinese Dynastic Histories* (1951) and *Sources of Japanese Tradition* (1958), compiled jointly with two former students, William Theodore de Bary and Donald Keene. *Donald KEENE*

Tsurezuregusa → Yoshida Kenkō

tsurigane ninjin

Adenophora triphylla var. *japonica*. A perennial herb of the Campanulaceae (bellflower) family which grows wild in mountain areas throughout Japan. Its height is 60–90 centimeters (24–35 in). The leaves generally grow in whorls around the stem and sometimes in opposite or alternate patterns; their shape varies greatly from ovate to linear-lanceolate. In autumn small drooping flowers with five bluish-violet petals bloom on the branch tips. The spring shoots have been known since ancient times as a delicacy. See also KIKYŌ. *MATSUDA Osamu*

Tsuru

City in southeastern Yamanashi Prefecture, central Honshū; on the river Katsuragawa. Tsuru has been known since the Edo period (1600–1868) for its silk textiles, especially covers for *zabuton* (cushions) and Japanese-style bedding. Pop: 32,901.

tsuru → cranes

Tsuruga

City in southern Fukui Prefecture, central Honshū, on Wakasa Bay. In the Edo period (1600–1868) it prospered as an intermediate port between the ports of the Sea of Japan and the Ōsaka area. Today it mainly imports lumber from Siberia. Principal industries are synthetic textiles, lumber processing, chemicals, cement, and marine food processing. Attractions are the Kehi Shrine, Shibata Garden, and Kehinomatsubara, a stretch of pines on Wakasa Bay. Pop: 61,844.

Tsuruga Bay

(Tsuruga Wan). Part of eastern Wakasa Bay, southwestern Fukui Prefecture, central Honshū. The port of Tsuruga, an excellent natural port with deep waters, is located on this bay. Coastal fishing is carried out here. The bay area is dotted with swimming beaches. Part of the Wakasa Bay Quasi-National Park.

Tsurugaoka Hachiman Shrine

Shintō shrine in Kamakura, Kanagawa Prefecture, dedicated to the spirits of the legendary emperor ŌJIN, who was deified as HACHIMAN, the legendary empress JINGŪ (Ōjin's mother), and Ōjin's spouse Himegami (also known as Hime Ōkami). It was originally established as an extension of the IWASHIMIZU HACHIMAN SHRINE in 1063 in nearby Yuigahama by Minamoto no Yoriyoshi (988–1075), who won fame as an archer in his campaigns against rebel forces in northern Japan. The shrine was moved to its present site in 1191 by Yoriyoshi's descendant, the founder of the Kamakura shogunate, MINAMOTO NO YORITOMO (1147–99), a devout patron of the shrine. Adopted as the tutelary shrine of the MINAMOTO FAMILY, the Tsurugaoka Shrine was richly supported by a succession of warrior families, including the Hōjō, Ashikaga, Toyotomi, and Tokugawa. It has numerous subshrines, known as Hachiman-sama, in the Kantō and Tōhoku regions. Its annual festival on 15 September is followed the next day by an exhibition of mounted archery (YABUSAME). *Stanley WEINSTEIN*

Tsurugidake

Mountain in eastern Toyama Prefecture, central Honshū, in the northern part of the Hida Mountains. It is composed of diorite and has sharp cliffs and stony peaks with snowy ravines in between. Along with HOTAKADAKE, it is one of the most popular rock climbing areas in the JAPANESE ALPS. Part of Chūbu Sangaku National Park. Height: 2,998 m (9,833 ft).

Tsurugisan

Mountain in west-central Tokushima Prefecture, Shikoku; a major peak in the SHIKOKU MOUNTAINS and the second highest peak in Shikoku after ISHIZUCHISAN. It is composed chiefly of limestone. A holy mountain since ancient days, many pilgrims still climb it today. Alpine flora abound. It is part of Tsurugisan Quasi-National Park, together with the gorges called IYADANI and ŌBOKE. Height: 1,955 m (6,412 ft).

Tsurumi Yūsuke (1885–1973)

Social critic and writer. Born in Gumma Prefecture and graduated from Tōkyō University in 1910, Tsurumi worked for the Railway

Tsushima——Izuhara

The largest port on Tsushima, Izuhara is located on the island's southeastern coast.

Ministry until 1924. Like his mentor NITOBE INAZŌ, Tsurumi was an exponent of liberalism and international cooperation. He assisted his father-in-law, GOTŌ SHIMPEI with the Political Ethicization Movement (Seiji Rinrika Undō) of the mid-1920s and published the journal *Shin jiyū shugi* (The New Liberalism) from 1928 to 1935. An eloquent speaker, he made extensive lecture tours in Japan and in North America in the 1920s and 1930s. His interest in people-to-people diplomacy and in the development of the Pacific region led him to help organize the Japan committee of the INSTITUTE OF PACIFIC RELATIONS (IPR) and to participate in the first six IPR conferences (1925–36). The Taiheiyō Kyōkai (Institute of the Pacific), which he founded in 1938, came to be consulted by government policymakers. Several of Tsurumi's books, including *Hokubei yūzeiki* (1927, A Stumping Tour of North America), a description of his American speaking tour of 1924–25; *Eiyū taibōron* (1929, Awaiting Heroes), an analysis of international affairs and an appeal to youth; and his novel *Haha* (1930; tr *The Mother*, 1932) were best-sellers for many years. He was elected to the lower house of the Diet in 1928 and four times subsequently. He served in the House of Councillors from 1953 to 1959 and as minister of welfare (1954–55) in the Hatoyama Ichirō cabinet. His son Shunsuke (b 1922), a philosopher, and his daughter Kazuko (b 1918), a sociologist, became prominent in the postwar period. *William R.* CARTER

Tsuru nyōbō

(The Crane Wife). Folktale about an honest man who rescues a crane that has been shot with an arrow by a hunter. The crane returns as a beautiful woman and becomes his wife. Out of her own plumage, she secretly weaves rich brocades that bring great wealth to her husband. When he breaks his promise not to watch her weaving and discovers her true nature, she leaves him in sorrow. The folktale combines the motif of an animal repaying human kindness with that of marriage between a human and an animal. Its numerous variants have a clam, a fish, a fox, or a pheasant becoming the wife, or a monkey or water sprite (KAPPA) becoming the husband. *SUCHI Tokuhei*

Tsuruoka

City in northwestern Yamagata Prefecture, northern Honshū, on the Sea of Japan. Tsuruoka flourished as a castle town from the 14th century. The Shōnai Plain, on which the city is located, is a major producer of rice. Industrial products include silk, synthetic textiles, and farm machines and implements. The Yunohama and Yudagawa hot springs are located here, as is the Chidō Museum, which houses historical materials and local folk art. Pop: 99,751.

Tsuruta Yoshiyuki (1903–)

Former Olympic swimmer; born in Kagoshima Prefecture. In the 1928 Amsterdam Olympics he set a new Olympic record of 2:48.8 in the 200-meter breast stroke and was the first Japanese swimmer to win a gold medal. In the next meet in Los Angeles in 1932, Tsuruta

won the championship with a new Olympic record of 2:45.4. He is the only Japanese swimmer to take firsts in two successive Olympics. *TAKEDA Fumio*

Tsuruya Namboku (1755–1829)

KABUKI playwright of the late Edo period. The most noted dramatist of the Bunka–Bunsei eras (1804–30) and one of the most important writers of Japanese classic theatrical literature. He left more than 120 dramatic works of which the best were written late in his life.

Namboku's real name was Ebiya Genzō, and he was the son of a dyer in Edo (now Tōkyō). He grew up in the Nihombashi district, where his father's shop was located, not far from the busy kabuki theaters of the time, where the young Namboku frequently went to watch the actors in their dressing rooms. As a result of this interest, he left his father's shop and the dyeing trade at about age 20 and apprenticed himself to a team of playwrights at one of the kabuki theaters. He later married the daughter of a kabuki actor by the name of Tsuruya Namboku III who specialized in comic roles. After having used many other pen names, he eventually took to using his father-in-law's name and called himself Tsuruya Namboku IV. In his prime, he was most commonly referred to as "Namboku the Great."

Namboku created a new type of Edo kabuki drama in the style known as *kizewa kyōgen,* a naturalistic form related to the *sewa kyōgen* of the Kamigata, or Ōsaka theaters. The *sewa kyōgen* depicted the world of the townsmen (CHŌNIN), and within accepted social limits, focused on conflicts arising notably around money. Whereas the *sewa kyōgen* do not pretend to be critical of society, the *kizewa kyōgen* of Namboku describe a society decaying as a whole, one in which no social ethics remained effective. The plays of Namboku are characteristic in the way he portrayed those who have fallen from social status and who are driven by an unquenchable thirst for money and power, or by lust. This thirst is the very one condemned by Buddhism as the core of all human suffering. Whether or not Namboku was a true Buddhist, his plays are in fact impregnated with popular Buddhist beliefs and often refer to the texts of the NICHIREN SECT.

The climax of his plays is most often achieved by the juxtaposition of opposing characters, tormentors against their victims, who meet and argue in such places as lowly city dwellings, cemeteries, mountains, or brothels. The skillfully written dialogue in these situations mixes language from the highest forms of literature and poetry with the coarsest speech of gangsters and prostitutes. His dramas also depict the decay of the warrior and clergy classes at the end of the Edo period. Thus, Namboku is said to be a characteristic writer of the decadent times, prophesying the fall of the feudal government. His major plays include *Tenjiku Tokubei ikokubanashi* (1804, Tokubei of India: Tales of Strange Lands), *Kokoro no nazo toketa iroito* (1810, Riddles of the Heart Unraveled in Colored Threads), *Sakurahime azuma bunshō* (1817; tr *The Scarlet Princess of Edo,* 1975), and TŌKAIDŌ YOTSUYA KAIDAN (1825, The Ghost Story of Tōkaidō Yotsuya), his most famous play dealing with ghosts and horror, a genre for which he was also noted.

■——Tsuruya Namboku, *Dai Namboku zenshū,* 17 vols (Shun'yōdō, 1925–28). Tsuruya Namboku, *Tōkaidō Yotsuya kaidan* (1825), tr Jeanne Sigée as *Les Spectres de Yotsuya* (1979). *Jeanne* SIGÉE

Tsūsanshō → Ministry of International Trade and Industry

Tsushima

City in western Aichi Prefecture, central Honshū; 16 km (10 mi) west of Nagoya. Tsushima developed as a shrine town around the Tsushima Shrine. Its principal industry is woolen textiles. The River Festival of Tsushima Shrine attracts visitors each July. Pop: 59,049.

Tsushima

Island in the Korea Strait, between Korea and northwestern Kyūshū, 50 km (31 mi) southeast of Korea. It is divided into Kamishima (Upper Island) to the north and Shimoshima (Lower Island) to the south; it is administered by Nagasaki Prefecture. The island is made up of an uplifted peneplain averaging approximately 400 m (1,312 ft) in elevation, and the coast forms conspicuous drowned valleys. Tsushima has long been a vital point of transportation between Japan and the Asian continent. Forestry is the chief industry, with 84 percent of the island covered with forests. Only 4 percent of the island is arable. Principal agricultural products are *shiitake* (a species of mushroom), millet, buckwheat, and soybeans. Marine products include squid and cultured pearls. The island is part of the Iki–Tsushima Quasi-National Park and is the site of numerous historic remains. Asō Bay is particularly beautiful. Area: Kamishima, 255 sq km (98.4 sq mi); Shimoshima, 450 sq km (174 sq mi); pop: 50,804.

Tsushima, Battle of

(known in Japan as Nihonkai Kaisen, literally, Battle of the Sea of Japan). Greatest naval engagement of the Russo-Japanese War, in which Japan's combined fleet under Admiral TŌGŌ HEIHACHIRŌ annihilated most of Russia's Baltic squadron in the Tsushima Strait on 27–28 May 1905. In an attempt to restore Russian naval power in the Far East and to relieve Port Arthur (Ch: Lüshun, now part of Lüda), then under siege by the Japanese, 45 warships of the Baltic squadron under Vice Admiral Zinovii Rozhestvenskii embarked from the Gulf of Finland in October 1904 on a 220-day odyssey around Africa, across the Indian Ocean, and through the Malacca Straits toward Vladivostok. As this unwieldy squadron entered the Tsushima Strait between Japan and Korea on 27 May, it was intercepted by Tōgō's fast British-built battleships, cruisers, and scores of torpedo boats. In a daring maneuver, Tōgō succeeded in "crossing the T" of the approaching Russian column and subjected each of Rozhestvenskii's lead ships to concentrated fire. Many crippled Russian ships were dispatched by torpedo boats that night. By the next day, the Russians had lost 34 warships (including all of the squadron's battleships), and had suffered heavy casualties, 4,830 dead and 5,917 prisoners (among them Rozhestvenskii). Only three Russian vessels reached Vladivostok intact, others being scuttled at sea or interned at neutral ports. Japanese losses were three torpedo boats and 110 dead. The battle confirmed Japan's naval supremacy in waters off northeast Asia and created an opportunity for Japan to seek President Theodore Roosevelt's good offices for arranging peace negotiations with Russia. Until 1945, 27 May was celebrated as Navy Day (Kaigun Kinembi) in memory of the victory.

——J. N. Westwood, *Witness of Tsushima* (1970).

John J. STEPHAN

Tsushima Current

(Tsushima Kairyū). A warm ocean current which branches out of the KUROSHIO current south of Kyūshū and flows into the Sea of Japan by way of the Tsushima Strait. The current splits apart in the Sea of Japan but merges again near the Noto Peninsula. Most of the current eventually flows into the Pacific by way of the Tsugaru Strait. Being a warm current, it does not provide abundant fishing grounds.

Tsushima Incident

(Tsushima Jiken; also known as Tsushima Senryō Jiken or Roshia Gunkan Tsushima Senryō Jiken). Attempt by a Russian warship to obtain a base on the island of Tsushima in 1861. Strategically located between the Sea of Japan and the East China Sea, Tsushima was coveted as a base by several Western powers. Under the pretext of stopping for repairs, in February 1861 the warship *Posadnik* made surveys and anchored in the Osaki and Imazato coves of Asō Bay on the Western side of Tsushima. Its crew proceeded to build barracks on shore, while its captain demanded supplies and women as well as a long-term land lease. The local villagers resisted the Russians, but their efforts were discouraged by the frightened *daimyō* of Tsushima, Sō Yoshihira, and by the *gaikoku bugyō* (foreign affairs commissioner) OGURI TADAMASA, who was sent there by the Tokugawa shogunate in the hope of reaching a peaceful settlement. Finally, the British envoy Sir Rutherford ALCOCK dispatched two British warships to the area, and the *Posadnik* departed after a stay of over six months.

Tsushima Strait

(Tsushima Kaikyō). Between the islands of Tsushima and Iki, Nagasaki Prefecture, Kyūshū. In the broad sense also includes the Korea Strait between Korea and Tsushima. The strait connects the Sea of Japan and the East China Sea. Long an important artery in transportation between Japan and the continent, it is also the site of the battle

of TSUSHIMA, a famous naval engagement in the Russo-Japanese War. Narrowest point: 50 km (31 mi); deepest point: 130 m (426 ft).

tsūshō kaisha

(commercial companies). Companies formed in 1869 under the aegis of the Meiji government to foster foreign trade. Together with the KAWASE KAISHA, the banking facilities established to finance their operations, the *tsūshō kaisha* were the first Japanese enterprises organized as joint-stock companies (kabushiki kaisha). They were set up in eight key cities by MITSUI, ONO-GUMI, the KŌNOIKE FAMILY, and other wealthy merchant houses (see SEISHŌ) under the supervision of government commercial offices (tsūshōshi). The *tsūshō kaisha* promoted the establishment of subordinate trading companies for which they served as commodity exchanges, financial intermediaries, shipping agents, and chambers of commerce. After the abolition of the coordinating government offices in 1871, several of the *tsūshō kaisha* were converted into rice exchanges, and the rest were disbanded.

Tsutsui Junkei (1549–1584)

Daimyō of the Azuchi–Momoyama period (1568–1600). In the Muromachi period (1333–1568) the Tsutsui family played a prominent role in the military organization (kampu no shūto) of KŌFUKUJI, the Buddhist monastery of the Hossō sect that had occupied the position of military governor (shugo) of Yamato Province (now Nara Prefecture) since the Kamakura period (1185–1333). After struggles with their superiors in Kōfukuji and their rivals among the shūto, the Tsutsui emerged in the Tembun era (1532–1555) as a SENGOKU DAIMYŌ house and the leading power in Yamato. When the warlord Matsunaga Hisahide (1510?–77) seized control of the province in 1559, however, the young Junkei was displaced from Tsutsui Castle and reduced to seeking the support of Hisahide's enemies in a world of shifting alliances. In 1577 Hisahide unwisely turned against the hegemon ODA NOBUNAGA; Nobunaga destroyed him and installed Junkei, who had served Nobunaga in several campaigns, in his place. Junkei was confirmed as Nobunaga's governor of Yamato, with his seat at Kōriyama Castle, upon the completion of a land survey (KENCHI) and the destruction of local fortresses in that province in 1580. In this survey and in other actions Junkei was intimately associated with Nobunaga's vassal AKECHI MITSUHIDE. Mitsuhide called for Junkei's assistance after destroying Nobunaga in the HONNŌJI INCIDENT of 1582, but Junkei adopted a wait-and-see attitude and adhered to the national unifier TOYOTOMI HIDEYOSHI when the latter defeated Mitsuhide at the Battle of YAMAZAKI shortly afterward. Although he served Hideyoshi faithfully thereafter, Junkei is remembered, perhaps unfairly, as the proverbial opportunist.

George ELISON

tsutsuji → azaleas

Tsutsumi Chūnagon monogatari

(Tale of the Tsutsumi Middle Counselor). A collection of 10 narrative episodes, mostly anecdotal, derived from incidents at the courts of the latter part of the Heian period (794–1185) through the early part of the Kamakura period (1185–1333). The title refers to no one character named in the text, but may be an attempt by the compilers to lend historical authenticity and novelistic intensity to a series of love affairs and court observances in which a highly attractive and amorous gentleman is always the initiator of strange and humorous events. "Tsutsumi Counselor" was a sobriquet of the poet FUJIWARA NO KANESUKE (877–933), but there is no known connection between him and the *Tsutsumi Chūnagon monogatari*. The narrative style, consisting of elegant prose introductions to poem exchanges, is similar to that of the 10th-century ISE MONOGATARI (tr *Tales of Ise*, 1968). The fifth episode, considered the oldest in the collection, may be reliably dated 1055, and its author is the otherwise unknown lady Koshikibu. Authorship of the other episodes is unknown. The 10th episode seems the most recent of the collection and may have been written in its present form as late as 1385.

In most editions, the episodes are arranged in a seasonal sequence from spring to winter as follows: (1) "Hana sakura oru shōshō" (The Captain Who Broke the Branches from the Flowering Cherries), (2) "Kono tsuide" (On This Occasion), (3) "Mushi mezuru himegimi" (The Lady Who Loved Insects), (4) "Hodo hodo no kesō"

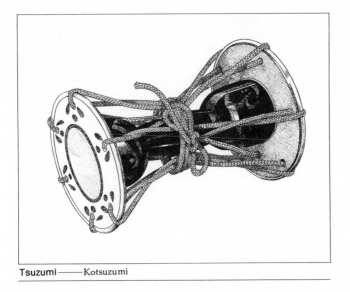

Tsuzumi —— Kotsuzumi

(Each to One's Own Love Letters), (5) "Ausaka koenu gonchūnagon" (The Counselor Who Failed to Pass the Meeting Gate), (6) "Kaiawase" (Shell Game), (7) "Omowanu kata ni tomari suru shōshō" (The Captain Who Spent Nights in an Unforeseen Place), (8) "Hanada no nyōgo" (Ladies with Flower Names), (9) "Haizumi" (Mascara), and (10) "Yoshinashigoto" (Things That Do Not Matter).

📖 —— *Tsutsumi Chūnagon monogatari*, tr Umeyo Hirano (1963). "Mushi mezuru himegimi," tr Arthur Waley as "The Lady Who Loved Insects" (1929). Edwin O. Reischauer and Joseph Yamagiwa, *Translations from Early Japanese Literature* (1951).

Kenneth L. RICHARD

Tsutsumi ware

(*tsutsumi-yaki*). Folk pottery of Tsutsumi, near Sendai, in Miyagi Prefecture, flourishing mainly in the early years of the 19th century. Local ceramic production dates back to 1695, when the RAKU WARE potter Uemura Man'emon was brought from Edo (now Tōkyō) to make TEA CEREMONY wares for the local *daimyō*. The Tsutsumi kilns were soon producing mainly folk-style kitchenware for the local populace. The domainal government in the meantime tended to patronize the nearby (but unrelated) Kirigome porcelain kilns.

Tsutsumi wares were made from granular, reddish brown clays. Most of the items produced were for household use, including mortars, bowls, and plates, but especially typical were the storage jars, varying in height from 10 centimeters (4 in) to a meter (3.3 ft). Traditional Tsutsumi pottery had a black or brown glaze, usually glossy, with a bluish or greenish white-flecked overglaze splashed on the rims or sides. Some pieces were glazed in the ordinary honeycolored (*ame*) translucent glaze.

After the BOSHIN CIVIL WAR (1868), the military conflict accompanying the MEIJI RESTORATION, the industry suffered greatly, and since the 20th century has switched mainly to the manufacture of tiles and drainage pipes. However, the Haryū family, in an effort to reestablish Tsutsumi pottery, is still producing some work in the traditional style.

David HALE

Tsutsumi Yasujirō (1889–1964)

Politician and entrepreneur. Born in Shiga Prefecture and a graduate of Waseda University, Tsutsumi was elected to the House of Representatives 13 times beginning in 1924, and acted as speaker in 1953 and 1954. Also active in the business world, he established a number of companies, including SEIBU RAILWAY CO, LTD, and created the Seibu group based on the railway, real estate, tourism, and bus transportation.

TANAKA Yōnosuke

tsutsushimi

(seriousness of mind; also pronounced *kei*; Ch: *jing* or *ching*). A philosophical concept especially important in the moral thinking of the Chinese Confucian philosopher Zhu Xi (Chu Hsi; 1130–1200; see SHUSHIGAKU). Zhu Xi elaborated on the concept of *jing* as formulated in the phrase *cunxin chijing* (*tsun-hsin ch'ih-ching*; J: *sonshin*

jikei), "preserving one's mind/heart and maintaining seriousness." This phrase refers to a state of mind in which clear judgment (*cunxin*) is possible and concentration of mind is exercised both internally and externally (*chijing*) to achieve it. "Maintaining seriousness" (*chijing*) is a moral method and not an attained state of virtue; it involves as a prerequisite "investigation of principles in things and extension of knowledge" (*gewu zhizhi* or *ko-wu chih-chih*; J: *kakubutsu chichi*). The notion of *chijing* was first brought to attention in Japan by Zen Buddhists, but it differs from Zen's more direct method of attaining calmness of mind in that it involves objective knowledge. Among Japanese thinkers of the Edo period (1600–1868) there were essentially two views concerning *jing* or *tsutsushimi*. The school of YAMAZAKI ANSAI regarded it as the cardinal moral principle of Confucianism that regulated every aspect of daily conduct, while the school of ITŌ JINSAI insisted on liberation from moral rigorousness and regarded *jing* only as a moral method. In everyday parlance in Japanese, the native word *tsutsushimi*, which is used to translate the Chinese concept *jing*, has a range of other meanings, including "modesty," "discretion," and "self-restraint."

MIYAKE Masahiko

tsuwabuki

Ligularia tussilaginea or *Farfugium japonicum;* also called *tsuwa*. An evergreen perennial herb of the chrysanthemum family (Compositae), which grows wild on the warm seacoasts of Kyūshū, Shikoku, and west of the Kantō region in Honshū. It is also widely planted as an ornamental. Long leaf stalks grow from the underground stems. Leaves are thick, roundish to kidney-shaped, and the edges are slightly wavy; the upper surface is dark green and shiny, and the lower surface is a lighter green and slightly hairy. From fall to early winter it grows a flower stalk of about 60 centimeters (2 ft) and bears composite yellow flowers in loose clusters. There are cultivated varieties such as the *ōtsuwabuki* (*L.t.* var. *gigantea*) with large leaves. The leaf-stalk is edible. Infusions from the dried leaves or juice squeezed from raw leaves has been used as an antidote for poisonous fish.

MATSUDA Osamu

Tsuwano

Town in western Shimane Prefecture, western Honshū. *Samurai* residences from its days as a castle town remain. It is now a distribution center for lumber and Japanese paper (*washi*). Tourist attractions include the former residences of the men of letters MORI ŌGAI and NISHI AMANE. Pop: 7,850.

Tsuyama

City in northern Okayama Prefecture, western Honshū. Tsuyama flourished as a castle town of the Matsudaira family during the Edo period (1600–1868). Local products are textiles, handmade Japanese paper (*washi*), and paper goods. The cherry blossoms at the site of Tsuyama Castle, now a park, attract visitors. Pop: 83,140.

Tsuyama Basin

(Tsuyama Bonchi). In northern Okayama Prefecture, western Honshū. One of a series of basins between the Chūgoku Mountains and the highlands known as the Kibi Kōgen and situated in the area drained by the river Yoshiigawa. The area's main products are rice, wheat, fruit, and dairy produce. The major city is Tsuyama. Area: approximately 200 sq km (77.2 sq mi).

tsuzumi

A traditional hourglass-shaped drum; it consists of two leather skins each sewn onto an iron ring larger in diameter than the drum body, then laced with ropes onto the lacquered wooden drum. Several kinds of hourglass drum were introduced into Japan from the continent prior to the Nara period (710–794). The *ikko* and *san no tsuzumi* still used in the traditional court music of GAGAKU preserve in some measure their Nara-period shapes; these are played with one or two sticks. Today, however, the word *tsuzumi* generally refers to the *ōtsuzumi* (big *tsuzumi*) and *kotsuzumi* (small *tsuzumi*) used in the NŌ and KABUKI drama. Both are played with the right hand and fingers; the *ōtsuzumi* player, however, usually wears thimble-like papier-mâché finger guards on the middle and ring fingers to produce a sharper sound, and a leather palm guard. The *ōtsuzumi* is about 28 centimeters (11 in) long with cowhide heads; it is tightly laced and is held on the left thigh with the left hand. The heads are heated before each performance, contributing to the high, dry sound. The *kotsuzumi* is about 25 centimeters (10 in) long and has horsehide heads loosely laced. The drum is reassembled at every performance to obtain the proper tension. It is held on the right shoulder with the left hand; by squeezing the laces with the left hand, the player can alter the tone. *KOJIMA Tomiko*

tsuzura

(clothes box). An old-fashioned piece of furniture used for storing clothes. It is made of woven vines, bamboo, or other flexible materials reinforced with tanned or lacquered paper. The *tsuzura* came into popular use during the Muromachi period (1333–1568). These boxes were originally made from vines of *tsuzurafuji*, a variety of the Menispermaceae family from which the name derives. Although the *tsuzura* is basically rectangular in shape and comes with a lid, there are many varieties, ranging from simple to highly elaborate; some have refined lacquer work decorations (MAKI-E) or golden family CRESTS. *MIYAMOTO Mizuo*

tsuzure-ori

(tapestry weave). Type of figured brocade and the technique for weaving it, brought to Japan from China circa 1400. Sometimes referred to as "fingernail weaving," since the weavers use their nails, filed to catch the threads, to execute the designs. This form of weaving has been used in the making of large decorative panels, temple hangings, and some religious clothing. Today it is used mainly for the type of sash known as Nagoya *obi* (see OBI) and for special-occasion wedding or family-crest gift covers called *fukusa*. *Barbara PORTER*

Tuan Ch'i-jui → Duan Qirui (Tuan Ch'i-jui)

Tule Lake Relocation Center

A wartime relocation facility for Japanese Americans, located near Newell, Modoc County, California, in operation from 27 May 1942 until 20 March 1946. It held a maximum of 18,789 inmates at any one time; 29,000 persons were confined there in all. Originally a "normal" camp receiving inmates from central California, southwestern Oregon, and western Washington, it became largely a concentration camp for those whom the government considered disloyal. There was more bloodshed and disorder at Tule Lake than at all the other centers combined. See also JAPANESE AMERICANS, WARTIME RELOCATION OF; WAR RELOCATION AUTHORITY.
▨——Gary Okihiro, "Tule Lake Under Martial Law," *Journal of Ethnic Studies* 5 (1977). Dorothy S. Thomas et al, *The Spoilage* (1974). Rosalie H. Wax, *Doing Fieldwork* (1971). *Roger DANIELS*

tuna

(*maguro*). In Japanese, *maguro* is the common name for saltwater fish of the class Osteichthyes, order Perciformes, family Scombridae, genus *Thunnus*. Best known in Japan is the large and tasty *homma-guro* or *kuromaguro* (North Pacific bluefin tuna; *Thunnus thynnus orientalis*), which grows to 3 meters (10 ft) in length, weighs over 300 kilograms (660 lb), and is found, among other places, in the waters off the west coast of North America. Like other tuna species, its meat has a reddish color and is used for *sashimi* (sliced raw fish) and *sushi* (raw seafood over rice-balls). *ABE Tokiharu*

In ancient times, tuna was known as *shibi* and appears in the *Kojiki* (completed in 712), Japan's oldest chronicle, and the poetic anthology *Man'yōshū* (completed in the latter half of the 8th century). For a *sushi* menu, *maguro* is indispensable; the fatty meat around the pectoral fins near the head, called *toro*, is particularly favored. In recent years, much of the tuna consumed in Japan has come from foreign sources. *SAITŌ Shōji*

turtles

(*kame*). In Japanese *kame* is the general name for reptiles of the order Chelonia. Four families are found in Japan: families Chelonidae and Dermochelyidae (marine); family Testudinidae (terrestrial or freshwater); and family Trionychidae (freshwater). Turtles of all four families are frequently found from Honshū southward, but in Hokkaidō only marine species are found. Among the marine turtles the *akaumigame* (*Caretta caretta*) is comparatively numerous; it lands on the Pacific coast of southwestern Japan and lays eggs in June or July. The *aoumigame* (*Chelonia mydas*), another species commonly seen in the waters of Japan, lands on the OGASAWARA ISLANDS to lay eggs. The most common turtle in freshwater areas is the *ishigame* (*Clemmys japonica*), which is often kept as a pet. The *suppon* (*Trionyx sinensis*) is raised for its tasty meat. The *semaru hakogame* (*Cyclemys flavomarginata*), nearly completely terrestrial, lives in Okinawa Prefecture. *IMAIZUMI Yoshiharu*

As the proverb "a crane lives a thousand and a turtle ten thousand years" indicates, the turtle has traditionally been regarded as a symbol of longevity and accordingly as a bearer of good fortune as well. Marine turtles with algae growing on their shells were regarded as most auspicious, since the algae waving in the water reminded viewers of an old bearded man and, thus, longevity. In Japan there persisted until recently the custom of giving drinks of *sake* to *aoumigame* that landed on the seashore, presumably in honor of their supposed great age or because the turtle was believed to be a messenger of the sea god. Turtles appear in many Japanese folk tales, among which the story URASHIMA TARŌ is the most famous. Shells of the *taimai* (*Eretmochelys imbricata*) have been utilized for tortoiseshell work (*bekkō*) since ancient times. *SANEYOSHI Tatsuo*

Twenty-One Demands

(Taika Nijūikkajō Yōkyū). Set of 21 articles presented by the Japanese government in early 1915 to YUAN SHIKAI (Yüan Shih-k'ai), the president of the new and weak Republic of China; the articles mainly specified the extension or introduction of Japanese privileges in China. Lengthy negotiations between the two governments ensued and reached their climax with a Japanese ultimatum in May 1915 for acceptance of a modified version of the original articles. The Chinese president capitulated, but in an atmosphere of popular outrage at the Japanese demands and the high-handed manner in which they had been pressed.
Japanese Aspirations in China——With its successes in the SINO–JAPANESE WAR OF 1894–1895 and the RUSSO–JAPANESE WAR of 1904–05, Japan had joined the ranks of imperialist powers in China. In addition to acquiring Taiwan as a colony, it inherited part of the tsarist Russian position in northeast China, especially in what was sometimes called South Manchuria (present-day Liaoning and Jilin [Kirin] Provinces). The position included control of the SOUTH MANCHURIA RAILWAY and administration of the GUANDONG (KWANTUNG) TERRITORY on the Liaodong (Liaotung) Peninsula. After the 1911 Revolution, when China abandoned imperial for republican forms of government, leading Japanese became increasingly interested in redefining Japan's role in China. The legal arrangements inherited from Russia were due to expire, the earliest as soon as 1923. It was felt that these should be extended in time and expanded in scope. There was also concern about Japan's relative weight in China's affairs among the imperialist nations. At the time of the 1911 Revolution, Britain kept the other foreign powers in line behind its policies of neutrality during the conflict and support for Yuan Shikai, afterwards. Japanese with particular interest in China found their initiatives blocked and felt frustrated, even bitter. Some, despite the ANGLO–JAPANESE ALLIANCE, wished to check or even displace Britain's predominance. One common argument turned on the need for a stronger Japanese base in China as preparation for Japanese leadership in some future racial showdown between Asians and Europeans or Americans. Even policy makers who did not share this dire vision agreed that Japan deserved a special role in Chinese affairs for reasons of propinquity, historical ties, and the Japanese blood and treasure expended in China during the recent wars.

The outbreak of general war in Europe at the beginning of August 1914 was immediately recognized by Japan as an unparalleled opportunity to advance its position in China. Other major powers became preoccupied with the European conflict. Britain, which had been using its superior political and financial strength in the first months of 1914 to increase its lead over Japan in Chinese railway concessions, had to concentrate its resources closer to home. The dictatorial Yuan, whose sturdiest backer was Britain, could no longer count so heavily on Western help and might more readily accommodate Japanese desires.

The Japanese government quickly declared entry into the war on the Allied side. A military expedition, overwhelmingly Japanese, though with token British participation, attacked Germany's leased territory in China's Shandong (Shantung) Province, centered at the port of Qingdao (Tsingtao) on Jiaozhou Bay (see JIAOZHOU [KIAO-CHOW] CONCESSION). The Germans surrendered on 7 November 1914. Through military action, Japan had acquired another foothold on Chinese soil, either to bargain with or to keep.

Content of the Demands —— Even as Japan was entering the war and occupying parts of Shandong, the government in Tōkyō was preparing its agenda for Sino-Japanese negotiations. With the German surrender at Qingdao, the forceful foreign minister KATŌ TAKAAKI secured the necessary clearances from the GENRŌ (elder statesmen) and the emperor to proceed. The Japanese minister in Beijing (Peking), Hioki Eki (also known as Heki Eki; 1861–1926), delivered a list of 21 desiderata to President Yuan on 18 January 1915, with warnings of retaliation if Japanese desires were not served.

The 21 articles were divided into five groups. The first concerned Shandong Province and the recently seized German holdings there. The possible reversion to China of these holdings was offered during the negotiations as an inducement to the Chinese to accept the rest of the demands, but the Chinese negotiators were not swayed. Japan pressed for the original articles in this group, which left Japan in possession of its recent acquisitions in Shandong. Ultimate disposition was to be settled between Japan and Germany in some postwar settlement. In addition, an expanded railway network under Japanese control was provided for, and a general sphere of Japanese influence in Shandong was implied.

From the Japanese point of view the most essential demands lay in the second group, dealing with South Manchuria and eastern Inner Mongolia. The various railway and leasehold agreements that underlay Japan's dominance in South Manchuria were to be extended to the end of the 20th or into the 21st century. A novel privilege was to be introduced: that Japanese, retaining immunity from Chinese law, would be allowed to rent or own land and buildings outside the treaty ports and leaseholds for the purposes of trade, manufacturing, or agriculture. The privileges that Japanese enjoyed in South Manchuria were also to apply to eastern Inner Mongolia, where previously the Japanese had held no special rights. This section of the demands also called for Japanese priority in the same regions with respect to railway construction, loans, and advisers.

The third group looked to Japanese participation as joint owners of the Hanyeping (Han-yeh-p'ing) Company, a mining and metallurgical complex in central China already heavily in debt to the Japanese. It further stipulated that the company should have first rights to all mines in its vicinity.

The fourth division consisted of only one article, barring China from making further cessions or leases of its coastal harbors or islands to any foreign country but Japan. The intent of this provision, it turned out, was to keep the United States out of Fujian (Fukien) Province, where Japan was nurturing a sphere of influence based on its proximity to Taiwan.

The fifth group, which Japan initially concealed from its British allies, contained a miscellany of far-reaching desiderata. Stipulations on the appointment of Japanese advisers to the Chinese government, on Japanese participation in administering Chinese police departments, and on a fixed and substantial percentage of Chinese arms and procurements to be from Japan—these articles lent substance to the charge that Japan sought to make all of China into some sort of colony or protectorate. Another article in this group provided for extensive railway rights in the Yangzi (Yangtze) region and farther south, areas where the British asserted a special interest. As the secrecy was unraveled, the Japanese government tried to soften the impact by stressing that the fifth group contained only "requests" or "desires," in contrast to the "demands" of the first four. But the Japanese negotiators continued to press the fifth group in one form or another during the three months of the negotiations.

Response to the Demands —— The Chinese response took both official and popular forms. The government's strategy was to procrastinate while appearing ready to discuss the less offensive articles. It was thereby able to discover Japan's real intentions regarding the various articles, to seek modifications, and to stir up other nations' opposition to the demands. The popular reaction was an outpouring of patriotic sentiment on a scale unprecedented in China. Its most potent form was a widespread boycott of Japanese goods and ship-

ping, which the government officially forbade but actually tolerated and exploited in the negotiations.

Despite the urgent messages of the American minister in Beijing, Paul S. Reinsch, Washington only gradually came to understand the seriousness of the crisis. Secretary of State Robert LANSING's remonstrations were of little help to China and, ironically, at one stage even fortified the Japanese position. Official American statements took on a clearly anti-Japanese edge only after the negotiations had been concluded. London was also slow to protest; but the Foreign Office noted specific intrusions into areas of established British claims and warned Japan that a rupture in Sino-Japanese relations over the fifth group of articles might fatally damage the Anglo-Japanese Alliance.

The Japanese Ultimatum —— After China had rejected Japan's 26 April revised version of the original demands, the Japanese cabinet approved the Foreign Ministry's plan for delivering an ultimatum to the Chinese. The genrō, who had become increasingly irritated over Foreign Minister Katō's methods, insisted on deleting from the ultimatum the main articles of the fifth group, which had achieved a special notoriety. On 7 May the Chinese government was given two days to accept the reduced list. Japan redoubled its large garrisons in China. With the fifth group withdrawn, the British government urged the Chinese to accede. President Yuan did so, and a series of treaties and notes between China and Japan were signed on 25 May 1915.

Japan gained from this episode little it did not already have. Subsequent Chinese governments were inclined to deny the legitimacy of these coerced agreements. In popular Chinese attitudes, the experience marked Japan as the most overbearing and dangerous of the imperialist countries. The disenchantment in Britain and America with Japan's approach to China was pronounced.

—— Madeleine Chi, *China Diplomacy, 1914–1918* (1970). Roger F. Hackett, *Yamagata Aritomo in the Rise of Modern Japan, 1838–1922* (1971). Marius B. Jansen, *The Japanese and Sun Yat-sen* (1954). Tien-yi Li, *Woodrow Wilson's China Policy, 1913–1917* (1952). Arthur S. Link, *Wilson: The Struggle for Neutrality, 1914–1915* (1960). Peter Lowe, *Great Britain and Japan, 1911–1915: A Study of British Far Eastern Policy* (1969). Ian H. Nish, *Alliance in Decline: A Study in Anglo-Japanese Relations, 1908–23* (1972). Horikawa Takeo, *Kyokutō kokusai seiji shi josetsu: Nijūikkajō yōkyū no kenkyū* (1958). Kikuchi Takaharu, *Chūgoku minzoku undō no kihon kōzō: Taigai boikotto no kenkyū* (1966). Usui Katsumi, *Nihon to Chūgoku: Taishō jidai* (1972). Yamamoto Shirō, "Sansen nijūikkajō yōkyū to rikugun," *Shirin* 57.3 (1974). *Ernest P.* YOUNG

Twenty-Six Martyrs

The Twenty-Six Martyrs is the collective name given to the Japanese and foreign Christians crucified at Nagasaki on 5 February 1597 by order of TOYOTOMI HIDEYOSHI. Hideyoshi's motives for issuing this order are not clear, but they appear to have been connected with the seizure of the cargo of a Spanish ship that had run aground at Tosa (now Kōchi Prefecture) in the previous December (see SAN FELIPE INCIDENT). The martyrs were made up of six Franciscan missionaries (see FRANCISCANS), three JESUITS, and 17 laymen, including three young boys. This was the first time any Europeans had been put to death in Japan for professing CHRISTIANITY.

Michael COOPER

typhoons

(taifū). Tropical storms occurring in the western Pacific. The Pacific equivalent of the hurricanes of the Western hemisphere, these tropical storms are prevalent in Japan during the late summer and early autumn. Typhoons originate with low atmospheric pressure systems in the tropics between the central Pacific (around longitude 180°E) and the northwestern region of the Pacific. They then travel to Japan and the other Asian countries in the temperate zone bordering the North Pacific. Typhoons are characterized by a wind velocity exceeding 17 meters (56 ft) per second at their center. They are capable of releasing tremendous energy, and almost every year Japan suffers the loss of hundreds of lives and damages amounting to several hundred billion yen.

A number of typhoons appear in the historic record, including those that thwarted the MONGOL INVASIONS OF JAPAN in 1274 and 1281. Typhoons during recent history that have been exceptionally destructive include the Muroto Typhoon of 1934, the typhoon asso-

Ranking	Name	Date	Maximum speed or total rainfall (place of measurement and prefecture)	Number of dead or missing	Number of buildings damaged	Damage to cultivated land (in hectares)
1	Ise Bay Typhoon	26 Sept. 1959	45.4 m/sec (Irago, Aichi)	5,098	1,352,717	210,859
2	Makurazaki Typhoon	17 Sept. 1945	47.7 m/sec (Kirigamine, Nagano)	3,746	446,897	167,131
3	Muroto Typhoon	21 Sept. 1934	48.4 m/sec (Kizugawa, Ōsaka)	3,066	488,897	—
4	Typhoon Kathleen	15 Sept. 1947	753.8 mm (Ashinoyu, Kanagawa)	1,910	394,041	292,440
5	Tōya maru Typhoon	26 Sept. 1954	38.0 m/sec (Sukumo, Kōchi)	1,761	371,043	66,645
6	Kanogawa Typhoon	26 Sept. 1958	37.8 m/sec (Nagatsuro, Shizuoka)	1,216	542,828	89,236

SOURCE: Kishōchō (Meterological Agency), Kishō nenkan (annual): 1981.

Typhoons —— Major typhoons in Japan and resultant damage

ciated with the TŌYA MARU DISASTER of 1954, the Kanogawa Typhoon of 1958, and the Ise Bay Typhoon of 1959. Each of these resulted in over 1,000 dead and missing. The Muroto typhoon is described in TANIZAKI JUN'ICHIRŌ's Sasameyuki (1942–48; tr The Makioka Sisters, 1957). These typhoons were named for their place of entry into Japan or the area of heaviest damage. The former American convention of using female names for typhoons was observed during the Allied Occupation. Beginning in 1953 serial numbers have been assigned to typhoons by year and order of formation. For example, the Ise Bay Typhoon is also called Typhoon No. 5915 (i.e., 59-15), as it was the 15th typhoon to form in 1959.

The word taifū is traced to two possible sources. According to one etymology, the word was originally Chinese and meant "strong wind off the coast of Taiwan." Alternately, taifū, together with the English word typhoon, is seen to derive from Arabic. Traditional Japanese names for typhoons include nowaki ("wind that levels fields"), a season word used in haiku to evoke the late summer. Traditional Japanese almanacs referred to the storms as nihyakutōka and nihyakuhatsuka (the "210th day" and "220th day" of the year, respectively, in the old calendar) to denote the prevalence of typhoons in early September at the peak of the rice-flowering season.

Structure —— Typhoons are small in comparison with storms outside the tropics. Their diameters are typically 500 kilometers (310 mi), though they sometimes reach 1,000 kilometers (620 mi). The pressure at the center of a typhoon can fall below 900 millibars. This extreme low pressure distinguishes tropical cyclones from temperate zone storms, as does the presence of a calm area—the eye— 20 to 50 kilometers (12–31 mi) in diameter around the center of the storm. The typhoon storm rages near the central region with a maximum wind velocity often in excess of 50 meters (160 ft) per second directly outside of the eye. Variations in the strength of the ascending current that supplies the typhoon with water vapor creates rows of rain clouds (rainbands) around the central region. These spirals of rain clouds send intermittent showers in advance of the typhoon storm.

Development and Course —— Most typhoons are formed in the Pacific Ocean east of the Philippines between latitude 5°N and 25°N. The water in this region remains at a constant high temperature throughout the year and releases a vast amount of water vapor into the air. The water vapor rises, leaving behind a low-pressure area and an updraft for additional vapor. Hot vapor then condenses in the upper atmosphere and falls as rain. Soon after formation, the typhoon is pushed by easterly winds and travels to the west or westnorthwest at a speed of 20 to 30 kilometers (12–19 mi) per hour. When it reaches the North Pacific it hits a high-pressure zone moving southwest of Japan. In the summer months in particular, this high-pressure zone often extends far out to the west and thus deflects northwest-bound typhoons to the west toward the Philippines, the South China Sea, and the southern coast of China. When not deflected in this manner, the typhoon gradually moves northnorthwest along the periphery of the high-pressure zone and eventually approaches the southern coast of Japan.

Determination of the point of deflection by the North Pacific high-pressure zone, called the recurvature point, is very important for forecasting the course of the typhoon. The location varies depending upon immediate atmospheric conditions, but it may be closely approximated from the observed center of the high-pressure zone. The high-pressure zone that is often near Honshū in the summer has a recurvature point off the coast of western Kyūshū which deflects typhoons to the north, toward the Sea of Japan and the Korean peninsula. However, the high-pressure zone common in the autumn deflects typhoons toward Okinawa and the southern coast of the main islands. A typhoon that travels in a northeasterly direction past its recurvature point will gradually accelerate in speed until it reaches 70 to 80 kilometers (45–50 mi) per hour.

The intensity of a typhoon varies over its course, but a medium-size typhoon exerts an average of 10^{25} ergs, an amount comparable to the energy released by 100 hydrogen bombs of the megaton range. The intensity is strongest at the recurvature point. It falls off gradually if the typhoon continues on toward the northeast, where the lower surface temperature of the seas reduces the energy supplied to the typhoon. Typhoons that pass over Honshū lose a great deal of energy in confronting surface friction. The intensity decreases rapidly when a typhoon hits the mountains of central Japan, where its center is usually split in two. The intensity is so diminished in typhoons that reach Hokkaidō or the sea east of Hokkaidō that they become weak tropical storms. In autumn they combine with a cold air mass coming from Siberia and proceed northeast as extratropical storms which dissipate in the vicinity of the Aleutian Islands.

Observation and Forecasting —— Accurate forecasting of a typhoon requires detailed observation of a considerably wide area, including the typhoon and its surroundings. The Japanese METEOROLOGICAL AGENCY (Kishōchō) performs many of the essential observation and forecast services. It collects data from about 150 meteorological observatories and stations all over Japan and prepares weather charts for making forecasts. Observations of atmospheric pressure and temperature and of wind conditions are made either four or eight times a day and sent via high-speed telecommunications to Tōkyō. Similar meteorological observations are reported from ships at sea and meteorological agencies of foreign countries, such as the Soviet Union and China. The Meteorological Agency immediately charts these observations, and a weather chart covering a wide region including the typhoon area is completed within one to two hours.

Forecasting of a typhoon requires knowledge of meteorological conditions at high altitudes as well. High-altitude meteorological observatories in Japan and neighboring countries conduct twice-daily observations using radiosondes and rawinsondes that provide information up to 12 kilometers (7.5 mi) above ground. An ocean weathership supplements the island observation posts in watching for typhoons approaching from the south of Japan. The ship conducts high-altitude observations at a point 450 kilometers (280 mi) south of Shikoku for six months from May through early November. The extreme scarcity of Japan's observation points in the southern seas is supplemented by the use of American meteorological satellites and typhoon forecasting. Japan has also recently started to utilize its own meteorological satellite, the Himawari (Sunflower).

Typhoon forecasts are announced on radio, television, and in the press. On the basis of radar reports, advisories and warnings are issued to prefectures threatened with damage from typhoon winds and heavy rains.

SUDA Ken

U

ubasoku

A Buddhist layman. The equivalent term for laywoman is *ubai*. As a transliteration of the Sanskrit *upāsaka*, *ubasoku* refers technically to any man who has taken the three refuges (in the Buddha, the DHARMA, and the *saṃgha*) and keeps the five precepts (against killing, stealing, sexual misconduct, lying, and drinking intoxicants). In this orthodox sense, the term was used early in Japanese Buddhism to refer to those who formed groups *(chishiki)* to erect temples or otherwise support Buddhism, or to men who practiced austerities, learned incantations, or studied scriptures in preparation for their formal application to become monks.

From this latter meaning, however, the term was applied broadly to unordained holy men, who, in the Nara (710–794) and early part of the Heian (794–1185) period, brought Buddhism to the common people. In spite of government attempts to suppress them on several occasions, they flourished. By combining Buddhist magical powers with those of Taoist immortals and the native shamanism, they established a tradition for later groups of ascetics and holy men, such as HIJIRI and SHUGENDŌ. They also developed a mode of mountain austerities which served as an alternative for those who sought personal salvation outside the official, and often corrupt, Buddhism of Nara. Although the word *ubasoku* remains as a fundamental Buddhist term, it ceased to mean members of any significant social group or religious movement by the late Heian period.

James H. FOARD

Ube

City in southwestern Yamaguchi Prefecture, western Honshū, on the Inland Sea. Ube grew rapidly as a mining and industrial town with the opening of coal mines in the Meiji period (1868–1912). The mines were closed in 1967. Steel, cement, fertilizer, and petrochemical plants are located on reclaimed land. Parks and green belts have been established as part of city planning. Yamaguchi University's schools of medicine and engineering are here. Pop: 168,960.

Ube Industries, Ltd

(Ube Kōsan). Comprehensive chemical company manufacturing petrochemical, chemical, cement, and machinery products. Ube Industries was established in 1942 through the merger of four companies: Okinoyama Coal Mining, founded in Ube, Yamaguchi Prefecture, in 1897, which was the mainstay; Ube Iron and Steel Works, which manufactured coal-mining machinery; Ube Cement Manufacturing, which utilized the clay produced by Okinoyama Coal Mining; and Ube Nitrogen Industry, which produced ammonium sulfate. After World War II, with the deterioration of the coal-mining industry in Japan, the company switched operations from the chemical to the petrochemical field and started production of polyethylene, polypropylene, and polybutadiene. Its cement and machinery departments are expanding steadily. Sales for the fiscal year ending March 1982 totaled ¥222.3 billion (US $923.5 million), of which cement provided 40 percent, chemical products 40 percent, and machinery 20 percent. In the same year the export ratio was 19 percent and the company was capitalized at ¥38.4 billion (US $159.5 million). The head office is in Tōkyō.

ubusunagami

The protective deity of one's birthplace. The term occurs as early as the 8th century in the chronicle NIHON SHOKI (720) and several provincial gazetteers (FUDOKI). At present the category of *ubusunagami* has become confused with that of UJIGAMI, the local tutelary deity, and in many locales the former term does not occur. In theory, the *ujigami* is the god of a consanguineous family or people,

while the *ubusunagami* is the deity of a geographic territory. In the period when the families of a village were all related by blood, this distinction was irrelevant, but as unrelated families came to occupy the same village, a need was felt for a deity who could protect all the inhabitants. The newly adopted territorial deity was usually called *ubusunagami* or CHINJU NO KAMI and was responsible for a larger territory than that of the *ujigami*. The worshipers of a single *ubusunagami* came to be called its *ubuko*, since the *ujigami*'s worshipers were termed *ujiko*.

Ōtō Tokihiko

Uchida Ginzō (1872–1919)

Historian. Specialist in the history of the Edo period (1600–1868) and pioneer of the modern study of Japanese economic history. Born in Tōkyō, he graduated from Tōkyō University in 1896 and became a member of its faculty in 1899. His course on Japanese economic history was the first of its kind in Japan. After a four-year stay in Europe, he was appointed to a professorship at Kyōto University, where he helped to establish the history curriculum. Uchida is particularly known for his multifaceted research on the history of the Edo period and for his introduction of rigorous empirical and comparative approaches to the study of Japanese economic history (see HISTORIOGRAPHY). His major works include *Keizaishi sōron* (1912, Introduction to Economic History) and *Kinsei no Nihon* (1919, Japan in the Edo Period).

Uchida Hyakken (1889–1971)

Novelist; essayist. Real name Uchida Eizō. Born in Okayama Prefecture. Graduate of Tōkyō University. Uchida taught German at several schools, including Hōsei University, before turning to professional writing at the age of 45. Although he wrote some novels, he is better known for his numerous essays written under an alternate pen name Hyakkien. One of the many disciples of NATSUME SŌSEKI, Uchida worked as an editor and proofreader when Sōseki's complete works were published. Principal works include *Meido* (1922) and *Ahō ressha* (1952).

Uchida Kōsai (1865–1936)

Diplomat and politician. Born in what is now Kumamoto Prefecture. A graduate of Tōkyō University, he entered the Ministry of Foreign Affairs and served as ambassador to Austria and the United States before being named foreign minister in the second SAIONJI KIMMOCHI cabinet (1911–12). After a stay as ambassador in Russia during the Bolshevik Revolution, he was again named foreign minister, first in the HARA TAKASHI cabinet (1918–21), then in the TAKAHASHI KOREKIYO (1921–22) and KATŌ TOMOSABURŌ (1922–23) cabinets. In 1931 Uchida became president of the SOUTH MANCHURIA RAILWAY. When the MANCHURIAN INCIDENT occurred that year, he put the entire railway at the disposal of the Japanese GUANDONG (KWANTUNG) ARMY to facilitate its conquest of Manchuria. As foreign minister again in the SAITŌ MAKOTO cabinet (1932–34), he called for the recognition of MANCHUKUO, the puppet state created by the Guandong Army, and for withdrawal from the League of Nations following its censure of Japan's conduct in Manchuria (see LYTTON COMMISSION). Uchida's conduct of foreign policy was in marked contrast to the "internationalism" of SHIDEHARA KIJŪRŌ, a contemporary who also served as foreign minister in several cabinets.

Uchida Roan (1868–1929)

Critic; novelist. Real name Uchida Mitsugu. Born in Tōkyō. As a child, he was influenced by Christianity, later contributing to JOGAKU ZASSHI, Japan's first magazine for women. In 1889 he was profoundly moved upon reading Dostoevsky's *Crime and Punish-*

ment, which he was later the first to translate into Japanese. A major polemist against the popular writing of his day, he advocated broadening the scope of popular literature by incorporating social dimensions and issues. His writing includes essays on and translations of modern European literature, which helped pave the way for the so-called naturalist school of the early 20th century. His main works include the essay "Bungakusha to naru hō" (1894), the novel *Kure no nijūhachinichi* (1898), and his memoirs *Omoidasu hitobito* (1925).

Uchida Ryōhei (1874–1937)

Ultranationalist leader. Born in Fukuoka Prefecture. As a youth he entered the GEN'YŌSHA, a right-wing nationalist society based in Fukuoka, and soon became the leading disciple of its founder, TŌYAMA MITSURU. When the TONGHAK REBELLION broke out in Korea in 1894, Uchida went with fellow Gen'yōsha members to help the rebels, thus beginning over a decade of direct personal action on the Asian continent (see TAIRIKU RŌNIN). In 1901, after returning to Japan from an intelligence-gathering trip through Siberia, he founded an ultranationalist organization, the AMUR RIVER SOCIETY, to press the government to adopt a strong policy toward Russia. In 1903 he joined the TAIRO DŌSHIKAI, a political association formed to advocate war with Russia. Following the Russo-Japanese War of 1904–05, Uchida called for the annexation of Korea and engaged in political intrigues there to promote that end (see KOREA, ANNEXATION OF). During the Taishō (1912–26) and early part of the Shōwa (1926–) period, he turned his attention to attacking liberal currents at home and rousing public opinion in unsuccessful attempts to prevent passage of the Universal Manhood Suffrage Bill in 1925 and ratification of the London naval armaments limitation treaty in 1930 (see LONDON NAVAL CONFERENCES). He was arrested in 1925 on suspicion of plotting to assassinate Prime Minister KATŌ TAKAAKI, but was found innocent.

Uchida Tomu (1898–1970)

Film director. Before the war he was a pioneer of realistic cinema, of which his acclaimed masterpiece *Tsuchi* (1939, Earth) is a leading example. After the war and 13 years of inactivity he specialized in period pieces.

Uchida started his career as a comic actor and production assistant to American-trained director Thomas Kurihara. He later joined NIKKATSU CORPORATION as an assistant director. The first few years of his directorial career were spent making silent comedies. In the mid-1930s he became increasingly involved with movements toward greater realism in film and more cinematic adaptations of literature. He made *Tsuchi,* from a novel by NAGATSUKA TAKASHI, in 1939 against the wishes of his production company and even had to complete the picture in secrecy. *Tsuchi* was daring because, though a fiction film, it attempted documentary realism in portraying the lives of a farming family that loses everything and then struggles to recover. Uchida attained his documentary effect by faithfully recording all the seasonal rites of Japanese agriculture over the course of a year, a painstaking process for his actors and crew.

After the outbreak of World War II, Uchida was sent to China, where he remained a prisoner until 1954. Upon repatriation to Japan he joined the TŌEI CO, LTD. There he specialized in remaking many classic period pieces. His postwar masterpiece, *Kiga kaikyō* (1965, The Straits of Hunger), is, however, in a genre known as the "humanistic thriller" for its sympathetic examination of a criminal's motives. In a poll celebrating the 60th anniversary of the movie magazine *Kinema jumpō, Kiga kaikyō* was voted third place on a list of the greatest Japanese films ever made.　　　*David OWENS*

uchikowashi

(literally, "smashing"). Urban riots of the Edo period (1600–1868). In protest against exorbitant rice prices, starving mobs destroyed the storehouses of rice merchants and pawnbrokers. Similar riots by farmers against village officials are called HYAKUSHŌ IKKI. *Uchikowashi* occurred sporadically during the 18th and 19th centuries in various cities. A food riot in Nagasaki in 1713 is one of the earliest examples. A large-scale riot took place in Edo (now Tōkyō) in 1733, when some 1,700 people attacked a rice store. *Uchikowashi* grew increasingly frequent toward the end of the Edo period. The riot in Ōsaka led by ŌSHIO HEIHACHIRŌ in 1837 set off a series of urban disturbances in other parts of the country. The extensive riots of 1866 in Edo and Ōsaka helped to hasten the collapse of the Toku-

gawa shogunate. Modern examples of *uchikowashi* are known as *kome sōdō;* the RICE RIOTS OF 1918 are particularly famous for their nationwide scale and political impact.　　　*Yoshiyuki NAKAI*

Uchimura Kanzō (1861–1930)

Christian leader, essayist, and editor. Born in Edo (now Tōkyō) in the compound of the *daimyō* of Takasaki, whom his father served, Kanzō showed an early ability in languages, a talent which his parents encouraged by starting him on English lessons at the age of 11. By 1877 he was able to gain admission to the Sapporo Agricultural College (now Hokkaidō University), where most lectures were in English. There, while studying fisheries science, he was converted to Christianity along with his friend NITOBE INAZŌ, under the influence of the American Merriman C. HARRIS and, indirectly, William S. CLARK. After graduation in 1881, he worked as a scientist until he went to study in the United States after an impetuous and short marriage. There he cared for retarded children, studied at Amherst College, and studied long enough at Hartford Theological Seminary to decide he did not want to become a pastor. He returned to Japan in 1888.

Back home, he found his Christian training had given him ideals he could not implement. He taught in a number of schools, but in each case left after disagreement over principles. The most famous confrontation was at the First Higher School, where he did not show, in the opinion of his colleagues, sufficient respect to the signature of the emperor appended to a copy of the new IMPERIAL RESCRIPT ON EDUCATION. Realizing that he could not continue as a teacher, Uchimura started to write and discovered that he could command a regular audience. By 1897 his critical essays had earned him a post as the senior editor of the YOROZU CHŌHŌ, which under his leadership became the largest newspaper in Japan. His colleagues there included KŌTOKU SHŪSUI, together with whom he became an outspoken pacifist. Both men resigned when the publisher of the *Yorozu* approved the government's warlike policies against Russia on the eve of the Russo-Japanese War.

When Uchimura resigned from the newspaper, he had already been publishing his own monthly, *Seisho no kenkyū* (Study of the Bible), for three years. Now he turned his full energies to this journal and published 357 issues before his death. At the same time Nitobe Inazō, now head of the First Higher School, sent some of his students to meet with Uchimura on Sundays for lectures on the Bible and ethics. Uchimura interrupted this quiet, studious life for widespread public lectures as World War I convinced him that renewed evangelical efforts were needed. For five years he addressed weekly audiences of five to seven hundred in downtown Tōkyō on the books of the Bible—for instance, 31 lectures on Job, 60 on Romans, and 71 on the life of Christ. His followers came to identify with Uchimura's attitude toward ecclesiastical organization—that the church is unnecessary and at times a hindrance. His word to describe his point of view, MUKYŌKAI, is still used to distinguish his tradition.

Uchimura's writings fall into three main categories: autobiographical works which detail the problems of an individual who tries to implement his ideals; polemics which present vigorous points of view in the secular forum of ideas; and pastoral views aimed at deepening the faith of fellow Christians. By far, the most popular have been the autobiographies, whose intense introspection is reflected in the titles of three works that were all first published in 1893: *Kyūanroku* (Search after Peace), *Kirisuto shinto no nagusame* (Consolations of a Christian), and *How I Became a Christian.* They seem to have appealed to readers in much the same way as the later confessional I-NOVELS of other Japanese authors. The most important among the polemics are those written about 1900. The biting satire of "Jisei no kansatsu" (1896, Observations on the Times) lampooned the bibulous optimism which followed the Sino-Japanese War, while the pacifist essays of 1903 still move the reader long after the emotions which inspired them are forgotten. *Japan and the Japanese* (1894) represents a separate subgenre in which Uchimura used his remarkable English-language skills to teach Westerners about Japan—in this case, great men in its history. An English-language monthly, *The Japan Christian Intelligencer* (1926–28), pursued similar themes late in his career. The pastoral works, best represented by the long series of lectures on various books of the Bible, were addressed to those within the faith or at least seriously interested in it. Almost unstudied, they provide a rich source of Christian interpretation in a society otherwise apparently little affected by Western faith.

All of Uchimura's writings expressed his Christian faith in ways which commend it to a person nurtured in the Confucian system. The autobiographical works fitted in with the tradition of a diary and later reflection on its contents. Introduction of Japan to the West and criticism of Japan's government reflected the *samurai*'s duty to instruct those in ignorance and to rebuke the folly of unwise rulers. And the studies of the Bible stressed the ethical imperatives inherent in Christian belief. Thus Uchimura presented Japanese Christianity as faith in one God engrafted onto his concept of BUSHIDŌ.

📖 ——Uchimura Kanzō, *Uchimura Kanzō zenshū* (Iwanami Shoten, 1932–33), vols 15, 16, and 20 contain Uchimura's English-language writings. John F. Howes, "Uchimura Kanzō," in Dankwart A. Rustow, ed, *Philosophers and Kings: Studies in Leadership* (1970). John F. Howes, "Uchimura Kanzō: The Bible and War," in Nobuya Bamba and John F. Howes, ed, *Pacifism in Japan: The Christian and Socialist Tradition* (1978). Masaike Megumu, *Uchimura Kanzō* (rev ed, 1977). Shinagawa Tsutomu, *Uchimura Kanzō kenkyū bunken mokuroku* (rev ed, 1977). Ōta Yūzō, *Uchimura Kanzō: Sono sekai shugi to Nihon shugi o megutte* (1977).   *John F. HOWES*

Uchimura Naoya (1909–)

Playwright. Real name Sugawara Minoru. Born in Tōkyō; graduate of Keiō University in economics. He studied drama with KISHIDA KUNIO and began publishing plays in the late 1930s. His long-run serial drama, "Eriko to tomo ni" (Together with Eriko), was an enormous success with radio audiences after World War II. Besides writing for radio and television, Uchimura has published numerous in-depth studies about the dramatic arts and the mass media, such as *Doramatorugī kenkyū* (1957, Dramaturgy Studies) and *Atarashii doramatorugī* (1963, New Dramaturgy).

Uchinada

Town in central Ishikawa Prefecture, central Honshū, on the Sea of Japan. The textile industry has replaced fishing as its chief industry. The city was the center of controversy in 1953 when local residents opposed the construction of a shooting range by American Occupation Forces. Pop: 20,815.

Uchinada Incident

(Uchinada Shishajō Hantai Undō). A movement in 1952–53 protesting the location of an American armed forces firing range in the village of Uchinada, Ishikawa Prefecture. The first of many protests against the presence of American bases in Japan (see UNITED STATES MILITARY BASES, DISPUTES OVER), it rapidly expanded from the village's outcry over the initial United States–Japan announcement of the range in September 1952 to become a prefectural and finally a national issue. The installation was completed by February 1953 and opened in March to train American personnel for the Korean War. The continuing protest led to the defeat of the cabinet minister Hayashiya Kamejirō by a vocal critic of the range in the election for the House of Councillors held in April. Even when the range was temporarily closed in May, railwaymen staged a 48-hour protest strike. It was reopened the following month, and after negotiations with the government the villagers agreed to accept financial compensation in September. By November local opposition had died away, and in 1957 the firing range was turned over to the Japanese government.

Uchinoura

Town in southeastern Kagoshima Prefecture, Kyūshū. Uchinoura was until recently a backward agricultural region where farmers supplemented their incomes with fishing and charcoal making. Its economy has improved somewhat with the building of the Tōkyō University Kagoshima Space Center. Pop: 6,863.

Uchiura Bay

(Uchiura Wan). Inlet of the Pacific Ocean, on the eastern coast of the Oshima Peninsula, southwestern Hokkaidō. A circular bay with a diameter of approximately 50 km (31 mi). Muroran, located at the northeastern end of the bay, is a major port and industrial center. Principal activities are the catching of squid and the cultivation of scallops.

uchiwa → fans

Uda, Emperor (867–931)

The 59th sovereign *(tennō)* in the traditional count (which includes several nonhistorical emperors); reigned 887–897 before abdicating in favor of his son Emperor DAIGO. Son and successor of Emperor Kōkō (830–887; r 884–887), Uda was not closely related to the FUJIWARA FAMILY and was determined to curb their influence. Although he was brought to the throne by the regent *(kampaku)* Fujiwara no Mototsune, Uda immediately challenged him in the AKŌ INCIDENT of 887. After Mototsune's death Uda refused to fill the regent's post, and he tried to counteract Fujiwara power further by promoting men of other families, most notably SUGAWARA NO MICHIZANE. On his abdication he presented Daigo with a book of precepts for ruling, called *Kampyō goyuikai.* Uda retired to the temple NINNAJI and became a priest, but he remained influential in state affairs throughout his son's reign. Fragments of his diary, UDA TENNŌ GYOKI, survive.   *G. Cameron HURST III*

Udagawa Yōan (1798–1846)

Scientist, physician, and scholar of WESTERN LEARNING. Born in the Ōgaki domain (now part of Gifu Prefecture), he was adopted by Udagawa Shinsai (1769–1834), a doctor of Western medicine and translator of Dutch medical manuals. Interested in natural history from an early age, he studied Dutch under Baba Sajūrō (1787–1822), an interpreter attached to the Tokugawa shogunate. In 1826 Udagawa was put in charge of translation in the shogunate's department of astronomy and participated in the project to translate a Dutch encyclopedia (see KŌSEI SHIMPEN). Besides Dutch, Udagawa read German, English, and Latin, and he published many works introducing Western science to Japan. Among the more important were *Shokugaku keigen* (1833), a treatise on Western botanical science (some of his terminology is still in use), and *Seimi kaisō* (1837), a translation of William Henry's (1775–1836) *Elements of Experimental Chemistry.*

Uda Tennō gyoki

The diary of Emperor UDA (r 887–897); also known as *Kampyō gyoki,* after the Kampyō era (889–898). Much of the original 10-volume work is lost, and what remains today was compiled in the Edo period (1600–1868) by Nakatsu Hirochika from fragments quoted in other works. It is a useful source of information about the court ceremony of Uda's time and the antagonism between him and the FUJIWARA FAMILY.   *G. Cameron HURST III*

Udo Shrine

(Udo Jingū). Shintō shrine in the city of Nichinan, Miyazaki Prefecture, Kyūshū, dedicated to Ugayafukiaezu no Mikoto and five other deities. The shrine is said to mark the birthplace of Ugayafukiaezu, the father of the legendary first emperor, Jimmu. According to tradition, the Udo shrine was erected in the time of Empress Suiko (r 593–628). At the end of the 8th century a Buddhist monk, acting under orders from the court, repaired the shrine and made it subordinate to a Buddhist temple, the Ninnō Gokokuji. After the formal separation of Buddhism and Shintō in 1868, the name of the shrine was changed from the Buddhistic Udo Gongen (Udo Incarnation) to the Shintō Udo Jingū (Udo Imperial Shrine). The annual festival is held on 1 February.   *Stanley WEINSTEIN*

Ueda

City in eastern Nagano Prefecture, central Honshū, on the river Chikumagawa. In ancient times Ueda was the seat of the provincial capital *(kokufu)* of Shinano Province and the provincial temple *(kokubunji).* It developed as a castle town of the Sanada family from 1583. It was known until World War II for its sericulture. Present industries include textiles and electric appliances. Rice, apples, and walnuts are cultivated. The remains of the provincial temple and Ueda Castle, as well as the temples Anrakuji and Jōrakuji, and the Bessho Hot Spring are of interest. Pop: 111,540.

Ueda Akinari (1734–1809)

Scholar, poet, and writer of fiction; preeminent literary personality of late-18th-century Japan; best known for his collection of nine tales of the supernatural, *Ugetsu monogatari* (1776; tr *Tales of Moonlight and Rain*, 1974).

Early Life——Born of an unmarried woman in the Ōsaka gay quarter, Akinari never knew his true father's identity. He was adopted at the age of three by a former *samurai* named Ueda, who worked as an oil and paper merchant. As a young boy he suffered from smallpox (1738), and one finger on his right hand was crippled. Perhaps this is why he never became a master calligrapher or painter. Otherwise, he gained fame in everything he tried.

He attended a private academy, the KAITOKUDŌ, did classical studies, and took part in a HAIKU (17-syllable poetry) circle. In 1755 Akinari became responsible for his adopted family's business. In spite of his father's initial opposition, he married in 1760 a woman named Otama, who had been serving for several years in the Ueda household. After his father's death in 1761, he continued to work for 10 years as a merchant. In his spare time he wrote prose fiction in the manner of SAIKAKU (1642–93), EJIMA KISEKI (1666–1735), and the UKIYO-ZŌSHI ("tales of the floating world").

Writer for the Hachimonjiya——Akinari published two collections of short stories in the popular manner of the *katagi-mono* ("character sketches"), a subgenre of the *ukiyo-zōshi*. The first of these, *Shodō kikimimi sekenzaru* (1766, The Worldly Monkey Who Knows All the Arts), was issued under the pseudonym, Wayaku Tarō ("Tarō, the Joker"). It was published by the Hachimonjiya ("Figure Eight Shop"), the leading bookseller of popular fiction, in five thin volumes, each with three droll and faintly satirical tales about townsmen. A short, witty preface tells that the book was based on gossip and compiled with the proverbial monkeys in mind who speak no evil, see no evil, and hear no evil. There is also reference to a legendary monkey that laughs at its fellow creatures' red behinds, blissfully unaware of its own. The inspiration in *Sekenzaru* came partly from contemporary persons and events and partly from Chinese and Japanese literary sources, the influence of which gives it a pedantic tone. Still, Akinari adapted what he borrowed for his own purposes. As a narrator he took a detached viewpoint and laughed at human imperfection and individual misfortune. Often he mixed pathos with his humor, and he showed sympathy toward some of his characters.

In the first tale of volume 2, for instance, he criticizes a social system that forces a dutiful son to support an undeserving family. The first tale of volume 3 relates how a lecherous man tries to seduce a young and beautiful nun in a temple. Skilled in the martial arts, she fends him off, and he flees, terrified, into the pouring rain. Such ironic twists occur in several of the tales. In *Sekenzaru* the characterization is skillful, the style fresh and lively. Akinari's second collection, *Seken tekake katagi* (1767, Sketches of Worldly Mistresses), deals more with women than men. *Sekenzaru* was reprinted at least twice during the Edo period (1600–1868). Of all Akinari's works only *Ugetsu* was more widely read.

Ugetsu Monogatari——By virtue of its poetic style, its eerie beauty, and skillful use of literary archetypes, Akinari's *Ugetsu monogatari* ranks among the best-known works in the classical tradition. Classified in the genre known as YOMIHON ("reading book"), it exemplifies the highest artistic level reached by the supernatural tale in Japan. With elegant diction, Akinari exploits the technical devices of traditional poetry and drama. Unlike his earlier tales, each story is set in times past and employs a network of references and allusions to historical persons, places, and events. Besides indebtedness to older Japanese texts, there are influences from the Chinese classical and popular traditions alike. One of Akinari's techniques in *Ugetsu* is to naturalize a Chinese tale by resetting it in ancient or medieval Japan and by ascribing to the characters Japanese attitudes and backgrounds. This feature came to characterize the *yomihon*, especially those by BAKIN (1767–1848).

In Japan the ghostly tale takes three basic forms. The strange doings of animals or nonhuman creatures reflect the Shintō inspiration. From Buddhism come stories of retribution or the power of karma. Last of all, there is a characteristically Chinese type. Each tale in *Ugetsu* may be analyzed in such terms, though there is some overlapping. Although each tale is complete in itself, the collection as a whole reveals an aesthetic unity, like an imperial anthology of court poetry, a sequence of linked verse, or a complete program of Nō plays. Natural imagery and human emotion are blended in a manner found in the Japanese classics. Skillful use of diction, rhe-

torical devices, and mood imparts to all the tales a powerful psychic force.

Poetry and Scholarship——After his effort to recreate the spirit of the classics in fictional form, Akinari tried to interpret it in scholarly terms. He thought of himself as a poet and scholar, not a writer of tales. While participating in haiku circles during his youth, he became interested in WAKA (31-syllable poems) and the scholarly tradition known as KOKUGAKU (National Learning). When his home and business were destroyed by fire in 1771, he turned to the study of medicine, quitting the world of commerce. He wrote an essay on the grammatical particles in haiku (1774), and he drew especially close to BUSON's (1716–84) circle of poets, two members of which, TAKAI KITŌ (1741–89) and MATSUMURA GOSHUN (1752–1811), also known as Gekkei, remained lifelong friends. He used the pen name Muchō ("crab"), referring to his deformed hand and to his solitary habits. The name suggests an outwardly stern but inwardly gentle disposition.

While studying literature and medicine, Akinari supported himself by teaching, editing, and writing commentaries on classics he especially admired. He opened his own medical practice in 1776 and continued in it for 11 years before retiring, perhaps from remorse at making a bad diagnosis of a young girl's illness and having her die.

The most dramatic episode in Akinari's career as a scholar was his dispute with the Kokugaku scholar MOTOORI NORINAGA (1730–1801). Their quarrel covered two distinct topics, phonology (centering on whether archaic Japanese had an "n" sound) and the nature of the Japanese state in relation to the rest of the world. For Norinaga, the classics embodied absolute authority. Akinari argued in deductive terms and warned against being misled by the ancient writing system. To Motoori, Japan was superior to all other countries because the sun goddess (see AMATERASU ŌMIKAMI) had been born there. Akinari observed how small Japan was and ridiculed the idea that it was the source of all civilization. He believed that each country had its own traditions and that without supporting evidence people ought not take those of any one country to be true and assume all others to be false.

Especially after retiring from medical practice and moving to Kyōto (1793), Akinari composed many *waka,* and the *waka* poet OZAWA ROAN (1723–1801) became his closest friend. In all, Akinari left 2,454 verses; these have been collected (1969), and he deserves to be counted among the best *waka* poets of his age.

Harusame Monogatari——Toward the end of his life Akinari again turned to prose fiction, leaving a posthumous collection of tales, *Harusame monogatari* (1808; tr *Tales of the Spring Rain,* 1975). Although it belongs, loosely speaking, to the *yomihon* genre, it has almost no supernatural element. The 10 tales that comprise it are uneven in length and literary quality. Still, it is a valuable revelation of Akinari's philosophical and moral outlook and covers a wide range of subjects—historical events, literature and literary conventions, religion, ethics, and social problems. Like *Tandai shōshin roku* (1808–09, Undaunted and Faint-Hearted Jottings), it stands as a kind of last testament. Some scholars believe its spontaneous informality makes it superior to the highly polished *Ugetsu,* which they criticize as too artificial.

Prose fiction was not Akinari's vocation, just as poetry was not Coleridge's. His ambitions lay in the scholarship of ancient Japanese literature and extended even to such topics as tea, on which his treatise, *Seifū sagen* (1794, Clean Air, Few Words), is still widely read and quoted. Clay utensils that he himself made are preserved in private collections. Akinari was a man of Renaissance temperament, and to the end of his days he tried to verify his findings and speculations by the most direct means of all—his own personal experience and imagination.

📖——Asano Sampei, *Akinari zenkashū to sono kenkyū* (1969). Donald Keene, *World Within Walls* (1976). Ueda Akinari, *Ugetsu monogatari,* tr Leon M. Zolbrod as *Ugetsu Monogatari: Tales of Moonlight and Rain* (1974). Ueda Akinari, *Harusame monogatari,* tr Barry Jackman as *Tales of the Spring Rain: Harusame Monogatari* (1975).   Leon M. ZOLBROD

Ueda Bin (1874–1916)

Poet; literary critic; translator. Born in Tōkyō. Graduate of Tōkyō University, where he studied English literature. He later became professor of English literature at Kyōto University. Ueda translated much European poetry into Japanese, as well as publishing his own original poems. Among his translations are numerous poems from the French of the Parnassians and symbolists. He is best known for his *Kaichōon* (1905), a collection of poems translated from English, French, German, and other languages. This volume, which includes his translation of Baudelaire's "L'Albatros" and Verlaine's "Chanson d'automne," had a profound influence on the emerging symbolist poetry movement in Japan in the early 20th century. *Kaichōon* also includes poems from Robert Browning's *Pippa Passes*. Other works include *Uzumaki* (1910), a novel, and *Bokuyōshin* (1920), a collection of his own and translated poems.

Ueda Kazutoshi (1867–1937)

Also known as Ueda Mannen. Scholar of the Japanese language and father of novelist ENCHI FUMIKO. Born in Tōkyō, he graduated from Tōkyō University where he was especially influenced by his studies with Basil Hall CHAMBERLAIN. He went on to study in Germany and France from 1890 to 1894. He introduced Western linguistic research methods into the study of Japanese language, linguistics, and literature. While a professor at Tōkyō University and a member of the National Language Research Committee (Kokugo Chōsa Iinkai)—now the COUNCIL ON THE NATIONAL LANGUAGE (Kokugo Shingikai)—he trained researchers and contributed to national language policies. His works include *Kokugo no tame* (For a Japanese Language), written in two volumes between 1895 and 1903, *Kokugogaku no jukkō* (1916, Ten Lectures on the Japanese Language), a Chinese-character dictionary entitled *Daijiten* (1917), and, in collaboration with Matsui Kanji (1863–1945), a well-known Japanese language dictionary entitled DAI NIHON KOKUGO JITEN (1915–19).
SHIMADA Masahiko

Ueda Teijirō (1879–1940)

Scholar of business management. Born in Tōkyō, he graduated from Tōkyō Higher Commercial School (now Hitotsubashi University) in 1900 and soon after became a professor there. When the school was upgraded to become the Tōkyō University of Commerce in 1920, he was made professor and became president of the university in 1937. He also served as a representative director of the Dai Nihon Keiei Gakkai, a pre–World War II business-management academic society. Ueda's *Kabushiki kaisha keizai ron* (1937, Economics of Joint Stock Corporations) analyzed the national economy under capitalism; his *Shōkō keiei* (1930, Commercial and Industrial Management) and *Keiei keizaigaku sōron* (1937, Introduction to Business Economics) established the foundation of business management in Japan. He was also the author of a noted book on the industrial revolution in England, *Eikoku sangyō kakumeishi ron* (1923).
YAMADA Katsumi

Uehara Yūsaku (1856–1933)

Army general and field marshal who served as army minister, chief of the Army General Staff Office, and inspector general of military education. Born in Hyūga Province (now Miyazaki Prefecture), the son of a *samurai*, he graduated from the Army Academy in 1879 and studied in France from 1881 to 1885. Named army minister in May 1912, he resigned when his demand for an increase of two army divisions was rejected by the SAIONJI KIMMOCHI cabinet. The cabinet in turn was forced to step down when the army refused to nominate a replacement for Uehara.
KONDŌ Shinji

Uejima Onitsura (1661–1738)

Haikai (see HAIKU) poet of the early Edo period. Real name Uejima Munechika. Onitsura was known for advocating the concept of *makoto* (sincerity) as the very essence of *haikai*, thus reasserting the emphasis on mental attitude rather than technique that has always been the predominant strain in classical Japanese poetics. Born in Itami in Settsu Province (now Hyōgo Prefecture), he began to compose *haikai* at a very early age and at 15 was already a disciple of NISHIYAMA SŌIN. His *haikai* is distinguished by a complete absence of artifice and an almost conversational tone. His major works include the essay collection *Hitorigoto* (1685) and the *haikai* anthology *Taigo monogurui* (1690).

Ueki Emori (1857–1892)

Political leader and thinker associated with the FREEDOM AND PEOPLE'S RIGHTS MOVEMENT of the 1880s. The son of a *samurai* of the Tosa domain (now Kōchi Prefecture), he studied at the domainal school, Chidōkan, and briefly, in 1873, in Tōkyō. He came under

the influence of ITAGAKI TAISUKE, also from Tosa, and helped him to organize the political groups RISSHISHA, AIKOKUSHA, Kokkai Kisei Dōmei (LEAGUE FOR ESTABLISHING A NATIONAL ASSEMBLY), and eventually the JIYŪTŌ, Japan's first political party. In 1879 he wrote a popular pamphlet, *Minken jiyū ron* (On People's Rights and Liberty), expounding the theory of naturally endowed human rights, the people's right to political independence and freedom, and the necessity of constitutional government. In 1881, in response to the government's pledge that a national assembly would be established by 1890, Ueki wrote a draft constitution in which he argued for popular sovereignty, a unicameral parliament, and the right to vote for all who paid taxes. As editor of the newspaper *Jiyū shimbun*, the organ of the Jiyūtō, he traveled tirelessly throughout the country promoting the people's rights movement. In the first national election (1890) he won a seat in the Diet. He died suddenly at the age of 35; some suspected that he had been poisoned.

Unlike many of the leading thinkers of his day, Ueki never studied abroad and had to rely exclusively on translations of Western works; he read widely in English, French, and American history, politics, and economics. He attended lectures by scholars associated with the MEIROKUSHA, seeking out men like NISHI AMANE and NISHIMURA SHIGEKI. Ueki was critical, however, of FUKUZAWA YUKICHI, the man who had awakened in him an awareness of political problems, for stressing national sovereignty over popular rights. Indeed, in his constitutional draft, *Nihonkoku kokken an*, Ueki advocated the people's right to resist and rebel. After Itagaki, who feared the tendency of some Jiyūtō members to violence, disbanded the party in 1884, Ueki became increasingly conservative. Although he still wrote and lectured on changing the traditional family system, the emancipation of women, and other social questions, he seemed almost to despair of Japan's politics and politicians.
HIJIKATA Kazuo

Uemura Kōgorō (1894–1978)

Businessman. Born in Tōkyō. After graduating from Tōkyō University, Uemura immediately joined the Ministry of Agriculture and Commerce (now the Ministry of International Trade and Industry; MITI), became director of the Coal Control Board in 1941, and concentrated on coal production and procurement during the war. He was purged by the Allied OCCUPATION after World War II but was asked to become vice president of KEIDANREN (Federation of Economic Organizations) after being rehabilitated. Uemura tried to avoid collusion between big businesses and the government by attempting to abolish the practice of direct corporate contributions to political parties. He became Keidanren's president in 1968. Uemura strengthened the economic organization's staff and established a collective management system. While in office, he devoted himself to negotiations regarding textile trade between Japan and the United States and to the solution of pollution problems. *YUI Tsunehiko*

Uemura Masahisa (1858–1925)

Church leader, essayist, and translator. Born into a wealthy family of retainers (HATAMOTO) to the shōgun. The comfort of Uemura's earliest years contrasted greatly with the penury of his teens. At 13 he studied English with the missionaries S. R. BROWN and James Ballagh, and under their influence became a Christian, going on to a mission school of theology in Yokohama and graduating in 1879. In 1880 he was ordained a minister of the Presbyterian Church.

While still a student, he had already started his career as an editor of numerous journals, and in 1880 was one of the founders of the *Rikugō zasshi* (The Universe). Over the next decade he published *Shinri ippan* (On Truth), a pivotal exposition of Christian belief aimed at counteracting the dominant utilitarianism of FUKUZAWA YUKICHI; founded a church, the Fujimichō Kyōkai, which became under his pastorate the second largest in Japan with more than 1,000 members; served with other church leaders on numerous committees including those for a hymnbook and the translation of the Old Testament; and helped found MEIJI GAKUIN UNIVERSITY. In 1890 he launched his own literary journal, *Nihon hyōron*, and the Christian weekly *Fukuin shūhō*, which under the later name *Fukuin shimpō* continued even after his death. He also lectured frequently on English literature to audiences which included young authors such as SHIMAZAKI TŌSON, KUNIKIDA DOPPO, and MASAMUNE HAKUCHŌ. In 1901–02, he engaged in a rigorous debate with EBINA DANJŌ over the nature of Christianity and its relation to Japanese nationalism. After a disagreement with missionaries over theological training, in 1904 he founded one of the schools which eventually became Tōkyō Union Theological Seminary. He traveled 3 times to the West and 22 times to Manchuria, Korea, and Taiwan. He died suddenly in 1925. One of his daughters, UEMURA TAMAKI, continued the Uemura family name as Japan's first ordained woman minister.

The main theme of Uemura's writings was the importance of the individual in society and the nurturing of Christians who could stand firm against social pressures. With the conviction that Western literature served to develop such people, he introduced a different writer in each issue of *Nihon hyōron*, particularly showing admiration for the poets Tennyson, Wordsworth, and Browning. His translations of the Psalms, Song of Songs, Isaiah, and hymns became modern Japanese classics. The use of an alternating eight and six-syllable meter in the hymns meant they could be sung to the original melodies, unlike other translations which used the standard Japanese seven- and five-syllable meter.

Though his literary accomplishments have earned Uemura recognition, he is best known as a church leader. He established the Presbyterian tradition in Japan with an emphasis on independence from missionary control. In contrast to his friend UCHIMURA KANZŌ, Uemura stressed the need for church organization but did not confine his work within narrow denominational bounds.

Uemura's square-set, stocky figure and halting speech contrasted greatly with his flowing prose in both Japanese and English. His defense of Uchimura after Uchimura's hesitation to bow before the IMPERIAL RESCRIPT ON EDUCATION in 1891 and Uemura's memorial service for a parishioner executed in 1911 because of his part in the HIGH TREASON INCIDENT OF 1910, an alleged plot to kill the Meiji emperor, demonstrated Uemura's courage in a society which demanded ever-increasing conformity.

📖——Uemura Masahisa Zenshū Kankōkai, ed, *Uemura Masahisa zenshū* (1933–34). Aofusa Katsuhira, *Dr. Masahisa Uemura: A Christian Leader* (1951). Kindai Bungaku Kenkyūshitsu, ed, *Kindai bungaku kenkyū sōsho* 23 (1970). Kyōgoku Jun'ichi, *Uemura Masahisa* (1966). Sawa Wataru, *Uemura Masahisa to sono jidai* (1937–44).   *John F.* HOWES

Uemura Naomi (1941–   )

Mountaineer; polar explorer. Born in Hyōgo Prefecture. From the time he enrolled in Meiji University he was active in its Alpine Club. He scaled the highest peaks on five continents (Everest, Kilimanjaro, Mont Blanc, Aconcagua, and McKinley) and, with the exception of Everest, he climbed alone. In 1968 he made the first recorded solo trip by raft down the Amazon. In 1978 he reached the North Pole by dogsled and is acknowledged as the first person in history to have made an overland traverse of Greenland's midsection.

TAKEDA Fumio

Uemura Shōen (1875–1949)

Painter; famous for her paintings of beautiful women. She was born Uemura Tsune in Kyōto, the second daughter of a tea merchant. Her father died two months before her birth, leaving her mother to raise the two girls and manage the family business alone. Shōen's painting genius was recognized early, and her mother encouraged her to continue the study of art.

After finishing elementary school Shōen went to the Kyōto Prefectural Painting School, where she studied with Suzuki Shōnen (1849–1918), a Chinese-style landscape painter from whose name Shōen's own is derived. In 1894 she began studying under KŌNO BAIREI. Following his death she became a student of TAKEUCHI SEIHŌ, Bairei's most outstanding disciple. She won her first award in the 1900 joint exhibition of the Japan Painting Association (Nihon Kaiga Kyōkai) and the JAPAN FINE ARTS ACADEMY (Nihon Bijutsuin), taking a silver medal along with Suzuki Shōnen, HISHIDA SHUNSŌ, and YOKOYAMA TAIKAN. With the inauguration of the BUNTEN exhibitions in 1907, these government-sponsored exhibits became the main stage for her work, where she won numerous awards.

Early in her career Shōen had shown great skill in figure painting, and her mature works are exclusively figures. While historical and traditional subjects make up a large portion of her oeuvre, she is best known as a painter of women. In these paintings she combined elements of MARUYAMA-SHIJŌ SCHOOL realism with UKIYO-E inspired design. Paralleling her own growth, her early figures of youthful innocence and charm later gave way to women of greater

warmth, substance, and maturity. Whether engaged in mundane activity or caught in moments of surprise, quiet reflection, or repose, Shōen's women are always studies in elegance and self-possession.

In 1941 she became a member of the Imperial Art Academy and in 1944 a court artist *(teishitsu gigein)*. In 1948 she became the first woman to receive the Order of Culture.   *Margo* STIPE

Uemura Tamaki (1890–   )

Christian activist. Born in Tōkyō, the daughter of the prominent Christian leader UEMURA MASAHISA. She attended Wellesley College in Massachusetts; then, widowed after a brief marriage, she began teaching at Joshi Eigakujuku (now Tsuda College). She helped HANI MOTOKO establish the school Jiyū Gakuen in 1921. She then studied theology at the University of Edinburgh and returned to Japan to found and serve as minister (she was Japan's first woman minister) for the Kashiwagi Church of the Nihon Kirisuto Kyōkai (Japan Christian Church, the influential union of Protestant sects founded in 1872). She was also active in Japan's Young Women's Christian Association (YWCA) and in peace movements after World War II as a member of the COMMITTEE OF SEVEN TO APPEAL FOR WORLD PEACE.

Ueno

City in western Mie Prefecture, central Honshū. Ueno developed as a castle town of the Tōdō family in the beginning of the 17th century. A well-known local product is IGA WARE (so called from the old provincial name of the area). The *haiku* poet BASHŌ was born here, and there are several sites associated with him, including his house. The area is also known as the place where the school of martial arts known as Iga Ninjutsu (see NINJUTSU) originated. Pop: 60,829.

Ueno Basin

(Ueno Bonchi). In western Mie Prefecture, central Honshū. Also known as the Iga Basin. It is surrounded by fault scarps and consists of the flood plain of the upper reaches of the river Kizugawa, a tributary of the Yodogawa. The area, a rice-producing region, is famous for sudden changes in temperature and for thunderstorms and thick fog. The major city is Ueno. Length: 30 km (19 mi); width: 15 km (9.3 mi).

Ueno Park

(Ueno Kōen). In Taitō Ward, Tōkyō. The park contains the Tōkyō National Museum, the Tōkyō Metropolitan Art Museum, the National Science Museum, the National Museum of Western Art, the Ueno Zoological Garden, the Tōkyō Metropolitan Festival Hall, the Japan Art Academy, Ueno Library, and the Tōkyō University of Fine Arts and Music. Shinobazu Pond is known for its waterfowl, lotus blossoms, and boating facilities. Kan'eiji, the Tokugawa family temple in the Edo period (1600–1868), is located in the park. Opened to the public in 1873.

Ueno Park, modern architecture in

There are a number of buildings in Ueno Park, Tōkyō, noteworthy for their place in the history of modern Japanese architecture. Although the Japanese quickly adopted Western building methods early in the Meiji period (1868–1912), a return to traditional forms has been a recurrent theme. The rising nationalist sentiment of the 1930s found architectural expression in Eastern-inspired forms; the rules for the design competition for a new Imperial Household Museum (now the Tōkyō National Museum) in Ueno Park had a clause stipulating that the design was to be oriental with Japanese overtones. MAEKAWA KUNIO, who had worked for the French architect Le Corbusier (1887–1965), deliberately ignored this stipulation and submitted instead a modern architectural entry. It was rejected, and the museum was built in 1937, based on a design by Watanabe Hitoshi (1887–1973) that satisfied the rule.

By the time the National Museum of Western Art was built (1959), however, modern architecture had seemingly won, and the design was by Le Corbusier. It was executed by three of his former pupils, SAKAKURA JUNZŌ, Maekawa, and Yoshizaka Takamasa (b 1917).

Across a promenade from this building is Maekawa's Tōkyō Metropolitan Festival Hall. Built in 1961, it is in exposed concrete and precast concrete panels and has distinctive curved eaves that wrap the disparate elements together and create a bold but unified ensemble. It belongs to the "heroic-brutalist" style—so called because simple, unadorned materials, particularly exposed concrete, were preferred—an international phenomenon of the period.

WATANABE Hiroshi

Ueno Riichi (1848–1919)

Newspaperman; managing executive of the newspaper ASAHI SHIMBUN. Born in Kyōto Prefecture, he joined the *Asahi shimbun* in 1880, its second year. The following year he became one of its managers by providing one-third of the newspaper's capital; the other two-thirds were supplied by MURAYAMA RYŌHEI. After 1908, when the *Asahi* was incorporated, Murayama and Ueno served as president in alternate years. While Murayama was an expansionist, Ueno was said to be a steady, practical businessman.

ARIYAMA Teruo

Ueno Zoological Garden

The first and most famous of Japan's ZOOLOGICAL GARDENS. Located in the Ueno district of Tōkyō. Founded in 1882 as part of the national museum at Ueno (now TŌKYŌ NATIONAL MUSEUM). After the Meiji Restoration of 1868 there was widespread recognition of the need for museums and zoological gardens in Japan. TANAKA YOSHIO and others made a study tour of Europe and the United States, and the facilities at Ueno were the result. Since 1924 Ueno Zoo has been managed by the Tōkyō metropolitan government. It houses more species of animal than any other zoological garden in Japan. It serves both as a learning and a recreational facility.

SUZUKI Zenji

Uesugi family

1. Territorial warlords (SHUGO DAIMYŌ) of the Muromachi period (1333–1568) who dominated the Kantō region for 100 years. The family founder, Uesugi Shigefusa, was descended from a cadet branch of the FUJIWARA FAMILY; his granddaughter became the mother of ASHIKAGA TAKAUJI, founder of the Muromachi shogunate. From the time of Uesugi Noriaki (1306–68) the Uesugi served as hereditary shogunal deputies for the Kantō (KANTŌ KANREI). In 1416–17 the Kantō deputy Uesugi Zenshū rebelled against the shogunate (see UESUGI ZENSHŪ, REBELLION OF). Under UESUGI NORIZANE the family consolidated its control of the Kantō, but toward the end of the Sengoku period (1467–1568) all four branches of the family fell from power, victims of the internecine struggles among the territorial lords and of the growing strength of the Later Hōjō family (see HŌJŌ FAMILY) in the region.

2. Late-Sengoku- and Edo-period (1600–1868) daimyō family. The last of the Uesugi Kantō deputies, Uesugi Norimasa (1523–75), fled to the north and took refuge with the warrior Nagao Kagetora (1530–78), on whom he bestowed his family name and official title. Under the name UESUGI KENSHIN, Kagetora became the most powerful daimyō in northern Japan. His adopted son UESUGI KAGEKATSU, however, fought against the future shōgun TOKUGAWA IEYASU in the Battle of SEKIGAHARA (1600). Although their domain was replaced by a much smaller one, the Uesugi endured as hereditary lords of Yonezawa in Dewa Province (now Yamagata and Akita prefectures) until the close of the Edo period. The family's most prominent leader during that time was UESUGI HARUNORI, who carried out many reforms in the domain.

Uesugi Harunori (1751–1822)

Tenth *daimyō* of the Yonezawa domain (now part of Yamagata Prefecture); also known as Uesugi Yōzan. His successful reforms earned him a reputation as one of the model lords *(meikun)* of the Edo period (1600–1868).

The second son of the daimyō of Akizuki (in what is now Miyazaki Prefecture), he was adopted into the Uesugi family and in 1767 became daimyō of Yonezawa. At that time the domain, like others, was in severe financial straits. Harunori issued sumptuary edicts; ordered the development of new industries such as silk, textiles, pottery, and livestock breeding; encouraged land reclamation; established grain reserves; and opened a school, the Kōjōkan, employing the Confucian scholar HOSOI HEISHŪ as its head. Harunori himself set an example, practicing frugality and reducing the number of his consorts. The first set of reforms was marked by its severity; officials who opposed the new measures were imprisoned or executed. As a result of these reforms, during the TEMMEI FAMINE of the 1780s it was said that Yonezawa did not suffer a single death from starvation. The famine did bring reform efforts to a halt, however, and undid much of what had been accomplished. Although Harunori and his coterie were forced to resign from office, he remained in actual power.

During the Kansei era (1789–1800) Harunori launched another series of reforms, closely aided by Nozokido Taika (1735–1803), who had assisted him in the earlier reforms. Of the many domainal reforms carried out during this period (see KANSEI REFORMS), these were considered the most effective.

Uesugi Kagekatsu (1555–1623)

Daimyō of the Azuchi-Momoyama period (1568–1600) and early part of the Edo period (1600–1868). Kagekatsu, the son of Nagao Masakage (d 1564), a provincial baron of Echigo (now Niigata Prefecture), was adopted by UESUGI KENSHIN, the great daimyō of that region. After Kenshin's death, he fought for the succession with another adopted son, Kagetora, driving him to suicide in 1579. Much of Kagekatsu's first years in the lordship was spent in a desperate struggle to check the advance of ODA NOBUNAGA on the southwestern flank of his territories; after Nobunaga's death he allied himself with the new hegemon, TOYOTOMI HIDEYOSHI, and in 1586 was confirmed by him in a vast domain of 550,000 *koku* (see KOKUDAKA) centered on Echigo. Kagekatsu participated in Hideyoshi's ODAWARA CAMPAIGN (1590) and invasion of Korea (1592), was appointed to the position of great elder *(tairō)* in 1597, and thereby rose to a central position in the Toyotomi regime; in 1598 he was transferred to a 1,200,000-*koku* domain at Wakamatsu in Mutsu Province (now the city of Aizu Wakamatsu, Fukushima Prefecture), becoming Japan's fourth greatest daimyō. In the great conflict which led to the Battle of SEKIGAHARA (1600), however, he ranged himself against the future shōgun TOKUGAWA IEYASU, and after Ieyasu's victory was in 1601 transferred to Yonezawa in Dewa Province (now Yamagata and Akita prefectures), his estate diminished to a quarter of its previous size. Service in Ieyasu's Ōsaka Campaign of 1614 was Kagekatsu's last exploit; he died in Yonezawa of disease.

George ELISON

Uesugi Kenshin (1530–1578)

Prominent *daimyō* of the Sengoku period (1467–1568) and the Azuchi-Momoyama period (1568–1600). Uesugi is one of the greatest names in the history of the Muromachi shogunate (1338–1573): successive members of the family held the high position of KANTŌ KANREI, the shogunate's executive officer for the Kantō region, and were military governors *(shugo)* of several provinces in that region as well as of Echigo (now Niigata Prefecture) on the coast of the Sea of Japan. Kenshin himself, however, was not of Uesugi stock but came from the Nagao family, who had since the 1340s served the Uesugi as deputy governors *(shugodai)* of Echigo.

During the Sengoku period, especially after Kenshin's father Nagao Tamekage (d 1537) rebelled against his Uesugi overlords in 1507, this typical *shugodai* family sought to expand its own power by usurping the authority of the *shugo* over the province and subordinating its many petty barons *(kokujin)*. Tamekage, who was in fact if not in name the *daimyō* of Echigo, was succeeded at his death on 4 February 1537 (Tembun 5.12.24) by Kenshin's elder brother Harukage (d 1553). Harukage proved unable to deal with the recalcitrant provincial barons, including rival branches of the Nagao family, and Kenshin assumed the military leadership of his house in 1546. The brothers came into conflict, but peace was restored and the appearance of an orderly succession was maintained by having Harukage adopt Kenshin as his son. On the last day of the year Tembun 17 (28 January 1549), Kenshin was installed in the lordship in Kasugayama Castle in Takada (now Jōetsu City). He was at the time known as Nagao Kagetora.

In 1561 Uesugi Norimasa (1523–75), who had fled to Kagetora's protection three years previously, passed on to him the headship of the Uesugi family's Yamanouchi branch and the post of Kantō *kanrei*; Kagetora now assumed the name Uesugi Masatora, also being addressed as Lord Yamanouchi. In 1562, the shōgun Ashikaga Yoshiteru (1536–65) honored him with a character from his own name, and he was thereupon called Terutora. Kenshin is the name he bore as a Buddhist lay monk *(nyūdō)*; its known use dates from January 1571.

Kenshin's career was marked by conflict with the two great daimyō houses of the Kantō, the TAKEDA FAMILY of Kai Province (now Yamanashi Prefecture) and the Later Hōjō (see HŌJŌ FAMILY) of Odawara. His rivalry with TAKEDA SHINGEN is famous, and their series of encounters at KAWANAKAJIMA in northern Shinano (now Nagano Prefecture) between 1553 and 1564 is a celebrated chapter of Sengoku history. These combats were inconclusive, as were Kenshin's repeated attacks on the Hōjō, the hereditary enemies of the Uesugi. Kenshin first sent troops into the Kantō in 1552, in the vain hope of saving Uesugi Norimasa's foothold in Kōzuke Province (now Gumma Prefecture) from the Hōjō; he mounted yearly expeditions against them from 1560 to 1566, without strategic success; his month-long siege of Odawara Castle in 1561 failed. In 1569 he finally made peace with the Hōjō; this rapprochement, directed against the sometime Hōjō ally Takeda Shingen, lasted until the end of 1571.

Stalemated in the Kantō region, Kenshin turned westward, invading Etchū Province (now Toyama Prefecture) in 1568. By 1573 he had subdued the armed adherents of the Buddhist Jōdo Shin sect (see IKKŌ IKKI) in that province and was attacking their coreligionists in northern Kaga and Noto provinces (parts of what is now Ishikawa Prefecture). This advance intruded into the sphere of interest of the hegemon ODA NOBUNAGA, whose forces entered southern Kaga that same year. The two powers avoided armed conflict until 1576; the next year, both sent major forces into Kaga, with Kenshin maintaining the upper hand. Early in 1578, Kenshin ordered the general mobilization of his vassals, ostensibly for another campaign against the Hōjō in the Kantō. Whether his objective was to march westward and destroy Nobunaga remains a mystery, for Kenshin died in the middle of the preparations on 19 April 1578 (Tenshō 6.3.13). His death brought on a situation reminiscent of that which had followed his father's: his adopted sons UESUGI KAGEKATSU and Kagetora (1553–79) fought for the succession. This second Kagetora, however, committed suicide in 1579 and Kagekatsu bore the fortunes of the house into the Edo period (1600–1868).

■ ——Fuse Hideharu, *Uesugi Kenshin den* (1917). Inoue Toshio, *Kenshin to Shingen*, in *Nihon rekishi shinsho* (Shibundō, 1964). *Dai Nihon komonjo, Iewake 12: Uesugi-ke monjo*, 3 vols (1931–63).

George ELISON

Uesugi Norizane (1411–1466)

Military leader of the Muromachi period (1333–1568); member of the warrior UESUGI FAMILY, which had held the powerful office of KANTŌ KANREI (shogunal deputy for the Kantō region) since 1363. Norizane was appointed to that post in 1419 to assist Ashikaga Mochiuji (1398–1439), the Kamakura *kubō* (governor-general of the Kantō region; see KUBŌ). Mochiuji had on several occasions taken action independent of the Muromachi shogunate, and when ASHIKAGA YOSHINORI became shōgun in 1429, Mochiuji's antagonism toward the shogunate intensified. Norizane tried to mediate between his superior and the shōgun in Kyōto but only incurred the former's distrust. Persecuted by Mochiuji in 1438 (Eikyō 10), Norizane left Kamakura and took refuge in Kōzuke Province (now Gumma Prefecture). Mochiuji sent an army to pursue him, but it was intercepted by shogunal forces, and Mochiuji was captured and eventually forced to commit suicide. (This incident is known as the Eikyō Rebellion.) Norizane returned to Kamakura and briefly resumed his office, but he soon took Buddhist orders and spent the rest of his life as an itinerant monk. Norizane is known also for his patronage, while still in office, of the ASHIKAGA GAKKŌ, a school founded by a member of the Ashikaga family in the 12th century, which he revitalized in 1439 by reforming its course of instruction, commending land, appointing as its director the learned Zen monk Kaigen (d 1469), and enriching the library.

Uesugi Shinkichi (1878–1929)

Scholar of constitutional law; nationalist leader. Born in Fukui Prefecture. On his graduation in 1903 from Tōkyō University, where he had studied under HOZUMI YATSUKA, Uesugi joined its faculty and in 1912 became a full professor. From 1906 to 1909 he studied in Germany under Georg Jellinek (1851–1911) and other scholars. In 1912–13 he argued against MINOBE TATSUKICHI's theory that the emperor was simply an organ of the state (see TENNŌ KIKAN SETSU), contending that the sovereign, as defined in the 1889 CONSTITUTION, was absolute. Thereafter he became active in politics, associating with the conservative YAMAGATA ARITOMO clique and forming

right-wing student organizations such as the Shichiseisha (Seven Lives Society) at Tōkyō University. After Yamagata's death in 1922, Uesugi served as political adviser to the SEIYŪ HONTŌ (True Seiyū Party) and with TAKABATAKE MOTOYUKI formed a national socialist organization, the Keirin Gakumei (Statecraft Study Association), which asserted that the state embodied the highest morality. His works include *Teikoku kempō* (1922, The Imperial Constitution) and *Kempō tokuhon* (1928, A Reader on the Constitution).

NAGAO Ryūichi

Uesugi Yōzan → Uesugi Harunori

Uesugi Zenshū, Rebellion of

(Uesugi Zenshū no Ran). Rebellion led by Uesugi Zenshū (or Uesugi Ujinori) in 1416–17 against Ashikaga Mochiuji (1398–1439), who was then governor-general of the Kantō region (Kamakura *kubō*; see KUBŌ) under the Muromachi shogunate (1338–1573). Zenshū served as shogunal deputy for the Kantō (KANTŌ KANREI), a post held for generations by members of the UESUGI FAMILY; but in 1415 he was forced from office by Mochiuji, his superior, who replaced him with a rival kinsman. Zenshū thereupon enlisted the aid of two other political malcontents—the shōgun Yoshimochi's (1386–1428) younger brother Ashikaga Yoshitsugu and Mochiuji's uncle Ashikaga Mitsutaka—and took up arms late in 1416. He was also able to enlist the support of landowning warriors in the area, and the conflict soon took on the aspect of a rebellion rather than an intrafamily feud. Although Zenshū and his allies succeeded in driving Mochiuji out of Kamakura, their insurrection was suppressed by the shogunate early in 1417, and they all either committed suicide or were killed.

Uetsuka Shūhei (1876–1936)

Leader of the Japanese immigrant community in Brazil. Born in Kumamoto Prefecture, he studied law at Tōkyō University. In 1908 Uetsuka went to Brazil as the agent of a colonization firm which was sponsoring the first group of Japanese emigrants. In the early years of Japanese emigration to Brazil, when settlers were yet to adjust to a foreign culture and language, Uetsuka made a great contribution by advocating independent farming and helping to found numerous Japanese agricultural settlements. He led a modest life, composing HAIKU poetry as a pastime.

SAITŌ Hiroshi

Ugaki Kazushige (1868–1956)

General and army minister, highly influential in army circles in the 1920s and in political circles from the 1920s through World War II. Born in what is now Okayama Prefecture, he entered the newly established Imperial Army Academy in 1887. His graduation in 1900 from the Army Staff College initiated three decades of service in the military elite. He studied military science in Germany for four years before and after the Russo-Japanese War (1904–05). Appointed head of the military section in the Army Ministry in 1911, he strongly advocated the creation of two more army divisions during the TAISHŌ POLITICAL CRISIS. In 1916 he was appointed head of the first section of the Headquarters Staff Office, where he drafted a plan for the SIBERIAN INTERVENTION. After World War I he returned to the Army Staff College as its principal and was made commander of the Tenth Division. In 1923 he was appointed vice-minister of the Army Ministry headed by TANAKA GIICHI.

In 1924 Ugaki entered the KIYOURA KEIGO cabinet as army minister, a post he retained in the succeeding cabinets of KATŌ TAKAAKI and WAKATSUKI REIJIRŌ. He was later army minister in the HAMAGUCHI OSACHI cabinet and thus held the post for a total of about five years. During this time he formed his own personnel network, the "Ugaki faction," which was largely independent of the Satsuma-Chōshū faction (HAMBATSU) that had dominated the Japanese army since the Meiji Restoration. His decision to reduce the number of army divisions from 21 to 17 was acclaimed by the general populace and senior politicians. The appropriations saved by this cut, however, he used to create air and tank forces. Furthermore, demobilized soldiers were assigned to give regular military instruction in middle and upper schools. These measures Ugaki instituted in order to prepare the country for war.

In 1931 Ugaki refused to cooperate in the MARCH INCIDENT, an attempted coup d'etat by young army officers and nationalistic civilians who had intended to make him prime minister in a future military regime. His failure to punish the insurgents, however, cost him the support of the rest of the army and impaired military discipline. He thereupon left the army to become governor-general of Korea, where he strove to develop an industrial base, especially in mining and hydroelectric power, for a Japanese invasion of China.

A leading candidate for the prime ministership since the fall of the Hamaguchi cabinet in 1931, Ugaki was finally nominated to that post upon the resignation of HIROTA KŌKI in January 1937. However, ISHIWARA KANJI and other middle-ranking army officers dedicated to Japan's continental expansion prevented him from appointing an army minister. Having failed to complete a cabinet, he withdrew and in May 1938 became foreign minister in the cabinet of KONOE FUMIMARO. His plans to negotiate peace with the Nationalist government in China were blocked by the Japanese army, and he resigned after only four months. Throughout World War II disgruntled military and political groups, including those who sought to overthrow the ultramilitaristic TŌJŌ HIDEKI cabinet, considered making him prime minister. After the war he was purged and detained by Occupation authorities. Rehabilitated, in 1953 he led all contenders in the national constituency vote for the House of Councillors. A member of the RYOKUFŪKAI, he was prevented by illness from engaging actively in politics during his final years.

■——Inoue Kiyoshi, *Ugaki Kazushige* (1975). Nukada Hiroshi, *Hiroku Ugaki Kazushige* (1973).   *Matsuo Takayoshi*

Uge no hitokoto → Matsudaira Sadanobu

uguisu → bush warbler

Uji

City in southern Kyōto Prefecture, central Honshū, on the river Ujigawa. Mentioned in many literary works since the Heian period (794–1185), it is now a residential suburb of Kyōto. Uji is also known for its fine tea. There is a synthetic textiles industry. Of special interest are the temple BYŌDŌIN and Mampukuji, a 17th-century Zen temple built by the Chinese monk INGEN. Pop: 152,689.

uji

Political groups in the ruling stratum of Japanese society before the Nara period (710–794); often translated as clan or family, but more accurately rendered as lineage group. Unlike *ujizoku*, the exclusively blood-related groups of an earlier age, *uji* included among their members not only lineal and collateral kinsmen but also their workers. An *uji* was typically composed of the *uji no kami*, the head of the prime lineage, *uji-bito* (lineage members), and *kakibe* or BE, consisting of subordinate laborers who worked on the lands that constituted its economic base. The *uji no kami* officiated at the worship of the tutelary god and, as the leader of his group, served the YAMATO COURT. He was given a hereditary title (KABANE) according to his position and duties at the court. See also UJI-KABANE SYSTEM.   *Hirano Kunio*

ujigami

Originally, the tutelary deity of an UJI or "clan." Early Japanese society was composed of many *uji*, the members of which believed themselves to be descended from a common ancestor who was thought to look after their interests and general well-being (see ANCESTOR WORSHIP). This deified ancestor, designated *ujigami*, was worshiped at a shrine under the exclusive control of the *uji*. Thus the Mononobe *uji* venerated the deity Nigihayahi no Mikoto as its ancestor and *ujigami*; the Ōtomo *uji* venerated the deity Amanooshihi no Mikoto as its ancestor; the Nakatomi (later Fujiwara) *uji* venerated the deity Amenokoyane no Mikoto as its ancestor, and so forth. Similarly, the imperial ancestress, Amaterasu Ōmikami, may be regarded as the *ujigami* of the imperial family, although she is never formally described in this fashion.

Occasionally, the *ujigami* was not the direct ancestor of an *uji*, but rather a deity closely connected with it, as is the case with the deities of the Kashima and Katori shrines who are venerated by the Fujiwara at the Kasuga Shrine along with the Fujiwara's divine ancestor Amenokoyane no Mikoto. Likewise, the Minamoto (Genji), a famous warrior *uji*, adopted as its *ujigami* the deity HACHIMAN, who is associated with military prowess.

Only members of the *uji* were entitled to worship the *ujigami*. When the *uji* shrine was of such prominence that the court deemed it politic to present an annual offering, it was customary for the court to choose as its representative a member of the *uji* to make the offering on behalf of the court. The services at the *uji* shrine were led by the nominal head of the *uji*. This privilege was carefully guarded, as is shown in the case of the ISE SHRINE at which, prior to the 11th century, even the crown prince could not make an offering without specific approval of the emperor, who was the head of the imperial family. The festival to honor the *ujigami*, called *ujigami matsuri*, was normally held twice a year, in the second (or fourth) month and in the eleventh month. Members of the *uji* serving in the upper levels of the bureaucracy were automatically granted leave to return to their home province at state expense, so that they could participate in the rites.

As the *uji* system began to decline in the medieval period (13th–16th centuries), the term *ujigami* was used increasingly to refer to the *ubusunagami* (or *chinju no kami*), i.e., the local deity who protects all the inhabitants of a particular region without respect to their individual family lineages. In current usage, *ujigami* denotes this regional tutelary deity rather than an ancestral deity. Supporters in the region of an *ujigami* are called *ujiko* (*ko* meaning children, underlings), and shrines of *ujigami* thus differ from shrines that attract devotees *(sūkeisha)* from beyond local boundaries. In line with this change, priesthood shifted to professional priests (see KANNUSHI) or, where there was a ritual organization (MIYAZA) in the community, to a household head chosen yearly *(tōya)*. The Meiji government attempted in 1871 to use the *ujigami-ujiko* relationship as the basis for a register to replace the Buddhist temple register (TERAUKE) of the Edo period (1600–1868), which was soon superseded by the modern family register system. In some areas of rural Japan today, particularly northern Honshū and southern Kyūshū, *ujigami* is used as a synonym for *yashikigami* ("household deity"), which refers to a specific deity enshrined at a small outdoor shrine *(hokora)* located in the northwest corner of the family plot. The *yashikigami*, which may be INARI, Hachiman, or some other well-known Shintō deity, is believed to afford special protection to a particular household and its land.   *Stanley Weinstein*

Ujigawa

River in Kyōto Prefecture, central Honshū. The name is applied to the middle reaches of the YODOGAWA, that is, the part from the border of Shiga and Kyōto prefectures to where it joins the KIZUGAWA at the town of Ōyamazaki. Numerous gorges are located on the upper reaches, as well as the Ujigawa Rhine and Amagase Dam. It was the site of a number of well-known battles in ancient times. Length: 30 km (19 mi).

uji-kabane system

Also known as the *shisei* system. The predominant mode of organization among the Japanese political elite during the century-and-a-half preceding the TAIKA REFORM of 645. The *uji* was a corporate group of households that were considered as a single extended kinship unit and that shared a common heritable *uji* name. Within this group were one or more lineages bearing an additional hereditary title, the *kabane*, which carried with it eligibility for the chieftainship of the *uji* and the privilege of performing some function in the Yamato ruler's court. The *uji* was, in a very real sense, a kind of asset allowing the chief to play a role in the court and the *kabane* defined his status there. The *uji* was thus as much a projection of the king's power as it was of preexisting social custom. *Kabane*-bearing *uji* chiefs were entrusted with the control of socially designated communities or groups, generally called *be*, whose members were required to render goods or services to the court, and it is quite likely that the institution of *be* was the beginning of the *uji*.

Although the precise origins of the *uji* are disputed, it seems to have first taken form during the 5th century among certain client groups serving the Yamato king's household and then to have spread to include regional chiefs who accepted the king's superior authority and assumed *kabane* titles expressing that submission. By the opening of the 6th century, the higher *kabane* holders had coalesced into a well-integrated court structure capable of surviving dynastic change and possessing a rudimentary fiscal administration. These high nobles were divided into two main groups, called *omi* and *muraji*. Nobles of the *omi* class were descended from regional grandees, and their duties were of a ministerial nature, not limited to any specific service function. Members of the *muraji* class were typically bound to some particular task, connected either with the religious and ritual aspects of sovereignty or the leadership of armed forces. As the *uji-kabane* system diffused through lower orders of court and local aristocracies, however, the distinction between ministerial and service nobles became less clear. By the early 7th century, the use of *kabane* and *uji* names was common even among village headmen, who might claim that their villages were *be*.

The *uji* and *kabane* names were usually combined and used as a hereditary court title, as, say, in the case of the 7th-century official Imbe no Obito Komaro. Here, the *uji* name Imbe, meaning "abstainers' division" is connected by *no*, the possessive particle, to the *kabane, obito* (probably "headman"), and Komaro is simply the individual's personal name. The entire name could also, at times, be expressed in a different sequence with the *kabane* last, as Imbe no Komaro no Obito. The *uji* name Imbe clearly indicates the ritual functions of the bearer, marking him as a service noble. An ordinary member of this *uji* would have no *kabane* and would be referred to by the *uji* name followed by the given name, as in Imbe no Konomi, another 7th-century figure. Typical of the ministerial nobility were the Izumo no Omi line. The *uji* name Izumo refers to an area of western Honshū that was once an autonomous chiefdom. Despite a tradition of former hostility to Yamato, the main line of the Izumo no Omi resided in Yamato as subject nobles, and a presumably related line continued as chiefs of Izumo.

The Structure of the Uji——The Imbe may be considered as fairly typical of the service corporation, probably the oldest form of *uji*. Such groups were sometimes referred to as *tomo*, "followers" of the king. The chiefly line (or lines) resided in Yamato, where they presided over their own village of *uji* members. There were, however, other Imbe villages subject to their authority. Four or five of these, called *tomobe*, were obliged to aid the Imbe chief in the discharge of his obligations. Each one consisted of a few hundred persons, and each had specific duties. The Imbe of Kii, for example, located in a forested area to the southeast of Yamato, were expected to supply timbers for palace construction, which was included among the ritual duties of the Imbe no Obito. Other *tomobe* villages were located in Izumo, over 200 miles to the west, and on the island of Shikoku. These communities provided the ritualists and other assistants needed by the chief at the Yamato king's headquarters. Finally, the chief, with the assistance of his *uji* members, controlled other villages whose inhabitants took no part in the conduct of his priestly office. Called *kakibe*, these agricultural communities, regarded as a kind of property, could be freely exploited by the chief and his kinsmen. Despite the differences of status between the Imbe of Yamato and the *tomobe,* and the *tomobe* and *kakibe,* all bore the name Imbe, signifying that, whatever their actual family ties were, all "belonged to" this corporate group.

Despite considerable variation, all *uji* conformed to this basic pattern, in which a subject chief and his kindred are endowed with the hereditary authority to direct the conduct of a designated group of royal subjects in the monarch's service. The *uji* chief in this way could enjoy a designated share of royal authority while at the same time being so utterly subordinate to the king's power as not to rival it. This was just as true of the ministerial nobles as it was of *tomo* chiefs like the Imbe leader. The Izumo no Omi line of Yamato, for example, seems to have had the responsibility for administering certain rice fields in Yamato that were considered to be royal demesne, while maintaining an extended family in its territorial base in Yamato and retaining ties of kinship and obligation with the local chiefs of Izumo to the west. All *uji* chiefs performed customary services for the ruler or court, and all were required to make the labors of certain of their dependents available. The Ki no Omi were a somewhat similar group, living in Yamato but maintaining ties with *uji* members in the Kii area southeast of Yamato, including the local chiefs there. Very active in the affairs of Yamato's allies in southern Korea, the Ki no Omi had control over a naval force and controlled a number of landing sites along the Inland Sea and the Korean coast. These were organized as *be* and placed under the direction of branch lineages of the Ki no Omi, some of whom also held official rank in the Korean state of PAEKCHE.

It must be pointed out that in the cases of nobles like Ki no Omi or Izumo no Omi, only a small portion of the inhabitants of the home area, such as Kii (or Ki) or Izumo, would be included as *uji* members or *be*. The system affected only certain communities within those large territories at first, although increasing numbers were absorbed into it during the 6th and 7th centuries. The territorial *uji* names of the ministerial nobility contrast sharply with the

functional *uji* names of the service nobles, and the *uji* form of corporate organization seems to have spread from the service nobility to the regional chiefs. There was a definite difference in *kabane* status between the two types. The *omi* type ministerial nobles frequently intermarried with Yamato royalty, but this was almost never true of the *muraji* type service nobles. *Muraji* nobles could, nevertheless, wield great power. The leader or the Ōtomo, or "great following," *uji* vied in proconsular power with the Ki no Omi and others in Korea at the beginning of the 6th century. This *uji* had the obligation of taking charge of a number of *be* that provided military retainers, and its leader Ōtomo no Muraji Kanamura is said to have had the decisive voice in installing a new king, Emperor Keitai, when, at the end of the 5th century (the early 5th century according to some scholars), the older line of monarchs became extinct.

The difference between the service nobles and the *omi* group seems to have been largely a historical one. The *muraji* originated as the king's clients and received their *be* from him, while the *omi* were descended from fellow chiefs who, submitting to the Yamato ruler, dedicated *be* to his service. There was, at any rate, a distinct inner-outer contrast between the two orders of high nobility, which may explain why the *muraji* type nobles monopolized all important functions at enthronement ceremonies, but only the *omi* type, along with certain royal collaterals, could provide the throne with heir-producing consorts. Despite this distinction, nevertheless, all members of the high nobility were equal in the sense that each had a direct share in the exercise of royal power.

There is a good deal of controversy about the origin of the *be* or "divisions," and the time when they were first instituted. It seems certain, however, that the development of the institution was stimulated by Korean examples, particularly that of the state of Paekche, which had arisen in southwestern Korea during the 4th century. There, the rulers had organized twelve divisions of palace functionaries, with titles such as grain division, meat division, storekeeping division, etc, and ten divisions of the government at large under headings like land, taxation, and law. The palace divisions, placed under the hereditary control of noble lines, probably date from the late 5th century, the very time when large numbers of Korean technicians were entering the Yamato king's service. The organization of naturalized Korean groups into *be* for the production of fine fabrics, the keeping of stables, the manufacture of iron tools and the like, and the placing of these under the hereditary supervision of other immigrant lines was almost certainly an imitation of the Paekche pattern. *Tomo* of the Imbe type, nonetheless, probably antedated these developments, at least in some respects, although there is little doubt that they must have affected the form finally assumed by the Imbe *uji*. It is nearly certain, moreover, that the term *be* was introduced to Japan by Korean scribes.

The word *uji* is itself uncertain, both as to origin and meaning. The 8th-century texts on which we largely depend are not consistent in their use of the term. Sometimes it means a patriline in the strict sense, but elsewhere, it clearly indicates a diffuse corporate group of persons related to one another by unspecified kinship ties and, sometimes, common residence. The word *uji* has often been translated into English as clan, with the proviso that the strict patrilineal descent and exogamy characteristic of Chinese clans is not implied. Membership in the corporate *uji*, it should be added, did not depend on the automatic operation of specific kinship rules. In a society where married women might remain in their natal homes and children might be reared by either the mother's or the father's kin, membership in corporate groups could be acquired through the mother as well as the father, a situation reflected in legends centering on conflicts over which parent a child "belongs" to or whose "name" he will assume.

This ambilineality was apparent in the organization of the 6th-century royal house. The founder, King Ohodo (pronounced Ōdo in modern Japanese), Emperor Keitai in later histories, was married to a princess of the former dynasty on his arrival in Yamato, and their child eventually overcame his rivals to be installed as successor. At a later date, historians felt it necessary to trace Ohodo's patriline back five generations to a much earlier Yamato king, but during the 6th century, the maternal link of Ohodo's heir to former kings was probably deemed sufficient grounds for legitimacy. In addition to this, a number of local chiefs from the regions around Lake Biwa, Ohodo's home area, were recognized as royal princes, even though many of them were linked to him only by marriage or maternal kinship.

The *uji* chief *(uji no kami)* most probably owed his position to recognition by his kindred as well as by the court. If his legitimacy were challenged, the Japanese histories suggest, resort might be had to trial by ordeal. According to a once prevailing theory, the *uji no kami's* power derived ultimately from his sacral authority as high priest of the *uji* deities. More recent scholarship, stressing the more overtly political factors of court status and control over *be*, has tended to deny this. The *uji* is no longer thought to be a mere outgrowth of the archaic rural village, where power to propitiate agricultural deities does seem to have been the chief expression of authority. Nevertheless, control over special cult centers and the worship of their deities was certainly an important duty for some *uji* chiefs, at least during the 6th and later centuries. The oldest documented case is that of the Isonokami Shrine, which by the mid-6th century at the latest, became the cult center of the Mononobe *uji*, a military group that rivaled the Ōtomo in power and prestige. The presiding authority at this shrine, however, was not the Mononobe leader himself, but a subchief of different ancestry called Mononobe no Obito, and the shrine seems to have started existence as an arsenal.

The religious role of the *uji* chief at court, if any, could differ from his sacerdotal relationship to his fellow *uji* members. For example, the chief court ritualists of the 6th and 7th centuries, called Nakatomi no Muraji, maintained the worship of certain deities that had little to do with their official functions but seem to have been more related to their establishment of private *be*. The question of *uji* deities is further complicated by the elaborate theogony presented in the 8th century materials. Those writings represent certain lines as originating in "heavenly" gods, and others, as descended from "gods of the land," all of which are interrelated in such a way as to legitimate the status and role of the various *uji* aristocrats. Deities ancestral to the Izumo line, for example, "surrendered the country" they had created to the divine ancestors of the Yamato kings. Such myths, with their emphasis on preordained descent status, resulted in large part as responses to the needs of a developing state. While the ruling stratum of the early 5th century was a loosely organized confederation of war chiefs, that of the middle 6th was a centralized aristocracy whose most eminent members all shared, in one way or another, in the hereditary exercise of royal power. The deities of the 6th century Yamato polity reinforced these privileges, and their legitimating function was of the highest importance. They were as much political symbols as they were expressions of folk religion.

The *uji* was not an unchanging unit, but could fragment into two or more branches, and separate groups could fuse into a larger one. The history of the Wani *uji* illustrates both phenomena. This group, whose home territory was in northeastern Yamato, was evidently among the earliest to associate itself with the kings of the late 4th century and may even have been considered royal at one time. By the end of the 6th century, the Wani had acquired *kakibe*, called Wanibe, in a great number of locations in western Honshū. The appropriation of regional farming communities on such a widespread basis, led, in most cases to the emergence of local hereditary chiefs called Wanibe no Omi. They probably were the descendants of local magnates, who, submitting to Wani control, developed affiliations with the Wani of Yamato. Significantly, no such *kakibe* were established in Izumo, Kyūshū, or northeastern Honshū, probably because those areas were more resistant to Yamato penetration during the 5th century. Early in the 6th, the paramount Wani chiefs in Yamato changed their name to Kasuga no Omi, leading to the establishment of new groups called Kasugabe, mostly in the home area, but in at least one instance, in the distant northeastern province of Mutsu. The adoption of the name Kasuga, after a particular site in the Wani base area, was linked to the establishment of one group of Wani residing there as a major consort family. From the late 5th century to the late 6th, a series of Kasuga ladies figured prominently among the numerous royal wives and dowagers. As the consort role was itself a crucial focus of power sharing, it could become subject to hereditary prerogative, and the dedication of lands and people, as Kasugabe, to the service of these queens undoubtedly stimulated the general change of *uji* name from Wani to Kasuga.

The weakening of the Kasuga by the emergent Soga *uji* during the later 6th century probably encouraged certain Kasuga lines to establish themselves as distinct units, again named after their residential seats, called Kakinomoto no Omi, Ono no Omi, or Awada no Omi. Still another branch, whose kinship ties to Mononobe leaders are unknown, became known as Mononobe no Obito and took charge of the Mononobe *uji* deities and the appurtenant *be* or "god households." Finally it must be noted that claims of common ancestry could, according to the dictates of political advantage, be easily

fabricated with the consent of both parties involved. It is thus somewhat unclear whether supposed branch lines were originally related to the main stem or not. The *uji-kabane* system was one in which kinship and prestige distribution were correlative factors; the former did not take priority over the latter.

During the 6th and early 7th centuries, the system of *uji* and *kabane* spread widely throughout regional aristocracy subject to Yamato control. It also proliferated among the ever increasing corps of craftsmen and palace functionaries attached to the royal court, many of whom were originally organized as *be*. Once surrounded by a following of kinsmen and clients and capable of asserting a hereditary claim, the chiefs of such groups could become *uji* heads. Such *uji*, however, unlike the Kasuga, Ōtomo, and other units of the high nobility, had no share in dynastic authority *per se*. On the contrary, these lesser groups derived their prestige from office holding in the strict sense. Their leaders, in other words, carried out specified duties not as agents or partakers of dynastic power but as agents of the state itself, or in some cases, as official retainers of specific queens, princes, or nobles.

These petty nobles and their *uji*, then, were creatures of an already centralized administration. By the early 6th century the king and his retinue of chiefs had formed a well integrated nuclear court structure with a rudimentary fiscal system. This government, whose development was both influenced and accelerated by extensive contacts with the older Korean kingdoms, embodied a distinction between the inner court, i.e., the king's domestic household, and the outer court or government at large, and each court had its own treasury. Most petty nobles were subject to the impersonal control of official boards, such as the treasuries, rather than to higher paramount chiefs.

During much of the 6th century, the treasuries seem to have been controlled by the dominant Soga *uji* leaders. They were staffed, however, by *kurabe*, "storehouse division (workers)," drawn from three or more settlements of immigrants residing in the Yamato area. The *kurabe* of the main treasury were drawn from the Hata group, led by a chief called Hata no Miyatsuko, and the Yamato no Aya, whose chief was the Yamato no Aya no Atae. Hata and Aya, allegedly Chinese but actually immigrants from Korea, provided a wide range of specialized services to the burgeoning economic administration or the court, including the manufacture of fine textiles. Service in the treasury was a duty imposed on designated households, which were required to produce one skilled warehouse keeper for a few month's work each year. Viewed as a whole, *kurabe* were a *be* without an *uji*, as the treasuries were government bureaus. Later, however, two separate *uji* were organized from Hata and Yamato no Aya components in the main treasury. The "horsekeepers' *be*," *umakaibe*, employed in the government stables, were drawn from a number of specially designated immigrant communities in the Yamato area. Each had its own chief, whose *kabane* was either *obito* or *miyatsuko*. Here again, service was rendered on an alternating basis.

Comparable to this class of government functionaries were certain service groups attached to the inner court, such as, for example, the *amabe*, whose duty it was to supply fish and shellfish for the royal table. These *be*, living in their own villages and subject to their own chiefs, were under the overall control of an *uji* chief in Yamato called Azumi no Muraji who, with certain others, was ultimately responsible for the presentation of cooked food to the king and princes.

Petty court functionaries of this type were called *tomo no miyatsuko*, a term used to distinguish them from the high nobility, whether of the service or regional type. By the early 6th century, after suppressing a number of local rebellions, the Yamato state succeeded in dividing the country into provinces called *kuni* and placing each of these under the authority of a *kuni no miyatsuko*, nearly always selected from the local aristocracy. These, too, with the encouragement of the central power, dedicated *be* and *tomo* to the use of court and nobility, while also securing private *kakibe* for themselves and establishing their own *uji*. It was this process of mutual appropriation that guaranteed the transcendance of the Yamato ruler over regions once commanded by nearly autonomous chiefs. Finally it enabled a variety of petty local village heads and *be* heads to assume *kabane*, as, for example, the numerous Wanibe no Omi mentioned above.

Uji chiefs in the late 6th century could, as a result of these developments, be grouped into four broad categories: *omi*, all regional chiefs of the high nobility; *muraji*, service group chiefs of the high nobility; *tomo no miyatsuko*, petty service chiefs; and *kuni no miya-*

tsuko, petty regional chiefs. This simple hierarchical order, it must be emphasized, was not the product of the *uji-kabane* system itself but of the total political process, in which the *uji* was merely one of several elements. Hierarchical *uji-kabane* structures, as exemplified by the Wani example given above, where local Wanibe no Omi presided over villages of Wanibe while being subject to the Wani no Omi in Yamato, were often older than the *kuni no miyatsuko* system, but under it, they developed more rapidly. It was common for the 6th-century court to command *kuni no miyatsuko* to establish service *be* for this or that purpose, to be directed by local chiefs, but under the overall direction of a specific noble or prince. The appropriation of service, often military, was usually carried out in this way. Other forms of appropriation, however, such as the designation of lands and granaries as official domains *(miyake)* had little to do with *uji* or *kabane,* although the workers in these lands were referred to as *be.* The *uji* system can be seen as one of several facilities used by the central nobility for the centralized control and distribution of economic and political assets. The *uji,* far more flexible than the Chinese patriclan for which it was named, facilitated power sharing by a numerous elite class with minimal reduction or centralized authority and helped that authority to monopolize strategic technical skills, coopt the power of local chiefs, and seize partial control over military and agricultural potential that would have otherwise been unreachable. The steady conversion of local communities into *be* and *tomo* undoubtedly reduced substantial numbers of the population to the Yamato regime, paving the way for the Taika Reform and the subsequent institution of a more bureaucratic mode of rule.

The Kabane —— The word *kabane* meant "bone" in old Japanese and was occasionally indicated by Chinese characters of that meaning. More frequently, however, it was represented by the character for "surname," indicating patrilineal descent. Altaic-speaking peoples of Northeast Asia commonly used the term "bone" to mean patrilineal descent, and in the Korean kingdoms royal and subroyal degrees of lineage status were called "bone rank." The use of the term *kabane* to mean "inherited status" and "inherited status title" was almost certainly the result of cultural borrowing from Korea, especially the kingdom of Paekche, usually a close ally during this period.

The *kabane,* as an element in a heritable name, dates from the late 5th century, in both Japan and Paekche. In both cases it facilitated the division of both high and petty nobility into distinct classes. *Miyatsuko,* for example, was never held by high nobles. Formal *kabane* status did not, however, indicate a precise location in a fixed status hierarchy. Bearers of the title *omi,* for example, did not necessarily rank higher than the *muraji* in the king's court, but their relationship to the ruler was qualitatively different. *Omi* were regarded as subchieftains, and *muraji,* as leaders of *tomo* serving the king.

By the middle of the 6th century, there were four general categories of official in the newly consolidated Yamato state. These were called, in order of formal precedence, *omi, muraji, tomo no miyatsuko,* and *kuni no miyatsuko.* In this usage, the term *omi* merely denoted all members of the high nobility, with the exception of certain royal princes, who were not service nobles, for whom *muraji* was the general term. Thus not all members of *omi* and *muraji* classes used those terms as *kabane. Tomo no miyatsuko,* tomo heads of the "official" type, serving the court rather than the throne directly, could have any one of several *kabane,* including *muraji,* and a similar variety appeared among the *kuni no miyatsuko.* Each of the major *kabane* was nevertheless primarily associated with one of the four classes of official nobility.

Nobles of the *omi* type, as already indicated, did not serve primarily as *tomo* heads and were well represented among the ruler's many consorts. Most members of the class held either *omi* or *kimi* as *kabane. Kimi,* a Japanese word meaning "lord" or "sovereign," was used for royal kindred, chiefly lines residing in areas distant from the power center in Yamato, and two old Yamato-based families called Miwa no Kimi and Kamo no Kimi. The princely lords were all either descendants of King Ohodo or his collateral affiliates, whose genealogy is far from clear. The regional chiefs were mostly frontier lords living in the far northeast (from modern Tōkyō northwards), the coast of the Sea of Japan or the island of Kyūshū, all places almost completely autonomous when King Ohodo came to power. These lords, mostly *kuni no miyatsuko* by the late 6th century, were still imperfectly subjected tributary chiefs. Kamo no Kimi and Miwa no Kimi, despite their Yamato residence, seem also to have been regarded as outsiders. They took charge of propitiating

certain local deities that might otherwise harm the regime and were linked ancestrally, at least by tradition, to an earlier dynasty of rulers.

Of those high nobles with the *omi kabane,* most belonged to one of two Yamato-based groups. The Wani group discussed earlier were concentrated in the northeastern corner of the Yamato Plain, and another *omi* group, including the Heguri no Omi and Soga no Omi, lived to the southwest. Nearly all *omi* resided in or near Yamato, but there were a few exceptions, notably the Izumo no Omi and the Kibi no Omi and their affiliates in what are Shimane and Okayama prefectures. The distinguishing feature of the *omi* group was a close and long-standing hereditary affiliation to the Yamato rulers, and a recently discovered inscription attests the use of *omi* by a subject chief from the northeast who served a late 5th-century Yamato king. The term indicated status as a "minister" of the ruler, as a subordinate sharer of royal power. Perhaps of Korean origin, it seems to have had a basic meaning of "noble."

Most high *tomo* chiefs bore the title *muraji,* but, as in the case of the Imbe no Obito, there were exceptions. There were also a few *muraji,* like the Owari no Muraji, who were territorial lords with no recognizable *tomo* obligations. Most *muraji,* however, did have such obligations, and the most powerful of these had either military functions, like the Ōtomo no Muraji and Mononobe no Muraji, or priestly roles, like the Nakatomi no Muraji and Imbe no Obito. Others were the Yamabe no Muraji, in charge of the forest keepers' *be,* and the Haji (or Hanishi) no Muraji, in charge of the clay workers' *be* and also of certain aspects of royal funerals in which ritual figurines were used. The term *muraji,* of very obscure origin, probably meant "high chief." Its use as a *kabane* title is difficult to date but probably did not begin before the 6th century.

Nobles in the third official class, *tomo no miyatsuko,* commonly used the term *miyatsuko* as a *kabane.* In this way they were held distinct from the *muraji* of the high nobility, most of whom also headed *tomo.* It is, indeed, very likely that the adoption of *muraji* as a *kabane* by the high *tomo* leaders resulted from the need to make this distinction clear. About half of the *tomo* heads with *miyatsuko* as a *kabane* were of Korean origin, as was the system of official *be* they presided over.

Bearers of the *kabane miyatsuko* usually fell into one of three categories. First were certain heads of foreign settlements in the Yamato area, like the Kudara no Atae (Kudara was the Japanese word for Paekche) or the Hata no Miyatsuko already mentioned. Next came the heads of occupational *be,* such as the various horsekeepers' *be* described above, and a great variety of other foreign specialists such as ironworkers, brocade makers, and so on, whose productive activities helped to secure the court's centrality in the system of economic distribution. In addition to these immigrant officials were some native Japanese occupational *be* heads who provided household maintenance services for the king, like the Moitori no Miyatsuko, whose *be,* made up of workers drawn from designated households and serving in rotation, took charge of supplying drinking water and ice to the palace and its officials. The most noteworthy feature of such *be* was not that they were often made of immigrant households but that they were taken from various unrelated settlements to serve the court as impressed workers. Headship of such *be* was typical of *miyatsuko,* as distinguished from *muraji.*

The third category of *miyatsuko* was made up of "namesake" heads. The "namesake" groups, *nashiro* and *koshiro,* so called because they bore the name of a king, prince, or empress, were often organized as military units, headed by either *muraji* or *miyatsuko.* Those headed by *miyatsuko,* however, were named after figures from the very late 5th century or the 6th, and those led by *muraji,* after earlier potentates. The *miyatsuko*-led groups were, furthermore, structurally distinct. They were usually *toneribe,* i.e., groups made up of soldiers contributed from a number of local magistrates' families for a term of service.

Official technicians of Korean origin had a variety of *kabane.* Some immigrants retained the titles they had used in Korea, like the Naniwa no Kishi, a family of medical experts who had been settled in Naniwa (in what is now Ōsaka) at the beginning of the 7th century. Kishi, in this name, was a Korean rank title meaning "lord," the equivalent of Japanese *kimi.* Others had *kabane* that indicated their profession, like *fuhito,* "clerk." The Shirai no Fuhito, for example, were established in the late 6th century to maintain household registers (possibly the first ever kept) on certain official domains, *miyake,* in the Kibi area called Shirai no Miyake. The Shirai no Fuhito, who continued to reside in Yamato, merely visited the *miyake* periodically, initiating a system of taxation from the center that was to be generalized on a nationwide basis a century later.

On the fourth level of Yamato officialdom were the provincial magistrates called *kuni no miyatsuko*. The consolidation of power in the early 6th century by the Yamato court permitted it to divide its realm into about 120 provincial units called *kuni*. The system was far from uniform, and the distinction between *tomo no miyatsuko* and *kuni no miyatsuko* was sometimes blurred, especially in the northeast, where the *kuni* magistrate's principal duty was to provide soldiers for service at court and elsewhere in Japan. Most *kuni no miyatsuko* were probably descended from earlier local chiefs, of whom some regarded the Yamato king as a mere *primus inter pares* and others were completely autonomous. As already stated, the most formidable of these were called either *omi* or *kimi*, depending on the degree of integration into the court structure.

There was, however, a *kabane* that was unique to the *kuni no miyatsuko* and certain other local administrators. This was *atae* (or *atai*), another term of disputed origin perhaps meaning "superior." The earliest recorded use of this title, from the late 5th century, related to Kōchi no Atae, magistrates of Kōchi (or Kawachi), west of Yamato on the Ōsaka Plain. The title was also used by the Yamato no Aya no Atae, chiefs of the immigrant residents of Yamato called Aya from among whom *kurabe* and other official workers were drawn.

Both the Kōchi no Atae and Yamato no Aya no Atae were of continental origin, as was, perhaps, the title *atae*, but most bearers of the *kabane* in the 6th century were native regional chiefs. *Atae* clearly expressed a greater degree of subjection than either *omi* or *kimi*. In the regions to the west of Yamato, *ohoshi* (pronounced *ōshi* in modern Japanese) *no atae*, "overall *atae*," was a common *kabane* that seems to have indicated an amalgamation of previously separate districts. Two examples of this were Aki no Ohoshi no Atae in Aki (now Hiroshima Prefecture) and Tosa no Ohoshi no Atae in Tosa (now Kōchi Prefecture). In contrast to this, the Kusakabe no Atae were the hereditary magistrates of the Izu Peninsula. Direction of this military namesake group was this eastern magistrate's primary duty, at least from the Yamato court's viewpoint. The Ki no Atae, a group whose relationship to the Ki no Omi was, in the Japanese chronicles, based vaguely on maternal kinship, were the magistrates of Kii, where they oversaw the interests of the Ki no Omi as well as those of the court at large. Sometimes, *kuni no miyatsuko* were women.

The *kuni no miyatsuko*'s *uji* members probably never exceeded a few hundred persons, and his relationship to the vast majority of the inhabitants of his district was strictly political and territorial. Most of the people, moreover, had neither *uji* nor *kabane*. But the *kuni no miyatsuko*, by providing court and nobility with a ready avenue for the appropriation of local resources, contributed substantially to the spread of the *uji-kabane* system locally. Demands from the central government and its high nobles required the *kuni* magistrates to convert more and more of the local inhabitants into *be* or *tomo*. This very often prompted him to have his own kin designated as local *be* heads, but the new heads might also be selected from other local notables. Sometimes these newly created local *be* chiefs adopted the *kabane* of their high chief in the capital, as was the case with the numerous Wanibe no Omi. Sometimes, if they were related to the local *kuni no miyatsuko*, they retained his *kabane* while using the name of the *be*, sometimes preceded by the area name, as their *uji* title. When, for example, the Shirai official domains were opened in Kibi, a local line called Shirai no Omi appeared, most probably basing its *omi* title on presumed kinship with the Kibi no Omi group. Shiragabe no Omi in the same region, were local *tomo no miyatsuko* of a "namesake" group established late in the 5th century. A Mononobe no Atae family appeared in Tamba, whose *kuni no miyatsuko* had the title *atae*. The result of this kind of interaction was that local *be* heads could have any of the various *kabane* that once distinguished the high nobility. The appropriation of local resources and the proliferation of *kabane* went hand in hand.

The *kuni no miyatsuko* thus became the chief intermediary between the local *be* heads and the Yamato authorities, and the major *be* heads became important members of his administrative staff. Yet there were still a number of village and community chiefs who remained outside the *uji-kabane* network well into the 7th century. Village heads and other local chiefs could, especially when given some official role, assume *kabane* status. *Obito*, "head," was the most common *kabane* for a village chief; it could be assumed, for example, if the village concerned were designated as part of an offi-

cial domain or *miyake*. *Inaki* (or *inagi*), "rice keeper," was another fairly common hereditary title. Management of granaries and distribution of seed rice (SUIKO) was, in ancient Japan, associated with the propitiation of local deities as a leadership function. *Agatanushi*, "district chief," a title of uncertain origin sometimes equated with *inaki*, became, like *inaki* itself, a *kabane* of local magnates incorporated into the *kuni no miyatsuko*'s administration.

Throughout this hierarchy of high and petty nobles, possession of a *kabane* indicated a claim to some kind of ancestral prerogative. There was no dogmatic insistence on patrilineal inheritance and the fictive nature of many descent affiliations was probably openly recognized. Even surviving genealogies sometimes blandly group lines differing in both *uji* and *kabane* as descended from the same first ancestor.

By the late 7th century, when the *uji-kabane* system was being displaced by a more bureaucratized form of aristocratic rule, most major lines of high and petty nobles had contrived to trace their ancestry to divine beings or legendary Yamato kings. Significantly, most high nobles of the *omi* class then claimed descent from ancient kings, while the highest *muraji* usually traced their ancestry to deities who helped the royal ancestors establish the kingdom. Ancestry, however, was not the only factor. The tracing of descent to legendary figures of the remote past was practiced by Japanese nobles of the late 5th century, as a surviving inscription demonstrates. Yet genealogies and legends could easily be altered. It is fairly clear, for instance, that when northeastern Japan was finally subdued in the 6th century, native aristocrats there revised their ancestral myths so as to include a legendary Yamato conqueror. Maternal lineage was sometimes very important. King Ohodo's maternal forebears were recorded with particular care in his genealogy. The property of the Mononobe no Muraji leader, confiscated after the civil war of 582 by the victorious Soga no Omi Umako, was later deposed on a descendant of Umako by a sister of the defeated chief. The name Mononobe no Muraji was then assumed by the new holder of the benefices. Specific obligations were impressed on the inheritor of *be* and *tomo* bearing the Mononobe stamp, and it appears that succession to them, whether through maternal or paternal inheritance, justified the use of the appropriate *uji* name and *kabane*.

History of the System —— The history of *uji* and *kabane* can be divided into three major periods: the formative period, extending from the early 5th to the early 6th century; the period of highest development, from the early 6th century to the mid-7th; and the period of formalization and decline, which may be considered as continuing until the early 10th century. The system may best be regarded as representing an intermediate stage in the development of the Yamato polity from a loosely organized hegemony of regional chiefdoms to the centralized RITSURYŌ SYSTEM of the 8th century. The *be* and *tomo* which underlay the *uji* were, during the early and middle periods, the principal means by which the Yamato dynasty was able to marshal the resources necessary to move from mere paramountcy to unquestioned sovereignty. Once the court structure had crystalized and regional autonomy was eradicated, hereditary power over *be* and *tomo* became a hindrance to further centralization. Nobles of the central court intent on bureaucratic consolidation on the Chinese model seized control in the Taika coup of 645, and thereafter most *be* and *tomo* were converted into "public subjects" (*kōmin*), the use of *uji* names became nearly universal, and the *uji* itself survived as an extended family group under the chieftainship of a high rankholder in the official bureaucracy.

During the first of the three periods postulated above, the proliferation of *tomo* and *be* in the household organization of the Yamato king resulted in a large and complex administrative structure which relied almost as much on principles of power sharing as on delegation and hierarchy. Besides making available to the throne new and reliable sources of military and agricultural equipment, luxury fabrics, and specialized administrative personnel, this system accommodated large numbers of regional leaders in the Yamato area as they took charge of the various service units and thereby joined the growing corps of subject nobility. At the same time, the office of king was gradually divested of all particularistic associations with the instruments of power, whether religious, military, or economic.

The *uji* was one result of these developments. Superintendence of scattered *tomo* villages of ritualists and foresters, for example, enabled the Imbe leader to acquire command over other villages as virtual fiefs and to distribute economic benefices among his kindred and affines, who by virtue of their dependent relation to him became his *uji* members. The *be* and *tomo*, accordingly, must have antedated the *uji* as an institution. Probably the *tomo* of military retainers, ritualists, and makers of military and ritual articles were among the earliest of these, and it is quite likely that they originally performed their services without the mediation of an *uji* leader. In the late 5th century, certain *be* leaders who were not themselves *uji* chiefs were classed as *tomo* and developed *uji* of their own later.

The early system of *tomo* was rapidly expanded in the late 5th century to include large numbers of foreign craftsmen, who were divided into *be*, or "sections" in imitation of Korean practice and placed under the direction of other literate foreign settlers who, because of their importance as archivists and clerks, had already acquired *tomo* status. These new economic monopolies, coupled with the numerous adherents and wide territories already under control, made the king less reliant on the allied regional chiefs, who could then be permanently subdued. The appropriation of more holdings by the *tomo* chiefs and the consequent growth of the *uji* served to accelerate the growth of royal power in a way that mere clientage could never have done.

At the beginning of the 6th century, the Ōtomo no Muraji, thanks to his command of palace garrisons, was able to confer the throne on a new dynasty. This event, so familiar to students of monarchical regimes, demonstrates not weakness but institutional strength on the part of the Yamato court. The systematization of *kuni no miyatsuko* as local administrators and the consequent diffusion of the *uji* system to areas far from Yamato give additional proof of the basic stability of the court structure.

The use of *kabane* titles, like the division of political jurisdictions into *be*, was adopted from Paekche in the late 5th century. Titles of authority were in use among Japanese long before the 5th century, and some that appear in Chinese descriptions of 3rd-century Japan, such as *hiko, tama,* and *mimi*, recur in the names of real and legendary kings of the Yamato genealogy. As indications of chieftainship, such titles may be regarded as "primitive *kabane*." Fifth-century Japanese royal genealogies, however, show that these titles were not used in combination with *uji* names as true *kabane*. The *kabane* may nonetheless have slightly antedated the *uji*, as it is possible that the earliest *tomo* heads had such titles. *Abiko*, an early title held by administrators of palace lands and probably etymologically linked to *hiko*, "prince," was, in this sense, a primitive *kabane*. *Sukuri* or *suguri*, a Korean term meaning "village head," became the *kabane* of several immigrant *be* chiefs probably before they became *uji* leaders with *be*. The use of distinctive *kabane* titles as portions of hereditary names did not begin in Paekche until the late 5th century, and it is quite improbable that they were employed in Japan in earlier times.

In the period of highest development, the second in the sequence outlined here, the court structure was further refined by distinguishing between the household or palace organization and the so-called "outer court," which was in fact the national government at large. High grandees of the *omi* and *muraji* classes continued to act on both levels, while lesser *kabane* holders like the *miyatsuko*, were confined to either one or the other. This distinction, another adaptation of Paekche institutions, made room for the development of more purely political offices in the national administration at the same time that *be* and *tomo* structures were growing in the *kuni no miyatsuko* territories, and Yamato *uji* developed widely scattered local branches, as illustrated above by the Wani *uji*.

Clerks and treasurers of foreign origin were organized into *tomo* without *uji* heads and without direct links to the royal household. Organized instead into government bureaus, they were directed, it is supposed, by purely political appointees drawn from the high nobility. These grandees had never been utterly restricted by their inherited functions, and, particularly in the conduct of foreign affairs, had long been accustomed to carrying out political policies expressed in terms of royal command. The development of this rudimentary bureaucracy was assiduously promoted by the 6th-century noble Soga no Omi Iname, who also sponsored the official adoption of Buddhism at court.

The coexistence of *tomo* organizations and impersonal office functions is well illustrated by the establishment, already mentioned, of the official domains called Shirai no Miyake. In that case, the founder of the Shirai no Fuhito line, a resident of the capital, received the hereditary duty of periodically inspecting the Shirai lands and keeping the census registers of cultivators up to date. His descendants, besides carrying out that duty, held a number of temporary offices connected with foreign relations.

At this stage, there was a growing inconsistency between the basically egalitarian nature of the *uji* system, in which all the *omi* and *muraji* had a particulate functional share of state power, and the burgeoning activities of the ministerial officials supervising the trea-

sury and the conduct of foreign relations. The higher levels of that bureaucracy demanded hierarchical organization and regularized office holding by full-time civil officials. Appropriation of land and labor by *uji* heads became an obstacle to the marshaling of resources under the command of a theoretically absolute sovereign, an ideal made especially compelling by the reunified Chinese empire of the 7th century. A tentative step in the direction of official hierarchy was made in 604, when a series of twelve court ranks was promulgated, and most court officials were assigned a place in this new system.

The third and final period of formalization and decline began with an intense effort to rationalize the government of the sovereign into a rationalized hierarchy modeled on that of Tang (T'ang) dynasty (618–907) China. The most decisive step in that direction, the Taika coup of 645, succeeded in part because of the willingness of its leaders to exchange particularistic estate rights for magisterial power in a newly consolidated hierarchy with enhanced capacity for fiscal and political control over the subject populace. One of the first proclamations of the reform program inveighed against the enlistment of people into *be* or *tomo* as offenses against the natural family order. Other decrees announced the intention to do away with namesake groups and *kakibe* entirely.

In 664, the capital nobility were divided into three classes, "great *uji*," "small *uji*," and "*tomo no miyatsuko*." *Uji* heads were confirmed in their authority, including the possession of *kakibe*. This concession to vested interest was followed, in 670, by a nationwide census, in which all house-holds with *uji* and *kabane* titles were registered. Thereafter, all claims to *uji* and *kabane* status, unless based on a subsequent decree, could be tested against this record. Normally held every six years, later censuses had imputed *uji* names to nearly all free subjects by the early 8th century, even persons who had never been part of the system at all. In this way every ordinary subject was given a "surname," consisting of an *uji* name and very frequently, a *kabane* title. The surname, including the *kabane*, was thus made automatically heritable by male descent, thereby losing most of its original significance as an elite privilege.

The policy of the central government in the late 7th century was not to obliterate aristocratic prerogative but rather to adjust the claims of distinguished ancestry to the needs of autocractic monarchy. For this purpose, more elaborate schemes of progressively graded ranks were established to replace the twelve levels of rank established in 604. The older system, probably the first systematic attempt to create a uniform hierarchy of official prestige, made no allowances for regular promotion, but merely assigned a place to each noble depending on the prestige he already had. In 664, at the same time the three types of *uji* were officially distinguished, the number of rank grades was increased from 19 to 26.

In 685, rank gradations were again increased, this time to 48. The five years preceding this measure had been devoted to the careful registration of *uji* and *uji* leaders and to the revision of the entire *kabane* system. In 682, persons of uncertain *uji* status were made ineligible for rank or office. From 680 to 684, the *kabane muraji* was awarded to most *tomo* leaders of the central court, thereby wiping out the former distinction between *muraji* and *miyatsuko*. In 684 the most drastic step was taken. An edict of that year announced the complete replacement of all *kabane* by a new series of eight titles, *mahito, asomi* (or *ason*), *sukune, imiki, michinoshi, omi, muraji* and *inaki* (YAKUSA NO KABANE). This plan was never carried through completely, but very soon afterwards, nearly all of the capital nobility received one of the four higher grades. Those still retaining *omi* and *muraji* as *kabane* were thereby relegated to the petty nobility, although later records show that among capital officeholders, *muraji* was more frequent than *omi*.

Mahito was a newly devised *kabane* for princely lines originating from King Ohodo's affines or descendants, whose title was *kimi*, and it was thereafter routinely awarded to persons six patrilineal generations from a former ruler. One *mahito* line, Tajihi no Mahito, produced several high officials, but most dropped quickly into obscurity. ASON, the second in ceremonial dignity, was in fact the highest in real prestige. It was awarded almost immediately to 52 *uji*, mostly of the *omi* class whose original *kabane* had been *omi* or *kimi*. Two *muraji* lines, the very powerful Mononobe and Nakatomi, were also included. *Sukune*, an ancient title of obscure origin, was then given to 50 *uji* of the *muraji* type, and *imiki* was in the next year awarded to 11 *uji*, mostly of Korean origin, descended from *tomo no miyatsuko*.

By this means, the high and petty nobility were clearly distinguished. Eligibility for the higher offices and ranks was very largely limited to this group, plus the sovereign's royal kindred, probably about two or three hundred in number. An edict of 690 shows that the administrative code, or *ryō*, put into force the year before, required that *uji* prestige be a factor in considering officials for promotion in rank. Codes in force after 702 omitted references to high birth as a qualification for high rank but imposed a complex system which virtually guaranteed that the best positions would be filled only by children or grandchildren of high officials, and an ordinance of 728 provided that, with the exception of members of the noblest families, officials of lower fifth rank could not be promoted further without a special decree. The stated purpose of the rule was to assure that distinctions between "noble and base" be reflected in the composition of official society. Specially favored were the princes and about ten *uji* holding *kabane* status of *mahito, ason* or *sukune*. The original purpose of the eight-*kabane* system was, it seems, being abandoned, as the new rule divided the three highest titles into upper and lower categories.

From the late 7th century onwards, the *uji* was defined as a patrilineal descent group, all of whose members had the same *uji* name and *kabane*. The codes specified that *uji* chieftainship had to be confirmed by imperial edict, but existing records from the 8th century preserve only four such awards, all to persons of the fourth rank. Official status of third rank or higher seems in most cases to have been taken as the equivalent of *uji* chieftainship over one's kin.

The new view of the *uji* as purely a kinship group, derived from Chinese conceptions of clan and surname in the late 7th century, led to a classification of lineages by patrilineal descent. The Japanese chronicles, on which work was begun at about the same time as the promulgation of the eight new *kabane*, demonstrate that nearly all the *uji* awarded *ason* claimed descent from legendary emperors of the remote past, while the *sukune* grantees usually asserted that their first ancestors were deities of the legendary period. In a somewhat similar manner, some of the immigrant *uji* claimed to spring from ancient Chinese emperors. The classification of lineages as either imperial (*kōbetsu*), deity (*shimbetsu*), or foreign (*shoban*) was universalized in the 8th century and was employed by the editors of SHINSEN SHŌJIROKU (The Newly Compiled Register of Lineages), a compendious listing of offical families in the capital area and the ancestry claimed by each. This work, begun in the period 758–764, was later "corrected" and finally completed and officially approved in 815. Here, too, the influence of Tang China is apparent, as the editors clearly based their work on early Tang listings of lineages qualified for office. The emphasis in the 8th century had shifted almost totally from hereditary service and control of *be* or *tomo* to office and rank in the stipended bureaucracy.

Official positions in regional administrations below the provincial level were never intensively bureaucratized and were, as a matter of official policy, reserved for the *kuni no miyatsuko* lineages, which were officially registered early in the 8th century. Unlike the posts in the capital, the positions of the country magistrates' offices were held for life and carried certain permanent responsibilities, most important of which was the superintendence of government granaries. Those local administrations seem to have been the monopolies of extended bilateral kindred groups able to resist government efforts to further intensify bureaucratic control. The local chiefs thus preserved some features of the 6th century *uji* system that had disappeared in the capital.

Even among the high aristocrats, however, there were survivals. *Uji* slaves, for example, were dedicated to temples or shrines under the control of the *uji* chief, thereby preserving, in slightly altered form, the institution of *kakibe*. This practice continued through medieval times, as did the institution of *uji no chōja*, a later form of the *uji* chief, without whose recommendation a person of the same "surname" could not receive court rank. The archaic *tomo* and *kabane*, however, had disappeared forever.

——Abe Takehiko, *Uji-kabane* (1966). John W. Hall, *Government and Local Power in Japan: 500–1700* (1966). Hirano Kunio, *Taika zendai shakai soshiki no kenkyū* (1969). Richard J. Miller, *Ancient Japanese Nobility* (1974). Inoue Mitsusada, *Nihon kodai shi no shomondai* (1949). Naoki Kōjirō, *Nihon kodai kokka no kōzō* (1959). Ōta Akira, *Nihon jōdai ni okeru shakai soshiki no kenkyū* (1929). Robert K. Reischauer, *Early Japanese History*, 2 vols (1937). Takeuchi Rizō, *Ritsuryōsei to kizoku seiken*, 2 vols (1957). Tsuda Sōkichi, *Nihon jōdai shi no kenkyū* (1937).   Cornelius J. KILEY

Ujina

District in the southern part of the city of Hiroshima, Hiroshima Prefecture, western Honshū, on Hiroshima Bay. Construction of the port of Ujina, now the port of Hiroshima, was completed in 1889 and it served as a base for the area's development. Ujina flourished as a transportation center for the army during the Sino-Japanese War of 1894–95 and until World War II. Undamaged by the atomic bombing of Hiroshima, the district became a major commercial port after 1945 for Hiroshima and Inland Sea traffic.

Uji shūi monogatari

An anonymous collection of tales. It is similar to KONJAKU MONO-GATARI; indeed nearly half of the 197 stories in *Uji shūi* occur also in the larger *Konjaku*, in some cases with virtually the same wording. Though the standard texts are divided into 15 books, these are not, as in *Konjaku*, classified into groups of stories, nor do the tales have *Konjaku*'s uniformity in their opening and closing formulae. It was once thought that *Uji shūi* was based on *Konjaku*, but the combination of similarities and divergences shows clearly that this cannot be so.

Equally puzzling is the relationship of *Uji shūi* and *Konjaku* with other, less important, collections containing tales with close similarities. The standard view of *Uji shūi* is that it was compiled in its present form, with perhaps some later interpolations, sometime between 1180 and 1220, probably nearer the latter date, and that many of its tales are retellings of items from some text of the now lost *Uji dainagon monogatari*, "Tales of the Major Counselor from Uji," by Minamoto no Takakuni (1004–77), that is referred to in its preface. This *Uji dainagon monogatari* was traditionally identified with, but is now thought to have been simply one of the sources for, *Konjaku*.

The title of *Uji shūi* seems to mean "Gleanings from Uji," but the exact significance of this is not clear, and in any case it has been pointed out that the Chinese character compound with which the word "gleanings" is written was also used (in China) to mean "major counselor."

Of the tale collections made during or just after the Heian period (794–1185), *Uji shūi* and *Konjaku* are the most interesting, containing both secular and Buddhist tales. Whatever the purpose of *Konjaku*, *Uji shūi* must surely have been compiled simply as an interesting assortment of tales, being less stereotyped and repetitious and, despite its Buddhist element, less insistently moralistic. Stylistically, its language is less influenced by Chinese than that of *Konjaku*.

Its stories range from edifying accounts of miracles wrought by Kannon and of rebirth in Amida's paradise, through stories of the supernatural, like that of the coffin that obstinately refused to stay buried and returned to the home of its occupant, and stories of a folktale type, like that of the grateful sparrow or that of the old man whose facial wen is removed by demons (see KOBUTORI JIJII), to humorous and even salty or grotesque incidents about the everyday life of the people, high and low alike. Its characters range from great men and eminent divines to confident tricksters. Thus, like *Konjaku*, it gives us a view of Heian life such as does not appear in any other work of the time. It is an invaluable human document.

——D. E. Mills, *A Collection of Tales from Uji: A Study and Translation of "Uji shūi monogatari"* (1970).   Douglas E. MILLS

ukai → cormorant fishing

ukebumi

(literally, "request document"). A type of formal letter written during the ancient and medieval periods; also known as *sanjō*. It was written either as an acknowledgment of a superior's orders, a pledge to carry them out, or a report on having fulfilled them. The form varied considerably according to the period and the degree of formality required. Those with the word *ukebumi* written under the signature or with the sender's personal monogram (KAŌ) on the reverse side of the paper were considered particularly polite. After the Heian period (794–1185), Japanese of all social classes made use of this form of letter writing. In the Edo period (1600–1868) *ukebumi* also referred to letters of personal guarantee. See also DIPLOMATICS.

Ukita Hideie (1572–1655)

Daimyō of the Azuchi-Momoyama period (1568–1600). At the death of his father, Naoie (1529–82), Hideie succeeded to a large domain centered on Okayama in Bizen Province. Hideie was a favorite of the national unifier TOYOTOMI HIDEYOSHI, who gave him his adopted daughter Gō Hime (1574–1634; the natural daughter of MAEDA TOSHIIE) in marriage. He served in several of Hideyoshi's major campaigns: the conquest of Shikoku in 1585 and of Kyūshū in 1587, the ODAWARA CAMPAIGN in 1590, and the INVASIONS OF KOREA IN 1592 AND 1597. Through Hideyoshi's patronage, Hideie obtained high court ranks, becoming an imperial councillor *(sangi)* in 1587 and provisional middle counselor *(gon chūnagon)* in 1594; the following year he was appointed one of the "Five Great Elders" (Gotairō) of the Toyotomi regime, thereby ascending to the highest ranks of Japan's governing structure. In the climactic Battle of SEKIGAHARA in 1600, Hideie was one of the principals of the coalition opposing the future shōgun TOKUGAWA IEYASU; defeated, he lost his 574,000-*koku* (see KOKUDAKA) domain and fled for his life to Kyūshū, seeking the protection of the SHIMAZU FAMILY of Kagoshima. In 1603, however, the Shimazu delivered Hideie into the hands of the Tokugawa; his life was spared, but in 1606 he was exiled to the island of Hachijōjima in the Pacific Ocean, where he lived out the rest of his years. A cultivated man, Hideie was also known as an amateur of the tea ceremony and of poetry.

George ELISON

Ukita Kazutami (1859–1946)

Political scientist and educator. Born in the Higo domain (now Kumamoto Prefecture), he attended the KUMAMOTO YŌGAKKŌ, where he became a Christian under the influence of Leroy Lansing JANES, and then went to the Dōshisha (later Dōshisha University) in Kyōto. From 1892 to 1894 he studied political science and history at Yale University. Returning to Japan in 1894, he taught at the Dōshisha and in 1897 became a professor at the Tōkyō Semmon Gakkō (now Waseda University), where he taught for over 40 years. Besides contributing to KOZAKI HIROMICHI's influential review *Rikugō zasshi* (Cosmos), Ukita also served for a time as editor-in-chief of *Taiyō* (Sun), the popular magazine published by HAKUBUNKAN. His articles on politics and social criticism from a liberal Christian viewpoint had strong influence on the so-called TAISHŌ DEMOCRACY, notably affecting YOSHINO SAKUZŌ, its leading theorist.

ukiyaku

(literally, "floating tax"). A type of surtax, customarily collected in cash, that was levied during the Edo period (1600–1868); also known as *ukimononari*. *Ukiyaku* constituted a third category of tax, the other two being HONTO MONONARI (fixed taxes collected annually; i.e., the rice tax or NENGU) and KOMONONARI (taxes collected for the use of commonage, forests, rivers, and so forth). Unlike the other taxes, *ukiyaku* could be levied at any time, on any item, and at any rate; hence its name. Examples of *ukiyaku* were *yaku* (assessed on dyers, carpenters, and other craftsmen), *bun'ichi* (a percentage of crops other than rice and the products of cottage industries), UNJŌ (assessed on *sake* brewers, transporters, and so forth), and MYŌGAKIN (assessed on hostelers, pawnbrokers, and so forth). In some regions *ukiyaku* were included in the category of *komononari*, in which case the surtaxes were called *jōmononari*.

Ukiyoburo → Shikitei Samba

ukiyo-e

(literally, "pictures of the floating world"). The work of a school of artists that emerged in the early part of the Edo period (1600–1868) and built up a tremendous popular market among the newly prosperous middle classes. The genre is composed mostly of woodblock prints, but also includes paintings. The subject matter tends to focus on the entertainment centers of its patrons, the brothel districts, and the KABUKI theaters. *Ukiyo-e* formats include albums and book illustrations, single-sheet prints, and greeting cards, and range from inexpensive large editions to elegant and costly, privately commissioned works. *Ukiyo-e* flourished throughout Japan, attaining its most characteristic form of expression in the woodblock prints produced in Edo (now Tōkyō) from about 1680 through the 1850s.

Early Ukiyo-e——The origins of *ukiyo-e* can be traced back to the early years of the 17th century, when peace had only recently been established after years of upheaval and war and the Tokugawa rulers were still in the process of consolidating their power. The full brunt of their repressive policies would not be felt for some years to come. In the cities of Kyōto and Ōsaka, the distinctive milieu from which *ukiyo-e* would emerge was flourishing as early as the Kan'ei era (1624–44). Several well-known genre paintings (see FŪZOKUGA) of the time depict the entertainment districts that had sprung up along the river Kamogawa in Kyōto; these screens depict throngs of plea-

Ukiyo-e——Moronobu

First in a series of 12 prints by Moronobu, most prominent of the early *ukiyo-e* artists, for a *shunga* album completed sometime between 1661 and 1672. Two young lovers are shown embracing behind a screen. *Sumizuri-e;* colors added by hand. *Ōban* size; 30.6 × 36.8 cm. Mid-17th century. Riccar Art Museum, Tōkyō.

sure seekers partying, squabbling, parading their finery, or watching the many sideshow attractions. Such scenes reflect a society intent on the pursuit of pleasure, a pursuit in which every social class—priests, warriors, the highborn, the lowly—seem to take equal part. This was the subject matter for which, somewhat later, *ukiyo-e* artists would be best known and from which, in fact, the term *ukiyo-e* derived (from the last part of the 17th century the boisterous, freewheeling life of the entertainment districts was known as the *ukiyo,* the "floating world").

Though *ukiyo-e* undoubtedly found its most characteristic form of expression in the print medium, certain major figures in the history of *ukiyo-e* (MIYAGAWA CHŌSHUN, for instance) were painters who rarely, if ever, designed prints. In fact, before the second half of the 17th century, the history of *ukiyo-e* can only be traced through the study of *ukiyo-e* painting (called *nikuhitsu ukiyo-e*). The first *ukiyo-e* works of consequence to use woodblock appear around 1660, though the art of woodblock printing had been known and practiced in Japan for centuries before this (see PRINTING, PREMODERN). It would not be until the early 18th century that prints would truly begin to eclipse paintings in importance in *ukiyo-e.* And it was not until around 1745 that a technique for color printing was developed. Until that time, any color used was added by hand.

Sex manuals and courtesan critiques were among the earliest types of printed *ukiyo-e.* The sex manuals seem to have been based to some extent on Chinese prototypes imported into Japan during the early years of the 17th century. Appearing sometimes as books, sometimes as albums, they consisted of a series of highly explicit love scenes involving robed or partially clad couples (rarely are the figures completely naked). Touches of humor are frequent. Unfortunately, very few examples of the earliest of these so-called "spring pictures" (SHUNGA)—those dating from 1660 or shortly after—have survived, and since none of these early *shunga* albums and books are signed, the artists remain unknown. Hishikawa MORONOBU and SUGIMURA JIHEI are the first recorded artists to whom individual works can be assigned with any degree of certainty.

The importance of *shunga,* both as works of art and in the history of *ukiyo-e,* has been generally overlooked; nevertheless, from the late 17th century on, *shunga* became part of the *ukiyo-e* artist's stock in trade. Every *ukiyo-e* artist of consequence tried his hand at the genre at one time or another, and for more than a few it constituted a major portion of their total oeuvre.

The "courtesan critiques" *(yūjo hyōban ki),* essentially picture books with added commentary, appeared at about the same time as the first printed *shunga.* The pictures, though purporting to be portraits of the leading courtesans of the day, were drawn completely from the imagination. Typically, the courtesans are shown at ease, engaged in some playful or essentially trivial pursuit, reading, perhaps, or adjusting their hair. The real interest of such scenes is not in the actions depicted but in the poses and consequent display of draping that result. The same emphasis would be found in innumerable later books, albums, and print series dealing with courtesans; and in this respect, these early "critiques" stood at the start of

Ukiyo-e——Utagawa Kunisada

Detail of a full-color woodblock print *(nishiki-e)* in triptych form by Kunisada, showing the various stages of printmaking. Although women are portrayed in place of the usual male artisans, the work is an accurate depiction of printmaking. *Ōban* size; 36.0 × 25.1 cm (left), 36.0 × 25.2 cm (center), 36.0 × 25.1 cm (right). 1857. Private collection.

a long-lived tradition that would include such masterpieces as TORII KIYONOBU I's *Keisei ehon* (1700), Suzuki Harunobu's *Ehon seirō bijin eawase* (1770), and Kitao Masanobu's *Yoshiwara keisei shin bijin awase jihitsu kagami* (1784). They also almost certainly inspired by analogy the "actor critiques" *(yakusha hyōbanki)* that began to appear a generation or so later.

Related to the "courtesan critiques" are the pictures of beautiful women *(bijin-e)*. Most frequently depicted were the higher-ranking courtesans, especially the *tayū*, popularly known as *keisei*, or "castle breakers," in half-humorous allusion to the devastation wrought by their charms. One of the most enduring images of all of *ukiyo-e* is that of the well-known courtesan, arrayed in all her finery, parading through the YOSHIWARA district of Edo or the Shimabara district of Kyōto, flanked by two young female attendants. She is sometimes shown preceded by an elderly maid who carries a lantern and followed by a manservant who holds an umbrella over her. The hauteur of the leading courtesans, their elegance, and their refinement provided inspiration to successive generations of artists (see GEISHA). The Kaigetsudō masters (see KAIGETSUDŌ SCHOOL) working in the early years of the 18th century rarely turned to any other subject, and many of Utamaro's most memorable prints of the 1790s were also of these stylish beauties.

Woodblock Printing——Albums and books of the kinds described above seem to have antedated independent, single-sheet prints by perhaps as much as 20 years, though there is some question as to precisely when the first single prints appeared. Individual album sheets, found separately, have often been mistaken for (or passed on as) independent prints, and the same thing has been known to happen with book illustrations. A closer look at the craft of woodblock printing as it was actually practiced in the 17th century in Japan will explain how this might occur.

Book pages and prints were produced in essentially the same way: from engraved or carved wooden blocks (actually thin boards, generally of cherry wood), from which impressions were taken by hand without the use of a press. A single side of a block usually accommodated two book plates, which would be used to print the front and back of a single page (one side of a sheet of paper folded over and bound). With the single-sheet format, only rarely was there more than one "plate" per block. Pages of text were carved and printed in the same way as illustrations. This required skill of a very high order on the part of the carver, since the script generally favored was a highly cursive form of *hiragana* (see KANA). Though movable type was not unknown, its use tended to be restricted to relatively obscure works on Chinese or Buddhist subjects, where separate, square-style Chinese characters were used. In general, it can be said that books were reproductions of manuscripts very much in the same way as prints were reproductions of drawings. Print and book publishing were closely allied enterprises, so much so that it was quite common for many of the better-known publishers to be involved in both. A result of this close alliance was the appearance from time to time of works that combined in some way elements that were previously found only in prints or books separately.

The publishers of *ukiyo-e* were, originally at least, primarily book publishers. They were a special breed of book publishers, however, called *jihon toiya*, "wholesalers of *jihon*." (*Jihon* was a term coined to distinguish the popular picture books and novelettes produced in Edo from similar books published elsewhere or more difficult reading, such as scholarly books or classics.) The *jihon toiya* were enterprising businessmen and were quick to keep current with the changeable tastes of their public. The market for illustrated books (*ehon*) grew steadily throughout the Edo period (evidence of the remarkable increase in literacy throughout the country), and the *jihon toiya* catered to this market with considerable success. They brought out books on almost every conceivable subject, but, as one might expect, the more popular works reflected the same interests and preoccupations as the prints and were presumably intended to appeal to the same public. Some of these illustrated stories (SHAREBON) took the Yoshiwara as their locale and the *tsūjin*—the sophisticated man-about-town—as their hero and, in so doing, added further to the mystique of the "floating world." Others, more satirical in character, drew from a greater variety of experience (see KIBYŌSHI).

The publishers were even more enterprising when it came to prints. Here also they played a central role, gauging the market, determining subject matter, commissioning the artists. It was the publishers and not the artists who worked with the engravers and printers and oversaw the actual production of the prints. The artists simply supplied the working drawings or designs. A strict division of labor was involved in producing an *ukiyo-e* print and more often than not the artists were no more than contributors to a collaboration in which the publishers had the final say.

By the late 17th century, the center of the work of *ukiyo-e* had shifted from the Kamigata (Kyōto and Ōsaka areas) to Edo, where it would henceforth remain. There were several reasons for this, one being that Edo had finally become established as the principal urban center of the country. Of even greater importance, however, was the remarkable development of print publishing in Edo. Though books continued to be published in great numbers in the Kamigata, the single-sheet print seems to have become an Edo specialty. So strong was the Edo monopoly, in fact, that Ōsaka publishers did not even attempt to challenge it until the 1790s. The single-sheet print attained its first real popularity during the closing years of the Genroku era (1688–1704). The large format of these first single-sheet prints suggests that they were intended to be mounted on scrolls, as substitutes for paintings; in fact, many of them show evidence (horizontal folds and tears) that they were once so mounted.

The development of the single-sheet print marks a major turning point in the history of *ukiyo-e* with which certain other important changes are also associated. One of these is the new pride and self-assertiveness evinced by many *ukiyo-e* artists. The Kaigetsudō masters, for instance, signed their work with a flourish that would have seemed unthinkable a scant generation earlier.

Edo Ukiyo-e——The Genroku era was decisive in the development of both kabuki and *ukiyo-e*, marking the coming of age, as it were, of both art forms. By the 1690s, most of the conventions that would characterize kabuki for the remainder of its history had already been established and most of the standard roles created. Ichikawa Danjūrō I (see ICHIKAWA DANJŪRŌ), the founder of the famous Ichikawa line of actors, had a major part in this development. He invented a vigorous, bombastic form of acting, involving much posturing and glowering, known as *aragoto* ("rough stuff"). *Aragoto* became immensely popular in Edo—it met with considerably less favor in the Kamigata—and by 1700 had come to be recognized as a specialty of the Edo stage. Meanwhile, portrayals of actors *(yakusha-e)* in popular roles had already become part of the standard subject matter of *ukiyo-e;* it remained, however, for the TORII SCHOOL to successfully meet the challenge of rendering the pyrotechnics of an *aragoto* performance in graphic terms. The resulting prints stand out decisively from anything done previously. Two artists—their exact relationship with one another is unknown, though they clearly belonged to the same school—are associated with this development: Torii Kiyonobu I and TORII KIYOMASU I. The style they perfected, with its vigorous use of line and robust, swollen forms, seemed particularly appropriate for theatrical subject matter, and the Torii school soon acquired a virtual monopoly of commissions in Edo for painted theater posters *(kamban)*, illustrated program notes *(ebanzuke)*, and announcements, a monopoly it was to maintain, though not without challenge, for three or four generations.

From the 1690s on, the relationship between kabuki and *ukiyo-e*

Ukiyo-e——Torii Kiyomasu I

Tan-e print showing the *kabuki* actor Ichikawa Danjūrō as folk hero Soga no Gorō uprooting a bamboo. The figure's bold *aragoto* pose is characteristic of Torii-school works. Red-orange and yellow colors added by hand. *Ōban* size; 54.6 × 32.0 cm. 1697. Tōkyō National Museum.

Ukiyo-e——Kaigetsudō Ando

This example of *ukiyo-e* painting *(nikuhitsu ukiyo-e)* by the founder of the Kaigetsudō school portrays a beautiful woman placing a comb in her hair. The *bijin-e* (pictures of beautiful women) theme is typical of the school. Colors on silk. 110.8 × 48.6 cm. Ca 1700. Idemitsu Art Gallery, Tōkyō.

became even closer. A pose or entrance popularized by a particular actor would be recorded and further popularized by the prints brought out to commemorate his performance. *Ukiyo-e* thus became a kind of visual catalog of kabuki conventions and so helped to establish the kabuki tradition. (A separate theatrical print style arose in Ōsaka; see ŌSAKA SCHOOL).

The finest prints of the Torii school are in the large, *kakemono-e* (hanging scroll picture) format and are either uncolored *(sumizuri-e,* "ink printed pictures") or sparingly painted in red-orange and yellow *(tan-e).* A marked falling off in quality is apparent in work produced after 1718, and the generous *kakemono-e* format was abandoned, developments which may have had their origin in sumptuary edicts.

Contemporary with these early Torii masters was a school of artists that specialized in pictures of courtesans, the Kaigetsudō school. Primarily painters, what few prints they did design (only a handful have survived) were probably intended, even more so than other prints of the time, as inexpensive substitutes for paintings, since they are all in the painting-size *kakemono-e* format and all reproduce, with extraordinary fidelity, mannerisms and stylistic details that clearly have their origin in painting. Courtesans of the Kaigetsudō type, tall, regal, somewhat haughty figures, were immensely popular during the first two decades of the 18th century, and for a while even the Torii artists came under the Kaigetsudō influence. The school had its most lasting impact, however, on painting, and on artists such as Miyagawa Chōshun, Baiōken Eishun (fl 1704–63), and Kawamata Tsuneyuki (1676?–1741?), who never designed prints.

Painting would never again have such influence on the history of *ukiyo-e.* To be sure, all the great print designers were also painters (some, like HOKUSAI, even producing a considerable oeuvre of album sheets, scrolls, and screens), and there continued to be artists who specialized in painting. But from the 1720s on, all the major stylistic changes in *ukiyo-e,* all the real innovations, seemed to occur first in prints.

Another major contemporary of the Torii masters is OKUMURA MASANOBU, some of whose earliest work is very difficult to distinguish from that of the Torii. His career lasted a long time, however, and he was probably more consistently creative over a longer period of time than any *ukiyo-e* artist other than Hokusai. Unlike so many other *ukiyo-e* artists of his time, he did not limit himself to one kind

of subject matter, nor did he even limit himself to the usual *ukiyo-e* subjects. He was especially fond of *mitate-e,* parodies of classical subject matter, a genre that obviously gave freer rein to his imagination than was possible with pictures of actors or courtesans, though he did turn his hand to these as well. He was also a publisher and in that role was associated with several of the major technical innovations that occurred in printing during his lifetime, such as the development of *urushi-e* ("lacquer prints"), which used a coating of transparent glue to give a lacquer-like gloss to the blacks, and *uki-e,* which used Western perspective and must have been regarded as a great novelty when they first appeared around 1740.

Uki-e were apparently very popular from 1740 to about 1745 but then gradually fell out of fashion, though they enjoyed brief periods of vogue subsequently, most notably during the 1770s. The *uki-e* of the 1740s are almost all interior scenes that rely heavily on the geometry of the architecture to control the sense of perspective, and most of them, as a result, seem somewhat mechanical and contrived. Later *uki-e,* especially those of UTAGAWA TOYOHARU, include landscapes as well and are much more sophisticated. By the 19th century, Western perspective had been fully absorbed into the mainstream of *ukiyo-e* and naturalized to the point where it could become a factor in the emergence of landscape prints in the 1820s.

It was just after the first *uki-e* had become popular that the first prints with printed color appeared. From about 1745, when a technique was invented for successfully registering successive blocks, color began to be used. For a long time only two- or occasionally three-color blocks were used, and the resulting prints were called *benizuri-e* ("safflower printed pictures") because of their extensive use of a shade of pink derived from the safflower *(beni).*

In spite of the predominance of Edo *ukiyo-e* artists, one of the most influential figures of the second quarter of the 18th century lived in Kyōto: NISHIKAWA SUKENOBU. Primarily a painter (no single-sheet prints by him are known), his influence was due almost entirely to the extraordinary popularity enjoyed by his illustrated books which were distributed throughout the country by publishers with outlets in both Edo and the Kyōto–Ōsaka area. The books dealt with the most diverse topics, from scenes of everyday life to classical poetry, and this catholic approach to subject matter undoubtedly had an effect on later *ukiyo-e.* Stylistically, Sukenobu's work is characterized by a delicacy that sets it apart decisively from contemporary work in Edo; in this respect, too, it was not without its effect on subsequent *ukiyo-e.*

Ukiyo-e———Nishimura Shigenaga

A moon-viewing party at a teahouse in the Yoshiwara pleasure quarter as portrayed by Nishimura Shigenaga (d 1756). An example of *uki-e*, the term for prints using a Western sense of perspective. Detail of a *sumizuri-e*; colors added by hand. *Ōban* size; 33.2 × 46.5 cm. Mid-18th century. Tōkyō National Museum.

Ukiyo-e———Harunobu

Full-color woodblock print *(nishiki-e)* featuring the tea stall girl Osen (right), a popular beauty of Harunobu's day. Here she is shown examining a fan vendor's wares, which bear the likenesses of *kabuki* actors. *Chūban* size; 27.4 × 19.5 cm. Ca 1769. Tōkyō National Museum.

Full-Color Printing———The year 1764 marks one of the major turning points in the history of *ukiyo-e*, for it is at this time that the work of Suzuki HARUNOBU came into vogue. Little is known of Harunobu's life prior to 1764. It is possible that he studied in Kyōto. Certainly some of his best work shows the influence of Sukenobu, though the few nondescript prints he produced prior to 1764 seem to owe more to TORII KIYOMITSU I. One would be hard pressed to discern in these early prints any of the qualities that were to have such a profound impact on the future course of *ukiyo-e*. But by 1766 almost every *ukiyo-e* artist was working in the style of Harunobu. The change in style was all the more dramatic because it coincided with and was probably inseparable from the change from two-color or three-color prints *(benizuri-e)* to full-color prints *(nishiki-e)*.

Tentative steps toward the introduction of full-color printing had already been made in the years just prior to 1765; certain prints from these years show blue and yellow added to the basic pink and green *benizuri-e* palette, but the added colors barely change the essential look of these prints. When full-color printing appeared in 1765, color was handled in an entirely different way.

The first full-color prints seem to have been commissioned privately for limited distribution, but within a short time many of the same prints appeared in second, larger editions, and the craze for full-color printing began. Their novelty alone must have been a great attraction, but more important, they opened up a whole new world of expressive possibilities. *Benizuri-e*, by contrast, came to seem old-fashioned and limited; and, in fact, only a few *benizuri-e*—all actor prints—were published after 1765.

Among the other innovations that occurred at this time was a change in the standard print size, from the narrow *hosoban* shape, which continued to be used for most actor prints, to the squarer *chūban* format. *Hashira-e* or pillar prints continued to be produced; much of Harunobu's work in this format reveal a racy, somewhat worldly side of his personality.

The stylistic revolution brought about by the development of full-color printing soon affected even such traditional genres as actor portraits. The foremost innovators in this field were KATSUKAWA SHUNSHŌ and IPPITSUSAI BUNCHŌ. Early prints by both men are datable to the later 1760s, and they were already producing characteristic work by the 1770s, when they collaborated in the publication of *Ehon butai ōgi* (Book of Fan Pictures of the Stage). What was new about their actor portraits was the way they took advantage of full-color printing, and the greater range of descriptive means it provided, to bring a new sense of realism to their depictions. For the first time actors were presented as individuals; one actor will be depicted with skinny legs and aquiline features; another with broad shoulders and a barrel chest. "Portraits" of a generation earlier do not show this degree of differentiation, and it is usually only by means of his crest *(mon)* that one is able to determine an actor's identity.

Bunchō's period of greatest activity seems to have been around 1770, and he seems to have produced little or no work after that.

Shunshō, on the other hand, continued to work until only shortly before his death in 1793. Moreover, he attracted a great many pupils, some of whom, such as KATSUKAWA SHUN'EI, Katsukawa Shunchō (fl 1780–95), and—most notably—Hokusai, became artists of note in their own right. Shunshō's importance as an innovator and teacher can hardly be overestimated. The changes he set in motion prepared the groundwork for the work of SHARAKU and all later actor prints.

Mitate-e, Kyōka, Kibyōshi, and Surimono———Although many of Harunobu's prints are imbued with a gentle nostalgia for the past, there was another side to his temperament apparent in some of his prints. The so-called *mitate-e* reflect an irreverent, worldly spirit more typical of *ukiyo-e*. The term *mitate* means to compare or liken, and *mitate-e* are pictures that parody or mimic the subject matter of classical art or literature by translating it into contemporary equivalents. A courtesan about to write a love letter might be likened, for instance, to MURASAKI SHIKIBU composing the TALE OF GENJI; or a pair of figures, one with a broom and the other with a letter, would be compared with the Zen monks KANZAN AND JITTOKU. As obscure as such comparisons might seem, they were probably fairly obvious to the literate Japanese public of the time, which clearly had a taste for such picture puzzles and knew what clues to look for. *Mitate-e* had already been popularized to some extent a generation or so earlier by Kitao Masanobu (1761–1816), and these elaborate parallels, often strained, remained a feature of *ukiyo-e* throughout its history.

From the 1770s on there were close ties between *ukiyo-e* artists and many of the leading poets of KYŌKA, a kind of comic verse that was becoming increasingly popular in the 1760s. This is hardly surprising, given that much of the literary and artistic life of the time centered on the pleasure quarters. If shared interests drew them together, so did collaboration on various publishing projects. Many of the *kyōka* poets also wrote *kibyōshi* and *sharebon*, which were almost always illustrated by *ukiyo-e* artists, and at least one talented individual achieved success both as an author and as an artist: the writer SANTŌ KYŌDEN, who, under the artist-name Kitao Masanobu, designed a number of distinguished prints in the 1780s. The *kyōka* poet Shokusanjin (ŌTA NAMPO) was a collector and acknowledged connoisseur of *ukiyo-e* and is thought to be the author of the first serious book on the subject, *Ukiyo-e ruikō*, which was written in the 1790s.

Ukiyo-e——Torii Kiyonaga

Statuesque beauties enjoy the cool of evening in a full-color woodblock print *(nishiki-e)* by Kiyonaga. The use of Western perspective in rendering background is typical of this artist. One print of a diptych. *Ōban* size; 39.0 × 25.5 cm. Ca 1784. Riccar Art Museum, Tōkyō.

Ukiyo-e——Utamaro

Portrait of the celebrated beauty Tomimoto Toyohina by Utamaro. A full-color woodblock print *(nishiki-e)* in the *ōkubi-e* (close-up) format, it is one of a set of six beauties satirically presented as the Six Poetic Sages (Rokkasen). *Ōban* size; 37.5 × 25.8 cm. Late 18th century. Tōkyō National Museum.

Such relationships help to account for the appearance, from time to time over the next generation or two, of some extraordinarily handsome books combining *kyōka* with illustrations by *ukiyo-e* artists. For some of these, "illustrations" is an inadequate word; poems and pictures are perfectly matched, the one subtly enhancing the other in a way that is possible only through the closest collaboration between the artist and the contributing poets. One such work is Utamaro's deservedly famous *Insect Book (Ehon mushi erami)*, published by Tsutaya Jūzaburō (himself a *kyōka* poet of some note) in 1788.

The pages of the *Insect Book* look remarkably like SURIMONO, which are prints that combine *kyōka* with pictures by *ukiyo-e* artists. Undoubtedly, the success of *kyōka* albums such as the *Insect Book* helped to lay the groundwork for the emergence of the *surimono* as a popular print form in the mid-1790s.

Surimono were commissioned for special occasions and issued in limited editions for use as announcements or invitations or to be presented as gifts; they circulated privately and were not available for purchase in shops. They combined *kyōka* verse with related imagery and so could be enjoyed both as literature and as works of visual art. In the most successful examples, these two elements are exquisitely matched. Much of this elaborate interplay—some of which may well have been obscure to all but a few *cognoscenti*— must inevitably elude modern viewers. The elegance and refinement of the printing makes it clear at once, however, that these are no ordinary works of art. Technically, they are quite extraordinary, making frequent use of *gauffrage* (blind printing) and burnished metallic pigments. Their deliberate artistry and restrained elegance indicates they were made for a highly sophisticated clientele.

Surimono and *kyōka* books were not the only genres in which *ukiyo-e* artists and writers collaborated. Mention has already been made of *kibyōshi*. These rather slight "novelettes" were, in many respects, not unlike comic books. As with comic books, the pictures were every bit as important as the text. The text, consisting of narrative interspersed with snatches of dialog, actually interacts with the pictures, taking up much of the upper third of the illustration and filling many of the empty spaces between figures.

The Golden Age of Ukiyo-e——In the 1780s the tentativeness that characterized the work of a generation earlier disappeared, and there was as yet none of the straining for effect that would be apparent a few years later. It was, on the whole, a period of consolidation rather than innovation, and such changes as did occur evolved easily

and naturally from prior developments in the direction of greater elaboration or amplification. The *chūban* format, which first appeared in the 1760s, was gradually supplanted by the more generous *ōban* format, and the development of *ōban* diptychs and triptychs soon made even more complex compositions possible.

One artist above all others is associated with this period: TORII KIYONAGA. He created, or at any rate perfected, an ideal of feminine beauty—tall, stately figures of unusual dignity and composure—that dominated the 1780s and remained influential until well into the following decade. His compositions, with their deliberate massing of volumes and studied balancing of opposites seemed to delight in playing off verticals against horizontals and are some of the most masterful in the history of *ukiyo-e*. Yet seldom has an artist so clearly displayed the defects of his virtues; the restraint that was such a notable feature of his work could only too easily degenerate into dullness, and occasionally it did. The work of some of his contemporaries, though lacking his assurance, often seems more daring by contrast. Among Kiyonaga's more prominent contemporaries were Kitao Masanobu, Katsukawa Shunchō, and KUBO SHUMMAN. Masanobu, though active as an artist only briefly, actually rivaled Kiyonaga for a time; his *Yoshiwara keisei shin bijin awase jihitsu kagami* (A Mirror Comparing the Handwriting of New and Beautiful Courtesans of the Yoshiwara), printed in 1784, may well antedate similar work by Kiyonaga in the commanding stature of its figures, the sumptuousness of its costumes, and the richness of its settings.

A subtle but distinct change occurred in *ukiyo-e* after 1790. Images acquired a new intensity, artists seemed more willing to take chances, and styles began to succeed one another with greater rapidity. The archetypical artists of the period are UTAMARO and Sharaku, both of whom produced, at their best, images of extraordinary power and daring. Both brought a new sense of realism to their work, a heightened sense of contact with their subject matter, using the device of the *ōkubi-e*, or close-up bust portrait. They were interested in the physical attributes of their subjects to a greater extent than any of their predecessors. Utamaro's women are often sensuous, even sensual, to an extreme, and Sharaku's big-boned female impersonators (ONNAGATA) are only too obviously masculine. Utamaro had a superb sense of design and constantly devised new, daring ways to arrange his figures. He was one of the first to isolate his figures against a brilliant, mica background and did so with a flair that other artists of the time, such as HOSODA EISHI, UTAGAWA

Ukiyo-e ——— Sharaku

Full-color woodblock print *(nishiki-e)* portraying *kabuki* actor Ōtani Oniji II as the rogue Yakko Edobei. One of a set of 28 prints depicting kabuki actors in various roles. Printed on a dark mica ground. *Ōban* size; 38.1 × 25.1 cm. 1794. Tōkyō National Museum.

Ukiyo-e ——— Hokusai

Detail of one print in Hokusai's series *Thirty-Six Views of Mount Fuji.* A full-color woodblock print *(nishiki-e)* in which the mountain is depicted in vermilion red, it is popularly known as *Red Fuji. Ōban* size; 25.5 × 38.0 cm. Before 1831. Tōkyō National Museum.

TOYOKUNI, or Momokawa Chōki seldom managed to equal. However, there was a discernible decline in the quality of his work after 1800.

Another shift occurred shortly after 1800—a discontinuity that, though variously described and interpreted, is unmistakable. It took place on at least two levels: on the basic level of design there was a distinct faltering of inspiration and a radical change, if not an actual decline, in taste; on the technical level, a visible deterioration in the quality of printing began to be seen, and for the first time poor impressions, showing faulty registration and other marks of carelessness, are found in considerable numbers.

The likeliest explanation for the change is that the print-buying public had changed. It had almost certainly grown larger and probably less discriminating. Prints were issued in greater numbers and with greater haste to meet the increased demand. However, the flagging creativity and lack of inventiveness on the part of the artists is harder to account for. The depictions of the tall, elegant "beauties" of the 1770s had by 1810 been replaced by a much shorter type, with hunched shoulders and sharp features. Extreme and sometimes even contorted postures seemed to become increasingly popular and KIMONO patterns became coarser and more strident. Pictures of actors followed suit, displaying a tendency to become even more exaggerated, if not downright grotesque.

Landscape ——— The emergence of the landscape print was a relatively late phenomenon in the history of *ukiyo-e*. The first of Hokusai's *Thirty-Six Views of Mount Fuji* appeared in 1823. Prior to that, landscape, as independent subject matter for *ukiyo-e,* was virtually unknown. Although many of Toyoharu's *uki-e,* some of which were designed as early as the 1770s, could be described as landscapes, *uki-e* are a separate genre and probably appealed only to a fairly select public interested primarily in the curious and exotic. Some of Utamaro's illustrations for *kyōka* books, such as *Ginsekai* (1790, Silver World), might also be described as landscapes; but these, too, were designed for a limited, fairly sophisticated clientele. The *Thirty-Six Views* were aimed at a broader public, and the impact must have been little short of sensational. Within a brief time other artists were following Hokusai's lead, and landscape achieved a degree of popularity that rivaled that of established genres such as portraits of actors and courtesans.

Part of this sudden popularity of landscape was undoubtedly attributable to Hokusai and his extraordinary ability to command attention and attract followers. Hokusai's was a forceful personality, and the imagery of the *Thirty-Six Views* must have been as powerful and arresting to the Japanese public of the 1820s as it is today.

By the 1830s the Japanese print-buying public was much larger than it had been three decades earlier and was apt to include provincial shopkeepers and housewives as well as urban sophisticates and youths with pretensions to being men-about-town. The novel-buying public had similarly expanded, and popular literature was quick to reflect the change. The wit and urbanity that had characterized the *kibyōshi* and *sharebon* of the 1780s had little appeal for a public that preferred coarse humor, pathos, or swashbuckling adventure.

The niceties of Yoshiwara etiquette or the fine points of kabuki acting were hardly matters of great moment to the majority of this new public. Pictures of courtesans and actors continued to be made in great numbers but they tended to be garish or carelessly printed. This could only reflect a more casual, less exacting attitude on the part of the purchasers, who were almost certainly no longer habitués of the pleasure quarters or knowledgeable patrons of the stage. The interests of this new public were wider, if somewhat shallower. Voracious readers, they devoured travel books and were fascinated by tales of the bizarre and unusual. They were hungry for novelty; and when the first landscape prints appeared they responded enthusiastically.

By the 1820s Hokusai had been active as an artist for some 40 years and developed a highly individual, even idiosyncratic, style combining Chinese and Western influences with elements drawn from the native KANŌ SCHOOL, TOSA SCHOOL, and RIMPA styles in addition to *ukiyo-e*. He had shown himself capable of using landscape effectively as a backdrop or setting for figure subjects, as in some of his *surimono* of the late 1790s, for instance, or in illustrated books such as *Tōto shōkei ichiran* (Fine Views of the Eastern Capital at a Glance), which was published in 1800.

Hokusai's protean talents also found expression in painting and drawing. His earliest paintings all seem to be of standard *ukiyo-e* subjects, such as courtesans, and are in a style that clearly derives from Shunshō. His later paintings, however, recognize no limitations of subject matter and show growing stylistic freedom along with increased evidence of Rimpa influence. Hokusai was a prolific draftsman, as the famous 14-volume *Hokusai manga* (which reproduces only a portion of his drawings) proves. He would draw anything, and the world of imagery contained in the *Manga* is overwhelming in its variety. In technique, too, the drawings are surprisingly varied; some are drawn with a dry, precise brush; others use wash; still others employ a mixture of approaches.

Hokusai's only true rival in the field of landscape, Andō HIROSHIGE, was relatively slow to find himself artistically. He had turned to landscape by around 1830, or possibly even a year or two earlier, but it was his great Tōkaidō series of 1834 that first brought him fame and a host of imitators. Hiroshige was concerned, to a much greater extent than Hokusai, with atmosphere, light, and weather. The moonlight in his panoramic triptych *Night View of Kanazawa in*

Musashi Province suffuses the landscape in a way that almost seems to defy the limitations of the woodblock medium, and his rain and snow scenes are deservedly famous. Hiroshige's landscapes seem less exotic, more essentially Japanese, than Hokusai's. To some extent they bear a resemblance to the "one-corner" landscape paintings of the Southern Song (Sung) dynasty (1127–1279). This is not as surprising as it may seem; by Hiroshige's time Southern Song painting traditions had long since been absorbed and "naturalized" by Japanese painters of many different schools. To these Chinese elements, Hiroshige added others derived from the contemporary MARUYAMA–SHIJŌ SCHOOL and Western realism, creating a style uniquely his own.

UTAGAWA KUNIYOSHI stands out among Hiroshige's contemporaries for his energy and vivid imagination as well as his occasional, and generally quite successful, use of Western perspective and chiaroscuro.

By the 1860s *ukiyo-e,* like all traditional schools of Japanese art, had begun to feel the effects of increased contact with the West. *Ukiyo-e* was too much a part of the Edo-period society it mirrored to outlive that society's demise, and the radical transformation of Japan that began in the 1860s marked the beginning of the end of *ukiyo-e.* However, a great many talented artists trained in the *ukiyo-e* tradition continued to work on into the second half of the 19th century. Two of the most outstanding of these, TAISO YOSHITOSHI and KOBAYASHI KIYOCHIKA responded in very different ways to the social and cultural cross-currents of the time. Kiyochika broke decisively with the past to produce work that, though still unmistakably Japanese in feeling, used all the devices of Western pictorial realism to describe the world of his day as he actually saw it. Yoshitoshi preferred traditional subject matter, particularly of the more lurid variety, such as ghost stories and tales of revenge, and used Western techniques only insofar as these served to heighten the macabre or melodramatic effects that especially fascinated him.

◼ —— There are a large number of publications on *ukiyo-e* both in English and in Japanese. For specific citations, see the bibliographies appended to articles on individual artists. A major source in Japanese is: Yoshida Teruji, *Ukiyo-e jiten,* vols 1 and 2 (1965); vol 3 (1971); vols 1–3 (1974).   *Donald* JENKINS

ukiyo-zōshi

(books of the floating world). A generic term for popular fiction written between the 1680s and 1770s in Kyōto and Ōsaka. *Ukiyo,* in the medieval Buddhist context, refers to the "world of sorrows" (*uki* meaning "painful" or "hateful") but here (where *uki* is a homophone meaning "floating") it is used to mean "contemporary," or "amorous." SAIKAKU's *Kōshoku ichidai otoko* (1682, Life of an Amorous Man) is considered the first work in the genre. During Saikaku's time, all popular fiction was referred to as KANA-ZŌSHI; it is not until about 1710 that one finds mention of *ukiyo-zōshi* as a genre. Even then, the term was used only in reference to the amorous fiction earlier known as KŌSHOKUBON. It was only in the Meiji period (1868–1912) that the Edo-period (1600–1868) literature describing the tribulations of this world was called *ukiyo-zōshi.*

The *ukiyo-zōshi* come in a variety of forms and styles, but they generally fall into categories established by Saikaku in his major works. These include the *kōshoku-mono,* or amorous pieces centered around the pleasure quarters as in *Life of an Amorous Man.* The second category, called *chōnin-mono,* deals with the economic life of townsmen as represented in such works as *Nippon eitaigura* (1688; tr *The Japanese Family Storehouse,* 1959). The third category, called *setsuwa-mono,* include tales of the strange and curious gathered from various legends and folklore, as seen in *Saikaku shokokubanashi* (1685, Saikaku's Stories from the Provinces). The fourth and final category, known as *buke-mono,* deals with various aspects of *samurai* life as found in such works as *Buke giri monogatari* (1688, Tales of Samurai Honor).

Following Saikaku's death in 1693, the *ukiyo-zōshi* tradition was carried on in Ōsaka by such writers as NISHIZAWA IPPŪ, MIYAKO NO NISHIKI, and HŌJŌ DANSUI. For the most part, however, these writers were pale imitations of Saikaku and did not develop a new or distinct style.

From around 1700, the center stage for popular literature shifted to Kyōto, where the writer EJIMA KISEKI and the bookseller Hachimonjiya Jishō (d 1745) assumed leadership of the literary circle. Beginning in 1701 with *Keisei irojamisen* (The Courtesan's Sensual Samisen), the team of Kiseki and Jishō produced numerous *ukiyo-zōshi* that served to make the genre more popular and accessible.

Ukiyo-e —— Hiroshige

Detail of the middle sheet of a full-color woodblock print *(nishiki-e)* triptych entitled *Night View of Kanazawa in Musashi Province.* This moonlit panorama is typical of Hiroshige's concern with atmosphere and light. *Ōban* size; 37.6 × 25.4 cm. Ca 1835–36. Tōkyō National Museum.

The books that Kiseki wrote and Jishō published were known as HACHIMONJIYA-BON.

The *hachimonjiya-bon* enjoyed great popularity for a number of years. However, since Jishō signed his name to all of Kiseki's works and claimed credit for them, Kiseki left the Hachimonjiya and established his own publishing house, the Ejimaya, in 1711. Seven years later, the two reconciled and began their partnership anew.

In the meantime, Kiseki had developed a kind of *ukiyo-zōshi* known as the *katagi-mono,* or sketches of various types of townsmen. These *katagi-mono,* represented by such works as *Seken musuko katagi* (1715, Characters of Worldly Young Men), were immediately successful and propelled Kiseki to the forefront of popular literature, which had suffered since Saikaku's death. However, in the 1720s, owing to strict government censorship of frivolous or licentious literature, Kiseki turned primarily to writing texts for JŌRURI puppet plays and KABUKI. In 1766, after the deaths of both Kiseki and Jishō, the Hachimonjiya publishing house was sold, and *ukiyo-zōshi* ceased to be produced.

ultranationalism

(chō kokka shugi). In modern Japanese history the term ultranationalism refers to an extreme form of patriotism encompassing such varied movements as PAN-ASIANISM, Japanism (NIHON SHUGI), agrarian nationalism (NŌHON SHUGI), and restorationism (see "SHŌWA RESTORATION") that purportedly served as the chief ideological prop of Japanese military expansion overseas and political regimentation at home during the years 1931–45.

Ultranationalism is a useful word for calling attention to the rhetorical inflation of Japan's political ambitions and sense of destiny in the hectic decade of the 1930s. In content, however, ultranationalism differs little from the nationalism (kokka shugi) that spawned it. There is no clear line dividing the substance of Japanese nationalism from that of ultranationalism. Since the course of events at home and abroad grew more intense but did not shift in any basic way, it is hard to see why the term ultranationalism came to be used at all. It appears to be an epithet employed mostly after World War II to defame the propagandists of Japan's war hysteria, Japanese incursions into Asia, and the trend toward monolithic domestic politics. Used in this way, it remains a viable standby in the vocabulary of modern Japanese history, but it would be wrong to think that it marks a sharp turn in Japanese ideology.

Ukiyo-e ——— Utagawa Kuniyoshi

Full-color woodblock print *(nishiki-e)* in triptych form depicting legendary swordsman Miyamoto Musashi subduing a whale. The heroic theme and triptych format are typical of Kuniyoshi's work. *Ōban* size; 37.0 × 25.4 cm (left), 37.0 × 25.0 cm (center), 37.0 × 25.4 cm (right). 1849–50. Private collection.

Genesis of Ultranationalism ——— Japanese nationalism dates from an early stage in the country's recorded history. No one doubts the permeation of 20th-century Japanese public mores by nationalist ideas through the school system and the prevailing work ethic, buttressed by the rise of mass culture and modern communications media. The signs of nationalism were ubiquitous throughout Japan after the MEIJI RESTORATION of 1868, but in the 1930s the rhetoric of nationalism became so inflamed that ultranationalism was born.

It arose from an intensification of Japanese involvement abroad and the concurrent domestic social turmoil after World War I. At a time when various social groups sought new and more strident ways to promote their goals and the nation became more embroiled in military confrontations on the Asian continent, ultranationalism signified the upsurge in passion and the public's willingness to resort to drastic measures, such as all-out war with China if necessary, to achieve Japanese purposes. This whole situation, in turn, derived from Japan's new power and influence—the result of the ravages of World War I among European nations.

Until 1915 Japanese strategic objectives abroad centered on constructing a stable and defensible sphere that would give the nation a foothold on the continent. To mobilize a domestic economic base for this purpose, the government facilitated capital formation and an increase in industrial jobs. Agriculture fueled industrial development, and high growth rates across the economic spectrum characterized most of the Meiji period (1868–1912). Both public and private opinion makers supported the status quo, and the government overcame short-term shocks such as the 1895 TRIPARTITE INTERVENTION by further developing Japan's new empire.

World War I changed the situation in three ways. The "great powers" withdrew from Asia to fight in Europe, leaving a vacuum, especially in a fragmented China. Wartime exhaustion precluded the European powers' return to their former high levels of activity. Finally, the Russian Revolution produced the Soviet Union, with its radical ideological challenge to the rationale of the established world order.

Japan reacted throughout the 1920s more by expediency than by plan. Determined to secure a larger empire suitable to its new great-power status, the government explored novel and indirect means of exercising influence in China, particularly in Manchuria with its fertile south and vast industrial raw-material base. Desirous of restoring international stability, the government also participated in negotiations to limit the build-up of armaments. Such negotiations required give-and-take, and the prospect of slowing Japan's ascent to world power alarmed patriots who opposed "internationalism," full self-determination for former colonial peoples, and other imagined threats to Japan's well-being.

The dislocations of World War I also led to troubles in the Japanese economy. Serious and widespread disorders, ranging from agricultural impoverishment and riots to industrial shutdowns, marked the 1920s. A new host of critics appeared, demanding relief and the restoration of unbridled economic growth.

These objective conditions gave rise to vehement demonstrations of dissatisfaction with government policies. Military officers joined civilians in secret societies that often appealed to the public in the 1930s, though not achieving mass support, in attempts to compel Japan into adopting a more aggressive posture abroad and carrying out a reorganization of priorities at home. Terror and the threat of revolt entered their ideological arsenal and methods of operation. These groups typically cited communism and socialism as a collective *bête noire*, but their real enemies were the established political parties and the civil and military bureaucracies that set government policies. Young military officers planned coups d'etat by the dozen and at least on three occasions tried to carry them out (see OCTOBER INCIDENT; MAY 15TH INCIDENT; and FEBRUARY 26TH INCIDENT). These attempts demonstrated that existing institutions, rather than the minute bands of intellectuals who propounded leftist doctrines, were their target.

Contradictions in Interpretations of Ultranationalism

Commentators on ultranationalism are commonly prey to weaknesses in two principal areas of definition: temporal and "occupational." The first refers to the problem of establishing when nationalism shaded into ultranationalism. Even if we concede that ultranationalism represented an outgrowth of the main nationalist impulse, it is difficult to pin down the origins of the extreme or transcendent version of Japanese nationalism.

Patriotic and chauvinistic societies in modern Japan date back to the GEN'YŌSHA (1881) and AMUR RIVER SOCIETY (1901). Their members included would-be rebels against Meiji-government policies in both Asia and Japan. Though the members tended to be men of means, they were not above advocating terrorist tactics. In the 20th century we encounter "right-wing" terrorism long before the 1930s. For example, in 1921, Asahi Heigo (1890–1921) assassinated the financial magnate YASUDA ZENJIRŌ on behalf of a radical platform of antiestablishment goals. KITA IKKI and ŌKAWA SHŪMEI joined forces in 1919 to form the YŪZONSHA, a society dedicated to the radical reconstruction of Japanese foreign policy and internal social structure. They consorted with like-minded military officers from early in the 1920s, and these early contacts prefigured the notorious uprising of February 1936, when army officers seized central Tōkyō for half a week. Such problems reveal a flaw in the chronology of nationalism.

"Occupational" definition refers to the problem of establishing what kinds of actors took part in ultranationalist, as opposed to nationalist, activities. The primary predicament in this area involves a distinction between public and private action. When ultranationalism is discussed, a confusion of government and nongovernment actors usually ensues. There is an assumption that the Japanese government and a variety of nongovernmental organizations and individuals shared a common commitment to ultranationalist goals. Nothing could muddy the issue more.

If ultranationalism as a term has a valid meaning, it turns upon the ideas and actions of those out of office who sought to reorient the power structure, Japan's domestic and international policies and its internal social relations, or some combination of these elements. The ultranationalists chafed at the status quo. Rural agitators such as GONDŌ SEIKYŌ and TACHIBANA KŌZABURŌ represented the interests of economically depressed farmers, whereas more cosmopolitan plotters like Ōkawa Shūmei and Kita Ikki sought a reshuffling of people in authority or institutional reorganizations. But along with the rebels of the February 1936 uprising, they all shared a conviction that under its current leadership Japan was headed for disaster.

Prominent figures in government rarely sympathized with the ultranationalists. There were exceptions, such as the enigmatic General ARAKI SADAO, but most high civilian and military leaders steered away from ultranationalist jingoism. On the question of reorganization, perhaps General ISHIWARA KANJI was favorably disposed, but he too was a solid member of the establishment. Ultranationalism in the sense of a sudden and sharp deviation from prevalent ideas may have characterized some movements outside of government but never those at high government echelons.

A secondary predicament in this area weighs on the social definition of ultranationalism. The popular base of nationalist activity in the 1930s allegedly shifted from the upper classes to downtrodden farmers and workers as well as the petty bourgeoisie—teachers, small businessmen, resident landlords, and the like. But no basis exists for doubting that such people had been supporting nationalism since the Meiji period. Their numbers increased as Japanese society became more complex and urbanized, but there is no evidence that they shifted ground or that any powerful movement came to them for support.

Nationalism and Ultranationalism —— These temporal and occupational qualifications compromise the utility of dividing ultranationalism from nationalism in the modern Japanese experience. The characteristics attributed to ultranationalism blend into those associated with the numerous manifestations of evolving Japanese nationalism. The injection of increasingly radical methods into the repertoire of a few firebrands scarcely marks a fundamental change in either nationalism's ideological basis or its hold on the vast majority of the populace. The basis and appeal of nationalism in a world made up of competing nation-states continued largely unchanged from the Meiji period into the 1930s and the heated atmosphere of wartime Japan.

📖 ——Masao Maruyama, *Thought and Behaviour in Modern Japanese Politics* (1963). Ivan Morris, *Nationalism and the Right Wing in Japan* (1960). Richard J. Smethurst, *A Social Basis for Prewar Japanese Militarism* (1974). Richard Storry, *The Double Patriots* (1957). George M. Wilson, *Radical Nationalist in Japan: Kita Ikki* (1969). George M. Wilson, "A New Look at the Problem of 'Japanese Fascism,'" *Comparative Studies in Society and History* 10.4 (July 1968). Hashikawa Bunzō, ed, *Chōkokka shugi*, in *Gendai Nihon shisō taikei*, vol 31 (Chikuma Shobō, 1964). Hata Ikuhiko, *Gun fashizumu undō shi* (1962). Takeuchi Yoshimi, ed, *Ajia shugi*, in *Gendai Nihon shisō taikei*, vol 9 (Chikuma Shobō, 1963). Tsukui Tatsuo, *Uyoku* (1952).　　　　　　　　　*George M.* WILSON

Umarete wa mita keredo

(Foreign release title: *I Was Born, but . . .*). A 1932 silent film directed by OZU YASUJIRŌ about two young boys learning to cope with the dictates of society. The boys move with their parents to a neighborhood in Tōkyō near the home of their father's employer. The two must adjust to the neighborhood, their new school, and new playmates. As outsiders they are teased at first by the other boys but gradually win acceptance through their own strength and guile. And though they are anxious to please their father, they cannot understand why he insists that they be nice to the company president's son, also a member of the neighborhood gang, who is not half as smart or tough as they are. They cannot fathom the relationship between employer and employee, a problem that for a time turns them against their father. Gradually they come to understand the order of things and at the end they have accepted the adult code of behavior that demands greater honor for position than for ability, thereby marking their loss of innocence.

In this early film Ozu had not yet settled into the understated refinement and simplicity of shot composition that characterizes the main body of his work. Here he moves his camera frequently, tracking with the boys at play, or down a row of desks at the father's office.

Umarete wa mita keredo is considered the first work of social criticism in Japanese cinema. One of its central themes is the tension between work and family life, a theme that Ozu returned to in many of his films. Yet at heart, the film is a comedy. Many of its comic scenes are richly reminiscent of the American *Our Gang* comedies, with the feats of prowess and ritual observances that young boys put each other through. This major motif, though bearing serious undertones, gives the film a prevailing sense of boyish mischief. Ozu made *Ohayō* (1959, Good Morning) as an updated variation on this film.　　　　　　　　　*David* OWENS

umbrellas, traditional

(kasa). Umbrellas in Japan are divided into two types: *higasa* (sun umbrellas) and *amagasa* (rain umbrellas). Silk umbrellas were first introduced to Japan during the mid-6th century from the Korean kingdom of Paekche; they were used exclusively by the aristocratic class as sunshades. It was not until the Edo period (1600–1868) that common people started to use umbrellas. In the Genroku era (1688–1704) a variety of rain umbrellas made of oiled paper stretched over a bamboo rib frame became the popular fashion. These included the *janomegasa* ("snake-eye umbrella"), which were black, red, or navy in color with a center ring of white, resembling the eye of a snake; the *bangasa*, with wide ribs; and the *momijigasa*, which had rattan handles. Paper parasols also became popular, particularly the *ehigasa* painted with pictures of birds and flowers. Today these traditional paper umbrellas are rather expensive and have been largely replaced by Western-style rain umbrellas and cloth parasols. See also RAINGEAR, TRADITIONAL.　　*ENDŌ Takeshi*

ume —→ plum, Japanese

umeboshi

A food item made by salt-curing the fruit of the *ume* (Japanese apricot; see PLUM, JAPANESE) and sun-drying it for several days together with beefsteak plant *(shiso)* leaves to add red color. The Japanese have valued it from ancient times and have attached importance to its medicinal properties. The acid taste of *umeboshi* aids digestion; it is thought to stimulate appetite and to be effective against fatigue. Because of its supposedly germicidal properties, it is included with rice in box lunches and in *nigirimeshi* (rice balls) to prevent spoiling.　　　　　　　　　*TSUJI Shizuo*

Umeda Umpin (1815–1859)

Imperial-loyalist *samurai* of the late part of the Edo period (1600–1868). Born in the domain of Obama (now part of Fukui Prefecture); real name, Umeda Genjirō. He studied Confucianism in Edo (now Tōkyō) from 1829 to 1840, and after traveling to Kyūshū, where he met YOKOI SHŌNAN, he opened a school in Kyōto. There, he became acquainted with YANAGAWA SEIGAN and Rai Mikisaburō (1825–59), the son of RAI SAN'YŌ, and joined them in the SONNŌ JŌI movement to overthrow the Tokugawa shogunate and restore imperial rule. In 1852 he was stripped of samurai status for criticizing domainal policy and presuming to speak out on national defense. He then roamed around the Kyōto–Ōsaka area enlisting sympathizers for the proimperial movement and negotiating between the loyalist Chōshū domain (now Yamaguchi Prefecture) and Kyōto–Ōsaka merchants. He was arrested in the 1858 ANSEI PURGE and died the following year in prison.

Umehara Ryūzaburō (1888–　　)

Western-style painter. Born in Kyōto, he studied painting under ASAI CHŪ at the Kansai Art School. From 1908 to 1913 he lived in Europe, studying in Paris at the Académie Julian and then with Renoir. He was also influenced by the work of Matisse, Gauguin, and the German Expressionists. In Tōkyō he helped to found two artist groups—Nikakai in 1914 and Shun'yōkai in 1922—and joined the Western-art section of another artist group, Kokuga Sōsaku Kyōkai, in 1926. He returned to France in 1920–21, visited China in 1929 and Taiwan in 1933–35, and then stayed in Beiping (Peiping; now Beijing or Peking) from 1939 to 1943. From 1944 to 1952 he was a professor at the Tōkyō Bijutsu Gakkō (now Tōkyō University of Fine Arts and Music). His paintings range from nudes and still lifes to Beijing street scenes and palaces. His use of color and sense of design have made him one of the foremost Western-style artists of his day. A member of the JAPAN ART ACADEMY (Nihon Geijutsuin), in 1952 he received the Order of Culture.

Umehara Sueji (1893–1983)

Archaeologist. Born in Ōsaka. After graduating from Dōshisha Middle School in Kyōto, he found employment as an assistant at the newly established archaeological exhibit hall at Kyōto University. In 1921 he served on the committee for the investigation of Korean sites. After an extended period of study in Europe between 1925 and 1929, he returned to become a member of the Kyōto Institute of the Academy of Oriental Culture (now Kyōto University Research Institute for Humanistic Studies) and a lecturer at Kyōto University, attaining full professorship in 1939.

Umehara's first interest was the mounded tombs (KOFUN) of Japan and Korea. Later he turned specifically to the BRONZE MIRRORS found in the tombs and then to the bronze culture of the Asian continent. His hypothesis concerning the distribution of mirrors among Kofun-period (ca 300–710) rulers (see ARCHAEOLOGY) is important to the understanding of early political development. Umehara's publications include *Kodai hoppōkei bumbutsu no kenkyū* (1938, Studies on Ancient Northern-Style Civilization), *Shina kōkogaku ronkō* (1938, Thoughts on Chinese Archaeology), *Nihon kōkogaku ronkō* (1940, Thoughts on Japanese Archaeology), and *Chōsen kodai no bunka* (1946, Ancient Korean Culture).

Gina Lee BARNES

Ume Kenjirō (1860–1910)

Legal scholar. Born in Shimane Prefecture. He graduated from the law school attached to the Justice Ministry in 1884 and became a professor at Tōkyō University in the following year. He then studied at the University of Lyons, and after receiving a doctoral degree, studied for a year at the University of Berlin before returning to Japan in 1890. He taught civil and commercial law at Tōkyō University until his death. In the so-called CIVIL CODE CONTROVERSY, he strongly urged the immediate enforcement of the civil code drawn up in 1890 by Gustave BOISSONADE DE FONTARABIE and others; when it was decided in 1892 to delay its enforcement, he appealed to Prime Minister ITŌ HIROBUMI, to establish a committee to prepare a new draft. In 1893 he was appointed to the new body, together with HOZUMI NOBUSHIGE and TOMII MASAAKI; the CIVIL CODE was put into effect in 1898 and, although extensively revised after World War II, remains in use to the present day. Ume was also responsible, together with Tanabe Kaoru (1860–1936) and OKANO KEIJIRŌ for the 1899 COMMERCIAL CODE; this too, although radically revised from time to time, remains in force. Apart from his teaching duties, he was also director of the Cabinet Legislative Bureau (Hōseikyoku) and from 1906 legal adviser to the Korean government. His principal work, *Mimpō yōgi* (5 vols; 1896–1900, Essentials of Civil Law), is still used as a reference book.

KATŌ *Ichirō*

umemodoki

Ilex serrata var. *sieboldii*. Deciduous shrub of the family Aquifoliaceae; found wild in wet areas in the mountains of Honshū, Shikoku, and Kyūshū. It is also cultivated as a decorative plant because of the beauty of its fruit. It grows to a height of several meters and hairs grow on the young branches. The leaves are alternate, emerging either as ovals or as egg-shaped lanceolates, and are serrated on the edges. The shrub is dioecious. In June light purple flowers appear and bloom in a cluster near the leaf axil, followed by crimson ball-shaped berries. This fruit remains on the branches in late fall and early winter after the leaves have fallen off.

Among variant species there are the *kimino umemodoki*, with yellow fruit, the *shiro umemodoki*, with white fruit and flowers, and the *koshō umemodoki*, with its relatively small leaves and berries. These varieties are grown mainly for use in BONSAI. Wild varieties of the ilex include the *inu umemodoki* (*Ilex serrata* var. *argutidens*) and the large-leaved *ōba umemodoki* (*Ilex nemotoi*). The umemodoki receives its name from its leaves, which resemble those of the *ume* or Japanese apricot.

MATSUDA *Osamu*

Umezaki Haruo (1915–1965)

Novelist. Born in Fukuoka Prefecture. Graduate of Tōkyō University. He was drafted into the navy toward the end of World War II

and later gained recognition as one of the so-called first wave of postwar Japanese writers. His story "Sakurajima" (1946), based on his war experiences, deals with the fear of death and the sense of emptiness of human existence faced by a young intellectual soldier. These themes pervade his early works. He later turned to writing light satire, describing the lives of the common people in such stories as "Boroya no shunjū" (1954), which was awarded the 32nd Naoki Prize. His novels include the semiautobiographical *Kuruidako* (1963) and *Genka* (1965).

Umezawa Hamao (1914–   )

Microbiologist. Born in Fukui Prefecture; graduate of Tōkyō University. Umezawa is known as one of the world's foremost experts on the development of such antibiotics as sarcomycin, kanamycin, and bleomycin. He taught at Tōkyō University and served as director of its Institute of Microbial Chemistry. He received the Order of Culture in 1962.

SŌDA *Hajime*

Umezu Masakage nikki

The diary of Umezu Shume Masakage (1581–1633), a key administrator of the SATAKE FAMILY's Akita domain in Dewa Province (now Akita Prefecture); it covers, with some interruptions, the years from 1612, when Masakage reassumed his duties as commissioner of the rich silver mine at Innai, to 1633, when he had risen to the posts of his domain's general commissioner of mines, commissioner of finance (KANJŌ BUGYŌ), and senior councillor (KARŌ). Although Masakage could boast some military accomplishments, he is primarily an example of a new bureaucratic or even technocratic type of *samurai* that emerged in the early part of the Edo period (1600–1868). His diary is an important source on domanial administration at a time when the Tokugawa BAKUHAN SYSTEM of government was taking shape and is of particular interest for the insights it offers into the period's mining and civil engineering technology (Masakage was also involved in a major aqueduct project and was allotted salary lands in the area reclaimed thereby).

George ELISON

Umezu Yoshijirō (1882–1949)

Army general and last chief of the ARMY GENERAL STAFF OFFICE. Born in Ōita Prefecture. Graduate of the Army Academy in 1903. He later served as commander of the Japanese forces in Tianjin (Tientsin) in North China, where in June 1935 he concluded the HE-UMEZU (HO-UMEZU) AGREEMENT with General HE YINGQIN (Ho Ying-ch'in) of the Beijing (Peking) Military Council of the Guomindang (Kuomintang), banishing the Guomindang and CHIANG KAISHEK's Nationalist Army from Hebei (Hopeh) and allowing the Japanese army to make advances into the province. Under Umezu's command in the early 1940s, the Japanese GUANDONG (KWANTUNG) ARMY settled all disputes over the Outer Mongolian–Manchurian border. Succeeding General SUGIYAMA HAJIME as chief of the Army General Staff Office in 1944, he served until the end of World War II. On 2 September 1945 he represented the Imperial High Command in signing the formal documents of surrender on board the USS *Missouri* (see SURRENDER, INSTRUMENT OF). Found guilty as a class A war criminal at the WAR CRIMES TRIALS, he was sentenced to life in prison, where he died from illness in 1949.

KONDŌ *Shinji*

Unazuki

Town in eastern Toyama Prefecture, central Honshū; on the river Kurobegawa. Its hot springs, skiing facilities, and scenery, especially the Kurobe Gorge, attract many visitors. Pop: 7,653.

uneme

Female attendants in ancient times who served the ruler's daily needs. Such women first appear in records referring to the 6th century. They were selected from among the sisters and daughters of local chieftains (KUNI NO MIYATSUKO) and presented as tribute to the sovereign at the YAMATO COURT (ca 4th–mid-7th centuries). Some historians have asserted that the custom began as a means to ensure the loyalty of provincial leaders to the court. By the time of the TAIKA REFORM (645) the acquisition of *uneme* was firmly established as an imperial prerogative. These women held much lower status than the sisters and daughters of the pedigreed Yamato aristocracy, who might expect to enter the palace as junior consorts (or concubines, *nyōgo*) and eventually to become empresses (KŌGŌ or CHŪGŪ).

📖——Kadowaki Teiji, *Uneme* (1965).　　　*Michiko Y. AOKI*

unemployment

(*shitsugyō*). Compared with other industrialized countries, Japan's unemployment rates are very low; in the 1970s they hardly ever exceeded 2 percent. However, official statistics which show almost total employment do not reflect the true situation; they may result from including much substandard employment. Because of vast wage differentials among industries, many workers actually earn very little, and should thus be considered underemployed. Other employees work less than the usual full working hours; they too may be considered partially unemployed.

The ratio of farmers in the Japanese working population is high compared to that of other developed countries. When workers who are originally from farming areas find themselves out of work in urban settings, they often return to their homes. This hidden unemployment could be one of the reasons for the large farming population. The practice also helps to keep the unemployment figures down. The widespread phenomenon of working far away from home (DEKASEGI) is another reason why unemployment is kept low. The high percentage of those receiving higher education indicates, moreover, a tendency to continue in school if desirable employment is not found.

Because of the large wage differentials between ages in Japan, enterprises prefer to hire young people; unemployment is high among workers in the upper-age groups, who receive very few work offers. This is in marked contrast to the high rate of unemployment among youth in the United States and in Europe. The existence of a gap between customary retirement at age 55 and the age at which one becomes eligible for a pension (about age 60) causes workers to look for reemployment after their first retirement. These jobs tend to be insecure, and during a recession unemployment among these older workers will increase.

The rate of unemployment, which had been at or below 1 percent during the 1960s, jumped to close to 2 percent after the OPEC-induced recession began in 1973. A system of insurance, paid for jointly by employees and employers, is available for unemployed workers. Those unemployed individuals who are looking for a job can receive benefits for between 90 and 300 days, depending on their age. See SOCIAL SECURITY PROGRAMS.　　　*KURITA Ken*

unemployment insurance → social security programs

Unequal Treaties, revision of

(*jōyaku kaisei*; literally meaning "treaty revision"). The term *jōyaku kaisei* refers to the extended diplomatic negotiations following the Meiji Restoration of 1868 in which the Japanese government sought to revise and eventually replace the so-called Unequal Treaties concluded with the Western powers during the 1850s and 1860s. To the Japanese of that day treaty revision was a national goal. A standing item on the government's agenda for a quarter century, it figured prominently in domestic politics as well. As a functional and emotional heir to the "expel the barbarians" refrain of the latter part of the Edo period (1600–1868), it offered a patriotic alternative to indiscriminate antiforeignism, provided justification for social reforms, and supplied critics of the regime with an effective political weapon.

Treaties and Problems——The foundations of the treaty system had been laid by the Tokugawa shogunate's ANSEI COMMERCIAL TREATIES with the United States, the Netherlands, Russia, Britain, and France. Beginning with the commercial treaty that Townsend HARRIS had wrested from the shogunal negotiators on 29 July 1858, these agreements expanded upon earlier pacts that had opened the ports of Shimoda, Nagasaki, and Hakodate and provided for the opening of the ports of Kanagawa (now Yokohama), Niigata, and Hyōgo (now Kōbe) and the cities of Edo (now Tōkyō) and Ōsaka. They also established tariffs on a sliding scale, ranging from 5 percent on raw materials to 20 percent on most manufactured goods (35 percent in the case of alcoholic beverages), and acknowledged the right of foreigners to be tried in consular courts according to their own laws.

These treaties had provided for revision after 1 July 1872, but before that date they had been considerably modified. Outbreaks of antiforeign violence had put the shogunate on the defensive and had led to a series of tariff reductions that culminated in the Tariff Convention of 1866 (see KAIZEI YAKUSHO). This convention limited tariffs to 5 percent on most items and set low specific duties on others. The Western powers also took advantage of the loosely worded treaties and most-favored-nation clauses to expand their privileges in other areas.

The negotiations drew their dynamic from the West's desire for the opening of all of Japan to foreign residence and to economic activity and from the Japanese quest for abolition of extraterritorial privilege and conventional tariffs. In these questions, national honor, national interest, and the domestic standing of the new government were to become closely intertwined. The conventional tariffs represented both an affront to national sovereignty and the loss of a much-needed source of revenue. At the same time, they increased dependence on other taxes and denied protection to native handicrafts and industries, thereby leaving the government open to domestic criticism.

The extraterritoriality question had similar contours. Given the inadequacy of Japan's traditional legal codes, consular jurisdiction may have offered a reasonably convenient means of administering treaty-port affairs, but European clichés about the savagery of Oriental justice hardly inclined the Japanese to expect equal treatment in their dealings with foreigners. National weakness was underlined by the Western powers' refusal to acknowledge the authority of Japanese administrative law. Perhaps the best-known of the humiliating incidents to which this gave rise occurred in 1879. Fearing cholera, the government attempted to quarantine the German steamer *Hesperia* at Yokohama, but the German consul refused to countenance the directive and had the vessel escorted to port by gunboat. Thus, the Japanese often found the line between extraterritoriality and exemption from all jurisdiction rather thin.

Initiatives and Negotiations——From a Japanese perspective, the negotiations can be conveniently divided into five periods.

1868–1874. The new Meiji government's first official response to the treaties (on 8 February 1868) was to accept them. While it may seem that they had little alternative, the act itself was a positive one, taken in the interest of asserting control over foreign affairs and winning international support. A domestic statement pointed toward an even broader acceptance of international proprieties: the treaties were to be corrected through discussion, foreign relations conducted in accordance with a "law of nations," and the treaties observed as the law of the land. Having reestablished "legitimate rule" and initiated reform at home, imperial officials at first hoped that revision might be easily obtained once domestic stability had been achieved. By the time of the IWAKURA MISSION in 1871, however, the dimensions of the burden they had incurred began to be visible and the notion that revision would depend on internal reform was generally acknowledged. This link between reform and revision completed the basic framework within which the treaty revision process would develop.

1875–1879. Recognizing the difficulty of recovering all of Japan's rights at once, Foreign Minister TERASHIMA MUNENORI pushed forward with an attempt to gain control over tariffs. Speaking the language of sovereignty, he presented documents that showed that actual tariff rates averaged only 3.4 percent and offered the opening of more ports in return for tariff autonomy. Although the United States agreed to this proposal in 1878, Britain did not, and it came to nothing. Thus, a decade after the Restoration, Japan was still saddled with treaty conditions worse than those originally imposed under the Ansei treaties.

1880–1887. In 1880, Terashima's successor INOUE KAORU offered new proposals couched in less sweeping terminology but aimed at increasing both tariff rates and Japan's jurisdiction over foreigners. Although these proposals also proved unacceptable to the British, they did lead to joint preliminary talks in Tōkyō among representatives of the treaty states in 1882. These talks prepared the way for a further round of negotiations that began in 1886 and envisaged agreement on the following terms: extraterritoriality was to be abolished, the entire country opened, and foreigners granted equal rights with Japanese. Japan, however, was to establish a legal system based on Western principles, provide translations of its codes for Western perusal, and set up a system of "mixed courts" that would have primary jurisdiction in all cases involving foreigners. To Inoue this seemed a major achievement. To the French jurist and longtime government adviser Gustave Emile BOISSONADE DE FONTARABIE and prominent traditionalists like General TANI KANJŌ, however, the formal gains masked an intrusion of foreign

Uniforms

Students wearing typical school uniforms in a public junior high school in Saitama Prefecture.

authority and influence that Japan might never be able to overcome. When the contents of the proposed treaty became known during the summer of 1887, these objections sparked widespread opposition that proved a boon to the flagging FREEDOM AND PEOPLE'S RIGHTS MOVEMENT and soon grew to major proportions (see SANDAI JIKEN KEMPAKU MOVEMENT). Negotiations were suspended and Inoue resigned.

1888–1889. The government now turned to ŌKUMA SHIGENOBU as foreign minister, and he returned to dealing with the powers separately. Negotiations were reopened in November 1888, agreements were soon signed with Germany and the United States, and talks with England were under way when treaty revision once again ran afoul of public opinion. Ōkuma had removed some of the more objectionable features of the Inoue plan but the public was in no mood for details. A draft of the proposed treaty obtained by the newspaper *Nihon* rekindled opposition. This time the issue split both the party movement and the cabinet, and when Ōkuma was attacked and seriously injured by a nationalist fanatic, the negotiations were broken off.

1890–1894. Discussions were renewed in February 1890, but little progress was made until MUTSU MUNEMITSU became foreign minister in August 1892. By this time, the government was again under considerable pressure, both from hardliners in the newly established Diet and from a broader stream of patriotic sentiment that had begun to run sour. In a failure of nerve that reversed the whole thrust of Meiji Japan's drive toward revision, the public seemed increasingly persuaded that the existing treaty port system was preferable to the dangers of racial and cultural extinction that opening the country to mixed residence (NAICHI ZAKKYO) would bring. In the end, however, the government turned this outpouring of popular sentiment to its advantage, offering it as justification for a tougher negotiating stance. It was this show of determination, together with Japan's undeniable social and institutional progress and British interest in securing an ally in East Asia, that provided the formula for success. The ANGLO-JAPANESE COMMERCIAL TREATY OF 1894 (Aoki–Kimberley Treaty), initialed on the eve of the first Sino-Japanese War, was written in the language of reciprocity and provided for the abolition of extraterritoriality in five years. By 1897 similar treaties had been signed with the other major treaty nations. New treaties restoring tariff autonomy to Japan were concluded with the major nations in 1911.

Given this complex of events and emotions, one may wonder whether the term "treaty revision" is of sufficient scope to convey the drive for full independence that was its motive. Indeed it often seems inadequate to describe what was really at stake in the negotiations. For though the specific aggravations of extraterritoriality and the liabilities of the treaty tariffs were real enough, the fundamental issue was the establishment of a relationship that would certify Japan's attainment of an equal station in the civilized company of a European-dominated world.

——W. G. Beasley, *The Meiji Restoration* (1972). Inoue Kiyoshi, *Jōyaku kaisei* (1955, repr 1978). F. C. Jones, *Extraterritoriality in Japan* (1931). *Meiji bunka zenshū,* vol 6, *Gaikōhen* (Nihon Hyōronsha, 1928). Kenneth Pyle, *The New Generation in Meiji Japan* (1969). *Jerry* DUSENBURY

UNESCO activities in Japan

Japan was admitted to the United Nations Educational, Scientific, and Cultural Organization (UNESCO) in 1951, signaling its return to the community of nations after World War II. UNESCO work in Japan is now handled by the Japanese National Commission for UNESCO. The commission's educational activities cover such fields as the natural sciences, social sciences, and cultural affairs. It promotes such projects as educational assistance in the developing countries of Asia and the Pacific, the research work of the Center for East Asian Cultural Studies, and the activities of the Asian Cultural Center for UNESCO. In addition the commission cooperates actively in the affairs of the United Nations University. On the nongovernmental level, there is a National Federation of UNESCO Associations with more than 220 affiliates, which sponsors various activities throughout the country. Contributions by Japan to UNESCO in 1981–83 were the third largest in the world and amounted to $56,641,104 (9.48 percent of the total). See also UNITED NATIONS AND JAPAN. *YAMAGUCHI Makoto*

unfair labor practices

Activities of an employer that infringe upon a worker's right to organize, bargain collectively, and engage in concerted action. These three FUNDAMENTAL LABOR RIGHTS are guaranteed by article 28 of the 1947 constitution. In addition, the Labor Union Law (Rōdō Kumiai Hō) prohibits typical violative activities by employers as unfair labor practices and provides a remedial system based on LABOR RELATIONS COMMISSIONS.

The prohibited practices are similar to those found in the Wagner Act in the United States: (1) the dismissal, transfer, demotion, or other adverse treatment of a worker in retaliation for the organization of a union, membership in a labor organization, collective bargaining, strikes, or other legitimate union activity; (2) the requirement that a worker sign, as a condition of employment, a promise to withdraw from or not to join a union (a "yellow dog contract"); (3) refusal by an employer, without sufficient cause, to bargain collectively; (4) control of or interference in the formation or administration of a union, including the provision of financial assistance to the union; and (5) dismissal or other adverse treatment of a worker for requesting relief from unfair labor practices through a labor relations commission or for testifying before such a commission.

The Labor Union Law initially contained penalties for employers who committed unfair labor practices, but a 1949 amendment to the law substituted the principle of returning a situation to its original condition, without the unfair practices. When an employer violates a relief order issued by a labor relations commission or an emergency order from a court, a fine of up to ¥100,000, one year's imprisonment, or both may be assessed. See also LABOR LAWS. *KATŌ Shunpei*

Unification Church → Holy Spirit Association for the Unification of World Christianity

uniforms

(seifuku). It was not customary in premodern Japan to wear uniforms to provide identification or to differentiate among occupations of groups in daily life. Only when Japan began to be influenced by Western thought and culture in the late 19th century did uniforms come into wide use. About the time the Chinese-inspired RITSURYŌ SYSTEM of government was adopted in the 7th century, however, certain rules regulating clothing were laid down, and in one sense these clothes may be considered uniforms.

In 604, for example, Prince SHŌTOKU, in imitation of China, devised a system of 12 court ranks (KAN'I JŪNIKAI) and designated the color of the headdress and clothing for each rank, ranging from purple for the highest to green, red, yellow, white, and black in descending order. The TAIHŌ CODE (701) and YŌRŌ CODE (718; effective 757) also meticulously prescribed for each rank the headwear, clothing, and accessories to be worn by male and female visitors to the imperial court. Ceremonial dress for special events such as the enthronement of the emperor was known as *raifuku;* dress worn by those who came to work daily at the court as *chōfuku;* and clothing worn by officials without rank or by scholars in attendance at the court as *seifuku.*

During the Heian period (794–1185) the clothing of the nobility continued to be heavily influenced by China, but once embassies to China were abolished at the end of the 9th century, it gradually became nativized. *Raifuku* and *chōfuku* for women evolved into the *karaginumo* and *uchiki,* later called the *jūni hitoe* ("12-layered garment"). The wearing of ceremonial dress by men fell into disuse, and the *chōfuku* evolved into the *sokutai.* During and after the Kamakura period (1185–1333), garments worn by the rising warrior class acquired prestige. By the 15th century the *hitatare,* originally apparel worn by lower-ranking warriors, became the ceremonial dress of higher-ranking warriors. In the Edo period (1600–1868), the *hitatare* was simplified into the *kamishimo,* a less formal ceremonial dress. *Raifuku,* although not worn often, remained the prescribed clothing for the most important occasions until the end of the Edo period. The *kosode* was the main ceremonial dress for women from the Kamakura through the Edo periods.

After the Meiji Restoration in 1868, uniforms were adopted for the military, police, students, factory workers, nurses, and so forth. Today uniforms are usually worn by students from kindergarten through secondary school and rarely in college. Some occupations require uniforms, as in Western countries, but many Japanese firms also oblige certain women employees to wear uniforms in the belief that the practice promotes a sense of group identification. Although not limited to any particular industry, the practice is most noticeable in banks and department stores. See also CLOTHING.

📖——Roy Dilley, *Japanese Army Uniforms and Equipment, 1919–1945* (1970). Tsutomu Ema, *A Historical Sketch of Costumes and Customs* (1936).   ŌTA Rin'ichirō

Union of New Religious Organizations of Japan

(Shin Nihon Shūkyō Dantai Rengōkai, abbreviated Shinshūren). Association of 81 religious organizations as of 1980; with headquarters in Tōkyō and local branches. It was established in 1951 by 24 recently founded religious organizations (the so-called NEW RELIGIONS) to promote mutual communication and cooperation, especially in defense of religious freedom. Since its establishment several organizations, such as REIYŪKAI and SEICHŌ NO IE, have withdrawn, and other organizations have joined. Membership in 1980 included the RISSHŌ KŌSEIKAI, and the PL Kyōdan. The union is a member of the Japan Religious League.

Union of Soviet Socialist Republics and Japan → Russia and Japan

United Church of Christ in Japan

(Nihon Kirisuto Kyōdan). Protestant Christian denomination formed during World War II (1941) as a union of most Protestant denominations and other groups, partly to brace themselves against the mounting ideological and political pressures on Christians from the militarist government, which imposed nationalistic Shintō doctrines and restricted the religious activities of all Japanese through the Religious Organizations Law (1939–45). The church absorbed more than 30 denominations and organizations, including the SALVATION ARMY, some of the Anglican-Episcopal churches, and the YMCA and YWCA. Although the Salvation Army, the YMCA, and YWCA, along with many denominations, such as the Anglican-Episcopal, Lutheran, and some Baptist and Methodist denominations, withdrew from the union after the war when the law was rescinded, it remains the largest Protestant denomination in Japan. In 1946 the church stipulated a charter and in 1954 formulated its own creed. The church is governed by a general assembly and a standing executive committee. Nationwide, the church is divided into 16 districts with 1,385 churches, 135,250 members, and 2,811 Japanese and 244 foreign clergy (1978).

📖——Richard H. Drummond, *A History of Christianity in Japan* (1971).   Kenneth J. DALE

United Kingdom and Japan

The British were among the first Westerners to have contact with Japan in the early 17th century, but full relations between the two countries were established only after the opening of Japan in the mid-19th century. Britons played key roles in the modernization of Japan, and the two countries were allied during the early 20th cen-

tury. Relations suffered from colonial competition in East Asia and were broken off during World War II. In the postwar period, good relations have been resumed and trade between the two nations is active.

Early Contacts——British perceptions of Japan, like those of other Europeans, go back to the age of the navigators at the end of the 15th century. Along with dreams of sailing to the Indies and Cathay, the navigators also aspired to sail to Japan. But in those days Japan was a mythical land of which little of substance was known. The Venetian navigator John Cabot (1450–98), who sailed out of Bristol and across the Atlantic in 1497, was described as intending "to go on until he shall be over against an island, called by him Cipango (Japan), where he thinks all the spices in the world and also all the precious stones originate."

It was early in the 17th century, in the days of the merchant adventurers rather than the navigators, that the first real contacts took place. Britain's early contacts are associated with the name of William ADAMS, who joined a Dutch expedition of which the remnant eventually limped into Japanese harbors in 1600. Arms from the ship assisted TOKUGAWA IEYASU in his victory at the Battle of SEKIGAHARA in that year. Ieyasu valued Adams's skills in shipbuilding and gunnery and granted him privileges and estates. As Ieyasu's adviser on foreign trade matters, Adams may have played a part in breaking the Portuguese trade monopoly and obtaining trade privileges for the Dutch. In 1609 the Dutch trading post at Hirado was set up; and it was only a matter of time before Adams wrote to the English East India Company asking for trading ships to be sent to Japan. In fact, Captain John SARIS was already on his way with three ships, and he obtained trading privileges upon arrival in Japan. Contrary to Adams's recommendation, Saris located his first trading post under Richard COCKS at Hirado, remote from the capital of Japan. Adams was much less influential under Ieyasu's successor and died in 1620. In consequence, the British outpost did not prosper and was closed three years later. The British faced the rivalry of foreign traders, and attempts to reopen the trade fell foul of the NATIONAL SECLUSION policy of the Tokugawa shogunate (1603–1867).

Over the next 230 years, while Japan was closed to the outside world, reports about Japan continued to filter out through the Dutch enclave at DEJIMA. Sporadic efforts were made to reopen the English trading post, but nothing materialized. In 1853, arriving with four American warships, Commodore Matthew PERRY demanded trading facilities for the United States. Soon after, the commander-in-chief of Britain's China squadron, Admiral Sir James Stirling (1791–1865), visited Japan and signed a limited arrangement with the magistrate of Nagasaki. Later, Sir John Bowring (1792–1872), superintendent of British trade in East Asia, asked the shogunate for the opening of trade but received no reply. After the Anglo-French expedition against North China, James Bruce, the eighth Lord Elgin (1811–63) visited Japan and was ultimately granted trading rights by the Treaty of Edo (Tōkyō) of 26 August 1858 (see ANSEI COMMERCIAL TREATIES). Emissaries were exchanged between the two countries and Britain assumed it had secured the opening of ports at Nagasaki, Kanagawa, Hakodate, Hyōgo, Niigata, Ōsaka, and Edo. The shogunate, however, facing widespread domestic opposition, urged Britain not to proceed with the opening of all these ports. In any event, the treaty did not receive the emperor's assent until 1865 and then was held over for three more years. British consuls with extraterritorial jurisdiction were installed at the various ports; and British merchants became quite numerous in the foreign settlements, primarily at Yokohama (which had been substituted for Kanagawa at Japan's request), Nagasaki, and Hakodate. The presence of foreigners led Japanese who were hostile to foreign trade to register their disapproval by assaulting foreigners or attacking their property. Although the Japanese sometimes had provocation from the undisciplined foreign community, these attacks reflected a malaise of late Tokugawa society. Disagreements between the emperor's court and the Tokugawa authorities were coming to the surface and often took the form of antiforeign agitation. The nationals of Britain, like the nationals of other foreign countries, became a frequent object of attack, as in the RICHARDSON AFFAIR.

With the political forces in Japan so delicately balanced, Britain faced the difficult question of whether to favor the established shogunate or the reforming elements. Traditionally, Britain had signed its treaties with the shogunate, but British attitudes were changing, in part because of the influence of the young student-interpreter, Ernest SATOW, who reached Yokohama in 1862. During his travels and investigations throughout the country, Satow came to believe that Tokugawa rule was decadent and rigid, and that drive and capacity lay with *tozama* ("outer") domains like Chōshū (now Yama-guchi Prefecture) and Satsuma (now Kagoshima Prefecture). He openly advocated reform of the shogunate and the greater involvement of these domains in administration and treaty making. There was little likelihood that either London or Harry PARKES, who served as British minister from 1865 until 1883, would be swayed by the observations of a mere interpreter in his early twenties. But Satow may have planted ideas which influenced his superiors and may also have impressed important Japanese who saw in Satow the Japanese-speaking mouthpiece of the British minister. In fact British policy in support of the shogunate was probably less fixed than many imagined. During the BOSHIN CIVIL WAR Britain remained neutral, acting correctly but circumspectly toward the new government that emerged with the MEIJI RESTORATION in 1868. This indicated that Britain's stance was much less partisan than people in Japan commonly imagined.

Britain's Role in Japan's Modernization——As the pioneer of the industrial revolution, Britain naturally had a part to play in the effort to modernize Japan, to which the new Meiji leaders turned after the civil war. Britain was regarded as one of the models for the building of factories, railways, lighthouses, and other elements of a modern economy. It was for this reason that the Japanese mission of inspection, headed by Prince IWAKURA TOMOMI, spent four months in Britain in 1872, studying governmental and industrial establishments in the course of a world tour (see IWAKURA MISSION).

The lessons of Britain's industrial experience reached Japan in two other ways during the Meiji period (1868–1912). The first was through the group of students sent abroad for study in Britain. Some young, ambitious Japanese had been there before the Restoration despite the prevailing ban on leaving the country. Under domain auspices ITŌ HIROBUMI and INOUE KAORU from Chōshū had visited Britain for study in 1863–64, and MORI ARINORI of Satsuma had studied science and mathematics there. As representatives of the *tozama* domains, all three rose to important positions in the post-Restoration government. Later examples of students sent abroad were MUTSU MUNEMITSU, who came to hold important government offices, and BABA TATSUI, who made major contributions to the establishment of political parties and to education.

The second way in which Japan drew on British experience was through employing British nationals as *oyatoi gaikokujin* (FOREIGN EMPLOYEES OF THE MEIJI PERIOD). The Meiji government offered contracts to foreigners for service as government advisers. These posts were divided among various countries that were prominent at the time and fell into widely differing categories, ranging from diplomatic advisers to specialists in new technologies. Most of those contracts connected with the navy, railways, and some aspects of education went to British nationals.

In the field of naval education, for example, Harry Parkes arranged for a mission to be sent to Japan prior to the Restoration under Commander R. E. Tracey. The mission set up an academy in Edo and began the instruction of 71 cadets, but the collapse of the shogunate forced it to close. Shortly after the Restoration, Lieutenant Albert G. S. Hawes and Lieutenant Francis Brinkley began to instruct young Japanese aspirants. This effort was superseded in 1873, when Britain sent out a larger mission under Commander Archibald Lucius Douglas with over 30 officers and men under a three-year contract. Douglas took charge of the Naval Academy that was established in Tōkyō.

There was also a flow in the opposite direction: Many Japanese in the former domainal navies sought their fortune by going to Britain for training. One was TŌGŌ HEIHACHIRŌ of Satsuma, who went as a cadet to Britain in 1871. After some tutorial instruction at Cambridge, he spent several years on training ships, notably the *Worcester*, and undertook a voyage of seven months aboard a sailing ship to Australia and back. He was then instructed to oversee the construction of the corvette *Hiei*, which was being built for Japan at Pembroke. Tōgō returned to Japan in January 1878 to find the Imperial Navy a new, disciplined organization, the result of British training.

These are examples of the "two-way traffic" of the modernization process in which Japan and Britain (among others) were engaged. It was most active in the 1870s. After 1880 a reaction set in: excessive imitation by Japan of foreign models was criticized from the nationalist standpoint, while the Meiji government had in any case to curb such spending in the interests of economy.

Teachers tended to survive longer. Here again the Japanese government made carefully balanced choices to avoid focusing on any one country as its source. Among British educators, mention should be made of Dr William WILLIS, who traveled widely in Japan, served

both sides in the civil war, and ultimately took charge of the Igakkō in Tōkyō, which incorporated a former medical school with a new hospital. Willis then received a contract to organize the medical school and general hospital at Kagoshima in Kyūshū. An educator of a different stamp was Basil Hall CHAMBERLAIN, who taught English at the Tōkyō Naval Academy from 1874 to 1882. He transferred in 1886 to the government teaching service, becoming adviser to the Ministry of Education on the systematic teaching of Japanese and serving concurrently as professor of Japanese at Tōkyō University.

In the field of science and technology, George Henry Dyer from Glasgow held the appointment of principal of the Kōgakuryō (Technical College; renamed Kōbu Daigakkō in 1877) in Tōkyō from 1873 to 1883 and became professor of engineering at Tōkyō University and adviser to the Ministry of Public Works (Kōbushō). It was Dyer who introduced the Japanese to systematic instruction in civil and mechanical engineering and naval architecture. Another teacher at the Kōbu Daigakkō was John MILNE, who went to Japan in 1876. Despite his general teaching, he began to concentrate on seismology and became the father of earthquake research in Japan. After his transfer to Tōkyō University, Milne became professor of seismology and served there until his retirement in 1894.

These examples indicate the role of the British (among other foreign specialists) in helping to create some of the institutions of modern Japan. They were only part of a much bigger pool, ranging from advisers to the Japanese government like Sir Francis Taylor Piggott to missionaries and missionary-teachers like Arthur Lloyd and Walter Dening.

Trade and Diplomacy during the Meiji Period——There was a regular and expanding trade between Britain and Japan in the Meiji period. Japanese exports to Britain amounted to £573,136 in 1874 and £385,791 in 1875, while imports from Britain totaled £1,584,517 in 1874 and £2,460,227 in 1875. For most of the Meiji period, Japan's imports from Britain greatly exceeded exports. While there were certain staples of the trade, the figures were rather unstable because the amount of capital equipment that the Japanese brought from Britain varied from year to year. Thus, of the 28 warships that the Japanese navy operated in 1883, 19 had been built in British yards and imported. This trend continued down to the end of the century, when Japan developed its own shipyards.

Another sphere of enterprise in which Britain helped was railway building. T. B. GLOVER, a prominent British merchant in Nagasaki, demonstrated a 762-millimeter-gauge steam engine called the *Iron Duke* in 1865. In 1869 a Scottish adviser named Henry BRUNTON suggested the building of a line from Tōkyō to Yokohama. In the following year a loan for £1 million was raised in London at 9 percent interest for this purpose. A team of 19 engineers was sent out; the section from Shimbashi to Yokohama was built and went into operation in 1872. The next line to be opened ran from Ōsaka to Kōbe and was completed in May 1874. By this time there were 104 foreign railway engineers in Japan, of whom 94 were British. One of these, the grandson of the great Cornish engineer Richard Trevithick, organized the building of the first steam locomotive to be made in Japan. It was a corollary of the employment of British engineers that they made use of British products that were familiar to them and had a reputation for reliability and durability. It is reported that British-made rails used by Japanese railways were still in good condition after 30 year's use, whereas American and German rails did not survive as long.

In the political sphere, the major effort in the first two decades of the Meiji period was the revision of the "Unequal Treaties," as the Ansei Treaties came to be called. With a sizable slice of Japan's trade and the largest number of nationals in the treaty ports, Britain was intimately involved in this issue. While sympathizing with Japan's desire to renegotiate the treaties in which Japan had given foreigners rights of consular jurisdiction in both civil and criminal cases and which limited the rate of duty on imports to 5 percent *ad valorem*, Britain declined to give up its extraterritorial privileges until Japan's domestic law codes were amended. This attitude was one of the factors that contributed to serious public outcry against the British sparked in 1886 by the sinking of the *Normanton* off Wakayama Prefecture (see NORMANTON INCIDENT). These riots formed a backdrop to the negotiations that were then proceeding and were a warning to Britain about what might happen if it insisted on holding on to its existing privileges. The Japanese government, for its part, was showing willingness to revise and modernize the various legal codes.

A breakthrough came when Mutsu, who had himself been a student in Britain and had translated Jeremy Bentham's *Principles of*

Morals and Legislation, became foreign minister. He decided to negotiate with individual countries and to open talks in London. Despite setbacks, a new commercial treaty was devised and signed on 16 July 1894 (see ANGLO-JAPANESE COMMERCIAL TREATY OF 1894). It prescribed that the extraterritorial rights of foreigners would be terminated when the new law codes came into force, as they did in 1899. While Japan's position over tariffs was improved, complete tariff autonomy was not attained until the commercial treaties were revised afresh in 1911. For Mutsu the British treaty was the thin end of the wedge. Having obtained Britain's agreement in principle, he was able to negotiate favorably with most other governments. Moreover, the British treaty came at just the right time—in the fortnight of crises just before Japan declared war on China on 1 August 1894 (see UNEQUAL TREATIES, REVISION OF; SINO-JAPANESE WAR OF 1894–1895).

The Alliance Period——A treaty establishing the ANGLO-JAPANESE ALLIANCE was signed by HAYASHI TADASU, the Japanese minister, and Foreign Secretary Lord Lansdowne in London on 30 January 1902. It was limited to the "extreme east" and was due to last for 5 years. It was not invoked during the RUSSO-JAPANESE WAR (1904–05), but during the final stages of the war, negotiations were begun to renew and revise the alliance. This was accomplished in the second Anglo-Japanese treaty, which was signed by the same officials in London on 12 August 1905. It had a wider scope than the earlier alliance and was due to last for 10 years. Opinion in both countries became reserved about certain aspects of the alliance, and negotiations for a further revision took place in 1911. The third Anglo-Japanese treaty was due to last for 10 years and was less far-reaching than its forerunner. During its term there was some cooperation between the two countries in military operations in China, in naval operations in the Mediterranean, and at the Paris Peace Conference.

There were commercial undertones to the alliance that became more pronounced as the alliance developed. The alliance benefited both parties by helping to ensure financial loans to Japan and by increasing the volume of commerce in the period to 1914. An Anglo-Japanese commercial exhibition held in London in the summer of 1910 created a favorable impression of Japan's products and prospects. From the turn of the century the items of trade changed considerably, but the balance of trade remained in favor of Britain. Thus, Japanese imports from Britain in 1900 were £9.8 million while exports were £1.5 million; in 1904, the figures were £4.9 million and £2.3 million; and in 1913, £14.5 million and £4.4 million. These figures are slightly distorted by Japanese imports of arms, ammunition, and ships, which occur only occasionally. It is clear that the volume of trade by value was increasing and that the balance was held by Britain. When, however, we look at the goods traded in, we find that the quantity of cotton yarn imports into Japan remained static. It was already clear that the Japanese themselves would gradually be able to provide the bulk of their own needs in cotton.

After 1919 world opinion grew hostile to the existence of alliances, and criticism of the Anglo-Japanese Alliance was heard in the United States, China, and Canada. During the WASHINGTON CONFERENCE in 1921–22, the future of the alliance was discussed in informal sessions between the parties; and it was agreed to merge the alliance into a more noncommittal FOUR-POWER TREATY, in which the former allies were to be joined by the United States and France. When ratification of the Four-Power Treaty was completed in 1923, the alliance lapsed.

Interwar Period——The former allies drifted apart, even though there were no serious disagreements until the 1930s. One factor that bound them together was that China was in a state of chaos for most of the 1920s, and both allies suffered from the nationalist movement there. Britain, therefore, saw Japan as a stabilizing force in East Asia and as a nation weakened by the great earthquake of 1923. Britain defined its policy toward Japan in 1926 as "giving her no excuse for aggression, while affording her the maximum scope for her economic development." However, when Japan made its moves in Manchuria in 1931 (see MANCHURIAN INCIDENT), there was little in the way of a special relationship that survived. Surrounded by political and economic problems in Asia and the Pacific, Britain was prepared to reach minor accommodations with Japan, but none of these in fact materialized in the 1930s.

Most of the divisive issues between Britain and Japan were played out on the international stage and need not concern us here (see WORLD WAR II). Other issues were exclusive to Britain and Japan, prominent among them trade disputes. It was not so much Anglo-Japanese trade that was at issue, though Britain was gradually losing its favorable balance and was indeed losing out to its most serious competitor, the United States. It was, rather, competition in third markets, particularly in the British empire that caused tension. During World War I Britain's industries were forced to concentrate on war production, and the usual markets for British products were neglected. This afforded an opportunity to other countries not so deeply involved in the war to develop their trade to the detriment of Britain. This continued after the war and led to rivalry in China and Southeast Asia in the 1920s. Moreover, Japan made a transition from being an international debtor nation to supplying overseas capital, despite the difficulties faced by its banks in the 1920s.

After the Manchurian Incident trade tension became more intense. In the 1930s this manifested itself in the competition in cotton that affected equally the older Lancashire industry and the developing textile industry in India (see INDIA AND JAPAN). At the Ottawa Conference in 1932 Britain had accepted proposals for imperial preference in trade with its colonies, and this of necessity affected Japan's trade adversely, even if Japan was not intended as the sole target of the preference. When Japanese and British delegations met in London in January 1934, they could find no formula that would break the impasse. After a while these commercial disputes were dwarfed by the outbreak of the SINO-JAPANESE WAR OF 1937–1945.

The vulnerability of the British empire in Asia and the Pacific came to the fore again after KONOE FUMIMARO's announcement of Japan's New Order in East Asia (TŌA SHINCHITSUJO) in November 1938. The issue had first been discussed with the leaders of the empire at the dominion conference in May of the previous year, and Australia had put forward the idea of a Pacific pact, but this did not commend itself to the Japanese. In 1939 the various disputes moved to a political plane with the outbreak of the war in Europe. In China, Japan regarded Britain as being obstructive through its concessions, treaty ports, and colonies, and as the major abettor of Chiang Kai-shek in his resistance. The Japanese were careful not to overplay their hand since they thought that Britain might act as mediator between Tōkyō and Chongqing (Chungking). But a number of developments, including the Tianjin (Tientsin) Incident (in which residents of the British concession in Tianjin were humiliated by Japanese soldiers in 1939) and the closing of the Burma Road, were signs that Britain had lost the power of retaliation and resistance to Japan.

Two factors in the situation carried with them special menace. One was the TRIPARTITE PACT of September 1940, in which Japan sided with Britain's two enemies in Europe, Germany and Italy, at a particularly difficult juncture in the European war. The other was the occupation of southern Indochina, which was approved by the Japanese army and navy in mid-1941 and carried out soon after. Hitherto Britain had placed some reliance on the Japanese navy as a restraint on the Japanese army and as a force that was more sensitive to British and American thinking. In 1941 the naval leadership changed, seized the initiative from the army, and succeeded in diverting Japan's expansion from north to south. When Japan acquired rights of military occupation in southern Indochina, it was an ill omen for the security of British Malaya.

When Japan declared war on 8 December 1941, it was declared against the United States and the British Empire. In Southeast Asia the Japanese armies attacked Britain's colonies. They overran Malaya from the north and captured Singapore on 15 February 1942. Previously Japan had launched an attack against Burma that continued successfully until the setback in the IMPHAL CAMPAIGN between March and July 1944 and the recapture of Myitkina (August 1944). These encounters caused immense casualties on both sides and the Japanese high command, which did not have the advantage of air superiority, pulled out of northern Burma. They went into retreat and lost Rangoon in May 1945. In Malaya, however, they held out until the end of the war, as the British did not attempt a landing until the recapture of Penang on 3 September.

When Japan attacked British territories in 1941, it was the end of a long road of latent hostility and came as no real surprise to Britain. It revealed the vulnerability and unpreparedness of Britain's colonial territories. But the Japanese armies overextended themselves militarily and were not generally successful in winning the allegiance of the occupied countries.

Post–World War II Relations——Under the Allied OCCUPATION of Japan, the British Commonwealth was invited and agreed to send a force. From February 1946 it contributed a force of 36,000 troops, of which the British and Indian contingents were withdrawn in 1947. The BRITISH COMMONWEALTH OCCUPATION FORCE (BCOF) had its headquarters in Kure, and its occupation area covered Shikoku and the Chūgoku region (Hiroshima, Okayama, Shimane, Tottori, and

United Kingdom and Japan

UK Balance with Japan (in millions of US dollars)				
	1966	1969	1972	1975
British imports	223	344	955	2,022
British exports	164	372	539	927
Visible trade balance	−59	+28	−416	−1,095
Invisible balance	+240	+397	+466	+750
Overall balance	+180	+424	+51	−345

Yamaguchi prefectures). In these prefectures they performed the normal duties of a garrison and worked in conjunction with the American military government teams operating in the prefectural capitals. The British force did not have governmental responsibilities in its occupation zone.

Britain also played a role in the FAR EASTERN COMMISSION in Washington, where it was initially represented by Sir George SANSOM, and in the Allied Council for Japan, where it was represented by MacMahon BALL of Australia. These bodies were of marginal importance in the task of administering Japan, and it must be concluded that Britain's role in the Occupation was peripheral and in some respects an irritant to the Americans.

Britain did not have much say over the destiny of Japan, which was at the time very much in the shadow of the United States. But the Labour government followed a remarkably independent line. Britain became in 1947 a strong advocate of an early peace treaty with Japan. This was because the goals of the Occupation as laid down in the wartime conferences seemed to have been achieved, and the costs of military occupation and its responsibilities were crippling. For these and other reasons, London, with the support of Commonwealth countries, pressed for early negotiations with Japan but did not get its way.

As a member of the Far Eastern Commission, Britain had been allocated a special role in the peacemaking with Japan and could not therefore be relegated to a secondary role as had happened with the Occupation. Moreover, Britain had grave differences of opinion with the United States over the political situation in East Asia. Especially important was its recognition of the People's Republic of China in January 1950. While the United States was frankly indecisive over the peace treaty, Britain was anxious to grasp the initiative by preparing a draft. It was probable that Britain would want Japan to have an open choice of concluding peace with the government of Beijing (Peking). When, however, the Chinese communists intervened in the Korean War, Britain came round to cooperating with Washington. To sidestep the problem of inviting communist China to the peace conference, it was decided to avoid inviting either the communist or the Nationalist Chinese government. After the conclusion of the SAN FRANCISCO PEACE TREATY, Japan had to choose how to make its peace with China. Once more Britain wanted the Japanese government to have unfettered freedom of choice after the multilateral treaty came into force in 1952. But the United States, for domestic political reasons, favored the peace being made between Tōkyō and Taipei. Here again the British view was not supported by the Japanese government.

British opinion was deeply divided over Japan's return to international markets in the 1950s. When Japan was admitted to the General Agreement on Tariffs and Trade (GATT) in 1955, 14 countries, including Britain, withheld most-favored-nation status. Nonetheless both countries tried from time to time, notably in 1956, to negotiate a trade treaty. This was assisted by the Anglo-Japanese cultural agreement concluded in 1960. When visits by trade delegations had broken down the walls of distrust, the trade treaty was signed in November 1962 after seven years of negotiation. While Britain took confidence from the fact that there were safeguard clauses and certain "sensitive" imported goods were specified, Japan gained the point that the terms of the treaty were reciprocal, and Britain was required to apply the GATT rules to Japan.

Improvement in air transport in the 1960s led to an increase in the number of visits exchanged between the two countries at all levels, political, scholarly, and touristic. Perhaps as a symbol of this

improved communication, there was an exchange of royal visits. In October 1971 the Japanese emperor, accompanied by the empress, visited Britain. It was the year of the 50th anniversary of his earlier visit as prince regent in 1921. The visit was returned when Queen Elizabeth II made a ceremonial tour of Japan in May 1975.

The two countries clearly have a bond in being constitutional monarchies. They share a historic relationship through the early alliance in which Britain placed its weight behind Japan at a critical stage in Japan's development. Against these have to be set the trade disputes that have distorted relationships between the two countries in the 1970s.

As recently as the 1950s Britain earned a surplus in the trading account between the two countries. During the latter half of the 1960s, however, there were years when Britain ran a deficit in the bilateral trade. In the 1970s this deficit was multiplied many times and alarmed those who were concerned with the survival of Britain's staple industries, such as automobiles. The Japanese argue that one must set off against these surpluses what they spend on services such as insurance and shipping, of which a large amount goes to the city of London. As the accompanying table shows, trade between the two countries represents a rather intractable problem that will color their future relations. During the 1970s British exports to Japan have tended to be strongest in the categories of machinery (tractors, aircraft engines, and textile machinery) and beverages (primarily whiskey). The leading items in Japan's exports to Britain have been transport equipment (cars, motorcycles, and vehicle parts) and electrical goods (television sets, radio equipment, and accessories).

——Kajima Morinosuke, *Nichiei gaikō shi* (1957). P. C. Lowe, *Great Britain and Japan, 1911–1915* (1969). Ian NISH

United Nations and Japan

Japan was admitted to the United Nations on 18 December 1956. Since that time Japan has consistently followed a foreign policy that includes "the centrality of the United Nations" as one of its basic guidelines, and has made special contributions to the activities of that organization.

As of 1982 Japan maintained ten UN organs, including the UN University. The country's activities at the UN center on political issues such as disarmament and the Korean problem, as well as socioeconomic concerns including Third World problems, economic assistance, and human rights. Japan has also played important roles in such issues as the peaceful use of outer space, the law of the sea, and the environment. It participates actively in all special agencies of the United Nations, including the International Labor Organization (ILO), the International Monetary Fund (IMF), and the United Nations Educational, Scientific, and Cultural Organization (UNESCO). In addition, it is a member of almost all UN committees and special committees, with its roles in the Security Council and Economic and Social Council receiving special emphasis.

Centrality of the United Nations——Japan's first application for admission to the United Nations in 1952 was vetoed by the Soviet Union because of the cold war. In 1955 Japan was once again denied admission because of Soviet opposition. Following the SOVIET-JAPANESE JOINT DECLARATION of 1956, a recommendation to admit Japan was approved by the Security Council on 12 December, and the General Assembly admitted Japan on 18 December. Immediately after its admission, Japan announced its Three Principles of Foreign Policy. These are the centrality of the United Nations, cooperation with the economically advanced Western nations, and its identity as an Asian nation.

Japan has a unique position in the United Nations both as an industrialized nation and as a part of Asia, which is still a developing area. This position should ideally put it in the role of a mediator, but has more often led to conflict.

Japan's military situation has led to another anomaly. While recognizing the importance of the United Nation's function as a preserver of peace, Japan is unable to send troops to participate in UN peacekeeping operations because of its renunciation of arms as embodied in article 9 of the Japanese constitution. Thus, when Secretary-General Dag Hammarskjöld requested that Japan send 10 officers from its Self Defense Forces to join the UN Observation Group in Lebanon in 1958, the Japanese government felt obliged to turn down the request. Japan has endeavored to give economic assistance in place of such military assistance.

UN Agencies and UN Nongovernmental Organizations in Japan——At present there are ten UN agencies operating in Japan: the UN Information Center, the UN University Center, the Statistical Institute for Asia and the Pacific, the UN Center for Rural Development, the ILO Tōkyō Branch Office, the Tōkyō Office of the International Bank for Reconstruction and Development and the International Development Association, the United Nations Children's Fund (UNICEF) Office in Japan, the branch office in Japan of the United Nations High Commissioner for Refugees (UNHCR), the United Nations Development Program (UNDP) Tōkyō Liaison Office, and the United Nations Industrial Development Organization (UNIDO) Investment Promotion Service of Tōkyō.

The UN University is the single largest agency of this group. Plans for creating it were ratified at the 27th meeting of the General Assembly in 1972, and it began its activities in Tōkyō in 1974. The university is unique in that it has no student body, maintaining instead a large network of research facilities. It also has an autonomy not found in other UN agencies. The university has established the problems of hunger, individual and social development, and the use and control of natural resources as primary research areas, and is now engaged in research activities with the assistance of 21 cooperating agencies. Funds for maintaining the university come from governments, foundations, universities, and individuals in member nations of the United Nations. As host country, Japan has pledged a total of $100 million for the operation of the facility.

The importance that Japan places on the role of the United Nations is also reflected in the 12 nongovernmental organizations registered with the United Nations in Japan. These include the Japan Red Cross Society, the UN Association of Japan, the National Federation of UNESCO Associations in Japan, and the Japanese Committee of the World Conference of Religion for Peace. In 1954 the UN Association of Japan, responding to the strong desire among the Japanese people for world peace, cast and donated a "Peace Bell" to the United Nations. The bell is now exhibited in the UN Headquarters Building in New York.

Japan's Activities at the United Nations—— In order to perform its activities at the United Nations smoothly, Japan has established a UN Bureau at the Ministry of Foreign Affairs and a Permanent Mission to the United Nations based in New York, as well as a permanent delegation to the United Nation's European subheadquarters in Geneva, Switzerland.

In the area of disarmament, as the only nation to have experienced nuclear attacks, Japan has a special interest. It has thus pleaded for an effective international effort to achieve total disarmament and participated in the 1963 Nuclear Test Ban Treaty and the 1968 Nuclear Nonproliferation Treaty. In addition, Japan has attended all UN disarmament conferences and played an active role in both the Committee on Disarmament in Geneva and the 1978 Special Session of the General Assembly devoted to disarmament. Japan's contributions toward disarmament also include a proposal to establish an earthquake data exchange network as a means of verifying nuclear tests and research to solve technical problems involved with forming such a network. Through participation in the International Nuclear Fuel Cycle Evaluation (INFCE) and the Review Conference of the Parties to the Treaty on the Nonproliferation of Nuclear Weapons, Japan has sought technical measures to prevent nuclear proliferation and promote the peaceful use of atomic energy.

As an advanced industrial nation, Japan has actively participated in discussions on economic questions involving the Third World, natural resources, energy, food supply, and population. Japan also participates in economic development activities like the UN Development Program (UNDP).

With its concern for problems of human rights, Japan participated in May 1979 in the International Covenant on Economic, Social, and Cultural Rights. Japan also attended the August 1979 World Conference to Combat Racism and Racial Discrimination, in which 123 nations, as well as agencies of the United Nations, participated. Japan has shown unswerving opposition to the apartheid policies of South Africa while at the same time encouraging the peaceful abolition of such practices. Other areas of Japanese participation have included the UN conferences on the peaceful use of outer space, the law of the sea, the human environment, and the position of women.

Japan is exceeded only by the United States and the Soviet Union in its allotment for UN expenditures; in 1980 its share accounted for 9.6 percent of the total. It also made a separate contribution of $10 million in 1974 to help offset the organization's deficit.

The relatively small number of Japanese serving on the staff of the United Nations compared to the size of its contributions has been a continuing source of concern, and the Japanese government has presented its case to the secretary-general. The 33rd session of

the General Assembly accepted a resolution to fill 40 percent of all vacancies during 1979–80 with nationals from unrepresented and under-represented countries, opening the door for a possible increase in Japanese representation. See also LEAGUE OF NATIONS AND JAPAN; INTERNATIONAL RELATIONS.

📖——Akashi Yasushi, Kokusai rengō, 2nd ed (1975). Gaimushō, Waga gaikō no kinkyō 23 (1979). Iguchi Sadao, ed, Kokusai rengō, vol 32 of Nihon gaikōshi (Kajima Shuppankai, 1972). Saitō Shizuo, Kokusai rengō ron josetsu, 3rd ed (1981). SAITŌ Shizuo

United Social Democratic Party

(Shakai Minshu Rengō). Political party established in March 1978 by the merger of two groups led by people who had broken with the JAPAN SOCIALIST PARTY: (1) the Shakai Shimin Rengō (Socialist Citizens' League), which had been created by EDA SATSUKI in May 1977 to carry on the ideals of his father EDA SABURŌ; and (2) a group led by DEN HIDEO and Hata Yutaka (b 1925), both of whom had broken with the Japan Socialist Party in September 1977. The party calls for the establishment of a free socialist democratic society. Its leader in 1982 was Den Hideo.   Daniel A. METRAUX

United States and Japan

The United States has played a unique and important role in the history of modern Japan. The American people, their ideas, institutions, and tastes have exerted tremendous influence upon the Japanese people. The Japanese, too, have shaped the course of American history, most dramatically by threatening the national security of the United States but also through immigration and economic transactions. At various times during the 130-year history of direct encounter, the relationship between the two countries has been characterized by exclusiveness, separation, power, and antagonism on the one hand, and by shared aspirations, accommodation, understanding, and compatibility on the other. The story, which is still being written, forms a unique chapter in the history of cross-cultural relations.

The Opening of Relations (1853–1890)—— The first direct encounter between the United States and Japan occurred with the arrival of Commodore Matthew PERRY and his fleet off the coast of Japan in July 1853. Formal relations began the following year with the signing of the KANAGAWA TREATY, the first of Japan's treaties with the West that marked the OPENING OF JAPAN. In 1858 the HARRIS TREATY, negotiated by American consul Townsend HARRIS, began the process of opening Japanese ports to Western traders. Thus, the United States spearheaded the effort to break down Japan's NATIONAL SECLUSION and inaugurate the era of modern international relations. In 1860 the KANRIN MARU, the first modern warship under Japanese command, accompanied the American warship that carried a shogunate mission to ratify the Harris Treaty.

No two societies could have been more different in the mid-19th century than Japan and the United States. Japan was a society with little international contact, where peace and relative stability had been ensured through an elaborate system of government, and where a sense of unity and cohesiveness had been fostered through racial homogeneity, Confucian orthodoxy, and a widespread system of education. The inhabitants had to live with limited natural resources, with no prospect of migration beyond their boundaries, and little thought that they could effect fundamental social change. The United States, by contrast, was a country of immigrants and of expanding geographical horizons. It had been an independent political entity for barely 70 years and its future was by no means determined. Sectional, racial, and economic conflicts were prevalent. At the same time, the people—except for slaves—enjoyed an abundance of resources, opportunities, and rights. They assumed that the country would grow in size, population, and culture, and would soon emerge as the most advanced in the entire world.

Although it was little more than an accident that the United States, rather than another Western country, was instrumental in causing the end of Japanese seclusion, this fact was of crucial significance for the subsequent development of Japan. For one thing, the American obsession with material progress and mechanical arts brought about an infusion of Western technology about which the Japanese had known but little. Japan was able to obtain the most up-to-date of modern products from the United States. The Japanese also became interested in the history of the country that had opened Japan's doors to the world. Japanese leaders were fascinated with the story of the founding of the American republic, and with its political and economic institutions. As more and more American sailors, merchants, and diplomats arrived from across the Pacific, the Japanese became conscious of the importance of the ocean to their position in the world. In addition, since the primary interest of the United States during the 1850s was commercial, not political or territorial, American traders went to Japan to enjoy their universally acknowledged right to engage in commerce. In doing so, they laid the foundation for a mode of international intercourse that would be critically important to the Japanese.

Especially after the Meiji Restoration of 1868, Japan's new leaders were preoccupied with the question of ensuring domestic stability even as they instituted political and social changes. They were eager to effect orderly change at home so as to maintain a stable environment for initiating programs for economic development and cultural modernization. In all these respects the United States had much to offer, as a model and as a provider of technology. The American political process of orderly transfer of power, as exemplified by George Washington's peaceful retirement and replacement by John Adams—an instance that was cited on numerous occasions by Japanese writers—was a major discovery that made a deep impression on the Japanese of the 1860s. Although the American Civil War was, in a sense, a failure of the system to accommodate dissent, the Japanese admired the way in which the United States emerged from the turmoil as one entity, apparently even more strongly united than before. In the postbellum years, rapid industrialization and urbanization added a new dimension to Japanese understanding of the United States. Japanese diplomats, businessmen, and students admired the energies of an industrializing America as well as the various social movements it was giving rise to. Although Japan's political and economic problems were quite different from those in the United States, travelers and students who visited America were attracted to various social theories that were being developed there to cope with the complex issues of industrialization and urbanization. For those Japanese who felt alienated from the course of Meiji politics, "the sacred land of liberty" offered an inviting prospect.

Even more important in the Japanese view was the American way of conducting external relations. The Japanese in this period, especially after about 1880, became obsessed with the Darwinian contest that seemed to characterize world affairs and with the seeming nonchalance with which the mighty nations went about subjugating the weak. Few Japanese leaders argued initially that their nation should emulate the great powers; they knew all too well that Japanese pretensions to being a great power would simply be scorned. Moreover, overseas adventures could exacerbate domestic tensions, and what the country needed first of all was to effect necessary changes at home. But the United States impressed them as somewhat different in orientation from the other Western powers. Americans did not seem as intent on acquiring territory or subjugating peoples overseas. Instead, their external affairs were largely an extension of domestic private activities, both economic and religious. They were extending their commercial interests and cultural influences as they went abroad as merchants, missionaries, and tourists. Very few overseas Americans were in the armed forces, and none was in the colonial service. Thus American foreign affairs were essentially private, peaceful, and informal. The Japanese referred to this type of external activity as "peaceful expansionism," to distinguish it from more blatant cases of aggression and avarice. Not that peaceful expansionism was any less expansionist, or that economic competition was any less competitive. But the Japanese were more impressed with American-style expansionism because it was not overtly supported by gunboats, because its success depended on the vitality and resourcefulness of individual citizens, and because the country could compete with others without having to build large-scale armed forces. This, wrote many Japanese during the 1880s, was what Japan too should do in its external affairs. The United States appeared to be a model of an enterprising nation that, through the process of commercial and cultural expansion, promoted domestic economic and social development, while at the same time contributing to the peace and well-being of other peoples.

At first there were more Americans in Japan than Japanese in America. Many of these Americans were school teachers, government advisers, missionaries, and educators who were instrumental in imparting to eager Japanese the essence and secrets of Western civilization. Young Japanese men and women acquired their first knowledge of Western history, geography, mathematics, sciences, and religion from foreign teachers and visitors, among whom Americans were numerous, especially Protestant missionaries and secondary-school teachers (see FOREIGN EMPLOYEES OF THE MEIJI PERIOD). Meiji Japanese officials and intellectuals assumed that state initiatives would not be sufficient in the development of a new national identity. Much more crucial would be the roles of individuals and private associations in learning from, and trying to approximate, the material culture and spiritual developments of Europe and America, so that in time Japanese and Westerners would come to share similar outlooks and orientations. This type of reasoning led a growing number of Japanese to advocate migration to the United States, and already by 1890 several thousand had reached Hawaii and the West Coast (see EMIGRATION; JAPANESE AMERICANS IN HAWAII). Although most of them were lured primarily by the prospect of gaining riches quickly, the emigration was a major landmark in that it signified a departure from the tradition of exclusiveness and self-isolation. There was optimism that Japanese would do as well overseas as at home, that in time they would become thoroughly Westernized and exemplars of world progress. As Japanese emigrants learned from their hosts and evolved as modern citizens of the world, they would in time be able to make a significant contribution to peace and prosperity in the Pacific area. Some writers were so sanguine as to assert that in the not too distant future Japanese and Americans would become the leaders in mankind's perpetual progression toward material and cultural fulfillment.

Power Relations in Asia (1890–1920)——Unfortunately, this notion proved to be a grand illusion. In the decades after 1850 stress had been placed on similarities and closeness rather than differences and separation between the Japanese and American people. A transformation took place after 1890, and for a variety of reasons—many of them, it should be noted, related to domestic developments in each country—Japan and the United States began to stress the power factor in their external affairs. Both countries began acquiring large arsenals and strengthening their armed forces, became more assertive toward their weaker neighbors, obtained overseas territories, and entered into world politics. The roots of Japanese and American imperialism had little to do with their bilateral relations before 1890, but once the two governments decided to join the game of power politics, a new theme was inevitably added to these relations. The old theme of private intercourse and peaceful competition never disappeared and would continue to represent one current in US-Japanese relations. Alongside this, however, would develop another current characterized by naval rivalry, collision and collusion over China, and the threat of military conflict. Much of this developed because the two countries were Pacific nations, both coveting, or intent upon denying to the other, such territories as Hawaii and the Philippines. Both were concerned with the fates of Korea and China, and frequently one nation's gain there was viewed as the other's loss.

Economic and emigration matters, too, came to be viewed within the framework of power relations. With Japan launching a program of industrialization after the Sino-Japanese War (1894–95) and the United States overtaking Great Britain and Germany as the world's major manufacturing nation, the stage was set for a commercial rivalry in the underdeveloped areas of the world, particularly in China. With the establishment of Japanese colonial administration in southern Manchuria after the Russo-Japanese War of 1904–05 and in Korea in 1910, Japanese merchants and industrialists enjoyed preferential treatment there, to the chagrin of their American competitors. The United States, on its part, gave special privileges to its own traders in Hawaii and the Philippines. The sense of power rivalry likewise affected Japanese emigration to Hawaii and the United States. Tens of thousands of emigrants to Hawaii came to be seen as a threat to the interests and power of the islands' white minority, of whom Americans were most numerous. The movement for annexation to the United States, which was successfully consummated in 1898, was in part motivated by a desire to prevent a Japanese takeover. Similar reasoning underlay opposition to Japanese immigration on the West Coast, where the number of Japanese increased from just over 20,000 in 1900 to over 125,000 in 1907. Although still a small fraction of the population of the West Coast states, they appeared to some to be the spearhead of a far more substantial migration. Japanese themselves were saying that as many as one million immigrants would settle in California and transform it into a region with strong Japanese connections. The California legislature attempted to restrict this immigration by enacting the Alien Land Act in 1913 (see ALIEN LAND ACTS). Although the number of Japanese immigrants was small, it gave rise to serious concern for American security—a concern that was shared by such knowledgeable public figures as President Theodore ROOSEVELT and Secretary of State Elihu Root—while millions of newcomers from Europe were being accepted with equanimity. This disparity in attitudes indicated that American society, no less than Japanese, valued homogeneity and reacted strongly to the entry of "alien" elements. Most Japanese immigrants, to be sure, did not consider themselves alien forces but were eager to adapt to the American environment and to contribute to the economic and cultural development of the new land. But the more they succeeded in doing so, the more troubling their presence was to Americans concerned with security. In an age when the powerful nations were expanding in all directions, it was not surprising that the immigration question became bound up with the American-Japanese imperialist rivalry. See also "YELLOW PERIL."

Imperialism and power politics, however, can also give rise to stable relationships among nations. In place of a continuous struggle for supremacy, an equilibrium sometimes develops based on the recognition of preserves of rights and interests. The United States and Japan followed this pattern. While they came to view their relationship as that of two rival powers, they were also interested in a stable balance in the Pacific region. The United States gave up its extraterritorial rights in Japan in 1895 (see UNEQUAL TREATIES, REVISION OF), and after the turn of the century a number of agreements were made to respect the status quo and to honor respective spheres of influence. The KATSURA-TAFT AGREEMENT of 1905 and the TAKAHIRA-ROOT AGREEMENT of 1908 were both designed to assure the two countries that their positions and interests in Asia and the Pacific would not be threatened through unilateral action. Roughly speaking, these and similar understandings amounted to endorsing Japan's continental expansion, while recognizing America's position as a major colonial and naval power in the Pacific. Japan also agreed to restrictions on emigration to the United States, particularly in the GENTLEMEN'S AGREEMENT of 1907 and 1908.

Whatever the merit of these agreements, some Japanese were bitterly resentful of the Americans for having rejected them as immigrants. They became so affected by what they took to be insurmountable barriers separating the two peoples thay they turned to philosophical and cultural fatalism, believing that conflict, not convergence or harmony, was inevitable in US-Japanese relations. Some observers put the idea in the context of PAN-ASIANISM, the view that there was something unique about Japan and other Asian countries that set them apart from the West. In this perspective, East and West were mutually incompatible and incomprehensible, and Japan and the United States could never hope to share common interests, much less come to understand each other fully. This pan-Asianism was a product of the Japanese experience in North America at the turn of the century, and was a reaction not only against the exclusionist movement in the United States but also against Meiji Japan's Westernizing efforts. At the level of cultural relations, many Japanese were coming to the view that the vaunted success of modern Japanese transformation had simply made the nation more like, but not exactly identical with, a Western country; this implied that the West's superior power had defined the nature of Japan's cultural self-image. If Japan were to overcome its sense of inferiority, this line of thinking went, it would be necessary to assert its cultural independence, in addition to strengthening itself as a power.

Such thinking had a logic of its own, and it was revived from time to time whenever Japanese spokesmen wanted to justify a unilateral action in Asia, or when they sought to explain why they were not totally accepted by Westerners. And yet pan-Asianism never became the predominant theme in US-Japanese relations. Even during the height of the immigration crisis and of Japan's continental expansionism, the idea of the nation's separate identity—both culturally and physically—appealed only to a small minority of ideologues and exponents of military preparedness against the West. Government officials, businessmen, and intellectuals refused to believe that conflict, fatal incompatibility, and separate existences doomed Japanese relations with Europe and the United States, for to do so would have implied giving up all attempts at economic and political transformation, an objective to which they continued to commit themselves. They were disappointed by the American rejection of Japanese immigrants, but this did not, in most instances, lead them to advocate retaliation by ejecting Americans from Japan, or severing all ties between the two countries. Some writers argued, not that Americans and Japanese were racially and culturally too far apart to live in harmony, but that they should continue to strive for achieving the goal of mutual accommodation and cooperation. They pointed out that the Americans who rejected Asian immigrants were betraying the very principles upon which their forefathers had established their own country. If only they remained true to those principles, there would be the genuine possibility of cooperation between the two peoples in building an earthly paradise. The Japanese, according to such writers, should remind the Americans of their own heritage of tolerance and freedom, rather than castigate the whole of American society.

Such a nonfatalist, cooperationist view of US-Japanese relations was not just an abstract idea. It was a product of the major orientations of early-20th-century Japan, which stressed economic growth and cultural change. The United States was becoming important as a supplier of capital and technology for Japan and as a market for Japanese exports. After the Russo-Japanese War, in particular, loans totaling nearly $100 million were provided by American banks and investors to help Japan's "postwar management," and the United States consistently purchased more than 30 percent of Japan's exports, mostly silk products. Moreover, in Japanese politics a new breed of businessmen—oriented toward the wider world of financial transactions and forming close personal as well as business ties with their counterparts in New York and London—was emerging and gaining influence. Their perspective, stressing the nation's economic dependence on the United States and the consequent need to maintain stable, orderly relations, provided an important corrective to the fatalistic and pan-Asianist viewpoints. The signing of a treaty of commerce with America in 1911, in which Tōkyō and Washington shelved the immigration issue and concentrated on provisions for further growth of trade, represented a victory for this position.

The years of World War I (1914–19) saw these various perspectives vying with one another for influence over Japanese politics and foreign policy. The Taishō period (1912–26) began with the death of the Meiji emperor, symbolizing the changing of the guard between the old oligarchs and men who had not experienced the turmoil of the 1850s and 1860s. For a time these new leaders were seriously divided over the direction of the country's domestic and external affairs. Those who saw international relations primarily in power terms—notably army and navy officers, members of patriotic societies, and those with a vested interest in maintaining a large-scale military establishment and colonial service—undoubtedly felt vindicated in their perceptions when war broke out in Europe, seemingly reducing international relations to questions of naked armed combat, opportunistic alliances, unconcealed national egoism, and territorial aggrandizement. From a power point of view, the European war gave Japan a great opportunity to solidify and expand its hold on the continent of Asia (see TWENTY-ONE DEMANDS) and its position in the Pacific Ocean. With little effort it attacked and took possession of the German strongholds in the Shandong (Shantung) region of China and the Pacific, making Japan undisputably the major power in East Asia (see SHANDONG [SHANTUNG] QUESTION). Japan thus was pitted against the United States, which was also emerging as one of the principal naval powers of the world. The two nations became allies during the brief war period (1917–18) and signed a pledge (see LANSING-ISHII AGREEMENT) to respect the status quo, but the sense of rivalry was not dissipated. The two navies made contingency plans for warfare against each other, and even when their armed forces collaborated, as they did during the SIBERIAN INTERVENTION in 1918, their mutual animosity was only thinly disguised. It appeared as if the two nations' rivalry and competition would come to define the future of Asia's international politics.

Yet, at the same time, the theme of economic interdependence did not disappear during the war years, but grew even stronger. The overall trade of the two countries more than tripled, and they were selling four or five times as much to each other as before the war. While military strategists and some civilian chauvinists talked of a possible conflict in the Pacific after the European war was concluded, businessmen and politicians never lost sight of the economic relationship. Moreover, the domestic political situation was such that a leadership dedicated to warfare could not have emerged either in Tōkyō or in Washington. In Japan particularly, Taishō politics were characterized by growing restlessness with oligarchic rule and militaristic orientation, and by increasing assertiveness of the political parties and the business community, which were closely linked. For the first time in modern history, moreover, economically disadvantaged groups, workers, and farmers showed interest in national politics and organized themselves, through the help of intellectuals, into a movement against the establishment. Under those circumstances stability became a major preoccupation of the government and business elites. In time army and navy leaders, too, came around to accepting the need for domestic peace. The time, then, was not opportune for a military dictatorship, which would have been needed if Japan were to have seriously planned for war against the United States. Instead, it was considered better to avoid conflict and to continue extending commercial ties with America and other countries. For example, Admiral KATŌ TOMOSABURŌ, who played a key role in the 1917 war plan in the Pacific, became an advocate of accommodation and economic cooperation with the United States four years later. He argued that Japan simply could not afford to go to war with the rich and powerful country.

More than economic considerations were bringing the two countries together. In the United States and Japan there were sentiments favoring redefinition of national objectives to make a definite contribution to international peace and amity. In the United States, President Woodrow Wilson clearly took the lead in giving concrete form to such sentiments. He called upon his countrymen, and all peoples throughout the world, to consider the indivisible nature of peace and prosperity. Instead of pursuing selfish goals and strengthening themselves at the expense of others, all should join together in the common task of maintaining a stable world order so that each could mature politically and develop economically. Domestic and international developments were thus inseparably linked in Wilson's conception. It followed that voluntary cooperation at home among various groups and individuals would be matched by cooperation among countries of the world, in particular by cooperative action among the advanced industrialized countries to promote economic interdependence and to develop other parts of the world. In such a scheme, military build-up and power games would no longer be as important as broadly defined cultural pursuits.

Wilson's perspective was articulated at a critical moment in Japanese history when the country's leaders were groping for new ways to define national objectives, going beyond the augmentation of military and economic power which had provided the basic framework for national action during the preceding decades. Reflecting the intensifying movements against continued oligarchic rule and for democratization of politics, some Japanese leaders began to call for a new sense of national identity in the international environment. Instead of merely trying to catch up with the Western powers, or reacting to their actions, Japan should, they asserted, establish a definition of itself as a nation committed to larger international objectives. Rather than pursuing particularistic military or economic goals, the Japanese should couch their aspirations in terms of international cooperation and interdependence. This was how men like Prime Minister HARA TAKASHI and the delegates to the Paris Peace Conference—MAKINO NOBUAKI, SHIDEHARA KIJŪRŌ, and others— came to embrace the emerging internationalism of the postwar era. These ideas and movements were "the trends of the times," Makino observed, and Japan had little choice but to identify with them. That was the only way to make national existence viable and national identity meaningful. It was no accident that such a view coincided with a new pattern of US-Japanese relations that would stress their cooperation and partnership in building a better world, not their conflict and incompatibility in a competitive and imperfect world. See also TAISHŌ DEMOCRACY.

The Interwar Period (1920–1930) —— The above pattern was given promising institutional form during the WASHINGTON CONFERENCE (1921–22). The conference dealt with many of the bilateral and multilateral issues that had not been settled at the Paris Peace Conference. The FOUR-POWER TREATY (1921) did away with the ANGLO-JAPANESE ALLIANCE and substituted for it a consultative pact among the United States, Japan, Britain, and France; the WASHINGTON NAVAL TREATY OF 1922 established a ceiling for the navy of each of these countries and Italy; and the NINE-POWER TREATY (1922) pledged joint action by several nations in China so as to assist the latter's gradual evolution as an equal member of the international community. These agreements were quintessentially "liberal-capitalist-internationalist"; that is, they were concluded among nations oriented toward the preservation and stabilization of a capitalist world order on the basis of unfettered economic development and interdependence. They were also products of the postwar liberal imagination, envisioning a world without an armament race where goods and ideas traveled freely and where peace was ensured through a commitment to orderly social change.

Although the United States Senate rejected the League of Nations, delivering a severe political setback to Wilson's leadership, the success of the Washington Conference kept his vision alive. Indeed, the Republican administrations of presidents Warren Harding, Calvin Coolidge, and Herbert Hoover were no less committed to liberal internationalism than Wilson's. They shared his linking of domestic and international developments, both of which were to be oriented toward stability and harmony. At the same time, international relations became closely bound up with intercultural relations. The country's more formal, power-based relations with others were to approximate its more informal economic and cultural ties with them. Such a development was a reflection of the economic power and cultural influence of the United States during the 1920s. American technology, business methods, mass culture, and popular values spread to other lands, and there was a sense that order and stability in one country depended on order and stability in others.

The Japanese generally fitted themselves into this scheme of things. The Tōkyō government accepted the Washington agreements with alacrity and embraced such foreign policy goals as disarmament, equal economic opportunity, noninterference in affairs of other countries, peaceful resolution of conflict, cooperation in China, and active participation in League of Nations affairs. The new tendency was to identify Japan as a partner in the building of a more peaceful, stable, and prosperous international society. This was a vision that appealed to those who had become weary of the old slogan about enriching and strengthening the state; instead, they came to talk of "Japan in the World," and of the need for Japanese to become "world citizens." But these ideas were more than just abstract idealism. The new internationalism provided a framework within which economic relations with the United States would become closer. Indeed, the decade was characterized by an impressive flow of American capital and technology into Japan, so that by 1929 the latter had become an advanced country in terms of modern industrial equipment, mass production, and sophisticated systems of banking and finance. American assistance was particularly needed to rebuild Tōkyō after the earthquake of 1923, an event that also marked a point of departure for the Americanization of Japanese culture. Movies, jazz, radio, mass-circulation journalism, department stores, and ice cream parlors epitomized the Japanese borrowing from America's mass culture, while the popularity of John Dewey (1859–1952), Thorstein Veblen (1857–1929), and others signified the impact of American higher learning on Japan. Close friendships were formed between bankers, politicians, journalists, and even admirals of the two countries. The American press reported glowingly of Japanese "liberalism."

Not everything, of course, was conducive to optimism. The twenties, after all, was in the United States the decade of Prohibition, the Scopes trial, and the Ku Klux Klan, and in Japan, of the assassination of Prime Minister Hara (1921), the massacre of many Korean residents in the wake of the Tōkyō Earthquake, and the repressive PEACE PRESERVATION LAW OF 1925. These exemplified the illiberal, exclusionist, and chauvinistic tendencies in the two societies. The Immigration Act of 1924 (often called the Japanese Exclusion Act), passed by the US Congress despite pleas by both Japanese and American officials, provoked anti-American outbursts in Japan, resulting in the mushrooming of right-wing associations (see UNITED STATES IMMIGRATION ACTS OF 1924, 1952, AND 1965). Japanese nationalists condemned the policies of disarmament, economic interdependence, and international cooperation as mere replicas of American ideas. They bemoaned the spreading influence of American culture, which they said was turning Japanese into Westernized robots. They particularly resented what appeared to be the constraint exercised over Japan's China policy by the United States, making Japan unable to respond to growing Chinese nationalism that was challenging foreign, especially Japanese, rights and interests. They preferred unilateral action to protect these interests, and in this determination they were supported by Japanese in China and Manchuria, among whom the most powerful was the GUANDONG (KWANTUNG) ARMY. The army's complete indifference to the idea of international cooperation was demonstrated when some of its officers assassinated ZHANG ZUOLIN (Chang Tso-lin), the Manchurian warlord, in 1928, in an attempt to create turmoil in the region and thereby provide a pretext for quick military action.

Despite all such manifestations of illiberalism and anti-internationalism, the decade established a framework for US-Japanese ties that were to prove durable. Japan's economy and culture became almost irreversibly oriented toward the United States, while in the United States there emerged a view of Japan as basically peaceful and cooperationist in outlook. This did not mean that the differences between the two peoples disappeared. The so-called Japanese Exclusion Act showed that American society continued to view Japanese immigrants unfavorably. However, such instances of mutual incompatibility and antagonism were not allowed to define the prevailing pattern of US-Japanese relations. They constituted but a minor series of events and not a major theme in these relations, at least in the minds of those Japanese who dominated the country's political, economic, and cultural life. These leaders preferred to stress more positive images of the United States in order to foster domestic stability and development. Although the exclusion of the Japanese was unfortunate, they did not want the episode to provoke the latent chauvinism of the Japanese toward the United States, and they preferred to think that the two peoples shared the same fundamental commitment to development and orderly political change, which in turn contributed to world peace and interdependence. YOSHINO SAKUZŌ, NITOBE INAZŌ, and other leading intellectuals reiterated the theme that Japan's Americanization was a good and necessary development simply because it was the inevitable trend of the modern world.

The decade of the 1920s was also significant because the Japanese who grew up in those years and were affected by the Americanizing tendencies of the nation's life were precisely those who would emerge as the leaders in post–World War II Japan. Party politicians, businessmen, academic figures, journalists, bureaucrats, labor union leaders, and students who began their careers, or were in their middle careers, during that decade would reemerge after 1945 and be instrumental in redefining national life. They would remember the time when US-Japanese relations had been founded on political, economical, and cultural cooperation. They would also realize that such a pattern of relations had been dependent on, and conducive to, a system of orderly change and cultural progression in Japan. Although their American counterparts did not share the sense of the overriding importance of US-Japanese relations, they too would come to recall the 1920s fondly. This common point of departure would be extremely important in the postwar development of the United States–Japan relationship. But first came the interlude of WORLD WAR II hostilities.

War Period (1930–1945) —— Some Japanese historians have called the period of 1930 to 1945 "the fifteen years' war." There is little question that, despite the apologetics and revisionist scholarship on the subject, the Japanese nation committed acts of unjustifiable aggression on other peoples. It is also true that in this period the Japanese military and its civilian supporters often couched their aggression in the language of a new Asian order. Japan, according to this conception, was to take the lead in ridding Asia of Western imperialism so that the East would rise again, true to its ancient legacy of harmony and unity, liberated from the bane of Western materialism and individualism. The United States, as the major capitalist and liberal democracy, came to symbolize the power, philosophy, and ambitions of the West. Although these were the very factors that had earlier induced the Japanese to try to emulate American culture and bourgeois lifestyles, after 1930 they came to mean something evil against which the nation must struggle. Differences between the two societies were now emphasized, and the unpleasant experiences of Japanese exclusion were recalled afresh. Instead of couching Japanese foreign policy in the framework of cooperation, it was argued that the nation should act boldly and unilaterally in defense of its own interests, regardless of how it was viewed by outsiders.

In the history of US-Japanese relations two causes for this shift in particular may be mentioned. First, the world economic crisis, starting with the Wall Street crash of 1929, undermined the foundations of capitalist interdependence. Because cooperative US-Japanese ties had been an aspect of, and had been sustained by, the capitalist international order, this crisis obviously affected bilateral relations. The economic aspect of their respective foreign affairs, hitherto the dominant theme, no longer defined the overall structure of US-Japanese relations as both governments began initiating policies—high tariffs, quotas, exchange control, devaluation, gold embargoes—that were motivated by nationalistic policies. Some leaders in the two countries, most notably Herbert Hoover in the United States and INOUE JUNNOSUKE in Japan, valiantly tried to stem the tide and to revive economic internationalism, but the former was defeated by Franklin Delano ROOSEVELT in the presidential election of 1932, and the latter was assassinated by a right-wing fanatic in the same year. After 1933 there were occasional attempts by Washington to put an end to the worldwide trend toward particularistic, autarkic economic policies, but those efforts were doomed to be subordinated to the increasingly more serious issues of security and survival.

These issues did not initially arise in US-Japanese relations, but they were the driving force behind the Japanese military's decision to act unilaterally. Both the army and navy judged that the nation was justified in resorting to forceful measures in order to protect its vital interests on the Asian continent and in the Pacific Ocean. More specifically, the army was determined to establish permanent control over Manchuria and, to a degree, over northern China; the navy

wanted parity with the naval strengths of the United States and Great Britain and pushed unsuccessfully toward this goal in the LONDON NAVAL CONFERENCES in 1930 and 1935–36. Theirs was the language of power and had a logic of its own. Certainly it seemed justifiable to use force and augment power when few obstacles stood in their way and when economic considerations seemed less and less relevant in determining foreign policy. Although such action did not immediately pose a threat to American security, in time it could not fail to do so, given the habit of thought that reduced bilateral relations to power equations. So long as Japan was engaging in its aggressive acts and military build-ups alone, the United States had little cause to be unduly alarmed. After 1938, however, the possibility grew that Japanese power might be combined with that of Germany and Italy as well as of conquered China. The possibility became a reality when the TRIPARTITE PACT was signed in 1940, and even more ominous when Tōkyō and Moscow concluded a neutrality pact in April 1941. The architects of these arrangements, notably MATSUOKA YŌSUKE, may not have necessarily wanted to threaten the United States; in fact, they continued to assert that a balance of power between the United States and the Axis partners was the best guarantor of world stability and peace. But this was not how the situation was perceived in Washington. Given Germany's military successes against the European countries during 1940 and 1941, the United States finally came to take the Japanese menace seriously. It began preparations for war against the Axis powers, and in the Asian-Pacific region took such steps as giving military aid to China, fortifying the Philippines, and keeping the bulk of its naval fleet in the Pacific Ocean.

Side by side with these external developments, there were changes within Japan that provided the second major cause of the growing hostile attitude toward the United States. After 1930 the party politicians, financiers, industrialists, civilian bureaucrats, and intellectuals steadily lost their influence as the country's economic crisis worsened. Sentiment grew in favor of a drastic change in the domestic political and economic orientations to put an end to the crisis. The series of assassinations (FEBRUARY 26TH INCIDENT; MAY 15TH INCIDENT), which eliminated some of the leaders of the existing arrangements, were accomplished with relative impunity because there was a psychological readiness to accept them. Right-wing groups and military officers, who had never been committed to the idea of a cooperative international order, were beneficiaries of this situation. Through terrorism, intimidation, and propaganda they steadily transformed the structure of leadership, so that by the middle of the 1930s the political parties had lost their influence, and their business allies were looking elsewhere for support. In justifying these acts and trying to consolidate their gains, the proponents of change found it convenient to couch them in anti-Western, pan-Asianist language. They asserted that bourgeois liberalism and capitalist democracy had been tested and found wanting, that they could not solve the grave economic and social ills of Western countries or of Japan, and that the only alternative for the nation was to repudiate Western values and to transform national politics, economy, and culture along non-Western lines. Although most pro-American leaders had been assassinated, silenced, or intimidated into collaboration with the exponents of the new domestic arrangements, the anti-American group thought it necessary to deal pro-Westernism a coup de grace by instituting educational and cultural reform programs. The schools were to emphasize "the essence of the national entity," the intellectuals were to cleanse themselves of vestiges of Western influences, and the whole nation was to dedicate itself to the establishment of a new Asian order with Japan as its undisputed spokesman. See also MILITARISM.

The result of these developments was that by 1941, when US-Japanese tensions were mounting as the two powers confronted each other in the Asian-Pacific region, there was self-consciousness about the cultural aspect of that confrontation. It was, according to Japanese spokesmen, the struggle of Asia to liberate itself from the West and, in the eyes of Americans, the last stand of Western civilization. When war came in December 1941, therefore, it was hardly surprising that the government and press of each country pounded on the theme of basic incompatibility. Campaigns of hatred, symbolized by such acts as the burning of American dolls that had been sent to Japanese villagers as tokens of friendship in more peaceful days, and the American relocation of Japanese residents on the West Coast, many of whom were United States citizens, to detention camps (see JAPANESE AMERICANS, WARTIME RELOCATION OF), were more than instances of wartime hysteria. They filled a psychological need to understand the nature of the war in terms of history and culture, and they expressed a resentment that had been building up in each country over what appeared to be the growing influence of the other.

It would be wrong, however, to focus solely on the incompatibility of the United States and Japan as powers and as cultures in accounting for the war. The two Pacific powers could have opted for an accommodation, however temporary and uneasy, on the basis of some definition of the status quo. This was what the two sides were groping to achieve in the summer and fall of 1941. Moreover, despite the rhetoric of pan-Asianism, Japanese policy before 1941 had never seriously entertained the idea of detaching the region totally from the rest of the world. Such a task had not seemed feasible at a time when Japan was still dependent on the American supply of petroleum, and regional economic development was never envisioned as a completely self-sufficient process. In fact, although the Japanese spoke a great deal about the new Asian order, there had been virtually no specific planning for its implementation until just prior to the attack on Pearl Harbor. This attack, then, should be viewed not as a premeditated first step for the building of a pan-Asianist order, but as a reaction to what the Japanese leaders considered to be the evolving realities of power relations in the Asian-Pacific region. They saw the country becoming increasingly "encircled," its very security and existence threatened by a formidable combination of the United States and its European allies. The only way to break out of this hostile environment, they asserted, was to try to destroy it. In retrospect, their fears may appear vastly exaggerated, and it certainly was not the intention of the United States or any other country in late 1941 to threaten the Japanese empire, let alone the security of the Japanese homeland. But such perception was bound up with the raison d'être of the military establishment of the country, and to concede the possibility of accommodation with the West would have been tantamount to relinquishing military control of politics. War was apparently the only choice for the military in Japan.

Once the war came, its development naturally hinged on the actual fighting in the Pacific Ocean, on the numerous islands and atolls, in the jungles of Burma, and in the skies of East Asia. It was a simple struggle for power, and the two sides gave it all they had. The outcome was a foregone conclusion, even to the Japanese high command who, in the aftermath of Pearl Harbor, admitted that the initial successes would not endure and that the enemy would soon launch a counterattack. The counterattack came sooner than expected, and within a year after Pearl Harbor, the Japanese leadership was conceding the possibility of failure because of US superiority in shipping, aviation, and natural resources. Much of the history of wartime US-Japanese relations, therefore, was concerned with the cessation of hostilities. Because Japanese victory was out of the question, the war would be terminated either as a draw or as a clear American victory. The former possibility was advocated by some in Japan who believed that the only realistic outcome of the conflict would be a partitioning of the Pacific Ocean into two spheres, with Japan establishing its control over the southwestern Pacific and the continent of Asia. But such a solution was unacceptable to the United States, because it would mean the sacrifice of its Chinese, British, Dutch, and other allies. From the American point of view, Japanese power would have to be eliminated completely from the ocean and its overseas domains liberated. This was accomplished within four years of the initial fighting.

The nonmilitary aspects of the war were more complicated. This becomes evident when one takes a close look at the two countries' war aims (or peace objectives). Wartime propaganda, to be sure, stressed their conflicting aims, the United States standing for such ideals as peace, liberty, and democracy enunciated in the Atlantic Charter, and the Japanese continuing to talk of "liberating greater East Asia from the yoke of the Anglo-American powers." In actuality, however, their ideas were not very different. After all, the Japanese idea of a new Asian order was often couched in idealistic, universalistic language; it was to be a regional system of economic development and prosperity, equality and reciprocity, and cooperation and understanding. Wartime Japanese pronouncements were filled with these and similar concepts that could have been lifted out of American declarations. This was fundamentally because Japanese officials who sought to define war aims had grown up during the 1920s and lived with the vocabulary of American and Western internationalism. Although there had been a halt to this Americanizing process after 1930, it had by no means been eliminated. One could further argue that in some respects the Americanization of Japanese life proceeded uninterrupted even during the war. This was certainly true of such activities as scientific development, urbanization,

mobilization of female workers, and even music. Americans who interrogated Japanese prisoners of war were often amazed to note that they seemed to know far more about the United States than about any other country in the world.

Although rhetorical similarity and cultural coincidences did not tell the whole story of the war, once American power crushed Japanese, the termination of hostilities was achieved with relative ease precisely because the two sides saw it in almost identical terms, that is, as the defeat of Japan's militaristic and Asianist orientation and its return to a more peaceful, cooperationist outlook at home and abroad. In other words, postwar Japan would be reintegrated into a system of interdependent international relations. US-Japanese cultural relations, which had been subordinated to but not completely eliminated by the power struggle, would reemerge as the key to the two countries' association. All of this may indicate that culturally the two countries had not really diverged much after 1930.

Postwar Relations (1945–1980)——The change in US-Japanese relations from wartime hostility to postwar accommodation and cooperation was not really a reversal; it was more a reaffirmation of deeper cultural orientations that had been part of modern Japanese life. At the same time, in an ironic twist of history, postwar Japanese foreign policy came to approximate capitalist internationalism, which had first been inspired by the United States, while the United States often diluted this principle to fit power-oriented cold war strategies.

Not that the power factor was absent from postwar US-Japanese relations. The mere fact that Japanese military power had been destroyed necessitated new arrangements for the maintenance of order and security in the Asian-Pacific region, and the United States became a major architect of the new system in constructing a series of agreements at the YALTA CONFERENCE (1945). In the Asian-Pacific region, as in Europe, a stable relationship among the United States, the Soviet Union, and Britain was envisaged on the basis of the acceptance, tacit or explicit, of their respective spheres of influence. The United States would be the predominant power in the Pacific Ocean, including the Philippines, OKINAWA (to be detached from Japan proper for the time being), and Japan; the Soviet Union would extend its sway over northeast Asia by regaining SAKHALIN and the Kuriles; and Britain would be restored to the colonial areas that had been invaded and occupied by Japanese forces. China would be freed of Japanese control and emerge as a sovereign power, joining the other three in establishing a trusteeship over Korea. These were the power-political arrangements, sometimes known as the Yalta system, that provided a framework of stability during the immediate postwar years. Japan was clearly within the American sphere of influence, a fact that was not seriously challenged by the Soviet Union or other countries.

American officials, however, were not satisfied with a power arrangement alone. They were also eager to push for the realization of a more truly interdependent world of multilateral transactions. This, they believed, would ensure global economic growth, a basic prerequisite for domestic political stability, international order, and prosperity. Japan, because it was under the American OCCUPATION and because its role as a military power had been ended, was a natural place to put these ideals into effect. The Occupation forces soon launched an extensive program of democratizing reform. The task was facilitated by the reemergence of a moderate, internationalist leadership that had been silenced during the preceding period. Architects of postwar Japanese policy such as Shidehara, YOSHIDA SHIGERU, and ASHIDA HITOSHI were well aware of the experiences of the 1920s and were determined to rehabilitate Japan as a peaceful member of a community of economically interdependent nations. Even the Occupation-imposed reform measures confirmed the hopes of these leaders and their followers in the new stability, for they were returning to an old definition of US-Japanese relations as the basic framework for national life.

From 1948 on the United States came to stress Japan's economic rehabilitation and reconstruction rather than decomposition and reform (see DODGE LINE). But this was not really a "reverse course," for it simply confirmed the return to an old, internationalist definition of US-Japanese relations. The basic thrust of American policy, namely, to promote "democratic forces and economic stability" in Japan (as a 1949 memorandum of the National Security Council stated), was nothing new. A liberal and reformist Japan, pursuing active economic and cultural transactions overseas, would be a force for peace and order in Asia, it was believed in Washington, and could be counted upon to resist pressures on regional equilibrium.

Japan's political leaders were in complete agreement and worked assiduously to solidify their control over national policy and politics.

The core of this postwar Japanese position remained remarkably constant, even after the SAN FRANCISCO PEACE TREATY was signed in 1951 and the Occupation ended in 1952. It was a liberal-capitalist-internationalist consensus that sought economic prosperity and political stability at home, gave top priority to scientific and technological development, stressed culture over power, and eschewed military or political roles in the international arena. At the same time, this position continued the nation's subordination to the United States in security matters. Japan remained under the American "nuclear umbrella," and its security was dependent not so much on its modest-scale SELF DEFENSE FORCES as on the UNITED STATES–JAPAN SECURITY TREATIES. In all respects, then, postwar Japan was even more closely linked to the United States than ever before. While a sense of confrontation with the Soviet Union and China often gave power considerations in the United States precedence over purely economic and cultural pursuits, in Japan the more traditionally "American" ideal of private initiative, equal economic opportunity, and cultural interchange was pushed with vigor. For instance, under the slogan, "separation of economics from politics," the Japanese chose to subordinate political questions to economic profits in dealing with the People's Republic of China, unlike the United States whose economic policy toward China derived from the strategy of containment. Japanese foreign policy was thus fairly predictable because those who controlled political and economic affairs had a stake in a stable and liberal international order and because the United States and other countries on the whole tolerated such orientations in postwar Japan. Even the riots and mass movements directed against the new United States–Japan Security Treaty of 1960 (see PEACE MOVEMENT) failed to alter the situation since the Japanese were aware that the military alliance was but one aspect of the country's foreign policy and that the leadership was equally committed to the more popular objectives of economic growth and expansion. The 1961 appointment of Edwin O. REISCHAUER as US ambassador to Japan and the IKEDA-KENNEDY AGREEMENTS of the same year helped strengthen the ties.

By 1970, 25 years after the end of the war, these postwar Japanese orientations had become solidified. In a survey conducted that year, an overwhelming majority of those polled said that Japan should continue to stress economic development and social welfare as the most worthy national goals. Two years later, another survey found that the Japanese wanted to base their security on economic cooperation with all countries, active diplomatic negotiations, the improvement of the people's livelihood, and the promotion of cultural exchanges, but not on the use of military power. In these and other opinion polls, an overwhelming majority approved of the general pattern of postwar life and favored continued close ties with the United States. There was frequently a correlation between the way postwar Japan and the United States were perceived. These opinions indicated that what was "postwar" had now become the norm. To have an affirmative view of the recent past was to reaffirm the economic and cultural aspects of Japanese relations with the United States. It was also to recognize the fact that domestic developments in each of the two countries had an important bearing on the other through the medium of a world order which they sought to construct and which facilitated their expanding interactions. The negotiated return of the OGASAWARA ISLANDS in 1967–68 and the agreement to return Okinawa to Japanese control, announced in the SATŌ-NIXON COMMUNIQUE in 1969, eliminated two sources of anti-American sentiment in Japan.

During the 1970s, however, there were indications that some of these familiar assumptions might no longer be tenable. The pattern of cooperation, and interdependence in US-Japanese relations had developed within a framework of liberal internationalism, which in turn had functioned in a global system of abundance and certain shared values. As the decade wore on, it became increasingly clear that oil and other energy resources were limited, that many new nations had no commitment to liberalism or internationalism, and that in advanced democracies, as well as in socialist and developing countries, larger and larger portions of national budgets were being diverted to military purposes. Often there was a paralysis of government, where state authority was unable to cope with conflicting demands of interest groups, with mounting issues of pollution and waste, and with individual and group terrorism. In both the United States and Japan, public attention was turning inward, and movements for consumer protection, women's and minority rights, and public health tended to overshadow concern with external affairs. In

the realm of power, after the change in the position of the United States in Asia occasioned by the Vietnam imbroglio and the subsequent rapprochement with China, serious questions were being raised about the future of the US-Japanese alliance and about Japan's defense posture. Some politicians in the two countries were calling on Japan to assume a more assertive, military-oriented role in the face of growing Soviet power. Economically, too, trade disputes, exacerbated by fluctuating rates of exchange between dollar and yen, were turning into a political issue, and it no longer appeared sufficient to restate a commitment to liberal principles (see UNITED STATES, ECONOMIC RELATIONS WITH). Economic internationalism was losing some of its appeal in an era of controlled growth and in a world where developing countries were intent on liberating themselves from a world order that had been defined for them by the rich nations. Incidents such as the LOCKHEED SCANDAL of 1976 also soured the relationship. In the sphere of culture, a parochial nationalism as well as an interest in non-Western countries grew in Japan. Instead of identifying with the United States or Europe or posing the old dichotomy of East versus West, some Japanese were arguing that Japan must rediscover its own tradition, others that it must turn neither to the rich and powerful West nor to a parochial East, but to the multiplicity of small and medium-sized countries that make up the bulk of mankind.

US-Japanese relations in the early 1980s, then, have clearly reached a point where reappraisal is inevitable. At issue is whether the ideas and orientations that have served Americans and Japanese well in the past will continue to be viable or whether they may have to look for alternative ways of defining national and international objectives. Whatever the outcome of this reappraisal, the very need for it indicates the enormous importance of US-Japanese relations to both countries. Despite periods of confrontation and crisis, their political, economic, and cultural interpenetration since the 1850s has been a theme, and in postwar Japan the most important thread, in their domestic and external affairs. The relationship has shown that a commitment to economic interchange, cultural openness, and intellectual freedom need not be confined to a Western society but can inspire others as well. Modern Japan has benefited enormously from a world environment that has cherished these objectives. The future of US-Japanese relations will perhaps depend largely on the determination and ability of the Japanese people to dedicate themselves to preserving and strengthening a more open international community.

📖——Akira Iriye, *Across the Pacific: An Inner History of American-East Asian Relations* (1967). Akira Iriye, ed, *Mutual Images: Studies in American-Japanese Relations* (1974). Charles E. Neu, *Troubled Encounter: The United States and Japan* (1974).

Akira IRIYE

United States armed forces in Japan

American military forces stationed in Japan under the provisions of the United States–Japan Security Treaty (see UNITED STATES–JAPAN SECURITY TREATIES). Article 5 of the treaty of 1960 states: "Each party recognizes that an armed attack against either party in the territories under the administration of Japan would be dangerous to its own peace and safety . . ." This provision is the basis of the United States' obligation to render military assistance for Japan's defense and Japan's obligation to provide the Americans with the necessary land facilities for bases and services.

As a result of the 1957 Kishi-Eisenhower joint declaration regarding the early withdrawal of United States military forces stationed in Japan, the United States Army withdrew its fighting divisions from Japan, leaving only supply and maintenance corps. The Fifth Air Force, which is responsible for the air defense of Japan and South Korea, is stationed at Yokota. The Seventh Fleet maintains two supply and repair bases at Yokosuka and Sasebo. In November 1969 the joint United States military command and Fifth Air Force command moved from Fuchū to Yokota. Army headquarters are in Zama, navy headquarters in Yokosuka. The commander of the United States Armed Forces in Japan represents the three branches of the military and coordinates their activities. In 1952, when the security treaty was put into effect, 260,000 American military personnel were in Japan, not counting Okinawa. When the treaty was revised in 1960, the number was reduced to 46,000; in 1979 there were 15,700 United States servicemen in Japan. If Okinawa is included, however, the number was 46,400. The breakdown was as follows: 2,500 army, 7,000 navy, 22,600 marines, and 14,300 air force. Between 1952, when the SAN FRANCISCO PEACE TREATY went into effect, and 1977, the number of incidents and accidents involving United States military personnel on duty was about 36,000 (chiefly traffic accidents); off-duty incidents numbered 110,000 (chiefly assaults and homicides). The number of Japanese killed as a result of on-duty and off-duty accidents was about 500. The American military has jurisdiction over cases involving on-duty servicemen, and Japan has jurisdiction over those involving off-duty servicemen.

At the insistence of the Japanese, the United States forces have gradually reduced the number of bases in Japan. However, in January 1976 the chairman of the Joint Chiefs of Staff announced in a published report that the United States was opposed to further cuts. The United States has asked that Japan take responsibility for part of the expense of maintaining Japanese employees on American bases, and Japan has increased its financial burden. See also UNITED STATES MILITARY BASES, DISPUTES OVER. *Mutsu Gorō*

United States, economic relations with, 1945–1973

Near the close of World War II and again shortly after its conclusion, the legal framework of the postwar international economic system began to take shape. In the wake of the war experience and the intellectual currents of the previous 25 years, the commitment shown at the great conferences on the postwar economic order was truly remarkable. With the exception of the Soviet Union, which soon withdrew from the system, the major participants in the conferences that shaped the General Agreement on Tariffs and Trade (GATT) in 1947 and the Bretton Woods agreement in 1944 all shared, or unfailingly gave lip service to, a central paradigm: the unrestricted flow of goods and services across national boundaries should be the ultimate aim of foreign economic policy. Like their mid-19th-century counterparts, postwar elites assumed that free trade at equilibrium exchange rates would lead to maximum world welfare, and this would occur without any country being made worse off.

Even in their framing, however, the great postwar international economic agreements fell short of liberal economic goals. Repeated de jure and de facto recognition of the special economic and political interests of the major signatories sapped the force of the bold general principles enunciated in each agreement. Nonetheless, the outcome of the new arrangements was a giant step away from the economic nationalism and bloc regionalism of the 1930s. Although not fully achieved, the goal of future economic diplomacy was still unfettered international economic exchange.

The framers of the early postwar world order did not expect that the increase in international commerce, by itself, would be enough to harmonize the varied interests of the world's nation states. The Bretton Woods and GATT arrangements were considered the economic buttresses of the world federalism that emerged with the San Francisco conference and the birth of the United Nations. It was hoped that the separation of economic transactions from the political arena would make it possible for an incipient world federal structure, such as the United Nations, to cope with a manageable level of international political transactions.

With the onset of the cold war, however, participation in international economic institutions became circumscribed, and the system that had been intended to harmonize the economic interests among all nations took on a different cast. Free trade and the multilateral clearing of all financial transactions among the noncommunist nations remained the goal of policymakers, but the system as a whole acquired decided security overtones. The International Monetary Fund (IMF) and the GATT became structures for shoring up the weaker economies of the anticommunist alliance. Analogously with the military security system, the international economic system became American-managed and -financed.

Japan in the Early Postwar Order ——— Changing American policies toward occupied Japan reflected the changing views on international political and economic relations. By 1949, the early OCCUPATION goals of reforming and democratizing the Japanese economy had given way to policies aimed at its full economic recovery so that it could serve as a vital building block in the newly envisioned American–East Asian security system. To this end, American policymakers accorded Japan special treatment in the American-sponsored postwar economic system. Like Western Europe, Japan was allowed to restrict severely the access of American products to its market while retaining relatively free access to the American market. During the 1950s, however, strenuous efforts were made to encourage Western Europe to accept commercial and financial policies consistent with a liberal international system. No comparable pressure was exerted on Japan, in part because Japan was relatively less developed. See also ECONOMIC HISTORY: Occupation-period economy.

European policymakers, however, were reluctant to accord Japan special privileges because of its semideveloped state and strategic position in East Asia. They were disinclined to allow unfettered Japanese participation in the international economic system—especially in view of continuing Japanese reluctance toward entering such a system on the same basis as the United States and Europe. Thus, Japan was not allowed to enter the GATT until 1955. Even then, European and other nations (comprising one-third of world trade) invoked article 55 to maintain special restrictions on imports from Japan. As late as 1960, when trade among the nations of Western Europe and the United States had been substantially liberalized, goods of Japanese origin remained subject to considerable discrimination. For example, of the 1,097 products designated in the Brussels Tariff Nomenclature, France discriminated against 357 Japanese products, Italy discriminated against 228 Japanese products and West Germany discriminated against 34 products.

Notwithstanding the weakness of many links in the multilateral commercial relationships among noncommunist nations, the period from the late 1940s through the mid-1960s did see a great liberalizing of commercial relations. American encouragement, as well as pressure on Western Europe, was relatively successful, and a series of reciprocal tariff reductions on manufactured products reached its culmination in the reductions negotiated in the Kennedy Round agreements in 1967. During these negotiations, for the first time, Japan participated as a major actor. As trade in manufacturing products was being liberalized, however, Europe and Japan exhibited considerable reluctance on liberalizing trade in agricultural products. Indeed, the establishment of the European Economic Community's Common Agricultural Policy in 1962 suggested increasingly illiberal trade in such commodities. Although the United States had once permitted a lack of reciprocity in particular commodities to its own disadvantage, by the end of the Kennedy Round the United States had reestablished the principle of reciprocity. Washington did, however, continue to contribute to European integration and Japanese political stability by assenting to international commercial arrangements that permitted relatively free trade in areas where the United States did not have a comparative advantage and to relatively and increasingly restrictive trade in commodity groups in which it did have a comparative advantage.

The Primacy of the Dollar: Advantages and Disadvantages for Japan ——— The Bretton Woods system was built with the experience of the 1930s in mind: nations should be able to participate in a liberal international trading system without having it cause cyclical unemployment. As national participation in the Bretton Woods system required that the international demand and supply for the national currency be in balance to correct cyclical imbalances, national central banks were permitted to buy and sell national currency in exchange for international reserve assets. Given the interwar experience of national attempts to export unemployment through competitive devaluation, the postwar system sought to limit exchange-rate adjustment to instances of secular disequilibrium.

This basically cyclical view of the international economy made it impossible for the architects of the postwar financial system to foresee the central problems of the system they had constructed. From the system's inception, gold and the US dollar served as the key reserve assets. Additions to the world gold stock from mining operations, however, proved insufficient to provide adequate liquidity for the rapidly expanding international economy. Growing industrial uses for gold exacerbated this problem. Under these circumstances, increases in international reserves could only come about through deficits in the American balance of payments. So great was the confidence in the American economy that continuing deficits in the late 1940s and early 1950s were viewed from all sides as a highly desirable means of adding desperately needed liquidity to the world economy.

Although stability between the dollar and gold was the foundation of the system in the 1950s and early 1960s, the same cyclical view that ignored the need for growing liquidity also ignored the need for relatively frequent exchange-rate adjustment. If anything, the specter of competitive devaluation led to official language that positively discouraged exchange-rate adjustment. Given the political difficulties inherent in parity changes because of their uneven impact across a national economy, an international monetary system that does not encourage such changes will likely undergo fewer than are economically necessary. Deficit nations must have international cooperation or they must devalue. Only the largess of other nations enabled the deficit United Kingdom to maintain the value of the pound in the mid-1960s. Surplus Japan needed no international help to maintain an undervalued currency through August 1971. See also BALANCE OF PAYMENTS.

As the exchange-rate adjustments were made with respect to reserve assets, the system worked to secularly appreciate the dollar. Thus, the economic imperatives of the cold war led to American responsibility for international financial management which, although giving fairly free financial scope to American international activities, handicapped the development of American export industries and encouraged more American overseas investment than would have been the case if the foreign exchange value of the dollar had been kept in equilibrium. Japanese and Western European industries that were in competition with American industries benefited from this overvaluation of the dollar. In Europe, this improved performance came at the price of increasing susceptibility to a takeover by American interests. Japan's tight restrictions on direct foreign investment enabled it, through the mid-1960s, to avoid substantial American equity in its industrial advance.

American Foreign Investment and Japanese Restrictions

Although the American experience of managing international commerce and finance was not without precedent, the character of the American-based international manufacturing corporation in the postwar period remains unique. What was unique was not that there was large-scale migration of capital, entrepreneurship, and technology but rather that large American corporations increasingly sent these elements abroad as part of a centralized global market strategy. What made this a key feature of the postwar world economy was not so much the dollar's role as international money (though this was clearly facilitating) but (1) the growing postwar gap in technology between the United States and other advanced countries; (2) the complexity and malleability of the new technology, which made it difficult for a corporate developer of a new technology to recapture fully the rents associated with its successful development in one country except by direct participation in the use of the technology in other countries; and (3) the improvements in communication which made the efficient execution of a centralized global corporate strategy possible. Thus, through the 1950s and into the 1960s, American actors probably effected the most important transfers of technology through the instrumentality of foreign direct investment.

Japanese reaction to this worldwide transfer of American technology contrasted sharply with the policies of Western Europe. Europe at first welcomed the advent of American corporations, but Japan sought to prevent their entry initially with the encouragement of the American Occupation. Although the earliest restrictions were designed to prevent the transfer of Japanese assets to Americans at fire-sale prices, the restrictions in the 1950s were framed largely with an eye to the still precarious Japanese balance of payments. Through the late 1950s, Japan controlled the flow of direct foreign investment by allowing repatriation of earnings only from foreign investments that had been validated by the government at the time of their entry. As such validation was given sparingly, only IBM's willingness to forego the possibility of repatriating its earnings (together with Japanese appreciation of the extraordinarily sophisticated nature of its technology base) allowed IBM JAPAN, LTD, to flourish and dominate Japan's substantial computer market. See also FOREIGN EXCHANGE CONTROL.

With Japanese assumption of advanced-country status in the IMF and full membership in the Organization for Economic Cooperation and Development (OECD) in 1964, the rationale and the legal and administrative framework for restricting and guiding foreign investment in Japan changed. Japanese officials, particularly in the MINISTRY OF INTERNATIONAL TRADE AND INDUSTRY (MITI), tended to stress the danger that substantial foreign direct investment would dampen the exceptionally rapid structural transformation of the Japanese economy. They suggested that, for largely cultural reasons, foreign management operating in such key Japanese industries as automobiles and heavy electrical equipment would find it difficult to take full advantage of the special dynamic opportunities offered by the transformation. Indeed, because it was widely recognized in Japan that foreign-based international corporations often acted in the interest of the home country, there was fear that foreign management would consciously choose not to take full advantage of Japanese opportunities. At the same time, the great international corporations, by their very nature, largely operated in those indus-

tries whose technology dictated oligopolistic market structures. Thus, an entrenched foreign presence in a major Japanese sector could prevent the growth of a Japanese competitor who did attempt to take advantage of such opportunities. See also FOREIGN INVESTMENT IN JAPAN.

More fundamentally and most particularly in the mid-1960s, major figures in the Japanese government chose to justify restrictions on foreign investment on the grounds that large Japanese-based-and-dominated international corporations were necessary for the future survival of Japanese national identity. The proposition was widely accepted that important advances in technology were developed only in the largest corporations and that such advances, being of exceptional value, were diffused exclusively within the corporation. The large corporations, as the carriers of the most progressive technology, would come into economic, political, and cultural dominance in the last third of the 20th century, and their international flexibility and organizational competence would come to attenuate the sovereignty of other institutions. Thus, if Japan was to participate in this new world order, restrictions on foreign direct investment were in order. Opportunities for growth within the Japanese market were to be reserved for nascent Japanese-based international corporations.

The Japanese regulations and restrictions meant that if rents for the development of technology were going to be earned from the Japanese economy, they would most likely be gained through the vehicle of a licensing agreement. Thus, many American corporations, although negative to the idea of licensing and quite capable of successfully exploiting their technology in Japan, agreed to license their technology to Japanese firms. Indeed, after standardizing for size, Japan was the world's preeminent licensee in the 1950s and early 1960s.

Although it is certainly true that the transfer of technology to Japan was diminished by restrictions on foreign direct investment, the extent of the diminution was limited because (1) much of the technology Japan wanted during this period was already widely available, and, typically, licensers did not seem to feel that they were giving up important proprietary opportunities; and (2) most technological transfer between Japan and other countries did not appear to flow through proprietary channels at all. Although various sources attribute as much as 30 to 60 percent of postwar Japanese economic growth to technological improvement and assimilation, as late as 1970, Japanese firms were paying no more than $500 million in licensing fees and royalties. It is impossible to rationalize this small figure by assuming massive mistakes by foreign licensers or overwhelming monopsony power or both by Japanese licensees acting in concert with the Japanese government. It seems more likely that most technology and technological information either reached Japan through nonproprietary channels or was produced by the Japanese themselves. Thus, Japan's special position within the American-sponsored international commodity trading system was achieved at relatively little economic cost. See also TECHNOLOGY TRANSFER.

Transition to a New International Economic System —— The American-sponsored-and-managed international economic system was highly successful in achieving the goals for which it had been constructed. The efficacy of international economic institutions had much to do with the widespread economic growth and improved national well-being that were characteristic of all noncommunist developed countries in the postwar period, and that led inevitably to the demise of those very international economic institutions. In the early postwar world, capital stock, advanced technology, international reserve assets, and, to a somewhat lesser extent, natural resources had been concentrated in the hands of the United States, but by the mid-1960s other major centers of economic power had arisen. Where once the cost of economic leadership had been small and the legitimacy of such leadership unchallengeable, the emergence of other major economic centers changed this. American corporate and union groups began to question America's unequal trade relations with some of its major trading partners. In turn, other major participants in the Bretton Woods system began to challenge the primacy of the dollar in international economic relations, suggesting in increasingly impatient terms that economic conditions in the United States and elsewhere no longer justified the special advantages conferred on the dollar. Similarly, the worldwide diffusion of advanced technology as well as the institutions for producing it increased host-country reluctance to give American-based corporations free reign to operate within their boundaries.

For much of the postwar period, the domestic American economy's insulation from the international economy (at the same time that there was extensive American participation in the international economy in absolute terms) was widely appreciated and the foreign sector was not blamed for economic ills. In the late 1960s and early 1970s, however, a cyclical downturn in the American economy coincided with a large shift from surplus to deficit in the American balance of trade and the presence of large quantities of manufactured imports from the new industries of America's leading trading partners. These new developments did much to undermine the American sense of international economic paternalism, which had sprung from relative and absolute economic strength. Although evidence was almost entirely lacking, the belief became widespread in the United States that import competition was pushing structural transformation at a pace that was socially intolerable. Liberal trade policies required that resources flow in and out of national industries in accordance with comparative advantage. As long as this process proceeds slowly, little social harm is done. When this process accelerates rapidly, considerable social harm becomes a possibility. As American union leaders have been fond of pointing out, the history of economic policy in the 20th century, and perhaps more so at other times, is the history of attempts to mitigate the unfettered ravages of the market economy. Intervention and protection are common when the determinants of structural change are domestic; should social conscience be suspended when the determinants are external?

The Emergence of American Protectionism

—— In the early 1970s, protectionist sentiment came to focus on the large, rapidly growing, export-oriented Japanese economy. Japanese exports to the United States had been growing far more rapidly than those of any other major US trading partner. Indeed much of the change in the overall US balance of trade can be attributed to the change during the 1960s of the American bilateral trade balance with Japan, from surplus to very substantial deficit. As the volume and structure of Japanese exports to the United States were growing and changing, however, legal and administrative barriers, both explicit and implicit, continued to hinder the export of American products to Japan. Although popular American concern about the impact of both imports from Japan and Japanese restrictions of American exports was rooted in misinformation and hysteria, the slowness of the Japanese in removing these restrictions probably dealt a mortal blow to the implicit principle of lack of reciprocity in American trading relations with other noncommunist advanced economies. American willingness to accept lack of full reciprocity, already shaken by political détente, became a dead letter in the wake of Japanese inaction in the late 1960s and early 1970s.

The new American attitudes regarding continued discrimination against American products, and related social and economic threats posed by foreign and particularly Japanese imports, became manifest in 1971 with (1) the diplomatically unhappy resolution of the Japan-American synthetic textile dispute; (2) the imposition of a special 10 percent tariff surcharge on all imports as part of President Richard Nixon's New Economic Policy; and (3) the introduction of and the widespread union support for the Burke-Hartke bill, which would have frozen foreign-manufactured products' share of American markets at the levels of the late 1960s. Although improvement in the unemployment situation in the United States in 1972 and early 1973 took the edge off rhetoric and killed the Burke-Hartke legislation, 1971 was truly a watershed in American foreign economic policy. Secretary of the Treasury John Connally, moving in tandem with the Nixon-Kissinger conception of American self-interest in a multipolar world, broke sharply with the previous major themes in American foreign economic policy.

The persistence of the hitherto unusual American posture of aggressively asserting a narrowly circumscribed view of self-interest in international trade relations during this period can be seen most clearly in (1) the unusually large number of investigations and actions undertaken in 1971–74 against foreign products by the US Treasury Department and the US Tariff Commission under the provisions of antidumping statutes; (2) the unilateral American export embargo on soybeans in June 1973; and (3) the lack of real American initiatives in the so-called Tōkyō Round of negotiations on the reduction of tariff and nontariff barriers, except in regard to European and Japanese commitments on trade in agricultural commodities. See also NIXON SHOCKS.

Enormous American diplomatic pressure—together with a growing appreciation of the benefits Japan might derive from full participation in a liberal, multilateral commodity trading system and a fuller recognition that most restrictions on manufactured imports would have an extremely small impact on the Japanese economy given its stage of development—prompted major changes in Japan's policy. Japan took active steps to remove remaining legal and administrative bars hampering the import of manufactured products

and positive action to encourage American imports. American pressure also had considerable influence on the direction of Japanese exports. In keeping with the general American diplomatic posture of attempting to reduce foreign pressure on its domestic markets, the United States encouraged members of the European Community to reduce their remaining, and not inconsiderable, barriers to the import of Japanese manufactured products. The partial success of this policy was one important element in the large increase in the share in total Japanese exports directed to Western Europe during 1972, 1973, and early 1974.

International Monetary Crisis and Yen Revaluation

—— American unhappiness with the way the international trading system had evolved by the early 1970s was matched by European and Japanese impatience with the increasingly onerous asymmetries in the international financial system. By the late 1960s, many foreign economies that had once viewed deficits in American balance of payments as desirable now found themselves awash with American-created liquidity and therefore saw the American deficits as highly unattractive dollar imperialism. With the increasing inroads of American-based corporate control in strategic sectors of the West European economies and the increasing unpopularity of American overseas military activities, lack of formal economic constraints on American international activities and apparent lack of American interest in bringing its balance of payments into equilibrium became almost intolerable.

Despite the absence of a liquidity problem, the Americans accepted the necessity of their balance of payments returning to equilibrium. Official American reaction, however, rejected the contention that the economic and political burdens of such an adjustment should essentially fall on the United States. Moreover, it vigorously defended the acquisition activities of American-based international corporations and the interventionist posture of American national security. From the American perspective, the problem with the Bretton Woods system was that its workings made increasingly difficult the United States' creation of sufficient external demand for dollars through foreign sale of goods and services. The failure of nations with a secular surplus in their balance of payments to appreciate their currency while deficit nations were forced to devalue was, over time, working to appreciate the dollar, the system's unit of account. American policymakers laid the blame for international financial difficulties at the doorstep of the surplus nations, in particular, Japan.

The Japanese government was aware of the American government's attitude on the need for correction of the Japanese surplus. While explicitly and quite rightly rejecting full Japanese responsibility for the malaise in the international financial arrangements, the government of Satō Eisaku preferred to adjust the Japanese balance of payments through (1) liberalizing import quotas and tariffs and removing a variety of export subsidies, thereby also responding to another set of insistent American demands; (2) encouraging substantial direct and portfolio investment by Japanese enterprise abroad, thereby ensuring Japanese international economic involvement proportionate to the growing size of the Japanese economy; and (3) reflating the domestic economy via government expenditures in the long-neglected areas of social welfare and social infrastructure. When this program was announced in June 1971, American government and business circles greeted it with considerable skepticism. The total package did not seem to have sufficient impact to offset quickly and substantially the burgeoning Japanese surplus and the attendant speculative pressure on the dollar. By the summer of 1971, Japanese and American attitudes had reached the classic impasse of the Bretton Woods arrangements—the surplus balance of payments nation feeling no need to move quickly and the reserve asset nation feeling unable to act. The real crisis, however, was the near impossibility for patient negotiations to resolve this deadlock. If Japan would not appreciate, the United States would not devalue, and since persistent negotiation was out of the question, the old system had to fall. The same worldview that had spawned an aggressive assertion of "American interests" in international commercial policy now prompted a related assertion in the international financial system. As part of the August 1971 New Economic Policy, the dollar's convertibility into gold was formally ended, and Japan and other surplus nations were bludgeoned into appreciating their currencies by official ultimata. The imposition of a surcharge on foreign imports and a new investment tax credit discriminating against producers' goods of foreign origin were also undertaken— two policy steps that would be rescinded only after surplus countries had responded in a fashion deemed appropriate by the American government. The American tactics worked; by December 1971, the

Smithsonian Agreements ratified the substantial revaluation of the yen and the mark.

Official American dissatisfaction with the yen parity did not end with the Smithsonian Agreements. Feeling that the yen was still undervalued, the US continued to press for further Japanese revaluation. The initial but predictably slow response of American trade flows to the worldwide changes in exchange rates strengthened American resolve. Finally in February 1973, in the midst of continued speculation against the dollar, the United States unilaterally devalued the inconvertible dollar against gold. Shortly thereafter, all major currencies began to float against the dollar. The Bretton Woods era was finally over.

The Yen in a New Era of International Financial Relations

Although the strength of the yen finally undermined the old system, Japan and its currency did not play a major role in the discussions surrounding the establishment of a new international monetary system. This was largely, but not entirely, the result of a radical change in Japan's international position after February 1973. Earlier, after Japan's first revaluation, the Satō government had inaugurated an unusually relaxed monetary policy in an effort to avoid the deflationary consequences of slackening export demand. This proved to be a bad miscalculation. The Nixon administration, with an eye to the 1972 election, employed far more expansionary policies than anyone in Europe, Japan, and possibly the United States expected. An unanticipated boom in world exports ensued, and in 1973, prior to the onset of the oil embargo, wholesale prices in Japan were accelerating at a rate of more than 22 percent annually. Although the Japanese government began to restrict aggregate demand in an effort to cope with soaring inflation, effective capacity began to contract even more rapidly because of reduced oil shipments from the Middle East. Inevitably, prices accelerated still faster. Thus, relative to other balance-of-payments surplus nations of the early 1970s, Japanese monetary policy was unduly inflationary. These monetary problems, together with a sharp increase in oil prices (probably affecting Japan more than any other country, with the possible exception of Italy) and the changing Japanese regulations on overseas investment, made the history of the yen after 1973 quite different from that of the German mark, the Swiss franc, the Dutch guilder, and the French franc, not to mention a number of Middle Eastern currencies.

As of the late 1970s there seemed small prospect in the foreseeable future that the world economy would return to an American-dominated liberal system. American banks and corporations were materially incapable of regaining their previous dominant role, and the American government was politically incapable of maintaining the self-restraint necessary to accommodate the economic needs of other nations. It was also unlikely that the world economy would break down into antagonistic regional blocs. The enormous trade in manufactured products among industrialized countries, the universal desire for access to the American market, and the increasing trade between Japan and Western Europe, together with the near-necessity of American-led cooperation among industrialized nations on international energy policy, made such a development most improbable. Japan would be economically preeminent in the western Pacific and the Common Agricultural Policy of the European Economic Community would survive, but these conditions would be but one facet of the industrialized economies' relations with one another and the rest of the world. More likely, the evolving international economic system would come to resemble 20th-century pluralism rather than either 19th-century liberalism or the regionalism of the 1930s. As under 19th-century liberalism, participation in the international economic system would become increasingly global. As under the regionalism of the 1930s, the increasing lack of shared values among major participants would leave the coordination of international economic activity less in the hands of markets and private initiative than had been the case throughout much of the postwar period. An increasingly narrower conception of national self-interest and an increasingly greater appreciation of the role of international oligopoly and international cartel would mean greater political intervention in international economic relations and, in consequence, an inevitable intermeshing of international economics with other international issues.

Pursuing a relatively narrow conception of national self-interest in the context of national goals of autonomy and stability does not necessarily mean doing violence to clearly beneficial international interaction. It means that the United States and other nations will act in the future as Japan has acted throughout much of the postwar period. It also means that an increasing variety of issues will be treated at the highest levels of government. With international economic issues once again requiring the attention of national political leaders and with issue-linkage acquiring a new legitimacy, one can expect national participation in an increasing variety of shifting international coalitions. Optimistically, one can hope that these new bases for occasional international alliance will serve, in pluralistic fashion, the cause of global integration and global stability. See also FOREIGN TRADE; FOREIGN TRADE, GOVERNMENT POLICY ON.

Gary R. SAXONHOUSE

United States education missions to Japan

(Amerika *kyōiku shisetsudan*). Missions that visited Japan in March 1946 and August 1950, at the invitation of the OCCUPATION authorities, to evaluate the Japanese educational system. Their reports contributed greatly to postwar educational reform (see EDUCATIONAL REFORMS OF 1947). The first mission was composed of 27 educational specialists headed by G. D. Stoddard. It relied largely on data prepared by the CIVIL INFORMATION AND EDUCATION SECTION OF SCAP, but through the cooperation of a Japanese group that later became the EDUCATION REFORM COUNCIL, it was also able to inspect the schools at first hand. In its report the mission recommended: greater flexibility in the educational system to meet the needs and abilities of individual students; greater emphasis on learning through experience; the establishment of local school administrations independent of the central government; the adoption of a 6-3-3 system on the American model; the adoption of coeducation; and the opening up of higher education to the general public. The second mission, composed of five members of the first mission and headed by W. E. Givens, studied the implementation of the reforms recommended four years earlier. It made a positive evaluation but recommended larger budget appropriations for education.

TAKAKURA Shō

United States Immigration Acts of 1924, 1952, and 1965

Prior to the passage of the Immigration Act of 1924, immigration from Japan to the United States was governed largely by the GENTLEMEN'S AGREEMENT of 1907–08. The so-called "barred zone" act of 1917, which kept out all other Asians except Filipinos, did not affect Japanese. As originally drafted, the legislation that became the 1924 act treated Japan as it treated non-Asian nations: all such were granted an annual quota based upon the presumed number of natives and their descendants who were resident in the United States at some previous date, 1890 being eventually chosen. With that date as a base point, the annual Japanese quota would have been 100, which was the minimum. But even this tiny annual addition was too much for Japanophobes, and a West Coast congressional bloc, organized by Senator Hiram W. Johnson of California, worked diligently to eliminate the Japanese quota and abrogate the Gentlemen's Agreement. The Coolidge administration supported a Japanese quota, and in the course of trying to marshal congressional support, Secretary of State Charles Evans Hughes prevailed upon Japanese Ambassador Hanihara Masanao (1876–1934) to write him a letter, for congressional consumption, expressing the views of the Japanese government. This Hanihara did. In the course of a long letter, which was patently friendly, the ambassador mentioned the possible "grave consequences" that might ensue were an anti-Japanese version of the bill enacted. The State Department released the letter as part of its lobbying effort, but it backfired badly. Senator Henry Cabot Lodge of Massachusetts (1850–1924) wrenched the phrase out of context and made it appear that the letter was improper and represented a "veiled threat" to the United States. The final legislation, passed overwhelmingly, resorted to the use of the concept of "aliens ineligible to citizenship," derived from the naturalization act of 1870, to deprive Japan of a quota by making all such aliens inadmissible as permanent immigrants. This provision of the law was based upon race, not nationality. A citizen of Canada of Japanese birth or ancestry was not admissible, even though Canadians, along with other Western hemisphere residents, were not subject to a quota at all.

Japanese were thus in effect barred from immigration to the United States from 1924 until the passage of the so-called McCarran-Walter Act of 1952. That act retained a modified form of the national origins quota system established in 1924 but amended the nationality act so that neither race nor ethnicity were bars to becoming an American citizen. (Because of a provision in the 14th amendment to the Constitution of the United States adopted in 1868—"all persons born . . . in the United States . . . are citizens of the United States"—children of Japanese immigrants, who were born in the United States or its territories, the *nisei,* were and remained citizens.) Japan was given an annual quota of 100. However, the same 1952 act provided for several categories of persons who were to be treated as "nonquota" entrants. This category included wives of American citizens, who were mainly war brides, or more properly Occupation brides, and certain close relatives of American citizens. As surviving *issei,* or first-generation Japanese Americans, flocked to courts to become naturalized citizens, they also made many of their relatives in Japan potential nonquota immigrants. During the period from 1952 to 1960, when only 800 quota spaces were allocated to Japan, some 40,000 Japanese actually migrated to the United States.

The 1965 immigration act scrapped completely the national origins quota system while limiting annual immigration to about 400,000 per year. The essence of this act, which retained provisions giving preferred status to close relatives of citizens, was to place emphasis not on race, ethnicity, or nationality, but rather on skills and training. Under its provisions, immigration from Japan has been between 10,000 and 20,000 annually. This does not include either the tens of thousands of Japanese businessmen and their families who have come to the United States on nonimmigrant visas to work in Japanese-owned businesses and factories, or students attending American colleges and universities on student visas. See also JAPANESE AMERICANS.

▬——Roger Daniels, *The Politics of Prejudice: The Anti-Japanese Movement in California and the Struggle for Japanese Exclusion* (1962; 2nd ed, 1978). Roger Daniels, *Racism and Immigration Restriction* (1974). Robert A. Divine, *American Immigration Policy, 1924–1952* (1957). *Roger DANIELS*

United States–Japan Administrative Agreement

(Nichibei Gyōsei Kyōtei). Formally entitled the Administrative Agreement under article 3 of the Security Treaty between the United States of America and Japan. An agreement concluded under the security treaty between the United States and Japan concerning the status of the US armed forces stationed in Japan under the treaty. The agreement was signed on 28 February 1952 and became effective together with the security treaty on 28 April 1952. Japan agreed to grant the United States the use of facilities and land necessary to carry out the treaty. The agreement also specified the rights, powers, and authority of the United States in its military facilities, conditions for the entry into Japan of vessels, aircraft, members of the armed forces, civilians attached to the military and their dependents, exemption from customs duties and taxes, the extent of criminal and civil jurisdictions, and other matters.

The agreement became the subject of public controversy in Japan. Critics believed it conferred excessive freedom of action on the US armed forces in carrying out article 1 of the security treaty, which provided that armed forces in and about Japan may be utilized to contribute to the maintenance of peace and security in the Far East and to the security of Japan against armed attack. A broad provision of the agreement required consultation between the US and Japanese governments in the event of hostilities or the imminent threat of hostilities, but critics argued that Japan would not have the power to restrain the United States from taking action and that Japan could become involved in a conflict it did not support. In addition, the jurisdictional privileges accorded the United States were broader in scope than those contained in similar US agreements with NATO countries. Finally, it was argued that the agreement had not been submitted to the Japanese Diet for approval on the grounds that it was an executive agreement not requiring the parliamentary approval prescribed for international treaties under the Japanese constitution.

A number of these problems were resolved in the years following the signing of the agreement. In a protocol signed on 29 September 1953, the scope of criminal jurisdiction was revised to conform to the NATO agreements. Negotiations for the revision of the security treaty and the administrative agreement started in 1958, and new documents were signed on 19 January 1960. These became effective on 23 June of the same year after being approved by the Diet. The new arrangements, which comprise the Treaty of Mutual Cooperation and Security and the Agreement regarding Facilities and the Areas and the Status of United States Armed Forces in Japan, known as the Status of Forces Agreement or SOFA, more

clearly specify the requirement of prior consultation before the activation of US forces based in Japan, although critics still contend that Japan does not have the power to restrain the United States from involving Japan in a conflict. See also UNITED STATES ARMED FORCES IN JAPAN; UNITED STATES–JAPAN SECURITY TREATIES; UNITED STATES MILITARY BASES, DISPUTES OVER.

OWADA Hisashi

United States–Japan Commercial Treaty of 1858 → Harris Treaty

United States–Japan Mutual Defense Assistance Agreement

(Nichibei Sōgo Bōei Enjo Kyōtei). Often called the MSA or Mutual Security Agreement, signed on 8 March 1954 in Tōkyō. Intended to reinforce the United States–Japan Security Treaty of 1951 (see UNITED STATES–JAPAN SECURITY TREATIES) and to provide a legal basis for the United States to furnish Japan with military equipment and technology, the agreement stated that the United States would make available military equipment and services to help Japan assume increasing responsibility for its own defense. Japan agreed in article 8 "to make, consistent with the political and economic stability of Japan, the full contribution permitted by its manpower, resources, facilities, and general economic condition to the development and maintenance of its own defensive strength and the defensive strength of the free world . . ." Pursuant to the agreement, the United States established a military assistance advisory group in Japan. Under a related agreement, the United States granted to Japan $10 million from the sale of agricultural commodities to assist Japan's defense industry and to help develop Japan's economic capacities. The Mutual Defense Assistance Agreement was considered to be an important step in linking Japan's defense efforts with those of the United States.

▬——Martin E. Weinstein, *Japan's Post-War Defense Policy, 1947–1968* (1971). US, Department of State, *Bulletin,* 5 April 1954. *Richard B. FINN*

United States–Japan security treaties

The United States–Japan Security Treaty (Nichibei Anzen Hoshō Jōyaku, abbreviated Ampo Jōyaku) signed at San Francisco on 8 September 1951 and implemented on 28 April 1952, and the successor Treaty of Mutual Cooperation and Security between the United States and Japan (Nichibei Sōgo Kyōryoku Oyobi Anzen Hoshō Jōyaku) signed at Washington on 19 January 1960 and in effect since 23 June 1960.

The Treaty of 1952 —— This treaty is inseparable from the SAN FRANCISCO PEACE TREATY and was the offspring of the cold war between the United States and the Soviet Union.

In the first period of the postwar Allied OCCUPATION General Douglas MACARTHUR, as Supreme Commander for the Allied Powers (SCAP), thoroughly carried out the complete disarmament of Japan required by the Potsdam Declaration. The primary motivation was "that Japan will not again become a menace to the peace and security of the world." The trauma of defeat and destruction in World War II had rendered most Japanese unexpectedly open to psychological as well as physical disarmament. This spirit of PACIFISM found unique expression in article 9 of the new constitution, which renounced war and prohibited the maintenance of armed forces. In 1947, MacArthur announced that the objectives of the Occupation had been essentially achieved and that it was time to prepare a treaty of peace with Japan. While such a proposal was considered premature by Allied and American critics, it illustrates an important change in the attitude of the United States toward Japan: the now-defenseless former enemy had become an ally who in its own interest and in conformity with United States foreign policies should be enabled to defend itself if and when attacked.

The first feelers from the United States for an early peace treaty came to nothing because of serious procedural differences with the Soviets. Hence, no peace treaty was prepared, much to the dissatisfaction of MacArthur, who believed that military occupations degenerate when maintained over long periods of time.

With the deterioration of relations between the two superpowers, American concern focused increasingly on the question of how to assure Japan's post-Occupation security from direct or indirect attack. Rearmament was unpopular within Japan, and its constitutionality—even for self-defense—had not yet been determined by the Supreme Court. A guarantee by the Allied nations of the security of a neutral Japan appeared too risky as long as mistrust prevailed between the United States and the Soviet Union. Nor did the United States appear to be sufficient protection in case of an armed conflict. The remaining option was the retention of American forces in Japan after it regained sovereignty. Continuation of the American military presence in Japan was, however, certain to be unacceptable to the communist nations. It could therefore be chosen only if the idea of a general peace treaty was given up in favor of a separate pact in which only Western nations participated. To some critics, however, it appeared absurd to conclude a peace treaty with Japan without including the biggest Asian nations.

In Japan the idea of "inviolable neutrality" guaranteed by the victor nations was favored by the people and, initially, by the government. The JAPAN SOCIALIST PARTY established four principles of peace, namely, settlements with all former enemies, neutrality, no military treaties with any country or military bases in Japan of another country, and no rearmament.

The outbreak of the Korean conflict in 1950 influenced American as well as Japanese thinking about a peace treaty. Negotiations between John Foster DULLES, who had been appointed President Harry Truman's personal representative, and Prime Minister YOSHIDA SHIGERU led to a basic agreement on the retention of US forces on bases in Japan under terms to be stipulated in a separate bilateral security treaty which would come into effect at the same time as the peace treaty. This solution became more palatable to the majority of the Japanese people who decided, after the events in Korea, that the idea of neutrality had been unrealistic. Since the bulk of the Occupation forces had been transferred to the Korean front, leaving Japan unprotected, SCAP authorized the creation of the Police Reserve, a nucleus of Japanese armed forces. The Socialists and more radical labor unions stuck, however, to their four principles. They and pacifist groups and individuals stressed the danger that a security treaty with the United States would alienate the communist nations. Moreover, in their view, trade with Mainland China was essential to Japan's economic development. On the other hand, the conservative, pro-American government was well aware of the enormous benefit the American military umbrella meant to Japan's economy. Furthermore, inasmuch as the peace treaty was generally regarded as magnanimous, many took the pragmatic approach of looking at the security treaty as the price to be paid for ending the Occupation and resuming sovereignty.

The Soviet Union, Poland, and Czechoslovakia did not sign the San Francisco Peace Treaty. India and Burma declined to take part in the treaty conference, though invited. Because of the confusion over the two-China issue neither Mainland China nor Taiwan had been invited to participate. The treaty was signed in San Francisco on 8 September 1951 by 48 nations. Its article 6a provided for the withdrawal of all Occupation forces of the Allied powers from Japan after the implementation of the peace treaty but explicitly left the door open to the "stationing or retention of foreign armed forces in Japanese territory under or in consequence of any bilateral or multilateral agreements which have been or may be made between one or more of the Allied powers . . . and Japan." This practically meant that most Occupation forces would remain in Japan as US security forces. An American pacifist called this a continuation of the Occupation in disguise.

The security treaty was an extremely short framework of general principles, while the most difficult details were spelled out in the accompanying UNITED STATES–JAPAN ADMINISTRATIVE AGREEMENT. The treaty shows a manifest endeavor to assure compliance with the charter of the United Nations. The preamble, emphasizing the danger an insufficiently armed Japan faces, states that it therefore desires to conclude a security treaty with the United States simultaneously with the peace treaty. The maintenance of US armed forces in and about Japan is legally justified by Japan's right to enter into collective security arrangements and the principle of the United Nations charter that all nations possess an inherent right of individual and collective self-defense. The United States declares its willingness to maintain its presence but not without expressing its expectation that Japan will increasingly assume responsibility for its own defense. A warning that Japan should always avoid any armament which could be an offensive threat was included, perhaps in an effort to reassure third nations regarding Japan's peaceful intentions and Japan regarding the constitutionality of the arrangements.

The main part of the treaty consists of five articles. Article 1 sets forth the agreement to station US forces in and about Japan to con-

tribute to the maintenance of international peace and security and to the security of Japan against armed attack from without. This protection is extended to include assistance at the request of the Japanese government in case of internal riots and disturbances caused by an outside power. Article 2 prohibits Japan from granting any bases or other military privileges to any third power without prior consent of the United States. Article 3 delegates the implementation of the treaty pertaining to the stationing of American forces to administrative agreements. Article 4 makes the expiration of the treaty dependent upon agreement by both countries that United Nations arrangements or other security provisions which will provide for the maintenance of Japan's security have come into force. Article 5 stipulates that after ratification by the two nations the treaty will come into force when instruments of ratification have been exchanged at Washington.

Ratification by the Japanese Diet took place on 19 November 1951. Within the Socialist Party the prior unity of purpose no longer prevailed: the left wing rejected both treaties, while the right wing voted for the peace treaty but against the security treaty. The dissension over this important issue resulted in the split of the two wings, which reunited only in 1955. In the United States the president ratified the treaties on 15 April 1952 after the Senate had given its advice and consent. The exchange of ratifications took place on 28 April 1952, the date both pacts took effect.

Dulles had declared to the Senate Committee on Foreign Relations that the West needed Japan just as Japan needed the West. In the security treaty nothing of such reciprocity can be found, and the Japanese became increasingly aware that they were the inferior partner in an "unequal treaty." The lack of reciprocity was even recognized by the State Department. The following features appeared particularly objectionable: the absence of an explicit obligation of the United States to defend Japan, if attacked; the broad authorization to use US forces in Japan (without prior consultation) for the maintenance of international peace and security in the Far East which, the Japanese feared, empowered the United States to launch from Japan a military action involving Japan in a conflict related to American foreign policy rather than to Japan's interests; the prospect of the United States interfering in case of domestic riots, which appeared humiliating to a sovereign nation; the likewise humiliating prohibition of the granting of military rights to a third nation without the prior consent of the United States; the mode of ending the treaty, whose expiration was dependent on mutual agreement so that it could not be terminated by Japan; omission of any right for Japan to veto the introduction of weapons into Japan, a sensitive issue in light of Japan's aversion to nuclear weapons.

The Administrative Agreement of 28 February 1952 was not much more reciprocal than the security treaty; it even provided for extraterritoriality of members of the United States forces, the civilian component, and their dependents. This was, however, changed, as promised, on 29 September 1953 to conform to the Atlantic Treaty arrangements.

The Treaty of 1960—— In the fall of 1958, the Japanese government under the premiership of KISHI NOBUSUKE proposed a liberalization of the security treaty. By this time, Japan was no longer a weak nation. It had achieved a considerable economic recovery, strengthened its military power, though not to the extent the United States would have liked, through the establishment of the SELF DEFENSE FORCES, and been admitted to the United Nations. These things brought about a reawakening of national pride. The United States, recognizing the need to render the treaty more equal and reciprocal, concluded with Japan a new treaty of Cooperation and Security, which was signed in Washington on 19 January 1960 and implemented on 23 June 1960. An improved Status of Forces Agreement replaced the Administrative Agreement. It no longer required Japan to contribute to the costs of the stationing of the US Forces in Japan.

The preamble of the treaty expresses the desire of the partners "to strengthen the bonds of peace and friendship traditionally existing between them and to uphold the principles of democracy, individual liberty, and the rule of law." Economic cooperation is added as another objective. Emphasis upon adherence to the principles of the United Nations and upon peaceful intentions is even stronger than it was in the 1952 treaty.

The main part omits the most objectionable features of its predecessor, such as interference in case of domestic riots and the ban on granting military rights to third nations. It explicitly commits the United States to "act to meet the common danger" in case of an armed attack in Japanese territories, or in other words to defend

Japan. It provides that the parties will consult from time to time regarding the implementation of the treaty, or at the request of either party whenever the security of Japan or international peace and security in the Far East are threatened. In consideration of Japanese sensitivity to atomic weapons, prior consultation was also agreed upon by exchange of notes in case of "major changes in the deployment into Japan of US armed forces, major changes in their equipment and the use of facilities and areas in Japan as bases for combat operations to be undertaken other than those conducted under article 5 of the said treaty" (for the defense of Japan against armed attack). The concern of the Japanese government for the people of the Ryūkyū Islands, which remained under American occupation, is taken into account by an agreed minute obliging the US government to consult at once with its Japanese counterpart in the event of an armed attack against these and other islands of comparable status, defend them, and secure the welfare of the islanders.

The United States–Japan Joint Committee, the consulting instrument for the Administrative Agreement, was continued under the Status of Forces Agreement. A higher-level Security Consultative Committee for the treaty replaced a similar one established in 1957. It is composed of the minister of foreign affairs and the director-general of the Defense Agency on the Japanese side, and the American ambassador to Japan and the commander in chief, Pacific, on the United States side.

Finally, the expiration of the treaty is no longer dependent upon mutual agreement. Beginning 10 years after the implementation of the treaty, either party may give notice to the other of its intention to terminate it, and expiration will become effective a year later.

Doubtless, the new treaty represented an essential improvement in equalization. Instead of the welcome expected by the Kishi government, however, a thoroughly organized opposition developed and escalated into a furor that reached its peak after the treaty was approved by the House of Representatives. This time large numbers of usually moderate people joined the Left in opposition. The main argument of the opponents was again that the close alliance with the United States could easily arouse the hostility of the neighboring communist nations and involve Japan in a possible nuclear war. A major difference between the original security treaty and the new one was that the former was more or less imposed upon Japan as inseparable from the yearned-for peace treaty, while the latter was concluded by a sovereign government. The risk of this voluntarily established partnership was, in the view of the dissenters, increased rather than diminished by the new device of consultation. In the case of an armed conflict, they asserted, an enemy might identify Japan with its treaty partner because of the prior consultation, even if Japan had objected to the intended action. The fear was also expressed that the persistent pressure by the United States upon Japan to strengthen its defense capacity would restore the power of the military-industrial complex and lead to a violation of the constitution. Moreover, opponents were motivated by a traditional feeling of affinity toward China and by the hope of profitable trade relations with it.

Still, all these objections might not have brought about Japan's most serious postwar political crisis without the turbulent events during the session of the House of Representatives on 19 and 20 May 1960. The date of assembling the House was chosen in expectation of the visit of President Dwight Eisenhower to Tōkyō, scheduled for 19 June. Since ratification by the Diet would automatically become effective after 30 days, Prime Minister Kishi was eager to obtain it on 20 May at any price. There was continuous wrangling in various Diet committees; for several hours the Speaker of the House was held captive by a sitdown of the Socialists and was finally forced to call the police into the Diet building to free him. Kishi finally "rammed" the approval through in a plenary session shortly after midnight on 20 May while the opposition parties were unaware that the majority party was voting for the treaty and without providing an opportunity for counterarguments.

This surprise move provoked a wild uproar, and now the target was not only the treaty, but also the premier, whose procedure in the Diet was widely condemned as sly and undemocratic. Even some members of his Liberal Democratic Party disapproved of it. The intense interest of the people had been aroused by the constant antitreaty propaganda, and the Diet procedures had been observed on television. The streets of Tōkyō were suddenly filled with mass demonstrations by hundreds of thousands of ordinary citizens, housewives, unionists, etc. The radical ZENGAKUREN (a federation of student associations) organized the most extensive and vociferous protests. There was no violence, although one person was accidentally trampled to death. Nevertheless, at times the situation seemed chaotic and the government had to cancel Eisenhower's visit, since his security could not be guaranteed. Kishi, against whom an assassination attempt had been made, flew to Washington, where the exchange of the instruments of ratification took place. Upon his return, in the face of continuing criticism from the media and the opposition movement, Kishi announced his resignation.

Anti-Americanism would be too simplistic an explanation for the mass protests against the treaty. To be sure, radical leftists as well as ultranationalists could be labeled anti-American, but what antitreaty elements objected to most was the continuous American military presence. Landowners were affected by the procurement of their property for the bases. Offenses committed by American military personnel and accidents caused by them had an irritating effect, as in the GIRARD CASE, when an American soldier shot and killed a Japanese woman during a military exercise. The different lifestyle of the US forces, with their post exchanges, commissaries, and clubs, annoyed the Japanese. Other events not directly connected with the American forces in Japan, such as the fallout in 1954 from an American nuclear test at Bikini resulting in the death of a Japanese fisherman, caused further ill will (see LUCKY DRAGON INCIDENT). Finally, the Ryūkyū situation remained a serious source of friction between the two nations. Although residual sovereignty of Japan over the Ryūkyūs had been recognized, the United States continued to exercise unlimited governmental power over the area, which it had built up as a huge military fortress. American control, denounced by the Japanese as colonial, was continued after the Japanese government resumed sovereignty in 1952 because the American military felt that they needed complete freedom of action so near to the potential enemy without being restrained by the requirements of the security treaty and the Administrative Agreement. Out of this conflict arose a strong reversion movement, which succeeded only in 1972. (See OKINAWA.)

After the treaty came into force and Kishi was replaced as prime minister by IKEDA HAYATO, the storm of protest dissipated surprisingly quickly, and the United States–Japan alliance grew more stable. After the escalation of US involvement in the Vietnam War, however, opposition to the treaty became linked with the antiwar movement and the effort to win the return of the Ryūkyūs. Between 1965 and 1970, numerous large demonstrations were held against the treaty; these activities escalated in 1969 in anticipation of the 1970 renewal of the treaty. However, the protests were largely confined to the radical student movement and the citizens' movement known as Beheiren (see PEACE FOR VIETNAM COMMITTEE), and they never approached the level of popular involvement that the 1960 protests had reached. The SATŌ–NIXON COMMUNIQUÉ, issued in 1969, defused the protests by announcing the agreement to return the Ryūkyūs to Japan. The communiqué also reaffirmed US-Japanese ties in the region by announcing Japan's recognition that the security of Taiwan and South Korea is closely linked to its own security. Although the Japanese government could have given notice of its desire to terminate the treaty, it chose not to do so, the treaty was automatically renewed, and a parliamentary and political battle over the treaty's extension was avoided. American military presence has since been substantially reduced and made less conspicuous, thus relieving tensions, and the end of the Vietnam War has further defused the security treaty as a controversial political issue. See also PEACE MOVEMENT; UNITED STATES MILITARY BASES, DISPUTES OVER.

English Text of 1952 Treaty, in *The Japan Yearbook* (1949–52). English Text of 1960 Treaty, in *The Japanese Annual of International Law* (1961). Robert A. Feary, *The Occupation of Japan, Second Phase: 1948–50* (1950). George R. Packard, III, *Protest in Tokyo: The Security Treaty Crisis of 1960* (1960). Edwin O. Reischauer, *Japan: The Story of a Nation* (1970). Yoshida Shigeru, *The Yoshida Memoirs,* tr Yoshida Kenichi (1962). Alfred C. OPPLER

United States–Japan Security Treaty, movement against → peace movement

United States–Japan Treaty of Amity, 1854 → Kanagawa Treaty

United States military bases, disputes over

(*kichi mondai*). In Japan as of 1978 there were 118 American military bases occupying a total of 482 square kilometers (186 sq mi)—

concentrated in Okinawa—and 2,785 Japanese SELF DEFENSE FORCES bases, covering 1,102 square kilometers (425.4 sq mi). The most important American military bases included the air bases at Yokota, Atsugi, Iwakuni, Kadena, and Futemma; the naval bases at Yokosuka and Sasebo; the maneuver area at Fuji; and the communications bases at Sobe, Misawa, Tokachibuto, and Iōjima.

Until Japan's defeat in 1945, popular opposition to the establishment of military bases in the country was not tolerated. Nonetheless, the government felt compelled to extend large subsidies to affected areas in order to mollify local residents. With the adoption of the 1947 constitution and the renunciation of war and arms, the government abolished the clause in the land expropriation law of 1900 that pertained to land for military purposes. In fact, however, most of the Japanese military bases were taken over by the OCCUPATION authorities, that is, the American military, which also established new bases which were used during the Korean War (1950–53) for logistical purposes. Since rents for use of the bases and subsidies to surrounding areas were minimal, the discontent of the residents was great.

Even after the signing of the San Francisco Peace Treaty in 1951, under the terms of the UNITED STATES–JAPAN SECURITY TREATIES the American military continued to maintain bases in Japan. The few that were returned were taken over by the NATIONAL POLICE RESERVE, newly formed in 1950, since the government had no legal grounds for otherwise appropriating land. (The National Police Reserve was reorganized as the NATIONAL SAFETY FORCES in 1952 and as the Self Defense Forces in 1954.) At the same time, the American military continued to press for new bases, and the Japanese government enacted a special law allowing land appropriation for US military use in 1952. However, it also recommended the curtailment and geographical concentration of American military personnel and bases, with a view to replacing them eventually with the Self Defense Forces.

As of the late 1970s, apart from some marines, there were hardly any American ground troops stationed in Japan proper, and naval and air operations had been reduced to a minimum. In reaction to President Carter's announcement in 1977–78 of a policy of gradual withdrawal of US ground forces from South Korea, the Japanese government had increased its contribution toward the cost of maintaining American bases and had requested that American forces remain in Japan.

Public opinion did not always seem to be in agreement with such government policies, although the base issue was now less intense. With the memory of the atomic bombing of Hiroshima and Nagasaki still strong and the persistence there of radiation sickness, opposition to the introduction of nuclear weapons into Japanese territory was widespread. (Angry demonstrations in 1968 against the entry of the nuclear-powered aircraft carrier *Enterprise* into Sasebo resulted in hundreds of injuries.)

Incidents involving US military aircraft, especially in the greater Tōkyō area, gave rise to further conflict. There were 33 casualties from the crash of an RF8A in the city of Machida, a suburb of Tōkyō, and 10 casualties from an F8U crash in the city of Yamato, Kanagawa Prefecture, both in 1964, while an RF4B crash in Yokohama in 1977 killed or injured 9 Japanese. All three accidents also involved the destruction of private homes and factories. According to the Status of Forces Agreement, compensation for accidents solely the responsibility of American military operations was to be borne 75 percent by the United States and 25 percent by Japan; the ratio was 50:50 when both sides are responsible. Thus far, however, the causes of the accidents had never been made clear, since the United States had refused to reveal the results of its investigations, and the Japanese government alone had paid compensation to the victims. Dissatisfied with the settlements (calculated according to undisclosed methods), heirs and survivors had sometimes taken their cases to court.

Another problem was the noise from the aircraft using bases. Residents had brought numerous suits to limit flights by American military aircraft which, they claimed, were too frequent, too late at night, and exceeded the maximum permitted noise level of 90W (WECPNL or weighted equivalent continuous perceived noise level). The offending aircraft were said to be responsible for the high incidence of hearing loss in primary school pupils and cracked windows in areas close to bases.

Popular opposition and resentment were strongest in Okinawa, which had remained under military occupation until 1972 and where US bases had been used as staging areas at the height of American involvement in the Vietnam War (1965–73). In ratifying the return

of Okinawa from the United States, the Japanese House of Representatives in 1972 had passed a resolution extending the Three Non-nuclear Principles (not to manufacture, possess, or allow the introduction of nuclear weapons; see HIKAKU SANGENSOKU) to Okinawa, a resolution that included a demand for reduction of the number of US bases there. The United States had accordingly removed Mace B missiles and B52 bombers before reversion took place in May 1972. There was less confidence in US compliance after subsequent revelations by informed American sources (e.g., retired Rear Admiral Gene R. LaRocque in 1974 and former ambassador to Japan Edwin O. REISCHAUER in 1981) that nuclear weapons had been secretly stored at the Iwakuni marine base and bases on Okinawa and that the aircraft carrier *Midway* did not off-load its nuclear weapons before entering its home port of Yokosuka. Many critics charged that poison gas and germ warfare canisters were covertly stored on Okinawa despite US disavowals. Frequent "war games" in Okinawa using live ammunition frightened and occasionally injured residents, and there were numerous incidents of troops parachuting onto agricultural land and damaging crops. US bases remained a sensitive and potentially divisive issue in both United States–Japanese relations and Japanese national politics. See also UNITED STATES ARMED FORCES IN JAPAN. *Fukushima Shingo*

United States, mission of 1860 to

(Man'en Kembei Shisetsu). The 81-man shogunate mission sent to Washington DC to exchange ratifications of the United States–Japan Treaty of Amity and Commerce of 1858 (HARRIS TREATY). The group of shogunate officials and domain representatives, led by the commissioners of foreign affairs (gaikoku bugyō) SHIMMI MASAOKI and MURAGAKI NORIMASA and the intelligence agent (metsuke) OGURI TADAMASA, left Japan in January 1860 aboard the American warship *Powhattan*. The KANRIN MARU, a Dutch-built ship with KATSU KAISHŪ as captain, accompanied the *Powhattan* as far as San Francisco to guard the mission and to take advantage of the training the voyage offered. Katsu and his Japanese crew were assisted by the American lieutenant John M. BROOKE and 10 of his seamen, who had been shipwrecked in Japan the previous summer. The young FUKUZAWA YUKICHI also went on the *Kanrin maru*.

In Washington the mission met with President James Buchanan and exchanged documents on 17 May. The occasion gave the Americans a glimpse of Japanese ceremonial attire and the Japanese an opportunity to observe American customs. Of particular interest to the Japanese during their two-month stay was the impending presidential election that was to result in victory for Abraham Lincoln; they were greatly impressed by the ballot system. The mission left the United States in early summer on the warship *Niagara;* sailing around the Cape of Good Hope, the *Niagara* reached Japan in the fall. The travel logs and diaries of the members of the mission have been collected in Nichibei Shūkō Tsūshō Hyakunen Kinen Gyōji Un'eikai, ed, *Man'en gannen kembei shisetsu shiryō shūsei*, 7 vols (1961).

Unitika, Ltd

(Yunichika). Comprehensive textile company engaged in the manufacture of cotton and woolen yarn and synthetic fibers. A member of the Sanwa Bank group, it is the second largest producer of nylon in Japan. It was founded through the merger of Nichibō, Ltd, and Nippon Rayon Co, Ltd. The forerunner of Nichibō was Amagasaki Spinning Co, Ltd, a cotton-spinning firm founded in Hyōgo Prefecture in 1889. The company absorbed smaller spinning enterprises and in 1918 changed its name to the Dai Nippon Spinning Co, after which it branched out into the production of cotton, wool, and silk yarn to become a comprehensive textile maker. In 1926 the company established a subsidiary firm called Nippon Rayon Co, Ltd, which started production of rayon filament yarn, spun rayon yarn, nylon, and polyester. Nichibō and its subsidiary merged to form Unitika in 1969. The company has joint ventures in Brazil, Thailand, Indonesia, and Hong Kong. Sales for the fiscal year ending March 1982 totaled ¥214.6 billion (US $891.5 million), of which 29 percent came from polyester, 25 percent from nylon, 9 percent from cotton yarn, 9 percent from secondary products, 7 percent from woolen yarn, and 21 percent from other products. It was capitalized at ¥23.8 billion (US $98.9 million) in the same year. The main offices are in Tōkyō and Ōsaka.

Universal Manhood Suffrage Movement

(Futsū Senkyo Undō). Movement to extend to all adult males in Japan the vote in elections for the House of Representatives in the pre–World War II IMPERIAL DIET. In practice, the principal aim was to eliminate the tax-payment qualification for voting, thus enfranchising a large majority of adult males. The movement did not always rule out minor disqualifications and did not for the most part aim at lowering the voting age (set at 25 from 1889 to 1946) or at the enfranchisement of women. (The latter was usually regarded as the object of a separate movement—the Fujin Sanseiken Undō or WOMEN'S SUFFRAGE Movement—and the franchise was not extended to women until December 1945.)

The first election law (1889) had limited voting for the House of Representatives to adult males who paid direct national taxes of ¥15 or more annually. This enfranchised about 450,000, roughly 1 percent of the total population. A movement for universal suffrage took shape in the 1890s and continued until the 1925 revision of the election law, which removed all tax qualifications for the vote, increasing the electorate from approximately 3 million to 12 million people, or 20 percent of the population.

Beginnings, 1897–1911 —— A sustained campaign for universal manhood suffrage dates from 1897 with the appearance of the League to Petition for Universal Suffrage (FUTSŪ SENKYO KISEI DŌMEIKAI, later called simply Futsū Senkyo Dōmeikai or Universal Suffrage League). For many of those involved, the campaign reflected a wish to forestall the social dislocation that was seen, on the analogy of developments in Europe, as a consequence of industrialization in Japan. Some early figures in the Universal Suffrage League, including its leader, Nakamura Tahachirō (1868–1935), were also motivated by the belief that Japan could have better resisted European pressure (the so-called TRIPARTITE INTERVENTION) to relinquish its territorial gains in the recent Sino-Japanese War (1894–95) if the populace at large had had a voice in politics and thus felt it had a stake in national affairs. The cause attracted a following both from socialists and from nonsocialist liberals (Nakamura Tahachirō was one) who sought a greater popular role in politics.

At this stage, the Universal Suffrage League tried to gain public understanding and support through discussion groups, speech meetings, and periodicals, including its own organs. The league, most active in Tōkyō, organized branches in some provincial cities, but it did not attempt to develop mass popular support. Starting in 1900 it presented a number of petitions for universal suffrage to the Diet.

Early Diet Activity —— Although the league itself was an extraparliamentary organization, a Diet member associated with the movement presented the first, unsuccessful universal suffrage bill in 1902. Bills were again presented unsuccessfully in 1903, 1908, 1909, and 1910. Members of various parties as well as independent legislators supported universal suffrage in the House of Representatives, but the movement was not identified with any party as such. Some, but apparently not all, supporters in the Diet were associated with the league.

The movement reached a premature climax in March 1911, when a bill for universal suffrage passed the House of Representatives. It is not clear from the record how the bill gained the necessary votes, but it appears to have passed with a bare quorum present. It has been speculated that many members voted for the bill anticipating that it would fail to pass the House of Peers, where in fact it was summarily rejected.

Eclipse and Revival, 1911–1919 —— The movement then went into eclipse until late 1918, largely because of active government hostility. Some of the government's alarm may have been caused by the near passage of the 1911 bill. Perhaps more important, government surveillance of radical groups had broadened to include the universal suffrage movement since the so-called HIGH TREASON INCIDENT OF 1910, in which several socialists and anarchists were executed for plotting to assassinate the emperor. Activities for universal suffrage continued after 1911, but in a less organized and visible way.

A number of circumstances by late 1918 encouraged a revival of support for the universal suffrage movement. The Allied victory in World War I gave prestige to the democratic cause in Japan; the Bolshevik revolution stimulated those who favored political and social change and alarmed those who feared that such change might come violently. Longer-term trends, such as the steady increase in the urban population and the sudden growth of factory industry and labor unions in the years leading up to 1918, were also cited as reasons for supporting universal suffrage.

In 1919 universal suffrage emerged as a major topic in journals of opinion and political discussion. Labor and student organizations, sometimes jointly, began early in the year to stage well-publicized demonstrations for universal suffrage in Tōkyō and other major cities. Agitation for it within political parties had appeared in late 1918; while much of the activity initially transcended party lines, it had become a partisan issue a year later. In December 1919 the major opposition party, KENSEIKAI, as well as the smaller RIKKEN KOKUMINTŌ, endorsed universal suffrage, and the government party, RIKKEN SEIYŪKAI, took a firm negative stand that was to continue for several years.

Arguments for Universal Suffrage —— Some proponents argued that universal suffrage was essential if Japan were to keep up with the world trend toward democracy; others reasoned that it would make such abuses as bribery of voters prohibitively expensive. Still others, echoing Nakamura Tahachirō, asserted that Japan could take a stronger stand in international politics if the masses were actively involved in national affairs.

Many politicians who favored universal suffrage or liberal expansion of the franchise specifically urged wider enfranchisement of the urban population. They claimed that the government law of 1919, which extended the franchise by lowering the tax qualifications, had increased the rural electorate disproportionately to the urban and noted that most of those getting the vote under that law paid the land tax rather than other direct national taxes. Since further reduction—short of elimination of the tax qualification—would have favored payers of the land tax even more, concern for increasing the urban electorate was naturally linked to advocacy of universal suffrage.

Many people also argued that universal suffrage would provide a safety valve for mass discontent, although they differed widely as to how much of a safety valve was necessary. Some doubted that it could be effective unless it genuinely met popular needs. Conversely, some Seiyūkai opponents of universal suffrage argued that, far from being a safety valve, it would make mass discontent more explosive.

There is reason to believe that the Kenseikai leadership sympathized with proponents of urban enfranchisement and the safety-valve argument, but it was internal party pressure—fear that the universal suffrage lobby within the Kenseikai might secede if not satisfied—rather than the arguments that persuaded the leadership to adopt universal suffrage as party policy.

Apathy and Success, 1920–1925 —— Popular demonstrations for universal suffrage declined in scope and intensity after mid-1920, possibly reflecting disappointment when the Seiyūkai government won an overwhelming election victory on an explicitly anti–universal suffrage stand. There were in fact signs of a growing feeling that parliamentary government and universal suffrage were irrelevant, as socialist and labor groups turned to anarcho-syndicalism and the emerging Communist Party rejected universal suffrage. After 1920 the issue was kept alive mainly by the opposition parties and therefore primarily in the parliamentary arena. These parties now assumed a more prominent role in the movement, such as it was.

The nonparty cabinets that governed from 1922 on were more receptive to universal suffrage than the Seiyūkai, and organized labor as well as socialists and communists also showed a more positive attitude. In 1924 a Kenseikai alliance with part of the Seiyūkai scored an electoral victory against the nonparty government of KIYOURA KEIGO (see MOVEMENT TO PROTECT CONSTITUTIONAL GOVERNMENT). KATŌ TAKAAKI, the head of the Kenseikai, became premier. The Seiyūkai accepted Kenseikai policy on universal suffrage as a price of the coalition, and a government bill was passed by the Diet in 1925. The first national elections under universal manhood suffrage were held on 20 February 1928. See also TAISHŌ DEMOCRACY.

—— John H. Boyle, "The Role of the Radical Left Wing in the Japanese Suffrage Movement," in Robert K. Sakai, ed, Studies on Asia, 1965 (1965). Peter Duus, Party Rivalry and Political Change in Taishō Japan (1968). Edward G. Griffin, "The Universal Suffrage Issue in Japanese Politics, 1918–1925," Journal of Asian Studies 31.2 (1972). Koizumi Matajirō, Fusen undō hishi (1928). Matsuo Takayoshi, "Taishō demokurashī ki no seiji katei: Futsū senkyo mondai o chūshin ni," Nihonshi kenkyū 53 (March 1961). Matsuo Takayoshi, Taishō demokurashī no kenkyū (1966). Matsuo Takayoshi, "Futsū senkyo undō no shiteki kōsatsu," in Inoue Kiyoshi, ed, Taishōki no seiji to shakai (1969). Miyachi Masato, Nichiro sengo seiji shi no kenkyū: Teikoku shugi keisei ki no toshi to nōson (1973).

Edward G. GRIFFIN

universities and colleges

(daigaku). The first modern universities in Japan were established by the national government, beginning with Tōkyō University in 1877 and followed by universities in Kyōto in 1897, Tōhoku in 1907, and Kyūshū in 1910 (see IMPERIAL UNIVERSITIES). Private colleges were also established, but private university status was not authorized until 1918, and these colleges were classified as "professional schools" (SEMMON GAKKŌ). By 1935 there were 45 universities in Japan. The university system was thoroughly reformed after World War II, and the number and quality of Japan's institutions of higher learning has increased dramatically.

History of Japanese Universities—— When a modern educational system was established in Japan after the Meiji Restoration of 1868, the university systems of Europe and the United States were used as models. Tōkyō University, the first comprehensive university, was founded in 1877 to train leaders needed for the modernization of the country in the advanced learning of the United States and Europe. The university had four departments (jurisprudence, liberal arts, natural science, and medicine), and the faculty was initially composed of Europeans and Americans, who taught in their own languages. A long preparatory period, mainly in foreign languages, was required prior to entrance.

In 1886, the government issued the Imperial University Order, reorganizing the university as the Imperial University (later renamed Tōkyō Imperial University after the establishment of other imperial universities) and creating five higher middle schools (later HIGHER SCHOOLS) in various parts of the country as preparatory schools for the university. Under the new system, the Imperial University had as its objectives scientific research and the training of personnel to meet the needs of the nation. The university now comprised six schools: medicine, law, engineering, liberal arts, natural science, and agriculture; each school established a course of study, and there was also a graduate school.

By the late 1890s, the university was employing Japanese instructors to teach classes in Japanese; the quality of instruction and research gradually improved. A second imperial university was established in Kyōto in 1897. In addition, there were the institutions of higher learning called semmon gakkō (professional schools). The entrance requirement for semmon gakkō was graduation from middle school or girls' higher school, and their aim was to provide high-level academic training.

Semmon gakkō received official authorization in the Professional School Order (Semmon Gakkō Rei) of 1903, and the number of such institutions increased. Higher education thus came to have a multilevel structure, composed of two types of institutions, universities and semmon gakkō. As the quality of the facilities of the semmon gakkō increased, pressure was exerted to raise their status to that of the universities. In 1918 the Ministry of Education promulgated the University Order (Daigaku Rei), which recognized the establishment of public and private universities in addition to the imperial universities. Influential private semmon gakkō thus became universities, while some of the government semmon gakkō became colleges. In 1935 there were 45 universities, classified as follows: 6 imperial universities, 12 national colleges, 2 public universities, and 25 private universities.

The number of universities gradually increased after 1918, and there were growing demands for freedom from government interference in the pursuit of learning and research. Conflict with government authority grew, and control over the universities was increased after the Manchurian Incident of 1931; this control was maintained throughout the 1930s and World War II.

After World War II, the Allied Occupation attempted a radical reform of the education system as an important element of the effort to democratize Japan. The reform aimed at the fundamental reorganization of the multilevel educational structure and the unification of institutions of higher learning (universities, higher schools, semmon gakkō, and normal schools) into four-year colleges and universities. The reform plan was put into effect along with reforms in the public school system in 1947. See EDUCATIONAL REFORMS OF 1947.

The greatest change was seen in the national institutions of higher learning. The 6 imperial universities became national universities, and, under the slogan of one national university per prefecture, various national institutions of higher learning within any one prefecture were combined into one university for that prefecture. As for private universities, those remaining from the old system continued to operate as universities, while most private semmon gakkō were elevated to university status. Some of the professional colleges lacked the facilities and staff to qualify as universities, and they were thus temporarily accredited as two-year JUNIOR COLLEGES; permanent accreditation of junior colleges was extended in 1964. Public semmon gakkō and most of the public universities were reorganized as four-year universities, and some of them became national universities. As a result, by 1949 a total of 173 new universities had been created: 68 national, 13 public, and 92 private universities.

Unlike the prewar system, in which universities were reserved for the privileged elite, postwar universities opened their doors to all, with the mission of providing general and technical education to train the leaders of a democratic society.

Present Status and Problems—— When numerous universities were established during the confusion of the postwar period, the MINISTRY OF EDUCATION set minimum standards but left improvements in quality to the universities. The power to accredit institutions was invested in the University Chartering Council (Daigaku Setchi Shingikai), which was composed of university authorities. It became very easy to establish private universities, and many were created. This resulted in great differences among the universities in quality of education and research. Also, since some universities were created from various prewar institutions that already varied in their facilities and teaching staff, a type of hierarchy developed within the four-year university system. At the top of the hierarchy are the national universities, with private institutions ranging below, along a continuum of decreasing quality.

The financial foundation of private universities is weak, because they are dependent upon student tuition and entrance fees for their operational base. Most Japanese private institutions do not have the large university endowments that provide financial strength for private universities in the United States. Government assistance to private universities began in the 1970s, but the amount they receive is small compared to support for the national universities. There is a great difference between the tuition fees of national and private universities, and among private universities themselves. The average annual tuition for private schools was double the approximately ¥150,000 (about US $700) at the national universities in 1978. The medical schools of a number of private universities charge more than ten times the tuition of their national counterparts and require a large entrance fee in addition. Most educational expenses are covered by the student's parents; contributions from student employment and scholarships are minimal (see FINANCIAL AID FOR STUDENTS).

Differences among schools are reflected in the difficulty of entrance examinations, the quality of students, and the opportunities for employment after graduation, all of which translates into a generally recognized ranking of the various universities in terms of prestige. This has led to intense competition in ENTRANCE EXAMINATIONS among those trying to enter higher-ranked universities, to the phenomenon of the so-called shiken jigoku (examination hell), and to the appearance of rōnin (the term for masterless samurai is applied to students who, having failed to enter the college of their choice, continue studying at CRAM SCHOOLS in preparation to retake the examination). The university entrance examination issue is now a major social problem.

As of 1979 there were 443 colleges and universities (92 national, 33 public, and 318 private) and 518 junior colleges in Japan. The number of students at universities was about 1.8 million and at junior colleges 374,000. Classified by type of institution, 21 percent attended national universities, 3 percent public universities, and 76 percent private universities. At national universities, the 2 largest subject areas in terms of enrollment were the natural sciences (42 percent) and education (25 percent); at private universities these were the social sciences (48 percent) and the humanities (15 percent). Some 22 percent of all students were women, more than half of whom were either in the humanities or in education departments. There were 80 women's universities. Of all 18 year olds, 37.9 percent entered universities or junior colleges. The basic requirement for admission is graduation from high school, and each university selects students on the basis of its own test of scholastic ability. Compared to the rigors of the entrance examinations, advancement after entrance is easy, and three-fourths of the students graduate after the prescribed four-year period.

In universities the school year starts in April and follows the semester system. Universities are composed of schools, and schools are composed of departments; at the time of entrance, students generally enroll in a particular school and department. Transfers to another department or school, or to another university, are allowed only in very exceptional cases, and students usually spend four years at the same university in the same school.

The curriculum is divided into general requirements and specialized courses; at most universities the first two years are spent on general requirements and the last two years on specialized courses. Programs in medicine and dentistry require six years of attendance, four of which are applied to professional education. Following the credit and elective system, the student is awarded a bachelor's degree after fulfilling the credit requirements.

The vast majority of students are employed as soon as they graduate. According to a 1979 survey, 73.6 percent of all university graduates were employed and 4.4 percent went to GRADUATE SCHOOLS. Of those employed, 39 percent were in professional or technical occupations, 41 percent in clerical work, 15 percent in sales, and 5 percent in other fields. Classified by industry, the largest percentages were: 26 percent in manufacturing, 23 percent in service industries, 15 percent in wholesale and retail, 14 percent in finance and insurance, and 8 percent in government. Most were either white-collar workers or otherwise employed in nonmanufacturing fields.

In national universities, teaching and research are basically organized on the basis of either chair (kōza) or subject (gakkamoku); private universities are primarily organized by subject. The chair system places stress on research and is most often found at universities that have graduate schools. A chair ordinarily consists of a professor, an assistant professor, and an assistant, and the budget for educational research is allotted per chair. In contrast, the subject system is primarily found in universities whose main function is education rather than research; posts of professor and assistant professor are set up and a budget is allotted for each instructor. Chair and subject are organized by department within the school. The schools have a rather large amount of autonomy. In private universities, the highest decision-making bodies are the board of directors and the board of trustees, but in many cases, the election of the president and deans of the school rests with the faculty council. In national universities the board of directors is the highest decision-making body, but all the members are elected by the faculty councils of the various schools and research institutes. The president and deans of the schools are elected by vote of the members of the faculty council. See also ACADEMIC FREEDOM; GAKUBATSU.

■ ——Makoto Asō and Ikuo Amano, *Education and Japan's Modernization* (1972). William K. Cummings, Ikuo Amano, and Kazuyuki Kitamura, ed, *Changes in the Japanese University* (1979). William K. Cummings and Ikuo Amano, "Japanese Higher Education," in Philip G. Altlack, ed, *Comparative Higher Education: Bibliography and Analysis* (1976). Kokusai Bunka Shinkōkai, ed, *Higher Education and the Student Problem in Japan* (1972). Michio Nagai, *Higher Education in Japan: Its Take-off and Crash* (1971). Organization for Economic Cooperation and Development, *Reviews of National Policies for Education: Japan* (1971).   AMANO Ikuo

university autonomy

(daigaku no jichi). A university's independence in administering its own affairs, without which ACADEMIC FREEDOM cannot be guaranteed, since a university's distinctive function is to conduct research and disseminate knowledge. University autonomy is as necessary as academic freedom for successful research, study, and teaching, as well as for the intellectual growth of students and professors. University autonomy in post–World War II Japan was established and strengthened by several official acts. A 1950 notice from the Ministry of Education and the resulting Tōkyō Metropolitan Police Ordinance of 1953 required that police obtain prior university approval for intelligence and public security activities on university campuses. The principle of university autonomy was further supported by the Educational Public Employees Special Law and the Basic Law Concerning the Execution of Duties by Police Officials. But in the case of an emergency affecting the public welfare, the police may enter a university campus without prior university approval. Thus a precarious balance exists between the university's need for self-government and society's need for the maintenance of peace and order, making the exact limits of academic freedom and university autonomy difficult to determine. The POPORO PLAYERS CASE (1963) showed students indirectly participating in decisions concerning university autonomy, while the violent student movements of the late

1960s led to active student participation in the making of university policy on autonomy, once the sole prerogative of faculty governing bodies.   Hiroshi ITOH

university upheavals of 1968–1969

Strikes and other incidents affecting many Japanese universities in 1968 and 1969. The academic year 1968–69 witnessed a nearly total paralysis of the university system in Japan, as a majority of the nation's 377 universities were beset with student strikes, boycotts, and violence. The campus disturbances represented profound student discontent with the Japanese system of higher education, but they were also linked with and exacerbated by the broader student political movement in opposition to what was viewed as Japanese and American imperialism, particularly the latter in Vietnam. In this sense, the crisis of 1968–69 in Japan was one part of an international wave of student protest.

The specific issues in the university disturbances of the late 1960s were diverse, and any given protest typically involved several complaints. The most common points of dispute were increased tuition fees, jurisdiction over student dormitories and meeting halls, demands for greater student participation in university governance, charges of corruption among university officials, demands for the revocation of disciplinary measures, and specific demands for the reform of such educational programs as the medical intern system.

While such epidemics of disruption had swept through Japanese higher education before (notably in 1930–32), the disturbances of 1968–69 were distinguished by their unprecedented scale, and systematic violence. Abetted by factional infighting among the students, the physical destruction was considerable; at Tōkyō University alone, damage was estimated at about ¥136 million (US $380,000).

The first major disturbance of 1968–69 broke out in April 1968 at Nihon University over the alleged misuse of funds by university officials. Two months later a dispute in the Faculty of Medicine at Tōkyō University over reform of the intern system led to the closure of the university by student strikers, who barricaded buildings throughout the campus. These two great strikes sparked a contagion of protests throughout the fall of 1968 that by the end of the year had affected 110 schools, 65 of which remained unresolved. Incidents of confrontation, frequently violent, between students and police, students and faculty, and among rival student factions became increasingly common.

The turning point in the paroxysm of 1968–69 was the massive assault by riot police on 18–19 January 1969 against the student radicals at Tōkyō University. After two days of spectacular battling with stones, shields, staves, and firebombs, the last bastion in the Yasuda Amphitheater gave way. This setback stemmed, but did not stop, the wave of student protest, which resulted in the almost total cancellation of university entrance examinations in March 1969 and the consequent lack of one graduating class. Strikes and demonstrations continued through the spring of 1969, resulting in a cumulative record for 1969 of 152 universities on strike, 10,000 student arrests, 873 riot police mobilizations, and the confiscation of 12,000 staves, 4,000 Molotov cocktails, and 4,000 iron bars.

By the late spring of 1969, however, the tide had decisively turned. The Okinawa Day demonstration of April 28 was a failure, a major setback for the movement against the United States–Japan Security Treaty (see UNITED STATES–JAPAN SECURITY TREATIES). The movement both on and off campus was beset by exhaustion. Both public and official sentiment turned increasingly against the students, resulting in the passage of the University Law. This law provided for sanctions against universities that failed within a certain time to resolve campus disputes, there being 70 when the law went into effect on 10 August 1969. The University Law also generated much debate over university reform, but in the end only very limited changes were made on most campuses. See also STUDENT MOVEMENTS; ZENGAKUREN; UNIVERSITY AUTONOMY.

■ ——Stuart Dowsey, ed, *Zengakuren: Japan's Revolutionary Students* (1970). Kyōdai Shimbunsha, ed, *Kyōdai tōsō: Kyōdai shinwa no hōkai* (1969). Nihon Daigaku Bunri Gakubu Tōsō Iinkai Shokikyoku, ed, *Hangyaku no barikēdo: Nichidai tōsō no kiroku* (1969). Tōdai Zengaku Joshu Kyōtō Kaigi, ed, *Tōdai zenkyōtō* (1969).
          Henry D. SMITH II

unjō

A fee collected from urban tradesmen and craftsmen, hunters, fishermen, etc, during the Edo period (1600–1868). From the 12th to the

16th centuries *unjō* referred to the shipment of goods to Kyōto as tax payments. Belonging to the category of miscellaneous taxes (KOMONONARI), it was generally paid in cash. Since the tax base and rate varied from year to year, *unjō* was considered one of the "floating taxes" (UKIYAKU). In contrast to the other major levy collected from businesses at this time—MYŌGAKIN ("offertory money"), which in theory was a voluntary cash donation—*unjō* was generally a fixed obligation; however, the two kinds of tax sometimes became confused.

The procedure for assessing *unjō* was determined by each domainal (HAN) government. In some cases *unjō* was more like a license fee than a tax. The Tokugawa shogunate appointed specialists, called *unjōkata,* to supervise the collection of these taxes in the shogunal domains (*tenryō*). Those *unjōkata* who were located in ports opened to European traders after 1854 became customs officials under the Meiji government in 1868.   *Philip* BROWN

unjust enrichment

(futō ritoku). Legal term referring to benefits that have been obtained without just legal cause, as well as the system by which the person in receipt of the benefit returns the benefit (unjust enrichment) to the injured party. If person A receives a benefit from person B's property or labor without just cause, and B, for that reason, sustains a loss, A has the duty to return the actual value of the benefit to B as unjust enrichment (Civil Code, art. 703). When A, the party benefited, has acted in good faith, unaware of the lack of just cause for this benefit, he must return only the actual value of the benefit. If he has acted in bad faith, knowing that he lacked just cause, he must return the value of the original benefit with interest, and in addition compensate the injured party for any damages sustained (Civil Code, art. 704).

One example of a situation where a claim of unjust enrichment may arise is found where there exists a contractual relationship between the parties, on the basis of which money or goods have passed from B to A, and subsequently the contract ceases to exist due to nullification, revocation, cancelation, or the like. In addition, unjust enrichment may arise in a variety of other situations, but a duty to return the unjust enrichment would be recognized only exceptionally where no contractual relation exists. However, the system of unjust enrichment is an important mechanism that may be applied to ensure fairness between the parties.   KATŌ *Ichirō*

unka → plant hopper

Unkei (?–1223)

Sculptor of Buddhist images in the early part of the Kamakura period (1185–1333). Son of KŌKEI, colleague of KAIKEI, and father of TANKEI, all of the KEI SCHOOL of sculpture. He was based at the temple Kōfukuji in Nara; his masculine and dynamic style appealed to the warriors of the Kamakura period. Among his extant works are the Dainichi Nyorai (Skt: Mahāvairocana) at Enjōji in Nara and an Amida Triad, a Fudō Myōō (Skt: Acala), and a Bishamonten (Skt: Vaiśravaṇa) at Jōrakuji in Yokosuka, Kanagawa Prefecture. Considered the greatest master of the Kei school, Unkei revitalized the art of sculpture with his realistic and dynamic renditions of Buddhist figures.

Unkoku school

A line of painters who traced their ancestry to the illustrious artist SESSHŪ TŌYŌ (1420–1506). Founded by UNKOKU TŌGAN (1547–1618), who appropriated the name of Sesshū's painting studio, Unkokuan, in order to establish this artistic descent.

Tōgan, a native of western Japan and a retainer to the MŌRI FAMILY of the Chōshū domain (now Yamaguchi Prefecture), at first studied the established KANŌ SCHOOL painting methods in Kyōto but then left the capital to follow the brush manner and themes of Sesshū, whose paintings survived in the western provinces. When he called himself the "grandson of Sesshū," he was challenged by a contemporary, HASEGAWA TŌHAKU, who also maintained a claim to using Sesshū's name. Tōhaku seems to have deferred to Tōgan, however, and took to signing his paintings "the fifth-generation Sesshū."

Unlike Tōhaku and the Kanō masters, Tōgan worked principally outside the environs of Kyōto, although he maintained ties with

Unkoku Tōgan

Detail of one of the 14 sliding-door panels of Tōgan's celebrated cycle of paintings entitled *West Lake.* Executed for the Ōbaiin, a subtemple of Daitokuji in Kyōto, in the late 16th century. Ink on paper. Each panel 180.0 × 141.5 cm. Ōbaiin, Daitokuji, Kyōto.

several monastic institutions in the Kyōto area that were supported by his patrons in western Japan. His sons and followers did likewise. Unkoku Tōeki (1591–1644), a son of Tōgan, studied and collaborated with his father on a number of projects both around Kyōto and in the Yamaguchi region. His large-scale *fusuma-e* (sliding-door painting) and *byōbu* (screen) compositions are numerous and successful. The work of Tōgan's elder son, Tōoku (d 1615?), is relatively unknown, as is that of several later followers.

Tōeki, who called himself the fourth-generation Sesshū, and his sons set the standards for Unkoku school painting in the 17th and early 18th centuries. Combining the colorful Kanō-school painting canons with Unkoku ink-painting techniques, they forged a distinct approach to traditional painting themes. However, the increased reliance by Tōeki's pupils upon an established set of Sesshū- and Tōgan-derived images precipitated a loss of creativity apparent in Unkoku painting from the third quarter of the 17th century. The school nevertheless lasted into the 19th century.   *Michael* CUNNINGHAM

Unkoku Tōgan (1547–1618)

Ink painter and founder of the UNKOKU SCHOOL. Born into a *samurai* family from Hizen Province (now parts of Nagasaki and Saga prefectures) in Kyūshū; his real name was Hara Jihei Naoharu. After the death of his father, he entered the service of the powerful MŌRI FAMILY in western Honshū. According to various records, he studied painting in Kyōto at the KANŌ SCHOOL atelier, but of this phase of his life little is known. He left Kyōto to work for his patron, Mōri Terumoto (1553–1625), who resided at Hiroshima Castle.

Mōri Terumoto owned a landscape handscroll (*Landscape of the Four Seasons;* Mōri Collection), dated 1486, by the renowned ink painter SESSHŪ TŌYŌ (1420–1506), who had resided in western Japan most of his life and had also been in the service of the Mōri family. According to an inscription appended to the handscroll by Tōgan in 1592, this painting was entrusted to Tōgan so that he might revive Sesshū's painting style, which had passed out of favor by the mid-16th century. In the same collection is a faithful copy of this masterpiece, usually attributed to Tōgan. Around this time Tōgan began using his professional name, "Unkoku" being a reference to Sesshū's studio-retreat known as the Unkokuan (Cloud Valley Retreat). Tōgan even established his own studio at the same site.

Tōgan traveled widely. Extant paintings and records associated with his name chart his activities in western Honshū, Kyūshū, and the Kyōto–Ōsaka area. Perhaps his most famous cycle of paintings is a *West Lake* scene and *Seven Sages* group of *fusuma-e* (sliding-door paintings) executed for the Ōbaiin, a subtemple of Daitokuji in Kyōto. These *fusuma-e* are generally considered Tōgan's masterpieces in the Chinese painting manner.

Other paintings attributed to Tōgan, on more Japanese themes, include the *Mt. Yoshino* screen (formerly Masuda Collection), the *Hunting Party* screen (MOA Museum of Art), and the *Portrait of Sugawara no Michizane* (Mōri Collection). A magnificent set of six large *fusuma-e* depicting *Crows in Plum Tree* (Kyōto National Museum) with gold foil background has also been assigned to Tōgan's hand, as have numerous scrolls depicting the Buddhist patriarch Daruma; HABOKU landscapes; and screens with Zen figural, landscape, and bird-and-flower subjects.

Tōgan's talent was in his own time considered equal to that of HASEGAWA TŌHAKU and the Kanō painters KANŌ SANRAKU and KANŌ SANSETSU. In fact, his reputation exceeded Tōhaku's, owing no doubt to his backing by several politically prominent families and by his allegiance to Sesshū. A mid-Edo-period (1600–1868) anecdote relates that Tōgan engaged in a legal dispute with Tōhaku over the right to use Sesshū's name and to claim authentic artistic lineage. Tōgan reportedly won the suit.

📖 ——Kawai Masatomo, *Yūshō/Tōgan,* vol 11 of *Nihon bijutsu kaiga zenshū* (Shūeisha, 1978). Tanaka Tsukeichi, "Unkokuha no hito to sakuhin," *Kokka* (July 1960; January 1961; February 1961; March 1961). Michael CUNNINGHAM

unlimited partnership company

(gōmei kaisha). A type of company incorporated under the COMMERCIAL CODE that is composed entirely of unlimited liability partners. It is similar to an unlimited partnership in Anglo-American law. Partners have a duty to contribute a specified amount of capital to the company and jointly and severally bear direct and unlimited liability to its creditors in the event that the property of the company is insufficient to meet its obligations. Contributions are generally in the form of cash or other property, but contributions of services and credit are also allowed. Because they are exposed to substantial liability, partners have the right to administer the affairs of the company and to represent it but are not allowed to engage in business activities that compete with it.

The consent of all partners is required for such actions as amendment of the articles of incorporation, mergers, dissolution of the company, or transfers of partnership interests. Articles of incorporation containing the trade name (which must expressly state that the company is an unlimited partnership), the purpose of the company, locations of the head and branch offices, names and addresses of the partners, and the type and value of each partner's contribution must be prepared and registered with the appropriate registry office. Partnership contributions need not be fully paid in at the time of the formation of the company. Liquidation may be either by consent of all partners or by court order.

Of the four types of corporation in Japan (the others being the JOINT-STOCK COMPANY, the LIMITED LIABILITY COMPANY, and the LIMITED PARTNERSHIP COMPANY), the unlimited partnership company is the least common; in 1978 there were only 20,000 unlimited partnership companies in Japan. See also PARTNERSHIP.

KITAZAWA Masahiro

Uno Chiyo (1897–)

Novelist. Born in Yamaguchi Prefecture. She first earned recognition when she won a prize in a newspaper fiction contest with her short story "Shifun no kao" (1921, A Face with Makeup). After the breakup of her first marriage she turned to professional writing. In the 1920s, she associated with many literary celebrities while living with the novelist OZAKI SHIRŌ and later with the painter Tōgō Seiji (1897–1978), on whom she based her novel *Irozange* (1933–35, Confession). She was married for the second time (from 1937 to 1964) to the novelist KITAHARA TAKEO, with whom she published the magazine *Sutairu* (Style). Her works, often drawn from her own life, feature delicately sensual descriptions of women's psychology. Among her best-known works are *Ohan* (1957; tr *Ohan,* 1961), the autobiographical *Aru hitori no onna no hanashi;* (1971, One Woman's Story), and the story "Kōfuku" (1924; tr "Happiness," 1982).

unohana

Deutzia crenata. Also known as *utsugi.* A deciduous shrub of the saxifrage family (Saxifragaceae) growing wild in mountainous regions throughout Japan and also planted near homes for hedges. It reaches a height of about 2 meters (6.6 ft) and has a hollow stem with shredded bark and numerous branches. The alternate leaves are ovate to broadly lanceolate in shape with serrated edges and rough undersides. The *unohana* or *utsugi* blooms from May to June, bearing five-petaled white flowers in clusters at the ends of the branches. A double-flowered variety is known as *yaeutsugi.* About 18 species of the genus *Deutzia* grow wild in Japan, including *himeutsugi* (*D. gracilis*), with smaller flowers blooming earlier than those of the *unohana,* and the pink-flowered variety, *akebono utsugi,* which is also raised as an ornamental. As a flower of early summer fields and mountains the *unohana* has supplied themes for Japanese poets. In ancient times the quality of the year's harvest was said to have been forecast by how this flower bloomed, perhaps because the white blossoms were likened to grains of rice. As the wood is tough and hard to split, it was formerly used for pegs, toothpicks, inlay work, and so forth; it is still a preferred material for wooden pegs. MATSUDA Osamu

Uno Kōji (1891–1961)

Real name Uno Kakujirō. Short-story writer, novelist, and essayist. Born in the city of Fukuoka and brought up in Ōsaka, Uno attended Waseda University to study English literature but left before graduating. He took up writing as a full-time profession, though during his life it paid him little. He spent his adult years in Tōkyō, had several live-in love affairs, fathered one son, traveled frequently with writer friends, and was married twice.

Uno Kōji's writing is representative of a certain middlebrow element in modern Japanese literature. A popular and prolific practitioner of the magazine story of his period, he first wrote using techniques of Japanese NATURALISM *(shizen shugi);* for example, the use of first person confessional or semiautobiographical format and subject matter modeled on either personal or secondhand experience. Friend and fellow-writer HIROTSU KAZUO helped him publish his best early short story, "Kura no naka" (1919, In the Storeroom), a humorous tale of a down-and-out writer's visit to the local pawn shop out of longing to see his kimonos, which he had pawned. Waggish humor and a discursive style became the trademark of his early writing. He turned out a stream of stories in the 1920s as a regular contributor to mainstream literary magazines like CHŪŌ KŌRON. Particularly good are "Ku no sekai" (1919, World of Woe), recounting the troubles of an artist (Uno in disguise) and his hysterical lover; "Ren'ai kassen" (1920, Love Wars), on the theme of competition for a lady's favors; and "Ko o kashiya" (1923; tr "Children for Hire," 1963), a tale about a hapless man trapped into hiring out children to prostitutes.

By the late 1920s Uno was ill from nervous exhaustion and upset by the suicide of his friend AKUTAGAWA RYŪNOSUKE. He gave up creative writing and spent some time in a mental institution, but was forced by poverty to publish essays and book reviews. The short story "Kareki no aru fūkei" (1933, Landscape with Dead Tree) signaled his writing comeback. Its depressed, introspective tone is taken as the dividing line in Uno's writing style: from the 1930s on, his stories are serious and mostly autobiographical, as in "Ningen ōrai" (1934, Human Comings and Goings) and "Kiyō bimbō" (1938, Clever Poverty).

During the repressive war years Uno maintained his artistic integrity by publishing critical studies like *Bungaku no sanjūnen* (1940, Thirty Years of Literature). The best of his postwar works are the novella *Omoigawa* (1948, Love Stream), a story of unfulfilled love between a married writer and a *geisha,* which received the Yomiuri Literary Prize for 1951, and his now largely neglected novel *Ku no sekai* (1949, World of Woe), based on the earlier short story. It is an exquisite work: a gentle, delicate blend of humor, pathos, and nostalgia which perfectly evokes the atmosphere of much of Uno's life. Years before his death from complications caused by tuberculosis, Uno eulogized his better-known writer friend in a book-length dialogue-essay entitled *Akutagawa Ryūnosuke* (1953).

Dennis M. SPACKMAN

Uno Kōzō (1897–1977)

Marxist economist and originator of theories which exerted a great influence on the Japanese academic world after World War II. Born in Okayama Prefecture and a graduate of Tōkyō University, Uno joined the ŌHARA INSTITUTE FOR SOCIAL RESEARCH, then went to Germany for further study. Upon his return to Japan, he joined the faculty of Tōhoku University and lectured on economic policy. Indicted for leftist beliefs in 1938, Uno was eventually acquitted but left the university and joined a private economic research institute. After World War II he joined the faculty of the Social Science Research Institute of Tōkyō University, where he organized joint studies on agricultural problems. After his retirement from Tōkyō University, he became a professor at Hōsei University. Uno's economic theory sought to separate economics from ideological debates on social class and establish the field as a purely objective science. He divided his studies of Marxist economics into three stages: theory, studies of stages of development, and analysis of current conditions. In his theoretical stage, Uno worked out a bold revision of ideas in Marx's *Das Kapital* and formulated a unique theory regarding financial crises which emphasized capital surplus. His main works are collected in *Uno Kōzō chosakushū* (1973–74).

SUGIHARA Shirō

Untei

(Pavilion of Fragrant Herbs). Library of the 8th century. It was among the most famous *kuge bunko*—private libraries assembled by court nobles, including the Kōbaidono of SUGAWARA NO MICHIZANE and the Gōke Bunko of ŌE NO MASAFUSA. The Untei was built by ISONOKAMI NO YAKATSUGU, probably in the decade 770–780, and stood at a corner of his residence, which he had converted into a temple. Yakatsugu is said to have shared his extensive collection of Buddhist commentaries and Chinese classics with "all who loved learning," among them the most distinguished scholars of his day. The library was probably named for the aromatic herbs used to prevent destruction of paper and cloth by insect larvae. The Untei continued to flourish as a center of learning for a decade after Yakatsugu's death (781) and may have survived for an additional half-century before it fell into disuse. *Theodore F.* WELCH

U Nu → Nu, U

Uny Co, Ltd

(Yunii). Retail chain based in the Nagoya area. Established in 1971 through the merger of the Hoteiya and Nishikawaya chains, it handles all types of merchandise, including clothing, food, household appliances, and leisure items. It is also involved in fast food sales. Uny has a total of 101 stores in the Chūbu and Kantō regions. Future plans call for the establishment of a network of medium-sized stores with an average floor space of 5,000 square meters (5,980 sq yd) and unusually ample, by Japanese standards, parking space in the suburban areas of the same regions. In order to compete successfully in the international market, Uny is endeavoring to reinforce its capital structure and merchandising ability. Sales for the fiscal year ending February 1982 totaled ¥357.3 billion (US $1.5 billion), with the following breakdown: food 40 percent, clothes 34 percent, household goods 23 percent, and others 3 percent. It was capitalized at ¥6.4 billion (US $27.2 million) in the same year. The head office is in Nagoya, Aichi Prefecture.

Un'yushō → Ministry of Transport

Unzen–Amakusa National Park

(Unzen–Amakusa Kokuritsu Kōen). Situated in western Kyūshū, in Nagasaki, Kumamoto, and Kagoshima prefectures. The park features volcanoes, islands, sheer cliffs, and hot spring resorts. UNZENDAKE, an active volcano whose highest peak is Fugendake (1,359 m; 4,458 ft), lies in the center of the SHIMABARA PENINSULA. Unzen Hot Spring is on its slopes; in spring and fall the mountain is covered with colorful wild Kirishima azaleas *(miyama kirishima)* and maples; in winter trees with frost-covered leaves are a particular attraction. South of the volcano in the YATSUSHIRO SEA are the 120 AMAKUSA ISLANDS, whose coastal regions are included in the park. These islands are characterized by hills, white-sand beaches, and sea cliffs. In 1966 the Five Amakusa Bridges were completed, linking the larger islands, among them Shimoshima and Kamishima, to one another

and to Kyūshū at MISUMI in the north. In both the Unzen and Amakusa areas, Christianity spread quickly when it was introduced in the 16th century. The persecutions that followed its proscription culminated in the SHIMABARA UPRISING of 1637. Area: 256.7 sq km (99.1 sq mi).

Unzendake

Group of composite volcanoes, Shimabara Peninsula, Nagasaki Prefecture, Kyūshū. It includes Fugendake (1,359 m; 4,458 ft), Kunimidake (1,347 m; 4,418 ft), and Myōkendake (1,333 m; 4,372 ft). It is known for its tracts of *miyamakirishima* (a kind of azalea), numerous hot springs, and scenic beauty. It is the main feature of Unzen–Amakusa National Park.

U Ottama → Ottama, U

Uozu

City in northeastern Toyama Prefecture, central Honshū; on Toyama Bay. It first developed as a castle town and then as a fishing port from the Edo period (1600–1868). Besides fishing, it has carbide, textiles, and machinery industries. Pop: 49,511.

Uraga

District in the city of Yokosuka, on the Miura Peninsula, Kanagawa Prefecture, central Honshū. In the Edo period (1600–1868) there was a magistrate's office here for the inspection of vessels entering and leaving Tōkyō Bay. Commodore PERRY landed here in 1853. The site of the Kannonzaki lighthouse and one of the largest shipbuilding industries in Japan.

Uraga bugyō

(commissioner of Uraga). One of the *ongoku bugyō* (commissioners for distant provinces) under the TOKUGAWA SHOGUNATE (1603–1867), the Uraga *bugyō* presided over the port of Uraga (now part of the city of Yokosuka), then the gateway to the shogunal seat at Edo (now Tōkyō). His duties included the administration of the city and the inspection and taxation of all ships entering Edo Bay. The office was established in 1720 to guard the sea approach to Edo; it was filled by one or two men at a time, who were directly responsible to the senior councillors (RŌJŪ) in Edo. As a result of the increase of foreign ships in Japanese waters after 1800, the commissioner's staff grew from about 60 men to about 150 in 1845.

Uraga Channel

(Uraga Suidō). Between the Miura Peninsula, Kanagawa Prefecture, and the Bōsō Peninsula, Chiba Prefecture, connecting Tōkyō Bay with the Pacific Ocean. It is an important artery, since all of the commercial traffic to the Tōkyō and Yokohama area passes through it. During the Edo period (1600–1868) ships were inspected here before being allowed to enter Tōkyō Bay; Commodore Perry passed through Uraga Channel with his "black ships" (KUROFUNE) in 1853. The coasts along this channel are popular for fishing and swimming. Width: about 10 km (6.2 mi).

Uragami family

Powerful landholders who took their name from the Uragami estate in Harima Province (now part of Hyōgo Prefecture); descendants of the scholar-official Ki no Haseo (845 or 851–912). During the Muromachi period (1333–1568) they rose in service to the AKAMATSU FAMILY, military governors *(shugo)* of Harima, whose power they later usurped. Following the ŌNIN WAR (1467–77), Akamatsu Masanori (1455–96) was made head of the Board of Retainers (Samuraidokoro) in Kyōto, and Uragami Norimune (1429–1502) became his deputy. Norimune's son Munesuke established a power base in Bizen Province (now the southern part of Okayama Prefecture), and in 1521 his son Muramune (d 1531) assassinated Akamatsu Yoshimura (Masanori's son) and became lord of Harima, Bizen, and Mimasaka (now the northern part of Okayama Prefecture). In 1561 the Uragami were overthrown and destroyed by their vassal Ukita Naoie (1529–81). *John W.* HALL

Uragami Gyokudō——"Mountains and Autumn Foliage"

A painting from the *Album of Misty Landscapes (Enkajō)*. Colors on paper. 29.1 × 22.4 cm. 1811. Umezawa Memorial Gallery, Tōkyō.

Uragami Gyokudō (1745–1820)

BUNJINGA (literati painting) artist; better known in his day as a musician and poet. Born into a *samurai* family in Bizen Province (now part of Okayama Prefecture), he studied Confucianism and, during his stay in Edo (now Tōkyō) as personal attendant to his domainal lord, he learned to play the Chinese zither (Ch: *qin* or *ch'in*; J: SHICHIGENKIN), compose poetry, and paint. His art name, Gyokudō Kinshi ("Jade Hall Zither Master"), was taken from the name of a Ming-dynasty (1368–1644) zither that he owned.

After the death of his lord in 1768, Gyokudō devoted himself to scholarship and the arts. In his music Gyokudō revived SAIBARA, the ancient folk songs of Japan that had been incorporated into formal court music. Gyokudō set *saibara* poems to revised melodies with zither accompaniment. Working within a limited range of musical and technical possibilities, he wrote long, chant-like melodies over complex overlapping rhythmic structures. He wrote a number of books on the zither.

Gyokudō's poetry is written entirely in Chinese five- or seven-character regulated verse. The poems range from 2 to 16 lines in length and celebrate his love for the zither, nature, *sake,* and solitude. His music and poetry were both published when he was in his 40s, around the same time that he began to paint landscapes in the literati style.

In 1794, two years after the death of his wife, he gave up his hereditary position and became a wanderer with his two sons, URAGAMI SHUNKIN and Shūkin. Carrying his zither, he traveled through Japan visiting literati friends. During these years he began to paint seriously, while making his living through his knowledge of medicine and talent in music. In 1811 he settled down in Kyōto with Shunkin; during his final decade he painted most of his masterworks. Among his circle of literati friends in Kyōto and Ōsaka were AOKI MOKUBEI and TANOMURA CHIKUDEN.

While still an official, Gyokudō painted mostly small-scale works in a style much like that of his friend TOTOKI BAIGAI. After 1794 he painted with greater energy on both small- and medium-sized hanging scrolls. Working in paper and monochrome ink, he developed a technique of overlaying gray and black ink, wet and dry brushwork, and often relied exclusively upon complex rhythmic patterns of horizontal dashes, rounded lines, short jabbing strokes, and vertical dots. His compositions are usually dominated by tall central mountains rising over a screen of trees in the foreground. Frequently, a tiny figure of a sage appears, reading in a hut or crossing a bridge, and sometimes carrying a zither. Only in this century have his landscapes been given the recognition they deserve. *Stephen* ADDISS

Uragami Shunkin (1779–1846)

BUNJINGA (literati painting) artist; the eldest son of URAGAMI GYOKUDŌ. Shunkin was born in Bizen Province (now part of Okayama Prefecture), where his father served as a *samurai* official. When Shunkin was 15, Gyokudō began a life of travel with his two sons, who became well-versed in music, poetry, calligraphy, and painting under their father's tutelage. The youngest son, Shūkin (1785–1871), concentrated on music and eventually accepted a post in the Aizu domain (now part of Fukushima Prefecture). Shunkin devoted himself to painting.

After almost two decades of travel, Shunkin married and settled down in Kyōto in 1811; he was joined by his father. Influenced by the literati circle of RAI SAN'YŌ, Shunkin developed a conservative painting style based on orthodox Chinese traditions, though his oeuvre extended beyond the conventional literati repertoire to bird-and-flower and figure paintings, including a portrait of his father. His work is close in technique and spirit to that of his friends OKADA HANKŌ, NAKABAYASHI CHIKUTŌ, and YAMAMOTO BAIITSU. The majority of his works, however, consist of landscapes. These show the influence of Huang Gongwang (Huang Kung-wang; 1269–1354), a Chinese Yuan (Yüan) dynasty (1279–1368) painter whose works filtered into Japan through Ming dynasty (1368–1644) woodblock prints and other copies.

One may note in Shunkin's work short, overlapping brushstrokes with darker ink overlaying grayer tones, clusters of dots to suggest vegetation, and pale color washes to soften the rocks and mountain forms. In his own day, Shunkin's well-composed and competently brushed paintings were preferred over his father's bolder and more imaginative works. *Stephen* ADDISS

Urakami kuzure → persecutions at Urakami

Ura Nihon

Term for the sections of Honshū along the Sea of Japan. "Ura" (rear) connotes the industrial and cultural "backwardness" of this part of Japan compared to the more "advanced" areas along the Pacific coast (OMOTE NIHON), and there are objections to the use of the term.

Uranouchi Bay

(Uranouchi Wan). Inlet of western Tosa Bay on the coast of south-central Kōchi Prefecture, Shikoku. The chief activities are pearl culture and yellowtail cultivation. Popular for swimming and gathering shellfish, the bay has been designated a prefectural natural park. Length: approximately 12 km (7.5 mi).

Urashima Tarō

Folktale. In the standard version a man named Urashima Tarō rescues a turtle that is being ill-treated by children. The turtle changes into a young woman, who invites him to the sea-god's palace (*ryūgū*), where he spends three happy years with her. Finally returning to his village, he finds himself a stranger. At a loss, he opens a box that she has given him but has forbidden him to open. White smoke rises from it and instantly he becomes a hoary old man; it has been 300 years since he left. Folktales of the same motif are found throughout Japan. The earliest extant version, in which the man is referred to as Shima no Ko, appears in the *Tango fudoki itsubun* (Local Records of Tango Province; see FUDOKI). Other early sources such as the NIHON SHOKI (720) and the MAN'YŌSHŪ (ca 759) refer to the man as Urashima no Ko. *SUCHI Tokuhei*

Urasoe

City on the island of Okinawa, Okinawa Prefecture. During the 12th–14th centuries Urasoe was the political, economic, and cultural center of the Ryūkyū kingdom (see OKINAWA). It was a major battleground during World War II. Automobile dealers and repair firms, construction companies, and foreign trading concerns are located here. The graves of several Ryūkyū kings may be seen at the site of Urasoe Castle. Pop: 70,286.

Urawa

Capital of Saitama Prefecture, central Honshū. In the Edo period (1600–1868) it developed as a POST-STATION TOWN on the highway

Nakasendō. Now a satellite city of Tōkyō, it has large housing complexes and foodstuff, machinery, and metal industries. The primroses (sakurasō) at Tajimagahara draw visitors in May. Pop: 358,180.

urayaku

1. Tax levied on coastal villages during the Edo period (1600–1868); also called kakoyaku. Originating as a kind of labor-service obligation (BUYAKU), during the Edo period it entailed rescuing vessels in distress, transporting government goods by sea, and expediting the passage of daimyō traveling to the shogunal capital of Edo (now Tōkyō) to fulfill their obligations of alternate-year attendance (SANKIN KŌTAI). Urayaku was subsequently commuted to a currency or rice payment and was classified as a type of miscellaneous tax (KO-MONONARI).

2. A government official placed in port towns and fishing villages during the Edo period. Also called hamayaku or hamagakari. He kept a register of ships, handled the disposition of wrecked vessels, and supervised launchings. As administrator of the fishing grounds, he was empowered to suspend the fishing rights of those who failed to observe regulations.

Urayasu

City in northwestern Chiba Prefecture, central Honshū. In the Edo period (1600–1868) it was a thriving fishing village under the direct jurisdiction of the Tokugawa shogunate. Seaweed (nori) and short-neck clams were once cultivated here, but since the completion of a land reclamation project, the city has become industrialized. Pop: 64,673.

urbanization

Process whereby a society increasingly assumes an urban character as urban population increases in absolute number and in proportion to rural population, either through increase in population of existing cities or through growth of new ones. Urbanization also occurs as rural people assume urban ways of thinking and behaving, and as urban institutions and services move into rural areas.

In Japan urbanization began when the first permanent capitals, HEIJŌKYŌ (now Nara) and HEIANKYŌ (now Kyōto), were built in the Nara (710–794) and Heian (794–1185) periods. Kyōto had a population of at least 100,000 in the Heian period. Soon other urban centers were built, primarily for political and military purposes; an example is DAZAIFU in northern Kyūshū. Still other urban centers grew to serve the needs of travelers, prominent among which are Naniwa (now Ōsaka) and Ōtsu (in what is now Shiga Prefecture). In northern Japan, HIRAIZUMI, which was established during the late Heian period, became known as "the Kyōto of northern Japan" because of its elegance and grandeur. The establishment of KAMAKURA as the seat of the Kamakura shogunate (1192–1333) brought about the rapid growth of this erstwhile rural community. By the middle of the 13th century Kamakura had a population of over 10,000.

While these political centers also performed important commercial and religious functions, urban centers with a specifically commercial or religious origin also grew up in many parts of Japan. For example, Hakata (now FUKUOKA) in nothern Kyūshū was an important commercial port city. Uji-Yamada (now the city of Ise), east of Nara, was a major center of Shintō, being the location of the ISE SHRINE, and ZENKŌJI was a major Buddhist temple in what is now Nagano Prefecture which attracted pilgrims from all over central Japan (see MONZEN MACHI; JINAICHŌ).

As the central authority of the military government declined in the 15th and 16th centuries, DAIMYŌ (regional warlords) began to develop their own regimes in their petty fiefdoms. Commercial and industrial activities flourished around the castles where these lords lived. These CASTLE TOWNS (jōka machi) grew up all over Japan, with populations reaching to the thousands and sometimes tens of thousands. The castle towns were of precarious existence as they were subject to destruction in warfare, the losing side often resorting to systematic burning of the city.

With the establishment of the Tokugawa shogunate early in the 17th century, castle towns began to enjoy peace and security, with consequent growth in population. EDO, now called Tōkyō, had a population of over one million by the middle of the 18th century, and was probably the largest city in the world at the time. Ōsaka, which had developed as the major commercial center of Japan,

boasted a population of 350,000 by the early 18th century. Ōsaka served as the distribution center of agricultural and manufactured goods throughout the Edo period (1600–1868), and has carried the tradition into modern times.

Major shifts in the urbanization process took place as Japan began rapid modernization in the latter part of the 19th century. Early in the Meiji period (1868–1912), there were 29 cities with a population over 30,000; thirty years later there were 33. In 1888 only 7.3 percent of the population lived in cities of 50,000 or more. In less than 20 years, 16.4 percent were living in cities of this size. Somewhat different statistics show that in 1920, 6.2 percent of Japanese lived in cities of one million or more; this increased to 17.2 percent in 20 years. In 1975 the number of those living in cities of over 50,000 (who may be regarded as constituting Japan's urban population) was almost 85 million, up 8.7 percent from 1970 and comprising about 75 percent of the total population of the country. In 1980 an estimated 80 percent of the population was living in cities.

This trend toward increasing urbanization can also be seen in the rapid diminution in the number of administrative villages (mura) and in the increasing number of those being absorbed into neighboring townships and municipalities. In 1940 there were 9,614 villages, 1,706 towns (machi) and 178 cities (shi). In 1976 the number of villages was 635, and the numbers of towns and cities had increased to 1,978 and 644, respectively.

The government census office has introduced the concept of "densely inhabited district" (DID), defining it as an area composed of a group of contiguous census tracts, each of which has a population density of about 4,000 inhabitants or more per square kilometer and a total population of over 5,000. In 1975, DID population constituted 57.0 percent of the total Japanese population (compared with 43.7 percent in 1960), and this population lived in 2.2 percent of the total land area of Japan.

The urbanization process in Japan has been particularly rapid in the years since World War II, as can be seen from the DID figures quoted above. Since rural areas are characterized by primary industry, and urban areas by secondary and tertiary industries, increase in the latter, particularly in the tertiary industries, is yet another index of urbanization. In the 25-year period from 1950 to 1975 the proportion of those engaged in primary industry decreased from 48.5 to a mere 13.9 percent, while those in tertiary industries steadily increased from 29.0 to 51.7 percent. These figures are corroborated by the fact that as many as 25 "rural prefectures" lost population in both of the consecutive 5-year periods of 1955–60 and 1960–65.

Cities are not only growing in size; they are also growing younger. Since the immigrant population is generally young, being greatest in the 15–25 year bracket, Japan's urban population is becoming younger, compared with its rural population, which is losing its younger people.

There are indications that in the 1960s the process of urbanization had slowed down and that even small reversals of urbanization were taking place. Migration into the Tōkyō metropolitan area, for instance, peaked in 1962 at 364,000 in net increase for that year. Ever since then, the net increment per year has been on the decline. Similarly, for the Kyōto-Ōsaka-Kōbe area, the peak year of population increase was 1961, and for Nagoya, 1963. Thus urban migration and concomitant rural depopulation, while not entirely ceasing, are not continuing at the same rate as before.

The so-called U-turn and J-turn phenomena are also part of this trend. Many of those who migrated to urban centers are finding city life dissatisfying and are returning to their home towns (a process referred to as the "U-turn" phenomenon) or to the prefectures of their origin (the "J-turn" phenomenon). Also, disenchantment with life in urban centers—the high cost of housing, pollution, and other problems—has driven many residents to satellite cities, from which they commute to the inner city. In 1970–75, central sections of Tōkyō and Ōsaka lost as much as 20 percent of their populations, while surrounding areas gained as much as 30 percent. Consequently, the population densities of central Tōkyō and Ōsaka, which would essentially count only those who sleep there at night, is comparable to the density in the hinterlands of Kyūshū or the Tōhoku region, whereas the suburban areas are marked by the highest densities in the country. This density pattern has been referred to as the "doughnut phenomenon." The size of this "doughnut" is enlarging every year, as is reflected in the increase in the number of commuters living in one city and going to another for work or schooling, or even crossing prefectural boundaries to get to work or school. The number of those who work or go to school within the city in which they live is correspondingly decreasing.

At the same time a minor counter-reversal has been discernible, in which some residents of satellite cities, weary of long commuting, are moving back into the middle of the city. Increasing affluence among the general population has made it possible to afford expensive housing in cities. These high housing costs are offset by the rapidly increasing costs of transportation. Also the success of pollution-control measures has made the urban environment somewhat more attractive.

One of the negative results of rapid in-migration and distant commuting has been a lack of the traditional Japanese neighborliness in the larger cities. Elderly people living alone tend not to be looked after by neighbors and may be neglected in an emergency. Crime may take place without neighbors' either noticing or caring. But these tendencies, while a cause for alarm, are still relatively minor compared with the magnitude of similar problems in the West. A surprising number of immigrants into Japanese cities manage to fit themselves into social relations there through relatives and work-related networks. In many ways Japanese cities remain vastly more livable than some of their Western counterparts.

Urbanization as a concept refers not only to the process of urban population increase, to which demographic sociologists have given much attention, but also to diffusion of urban ways of life into rural areas. Quantitative data are not as readily available for this process, since the measure is not the number of people moving (which is relatively easy to count), but the qualitative, cultural indices.

In the post-World War II era, this aspect of the urbanization process has been particularly accentuated by revolutionary changes in transportation and communication. Improved public transportation systems, new and better roads, and availability of automobiles to virtually every farm household, have readily made possible travel to and from urban centers seldom reached in prewar days. Television sets, which have practically replaced radios as the principal medium for obtaining news and learning about urban culture, are universally present in rural households.

The difference between rural and urban areas in terms of standards of living, attitudes toward life, and the like is thus diminishing, with the consequence that urbanism as a way of life is no longer a monopoly of urbanites, but is to a considerable measure shared by their rural brothers and sisters.

———David Kornhauser, *Urban Japan, Its Foundations and Growth* (1975). Robert J. Smith, "Preindustrial Urbanism in Japan," *Economic Development and Cultural Change* 9 (1960). James W. White and Frank Munger, ed, *Social Change and Community Politics in Urban Japan* (1976). Takeo Yazaki, *Social Change and the City in Japan* (1968).   Harumi BEFU

urban life

Japan became highly urbanized before the contemporary period. Indeed, much of its culture has developed in urban settings. Although the modern Japanese city has many characteristics in common with its counterpart in industrialized Western nations, the Japanese city also retains certain unique features that have their origins in Japan's premodern past.

The Functions and Development of Cities ——— The earliest Japanese cities developed to serve a number of functions, the most important of which were political and administrative, religious, and educational. The first cities were the capitals of ancient Japan: HEIJŌKYŌ (Nara) was completed in 710, and HEIANKYŌ (Kyōto) replaced it as the permanent imperial capital from 794 to 1868. These cities served as the residence of the imperial court, which consciously modeled itself on the Tang (T'ang) dynasty of China (618–907); the cities were built on a formal grid pattern, like the Chinese capital, with the imperial residence in the center.

The early cities were, from their inception, religious and ceremonial centers, representing the close relationship between sacred and secular rule that is found in many early cultures. Large and beautiful shrines and temples were constructed; the priests who inhabited them formed an elite stratum of society in ancient Japan.

The function of cities as educational centers was also evident in ancient Japan. In the ancient capitals, Japanese civilization achieved a considerable continuity through recorded histories that were the product of scribes and specialists who were capable of writing. It is somewhat difficult to separate religious beliefs and practices from secular educational pursuits, since most educational functions were concentrated in temples. Nevertheless, some universitylike institutions were established in Heiankyō in emulation of Tang society; these were never to play as important a role in Japan as the universities that appeared in medieval Europe.

A small number of other cities developed during the ancient period; these were primarily military or administrative centers, stopover points for travelers, PORT TOWNS, and market centers near temples and shrines (MONZEN MACHI). Most other Japanese cities evolved later out of feudal bastions—CASTLE TOWNS with a central moated area. The territory surrounding the castles was laid out for protection as well as for governance. SAMURAI served the dual roles of warriors and administrators in a unique blend not found in other cultures. Religious and edifying arts were cultivated by warriors guided by priests who specialized in architecture, landscaping, poetry, and esthetic ceremonials that derived from earlier imperial court traditions. Artistic activities as well as the martial arts were pursued in some respects as a legitimation of authority.

Development of Commerce and Urban Culture ——— In the castle towns, a fourth basic function of cities—marketing and commerce—developed some unique Japanese features. Reflecting the stratified structure of feudal society, which ranked samurai, farmers, artisans, and merchants in a descending hierarchy of classes (see SHI-NŌ-KŌ-SHŌ), specific districts of the castle towns were set aside for the various classes. Some special artisan and entertainment areas were ghettos allocated to various groups of outcastes, including the *eta* and HININ. The former were hereditary pariah artisans, engaged in such work as slaughtering animals and working with leather (see BURAKUMIN). The *hinin*, or "nonpeople," consisted of those who had dropped from proper social strata, through criminal activity, for example.

A fifth function of cities is their role as centers for transportation and communication. In feudal Japan, the growth of cities was spurred by the adoption of the SANKIN KŌTAI system during the Edo period (1600–1868), under which regional warlords (DAIMYŌ) were required to reside for long periods of time in the shogunal capital at EDO (now Tōkyō). As the daimyō and their entourages traveled from outlying regions into Edo and back, trade began to flourish along the main routes. Trade grew as patterns of transportation and communication became better established, linking the various parts of the country.

Entertainment, a final major function of cities, also developed a characteristic Japanese flavor related to the flow of travelers. Entertainment zones were strung along the roadways of entry and exit to most Japanese cities. In addition to legitimate inns, so-called gay quarters which housed prostitution and gambling served the passing traveler as well as the townspeople. With increasing economic surplus, Japanese society could afford a large number of specialists in the production of art and entertainment. Beginning at that time and continuing to the present, the Japanese city has had more inhabitants per capita engaged in entertainment than any other urbanized culture. As in all cultures, concepts of entertainment ranged from those considered lowly and improper to those considered lofty. Japanese art forms still extant represent all levels.

The CHŌNIN, or townsmen, evolved an urban way of life quite different from that of the samurai. The samurai class was expected to attend more edifying forms of entertainment, such as NŌ, but warrior-administrators were prone to frequent—when it was possible for them to do so without being sanctioned—the more popular forms of entertainment found in the *chōnin*'s gay quarters. These quarters were sequestered in particular sections of the city by a puritanical administration, which reckoned that if it could not stamp out prostitution entirely, it could exercise forms of social control through a supervisory network.

The emotional as well as economic vitality of the merchant culture was especially evident in these areas. Here groups of artist-artisans and performers developed that set social fashion. Women entertainers who lived here were ranked in various grades: GEISHA, who were specialists in various forms of artistic entertainment, would approximate in reputation and popularity the singers and performers that now appear on Japanese television; prostitutes ranked from the high-status *oiran*, who could be compared to the courtesans of ancient Greece, to prostitutes serving the common customer (see PROSTITUTION).

GAMBLING was also very popular. It was carried out by organized networks of gamblers, who would operate in the entertainment areas of the cities and in the stage stops along the major transportation routes, such as the TŌKAIDŌ, that linked Edo with the older cities of ŌSAKA and Kyōto. The tradition of these underworld figures, the YAKUZA, has been romanticized, both in some of the plays developed on the KABUKI stage and now in contemporary films and novels. Forms of sport where one could bet on the outcome were also popular: for example, SUMŌ wrestling has preserved a popularity that extends back to premodern days.

These entertainment centers somehow survived periodic crackdowns and developed a modus vivendi that proved useful to the distrustful government, which would people these quarters with police informers. Within the gay quarters there was a relaxation of the strict regard for formal rank. Commoners and samurai mixed freely, and modes of gaining prestige were totally unrelated to those constraining the individual in everyday life. Successful entertainers, leaders of gambling gangs, and proprietors of exceptionally popular houses of prostitution were an informal elite within the demimonde. There one found also itinerant *hinin*, traveling monks, and RŌNIN (masterless samurai). Parts of Japanese cities, then, were gathering places for displaced individuals, as was the case in medieval Europe.

Emergence of Edo—— The development of the city of Edo (now Tōkyō) illustrates how the various functions of the Japanese city played their part in the pattern of urbanization. Edo became important as an urban center when the seat of government was moved there by the Tokugawa shogunate in 1603. In setting up the administrative capital in Edo, the shogunate emulated some of the features of Heiankyō, the ancient seat of secular and sacred power. More importantly, Edo embodied the basic features of the castle town as a defensive bastion. Located in the northeastern section of the city were the settlements of the artisans and merchants, as well as the squalid hovels of the *eta* and *hinin* and the execution grounds for criminals and the politically disfavored. Over 200,000 were reportedly executed here during the Edo period.

The SHITAMACHI (literally, "downtown") was located partially on land filled in along the edge of Tōkyō Bay. The samurai class was settled on higher ground *(yamanote)* that spread out to the west of the castle. The social segments of the premodern city were separated geographically, but the entertainment quarters of the *chōnin*, the YOSHIWARA gay quarters, attracted many samurai, who sometimes disguised themselves in order to visit the area. The gay quarters were the setting for many of the UKIYO-E, wood-block prints that recorded the personalities and the life of the *ukiyo* (literally, "floating world").

The surplus population of rural regions—the second and third sons and younger daughters—migrated to the cities and contributed to their steady growth throughout the Edo period and into the modern era. Using the route of apprentice training, those who were considered an economic burden at home would be sent out to become *chōnin* in the cities. Some boys came as youthful apprentices attached to a household of artisans or merchants. Dependent on their master, some might remain apprentices without independent adult status until after 35 years of age. See APPRENTICE SYSTEM.

Rural girls often entered the city by working as maids to learn the better manners and domestic arts of the urban world. Less fortunate girls from impoverished families might be sold into transitional careers as prostitutes in the brothels of the gay quarters. Some apprentices would be married off or adopted by considerate mentors, who would arrange for their placement into the appropriate status level. Likewise, young prostitutes were often bought out of bondage to become wives or mistresses.

The population of Japanese urban centers in premodern times was reportedly greater than European or American counterparts. For example, during the middle of the 17th century, the population of Edo was estimated at about 600,000, far larger than the estimated 200,000 of London or the 50,000 of New York during the same period. Because of population density, Japanese cities were subject to frequent outbreaks of fire, which could quickly consume vast areas of flimsy wooden houses. One particular disaster in 1657 is reported to have left over 100,000 people homeless. Because of concern over fire, there was a great deal of organized local vigilance in the premodern city, with fire towers and voluntary firemen, who could be mobilized quickly. After each fire, the small wooden structures that constituted most of the city were rebuilt, each time accommodating an ever larger population.

The internal trade and transportation networks of Japan supported a bustling economy from an early date. Towns were settings in which the economic surplus could in many instances be better enjoyed by the wealthier townspeople than by the samurai, who were often given status but very little in the way of economic benefits. Since wealthier merchants and artisans in the cities were motivated toward acquiring literacy and proficiency in the arts for practical and prestige purposes, there was great demand for education, which was provided in village schools called TERAKOYA; the

elite class educated their children in official government schools. See also EDUCATION: Edo-period education.

Owing to the high level of interest in education, some have estimated that the literacy rate in premodern Japan must have been higher than that of most areas of premodern Europe. Consequently, most townsmen were readers of popular fiction by such writers as SAIKAKU. Dramatic performances—puppet as well as live performances—reached everyone, literate or not. Nō dramas performed at temples and shrines were both informative tracts and lyric poetic expressions, and the BUNRAKU puppet stage and kabuki presented history and dance by dramatizing events in the lives of the *chōnin*.

The Modern City—— Japanese urban centers today are bound together by land transportation; RAILWAYS and motor EXPRESSWAYS are the major modes of travel between cities. The railroad station in most Japanese cities was built in the *shitamachi* (downtown) and spurred the development of new, large commercial structures and underground shopping centers. It is surprising, however, that the introduction of railroad stations did not fundamentally alter the existing pattern of most cities, although entertainment centers came to be located near public transportation centers, an adaptation from the pattern of their development along the post roads of the past.

Today in some cities one still finds an awareness of a split between the lifestyle of people of higher status and the residents of "downtown." The urban growth patterns of modern Japanese cities differ from those found in the West. Under a modern veneer, in the center city one finds a continuity of premodern lifestyles and traditions, with some of these traditions transformed and adapted to fit new molds. While some sections of the original downtown areas have been preempted by modern business enterprises, the occupational groups that date back to the *chōnin* have maintained a tenacious hold on the center of the city, where small enterprises still flourish.

It is interesting to note that cottage industries and home factories that predominate in the downtown area have retained an economic viability despite the predictions of economists over the post–World War II decades that small-scale factory units would not survive. The dual economy, with small enterprises sustained by subcontracting work (see SUBCONTRACTORS) from larger factories, still persists in the *shitamachi* of Tōkyō and other cities. In the ARAKAWA WARD of Tōkyō, for instance, most merchants and artisans ran enterprises with fewer than 10 employees in the early 1970s. Some of these enterprises were interconnected in a network of subcontracting operations, with work performed in the home. Part of the residence contains a few machines on which family members work long hours along with one or two outsiders. To the uninitiated, these areas of Tōkyō look like vast warrens of tiny houses opening onto narrow lanes. They are inhabited by modest entrepreneurs, who think of themselves in capitalist terms, producing on machines they own without concern for wages and hours while seeking to maximize profit. Large-scale industrial development has increased land values, but this has not broken into these neighborhoods or driven these people out to the periphery of Japanese cities, as has happened in other economies. There are evidently economic counterforces that help these individuals maintain their foothold in the center of the city. In contrast, the *yamanote*, or "foothill," sections of large cities have been suburbanized in a way not unlike the patterns found in American cities. There, the modern SARARĪMAN (salaried men)—middle-class, white-collar workers for commercial firms or government offices—are moving into high-rise apartment structures or into the suburbs growing along the rail lines that lead out from the center city. Many of the better-off residents of these areas now own cars, and some have taken to the increasingly difficult task of commuting by car instead of crowding into the already saturated public transportation networks. By some estimates, close to three million people flow in and out of the heart of Tōkyō every day, commuting up to two hours each way.

The inhabitants of these newly suburbanized areas are the modern industrial, commercial, and service personnel of the Japanese economy. In this respect they are the descendants of the samurai bureaucracy; they now range in status through the various new forms and strata of the Japanese middle class. Here and there among the dwellers of the apartment complexes *(danchi)* and the higher-status condominiums *(manshon),* one occasionally finds older-style merchants still wedded in other ways to past traditions. They have, however, compromised with modernization by no longer living at their place of business. Instead they have moved to new residences built several stories above shopping centers, and elevators take them up to their new high-rise apartments.

The merchants and artisans who reside in the more densely populated, smaller areas of the city use the neighboring streets as part of their living area. Children spill out into tiny alleyways, and the housing is so close that there is very little privacy from neighbors. In the *yamanote* district, where private residences still exist, there is the possibility of separating off one's dwelling with a tiny garden and fences; in many instances, the gate *(mon)* has been replaced by a tiny area sheltering a car. Apartments, however, are becoming the dominant form of dwelling in denser parts of the city, to such a point that almost no single residences are being built. A typical apartment has a tiny kitchen, usually Western style. The rooms, too, are commonly Western, that is, with solid floors and chairs replacing the traditional *tatami* mats. If there is one remaining *tatami* room, it is often inhabited by an aged grandmother or older relative.

Leisure and Entertainment —— It is in the more dense urban areas that one still finds scenes reminiscent of the past. One can still witness on a summer evening in downtown Tōkyō men wearing light cotton, knee-length underwear on a leisurely stroll. Many still wear a wool bellyband *(haramaki)* to keep the stomach warm—a surviving belief that a warm stomach will preserve one's health. Individuals may be sitting on benches brought out where the breeze passes, using paper fans to cool themselves, perhaps with a mosquito coil burning beside them. There might be groups playing traditional games such as GO or SHŌGI outdoors, and one might hear the clacking of MAH-JONGG pieces from a game being played indoors. One also finds groups gathering in nearby noodle shops or bars to watch baseball, *sumō*, kick-boxing, or some other sports event on television, while drinking beer and eating snacks.

Living on a tight budget, most families do not have much to spend on outside leisure. Whatever the budget, some money will go to purchase beer and *sake:* the Japanese in general drink a great deal of alcoholic beverages, and their beer consumption rivals that of the major drinking countries of Europe. The *shitamachi* resident may use a neighborhood bar but every so often will find it cheaper to have his *sake* at home. Middle-class suburbanites who have to commute long distances are more apt to stop over in bars at the various transportation centers that ring the heart of the city. One of the attractions of drinking at a bar is the attendance of professional hostesses, who inflate the customer's ego. Sometimes it is more the ego boost than the alcohol that the man seeks in drinking at a bar. "Bar girls" are, in effect, a continuation of the women entertainers of the premodern period. Young girls entering the entertainment business may do so as an alternative to marriage. A good proportion of them do not marry or have been divorced and no longer aspire to the role of wife and mother.

Perhaps the most outstanding feature of present-day social life for modern urban middle-class Japanese is the commercial markets and forms of entertainment located around transportation connections. Shinjuku, the largest transportation hub in Tōkyō, is now the largest nightlife area. These areas are the modern version of the premodern staging areas that were located on the major arteries leaving the city of Edo. Now, instead of traveling the Tōkaidō, the weary, middle-class commuter arrives home late and leaves early. Except on weekends, when the family may make an excursion to a park or take a drive in the country, there is very little contact between a husband and his wife and family. The absentee fathers are replaced by a range of women's voluntary groups that maintain a form of neighborhood solidarity. Most of these groups are related to children's or neighborhood activities within the apartment complexes.

In *shitamachi,* on the other hand, one finds a very thick network of voluntary organizations related to business or to some form of public service. Social and recreational activities often include families related to one another in the complementary work network of subcontracting; individuals doing directly competitive work in the same area never meet in such recreational groups. The various voluntary networks formed by merchants and professionals, including the Kiwanis, Lions, and Rotary clubs, also avoid bringing together direct competitors.

Television is perhaps the dominant form of entertainment in urban life. With the highest per capita ownership of television sets in the world, the Japanese go less frequently to movie houses. The number of films made has fallen off dramatically from the 1960s, when Japan ranked first in the number of films produced annually.

Favorite TV programs include soap operas, quiz shows, situation comedies, popular music programs, and sports, including baseball, *sumō,* soccer, boxing, and Thai-style kick-boxing. Professional wrestling matches between Japanese and foreigners and kick-boxing are among the most popular programs for children and young adults. An extraordinary mélange of programming, from pop music and quiz shows, to samurai dramas and American Westerns flow into the Japanese household.

There is an increasing concern in Japan that the reading skills of children have dropped over the years. Although this is partly blamed on television, it is also attributed to the large number of comic magazines that cater to both children and adults. The content of some of these is explicitly sexual and even scatalogical, and acts of violence that are not commonly found in Western counterparts are depicted. Rental bookstores are heavily utilized in downtown areas, while middle-class Japanese are more apt to buy books and display them in a library collection. Newsstands at every transportation station carry a large variety of newspapers and weekly magazines, along with comic magazines. People riding trains and subways, whether sitting, standing, or leaning against one another, read avidly on their daily commute.

Downtown residents, more than the middle class, are apt to go to horse, bicycle, or motorboat races, where gambling is allowed. Mah-Jongg is a very popular indoor form of gambling, especially among the working class. Small Mah-Jongg parlors are scattered throughout the city, where one pays a nominal fee per hour to play. What strikes a visitor to a Japanese city more forcefully, however, are the more visible PACHINKO (pinball) parlors found in every commercial neighborhood. One sees hundreds of people standing or sitting in front of long rows of glass-fronted, upright pinball machines, incessantly flipping the metal bar that propels the balls. The entire hall resounds with the metallic clinking and clanking of rolling balls and the blare of popular songs from the loudspeaker. See also LEISURE-TIME ACTIVITIES; SOCIETY; LIFE CYCLE; URBANIZATION; SOCIAL PROBLEMS.

Ronald Dore, *City Life in Japan* (1958). Charles Dunn, *Everyday Life in Traditional Japan* (1969). Gilbert Rozman, *Urban Networks in Ch'ing China and Tokugawa Japan* (1973). Ezra Vogel, *Japan's New Middle Class* (1963). Takeo Yazaki, *The Japanese City* (1963). Hiroshi Wagatsuma and George DeVos, *The Heritage of Endurance* (1982). George DeVos

urban planning

Planning of the physical form, land development, and major public facilities of a city. In recent years, decision making concerning social, economic, financial, and administrative matters has also increasingly come to be identified with urban planning.

The planned development of urban settlements in Japan started in the 7th century in the Kinki region (Kyōto–Ōsaka area). Administrative capitals built at the time were patterned after the grid design of the Chinese capital of Chang'an (Ch'ang-an) built during the Tang (T'ang; 618–907) dynasty. One of these cities was the capital city of HEIJŌKYŌ, established in 710 at the site of present-day Nara. It flourished as the first large-scale city in Japan, with an estimated population of 200,000. The city had a checkerboard-type layout measuring about 4.3 by 4.8 kilometers (2.7 by 3.0 mi), with the emperor's palace situated in the north end of the city. A second large-scale city, HEIANKYŌ, was founded at the site of present-day Kyōto; the capital was transferred there in 794. Heiankyō was also planned after continental patterns, measuring 4.5 kilometers (2.8 mi) from east to west and 5.2 kilometers (3.2 mi) from north to south.

As the ancient political system was gradually replaced by the feudal system, new types of urban settlements appeared. Among these were temple towns (MONZEN MACHI), POST-STATION TOWNS *(shukuba machi),* PORT TOWNS *(minato machi),* MARKET TOWNS *(ichiba machi),* and, by far the most prominent of all, CASTLE TOWNS *(jōka machi).* While early castles tended to be situated on hilltops, population growth eventually forced transfer of the castles to open plains. As the residence of the feudal lord (DAIMYŌ), castle towns gained importance not only as political and military centers, but also as centers of distribution and exchange. Early castle towns were not planned but expanded spontaneously as their functions multiplied. In the stratified society of the Edo period (1600–1868), however, towns were laid out with clear divisions of land uses according to function and social status, i.e., *samurai,* merchants, or craftsmen. Roads were often laid out with defensive needs in mind, adopting such devices as T-shaped or crooked intersections to restrict visibility and maneuverability.

At the beginning of the Meiji period (1868–1912), the urban population in Japan was fairly evenly distributed throughout the country, reflecting the Tokugawa policy of dividing the country into small, self-sufficient domains. However, the replacement of the domain system by a centralized prefectural system and the modernization of transportation and industrial production gradually changed the feudal equilibrium into a nationally integrated system of cities based on specialization. New cities arose around military bases, international trade centers, and factories. Rapid expansion of industry in urban areas was accompanied by the penetration of the commodity economy throughout rural society and by a massive influx of rural peasants into the cities. While the percentage of total population in cities of more than 10,000 was only 11 percent in 1879, it increased to 32 percent by 1920. This rapid URBANIZATION prompted the introduction of city planning after the European model.

The first city planning measure to improve conditions in Tōkyō was included in the revision of the Tōkyō Municipal Ordinance (Tōkyō Shiku Kaisei Jōrei) in 1888. The revision, aimed mainly at the development of an infrastructure in the capital, created a city planning board which came under the direct control of the HOME MINISTRY of the national government. The provision was extended in 1918 to apply to five other cities: Kyōto, Ōsaka, Yokohama, Kōbe, and Nagoya.

In 1919 the Urban Planning Law (Toshi Keikaku Hō) was enacted, followed by the Urban Construction Law (Shigaichi Kenchikubutsu Hō). The Urban Planning Law stipulated that all city planning decisions in municipalities where statutory city planning was practiced were to be referred to the city planning board under the Home Ministry. All plans were sent for the approval of the cabinet, even though most of the financial burden for their implementation had to be borne by the municipalities.

Following the enactment of the Urban Planning Law, land readjustment (kukaku seiri) served as the major instrument of statutory city planning for the construction of basic public facilities on the urban fringe. Under the land readjustment scheme, a certain portion of designated areas was assigned for public uses such as streets and parks, and the lot lines of the remaining properties were adjusted in proportion to the value of their original share. The reduced portion was supposed to be compensated for in kind by the increased value of the readjusted property.

By the end of World War II, most major cities had been devastated by air raids. Production and communication facilities were mostly defunct. Meanwhile, the urban population increased with the repatriation of military personnel and civilians from abroad. In the following decade, all available resources were invested in revitalizing basic industry, and few resources were devoted to the reconstruction of cities.

In 1950 the Comprehensive National Land Development Law (Kokudo Sōgō Kaihatsu Hō) was enacted. The law provided for the designation of "specified development areas" (tokutei kaihatsu chiiki), in which the central government would assist development in order to reduce regional inequality. As a result of intensive lobbying by competing regional interests, 19 underdeveloped areas, covering almost the entire country except major metropolitan areas, were designated specified development areas by the end of 1951. This diluted the impact of the special assistance; economic recovery continued to center on the advanced areas.

Sustained economic growth in the following years gradually exposed many structural deficiencies, such as a shortage of social overhead capital, environmental pollution, and the widening of regional inequality. In 1960 the INCOME-DOUBLING PLAN (Shotoku Baizō Keikaku) was formulated, aiming at a doubling of per capita income by the end of the decade. As a physical embodiment of the plan, the COMPREHENSIVE NATIONAL LAND DEVELOPMENT PLAN (Kokudo Sōgō Kaihatsu Keikaku) was adopted in 1962. It was proposed that industry be dispersed throughout the Pacific Coast belt and that investment in social overhead capital be concentrated on the belt to improve public facilities such as ports, highways, and railways.

As for areas outside the belt, it was proposed that growth poles be selected at strategic locations for industrial development as NEW INDUSTRIAL CITIES (shin sangyō toshi) or industrial development areas (kōgyō seibi tokubetsu chiiki). Between 1963 and 1966 cities in 15 zones were given the former designation, and 6 areas were given the latter.

Together with economic recovery, the reconstruction of Tōkyō was an enormous problem, and in 1950 a capital city construction law was enacted to cope with the problem. Soon the necessity to coordinate planning for the metropolitan region beyond Tōkyō's prefectural boundaries became evident, and in 1956 a new law established the cabinet-level Capital Region Development Commission. A master plan, modeled after the Greater London Plan, was adopted in 1958. The first Capital Region Development Plan envisaged creating a green belt zone in areas 15 to 25 kilometers (9.4 to 15.6 mi) from central Tōkyō, constructing satellite cities outside the zone and thus preventing the horizontal expansion of built-up areas. In the period of rapid economic growth in the 1960s, however, Tōkyō outgrew the framework. In 1965 the master plan was revised to redesignate the green belt zone as the suburban development zone.

The advance of urbanization and industrialization proceeded unabated, and, by the mid-1960s, problems associated with rapid growth came to be felt more keenly. In 1969 a new development plan (Shinzensō) was formulated to respond to this new awareness. The plan envisaged developing networks of bullet railway lines and expressways throughout the country in order to lay the foundations for further economic development.

Provisions of the Urban Planning Law of 1919 became totally inadequate to cope with the rapid urbanization of the postwar years. After a series of amendments, the law was finally replaced by the new URBAN PLANNING LAW of 1969. An innovative feature of the 1969 law was the division of a city planning area into urbanization promotion areas (shigaika chiiki) and urbanization control areas (shigaika chōsei chiiki); no building permits would be issued in the latter districts. The primary aim of this provision was to contain urban sprawl. The new law modified the centralized decision-making system of the old law by delegating more authority to local autonomous bodies. Policy making and coordination are handled by the City Bureau of the MINISTRY OF CONSTRUCTION.

Various measures to improve existing quarters in the city were consolidated in the Urban Redevelopment Act (Toshi Saikaihatsu Hō) in 1969. Among other provisions, it stipulates that a redevelopment operation can be organized if two-thirds of property owners and leaseholders agree to the operation; it also stipulates that involved parties will be compensated with floor space in the new building or buildings in proportion to the value of their original share.

The limited availability of natural resources and fossil fuel was keenly felt after the Arab oil embargo in 1973. Consequently, new attention was paid to the quality of life rather than the growth rate of the gross national product. The third national development plan (Sanzensō) was formulated in 1977 against this background. A key concept of the third plan is the fostering of "settlement regions" (teijūken) throughout the country. A settlement region is envisaged as a regional unit of 200,000 to 300,000 residents, where a balance would be achieved among the natural environment, the human settlement, and production facilities. See also ECONOMIC HISTORY; POPULATION REDISTRIBUTION; LOCAL GOVERNMENT.

MERA Kōichi

Urban Planning Law

(Toshi Keikaku Hō). A law promulgating necessary measures regarding the substantive and procedural limitations of city planning to facilitate the sound and orderly development of cities. Enacted in 1968, the law was passed as a substitute for the old Urban Planning Law of 1919, which was not responsive to the era of urbanization. The main provisions of the law are as follows. First, city planning, as specified by this law, means that those plans established pursuant to this law relating to land use, maintenance of city facilities, and urban development projects are all undertaken with the goal of facilitating the stable and orderly growth of the cities. Second, it applies only to city planning areas designated by the prefectural governors. Third, the law divides the urban areas, establishing urbanization promotion areas and urbanization control areas, in order to prevent unstructured urbanization and to promote planned growth. Fourth, in order to undertake development activity within an Urbanization Promotion Area or an Urbanization Control Area it is necessary to receive development approval from the prefectural governor in advance. Fifth, city planning includes city structures (streets, high-speed city railways, parks, plazas, and water pipes above and below ground), as well as urban development projects (land regulation projects, new city residential development projects, and urban redevelopment projects). Sixth, decision-making authority for city planning is delegated to the city, town, and village mayors, the prefectural governors, and the minister of construction. Seventh, the law establishes an approval system for city planning projects and establishes administrative procedures for obtaining approval in such matters as building restrictions, expropriations, land purchases, and the financial responsibilities of applicants.

NARITA Yoriaki

urban subcenters

(fukutoshin). Secondary commercial centers which developed along with the expansion of large cities. These subcenters are usually located around major railway terminals and consist of department stores, specialty stores, markets, amusement and cultural facilities, restaurants, banks, and more recently, high-rise office and apartment buildings. Underground shopping complexes connected with railway stations are also an important feature of many of these areas. Shinjuku, Shibuya, and Ikebukuro are major subcenters of Tōkyō, as are Umeda, Namba, and Tennōji of Ōsaka.

NISHIKAWA Osamu

Ureshino

Town in southwestern Saga Prefecture, Kyūshū. Ureshino has long been known as a hot spring resort and producer of tea. A national hospital is located here. Pop: 20,394.

Urikohime

(The Melon Princess). Folktale, somewhat resembling MOMOTARŌ. An old childless couple find a melon drifting downstream. Upon slicing it, they find a baby girl. She grows into a beautiful maiden and is betrothed to a prince, but a devil (AMANOJAKU), disguised as the princess, attempts to take her place at the wedding. A sparrow discloses the ruse, and the princess is properly married.

SUCHI Tokuhei

urushi → lacquer tree

urushi-e

(lacquer pictures). A technique employing lacquer as a painting medium on a paper or a lacquer surface. The term is used to denote painted designs executed in a compound of lacquer and color pigments, in contrast to water and ink or water and pigments, the usual media for traditional Japanese painting. *Sabi,* a grinding powder, is sometimes added in order to give more body to the compound and thereby to impart a greater clarity to the brushstrokes. Owing to the chemical properties of lacquer, the range of colors has, until recently, been restricted to red, black, brown, green, and yellow. SHIBATA ZESHIN, a noted 19th-century lacquer artist and painter, is the most famous exponent of *urushi-e.* The oldest surviving example of *urushi-e* and undoubtedly the most famous is the mid-7th-century Tamamushi Shrine in the Nara temple HŌRYŪJI, with figural and landscape subjects executed in colored lacquer. The term *urushi-e* is often mistakenly extended to include other types of painting on a lacquer surface, such as *jōhana-nuri,* a technique that makes use of oil, or oil mixed with lacquer, as the binding agent (see MITSUDA-E).

Julia HUTT

Uryū, Lake

(Uryūko). Also known as Lake Shumarinai. Artificial lake in northwestern Hokkaidō. Composed of two lakes, it was created in 1943 by damming the upper reaches of the Uryūgawa, a tributary of the Ishikarigawa, to construct a hydroelectric power station. Catches include carp, crucian carp, and dace. Area: 23.7 sq km (9.1 sq mi); depth: 31 m (102 ft).

Usa

City in northern Ōita Prefecture, Kyūshū. Usa developed as a shrine town around the USA HACHIMAN SHRINE, the head shrine of Hachiman shrines scattered throughout Japan. Farm products include rice, vegetables, and mandarin oranges. Industrial products include machinery, textiles, and processed marine foods. Pop: 51,579.

Usa Hachiman Shrine

(Usa Hachimangū). Also known as Usa Jingū. A Shintō shrine in the city of Usa, Ōita Prefecture, Kyūshū, dedicated to the legendary emperor Ōjin, his mother, the legendary empress Jingū, and his deified wife, Hime Ōkami. The shrine first appears in historical records in the Yōrō era (717–724), when the deity HACHIMAN (the spirit of the deified emperor Ōjin) is said to have assisted the imperial forces in their campaign against the HAYATO rebels in Kyūshū. Hime Ōkami was enshrined soon after the establishment of the shrine. Hachiman is also said to have frustrated DŌKYŌ's plot to usurp the throne when, in 769, the deity delivered an oracle to WAKE NO KIYOMARO proclaiming the inviolability of the imperial line. Because of Hachiman's vow to oversee the construction of the Great Buddha image (completed in 752) in TŌDAIJI, a Buddhist temple in Nara, he has been thought of as a Japanese incarnation of a Buddhist divinity and was popularly called Hachiman Daibosatsu (Great Bodhisattva Hachiman). Thus, the shrine increased its royal prestige, which was regarded as second only to that of the Ise Shrine. In 823 Empress Jingū was enshrined in addition to Emperor Ōjin and Hime Ōkami, and in 859 a branch of the Usa Shrine was built in Kyōto (see IWASHIMIZU HACHIMAN SHRINE). As a guardian deity of warriors and a protector of the land, Hachiman has a large following. The Usa Hachimangū is regarded as the central shrine for some 25,000 Hachiman shrines scattered throughout Japan. Its main building is noted for its Hachiman-style architecture (see SHINTŌ ARCHITECTURE). The annual festival is held on 18 March, and the Shinkōsai festival, with its famous procession of *mikoshi* (portable shrines), is held from 31 July to 2 August. See also HONJI SUIJAKU.

Stanley WEINSTEIN

Ushibuka

City in Kumamoto Prefecture, Kyūshū. On the island of Shimoshima, one of the Amakusa Islands. The city is a fishing port with an abundant catch of sardines, horse mackerel, and sea bream. There is a major seafood processing industry. Beds for cultivating pearls are also maintained. The city's coastal area is part of the Unzen–Amakusa National Park. Pop: 24,003.

ushin

(literally, "having heart, feeling"). An aesthetic term used from about the Kamakura period (1185–1333), particularly to distinguish serious, elegant WAKA or linked verse (see RENGA AND HAIKAI) from the light or comic forms thereof (see KYŌKA), for which the term MUSHIN ("lacking heart or depth of feeling") was used. Formerly referring to discretion or discernment, the word gradually came to mean having refined taste and aesthetic sensitivity. The noted *waka* poet FUJIWARA NO SADAIE applied the term to one of several styles of serious poetry, and while his exact meaning is disputed, it is often interpreted as "having both elegance and depth of feeling." In Buddhism *ushin* refers to worldly attachment as opposed to *mushin,* which means detachment or emptiness (enlightenment).

FUKUDA Hideichi

usu

A mortar used in the threshing, refining, and milling of grain, and in pounding cooked glutinous rice *(mochi).* The *usu* was probably introduced to Japan along with rice cultivation early in the Yayoi period (ca 300 BC– ca AD 300); several bronze bells (DŌTAKU) from this period depict people using *usu.* Types of *usu* vary according to their function and shape.

Pounding mortars (tsukiusu). The *tateusu* is a vertical mortar used with a vertical or hafted pestle called a *kine. Yokousu* are horizontal trough-shaped mortars. The pestle of the *fumiusu* (stepping mortar) or *karausu* (Chinese mortar) is fixed at one end of a long pole and is operated by stepping on the other end of the pole. *Tsukiusu* are usually made of stone or wood; most commonly, wooden pestles are used in conjunction with stone mortars.

Grinding mortars (suriusu). The lower section of the mortar is fixed, while the upper section rotates around a vertical shaft. *Suriusu* are made of stone, wood, or clay, and are used for threshing, refining, or milling.

A variety of folk customs and rituals have developed around the use of the mortar and pestle. As the *usu* is traditionally likened to females and the *kine* to males, they have played a role in many rituals related to occasions such as marriage and childbirth.

INOKUCHI Shōji

Usui Pass

(Usui Tōge). Located on the border of Gumma and Nagano prefectures, central Honshū. Extends from Yokokawa station to the resort town of Karuizawa and has been known since ancient days as one of the most tortuous routes on the highway Nakasendō. The pass is noted for its natural beauty and panoramic views. A railway and a national highway both feature numerous steep slopes and hairpin turns. Altitude: 956 m (3,136 ft).

Usui Yoshimi (1905–)

Critic. Born in Nagano Prefecture. Graduated from Tōkyō University. As editor-in-chief of the magazine *Tembō* after World War II, Usui introduced into the literary world such figures as SHIINA RINZŌ and Gomikawa Jumpei (b 1916). His major critical essays have been collected in the 12-volume series called *Sengo* (1965–66, After the War). He also wrote a novel, *Azumino* (1964–74).   *ASAI Kiyoshi*

Usuki

City in southeastern Ōita Prefecture, Kyūshū. Usuki developed as the castle town of the Christian *daimyō* ŌTOMO SŌRIN, who built a castle in 1563. Traditional products are soy sauce and *miso* (bean paste). Whiskey distilleries and shipyards are also located here. A cluster of some 75 stone Buddhas carved into the mountainside, most dating to the latter part of the Heian period (794–1185), has been designated a national historic monument. The city's coastal area is part of the Nippō Coast Quasi-National Park. Pop: 39,753.

Usuzan

Active double volcano, in the Nasu Volcanic Zone, northeast of Uchiura Bay, western Hokkaidō. Its central cone is on the crater rim of the Lake Tōya caldera. It erupted in 1663, 1822, 1943, and 1977. Meiji Shinzan and SHŌWA SHINZAN, new volcanoes, are on Usuzan's slopes. Height: 727 m (2,385 ft).

uta-awase

(poetry match). A literary competition in which poems composed on assigned themes by members of two opposing teams were paired and judged for superiority. Poetry matches emerged in the late 9th century, reached their greatest popularity in the 12th and early 13th centuries, and declined thereafter, though they continued to be held through the early years of the 20th century.

The origins of poetry matches are not clear, although they seem to have been related to other ritualized contests that involved the matching of various objects, including pictures, chrysanthemums, roots, and shells, often accompanied by poems. By the late 9th century the matching of poems had become a separate form of entertainment, complete with its own elaborate ceremonial. The oldest recorded poetry match was the Zai Mimbukyō no Ie no Uta-awase held at the mansion of Ariwara no Yukihira (818–893) between 884 and 887. Emperors Kōkō (r 884–887) and Uda (r 887–897) encouraged the activity as part of their revival of native verse. The Teijiin no Uta-awase in 913 was one of many poetry matches sponsored by Uda and is the earliest competition for which there exist detailed records of the proceedings and judgments. In the early competitions the poems were composed extemporaneously, and the atmosphere casual and congenial, the emphasis less on the literary aspects of the contest than on the social and ceremonial. By the 11th century poets felt their reputations to be at stake, and the matches were conducted in an atmosphere of desperate seriousness. Themes were assigned ahead of time, and more attention was paid to the critical judgments.

Preparation for a match might begin several months in advance with the selection of contestants for the left and right teams, team captains, assistants, readers, judges, and a scorekeeper. The match consisted of a predetermined number of rounds, sometimes as few as 20, sometimes as many as 600 or even 1,500, all conducted according to elaborate rules of etiquette. At the beginning of a round the assistant would present his team's entry to the team reader, who would chant it, the process then being repeated on the opposing side. Sometimes the contestants would attack and defend the poems before the judge finally designated the winner or declared a draw. The first round always began with the entry from the left team, and since this was customarily composed by the sponsor of the match or

Usuki

Some of the stone Buddhas at Usuki. Most of the images at this site were carved during the late Heian period.

a person of high rank, there was an unwritten rule that it should win or at least be granted a draw. Each succeeding round began with the poem by the side that had lost the round before, and in case of a draw, the previous order was repeated. At the end of the match the winning team performed a victory dance, which was followed by a banquet, music, and the presentation of awards.

The poems were judged by all the participating poets or by an assigned judge who was a master poet. Multiple judges were in use by the early 12th century, and in the Sengohyakuban Uta-awase of 1201, there were 10 judges, each judging 150 rounds. Disgruntled contestants could appeal a judgment, and there was often heated debate, sometimes ending in the revision of a judgment. By the 12th and 13th centuries poetry matches had become the most important formal social occasion for the composition of poetry, and decisions by judges like FUJIWARA NO TOSHINARI (or Shunzei, 1114–1204) were instrumental in shaping poetic standards. Judges usually concentrated on finding some technical flaw or violation of precedent, and their judgments tended to be negative and conservative, thus discouraging innovation. Some of the earliest rules were not literary at all but involved ceremonial and social etiquette. In addition, standards of decorum developed that affected diction, conception, and style. Poems could not be excessively personal or emotional, nor could they contain inauspicious elements or vulgar language.

The oral nature of the poetry match dictated a certain style of poetry. Since the poem was heard and not read, it was important to use familiar words and place names, avoid complicated puns, and structure the poem for easy comprehension. The matches, providing a formal occasion for the composition of poetry, produced vast quantities of poems, many of which were included in the imperially commissioned anthologies, and the judgments became the backbone of poetic criticism. Since the participants also vied in their dress and other furnishings, the activity had a lasting cultural significance as an integrated artistic experience. Poetry matches also gave rise to several variant forms, including the *jika-awase* "personal poetry match," a type of poetic sequence that developed in the 12th century in which a poet selected his own themes, composed one or more rounds on each, and sometimes sent the "match" to a friend for judgment.

■——Hagitani Boku and Taniyama Shigeru, ed, *Uta-awase shū*, vol 74 of *Nihon koten bungaku taikei* (Iwanami Shoten, 1965). Minegishi Yoshiaki, *Uta-awase no kenkyū* (1958).

Susan Downing VIDEEN

uta-e

(literally, "poem-painting"). A decorative art form in which pictorialized letters of the Japanese syllabary (KANA) are employed along with natural imagery to allude to a poem. Such paintings, which often offered only a few cleverly disguised clues to the complete poem, achieved their most sophisticated development during the latter part of the Heian period (794–1185). The meanings of these cryptic picture-puzzles were often forgotten even in the Heian period, however, and today there are only a handful of *uta-e* whose hidden poems can be read with confidence. An outstanding example is the illustrated frontispiece of chapter 5 of the *Kunōji kyō*, a decorated manuscript of the LOTUS SUTRA datable to 1141. In this painting two Heian noblemen caught in a sudden spring shower take shelter under an umbrella in a simple landscape setting. The imagery of rain clouds, flowering trees, and grasses is well suited to the theme of this chapter of the Lotus Sutra, wherein the Buddha is likened to a great cloud from which the merciful rain of the law (DHARMA) falls to nourish all plant life in the universe. Additional pictorial elements in the *Kunōji kyō* painting suggest that it is also an *uta-e* based on a contemporary Buddhist poem by Shunzei (FUJIWARA NO TOSHINARI, 1114–1204):

Harusame wa	The spring rain
Kono mo kano mo	Falling here and there
Kusa mo ki mo	On grass, on trees
Wakazu midori ni	Without distinction
Somuru narikeri	Dyes them green.

The grouping of wheel, crane, and rock in the foreground of the painting form the three syllables of the word *wakazu*, "without distinction": the wheel can be read as the syllable *wa*, "wheel," while the rock takes the form of the *kana* symbol *ka*, and the crane *(tsuru)* signifies the syllable *tsu* or *zu*. Similarly, a cluster of three birds *(mitori)* flying above may be read as the homonym *midori*, "green." Thus each pictorial element in the painting represents part of Shunzei's poem. See also ASHIDE.   *Julia* MEECH-PEKARIK

utagaki

Also known as *kagai*. A festival of ancient origin, practiced before and during the Nara period (710–794), in which men and women gathered on mountaintops or at the seashore to sing, dance, eat, and exchange poems. These gatherings, which took place in the spring and autumn, are thought to have originated as fertility rites, and came to be characterized by a considerable amount of sexual license. Poems said to be from these festivals are included in the MAN'YŌSHŪ and other ancient writings.

Utagawa Kunimasa (1773–1810)

UKIYO-E artist. Born in Aizu in Iwashiro Province (now part of Fukushima Prefecture), Kunimasa went to Edo (now Tōkyō), where he worked as a craftsman in a dye shop. There his talent was recognized by the *ukiyo-e* master UTAGAWA TOYOKUNI, whose favorite pupil he became. Kunimasa specialized in portraits of KABUKI actors *(yakusha-e)*. His best work, however, is in the *ōkubi-e* format, portraits focusing on the head and shoulders. He also designed full-length actor portraits and *bijinga*, pictures of beautiful women.   *Anne Nishimura* MORSE

Utagawa Kunisada (1786–1864)

UKIYO-E woodblock print designer and book illustrator, specializing in figures of women and portraits of KABUKI actors.

Kunisada was born in the Honjo district of Edo (now Tōkyō) on the west side of the Sumida River in 1786. His childhood name was Tsunoda Shōzō. His father, Shōbei, who managed the Itsutsume ferry in Honjo and wrote HAIKU poetry under the pen name of Gokyōtei Kinrai, died when his son was a year old, and soon afterward the family moved to the vicinity of the Tenjin Shrine in Kameido. Shōzō showed an early interest in pictures and in his teens entered the studio of the print designer UTAGAWA TOYOKUNI. From his teacher he received the name Kunisada, and although his name appears in a privately printed book in 1807, he made his public debut with two illustrated books and a portrait of the Ōsaka kabuki actor Nakamura Utaemon III (see NAKAMURA UTAEMON) in 1808. From this date until his death 56 years later, Kunisada worked tirelessly, producing more than 20,000 single-sheet prints and many illustrations in a wide variety of styles, all marked with a quality of professional excellence that sets his work, however repetitive it may seem at times, apart from that of his many pupils and imitators. His early actor prints often exceeded his master's in originality and daring force. His series of half-length portraits of kabuki actors, *Ōatari kyōgen* (Successful Plays), for example, published in the mid-1810s, were the first prints since the 1790s to use mica backgrounds, and the artist may have been deliberately inviting comparison between his work and that of SHARAKU. His early prints of women were more graceful than those of his contemporaries and did much to establish the new pictorial type of female beauty that was popular in the middle of the 19th century.

Kunisada was acquainted with most of the important prose writers of his period, and with many poets and actors as well, illustrating

the fiction of the one group, and designing privately published SURIMONO for the others, including several hundred *surimono* portraits of the actor Ichikawa Danjūrō VII (see ICHIKAWA DANJŪRŌ) to whom he felt particularly close.

Although principally a figure artist, Kunisada designed a series of framed Western-style landscapes with figures of women in the 1820s, and another series of landscapes, mostly without figures, which was published in the early 1830s. Several of these last were based on designs by the MARUYAMA-SHIJŌ SCHOOL painter Kawamura Bumpō. He also introduced landscapes as backgrounds for many sets of figures, notably a series of illustrations of stations along the Tōkaidō with beauties posed before scenes taken from HIROSHIGE's first Tōkaidō series. Kunisada's late work is bold and brilliantly colorful, although its excellence often lies more in the realms of splendor, competence, and craft than in warmth or feeling.

During his career Kunisada used many secondary names. The most common, Gototei, which was derived from the name of his father's ferry, appears in books from 1811, and on prints through the 1830s. Ichiyūsai appears in books and on prints for a few years from the middle of 1811, Gepparō occasionally from 1811, and Kinraisha, derived from his father's poetry name, from 1813. In the late 1810s or early 1820s he seems to have begun using the name Kōchōrō, which appears frequently on his work through the early 1840s. He also used the names Tōjuen and Hokubaiko. In 1844 the artist, as though scorning to recognize the existence of the artist Toyoshige, who had used the name Toyokuni for a decade after the death of their common teacher in 1825, began signing his prints as Ichiyōsai Toyokuni II, occasionally with the secondary name Kokuteisha (Kunisadasha). He is now usually referred to as Toyokuni III. In 1845 he took orders as a lay priest and moved from Kameido to Yanagishima where he lived for the next 20 years. From around 1850 on he placed the signature of Toyokuni within an oval device with an irregularity in the upper right corner like a caterpillar. This was the cursive form of the character for *toshi* or year, which had been given to his teacher Toyokuni as a seal by a pupil who was a wealthy nobleman.

Kunisada had three daughters. The first and third respectively married the artists Kunisada II and Kunihisa (1831–90), while the second died at an early age. In the course of his long career Kunisada trained many pupils, the most illustrious, perhaps, being the theatrical portraitist Toyohara Kunichika (1835–1900). He also influenced the figure style of many contemporaries, including Hiroshige, UTAGAWA KUNIYOSHI, and most artists of the ŌSAKA SCHOOL.

Kunisada II (1823–1880) ——— The son of a farmer and a pupil of Kunisada who signed his early work Baidō Kunimasa III. In 1846 he married his master's eldest daughter and was allowed to use the name Kunisada II. Around 1870, after his master's death, he changed his name to Toyokuni III; he was the fourth and last artist to use this name and is now usually referred to as Toyokuni IV.

Kunisada III (1848–1920) ——— Eldest son of a family of four, he entered Kunisada's studio at the age of 10 in 1858 and continued studying with Kunisada II after the master's death. His early work was signed Baidō Kunimasa IV and Baidō Hōsai. In 1889 he took the name Kōchōrō Kunisada III. He specialized in portraits of kabuki actors.

🔖 ———Oka Isaburō, *Makki ukiyo-e* (1969), tr John Bester as *The Decadents* (1969).   *Roger* KEYES

Utagawa Kuniyoshi (1798–1861)

A leading color-print designer, book illustrator, and UKIYO-E painter. Born in Edo (now Tōkyō) on 1 January 1798, the son of Yanagiya Kichiemon, a silk dyer; his personal name was Igusa Yoshisaburō (later Magosaburō). In 1811 he was apprenticed to Utagawa Toyokuni I (see UTAGAWA TOYOKUNI), having struck up a friendship with Utagawa Kuninao (1793–1854), a pupil of Toyokuni's with whom he shared quarters, and in 1814 he was given the professional name of Kuniyoshi and set up on his own. His first illustrated book, *Gobuji chūshingura*, dates from that year, and his first recorded actor prints appeared in 1815. In this type of work, the specialty of the UTAGAWA SCHOOL, he naturally followed his master's style closely. But in the face of the established reputations of Toyokuni and his senior pupil UTAGAWA KUNISADA, Kuniyoshi at first found it difficult to make his way. In his early years he had studied the works of KATSUKAWA SHUN'EI, Katsukawa Shuntei, KITAO SHIGEMASA, and Kitao Masayoshi (SANTŌ KYŌDEN), and this helped to form the individual style of the heroic compositions for which he later became famous. An anecdote, which appears in various forms, says that a passing sneer from Kunisada was the stimulus that drove Kuniyoshi to vie with Kunisada and eventually to surpass him.

In 1818 Kuniyoshi designed his first heroic triptych, *The Ghost of Tomomori,* for the publisher Azumaya Daisuke, and this led to a few more commissions for prints of actors and heroic scenes in which Shuntei's influence is clearly seen. But it was not until 1827 that Kuniyoshi made his name with the *Suikoden* series, a set of 108 large and forceful figures of Chinese warrior bandits featured in a translation by BAKIN from the Chinese novel *Shuihuzhuan* (*Shui-huchuan;* The Water Margin). These gained immediate and immense popularity, being unlike anything that had appeared before, and established Kuniyoshi in popular favor; they were even imitated by Kunisada.

His rising star gave Kuniyoshi confidence to extend his range. In the early 1830s, as well as theatrical prints and heroic subjects, we find some fine SURIMONO and landscapes bearing his signature. The latter were probably prompted by HIROSHIGE's success in the field but are quite different, showing strong originality and some striking features derived from European prints, of which Kuniyoshi is said to have had a considerable collection. Indeed, he experimented with Western ideas throughout his career. His landscapes mostly represent views of Edo and its environs and are noteworthy for many touches of human interest—the concentration of an angler, the roving eye of a *samurai,* or three coolies crowding beneath a single inadequate umbrella. In these years Kuniyoshi also designed historical and legendary scenes of horizontal format *(yoko-e)* with a strong landscape element, depicting the lives of the Buddhist saint NICHIREN, the early Japanese statesman Prince SHŌTOKU, and the 24 (Chinese) Paragons of Filial Piety.

The years 1835 to 1850 were Kuniyoshi's greatest period, when he shared the highest rank in *ukiyo-e* with Hiroshige and Kunisada, collaborating freely with both on a number of occasions. Heroic triptychs and series of historical biographies poured from his brush, many of them of startling originality. The TAIRA–MINAMOTO WAR of the late 12th century, the revenge of the Soga brothers, the patriotic struggles of the Nitta and the Kusunoki warrior families, and the mid-16th-century battles at Kawanakajima provide the bulk of his subjects, but he also devoted series to the HYAKUNIN ISSHU (One Hundred Poems by One Hundred Poets) and the *Chūshingura,* a drama by Chikamatsu Monzaemon about the FORTY-SEVEN RŌNIN INCIDENT. But although these heroic subjects were undoubtedly his favorites and contain much of his best work, he also produced charming prints of women, and of cats, for which he had a passion, as well as comic subjects, fan prints, and *surimono.*

From about 1852 the beginning of a decline may be detected in the quality of Kuniyoshi's work, though he could still design a stirring triptych on occasion. His health also declined, especially from 1855 when he survived the terrible Ansei Earthquake but was severely shocked. In 1858 he suffered a paralytic stroke and died on 14 April 1861.

Vigor and versatility are the outstanding characteristics of Kuniyoshi's work. He seems to have been a bluff, genial, independent person, who was in trouble more than once with the authorities for suspected political satire. Besides innumerable color prints of every kind, he left a mass of drawings and sketches and a number of hanging-scroll paintings *(kakemono).* These latter mostly depict women, and several are of very high quality. He illustrated some 300 books. He had two daughters, both of whom became artists, and he trained more than 50 pupils, all of whom took *yoshi* as the first element of their names.

📖 ——B. W. Robinson, *Drawings by Utagawa Kuniyoshi* (1953). B. W. Robinson, *Kuniyoshi* (1961). B. W. Robinson, *Kuniyoshi: The Warrior-Prints* (1982). B. W. ROBINSON

Utagawa school

An important school of UKIYO-E artists active from the late 18th to the late 19th century, who specialized in landscapes, portraits of KABUKI actors, and historical subjects. The founder of the school, UTAGAWA TOYOHARU, studied painting with Toriyama Sekien and may have studied *ukiyo-e,* judging from his name, from ISHIKAWA TOYONOBU. His first prints, portraits of actors and pictures of beauties, seem to have been published in the late 1760s, but he achieved popular success as a designer of landscapes and interiors using Western perspective techniques, which began to appear around 1770. His first designs in this genre were made for hand-held optical viewing devices and were so popular that he repeated many of them in later years as full-sized landscape prints.

In the 1780s, apparently after he had stopped designing prints himself, Toyoharu taught UTAGAWA TOYOKUNI and allowed him to take the family name Utagawa. Quite independent of his teacher, Toyokuni invented a style of actor portraiture that was continued through the end of the 19th century by an unbroken string of artists whose names begin with the last two syllables of Toyokuni's name: UTAGAWA KUNIMASA, UTAGAWA KUNISADA, and Kunichika (1835–1900) being the best known. Toyokuni and Kunisada also influenced the formation of a school of over 200 designers of actor portraits in the city of Ōsaka (see ŌSAKA SCHOOL). Another pupil, UTAGAWA KUNIYOSHI, designed some actor prints and landscapes, but devised a style of his own suited to the heroic, legendary, and comic subjects in which he and his pupils specialized. The names of Kuniyoshi's pupils begin with the syllables Yoshi, and include Yoshitora, Yoshiiku (1833–1900), and TAISO YOSHITOSHI.

Toyoharu's second important pupil was UTAGAWA TOYOHIRO. Toyohiro was a more restrained artist than Toyokuni and produced less. He is remembered as the designer of a certain number of prints of women published in the 1790s and early 1800s, a few landscapes, some privately printed SURIMONO, and as the teacher of Andō HIROSHIGE.

Toyoharu, to judge from his work, was a repetitious and somewhat unimaginative artist, who took most of his ideas from previously published work. And yet, the works of his pupils, their pupils, and their pupils again, are numerous. Indeed, more than half the designs, and far more than half the surviving Japanese woodblock prints, are works of the Utagawa school, which he founded.

Roger KEYES

Utagawa Toyoharu (1735–1814)

UKIYO-E artist and founder of the UTAGAWA SCHOOL. Toyoharu first studied painting in Kyōto with the KANŌ SCHOOL artist Tsuruzawa Tangei (1688–1789). In the early 1760s he moved to Edo (now Tōkyō) and took up *ukiyo-e* printmaking. Rare early prints reveal the influence of ISHIKAWA TOYONOBU and possibly of the *ukiyo-e* artist and book illustrator Toriyama Sekien (1712–88). His prints and paintings after 1770 are numerous and include a series of landscape views of Edo that made him famous; these are probably based on a study of Dutch and German engravings and employ Western perspective *(uki-e).* Similarly inspired are several paintings of European landscapes, including views of Venice and the Roman Forum. In 1796 he was put in charge of the painters working on the official restoration of the Tokugawa family mausoleum at NIKKŌ. It is said that Toyoharu adopted the Utagawa name from the district in Edo where he had his residence. His two most famous disciples are UTAGAWA TOYOHIRO and UTAGAWA TOYOKUNI.

Anne Nishimura MORSE

Utagawa Toyohiro (1773–ca 1828)

UKIYO-E artist. Also known as Ichiryūsai; his real name was Okajima Tōjirō. Born in Edo (now Tōkyō), he was the disciple of UTAGAWA TOYOHARU and teacher of Andō HIROSHIGE. At Toyoharu's atelier he encountered UTAGAWA TOYOKUNI, a senior disciple, with whom he sustained a long and intense rivalry marked by occasional collaborative print publications such as *Toyokuni Toyohiro ryōga jūni kō* (ca 1800–1801, Illustrations of the Twelve Months) and *Ittsui otoko hayari no Utagawa* (ca 1810, Two Stars of the Utagawa School), the latter done at the suggestion of the writer SHIKITEI SAMBA. Toyohiro was Toyokuni's opposite in personality as well as artistic style; reserved where the other was flamboyant, and lyrical where the other was dynamic, Toyohiro's reputation was overshadowed by his rival during his lifetime. Toyohiro is known mainly for portraits of beautiful women *(bijinga)* and illustrated novelettes (KUSAZŌSHI), but it was his landscape series, such as *Edo hakkei* (Eight Views of Edo) and *Ōmi hakkei* (Eight Views of Ōmi), that made a deep impression on Hiroshige, his most illustrious disciple.

Anne Nishimura MORSE

Utagawa Toyokuni (1769–1825)

UKIYO-E print designer, book illustrator, and painter; inventor in the 1790s of a powerful and original style of actor portraiture that became the model for succeeding generations of *ukiyo-e* theater artists.

Toyokuni was born in Mishimachō in the Shiba district of Edo (now Tōkyō), the son of Kurahashi Gorobei, a celebrated sculptor of wooden dolls. His childhood name was Kumakichi, later Kumaemon. Early in his life he developed a love of painting and entered the studio of a neighbor, the *ukiyo-e* landscape print designer UTA-GAWA TOYOHARU, from whom he received his artistic family name, Utagawa, and the first two syllables of his working name. His first signed works were the illustrations for a novelette *Tsugamonai hanashi no oyadama* by Shinratei Manzō published in 1786, and his first woodblock prints were pictures of women said to have been published the following year. In the late 1780s and early 1790s Toyokuni continued to design book illustrations and pictures of women. The chronology of these early works is uncertain, but it is clear that Toyokuni turned, as did all his contemporaries, to the prints of TORII KIYONAGA, UTAMARO, and HOSODA EISHI for inspiration in the pursuit of a personal style.

In the spring of 1794, months before SHARAKU's first portraits appeared, an enterprising publisher named Izumiya Ichibei persuaded the young artist to design a few full-length portraits of KABUKI actors posed against light gray backgrounds. These portraits, in their format and intensity, were entirely unlike the conventional actor portraits of the day and became an enormous success. The publisher encouraged Toyokuni to continue, and over the next three years he designed over 50 prints for the Actors on Stage series (*Yakusha butai no sugata-e*). This success propelled Toyokuni from the ranks of the ordinary designers to the position of a star, and his newly found celebrity allowed him opportunities to design pictures of women, children, and comic subjects to rival his contemporaries Eishi and Utamaro. Toyokuni's confidence increased with his fame and his daring originality seemed to increase with his confidence. By the late 1790s Toyokuni had created an intense personal style, which, whether his subject was actors or beauties, was unmistakable.

The kabuki theater inspired Toyokuni with its tension and drama, and, as he strove to invest his prints with these qualities, he became more and more inclined to exaggerate expressions, gestures, and poses, and was increasingly interested in showing pairs of actors in dramatic involvement rather than as single figures. In 1795 he designed the first of his large heads of actors, a genre in which he excelled; in 1796 he designed a series of half-length portraits of pairs of actors; and in 1797 he designed for the publisher Eijudō the first of a series of 100 or more full-length portraits of pairs of actors, which continued through the early 1800s.

After the turn of the century, Toyokuni continued designing books and pictures of women, but his attention was increasingly directed to portraits of actors over which he and his pupils had assumed a virtual monopoly. There was an enormous increase in the number of publishers in Edo in the early years of the 19th century, and an equal increase in demand for prints. Designs by artists of Toyokuni's fame were eagerly sought after, and through a combination of haste, overwork, and lowered production standards, the quality of Toyokuni's work diminished greatly. All work suffered during this period, but Toyokuni was one of the few important designers of the 1790s who continued to work within the restrictions circumstance and necessity set for him. Toyokuni is honored in Japan for his perseverance in providing a broad, inclusive chronicle of one of the great periods of the kabuki theater. He should also be honored for his willingness to continue working under imperfect conditions, for the sake of those qualities that would come through in his work. In this he inspired not only UTAGAWA KUNISADA, his direct pupil, but HIROSHIGE and UTAGAWA KUNIYOSHI, who designed tens of thousands of single-sheet prints and book illustrations.

It is not known when Toyokuni married, but he had two children, a daughter (1810–71) who studied with her father and became a *ukiyo-e* artist, signing her work Kunikame, and a son, Naojirō, who became a wood sculptor. There is a story that Toyokuni disowned his son for profligacy, and it is believed that after his father's death Naojirō studied with Toyokuni II and signed some prints published in the 1830s as Toyotoshi.

Nearly all artists of the 1790s to 1830s whose names begin with the word *kuni* were pupils of Toyokuni. His first and perhaps most brilliant pupil was UTAGAWA KUNIMASA (1773–1810), who designed over 100 prints between 1796 and 1803, most of them portraits of actors. Toyokuni's most prolific and influential pupil was Kunisada (1786–1864).

Others with the Toyokuni Name—— Toyokuni II (1802–ca mid-1830s). Entered the studio of Toyokuni around 1820 and signed his early work Ichiryūsai Toyoshige. In 1824, Toyokuni adopted him and betrothed him to his daughter. In 1825, on Toyokuni's death, he inherited his name in spite of his youth and inexperience and designed pictures of actors and beauties, and an attractive series of eight landscapes titled *Meisho hakkei* (Eight Views of Famous Places). No work by Toyokuni II is known after the mid-1830s, and

he is thought to have died before Kunisada assumed the name in 1844.

Toyokuni III. See UTAGAWA KUNISADA: Kunisada II.

Toyokuni IV. See UTAGAWA KUNISADA: Kunisada III.

Hasegawa Toyokuni. Painter of a picture of a *geisha* in the style of KEISAI EISEN around the early 1830s. Perhaps the designer of a few stencil prints of geisha published in Kyōto around the end of the second decade of the 19th century.   *Roger* KEYES

Utakai Hajime —→ Imperial New Year's Poetry Reading

uta makura

Place-names appearing in classical Japanese poetry in connection with traditional associations and wordplays. The term *uta makura* originally referred to compendiums of poetic lore that served as handbooks for aspiring poets. Works such as the *Nōin uta makura* by the poet-priest NŌIN (b 988) contained commentary on poetic diction and explanations of MAKURA KOTOBA (conventional epithets, or "pillow words") as well as lists of place-names and their poetic associations. By the end of the Heian period (794–1185), the term *uta makura* referred exclusively to catalogs of place-names, and soon only to the toponyms themselves.

Though place-names in most of the poetry of the MAN'YŌSHŪ (compiled ca 759) lack traditional associations, by the late 9th century place-names had come to be associated with certain standard images and feelings. Poets and readers who might never have seen an actual place knew the literary traditions surrounding it from the earliest poem in which its name occurred. The poet, using a technique similar to HONKADORI (allusive variation), could enrich his poem by drawing on these conventional associations while demonstrating his originality by introducing subtle changes.

The use of place-names with standard associations was not limited to classical WAKA poetry. In the Edo period (1600–1868), the *haikai* (see HAIKU) poet Matsuo BASHŌ, for instance, visited famous *uta makura* along his route to the northlands and composed poems on each, combining his verses and the accompanying narrative in a sort of poetic travelogue called *Oku no hosomichi* (1694; tr *The Narrow Road to the Deep North*, 1966).   *Susan Downing* VIDEEN

Utamaro (1753–1806)

One of the most creative and influential artists in the history of the UKIYO-E ("pictures of the floating world") school. Full name, Kitagawa Utamaro. Utamaro is famed for his superbly conceived paintings and woodblock-print depictions of beautiful women from the shops, teahouses, and pleasure quarters of Edo (now Tōkyō). He received his initial artistic training during his adolescence under the supervision of Toriyama Sekien (1712–88), a minor artist who, although he belonged to the academic KANŌ SCHOOL tradition, worked more or less independently, drawing on the styles of various schools for his paintings and illustrated books. Utamaro's apprenticeship under Sekien seems to have been of short duration, and although some stylistic features and an occasional subject in Utamaro's oeuvre do appear to harken back to Sekien, his influence does not seem to have been significant.

Unlike TORII KIYONAGA (1752–1815), his great innovative predecessor in the development of the figure print, Utamaro's artistic career evolved in a gradual, tentative manner, and his distinctive creative talents did not become really apparent until he reached his mid-30s. The earliest group of designs from Utamaro's hand, beginning in the middle of the 1770s, consists of commonplace illustrations for cheap popular books, such as the librettos and guides to the theater produced for patrons of the KABUKI stage, or the vernacular farces or novelettes known as KIBYŌSHI. Toward the end of the decade he also began to design a few undistinguished single-sheet depictions of actors in the manner of KATSUKAWA SHUNSHŌ, under the name Toyoaki. About 1782 he took the name Utamaro. In the prints of this period one can see a greater vitality and latent ability. By the last years of the decade he was producing not only multisheet compositions of figures superbly composed in interior and landscape scenes, but also designing some of the most beautiful illustrated books in the history of *ukiyo-e*, works such as *Ehon mushi erami* (1788, Insect Book); *Kyōgetsubō* (1789, Moon-Mad Monk); *Ginsekai* (1790, Silver World), and in the same or following year *Shiohi no tsuto* (Gifts of Ebb Tide) and *Momo chidori kyōka awase* (Bird Book).

Utamaro's diptych and triptych prints from the last years of the Temmei (1781–89) and first years of the Kansei (1789–1801) eras demonstrate the mature artist's ability to compose figures into a continuous lateral framework that is convincing in its sense of spatial coherence. In their compositional ideas and figure canon, these prints often reflect the influence of Kiyonaga's multisheet works. By the end of the Temmei era, Utamaro seems already to have absorbed all of Kiyonaga's stylistic and compositional precepts for which he felt an affinity, and during the early years of the 1790s he proceeded to combine these with his own fertile ideas to create continuous multisheet depictions of a more personal and spatially sophisticated sort. Utamaro's early Kansei multisheet pieces therefore move well beyond Kiyonaga's much admired though often stylistically formularized works, for Utamaro brings a new inventiveness, a talent for combining figures into original but nonetheless visually plausible interrelated groups, that marks a new step forward in the history of *ukiyo-e*.

After a hiatus during the middle years of the Kansei era, when he concentrated his creative energies mainly on the problems of single-sheet composition, producing many of his most idiosyncratic and admired prints, Utamaro returned to multisheet designs, producing a group of works that demonstrated his continuing determination to experiment and create new and evocative visual ideas. Conceptually, these later works tend to be arranged in a shallower spatial context, and greater emphasis is usually placed on situating the figures in prominent foreground locations, one aspect of the artist's general preoccupation with viewing his subjects in a more immediate and intimate manner.

Utamaro's multisheet designs obviously constitute a significant aspect of his productive activities, but it is also important to recognize that his creative efforts during the Kansei era, when he produced his most distinctive and memorable designs, were devoted mainly to exploring the compositional potentialities of single-sheet prints. Here, within the arbitrary and restricted confines of a single continuous format, usually of modest size, he created his most effective and monumental compositions, the principal body of works on which his reputation is founded. Utamaro experimented with a variety of single-sheet formats, both vertical and horizontal in orientation, but he worked most often in the standard *ōban* (38 cm by 25 cm or 15 in by 10 in) size, vertically disposed, and it is here that one can observe his persevering and systematic investigation into the fundamental problems of pictorial art.

The figural subjects that appear in Utamaro's single-sheet prints of the 1790s range from full-figure to half-torso and close-up depictions. The number of individuals shown in a given composition may vary from group portrayals, where four or even five people appear occasionally, but where three is the usual number, to figures that are represented in pairs or singly. These prints of lovely courtesans and teahouse girls represent nothing less than the final and most complete realization of this quintessential subject in the history of *ukiyo-e*. They are, in fact, among the most accomplished and eloquent expressions of feminine beauty in Japanese art.

A salient aspect of Utamaro's conceptual preoccupation with women is his perennial interest in showing them in their most characteristic surroundings and revealing circumstances. Thus, a significant number of his full-figure prints show the popular beauties and demimondaines of the day situated either in their shops or in the great houses of pleasure in the YOSHIWARA district. Utamaro's artistic evolution is marked by a persistent interest in scrutinizing the daily activities of these women from ever greater proximity. Thus, he gradually narrows his focus, concentrating ever more closely on the intimate and personal aspects of their often glamorous but nonetheless sequestered lives. He is, for this reason, the premier artist of the Edo demimonde, and his prints constitute one of the most reliable and comprehensive sources of information on the activities that took place in the pleasure quarters, from the varying locations within the great Yoshiwara itself down to the less prestigious but flourishing unlicensed districts that dotted the great metropolis.

Another manifestation of Utamaro's interest in depicting his subjects from close range and in a meticulous, observant manner, are his half-torso and *ōkubi-e* (close-up or bust-depiction) prints. In these, the artist's talent for rendering anatomical detail is often augmented by his ability to capture the personality, mood, or circumstance of his subject. Although many of his representations of women are intended as idealized stereotypes, there are also a number of prints that qualify as portraiture. This quality is apparent in certain of his representations of the celebrated beauties of the period, elegant women such as Naniwaya Okita, Takashimaya Ohisa,

Utamaro

"The Face of Fickleness," one of Utamaro's *Ten Studies of Women's Physiognomies.* 37.7 × 24.2 cm. Ca 1792. Tōkyō National Museum.

Tomimoto Toyohina, or Ōgiya Hanaōgi, where subtle individual differences of physiognomy—the slight variation in the line of a nose, the fullness of a cheek, or the delicate contour of an eye—have been precisely and accurately rendered. These subtle, refined depictions form an interesting counterpoint to the powerful portraits of kabuki actors produced in the same period by SHARAKU (active mid-1794–early 1795), where physical and facial characteristics are emphasized to achieve immediate recognition and heighten visual impact. Utamaro's depictions of popular beauties are not, however, intended as realistic portraits. Rather, they reveal a persistent interest in idealization, a preocccupation with accentuating those features of face and physique that enhance feminine appearance, and a conscious disregard of any physical shortcomings that might detract from this objective. These subjects are therefore consistently portrayed in poses that show them to best advantage and emphasize not only their inherent comeliness, but their refined gentility as well.

There is, however, another aspect of Utamaro's creative activities in half-torso and *ōkubi-e* prints that one might call categorical realism. This is the artist's preoccupation with portraying either representative types of women drawn from different classes, or in delineating subtle varieties of feminine emotions or different manifestations of personality. Thus, many of his famous print series are devoted to an exacting depiction of women from the pleasure quarters, ranging from the gorgeous courtesans at the top of the demimonde hierarchy down to menial prostitutes; or, alternately, to portrayals of categories of women from a variety of social circumstances. In works like these Utamaro's intention is to present a convincing true-to-type representation of the category of the woman in question, to create a quintessential depiction. A different, more analytical interest may be seen in Utamaro's widely admired prints devoted to diverse manifestations of feminine personality and sentiment, such as the two related series of about 1792 or 1793, *Fujo ninsō juppin* (Ten Types of Feminine Demeanor) and *Fujin sōgaku juttai* (Ten Studies of Women's Physiognomies). Although it may be excessive to view these works as psychological inquiries, they are based on insights into emotions and behavior traditionally thought of as feminine, such as fickleness or conceit, or sentiments like impatience and petulance expressed in a revealing and eloquent manner. Utamaro's interest in the nuances of feminine emotion reaches an expressive high point in the remarkable series *Kasen koi no bu* (Selected Poems on Love), where he examines varying manifestations of love, providing the viewer with samplings of its benefits and frustrations.

Utamaro produced designs for many publishers over the years, but his closest relationship was with Tsutaya Jūzaburō (1750–97), who produced a significant number of his masterpieces. Tsutaya, the most celebrated Edo publisher of the period, played an influential role in the success of several *ukiyo-e* artists and popular writers, and it was Utamaro's good fortune to come under his guidance in the late 1770s and benefit from his discerning patronage until the time of Tsutaya's demise in 1797. Utamaro is thought to have resided with Tsutaya during these years, and it is obvious that he profited from the artistic ideas and competitive stimulus provided by the other talented *ukiyo-e* artists connected with Tsutaya, men such as Kitao Masanobu and Kiyonaga. Moreover, association with Tsutaya guaranteed an artist that the prints made from his designs would not only be faithful to the original, but also executed in the most meticulous and discerning fashion, for the wood engravers and printers who labored in Tsutaya's shop were unquestionably among the finest artisans of the day. These men established a standard of quality in executing woodblock prints and illustrated books unmatched in the annals of *ukiyo-e,* and the superb expressive line and captivating color schemes in Utamaro's prints would have been impossible without their inspired efforts.

During the decade of the 1790s Utamaro was the most widely emulated artist in *ukiyo-e.* However, a decline in the originality and creative vitality of his works set in at the end of this period, and after 1800 his prints were characterized by a growing dependence on repeated compositional formula, and few notable works appeared. The causes underlying this artistic retrogression remain to be clarified, but they probably have to do not only with a falling off of the artist's own conceptual powers, but also the increased number of works his popularity seems to have compelled him to produce, and the likelihood that certain of his students were involved in the execution of a substantial number of the prints of this period.

In 1804 Utamaro was imprisoned for depicting the great historical figure TOYOTOMI HIDEYOSHI (1537–98) in a manner that the authorities considered disrespectful and seditious. Although his incarceration was relatively brief, his failing creative energies seem to have suffered further as a result, and he died two years later at the age of 54.

Because of his eminent role in *ukiyo-e,* Utamaro attracted many students, such as Utamaro II, Yukimaro, Tsukimaro, Hidemaro, Kikumaro, and Isomaro, all using the Kitagawa family name, as well as a number of stylistic emulators, among them Bunrō, Kinoshita Sekijō, Harumasa Banki, and Kikukawa Eizan. Although some were men of creative ability, their works all failed to match Utamaro's in conceptual originality.

■——Jack Hillier, *Utamaro* (1961). Narazaki Muneshige, ed, *Kitagawa Utamaro,* in *Zaizai hihō,* vol 6 (1973).

Money HICKMAN

uta monogatari → monogatari bungaku

Utashinai

City in central Hokkaidō. Coal reserves (part of the Ishikari Coalfield) discovered in 1873 made Utashinai a mining town until the 1960s. It now has emerging textile and leather industries. Pop: 10,178.

Utility-Model Patent Law

(Jitsuyō Shin'an Hō). Japan is one of a few countries, including Germany, which have a system of what are called "utility-model" patents (Ger: *Gebrauchsmuster;* J: *jitsuyō shin'an*) as a supplement to the regular patent system. Japanese law provides protection for rights to devices invented for industrial purposes that do not qualify for regular patents. The first Japanese Utility-Model Law was enacted in 1905, patterned after a German law of 1891. Under the Utility-Model Patent Law enacted in 1959 (Law No. 123), a person who has made a device *(kōan)* may file an application for utility-model registration with the Patent Office. Device is defined as "the creation of technical ideas utilizing natural laws" (art. 2[1]). When compared with the definition of invention *(hatsumei)* under the PATENT LAW (Tokkyo Hō), it becomes clear that patentable inventions must be highly advanced, whereas technical ideas do not have to meet such a high standard in order to be qualified for utility-model registration.

In order to obtain utility-model registration, the device under application must meet the requirements of novelty, utility, and nonobviousness (art. 3). The Patent Office conducts a full examination

of applications, both as to substantive and procedural requirements. When the Patent Law was amended in 1970 in order to improve the examination procedure by adopting the early-disclosure and the examination-on-demand systems, the Utility-Model Law was also amended in order to incorporate these systems.

The owner of a registered utility-model enjoys an exclusive right to use the device in business for 10 years from the date of publication of the application (art. 15[1]) and is entitled to a civil remedy of injunction, damages, or a measure to restore his business reputation against infringers.

DOI TERUO

Uto

City in Kumamoto Prefecture, Kyūshū. During the Edo period (1600–1868), Uto was a castle town of the Hosokawa family. It produces rice and vegetables; *nori* (a kind of seaweed) is cultivated offshore. There is also an active chemical industry. Japan's oldest extant water system, the Todoroki Aqueduct, is located here. Pop: 32,954.

utokusen

(literally, "virtue money"). A medieval form of taxation; special impost levied on wealthy persons. The homophony of the characters for "virtue" and "profit," both pronounced *toku,* explains the oddity of the term. Commercialization and the growing use of money in the Japanese economy in the Kamakura period (1185–1333) led to the emergence of individuals who accumulated wealth by trading or usury; and efforts to identify such "men of worth" *(utokunin)* for tax purposes are attested in documentary sources from 1304, when the great Buddhist institution TŌDAIJI of Nara ordered its estate *(shōen)* managers to compile special lists of the rich. In the Muromachi period (1333–1568) tributes exacted from *utokunin,* most notably pawnbrokers (DOSŌ) and *sake* brewers (SAKAYA), formed a substantial source of income for the Muromachi shogunate, whose immediate domains were neither extensive nor secure enough to sustain its operations. In 1394 the shogunate ordered the "pawnbrokers and *sake* brewers scattered throughout Kyōto and its vicinity" to contribute the great sum of 6,000 *kammon* (6,000,000 coins) yearly toward the expenses of its administrative office; it also requisitioned contributions from moneylenders to pay for such events as the festive visit of the shōgun ASHIKAGA YOSHIMITSU to the Hie Shrine in 1394 and the visit of ASHIKAGA YOSHINORI to Hyōgo in 1434. As the shogunate's financial condition deteriorated after Yoshinori's assassination in the Kakitsu Rebellion of 1441, and especially during the rule of ASHIKAGA YOSHIMASA, it depended increasingly on this source of revenue and, in effect, became a debtor of the *dosō.*

George ELISON

Utsubo monogatari

(Tale of the Hollow Tree). Also known as *Utsuho monogatari.* A late 10th-century work of prose fiction in 14 chapters (divided into 20 fascicles, *kan*), of unknown authorship and date; believed to be the world's oldest extant novel.

The story deals with the lives of a nobleman, Kiyowara no Toshikage, and three succeeding generations of his family. Setting out for China on an official mission, Toshikage is shipwrecked on the shores of a strange land. He embarks on a series of fantastic adventures and is taught by a famous master to play the zither, or KOTO. Eventually he returns to Japan, bringing with him marvelous seven-stringed zithers (SHICHIGENKIN) and the musical knowledge he has gained during his journey. The focus then shifts to his descendants. His only daughter has a son, the filial Nakatada, who becomes one of the many suitors of the beautiful Atemiya. The tale describes the arduous efforts of Atemiya's suitors to win her hand, their disappointment when she marries the crown prince, and the power struggle that determines the successor to the throne.

The value of music, or the arts in general, seems to be the principal theme of the *Utsubo monogatari.* It appears in the first volume, runs through the greater part of the work as a contrastive motif, and dominates again at the end of the story. The chapters in between deal with love and political power, centering around the fair Atemiya with her numerous suitors (volumes 2–12) and the investiture of a new crown prince (volumes 13–18).

There is much debate over the authorship of the *Utsubo monogatari.* A 13th–century tradition attributes it to the lexicographer and poet Minamoto no Shitagō (also known as MINAMOTO NO SHI-

TAGAU). The 19th-century ascription to Fujiwara no Tametoki (947?–1021?), the father of Murasaki Shikibu, is even more doubtful. Although it is not known when the work was completed, allusions to *Utsubo* in the *Genji monogatari* (TALE OF GENJI), SEI SHŌNAGON's *Makura no sōshi,* and FUJIWARA NO KINTŌ's *Kintōshū* indicate that it was well known early in the 11th century, and therefore probably completed in the late 10th century. The oldest existing manuscript is dated 1651, but there is evidence through secondary tradition from the 13th to the 14th century that it preserves the original text.

The *Utsubo monogatari* does not exhibit a uniform style. The Toshikage story, probably based on preexisting literary material of legendary or fairy-tale character, contains elements reminiscent of oral storytelling and literary Chinese. It may have been conceived as an independent short novel and later revised to fit in with the following chapters, some of which are also believed to have been originally independent. Written in a different style, they portray mortal beings, and whether romantic or parodistic in tone, show a direct approach to reality. Poems are more important in the first half of the work than the second half. Only the second half exhibits the indirectness and refinement characteristic of the *Genji monogatari.* This development of the author's technique illustrates the transitional phase of the whole work, placing it stylistically after the TAKETORI MONOGATARI and the ISE MONOGATARI and before the *Genji monogatari.* See also MONOGATARI BUNGAKU.

——Edwin A. Cranston, "Atemiya: A Translation from the *Utsubo monogatari,*" *Monumenta Nipponica* (Autumn 1969). Gerhild Endress, "Zum Problem der kamakurazeitlichen Personennamen im Utsubo-monogatari," *Nachrichten der Gesellschaft fuer Natur- und Voelkerkunde Ostasiens* (1976). Fumiko M. C. Fujikawa, *A Study of the Dates and Authorship of the "Tale of the Hollow Tree"* (1977). Utsuho Monogatari Kenkyūkai, ed, *Utsuho monogatari ronshū* (1973). Gerhild ENDRESS

Utsukushigahara

Lava plateau, east of the city of Matsumoto, central Nagano Prefecture, central Honshū. The plateau provides a spectacular view of the surrounding area, including the Northern Alps (HIDA MOUNTAINS). Alpine flora bloom in summer, there is excellent hiking, and good ski grounds are available in winter. Part of Yatsugatake–Chūshin Kōgen Quasi-National Park. Average elevation: 2,000 m (6,560 ft); area: approximately 5 sq km (1.9 sq mi).

Utsunomiya

Capital of Tochigi Prefecture, central Honshū. The city developed as the base of the Utsunomiya family, military governors (shugo) of the area in the Kamakura (1185–1333) and Muromachi (1333–1568) periods. During the Edo period (1600–1868), it was a castle town of the Toda family. Principal manufactures are aircraft, tractors, and tele-

visions. Served by major railways and expressways, it has an active wholesale business. Attractions include the Futarasan Shrine and the Ōya Stone Buddhas, carved into a mountainside. Pop: 377,748.

Uwai Kakuken nikki

The diary of Uwai Kakuken (or Uwai Satokane; 1545–89), an important vassal of the powerful SHIMAZU FAMILY of Kyūshū; extant are fragments from the years 1574–76 and an almost uninterrupted set of entries dating from late 1582 to late 1586. Kakuken's adult life was spent in the service of the *daimyō* Shimazu Yoshihisa (1533–1611), under whose rule (1566–87) the power of the Shimazu expanded from Satsuma and Ōsumi provinces (now Kagoshima Prefecture) to cover practically all of Kyūshū. Since Kakuken was one of Yoshihisa's senior councillors (*rōjū*) and most trusted captains (from 1580 he was castellan of Miyazaki, a key fortress in Hyūga, charged with important administrative responsibilities in that newly conquered province), his diary contains many details of the Shimazu campaigns of conquest, providing much information on regional power alignments and occasional glimpses into national politics. Unfortunately, the text stops just before the great national unifier TOYOTOMI HIDEYOSHI invaded Kyūshū, defeated the Shimazu in June 1587 (Tenshō 15.5), and decisively altered the island's political configuration. War and affairs of state are not the diary's sole interest, however, for Kakuken pursued not only the military arts but also gentler pastimes, notably poetry. His casual reflections on what it takes to be an accomplished *samurai,* drafted in 1581, form a brief supplement to the diary. George ELISON

Uwajima

City in southwestern Ehime Prefecture, Shikoku; on the Bungo Channel. A castle town of the Date family during the Edo period (1600–1868), it is now a distribution center for marine products and lumber. The shipbuilding and food processing industries are active. Mandarin oranges are grown. Local attractions are the bullfighting and summer festival at the Warei Shrine and Uwajima Castle. Pop: 71,592.

Uwa Sea

(Uwa Kai). Inlet of the Pacific Ocean off the southwestern coast of Ehime Prefecture, Shikoku. Bounded by the Satamisaki Peninsula on the north, the Bungo Channel on the west, and the Pacific Ocean on the south. Has a heavily indented coastline. These waters are a good fishing ground for sardines and yellowtail. Pearl culture and yellowtail cultivation are also carried out here. Depth: 60–100 m (197–328 ft).

uyoku → right wing

V

Valignano, Alessandro (1539–1606)

Italian Jesuit who visited Japan three times to inspect the early Jesuit mission (see JESUITS). Born in Chieti in 1539, he studied law at Padua University and entered the Society of Jesus in 1566. Appointed visitor of the Jesuit missions in Asia (with the exception of the Philippines) in 1573, Valignano made three visitations of the Jesuit mission in Japan: 1579–82, 1590–92, and 1598–1603. During these visits he met several of the CHRISTIAN DAIMYŌ and was received in audience by both ODA NOBUNAGA and TOYOTOMI HIDE-YOSHI. An outstanding administrator, he reorganized the Jesuit mission and founded a novitiate at Usuki and two boys' schools at Funai and Azuchi. He promoted Japanese-language studies among the missionaries and urged adaptation to Japanese customs, compiling a remarkably perceptive manual of etiquette titled *Avertimentos y avisos acerca dos costumes e catangues de Jappão*. A large number of his unpublished letters, in which he spelled out in detail his plans for the Japanese mission, are preserved in the Jesuit archives in Rome. Valignano died in Macao on 20 January 1606.

Michael COOPER

Vaughn, Miles W. (1891–1949)

American reporter and correspondent for United Press International. Appointed correspondent for the Far East in 1924. His coverage of the LIUTIAOGOU (LIU-T'IAO-KOU) INCIDENT in 1931 received wide public attention. He was highly regarded by both Japanese and Americans as a veteran correspondent well informed on Japanese matters. He died in a boating accident on 30 January 1949. The Vaughn Prize, which was to become the most prestigious prize given to Japanese reporters in the field of international news, was established in 1950 by his Japanese friends. It is now known as the Ueda-Vaughn Prize in memory of Ueda Sekizō of DENTSŪ, INC, who died in the same accident with Vaughn.

HARUHARA Akihiko

vegetables, green

Among the many leafy vegetables used by the Japanese, cabbage, Chinese cabbage, and spinach are especially popular. Cabbage (*kyabetsu*) was introduced from the West in the Meiji period (1868–1912) and has been cultivated widely since then. It is produced in warm climates in the winter and in cool climates in the summer; it is also grown in truck gardens during spring and autumn so that there is a steady supply throughout the year. It is eaten in the same manner as in Europe and America, and is popular as a salad ingredient. Chinese cabbage (*hakusai*) was introduced from China in the Meiji period and its popularity spread rapidly starting in the Taishō period (1912–26). It is produced throughout the year, most being harvested from October through February. Its leaves contain few fibers and take on a sweet taste in winter. Used mainly for pickling, especially with salt, it is also cooked in various dishes. Spinach (*hōrensō*) has been cultivated since its introduction from China in the 17th century. It is often eaten boiled and flavored with soy sauce. Other leafy vegetables include varieties belonging to the genus *Brassica*, which are used mainly for pickling, although they are also cooked, as well as varieties of mustard with largish leaves, which are cultivated mainly in warm climates. These have a hot flavor and are used for pickling.

SUGIYAMA Tadayoshi

vegetables, Western

Vegetables introduced from Europe and the United States in the early part of the Meiji period (1868–1912) are known as Western vegetables (*seiyō yasai*) in distinction to those traditionally cultivated in Japan. Of these cabbage, onions, potatoes, and tomatoes have been assimilated so thoroughly into the Japanese diet that they are no longer distinguished as such. Among those still referred to as "Western vegetables," lettuce, cauliflower, celery, asparagus, and parsley have become especially popular.

SUGIYAMA Tadayoshi

vendetta → katakiuchi

venereal disease

(*seibyō*). First recorded in Japan in the early 16th century, venereal disease has been a problem at various times since, but vigorous government measures have resulted in a very low rate of venereal disease in Japan today. The earliest recorded instance of venereal disease in Japan is a 1512 report of syphilis, and venereal disease is thought to have entered Japan at about that time. In the Edo period (1600–1868) the prostitute quarters were a major source of infection, with venereal disease spreading throughout Japan. The first preventive measures taken seem to be the medical examinations of prostitutes conducted by J. L. C. POMPE VAN MEERDERVOORT in Nagasaki in 1860. After the Meiji Restoration in 1868, the new government established examination and treatment centers throughout the country (from 1871). In 1927 a venereal disease prevention law was enacted. Estimates give a venereal disease rate of 7–8 percent for the years before World War II, dropping to 3–3.5 percent during the war.

However, following the close of World War II, rates of venereal disease climbed once again and in 1945 approximately 60 percent of the prostitutes in Japan were thought to have contracted venereal disease. In 1948 the Venereal Disease Prevention Law (Seibyō Yobō Hō), designed to protect the general populace, was enacted, making tests for syphilis at the time of marriage and during pregnancy obligatory. A Stop Venereal Disease Week was also instituted, during which time blood tests for syphilis were given without cost and the afflicted immediately treated with penicillin. By 1950 a variety of antibiotics, including penicillin, were widely available at low cost for use in halting the spread of venereal disease.

In accordance with the Venereal Disease Prevention Law, a treatment program designed to reduce the rate of infection was introduced, and by 1952, aside from gonorrhea, the incidence of venereal disease had begun to decline. Then in 1958 the Prostitution Prevention Law (Baishun Bōshi Hō) abolishing government licensed prostitution was put into effect; the incidence of venereal disease continued to decline and government efforts for its prevention were discontinued.

In 1964 Japanese sailors serving on ships transporting war materials to the war zone in Vietnam became syphilis carriers, and for the next five years government and citizen organizations joined forces in the fight against venereal disease. Mass media campaigns concerning the consequences of syphilis were carried out, and by 1969 it had all but died out. In 1974, other than a small number of gonorrhea cases, there was very little communicable venereal disease in Japan, and syphilis was discovered in less than 0.01 percent of the pregnant women tested. Ministry of Health and Welfare figures show 9,819 recorded cases of venereal disease for 1980 (syphilis, 2,081; gonorrhea, 7,661; other, 77), and Japan now has one of the lowest rates of venereal disease in the world.

ONODA Yōichi

Verbeck, Guido Herman Fridolin (1830–1898)

Dutch-born American missionary. As one of the most important FOREIGN EMPLOYEES OF THE MEIJI PERIOD, he contributed to important government decisions in the years immediately following the Meiji Restoration of 1868. Verbeck was sent to Nagasaki in 1859 by the Dutch Reformed Church. In addition to his proselytizing activities he taught English, social sciences, and Western technology; his students included ITŌ HIROBUMI, ŌKUBO TOSHIMICHI, ŌKUMA SHI-

GENOBU, SOEJIMA TANEOMI, and others who were later prominent in the Meiji government. In 1869, recommended by Ōkuma, Verbeck went to Tōkyō, where he became assistant head of the Daigaku Nankō (a predecessor of Tōkyō University) and a trusted adviser to the new government. His recommendations contributed greatly to the establishment of the PREFECTURAL SYSTEM (1871), the sending of the IWAKURA MISSION to the West (1871), the EDUCATION ORDER OF 1872, and the CONSCRIPTION ORDINANCE OF 1873. After David MURRAY became adviser to the Ministry of Education in 1873, Verbeck worked as a legal consultant and official translator of law codes. In 1877 he left the government and devoted the rest of his life to missionary work.

📖 ——William Elliot Griffis, *Verbeck of Japan: Citizen of No Country* (1900). *SATŌ Hideo*

vermilion seal ship trade

(shuinsen bōeki). Licensed foreign trade, initiated in the 1590s by TOYOTOMI HIDEYOSHI and developed under the early Tokugawa shōguns (i.e., during the first three decades of the 17th century), in which ships carried licenses (*jō*) issued over the shōgun's vermilion seal *(shuin).* Since Chinese law kept Japanese out of China after 1547 and Chinese from going to Japan, Japanese merchants and seafarers sought trade in the Philippines and Southeast Asia. Hideyoshi and TOKUGAWA IEYASU tried to bring this trade under their control, as part of their drive for national unification, to help limit the activities of Japanese pirate-traders (WAKŌ), and to ensure the safety of Japanese shipping on the high seas, by issuing special licenses for foreign trade. Hideyoshi seems to have issued his first *shuinjō* for foreign trade as early as 1593, but it was Ieyasu who systematically developed the licensed trade after his rise to power in 1600. Typically, Ieyasu's *shuinjō*, issued from 1604 (according to some authorities, from 1602), authorized the holder to carry out one trading voyage, usually to a specified foreign port in Southeast Asia. In order to give the *shuinjō* international force, and to assure the safety of licensed Japanese shipping on the high seas, in 1601 Ieyasu began corresponding with rulers in Annam, the Spanish Philippines, and elsewhere in Southeast Asia, asking them to trade only with Japanese ships bearing *shuinjō* and to bar all others. They would thus be able to distinguish legitimate Japanese traders from *wakō.* Ieyasu also threatened sanctions against anyone who interfered with a vermilion seal ship (*shuinsen*, ship with a *shuinjō*). He sought thereby to guarantee the safety of licensed shipping abroad, which would also enhance his authority at home. In 1628, for example, the shogunate detained a Portuguese ship at Nagasaki in retaliation for a Spanish attack on a *shuinsen* in Siam (Thailand).

Shuinjō were issued to individuals and were not transferable; they were valid only for a specified period of time, and for only one voyage, to the destination named in the license. The *shuinjō* was subject to examination by authorities in foreign ports and guaranteed the inviolability of the ship. Even in war zones, *shuinsen* were neutral and not subject to attack, so long as they did not carry war matériel. These guarantees of neutrality even protected ships of belligerent countries, so long as they carried *shuinjō.*

Of over 350 licenses issued by the Tokugawa shōguns before they discontinued the system in 1635, most went to Japanese merchants favored by the shogunate, but some (37) were issued to *daimyō*, especially before 1611, to other *samurai* (10), and even to Chinese (43) and European (38) merchants. The 6 most common of the 17 recorded destinations are shown in the table.

Over 200 (57 percent) of the *shuinsen* voyages were to ports in Siam or the Indo-Chinese peninsula, where Japanese merchants had established resident trading communities and could trade with overseas Chinese merchants (see NIHOMMACHI).

The principal Japanese exports in the *shuinsen* trade were copper, silver, iron, Japanese craft items, and sulfur. The main imports were raw silk thread and silk cloth—by far the most important—as well as spices and medicines.

As the Tokugawa shogunate moved in the 1620s to control overseas Japanese activities more closely, perhaps reflecting increased fear of Christianity or greater hostility to foreign contact on the part of Ieyasu's successor, TOKUGAWA HIDETADA, the number of *shuinsen* decreased. From 1604 to 1618 an average of nearly 15 *shuinsen* had been licensed each year, but from 1619 to 1635 the average was fewer than 8.

After 1631, as the shogunate placed further restrictions on foreign trade, a patent from the *rōjū* (senior councillors) was required in addition to a *shuinjō*, and in 1635 all foreign voyaging by Japanese

---

Vermilion seal ship trade

Main Vermilion Seal Ship Destinations

	Number of voyages
Cochin China[1]	73
Siam (Thailand)	55
Luzon (northern Philippines)	54
Annam[2]	47
Cambodia	44
Taiwan	36

[1] The region now comprising southern Vietnam and southern Cambodia.
[2] Now central Vietnam.

SOURCE: Iwao Seiichi, *Shuinsen bōeki shi no kenkyū* (1958).

---

was prohibited except for specially licensed voyages to the Ryūkyūs and Korea. With that the vermilion seal ship trade came to an end, and Japan had to rely for much of its foreign trade on European or Chinese traders coming to the ports of Kyūshū (see NATIONAL SECLUSION). *Ronald P. TOBY*

Verny, François Léonce (1837–1908)

French engineer hired by the Tokugawa shogunate in 1865 at the urging of the French minister Léon ROCHES to supervise the construction of Japan's first lighthouse and a major government shipyard. Before the fall of the shogunate Verny had opened a pioneer foundry in Yokohama, expanded a small shipyard in Nagasaki, and picked the site for and begun construction on the new yard at Yokosuka. Following its victory in 1868 the Meiji government continued to employ Verny who, by 1870, had built four lighthouses at Kannonzaki, Nojimazaki, Jōgashima, and Shinagawa. After six years, the Yokosuka installation was officially opened by Emperor Meiji in January 1872.

In 1876 Verny returned to France, where he continued to assist the Japanese in hiring French engineers and procuring machinery. Despite the replacement of French engineers in signal work by British (see Richard Henry BRUNTON), the Japanese continued to use French lenses until nearly the end of the century. Most significant was the contribution of Verny and his 45 French coworkers in training the Japanese at Yokosuka to use Western architectural and industrial techniques such as stone construction, wood-frame brick building, Western roof trusses, steam machinery, iron casting, metal fitting, cement, and glass as well as the metric system. Verny's Shinagawa light, an Important Cultural Property, is now at MEIJI MURA in Aichi Prefecture. See also YOKOSUKA SHIPYARDS; NAGASAKI SHIPYARDS. *Dallas FINN*

Versailles, Treaty of

Treaty signed on 28 June 1919 at the conclusion of the Paris Peace Conference following World War I. The Japanese delegation, led by SAIONJI KIMMOCHI, sought to gain international recognition of its claims to former German privileges and property in the Shandong (Shantung) Peninsula of China and the Pacific Islands north of the equator. President Woodrow Wilson of the United States opposed Japan's claims, although he admitted that they were supported by valid treaties made in 1917 with Britain, France, and Italy. Japan acquired the Mariana, Caroline, and Marshall islands with little opposition but won Wilson's assent to its Shandong claims only when it threatened not to sign the treaty and promised to return Shandong eventually to full Chinese sovereignty. Wilson yielded because the League of Nations Covenant was a part of the Treaty of Versailles, and he believed that Japanese participation in the league was essential (see SHANDONG [SHANTUNG] QUESTION).

Japan also sought to insert an affirmation of the principle of racial equality into the League of Nations Covenant. Although it recognized the right of other countries to limit Japanese immigration, Japan had for many years protested discrimination against people of Japanese origin residing legally in Western countries. Japan claimed that the fundamental cause of the injustice perpetrated on these

Japanese was "racism"; the United States insisted that the cause was "economic competition." Japan considered racism a worldwide phenomenon and felt that the multiracial League of Nations must make a formal statement condemning it. Japan's attempt to insert a racial equality statement into the covenant failed on 13 February, largely because of British, American, and Australian opposition. A later attempt to insert a milder statement, omitting the word "race," into the preamble of the covenant was thwarted on 11 April by the same powers.

📖——Russel H. Fifield, *Woodrow Wilson and the Far East: The Diplomacy of the Shantung Question* (1952). Ikei Masaru, "Pari heiwa kaigi to sabetsu teppai mondai," *Nihon gaikō shi kenkyū* (October 1962). Ian Nish, *Japanese Foreign Policy, 1869–1942* (1977).

Frederick F. CZUPRYNA

vertical society

(tateshakai). Popularized by anthropologist Nakane Chie in her best-seller *Tateshakai no ningen kankei* (1967, Human Relations in a Vertical Society), the term is commonly used to distinguish Japan from presumably more egalitarian societies. Nakane argued persuasively that the essential building blocks of Japanese society are didactic relationships based on a presumption of hierarchical difference. Age, power, sex, rank, role, and experience are the outstanding qualities differentiating superiors and subordinates in most societies, but in Japan such differences do not inhibit the development of close personal ties. Hierarchical ties of this sort often prove to be quite central to informal small groups and thus to many kinds of larger Japanese organizations, both modern and traditional. Often, too, relationships between organizations will be explicitly hierarchical and phrased in terms of personal relationships of the sort Nakane underlines as most basic.

Typical of such personal ties are those between employer or supervisor and subordinate, teacher and student, elder and junior, parent and child, husband and wife. While some are clearly limited in their influence to particular institutions such as the family, others appear to have some relevance at all levels and in all arenas of Japanese life. Some, particularly parent-child and teacher-disciple, have been made central metaphors for various less clearly defined relationships. Both embody elemental values and emotions that are transferred and reinforced by the analogy implied. Subsidiaries are known as "child" companies, and political bosses can be honored by their subordinates with the title "teacher." The influence of Confucian social ethics and the traditional family system (IE) contained in the ideals implicit in these metaphors extends throughout many forms of hierarchical, personal relationships in modern society.

Applied indiscriminately, however, the implication that Japanese society is inherently and inevitably hierarchical can be misleading. Japanese often find hierarchy burdensome. They are quite selective about the creation of close relationships, knowing that hierarchy without the requisite empathy and mutuality can be autocratic and empty. In many groups hierarchical differences of age and rank in the formal system do not lead to positive, personal relationships at all. Hierarchy is not inherently personal; but when it is personal, it is much more powerful. In addition, the prominence of hierarchical ties should not be taken to mean that egalitarian ties are absent from Japanese society.

Nakane sees class consciousness and conflict as relatively undeveloped in Japan because of hierarchical ties that cut across class lines. Individuals have only a few such ties, however, and class differences can be significant in many less personal kinds of interaction. Yet, since hierarchical personal relations are often central to work, religious, and other community affiliations, they tend to dominate the character of key Japanese social relationships. See also SEMPAI-KŌHAI; OYABUN-KOBUN; SHUSHIGAKU; FAMILY; CONFUCIANISM.

📖——Nakane Chie, *Japanese Society* (1970).

Thomas P. ROHLEN

vice-ministers

(jikan). Government positions established in each ministry and agency that has a cabinet minister as its head official. The administrative vice-minister *(jimu jikan)* is the most important; his duties include assisting the minister, managing the affairs of the ministry or agency, and supervising each department, bureau, and affiliated organ. These officials are national public servants and are appointed and dismissed by their respective ministers. Such an official is nor-

mally referred to simply as vice-minister *(jikan)*. This office is the highest position in the government bureaucracy and thus carries great power. In contrast, parliamentary vice-minister *(seimu jikan)* refers to the vice-ministerial office within such ministries or agencies, the duties of which are basically political in nature. Parliamentary vice-ministers are appointed and dismissed by the cabinet and are usually chosen from among the members of the national Diet.

KOTANI KŌZŌ

Victor Co of Japan, Ltd

(Nippon Bikutā). Manufacturer of electronic audio and video products. Established under the name Victor Talking Machine Co, Ltd, as a wholly owned subsidiary of Victor Talking Machine Co, USA (RCA) in 1927, it assumed its present name in 1945. It is a member of the Matsushita group and a leader in the electronics industry. Its products include video cassette recorder/players (VHS), stereo components, color television sets, tape decks, videotapes, and phonograph records. The company's technical and engineering capacity for research and development is widely respected and has been applied to the opening of such new fields of technology as video discs. Exports have shown rapid growth and the company has nine subsidiaries in Europe, North America, and Southeast Asia. Its overseas brand is JVC. Sales for the fiscal year ending March 1982 totaled ¥494.3 billion (US $2.05 billion). The export ratio was about 71 percent and capitalization stood at ¥10.4 billion (US $43.2 million) in the same year. The head office is in Tōkyō.

Vietnam and Japan

The first Japanese to be mentioned in historical records as having been in Vietnam was ABE NO NAKAMARO. Abe, who had adopted a Chinese name (Chao Heng or Ch'ao Heng) and had become a Chinese government official, served in Vietnam (then ruled by Tang [T'ang] China) as a governor-general *(duhu* or *tu-hu;* J: *togo)* in the 760s. It was not until the 16th and early 17th centuries, however, that trade between Japan and Vietnam developed and Japanese traders formed NIHOMMACHI (Japanese quarters) in Faifo (Hoi An) and Tourane (Da Nang); these relations were cut in the 17th century with the adoption of the NATIONAL SECLUSION policy by the Tokugawa shogunate. See also NAMBAN TRADE.

Vietnam once again became significant to the Japanese with Japan's reemergence in international affairs during the Meiji period (1868–1912). When the French took over Vietnam during the Sino-French War (1884–85), several Japanese military officers and journalists published articles and books on the war and on Vietnam. Although Vietnamese nationalists looked to Japan as a possible source of support for their anticolonial struggle, Japanese leaders were concerned with maintaining good relations with the French colonists, and in 1907 the Japanese and French governments signed a treaty in which each promised to respect the other's sphere of influence in East Asia. This obliged the Japanese government to suppress the Vietnamese nationalist movement in Japan led by PHAN BOI CHAU in 1908. Meanwhile, trade between Japan and Vietnam stayed at a low level, partly because of French Indochina's tariff barrier against Japan, which was not abolished until 1932.

Japan began to expand its interests in Indochina with the establishment of consulates in Haiphong, Saigon, and Hanoi in the 1920s. Japan's military incursion into Indochina started well before the outbreak of the Pacific War, when in June 1940, just after the French surrender in Europe, the governor appointed by the Vichy government agreed to the Japanese demand to cut off Chiang Kai-shek's supply route through Indochina and accepted the presence of a Japanese observing mission. Japan then concluded an agreement with the French that permitted the stationing of Japanese troops in the northern half of Indochina in September 1940 and in the southern half in July 1941 (see INDOCHINA, JAPANESE OCCUPATION OF). Treaties of trade and navigation between Japan and Indochina were concluded in May 1941, and a Japanese embassy was opened in Hanoi in October 1941. Thus the Japanese received French cooperation without the use of force. In March 1945, afraid of arousing French resistance in the face of defeat, the Japanese disarmed the French and carried out a coup, having Emperor Bao Dai (b 1913) declare Vietnam's independence and form a new puppet cabinet but leaving real power in the hands of the Japanese. This new government proved incapable of winning popular support and of tackling the economic crisis that threatened North Vietnam. Under these circumstances the nationalist Viet Minh forces rapidly expanded their influence and finally replaced the Bao Dai government when Japanese "patronage" ended with Japan's surrender in August 1945.

In 1953 Japan established diplomatic relations with the French-backed Saigon government in the south but did not recognize the government in the north. In 1959 Japan signed a war reparations agreement in which it promised to provide South Vietnam with $39 million worth of goods and services, including the construction of a dam and the supply of commodities such as household electrical appliances, paper, and dyes. From the mid-1960s, the Japanese economy benefited from US military activity in Vietnam, with the Japanese government officially supporting American policy, but anti-war movements flourished among Japanese citizens and Vietnamese students in Japan (see PEACE FOR VIETNAM COMMITTEE).

Although official relations were not established between Japan and North Vietnam until 1973, trade between the two countries was conducted after 1956 through the Nichietsu Bōeki Kai (Japan-Vietnam Trade Association). Left wing groups in Japan, especially communists, also maintained close relations with the Hanoi government. The Nihon–Betonamu Yūkō Kyōkai (Japan-Vietnam Friendship Association) was established in 1955 to promote mutual understanding. The Japanese government took a serious interest in the normalization of diplomatic relations with Hanoi when it became clear that the United States and North Vietnam would arrive at a truce. In September 1973 the Tōkyō and Hanoi governments signed an agreement, but embassies were not actually opened until the end of the Vietnam War (the Japanese embassy in September 1975 and the Vietnamese embassy in January 1976). After the fall of Saigon in April 1975, the Japanese government attempted to develop better relations with Hanoi and in October 1975 signed an economic aid agreement to help Vietnam's postwar reconstruction. At that time, Japan entertained hopes for peaceful coexistence between the ASEAN and the Indo-Chinese countries, a hope articulated in the so-called Fukuda Doctrine declared by Prime Minister FUKUDA TAKEO in Manila in August 1977.

In the late 1970s, Vietnamese relations with Cambodia (under the Pol Pot regime) and with China worsened, culminating in Vietnam's invasion of Cambodia in January 1979 and China's invasion of Vietnam in February of the same year. The problem of Indo-Chinese refugees and the insecurity of the Thai-Cambodian border made the ASEAN countries increasingly critical of Hanoi. As a consequence, especially after visits by the Chinese leader Deng Xiaoping (Teng Hsiao-p'ing) to Tōkyō and Washington in January and February 1979, the Japanese ceased their efforts to establish closer relations with Vietnam and suspended economic aid; in addition, Japan joined an international anti-Soviet and anti-Vietnam bloc along with China, the United States, and the ASEAN countries.

📖——Gaimushō Ajiakyoku, ed, *Betonamu* (1967). Gotō Kimpei, *Nihon no naka no Betonamu* (1979). Iwao Seiichi, *Nan'yō nihommachi no kenkyū* (1940). Sugimoto Naojirō, *Abe no Nakamaro den kenkyū* (1940).   SHIRAISHI Masaya

Vining, Elizabeth Gray (1902–   )

American teacher who served as private tutor to Crown Prince Akihito from 1946 to 1950. A native of Philadelphia, Vining was known as an author of children's literature. She was selected to be private tutor to the crown prince and went to Japan in 1946. As she taught English to the then 12-year-old crown prince, she also stressed the necessity of his possessing a broad vision of society and the world and developing an outstanding personal character. She also lectured at Gakushūin University and Tsuda College. In this period shortly after the end of World War II, the Japanese were impressed not only by her learning but also by her strong pacifist convictions as a Quaker. After returning to the United States in 1950, she wrote a book about her experiences, *Windows for the Crown Prince* (1952).

TAKAKUWA Yasuo

violets

(*sumire*). Viola spp. Perennial herbs of the family Violaceae. Of the approximately 400 species of violet which grow wild in temperate zones throughout the world, over 50 are found in Japan. These Japanese species generally fall into two categories, those whose petioles (leaf stems) and peduncles (flower stalks) grow directly from the root, and those whose leaves and flowers grow from a main stem.

The name *sumire* is applied broadly to all the Japanese violets, but is also used to refer to one of the most common species of the former group, *V. mandshurica*. Its leaves are lanceolate with long petioles, and the blossoms are a deep purple. It reaches a height of 7 to 11 centimeters (3–4 in). Similar species grow wild in Japan including the *shirosumire* (*V. patrinii*), which grows in cold areas and has white flowers; the *kosumire* (*V. japonica*), smaller than the *sumire*, with pale purple flowers; the *fumotosumire* (*V. pumilio*), with purple-striped petals; the *nojisumire* (*V. yedoensis*), with pale bluish flowers which bloom before the *sumire*; and the *shihaisumire* (*V. violacea*), with wine-colored blossoms. Members of the latter group include the *tachitsubo sumire* (*V. grypoceras*), with purple-striped petals; the *nioi tachitsubosumire* (*V. obtusa*), with fragrant, wine-colored flowers; and the *tsubosumire* (*V. verecunda*), often seen in fields and home gardens, with white blossoms. All these native varieties grow wild; cultivated varieties are, strictly speaking, Western varieties.   MATSUDA Osamu

Viscaino, Sebastian (1551?–1615)

Spanish envoy to Japan in the early 17th century. In 1608 he was ordered by the viceroy of Mexico to explore the American Pacific Coast. In 1610 he was sent to Japan, ostensibly to thank the Tokugawa shogunate for its generosity to Rodrigo VIVERO DE VELASCO, a former governor of the Philippines who had been shipwrecked in 1609 and returned home earlier in 1610. Viscaino's ship was disabled in a storm, but he managed to reach the port of Uraga in 1611. He met with the retired shōgun TOKUGAWA IEYASU in Sumpu (now the city of Shizuoka) and his son TOKUGAWA HIDETADA in Edo (now Tōkyō) before returning to Mexico in 1613 with the mission led by HASEKURA TSUNENAGA.

Vivero de Velasco, Rodrigo (d 1631)

Colonial officer from New Spain (Mexico) who used his forced 10-months' stay in Japan to report on local conditions and tried to establish relations between Japan and Spain. A member of a noble family, Vivero had been a mining official in Mexico before becoming interim governor of the Philippines in 1608. In Manila he was contacted by William ADAMS, the English pilot and shogunal adviser, with the aim of establishing direct trade between the Tokugawa shogunate and New Spain, a project long favored by TOKUGAWA IEYASU. At the end of September 1609, while returning to Mexico, Vivero was shipwrecked near Iwada in Kazusa Province, on the east coast of what is now Chiba Prefecture.

After negotiations with the Tokugawa authorities, both sides drafted a treaty that proposed extraterritorial privileges for a Spanish shipyard and naval base in the Kantō region in exchange for trans-Pacific trade and Mexican silver-mining technology, then the most advanced in the world. Vivero's draft also called for the mapping of the Japanese coast, freedom for Christian missionary activities, and the expulsion of the Dutch, who had already won trading privileges.

Both sides' internal factionalism as well as their concern for ideological orthodoxy and national prerogatives precluded the success of the project. Yet when Vivero left Japan on 1 August 1610, on a ship built under Adams's supervision and in the company of a group of Japanese merchants, he did so as the highest-ranked, best-informed, and most sympathetic official of the Spanish empire to have trod upon Japanese soil.

📖——Lothar Knauth, *Confrontación transpacífica* (1972).

Lothar G. KNAUTH

vocational education

(*shokugyō kyōiku*). In Japan, vocational education is offered in high schools, technical colleges, miscellaneous vocational schools, public vocational training centers, and private industry.

In high schools, both public and private, vocational courses are offered in such areas as nursing, homemaking, business, industrial arts, agriculture, and fisheries as part of the school curriculum. Although an increasing number of Japanese high school students are concentrating on college preparatory courses and programs, a total of 1,239,000 students were enrolled in vocational courses in 1979.

TECHNICAL COLLEGES offer rigorous five-year programs to train technicians and engineers for Japan's rapidly growing industry. First established in 1962, technical colleges now number 62 and offer specialization in such areas as electrical engineering, mechanical engineering, architecture, and metallurgy. In 1979 a total of 46,000 students were enrolled in technical colleges.

Numerous private vocational schools offer courses in fields that are in great demand such as computer programming, communica-

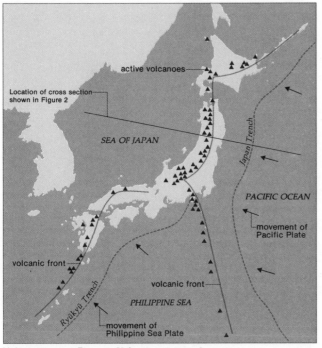

Volcanoes——Figure 1: Volcanic activity in Japan

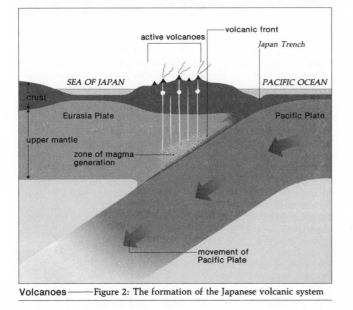

Volcanoes——Figure 2: The formation of the Japanese volcanic system

was enacted in 1958 and the present law in 1969. Prior to the enactment of the original law, the state had provided short-term vocational training for unemployed workers and guidance and assistance for the technical training of young workers. The original law consolidated these programs and set up a new system of vocational training to respond to the changes in the labor market caused by technical innovations. The law stipulated that any vocational training should not overlap with regular, formal education, that basic vocational training plans be established by the minister of labor and the prefectural governors, that standards for the training, as well as necessary facilities, be established by national and local public bodies and the Employment Promotion Corporation (Koyō Sokushin Jigyōdan) and that people who complete prescribed training programs and duly pass the tests be designated as certified skilled workers.

Katō Shunpei

volcanoes

(kazan). There are a large number of active volcanoes in Japan; more than 200 were formed during the Quaternary period alone. These volcanoes form a part of the so-called circum-Pacific volcanic zone, which surrounds the Pacific Ocean, one of the world's greatest areas of geological activity. Volcanic eruptions have had a significant influence on the life of the Japanese people since earliest times, frequently causing heavy loss of life. On the other hand, volcanoes have also produced beautiful natural views and features, provided fertile soil, and supplied a source of useful ore deposits.

Distribution and Makeup of Volcanoes——The volcanoes formed during the Quaternary period are located in a line that generally runs parallel to the Japanese archipelago (see Figure 1). The eastern edge of volcano distribution in Hokkaidō and northern Honshū forms a line running almost parallel to the central mountain range which forms the backbone of the archipelago; to the west of this edge line, called the volcanic front, volcanoes are distributed as far as the Sea of Japan. It is notable that there are no volcanoes at all east of this edge line, and that they are most densely distributed along the line itself and in the area immediately to its west. This distribution pattern is common to the entire circum-Pacific volcanic zone. The volcanic front turns abruptly southward in the northwest corner of the Kantō region of Honshū near Mt. Asama (ASAMA-YAMA), and by way of the YATSUGATAKE volcano group, FUJI-HAKONE-IZU NATIONAL PARK, and the eastern side of the Izu Peninsula, goes through the Izu Islands to the volcanic islands of the Marianas. In the southwestern part of Japan, the distribution is not so dense, but a volcanic front runs across western Honshū, extends southward to central Kyūshū, and is connected to the volcanoes of Taiwan by way of the Ryūkyū Islands. These two volcanic fronts are products of the underground structure of the lithospheric plates that form the skeleton of the Japanese archipelago.

The Pacific Plate, which occupies most of the bed of the Pacific Ocean, is moving westward at a speed of several centimeters per year, and subducts at the edge of the Eurasia Plate, which forms the Eurasian landmass (see Figure 2). The edge of this subduction of the Pacific Plate forms the Japan Trench. In the part of the Pacific Plate that has already subducted deeply underneath the Eurasia Plate, earthquake activity is relatively frequent. Magma seems to form directly above this deep seismic zone, and volcanoes are distributed along a line on the earth's surface directly above this magma-forming zone. Thus, the volcanic front is thought to arise over a zone where the Pacific Plate has subducted to a certain depth, and runs parallel to the axis of the Japan Trench.

The Pacific Plate has steadily advanced toward the eastern edge of the Asian continent for millions of years, and during this period there has been little change in the pattern of volcanic activity in the Japanese archipelago. Activity has been particularly great over the past 20 million years. At the beginning of this period (Miocene age of the Tertiary period), the Japanese archipelago was under water, and there was much submarine volcanic activity. Matter emitted by these submarine volcanoes accumulated in a thick layer, which is now found widely distributed on the Japanese land surface. Many deposits of useful mineral ores were also formed at this time by submarine volcanic activity, including the so-called black ores *(kurokō)* of lead, zinc, or copper, as well as metalliferous veins containing deposits of gold, silver, lead, zinc, or tin.

Structure and Activity of Japanese Volcanoes——Many Japanese volcanoes have a conical shape similar to that of Mt. Fuji (FUJI-SAN), which has become the symbol of Japan. These volcanoes, called stratovolcanoes, were formed by the alternate accumulation of

tions, and fashion designing. These schools have become very popular in recent years because they can train students to meet the demands of industry in a relatively short period of time (one to two years).

Government-sponsored vocational training centers offer programs that range from six months to a year in such areas as dressmaking, automobile maintenance, carpentry, and electronics. Aimed primarily at unskilled young people, these centers offer them a chance to seek better opportunities on the job market. Most on-the-job training is carried out in the private sector, with companies training their own employees in highly technical and supervisory positions (see CORPORATE TRAINING PROGRAMS).

Hosoya Toshio

Vocational Training Law

(Shokugyō Kunren Hō). A law that provides for trade-skill testing and vocational training in order to develop abilities necessary for the employment of skilled workers and, ultimately, to bring about the elevation of the position of laborers, the stabilization of employment, and the development of valuable workers. The original law two kinds of matter emitted from the summit crater: lava flows, and volcanic blocks and bombs. One characteristic of this type of volcano is its profile, which consists of a beautiful exponential curve with wide, gentle skirts. Stratovolcanoes, which grow by the repetition of moderately explosive eruptions, are the most common type in both Japan and the entire circum-Pacific volcanic zone. Mt. Fuji is the largest volcano in Japan with a volume of 300 cubic kilometers (10.6 million cu ft), but it grew to this size relatively rapidly (within the past 80,000 years), and in this sense is not typical of Japanese volcanoes. Together with HAKONEYAMA, a large, polygenetic volcano located nearby, Mt. Fuji emitted a large amount of ash, which was carried by westerly winds and fell over the Kantō Plain centered on Tōkyō, forming a volcanic ash layer ranging from several meters to several tens of meters in thickness. The rich farmland of this region owes much to the fertile topsoil produced by the eruptions of Mt. Fuji and Hakoneyama.

The maximum life of the average stratovolcano is several hundred thousand years. During its life its activity is not constant or even regular, and its dormant periods are much longer than its active periods. Although eruptions of over 80 Japanese volcanoes have been recorded, only a few are active to any degree at present. In general, a major eruption accompanied by the emission of large amounts of lava or pumice and significant growth in the shape of the volcano occurs only once in several hundred or one thousand years or more. For example, SAKURAJIMA, an active volcano in Kyūshū, started its activity about 13,000 years ago, but there have been only five instances of lava flow in the past 500 years. In recent years, however, this volcano has been emitting clouds of ash and experiencing minor explosions almost continually, causing great damage in the surrounding area.

The dimensions of the average stratovolcano are approximately 1,000–2,000 meters (3,300–6,600 ft) in height and ten to several tens of cubic kilometers in volume. In many cases, additional volcanic products from later effusions accumulate on all or part of the surface of an older volcano which has suffered from erosion, thus forming a new stratovolcano or creating a new volcanic group of complicated structure.

Many of the smallest volcanoes were formed by a single eruption and have never resumed activity. One such type, the pyroclastic cone, is usually formed over a period ranging from several days to several years by an effusion of pumice, scoria, and volcanic ash, which are piled into a cone-shaped volcano with a crater at its summit. Another type is the lava dome, in which highly viscous lava is gradually pushed up as a huge mass from the crater onto the ground, thus forming an umbrella hill. In many cases there is no explosive eruption, but a violent steam explosion may occur when highly heated lava comes in contact with the underground water. Most pyroclastic cones and lava domes are no more than 200 meters (656 ft) in height, and they often occur in groups. In the Izu Peninsula, for example, a group of about 70 such monogenetic volcanoes was formed in a period from several tens of thousands of years ago until three thousand years ago in an area of numerous fault movements and earthquakes. This is probably a result of movements in the earth's crust which created passages for large quantities of magma to rise to the surface.

Two other rarer kinds of eruption activity are known for their extremely destructive power. One is a large steam explosion, which is a characteristic feature of the stratovolcano toward the end of its life. One of the few recorded examples of this phenomenon in Japan was the 1888 eruption of Mt. Bandai (BANDAISAN), a medium-sized stratovolcano, in which a series of violent explosions lasting several minutes each were followed by a huge landslide in which a portion of the mountain estimated to measure 1.5 cubic kilometers (52,960 cu ft) in volume fell away at a speed of over 80 kilometers (50 mi) per hour. It blocked rivers, thus creating new lakes, buried villages downstream, and killed 70 people. On the north side of the volcano a huge explosion caldera was formed. Many old stratovolcanoes destroy themselves by this kind of explosive eruption (as do many lava domes in a smaller but similar way). It is known that there were even larger, more violent examples of this kind of activity in prehistoric times. This type of eruption is not caused directly by magma, but by the high pressure of the steam heated by the magma. The other type of destructive eruption is caused by the effusion of an enormous amount of magma onto the ground within a brief period. Since the andesite and dacite magmas characteristically found in the Japanese archipelago have a high viscosity, they cannot effuse rapidly in the form of large-scale lava flows. However, these magmas contain large quantities of gaseous components (mostly water vapor) which, under certain conditions during volcanic eruptions, separate

themselves from the magma in the form of foam, much like the foam of beer which rises when a bottle is opened. When a large-scale vesiculation occurs in an underground magma pool, the foamy magma splits into pieces and is violently ejected as a mixture of pumiceous rocks and volcanic gas. The eruption of Komagatake in Hokkaidō in 1929 is a small-scale example of this phenomenon. As the eruption continued for an entire day and night, a large volume (about 1 cubic kilometer or 35,310 cu ft) of pumice flowed down from the summit like an avalanche, covering the base.

The mixture of heated rocks, pumice, volcanic ash, and gas is called a pyroclastic flow. It is known that there were many pyroclastic flows in the Japanese archipelago in past geological ages. A pyroclastic eruption that occurred in the southern part of Kyūshū about 22,000 years ago emitted a total of 150 cubic kilometers (5.3 million cu ft) of pumice and volcanic ash in an extremely short time, and produced a volcanic ash layer several tens of meters thick over a very wide area. The volume of 150 cubic kilometers is equivalent to quite a large-sized stratovolcano in Japan. As the result of this eruption, a part of the underground magma pool was emptied and consequently the area around the crater collapsed in a ring shape. This collapsed part is called a caldera; there are more than 20 such calderas in Japan with diameters ranging from a few meters to over 20 kilometers (12.4 mi). Many of them contain beautiful lakes, and have been designated as national parks.

The Japanese People and Volcanoes —— The Japanese people in ancient times certainly must have witnessed smoking volcanoes and even occasional eruptions. Very few records or stories describing such volcanic activities have survived, but some people are of the opinion that some volcanic events are personified as figures in the Izumo myths. Unlike volcanoes in Hawaii, whose activity is not so explosive and which often are personified in a friendly manner in Polynesian folktales, the more violent Japanese volcanoes seem to have been classed with atmospheric phenomena such as thunderbolts and regarded as objects of fear or worship. From the period of the YAMATO COURT (ca 4th century–ca mid-7th century) on, volcano deities were given quite a high status in the Shintō pantheon. Many historical records reveal that special envoys were frequently appointed by the imperial court, apparently to soothe and pacify these volcano deities, especially when volcanic activity became intense.

Remains of human life dating back some 8,000 years have been found in stratigraphic examinations of the slopes of the Izu Ōshima volcano, located on the island of the same name 100 kilometers (62 mi) southwest of Tōkyō. This is an amazingly long history, even compared to other records of the prehistoric age in Japan. Furthermore, it is surprising that the people living on this remote island were able to maintain their communities despite the destruction of homes and loss of life in repeated major eruptions and lava flows. This volcano remains active today, and poses a continual threat to the lives and livelihoods of the islanders. At the same time, they consider it a sacred "divine fire" and, as long as its activity remains neither dangerous nor harmful, it serves as a unique sightseeing attraction.

The History and Present Situation of Volcanology —— When Western scholarship began to be introduced to Japan in the 19th century, the volcanoes in the Japanese archipelago immediately became the object of very active study. Geologists and geophysicists invited by the Japanese government from Germany and England climbed many volcanoes, wrote travel-sketch-type reports, and formulated general accounts of Japanese natural history. This was soon followed by more systematic study by Japanese scholars who had returned after studying in the West. Especially after the great Nōbi Earthquake of 1891, the need for research on earthquake and volcanic phenomena was fully realized, and a national committee was set up for this purpose. Systematic geological surveys of the main volcanoes in Japan were made by Kotō Bunjirō (1856–1935) and his students, and detailed seismological studies of volcanic eruptions were made by ŌMORI FUSAKICHI and others. The explosive activity of Mt. Asama was closely examined, and understanding of volcanic micro-earthquake phenomena was increased by the work of Minakami Takeshi and others who classified volcanic micro-earthquakes into two types and postulated that there is a distinct relation between the frequency of volcanic micro-earthquakes and the probability of a volcanic eruption. This enabled scientists to predict possible volcanic eruptions through close observation of volcanic earthquakes.

Following the great eruption of Sakurajima in 1914, when more than one cubic kilometer of lava flowed out of a crater on the side of the mountain, it was found that an equivalent volume of earth subsided in the area around the volcano. The sunken area was found to form a series of concentric circles with their center located in Kagoshima Bay about 10 kilometers (6.2 mi) north of Sakurajima volcano. It was estimated that the central portion of this area sank 2 meters (6.6 ft). This phenomenon was interpreted to have been caused by a huge magma reservoir which lay at a depth of about 10 kilometers directly below the center of the sunken ground. Due to the lava flow from this reservoir to the crater of the volcano, the pressure inside the reservoir dropped, causing the ground to sink. This explanation was later confirmed by many other examples.

In recent years, lithologists and geochemists have actively taken up the study of volcanoes, as the lava and gases emitted by volcanoes are actually brought out from deep inside the earth and thus offer significant geological information. The generation of magma in the Japanese archipelago is directly related to the subduction of the Pacific Plate (or the Philippine Sea Plate in southwestern Japan) underneath the Eurasia Plate. If magma is generated by the partial fusion of the earth's upper mantle at a depth of 100–200 kilometers (62.1–124.3 mi), its main constituent must be basaltic material containing little silicon dioxide (SiO_2), and it must be richer on the Sea of Japan side in alkali metals such as potassium oxide (K_2O) or sodium monoxide (Na_2O) and similar elements than it is on the Pacific side. In actuality, however, magma found in the Japanese archipelago has a relatively small amount of basaltic material. An overwhelming proportion is andesitic magma, richer in silicon dioxide. Therefore, another theory of magma generation was developed based on a partial fusion of the crust of the ocean bottom, which consists mainly of basaltic matter and constitutes the upper surface of the Pacific Plate. In addition, it was asserted that as the water released from the crust of the sea bottom passes into the mantle, it functions as flux, and thus andesitic, not basaltic, magma is generated directly from the upper mantle. Recently, it has become possible to reproduce artificially conditions equivalent to those in the mantle (a temperature of 1,500°C or 2,732°F and a pressure of 30,000 atmospheres), and it is gradually being determined that this form of magma generation is actually possible. At the same time it has been demonstrated that the incidence of alkali metals increases quite regularly from east to west across the Japanese archipelago, indicating that as the Pacific Plate moves west, its basaltic surface becomes a component of magma. It is now established as a certainty that the internal structure of the mantle is intimately related to volcanic activities. However, the actual process of magma being generated, rising to the surface of the earth, and causing volcanic emissions is quite complicated. Although a number of hypotheses have been presented, an overall view of volcanic activity in the Japanese archipelago, including the mechanism of magma generation, has not yet been developed as a coherent theory.

Disasters Due to Eruptions and Their Prevention—— In a country like Japan, where population density is high, it is inevitable that areas of human habitation have extended very close to active volcanoes. Thus, volcanic eruptions invariably become disasters which cause considerable damage. Volcanologists are faced with social demands to find ways of avoiding or reducing these disasters as well as doing basic research on the nature of volcanic activity.

The degree of immediate threat to human life posed by volcanic activity depends upon the size of the eruption. In a vulcanian eruption, which is the most common type of eruption in Japan, it is only rarely that volcanic rocks and bombs are ejected from the crater over a horizontal distance of several kilometers. As noted above, it is not difficult to foretell any explosive eruption by the observation of volcanic micro-earthquakes, and when these warning signals occur, entry into the danger area around the crater is prohibited. These responsibilities are carried out as part of the wide-ranging meteorological observation and forecast system of the METEOROLOGICAL AGENCY, and in recent years excellent results have been obtained. At a greater distance from the volcano than the range of volcanic bombs, damage to buildings, such as the breaking of windows due to shock waves at the time of the eruption, is a major concern. Even more dangerous, however, is the fall of lapilli and pumiceous rocks which have been blown high in the sky and drift with the wind to land in areas far from the crater. When dense and hard, even a single fragment with a diameter of 1 centimeter (0.39 in) can be deadly. In addition, if volcanic ash accumulates in a wide area, it can cause extensive damage to crops. In fact, damage from volcanic ash has brought the greatest economic loss among all the various disasters from eruptions. In the historical documents of the 10th century, there are numerous passages recording appeals made to the central government as a result of damage from fallen volcanic ash—appeals for the reduction of and exemption from taxes. Several tragic famines were caused by the destruction of rice paddies and fields following repeated volcanic eruptions, or by unseasonably cold weather

which resulted from volcanic ash floating in the sky and reducing the sunlight over a wide area.

Though very rare, a landslide that accompanies a steam explosion can bring about a much larger disaster. The explosion of Mt. Bandai mentioned above, is one such example. In the landslide of the Unzen volcano in 1792, the collapsed part of the volcano slid into the sea, causing a tidal wave which killed 1,500 people. It is extremely difficult to forecast such steam explosions accurately. Other eruptions in the Japanese archipelago in prehistoric times are known to have brought about much greater destruction. They were large-scale effusions of pyroclastic flows, accompanied by the formation of calderas. In southern Kyūshū, a pyroclastic flow eruption created a caldera with a diameter of 2 kilometers (1.2 mi) about 4,000 years ago, but the damage caused by this flow has not been clearly determined. It is known that there were at least 10 cases of extremely large pyroclastic flows with caldera formation in the Japanese archipelago over the past several tens of thousands of years. This means that such eruptions have occurred at an average rate of once every several thousand years. In light of the human history of 20,000 years in the Japanese archipelago, the consequences of this fact are extremely grave. However, there has been no eruption of this size in the historical age, the largest being the Kambara pyroclastic flow from Mt. Asama which killed about 1,200 people in 1783.

Preparedness to cope with volcanic disasters has recently been increased each time an eruption is experienced, and increasing amounts of know-how have also been accumulated. Today, microearthquakes and any change in the earth's crust (such as a tilt, rise, or subsidence) are observed regularly and continuously at more than 20 active volcanoes throughout Japan. The state of the crater, the amount of gas and its constituents, and any changes in hot springs or in the underground temperature are always watched, so that even small changes in volcanic activity are noticed immediately. Thus, it is very unlikely that a major and sudden eruption could occur without some forewarning. However, means of preventing disasters stemming from volcanic eruptions remain inadequate, as volcanic eruptions are natural phenomena involving the release of huge amounts of energy. Continuing efforts are nevertheless being made to understand the mechanism of volcanic eruption and to search for effective means of forecasting and avoiding these disasters.

ARAMAKI Shigeo

volleyball

Volleyball was introduced to Japan in 1913 by F. H. Brown, a YMCA worker from the United States. National volleyball championships began in 1921. The Japan Imperial Volleyball Association (later Japan Volleyball Association) was founded in 1927. The earliest volleyball teams in Japan consisted of 16 (later 12) players. In 1925 the team of 9 players was introduced, and this number—unique to Japan—was soon adopted throughout the country. Since World War II volleyball has become increasingly popular; the number of women players in particular has risen dramatically. In the 1950s, volleyball played with 6 players per team (according to international rules) was introduced, and the level of Japanese volleyball thereafter quickly reached the international standard. In the late 1970s the number of volleyball teams above the high-school level that were registered with the Japan Volleyball Association was nearly 11,600. A recent phenomenon is so-called housewives' volleyball; there are approximately 5,800 housewives' teams composed of 9 players each.

WATANABE Tōru

Vories, William Merrel (1880–1964)

Known in Japan as Hitotsuyanagi Mereru. Christian educator and businessman. Born in Kansas, USA, Vories became an active member of the YMCA while at the University of Colorado and went to Japan in 1905 as a Christian missionary. After working as an English teacher at Ōmi Hachiman in Shiga Prefecture, he started a successful architectural office in 1908, and in 1920 he founded Ōmi Sales. This became Ōmi Kyōdaisha in 1934; it marketed and later also produced the ointment Mentholatum. (Ōmi Kyōdaisha remains a unique self-supporting missionary enterprise.) In 1918 he established and led the Ōmi Mission, devoting himself to missionary work and education, establishing churches, schools, and a tuberculosis sanatorium. He married the educator Hitotsuyanagi Makiko (1884–1969) in 1917 and became a Japanese citizen in 1941. In 1958 he was designated the first honorary citizen of the city of Ōmi Hachiman.

MORI Masumi

W

Wa

The Japanese pronunciation of a Chinese character used originally in China and Korea to designate Japan and the Japanese (Ch: Wo). The earliest extant references to Wa (Wo) are brief geographical notations in the *Shanhai jing* (*Shan-hai ching;* Classic of Mountains and Waterways), date uncertain, and the *Han shu* (History of the Former Han Dynasty), a work of the 1st century AD. The first account of any length appears in the Eastern Barbarian section of the WEI ZHI (*Wei chih;* ca 297). According to the *Wei zhi,* the land of Wa (apparently the northern Kyūshū area) was divided into a number of petty kingdoms (e.g., NAKOKU; ITOKOKU) and was eventually unified by HIMIKO, the female ruler of one of them, YAMATAI. After the late 7th century, Chinese records reflect the adoption by the YAMATO COURT of Nihon (or Nippon) as the official name of Japan; however, Wa persisted as an epithet in some Chinese texts. The etymology of Wa is uncertain, but it eventually took on disparaging connotations, the most notable instance being its use in the word WAKŌ, referring to the Japanese pirates who raided the coasts of China and Korea during the 13th to 17th centuries. The Japanese themselves have from early times used this Chinese character interchangeably with another, also pronounced *wa* in Japanese (but *he* or *ho* in Chinese), as a prefix in a number of words designating things as Japanese rather than Chinese or Western (e.g., WAKA; WAKON KANSAI); however, the latter, which has more positive connotations (harmony and peace), was preferred and is now established.

wabi

An aesthetic and moral principle advocating the enjoyment of a quiet, leisurely life free from worldly concerns. Originating in the medieval eremitic tradition, it emphasizes a simple, austere type of beauty and a serene, transcendental frame of mind. It is a central concept in the aesthetics of the TEA CEREMONY and is also manifest in some works of WAKA, *renga,* and *haikai* (see RENGA AND HAIKAI). Its implications partly coincide with those of SABI and FŪRYŪ.

The word *wabi* was derived from the verb *wabu* (to languish) and the adjective *wabishii* (lonely, comfortless), at first denoting the agony of a person who fell into adverse circumstances socially, mentally, or both. But ascetic literati of the Kamakura (1185–1333) and Muromachi (1333–1568) periods developed it into a more positive concept by making poverty and loneliness synonymous with liberation from material and emotional worries, and turning the absence of apparent beauty into a new and higher beauty. These new connotations of *wabi* were cultivated especially by masters of the tea ceremony such as Murata Jukō (d 1502), Takeno Jōō (1502–55), and SEN NO RIKYŪ (1522–91), all of whom sought to elevate their art by associating it with the spirit of Zen and stressed the significance of creating richness in poverty, and beauty in simplicity. Jōō is said to have cited the following poem by FUJIWARA NO SADAIE (1162–1241) to suggest the essence of *wabi:*

> As I look afar
> I see neither cherry blossoms
> Nor tinted leaves:
> Only a modest hut on the coast
> In the dusk of autumn nightfall.

Such poets as SAIGYŌ (1118–90), SHINKEI (1406–75), and BASHŌ (1644–94) pursued similar ideals, although to them *wabi* was more a lifestyle than a poetic principle. It became an integral part of a poetic ideal only when it was absorbed into *sabi,* the main tenet of *haikai.*

━━━━Kazue Kyōichi, *Wabi: Wabicha no keifu* (1973). Mizuo Hiroshi, *Wabi* (1971). Mochizuki Shinjō, *Wabi no geijutsu* (1967). Okazaki Yoshie, *Bi no dentō* (1940). A. L. Sadler, *Cha-no-yu: The Japanese Tea Ceremony* (1963).   Makoto UEDA

Wacoal Corporation

(Wakōru). Company engaged in the manufacture and sale of high-quality women's lingerie and clothing. Wacoal was established in 1949 as Wakō Shōji, a retailer of women's accessories. Sales proceeds from women's underwear rank first in the industry. As styles changed from Japanese to Western clothing after World War II, Wakō Shōji was quick to grasp the trend and began production of underwear with original techniques. It provided foundations to department stores and gained a reputation as a quality manufacturer. In 1970 the company established joint ventures in South Korea, Taiwan, and Thailand; by 1980 it controlled the top share of the high-quality women's underwear market in Thailand. By floating American depositary receipts in 1977, Wacoal succeeded in raising overseas capital funds, and in the following year it concluded a capital tie-up with Olga Co of the United States. In 1979 it initiated production operations in China. Future plans call for the development of outerwear, interior decorating fabrics, and fashion clothing. Sales for the fiscal year ending August 1981 totaled ¥94.2 billion (US $427.2 million), of which foundations made up 40 percent, lingerie 34 percent, nightwear 16 percent, children's wear 5 percent, and others 5 percent. The company was capitalized at ¥6.9 billion (US $31.3 million). The head office is in Kyōto.

Wada

Town in southern Chiba Prefecture, central Honshū. Its mild climate makes it ideal for horticulture, mainly flowers and vegetables. There is also dairy farming and fishing. It is part of the Minami Bōsō Quasi-National Park. Pop: 6,878.

Wada Eisaku (1874–1959)

Western-style painter. Born in Kagoshima Prefecture. Studied painting in Tōkyō with HARADA NAOJIRŌ and Soyama Yukihiko (1859–92) and later with KURODA SEIKI. He graduated from the Tōkyō Bijutsu Gakkō (now the Tōkyō University of Fine Arts and Music) and began teaching there in 1896. From 1898 through 1903 he lived in France, studying with Raphael Collin. After returning to Japan he resumed his post at the Tōkyō Bijutsu Gakkō, where he served as director from 1932 to 1935. In 1943 he received the Order of Culture. His paintings display academic realism and reflect the influence of the Barbizon school of 19th-century France. See also YŌGA.

Wada Pass

(Wada Tōge). In central Nagano Prefecture, central Honshū. Located west of the highland Tateshina Kōgen, the pass is celebrated for its great beauty. It was an important route on the highway Nakasendō in premodern times. Relics of the Stone Age have been excavated near the pass. Altitude: 1,531 m (5,022 ft).

Wada Yoshimori (1147–1213)

Military leader of the early part of the Kamakura period (1185–1333). Grandson of the warrior Miura Yoshiaki (1092–1180), an early supporter of the MINAMOTO FAMILY, Yoshimori took the surname Wada from his village on the Miura Peninsula in what is now Kanagawa Prefecture. He joined MINAMOTO NO YORITOMO in 1180 in his rebellion against the TAIRA FAMILY and was rewarded with the post of administrator (*bettō*) of the Board of Retainers (SAMURAI-DOKORO). Having helped Yoritomo to establish his military government in Kamakura, Yoshimori went on to serve him in several campaigns that finally destroyed the Taira and led to the founding of the Kamakura shogunate. In 1203 he was ordered by the second shōgun, MINAMOTO NO YORIIE, to kill Yoriie's maternal grandfather, HŌJŌ TOKIMASA, who was on the point of seizing control of the shogunate. Yoshimori instead joined Tokimasa, and together they succeeded in replacing Yoriie with his younger brother MINAMOTO NO SANETOMO. Later the Hōjō came to fear Yoshimori because of his popularity among the Minamoto vassals. In 1213 Tokimasa's son HŌJŌ YOSHITOKI provoked him to revolt, and he was soon defeated and killed in a battle at Yuigahama, near Kamakura.

Wadō kaichin → Wadō kaihō

Wadō kaihō

(currency of the Wadō era, 708–715; also called Wadō *kaichin*). Japan's oldest coin, one of 12 types minted during the Nara (710–794) and Heian (794–1185) periods and known as KŌCHŌ JŪNISEN (12 coinages of the imperial court). The court established a minting office (the Chūsenshi) in 708 and began production of this coin in silver and then in copper; from 709 onward, only copper was used. Wadō *kaihō* were round with square holes in the center and with the four Chinese characters *wa, dō, kai,* and *hō* (the last sometimes read *chin*) arranged in clockwise fashion on the obverse. A mold used in minting these coins has been found in the remains of HEIJŌKYŌ, the seat of government in the Nara period, and molds, crucibles, and bellows have been excavated in such widely separated places as Kyōto and Yamaguchi prefectures. This and other archaeological evidence suggests that the coins, though not in wide use, were minted and circulated in all regions that were under control of the imperial court.　　　　　　　　　　　　　　*KITAMURA Bunji*

waegwan

(J: *wakan;* Japanese residence). Walled compounds reserved for Japanese conducting trade and diplomacy in Korea from the early 15th century until shortly after the Meiji Restoration of 1868. From the beginning of the 1400s, official contacts between Japan and the YI DYNASTY (1392–1910) of Korea were increasingly channeled through the SŌ FAMILY of Tsushima to the Korean ports of Pusanp'o (now Pusan) and Naeip'o (now Chep'o). The first *waegwan* was located in the latter port. After 1419 the port of Yŏmp'o, near modern Ulsan, was also opened to Japanese trade.

The Japanese population at these ports grew to several thousand and flagrantly violated trade limitation agreements; the Korean authorities closed the ports after an uprising by Japanese residents in 1510 and reopened only Naeip'o in 1512 (see SAMP'O INCIDENT). In 1521 Pusanp'o was also reopened. A confrontation between Korea and Tsushima closed the Naeip'o *waegwan* in 1544, but another was established at Pusanp'o in 1547. The Japanese INVASIONS OF KOREA IN 1592 AND 1597 put an end to normal trade, but after the conclusion of a peace treaty in 1609, the *waegwan* at Pusanp'o was reopened in 1618. In 1678 it was moved to Tongnae, just north of Pusan.

Just as Japan limited Dutch trade to the island of DEJIMA in Nagasaki harbor during the Edo period (1600–1868), Korea allowed the Japanese only a strictly regulated trade within the 50-acre walled compound of the *waegwan.* The 1609 treaty barred Japanese from visiting the Korean capital, Seoul, although Chinese were welcome there; in contrast, 11 Korean delegations visited Edo (now Tōkyō) between 1606 and 1763.

After the Meiji Restoration of 1868, Japan's new leaders sought expanded relations with Korea, and control of the *waegwan* was transferred from the Sō family to the newly formed Ministry of Foreign Affairs in 1872. But Korea refused to recognize the new government or to loosen the old trade limitations; this caused some Japanese to call for an invasion of Korea (see SEIKANRON) and led to Japanese "gunboat diplomacy" that resulted in the Western-style commercial Treaty of KANGHWA in 1876. The former *waegwan* thereupon became Japan's first consulate in Korea. See also KOREA AND JAPAN: premodern relations.　　　　　*C. Kenneth QUINONES*

Wagatsuma Sakae (1897–1973)

Legal scholar. Born in Yamagata Prefecture. After graduating from Tōkyō University in 1920, he studied civil law under HATOYAMA HIDEO. He was appointed to the faculty of his alma mater in 1922 and remained there until his retirement in 1957. Departing from Hatoyama's conceptual approach to civil law, Wagatsuma placed it in the context of social and economic realities and put special emphasis on judicial precedent. Besides training many students, as a member of numerous government commissions he participated in the drafting of the post–World War II CIVIL CODE, especially its section on family law, and other legislation. He received the Order of Culture (Bunka Kunshō) in 1964. Wagatsuma's works include *Mimpō kōgi* (7 vols, 1932–62, Lectures on the Civil Code), *Mimpō sōsoku* (1965, General Provisions of the Civil Code), widely regarded as the standard work on the code, and *Kindaihō ni okeru saiken no yūetsuteki chii* (1953, The Primacy of the Law of Obligations in Modern Law), a study that showed his interest in the larger question of the relation between capitalism and private law.　　*KATŌ Ichirō*

wage differentials

(*chingin kakusa*). There are two primary sets of factors by which wage differentials may be measured. One set consists of factors related to personal conditions, such as occupational category, sex, age, length of service, and education. The other is based on social conditions, including the industry, location, and size of the enterprise in which the worker is employed.

As a result of the development of management-labor wage negotiations on a nationwide scale during the rapid economic growth of the 1960s, wage differentials in Japan have been reduced considerably, although they are still greater than those found in other industrialized countries. One characteristic of Japanese wage differentials is that wage rates are not clearly defined by job or trade. Instead, the differential between a senior or junior employee is based on the worker's age and length of service (see SENIORITY SYSTEM). This is because there is very little movement between jobs in Japan, so that wages are usually determined by personnel rankings. Workers who are fresh out of school are placed in jobs based on educational background and sex. They will thereafter rise through the ranks to more advanced jobs. Leaving to join another enterprise usually causes the worker to earn lower wages because of the low valuation placed on his past experience. Wage differentials based on education, sex, and age increase among older groups of workers.

According to 1977 Ministry of Labor statistics for all industries, educational background made little difference in wage levels for 20 to 24 year-old male employees, but among 35 to 39 year-old male employees, high school graduates earned 16 percent more and college graduates 45 percent more than middle school graduates. Measurements of wage differentials based on age showed that 50 to 54 year-old workers of both sexes earned 86 percent more than 20 to 24 year-olds, while 35 to 39 year-olds made 71 percent more. In the breakdown of enterprises by the number of employees, if those with over 500 employees are considered 100 on an index, wages at firms with 100–499 employees measured 82; at firms with 30–99 employees, 66.8; and at firms with 5–29 employees, 59.8. In enterprises with over 10 employees, males aged 20 to 24 earned 23 percent more than females of the same age group; in the 35 to 39 age range, males earned 43 percent more; and in the 50 to 54 year-old group, males earned 47 percent more. See also WAGE SYSTEM; EMPLOYMENT SYSTEM, MODERN.　　　　　　　　　　　　　　*KURITA Ken*

wage level

(*chingin suijun*). Before World War II Japan had the lowest level of wages among industrial nations. The causes were several: (1) an abundance of workers recruited from small farming families in which living standards were very low; (2) severe government suppression of organized labor, which prevented workers from gaining negotiating power; and (3) the priority given to rapid capital formation and strong military development, which limited employee wages. After the war, however, these conditions were greatly changed. The removal of restrictions on labor union activities in particular, along with the development of the Japanese economy, improved working conditions. Immediately after the war, the Japanese level of wages went down to a subsistence level because of the deterioration of the economy, but by about 1948 it had improved, and by 1952–53 it had recovered to the level of 1934–36. Especially after 1955, when the Japanese economy was expanding rapidly and the demand for labor grew, the LABOR UNIONS achieved large wage increases through the SHUNTŌ (spring wage offensive).

During the worldwide recession in the 1970s, the growth rate of the Japanese economy declined, and the percentage increases in

Wage system ——— Table 1

Wage Differentials among Firms of Different Sizes							
Firms employing 100 or more				Firms employing 10–99			
Ages 18–19	Ages 20–24	Ages 30–34	Ages 40–50	Ages 18–19	Ages 20–24	Ages 30–34	Ages 40–50
1954	72	100	165	204	74	100	147	156
1958	79	100	186	238	74	100	143	155
1961	78	100	182	237	77	100	137	147
1964	81	100	162	214	78	100	132	138
1967	82	100	150	206	76	100	134	135
1970	85	100	144	179	80	100	137	134
1975	86	100	142	159	81	100	139	132

NOTE: Average wage for male production workers, ages 20–24, in manufacturing industries = 100.
SOURCE: For 1954: Rōdōshō (Ministry of Labor), *Kojimbetsu chingin chōsa kekka hōkoku* (annual): 1954. For 1958 and 1961: Rōdōshō, *Chingin kōzō kihon tōkei chōsa hōkoku* (annual): 1958 and 1961. For 1964–75: Rōdōshō, *Sengo rōdō keizai shi* (1966) and Nihon Seisansei Hombu (Japan Productivity Center), *Katsuyō rōdō tōkei* (annual): various years. Table reprinted from Takafusa Nakamura, *The Postwar Japanese Economy: Its Development and Structure* (1981).

wages also dropped sharply. Especially in the years after the OIL CRISIS OF 1973, the wage control policy of NIKKEIREN (Japan Federation of Employers' Associations) was successful in keeping percentage wage increases about equal with inflation. As a result, the level of real wages has not risen.

In the 1960s, the Japanese level of wages was one-sixth that of the United States, one-third that of West Germany and the United Kingdom, and half that of France, but the average percentage wage increases in 10 years were 4 percent in the United States, 7–10 percent in European countries, and 14 percent in Japan. In 1970 Japan reached the wage level of France. After the tremendous upward revaluation of the yen, the Japanese wage level increased to 60–70 percent of the American and West German levels in 1976, putting Japan third behind them. With the yen's continued strength, it appeared that the Japanese level of wages reached that of the United States and West Germany in 1977, but according to some accounts, the level of real wages in Japan is still less than 70 percent of West Germany's because of the high price of daily necessities and housing, and especially the price of land. KURITA Ken

Wagener, Gottfried (1831–1892)

Also known as Gottfried Wagner. German technical consultant and teacher who contributed to Japan's developing arts and industries, especially textiles and ceramics, in the Meiji period (1868–1912). An influential adviser to the government and craft industries on how to implement Western techniques, increase production, design goods for foreign trade and publicize Japanese wares abroad, he was also a pioneer in urging the Japanese to study, preserve, and practice their traditional arts and crafts.

Born in Hannover, Wagener graduated from Georg-August University in Göttingen and went to Nagasaki in 1868 to help build a factory. The next year he aided local authorities in improving the kilns for ARITA WARE. He went to Tōkyō to enter government service as a teacher in 1871. Over the years he taught physics, applied chemistry, and related courses at Daigaku Nankō and Tōkyō Kaisei Gakkō (predecessors of Tōkyō University) and from 1884 was head of the Pottery and Glass department of the Tōkyō Shokkō Gakkō (now Tōkyō Institute of Technology). He provided important planning and advice for the Japanese participants in the international exhibitions at Vienna in 1873 and Philadelphia in 1876. In his writings he urged the adoption of Western techniques to strengthen rather than replace traditional crafts—a suggestion which eventually became government policy. He was commissioned to build the first Western ceramic plant and also helped to establish a museum for Japanese art (now the TŌKYŌ NATIONAL MUSEUM). Wagener's other contributions include the introduction of a *champlevé* enamel technique to traditional CLOISONNÉ and the development of the distinctive ASAHI WARE. He also influenced Meiji artists and craftsmen in many fields. KURAUCHI Shirō

wage system

Wage determination has been one of the essential elements in the Japanese employment system, along with enterprise unionism, enterprise centeredness, and implicit "lifetime employment." The base salary in large firms is determined by a seniority wage principle and is supplemented by various allowances, welfare benefits, seasonal bonuses, and a retirement payment. Japanese wage policy has contributed to assuring workers' acceptance of technological innovation, job rotation, in-plant training, with a result of savings in company labor costs.

The origins of the seniority wage and lifetime employment systems may be traced to the early 1920s and to the response by firms to a shortage of skilled labor, mostly in the manufacturing and chemical industries. During 1939–41, government control over starting salaries and annual wage increases spread the system of wage levels and annual increments based on seniority throughout Japanese industry. This practice, complemented by the worker's confidence in continued employment, became increasingly prominent during the postwar years, serving to promote unity between labor and management at a time when firms were initially forced to reduce their wartime scale of operations and terminate the employment of large numbers of workers.

The system that has evolved in Japan since 1950 reflects differences in wage policy between large and small firms, as well as distinctions between permanent and nonpermanent workers. Large firms (1,000 or more employees) are characterized by the use of a permanent labor force, which constituted approximately 72.8 percent of their male workers in 1978. Nonpermanent workers (including women) were hired on a temporary basis or could be laid off in slow periods. Only permanent employees are members of the company-wide union and under the seniority wage and lifetime employment principles. The proportion of nonpermanent full-time workers has declined since the early 1960s because of labor shortages, permission to enter company-wide unions, and the increased numbers of female part-time workers.

In the 1950s, starting salaries for permanent workers in manufacturing industries were relatively low but rose sharply with age, especially in firms with 100 or more employees (Table 1). In the 1960s a leveling tendency for wages in all firms began, with higher starting salaries and comparatively lower payments to older workers. This contraction has been prominent in firms with 10 to 99 employees. In the 1950–75 period, real wages have overall more than quadrupled (Table 2). From about 1960, wages in firms with 100 to 499 employees have also become closer to those in larger firms, though compared to 1965, wages in firms with fewer than 100 workers have declined with respect to the larger firms. The widening discrepancy seen after 1965 between average wages in firms with 100 or more employees compared to smaller firms at least reflects differences in their seniority wage policies (see Tables 1 and 2).

The labor shortage experienced by Japanese industry after the 1950s most severely affected small firms, causing them to pay higher

Wage system——Table 2

Indexes of the Structure and Level of Wages

	Average wage index for all industries (1975 = 100)		Rate of increase in index (annual rates) (%)		Manufacturing industry wage differentials by size of operation (places of business employing 500 or more = 100)			
	Nominal	Real	Nominal	Real	500 employees or more	100–499 employees	30–99 employees	5–29 employees
1950	5.6	24.2	—	—	100	83.1	67.3	—
1955	10.1	32.8	12.5	6.0	100	74.3	58.9	—
1960	13.6	41.0	6.1	4.6	100	70.7	58.9	46.3
1965	22.0	49.4	10.1	3.8	100	80.9	71.0	63.2
1970	43.7	75.3	14.7	8.8	100	81.4	69.9	61.8
1975	100.0	100.0	18.0	5.8	100	82.9	68.7	60.2

SOURCE: Rōdōshō (Ministry of Labor), *Maitsuki kinrō tōkei chōsa hōkoku* (monthly): various issues. Table reprinted from Takafusa Nakamura, *The Postwar Japanese Economy: Its Development and Structure* (1981).

wages to attract and keep workers, either upon graduation from school or in mid-career. Thus, in firms with 10 to 99 employees, by 1970 wages for those in the 30–34 age bracket were even higher than rates for older employees (see Table 1). This phenomenon occurred while wage differentials for younger workers in all firms, but most notably in the smallest firms, were gradually reduced. Such changes in the wage system have been possible because small firms do not guarantee a wage based on seniority and lifetime employment, and large firms (500–1,000 employees or more) have modified their application of these principles. Large firms nonetheless maintain the concepts of seniority wage and implicit "lifetime employment" features, heralded as characteristic of Japanese management and still central to the postwar enterprise-wide union.

The Japanese wage system offers a base wage that is a relatively small percentage of an employee's total remuneration. For example, the real wage per man-hour in Japan was only about half that in the United States in 1978, though total labor costs per worker were more even. The total cash income of permanent blue- and white-collar workers in large firms can be divided into four components: base wage, 58.5 percent; nonstatutory and statutory allowances, 11.2 percent and 6.3 percent respectively; and seasonal bonuses, 24.1 percent (figures for 1975). The monthly salary includes the base wage and nonstatutory allowances. Primary factors determining the base wage are sex, seniority, and education. A secondary factor is merit rating.

Nonstatutory allowances reflect job position, skill, abnormal working conditions, employee performance, attendance, family size, housing, commuting expenses, and so forth. They recognize differences among individuals or groups of workers and raise salaries without increasing the base wage or distorting the seniority principle. Nonstatutory allowances can be terminated upon obsolescence.

Statutory allowances include overtime and shift-work premiums, as well as paid vacations. Over 90 percent of all firms do not pay more than the legal minimum of 25 percent of a worker's base salary for overtime. As a method of obtaining extra labor, overtime has been cost effective for Japanese employers. The overtime premium equivalent to the labor cost of adding a new employee was 55.3 percent ($55.3 > 25.0 \times 2$) in 1977.

Seasonal bonuses provide wage flexibility for the employer and offer motivation for the worker. These are paid in June and December to blue- and white-collar workers alike, regardless of whether the firm has been profitable. The standard bonus amount is determined through multiplying the monthly salary by a multiple that is itself based on the average number of days of regular attendance per month over several months. The payment is thus reduced by days absent from work and is modified according to the superior's assessment of each employee's performance. Contributions to the company on an individual and group basis over 6-month periods are thus recognized by the firm and rewarded. Company bonuses have served to increase flexibility in the wage system over the recent decade. The annual growth rate for bonuses in major companies in 1968–79 ranged from over 2 percent to 46 percent, and monthly salary gains averaged around 6 percent to 33 percent (see BONUS).

Retirement payments and all other nonwage benefits constituted 15.8 percent of total labor costs in 1975. The retirement bonus ac-

counted for some one-fifth of this percentage. This payment is computed according to the base wage, with a lower base wage resulting in a lower benefit. In place of a pension, this benefit is paid in one lump sum upon retirement, usually at 55–60 years of age. In 1975 the typical male permanent employee in a company with 1,000 or more workers, a middle school graduate, was ideally paid a retirement benefit of ¥8 million ($27,000) the equivalent of 35.4 months. The mandatory retirement age is enforced by penalizing both early and late retirement. An employee leaving before his age limit would receive approximately 80 percent of the normal retirement payment, regardless of years with the company. After reaching retirement age, workers often continue with the company at a reduced salary on a temporary basis or move to subsidiaries and affiliated firms. See also RETIREMENT.

Despite consistent growth in labor productivity, there are certain problems in the Japanese wage system. The seniority-merit formula and lifetime employment guarantee have limited application, and the system discriminates against most older workers and female employees, as well as workers in small firms. Wages of male production employees working beyond retirement age become roughly the same or even less than wages of employees aged 20–24 years. These older employees are no longer under the seniority wage principle, although they have received retirement payments, and in years of presumably greater family expenses (ages 35–55) salaries were accordingly higher. The young male employee suffers somewhat from a low starting salary, although less today than in past years. His expenses are also relatively low (for example, company dormitories are provided for single males), and he has assurances that his salary will rise at a rate different from his peers who entered the company in the same year if his performance is judged to be superior.

A serious wage gap is concentrated in older employees at small firms prior to retirement. Taking the average wage of permanent workers in large firms (1,000 or more employees) as 100, in 1975 the wage index of workers in the smallest companies (10–99 employees) was 97 at ages 25–29, 90 at ages 35–39, and only 82 at ages 45–49. Differences in salary between male and female employees also become greater with age, as women are not on the same seniority wage scale. A female production employee in a large firm in 1979 was paid about 80 percent of that of her male counterpart aged 25–29. At ages 35–39, her pay scale was around 60 percent, and at ages 45–49, only 53 percent. See also WAGE DIFFERENTIALS; WAGE LEVEL; EMPLOYMENT, FORMS OF; SENIORITY SYSTEM; EMPLOYMENT SYSTEM, MODERN.

——Ministry of Labor, *Rōdō hakusho* (yearly). Ministry of Labor, *Chingin ni kansuru shokakusa no jittai* (1978). Sakurabayashi Makoto, "Wage Administration in Japan," *Ostasiatisches Seminar* 2 (1979). SAKURABAYASHI Makoto

wagtails

(sekirei). Birds of the family Motacillidae, with a slender body about 20 centimeters (8 in) in length and a longish tail. Preferring to live near bodies of water, they forage on the ground, wagging their tails continually. Five species are found in Japan: the *kisekirei* (grey wag-

Wajū

A *wajū* community in the Aburajima area of Gifu Prefecture. One of many in this area, it lies between the rivers Ibigawa (left) and Nagaragawa (right). The treelined dike to the left, known as the Sembon Matsubara, forms Gifu Prefectural Natural Park.

tail; *Motacilla cinerea*), the *hakusekirei* (white wagtail; *M. alba*), and the *seguro sekirei* (Japanese wagtail; *M. grandis*) breed in areas north from the island of Kyūshū; the *tsumenaga sekirei* (yellow wagtail; *M. flava*) breeds only in northern Hokkaidō and the Iwami *sekirei* (forest wagtail; *Dendronanthus indicus*) only in Kyūshū and western Honshū. The black-backed, white-bellied *seguro sekirei* is peculiar to Japan. The Iwami *sekirei* is distinguished from the others by the sidewise bobbing of its tail and its choice of tree branches rather than the ground for nesting.　　　　　*Takano Shinji*

There is a passage in the *Nihon shoki* (720) relating how the male and female deities Izanagi no Mikoto and Izanami no Mikoto watched and then emulated a pair of mating wagtails, after which Izanami gave birth to the islands of Japan. For this reason a pair of wagtails is sometimes used as a decorative theme at weddings.
　　　　　Saneyoshi Tatsuo

Wainai Sadayuki (1858–1922)

Fish breeder. Known for his success at breeding trout *(masu)* in Lake TOWADA (northern Honshū), where it had been said that fish could not live. Born in Mutsu Province (now Akita Prefecture). Wainai introduced two varieties of carp into Lake Towada in 1884 without success. In 1902 he stocked the lake with *himemasu* from Hokkaidō's Lake Shikotsu. (This fish is a kind of native trout similar to the kokanee salmon of Alaska.) By 1905 he had succeeded in breeding the fish. Later introduced into other fishless lakes throughout Japan, it came to be known by his name as Wainai *masu* (Wainai trout).　　　　　*Aruga Yūshō*

Wajima

City in northern Ishikawa Prefecture, central Honshū. Principal industries are fishing, seafood processing, and the manufacture of *wajima-nuri* lacquer ware. Attractions include the Sosogi Coast, the terraced paddies at Semmaida, the morning market, and the female divers *(ama)* on the nearby island of HEGURAJIMA. Pop: 32,662.

Waji shōran shō

(Notes on the Rectification of Japanese Writing). A comprehensive study of *kana* (the Japanese phonetic syllabary) orthography written by KEICHŪ (1640–1701), a scholar of National Learning (KOKUGAKU), in the Edo period (1600–1868); published in five volumes in 1695. After carrying out research in old classical texts, Keichū corrected the Teika *kanazukai,* a long-practiced system of traditional *kana* usage attributed to FUJIWARA NO SADAIE (also known as Fujiwara no Teika). Arranging entries according to the old Japanese *iroha* syllabary order, he gave the corrected *kana* for problem words and cited the sources on which this was based. Most later studies of *kana* and historical *kana* usage up until World War II were based on his work. See also KANA.　　　　　*Uwano Zendō*

wajū

(literally, "within a circle"). A type of community, surrounded by embankments for protection from flooding (the embankments containing both the community and its fields); found in the delta area formed by the lower courses of the rivers Kisogawa, Nagaragawa, and Ibigawa. The area extends from the city of Ōgaki, Gifu Prefecture in the north to the mouths of the three rivers in Aichi and Mie prefectures in the south. The building of *wajū* in this area has a long history, the first dating as early as 1319. Although they are gradually disappearing, a total of 80 still exist.

waka

Traditional Japanese vernacular poetry in the classical forms: "Japanese poetry" or "Japanese song," as contrasted with *kanshi,* "Chinese verse." The term applies broadly to the tradition of classical poetry with its several forms developed over a period of some 1,400 years, from the oldest extant primitive song of about the mid-6th century to the present. In the narrower, more usual sense, *waka* designates the aristocratic poetry of the early literary, classical, and post-classical periods from the late 8th century to the early 20th, expressed primarily in the single dominant form, the TANKA (also called *uta*), or "short poem," consisting of five lines in 31 syllables in the pattern 5–7–5–7–7. In this sense *waka* is synonymous with classical *tanka,* and except for the primitive, early literary, and modern periods, this usage will be followed in the ensuing discussion.

General Characteristics —— Although it has demonstrated a remarkable capacity for development, renewal, and variety within closely restricted limits, *waka* of all periods may be said to share certain constant distinguishing characteristics. First is the prosodic fact, derived from the nature of the Japanese language, of syllabic meter, the basically open syllables of the language coming to be grouped in lines of five and seven syllables. Second is the equally distinctive fact of lyricism: *waka* is preeminently a lyrical tradition, developing, exploring, and expressing emotions, feelings, states of mind and being, and the affective qualities of experience. For the most part it is intellectually thin. Such a dominant concern with lyricism is in part the natural concomitant of the brief 31-syllable form; but in more positive terms, the brief form itself came to be thought the ideal vehicle for expressing the characteristic Japanese concern with the heart rather than the mind, with emotive rather than ratiocinative processes and responses.

Third is the fact of the social, contextual character of *waka*. To a degree unknown in the West, *waka* is social and occasional, the lyrical response to an event, a scene, or an observed aspect of nature or human affairs. Thus a poem is often impossible to treat as a single expression apart from its context or circumstances of composition. Such contexts varied from a lover's private plea to his cruel mistress to formal or informal social occasions calling for impromptu verse or elegant poems carefully prepared in advance. In sum, *waka* may be characterized as essentially a poetry of personal, private lyricism in an occasional, social context.

Fourth is the Japanese sense of the linguistic and cultural purity of the tradition. To an extent for which it is difficult to find parallels in the poetry of other civilizations, the Japanese retained over the centuries a consciousness of the special nature of *waka* as distinguished from the Chinese or other poetic traditions, maintaining an attitude, even in the most sophisticated literary periods, toward the native poetry as in part purificatory ritual, requiring an avoidance of the ugly and the unclean. Such an attitude derived from *waka's* earliest ancestors, the prayers and incantations of Shintō religious ceremonies. By the end of the 7th century, it had already led to certain limitations of subject matter and to the implicit understanding that the language must be "pure" Japanese, with all words of recognizably foreign (Chinese) origin excluded from the poetic vocabulary.

Fifth are the opposite motifs of increasing formal and structural simplification and fragmentation combined with growing rhetorical and technical sophistication. Thus, over the centuries an early variety of metrical forms was abandoned in favor of the single 31-syllable *tanka,* while the greater variety of subjects and concerns of early Japanese poetry and song was progressively restricted to a narrower range. With the growth of the literary tradition, poets were enabled to transcend the limitations of form and content and to express extremely fine gradations of feeling and subtle emotional and psychological states. Further, in time the brief *tanka* form itself tended to become divided into two or more formal and syntactic parts, while paralleling this internal fragmentation was an equally strong impulse to integration: the separate parts of single *tanka* were integrated by rhetorical, associational, and other means, while individual 31-syllable poems were integrated by techniques of association and progression into larger structures of sequences and anthologies.

Finally, there are the dual claims of invention and convention. To an extent little understood by many Western students, in the classical periods *waka* came to be governed by convention down to the smallest details of imagery and phrasing, while invention was restricted to a subtle adjustment of conventional elements into a new composition that displayed but a touch of originality. But at all times the best poets and critics were aware of the tension between convention and invention, between the impersonal and the personal, seeking to achieve balance and harmony between the two. Periods of high accomplishment were distinguished by the achievement of such a balance in terms significant to the age; periods of attenuation and decline were characterized by a loss of balance, the scales almost always tilting on the side of overconventionalism, loss of inspiration, and the flagging of invention. Radical departures from tradition were never tolerated, while even degrees of innovation that might be thought mild by Western standards were usually rejected in their own generation and only gradually and grudgingly accepted by later poets after a period of naturalization. Over the centuries of the *waka* tradition, cycles of innovation, harmony and balance, attenuation, and decline follow one another; these cycles may be understood in terms of the dual claims of convention and invention.

Prosody—— Although *waka* originated in a vaguely defined oral, bardic tradition dating as far back as the 6th century, and although it developed over some 14 centuries of linguistic as well as literary and poetic change, the present state of knowledge provides no evidence that the prosody has changed fundamentally since earliest times. Consequently, as far as is known, it is possible to read transcriptions of the most ancient songs in the pronunciation of the modern language without altering the meter or obscuring the proper scansion. This continuity in the case of Japanese prosody may be ascribed to the relatively simple phonological structure of the Japanese language, both ancient and modern. Assigned to the Altaic, or Ural-Altaic, group of languages, Japanese is closely related to no other tongue but shares certain structural features as well as a minimum number of cognate words with such other members of the group as Korean, Mongolian, and Tungus. Agglutinative and polysyllabic, Japanese, though a "tone language," is a language of little accent. Phonologically, Old Japanese is known to have been somewhat more complex than the later, classical language, having had seven vowels instead of the five to which the language has been reduced since the end of the 8th century. Although the possibility should be admitted of the conscious manipulation by ancient bards of tonal patterns, vocalic harmony, and the like, no clear evidence of such manipulation exists. In the final analysis one arrives at the conclusion that Japanese prosody of all periods (except for contemporary Western-influenced free verse) involves primarily a quantitative meter based upon the syllable or mora. A syllable consists of a single vowel; a consonant or consonant cluster plus a vowel; *m* or *n* preceding a consonant (except *y*) within a word; *n'* before either vowel or *y* within a word; or a final *n*. Long vowels count as two syllables.

The oldest extant songs display little prosodic regularity, although already there is a tendency for longer and shorter lines to alternate. No doubt a good deal of the metrical raggedness was smoothed out in singing or recitation to musical accompaniment, but in general, the older the text, the more irregular the meter. During the 7th century the number of syllables per line became standardized at five or seven, shorter lines usually alternating with longer lines in various combinations which defined the forms of ancient *waka*. Why the line lengths became fixed at five and seven syllables is not definitely known, although it seems likely that the Japanese fives and sevens were developed by analogy with the five- and seven-word lines of Chinese poetry. Although there is no similarity between the Chinese and Japanese languages, the vastly older Chinese civilization perforce became the fount of all literary culture for the preliterate Japanese, and during the 7th century when the line lengths of Japanese verse were regularized, the Japanese were beginning to undergo some two centuries of intensive Chinese cultural influence.

Probably by the middle of the 7th century the *tanka* form had already begun to establish itself as paramount. By the end of the 9th century it had become for all intents and purposes the unique form of literary poetry. Down to the middle of the 8th century, the prin-

cipal form besides the *tanka* was the *chōka* (also called *nagauta*), or "long poem." It consisted of an indefinite number of pairs of five- and seven-syllable lines with an extra seven-syllable line at the end, making the last five lines of the *chōka* identical in form with the *tanka*. The *chōka* was not especially long by Western standards— the longest is one in 149 lines by KAKINOMOTO NO HITOMARO (fl ca 685–705)—and at its shortest it might be a mere seven lines long. During the 7th century it became common practice to add to the *chōka* one or more short envoys (*hanka* or *kaeshiuta*), which were identical in form with the *tanka*. The increasing importance given the envoy was one of several factors which led to the decline of the *chōka* in the late 8th century and its virtual disappearance from the literary tradition by the end of the 9th.

Of the four other "forms" of early *waka*, all except the *renga*, or "linked poem," had died out by the end of the 8th century. The shortest form was the *katauta* ("half-poem") of three lines in the pattern 5–7–7 (or sometimes 4–7–7) syllables. It was not felt to be complete, and although it sometimes appears as an independent form, it was most often combined in pairs in dialogue. The *katauta* thus constituted half of a *sedōka*, or "head-repeated poem"—a form which owes its name to its repeated pattern in six lines of 5–7–7–5–7–7 syllables. The *sedōka* was most commonly used for dialogue, but some examples consist of a single sentence uttered by a single speaker. It was probably above all a song form: its even number of lines is typical of Japanese song of all periods, as contrasted with the odd number which became the rule in literary poetry, and it did not long survive the 7th century. The *Bussokuseki no uta*, or "Buddha's Foot-Stone poem," is named from a stone stele incised with the Buddha's footprint, with which most of the extant examples of the form are associated. It has six lines in the pattern 5–7–5–7–7–7, and may be regarded as a variant (or possibly, ancestor) of the *tanka*, for the last line is usually only a slightly varied repetition of the fifth. Finally, the *renga*, or "linked poem," was, in the early literary period and until the late 12th century, simply a *tanka* whose first three lines were composed by one person, the last two by another. It was usually playful and was employed in gallant exchanges or in games of verse-capping. However, it was the only one of the minor forms of early literary poetry to survive into the classical periods and must be recognized as an ancestor of the fully developed linked verse in 50 or 100 segments which became a major genre from the 14th century through the 18th.

The Japanese syllabic meter needed to be controlled by rhetorical and other means if it was not to become hopelessly sing-song and monotonous, especially in the *chōka*. The best poets often varied the *chōka* by marking divisions within the body of the poem by an extra seven-syllable line, or by inserting a short line of three or four syllables between the usual five- and seven-syllable pairs. However, in time the *chōka* became metrically fixed and increasingly monotonous. Again, by the 13th century the practice of adding or subtracting syllables to a line came to be strictly limited: it might be lengthened beyond the usual five or seven syllables only in the most exceptional circumstances, and it almost never had fewer than either five or seven syllables.

Alliteration, consonance, and assonance are found in the earliest Japanese songs and were used by poets of all periods to give richness, rhetorical complexity, and interest to their verse. The cadence might be freely varied with a syntactic pause at the end of any or all of the lines of a poem. Lines of five and seven syllables came to be grouped characteristically in pairs marked by syntactic pause at the end of the second line. In the early literary poetry, particularly in the *chōka*, the dominant cadence was 5–7 (called *goshichichō*); toward the middle of the 8th century, the *tanka* and even the *chōka* began to show a tendency to group lines in the opposite fashion, and the 7–5 cadence (*shichigochō*) began to gain ground. In time, *tanka* began to show a tendency to fall into two parts, with a caesura at the end of the third line: 5–7–5: 7–7. The division was often marked by a participle at the end of the third line; by reversing the syntax and placing in the last two lines the clause that would normally come first; or by dividing the poem into a generalization in the first three lines followed by a syntactically unrelated symbolic description— often terminating in a noun—in the last two, as in this poem by the priest JAKUREN (ca 1139–1202):

Sabishisa wa	Loneliness—
Sono iro to shi mo	Its essential beauty of a color
Nakarikeri	Not to be defined:
Maki tatsu yama no	Over the dark cedar trees, the dusk
Aki no yūgure	Gathering on autumn hills.

The classical critics called the two units created by the division of the *tanka* "upper verses" *(kami no ku)* and "lower verses" *(shimo no ku)* and recognized various ways of integrating them by rhetorical and other means, such as using in the lower verses images related to those in the upper ones. Critical disputes arose as to the relative merits of "closely related verses" *(shinku)* and "distantly related verses" *(soku)*: the innovating poets of the 14th century tended to favor the latter, the conservatives the former.

Rhetorical Devices——Such important transcending rhetorical techniques as parallelism, irony, and the like are shared by *waka* with Western traditions. Certain other techniques, however, characteristically and to an extent uniquely Japanese, are best described separately. These are the MAKURA KOTOBA or "pillow word," the JOKOTOBA or semi-metaphorical "preface," the UTA MAKURA or poetic place name, the KAKEKOTOBA or "pivot word," and the *engo* or "associated word." All of these techniques involve word play to a large extent, and to appreciate them it must be understood, first, that the Japanese language, with its large number of homonyms, is ideally suited to such uses, and second, that the pun, held in such low esteem by traditional Western critics, was from the very beginning employed by the Japanese for serious artistic purposes. The *makura kotoba, jokotoba,* and *uta makura* are historically the oldest of these devices, being found in the earliest extant primitive song; the last two became current in the early classical period, from the mid-9th century. It is a remarkable fact, however, that a technique, once invented, was never abandoned: instead, it was added to the cumulative store upon which successive generations of poets might draw for various poetic styles.

The *makura kotoba* is a stylized, semiimagistic epithet, normally of five syllables (often including a possessive particle), used to modify certain fixed words in a fashion similar to the Homeric epithets. Very often the connection between the pillow word and the word it modified involved word play, and in many cases the original meaning was lost, the epithet either losing any specific lexical meaning or else becoming glossed by folk etymology to yield an entirely different significance from its original one. In either case, the *makura kotoba* was used in older poetry partly as a formulaic, semiritualistic means of creating a solemn, elevated tone, and partly for metaphor half submerged in formality. These uses continued through the classical periods, but with the growth of the tradition, changes in the language, and new poetic styles, the *makura kotoba* came to be frequently employed by classical poets to create an archaic effect, often in a romantic-primitivistic way to evoke the atmosphere of a simpler, happier age. New pillow words continued to be invented through the early literary period, but from the 9th century the number became fixed, and the same ones were used over and again down to modern times.

The *jokotoba* (also called simply *jo*) was, like the *makura kotoba,* joined to the word modified or the "basic statement" of the poem by similar techniques of juncture: word play, similarity of sound, or an implied metaphorical relationship. However, it was of indeterminate length, sometimes taking up as much as the whole of the "upper verses," and was less fixed by convention. Characteristic of much primitive and early literary poetry, the preface was often only tenuously related to the statement, the word play at the point of juncture being paramount and the relationship between the two parts of the poem being, as in the case of many *makura kotoba,* more one of tonal metaphor than of sense. Like the pillow word, the preface was often used by classical poets to evoke the poetry and the world of the primitive and early literary periods. New ones might be freely invented in any age, although later classical poets seldom availed themselves of the privilege.

Uta makura, which literally means "poem pillow" was the name of a famous place—mountain, river, forest, field, lake, or seacoast—known primarily for its beauty, but also sometimes arbitrarily chosen because of its possibilities for word play. *Uta makura* had semi-metaphorical significance, often being associated with specific qualities of lyrical tone. They are found commonly in the most ancient verse but continued to play an even more significant part in the poetry of later periods. During the early classical period (late 8th through 12th centuries), the number of poetic place names became fixed, and catalogues and lists were compiled for the use of novice poets. Having rich evocative potential and associational qualities, *uta makura* became one extremely important means for integrating and linking sequences of individual *tanka* and the separate segments of the later linked verse.

The *kakekotoba,* or "pivot word," was both an important rhetorical device in its own right and was involved much of the time at the point of juncture between *makura kotoba, jokotoba,* and *uta makura* and the word or words with which they were associated. The pivot word was essentially a technique of using a series of sounds (all or part of a word) in two overlapping syntactical or semantic patterns, one meaning being evoked by what preceded the pivot, and the completely different meaning of a homophone in connection with what followed. The device might well be called a syntactic conceit, and it is significant that it came to its fullest development with the emergence in the early 9th century of the *tanka* as the preeminent form, for the 31-syllable poem needed, far more than the *chōka,* to transcend its limits by such techniques with the potential of saying much in little.

Engo was the use of a word that had, or created, an "association" with a preceding word or words, often but not always evoking a second, homonymic meaning in the associated word. The device was used throughout the classical periods for several important purposes: to give complex texture to the verse and transcend the limits of the *tanka* as in the case of the pivot; to convey allegorical meanings or *double entendres;* to pull together the upper and lower verses of a poem, which might otherwise be syntactically, modally, or imagistically disjunctive; to integrate separate *tanka* in sequences and anthologies by associations between words in contiguous poems.

Imagery and Metaphor——*Waka* of all periods characteristically employ an unusually high proportion of images, many of them drawn from nature. Thus, the poetry is notably particularistic and concrete in its functionings. Imagery is used for itself, for natural setting and description, and for tonal metaphor and symbolic description. Personification of natural images became increasingly important in the classical periods and frequently led to allegory, especially in the poetry exchanged in courtship and social discourse. Thus, a plea to the cuckoo to come and sing might actually be a reproach to an inattentive lover or a request to a friend for a visit. With the growth of tradition, repeated influences of Chinese poetry of different periods, and a deepening consciousness of the Buddhist world view, certain natural images came to be imbued with innate tonal and symbolic values, enabling sophisticated poets to convey in ostensibly "objective" description both a scene in nature and the emotional response to it. With respect to allegory, Japanese, unlike Western allegory, with its personified abstractions and battles between Good and Evil, tended to be concrete, private, and closed; natural images such as those of the cuckoo and the orange tree awaiting its visit stood for other physical beings (a lover and his lady) in poems which could equally well be merely taken at face value.

In spite of the importance and prevalence of imagery in much of *waka,* the number of natural images deemed suitably poetic came to be severely restricted in the early classical period; few new members were admitted to this elite group over the ensuing centuries and then only after much resistance and debate. Such stringent limitations on poetic diction seemed to offer the Japanese a kind of esoteric equivalent for the prosodic and other complexities of Chinese verse—a means of elevating and refining the poetic medium, for all its simplicity, to a status of equality with Chinese poetry.

Subjects, Themes, and Modes——To an extent unparalleled in Western poetry, the subjects and themes of *waka* came, like imagery and diction, to be restricted by tradition and convention to limited aspects of the world and human experience. Whereas in the earliest period the observable limitations of subject and theme appear to have been those of a primitive, unreflective social milieu and view of the world, after a period of relatively free experimentation with narrative, philosophical, and didactic modes under strong Chinese influence in the 7th and 8th centuries, *waka* came to concentrate upon the lyrical treatment of a handful of subjects and only a few, though basic and important, themes. Human affairs (celebration, separation, grief, and especially love) and nature (the four seasons in their changing aspects, the beauties of the natural scene) became by early classical times the two major subject areas; in the early 10th century this parallel importance of nature and human affairs as poetic subjects was symbolized in the structure of the first of 21 anthologies of vernacular poetry periodically compiled by imperial command between 905 and 1439. The major subject categories remained dominant through the classical and post-classical periods, although a few less important classifications were dropped and a few new ones added over the centuries.

Certain subjects commonly treated and expected in Western poetry are conspicuously absent from *waka* after the early literary period: war and battle, physical suffering, dying, and other "unclean" acts were banished, as were all ugly, low, or nasty images. Blood was never spilled even in the most ancient and primitive verse: instead, an auspicious ritual purity of language was maintained even when dealing with the most painful subjects; violence and death were treated either referentially or by means of harmless allegory.

The themes of *waka* came to be as restricted as its subjects, although these themes were expressed with a variety, subtlety, and evocative power seldom matched in Western traditions. From the early literary period, the lyric themes of beauty and sadness came increasingly to dominate the literary poetry; to a large extent these themes expressed an awareness of the overarching effects of time. Time was both a condition of existence and a threat to all human and natural values, a source of beauty and the cause of sadness. On the other hand, there were the themes that transcended the conflict with time: public events, religion, secular mysticism, cosmic irony, and a sense of human sympathy and identity. But with the growing dominance of a Buddhist world view holding all life to be ephemeral, all human passion and attachment to be an impediment to spiritual progress, the nature poetry came typically to express a lyric melancholy and poetry on love and most other human affairs, a poignant awareness of the impermanence and unreliability of all personal ties. Joy and pleasure in love, satisfaction in success, and rejoicing in good fortune were restricted to specific occasions usually of a ritualistic or public nature, and poems on these themes constituted but a small portion of the surviving classical poetry.

Sources —— From the early literary period, *waka* became so intrinsically a part of both the literature and the everyday social life of the ruling classes that just as every social event, public or private, was an occasion for poetry, so in a real sense all of the forms and genres of vernacular prose—the poetic diary, the lyrical tale, the commonplace book or miscellany, the "novel" or romance—developed from *waka*. Not surprisingly, all of these genres are typically a mixture of poetry and prose. In consequence, the sources of *waka* must be understood to embrace all of the literature of the court from the earliest period.

Most of the extant songs and poems of the earliest or primitive period (ca 550–685) are preserved in the early chronicles—the KOJIKI (712, Record of Ancient Matters), the NIHON SHOKI or *Nihongi* (720, Chronicles of Japan), the *Shoku nihongi* (797), and the like—in a few surviving local gazetteers, and a handful of other works. Such materials were intended to record important traditional materials—the myths and legends of the people, the divine origins of the imperial family and other powerful clans—and were not conceived of as collections of poetry as such, although they contain a great many poems, songs, and verse fragments. In the early literary period (630–784) was compiled the first extant anthology of *waka*, as well as the largest and in many respects the greatest. This was the MAN'YŌ-SHŪ (ca 759, Collection for Ten Thousand Generations or Collection of Ten Thousand Leaves). It consists of 20 books and contains 4,500-odd poems; of these, more than 4,000 are *tanka*, showing the early dominance of that form. In the early classical period (784–1100) was compiled the first of the 21 imperial anthologies of *waka*, the KOKINSHŪ (Collection of Ancient and Modern Times, 905); it was followed by the *Gosenshū* (GOSEN WAKASHŪ; Later Collection, ca 955) and the *Shūishū* (SHŪI WAKASHŪ; Collection of Gleanings, ca 996). These three early classical anthologies, called collectively Sandaishū, "the Collections of Three Eras," dominated the practice and defined the diction of later poetry throughout the classical periods. Subsequent imperial anthologies were compiled on an average of once every 50 years until the 21st and last, the *Shin zoku kokinshū* (New Collection of Ancient and Modern Times, Continued, 1439). Traditionally, the first 8 are designated the "Collections of Eight Eras" (Hachidaishū); the last 13, the "Collections of Thirteen Eras" (Jūsandaishū). The imperial anthologies vary considerably in size, quality, and relative importance, but in all periods they had a crucial public and social significance as the most important literary enterprises of their day.

By analogy with Chinese practice, from the early literary period poets made "personal collections" (*shikashū*) of their own poems, and these as well as other materials were drawn upon by the compilers of the *Man'yōshū* and the imperial collections, which are in large measure anthologies of anthologies. None of the sources used by the compilers of the *Man'yōshū* survive independently, although many are mentioned in headnotes and footnotes to the poems. From the early classical period, personal collections survive in growing numbers, along with the records of poetry contests (UTA-AWASE), which became increasingly popular from the early 10th century. Apart from these are a number of "unofficial" or private anthologies (*shisenshū*) of what was considered the best work distilled from

earlier imperial anthologies or contemporary poets, often used as source works demonstrating the correct treatment of poetic topics or materials, or as textbooks for aspiring poets. Thus, the *Kokin waka rokujō* (Six Books of Japanese Poetry, Ancient and Modern) of the late 10th century is a collection of some 4,500 poems classified under 30 major headings and 503 conventional poetic topics; collections called *Ruijū uta-awase* (Classified Texts of Poetry Contests) were compiled at least twice toward the end of the early classical and beginning of the mid-classical (1100–1241) periods.

These and many other similar materials accumulated over the centuries, amounting to a huge corpus of *waka* of scores of thousands of poems and hundreds of volumes in modern printed texts. The majority of these poems are neither great nor even very good, but such was the prestige, the importance, and the strength of the *waka* tradition that even in the post-classical periods, usually considered to be centuries of unrelieved decline, poets nevertheless put forth their best efforts and many good poems do in fact survive. The continuity and persistence of *waka* give cause for wonder, and the phenomenon is peculiarly Japanese. It is conservatism in the best sense—the desire to preserve the best of traditional culture, to be a part of that culture, and to hand on the tradition to later generations.

Primitive Song and Poetry (ca 550–686) —— Although *waka* usually designates the secular poetry of the literate culture—primarily the poetry of the court beginning in what has been called the early literary period—it is nonetheless firmly rooted in the oral tradition of primitive, preliterate song. The early sources contain all together somewhat more than 600 songs and poems. Inasmuch as they were not written down until the 8th century, after the Japanese had been subjected to considerable and increasing literary and civilizing influences from Korea and China, many of the traditional materials have obviously been revised, transformed, and forced into a narrative context which in most cases they probably did not originally have. Some of the longest as well as the best *chōka* form small narrative-dramatic sequences having a cast of characters and a narrator; the sequence on the wooing of Princess Nunakawa by the Deity of Eight Thousand Spears (*Kojiki*, 2–3) is a notable example. The sequence is, however, far from long by Western standards, being only some 66 lines. It may be taken as an extended, fictionalized example of the primitive *utagaki* or *utakagai*, a ritualized occasion of public courtship thought to have taken place in spring and autumn, in which youths and maidens sparred with one another by means of poetic exchanges. The practice survived in the sophisticated period of the court in the traditional institution of the New Year's mummers and, more important, in the continuing use of *waka* in amorous discourse and courtship.

The early materials display many characteristics which are expected from an oral tradition relayed in large part by groups of hereditary professional reciters (*kataribe*) and by entertainers or mummers (*wazaogi*): formulas; pillow words; repetition of words, lines and phrases; simple contiguous parallelism; interjections and refrain words. The subjects are those of daily life: love, grief, travel, feasting, drinking, boasting, war. The imagery, simple and homely, encompassed the entire range of experience (or consciousness of the world) of the primitive Japanese, with the exception of images of sickness, death, and other "unclean" things held in abhorrence by a people whose religious beliefs stressed ritual purity and freedom from pollution. Instead, harmless natural images were substituted metaphorically or allegorically for images of carnage and bloodshed: the enemy might be represented by a noxious weed in a millet field, to be rooted out and destroyed.

The essentially neutral imagery of primitive song—it could not be said to be either good or bad in itself—was limited in range and lacked any inherent feeling or tone. At the same time, the early bards had certain means to endow otherwise neutral images with value, usually of a sacred, ritual nature, in the form of a few ornamental prefixes: *i-* (sacred), *ma-* (true), *mi-* (fair, lovely), *tama-* (precious, jewellike)—so that such an act as pounding poles into a river might be rendered solemn and awesome. Some of these prefixes were passed on into the tradition of literate poetry, and their use became conventional, if optional, with certain words and *uta makura*, as in Mi-Yoshino (Fair Yoshino), *tama-mo* (gemlike seaweed), *i-gaki* (sacred fence). Pillow words, with which primitive poetry was plentifully endowed, were also used for similar effect—to give essentially neutral poetic materials a certain metaphorical importance or tonal majesty; indeed, a single song might consist almost entirely of a formulaic list of *uta makura* preceded by *makura kotoba*, and only the last two or three lines would contain a bald statement of the situation and the feelings of the speaker.

An important structural principle of early song is preparation-conclusion. This often involved a description of a place or sequence of places, sometimes stiffened by sequences of pillow words; a development of imagery from large to small, from the whole to the part, as in a song describing a palace, the surrounding trees, a particular tree, the upper, middle, and lower branches of the tree, the leaves on the branches, a single leaf that drops into a wine cup and makes an auspicious sound. In its most primitive manifestations, the technique is monotonously insistent, causing incantation nearly to swallow up song; in somewhat later poetry it seems to reflect an obsession with the rhetorical device of the *jokotoba* (preface). Thus, poem after poem among the anonymous verses in the *Man'yōshū* believed to be the oldest in the anthology consist of a preparatory descriptive statement which turns out to be a preface joined, often by word play, to a concluding declaration of feeling or intention. The editors of the *Man'yōshū* designated such poems as "verses expressing feelings by referring to things" (*kibutsu chinshi ka*), and it is quite certain that the technique developed from Chinese examples, which fact no doubt accounts in large measure for its popularity. Toward the end of the primitive age, the possibilities of the technique appear to have been seized upon primarily for love poetry, the "verses referring to things" in the *Man'yōshū* being a subcategory of *sōmon*, or "amorous exchanges." In the most pleasing examples, the preparation or preface serves as an appropriate metaphor for the feelings expressed in the conclusion or declaration; in the least satisfactory examples, the relationship is forced and far-fetched, although enthusiasts have extolled this very effect, proclaiming the imaginative freedom of association and the virtues of illogicality.

Generally in the early period, the basic mode of expression is simple declaration—the situation of a specific poetic speaker declaring his or her feelings on a specific occasion. The poetry is unreflective and only incidentally descriptive: the speakers see only events and objects and declare their immediate reactions to them. There is no probing of feeling, no search for a meaning to life or to the world around them. At the same time, this early *waka* has a vividness and immediacy, seeming to bring us to the very brink of the world of which it was a part, and above all, it established in terms which were constant and fundamental the characteristic norms of *waka* from which the later literate and sophisticated tradition was to grow.

The Early Literary Period (ca 610–784)——This period of roughly 130 years was an age of remarkable cultural development. Governmental, social, and cultural institutions, Buddhism and Buddhist monasteries, art and architecture flourished under strong Chinese influence as the dominant ruling elite embarked upon a vigorous campaign to "modernize" Japan by means of wholesale borrowing from China. Of all the arts, native poetry and written literature took longest to emerge in their new guise, requiring a writing system (the adaptation of the Chinese system to the totally different Japanese language). Survivals and crosscurrents complicate the gradual transition from a primitive oral literature to a fully developed, literary poetry. However, by the late 7th century it is possible to speak of individual poets and to distinguish new subjects, themes, modes, and techniques that clearly mark the new poetry as dramatically different from the anonymous compositions of the primitive bards. In view of the enormous impact of the Chinese example, it is remarkable that the vernacular poetry of this age remains incontrovertibly Japanese in language, style, emphases, and techniques. Japanese poetry in this period was transformed by the experience of cultural borrowing, not engulfed by it.

Nearly all of the extant poetry of the early literary period is preserved in the great early anthology, *Man'yōshū*. Much has obviously been lost, as many notes in the collection referring to this or that lost anthology or personal collection of some poet attest. Nevertheless, as an anthology of anthologies, the *Man'yōshū* probably provides a representative sampling of the poetic achievement of this remarkable age.

First Man'yō period. The first division of the early literary period as such, also known as the first *Man'yō* period, is usually said to encompass the years from 629 to 671. During these two score years, the court culture was only beginning to emerge from the clan society, and in conformity with traditional practice, the "capital" was frequently moved from one place to another, generally following the death of a sovereign, or as a result of the struggles attendant upon the development from clan rule to a relatively centralized political authority.

Much of the verse of this first period was composed by, or is attributed to, exalted individuals—emperors and empresses, members of the imperial family, and courtiers of high rank—rather than the literary professional poets of a few generations later. Most of it is preserved in the first two books of the *Man'yōshū*, whose roughly chronological structure suggests they were originally a separate anthology incorporated by the compilers into the larger one. Much of the poetry was supposedly composed in response to incidents and occasions in real life. Many poems show the characteristics of primitive song, employing direct declaration, traditional rhetorical techniques, and simple types of parallelism. Significant new developments are also evident at the end of this early period, especially the sudden appearance of nature poetry and of the descriptive mode, often combined with declaration. Expressed in the surviving verse of a handful of people, the new interest appears with dramatic suddenness; it is clearly due to the direct influence of Chinese nature poetry. It is not surprising that the same group who produced this new Japanese poetry were simultaneously reading and composing Chinese verse, of which some examples are preserved in the *Kaifūsō*, the first collection of *kanshi*, or Chinese verse composed by Japanese poets. In some cases, it is possible that the primary interest to poet and audience of ostensibly descriptive lines was a hidden message allegorically conveyed by images of nature. However, a *chōka* by Princess Nukata (or Nukada; NUKATA NO ŌKIMI) on the relative merits of spring and autumn is an elegant, sophisticated literary piece clearly inspired by an age-old Chinese literary "debate."

Other important developments in the first *Man'yō* period include the regularization of the line lengths of Japanese verse to five and seven syllables; the development of more sustained compositions in the *chōka* form; and the custom of adding one or more envoys, or *hanka*, to the longer poems. The practice was probably an adaptation of a similar Chinese practice, the *fanzi* (*fan-tzu*; "repeating words") that often accompanied the Chinese *fu*, or "rhyme prose," a form which exerted an important, though indirect influence on the poetry of this and the following period.

Second Man'yō period and Hitomaro. The second *Man'yō* period, covering the years 672–710, is dominated by the genius of one of Japan's greatest poets, KAKINOMOTO NO HITOMARO (fl ca 685–705). Despite the new developments of the preceding period, Hitomaro's emergence is so sudden and dramatic as to be unaccountable except as a happy confluence of genius with a favorable cultural milieu. In spite of his enormous importance, few poems agreed to be indisputably by this great poet survive—17 *chōka* and 62 *tanka*—although a good many others in the *Man'yōshū* as well as in later anthologies are attributed to him. Similarly, little is known of Hitomaro the man, except that he was an official of low rank who held at least two minor provincial posts, had at least one wife (probably two), and created a body of poetry that remains to this day the glory of the *Man'yō* age. Although he composed in all of the major contemporary forms, he is especially noted for his development of the *chōka* into a sustained, elevated poetic genre, a vehicle for both private lyricism and public poetry of high seriousness, solemnity, and grandeur. Emerging from the misty background of oral tradition, with its hereditary reciters, Hitomaro may be called Japan's first professional literary poet. He is the first *Man'yō* poet known to have accompanied his sovereign or other royal personages on journeys and excursions, composing poems on command, in the manner of Western poets laureate, to commemorate events of importance in the life of the court. His *chōka* include celebrations of imperial palaces and pleasances, laments and eulogies composed on the deaths of royal princes, elegies on visits to the ruins of former capitals. The longest *chōka* in the *Man'yōshū* is a 149-line composition by Hitomaro (*Man'yōshū* 199) on the death of Prince Takechi; its central portion is a narrative passage describing with some indirection the prince's victory over the rebel forces in the famous JINSHIN DISTURBANCE (672). As this length suggests, the *chōka*, even in the hands of its greatest master, was not really long by Western standards, but Hitomaro by his tonal integrity and technical mastery gave it a cohesion and integrity that were never matched. From the oral tradition he retained certain distinguishing features which gave his poems a striking simplicity, immediacy, and directness of effect. His language remains stubbornly Japanese, his imagery plain and homely—the lithesome beauty and yielding gentleness of his beloved, for example, are expressed in the metaphor of seaweed swaying in the ocean currents. At the same time, Hitomaro was uniquely resourceful and creative, developing and shaping the traditional forms and techniques, building upon the bardic word-hoard. Thus, although many of his pillow words were inherited from tradition, at least half appear to have been created by himself. In his hands the ancient technique not only evoked tradition and the quasi-religious effect of certain kinds of primitive verse but assumed a new importance, giving dignity and solemnity to his subjects.

Similarly, Hitomaro brought the use of complex, noncontiguous parallelism to a level of perfection in the *chōka* never equalled. His ultimate teacher of such techniques cannot have been other than Chinese poetry and mixed forms of poetry and prose, perhaps primarily the *fu*, although it is impossible to point to direct influence. At all events, complex Chinese techniques of parallelism are so thoroughly acclimatized to the genius of the Japanese language in his poetry that he succeeds in deriving the maximum benefit while suffering few if any of the disadvantages—artificiality, distortion, monotony. Syntactically, his *chōka* usually constitute either a single or at most two or three units, the breaks coinciding with what might be called stanzaic divisions of the poem. Exploiting the potential of the Japanese language for syntactic ambiguity, he uses verb and adjective inflectional terminations for expressing either a conclusive or attributive meaning. Consequently, an apparent break in the fluid syntax often proves to conclude a hypotactic construction that is attributive to a following substantive, and so over and again to the end of the poem. The reader is thus presented with a tightly integrated structure of experience embodying Hitomaro's theme—in the case of his poem on discovering the body of a man, for example, the inevitable but baffling reality of human suffering and death in a benign and divinely ordered world.

Complicated techniques, reflective themes and modes, and other elements are combined and harmonized in Hitomaro's *chōka* with the native simplicity and plain imagery of the traditional Japanese poetic language in such a way that in total effect he seems the most Japanese of poets. His ability to achieve impressive results comparable in their own terms with the rich vocabulary and many synonyms of the Chinese *fu*, but scarcely possible in the limited diction of the Japanese of his time, is nowhere more impressively demonstrated than in the solemn "overtures" or introductory passages of many of his *chōka*. Such passages typically begin with lines of joyous praise of the land, its divine origins, and its continued sanctity and beauty in the present. Reminiscent in some respects of the "land-praising songs" of primitive verse and employing diction and techniques inherited from the bardic tradition on the one hand, Hitomaro's overtures establish the setting for human events and situations—danger, suffering, sorrow, death—often in ironic contrast to the god-graced peace and beauty of the land. Sometimes the overtures establish an atmosphere of solemnity and worshipful awe leading to a description of an imperial pleasance or royal excursion. By this and other means—particularly, his tone of compassion, gentle irony, and broad human sympathy, and his transcendent themes—Hitomaro gave public significance to the most private subjects and endowed the *chōka* with a vitality and structural validity which it was never to know again.

Many of Hitomaro's most famous *tanka* are, in fact, envoys to his *chōka*. In these he expresses his personal feelings (or those of his poetic speaker) and emotional response to the situation set forth in the longer poem and often completes the syntax, as it were. The second envoy (*Man'yōshū* 137) to his *chōka* "On Parting from His Wife as He Set Out from Iwami for the Capital" may serve as a single example:

Akiyama ni	O colored leaves
Otsuru momijiba	Scattering upon these autumn hills—
Shimashiku wa	If only for a moment,
Na chirimagai so	Cease your troubled, restless fall,
Imo ga atari min	Let me see where my beloved dwells.

Third Man'yō period (710-735). The third division of the early literary period corresponds to the early Nara period, the generation following the establishment of Japan's first permanent capital at Nara in 710. Although no single individual attains the level of Hitomaro, an impressive number of poets of the first rank testify to the vigor of contemporary literary activity. Apart from the sovereigns and their immediate families, some of whom were accomplished poets, the important figures were, like Hitomaro, for the most part relatively low ranking courtiers or provincial officials. Some half-dozen individual poets are outstanding.

General developments include the ever growing importance of the *tanka*, while the *chōka* gives signs of shrinking and weakening and its emotional focus shifts to the envoys. Chinese influence is also more directly evident in certain poetic subjects than even in Hitomaro's laments on ruined capitals, although the poetry, like the

poetic medium—the language—remains, as ever, stubbornly Japanese.

ŌTOMO NO TABITO (665-731), the highest in official rank of the major poets of the period, belonged to a once strong military clan that had lost much of its hereditary power and prestige to the rising Fujiwara clan and its allies. Well-trained in Chinese literature, he wrote poetry and prose in Chinese, some of it preserved in the *Man'yōshū*, and he is famous for his literary pose of elegant sophistication and Taoist-inspired hedonism. Appointed in the late 720s as viceroy of the government headquarters at Dazaifu in northwestern Kyūshū—on its face an honorable appointment but in fact a kind of banishment from court—Tabito gathered about him a circle of literary-minded men with whom he drank wine and composed verse, celebrated such fashionably exotic occasions as the plum blossom feast, and behaved insofar as possible like a Chinese literatus in exile. The most famous, as well as the most "Chinese," of his verses are a set of 13 *tanka* on the pleasures of wine and the superiority of maudlin drunkenness to smug moral rectitude. He also composed on more ordinary subjects: his poems of grief on the death of his wife, for example, are simple, direct declarations of sorrow.

YAMANOUE NO OKURA (660-ca 733) was as "Chinese" in his poetic manner as Tabito but in a very different way. Indeed, the latest theory about him is that he was actually a Korean or a descendant of Korean immigrants. In his early forties he accompanied an embassy of government officials and students to China, where he remained for several years. After his return to Japan, he enjoyed a reputation as a scholar of Chinese, serving as tutor to the crown prince and eventually being appointed governor of the province of Chikuzen (now part of Fukuoka Prefecture) in Kyūshū, where he joined Tabito's literary circle.

Okura is renowned for his Confucian-inspired moral and ethical concerns, and of all Japanese poets is most famous for his didactic poems, his descriptions of the sufferings of the poor and destitute, and other works manifesting a social consciousness of patently Chinese inspiration otherwise scarcely to be found in the *waka* tradition. He also treats such universal themes as grief at the loss of his son and the destructive effects of time as it changes golden girls and boys into ugly, contemptible old wretches. The concern with time, already fundamental in Hitomaro's elegies on ruined capitals or poems of grief, comes from this period to permeate the developing *waka* tradition, becoming in the classical periods the most important theme.

Notwithstanding his Confucian didacticism and concern with the world he lives in, Okura characteristically responds with Buddhist-inspired resignation and acceptance. Passivity and resignation, instead of resistance and revolt, again are attitudes that came to dominate classical poetry. Such attitudes dull the edge of social criticism, diminish the possibilities for tragic conflict, and remove the responsibility for actions from the actors to an overwhelming movement of time and an ineluctable fate. Nevertheless, acceptance and resignation, suited to the tone of lyric melancholy found in the envoys even to Okura's most Confucian poems, give to the *waka* tradition as a whole much of its affective character, as in this envoy to his *chōka* on the death of his little son Furuhi (*Man'yōshū* 905).

Wakakereba	He is so young
Michiyuki shiraji	He will not know the road to take—
Mai wa sen	I will pay your fee,
Shitabe no tsukai	O courier from the realms below,
Oite tōrase	Carry him upon your back!

Apart from the intrinsic interest of his subjects and themes, Okura was an inventive, experimental technician and craftsman, showing a mastery of rhetorical techniques, of the most complex varieties of contiguous and noncontiguous parallelism, and of a logical, quasi-stanzaic structure. The stanzaic quality of his *chōka* is emphasized by syntactic breaks and metrical irregularities which underscore structural divisions. Such prosodic and structural experimentation was scarcely to be repeated after this period; it gives unusual strength and interest to Okura's verse.

YAMABE NO AKAHITO (d ca 736) is known to tradition as the great nature poet of the third *Man'yō* age, outshining his contemporary, KASA NO KANAMURA (fl ca 715-733), to whose pioneering efforts he is said to owe a debt. The *Man'yōshū* contains both *chōka* and *tanka* by Akahito, but it is in the latter that his poetic gift is at its best. His carefully wrought formal structures were esteemed by generations of poets for the beauty of their imagery and their quiet lyricism. They convey a vivid sense of a nature loved, revered, and perceived as wholly beneficent and harmonious with man. Such a tone infuses his second envoy to his famous *chōka* on the imperial lodge in the vale of Yoshino (*Man'yōshū* 925).

Nubatama no	As the jet-black night
Yo no fukeyukeba	Deepens among the birches
Hisagi ouru	On the river banks,
Kiyoki kawara ni	Again and again the plovers call
Chidori shiba naku	Above the pure bed of the stream.

TAKAHASHI NO MUSHIMARO (fl ca 730) is of somewhat lesser importance and is traditionally known for his poems on travel and on local myths and legends. His reputation rests upon a single *chōka* and envoy of indisputable authorship, and some 13 *chōka*, 18 *tanka*, and one *sedōka* indicated in the *Man'yōshū* as from the "Takahashi no Mushimaro Collection." If we assume them to be indeed by him, his verse treatments of such famous legends as the tale of Urashima (a young fisherman who spent what seemed a few fleeting hours with the Dragon King's daughter at the bottom of the sea but returned home to find himself an old man and all his friends and relatives long dead) make him unique among *Man'yō* poets.

Fourth Man'yō period and Yakamochi. The fourth and last *Man'yō* period is dominated by the famous ŌTOMO NO YAKAMOCHI (718?–785), eldest son of Tabito, and his literary circle—members of his family, friends, and intimates. A major poet in his own right, Yakamochi is believed to have been the last in a series of compilers of the *Man'yōshū* and its chief and final editor. It is therefore hardly to be wondered at that the anthology contains more of his poems than of any other person; indeed, his 479 poems (including 46 *chōka*) represent more than one-tenth of the entire collection; and its latest datable poem is one of his written in 759. During his bureaucratic career Yakamochi served as governor or vice-governor of several provinces, as an officer of the Ministry of Military Affairs, and in other capacities which enabled him to indulge his interests in collecting folk and provincial poetry and lore. He was one of the chief collectors of the famous "Songs of the Frontier Guards" (*sakimori no uta*), poems by common soldiers conscripted for military guard duty at Dazaifu and elsewhere in the western provinces facing Korea and China.

Yakamochi's poetry is marked by crucial differences from that of the earlier *Man'yō* periods, differences symptomatic of both the man and his age. Representing consolidation and maturity, Yakamochi and his circle also show signs of attenuation and lassitude, frivolity and inconsequence, along with other characteristics stemming ultimately from the new and increasing influence of Chinese poetry of the Six Dynasties (222–589) period. In general, with Yakamochi and his contemporaries, *waka* became largely private and personal, turning in upon itself in reflection and musing, becoming more introspective and subjective, more intellectual, contrived, and occasionally precious. Much of the poetry of this generation is also mere amorous gallantry of little substance and no depth—although the particular circumstances of Yakamochi's relation to the *Man'yōshū* are no doubt responsible for the preservation of so many of his bantering exchanges with various lady friends and relations.

Much of Yakamochi's lighter, more informal verse dates from his youth and early manhood. His flirtations included his aunt, Lady Ōtomo of Sakanoe (ŌTOMO NO SAKANOE NO IRATSUME; fl ca 728–746), as well as Lady Kasa and Lady Ki. Many of these poems are included in Books 17–20 of the *Man'yōshū*, which constitute, to a large extent, Yakamochi's personal poetic diary. In his middle period, from about 746, when he served first as governor of the province of Etchū (now Toyama Prefecture) and then as an official at Nara, his poetry is increasingly dominated by a tone of sadness, said to reflect his pessimism over the deteriorating fortunes of his clan and his personal reverses. At the same time, much of the verse from his early middle years is innovative, adapting from Chinese example new techniques and modes of subjective posturing and elegant confusion and at the same time quietly beautiful lyric description. It is said that the Chinese Chen (Ch'en) dynasty (557–589) anthology *Yutai xinyong* (*Yü-t'ai hsin-yung*; J: *Gyokudai shin'ei*; New Songs from the Jade Terrace), a collection of primarily Six Dynasties verse compiled by Xu Ling (Hsü Ling; 507–583) was the immediate inspiration for his famous set of poems on the damson trees in his garden, of which the following is one (*Man'yōshū* 4140):

Waga sono no	Lying in my garden,
Sumomo no hana ka	Are those blossoms of the damson tree,

Niwa ni chiru	Or patches of snow
Hadare no imada	Lately fallen in the courtyard,
Nokoritaru kamo	Lingering upon the ground?

The poem's extreme subjectivity, its pose of elegant confusion of the speaker's senses, expresses a new attitude toward man's relation to the external world. Though out of fashion in China, where high Tang (T'ang) culture was at its zenith in the mid-8th century, these styles were studied by Yakamochi and other Japanese literati in older Chinese anthologies which they considered authoritative and were probably tried first in their own poems in Chinese, later in their Japanese, verse. The pose of elegant confusion of Yakamochi in his middle years was passed on to the earliest classical poets, the "Six Poetic Geniuses" (ROKKASEN) and others of the 9th century, and came to dominate the new poetry of wit and courtly elegance which signified to the following age all that was modern and sophisticated.

Yakamochi's weaknesses as well as strengths have a wider significance, being characteristic not merely of the man but of the age. Heir to an established tradition of vernacular poetry, he could study and emulate the achievement of at least two previous generations—the generation of Hitomaro and that of Tabito, Okura, and Akahito. It is evident, particularly in his *chōka*, that he did not hesitate to borrow from these predecessors ideas, structures, techniques, metaphors, and imagery. Indeed, so much did he borrow and so little did he repay that many of his *chōka* can only be described as imitative and derivative: invention and innovation by Hitomaro and Okura received as convention by Yakamochi. Too often Yakamochi falls back upon clichés and stock phrases that seem merely decorative and perfunctory. He is also sometimes strangely uninvolved in his poems, standing back from his materials and observing them with the dispassionate eye of a scientist classifying specimens in the laboratory. Symptomatic of an apparent lack of emotional involvement is his willingness to use solemn forms and public modes for the most inappropriate purposes: his *chōka* on his favorite hunting hawk (*Man'yōshū* 4011–4015, 4154–4155) use a solemn public form for a private, almost trivial purpose, whereas his formal poems on state occasions merely echo, usually at shorter length, the phrases of his great predecessors. At the same time, Yakamochi is technically skilled, capable of a variety of artistic poses; he is the most sophisticated of early literary poets. Among his most moving poems are his *chōka* (*Man'yōshū* 4331–4333, 4398–4400, 4408–4412) sympathizing with or written in the pose of a frontier guard sent for perilous conscript duty in the western provinces.

Anonymous poems. Besides the poems by the some 530 individuals whose names are either mentioned in headnotes or otherwise ascertainable, more than a quarter of the 4,500-odd poems of the early literary period preserved in the *Man'yōshū* are by unknown authors. Much of this anonymous verse deals with immediate, everyday human situations—love, parting, travel, homesickness—and is in the simple mode of direct declaration of feeling. The "poems of the frontier guards" and the "poems of the east" (Azuma uta) have been particularly admired for their folk qualities. The poems of the frontier guards, it is said, convey poignantly the real feelings and genuine sorrows of men forced to leave wife, children, parents, and other loved ones behind to an uncertain future and to go off to an equally uncertain fate in a distant province; but the pathos of these poems is held to be offset by a genuine patriotism and devotion to country, sovereign, and duty. The "poems of the east" contain eastern dialect words, local eastern place names, and other features attesting to their provincial character and have, like the poems of the frontier guards, been esteemed as a lyric cry from the masses.

In fact, many of these and other anonymous poems were revised, prosodically regularized, and otherwise improved and smoothed out by the literary men—Yakamochi, Mushimaro, and others—who collected and wrote them down. It must also be emphasized that by the second quarter of the 8th century the convention of composing "in the manner of" or "on behalf of" another person, real or fictitious, had become well established. Inasmuch as Yakamochi, for example, is known to have composed some of his best and most moving poems in the role of a frontier guard, it may be easily imagined that the practice of assuming different poetic personae was more widespread than is often recognized and accounts for at least some proportion of the anonymous verse in the *Man'yōshū*.

The Early Classical Period (794–1100) —— The date 794 marks a political rather than literary event—the moving of the capital to Heiankyō (now the city of Kyōto)—but it is customary for literary, as well as cultural and political, historians to employ it as marking the beginning of a new era. Actually, it was toward the close of the early literary period, notably in the poetry of Yakamochi and his circle, that profound changes in the styles and modes of *waka* began to be evident. The period of change and the rapid development of new poetic styles lasted somewhat less than a hundred years, from the final completion of the *Man'yōshū* to the mid-9th century. The new styles and modes gave an indelible stamp to the *waka,* which it was to carry for nearly 1,200 years down to modern times; they led to a new poetic age, the period of the *Kokinshū* and the next three imperial anthologies. Taken as a whole, these 300-odd years constitute the early classical period of Japanese poetry.

Traditionally, literary historians have pointed to the period from the end of the *Man'yō* age to the emergence in the mid-9th century of the so-called Six Poetic Geniuses of Japanese classical poetry as a kind of literary "dark ages." Undeniably, it was a period of intense, almost frenzied, cultural borrowing from China, when the whole court seemed to become obsessed with Chinese fashions, costumes, art, music, and, above all, Chinese poetry. During this period, all the men, it was held, did nothing but compose poetry in Chinese, which was recited or sung at elegant banquets where everyone wore Chinese costume and Chinese music and dancing were performed. The *waka,* on the other hand, was relegated to the boudoir, where it managed to survive only because it was an essential means of communication in the elegant ritual of courtly love between gentlemen of fashion and the sequestered ladies in the women's quarters. Though exaggerated, such accounts are partially true. Women were not supposed, at least, to study Chinese or to compose Chinese verse, which was thought much too masculine and intellectually demanding a pursuit for their delicate minds and constitutions. And poetry did indeed probably continue unabated as an important means of social communication not only between the gentlemen of the court and their ladies but between cultivated men in the social give and take of daily life. At the same time, the Chinese vogue was pervasive, as is demonstrated by the fact that four important anthologies of verse in Chinese by Japanese poets were compiled between 750 and 830.

Influence on waka of Six Dynasties poetry. The mannered elegance, wit, subjective posing, intellectual reasoning and pseudologic, and precious conceits of the typical Six Dynasties "vanity-case style," as it was termed by contemptuous Tang critics, were avidly studied and then imitated by the Japanese literati in their own Chinese verse. Chief among Chinese sources was the *Wen xuan (Wen hsüan;* J: *Monzen),* or "Literary Selections," a vast classified anthology of many genres, particularly *fu* and *shi (shih),* covering a thousand years down to the time of its compilation in the first half of the 6th century by Prince Zhao Ming (Chao Ming) of the Liang. The 8th- and 9th-century Japanese courtiers composed verse in Chinese at every conceivable court feast, celebration, musical entertainment, or other ceremonial function. Some of the most beloved examples were set to music and are preserved in such important later Heian collections as the WAKAN RŌEISHŪ (Collection of Chinese and Japanese Poems for Singing), compiled by FUJIWARA NO KINTŌ (966–1041), and *Shinsen rōeishū* (New Collection of Poems for Singing), compiled by FUJIWARA NO MOTOTOSHI (ca 1056–1142?). Having mastered certain of the most important techniques of the new styles in Chinese, the courtiers then began to adapt them to their *waka.* Given the completely different linguistic medium, such an attempt might well have resulted in failure, had it not been that the potential of the highly inflected Japanese language, with its varied tenses, moods, and aspects, was especially suited to the expression of the cause-and-effect logic, witty speculation, and quasi-intellectual reasoning characteristic of the typical Six Dynasties styles. What was expressed by implication, by juxtaposition, or by syntactic means in the Chinese could be expressed overtly by inflectional categories in the Japanese. Unfortunate in many ways as was the historical accident of the profound impact on *waka* of Six Dynasties poetry, it did undeniably suit the capabilities of the Japanese language.

In adapting Chinese verse to the *waka,* the Japanese also made use of native rhetorical techniques not found in the Chinese to convey in uniquely Japanese terms the wit, surprise, and elegant cleverness which came to be regarded as "modern" *(imamekashi),* the epitome of "courtly elegance" *(miyabi).* Thus in the early classical period the techniques par excellence came to be the *kakekotoba,* or pivot word, and the *engo,* or association. Both to transcend the limitations of the *tanka* form—to say most in little—and to provide a distinctively Japanese vehicle for the wit and intellectual ingenuity *à la chinoise* prized as the new, "correct style" *(sama)* for the *waka,*

these techniques were effectively employed by the new generation of *waka* poets of the middle and late 9th century, the Six Poetic Geniuses and their generation.

The Kokinshū. The completion of the *Kokinshū* in 905 was an event of great significance. It indicated both a slowing down of the Chinese vogue and a recognition that Japanese poetry had been modernized and given the necessary stylish elegance to be accorded equality with the Chinese. Ordered by Emperor DAIGO (885–930; r 897–930), a sovereign who, like his father and predecessor on the throne, Emperor UDA (867–931; r 887–897), came to be regarded as a sage-emperor, patron of a golden age of Japanese culture, the *Kokinshū* was the first official imperial anthology of Japanese poetry. It was a concrete testimony not only that the *waka* had once again come into its own as an art worthy of official sponsorship, but that it was also (by analogy with the official status given poetry in China) now regarded as the highest of the arts.

The *Kokinshū, Gosenshū,* and *Shūishū* contain primarily the new poetry of the first century and a half of the early classical period. The *Kokinshū* is by far the most important of these three anthologies, the others being considered as essentially supplements to it. With 1,111, about 1,426, and 1,351 poems respectively, the first of these anthologies is a little less than, the other two a little more than, a quarter the size of the *Man'yōshū.* The poetry of the *Kokinshū* falls into three distinct periods, apart from a small number of older poems.

First Kokinshū period. The first *Kokinshū* age corresponds to the late Nara and early Heian periods. Most of the 450-odd anonymous poems in the anthology date from the earlier part of this period and overlap in time with *Man'yō* poetry of the third and fourth periods; the latter part of the period—the early 9th century—is represented by a half-dozen or so poets, of whom the most prominent are Emperor Heizei (774–824; r 806–809) and the courtier ONO NO TAKAMURA (802–852?). Most of these poems continue the older styles inherited from the early literary period, but there are a few striking exceptions which show the new influences: for example, Heizei's poem treating the autumn leaves on the river Tatsutagawa as a bright brocade that might be torn if stepped upon *(Kokinshū* 283*);* Takamura's poem declaring the scent of the plum blossoms to be a sure sign of their presence, even though the eye may confuse their white beauty with snowflakes (335).

Second Kokinshū period. The second *Kokinshū* period produced in many respects the most interesting and exciting early classical poetry. Known also as the Age of the Six Poetic Geniuses, the period covers approximately 30 years from about 860 to 890. The important poets include five of the Six Poetic Geniuses—ARIWARA NO NARIHIRA (825–880), the bishop HENJŌ (816–890), Lady ONO NO KOMACHI (fl mid-9th century), Fun'ya no Yasuhide (fl ca 860–880), and Henjō's son, the priest SOSEI (fl ca 859–923). To these should be added one or two more prominent individuals such as Ariwara no Yukihira (818–893). Of the poets of this second *Kokinshū* period, two especially, Narihira and Komachi, stand out. Narihira was said to be a handsome ladies' man and was long thought to be the lover-hero of the early *uta monogatari,* or collection of lyrical tales, ISE MONOGATARI (Tales of Ise), which indeed contains many of his poems. Like the other Poetic Geniuses, he is so called simply because KI NO TSURAYUKI mentions him by name in his famous Japanese preface to the *Kokinshū,* where he criticizes him for having an excess of feeling which his language is inadequate to express. No doubt Tsurayuki had in mind such examples as the following, Narihira's most famous poem, whose subjective view of the external world is shaped by an experience of ill-fated love *(Kokinshū* 747):

Tsuki ya aranu	Moon, are you not the same?
Haru ya mukashi no	Spring, can it be that you are not
Haru naranu	The spring of old,
Waga mi hitotsu wa	And I myself the only thing
Moto no mi ni shite	Remaining as it used to be?

The simple paraphrasable meaning of this poem has been a subject of critical debate over the centuries; still today half a dozen standard Japanese commentaries will yield as many different interpretations. With Narihira, indeed, the subjectivity of Six Dynasties verse is carried to such a pitch that on occasion the reader comes close to being excluded from the experience. Not so with Komachi: her poems have a passionate intensity equal to or even greater than Narihira's; yet, although her poetic texture is of a richness hardly matched by any other poet, her verse is never obscure. Tsurayuki's criticism of Komachi, that her verse is moving but lacks strength, like an elegant lady suffering from an indisposition, is not easy to reconcile with the reality of her poetry, as in the following famous example, in which the speaker's intense desire is conveyed by a series of pivot words and associations (*Kokinshū* 1030):

Hito ni awan	On such a night,
Tsuki no naki ni wa	When no moon gives us the chance to meet,
Omoiokite	I wake, my passion blazing,
Mune hashiribi ni	In my breast an uncontrollable fire
Kokoro yake ori	That utterly consumes my heart.

So intense is the feeling expressed, so uninhibited the rhetoric, that Tsurayuki and his fellow editors actually consigned this famous poem to the limbo of *haikai*, "unconventional verse," a category first found in this anthology and reserved for poems which were deemed excessive, even comical in effect and therefore not suitable for inclusion under more formal rubrics. Whether or not one agrees with the compilers about this particular poem, Komachi provides the prototype of an important poetic persona that was assumed by a series of major women poets throughout the classical periods: the passionate woman. For although it was always felt that poems by women ought ordinarily to have a feminine delicacy and restraint, when the subject was love, the frustrated passions and bitter resentment of neglected or rejected women were sometimes given vent in strikingly intense, even erotic, verse.

Third Kokinshū period. To the third *Kokinshū* period—the generation of the compilers, from about 885 to 905—belong the great bulk of the poems in the anthology. This is the period of consolidation and refinement of the subjective probing, self-conscious posing, and the like, which mark the *Kokinshū* style. By contrast with the poetry of the Six Poetic Geniuses, the verse of Tsurayuki and his fellow compilers of the *Kokinshū*—KI NO TOMONORI (fl ca 900), ŌSHIKŌCHI NO MITSUNE (fl ca 900), MIBU NO TADAMINE (fl ca 910)—is smoother, more restrained, more mellifluous; their diction and imagery more refined, more elegantly chaste; their emotion less passionate and intense. These men, all courtiers of middling or lower middling rank, and in this respect like Hitomaro, Okura, Akahito, or Yakamochi of the early literary period, are represented by more poems in the anthology than anyone else. Thus, Tsurayuki has 102 poems; Mitsune, 60; Tomonori, 46; Tadamine, 35. To these major poets among the some 122 named individuals of this period represented in the collection should be added the priest Sosei with his 32 poems, and Lady ISE (ca 877–940; a noted poet of the passionate style) with 22.

Poetics. Tsurayuki's Japanese preface to the *Kokinshū* is the first extant example of a distinctively Japanese poetics written in the vernacular language. Earlier tentative, only partially successful attempts to forge an aesthetic for *waka* by forcing it into a Chinese mold—the *Kakyō hyōshiki* (772) of Fujiwara no Hamanari (711–790) is the oldest and most important example—for the most part succeeded only in creating a host of difficulties for generations of later poets confronted with their lists of "poetic ills" (*kabyō, uta no yamai*) and things to be avoided. Most of the distinctions these earlier critics tried to make were essentially meaningless for the Japanese language and its poetry, and there is comfort in the thought that for the most part they were ignored. In his turn, Tsurayuki bases his poetics essentially upon Chinese sources: he borrows, for example, verse classifications ("principles" or "genres") and a concept of poetry's function as political and social criticism from the Chinese classic *Shi jing (Shih ching)*, or Book of Odes, especially its "Great Preface." At the same time, his famous opening sentence, "The poetry of Japan has its roots in the human heart and flourishes in the countless leaves of words," with its running metaphor of poetry as growing spontaneously like a tree from the irrepressible feelings of men, stresses the lyrical nature of the native genius and expresses the fundamental Japanese aesthetic in terms that were never challenged.

Another important contemporary work is Mibu no Tadamine's *Wakatei jisshu*, or "Ten Styles of *Waka*." In this brief treatise, Tadamine names each of 10 poetic styles, adds a few explanatory or cautionary remarks in Chinese, and then gives four or five illustrative Japanese poems. His work has the virtue of being founded much more directly upon the realities of Japanese poetic practice than its predecessors, and it has considerable historical importance as the first of a long line of Japanese poetic treatises distinguishing 10—or 18, or 30—styles, nine levels of excellence, and the like.

Poetry contests. The artistic self-consciousness of the early classical poets was further developed and refined by the poetry contest (UTA-AWASE), a custom derived from elegant parties at which the relative merits of such things as flowers, paintings, and other objects were disputed. The various entries were accompanied by poems proclaiming their superiority, and gradually the poems replaced the objects as the focus of interest, while more specifically poetic topics such as love were introduced. As the practice was developed and elaborated, the decorum of a particular contest became more or less formal, depending upon the place, the sponsor, and the occasion, but by the mid-9th century most contests had 10 or more participants divided into two sides, right and left, who pitted their poems against each other in a series of rounds consisting of one poem from each side, with the side winning the most rounds being the victor. The oldest poetry contest for which a written record survives in Japan is the so-called "Poetry Contest at the Residence of the Minister of Public Affairs," sponsored by Ariwara no Yukihira sometime between 884 and 887. For the next five centuries the poetry contests afforded one of the most important contexts in which accomplished poets might perform; as such they provided important material for the compilers of imperial anthologies. Indeed, headnotes to poems indicate that some half-dozen *uta-awase* texts were used as sources by the compilers of the *Kokinshū*. And although there are no indications that in the oldest *uta-awase* any formal decisions were made as to the winning poem in each round, as time went on, judges came to be appointed; the poetic topics (*dai*) on which poems were to be composed were sometimes assigned to the participants days, weeks, or even months ahead of time; and in general what began in the 9th century as a pleasant diversion had become by the 13th an occasion of the utmost seriousness and importance.

In his *Kokinshū* preface, Tsurayuki distinguishes between *kokoro*—spirit, feeling, or conception of a poem—and *kotoba*, the materials or diction. These terms became fundamental in Japanese poetic criticism of the early classical period, along with such other concepts as *sugata*, "total effect" or "shape," and (carrying Tsurayuki's nature metaphors further) the "blossoms" (*hana*) and "fruit" (*mi*) of poetic style. The ideal was harmony and balance between *kokoro* and *kotoba*, between the blossoms of technique, rhetoric, elegance and purity of diction, and surface effect, and the fruit of personalism, originality, sincerity, and a conviction of truth. Such principles were gradually applied in the decisions and critical pronouncements of the *uta-awase* judges; the decisions and comments came to be written down and carefully preserved, accumulating as a valuable store of critical precedent to be regarded—depending on the judge—as either a means of justifying new styles or of protecting the status quo.

As the poetry contests show, although by the early classical period virtually all poetry expressed in one form or another a private lyricism, the actual occasions for poetry were at the same time nearly all social in nature. Different social occasions required a different decorum for the verses deemed appropriate to them; these ranged from the strictly correct, auspicious, quasi-ritualistic lines proper to a New Year's celebration at court to the informal, private lines sent in a letter or message to a friend or lover or recited impromptu through the curtains of the women's quarters. Thus, although the distinction between public and private poetry, still very much a literary fact in the age of Hitomaro, practically disappeared in the early classical period, the formal-informal distinction became crucial in its place. Levels of formality helped create a consciousness of appropriate styles for different occasions: poetry contests, for example, though in one sense calling for the poet's most original and ingenious efforts, continued on the whole to preserve a strict decorum: each participant had to be certain that his verses suffered from none of the arcane "poetic ills" that might permit a watchful opponent to demand its disqualification on technical grounds. Such strict decorum made experimentation risky and innovation difficult, and it is hardly surprising that in the generations following the *Kokinshū* the general trend was in the direction of yet further refinement, conventionalism, and mannerism. The claims of the heart—the primacy of *kokoro* over *kotoba*—were to a certain extent maintained by the women poets, who carried on the tradition of the passionate woman from Komachi and Ise down to IZUMI SHIKIBU (fl ca 1000), Sagami (fl ca 1050), MURASAKI SHIKIBU (fl ca 1000), and others in the late 10th century and first half of the 11th. It should be remembered that this was the golden age of the woman writer in Japan—the time when Lady Murasaki was writing her great *Tale of Genji*, Lady SEI SHŌNAGON her inimitable *Pillow Book*, Lady Izumi her confessional verse-diary, and so on.

Influence of Bo Juyi (Po Chü-i) and Tang poetry. Along with the steady accumulation of tradition, example, and poetic precedent, by the late 10th century certain courtiers began to assume a special status as authorities and experts on poetry. Such a man was Fujiwara no Kintō (966–1041), a man of accomplishment in several arts, the dominant critic of his age, and compiler of the third imperial anthology, *Shūishū*. In most respects, Kintō was conservative, preferring the blossoms to the fruit, and carrying on the traditions and conventions of the *Kokin* styles of wit, ingenuity, and technical virtuosity. But in spite of the homogeneity, Kintō and his contemporaries were beginning gradually, grudgingly to respond to new classical models in the form of Chinese poetry of the Tang dynasty, particularly that of the famous Bo Juyi (called in Japanese Haku Rakuten; 772–846). Virtually the only Chinese poet whose works were introduced into Japan during his own lifetime, Bo had been known to the Japanese since the 9th century, and because he enjoyed such a vogue in China at that time, it was assumed that he had to be a great poet and his poetry worthy of emulation. However, Bo wrote in many styles, including the elegant, lapidary manner of the Six Dynasties, although he was particularly esteemed by the Chinese for his simple, intelligible, more descriptive poetry, whose plainness stands in striking contrast to the ornate conceits and paradoxes of the older styles. Bo's collected works (known in Japanese as *Haku-shi monjū*) were imported into Japan at an early date, but such was the hold the Six Dynasties intellectual styles had upon the Japanese that for nearly two centuries their admiration for Bo's plainer manner could not extend to emulation. Thus, although the *Wakan rōei-shū*, the influential collection of Chinese couplets and Japanese *waka* for singing made by Kintō, contains more verses by Bo Juyi than by any other Chinese poet, the Japanese poems in the collection are in the high *Kokinshū* or "Fujiwara" style.

At the same time, certain changes in the *waka* of Kintō's age may be interpreted as reflecting an effort to adjust to the newer models. Thus, the tendency in Kintō's critical preferences and personal poetic style toward an ever greater smoothness of texture and blandness of conventional expression may be taken as a kind of adjustment, albeit an unsatisfactory one, to Bo's simple intelligibility. Smoothly, even ritualistically conventional, the verse of Kintō and most of his contemporaries seems to affirm the status quo, to bolster symbolically the comfortable, self-confident belief in the stability of the Fujiwara and of their famous leader, FUJIWARA NO MICHINAGA (966–1028). But more striking changes were beginning to take place beneath the bland homogeneity of the *Shūishū* age. Certain of these changes are exemplified in the idiosyncratically experimental verse of SONE NO YOSHITADA (fl ca 985). A minor court official and unrepentant persona non grata, Yoshitada scandalized his conservative contemporaries with the unconventional diction of his poems, his tendency to use "rude," colloquial expressions and unconventional imagery. To a certain extent, Yoshitada's diction may have represented an effort to create a Japanese counterpart to Bo Juyi's plainer style, and in part it may have expressed, for him at least, a renewed interest in the by-now archaic, difficult, and to contemporary sensibilities, crude, rough, and inelegant language of the *Man'yōshū*. Yoshitada got no thanks for his pains—he was hooted out of court, so to speak—but a century or so later, the court poets had gradually begun to adapt themselves and their poetry to the descriptive mode and the innovative experimentation of Yoshitada.

Reemergence of descriptive poetry. By the time of the fourth imperial anthology, the *Go shūishū* (Go shūi wakashū; Later Collection of Gleanings), completed in 1086, new styles at last began to find their way into official compilations, for although in terms of the number of their poems chosen, FUJIWARA NO MICHITOSHI (1047–1099), compiler of the *Goshūishū*, gives preference to poets of earlier times, still, important innovating and contemporary poets are also represented, if sparsely: the priest NŌIN (b 988), MINAMOTO NO TSUNENOBU (1016–1097), ŌE NO MASAFUSA (1041–1111). Of these three poets, Tsunenobu and Nōin are of particular importance.

In the mid-classical period, Tsunenobu was looked up to as one of the great innovators for his revival of descriptive poetry and for bringing back to life certain simpler styles that had been buried for three centuries in a neglected *Man'yōshū*. Characterized by the great critic FUJIWARA NO TOSHINARI (Fujiwara no Shunzei; 1114–1204) as "a man who preferred a lofty style and the effect of older poetry," Tsunenobu anticipates the later descriptive poetry of lyric melancholy *(sabi)* in such a poem as this (*Kin'yōshū* 183), "Composed on 'The Autumn Wind at a House in the Rice Fields' when he and others went to visit Morokata's villa at Umezu":

Yū sareba	As evening falls,
Kadota no inaba	From across the fields of grain
Otozurete	Beyond the gate,
Ashi no maroya ni	The autumn wind comes rustling
Akikaze zo fuku	In its visit to the reed-thatched hut.

Nōin was the prototype of the itinerant priest-poet who finds inspiration and solace in nature, the spiritual forebear of the later and more famous SAIGYŌ (1118–90). His most famous poem illustrates a growing desire to move away from the ornate, rhetorically complex, and artificial Fujiwara style to a simpler, more honest poetry. Ostensibly, the poem was "Composed at the Barrier of Shirakawa on a journey to the Michinoku region."

Miyako oba	From the capital
Kasumi to tomo ni	I set forth with the rising haze
Tachishikado	Of springtime,
Akikaze zo fuku	But now the wind of autumn blows
Shirakawa no Seki	At the Barrier of Shirakawa.

Actually, Nōin is said to have composed the poem in Kyōto, but wishing it to be accepted as the product of "real feelings" on a "real journey," he secluded himself, gave out the story that he had gone off on a long trip to Michinoku, emerged after a suitable time, and triumphantly produced his poem. To the modern Westerner, the concern with "real circumstances" may seem excessive, but autobiographical "truth" and "sincerity" held a strong attraction in the context of a *waka* tradition that had become increasingly formal and fictitious. In fact, more and more poems in Nōin's time were *daiei*, "compositions on topics"—verses written at home or at poetry contests on prescribed topics. Such topics might, of course, permit a simple, descriptive mode of treatment, but at the end of the early classical period, poets faced the difficult problem of transcending the limitations of a poetic medium which seemed to allow less and less room for the vital personal element, the life blood of lyrical conviction. Gradually, building upon the experiments in descriptive poetry of Nōin, Tsunenobu, and others, the poets of the mid-classical period forged a new poetry and a new poetics that succeeded in restoring the crucial balance between *kokoro* and *kotoba*.

The Mid-Classical Period (1100–1250)——The century and a half from about 1100 to 1250 was a period of profound changes in *waka* and in the aesthetic attitudes and artistic commitment of the courtier-poets who carried on the tradition. The first hundred years or so of the period were marked by literary controversy, as conservative and innovating poetic factions, and later, rival poetic dynasties or schools, competed for official recognition, for imperial commissions to compile the periodic anthologies, and for appointments as participants and judges at the increasingly frequent *uta-awase*. By the year 1100, some three and one-half centuries had passed since the *Man'yōshū*, two centuries since the bulk of the poetry in the *Kokinshū* had been written. The growth of tradition meant the accumulation of a large body of knowledge, the development of many precedents, a progressive hardening of conventions. To be an accomplished poet in such an age meant for the seriously committed to be a scholar as well; even amateurs and dilettantes were expected to have a detailed knowledge of at least the Sandaishū (the *Kokinshū, Gosenshū* and *Shūishū*), and of numerous other classical works of Heian literature: collections of lyrical tales, a handful of the most important romances, numerous "unofficial" anthologies and individual collections of the poets. Tradition has it that the first example of a Japanese poet actually placing himself under the tutelage of a teacher, as Buddhist novice monks were put under the rule of a learned older priest, was the case of Nōin, who is said to have become a student-disciple *(deshi)* of the important conservative poet Fujiwara no Nagatō (fl ca 980) in the early 11th century. During the 12th and 13th centuries the practice became standard, especially for those most important poets, the courtiers of middling or lesser noble standing who saw in poetry a way to gain fame, honor, promotion, and a measure of worldly security in a society dominated by a single clan—a society in which ranks, offices, emoluments, and status were passed from one generation to the next according to virtually immutable hereditary principles.

In contrast to the early classical period, with its wit, reasoning, elegant posturings, ingenious conceits and paradoxes, the mid-classical was an age in which poets sought in the new mode of descriptive poetry to achieve depth and resonance, tonal complexity, and an atmosphere of exquisite beauty conveyed by romantic overtones, associations, and symbols. The prevailing sadness of tone of the new poetry was shaped and colored by a Buddhist-inspired fatalism, and, specifically, the doctrine of *masse* or *mappō*—a view of the present as a last age of human and institutional degeneration preceding the emergence of a new Buddha and the beginning of a new cycle. The 12th and 13th centuries in Japan were thought to coincide with such an age—a view borne out by contemporary events such as the civil wars at the end of the 12th century, worldliness and venality among the Buddhist priesthood, famines, floods, and other natural disasters. These events gave poignancy to the prevailing view of life as *mujō*, "impermanence." And in terms of literary influences, the fact that much late Tang Chinese poetry is characterized by a similar outlook no doubt gave to this classical model a special relevance to Japanese experience in this period.

Descriptive symbolism. With the growth of criticism and the development of terms expressive of the new ideals, such words as *aware* (pathos, wistful sadness, sad beauty) and SABI (loneliness) came to designate poetic tones and emotional and physical states considered desirable, to be sought out and cultivated. The ideal of *sabi* is especially identified with the great mid-classical poet SAIGYŌ. Saigyō presents with strong lyrical conviction the persona of a solitary itinerant priest wandering over fields and mountains, feeling himself, despite the harsh Buddhist commands against attachment to any person or thing, inevitably drawn to the beauty of nature, whether the fragile loveliness of cherry blossoms or the grays and blacks of a melancholy landscape at autumn dusk, as in this famous poem (*Shin kokinshū* 362):

Kokoro naki	While denying my heart,
Mi ni mo aware wa	Even I cannot but feel
Shirarekeri	This sad beauty:
Shigi tatsu sawa no	A longbill rising up in flight
Aki no yūgure	From a marsh at autumn dusk.

Sadness, loneliness, isolation, the pose of an exile, recluse or a homeless wanderer—the tone of such verse was felt to be most ideally conveyed by imagery of a drab, sere, monochromatic kind, like the ink-wash paintings of the Chinese artists. And the season of the year felt to be inherently most conducive to the mood of *sabi* was autumn, especially at the close of day. By the middle of the 12th century, such phrases as *aki no yūgure*, "autumn dusk," had come through poetic association to become symbols of emotional states, so that their use in a poem enabled the poet to evoke the atmosphere of *sabi* through description alone, without necessarily requiring the presence of a speaker in the poem declaring in so many words, "How lonely I am."

The evocative poetry of descriptive symbolism was, so to speak, the end product of a century or more, and many of its finest examples are to be found in the crowning artistic achievement of the age, the great eighth imperial anthology, SHIN KOKINSHŪ (New Collection of Ancient and Modern Times). In the first half of the 12th century, however, the literary scene was far from harmonious or settled into a new dominant style. The continuing disputes between exponents of the old and new are typified by the opposition between the arch-conservative FUJIWARA NO MOTOTOSHI (ca 1056–1142?) and the innovator MINAMOTO NO TOSHIYORI, (Minamoto no Shunrai; 1055?–1129). Stubborn and often wrong, Mototoshi insisted on the established precedent in everything, down to the most minute detail of diction or poetic treatment. His obsessive clinging to tradition and the Fujiwara style represented a common, if somewhat exaggerated, conservative interpretation of the principle of *hon'i*, the "essential nature" of a thing, the "correct handling" of a poetic topic, or the "proper attitude" for a poet to express. To Mototoshi, all of these things were decreed by tradition; the poet was permitted only the narrowest range of originality in expressing time-worn poetic clichés in ever so slightly new combinations. Shunrai, on the other hand, although like all innovating poets capable of the most conservative of poems when occasion demanded, practiced two contrasting innovative styles: in the one, he followed the example of the eccentric Sone no Yoshitada, using unprecedented, colloquial and vulgar or archaic diction in startling ways, carrying reasoning, ingenuity, and other intellectual characteristics of the Fujiwara style to extremes of eccentricity. In his other style, for which he was most admired by later poets, Shunrai carried on the descriptive tradition begun by his father, Tsunenobu, composing a number of celebrated poems which represent an important stage in the development of the fully realized descriptive-symbolist styles of the *Shin kokinshū*.

The struggle between conservatives and innovators. The opposition between Mototoshi and Shunrai was carried on openly in the arena of the poetry contest, which continued through the period to be the most important stage for the struggle between conservative and innovating factions. In the latter half of the 12th century, the conservatives were chiefly represented by the venerable Rokujō family—Akisuke, Kiyosuke, Kenshō, Suetsune, Tomoie, and others—a poetic dynasty that lasted from the late 11th century to the end of the 14th. They were opposed and bested by the Mikohidari (or Mikosa) family, a remarkable line of gifted innovating poets whose descendants eventually came to dominate *waka* from the age of the *Shin kokinshū* through the late classical and post-classical periods, and down to modern times.

Allying themselves with one or another august personage, and sometimes supported by the same patron either simultaneously or successively, the Rokujō–Mikohidari forces gathered supporters, disciples, and partisans from the most gifted poets of the age. Among the great patrons were Fujiwara no Kanezane (KUJŌ KANEZANE; 1149–1207); his son Go-Kyōgoku Yoshitsune (FUJIWARA NO YOSHITSUNE; 1169–1206); and the supreme patron of the age, the former emperor GO-TOBA (1180–1239; r 1183–98). Holding themselves above the rivalries of the professional poets—the officials or bureaucrats of middling rank, priests, and court ladies—the patrons retained the traditional aristocratic attitude toward poetry; in this view, poetry was, like music, calligraphy, and even learning, an art to know something about, but certainly not a vocation, not a quasi-religious calling that might dominate one's entire life.

The achievement of harmony and balance. In the age of the greatest Mikohidari poets, Fujiwara no Shunzei (Fujiwara no Toshinari; 1114–1204), and his son Fujiwara no Teika (FUJIWARA NO SADAIE; 1162–1241), the personal rivalries and poetic differences between the Rokujō and the Mikohidari were fought out in a series of important poetry contests in which the poetically more gifted Mikohidari were consistently on the winning side. The Rokujō partisans had a deserved reputation as scholars, learned authorities on poetic precedent and lore, and even experts on the obscurities of the *Man'yōshū*; the Mikohidari, comparative newcomers, were better poets than scholars and less tightly bound by tradition. The claims of convention and invention were brought into balance by the genial, kindly, but persistent and indomitable Shunzei. A serious student of meditative Buddhism, particularly the *shikan*, or "concentration and insight," a discipline of meditation practiced in the Tendai sect, Shunzei adapted to the practice of *waka* several of the most important mystical attitudes and meditative disciplines of esoteric Buddhism. To Shunzei—and his contemporaries among the lesser nobility—poetry had become a high calling, a *michi* or "way of life," requiring commitment equal to that of a priest for his sacred calling, and just as surely as religion a means to ultimate enlightenment and truth. This attitude of secular mysticism helped Shunzei and his followers to transcend the uncertainties and vicissitudes of an unstable age, while at the same time demanding of them the utmost in effort, concentration, and identification with the poetic materials, often represented by the topic, or *dai*. By concentration on the "essential nature," the *hon'i* of the experience, Shunzei and his followers sought to express through richly evocative descriptive poetry that which was quintessentially true in nature or human life. The poet must enter into the experience, achieve identification with it, and express it in a new way, achieving a poetic integrity and conviction of truth that restored the vital balance between the impersonalism of tradition and the personalism of the individual poetic vision.

"Old words, new treatment." In the course of his very long life of 90 years, Shunzei came to occupy a unique position of the highest honor and prestige as the "grand old man" of poetry. During this period he continued to advocate—modestly, politely, but steadily and unremittingly—certain crucial prescriptive and aesthetic ideals. Having a profound reverence for tradition, he based his poetry and his poetics squarely upon the classical heritage of the Sandaishū, which he saw as the source and inspiration for every new departure. The prescriptive ideal he developed was expressed in his famous phrase "old words, new treatment" (*kotoba furuku, kokoro atarashi*), that is, a serious elevated poetry couched in the purest classical language, but presenting a new poetic conception as a result of profound meditation and rigorous discipline. To Shunzei—and even more to Teika, who inherited his father's principles, modifying them in significant ways—an ideal means to achieve harmony between the old and the new was the use of poetic allusion. An increasingly popular practice, allusion to older poetry, was employed to give depth, romantic atmosphere, and tonal complexity to the new composition. An essential requirement was that the older poem be taken from the Sandaishū or similar canonical works, including such prose

classics as the *Tale of Genji*, and it must be easily identifiable, so that the montage effect was unmistakable. The technique was called *honkadori*, allusive variation, or "using a foundation poem," and it was especially advocated by Teika and his poetic circle in the late 12th and early 13th centuries. Allusive variation also conveyed the central thematic concerns of the age, particularly the passage of time, *mujō*, and the sad pathos of fragile beauty.

Aesthetic ideals. Closely related to Shunzei's neoclassical ideal of "old words, new treatment" was his preference for poetic effects of moving beauty *(aware)*, romantic evocativeness *(en)*, and especially of "mystery and depth" *(yūgen)*. These and other elements might be combined in a single poem, and the effects of *en* and *yūgen* were particularly well conveyed by allusion. A poem ("On Autumn") Shunzei is said to have liked best of all his own compositions may serve as an example of both the effect of *yūgen* and the technique of *honkadori (Senzaishū 258)*:

Yū sareba	As evening falls,
Nobe no akikaze	From along the moors the autumn wind
Mi ni shimite	Penetrates the heart,
Uzura naku nari	And the quail raise their cry
Fukakusa no sato	In the deep grass of Fukakusa.

The desolate scene at dusk (the *uta makura* or poetic place name Fukakusa means "deep grass") expresses the essential nature of autumn as a symbol of loneliness which can be felt by any reader. However, Shunzei has given this poem depth, romance, and an atmosphere of mystery by making it an allusive variation upon a famous poetic exchange recorded with a few lines of narrative in the famous collection of lyrical tales, ISE MONOGATARI (episode 123), and in the *Kokinshū* (971–972). The lover (perhaps the famous poet Narihira), having lost interest in the lady and on the verge of leaving her, recites this poem.

Toshi o hete	When I have gone
Sumikoshi sato o	From this village of Fukakusa
Idete inaba	After all these years,
Itodo Fukakusa	Will its deep grass grow ever taller
No to ya narinan	And it become a tangled moor?

The lady replies:

No to naraba	If it become a moor,
Uzura to nakite	Then like the quail I will raise my cry
Toshi wa hen	Through the long years,
Kari ni dani ya wa	For will you not return for one brief hour
Kimi wa kozaran	To cut the grass and hunt for me?

According to the story in *Ise monogatari*, the lady's poem so moved her lover that he changed his mind and stayed with her (at least for the time being). However, there are several mysterious things about the situation. It is not known who the man really was, or the lady, or how the affair ultimately turned out—although the sad ending to every love affair conventional in Japanese courtly love offers a clue. The romantic circumstances of the old poems and their story are shrouded in mystery, and the mystery is deepened by the passage of time. Shunzei's contemporaries would have recognized the story as from an old romance of nearly three centuries before, but obviously, whatever the outcome in the brief human span, time has had the victory: now both lover and lady are gone, and only the deep grass, the plaintive cries of the quail, and the melancholy autumn wind are left. The poem is on autumn to be sure, but on autumn as a symbol of the passing of time, of love, of youth and beauty, and even, perhaps, of the greatness of the courtly past. Shunzei uses key words and phrases from both older poems—just enough to evoke them in the minds of his audience, superimposing them upon his scene of desolation. Now the autumn wind is all that visits the melancholy place: it is a complex symbol of the grievous passage of time, for the suffering and loss, and an ironic metaphor for the departed lover. Not least, Shunzei's language is pure, his cadences lovely, with the caesura at the end of the third line and the poem terminating, like so many of the poems of the age, in a substantive *(taigendome)*. To an ideal extent the poem fulfills the requirements of "old words, new treatment."

The Age of the Shin Kokinshū——The generation after Shunzei was dominated by the personality and tastes of the former emperor Go-Toba, the greatest patron of the day, and by Teika, chosen by Shunzei to succeed to the Mikohidari poetic heritage. Short-

tempered, impatient, morose, and having withal a marked tendency to self-pity—in short, the complete opposite of his father—Teika appeared to others as a cold, forbidding, difficult man. In his dedication to the art of poetry, however, he was fully his father's son. After a long period of disappointments and reverses—his progress was blocked at every point by die-hard remnants of the Rokujō forces and his abrasive personality was not an asset—Teika was at last favorably noticed by Go-Toba, who in 1201 appointed him one of a committee of six compilers of the *Shin kokinshū*, the "New Kokinshū," whose very title announced the former sovereign's intention to restore to his own age the cultural and literary brilliance of Emperor Daigo's court, when the first great imperial anthology had been compiled.

Teika's styles. As scion of his house, Teika attracted the most gifted and interesting poets of the age, and although as time went on he became increasingly restrained and conservative, in his younger years he was quite daringly experimental, choosing among other models some of the more baroque exercises in wit and ingenuity of the eccentric Shunrai. But Teika, instead of deliberately using vulgar, colloquial, or unprecedented diction, followed his father's prescription of "old words, new treatment," trying in the "new treatment" such unprecedented—and to his critics allegedly incomprehensible—techniques as startling reversals of diction, transference of images, synesthesia, far-fetched word-play, and the like. The chief effect he sought was called *yōen*, "ethereal charm." It was related to *yūgen* but was more magical, more delicate, more romantically other-worldly, "like a celestial maiden descending to earth on a hazy moonlit night in spring." Allusion was central to creating the tonal depth and romantic atmosphere that distinguishes such a poem as the following (*Shin kokinshū* 38):

Haru no yo no	The bridge of dreams
Yume no ukihashi	Floating on the brief spring night
Todae shite	Is broken off:
Mine ni wakaruru	From the peak a wreath of cloud
Yokogumo no sora	Takes leave into the open sky.

Ostensibly on spring, the poem has romantic overtones of love conveyed in part by the personification of the cloud as a lover leaving his mistress at dawn. Tradition also had invested the words "dream" and "spring night" with romantic associations of lovers' visits or dreams of love cut off all too soon by the proverbial brevity of a night in spring. At the same time, the atmosphere of "ethereal charm" is in no small part conveyed by the second line, which literally means "floating bridge of dreams." The phrase is the title of the last chapter of the *Tale of Genji*—a chapter full of sadness, uncertainty, and the pathos of people and events at cross-purposes, cut off from each other by misunderstanding and suspicion. By alluding to the chapter title in his poem, Teika evokes the romantic associations of the ill-starred triangular relationship between the young men Niou and Kaoru and the lady Ukifune; their relationship is evoked by the scene at dawn before the speaker's eyes as he (or she) awakes too soon from a dream of love, and the whole complex experience is a symbol of the essential nature *(hon'i)* of spring: beautiful, erotic, delicate, fleeting, ineffably pathetic and sad.

In his middle years, Teika moved away from his aesthetic of *yōen* to an ideal of lyrical conviction or conviction of feeling (*ushin* or *kokoro ari*). Both an essential ingredient of every other style and a separate style by itself (in which case it often meant "intense feeling"), *ushin* was primarily an effect of lyrical commitment and sincerity, an integrity of tone. Largely an attempt to deal with the continuing problem of personal invention and "sincerity" in a tradition even more conventional and circumscribed, Teika's idea of *ushin* brought him in his later years to favor simpler styles: direct declaration, a toning down of word play and other elegant rhetoric, less complexity of tone, as in this poem on "Snow," composed when he was 70 years old (*Shūi gusō* 1425).

Oiraku wa	To be old—
Yuki no uchi ni zo	Now amid the winter snow
Omoishiru	I understand:
Tou hito mo nashi	No one comes to visit me,
Yuku kata mo nashi	There is no place to go.

In 1232–35 Teika compiled the ninth imperial anthology, *Shin chokusenshū* (New Imperial Collection), which contains verse on the whole of a more plain, less highly wrought kind than the characteristic styles of the Age of the *Shin kokinshū*. The preponderance of simpler styles no doubt reflects Teika's late preferences and his continuing commitment to the ideal of conviction of feeling. He may also have been influenced by new Chinese models, some of the more matter-of-fact narrative and descriptive styles of the Song dynasty. The stark simplicity in such a poem as Teika's on snow and old age had important implications for the new characteristic styles of the next and last classical age of *waka*, the late classical period.

Other poets. Among the outstanding poets of the two generations of Shunzei and Teika should be mentioned the priest Saigyō, whose 94 poems in the *Shin kokinshū* are the most for any single individual; Archbishop JIEN (1155–1225); FUJIWARA NO YOSHITSUNE (Go-Kyōgoku Yoshitsune; 1169–1206); Princess SHIKISHI (or Shokushi; d 1201); FUJIWARA NO IETAKA (1158–1237); the priest Jakuren (ca 1139–1202); and "Shunzei's Daughter" (FUJIWARA NO TOSHINARI NO MUSUME; ca 1171–1254).

Principles of association and progression. The *Shin kokinshū* is discussed in a separate article. The point to be stressed here is that the individual poems in the anthology are arranged into subgroups, groups, and larger wholes by complex principles of association and progression from poem to poem and from subject to subject. The larger principle is progression, especially evident in the books of poems on nature and human affairs, such as love, that undergo change and development through time. Thus, the nature poems are grouped into books following the progression of the seasons from earliest spring to the last day of winter, and within the seasonal books, poems follow the progression of flowers, birds, court festivals, and observances in their appointed time. The love poems are grouped according to the conventional stages of Japanese courtly love: the lover's first declaration of his passion, the lady's initial rejection of his suit, persistent wooing, surrender, infrequent clandestine meetings and sad partings as the lover must escape unobserved at dawn, increasingly frequent derelictions as the lover begins to lose interest, the lady's anxious nightly vigil as she vainly awaits him, her increasing misery, bitterness, and despair. Originally having nothing to do with each other, the separate poems were so selected and organized by the editors as to provide subprogressions as well—whether in terms of a set of older poems alternating with newer ones, say, or progressions of movement in a series of place names in successive poems as a leitmotiv carrying the reader from one place to another through an unfolding landscape. A concomitant important principle of arrangement involved the judicious placement of "design poems"—poems with strikingly beautiful imagery, ingenious rhetoric, and the like, against a background of more bland, conventional "background" poems. The *ji-mon*, or "design-background" alternation controls the tensions of the developing sequence, providing highs and lows to sustain interest and carry the reader along in a highly naturalistic manner suggestive of the peaks and valleys of normal human experience. The total cumulative effect of these techniques is to integrate the nearly 2,000 poems of the *Shin kokinshū* into a harmonious whole as a unit that might be considered a single long poem of some 10,000 lines.

The techniques of association and progression and design and background are already to be found in less refined form in the earlier anthologies; they are applied in the *Kokinshū*, for example, if only partially and inconsistently; they can even be found intermittently in the arrangement of certain groups of poems in the *Man'yōshū*; and in successive imperial anthologies from the *Gosenshū* on, they continued to be applied with greater or less care. Nevertheless, it was the great popularity of poetic sequences in the 11th and 12th centuries—20, 30, 50, or most typically 100 poems by a single poet—that gave impetus to the refinement of techniques of association and progression and their use in imperial anthologies. Together with the universal practice of *daiei*, composing poems on fixed topics, poetic sequences developed the sensibilities and literary expectations of poets and readers to the nuances and pleasures of harmoniously grouped poems. The poetic sequences are also clearly the most important direct antecedent of the extended *renga* or linked verse in 50 or 100 links that began to be composed in earnest during the early 13th century. An important effect of the integration of poems in structures was to transcend the limitations of length of the brief *tanka* form, providing a uniquely Japanese construction that emphasized episodic and linear development.

That the principles of integration were applied with such telling effect by the compilers of the *Shin kokinshū* must be largely credited to former emperor Go-Toba. Go-Toba participated actively in the selection and arrangement of the poems for his anthology, often overruling or revising the compilers' choices. And he continued to edit and re-edit the collection intermittently throughout his life.

Attenuation and decline. In his older age, Teika passed on his poetic prestige, authority, and public role to his son and heir FUJIWARA NO TAMEIE (1198–1275). Tameie lacked the abilities of his father and grandfather, and failed to provide inspiring leadership and excitement to the poetic world of his day. His own poetry is representative of the attenuation and decline that began to set in after the compilation of the *Shin kokinshū*: it is competent, bland, and, in a word, insipid. Espousing one of Teika's famous Ten Styles called *ken'yō*, or "the style of describing things as one sees them," instead of the intense *ushin* ideal, Tameie remained safely conventional, eschewing radical new departures or striking effects. In a sense he reverted to the tried and true Fujiwara style, and his verse is in some ways reminiscent of Kintō's; on the other hand, to do him justice, the very blandness of his poetry and his apparent choice of a rather humdrum style may have had a more positive inspiration: it may have been influenced in part by the example of Chinese Song poetry, some of which has a somewhat flat, prosaic quality. Such stylistic features were inherited, modified, and developed—even carried to an extreme—by Tameie's descendants and the innovating poets of their age. In consequence, their poetic practice is significantly different from that of the mid-classical period and of sufficient interest to merit separate treatment.

The Late Classical Period (1250–1350)

After the death of Teika, the harmony between competing poetic factions and rival schools began to disintegrate, and from the mid-13th century to the end of the 15th, battle was repeatedly joined between representatives of conservative and innovating poetic schools. Ironically, most of these bitterly divided factions were headed by the descendants of Teika and Tameie themselves—the Nijō, Kyōgoku, and Reizei families descended respectively from Tameie's older sons, Fujiwara no Tameuji (1222–86) and Fujiwara no Tamenori (1227–79), and from his youngest son, REIZEI TAMESUKE (1263–1328), the child of Tameie's second and favorite wife, the determined lady known to history as Abutsu the Nun (ABUTSU NI; d 1283). Honest poetic differences tended to be confused with personal animosities, political factionalism, quarrels over the inheritance of landed estates, and most important in the long run, possession of the library of precious manuscripts, treaties, and the like, passed on by Teika to Tameie as the family patrimony of poetic and literary knowledge. From the mid-Heian period, with the growth of secret traditions and the ideal of a Way of Poetry, such documents and treatises had tended to be treated increasingly as "proof" of poetic authority and expertise, to be handed down from father to son or master to disciple and to be kept away from outsiders. By the generation of Tameie's feuding children, it had become of utmost importance to possess such documents in order to bolster claims to legitimate poetic authority. It can be readily seen that given the strength of the hereditary principle in Japanese court society, poetic knowledge, taste, judgment, and even creative ability came to be regarded as tangible property to be willed to one's descendants and represented by the concrete evidence of documents. The confusion between poetic eminence and actual accomplishment was an important factor in the long decline of classical poetry and the increasing vitality of the new linked verse genres not so closely identified with the court class. At the same time, the established aristocratic schools of *waka* were infiltrated by commoners of dubious lineage, priests, warriors, and other upstarts who first became their pupils and partisans and then emerged as the creative element in the continuance of their traditions.

Tameie's descendants of the senior Nijō line represented the conservative side of the tradition. They quarreled publicly and acrimoniously with the allied junior branches, the Kyōgoku and Reizei lines, eventually losing a lawsuit brought to force Tameie's younger son, Reizei Tamesuke, to surrender to them the landed property and poetic documents willed to him by Tameie in his old age. However, the Nijō soon began to produce forged documents to support their position, and such was their prestige as the descendants of Tameie's eldest son and "legitimate heir" and their political influence at court that they were able to dominate the public, official side of poetic activity from the late 13th century to the mid-15th. Thus, of the 11 remaining imperial anthologies produced after Tameie until the practice ceased in the mid-1400s, 9 were compiled by his Nijō descendants, their adherents and successors; only 2—the *Gyokuyōshū* (GYOKUYŌ WAKASHŪ; Collection of Jeweled Leaves, 1312–14) and *Fūgashū* (Collection of Elegance, 1344–46)—by the junior Kyōgoku-Reizei poets.

In fairness, the poetic activities of generations of poets of the Nijō school cannot be simply dismissed out of hand. Most Nijō poets were at least competent, some rose significantly above the general mediocre level, all had what seemed persuasive reasons for writing as they did. The very fact of the durability of the classical tradition bespeaks the importance it continued to have, the seriousness with which it was taken. In general, however, the poetic practice of the conservative Nijō poets after Tameie essentially reflected his own preference for a style of bland simplicity, a diluted version of the high classical Fujiwara style. Excitement is found in this period almost exclusively in the poetry of the Kyōgoku–Reizei poets.

Although the Reizei line proved to be the most enduring, they remained mostly in the background during the literary and political struggles between rival factions in the 13th and 14th centuries. Establishing good relations with both the court in Kyōto and the military aristocracy in Kamakura, possessing the bulk of Teika's most valuable documents and some talented young poets, at first the Reizei allied themselves with the Kyōgoku branch, represented by Tameie's truculent grandson KYŌGOKU TAMEKANE (1254–1332). Tamekane quickly emerged as the leader of the dissidents, especially against NIJŌ TAMEYO (1250?–1338), another of Tameie's grandsons and head of the conservative wing.

In both theory and practice, the innovating poets, like their Nijō opponents, based themselves upon the past, taking for their chief models different aspects of Teika's example, especially his later style of ushin. The interpretation they gave this ideal, however, though borne out by a number of Teika's own poems, was carried by the Kyōgoku–Reizei poets beyond what Teika probably ever envisaged. Inspired in important ways by the practice of Song poets interested in philosophic issues and problems of human perception and psychological reality and concerned with inner truth and beauty concealed beneath a rough, even ugly surface, the innovators were also influenced by Neo-Confuciansim. Not least, they had, like many Song poets, a lively interest in Zen Buddhism. In sum, Teika's ideal of "conviction of feeling" was significantly modified by his Kyōgoku–Reizei descendants into the ideal of a "conviction of truth" (makoto). In practice, this ideal led to new and striking results in their poetry, especially their poetry on nature and on love.

The new late-classical styles. At first glance no poetry can be more difficult in its functionings than the nature and love poetry of the late-classical innovators. Their poetry on seasonal topics is all images: the descriptive symbolism of the mid-classical period, often expressed in combined generalization and description, is in their verse completely descriptive. Images and scenes in nature appear to be presented for themselves without reference to symbolic values or lyrical tone, apart from the underlying convention in Japanese poetry that nature is appreciated for its beauty. The Kyōgoku–Reizei poets appear to be so intent upon reporting accurately their observations that considerations of feeling, the inherent emotional and lyrical values of spring cherry blossoms or autumn evenings, seem to be passed over in favor of a quasi-scientific concern with detail. The poetry on love, on the other hand, is almost completely abstract, lacking concrete imagery for the most part, and almost exclusively concerned with the inner psychological and emotional states of people experiencing the successive stages of conventional courtly love. Nevertheless, when considered more carefully, the two disparate modes of imagistic nature poetry and image-free love poetry turn out to proceed from the same concerns and assumptions and to share a basic subjectivity. For although apparently almost coldly impersonal, reportorial and photographic, the nature poetry is in fact intensely concerned with time and change: the instant that a fading sunset begins to turn to dusk, the millisecond in which thousands of raindrops on the grass are brilliantly lighted by a flash of lightning. Again, the love poetry is absorbed in the exact depiction of change in the psychological state of a woman, for example, whose anxieties begin to shift from concern about gossip and her reputation to worries about the fidelity of her lover or whose growing bitterness against him begins to change to the blank numbness of despair.

Such a concentration upon time in flux and an almost fevered attempt to capture the precise moment in words gives the poetry of the Kyōgoku–Reizei poets an intensity that is at first not evident beneath the undeniably prosaic surface of much of their verse. Similarly, although these late classical poets characteristically eschew certain traditional techniques of waka, especially the pivot words and various kinds of conventional associations involving word play, study of their verse soon shows their ostensibly "objective" nature poetry to be in fact shaped by a perceiving sensibility, a poetic speaker who describes a phenomenon or a process in a carefully patterned sequence, using language in new metaphorical ways. Thus, a poem by the former emperor Go-Fushimi (1288–1336; r 1298–1301), "On a Winter Garden" (*Fūgashū* 739):

Shiguru to mo	The leaves are wet
Shirarenu niwa wa	In the garden where the drizzle
Ko no ha nurete	Falls imperceptibly,
Samuki yūhi wa	And the cold sun of evening
Kage ochinikeri	Has dropped behind the hills.

For drizzle to be imperceptible implies a human observer, and a cold sun dropping behind the hills is physically impossible, metaphorically true. The diction in this particular example is conventionally pure, but the combination of words in "the cold sun of evening" (*samuki yūhi*) creates a kind of metaphor found but rarely in the poetry of earlier periods: an unusual feature of Teika's youthful poetry, despised by the conservatives of his day as "Zen gibberish," now taken up by the late-classical poets and made into almost a mannerism, a hallmark of the new style. Again, to treat the sunlight as dropping behind the hills is a commonplace in English, a bold new use of words in *waka*.

Abstractions. Similarly, the innovating poets are given to a much more noticeable use of abstractions for sensual and psychological qualities such as coolness, coldness, loneliness, and longing, where earlier poets tended to use the corresponding adjectives. An example is this summer poem by Tamekane (*Gyokuyōshū* 419):

Eda ni moru	In the thinness
Asahi no kage no	Of morning sun filtering through
Sukunasa ni	Among the branches,
Suzushisa fukaki	The coolness is deep
Take no oku kana	Within the bamboo grove.

The metaphorical function of the abstractions in this poem perhaps saves it from the flat effect that characterizes many of the Kyōgoku–Reizei poets, especially former empress Eifuku (EIFUKU MON'IN; 1271–1342)—an effect much admired, it may be added, by modern taste, as in the following example (*Gyokuyōshū* 84).

Mine no kasumi	Haze on the peaks,
Fumoto no kusa no	Light green on the grasses
Usumidori	At the base:
Noyama o kakete	Spreading over fields and mountains
Harumekinikeri	Are the signs of spring.

An illustration of the abstract, imageless love poetry characteristic of the new styles is the following poem, again by former empress Eifuku, its speaker a lady who waits night after night for her faithless lover (*Fūgashū* 1052):

Ware mo hito mo	Both I and you,
Aware tsurenaki	How wretched we do make each other
Yonayona yo	Night after night!
Tanome mo yamazu	You never stop telling me, "Be patient,"
Machi mo yowarazu	And I will not give up this fruitless wait.

Other stylistic features. In their overriding concern for "truth," the Kyōgoku–Reizei poets shocked their opponents by carelessly disregarding such traditional poetic "don'ts" as repeating the same or similar words in a poem, permitting successive lines to end in the same vowel, or using "low" or vulgar diction. Again, the innovators lent liveliness to their verse by syntactic reversals and other unconventional means essayed by the youthful Teika but rejected by his Nijō descendants. The Kyōgoku–Reizei poets also made a virtue of structural fragmentation within the *tanka*, often relating upper and lower verses by juxtaposition rather than the traditional careful distribution of related words and images throughout the poem. Such juxtapositions were called *soku*, or distantly related verses, by contrast with *shinku*, or the closely related verses insisted upon by the conservatives. The innovators also often applied the principle of *soku* in their arrangement of poems in sequences and anthologies, so that a given pair or subsequence of poems in the *Gyokuyōshū*, for example, may seem at first glance to be haphazardly arranged, with no evidence of the techniques of association and progression developed to such perfection in the preceding age. In fact, the poems are usually related but frequently in "distant," subtle ways. A favorite technique was to create an association by juxtaposing two poems which taken together might suggest an allusion to a single older poem.

The Post-Classical Period (1350–1600)

——The 21st and last of the imperial anthologies of *waka* was completed in 1439 (Eikyō 11). Compiled by Asukai Masayo (1390–1452), a member of an important family hereditarily allied with the now defunct Nijō line, the collection is dominated by the orthodox conservative styles, a bias aptly reflected in its title, *Shin zoku kokin wakashū,* or "New Collection of Ancient and Modern Times Continued." Ordered by the emperor at the behest of the shōgun, the anthology symbolizes both the final decline of the great court tradition and the intrusion of outsiders into the "poetic garden." But for the most part, both newcomers and those nobles who continued to play a leading part in poetic activities merely perpetuated the forms and conventions of the Fujiwara style, which became increasingly attenuated, stereotyped, and sterile. The distinctions between conservatives and innovators, important in the late 13th and 14th centuries, had become largely meaningless by the 15th, as all schools and factions shared an awed veneration for the poetry and culture of High Heian, looked to the *Kokinshū* as orthodox scripture, and elevated Teika to the level of a divinity whose word was law. Among the courtiers who continued to play an important role in the preservation of traditional *waka* and contributed in vital ways to maintaining the prestige and attraction of court culture were men distinguished for their learning, if not for the originality of their verse. Such individuals were ICHIJŌ KANEYOSHI (Ichijō Kanera; 1402–81) and Sanjōnishi Sanetaka (1455–1537), as well as the successive heads and members of the Reizei line.

Anti-Nijō forces. Ironically, by the 15th century the most articulate opponent of the dominant Nijō school was not a member of the Reizei family but instead the vigorous IMAGAWA SADAYO, or Ryōshun (b 1326), a brave warrior with a distinguished record on the battlefield and a passion for poetry, who became a Buddhist priest in later life and brought his combative nature to bear in treatises and polemics aimed at the Asukai and other latter-day heirs of the Nijō. Ryōshun was succeeded by his pupil, the priest SHŌTETSU (1381–1459), a prolific poet and critic in his own right. Both men called for a return to what they considered to be the central ideals and practice of the divine Teika, thus in a sense seeking to establish a new orthodoxy to replace the Nijō doctrines. Indeed, in his most famous treatise Shōtetsu invokes the punishment of the gods and Buddhas on anyone who might dare take the great Teika's name in vain; and, like the conservatives, Ryōshun, Shōtetsu, and others venerated the *Kokinshū* as the fountainhead of *waka* and the source of all acceptable styles, even though Ryōshun also argued for a more liberal policy in admitting to the poetic vocabulary "pleasant-sounding" words and phrases not to be found in the *sandaishū*. For obvious political reasons, very few poems by these and other Reizei adherents found their way into the later imperial anthologies, and the verse of such comparatively original and interesting poets of the age is best studied in their personal collections, of which a considerable number survive. Characteristically traditional even at its most innovative, by attempting to emulate Teika's ideal of "conviction of feeling," the best verse of Ryōshun and Shōtetsu at least carries an emotional excitement not often found in the conservative verse. At the same time, the poetry of Shōtetsu in particular is often involuted, elliptical, and cryptic, and, like Teika's youthful "Zen gibberish," extremely difficult to understand.

Decline of court poetry. In the latter part of the 15th century, the imperial capital was devastated by the long Ōnin wars (1467–77), the entire city repeatedly reduced to ashes. Those courtiers who could sought refuge on their remaining country estates or under the protection of powerful warlords, to whom they taught the art of poetry or other traditional esoteric subjects. In general, however, the court culture suffered a staggering blow. Thus, although poetry contests continued to be held, especially during the years immediately following the Ōnin wars, imperial anthologies were no longer compiled: a vivid illustration of the court's loss of both intellectual vitality and material resources. Again, the growing importance of parvenu commoners *(jige)* in the cultural life of the age is represented by such an important figure as TŌ NO TSUNEYORI (1401–84), a descendant of provincial magnates in eastern Japan. Tsuneyori studied *waka* with both Nijō authorities and with Shōtetsu, and he is noted for having passed on the tradition of ritually transmitting to one's poetic heir certain secret teachings (many of them trivial) about the *Kokinshū*. The practice was known as Kokin Denju, "Transmission of the *Kokinshū*," and in Tsuneyori's case the favorite disciple was the priest SŌGI (1421–1502), a man of obscure origins who nevertheless became an important *waka* poet and a master of renga regarded as the greatest who ever lived. By virtue of his initiation by Tsuneyori, Sōgi was revered in his day as the sole surviving authority of the Nijō school. His mastery of both traditional *waka* and linked verse was typical of the outstanding renga poets beginning as

far back as the famous NIJŌ YOSHIMOTO (1320–88). Yoshimoto, Sōgi, and other renga poets adapted the ideals, techniques, and styles of *waka* to linked verse, elevating it and transforming into a courtly art what had begun as a playful game of verse capping. For both *waka* and renga they gathered about themselves numerous pupils and disciples of similar origins, and under the patronage of the shōgun Ashikaga Yoshihisa (1465–89), a number of poetry contests were conducted and a group project was even initiated (but never completed) to compile a vast compendium of existing knowledge about *waka* as a kind of compensation for the now abandoned tradition of the imperial anthologies.

After Yoshihisa's death, poetic activity at the shogunal court declined markedly. However, one of Sōgi's most important pupils was the *daimyō*-poet and scholar HOSOKAWA YŪSAI (1534–1610), author of a number of treatises and collections of lore. Yūsai had many pupils, including, ironically, a number of court nobles, for his knowledge of the art far exceeded theirs. He is often regarded as the founder of *waka* of the early modern period. And although most of its poetic vitality had been lost by the end of the 16th century, on the surface, at least, *waka* enjoyed a new popularity if not revival owing to the interest and patronage of the great general and flamboyant cultural parvenu TOYOTOMI HIDEYOSHI (1537–98). Hideyoshi's massive assaults upon the arts were as famous as his military successes; together with his marathon tea ceremonies for hundreds of participants, he sponsored numerous poetry parties at famous places around the country, often to celebrate his military victories. Participating in these occasions were many of Hideyoshi's chief allies among the great daimyō; like himself, most of them were indebted for their knowledge of *waka* to the teaching of Hosokawa Yūsai.

The Edo Period (1600–1868) —— Although in accordance with the common practice among Japanese literary historians, the Edo or Tokugawa period is called the early modern period in *waka* history, there are actually few signs of significant change until about the middle of the 17th century. In the early 1600s, disciples of Yūsai continued to teach and compose the traditional conservative verse, passing on to later generations the "secret teachings" and courtly ideals of the Nijō school. At the same time, indications of impending change in the aristocratic orthodox basis of *waka* conservatism began to appear. A distinctive feature of the age, no matter how backward-looking the ideals and practice of specific individuals and schools, is that to an extent unknown even in the post-classical period, *waka* was taken up by the commoners. Some of these commoners were low-ranking samurai, many were of much lower origins. The important figures, like the leading transitional poet KINOSHITA CHŌSHŌSHI (1569–1649), displayed a certain independence of thought. No longer bound by strict ties of loyalty and obedience to a family tradition or established poetic school, the new generations felt freer to select from the entire range of Japanese poetic tradition the styles and ideals they chose to emulate. Thus, Chōshōshi was a disciple of the conservative Yūsai, yet he also studied with the famous scholar of the Reizei family, FUJIWARA SEIKA (1561–1619), and he looked rather to the examples of Kyōgoku Tamekane and Shōtetsu in advocating greater freedom of style and a liberalization of poetic diction.

The new eclecticism and critical spirit were even more pronounced in such a representative figure as TODA MOSUI (1629–1706). Mosui was extremely critical of the traditional poetic schools, calling upon poets to free themselves from the restraints of both the Nijō and Reizei traditions and to open up new ground. A direct attack upon the established poetic schools, with their secret teachings, was made in 1742 by KADA NO ARIMARO (1706–51), nephew of the famous Shintō priest and classical scholar KADA NO AZUMAMARO (1669–1736), in a polemical treatise entitled *Kokka hachiron* (Eight Matters of Concern in the National Poetry). Like most of his contemporaries, Arimaro invoked the past to justify change in the present, calling for a return to the "true poetic values" of the age of the *Man'yōshū*.

The national scholars. Idealization of Japan's primitive past and of its earliest literature characterized the so-called national scholars (*kokugakusha*; see KOKUGAKU), beginning with SHIMOKŌBE CHŌRYŪ (1624–86) and the scholar-priest KEICHŪ (1640–1701). Keichū's vast exegetical edition of the *Man'yōshū* was a landmark in the revival of native learning and *waka* scholarship in the early modern period. Over the years the national scholars espoused different aesthetic ideals and poetic styles, depending upon the particular earlier work or works they chose as models. Thus KAMO NO MABUCHI (1697–1769), TAYASU MUNETAKE (1715–71), and KATORI NAHIKO (1723–82) composed in an archaistic style imitative of the *Man'yō-*

shū, which they admired extravagantly for its "manliness" *(masuraoburi);* MURATA HARUMI (1746–1811) and KATŌ CHIKAGE (1735–1808) looked to the *Kokinshū* and *Shin kokinshū.* KITAMURA KIGIN (1624–1705) and MOTOORI NORINAGA (1730–1801) were, like many of their contemporaries, far better scholars than poets. Kigin studied *waka* and *haikai* under several different teachers and produced some of the standard commentaries on the major classics, including an annotated edition of the first eight imperial anthologies still much in use today; his poetic style reflects the conservative predilections of his principal teachers. Norinaga imitated the characteristic styles of both the *Shin kokinshū* and the *Man'yōshū,* producing major exegetical editions of both these anthologies, together with a monumental commentary on the early chronicle *Kojiki.* In addition, he wrote the most original and penetrating premodern criticism of the *Tale of Genji.*

Though linked by a common interest in native Japanese cultural traditions (as distinguished from the traditions and literary genres influenced, and therefore in their view, corrupted, by Chinese influence), the national scholars were divided into groups or "schools" based upon a common teacher (the Agata school, comprising the disciples of Kamo no Mabuchi) or on regional differences (the Edo school, made up of scholar-poets residing in the shogunal capital city). At the same time, the court tradition, however weakened, survived in Kyōto among the descendants and partisans of the Reizei family, and such prominent poets as OZAWA ROAN (1723–1801) took lessons in composition and poetic ceremonial from them.

Independents. Roan's most important disciple, KAGAWA KAGEKI (1768–1843), followed his master's lead by looking for his poetic ideals to the *Kokinshū,* thereby standing in contrast to the majority of Mabuchi's followers. Kageki's disciples in turn formed the so-called Keien school, which was both prominent and powerful in the latter part of the Tokugawa period and the early years of the Meiji period (1868–1912), the beginning of the modern age. Apart from these representatives of the "poetic establishment," many other independent individuals, scattered among the many fiefs and provinces throughout Japan, produced with unflagging enthusiasm vast quantities of *waka* in a variety of styles imitative of earlier periods. Of these, TACHIBANA AKEMI (1812–68), Ōsumi Kotomichi (1798–1868), and HIRAGA MOTOYOSHI (1800–1865) are provincial poets whose reputations and influence have been felt into modern times. Most important of all, at least in the modern estimation, is the Zen priest RYŌKAN (1758–1831). Especially admired today for his Zen-inspired simplicity, unpretentiousness, and keen insight, Ryōkan is famous for both his poetry in Chinese and his *waka,* which are often written in an archaic *Man'yō* style suggestive of Mabuchi and his disciples.

The Modern Period (1867–present)——The accession of Emperor Meiji and the dissolution of the Tokugawa shogunate in 1867 signaled the beginning of a period of intense modernization and Westernization which utterly transformed Japan and its material and intellectual culture during the course of the next century. During the early years of the Meiji era, wholesale, indiscriminate borrowing from the West was carried on in nearly every sphere of life. Nevertheless, literature, and especially such an uncompromisingly traditional form of literature as *waka,* remained for a score of years or more largely unaffected. On the contrary, the more powerful early modern schools of *waka*—the Keien school founded by Kagawa Kageki, and the Palace school, consisting of the latter-day followers of the old Nijō, Asukai, and Reizei families of court poets—dominated poetic activities at the imperial palace, while on the popular level the old-fashioned teachers continued to give instruction in the old way. It was not until the 1880s that the established *waka* began to feel the effects of new forms and ideas from the West, zealously advocated by the young intellectuals.

The first stage in the "modernization" of *waka* came in the form of violent attacks upon it, especially by three young professors of Tōkyō University, who in 1882 published an anthology of Western-style poetry called "Selections of Poetry in the New Style" *(Shintaishi shō).* These young men and their partisans advocated the total abandonment of *waka* for the new, freer, more expansive forms recently introduced from Western poetry. By the end of the 1880s, however, a more moderate viewpoint began to be expressed, consonant with a growing cultural conservatism and a temporary reaction against frantic borrowing. In the modern view, the traditional forms of native poetry might be permitted to survive alongside the new, Western-inspired genres, but the old poetry had to be revolutionized and infused with new spirit. This more optimistic, programmatic outlook was notably expressed by two major figures of the new age:

YOSANO TEKKAN (1873–1935) and MASAOKA SHIKI (1867–1902). On the eve of the Sino-Japanese War of 1894–95, modern Japan's first adventure in military conquest, Tekkan published an essay called "Music of a Land About to Fall" ("Bōkoku no on"), in which he excoriated the traditional *waka* for its effeminacy, its languid spirit contrary to the courage and noble resolve required by the new times. What was needed, said Tekkan, was a robust virility, what the national scholar Kamo no Mabuchi had advocated as the ideal of "manliness." Tekkan's poetry only indifferently expressed his patriotic ideal, for the virility of his largely conventional poems was to be found chiefly in such startling images as tigers and swords, but he played an important role in inspiring a whole new generation of *tanka* poets—who now deliberately substituted the term *tanka* for *waka* in order to distinguish themselves and their "revolutionary" compositions from the established conservative schools.

The Myōjō school. In 1899 Tekkan founded the New Poetry Society (Shinshisha), and the society's journal, *Myōjō* (The Bright Star), was first published in 1900. The poets of the new *Myōjō* school attempted to imbue their verse with a spirit of individualism and freedom from conventional social restraints. The results were at times sensationally autobiographical and even ludicrously comic, but in the eight short years of its publication, *Myōjō* was the major journal of the important cult of romanticism and personal lyricism in the modern *tanka.* Tekkan's wife (originally his student), YOSANO AKIKO (1878–1942) especially gave voice to an uninhibited passion that shocked contemporary readers. Her romantic images of "tangled hair" and bedclothes rumpled from violent lovemaking scandalized Meiji society, still dominated as it was by two centuries and more of Confucian puritanism. In fact, her ultimate sources of inspiration were the passionate woman poets—Komachi, Ise, and others—of the early classical period.

Masaoka Shiki and shasei. Masaoka Shiki first directed his reforming zeal to *haikai,* turning to the *tanka* only somewhat belatedly, after Tekkan had published his "Music of a Land About to Fall." As a *haiku* poet and reformer, Shiki had gathered an enthusiastic following. His disciples were particularly attracted by his strong personality and qualities of leadership and not least by his courage in the face of the fatal tuberculosis that made him a pain-racked invalid during the last years of his short life. Shiki's own manifesto was published in the form of "An Open Letter to the *Tanka* Poets" ("Utayomi ni atauru sho") in 1898. A classic of modern Japanese literary polemics, Shiki's manifesto is a sweeping denunciation of the entire *waka* tradition from the *Kokinshū* on. Decrying the "shallow wit" *(rikutsu)* and "silly artifice" of Tsurayuki, Teika, and all their ilk, Shiki declared that no worthwhile poetry had been written in Japan since the *Man'yōshū,* with the exception of the *Man'yō*-style verses of the ill-starred third Minamoto shōgun, MINAMOTO NO SANETOMO (1192–1219), who was assassinated at the young age of 27, actually leaving scarcely a ripple on the surface of mid-classical poetic development. Shiki's adulation of the *Man'yōshū* and Sanetomo and his revulsion against the classical tradition was a form of romantic primitivism which he derived from Kamo no Mabuchi through two or three minor independent poets of his own day. Simultaneously, his ideals were importantly shaped by his *haiku* training and preference for descriptive poetry and by his earlier association with some young Western-style painters who were attempting to adapt contemporary European modes of realistic representation to the Japanese context. From one such acquaintance, Shiki borrowed the term *shasei,* "copying life," which he employed interchangeably with *shajitsu,* "copying reality," as a key term for a prescriptive ideal of "objective description" in poetry. As for the poetry of the *Man'yōshū* and Sanetomo, Shiki saw them as the uninhibited outpouring of sincere feeling—spontaneous, natural, artlessly simple.

The early twentieth century. Shiki's followers formed the Negishi Tanka Society, and in 1908 his disciples ITŌ SACHIO (1864–1913), NAGATSUKA TAKASHI (1879–1915), and others founded the poetry journal ARARAGI. Many younger poets joined them as Sachio elaborated the basic orthodoxy of *shasei* and the *Man'yō* ideal into a justification for poetry as a spontaneous *sakebi,* or lyric cry. *Shasei* was endowed in turn by Sachio's disciple SAITŌ MOKICHI (1882–1953) with the universal significance of "describing all of human life." The opposing *Myōjō* school, on the other hand, failed to retain cohesion in change, and the important younger poets it produced—the symbolist KITAHARA HAKUSHŪ (1885–1942), YOSHII ISAMU (1886–1960), and others—quickly left the group to pursue their separate ways. By contrast, the *Araragi* poets continued to dominate the *tanka* scene for the first two decades of the 20th cen-

Wakakusayama

View from Nara of the annual turf burning on Wakakusayama. The pagoda of the temple Kōfukuji is silhouetted against the flames.

tury, but the group became increasingly defensive and in-grown over the years, reacting to and also giving cause for the proliferation of independent splinter groups and societies. Outside the mainstream, such trendy experiments as "proletarian *tanka*," "anarchistic *tanka*," Dadaism, "*tanka* in free meter," "colloquial *tanka*," and so on, enjoyed a brief popularity as most of the traditional conventions of subject, treatment, diction, and cadence were defied in successive attempts to give contemporary relevance to this most ancient of Japanese traditional arts.

The contemporary scene. The judgment of most Japanese literary historians is that these efforts were unsuccessful and that the world of the *tanka* continued to deteriorate and stagnate, breaking up into ever smaller, more exclusive, local cliques. A temporary unity was imposed in World War II, when almost to a man Japan's *tanka* poets fell into line in the service of the fatherland, producing thousands of now forgotten patriotic verses extolling sacrifice in the imperial cause. With the end of the war, many of the old groups resumed activities on the old footing, and numerous new ones were formed as once again the *tanka* became a favorite activity for a large public of middle-class amateurs. But because of their wartime behavior, the *tanka* poets and the form itself were newly discredited in the eyes of many Japanese intellectuals. The old Meiji controversy as to the possible relevance of the *tanka* in the modern age was revived, this time in the allegation that it could be no better than "second-class art" (*daini geijutsu,* a phrase that had been applied to *haiku*), a mere hobby unworthy of the serious attention and irrelevant to the concerns of the world today. Thus, although in one sense the *tanka,* given its hundreds of societies and millions of practitioners, may be said to be in a flourishing state at present, the fact must also be faced that very few really outstanding poets take much interest in it, preferring instead the larger, more exciting possibilities and relative freedom from conventions of Western-style poetry. During the course of the 20th century, indeed, the *tanka* (i.e., *waka*) has been increasingly relegated to an ever less important function. In an age of journalism and the psychological novel, it seems unlikely that it will regain a dominant place.

■——Geoffrey Bownas and Anthony Thwaite, *The Penguin Book of Japanese Verse* (1964). Robert H. Brower and Earl Miner, *Japanese Court Poetry* (1961). Ian Levy, *The Ten Thousand Leaves: A Complete Translation of the Man'yōshū, Japan's Premier Anthology of Poetry* (1981–). Earl Miner, *An Introduction to Japanese Court Poetry* (1968). J. Thomas Rimer and Robert E. Morrell, *Guide to Japanese Poetry* (1975). Hiroaki Satō and Burton Watson, *From the Country of Eight Islands: An Anthology of Japanese Poetry* (1981). *Waka bungaku daijiten* (Meiji Shoin, 1962). Robert H. BROWER

wakadoshiyori

Junior councillors or "young elders"; also known as *shōrō* or *sansei.* Officials in this post stood second only to senior councillors (RŌJŪ) in the TOKUGAWA SHOGUNATE, although their power declined somewhat toward the end of the Edo period (1600–1868). Their main duty was to supervise direct vassals of the shōgun (HATAMOTO and GOKENIN), using the reports of the inspectors (METSUKE). The *wakadoshiyori* also dealt with administrative sectors outside the

control of the *rōjū,* such as the supervision of artisans, physicians, routine construction work, and of most of the shōgun's guard units (BANKATA). In the event of war, they were to lead the *hatamoto* into battle. The office was established in 1633, when MATSUDAIRA NOBUTSUNA appointed six men to this post, but the usual number varied from three to five, each (like the *rōjū*) serving for a month at a time on a rotating basis. They were chosen from among the FUDAI *daimyō.* Each daimyō domain also had a set of junior councillors to assist its senior councillors.

wakai

(compromise). Agreement between plaintiff and defendant to terminate a lawsuit. When an agreement is reached between parties in the course of civil litigation, the particulars of the agreement are presented to the court. In the event that the court records the particulars in a protocol, such a settlement protocol has the same effect as a final judgment (Code of Civil Procedure, art. 203). There is no dispute that a settlement protocol may be enforced in regard to all matters determined by compromise and that the lawsuit is terminated within the scope of the compromise, but scholarly opinion is divided on the *res judicata* effect of a settlement protocol. The Supreme Court of Japan has not clearly admitted such a *res judicata* effect.

A large percentage of lawsuits are disposed of by settlement. For example, in 1972, of 73,570 civil cases in Japanese district courts, 22,284 cases (30.3 percent) were terminated by settlement. The court may encourage a settlement between the parties at any stage of the proceedings (Code of Civil Procedure, art. 136) and so has extremely broad discretion as to the timing of the settlement. Generally speaking, negotiations take place in three stages. The first opportunity for settlement is when the issues have been framed and documentary evidence has been produced, immediately before trial. The second opportunity is after the main witnesses on important issues have been examined. The last opportunity is after the conclusion of the presentation of evidence. Many judges take the initiative in suggesting figures and recommending payment in accordance with the extent of the evidence. The traffic accident division of the Tōkyō District Court has established standard amounts of compensation for pain and suffering, nursing care, funeral expenses, and so on, and use them as an instrument of persuasion. In that division, one work day out of three is devoted to settlement conferences.

TANAKA Yutaka

Wakakusayama

Also called Mikasayama. Hill in the eastern part of the city of Nara, Nara Prefecture, central Honshū; composed of andesite. It is known for its elegant shape. The summit commands a view of the city of Nara. On the summit is a mounded tomb (KOFUN) called Uguisuzuka. The hill is covered with turf and is known for the turf burning that is conducted there every January. The hill is part of Nara Park. Height: 342 m (1,122 ft).

Wakamatsu Shizuko (1864–1896)

Translator and author. Born into a *samurai* family in Wakamatsu in the Aizu domain (now part of Fukushima Prefecture) as Shimada Kashi. After graduating from the Ferris Girls' School in Yokohama in 1882, she taught English there. In 1889 she married IWAMOTO YOSHIHARU, cofounder of the influential women's magazine JOGAKU ZASSHI. Her original works, reflecting Christian influence, and her translations from such authors as Longfellow and Tennyson were published in that magazine and several others, but she is best known for her translation of F. E. Burnett's novel *Little Lord Fauntleroy* (1886; tr *Shōkōshi,* 1890–92).

wakamono-gumi

A traditional male youth group found in rural communities. The *wakamono-gumi* played a central role in village society where distinctions based on age were paramount. At its height the *wakamono-gumi* system was stronger in western Japan than in the northeastern area. *Wakamono-gumi* activities included directing festivals and rituals, performing communal village work, acting as night watchmen and firemen, and participating in rescue work in emergencies. Members also received training in work skills and engaged in social activities with the *musume-gumi* (girls' organization). Most boys entered the *wakamono-gumi* at around 15 years of age, but in some cases only the firstborn son of a family or one boy from a family became a member. It was usual to leave the organization after marriage, although some married men remained members. Since membership in the *wakamono-gumi* meant that the youth was fully recognized as an adult by the villagers, strict initiation ceremonies were often performed. New members of the *wakamono-gumi* commonly lived together in communal lodgings called *wakamono yado*. From the end of the 19th century to the early part of the 20th century, the role of the *wakamono-gumi* was largely taken over by the *seinenkai* and the *seinendan* youth groups. Only vestiges of the *wakamono-gumi* exist today in the form of youths providing assistance for festivals, ceremonies, and other annual events.

Wakanoura

Coastal area in the city of Wakayama, Wakayama Prefecture, central Honshū. Forms the easternmost point of the Inland Sea National Park and is noted for the beauty of its beaches and surrounding scenery. Mentioned in the 8th-century poetry anthology *Man'yōshū*. The tourist areas of Shin Wakanoura and Oku Wakanoura are located on the coastline's western section.

Wakan rōeishū

(Collection of Chinese and Japanese Poems for Singing). Anthology of favorite Chinese couplets and Japanese *tanka* (31-syllable WAKA) for singing to fixed melodies, which were not included in the text. Compiled by the poet and critic FUJIWARA NO KINTŌ around 1013. It contains 587 couplets in Chinese by some 30 Chinese and 50 Japanese poets, including the very important and influential Tang (T'ang) dynasty poet, Bo Juyi (Po Chü-i; 772–846). Other Chinese poets featured are Yuan Shen (Yüan Shen; 779–831) and Xu Hun (Hsü Hun; fl ca 850); and of the Japanese poets of Chinese verse the most important are Sugawara no Fumitoki (899–981), SUGAWARA NO MICHIZANE, Ōe no Asatsuna (886–957), MINAMOTO NO SHITAGAU, and Ki no Haseo (845–912). The 217 Japanese *tanka* in the collection are by 80 poets, of whom the most important are KI NO TSURAYUKI, ŌSHIKŌCHI NO MITSUNE, and KAKINOMOTO NO HITOMARO (fl ca 685–705). Major sources for the work were Ōe no Koretoki's (888–963) collection of famous couplets by Chinese and Korean poets of the T'ang dynasty, *Senzai kaku* (ca 960, Superior Chinese Verses of a Thousand Years), and possibly his *Honchō kaku* (Superior Chinese Verses by Japanese Poets), not extant. For the Japanese *tanka*, the chief sources were the first three imperial anthologies *(chokusenshū)* of vernacular poetry compiled between the beginning of the 10th and the beginning of the 11th century. The work is divided into two books, poems on the four seasons occupying the first book and "miscellaneous" poems the second. Within these divisions, the poems are subclassified by common topics, Chinese couplets frequently alternating with Japanese *tanka* on the same subject.

The work had an enormous influence on later literary tradition and was especially instrumental in spreading knowledge of Bo Juyi's poetry throughout the court and establishing his reputation in Japan as the greatest of Chinese poets. The collection was widely memorized and its poems constantly alluded to in novels, diaries, miscellanies, plays, and even in popular literature of the 17th century and later. It was also used as a text for teaching composition, especially of Chinese verse, and as a copybook for writing practice. A two-volume supplement, entitled *Shinsen rōeishū* (New Collection of Chinese and Japanese Poems for Singing) was compiled by FUJIWARA NO MOTOTOSHI about a century later, around 1110.

■ ——Robert H. Brower and Earl Miner, *Japanese Court Poetry* (1961). *Robert H. BROWER*

Wakan sansai zue

(Japanese-Chinese Illustrated Assemblage of the Three Components of the Universe). Illustrated encyclopedia in 105 chapters edited by Terashima Ryōan, an Ōsaka physician; completed in 1712. Closely patterned on the Chinese work *Sancai tuhui (San-ts'ai t'u-hui;* J: *Sansai zue)* of 1607, each chapter covers a different topic, ranging from astronomy and geography to plants and animals to clothing and implements. The entries are written in Chinese prose *(kambun)*. The encyclopedia, which reached a wide audience, is useful for studying the material culture of the Edo period (1600–1868).

Wakasa Bay

The Ōi nuclear power facilities on Wakasa Bay. The plant's two reactors are the largest of their kind in Japan.

Wakao Ayako (1933–)

Film actress. Born in Tōkyō, she moved to Sendai during World War II, and as a high-school student was inspired to become an actress after seeing a performance by HASEGAWA KAZUO and his Shin'engiza troupe. She joined the troupe and later moved to the Daiei Motion Picture Company. Appearing in Shima Kōji's *Jūdai no seiten* (1953, Teenager's Sex Manual), *Chatarei fujin wa Nihon ni mo ita* (1953, Japan's Own Lady Chatterley), and Hisamatsu Seiji's *Jūdai no yūwaku* (1954, Temptation of Teenagers), she became a sex symbol. She also appeared in MIZOGUCHI KENJI's *Gion-bayashi* (1953, Gion Festival Music) and *Akasen chitai* (1956, Street of Shame). In such films as Masumura Yasuzō's *Tsuma wa kokuhaku suru* (1961, The Wife Confesses), *Manji* (1964), *Otto ga mita* (1964, The Husband Saw), *Seisaku no tsuma* (1965, The Wife of Seisaku), and *Nureta futari* (1968, Evil Duo), she excelled in portraying women who have to come to terms with their sexuality. Since the bankruptcy of Daiei, she has acted exclusively on stage and on television, apart from occasional appearances in the Shōchiku film series *Otoko wa tsurai yo* (It's Tough Being a Man), starring ATSUMI KIYOSHI. *ITASAKA Tsuyoshi*

Wakasa Bay

(Wakasa Wan). Inlet of the Sea of Japan on the northern coast of central Honshū, extending between Echizemmisaki, a cape in Fukui Prefecture, in the east and Kyōgamisaki, a cape on the Tango Peninsula, Kyōto Prefecture, in the west. It has a heavily indented coastline with numerous small bays and peninsulas. A good fishing ground, the bay also has many fine bathing beaches. An atomic energy plant is located here. Sections of the shoreline of the bay form the Wakasa Bay Quasi-National Park.

Wakatsuki Reijirō (1866–1949)

Politician; prime minister (1926–27; 1931). Born in the Matsue domain (now Shimane Prefecture). Graduated from Tōkyō University and entered the Finance Ministry. In 1912 he became finance minister in the third KATSURA TARŌ cabinet and joined the RIKKEN DŌSHIKAI, the political party formed by Katsura during the TAISHŌ POLITICAL CRISIS of 1912–13. He was again minister of finance in the second ŌKUMA SHIGENOBU cabinet. In 1914 he allied with KATŌ TAKAAKI and subsequently joined the political party KENSEIKAI, successor to the Rikken Dōshikai. Named home minister in the Katō coalition cabinet of 1924, he worked for the passage of the universal manhood suffrage bill (see UNIVERSAL MANHOOD SUFFRAGE MOVEMENT) and the PEACE PRESERVATION LAW OF 1925. He remained in the same post in the second Katō cabinet.

When Katō died in office in 1926, Wakatsuki took over as both prime minister and as president of the Kenseikai. A less skilled politician than his predecessor, he was unable to reconcile competing interests and was unpopular within the party. In 1927 Wakatsuki was forced to resign the premiership when the PRIVY COUNCIL, unhappy over his conciliatory foreign policy, blocked his proposal to give funds to the financially troubled Bank of Taiwan. As Japan's

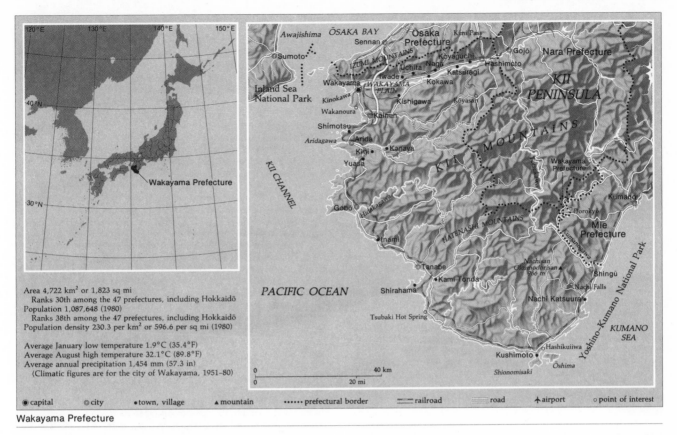

Area 4,722 km² or 1,823 sq mi
  Ranks 30th among the 47 prefectures, including Hokkaidō
Population 1,087,648 (1980)
  Ranks 38th among the 47 prefectures, including Hokkaidō
Population density 230.3 per km² or 596.6 per sq mi (1980)

Average January low temperature 1.9°C (35.4°F)
Average August high temperature 32.1°C (89.8°F)
Average annual precipitation 1,454 mm (57.3 in)
  (Climatic figures are for the city of Wakayama, 1951–80)

⊙ capital   ○ city   ● town, village   ▲ mountain   •••••• prefectural border   ═══ railroad   ═══ road   ✈ airport   ○ point of interest

Wakayama Prefecture

chief delegate to the 1930 London Naval Conference, he pressed for ratification of the proposed disarmament treaty despite opposition from rightists and the navy. After Prime Minister HAMAGUCHI OSACHI was shot by a right-wing extremist in 1930, Wakatsuki assumed the presidency of the RIKKEN MINSEITŌ, successor to the Kenseikai, and served once more as prime minister (1931). When the MANCHURIAN INCIDENT occurred in 1931, he worked hard to contain the hostilities but failed. He resigned in late 1931 when the cabinet became divided over Home Minister ADACHI KENZŌ's plan to form a Seiyūkai–Minseitō coalition cabinet. Although he retired from active politics, he continued to exercise power as a JŪSHIN (senior statesman). He opposed going to war with the United States and after World War II served as witness at the WAR CRIMES TRIALS.

Wakayama

Capital of Wakayama Prefecture, central Honshū, located at the mouth of the river Kinokawa. Its development began in 1585 with the construction of a castle by TOYOTOMI HIDEYOSHI. In the Edo period (1600–1868) it came under the rule of the Kii branch (see GOSANKE) of the Tokugawa family. Steel and chemical industries are active, along with traditional furniture making. Of interest are the temple Kimiidera, the Wakanoura coast, the Kada coast, and the island of Tomogashima in the Inland Sea National Park. Pop: 401,462.

Wakayama Bokusui (1885–1928)

TANKA poet. Real name Wakayama Shigeru. Born in Miyazaki Prefecture. Graduate of Waseda University. While still a student, he began composing *tanka* under the influence of the noted Meiji poet ONOE SAISHŪ (1876–1957). He established his name as a poet in 1910 with his collection of poems, *Betsuri*. A wanderer and a great lover of *sake,* he supported himself most of his life by writing numerous travel essays as well as poems. His style is generally that of the naturalist school of the early 20th century. His poems express the loneliness and sorrows of a traveler who often seeks comfort in drink; they are known for their mellifluous quality, which invites the reader to recite them aloud. His principal works are *Umi no koe* (1908), a collection of poems, and *Minakami kikō* (1924), a collection of travel essays.

Wakayama Plain

(Wakayama Heiya). Located in northern Wakayama Prefecture, central Honshū. Bounded by the Izumi Mountains to the north and the Kii Mountains to the south and situated along the Median Tectonic Line, this wedge-shaped plain bordering the Kii Channel consists of the flood plain of the river Kinokawa. A rice-producing area, it has numerous mandarin orange orchards on the surrounding foothills. The major city is Wakayama. Area: approximately 100 sq km (39 sq mi).

Wakayama Prefecture

(Wakayama Ken). Located on the southwestern side of the Kii Peninsula in central Honshū, and bounded by Ōsaka Prefecture on the north, Nara and Mie prefectures on the east, the Kumano Sea and the Pacific Ocean on the south, and the Kii Channel on the west. With the exception of the plain around the capital of WAKAYAMA, the prefecture is almost entirely occupied by mountains. It is cut off from the main transportation routes by its mountainous terrain and remote location. The climate is generally warm, although some of the inland mountain regions are comparatively cool.

Known after the TAIKA REFORM of 645 as Kii Province, the Wakayama area has long been noted for its Shintō and Buddhist holy places. The Kumano district in the south came to have a special importance in the Shintō religion (see KUMANO SANZAN SHRINES), while the monastery complex on Mt. Kōya (KŌYASAN) is still a major center of Japanese Buddhism (see KONGŌBUJI). In the Edo period (1600–1868) the area was the domain of a Tokugawa branch family. The present prefectural boundaries were established in 1871.

Apart from mandarin oranges, agricultural production has been declining. Fishing and forestry continue to be important. Industry is largely concentrated in the area around Wakayama, where it forms a continuation of the Ōsaka industrial district. Major products include steel and electrical equipment. Papermaking and spinning plants are scattered along the southern coast.

The Yoshino–Kumano and Inland Sea national parks span parts of the prefecture. The sandy beaches at Shirahama and rugged coves at Katsuura attract numerous vacationers from the Kyōto–Ōsaka–Kōbe area. Nachi Falls is one of Japan's largest waterfalls. Area: 4,722 sq km (1,823 sq mi); pop: 1,087,648; capital: Wakayama. Other major cities include Tanabe, Kainan, and SHINGŪ.

Wake no Kiyomaro (733–799)

Court official of the late 8th century; principal adviser to Emperor KAMMU. Born Iwanasu no Wake no Kimi, the son of a powerful chieftain in the Fujino district of Bizen Province (now part of Okayama Prefecture), he is thought to have entered service at the imperial palace as a military guard. In 764 he distinguished himself in the suppression of the rebellion of FUJIWARA NO NAKAMARO. He was appointed an officer of the third rank in both the Right Military Guards (Uhyōe) and the Imperial Guards (Konoe) and granted the honorific cognomen (*kabane;* see YAKUSA NO KABANE) *mahito;* he was subsequently known as Fujino no Mahito. In 769 he sought to thwart the ambitions of the powerful priest DŌKYŌ, favorite of Empress Shōtoku (Empress KŌKEN), to succeed to the throne, asserting that, contrary to Dōkyō's claim, the oracle of the USA HACHIMAN SHRINE disapproved of the proposal. Kiyomaro was exiled to Ōsumi Province (now part of Kagoshima Prefecture), but with the death in the following year of Empress Shōtoku and the accession of Emperor Kōnin (r 770–781), he was recalled to the capital and granted the hereditary title *ason.* In 784 he was appointed by Emperor Kammu, who had succeeded Kōnin in 781, to head successively the province of Settsu (now part of Ōsaka and Hyōgo prefectures), the Ministry of the Imperial Household, and the Ministry of Civil Affairs. In these offices he was responsible for improving the channel of the river Yamatogawa and for moving the capital, first to NAGAOKAKYŌ in 784 and then to HEIANKYŌ (Kyōto) in 794. At the same time he worked to improve regional civil administration. In accordance with his last wishes, a school, the Kōbun'in, was established for the education of male members of the Wake family.

📖 ——Hirano Kunio, *Wake no Kiyomaro* (1964).   YAGI ATSURU

wakiōkan

(side roads). Also called *wakikaidō;* secondary routes in the Edo period (1600–1868) that connected with the five main highways (GO-KAIDŌ). These roads included the Chūgokuji (from Ōsaka to Kokura in what is now Fukuoka Prefecture), the Mitoji (from the outskirts of Edo [now Tōkyō] to Mito in what is now Ibaraki Prefecture), the Sayaji (from Miya in what is now Aichi Prefecture to Kuwana in what is now Mie Prefecture by way of Saya in what is now Aichu Prefecture), and the Minoji (from Nagoya to Ōgaki in what is now Gifu Prefecture). Also included in the category of *wakiōkan* were two special routes reserved for official use: the Nikkō Onari Kaidō, used by the shōgun for pilgrimages to the Tokugawa family shrine in Nikkō, and the Reiheishi Kaidō, a branch of the NAKASENDŌ highway, used by imperial envoys from Kyōto to attend the annual memorial services at the Nikkō shrine.

Wakkanai

City in northern Hokkaidō, on the Sōya Strait. An ice-free port, Wakkanai flourished as a departure point for the island of Sakhalin until the end of World War II. It presently maintains ferry service to the islands of Rishiri and Rebun. It is a major fishing center, with abundant catches of crab, herring, cod, flatfish, and salmon. Major industries are marine food processing, lumbering, and dairy farming. Its coastal area is part of the Rishiri–Rebun–Sarobetsu National Park. Pop: 53,471.

Wakō

City in southeastern Saitama Prefecture, central Honshū. Once an agricultural area, it now has machine and automobile plants as well as many housing complexes. Pop: 49,718.

wakō

Japanese pronunciation of a term applied by Chinese and Koreans to Japanese pirates who pillaged the coasts of East Asia from the 13th century into the 17th century. Initially the pirate bands were composed of Japanese, but at times they included Koreans and Chinese as well as a few Portuguese and natives of Southeast Asia. The character for *wa* (read *wo* in Chinese and *wae* in Korean), meaning dwarf, was an ancient Chinese appellation for Japan; the character for *kō* (read *kou* or *k'ou* in Chinese and *ku* in Korean) means brigand or bandit. The earliest appearance of the term is on the KWANGGAET'O MONUMENT, a stela erected in 414 to the memory of King Kwanggaet'o (r 391–413) of the Korean state of KOGURYŌ,

which refers to Japanese military forces in Korea who were defeated by the king.

Wakō and Korea ——Japanese marauding against Korea may be divided into three phases. The first phase lasted from 1223 to 1265. The raids originated on the islands of TSUSHIMA or IKI and the northern coast of Kyūshū and were directed against the southern coast of Korea. After the 1223 raid, others followed in 1225, 1226, and 1227. The two raids of 1227 led to a Korean protest, and 90 pirates were executed by Kyūshū authorities in the presence of the Korean envoy. After a temporary halt, raiding resumed in 1259, but Korea was occupied in that year by the warlike Mongols (see MONGOL INVASIONS OF KOREA), and, with the exception of a raid in 1263 in which the Japanese seized government ships carrying tax rice and another in 1265, the attacks came to an end.

The second phase lasted from 1350 to 1419. The renewal of marauding on a much greater scale was due to a number of factors: the military weakness of the Mongols in China and Korea; the closing of Ningbo (Ningpo) and other Chinese ports south of the Yangzi (Yangtze) River by Mongol officials to Japanese merchants for breaches of the peace; the political and economic chaos in Japan resulting from the civil war between the NORTHERN AND SOUTHERN COURTS; and a series of natural disasters between 1346 and 1349. *Wakō* raids reached a peak in the late 1370s and early 1380s. Both coasts of Korea were ravaged, especially the rice-rich southern and eastern coastal valleys. Kaesŏng (then called Songdo), the capital, was threatened several times. Tax-rice flotillas were seized, and, when the Koreans decided to transport the rice by land, the *wakō* went inland and looted the granaries. Booty included other grains, cloth, captives, and coins. The loss of coins was so great that Korea returned to a barter economy. Coastal districts were evacuated and fishing and salt production ceased. Some poor Koreans even joined the *wakō* bands as guides. The Koreans sent diplomatic missions, the first in 1366, to protest to the MUROMACHI SHOGUNATE (1338–1573), but it was found to be more effective to negotiate directly with the feudal lords who controlled western Japan. The Korean army was improved under the leadership of Ch'oe Yŏng (1316–88) and YI SŎNG-GYE, and in 1380 warships equipped with cannons destroyed a *wakō* fleet of 300 to 500 ships at the mouth of the Kŭm River. By 1385 the naval initiative had passed to the Koreans, who began eliminating Japanese pirate bases on offshore islands. In 1389 Yi Sŏng-gye, who would found the YI DYNASTY three years later, ordered a punitive expedition against Tsushima in which 300 Japanese ships were burned and more than 100 Korean captives were recovered.

The early rulers of the Yi dynasty permitted trade, and Japanese feudal lords returned captives for profitable gifts. The Korean court conducted diplomatic relations through the lords of Tsushima (see SŌ FAMILY) and held them responsible for the good behavior of the Japanese. Raids declined, and when there were incursions in 1419, the Yi government responded by executing 737 Japanese traders and launching a punitive expedition against Tsushima. Some 128 ships were seized, 1,939 houses burned, 137 Chinese liberated, and 20 Japanese taken prisoner (see ŌEI INVASION). This ended the second phase. By this time, however, *wakō* bases in Japan had spread throughout Kyūshū and the coasts of the Inland Sea. Moreover, with navigational and shipbuilding techniques learned from the Chinese, the pirates could sail in any season.

The third phase was relatively minor. The authority of the Muromachi shogunate curbed *wakō* incursions into Korea. Korea gradually restricted trade to three ports, Naeip'o (now Chep'o), Pusanp'o (now Pusan) and Yŏmp'o (near modern Ulsan). As the authority of the Muromachi shogunate weakened, however, *wakō* again pillaged the southern coast of Korea in 1544, 1555, and 1589, but their main effort was at this time directed toward China.

Wakō and China ——Although *wakō* had already raided the Ningbo area sometime between 1308 and 1311, it was not until the 1350s that they began in earnest. In 1358 they raided the Shandong (Shantung) Peninsula and followed this with similar raids on other coastal provinces. In 1363 they met defeat in an engagement on the Shandong Peninsula.

Even after the founding of the Ming dynasty (1368–1644) the raids continued unabated and pushed south to Fujian (Fukien) Province. The Chinese built forts from Shandong to Fujian to discourage the Japanese marauders and forbade coastal trade and foreign voyages. The retired shōgun ASHIKAGA YOSHIMITSU entered into tributary relations with the Ming, mainly with an eye to the profits of trade, and in the TALLY TRADE that followed, the shogunate, the ŌUCHI FAMILY and the HOSOKAWA FAMILY, and other participants restrained the *wakō* based in their domains. Pirates who continued to raid were captured and sent to China, where they were executed. The authority of the Muromachi shogunate was greatly weakened after the ŌNIN WAR (1467–77). In 1523 China forbade foreign trade at Ningbo. This led to smuggling by Japanese along the Jiangsu (Kiangsu), Zhejiang (Chekiang), and Fujian coasts, and when the Chinese authorities attempted to suppress it, the Japanese resorted to piracy. With the assassination of ŌUCHI YOSHITAKA, who had controlled the Shimonoseki Strait, and the fragmentation of Japan into warring factions, the *wakō* once more sailed abroad in great numbers. Between 1552 and 1559 they raided from Jiangsu to Guangzhou (Canton), often penetrating deep inland and threatening Nanjing (Nanking), Suzhou (Soochow), and other major cities. In many cases these "Japanese pirates" were predominantly Chinese, led by men like Wang Zhi (Wang Chih), who operated from the Zhoushan (Chusan) Islands near Ningbo. After TOYOTOMI HIDEYOSHI conquered Kyūshū in 1587, he issued an edict prohibiting piracy. *Wakō* activity was drastically reduced in Japan, but by then there were several generations of Japanese freebooters living abroad.

Wakō and Southeast Asia——Little is known of *wakō* activities in Southeast Asia. From the late 16th century the *wakō* frequently used Portuguese pilots although they often found the Portuguese siding with the Chinese for economic reasons. By the 1580s *wakō* had also penetrated the Philippines, where they played a double game, most often cooperating with the Spanish. Most trade in Southeast Asia was conducted by legitimate merchants licensed by Hideyoshi or later by the Tokugawa shogunate (see VERMILION SEAL SHIP TRADE), but others traded illegally or preyed on the legitimate trade. The Spanish and Portuguese grew to fear the Japanese, *wakō* and traders alike, and in 1597 Portuguese authorities in Macao excluded all armed Japanese. The extent of Japanese penetration of Southeast Asia is apparent from the career of YAMADA NAGAMASA, a legitimate trader who gained favor at the Siamese court.

■——Benjamin H. Hazard, "The Formative Years of the Wakō, 1223–63," *Monumenta Nipponica* (1967). Benjamin H. Hazard, "The Wakō and Korean Responses," in *Papers in Honor of Professor Woodbridge Bingham* (1976). Ishihara Michihiro, *Wakō* (1964). Kwan-wai So, *Japanese Piracy in Ming China During the 16th Century* (1975). Mori Katsumi, "International Relations Between the 10th and the 16th Century and the Development of the Japanese International Consciousness," *Acta Asiatica* 2 (1961). Naganuma Kenkai, *Nippon no kaizoku* (1955). M. S. Seoh, "A Brief Documentary Survey of Japanese Pirate Activities in Korea in the 13th–15th Centuries," *Journal of Korean Studies* 1.1 (1969). Tanaka Takeo, *Wakō to kangō bōeki* (1961). Tomaru Fukuju and Mogi Shūichirō, *Wakō kenkyū* (1942). Yosaburo Takegoshi, *The Story of the Wakō, Japanese Pioneers in the Southern Regions* (1940).

Benjamin H. HAZARD

wakon kansai

(Japanese spirit, Chinese knowledge). The ideal of using knowledge gained from China in accordance with Japan's native cultural traditions. The phrase was traditionally attributed to the 9th-century scholar SUGAWARA NO MICHIZANE but may have been coined as late as the 18th century. In the Meiji period (1868–1912) it was modified to *wakon yōsai* (Japanese spirit, Western knowledge) and was advocated as a guiding principle for the adoption of Western culture.

Robert BORGEN

wakon yōsai

(Japanese spirit, Western knowledge). The ideal of adopting and applying Western learning and knowledge in conformity with native Japanese cultural traditions. The phrase was a modification of an earlier, similar sounding slogan, WAKON KANSAI (Japanese spirit, Chinese knowledge), said traditionally to have been coined in the 9th century to call attention to the importance of the native cultural heritage and the unique spirit inherent in Japanese civilization. In like fashion the phrase *wakon yōsai*, also based on this same notion, gained currency in the Meiji period (1868–1912) as Western knowledge and technology began to be adopted on a large scale in Japan. It also echoed the expression "oriental ethics (spirit), Western technique (science and technology)," of the *samurai* thinker SAKUMA SHŌZAN (1811–64). In the early phase of the modernization of Japan, the adoption of Western technology was an inevitable, necessary step toward the pursuit of envisioned national growth. The wish to maintain traditional moral values produced the position of

compromise known as *wakon yōsai*. This term exemplifies the process by which traditional Japanese culture and Western technology were woven together in modern Japanese civilization.

Suzuki Eiichi

Wako Shungorō (1890–1965)

Leader of the Japanese immigrant community in Brazil. Born in Nagano Prefecture. After working as a newspaper reporter, Wako emigrated to Brazil in 1913 and helped establish Japanese agricultural settlements such as Aliança and Tieté. He published a study on Japanese immigrants in the Bauru district in 1939. Later Wako devoted himself to the education of Japanese farmers' children, helping to build a student center and the Harmonia dormitory in São Paulo.

Saitō Hiroshi

Wakun no shiori

Japanese-language dictionary compiled by TANIGAWA KOTOSUGA (1709–76) in the latter half of the 18th century. A representative Edo-period (1600–1868) dictionary, the *Wakun no shiori* consists of 93 fascicles in 82 volumes which are subdivided into three parts. The first and second parts were published, after Tanigawa's death, during the period 1777 to 1862. The last part did not come out until 1887. The *Wakun no shiori* contains an extensive selection of word entries drawn from the ancient, classical, and colloquial vocabularies (including local dialects). It cites numerous usage examples from authoritative sources and gives informative explanations for each word entry. Words are arranged in the order of the standard "50-sound" chart (GOJŪON ZU) of the KANA syllabary. It is considered the prototype of the modern Japanese-language dictionary and is a valuable research tool for Japanese vocabulary studies. The *Zōho gorin wakun no shiori,* a revised and enlarged three-volume edition without the final section, is still used.

Uwano Zendō

Waley, Arthur David (1889–1966)

The translator who, more than any other, was responsible for introducing classical Chinese and Japanese literature to Western readers. Waley combined a thorough knowledge of the languages with remarkable literary gifts. His translations from the Chinese, beginning with *Chinese Poems,* privately published in 1916, spanned his entire career. A list of the most important might include *A Hundred and Seventy Chinese Poems* (1918), *The Way and Its Power* (1934), *The Book of Songs* (1937), *The Analects of Confucius* (1938), *Three Ways of Thought in Ancient China* (1939), and *The Life and Times of Po Chü-i* (1949). Almost all of his translations from Japanese, however, were produced over a relatively short period of time. These include *Japanese Poetry: The Uta* (1919; a selection of *waka* poems from the MAN'YŌSHŪ and imperial anthologies preceded by an eight-page grammatical note intended to make it possible for readers to enjoy the poems in the original), *The Nō Plays of Japan* (1921); the TALE OF GENJI (translation of the *Genji monogatari,* published in six volumes, 1925–33); *The Pillow Book of Sei Shōnagon* (1928; approximately a quarter of the text of *Makura no sōshi*; see SEI SHŌNAGON), and "The Lady Who Loved Insects" (1929, one story from the TSUTSUMI CHŪNAGON MONOGATARI). Waley also wrote extensively on Chinese and Japanese art and was one of the first Westerners to write on Zen Buddhism and its relation to art. His translations from the Japanese must be judged defective by present-day scholarly standards, owing in part to recent advances in scholarship but owing principally to the extreme freedom with which he treated his texts. His translation of NŌ plays obscures important structural features, while his *Tale of Genji* omits significant portions of the original text. Waley was a man of strong convictions and independent mind; he translated only works to which he was especially drawn and which he felt would go well into English without needing large numbers of explanatory notes. He was proud of the appeal of his work to lay readers and believed that an agreeable English style was as necessary to a translation as faithfulness.

Waley was born to an English-Jewish family originally named Schloss (the name was changed during World War I to avoid harassment as suspected enemy aliens). He attended Rugby (1903–06) and enrolled in a classical course at King's College, Cambridge (1907–10), which poor eyesight forced him to abandon before completion. Essentially self-educated in Chinese and Japanese, he began his activities as a translator while employed as an assistant at the British Museum. He never accepted a regular university appointment, and he refused to visit Asia. He enjoyed being called upon by visitors from Japan but never learned to speak Japanese and had little interest in modern Japanese literature. His personal life was abstemious; his principal recreations were music and skiing. His acquaintances included many outstanding figures in 20th-century British literature. His English translations have been translated into other European languages and influenced such major writers as Bertolt Brecht.

——Francis A. Johns, *A Bibliography of Arthur Waley* (1968). Ivan Morris, ed, *Madly Singing in the Mountains* (1970). Marian Ury, "The Imaginary Kingdom and the Translator's Art: Notes on Re-reading Waley's *Genji*," *Journal of Japanese Studies* 2.2 (1976).
Marian URY

wall painting → screen and wall painting

Wamyō ruiju shō

Also known as *Wamyōshō* or *Shitagau ga wamyō*. Chinese-Japanese dictionary compiled by MINAMOTO NO SHITAGAU around 934. There are both 10- and 20-volume editions extant, but the historical relationship between the two is unclear. Encyclopedic in nature, the work assembles the names of many objects and classifies them according to traditional categories (the *ruiju* of the title means "classified by categories"), e.g., heaven and earth, human relations, etc. Definitions in Chinese provide meanings, pronunciations, and literary sources. Entries also record the Japanese pronunciation (*wamyō*) of the term in *man'yōgana* (Chinese characters used phonetically). Sources cited include many documents no longer extant, so that the *Wamyō ruiju shō* serves as a valuable research tool for bibliographers and cultural historians of the Heian period as well as linguists.
UWANO Zendō

Wamyōshō → Wamyō ruiju shō

Wang Jingwei (Wang Ching-wei) (1883–1944)

(J: Ō Seiei; also known as Wang Zhaoming or Wang Chao-ming; J: Ō Chōmei). A Chinese Guomindang (Kuomintang; Nationalist Party) politician who collaborated with Japan as head of its puppet government in Nanjing (Nanking) during the SINO-JAPANESE WAR OF 1937–1945. Like many young Chinese in the years after the Russo-Japanese War (1904–05), Wang went to Japan for his university education. While a student at Hōsei University, he became an enthusiastic disciple of SUN YAT-SEN and helped organize the overseas Chinese community to support Sun's anti-Manchu cause. In 1910 Wang was catapulted into national attention for his part in a daring (though unsuccessful) attempt on the life of the Manchu prince regent. Long years of close association with Sun led many to think that Wang was the logical successor to the revered leader of the Guomindang. Wang, however, lacked a military power base and consequently did not fare well in the political struggles that ensued upon Sun's death in 1925. For the next 13 years Wang was alternately in and out of the government, which came to be increasingly dominated by his rival, CHIANG KAI-SHEK.

In the period after Japan's seizure of Manchuria in 1931, Wang and Chiang, despite their personal rivalry, agreed that the defeat of communism at home took precedence over—and necessitated a postponement of—a war of resistance against Japan. Even after hostilities broke out in 1937, Wang continued to advocate a negotiated settlement with Japan. In December 1938 he defected from the wartime capital of Chongqing (Chungking) and began a 16-month search to find a basis for collaboration with his nation's enemy. In March 1940 Wang became the head of the newly created REORGANIZED NATIONAL GOVERNMENT OF THE REPUBLIC OF CHINA, which he committed to cooperation with Japan. Although vilified by many for treason, Wang argued that it was a necessary and thankless task, negotiating with Japan to soften the harshness of the occupation, protect Chinese lives and rights, and preserve national integrity in the parts of China controlled by Japan. He died in Nagoya, Japan, in 1944. See also CHINA AND JAPAN: China and Japan after 1912.
John H. BOYLE

Wang Kemin (Wang K'o-min) (1873–1945)

(J: Ō Kokubin). Leader of Japanese-sponsored government in North China during World War II. After passing the provincial-level civil service examination, Wang was sent to Japan in 1900 to supervise Chinese students there. In 1902 he became a councillor to the Chinese legation in Tōkyō, a position he held until his return to China in 1907. In 1913 he became a managing director of the Sino-French Banque Industrielle de Chine, and in 1917 he was appointed governor of the Bank of China. He served briefly as minister of finance in 1918 and in 1924. In the 1930s Wang was a prominent pro-Japanese politician. After the SINO-JAPANESE WAR OF 1937–1945 broke out, Wang headed the collaborationist PROVISIONAL GOVERNMENT OF THE REPUBLIC OF CHINA in Beiping (Peiping; now Beijing or Peking). After that regime was superseded by the puppet government in Nanjing (Nanking) under WANG JINGWEI (Wang Ching-wei) in 1940, Wang Kemin played a role in the North China Political Council, which he headed from 1943 to 1945. Arrested at the end of the war, he died in prison.

——John Hunter Boyle, *China and Japan at War, 1937–1945: The Politics of Collaboration* (1972). Gerald E. Bunker, *The Peace Conspiracy: Wang Ching-wei and the China War* (1972).
Robert ENTENMANN

Wang Tao (Wang T'ao) (1828–1897?)

(J: Ō Tō). Best known as the founder of modern journalism in China, Wang Tao was a scholar and early advocate of reform whose book on his visit to Japan in 1879 was one of the earliest Chinese accounts of Meiji-period (1868–1912) Japan. Wang worked in Hong Kong as an editor and translator with English missionaries and for 10 years aided James Legge in his famous translation of the Chinese classics before pursuing a career in publishing and journalism. One of his books, *Pu Fa zhan ji* (*P'u-Fa chan chi*; The Franco-Prussian War), first published in 1877, was widely read in Japan and reprinted by the Japanese Army Ministry in 1878 and 1887. In 1879 a group of Japanese literary scholars, including NAKAMURA MASANAO, invited Wang to Japan. Wang met many literary, political, and journalistic figures, learning about the early reforms of Meiji Japan. His *Fusang youji* (*Fu-sang yu-chi*; A Record of Travels in Japan), was a result of his four-month visit. In his book Wang praised the Meiji Restoration (1868) for its selective use of Western institutions. He also expressed admiration for Japan's energetic study of the West and its success in limiting Western penetration into Japan. At the same time Wang was ambivalent, writing that in its eagerness to Westernize, Japan had lost its spiritual core. Later, Wang became distrustful of Japan's foreign policy and criticized Japan's seizure of the Ryūkyū Islands, using the DAI NIHON SHI (History of Great Japan) to support his argument that the islands belonged to China.

——Paul A. Cohen, *Between Tradition and Modernity: Wang T'ao and Reform in Late Ch'ing China* (1974). Fuse Chisoku, "Ō Shisen no Fusō yūki," in *Tōa kenkyū kōza* (December 1938). Sanetō Keishū, "Ō Tō no raiyū to Nihon bunjin," in *Kindai nisshi bunka ron* (1941). Wang Tao, *Fusang youji* (*Fu-sang yu-chi*; 1879).

Wang Yangming school → Yōmeigaku

Wang Zhaoming (Wang Chao-ming) → Wang Jingwei (Wang Ching-wei)

Wang Zhengting (Wang Cheng-t'ing) (1882–1961)

(J: Ō Seitei). Also known as C. T. Wang. Chinese diplomat and minister of foreign affairs. The son of a Methodist minister, Wang studied in Japan from 1905 to 1907 and then in the United States, where he graduated from Yale University in 1910. After returning to China he became a parliamentary leader in Beijing (Peking). In 1917 he joined SUN YAT-SEN's government in Guangzhou (Canton) and represented it at the Paris Peace Conference in 1919. In 1921 he was a member of the Chinese delegation to the WASHINGTON CONFERENCE, and in 1922 he represented China on a Sino-Japanese commission overseeing the withdrawal of Japanese troops who had been stationed in Shandong (Shantung) Province since World War I. He was minister of foreign affairs from November 1922 to March 1924 and briefly served as acting premier of the Beijing government. In July 1928 he joined the Nationalist government of CHIANG KAI-SHEK as foreign minister. Popular opinion blamed him for the Chinese government's lack of resistance to the Japanese occupation of Manchuria (see MANCHURIAN INCIDENT) and forced his resignation on 30 September 1931. He served as China's ambassador to the United States from 1936 to 1938. He died in Hong Kong.

Robert ENTENMANN

Wani (fl ca AD 400?)

Immigrant (KIKAJIN) who came to Japan from the Korean state of Paekche in about AD 400 and became a scholar and administrator in the service of the YAMATO COURT. According to the chronicles KO-JIKI (712) and NIHON SHOKI (720), Wani (or Wani Kishi) was sent by the Paekche king on the recommendation of an earlier scholar-immigrant to be tutor to a son of Emperor ŌJIN. He is said to have brought with him the Analects of Confucius and the "Thousand-Character Classic." The 9th-century historical work *Kogo shūi* states that, in the reign of the legendary emperor Richū, Wani and Achi no Omi, ancestor of the greater part of the immigrant AYA FAMILY, shared administrative responsibility for the Inner Treasury (Uchikura). The Kawachi no Fumi clan, who traced their ancestry to Wani, settled principally in what is now Ōsaka Prefecture. They were active in government service, horse breeding, and military affairs as well as scholarship and handicraft production. After their conversion to Buddhism in the 6th century, they built Sairinji, in what is now the city of Habikino, Ōsaka Prefecture, as their family temple. Perhaps Wani's best-known descendant was the itinerant priest and social activist GYŌGI (668–749). *William R. CARTER*

Wa no Goō → Five Kings of Wa

warabe uta → children's songs

Warabi

City in southeastern Saitama Prefecture, central Honshū. Warabi developed in the Edo period (1600–1868) as a post-station town on the highway Nakasendō. Principal industries are ceramics and electrical appliances. Pop: 70,876.

warabidemon → fern frond design

waragutsu

(straw shoes or straw boots). Also known as *yukigutsu* ("snow shoes"). Traditional footgear still widely used in the rural snowbound regions of northern Honshū. They range from straw sandals *(waraji)* with toe covers or straw slippers to low and high styles of boots, the latter being most typical. Because they can be easily slipped on and off, *waragutsu* are worn inside the home on packed dirt spaces such as kitchen floors, for going to outhouses, or for walking in the neighborhood. *MIYAMOTO Mizuo*

waraji

A traditional rough straw sandal, with a thong passing between the big and second toes; tied onto the foot with straw straps, which pass through a series of loops on the sides of the sole. Not to be confused with the finer straw sandal, *zōri*, which is held onto the foot by the thong alone. Materials used include plain rice straw, flax (ASA) fibers, wisteria or grape fibers, and straw interwoven with cloth strips. *Waraji* were used throughout Japan and worn when taking long journeys on foot. Their manufacture was one of the evening's tasks in a farm household; in many regions making *waraji* was the first task of the New Year. *MIYAMOTO Mizuo*

Warashibe chōja

(The Straw Millionaire). Folktale. A poor man prays to the bodhisattva Kannon (Skt: Avalokiteśvara) for good fortune and is told that the first thing he touches outside the temple shall be his. At the temple gate he stumbles on a stone and grabs a straw. He trades this straw for an orange and then trades each new acquisition for something more valuable (cloth, a horse, a field) so that he finally becomes wealthy. The story, widespread in Japan, appears in medieval works like the KONJAKU MONOGATARI and the UJI SHŪI MONOGATARI and is particularly associated with the statue of Kannon at the temple HASEDERA. *SUCHI Tokuhei*

war crimes trials

A series of quasi-legal military tribunals during and after World War II in which Japanese and German military and civilian leaders were tried by the victorious Allies for alleged war crimes; the trials of Japanese leaders culminated in the International Military Tribunal for the Far East (Kyokutō Kokusai Gunji Saiban), held in Tōkyō from 1946 to 1948.

The term war crimes denotes activity in wartime that contravenes recognized standards of military conduct. Theoretically it should include illegal activity by all participants and should exclude activity not clearly considered illegal. In the aftermath of the Pacific War, however, neither condition applied.

As regards the first condition, the various wartime and postwar trials and tribunals considered only Japanese acts, not acts committed by the Allies. American acts of dubious legality included the fire-bombings of major Japanese cities and the atomic bombing of Hiroshima and Nagasaki. Writing in 1960, 12 years after the end of the Tōkyō Trial at which he was the Dutch justice, Bernard V. A. Röling commented: "From the Second World War above all two things are remembered: the German gas chambers and the American atomic bombings." But the atomic bombings were not the subject of war crimes prosecution, and at the Tōkyō Trial evidence concerning the two bombs was declared inadmissible.

Similarly, the Russian attack on Japan on 8 August 1945 was a prima facie breach of the Soviet Union's nonaggression pact with Japan. To be sure, the Soviet Union had announced its intention not to renew the pact, but its expiration date was April 1946. Asked after the Tōkyō Trial about various Russian acts, the American prosecutor at Tōkyō commented: "The recipe for rabbit stew is first to catch the rabbit." The logic applies equally to American acts and American actors; and it explains why only Japanese acts and Japanese actors were prosecuted.

As regards the second condition, the bulk of the prosecution at the Tōkyō Trial rested on charges not clearly considered illegal. For example, the principal charge at Tōkyō was that of "aggression"; yet as recently as 1944, three of the Big Four (France, Great Britain, and the United States) had agreed that aggressive war was not a crime. On both scores, then, the war crimes prosecutions relating to the Pacific War are open to the charge, first made by some of the defendants, that they were victors' justice—revenge dressed up in the trappings of legality.

The distinction between war crimes and war crimes prosecutions is a critical one, but it is all too often ignored. Most references to war crimes mean war crimes that were brought to prosecution; the two major forms of such prosecution will be examined here. These are, first, the multitude of "minor" trials, which considered primarily alleged atrocities, committed either in battle, during military occupation, or against prisoners of war; and second, the one showcase trial at Tōkyō, which considered primarily the prewar and wartime policies of the Japanese government.

The "Minor" Trials —— The Allies tried some 6,000 Japanese in several thousand "minor" trials during and after the war. Of the accused, 920 were sentenced to death and executed. The records of these trials are fragmentary and scattered, and no systematic study has yet been published. Therefore, even the statistics are inexact, and general statements are difficult to make.

The most famous of the "minor" trials is that of General YAMASHITA TOMOYUKI in 1946. Commander of most Japanese forces in the Philippines at the time of the Allied reconquest, Yamashita was tried before a military commission of five American generals, none of whom had either combat or legal experience. The charge against him was that he "unlawfully disregarded and failed to discharge his duty as commander to control the operations of the members of his command, permitting them to commit brutal atrocities and other high crimes." Found guilty as charged, he was sentenced to hang. That sentence was upheld on appeal by General Douglas MACARTHUR; both the Philippine Supreme Court and the US Supreme Court (5–2, Justices Frank Murphy and Wiley B. Rutledge dissenting) refused to review the merits of the verdict. Justice Murphy's dissenting opinion indicates some of the legal issues raised by the Yamashita case and by many of the other "minor" trials. He wrote: "This petitioner was rushed to trial under an improper charge, given insufficient time to prepare an adequate defense, deprived of the

War crimes trials

The Tōkyō Trial: Defendants, Verdicts, Sentences, Paroles

Defendant	1	27	29	31	32	33	35	36	54	55	Sentence	Parole
Araki Sadao (1877–1966)	G	G	A	A	A	A	A	A	A	A	Life	1955
Doihara Kenji (1883–1948)	G	G	G	G	G	A	G	G	G	O	Death	
Hashimoto Kingorō (1890–1957)	G	G	A	A	A	—	—	—	A	A	Life	1955
Hata Shunroku (1879–1962)	G	G	G	G	G	—	A	A	A	G	Life	1954
Hiranuma Kiichirō (1867–1952)	G	G	G	G	G	A	A	G	A	A	Life	
Hirota Kōki (1878–1948)	G	G	A	A	A	A	A	—	A	G	Death	
Hoshino Naoki (1892–1978)	G	G	G	G	G	A	A	—	A	A	Life	1955
Itagaki Seishirō (1885–1948)	G	G	G	G	G	A	G	G	G	O	Death	
Kaya Okinori (1889–1977)	G	G	G	G	G	—	—	—	A	A	Life	1955
Kido Kōichi (1889–1977)	G	G	G	G	G	A	A	A	A	A	Life	1955
Kimura Heitarō (1888–1948)	G	G	G	G	G	—	—	—	G	G	Death	
Koiso Kuniaki (1880–1950)	G	G	G	G	G	—	—	A	A	A	Life	
Matsui Iwane (1878–1948)	A	A	A	A	A	—	A	A	A	G	Death	
Matsuoka Yōsuke (1880–1946)	Died during the trial											
Minami Jirō (1874–1955)	G	G	A	A	A	—	—	—	A	A	Life	1954
Mutō Akira (1892–1948)	G	G	G	G	G	A	—	A	G	G	Death	
Nagano Osami (1880–1947)	Died during the trial											
Oka Takasumi (1890–1973)	G	G	G	G	G	—	—	—	A	A	Life	1954
Ōkawa Shūmei (1886–1957)	Declared unfit for trial											
Ōshima Hiroshi (1886–1975)	G	A	A	A	A	—	—	—	A	A	Life	1955
Satō Kenryō (1895–1975)	G	G	G	G	G	—	—	—	A	A	Life	1956
Shigemitsu Mamoru (1887–1957)	A	G	G	G	G	G	A	—	A	G	7 years	1950
Shimada Shigetarō (1883–1976)	G	G	G	G	G	—	—	—	A	A	Life	1955
Shiratori Toshio (1887–1949)	G	A	A	A	A	—	—	—	—	—	Life	
Suzuki Teiichi (1888–)	G	G	G	G	G	—	A	A	A	A	Life	1955
Tōgō Shigenori (1882–1950)	G	G	G	G	G	—	—	A	A	A	20 years	
Tōjō Hideki (1884–1948)	G	G	G	G	G	G	—	A	G	O	Death	
Umezu Yoshijirō (1882–1949)	G	G	G	G	G	—	—	A	A	A	Life	

Count 1: overall conspiracy; Count 27: waging war against China; Count 29: waging war against the United States; Count 31: waging war against the British Commonwealth; Count 32: waging war against the Netherlands; Count 33: waging war against France; Count 35: waging war against the Soviet Union (Lake Khassan); Count 36: waging war against the Soviet Union (Nomonhan); Count 54: ordering, authorizing, or permitting atrocities; Count 55: disregard of duty to secure observance of and prevent breaches of laws of war. The other 45 counts were dismissed or not dealt with in the majority judgment.

G—guilty   A—acquitted   O—charged but no finding made

NOTE: On 7 April 1958, the Japanese Foreign Ministry announced the unconditional release of the 10 surviving parolees.

SOURCE: Adapted from Richard H. Minear, *Victors' Justice: The Tokyo War Crimes Trial* (1971).

benefits of some of the most elementary rules of evidence, and summarily sentenced to be hanged. In all this needless and unseemly haste there was no serious attempt to prove that he committed a recognized violation of the laws of war." If this tribunal, which was exceptional both in extent of preparations and in amount of press coverage, was flawed so grievously, it seems safe to assume that many of the less prominent "minor" trials were also drumhead justice.

The Tōkyō Trial ——— The Pacific counterpart of the first showcase trial at Nuremberg was the International Military Tribunal for the Far East, known more often as the Tōkyō Trial. Convened on 3 May 1946 after many months of preparation, the Tōkyō Trial involved charges against 28 political and military leaders of the prewar and wartime Japanese governments. Foremost among the defendants was TŌJŌ HIDEKI, prime minister during most of the war and general in the Imperial Army. Of the 28, 14 were generals, 3 were admirals, and 5 were career diplomats. On the bench were 11 justices, one each from the aggrieved and victorious nations and one each from the Philippines and India, which had not been independent at the time of the Pacific War. The trial lasted two and one-half years, and the justices announced verdicts and sentences in November 1948. (See table.)

The charges against the defendants at Tōkyō fell into three major categories: conspiracy to commit aggression, aggression, and conventional war crimes. Each charge involved serious problems, both legally and procedurally.

The crime of conspiracy did not exist in international law before 1945. The president of the tribunal, Sir William Webb of Australia,

wrote in his separate opinion that international law "does not expressly include a crime of naked conspiracy"; for the tribunal to create such a crime, he held, "would be nothing short of judicial legislation." However, the majority of the justices thought otherwise and convicted all but two defendants of conspiracy. Two of those so convicted were found guilty *only* on this charge; they were both sentenced to life imprisonment.

The charge of having committed aggression rested upon a similarly fragile legal foundation. First, no precedent existed for trying individuals for acts of state. As Chief Prosecutor Joseph B. Keenan (United States) stated in his opening speech, "We freely concede that these trials are in that sense without precedent." But of the justices, only Radhabinod Pal (India) held that individuals could not be held responsible for their acts as government officials. Second, no generally agreed upon definition of aggression then existed (or exists today). Third, aggression was not considered a crime in international law. The chief evidence summoned by the prosecution was the KELLOGG-BRIAND PACT (1928), which renounced recourse to war as an instrument of national policy; but that pact made no mention of crime, did not define aggression, and set up no tribunal to adjudicate in case of war. In 1944 both the United States and Great Britain had been signatories to a United Nations War Crimes Commission report that stated: "Acts committed by individuals merely for the purpose of preparing for and launching aggressive war, are . . . not 'war crimes.'" Still, all but two of the Tōkyō justices held that aggression was or should be a crime in international law; and the majority convicted all but three of the defendants on at least one charge of committing it.

The charge of conventional war crimes consisted of two counts: that some defendants "ordered, authorized, and permitted" conventional war crimes (count 54); and that they "deliberately and recklessly disregarded their legal duty to take adequate steps to secure the observance and prevent breaches" of the laws and customs of war (count 55). On count 54, borrowed from Nuremberg, five defendants were found guilty, and all five were condemned to death. Count 55 was new to international law at Tōkyō, although it had figured earlier in the trial of General Yamashita. On this count, seven defendants were found guilty; of these, four were condemned to death, two were sentenced to life imprisonment, and one received the lightest sentence of all: seven years. One defendant was found guilty *only* on count 55; he was condemned to death.

The Tōkyō Trial was beset also by procedural flaws. There were no judges from neutral nations. Only one judge (Pal, of India) had a background in international law. The Soviet judge understood neither official language of the trial (i.e., English and Japanese). The Philippine judge was a survivor of the BATAAN "Death March." The first American judge resigned in disgust in July 1946, and another was appointed to take his place. One judge (Pal) was simply not present during 20 percent of the court sessions. These 11 judges decided all issues by majority vote. For example, the vote to condemn one defendant (HIROTA KŌKI) to death was 6-5; the votes on the other death sentences were 7-4; and the vote to execute by hanging rather than by firing squad was 6-5.

In order to find the defendants guilty, the tribunal had to endorse a view of the Pacific War that carries little credence today. According to the tribunal's majority, the conspiracy charged by the prosecution did in fact exist, beginning as early as 1927, and was responsible for virtually all the events of the 1930s: the MANCHURIAN INCIDENT of 1931, the assassination of Prime Minister INUKAI TSUYOSHI in 1932, the FEBRUARY 26TH INCIDENT of 1936 (which defendant Tōjō had helped to put down), the TRIPARTITE PACT, the attack on Pearl Harbor, and so on. To the argument that Japan acted in significant measure from considerations of self-defense, the majority responded that it was "merely a repetition of Japanese propaganda issued at the time she was preparing for her wars of aggression."

The final judgment was a majority one, supported by 8 of the 11 judges. Five judges prepared separate opinions. These ranged from a call for stiffer punishment in a few cases (Deefin Jaranilla, Philippines), to an argument against the death penalties (Webb, Australia), to the dissents on legal issues of Henri Bernard (France) and Röling (Holland). The most thorough dissenter was Pal (India), who found all defendants innocent on all counts.

The defendants appealed the verdicts, first to General MacArthur and then to the United States Supreme Court. After hearing preliminary arguments, the court voted 6-1 (with one abstention and one opinion reserved) that it lacked jurisdiction. In a concurring opinion, Associate Justice William O. Douglas wrote that the Tōkyō Trial "acted as an instrument of military power of the Executive Branch of government . . . It took its law from its creator and did not act as a free and independent tribunal to adjudge the rights of petitioners under international law." Their appeals exhausted, the defendants condemned to death were hanged on 23 December 1948. Shortly after the trial the OCCUPATION authorities released the remaining class-A suspects who had spent the years 1945–48 in prison without indictment. Unlike Nuremberg, which witnessed a succession of trials, there was only one Tōkyō Trial.

From the vantage point of the early 1980s, the postwar trials of Japanese war criminals can be explained but not justified. Major elements of the explanation include the bitterness of the fighting in the Pacific and the racial and cultural differences between the Japanese and most of the Allies. But brutality was not confined to the Japanese side: Allied soldiers often took no prisoners, and torture and mutilation were not unknown. Moreover, it is striking that the victorious Allies executed many more Japanese than Germans on conventional war crimes charges. The Japanese total (including the Tōkyō Trial) was 927; the German total (the Dachau trials excepted) seems to have been less than 100.

Similarly, the Tōkyō Trial was perhaps inevitable. Indeed, one major argument in support of the trial is that "only" seven Japanese leaders paid with their lives, not the thousands who might have died in a nonjudicial bloodbath. Still, the Tōkyō Trial and its verdict represented an extension into the postwar period of the self-serving Allied explanation of the Pacific War: an irrational Japanese attack on the "world order." The principal legacy of the Tōkyō Trial thus lies in the realm of propaganda and popular images: that the Japanese cause was wrong and illegal; that the Allied cause was right and legal.

Thirty years after the Pacific War came to an end, the fall of Saigon in 1975 marked the end of the American adventure in Indochina. By then the My Lai massacre had been exposed, the Pentagon Papers published, and the secret bombing of Cambodia revealed. Allied condemnation of Japanese policies and acts in the Pacific War was easy in the early postwar years. It is not so easy today.

——John Alan Appleman, *Military Tribunals and International Crimes* (1954). Robert J. C. Butow, *Tojo and the Coming of the War* (1961). Sung Yoon Cho, "The Tokyo War Crimes Trial," *Quarterly Journal of the Library of Congress* 24.4 (1967), a bibliographical aid. Eugene Davidson, *The Trial of the Germans* (1966). Kojima Noboru, *Tōkyō saiban,* 2 vols (1971). Richard H. Minear, *Victors' Justice: The Tokyo War Crimes Trial* (1971). A. Frank Reel, *The Case of General Yamashita* (1949). B. V. A. Röling and C. F. Rüter, ed, *The Tokyo Judgement* (1972). Saburo Shiroyama, *War Criminal: The Life and Death of Hirota Koki,* tr John Bester (1976). Telford Taylor, *Nuremberg and Vietnam: An American Tragedy* (1970).

Richard H. MINEAR

warigo

A type of traditional lunch box, made of thin sheets of *hinoki,* or Japanese cypress. It probably came into use as early as the Nara period (710–794). The box, small enough to hold in one's hand, was of oval, triangular, oblong, or fan shape. It was usually discarded after use. Later, *warigo* came to refer also to MAGEMONO (wood-strip-craft containers) in general, or *kōri,* a type of suitcase made of woven strips of bamboo or willow bark. INOKUCHI Shōji

war literature

This article deals with Japanese literature produced as a direct result of the Sino-Japanese, Russo-Japanese, and First and Second World Wars. Although it is the successor to the classical genre of GUNKI MONOGATARI (military chronicles or tales), descriptions of battle or heroic deeds occupy a much less significant place in modern war literature, where emphasis has shifted from the fate of a people or society to that of the individual.

The character types of modern Japanese war novels are usually conscripts. They are not generals or other leaders as in traditional military chronicles. The basic dichotomy between consciousness and action which is brought out by the impossibility of controlling one's own fate and conditions makes modern war literature a highly introspective form of writing. Moreover, since individuals are reduced to mere tools serving the war effort, usually against their will, the question of protest and resistance, of moral responsibility and guilt, becomes one of the crucial motifs in modern war literature. This is particularly true of the literature produced in response to World War II. During this war, however, the strict censorship and police suppression of antiwar activities forced writers who were opposed to Japan's war effort to be silent or to write in a way that expressed their fundamental disagreement circuitously. Most writers, however, responded to World War II in a more ambivalent manner, mainly because the war was justified in the name of the emperor, and was supposedly fought for the sake of preserving the Japanese and the East Asian cultural tradition which was said to be threatened by the Western powers.

The existence of censorship and ruthless repression made it difficult for writers and intellectuals to form their own views and express them openly. Also, their complex attitude toward their cultural tradition was responsible for rendering the writers and intellectuals totally ineffectual as a critical, antiwar force, and robbed their writings of any epic perspective. For this reason, Japan's literary activities after World War II had to start anew. The writers were free to reexamine their attitudes toward the war and the role they, as modern intellectuals, played in it.

The SINO-JAPANESE WAR OF 1894–1895 was the first manifestation of Japan's imperialism justified in the name of national development. The newspapers carried many war stories, most of them enthusiastically supporting Japan's war effort. KUNIKIDA DOPPO, who covered the war as a journalist, wrote *Aitei tsūshin* (Letters to My Beloved Brother) in 1894. The work contains vivid descriptions of battle and is characterized by a strong nationalistic feeling in support of the war. *Sosei nikki* (1894–95, Westward Expedition Diary), the diary MORI ŌGAI kept during his service as a military doctor, and MASAOKA SHIKI's *Jinchū nikki* (1895, Battlefront Diary) also describe the writers' war experiences.

IZUMI KYŌKA, on the other hand, presents a strong criticism of Japanese militarism in *Kaijō hatsuden* (1896, Dispatch from Hai-cheng [Hai-ch'eng]), in which he describes the atrocities committed against the Chinese by Japanese soldiers. KITAMURA TŌKOKU led the pacifist campaign through his magazine *Heiwa* (Peace) from a Christian standpoint. TOKUTOMI ROKA's *Hototogisu* (1898–99, Cuckoo) used the war only as background, but in his collection of essays *Shizen to jinsei* (1900, Nature and Life) Tokutomi expresses his disgust with nationalism and jingoism.

The RUSSO-JAPANESE WAR, Japan's first modern war against an established Western power, marked perhaps the most significant turning point in the development of modern Japan and that of modern Japanese literature. Not only was the war a natural consequence of Japan's involvement in China and Korea, but also it fulfilled on a superficial level the immediate goal of Meiji modernization, making Japan a world military power. The conflict engendered a surge of nationalistic fervor and an outpouring of war literature. Many journals were established for the sole purpose of publishing writings on war. One such magazine was *Sensō bungaku* (War Literature), published by Ikueisha from February 1904 to February 1905, to which many noted writers such as YAMADA BIMYŌ, OGURI FŪYŌ, and Emi Suiin (1869–1934) contributed.

In the literary works on the Russo-Japanese War, one can see the most condensed and powerful expression of nationalistic feeling. Among the works produced, Sakurai Tadayoshi's (1879–1965) *Nikudan* (1906, Human Cannonballs) and Mizuno Hironori's (1875–1945) *Kono issen* (1911, This One Battle) stand out as two of the most popular and moving accounts of the war. Both works were written by young officers who had fought in the war themselves; the former deals with the attack on Port Arthur by the army and the latter with the navy's battle on the Sea of Japan (see TSUSHIMA, BATTLE OF). In these two works, although soldiers' and sailors' deaths are treated sympathetically from the standpoint of humanism, their tragedy appears not as a result of a conflict between the individual and the nation, but as the result of their selfless devotion to their country. Although the works are moving, the authors' identification of individual consciousness with national consciousness makes for the glorification of the tragedy, and the works do not transcend the realm of nationalistic war literature.

The work that attained the highest literary achievement at the time is TAYAMA KATAI's *Ippeisotsu* (1908; tr *One Soldier*, 1956). Katai, who accompanied the army as a journalist, had personally experienced the misery of war; his experiences are described in a diary entitled *Dai nigun jūsei nikki* (1905, A Diary of Service in the Second Army), in which he elaborates on the unnecessary sacrifices individuals had to make for the sake of a larger purpose. *Ippeisotsu* deals with the agony and meaningless death of a nameless private for whom the glory of nationalism has no relevance. Concentrating on a naturalistic description of the private's cruel death in a foreign land, a description that is tightly focused and unsentimental, Katai most powerfully reveals his view of the condition of modern man, whose fate is governed by a force beyond human control. At the same time, he reveals the brutality and senselessness of the war to the individual, a side of the Russo-Japanese War that was generally kept from the public.

Poets who wrote poems in response to the war included Noguchi Ichitarō (1867–1905) with his *Seiro sensei ki*, DOI BANSUI *(Hekireki)*, SUSUKIDA KYŪKIN *(Nijūgo gen*, 1905), YOSANO AKIKO and Mori Ōgai. Among their works, Yosano Akiko's poem "Kimi shinitamō koto nakare" (1904, Pray Thee Do Not Die) expressed a strong feeling against the war from a woman's perspective. The poem was attacked as anti-Japanese, and was hotly debated in the press. Mori Ōgai's *Uta nikki* (1907, Poetic Diary), on the other hand, is filled with unhesitating, powerful descriptions of the brave soldiers who fought the war, supported by their *samurai* spirit and love of the nation. Ōgai's sentiment was closer to that of General NOGI MARESUKE, one of the great heroes of the war, than to the common soldier. Although Ōgai's work contains lyrical passages of love and nostalgically treats the theme of soldiers away from home, this work is a product of the establishment perspective on the war and contrasts markedly with that of Tayama Katai in this respect. The TANKA poetry that dealt with the war—about 20 volumes were published in all, including *Seiro kashū* (1904, Punish Russia Poems)—contain nationalistic sentiments expressing a strong sense of loyalty.

The war was reflected in the works of many Meiji-period (1868–1912) writers, including many who did not actually participate in or witness it directly. NATSUME SŌSEKI's "Shumi no iden" (1906, The Heredity of Taste), which includes descriptions of the battle scenes of Port Arthur and of the return of the soldiers from Manchuria, as well as an account of an acquaintance's death, could be called

war literature. Sōseki's interest, however, is in the determination of the individual's fate by the uncontrollable force of history. Considering the slaughterhouse of war the absurd work of a crazy god, Sōseki expressed the dark feeling of apocalypse he sensed behind the victorious return of the Japanese army.

Tokutomi Roka's *Yadorigi* (1909, Parasite) is based on the notes of a young soldier who actually fought in the war. Although Roka was a nationalist at the time he wrote the novel, he presents a young soldier's skepticism about life as a soldier. In the work, he implicitly criticizes the army and reveals a complex view of the war itself.

As a part of the labor and socialist movements that emerged during the fourth decade (1897–1906) of the Meiji period, HEIMINSHA (Society of Commoners) was established, and KŌTOKU SHŪSUI led an active antiwar movement when the Russo-Japanese War started. UCHIMURA KANZŌ, a Christian philosopher, declared his antiwar stance openly in *Yo ga hisenronsha to nari shi yurai* (1904, The Reason Why I Became a Pacifist), and KINOSHITA NAOE did the same, linking his attitude to socialism. Both of his antiwar works, *Hi no hashira* (1904, Pillar of Fire) and *Ryōjin no jihaku* (1904–06, Confessions of a Husband), were serialized in the *Mainichi shimbun*. The fact that the newspaper carried antiwar novels during the war indicates that many writers shared this view, and also sheds light on the extent to which writers were allowed free expression.

Such magazines as *Shinsei* (The New Voice) and *Jidai shichō* (Trend of the Days) were consistently critical of those who wrote about the war out of blind patriotism or mere opportunism. They also criticized the limited literary merit of many of the works produced at the time. *Bungei kurabu* (Literature Club) serialized in 1904 the column "Writers' Views of the War," in which writers frankly expressed their feelings about the war. Japanese translations of Tolstoy's antiwar essays were also published at this time. Despite the strong sentiment of nationalism, the freedom of expression enjoyed by writers and intellectuals generally contrasts sharply with the situation that existed during World War II. Most writers, however, reflecting the nationalistic fervor of the Meiji period, did not go so far as to bring their loyalty into question, and sympathy for the enemy was seldom reflected in their works. AKUTAGAWA RYŪNOSUKE's "Shōgun" (1922, The General), dealing with General Nogi and written during the Taishō period (1912–26), KUROSHIMA DENJI's "Sori" (1927, Sleigh), written in the early years of the Shōwa period (1926–), and TOKUNAGA SUNAO's "Nihonjin Satō" (1950, Satō the Japanese), written after World War II, are examples of critical and cynical treatments of the Russo-Japanese War in retrospect.

Although Japan was one of the victors in World War I, it did not take part in much of the actual fighting. Therefore, the war was seldom treated in literature. MIYAMOTO YURIKO's *Nobuko* (1924–26) tells of the wild joy of the Americans in New York on the day the war ended in 1918. SHIMAZAKI TŌSON's *Sensō to Pari* (1915, War and Paris) presents the author's observations of Paris during the war and attempts to offer answers about the war. Natsume Sōseki presents in "Tentōroku" (1916, An Account of Nodding Approval) his critical analysis of German militarism in World War I. Most of the writers of the SHIRAKABA SCHOOL (MUSHANOKŌJI SANEATSU and others) opposed the war from the standpoint of humanism.

Japan sent its army to Siberia in 1918 to assist the antirevolutionary forces. Both Kuroshima Denji's "Uzumakeru karasu no mure" (1928, A Flock of Swirling Crows) and HOTTA YOSHIE's "Yoru no mori" (1955, The Forest of Night) are outspoken antiwar short stories criticizing Japan's invasion of Siberia.

The military development of Japan, which culminated in the SINO-JAPANESE WAR OF 1937–1945 and World War II, changed the writers' situation fundamentally. First, writers were deprived of the freedom of expression and thought, and imprisonment and torture were used to force those who were critical of the war to be silent or to change their views. Secondly, writers were deprived of information with regard to the war and the world situation in general, receiving only the distorted view of reality presented by the military government. They could not, therefore, readily form independent judgments as individuals. Thirdly, writers were reduced to nothing but ordinary citizens, subject to the draft and deprived of the privileges of the elite which they had enjoyed before. The government treated the writers as privileged only when they collaborated in the war effort.

The government set up an information center for the purpose of controlling cultural activities in promoting popular enthusiasm for the war. By the time World War II started in 1941, even those writers who had been critical of the war in China were affected by the notion of "the sacred war" that sought to create a GREATER EAST

ASIA COPROSPERITY SPHERE. About 350 writers attended the Patriotic Writers' Meeting in December 1941; and in 1942, a patriotic writers' group, NIHON BUNGAKU HŌKOKUKAI (Patriotic Association for Japanese Literature) was established. In the same year, a large-scale writers' meeting, Daitōa Bungakusha Taikai (The Conference of East Asian Writers), was held in support of the war, advocating both nationalism and PAN-ASIANISM. Writers were used actively as reporters and served as information officers in the army and navy.

Besides forming Nihon Bungaku Hōkokukai, the government forced about 80 existing little magazines to merge into 8 so as to make them more readily subject to its control. Such journals as Masurao (Strong Men) were published by the GUANDONG (KWANTUNG) ARMY for the same purpose. Thus governmental control over the publication of literary works contributed to the proliferation of war literature and war reporting.

Most of the communists and socialists who had initially stood against the war changed their views under censorship and police repression. Many of them eventually became supporters of the war. By the time of Japan's involvement in World War II, there existed no resistance movement to speak of, and with the exception of a handful of writers, including Miyamoto Yuriko and Kuroshima Denji, most writers silenced their criticism of the war and the government.

Most of the writers of war literature supported the war to the end. Yet, not all of their works lacked critical perspective or literary merit. NIWA FUMIO's Kaisen (1942, Sea Battle) and IBUSE MASUJI's Chōyō nikki (1943, The Diary of a Draftee) stand as representative personal accounts of the war by writers. In both works, the authors describe their fundamental alienation from the psychology of professional soldiers and depict the manner in which war distorts humanity. Yet none of these themes are pursued in depth, leaving the works no more than personal observations of the war. HAYASHI FUSAO's Sensō no yokogao (1937, A Profile of War) praises war as something that is beautiful and lauds the nobility and strength of the Japanese who sacrificed their lives for an ideal. KON HIDEMI's Firipin jūgun (1943, With the Army in the Philippines) also presents the nationalistic sentiment of the author, but it also offers a perspective that makes it possible for the reader to regard the war from the standpoint of the victims of Japanese militarism.

Among full-length novels, the best works include ISHIKAWA TATSUZŌ's Ikite iru heitai (1937, The Living Soldiers); HINO ASHIHEI's 1938 trilogy Mugi to heitai (1938; tr Barley and Soldiers, 1939), Tsuchi to heitai (1938; tr Mud and Soldiers, 1939), and Hana to heitai (1938–39; tr Flowers and Soldiers, 1939); Iwata Toyoo's Kaigun (1942, Navy); and TAKAMI JUN's Nōkana no koto (1943, A Note About Nōkana). Ishikawa's Ikite iru heitai traces the fate of Japanese troops transferred from the northern Chinese front to join the attack at Nanjing (Nanking) and describes the atrocities against the Chinese committed by the Japanese army. Although Ishikawa was not a critic of the war and had joined the army only because he was sent by the magazine Chūō kōron with an assignment to write about it, the book was immediately banned following its publication. The novel ruthlessly unveils the destruction of humanity by war, yet the author remains an uncommitted outside observer. Moreover, he never questions the war itself, the motives behind Japan's invasion of China, or the meaning of the Nanjing massacre. Nevertheless, Ishikawa was interrogated by the secret police for writing such a vivid account.

Hino Ashihei's Mugi to heitai also does not attempt to analyze the nature of the war, but basically attempts to celebrate the nationalistic spirit. However, the novel effectively presents the sadness and strength of ordinary citizens and soldiers attempting to live fully in a situation beyond their control. Iwata Toyoo, better known today as SHISHI BUNROKU, wrote Kaigun, dealing with one of nine young officers of a special submarine attack force killed in the attack on Pearl Harbor. Although the novel contains a vivid account of the attack, its emphasis is on the birth of a tragic young hero, tracing his growth as a sensitive, talented novelist. An enormously popular novel, it was serialized in the Asahi shimbun, dramatized by several groups and made into a film.

Many of the works written during the war do have a critical perspective, but most of them remained uncritical of the war itself and avoided the question of who was responsible for the war. The works of the proletarian writer Kuroshima Denji, who continued to write antiwar novels after his work on Japan's Siberian involvement, stand out as the strongest exception in this respect. Busō seru shigai (1930, The Armed City Streets), which deals with events leading up to the MANCHURIAN INCIDENT and the SHANGHAI INCIDENT, presents a Marxist analysis of Japanese militarism as a tool of colonial-

ism and imperialism. In Kuroshima's description, military atrocities are explicitly connected with capitalist exploitation. Not only was the novel banned when it first came out, it remained banned during the postwar Occupation.

Kuroshima also analyzed class divisions and differences in class consciousness among the Japanese in China, relating them clearly to Japanese racism. Presenting an antiwar, rebellious soldier as a positive hero and including cooperation between Japanese and Chinese intellectuals and citizens as one of its themes, his novel is perhaps the most analytical and committed antiwar, antiracist, and anticapitalist book written during the period.

While many poets collaborated in the war by writing poems and popular songs in praise of it, some poets, including Misako Genzo, who was sent to prison, wrote antiwar poems. The Nihon Puroretaria Sakka Dōmei (Japan Proletarian Writers' Association) also published special antiwar anthologies, including Akai jūka (1932, Red Gunfire) and Senretsu (1932, War Lines), among others, but they were all banned immediately after publication. One memorable book of antiwar poems was Chiisai dōshi (1931, Little Comrades); directed to the common people and especially to children, it was an attempt to counter the proliferation of propagandistic war songs.

Postwar literature began with the writers' reevaluation of their war experiences and their responsibility as intellectuals. Freed from censorship, the most significant war literature was written in the decade after the end of the war. UMEZAKI HARUO's "Sakurajima" (1946, Cherry-Tree Island), NAKAYAMA GISHŪ's "Teniyan no matsujitsu" (1948, The Last Day of Tinian), Hotta Yoshie's Sokoku sōshitsu (1950, The Loss of the Motherland), ŌOKA SHŌHEI's Nobi (1951; tr Fires on the Plain, 1957), NOMA HIROSHI's Shinkū chitai (1952; tr Zone of Emptiness, 1956), AGAWA HIROYUKI's Kumono bohyō (1955, The Tomb of Clouds), and Gomikawa Jumpei's (b 1916) Ningen no jōken (1956–58, The Condition of Man) are only representative of the many works that present literary treatments of the meaning of the war and of lives placed in extreme predicaments.

Ōoka Shōhei, whose other works on war include Reite senki (1967–69, Battle for Leyte), presents in Nobi an existential human condition in which man's basic ethics are tested. The novel deals with a soldier who, struggling to survive on a Philippine island, eats human flesh, and describes what the author refers to as "the lowest story of man." Noma Hiroshi, on the other hand, was more concerned with the social and organizational structures supporting the war. Shinkū chitai analyzes the nature and structure of the army as the basic social organization that fought and supported the war, and the one that committed itself to the destruction of humanity.

TAMURA TAIJIRŌ's Shumpuden (1947, An Account of a Prostitute), TAKEDA TAIJUN's Shimpan (1947, The Trial) and Hotta Yoshie's Jikan (1953, Time) deal with man's battle with himself in war, and with the sense of loss and devastation he feels after violating what he would normally accept as human law, thus denying the basis of his own humanity. Those novels were written after Japan's defeat when there was a general feeling of loss, and all are based on stories of atrocities committed against the Chinese and other Asians.

Gomikawa Jumpei's Ningen no jōken, in five parts, is an ambitious attempt at an epic in which man's relation to history and the test of humanism are pursued through the drama of a man forced against his will to become involved in the war. INOUE MITSUHARU's Gadarukanaru senshishū (1958, Poems on the Battle for Guadalcanal) recreates the fanatical atmosphere toward the end of the war in which a Japanese youth, who believed in ultranationalism yet hated the war, is sent off to the war to die.

Many accounts of the war were published after the fact, but among them, Kike wadatsumi no koe (1949, Listen to the Voice of the Sea God), a collection of notes and diaries of 76 student soldiers who had been used in kamikaze suicide attacks toward the end of the war, is the single most moving document of human tragedy. And although they do not deal with the actual fighting, Ibuse Masuji's Kuroi ame (1965–68; tr Black Rain, 1969), Ōta Yōko's (1906–63) "Hanningen" (1954, Half Human), Inoue Mitsuharu's Chi no mure (1963, A Group of Earth-Creepers) and Hayashi Kyōko's (b 1930) "Matsuri no ba" (1975, The Festival Ground) deal with the Hiroshima or Nagasaki atomic-bomb experience.

The new generation of writers born in the 1930s also dealt with the Japanese war experience as the starting point in their writing. Most often, they questioned the meaning of life in its relation to history. Most of ŌE KENZABURŌ's works, including Shiiku (1958; tr The Catch, 1959) and Aikoku shōnen (1959, Patriotic Boy), deal with the war as the core of his generation's childhood existence, making Japan's war experience a symbol in modern man's quest for the meaning of life. TAKAHASHI KAZUMI also pursued throughout his works analyses of ultranationalism and of the degradation of the intellectuals blinded by it.

Postwar poetry also faced the war experience as its starting point. The members of the modernist group Arechi (The Wasteland), to which such poets as Tamura Ryūichi (b 1923) and AYUKAWA NOBUO belonged, placed the war experience at the core of the disillusionment and self-alienation with which they felt they had to live in a modern wasteland. A collection of poems dealing with the Hiroshima holocaust, *Shi no hai shishū* (The Ashes of Death Poetry) was published in 1954.

🕮 ——Anthologies: Agawa Hiroyuki, Ōoka Shōhei, Okuno Takeo, Hashikawa Bunzō, and Murakami Hyōe, ed, *Shōwa sensō bungaku zenshū,* 15 vols plus 1 appendix vol (Shūeisha, 1964–65). Hirano Ken, Ōoka Shōhei, Yasuoka Shōtarō, Kaikō Ken, and Etō Jun, ed, *Sensō bungaku zenshū,* 6 vols plus 1 appendix vol (Mainichi Shimbunsha, 1971–72). Kimura Ki, ed, *Meiji sensō bungaku shū* (Chikuma Shobō, 1969).   *Noriko Mizuta LIPPIT*

Warner, Langdon (1881–1955)

Teacher, author, and oriental art expert; curator of the oriental collection at Harvard's Fogg Museum; widely believed in Japan to have saved Nara and Kyōto from aerial bombardment during World War II.

Graduating from Harvard in 1903, Warner was chosen in 1906 by Harvard University's president Charles Eliot to train for museum work in Asian art. He was apprenticed for several years under OKAKURA KAKUZŌ in Japan, where he formed lasting friendships with students who became leaders in the Japanese art world. Niiro Chūnosuke (1868–1954), a sculptor restoring older pieces at the Nara temple HŌRYŪJI, introduced Warner to the as yet little studied field of ancient Japanese sculpture.

In 1912 he was selected by Charles L. Freer, the collector of oriental art, to be director of the American School of Archaeology in Beijing (Peking). There he trained both Chinese and American specialists in the preservation and study of China's vast and neglected antiquities. At Harvard, also in 1912, he taught the first formal course in oriental art to be offered at an American university.

After brief service with the State Department during World War I, Warner became director of the Pennsylvania Museum of Art. Later he led two expeditions to China for the Fogg Museum, one of them to the grottoes of Dunhuang (Tun-huang) on the Turkestan border. In Shanghai he helped the Nelson Gallery of Kansas City acquire the large Northern Wei-period relief of *The Empress as Donor, with Attendants,* which was being vandalized and sold piecemeal on the Beijing market.

Warner was chiefly responsible for the exhibition at the San Francisco World's Fair of 1939 entitled "The Art of the Pacific Basin." For his efforts the University of California at Berkeley awarded him an honorary degree. With the approach of World War II he joined with professor ASAKAWA KAN'ICHI of Yale to persuade President Franklin Roosevelt to send a message directly to Emperor Hirohito to try to avert war. It was sent but delivered too late. During the war, Warner taught civil affairs officers, made shortwave broadcasts to Japan, and served with the Roberts Commission which was charged with the protection and salvage of artistic and historic monuments in war areas.

In March 1946 he went to Japan as a consultant to the Monuments, Fine Arts, and Archives Section of the Allied OCCUPATION headquarters. He was immediately hailed as the "savior" of Nara and Kyōto, largely because of an article by Yashiro Yukio (1890–1975), his oldtime colleague and friend. This role Warner immediately and consistently denied. Nara had never been a target, and Kyōto had been specifically stricken from the list of target cities by Secretary of War Henry L. STIMSON, with the concurrence of President Truman, and with no prompting from Warner or others. In 1950 Warner was asked by the Lowell Institute of Boston to give a series of lectures on Japanese art, which were published as *The Enduring Art of Japan* (1952). In 1952 he was named a member of a committee to select Japanese art works for an exhibit scheduled for 1953; his duties took him to Japan for the last of some 20 visits. Warner died in Cambridge, Massachusetts, on 9 June 1955. He was awarded the Order of the Sacred Treasure, Second Class, by the government of Japan.

🕮 ——Theodore Bowie, ed, *Langdon Warner through His Letters* (1966). Otis Cary, "Mr. Stimson's 'Pet City'—The Sparing of Kyōto, 1945," *Moonlight Series* 3 (Kyōto, Dōshisha University, 1975).
          Otis CARY

War Relocation Authority

The War Relocation Authority (WRA) was created in March 1942 by the US government to construct and administer the relocation centers needed to receive the more than 110,000 Japanese Americans whom the US Army was about to incarcerate in temporary assembly centers on the Pacific Coast. In addition, the goals of the WRA were to get as many Japanese Americans as possible, particularly the *nisei* (second generation), who were citizens, out of the camps and back into civilian life east of the Sierra Nevada Mountains. In these tasks the WRA was largely successful; by the end of the war, in August 1945, only 44,000 Japanese Americans remained behind barbed wire.

The civilian agency established relocation centers at 10 interior sites: TULE LAKE and MANZANAR in California; MINIDOKA, Idaho; TOPAZ, Utah; POSTON and GILA RIVER in Arizona; HEART MOUNTAIN, Wyoming; AMACHE, Colorado; and ROHWER and JEROME in Arkansas. Small guard detachments were provided at each center by the US Army. All the centers were in desolate and climatically inhospitable places. Conditions, although spartan by American standards, were essentially humane. At three centers, Manzanar, Topaz, and Tule Lake, there were shootings in which inmates were killed by guards. Camp populations, however, grew more by natural increase than they declined by deaths from all causes.

Originally there were no distinctions between the centers, but eventually Tule Lake became the place where the WRA sent persons whom, for one reason or another, it classified as disloyal. Many of these had refused to take a loyalty oath to the US government, while others had formally renounced their American citizenship or applied for repatriation or expatriation to Japan. Still others were sent to Tule Lake because they were regarded as "troublemakers." Not surprisingly, there was more violence at Tule Lake than at all the other centers combined.

A US Supreme Court decision, *Ex parte Endo,* 323 US 283, handed down on 18 December 1944, ruled that the WRA had exceeded its authority in detaining "conceded loyal" citizens against their will. The last center to close was Tule Lake, in March 1946, and the WRA was dissolved three months later. See also JAPANESE AMERICANS, WARTIME RELOCATION OF.

🕮 ——Leonard J. Arrington, *The Price of Prejudice* (1962). Roger Daniels, *Concentration Camps, USA* (1972). Milton S. Eisenhower, *The President is Calling* (1974). Arthur A. Hansen and Betty E. Mitson, ed, *Voices Long Silent: An Oral History of the Japanese American Evacuation* (1974). Alexander H. Leighton, *The Governing of Men* (1945). Dillon S. Myer, *Uprooted Americans* (1971). Douglas W. Nelson, *Heart Mountain* (1976). Edward H. Spicer et al, *Impounded People* (1969). Dorothy S. Thomas and Richard S. Nishimoto, *The Spoilage* (1946). Rosalie H. Wax, *Doing Fieldwork* (1971).   *Roger DANIELS*

Warring States period → Sengoku period

warrior government

(buke seiji). The form of government that prevailed in Japan for nearly 700 years, from the founding of the Kamakura shogunate in 1192 until the Meiji Restoration of 1868. For many, warrior government means FEUDALISM, within which certain stages can be distinguished. Indeed, feudal elements were present, if not predominant, throughout the 700 years. It is more useful, however, to divide the period into four phases of warrior rule: the KAMAKURA SHOGUNATE (1192–1333), the MUROMACHI SHOGUNATE (1338–1573), the rule (1568–98) of the national unifiers ODA NOBUNAGA and TOYOTOMI HIDEYOSHI, and the TOKUGAWA SHOGUNATE (1603–1867).

Three major regimes dominated the period of warrior rule—the Kamakura, Muromachi, and Tokugawa shogunates. These were, to a greater or lesser degree, nationwide warrior regimes organized on feudal or quasi-feudal principles of vassalage and headed normally by a warrior with the title SHŌGUN, short for *seii tai shōgun* ("barbarian-subduing generalissimo"). By contrast, the regimes of Oda Nobunaga and Toyotomi Hideyoshi were of short duration, and neither held the title of shōgun or founded a shogunate.

Rise of the Warrior Class —— The rise of the warrior class (*buke, bushi,* or *samurai*) occurred within the framework of the imperial state based on the RITSURYŌ SYSTEM. During the Heian period (794–1185), the small Kyōto-based court aristocracy lost control over coercive military power. As early as 792, the absence of any foreign threat or serious discontent among the populace led to the abandonment of conscript armies. Thereafter, military and police functions were handled on an ad hoc basis. The court dealt with provincial uprisings, piracy, and other outbreaks of violence by dispatching temporary commanders who recruited fighting men from among local able-bodied males (KONDEI). The lawlessness on the frontiers of Heian society, especially in eastern Japan, encouraged the development of a permanent arms-bearing class.

Powerful bands of warriors (BUSHIDAN) began to coalesce by the mid-Heian period, usually under the leadership of former provincial officials who had settled in the provinces after their tenure had expired. Local warriors came to function hereditarily as middle- and lower-level provincial officials and as administrative and police officers in estates (SHŌEN) owned by absentee court landlords. In public and private lands alike, they carved out substantial holdings for themselves, yet in both spheres they were subject to the authority of the court.

The Heian court increasingly relied upon such people to control local politics, particularly tax collection, and to supervise court-owned estates; and significant linkages between court nobles and provincial warrior leaders became common. Indeed, the greatest military leaders were members of the MINAMOTO FAMILY and the TAIRA FAMILY, descendants of imperial lineages who, by the late Heian period, had established strong patron-client relationships with certain noble houses and secured positions of importance within the court bureaucracy.

Hōgen and Heiji Disturbances—The degree to which warrior chieftains had become a part of court life was clearly demonstrated in 1156 and 1160 when two major factional disputes in the capital were decided by force of arms. In the HŌGEN DISTURBANCE of 1156, major rifts within the imperial family, the regent FUJIWARA FAMILY, the Taira, and the Minamoto pitted brother against brother and father against son. The matter was decided by warriors supporting Emperor GO-SHIRAKAWA and led by the generals TAIRA NO KIYO-MORI and MINAMOTO NO YOSHITOMO.

Angered at Kiyomori's receiving preferential treatment despite his own greater contribution to the victory, Yoshitomo joined other frustrated elements in a coup in 1160. Kiyomori crushed this so-called HEIJI DISTURBANCE, rushing back from a pilgrimage to Kumano, south of Kyōto. Yoshitomo was killed and his surviving offspring exiled. Minamoto influence was expunged from the court.

Kiyomori's career soared, and by 1167 he had risen to grand minister of state (dajō daijin). His daughters were married into the traditional nobility and the imperial family, his kinsmen infiltrated the noble council, and his grandson Emperor ANTOKU even became sovereign. While some regard Taira ascendancy as the establishment of the first warrior regime, Kiyomori clearly rose to power by traditional means of patronage, strategic marriage alliances, and domination of the imperial institution. The Taira thus made a skillful transition from provincial warrior-official to high court noble status.

The Kamakura Shogunate—The TAIRA-MINAMOTO WAR of 1180-85 resulted in the establishment of Japan's first warrior government. On the obvious level the war was a struggle between the Minamoto and the Taira, that is, between Yoshitomo's son MINAMOTO NO YORITOMO and Taira no Kiyomori. On another level, however, it was a socioeconomic revolution by warriors in eastern Japan who were kept from exercising full control over their homelands by absentee proprietors at the court. Most warriors joined the Minamoto or the Taira not because of loyalty but to establish firmer control over their holdings or to settle local grievances.

Yoritomo quickly seized most of eastern Japan in open rebellion and claimed the right to administer it. Establishing his headquarters at Kamakura in Sagami Province (now Kanagawa Prefecture), he set up three offices (see SAMURAI-DOKORO; KUMONJO; MONCHŪJO) to govern his expanding network of vassals and lands seized from vanquished enemies. A government in the field grew of necessity.

Later Yoritomo received legal sanction from the court legitimizing his de facto control. He was granted the right to station JITŌ (land stewards) in estates and SHUGO (constables; later military governors) in provinces and to impose commissariat levies (HYŌRŌMAI) on public and private lands. In effect, Yoritomo was entrusted with the police and military responsibilities of the state. When in 1190 he was appointed commander of the inner palace guards of the right (ukonoe no taishō), his residence in Kamakura came to be called a bakufu, a Chinese term meaning the camp of a commander in the field. After Yoritomo was granted the title of shōgun in 1192, any regime headed by someone bearing that title was called a bakufu, and the term is translated in this encyclopedia as shogunate.

The Kamakura period was one of divided authority between the court and the shogunate. The court delegated part of its authority to the shogunate; and even though Yoritomo and his immediate successors sought to limit their jurisdiction to supervision of warrior society, the shogunate was almost forced to assume greater powers as people increasingly turned to Kamakura for solutions to their problems, particularly land disputes. The crisis provoked by the MONGOL INVASIONS OF JAPAN of the 1270s and 1280s further strengthened warrior dominance.

Yet it would be incorrect to say that the shogunate controlled the entire warrior class, let alone all of Japan. Actually, it was a government of eastern warriors that penetrated the country through its network of stewards and constables and by reliance upon the SŌRYŌ SYSTEM, in which the family head apportioned land to family members. Vassalage and kinship ties were closely intertwined. Large numbers of warriors never even became direct vassals (GOKENIN) of the shogunate. Furthermore, after three brief generations of Minamoto control, shogunate leadership fell to 16 successive HŌJŌ FAMILY regents (SHIKKEN), none of whom enjoyed the same kind of personal vassalage network Yoritomo had.

Tied to the estate and public land systems of the imperial state, the shogunate was unable to develop an independent power base. Kamakura courts were involved in land disputes between central proprietors on whose estates Kamakura vassals, serving as stewards, were illegally encroaching. The shogunate's dilemma was whether to support its own vassals or to preserve the estate system upon which it depended. This was the limitation of the Kamakura shogunate: it remained somewhere between the old imperial state and a new, truly independent, military ("feudal") regime.

The Muromachi Shogunate—The Hōjō regents never completely recovered from the Mongol invasions despite Japan's victory: disgruntled vassals, unrewarded or at best insufficiently rewarded for their service and often in debt to moneylenders, grew impatient with shogunate leadership. When Emperor GO-DAIGO attempted to unseat the Kamakura regime, many warriors, including Kamakura vassals, supported him. Go-Daigo's KEMMU RESTORATION proved anachronistic, however; and ASHIKAGA TAKAUJI, having betrayed his Hōjō overlord and destroyed the shogunate in 1333, turned on Go-Daigo and drove him south into the mountains of Yoshino. Takauji enthroned his own puppet emperor in Kyōto (the Northern Court) to legitimize the establishment of his own shogunate in 1338. This regime is known from the shogunal house as the Ashikaga shogunate or as the Muromachi shogunate, from the name of its Kyōto location.

The Ashikaga destroyed the dual rule of Kamakura times. Takauji and his successors not only reduced Go-Daigo's Southern Court but rendered the Northern Court powerless as well. Courtier rule was no longer a matter of consequence, and warrior government was the only effective authority in Japan.

The Ashikaga regime was different from its Kamakura predecessor. The latter had been largely an Eastern power, based upon large Kantō warrior houses, and was unable to bring all the land under its control. The Muromachi shogunate managed to bring the entire warrior class within its governmental framework. But this does not mean that Ashikaga power was greater than that of Kamakura; in fact, it was probably weaker.

The Ashikaga could not duplicate the direct lord-vassal relationship of Kamakura times. Instead, they tried to organize warrior society through the most powerful of the regional lords (SHUGO DAIMYŌ) who had emerged during the war between the Northern and Southern Courts. Thus there was an organizational framework of shōgun-shugo-samurai, a very structured, almost classlike feudal nexus. This was a symptom of Ashikaga weakness, not strength, since everything hinged upon the cooperation of the shugo daimyō.

The Ashikaga were only one of several powerful regional families, and they could not, as Yoritomo had done, reduce a large segment of warrior society to personal vassalage. After several decades there emerged about 11 major shugo houses, of which 6 were Ashikaga collateral branches and 5 were unrelated. Compared to the more centralized rule of the Kamakura regime, the Muromachi shogunate represented a delicate balance of power between the shogunal house and the shugo daimyō, whose loyalty was necessary to ensure Ashikaga hegemony.

A factional dispute arose over shogunal succession in the mid-15th century, however, and from 1467 to 1477 Kyōto was engulfed in the ŌNIN WAR, which destroyed much of the city and forced much of the populace to flee. The conflict spilled over into the provinces. Many of the great shugo daimyō families—who resided in

Kyōto—saw their domains seized by underlings with stronger personal ties in the region, and the Ashikaga shōguns lost the power to control regional barons.

For a century warfare swept Japan as vassal turned against lord (see GEKOKUJŌ). Powerful barons, intent upon wresting territory from each other, struggled for nationwide control. It was the height of feudal development, a period known in Japanese history as the Warring States (Sengoku) period. Although the Muromachi shogunate structure remained intact, the shōgun was a mere puppet, powerless to regulate society at all.

Nobunaga and Hideyoshi —— By 1568 one baron, Oda Nobunaga, had subjugated most of his rivals, and in 1573 he deposed the last Ashikaga shōgun. Although he created a regime more extensive than that of either Yoritomo or Takauji, Nobunaga did not establish a shogunate. By this time the tradition seems to have developed that only Minamoto descendants could legitimately form a shogunate. Yoritomo had established the first one; but his successors, the Hōjō—claiming Taira descent—created a regency to control the shōguns. Takauji had established a shogunate, since his was a branch family of the Minamoto. Without Minamoto genealogy, Nobunaga apparently felt unable to establish a shogunate.

When Nobunaga was killed by one of his generals, Toyotomi Hideyoshi avenged him and seized the reins of power. Hideyoshi rose from commoner to grand minister of state in this tumultuous age, but for reasons similar to Nobunaga's he did not organize a shogunate. His actual control of Japan, nonetheless, was more complete, and he even launched massive INVASIONS OF KOREA IN 1592 AND 1597 in an effort to conquer China.

The two brief warrior regimes of Oda Nobunaga and Toyotomi Hideyoshi are often subsumed under the term SHOKUHŌ SEIKEN or Oda-Toyotomi Regime, Shokuhō being a compound formed from alternate pronunciations of the first Chinese characters of their family names. They not only united the country out of feudal chaos but also, by eliminating the last vestiges of the estate system and carrying out a nationwide land survey (KENCHI), established the principle of legal ownership of land by farmers. Likewise, through confiscation of swords and other weapons from the peasantry (see SWORD HUNT), farmer and samurai were clearly distinguished and the latter were concentrated in the CASTLE TOWNS. Commercial ventures were also restricted to cities, foreign trade was encouraged, guilds were abolished (see RAKUICHI AND RAKUZA) and commerce was stimulated, so that for this brief interlude national power was enhanced, and Japan reached a high level of socioeconomic and cultural development. Even intercourse with the West was vigorous at the time.

The Tokugawa Shogunate —— Upon Hideyoshi's death, a power struggle broke out over succession to national hegemony. In the Battle of SEKIGAHARA in 1600, TOKUGAWA IEYASU defeated a coalition of generals and emerged as the undisputed heir to Hideyoshi's mantle. In 1603 he organized the third shogunate in Japanese history. Situated in the new city of Edo (now Tōkyō), it was known as the Edo or Tokugawa shogunate.

Unlike his two predecessors, Ieyasu felt qualified to establish a shogunate, since he could, after a fashion, claim Minamoto descent. He became shōgun, and the position was passed on through his descendants in 15 shogunal reigns until TOKUGAWA YOSHINOBU's resignation in 1867. The Tokugawa shogunate was thus the warrior regime of longest duration. The Tokugawa regime differed in other ways from earlier warrior governments. The Japanese refer to the balance of power between the shogunate at Edo and the various DAIMYŌ domains as "centralized feudalism." Professor John W. Hall has coined the term "military-bureaucratic" to describe this BAKUHAN SYSTEM (shogunate-domain system).

Ieyasu recognized the local base of the daimyō in return for their acknowledgment of shogunal authority. He also established Tokugawa family lands (TENRYŌ), perhaps 25 percent of the country, including jurisdiction over major cities like Ōsaka and Kyōto. The rest of the country was divided among the daimyō, who were either related to the Tokugawa, vassals of the Tokugawa, or enemies or neutrals who pledged fealty after Sekigahara. These were the SHIMPAN, FUDAI, and TOZAMA lords, respectively, numbering between 250 and 300 over the period. Daimyō were those warriors with an annual rice income of more than 10,000 koku (1 koku = about 180 liters or 5 US bushels; see KOKUDAKA).

Daimyō were allowed great autonomy within their own domains, and feudal ties of vassalage still bound together daimyō and samurai retainers. The central shogunate administration, staffed mainly by fudai retainers, was nonetheless far more complex and pervasive

than either the Kamakura or the Muromachi shogunate. Ieyasu instituted measures to ensure security and perpetuate Tokugawa rule. The shōgun could reassign daimyō at will, deposing recalcitrant lords (see KAIEKI) and surrounding them with pro-Tokugawa neighbors. An intricate police system of formal censors, inspectors, and spies kept constant surveillance on the daimyō (see METSUKE; ŌMETSUKE; OMMITSU). The system of alternate attendance (SANKIN KŌTAI) was initiated to keep the daimyō economically dependent and to force them into an outward show of loyalty. Under this system they were required to make periodic trips to Edo to serve at the shogunal court, necessitating expensive residences in Edo, where family members were kept as hostages when the lord returned to his domain.

Furthermore, Ieyasu's successors severed communication with much of the rest of the world by banishing Christians (mostly Catholics), proscribing CHRISTIANITY, and forbidding Japanese who had left the country to return (see NATIONAL SECLUSION). Only the Dutch, Chinese, and Koreans maintained intercourse with Japan. Moreover, there was strong institutional support of Neo-Confucianism (SHUSHIGAKU) to inculcate loyalty and obedience and to discourage movement between social classes. Consequently, numerous legal codes regulated the lives of the citizenry (see BUKEHŌ).

Thus, compared to earlier shogunates, the Tokugawa regime exercised greater central authority within what was still a "feudal" context. Society was certainly more ordered than at any previous time in Japanese history. The Tokugawa shōguns ruled for about 250 years, during which warfare was virtually unknown. As a result, the samurai were converted into local and shogunate bureaucrats, and society underwent tremendous structural changes. The toppling of the Tokugawa shogunate by certain warrior elements in 1867–68 paved the way for a dramatic period of industrialization along Western lines.

An Overview of Warrior Government —— Thus for 700 years warrior regimes controlled Japan. At no time, however, was the supreme position of the EMPEROR as the source of legitimacy questioned. No Japanese warrior set out to destroy the old order and make himself king in a new image. Warrior government was an institutional graft onto the body of imperial rule. Warrior regimes at first coexisted with imperial rule, then overshadowed it, but never completely replaced its institutions.

The imperial system was not rejected, but warrior government was nevertheless more oriented to Japan's social and political realities. Whereas the various forms of aristocratic rule tried to adopt ancient Chinese precedents to solve contemporary Japanese problems, warriors were less concerned with precedents than solutions. Thus, the institutions, laws, and ideals of warrior government were more "Japanese" and were also more pragmatic, rational, and more firmly rooted in the contemporary society.

■ —— Kan'ichi Asakawa, *Land and Society in Medieval Japan* (1965). John W. Hall, *Government and Local Power in Japan, 500 to 1700* (1966). John W. Hall and Jeffrey P. Mass, ed, *Medieval Japan: Essays in Institutional History* (1974). John W. Hall and Toyoda Takeshi, ed, *Japan in the Muromachi Age* (1977). Jeffrey P. Mass, *Warrior Government in Early Medieval Japan* (1974). Jeffrey P. Mass, *The Kamakura Bakufu: A Study in Documents* (1976). George B. Sansom, *A History of Japan*, 3 vols (1958–63). Minoru Shinoda, *The Founding of the Kamakura Shogunate* (1960). H. Paul Varley, *The Ōnin War* (1967). H. Paul Varley, *Imperial Restoration in Medieval Japan* (1971).   G. Cameron HURST III

warrior-monks

(sōhei or shūto). Armed monks attached to great Buddhist institutions from early times, and particularly from the middle of the Heian period (794–1185) onward. Although monks were strictly forbidden to bear arms—both by secular law and by their religion—armed monks and menials from temples and monasteries are known to have participated in civil disturbances as early as the 8th century. By the late 10th century, as religious institutions became proprietors of landed estates (SHŌEN), they frequently mobilized warrior-monks to support them in land disputes. By the 11th century, young men were recruited from these estates for military service; and because they shaved their heads in imitation of monks, they too were called sōhei. The sōhei often fought among themselves and at times threatened both the court and the shogunate with their military might. The warrior-monks of the temples ENRYAKUJI, KŌFUKUJI, and MIIDERA were especially feared. Their power was ultimately broken by ODA NOBUNAGA (see ENRYAKUJI, BURNING OF) and TO-

YOTOMI HIDEYOSHI and by the various prohibitions of the early part of the Edo period (1600–1868). See also GŌSO.

G. Cameron HURST III

war songs → gunka

wasan

Buddhist poems or hymns composed in Japanese praising Buddhas, bodhisattvas, and founders of sects. Verses or *gatha* appear in Buddhist sutras and texts from earliest times, and the *wasan* were modeled on the chanted hymns from China and other hymns already existing in Japan. In *wasan*, four lines of alternating seven- and five-syllable length form one stanza; a complete *wasan* may consist of up to 20 or 30 stanzas. From the early Heian period (794–1185) *wasan* became a prominent means for propagating PURE LAND BUDDHISM among the people. KŪYA (903–972), the saint of the marketplace, taught NEMBUTSU by singing the praises of the Buddha AMIDA. RYŌNIN (1073–1132), founder of the YŪZŪ NEMBUTSU SECT, employed Tendai ceremonial music in spreading his doctrine. Buddhist scholars and teachers of the TENDAI SECT and Pure Land sects such as ENNIN (794–864), GENSHIN (942–1017), and Senkan (918–984) produced numerous poetic works extolling Amida and his Pure Land. *Wasan* were also popularly employed in the JI SECT, founded by IPPEN (1239–89).

Among the various composers of *wasan*, SHINRAN (1173–1263), the founder of the JŌDO SHIN SECT, was the most prolific and influential. He penned more than 500 verses, deposited in several major collections. RENNYO (1415–99), the eighth patriarch, combined three texts by Shinran in the *Sanjō wasan* for use in worship services: the *Jōdo wasan* in 118 verses, the *Kōsō wasan* in 119 verses, both completed in 1248, and the *Shōzōmatsu wasan* in 116 verses which appeared in 1257. The content of the *Sanjō wasan* corresponds generally to the teachings presented in the scholarly KYŌGYŌSHIN-SHŌ, Shinran's major treatise on Jōdo Shin doctrine. The *Jōdo wasan* summarizes the teachings of the three Pure Land sutras, while the *Kōsō wasan* reviews the doctrines of the seven patriarchs to whom Shinran looked as the source of his teachings. However, in the *Shōzōmatsu wasan*, based on the theory of three stages in Buddhist eschatology, Shinran sets forth his personal criticism of the religion and society of his time, as well as confessions of personal imperfection. It also contains verses in praise of the Buddha of Zen-kōji. In addition to these works, Shinran composed poems in praise of Prince SHŌTOKU in the *Kōtaishi Shōtoku hōsan* in 75 verses in 1255 and the *Dainihonkoku zokusannō Shōtoku taishi hōsan* in 114 verses dating from about 1257. In these latter texts Shinran gained inspiration from the cult of Prince Shōtoku whom he exalted as a manifestation of KANNON (Skt: Avalokiteśvara) and the founder of Japanese Buddhism, as well as its protector against all enemies.

Shinran's lyrical style was particularly designed to appeal to the unlettered, ordinary person, in contrast to his more scholarly works and poems in Chinese literary style. In order to make his teachings easily available and understood, Shinran used the popular seven-five syllabic pattern. In later editions he revised and clarified terms to make them more understandable. Shinran urged his followers to sing these verses when they recited the *nembutsu*. In this way his teachings could be easily recalled and faith merged with the daily routine of life and labor.

📖 ——Hompa Hongwanji Mission of Hawaii, ed, *The Shinshū Seiten* (1955). Ikuwa Kammyō, *Shinran shōnin senjutsu no kenkyū* (1970). Inoue Mitsusada, *Nihon jōdokyō seiritsushi no kenkyū* (1956). Ryūkoku Translation Series 4, *The Jōdo Wasan: The Hymns on the Pure Land* (1965); 6, *The Kōsō Wasan: The Hymns on the Patriarchs* (1974). Alfred BLOOM

wasan

(traditional Japanese mathematics). The system of mathematics developed in Japan before the Meiji Restoration (1868), chiefly during the Edo period (1600–1868). The term is used in contrast with *yō-san*, or mathematics introduced from Europe.

Formal mathematics was first introduced to Japan from China sometime between the 7th and 8th centuries, but except for basic mathematical tools such as the multiplication table, most of this knowledge was later lost. Mathematical knowledge was imported anew from China in the 16th century in the form of simple arithmetic, such as calculation on the ABACUS. With the support of the samurai and merchant classes, who recognized the usefulness of this new mathematics, a uniquely Japanese system was soon developed.

The oldest extant treatise on mathematics by a Japanese is Mōri Shigeyoshi's *Warizansho* (Writings on Division), published around 1620. The book *Jinkōki*, published in 1627 by his disciple YOSHIDA MITSUYOSHI, greatly contributed to the spread of computation for practical purposes, and this title was long used as a generic term for arithmetic textbooks. Around this time, *tengenjutsu* (Ch: *tianyuan-shu; t'ien yüan shu*), a method of calculating with sticks, was introduced from China; this technique could be used to solve algebraic equations with one unknown, but was too cumbersome to handle simultaneous equations. A breakthrough did not come until SEKI TAKAKAZU, later revered as the "god of *wasan*," developed a workable system of algebraic notation. Seki also developed a theory of determinants as well as a formula for calculating the circumference of a circle, and generally laid the foundation of *wasan*.

His disciple TAKEBE KATAHIRO, in his work *Tetsujutsu sankei* (1722), developed theories of series expansion and convergence speed. Kurushima Yoshihiro (d 1757), a mathematician known for his eccentricity, discovered both Laplace's expansion theorem and Euler's function before European mathematicians did. Matsunaga Yoshisuke (ca 1690–1744) accurately computed the value of pi (π) to the 50th place, and together with Kurushima systematized the entire body of mathematics that had been developed by Seki and his disciples. This work was continued by Yamaji Nushizumi (1704–72). One of Yamaji's students, Arima Yoriyuki (1714–83), the *daimyō* of the Kurume domain (now part of Fukuoka Prefecture), helped to popularize *wasan* by compiling the *Jūki sampō* (1769), a compendium of the major body of *wasan* principles.

Another student of Yamaji, Ajima Naonobu (1732–98), developed the study of arcs and circles into a theory of integral calculus. Ajima's work was further developed by Wada Nei (1787–1840), a student of one of his disciples, who devised a table of definite integrals, culminating in a system much like Western differential and integral calculus.

Although most *wasan* scholars of the 17th and 18th centuries were of the samurai class, the first half of the 19th century saw an increase in the number of mathematicians and the inclusion of many amateurs from the merchant class. But there was little real progress in mathematical theory, and the focus was on needlessly intricate techniques. Moreover, the field tended to be beset with factionalism. Aida Yasuaki (1747–1817), for example, founded a school that he called the Mogamiryū (also known as Saijōryū), and for more than 20 years engaged in a debate with Yamaji's disciple, Fujita Sadasuke (1734–1807). The argument, unfortunately, revolved around claims for superiority made by each school, rather than mathematics itself.

The study of geometric figures became popular toward the middle of the 19th century. Mathematicians, along with those concerned with naval science, welcomed from Europe new concepts in astronomy, calendrical science, trigonometry, logarithms, and other aspects of mathematical knowledge useful for navigation and other practical applications.

In the early part of the Meiji period (1868–1912), *wasan* scholars helped set up the mathematics curriculum within the new school system. When Japan's oldest academic society, the Tōkyō Sūgaku-sha (forerunner of the present Mathematical Society of Japan, or Nihon Sūgakkai) was founded in 1877, more than half of its members were scholars trained in *wasan*. By the end of the century, however, *wasan* had given way to Western-style mathematics. Apart from the abacus and a few special terms, it has survived only as a subject for historians of science.

It must nevertheless be acknowledged that *wasan* reached on its own an unusually high level, even by world standards, and that it anticipated—however unsystematically—European mathematical developments in several respects. There is evidence that in its early phase *wasan* scholars carried out joint research and applied their work to astronomical calculations, calendrical science, and surveying. However, the theories of *wasan* were never applied to other disciplines, such as mechanics; and *wasan* lacked an interest in rigorous proofs, tending to degenerate into a sterile intellectual pastime. Again, the climate of scientific inquiry found in the learned societies of Europe was notably lacking, and given the tendency of later *wasan* scholars to keep their knowledge as their own exclusive property rather than to publicize it, an eventual loss of creativity was inevitable.

Recently there has been a movement to see *wasan* as a valuable heritage and to evaluate and present it accordingly. For example, local historians have undertaken the study of *sangaku*, or votive plaques inscribed with mathematical problems and solutions, which were offered by *wasan* scholars at shrines and temples. Many achievements of *wasan* scholars are interesting from the perspective of modern mathematics, and incorporating their spirit into present-day mathematical education has a relevance that goes beyond mere antiquarian curiosity. *HITOTSUMATSU Shin*

Waseda bungaku

(Waseda Literature). The literary journal of Waseda University (known until 1902 as Tōkyō Semmon Gakkō), *Waseda bungaku* has been issued in eight series, the first two series being the most significant. Founded and edited by the eminent writer-critic TSUBOUCHI SHŌYŌ, the first series of *Waseda bungaku* appeared between October 1891 and October 1898, first as a semimonthly and later as a monthly. It was the first specialized literary magazine of its kind and was to be modeled on Western literary magazines like the *Westminster Review*. In 1894, the year Shōyō took over as publisher, original prose works and poetry were added to the original fare of commentaries, critical articles, and translations. Among its contributors were SHIMAMURA HŌGETSU, TAKAYAMA CHOGYŪ, MORI ŌGAI, MASAOKA SHIKI, and KOSUGI TENGAI.

The second series of *Waseda bungaku* was published from January 1906 to December 1927. Under the editorship of Shimamura Hōgetsu, one of several members who had worked on Shōyō's journal, it quickly became a major vehicle of the so-called Japanese naturalism and assumed a central role in the development of Japanese naturalist literature and theory. It was opposed by rival Keiō University's MITA BUNGAKU, edited by NAGAI KAFŪ, a leader of the antinaturalist camp. The list of contributors during this period is a long one; it included such writers as HASEGAWA TENKEI, MASAMUNE HAKUCHŌ, TAYAMA KATAI, CHIKAMATSU SHŪKŌ, IWANO HŌMEI, and SHIMAZAKI TŌSON. Writers like HIROTSU KAZUO, UNO KŌJI, and KASAI ZENZŌ helped maintain the journal's reputation in the postnaturalist years, but by 1920 *Waseda bungaku's* literary influence had waned. It ceased publication in 1927.

The third series of *Waseda bungaku*, published from June 1934 to February 1949, is noted chiefly for editor Tanizaki Seiji's (1890–1971) skill in avoiding government censorship. Members included KINOSHITA NAOE, NIWA FUMIO, and IBUSE MASUJI. It put out a number of special issues devoted to critical articles on the works of FUTABATEI SHIMEI, NATSUME SŌSEKI, ARISHIMA TAKEO, and AKUTAGAWA RYŪNOSUKE.

Series four, five, and six appeared at intermittent intervals over a 10-year span from 1949 to 1959. New members were added to the long list of contributors, with Niwa Fumio, ISHIKAWA TATSUZŌ, and HINO ASHIHEI acting as joint editors of series six. Series seven comprised 72 issues published from 1969 to 1975. One of the outstanding features of this series was the criticism of Akiyama Shun (b 1930). He was joined by young writers like Gotō Meisei (b 1932) and MIURA TETSUO. Series eight began publication in June 1976 and was still in existence in the 1980s. *Theodore W. GOOSSEN*

Waseda University

(Waseda Daigaku). A private, coeducational university located in Shinjuku Ward, Tōkyō. Established in 1882 by ŌKUMA SHIGENOBU as the Tōkyō Semmon Gakkō; renamed Waseda University in 1902. One of the representative private universities of the early modern period, its graduates include many outstanding writers, politicians, and journalists. It has faculties of political science and economics, law, letters, education, commerce, science and engineering, and social sciences as well as a night curriculum in the social sciences and in literature. It also maintains an international division, where approximately 100 foreign students study each year. Waseda also maintains the following facilities: Casting Research Laboratory, Institute for Research in Contemporary Political and Economic Affairs, Institute of Comparative Law, Institute of Language Teaching, Science and Engineering Research Laboratory, System Science Institute and the Institute for Research in Business Administration. Waseda is known for its keen baseball rivalry with Keiō University. The Waseda Daigaku Tsubouchi Hakushi Kinen Engeki Hakubutsukan (Tsubouchi Memorial Theater Museum, also known as Empaku), was established in 1928 to commemorate the writer TSUBOUCHI SHŌYŌ's 70th birthday and his translation of the complete works of Shakespeare. It is the only museum of theater in Japan. Enrollment was 34,450 in 1980. *FUJIKAWA Kinji*

washi

The collective term for Japanese hand-molded paper made principally from *kōzo* (paper mulberry; *Broussonetia kazinoki*), *gampi* (*Wikstroemia sikokiana*), or *mitsumata* (*Edgeworthia papyrifera*). Other bark fibers, such as *asa* (hemp; *Cannabis sativa*), have been used at various times, and today wood pulp is frequently added to the stocks of the cheaper range of papers.

Invention and Transmission —— The invention of paper in China dates from ancient times. Recent excavations in Shaanxi (Shensi) Province have yielded examples of true paper, made by the aqueous deposition of macerated plant fiber, which have been dated to the mid-2nd century BC, some two and a half centuries before the traditional date AD 105, when, according to the *Hou Han shu* (History of the Later Han Dynasty), Cailun (Ts'ai Lun), a eunuch in the court of Emperor Ho, is credited with the invention. It was probably not used as stationery until the 1st century AD.

Establishing a date for the introduction of papermaking into Japan has been hindered by the acceptance of a traditional rather than factual date. The 8th-century NIHON SHOKI (Chronicle of Japan) states that the monk Donchō (Kor: Tam-chi), who arrived from Korea in 610, knew the art of making pigments, ink, and paper. It is not clear that he introduced papermaking into Japan, but that is the traditional interpretation. Little factual evidence is available, but it seems likely that paper first reached Japan during the late 5th century. The fact that the *Nihon shoki* cites a census from as early as 540 suggests that by this time papermaking was known in Japan, because the distribution of hempen cloth or imported Chinese paper for this purpose would have been too costly. It might be said that without an established supply of home-produced paper such things as the TAIKA REFORM of 645 could not have been put into effect, for the quantities of paper required for the compilation of a national census and accounts would have been considerable.

Nara Period (710–794) —— The Nara period may be thought of as being the first age of papermaking in Japan. The centralization of political authority, the establishment of the imperial court at Nara with its attendant bureaucracy, and the dramatic expansion of the Buddhist priesthood created a new and heavy demand for paper.

The finest examples of paper of this age are to be found in the SHŌSŌIN, the 8th-century imperial repository of the temple Tōdaiji in Nara, where the oldest examples of Japanese paper have been collected. The collection is made up of items from the archives of the central and regional governments, paintings, drawings, sample books, and single unused sheets. The oldest examples are census registers from the provinces of Mino (now part of Gifu Prefecture), Chikuzen (now part of Fukuoka Prefecture) and Buzen (now parts of Ōita and Fukuoka prefectures), and clearly date to 701. The papers were made in the provinces in which the census was compiled. All were molded from *kōzo* fiber by the *tamezuki* method, a technique in every respect the same as that used in the West and which is the oldest of the two methods employed in Japan. All are of fine quality, indicating that papermaking was well established in areas some distance from the capital.

Altogether the Shōsōin archive cites some 233 different types of paper. The names tell us where they were made, e.g. Mino *kyōshi* (paper from Mino Province for sutra copying); the material used, e.g. *mashi* (hemp paper); the color, e.g. *benigami* (crimson paper); or the method by which they were decorated, e.g. *kinjin ryokushi* (green paper dusted with gold). Twenty-one provinces are mentioned as producing paper.

The principal raw materials for papermaking during this period were hemp, *kōzo*, and *gampi*, but many other fibers were being experimented with, most in combination with *kōzo*. Varieties of decorated paper, used mainly for sutra copying, were very numerous, ranging from simple dyed sheets to those exhibiting a number of techniques used together, such as stamping, stenciling, gilding with small pieces of gold or silver leaf, and washline drawing. The fact that many of the documents have writing on both sides, a practice which was to disappear as paper became more available, shows that it was still relatively scarce and available only to official government bodies and Buddhist temples.

Heian Period (794–1185) —— The Heian period was the "golden age" of papermaking, not so much for quantity but for quality and variety. With the flowering of courtly culture and a break from the Buddhist dominance of the previous age, there developed a wider demand for both official papers and luxuriously decorated sheets on which to keep diaries, write poems, and so forth. Little, if any, however, found its way into the hands of the common people. Demands were so great that the central government felt it prudent to establish its own mill, and this, the Shiokuin (also called Kan'yain), was set up during the period 806–809 on the banks of the river Kamiyagawa (also pronounced Kan'ya) in Kyōto. The raw materials for the mill were supplied as tax in kind by some 23 provinces and Dazaifu, the government headquarters in Kyūshū. Many of these also supplied the court with the finished product. The four molders or vatmen of the official mill produced between them some 270,000 sheets annually. Three main types of paper were molded there, made from freshly prepared hemp fiber or macerated hempen cloth, kōzo, and gampi. Another type, made from or containing the bark fibers of the kurara shrub (Sophora angustifolia) and called kujinshi, was also prepared. This contained a natural insecticide, which made it ideal for the preservation of records and important papers. Collectively the papers of the mill were called kan'yagami. Tinted papers called kan'ya no shikishi were also produced. Toward the end of the period the mill found it increasingly difficult to acquire raw materials and was forced to make paper from recycled waste. This was known as shukushi. It was tinted grey because it was difficult to remove the ink; thus it was called usuzumigami ("pale ink paper") or suiunshi ("water cloud paper"), depending upon its tone. Initially this was used by the court but later became popular with calligraphers. During this period another paper came into vogue, namely michinokugami (Michinoku paper), which is thought to have been made in the vicinity of Hiraizumi in what is now Iwate Prefecture. This was the forerunner of danshi ("creped" paper) and was made from mayumi (spindle tree; Euonymus sieboldianus). It was white, plump, and smooth, not creped like modern danshi made of kōzo. It was considered a rather formal, masculine paper. Variously dyed papers continued to be made, numerous tints being available, many unique to Japan. One of the innovations of the age was the production of colored papers molded from pulp dyed in vats. The most representative of these are the so-called cloud papers uchigumori (hanging cloud) and tobigumo (floating cloud). Cloudlike patterns were produced either by overmolding or dripping blue stock onto a freshly molded sheet of white gampi paper, usually containing some form of filler such as white clay. Strips of these were much used as tanzaku, narrow strips of paper used for poem writing. SUMINAGA-SHI, an early type of marbled paper, also made its appearance during this period and was made by placing a piece of white loaded gampi paper in a shallow tray and covering it with water. Ink was then dripped onto the surface and agitated with a brush or stylus until a marbled effect was achieved. The paper was then lifted through the ink, which was deposited on the surface of the sheet.

Papers decorated with gold and silver leaf continued to be made in ever-increasing variety. Fine mica powder was also added to the list of pigments. The finest papers available in late Heian times may be seen among the pages of the NISHI HONGANJI's copy of the Sanjūrokunin Kashū (Collection of Thirty-Six Master Poets), a collection of verse compiled in the 12th century. Every imaginable type of paper was used to make this book, each sheet carefully chosen for its decorative quality or to reiterate the sentiment of the verse that was written upon it.

Kamakura, Muromachi, and Azuchi-Momoyama Periods (1185–1600)

The rise of the warrior class with a change to a feudal form of government and the decline in the economic and political fortunes of the imperial court reduced the demand for fancy paper but stimulated increased production of good quality utility paper. The development of printing, markets, and the freer use of paper in architecture for screen and partition covering added a new dimension to paper consumption.

Danshi was still highly prized as a formal stationery but increasingly came to be called hikiawase, possibly because twists of it were used to seal the joints in samurai armor. Papermaking in general made great strides and many new as well as improved older types made their appearance.

Sugiharashi, a white, soft, and pliable paper, first produced for private consumption at the manor of the KONOE FAMILY in Harima (now part of Hyōgo Prefecture), was less formal and somewhat cheaper than danshi and soon found favor among the warrior class. Hōsho, a white danshi-type paper produced in Goka in Echizen (now part of Fukui Prefecture), also became popular as a formal stationery. It was in Echizen too that torinoko (eggshell) was produced. This was a stout paper, having a tone and texture resembling eggshell and is without doubt the most famous of the gampi papers.

It was much favored by calligraphers and many of the finest manuscripts of the age are written upon it.

Mino perhaps produced more paper than any other province at the time and, able to keep the quality high and the price down, it was able to satisfy popular demand, so much so in fact that the word minogami became synonymous with paper. Senkashi from Iyo (now Ehime Prefecture), shuzenjigami from Izu (now part of Shizuoka Prefecture), and yoshinogami from Yamato (now Nara Prefecture) were also in great demand. Towards the end of the 16th century, mitsumata bark fiber was discovered to be suitable for papermaking. Although not produced in quantity until much later, it came to replace hemp, which had lost favor during the late Heian period as one of the three basic raw materials of the craft.

Edo Period (1600–1868)

At the beginning of the politically stable Edo period, the pursuit of learning, which had suffered greatly during the Sengoku period (1467–1568), was revived. The Tokugawa shogunate established an official publishing house in Suruga (now part of Shizuoka Prefecture) and this in turn stimulated the opening of provincial printing centers. Publishing in general reached new heights and for the first time both books and paper ceased to be for the exclusive use of the ruling classes and became freely available for all.

The Tokugawa shogunate adopted hōsho and shuzenjigami as its official paper, thus influencing daimyō feudal lords to establish papermaking centers in their own domains so that they could have a personal source of supply. Many centers produced more than was locally needed and much surplus paper found its way into the markets of Edo (now Tōkyō), Ōsaka, and Kyōto. Echizen hōsho and torinoko were still considered the finest papers but with time many other centers also became famous. Most of the papers produced were of the danshi and hōsho types, but hanshi, produced in most parts of Japan, soon became popular. The best-known examples are Yanagawa hanshi from Chikugo (now part of Fukuoka Prefecture), Yamashiro hanshi from Nagato (now part of Yamaguchi Prefecture), Tokuji hanshi from Suō (now part of Yamaguchi Prefecture), Sekishū hanshi from Iwami (now part of Shimane Prefecture), Ōzu from Iyo, and Mino hanshi from Mino. All of these were made from kōzo. Suruga hanshi from Suruga (now part of Shizuoka Prefecture), however, was molded from mitsumata. It first appeared during the mid-18th century and marked the first time that mitsumata had been used on any scale. Mino hanshi was much used by printers, so much so that Mino paper sizes became the standards for printed books. Another important outlet for the craftsmen of Echizen was supplying the UKIYO-E print makers with hōsho, which they commonly used, almost to the exclusion of all other types of paper.

Meiji Period (1868–1912) to the Present

In order to satisfy the demands of the age of modernization, Western papermaking technology was introduced into Japan in the 1870s. Craftsmen papermakers, however, were still able to hold their own, at least until the first decade of the 20th century. Since industrially produced paper could be made in greater quantities and was increasingly cheaper than the handmade variety, families engaged in the craft have found it more and more difficult to compete. In 1928, 28,532 families were recorded as engaged in papermaking, but by 1973 the number had dropped to 851. In spite of this the craft endures, and there is today an increasing demand for fine quality handmade paper, whatever the cost. There are qualities of strength and durability to be found in the handmade product which can only come from the hands of craftsmen skilled in the traditional techniques that have evolved over a period of some 1,400 years and that cannot be reproduced by industrial methods.

Techniques of Papermaking

The bark fibers of three shrubs, kōzo, gampi, and mitsumata make up the papermaker's basic raw materials. All occur naturally in most parts of Japan with the exception of Hokkaidō and the northernmost tip of Honshū. Kōzo and mitsumata shrubs are cultivated, but gampi bark is always gathered from the wild plant. Before bark is turned into paper it must be cropped, stripped, bleached, boiled in lye to remove the nonfibrous materials, washed, graded, and finally pulped. Techniques vary slightly for each of the raw materials but those pertaining to the production of kōzo pulp are most typical.

The annual crop of branches is cut from the squat trunks of the shrubs in late autumn. Cutting is done with a sharp sickle as near to the ground as possible. Shrubs of from three to eight years old produce the best bark, but after the first two years of free growth branches may be cropped annually. Removal of the bark from the branches is facilitated by steaming. This is done by placing bundles of branches inside a large steamer or tub that is placed inverted over a cauldron of boiling water. After three hours these are removed and soaked in cold water to allow handling. Bark is then removed by loosening it from one end of the branch and peeling in a single action. At this stage it is called "black bark." The white inner layer of fiber is used for paper; the outer flakey waste material is removed by scraping. The white inner layer is called "unbleached white bark." Any greenish tinge is then removed by natural bleaching. Bundles of bark may be pegged in a shallow stream of cold, clean water (river bleaching), packed under snow (snow bleaching), or hung out in the cold night air (night bleaching). This operation takes two or three days and when completed the bark is called "bleached bark" or "white bark" and represents approximately 8 percent by weight of the original branch crop. The nonfibrous element is then removed by boiling in lye, traditionally made by dissolving wood ash in water. After this the lye and waste material are washed away and the fiber is carefully cleaned of dirt. The fiber is then pulped either by beating with wooden batons or mallets, or by crushing it in a hand or water-driven mortar. Today these may be electrically powered. The pulp is then placed in a large vat of fresh, clean water to produce the "stock."

Molding Paper —— There are two methods of molding employed in Japan: *tamezuki,* which was introduced into Japan from China, is essentially the same method as that used in the West; *nagashizuki,* the alternative and most commonly used method, is peculiar to Japan and probably evolved during the 8th century. In the case of *nagashizuki,* the stock or pulp water mix contains a mucilage, obtained from one of several plants. *Tororo (Abelmoschus manihot)* or *noriutsugi (Hydrangea paniculata)* are those most commonly used. The inclusion of mucilage produces an emulsion in which the fibers are suspended and ensures that they do not knot. It also effectively thickens the liquid and delays its draining time as it passes through the mesh of the mold, allowing the vatman greater control in the determination of paper thickness. Similarly, it acts as a buffer between sheets when these are couched, no interleaving felts being used as in the case of *tamezuki.* The main differences between the two methods are that in *tamezuki* all excess liquid is allowed to drain through the mold, while in *nagashizuki* most of it is cast out. Each sheet or waterleaf requires several dips into the vat of stock. In the case of *tamezuki* the "face" or "right side" of the sheet is produced first, while in *nagashizuki* it is produced by the final dip. After molding some four to six hundred sheets, or one "block," the sheets are pressed to remove excess water and separated and brushed into fine grained wooden boards to dry. Finally the sheets are gathered, cut to size, packed, and marketed. Hand crafted paper is made in most parts of Japan, but the major centers are: TŌYO and KAWANOE in Ehime Prefecture; Imadate and OBAMA in Fukui Prefecture; YAME in Fukuoka Prefecture; Adachi in Fukushima Prefecture; MINO and Kawai in Gifu Prefecture; Ino and TOSA in Kōchi Prefecture; Ayabe in Kyōto Prefecture; IIDA in Nagano Prefecture; Yoshino in Nara Prefecture; Ogawa in Saitama Prefecture; Misumi and Yakumo in Shimane Prefecture; Saji and Aoya in Tottori Prefecture; and Nakatomi in Yamanashi Prefecture.

📖 —— Abe Eishirō, *Washi sammai* (1972). Fujita Sadao, *Sugiharashi* (1970). Brian F. Hickman, "Japanese Handmade Papers: Materials and Techniques," *The Japan Society of London Bulletin* (March 1977). Sukey Hughes, *Washi* (1978), contains an extensive bibliography. Ikeda Hideo, *Washi nempyō* (1974). Jugaku Bunshō, *Nihon no kami* (1946). Jugaku Bunshō, *Washi no tabi* (1973). Katō Kiyoharu, *Washi* (1966). Kume Yasuo, *Washi no bunka shi* (1976). Kunisaki Jihei, *Kamisuki chōhōki* (1798), tr Charles E. Hamilton as *Kamisuki chōhōki—A Handy Guide to Papermaking* (1948). Machida Seishi, *Washi bunka* (1977). Seki Yoshikuni, *Tesukigami shi no kenkyū* (1976). Washi Kenkyūkai, ed, *Washi kenkyū,* 12 vols (1939–45).   Brian HICKMAN

Washington Conference

(Washinton Kaigi). An international meeting held from November 1921 to February 1922 in Washington DC to limit naval armaments and resolve outstanding East Asian international political problems. The conference produced treaties that ended the ANGLO-JAPANESE ALLIANCE of 1902, limited naval construction, and reaffirmed the principles of Chinese political and territorial integrity.

Origins —— The need for such a conference arose from changes brought about by World War I. That conflict destroyed German and Russian influence in East Asia, greatly weakened British and French strength in the region, and left Japan and the United States at odds

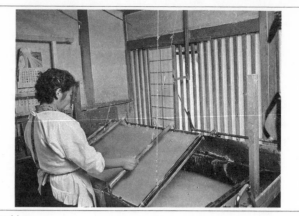

washi

Casting out excess liquid by shaking the mold in the *nagashizukuri* method of molding Japanese handmade paper.

over Japan's occupation of parts of Siberia following its intervention in the Russian Revolution (see SIBERIAN INTERVENTION), Chinese problems, and disposition of former German Pacific territories. In addition, the war committed Japan, Great Britain, and the United States to naval expansion programs that threatened to disrupt harmonious relations. The American naval program of 1916, designed to build a navy second to none, and Japan's "eight-eight fleet" (HACHIHACHI KANTAI) scheme of 1920, the largest and most costly in its history, convinced many observers that the two Pacific powers were on a collision course.

This state of affairs worried political leaders already troubled by postwar economic recession and the fragmentation of wartime political coalitions. Prodded by Congress, President Warren G. Harding on 11 July 1921 invited Japan, Great Britain, France, and Italy to send delegates to Washington to discuss naval and East Asian problems.

Japan's Response —— Prime Minister HARA TAKASHI regarded Harding's invitation as a threefold opportunity. Naval limitation by international agreement might reduce defense costs and yet leave Japan secure in the western Pacific. The conference might also provide an opportunity to resolve pressing diplomatic problems. While Hara preferred to retain the Anglo-Japanese Alliance or expand it into a tripartite entente with the United States, he was prepared to abandon it so as to improve relations with Washington. He also saw the naval limitation issue as a means of cementing a domestic political alliance between his RIKKEN SEIYŪKAI party and the navy.

On 27 September 1921 Navy Minister Admiral KATŌ TOMOSABURŌ, Ambassador SHIDEHARA KIJŪRŌ, and Prince TOKUGAWA IESATO were appointed delegates to the Washington Conference. They were given instructions endorsing naval limitation and leaving ample room for compromise in securing it.

Negotiations —— American Secretary of State Charles Evans Hughes opened the meeting on 12 November 1921 by offering to scrap 30 American capital ships if Great Britain would abandon 23 and Japan give up 25. This proposal was referred to naval experts while the diplomats dealt with Hughes's demand for termination of the Anglo-Japanese Alliance. American, British, and Japanese negotiators then fashioned a replacement for it, the FOUR-POWER TREATY, by which their nations and France pledged to respect the status quo in the Pacific and to confer if it were threatened.

Naval limitation demanded a more complex, compromise-filled agreement. Katō Tomosaburō overcame his subordinate KATŌ HIROHARU's insistence on a 10:10:7 capital-ship strength ratio for the United States, Great Britain, and Japan. He convinced Hughes to permit the Imperial Japanese Navy's retention of its newest capital ship, the *Mutsu,* and persuaded British and American delegates to accept the principle of preserving the status quo of designated western Pacific fortifications. This bargain placated opposition within the Imperial Navy and enabled the TAKAHASHI KOREKIYO cabinet, a weak, faction-ridden group that lacked the leadership skills of its predecessor, the Hara cabinet, to argue that a 10:10:6 ratio was acceptable.

The Washington Conference also established a new order of China diplomacy. Chinese and Japanese delegates met separately to resolve differences over the SHANDONG (SHANTUNG) QUESTION. To clear away past misunderstandings generated by the TWENTY-ONE DEMANDS of 1915 and the LANSING–ISHII AGREEMENT of 1917, Japan and the United States joined seven other powers in two treaties. One provided for joint regulation of Chinese tariffs, and the other reaffirmed the principles of Chinese political and territorial integrity and of equality of economic opportunity in China.

Consequences for Japan —— The conference concluded on 6 February 1922 with the signing of the five-power naval agreements (WASHINGTON NAVAL TREATY OF 1922) and the China treaties (see NINE-POWER TREATY). (The Four-Power Treaty had been signed on 13 December 1921.) These accords profoundly influenced Japanese diplomacy and domestic politics for a decade. They laid the basis for the "cooperative diplomacy" subsequently practiced by Shidehara Kijūrō. The naval treaties gave Japan maritime predominance in the western Pacific and made possible significant reductions first in navy, then in army, expenditures. Finally, the Washington Conference solidified the alliance between politicians and admirals that Hara had fashioned in 1921. Their cooperation in constraining army political power at home and activism abroad was an essential feature of "TAISHŌ DEMOCRACY."

📖 ——Bōeichō Bōei Kenshūjo Senshishitsu, ed, *Daihon'ei kaigumbu rengō kantai,* vol 1 (1975). Roger Dingman, *Power in the Pacific* (1976). Gaimushō, ed, *Nihon gaikō bunsho: Washinton kaigi kyokutō mondai* (1975). Kajima Heiwa Kenkyūjo, ed, *Washinton kaigi oyobi imin mondai,* in *Nihon gaikō shi,* vol 13 (1971).

Roger DINGMAN

Washington Naval Treaty of 1922

(Washinton Kaigun Gunshuku Jōyaku). An agreement concluded on 6 February 1922 by Japan, France, Great Britain, Italy, and the United States to limit the size, armament, and deployment of capital ships of war.

Origins —— The idea of limiting navies by international agreement became a reality immediately after World War I. The victors imposed naval limitation on defeated Germany and pledged to seek arms limitation themselves in article 8 of the League of Nations Covenant. At the December 1920 League meeting in Geneva, Japanese Ambassador ISHII KIKUJIRŌ hinted that Tōkyō might follow suit if Washington and London ceased to build capital ships. US Senator William E. Borah took this opportunity to secure passage of a congressional resolution calling for an arms limitation conference. On 11 July 1921 President Warren G. Harding invited Japan, Great Britain, France, and Italy to a conference in Washington to discuss naval limitation and East Asian international political problems (see WASHINGTON CONFERENCE).

Japan's Position —— Ten days after receiving the invitation, Japanese naval experts presented Navy Minister Admiral KATŌ TOMOSABURŌ with the first of several reports favoring naval limitation. By September 1921 they concluded that an agreement was both feasible and desirable, that capital-ship construction should cease by 1 January 1922, and that the Imperial Japanese Navy could accept inferiority in numbers and total tonnage of capital ships if it were agreed that possible adversaries would not develop advanced-base facilities in the western Pacific. Although technical experts argued for a 70-percent strength ratio in relation to the US Navy, Admiral Katō, whom Prime Minister HARA TAKASHI named delegate to the Washington Conference, accepted formal negotiating instructions that did not mention this figure.

Negotiations —— US Secretary of State Charles Evans Hughes opened the negotiations on 12 November 1921 by proposing reductions in capital ships, both built and under construction, that would establish a 10:10:6 strength ratio for the American, British, and Japanese navies. He also called for limitations on auxiliary surface craft and submarines, as well as cessation of capital-ship construction. The Japanese delegates accepted these ideas in principle but objected to the specifics. Rear Admiral KATŌ KANJI, the senior technical expert, who wished to retain a 10:10:7 ratio, disputed American calculations of capital ships built and insisted upon retention of Japan's newest battleship, the *Mutsu.* Senior delegate Katō Tomosaburō then cabled Tōkyō for instructions, listing alternatives ranging from insistence on the 70-percent ratio, through compromise on a 10:10:6.5 or 10:10:6 ratio with retention of the *Mutsu,* to simple acceptance of the American proposal. The TAKAHASHI KOREKIYO cabinet, which had succeeded the Hara cabinet, favored the first two choices and directed that any compromise be compensated for by an agreement on base fortifications in the western Pacific.

Katō Tomosaburō then negotiated a broad agreement allowing for a 10:10:6 ratio, retention of the *Mutsu,* and limitation of bases.

Terms —— After the failure of efforts to broaden the agreement on capital ships to include auxiliary surface craft, the Five-Power Treaty on capital-ship limitation was signed on 6 February 1922. The treaty, which was to remain in effect for 15 years, specified the ships to be scrapped and limited, in size and armament, all capital ships built and under construction. Article 19 required maintenance of the status quo of specified fortifications in the western Pacific. The agreement provided for subsequent meetings for its revision and updating; these were held at Geneva in 1927 and at London in 1930 and 1935–36 (see LONDON NAVAL CONFERENCES). A separate instrument pledged the signatory powers to observe certain rules in the use of submarines and noxious gases. After considerable debate in the Diet, Japan ratified the treaty on 5 August 1922; it became effective 17 August 1923, following the deposit of ratifications at Washington.

Significance —— The Washington Naval Treaty sparked debates within the Imperial Japanese Navy that led to a major political controversy in 1930 and to Japan's decision in 1934 to abrogate the agreement. Nonetheless, the treaty has come to be regarded as the first example of strategic arms limitation by international agreement.

📖 ——Bōeichō Bōei Kenshūjo Senshishitsu, ed, *Daihon'ei kaigumbu rengō kantai,* vol 1 (1975). Roger Dingman, *Power in the Pacific* (1976). Kajima Heiwa Kenkyūjo, ed, *Washinton kaigi oyobi imin mondai,* in *Nihon gaikō shi,* vol 13 (1971). Kobayashi Tatsuo, "Kaigun gunshuku jōyaku," in Tsunoda Jun, ed, *Taiheiyō sensō e no michi,* vol 1 (1963).

Roger DINGMAN

Washiuzan

Also known as Washūzan. Hill in the southern part of the city of Kurashiki, Okayama Prefecture, western Honshū. Weathered granite rocks protruding from Washiuzan form grotesque figures. Its summit commands a view of the Inland Sea. At its foot is Ōhama swimming beach. Washiuzan, part of the Inland Sea National Park, attracts crowds of tourists throughout the year. Height: 113 m (370 ft).

wasps → bees and wasps

watakushi shōsetsu → I-novel

Watanabe Jōtarō (1874–1936)

Army general. Born in Aichi Prefecture; graduated from the Army Academy in 1896; became a general in 1931. Watanabe was known as an authority on military history and was named inspector general of military education when a leader of the KŌDŌHA faction, MAZAKI JINZABURŌ, was dismissed in 1935. Thereafter regarded as a leader of the rival TŌSEIHA faction in the army, he was assassinated by Kōdōha officers in the FEBRUARY 26TH INCIDENT of 1936.

HATA Ikuhiko

Watanabe Kazan (1793–1841)

Scholar of WESTERN LEARNING and painter; real name, Watanabe Sadayasu. Pupil of TANI BUNCHŌ. Most famous for landscapes in the BUNJINGA (literati painting) style and for realistic portraits, he also did bird-and-flower paintings and figure and nature studies.

Kazan served as a high-ranking official of the small Tawara domain (now part of Aichi Prefecture), working to improve its economic conditions and coastal defense system. In his early 30s he became fascinated with Western Learning, and with other *rangakusha* (scholars of "Dutch studies") in Edo (now Tōkyō) formed the study group SHŌSHIKAI. He also wrote a pamphlet criticizing the shogunate's NATIONAL SECLUSION policy (see SHINKIRON). Kazan came under the suspicion of the Tokugawa government for advocating closer relations with the West and, along with other *rangakusha,* was arrested in 1839 on a false charge of conspiracy (see BANSHA NO GOKU). His death sentence was commuted to life imprisonment, which he was later allowed to serve in his home domain. He lived there for two years, painting, reading, and writing. On 11 October 1841, worried lest he cause trouble to his *daimyō* or those close to him, he committed suicide.

An eclectic painter, Kazan worked in styles based on traditional Chinese and Japanese as well as Western models. His work ranges from delicate bird-and-flower studies to strong, decisively rendered landscapes and portraits. He was an acute observer of everyday life and filled travel diaries and notebooks with sketches, capturing with quick, deft lines the gestures and costumes of all types of people. Although he experimented with Western techniques of modeling and perspective, his works retain an emphasis on brushwork and line. It is this combination of Western and Japanese methods that makes his painting distinctive. Kazan made his greatest innovations in PORTRAIT PAINTING. He worked from sketches done from life and tried to capture the personality as well as physical likeness of his subjects. In his 1837 painting of the scholar and shogunal official Takami Senseki (1785–1858) now in the Tōkyō National Museum, and his undated sketch of the physician Takenaka Genshin (dates unknown), fluid line and shading give a sense of anatomical structure and solidity new in Japanese portraiture. *Carol* MORLAND

Watanabe Masanosuke (1899–1928)

Labor-movement activist and communist leader of the Taishō period (1912–26). Born in Chiba Prefecture, he received only an elementary-school education. While working at a celluloid factory in Tōkyō, Watanabe came into contact with members of the SHINJINKAI, a socialist study group at Tōkyō University, and with their help formed a union in the factory. In 1922 he joined the newly formed JAPAN COMMUNIST PARTY but was arrested along with other leftists in the following year. After his release from jail in 1924, he returned to labor-union activities and in the same year married TANNO SETSU, who had also devoted herself to the cause of labor. Active for a while in the left-wing faction of the SŌDŌMEI (Japan Federation of Labor), he was expelled for being too radical. In 1926 he joined the Central Committee of the Japan Communist Party, which had been reestablished the year before. He went to Moscow in 1927 for a Comintern meeting on party strategy and tactics, and helped to draft the so-called 1927 Thesis on Japan. He escaped arrest in the mass roundup of leftists known as the MARCH 15TH INCIDENT of 1928, although his wife was imprisoned. In the autumn of the same year he went to Shanghai to attend a trade-union conference; on his way back to Japan he committed suicide while trying to escape police in Jilong (Keelung), Taiwan.

Watanabe Nangaku (1767–1813)

Painter of the MARUYAMA-SHIJŌ SCHOOL. Real name Watanabe Iwao. Born in Kyōto. He studied under MARUYAMA ŌKYO and possibly under another of Ōkyo's disciples, Komai Ki (1747–97). Nangaku's range was wide and his subjects included figures, flowers, and animals. He was especially esteemed for his pictures of beautiful women *(bijinga)*, his drawings of carp, and his impromptu sketches. The influence of KŌRIN and the RIMPA style of painting can be detected in his later work, which often displays a decorative style and color as well as a notably delicate brush stroke. Nangaku spent three years teaching painting in Edo (now Tōkyō) and so provided Edo with its first real introduction to the Maruyama-Shijō style. Among his students was Ōnishi Chinnen (1792–1851).

C. H. MITCHELL

Watanabe Sadao (1933–)

Jazz alto saxophonist. Born in Tochigi Prefecture. In the early 1950s he played in the Cozy Quartet with AKIYOSHI TOSHIKO. While studying at the Berklee College of Music in Boston from 1962 to 1965, he became interested in the bossa nova, African music, and fusion music. He carried these new musical forms back to Japan, where, now nicknamed "Nabe Sada," he exerted great influence upon younger musicians. His performances, characterized by a strong jazz spirit allied with a fluid expressive power, have won him critical acclaim in both Japan and the United States. *Abe Yasushi*

Watanabe Shikō (1683–1755)

Artist of the RIMPA school. He was born and lived in Kyōto. Real name Watanabe Motome. A retainer of the court noble KONOE IEHIRO, he began his artistic career by studying the painting style of the KANŌ SCHOOL. He is said by some to have studied under KŌRIN and is counted, along with TATEBAYASHI KAGEI, as one of Kōrin's most important followers. He is noted for his paintings of mountain landscapes and trees and flowers.

Watanabe Tetsuzō (1885–)

Businessman and politician. Born in Ōsaka; graduated from Tōkyō University. Watanabe became assistant professor at Tōkyō University in 1913 and was later promoted to full professor. He was elected to the House of Representatives in 1936. After the outbreak of the Sino-Japanese War of 1937–45, Watanabe became active in the movement against militarism. From 1947 he served as president of the Tōhō film company and worked to settle the TŌHŌ STRIKE. After leaving Tōhō in 1950, Watanabe became active in anticommunist and prorearmament movements. *Maeda Kazutoshi*

Watarai Shintō

Also called Ise Shintō, Gekū Shintō. An important school of Shintō founded by and transmitted within the Watarai family, who were the hereditary priests of the Outer Shrine (Gekū) of ISE SHRINE. According to tradition, the Inner Shrine (Naikū), which is dedicated to the imperial ancestress and sun goddess AMATERASU ŌMIKAMI, was established at Ise in 4 BC. The Outer Shrine, which honors the food deity Toyouke no Ōkami, was moved to Ise from Hiji in Tamba Province (now part of Hyōgo Prefecture) in 478 so that its deity might directly serve Amaterasu.

The inequality between the two Ise shrines began to diminish under the influence of RYŌBU SHINTŌ, which held that the Inner and Outer Shrines were two aspects of a single reality, just as were the two mandalas in Shingon Buddhism. Resentful of the inferior position to which the Outer Shrine had been relegated, Watarai Yukitada (1236–1305), the first major exponent of this school, basing himself on the ideas of Ryōbu Shintō, proclaimed the equality and interdependence of the two shrines, which were likened to the sun and moon or heaven and earth. By the 13th century Watarai Shintō had produced a sacred corpus called the *Shintō gobusho* (Five Books of Shintō), which were attributed to semilegendary figures in order to provide authority for the views of the school that were then taking shape.

Not content to assert the mere equality of Toyouke with Amaterasu, some Watarai scholars developed a complex theology suggesting the ultimate superiority of Toyouke over all other deities, including Amaterasu, by identifying Toyouke with Amenominakanushi no Kami ("The Deity Who Is the Lord at the Center of Heaven"), which is the name of the first deity mentioned in the KOJIKI (712, Records of Ancient Matters). Using dubious etymologies and drawing on Chinese cosmological theories, the Watarai scholars linked Toyouke (also known as Miketsukami) with the element water by interpreting the *mi* in Miketsukami as *mizu* (water). Since, in their view, water was the source of heaven and earth and predominated over fire, which was regarded as the essence of the sun deity Amaterasu, Toyouke emerged as the supreme deity of Shintō. Watarai scholars also rejected the widely held view that Shintō deities were Japanese manifestations of Buddhist divinities (HONJI SUIJAKU), asserting on the contrary that it was the Buddhas and bodhisattvas who were the transformations of eternal Shintō deities.

With its emphasis on the supremacy of the Ise Shrine over all other shrines, the divine origin of the imperial family, and the superiority of Shintō over Buddhism, Watarai Shintō strongly influenced other Shintō schools such as the Yoshida and Suika and contributed to the development of nationalist thinking, as reflected in the writings of the loyalist KITABATAKE CHIKAFUSA (1293–1354). Yet despite its bias against foreign ideas, Watarai Shintō relied heavily on Buddhist and Confucian concepts in the formulation of its own doctrines, for which fact it was criticized in the Edo period (1600–1868). *Stanley* WEINSTEIN

Watarasegawa

River in central Honshū, originating in the mountains of western Tochigi Prefecture, flowing through the eastern part of Gumma Prefecture, and joining the TONEGAWA in northeastern Saitama Prefecture. A multipurpose dam has been constructed on the upper reaches. Water pollution by the Ashio Copper Mine, in operation until 1972, had been a problem since the Meiji period (1868–1912; see ASHIO COPPER MINE INCIDENT). The water is utilized for irrigation and electric power as well as for drinking by the cities of Ōta, Ashikaga, and Kiryū. Length: about 94 km (58 mi); area of drainage basin: 2,612 sq km (1,008 sq mi).

water lily

(*suiren*). Of the more than 50 known species of the water lily family (Nymphaeaceae) in the world, the only one native to Japan is *Nymphae tetragona* var. *angusta,* a freshwater perennial found in ponds and marshes. Its stubby rhizome grows up to the water surface from roots and base leaves buried in a pool or marsh bed. Its leaf stalks are long, slender, and cylindrical, and the thick, oval leaf blades are green on top and dark purplish underneath. Each leaf is shaped like an arrowhead, with a slit from its bordered edge to its center. In July or August a white flower about 5 centimeters (2 in) in width blossoms atop a long, thin stalk that rises above the water. Since Japanese water lilies normally open their blossoms at about 2:00 PM, the hour of the sheep in the traditional Japanese calendar (see JIKKAN JŪNISHI), they are also called *hitsujigusa* (sheep plant).

Most of the species known as *suiren* in Japan today are actually of Western origin. Unlike the indigenous species they have relatively large leaves and bloom at different times from summer to autumn in a variety of colors, including white, yellow, pink, red, and purple. See also LOTUS. MATSUDA Osamu

Water Resources Development Public Corporation

(Mizushigen Kaihatsu Kōdan). Corporation established by the Japanese government in 1962 to meet the increased demand for water by cities and industries and to carry out comprehensive development and utilization of water resources. Up to 1962, flood control projects were under the jurisdiction of the Construction Ministry, waterworks under the Welfare Ministry, industrial waterworks under the Ministry of International Trade and Industry, and agricultural waterworks under the Ministry of Agriculture and Forestry. Since that year, however, the corporation has been given the job of constructing dams, dikes, multipurpose irrigation channels, and other facilities in accordance with the Basic Plan for the Development of Water Resources. Its main objective is to rectify such problems as the shortage of water, which necessitates limiting the supply of water to households, and the problem of land subsidence resulting from excessive pumping of groundwater. The corporation has centered its development efforts on the six major river systems: the Tonegawa, Arakawa, Yodogawa, Kisogawa, Yoshinogawa, and Chikugogawa. The principal dams and irrigation projects already completed by the corporation include the Aichi Irrigation Project and the Yagisawa Dam. In 1968 the corporation absorbed the Aichi Irrigation Public Corporation. HIRATA Masami

Waters, Thomas James (1830–?)

English architect and engineer who, arriving in Japan at the beginning of the Meiji period (1868–1912), produced some of the nation's earliest foreign-designed buildings. His main accomplishments were to promote the local production and extensive use of brick for construction, to build one of the first modern foundries, the Ōsaka Mint, and to execute the new government's first urban plan by reconstructing the Ginza area in Tōkyō after a disastrous fire in 1872. Less visible but equally innovative was his introduction of modern waterpipes and sewage systems.

Between his arrival in about 1865 and his departure about 1880, Waters built the Ōsaka Mint and its reception hall (Sempukan), 1870; the Takehashi Imperial Barracks and the Museum of Commerce in Tōkyō, 1871; the British Legation, 1872; and the colonnaded brick- and stone-faced buildings lining Japan's first Western-style street, the Ginza, in 1873. His favorite style was classic revival as can be seen in the two Ōsaka Mint buildings still preserved as important cultural properties and in the many Meiji-period woodblock prints of the then spectacularly modern Ginza. Dallas FINN

waterwheels

(*suisha*). The first mention of a waterwheel in Japan is found in the chronicle NIHON SHOKI (720) which states that DONCHŌ, who came to Japan from the Korean kingdom of KOGURYŌ in AD 610, made Japan's first millstone, which hulled rice by water power. However, the shape and mechanics of this mill are unknown. Government records of 829 state that "orders were given to all the provinces that waterwheels be built." These were wheels used to lift water for irrigation purposes and were run by human or animal power. This kind of waterwheel was developed in agricultural areas throughout

the medieval period (13th–16th centuries), and by the Edo period (1600–1868), it had become widespread, as had the water-driven mill wheel, which was employed in producing textiles, oil, wheat, flour, and polished rice. In modern times, with the increased availability of electricity, waterwheels came to be used much less frequently. According to a survey made by the National Science Museum, there were in 1980 about 800 waterwheels in the country, of which about 500 were in use.

Watsuji Tetsurō (1889–1960)

Philosopher and cultural historian noted for his systematic studies of ethics and his inquiry into the particular philosophical components of Japanese culture. Born in Hyōgo Prefecture, Watsuji graduated from Tōkyō University. A prolific writer, whose collected works comprise 20 volumes, his earliest works dealt with Western thinkers; he published a study of Nietzsche in 1913 and one of Kierkegaard in 1915. Then he underwent what he himself called an intellectual "about-face," something he described in *Gūzō saikō* (1918, Resurrecting Idols) as a renewed "appreciation for Buddhism and the Buddhist art of the Asuka and Nara periods." From this point on Watsuji concentrated primarily on the intellectual roots of Japanese culture. Between 1920 and 1923 he wrote essays on DŌGEN, important because they revived interest in this neglected 13th-century Zen master and stimulated widespread interest in the structure and value of Dōgen's philosophy. From 1925 until 1934 Watsuji taught ethics at Kyōto University, a position which made him a colleague of NISHIDA KITARŌ and gave him the context for beginning work on his major project, *Rinrigaku,* a systematic treatise on ethics, the first volume of which appeared in 1937. From 1934 until his retirement in 1949 he taught at Tōkyō University.

Watsuji was not merely a reactionary thinker; it is clear that he wished to articulate a particularly Japanese alternative to modern Western thought. He held, for instance, that the native intellectual traditions of the Japanese contained the basis for a more sound and balanced ethics; he insisted that the word for man in Japanese (*ningen*) demonstrates this balance because it simultaneously defines man as an individual and as part of society. Western thought, by contrast, was seen by Watsuji as one which overemphasizes man's existence as an individual. Accordingly, Watsuji cited and examined certain classical aesthetic forms of Japan, especially the TEA CEREMONY (*chanoyu*) and linked verse (see RENGA AND HAIKAI), because of the special way in which they express the interdependence of the individual and society. Throughout all his work the close link between ethics and the arts of Japan is evident.

📖 ——*Watsuji Tetsurō zenshū,* 20 vols (Iwanami Shoten, 1961–63). Watsuji Tetsurō, "The Significance of Ethics as the Study of Man," tr David A. Dilworth, *Monumenta Nipponica* 26.3-4 (1971). Robert N. Bellah, "Japan's Cultural Identity: Some Reflections on the Work of Watsuji Tetsurō," *Journal of Asian Studies* 24.4 (1965). William R. LaFleur, "Buddhist Emptiness in the Ethics and Aesthetics of Watsuji Tetsurō," *Religious Studies* 14 (June 1978). William R. LaFLEUR

wax-resist dyeing

(*rōketsu* or *rōkechi*). A textile dyeing process. The earliest known examples of Japanese wax-resist dyeing are four folding screens in the 8th-century SHŌSŌIN repository in Nara. These screens show a strong Indian influence and were done in a technique, then called *rōkechi* (see SANKECHI), which came to Japan from India via China during the Tang (T'ang; 618–907) dynasty. The designs were achieved by use of a wooden block print stamped onto the fabric, a system of pattern repetition that by this time had been perfected. During the ensuing Heian period (794–1185), however, Japan isolated itself from foreign cultures, and the Japanese began to favor clothing without printed patterns; consequently Tang-style *rōkechi* soon died out. The process (now pronounced *rōketsu*) was revived in the Taishō period (1912–26) and it has been very popular since then, largely owing to the perfecting of chemical dyes and the addition of many new colors to the ancient spectrum of natural browns, blacks, and indigos.

In the *rōketsu* process, wax-resist and dye are applied to the fabric with a brush, in contrast to Indian and Indonesian batik, which utilizes a dipping process followed by wax-resist applied with a *tjanting* tool. In modern *rōketsu,* the fabric generally goes through several repetitions of the waxing-dyeing process, then the wax is removed chemically, and the dye is fixed into the fabric by steaming before a final washing. A characteristic and highly original effect is created through the cracking of the wax during the wax-resist process. Two different types of wax may be used: microwax is used to resist the dye, and beeswax or paraffin to achieve cracking. They may be used together or separately.

Not all resist-dyeing methods require wax for cracking or for resisting dyes. The YŪZEN dyeing technique, for example, uses rice starch (nori) instead of wax. The difference is that wax allows for a freer application of brush strokes, much as in painting, achieving a startling effect that is impossible in yūzen. A further advantage of wax is that it allows for a fuller permeation of the dye into the fabric.

Modern rōketsu motifs range from the traditional flowers and birds to abstract designs. Rōketsu is common in Japanese daily life in such diverse items as CLOTHING (mainly KIMONO), folding screens, framed pictures, NOREN curtains, and pillow covers.

——Miwa Masatada, Rōketsuzome no hanashi 9 (1962). Sano Takeo, Senshoku nyūmon (1973). Yasuko YABE

wayo

(literally, "peaceful giving"). Originally, the free and voluntary transfer of property and rights to either relatives or nonrelatives (in the latter case, it was called tanin wayo); by extension it came to mean a peaceful out-of-court settlement between two disputants. Wayo (or, more correctly, wayo chūbun) settlements on division of revenue between SHŌEN (estate) proprietors (HONKE AND RYŌKE) and shogunate-appointed land stewards (JITŌ) became increasingly common from the middle of the 13th century. In order to be legally binding, wayo settlements had to be reviewed by the shogunate, which issued a document of confirmation (gejijō). In many cases wayo worked to the advantage of the jitō, and thus became yet another instrument for his encroachment on the proprietary rights of estate owners. These private agreements reflected the Kamakura shogunate's (1192–1333) gradual retreat from jurisdictional control over its appointees. See also SHITAJI CHŪBUN.

weasels

The principal variety of weasel in Japan is the itachi (Mustela sibirica) of the family Mustelidae. Widely distributed in East Asia, it is native to all parts of Japan except Okinawa and Hokkaidō. In recent years it has been introduced into Hokkaidō for the extermination of rats and mice. The body of a large male measures roughly 35 centimeters (14 in) in length and its tail around 17 centimeters (7 in). Females are less than half the size of males. Except for the head, which is blackish brown, the body of both male and female is entirely brown. The itachi's customary habitat is near water and it is regularly seen in both mountainous areas and on the outskirts of cities. It feeds on small animals such as mice, frogs, and crayfish. The fur is of good quality and is exported under the name "Japanese mink." Related species of the same genus inhabiting Japan are the iizuna (least weasel; M. nivalis) and okojo (stoat; M. erminea). The itachi is noted for its malodorous spray, giving rise to the expression itachi no saigoppe ("the weasel's last resort").

IMAIZUMI Yoshiharu and SANEYOSHI Tatsuo

Webb, Sir William Flood (1887–1972)

Australian jurist and president of the International Military Tribunal for the Far East from 1946 to 1948. Born in Brisbane, Queensland, he had a distinguished legal career during which he occupied the positions of chief justice of Queensland (1940–46) and justice of the High Court of Australia (1946–58). While serving on the tribunal he was of the opinion that the guilt of those accused was mitigated by the prior responsibility of the emperor for the crimes of which they stood accused. He proposed that no capital punishment be imposed on any of the accused because they had only been obeying orders, whereas the emperor had escaped trial. His belief in the emperor's complicity brought him into serious disagreement with the chief prosecutor, the American Joseph B. KEENAN, as well as some of his fellow judges. Nevertheless, when the tribunal by majority decisions pronounced death sentences on seven of the accused, Sir William did not press his dissent, on the ground that he could not say that the death sentences were manifestly excessive. See also WAR CRIMES TRIALS.

——Richard H. Minear, Victor's Justice: The Tokyo War Crimes Trial (1972). J. A. A. STOCKWIN

weddings

Weddings are perhaps the most important rite of passage in Japan, and one of the four major ceremonial occasions referred to as kankon sōsai (coming-of-age, marriage, funerals, ancestor worship). For the uniting of a man and woman as husband and wife to be official a new family register (koseki; see HOUSEHOLD REGISTERS) must be compiled for the couple at the local administrative office, but social and public recognition of a marriage in Japan is secured by the purchase and display of large amounts of furniture and clothing, and by extravagant weddings with elaborate formal costumes and large receptions. Modern weddings have considerable variation, but usually include one or more old customs which have become simply required formalities today.

Traditional Weddings—— What is thought of today as a "traditional" wedding was established as a pattern during the Meiji period (1868–1912). Although the marriage procedure varied a great deal with locality, most weddings included the customs described below.

In cases where the parties had not met, the courting procedure began with an exchange of photographs (miai shashin). The next step was a meeting between the couple and their families (MIAI), arranged by a go-between (NAKŌDO) who served both as intermediary prior to the wedding, and as counselor to the young couple afterward. After the couple saw each other for the first time at the miai, one might refuse the marriage offer, or successive meetings might be held. Once an agreement was reached, the betrothal was sealed with a toast of sake between the participants, at which time the yuinō, or exchange of engagement presents, was discussed. These were gifts of food and sake (more recently they have included clothing accessories and money) brought by the bridegroom to the bride shortly before the wedding. She was often obligated to return gifts of half the value of the gifts received. Yuinō gifts were always returned in the event the engagement was broken, as were the jisankin (dowry) or household goods the bride took with her returned in the event of a divorce.

The day of the wedding was chosen carefully, to avoid inauspicious days as well as the period while the Shintō deities gathered for the annual October conclave at Izumo. Auspicious days were determined by Chinese and Japanese astrological traditions.

Traditional wedding rituals began the day before the wedding, when the bride prayed at the family shrine or temple, or had a parting banquet with neighbors and parents. On this occasion in some areas women blackened their teeth to indicate their new married status (see the section on ohaguro in COSMETICS). The wedding-day rituals primarily took place at the household of the groom, or at the household of the bride if the groom was adopted into her family in the kind of marriage called mukoiri. In cases where the bride entered the groom's household, she dressed in white as she took formal leave of her parents. The white was symbolic of the death of her natal ties to them. She might break a teacup on the threshold of her own home as a spell to ensure that she would not return. Friends paraded through the streets carrying her new household goods, and there might be up to seven days and nights of partying. At the household of the groom she appeared in a colorful furisode style KIMONO, wearing a cotton or silk head covering called tsunokakushi (literally, "horn-hiding"). The groom wore kimono with family CRESTS and the loose trousers called hakama (see the section on men's kimono in KIMONO).

Once at the home, various rites were performed, the most important being the couple pledge. This ritual exchange of sake is called sansan kudo (three-three-nine times), originally practiced in high-ranking households and now standard to weddings throughout Japan. It consists of three formal sips of sake by the bride and groom from a set of three cups graduated from small to large size. The pledge took place in front of relatives or representatives of both the bride and groom, usually their parents. Following the pledge, the introduction of the two households through a formal exchange of sake was held. At the reception afterward (the hirōen), traditional auspicious symbols were displayed in the form of clam soup (symbolic of a happy and inseparable union); decorations in the shape of butterfly bows (which also adorn the sake containers in the traditional threefold pledge); fans that unfold from a single fold to many and symbolize fruitfulness; and branches or pictures of pine, bamboo, or plum, which signify endurance, uprightness, and feminine virtue.

Three days after the ceremony the wife, and sometimes her husband, returned to her family home (a custom called satogaeri), bringing gifts for relatives and friends. The parents of the bride and groom might also visit each other, thus sealing the union and ending the marriage procedure.

Modern Weddings —— Traditional weddings were basically secular rites decided upon by local customs and personal preference. Weddings today are still determined by these considerations, but are more likely to include a religious ceremony, even when the couple has no particular belief or religious affiliation. Shintō weddings became popular after the Shintō marriage ceremony held for the Crown Prince in 1900. The priest ritually purifies the participants and invites the intercession of the deities while the couple sits before the altar with the go-between and his or her spouse, or two go-betweens (one chosen by each set of relatives). *Sansan-kudo* is performed before the priest. The ceremony might include dances by shrine dancers. Buddhist weddings have a similar format, but include the reading of sutras. Christian weddings are not unpopular.

The trend has been from weddings at homes to weddings in shrines, temples, and since World War II, hotels, restaurants, or special wedding halls, often furnished with special wedding chambers with Shintō architecture. Priests are engaged from local shrines. "*Miai* marriages" follow some of the traditional patterns, although the couple sometimes go out on dates. In the case of so-called "love marriages," the *nakōdo* might be a purely symbolic role played by a family friend or influential business contact of one of the families, and even a *miai* might be held for form's sake. The ritual and symbolic change of clothes (*ironaoshi*) of the traditional wedding has become merely an ostentatious display of the family wealth; because of the prohibitive cost of buying the costumes, they are often rented, but even the rental cost is phenomenal. The bride might first wear a white kimono, or white with gold and silver, then change to a colorful kimono, and finally to a cocktail dress or even a Western wedding dress. The groom may change from Japanese costume to morning coat. The importance of the ceremony is often overshadowed by the reception, where the traditional symbols associated with weddings are still displayed.

Although the custom of *satogaeri* might still be observed by some, most Japanese try to take a honeymoon of about three to five days, since they do not have the freedom of taking long vacations from work. The couple may make their ritual trip after settling into their new home. *Barbara Bowles* SWANN

weekly magazines

(*shūkanshi*). The first successful weekly magazines in Japan were both launched in 1922, the *Shūkan asahi* by the Asahi Shimbun Newspaper Company on 25 February, and the *Sandei mainichi* by the Mainichi Shimbun Newspaper Company on 2 April. They were preceded by *Shū* (Week, established 1917) and *Sekai shūhō* (World Weekly Report, established 1920), both published in Tōkyō, but neither of these earlier weeklies attained much influence. In the background of the appearance of the two weeklies was the spread of interest in government and society and a surge in general intellectual curiosity among the population at large. In response, the two newspaper companies drew upon their technical and economic resources, expanded the coverage and interest value of their daily columns, and produced these weekly magazines.

The subject matter of the early weeklies varied, ranging from such topics as current events, society, and the economy to women's and children's interests, serialized novels, and entertainment. Both the *Asahi* and *Mainichi* newspapers were based in Ōsaka, the commercial center of Japan at the time, and their magazines conveyed the spirit of that city. Their circulations were over 300,000 each, a large figure for the time.

The MANCHURIAN INCIDENT of 1931 was indicative of the growing role of the military in politics. The weeklies took on a nationalistic character, a tendency that became even more pronounced after the outbreak of the Sino-Japanese War in 1937. In 1940, in the midst of a paper shortage, the government directed the weeklies to change their format to a smaller size (152 × 257 mm; 6 × 10 in), one that remains the standard size of the modern weekly magazine.

After World War II, new weekly magazines made their appearance in rapid succession. The first group, including *Shūkan yomiuri*, *Shūkan Tōkyō*, and *Shūkan sankei*, were published by newspaper companies. The *Asahi gurafu* (Asahi Graphic), a pictorial weekly which had suspended publication during the war, reappeared and remains popular today. Book publishers also inaugurated weekly magazines, the most important of which was the *Shūkan shinchō*, published first in February 1956. Observing the success of this ven-

ture, other firms put out the *Shūkan bunshun*, *Shūkan kōron*, and *Shūkan gendai*.

In the last two decades, weekly magazines have become more specialized, catering to specific audiences such as women, children, young adults, and so forth. Total circulation for the weeklies more than doubled between 1959 and 1978, and the boom seems likely to continue.

The editorial content of the weekly magazines serves as an alternative to the homogeneous perspectives of the more traditional general-interest monthly magazines, the *sōgō zasshi*. The *sōgō zasshi*, including SEKAI (World) and CHŪŌ KŌRON (Central Review), tend to take an overly abstract and generalized approach to events and issues. Postwar popular weekly magazines, on the other hand, emphasize the concerns of the "average reader" and endeavor to show the public what influence events and issues have on their everyday lives. One such weekly, the *Shūkan shinchō*, has adopted as its motto the phrase, "All human affairs are rooted in lust and greed." It is a leader in the market. The success of the weekly magazines reflects the popular preference for reporting on the human side of daily affairs over the more restrained and factual reporting of the traditional magazines. See also MAGAZINES. *SHIMIZU Tetsuo*

weights and measures

Two completely standardized systems of weights and spatial measures have been used in Japan since the Meiji period (1868–1912). One of these is the metric system, which has long been in general use among scientists and for official purposes, and which in 1959 was decreed to be the only system allowed for other common uses. The metric units seem already to have moved a long way toward complete public acceptance, and the day is probably not far distant when they will have entirely replaced the units of the other modern system.

The other system may be referred to as native or Japanese. The names of the units in it are mostly of Chinese origin, but their values are not the same as those of the corresponding Chinese units. The native system has been standardized (i.e., defined in terms of the metric system) only since 1891.

The native system contains units of the following kinds: weight, length or distance, cloth measure, area, and volume or capacity. Units of cloth measure refer to lengths of standard bolts. (There are various widths of standard bolts. The most common of them are approximately 16 centimeters [6.3 in], 70 centimeters [27.6 in], and 140 centimeters [55 in].) Cloth measures employ many of the same words as ordinary linear measures, but confusingly have values exactly one-quarter longer than the ordinary units of length.

Premodern Units —— When one comes to deal with units of measurement in use before the Meiji period the situation becomes complex indeed. The fact that the terminology used is roughly the same as that of the native system, fully standardized after 1891, may lead the uninitiated into believing that problems are as simple of solution as with modern units. Such is not the case. The intrinsic difficulty of the situation stems from three causes. First, at any given time there was not necessarily a standard definition throughout Japan of the value of any particular unit of measurement. Second, within the same area, the values of specific units did not necessarily remain constant over long periods of time. Third, even with respect to different units of the same kind (e.g., units of weight, or of linear or volume measure) the ratios that existed at one time did not necessarily exist at another. Specific illustrations follow.

It is well known among modern students of measurements that there is a special value to be placed on the *ken* (the length of the standard architectural module) in certain parts of the Kansai region (Kyōto-Ōsaka-Kōbe area). That is, whereas the official definition of the *ken* makes it 1.82 meters (5.97 ft), a common Kansai use of the same unit takes it to be 1.97 meters (6.46 ft). A possible way of explaining the discrepancy is simply to say that that unit represents the unit of length that Japanese architects—in whatever part of Japan they may be—take as their basic measuring unit. The *ken* is thus the length of a TATAMI, or twice the width of one, or the distance between two successive vertical supports in a traditional building. It should be understood from this that the modular nature of Japanese architecture makes for uniformity in any locality in the values to be placed on the basic counting units used in constructing buildings. This does not mean, however, that the module was constant in different areas, and there is no assurance that even within the same general area there was absolute uniformity between the modules used by different artisans. The discrepancies among values assigned to other units of spatial measure and of weight were equally striking. In most cases measurement of particular objects was done by reference to instruments that were themselves unstandardized. That is, almost any manufacturer of foot rules, say, or of balance weights, could obtain from local authorities the right to define the exact dimensions of its own product.

It is to be expected that if the values of units varied considerably from place to place at any given time, they were not even constant in a single place over long periods of time. Variation might occur simply on account of gradual changes in dimension of the devices used for measuring, or they might occur because of sudden redefinitions of certain units. An instance of the imperceptibly slow kind of change is the fact that the standard span (distance between vertical supports) of Kamakura period (1185–1333) buildings in the city of Kyōto, which was called one *ken,* does not exactly correspond to the *ken* unit used in the same city in the Edo period (1600–1868). A famous example of the sudden kind of change was TOYOTOMI HIDEYOSHI's redefinition of the unit of area one *chō,* reducing it from 3,600 to 3,000 square *ken.* Hideyoshi is said to have effected this dramatic change in measure in order to raise the absolute amount of taxes collected on parcels of land without appearing to increase the amount levied on single measured units.

The last-named example shows that the ratios between different units of the same system did not necessarily remain constant over long periods of time. In fact at one and the same time there might be two or more sets of ratios in common use in different parts of the country. The *kin* is a unit of weight equivalent to 0.601 kilograms (1.32 lb) and now contains 160 *momme* (1 *momme* = 3.750 grams or 0.13 oz). Before standardization, however, the same unit varied with the objects being weighed. It might be 160, 180, or 220 *momme,* the value of the *momme* being more or less constant.

Japanese specialists have done considerable work in tracing the history of each unit of measure, but understandably they have not been able to compile easy reference sources that will answer all questions involving measures at every place and time. There is a good historical study of linear measures in Japan by Fujita Motoharu (*Shakudo sōkō,* 1929). There are also excellent brief definitions of the principal premodern units of measurement in the historical encyclopedia *Nihonshi jiten.* They are excellent because they are not more precise than the realities of premodern usages of the units warrant. It is also recommended that students consult the entries in general encyclopedias and historical encyclopedias (particularly the *Nihon rekishi dai jiten,* 1956–60) under *hakari, doryōkō,* and names of individual units.

Monetary Units —— The only common unit of Japanese currency today is the YEN, exchangeable from 1949 to 1971 at an official rate of 360 yen to one dollar and in 1981 at around 220 yen. The *sen* (0.01 yen) remains a theoretical unit of monetary value, but since the postwar inflation it has ceased being a practical unit for coinage or pricing.

The same caution applies to premodern units as to premodern weights and spatial measures. In fact the system of measuring economic value was in some ways even more complex because Japan's primary medium of exchange and measure of wealth until well along in the Edo period was not money at all, but bulk rice. Furthermore, money might be either metal or paper, and the former might be measured either as pieces with set values or by weight. Rates of exchange between rice and money sometimes fluctuated wildly, as did correspondences between different metals and between the piece and weight evaluations of coins of the same metal.

Meaningful conversions to present monetary units are impossible, and students are warned not even to attempt them. Nevertheless, certain other kinds of conversion are both fruitful and possible due primarily to the signal scholarly work in this field begun by the Japanese Finance Ministry 100 years ago: the *Dai Nihon kahei shi* (1876–83; rev 1925–26), the most inclusive source for all kinds of information on the history of Japanese currency. See also KOKU; MONEY, PREMODERN.

Herschel WEBB

Wei zhi (Wei chih)

(J: *Gishi;* The Wei Chronicle). A history of the Chinese Wei dynasty (220–265). Its section dealing with the "Wa people" (Ch: *wo-ren* or *wojen;* J: *wajin;* i.e., the Japanese) is of unsurpassed importance as a document giving us information on Japan in the second and third centuries. "Wajinden," the name commonly used in Japan for this section, refers to the subsection on the Wa people in the "Dongyi zhuan" (Tung-i chuan; literally, "Eastern Barbarian Ac-

Weights and measures

Traditional Weights and Measures as Standardized in 1891[1]			
		Approximate metric equivalents	Approximate US equivalents
Length [2]			
bu		3.03 mm	0.119 in
sun	10 *bu*	3.03 cm	1.193 in
shaku	10 *sun*	30.30 cm	11.930 in
ken	6 *shaku*	1.818 m	5.965 ft
chō	60 *ken*	109.09 m	119.30 yd
ri	36 *chō*	3.927 km	2.440 mi
hiro	6 *shaku*	1.818 m	0.994 fathom
kairi		1.852 km	1 nautical mi
Area			
tsubo (or *bu*)	(1 sq *ken*)	3.306 sq m	35.58 sq ft
se	30 *tsubo*	99.175 sq m	118.61 sq yd
tan [3]	10 *se*	0.099 ha (991.75 sq m)	0.245 a (1,186.11 sq yd)
chō (or *chōbu*)	10 *tan*	0.992 ha	2.451 a
Weight			(avoirdupois)
bu		0.375 gm	5.787 gr
momme	10 *bu*	3.750 gm	57.870 gr (0.132 oz)
kin	160 *momme*	600.00 gm	1.323 lb
kan (or *kamme*)	1,000 *momme*	3.75 kg	8.27 lb
Capacity			
shaku		18.039 ml	0.033 pt (dry) or 0.610 fl oz
gō	10 *shaku*	180.39 ml	0.328 pt (dry) or 6.100 fl oz
shō	10 *gō*	1.8039 l	1.638 qt (dry) or 1.906 qt (liquid)
to	10 *shō*	18.039 l	2.048 pk or 4.766 gal
koku	10 *to*	180.39 l	5.119 bu or 47.655 gal

[1] The table shows values for the units as standardized in terms of the metric system in 1891. Actual values in the premodern period differed from time to time and place to place.
[2] Less frequently used measures of length include the *rin* (0.1 *bu*) and the *jō* (10 *shaku*). When used for cloth measure the *bu, sun,* and *shaku* were 25% longer than indicated here. The standard bolt measure mentioned in the article was the *tan* (length 11 m or 12 yd).
[3] Before the late 16th century the *tan* equaled 360 *bu* (0.119 hectare or 0.294 acre) and the *chō* equaled 3,600 *bu* (see KENCHI).
NOTE: See also KOKU, RI, and RYŌ for premodern equivalents.

counts"; J: "Tōiden") section of the *Wei zhi.* The *Wei zhi,* one of the post-Han *Chronicles of the Three Kingdoms (Sanguo zhi* or *San-kuo chih)* was compiled in the late 3rd century by Chen Shou (Ch'en Shou, 233–297), an official of the Western Jin (Chin) dynasty (265–317).

The "Wajinden" is about 2,000 Chinese characters in length and can be divided into eight sections. The first section refers to the location of the various "countries" of the Wa people, as well as changes, from the Han through the Wei periods, in the number of countries maintaining a tributary relationship with China. The second section is a brief description of the Wa countries, including the distances of some of these from Daifang (Tai-fang), the Chinese commandery in west central Korea. The third section deals with the Wa people's customs and products, and matters of politics and social ranking are discussed in the fourth section. The fifth section relates the type of life led by HIMIKO, the female ruler of one of the countries, YAMATAI, to which almost all the other Wa countries are said to have given allegiance. The sixth section describes the existence of countries of "Wa ethnic stock" (J: *washu*) to the east of Yamatai, as well as countries across the sea to the south; it also touches on the geographical environment of the Wa countries. The seventh section describes chronologically relations between Wei China and Yamatai during the period 239–247; the eighth section is a concise account of Himiko's death and subsequent developments.

The locations of several of the Japanese kingdoms (*koku* or *kuni*) named in the "Wajinden" can be fairly well established, e.g., Tsushima (the Tsushima Islands, now part of Nagasaki Prefecture); Iki (the island of Iki, now part of Nagasaki Prefecture); Matsuro (the Higashi Matsuura district of Saga Prefecture); Ito (ITOKOKU; the Itoshima district of Fukuoka Prefecture); Na (NAKOKU; now part of the city of Fukuoka); Fumi (the town of Umi in the Kasuya district of Fukuoka Prefecture). Also listed are some 23 other kingdoms owing allegiance to Yamatai, including Tōma (or Toma) and Shima. Kuna (or Kunu), a country in political opposition to Yamatai, is also mentioned. In the case of several countries, mention is made of official titles, the numbers of houses, products, living conditions, and so on.

The information on Yamatai, the location of which has been debated extensively, is the most detailed. It is said to have had more than 70,000 houses and four ranks of officials. One official was permanently stationed in Ito and charged with inspecting various affiliated countries. Officials similar to the Chinese *cishi* (*tz'u-shih*; top officials of Chinese subprefectures; *zhou* or *chou*) were said to be dispatched to the various countries. Yamatai had at one time been under the control of a male ruler, but after warfare and political disturbances in the latter half of the 2nd century, the female ruler mentioned above, Himiko, was chosen. From 239 to 247 Himiko sent tributary envoys to Wei China. Yamatai became engaged in warfare with its old enemy Kuna. Himiko died during this time of disruption, and after a brief period of leadership by a male ruler, there began a period of rule by another female leader, named Iyo.

As for the particulars of Japanese lifeways, the "Wajinden" informs us that the men painted their faces and bodies. An account of this same folk custom is seen in an extant section of a Chinese historical work known as the *Wei lue* (*Wei lüeh*; J: *Giryaku*), edited by Yu Huan (Yü Huan), who lived roughly during the same time as the *Wei zhi*'s compiler Chen Shou. In light of this and other common accounts given in the two works, it was once thought virtually certain that the "Wajinden" was based on the *Wei lue*. However, a more recent theory holds that the "Wajinden" was most probably based on a nonextant historical work, the *Wei shu*, edited by Wang Shen (d 266).

🔖 —— Wada Kiyoshi and Ishihara Michihiro, tr and ed, *Gishi wajinden* (1951), a translation of the Chinese account into Japanese. Ryusaku Tsunoda and L. C. Goodrich, *Japan in the Chinese Dynastic Histories* (1951). Yamao Yukihisa, *Gishi wajinden: Tōyōshi jō no kodai Nihon* (1972). SAEKI Arikiyo

Welsh onion

(*negi*). *Allium fistulosum*; a biennial plant of the family Liliaceae which has long been an important winter vegetable in Japan. It was introduced to Japan from China before the 10th century. It is similar to the leek but smaller; its leaf base does not form an enlarged bulb, and its leaves and leaf sheaths are edible. In the eastern part of Japan, varieties which seldom grow in bunches are planted, and the stalks are covered high with earth to promote blanching. In western Japan, varieties which tend to bunch are grown and left relatively exposed for greater utilization of the green leaves. It is used mainly in fish and meat dishes and is indispensable to SUKIYAKI.

SUGIYAMA Tadayoshi

western Japan

(*nishi Nihon*). Term denoting the western half of Japan when the country is divided into two parts. Included in this term are the Kinki, Chūgoku, Shikoku, and Kyūshū regions as well as the five prefectures of Toyama, Gifu, Aichi, Ishikawa, and Fukui in the Chūbu region. Western Japan differs considerably from EASTERN JAPAN in local language and culture. It had long been the political and economic center of the country, but lost its position as a political center in the Edo period (1600–1868), and ranked second in economic importance to eastern Japan after World War II. Farming is carried out on a smaller scale than that in eastern Japan, which developed later.

Western Learning

(*Yōgaku*). The Japanese study of Western science and art during the Edo period (1600–1868). In the 16th century it was called the Learning of the Southern Barbarians (Nambangaku or Bangaku), since the Portuguese, Spanish, and Dutch who introduced this learning to Ja-

pan had come from their colonies to the south. For most of the Edo period, however, it was called Dutch Learning (Rangaku), because the Japanese learned of Western culture through the Dutch, the only Westerners with whom they were allowed to have commercial and cultural contact. The term Yōgaku came into common usage only in the late Edo period, when Japanese interest in and knowledge of the variety of Western Learning led them to learn Western languages other than Dutch.

In the 16th century Portuguese merchants and missionaries brought to Japan not only their Roman Catholicism but also a wealth of material culture. Clocks, arquebuses, copperplate engraving, oil painting, tobacco, and eyeglasses all found their way to Japan in Portuguese ships. Western methods of navigation, shipbuilding, and the manufacture of clocks and firearms were imitated, while Western medicine and surgery were avidly studied.

The Dutch in Japan —— On 19 April 1600 the ship LIEFDE (Charity) sailed into Usuki Bay in Bungo Province (now Ōita Prefecture). Only a score of the original crew of 110 had survived its 22-month voyage from Rotterdam. Despite the slanders of Portuguese merchants and missionaries, they soon won protection from Ōtomo Yoshimune (1558–1605), the *daimyō* of Bungo, and an audience at Ōsaka Castle with the new hegemon, TOKUGAWA IEYASU. Ieyasu retained the ship's English pilot, William ADAMS, as his adviser on astronomy, cartography, mathematics, and shipbuilding; and five years later the *Liefde*'s captain, Jacob Jansz Quaeckernaeck, through Adams's intercession, received from Ieyasu a permit (SHUINJŌ) for trade with Japan. Quaeckernaeck then sailed to the Dutch trading station in the Malay state of Patani, where he handed to Admiral Cornelis Matelieff de Jonge an official Japanese passport authorizing Dutch trade with Japan. Consequently, Abraham van den Broeck, commanding two ships, left Johore and cast anchor off the island of Hirado (now part of Nagasaki Prefecture) on 1 July 1609. On 24 August the Dutch were allowed to set up a trading post *(factorij)* there. Meanwhile, on 20 March 1602, the various Dutch Companies for Trade with Remote Countries had amalgamated into the United Netherlands Chartered East India Company to maintain a monopoly of all Dutch trade and navigation east of the Cape of Good Hope and west of the Strait of Magellan.

After the full implementation of the NATIONAL SECLUSION policy in 1639, the Dutch were to remain until 1854 the only Westerners allowed to trade with Japan. This privilege they owed to their fierce enmity toward the Portuguese and the Spaniards as well as their willingness to divorce trade from religious proselytizing. In 1641 the Tokugawa shogunate ordered them to move to DEJIMA in Nagasaki Harbor, and it was from this island that Dutch accounts of Western Learning made their way into Japan during the two succeeding centuries of Tokugawa rule.

The Beginnings of Dutch Learning —— Although Japanese authorities had severely restricted the import of Western books, even in Chinese translation, the Japanese thirst for knowledge of the West persisted, even among the authorities. In 1650 the physician of the East India Company on Dejima, Caspar Schambergen, accompanied the chief of the Dutch settlement *(Opperhoofd)* on his annual mission to Edo (now Tōkyō). Requested by the shōgun to stay on in the capital for a few more months, he instructed the shogunal physicians in Dutch medicine, thereby founding the so-called Kasuparuryū (Caspar school of medicine).

In the first century of seclusion, however, such contacts were rare, and it was principally the official Japanese interpreters of the Dutch language at Nagasaki who became versed in Western culture. But their posts were hereditary, and their linguistic ability and knowledge should not be overestimated. In 1695, however, the exceptionally gifted astronomer NISHIKAWA JOKEN compiled a book on the geography, products, manners, and customs of other countries, entitled *Kai tsūshō kō* (Study of Commercial Intercourse with the Chinese and Other Foreigners). Two works of the Confucian scholar and statesman ARAI HAKUSEKI, *Seiyō kibun* and *Sairan igen*, further described conditions in the West. An important figure in the subsequent development of Western studies was the shōgun TOKUGAWA YOSHIMUNE (r 1716–45). His deep interest in improving agriculture, the basis of Japan's economy, led him to order Nakane Genkei (1662–1733), a mathematician from Kyōto, to correct the traditional Japanese calendar. As a result of his research Nakane recommended the study of foreign books on this subject and induced Yoshimune in 1720 to end restrictions on the import of all Western books except those propagating the Christian faith.

In 1740 Yoshimune ordered AOKI KON'YŌ and NORO GENJŌ to study the Dutch language. Aoki later wrote a study of the Dutch monetary system and some treatises on the Dutch language, while Noro compiled a work on Dutch plants.

The active study of Western Learning began between 1750 and 1790 with the research and publication of MAENO RYŌTAKU, SUGITA GEMPAKU, and ŌTSUKI GENTAKU. Bangaku came to be replaced by a new term, Rangaku, "Dutch Learning." Just as the English terms "Sinology" and "Japanology" are very broad in scope, the appellation Rangaku referred to a wide range of sciences, of which medicine, astronomy, mathematics, botany, physics, chemistry, geography, geodesy, and military sciences, especially ballistics, were the most important. Scholars specializing in these studies were called Rangakusha, or "Hollandologists." Their success in adopting European science stemmed in large part from earlier advances made in these fields by the Japanese themselves.

Medicine —— Among the Western sciences imported into Tokugawa Japan, medicine was the most studied and appreciated. Since it sought to preserve human life, the Japanese authorities did not interfere with, and some times even officially supported, the import of Western medical treatises.

During the last four decades of the 17th century Western medicine was studied mainly by the Nagasaki interpreters. Medical doctors in the service of the Dutch East India Company often taught their Japanese colleagues during their annual visits to Edo. Unlike many ship's surgeons of the time, the Dejima physicians were highly accomplished. Indeed, they were carefully selected by the Dutch colonial government at Batavia to create good will in Japan. Willem ten Rhijne (1647–1700), Engelbert KAEMPFER from Germany, and Carl Peter THUNBERG, a Swede and pupil of Linnaeus, played important roles in the spread of Western medical learning in Tokugawa Japan.

In accounts of the development of Rangaku the publication of the *Kaitai shinsho* (New Book of Anatomy) by Sugita Gempaku in 1774 is invariably and rightly recorded as an epoch-making event. Nonetheless, more than a century earlier the chief interpreter at Nagasaki, Motoki Ryōi (1628–97), had already translated a Dutch book with anatomical diagrams. Also, at the beginning of the 18th century YOSHIMASU TŌDŌ had recognized that assumptions of traditional Chinese medicine *(kampō)* did not tally with anatomical facts. In 1754 YAMAWAKI TŌYŌ obtained permission from the shogunate to conduct the first Japanese dissection of a human corpse.

The most important teacher of Western medicine was Philipp Franz von SIEBOLD. In addition, Otto G. J. Mohnike (1814–87), who resided in Japan from 1848 until 1853, introduced smallpox vaccination and the stethoscope. In 1857 J. L. C. POMPE VAN MEERDERVOORT came to Nagasaki as a naval doctor and became director of the newly established Medical Institute (Igaku Denshūjo). In 1861 he opened a hospital, the Nagasaki Yōjōsho, where he treated 930 patients during the first year. By the time he left Japan in 1862, he had issued medical certificates to 61 Japanese doctors. Among them were Matsumoto Ryōjun and Satō Shōchū (1827–82), who were to become the mainstays of medical science in Japan.

Astronomy and Geography —— The study of astronomy also was encouraged by the authorities. The Jōkyō calendar, devised by SHIBUKAWA SHUNKAI, was officially adopted by the shogunate in 1684 (Jōkyō 1) to replace a Chinese calendar that the Japanese had used for 823 years. Shibukawa's calendar was, however, merely a revision of another Chinese calendar of 1281. Later, the shōgun Tokugawa Yoshimune would, as we have seen, promote research on Western calendars.

Ptolemaic astronomy had been introduced earlier by the Portuguese missionaries, but had no lasting influence. Copernican theories were first publicized by the Nagasaki interpreters Motoki Yoshinaga (1735–94) and SHIZUKI TADAO. Shizuki's *Rekishō shinsho* (1798–1802, New Book of Astronomical Calculations) was a translation of the Dutch version of the treatises on physics and astronomy, *Introductiones ad veram physicam et veram astronomiam* (1701 and 1718), by John Keill (1671–1721). The corrections of the lunar calendar in 1754, 1798, and 1842 were based on data provided by the Dutch.

Western maps of the world were first introduced by the Portuguese. By 1650, however, we find evidence of the influence of Dutch cartography, particularly the atlases by Blaeu, Goos, and De Witt. Nishikawa Joken's *Kai tsūshō kō* was followed by other geographical compendia, most notably *Seiiki monogatari* (1798, Tales of the West) by HONDA TOSHIAKI. Honda traveled extensively and had a sound knowledge of the islands north of Japan proper. His disciple MOGAMI TOKUNAI explored Karafuto (Sakhalin) and the Kuril Islands. Another important explorer was MAMIYA RINZŌ, who visited

Karafuto and eastern Siberia and left a description of his journey, *Tōdatsu kikō* (1810, Travels in Tartary). The land surveyor and cartographer INŌ TADATAKA spent about 20 years exploring Japan's coastline. Later studies found his geographical measurements to be quite accurate.

Mathematics —— Students of Japanese mathematics (WASAN) scorned Western mathematics. Although it was highly advanced, *wasan* served mainly as an intellectual pastime with little practical application. Thus it was students not of *wasan* but of Rangaku who studied Western mathematics for use in astronomy, geography, ballistics, and other sciences.

Botany, Physics, and Chemistry —— Botany, physics, and chemistry were, of course, closely related to the study of medicine. With regard to botany, one should mention the oldest Japanese book on Dutch plants, *Oranda honzō wage* (ca 1745, Dutch Botanicon Translated) by Noro Genjō, and Thunberg's influence on this discipline in Japan. Zoological studies, by contrast, were of little importance. The study of physics began to develop rapidly after the introduction of the theories of Newton and Napier in *Rekishō shinsho* by Shizuki Tadao. Another influential work on Western physics was *Kikai kanran* (1825, Beholding the Waves in the Sea of Ether) by the physician Aochi Rinsō (1775–1833). Chemistry was important for manufacturing medicine and explosives. Although no spectacular achievements in this field seem to have been made, UDAGAWA YŌAN achieved fame for his studies on chemistry as well as botany.

Military Science —— Many European firearms and huge quantities of other European munitions were imported into Tokugawa Japan, especially in the first decades of Dutch settlement on Hirado. Several Dutch gunners taught ballistics to Japanese. With the continuation of peace, however, interest in military science flagged, to revive only when Japan felt threatened from abroad in the early 19th century. Noteworthy is TAKASHIMA SHŪHAN, who studied gunnery in Nagasaki for five years and is considered a pioneer of modern Japanese military technology.

In 1855 the Naval Institute (KAIGUN DENSHŪJO) was established at Nagasaki by the shogunate, with a Dutch navy detachment under the command of Lt. G. C. C. Pels Rijcken in charge of instruction. In the same year King William III of the Netherlands presented the Japanese government with its first warship, the paddle-steamer *Soembing* (later renamed *Kankō maru*); to fuel this ship the first mine shaft was sunk at the MIIKE COAL MINES.

The Arts —— Before the period of national seclusion several Japanese artists had experimented with Western-style painting, but its influence soon faded (see NAMBAN ART). OKUMURA MASANOBU and MARUYAMA ŌKYO used perspective and other Western techniques, but they did not paint in the Western style. The versatile scholar and writer HIRAGA GENNAI made the first Japanese oil paintings, but he is known mainly as a teacher of this style. Among his pupils were the daimyō SATAKE SHOZAN and his vassal ODANO NAOTAKE (see AKITA SCHOOL). Another of Gennai's disciples, SHIBA KŌKAN, studied Dutch under Maeno Ryōtaku and Ōtsuki Gentaku and became the greatest Western-style painter of the Edo period. Finally, the art of the NAGASAKI SCHOOL was influenced by Western subject matter and materials (see WESTERN-STYLE PICTURES, EARLY).

Language Studies —— Knowledge of Dutch was at first transmitted orally, and interpreters and scholars made notes only for their personal use. Aoki Kon'yō's several treatises on the Dutch language, for instance, were never printed. In 1767 the interpreter Nishi Zenzaburō (1717–68) set out to compile a Dutch-Japanese dictionary, but he died a year later, having only reached the letter B.

But after 1774—the year of the publication of Sugita Gempaku's *Kaitai shinsho*—many books on the Dutch language appeared. In 1783 Ōtsuki Gentaku compiled his *Rangaku kaitei* (A Ladder to Dutch Learning). Printed five years later, it included a Dutch vocabulary list, a concise grammar, and an apologia for Rangaku. Ōtsuki also founded the first boarding school for students of Dutch Learning at Edo, the Shirandō. One of his pupils, INAMURA SAMPAKU (1758–1811), compiled the first Dutch-Japanese dictionary, HARUMA WAGE (Halma Explained in Japanese) in 1796. The strange title is due to the fact that it was based on the Dutch-French dictionary compiled by François Halma in 1708. *Haruma* later became a generic name for Dutch-Japanese dictionaries.

In 1815–16 the manuscript of a second *haruma* was completed, the *Dōyaku* (or *Zūfu*) *Haruma* (Halma Translated by Doeff). This dictionary was compiled by a group of Nagasaki interpreters under the supervision of Hendrik DOEFF, who had come to Japan in 1799 and was chief of the Dejima settlement from 1803 until 1817.

Japanese studies on the parts of speech in Dutch were written by SHIZUKI TADAO, his son Banri (1785–1837), and Fujibayashi Fuzan (1781–1836) of Kyōto. Tsurumine Shigenobu (1788–1859) was the first to apply Dutch grammatical principles to the Japanese language. In 1833 he published his *Gogaku shinsho* (New Book on Linguistics), a descriptive grammar of Japanese based on Western linguistic classifications. Several Dutch grammars were also reprinted in Japan.

Until 1870 Dutch remained the official language for negotiations with foreigners. Many Dutch words, in particular names of new ideas, objects, animals, and plants, were taken into Japanese as foreign LOANWORDS. Some examples of the more than 160 such words of Dutch origin still used regularly by Japanese are *bīru* (bier/beer), *kaban* (kabas/satchel), *kōhī* (koffie/coffee), and *randoseru* (ransel/knapsack). Many Dutch compounds, especially scientific, medical, and anatomical terms, were translated literally into Japanese. For example, the Japanese word for formic acid, *gisan*, like its Dutch etymon *mierenzuur*, translates literally into "ants" and "sour."

Rangaku Schools——Toward the end of the 18th century several Japanese scholars pointed out the impending threats to the country's independence, particularly from Russia. Prominent among those scholars was HAYASHI SHIHEI, who advocated in his *Kaikoku heidan* (1791, Discussion of the Military Problems of a Maritime Nation) a strengthening of coastal defenses and the building of a strong navy. At first the shogunate ignored such warnings and even took drastic measures against these "firebrands." In time, however, the authorities began to realize the necessity of acquiring more knowledge about the outside world. In 1811 *bansho wage goyōgakari*, government officials to translate foreign books, were appointed in Edo. Ōtsuki Gentaku and other prominent scholars were charged with the translation of a Dutch version of a French encyclopedic work. They produced 70 volumes in 28 years, but the project was never completed (see KŌSEI SHIMPEN).

In 1838 the physician OGATA KŌAN established in Ōsaka a Rangaku school for government officials and young men from all over Japan. The average number of students at one time was 1,000. Many of them, like FUKUZAWA YUKICHI, went on to play an important role in the modernization of Japan during the Meiji period (1868–1912).

In 1855 the shogunate established the Yōgakusho (Institute for Western Learning) at Edo, the name of which was changed to BANSHO SHIRABESHO (Institute for the Investigation of Barbarian Books) in 1856. Members of this institute studied Western sciences, taught foreign languages, and translated diplomatic documents. At first only Dutch was taught, but in 1861 English and French were added to the curriculum and in 1862 German and Russian. In 1862 its name was changed again to Yōsho Shirabesho and in 1863 to Kaiseijo. In 1877 it became TŌKYŌ UNIVERSITY.

The rise of Japan as a great power in the second half of the 19th century is, to a large extent, attributable to the swift adoption of Western techniques and sciences. For this process the foundations had been laid by the students of Western Learning. See also NETHERLANDS AND JAPAN.

▬▬——Arisaka Takamichi, ed, *Nihon yōgakushi no kenkyū*, 4 vols (1968–77). John Z. Bowers, *Western Medical Pioneers in Feudal Japan* (1970). C. R. Boxer, *Jan Compagnie in Japan 1600–1850* (rev ed, 1950). C. R. Boxer, *The Christian Century in Japan, 1549–1650* (1951). Cal French, *Shiba Kōkan: Artist, Innovator, and Pioneer in the Westernization of Japan* (1974). Grant Kohn Goodman, *The Dutch Impact on Japan (1640–1853)* (1967). Hirose Hideo, Nakamura Shigeru, and Ogawa Teizō, *Yōgaku*, vol 2: vol 65 of *Nihon shisō taikei* (Iwanami Shoten, 1972). Iwao Seiichi, *Sakoku*, vol 14 of *Nihon no rekishi* (Chūō Kōron Sha, 1966). Donald Keene, *The Japanese Discovery of Europe, 1830* (1969). C. C. Krieger, *The Infiltration of European Civilization in Japan During the 18th Century* (1940). Numata Jirō, Matsumura Akira, and Satō Shōsuke, *Yōgaku: I*, vol 64 of *Nihon shisō taikei* (Iwanami Shoten, 1976). Ōtsuki Nyoden and Satō Eishichi, *Nihon yōgaku hennenshi* (1965). F. Vos, "Dutch Influences on the Japanese Language," *Lingua* 12 (1963). Elizabeth P. Wittermans and John Z. Bowers, *Doctor on Desima: Selected Chapters from Jhr. J. L. C. Pompe van Meerdervoort's Vijf Jaren in Japan [Five Years in Japan], 1857–1863* (1970). Frits Vos

Western literature and Japanese literature

The Japanese began to translate Western literature into Japanese in the middle of the 16th century. These translations were mainly of books brought to Japan by Catholic missionaries. A portion of *Aesop's Fables* was published in the contemporary spoken language at Amakusa in Kyūshū in 1593, and by the 1830s this version had been reissued many times in Kyōto (see ISOHO MONOGATARI). Several translations of religious books were also published at the end of the 16th century, such as Luis de Granada's *Guia de Pecadores*, a translation of which was published in 1599. In addition, priests wrote books in Japanese as aids for their missionary work. However, in the first half of the 17th century, the country was closed to foreign trade and travel, with a few exceptions, and the translation of Western books came to an almost complete halt.

After more than two centuries of cultural isolation, the Meiji Restoration of 1868 provided the motivation for Japanese writers to create a more modern literature. A few literary works had been written about the awakening of the individual and his relationship to society during the latter part of the Edo period (1600–1868) but these works were quite different from those written on the same theme in the West at the same time. It was only after the Meiji Restoration that literature truly centered in the individual began to be written. At that time the mood of European literature was shifting from romanticism to realism, and Japanese writers were influenced by both movements. At the beginning of the 20th century, Western classical, medieval, and post-Renaissance literature were imported virtually at random and were read as if they were all the same sort of thing. It was under these chaotic conditions that modern Japanese literature came into being.

English and Irish Influences——The Meiji Restoration took place during the reign in Britain of Queen Victoria, a period when England was powerful and wealthy, and it was natural that the literature of such a nation should be introduced widely into Japan. In 1871 NAKAMURA MASANAO published a translation of Samuel Smiles's *Self Help*. Nakamura later also translated Smiles's *Character and Thrift*. Smiles found favor among the Japanese of the time because his utilitarianism emphasized endurance and diligence, qualities that are also found among the Confucian virtues. John Stuart Mill's *On Liberty* was also translated by Nakamura in 1872. Adapted versions and abridged translations of Shakespeare's plays appeared in the 1870s. During the 1880s John Milton's *Paradise Lost* and Daniel Defoe's *Robinson Crusoe*, as well as the poetry of William Wordsworth and Alfred Tennyson, were translated. Japanese of the educated class who could read English were also reading Charles Dickens and William Makepeace Thackeray in the original. Edward Bulwer-Lytton's political novel *The Last Days of Pompeii* (1834) was translated and became a best seller. Other political novels gained popularity, and, among these, the works of Benjamin Disraeli were widely read.

Of the many writers and their works introduced in Japanese during this period, Herbert Spencer's evolutionist philosophy and Shakespeare's plays greatly influenced Japanese literature. The preface to *Shintaishi shō* (1882), a well-known anthology of "new-style" poetry, written by YATABE RYŌKICHI and TOYAMA MASAKAZU, reflects Spencer's ideas. TAKADA SANAE, TSUBOUCHI SHŌYŌ, TAKAYAMA CHOGYŪ, and SHIMAMURA HŌGETSU referred to Spencer's ideas on evolutionist philosophy in publicizing their new theories of literature. Of the four, however, Takayama and Shimamura opposed Spencer's aesthetic theories.

Tsubouchi Shōyō was the writer most responsible for attempting to transplant English literature into Japanese soil. He translated Shakespeare's *Julius Caesar* in 1884; and by 1928 Shōyō had completed a 40-volume *Shēkusupia zenshū* (Works of Shakespeare). Shakespeare's influence on modern Japanese authors can be seen in such works as SHIGA NAOYA's *Kurōdiasu no nikki* (1912, The Diary of Claudius), DAZAI OSAMU's *Shin Hamuretto* (1941, New Hamlet), and FUKUDA TSUNEARI's *Horeishō no nikki* (1949, The Diary of Horatio).

Charles Dickens was read by Tsubouchi, TOKUTOMI ROKA, and NATSUME SŌSEKI, but his work did not have much influence on Japanese literature. Roka did, however, write an autobiographical novel *Omoide no ki* (1901; Record of Recollections; tr *Footprints in the Snow*, 1970) after reading *David Copperfield*.

Walter Pater's ideas were unfavorably received in his native England, but he attained great popularity in Japan. His works were introduced in Japan by HIRATA TOKUBOKU and UEDA BIN. In addition to writing several essays on Pater, Ueda wrote a novel, *Uzumaki* (1910), which included a detailed description of Pater's ideas. Pater is also mentioned in works by such eminent writers as Natsume Sōseki, TANIZAKI JUN'ICHIRŌ, and AKUTAGAWA RYŪNOSUKE. Among post–World War II authors, MISHIMA YUKIO was the most influenced by Pater. Pater's name is mentioned several times in Mishima's *Kinjiki* (1951–53; tr *Forbidden Colors*, 1968), and the aesthetic, hedonistic lifestyle of one of the main characters, Hinoki Shunsuke, greatly resembles Pater's own life. Elements of Pater's thought are also a part of several of Mishima's short stories.

Oscar Wilde first became known in Japan through MORI ŌGAI's complete translation of *Salomé* (1907–09) from a French translation. *Salome* is particularly admired in Japan and has been staged many times since 1920. Both Tanizaki Jun'ichirō and Mishima Yukio incorporated the spirit of Wilde's writing in their novels.

The works of Thomas Hardy found two completely different receptions. In the early 1900s he was considered a writer of "pastoral" fiction. Later his writing influenced "popular" writers with its theme of people whose lives are controlled by chance. KIKUCHI KAN in particular learned a great deal from *Tess of the d'Urbervilles,* and Tanizaki Jun'ichirō wrote that he was indebted to Hardy's "Barbara of the House of Grebe" for the idea for his *Shunkinshō* (1933; tr *A Portrait of Shunkin,* 1965).

James Joyce's influence on Japanese writers began with an essay on *A Portrait of the Artist as a Young Man* by NOGUCHI YONEJIRŌ in 1918. Akutagawa Ryūnosuke attempted to translate a portion of the novel. When *Ulysses* was translated in 1931–34, young writers focused their attention on Joyce's use of the interior monologue. ITŌ SEI's *Tsubomi no naka no Kiriko* (1930), KAWABATA YASUNARI's *Suishō gensō* (1931), and Tanizaki's *Manji* (1928–30) were all attempts at the use of Joycean interior monologue. After World War II, Itō Sei's *Narumi Senkichi* (1946–48) was written under the influence of *Dubliners* and NOMA HIROSHI's *Waga tō wa soko ni tatsu* (1960–61) under the influence of *A Portrait of the Artist as a Young Man.*

D. H. Lawrence was first translated in the 1920s and was first thought of as belonging to the same school as Joyce. This opinion was revised in the 1930s. Lawrence's name became widely known when Itō Sei's translation of *Lady Chatterley's Lover* was brought to court on charges of obscenity in 1951. The poet who most influenced Japanese poets and critics was T. S. Eliot. When Eliot's poems began to be introduced in the 1920s, he became the focus of attention of such poets as NISHIWAKI JUNZABURŌ. The dramatist George Bernard Shaw's *The Shewing-up of Blanco Posnet* was translated in 1909 by Mori Ōgai and staged at the Yūrakuza. It was followed by *The Man of Destiny* and *You Never Can Tell.* The most popular of Shaw's works in Japan is *Arms and the Man,* and after World War II *Pygmalion* was often staged.

American Influences —— Early in the Meiji period Protestant missionaries were responsible for the introduction of American literature and its widespread readership. Young educated Japanese were especially impressed with puritanism and the American "pioneer spirit." Because so much emphasis was being placed on the materialistic aspects of modernization, these intellectuals found Ralph Waldo Emerson's ideas concerning the pursuit of truth, self-reliance, and independence a refreshing change. KITAMURA TŌKOKU's interest in Emerson's concept of the "over-soul" led him to create a theory of romantic idealism. Tōkoku also wrote a biography of Emerson, published in 1894, which found a large audience. TOKUTOMI SOHŌ, who was influential in the publishing and literary circles of the time, published his translations of Emerson's letters serially in a magazine and in 1901 collected these letters in a book entitled *Emason no shokan.* In addition, IWANO HŌMEI published an analysis of Emerson's *Nature,* and KUNIKIDA DOPPO sought emotional solace in Emerson's thought. In 1917 a complete edition of the works of Emerson, *Emason zenshū,* was published in six volumes.

The work of Henry David Thoreau was also introduced in the first years of the 20th century. *Walden* especially was widely read and Thoreau's contemplative way of life drew the admiration of university students. Henry Wadsworth Longfellow's "The Psalm of Life" and "The Village Blacksmith" were translated in 1882 and became so popular that even today they are used in grade school textbooks. The poet who most greatly influenced scholars was Walt Whitman. Whitman was first brought to the notice of the Japanese in 1892 by Natsume Sōseki and is known to have inspired UCHIMURA KANZŌ and Takayama Chogyū. ARISHIMA TAKEO, who studied at Haverford College in Pennsylvania, became a fervent admirer of Whitman and published translations of his poetry (*Hoittoman shishū,* 2 vols, 1921 and 1923). In one of Arishima's most important novels, *Aru onna* (1911–13; tr *A Certain Woman,* 1978), the female protagonist is the embodiment of Whitman's ideas in the poem "Loafer." Poets Shiratori Shōgo (1890–1973) and Tomita Saika (b 1890) were both deeply influenced by Whitman. Kawabata Yasunari partly based his short story "Izu no odoriko" (1926; tr "The Izu Dancer," 1955) on Whitman's "To a Stranger" and incorporated the

first stanza of "To a Common Prostitute" in the short story "Inochi no ki" (1926).

Nathaniel Hawthorne's works were introduced to Japan early by Tsubouchi Shōyō, and until World War II his work was widely read in textbooks on English literature. Many writers like Tanizaki Jun'ichirō, SATŌ HARUO, and Akutagawa Ryūnosuke were drawn to the mystery and decadence of Edgar Allan Poe's stories and tried to create an atmosphere of the macabre in their works. The writer responsible for developing the mystery genre in Japan was EDOGAWA RAMPO, whose name (a pen name) is a punning reference to Poe's. The short stories of O. Henry were first translated in the 1910s. Akutagawa Ryūnosuke's "Yabu no naka" (1922; tr "In a Grove," 1952; used as the basis for the movie *Rashōmon*), is thought to have been influenced by Ambrose Bierce, but in his diary, letters, and notes, Akutagawa wrote that he was influenced by O. Henry's *Roads of Destiny.* O. Henry's short stories have also been widely used in school textbooks.

The American naturalists Theodore Dreiser and Upton Sinclair were introduced in the second decade of the 20th century. These novelists provided a new source of guidance for Japanese writers of the PROLETARIAN LITERATURE MOVEMENT. Impressed with Sinclair's *King Coal,* AONO SUEKICHI began advocating his own theory of "researched art." Maidako Hiroichirō, who translated Sinclair's *The Jungle* in 1925, insisted that the aim of the novel was to reveal human wickedness. In 1930 Hosoda Tamiki (1892–1972) published *Shinri no haru* (1930–31), which he based entirely on the theories of these proletarian writers.

Writers of the Lost Generation, including Ernest Hemingway and Scott Fitzgerald, were introduced in the 1920s. William Faulkner was also introduced at this time, but before his work could influence Japanese writers, World War II began and cultural relations were broken off. Various plays by Eugene O'Neill were translated in the 1920s and were frequently staged. They had a large impact on the development of SHINGEKI (the "new drama").

The influence of Hemingway's "hard-boiled" writing style can be found among the postwar writers. NIWA FUMIO imitated Hemingway's style in *Shadanki* (1952), a novel that describes unsettled human relationships immediately after the war. TACHIHARA MASAAKI attempted a translation of Hemingway's *A Farewell to Arms,* and his works show the influence of Hemingway's style and his way of portraying love. ISHIHARA SHINTARŌ's style bears a superficial likeness to Hemingway's. Kawabata Yasunari called Faulkner's novels a "literature of association," and it is thought by some that his own style, which depends heavily on the association of ideas, in some way resembles Faulkner's. At the end of World War II, NAKAMURA SHIN'ICHIRŌ and FUKUNAGA TAKEHIKO were much impressed with the French translations of *Sanctuary* and *The Sound and the Fury,* and Fukunaga used aspects of Faulkner's style in his own work. Among the younger writers, elements of Faulkner's style can be seen in OGAWA KUNIO's *Kokoromi no kishi* (1970) and Tsushima Yūko's *Ikimono no atsumaru ie* (1973).

Henry Miller, Norman Mailer, John Updike, J. D. Salinger, and Saul Bellow have all in some way influenced postwar writers. One example is SHŌJI KAORU's imitation of Salinger's style of writing dialogue. Mishima Yukio held discussions with Henry Miller and Norman Mailer on the art of writing, and ŌE KENZABURŌ has exchanged views with Updike.

Of the more recent American poets, William Carlos Williams, Carl Sandburg, Robert Frost, and Allen Tate had great influence on Japanese poets. Among playwrights, Arthur Miller, Tennessee Williams, and Edward Albee have been read and staged. Mishima Yukio was responsible for the introduction of many plays by Williams and Albee.

French Influences —— Immediately after the Meiji Restoration, French studies in Japan mainly centered on philosophy, law and sociology. Montesquieu's *L'Esprit des lois* was translated in 1876 and Jean-Jacques Rousseau's *Du contrat social* was translated in 1877. NAKAE CHŌMIN, the theorist of the FREEDOM AND PEOPLE'S RIGHTS MOVEMENT, was one of the first to introduce French culture and political theory to Japan. After Mori Ōgai translated portions of Rousseau's *Confessions* from a German translation in 1891, Rousseau began to influence Japanese writers. Later, SHIMAZAKI TŌSON was so deeply impressed by the *Confessions* that he wrote *Shinsei* (1918–19), a work that closely resembled it. Tōson was also indebted to Rousseau in writing *Hakai* (1906; tr *The Broken Commandment,* 1974) and *Yoake mae* (1929–35). Rousseau also influenced such Japanese naturalist writers as TAYAMA KATAI and

Kunikida Doppo. One must not overlook his influence on certain socialist essayists like SAKAI TOSHIHIKO, KINOSHITA NAOE, and ŌSUGI SAKAE.

ITAGAKI TAISUKE, the leader of the people's rights movement, met Victor Hugo in Paris in 1883. Itagaki brought back to Japan various novels by Hugo, and their translations were published in rapid succession. The Tokutomi brothers, Sohō (1863–1957) and Roka (1868–1927), Morita Shiken (1861–97), Hara Hōitsuan (1866–1904), and FUKUCHI GEN'ICHIRŌ were early admirers of Hugo. KUROIWA RUIKŌ's complete free translation of Les Misérables became a best seller and OZAKI KŌYŌ's translation of Notre Dame de Paris was also a popular success. The depth of Hugo's influence can be found in works by NAKAZATO KAIZAN and OSARAGI JIRŌ. Hugo's poems, with their novel imagery and power of sustained personification and vision, led DOI BANSUI to complete his famous Tenchi ujō (1899).

Émile Zola, the founder and leader of French naturalism, was a stimulus to certain young Japanese writers who established the naturalist school in Japan (see NATURALISM). Although they themselves did not employ Zola's writing method, older writers such as Nakae Chōmin, Tsubouchi Shōyō, and Mori Ōgai were responsible for calling attention to his technique, which was a combination of minute yet impersonal detail. Writers such as KOSUGI TENGAI, Tayama Katai, and NAGAI KAFŪ adopted Zola's theories from Le Roman expérimental. Among them, Kafū was the most ardent imitator in his early days. He wrote various essays on Zola, and he also published several short stories which vividly reflected Zola's technique. One can find Zola's influence in Tōson's Hakai, a novel that Shimamura Hōgetsu praised as the most representative naturalist work Japan has produced.

Guy de Maupassant and Alphonse Daudet were first introduced to Japan by Mori Ōgai, who labeled them the most popular writers in Europe. In the first years of the 20th century, Ueda Bin, Shimazaki Tōson, and Tayama Katai made attempts to translate Maupassant's short stories. Japanese novelists were eager to adopt Maupassant's style and tone. After four years in the United States and France, Nagai Kafū, who read Maupassant widely, published many short stories that clearly showed how much he was influenced by Maupassant's impersonal and dramatic style, as well as the structure and swiftness of his plots. Even after World War II, Maupassant's short stories continued to influence various writers, among them Mishima Yukio.

Zola's predecessor, Gustave Flaubert, was late in being introduced to Japan. Shimazaki Tōson read Madame Bovary (probably in an English translation) before his publication of a short story "Kyū shujin" (1902), but Flaubert's short stories only began to be translated in the first 10 years of the 20th century. With the publication of Madame Bovary, Salammbô, and L'Éducation sentimentale in the 1920s, the superb quality of Flaubert's theories, methods, and techniques were recognized by scholars, but writers found it difficult to make use of them in writing.

It is an interesting fact that great realistic novelists such as Stendhal and Honoré de Balzac were introduced to Japan later than the naturalist writers. These important writers were overlooked while the Japanese eagerly introduced later (and more contemporary) writers at the beginning of the Meiji period. Although Stendhal was discussed in writing in 1900 by Ueda Bin, his novels were left unstudied for more than 20 years. Tanizaki Jun'ichirō, whose work reflects Stendhal's influence, translated La Chartreuse de Parme and wrote an evaluation of Stendhal in his essay "Jōzetsuroku" (1927). After World War II, ŌOKA SHŌHEI, who systematically studied Stendhal, wrote Musashino fujin (1950), which was in some ways influenced by Le Rouge et le noir.

Balzac was mentioned briefly in the late 1880s by the politician OZAKI YUKIO and in the first years of the 20th century by Mori Ōgai. The real introduction, however, began in the second decade of the 20th century. The translations of La Comédie humaine and Contes drolatiques were read by many writers, but since his novels showed a predilection for the squalid and the unhappy, Japanese novelists were not highly impressed. Tanizaki was the only novelist who gave Balzac a favorable evaluation.

Prosper Mérimée influenced Akutagawa Ryūnosuke with the objectivity and conciseness of his style. Akutagawa's short stories such as "Karumen" (1926), "Chūtō" (1917; tr "The Robbers," 1964), "Kokui seibo" (1921), "Konan no ōgi" (1926), and "Aru ren'ai shōsetsu" (1924) reveal Mérimée's influence. However, Akutagawa's contemporaries, YOKOMITSU RIICHI and Kawabata Yasunari, showed more

interest in Paul Morand, finding his unusual, racy style very attractive.

The works of André Gide had been discussed by Ueda Bin, and Nagai Kafū was an avid reader, but Gide's influence upon Japanese writers really began in the 1930s. La Porte étroite (1909) was so beautifully translated in 1923 by Yamanouchi Yoshio (1894–1973) that it won a great number of readers. L'Immoraliste (1902) and Les Faux-Monnayeurs (1926) also became very popular in the 1920s. Influenced by the latter, Yokomitsu published an essay on the theory of the "pure novel" and a novel, Kazoku kaigi (1935), based on this theory.

Marcel Proust exerted a great influence on various writers in the 1920s and 1930s with his psychological accuracy and his exceptional gallery of characters. Jinzai Kiyoshi (1903–57) and HORI TATSUO, both of whom studied Proust, were impressed by his tremendous roman-fleuve. Hori published Utsukushii mura (tr Beautiful Village, 1967) in 1933, and it is a good example of the influence of Proust's technique. Among the earliest works to be influenced by Proust were Yokomitsu Riichi's "Kikai" (1930; tr "Machine," 1961) and Kawabata Yasunari's Suishō gensō (1931). Other noteworthy authors who were influenced by Proust include Itō Sei, TOKUDA SHŪSEI, TAKAMI JUN, Ōoka Shōhei, and NAKAMURA SHIN'ICHIRŌ.

Romain Rolland was introduced to Japan in the first decade of the 20th century, and a number of translations and studies of his work were published. Writers of the SHIRAKABA SCHOOL were lavish with their praise and so were the "idealist" writers ABE YOSHISHIGE, ABE JIRŌ, KOMIYA TOYOTAKA, and WATSUJI TETSURŌ. However, only the poet TAKAMURA KŌTARŌ, the novelist MIYAMOTO YURIKO, and the dramatist KUBO SAKAE actually brought Rolland's methods into their creations. It is especially in Miyamoto's novel Dōhyō (1947–50) that Rolland's theory of folk art can be seen.

Raymond Radiguet was first introduced in the 1920s and had the greatest influence on Hori Tatsuo and Mishima Yukio. A close examination of Hori's works shows how much he borrowed from Radiguet in the form of imitating Radiguet's expressions. "Suizokukan" (1930) shows the influence of Le Diable au corps, Mugiwara bōshi (1932) that of Denise, and Seikazoku (1930) and Naoko (1941; tr Naoko, 1967) that of Le Bal du comte d'Orgel. Of the postwar writers, Mishima Yukio was a most ardent admirer of Radiguet. In an important early work Tōzoku (1946–48) Mishima presents a summing up of his experience with Radiguet. Radiguet's influence extended to Kinjiki (1951–53; tr Forbidden Colors, 1968) and there is even a short story entitled "Radige no shi" (1953, Radiguet's Death), in which Mishima clearly set down the differences between Radiguet and himself.

Although André Malraux and Jean-Paul Sartre were introduced to Japan before World War II, it was the postwar writers who were most deeply influenced by them. Sartre's influence was especially widespread, and among those who seized upon Sartre's ideas were NOMA HIROSHI, and Ōe Kenzaburō. In the case of Malraux, although his work was widely read and a great deal of criticism has also been published, it is difficult to find evidence of direct influence. Rather, Malraux's influence was on scholars through his "literature of action." Albert Camus was introduced relatively late to Japan, but when translations of his work did appear they became the center of controversy. The 1951 publication of L'Étranger (1942) provoked a spirited debate between the novelist HIROTSU KAZUO and the critic NAKAMURA MITSUO. Of the younger writers, Ōe Kenzaburō showed an especially great interest in Camus.

The influence of French poets on modern Japanese poetry was very great. Charles Baudelaire has made a deep impression on many poets, beginning with Nagai Kafū. Baudelaire's thought and methods influenced such poets as IWANO HŌMEI, KAMBARA ARIAKE, KINOSHITA MOKUTARŌ, YAMAMURA BOCHŌ, ŌTE TAKUJI, and HAGIWARA SAKUTARŌ. Alfred de Musset, Paul Verlaine, Stéphane Mallarmé, and Émile Verhaeren played significant roles in the development of modern poetry in Japan. Of even greater influence however, were Arthur Rimbaud and Paul Valéry. Nagai Kafū's 1913 translation of Rimbaud's "Sensation" ("Sozoro aruki") drew praise for its freshness of expression. In the 1930s it was the critic KOBAYASHI HIDEO who first pointed out that Rimbaud was able to view history and nature purely objectively because he realized that he stood alienated from modern society. Around this period, NAKAHARA CHŪYA began to write poetry inspired by Rimbaud, which attracted many young readers. In Japan Valéry's reputation is that of a critic rather than a poet. In 1924 SAIJŌ YASO met Valéry while studying in Paris and it was he who introduced Valéry's poetry to Japan. In 1925 HORIGUCHI DAIGAKU translated poems by Valéry, and since then all of his poetry has been translated. However, it is almost impossible to find Japanese poetry that has been directly influenced by Valéry. It is Valéry's poetic theories that have drawn most of the attention and have provided the greatest influence.

The influence of French literature on modern Japanese literature has been of great importance. It must be remembered that beginning with the introduction of the naturalist writers in the first years of the 20th century and continuing through the 1930s, it was essentially French literature that provided the stimuli for the birth of new literary movements in Japan.

Russian Influences——Translations of Russian literature began to appear in Japan in the 1880s. The first of these was an abridged translation, published in 1883 by Takasu Jisuke (1859–1909), of Aleksandr Pushkin's *The Captain's Daughter.* The first quarter of Leo Tolstoy's *War and Peace* was translated by Mori Tai in 1886. Both translations concentrated on a faithful rendering of the plot line rather than on literary qualities. FUTABATEI SHIMEI was the first to introduce Russian literary theory in his *Shōsetsu sōron* (1886), which was based on Vissarion Belinsky's concept of realism. Futabatei's essay played a large part in urging young writers toward realism. Futabatei used self-interrogating interior monologues in his own novel *Ukigumo* (1887–89; tr *Ukigumo,* 1956), a technique he had found in Dostoevsky's *Crime and Punishment.* Futabatei also translated several pieces from Ivan Turgenev's *A Sportsman's Sketches.* His use of colloquial language rather than classical literary language in the Turgenev translations was to have great impact on young writers of the same period. Futabatei's Turgenev translations were influential in another way: they contained many lyrical descriptions of nature. The famous descriptions of the plum grove and seashore at Atami in Ozaki Kōyō's *Konjiki yasha* (1897–1902; tr *The Golden Demon,* 1905) were based on Futabatei's translations. Kunikida Doppo took hints on structure from Futabatei's 1897 translation of Turgenev's *Rudin* (entitled *Ukikusa*) in writing "Wasureenu hitobito" (1898; tr "Unforgettable People," 1972) and "Jonan" (1905; tr "Petticoat Dangers, 1913).

Another writer greatly influenced by Turgenev was Saganoya Omuro (1863–1947), whose novel *Hatsukoi* (1889) resembled Turgenev's "Rendezvous" in its plot. In the same year Saganoya also published *Ruten,* a work influenced by *Rudin.* In the 1890s Mori Ōgai translated several German translations of Turgenev and also used various Turgenev techniques in his own writing.

Dissatisfied with Futabatei's translations, Kunikida Doppo, Tayama Katai, Shimazaki Tōson, and others turned to Constance Garnett's English translations of Turgenev to search for material for their own creations. One example is Tayama Katai's "Jūemon no saigo" (1902), which took hints from the "The End of Tchertophanov" in Garnett's translation. By 1920 almost all of Turgenev's work had been translated. Among the writers who read Turgenev avidly were Nagai Kafū, Arishima Takeo, Tanizaki Jun'ichirō, and Akutagawa Ryūnosuke.

Mori Tai's abridged translation in 1886 of the first volume of Leo Tolstoy's *War and Peace* was in classical Japanese, and the title Mori used bears no resemblance to the original. It is not known how widely it was read. One writer upon whom Tolstoy made a profound impression was Tokutomi Roka. Tokutomi wrote about Tolstoy in 1890 in the magazine *Kokumin no tomo* and published a biography of him in 1897. Tokutomi's autobiographical novel *Omoide no ki* (1901; tr *Footprints in the Snow,* 1970), which had been inspired by *David Copperfield,* was also influenced by Tolstoy's trilogy *Childhood, Boyhood,* and *Youth.* Tokutomi even journeyed to Russia to meet Tolstoy and recorded his impressions in a travelogue. Another writer responsible for introducing Tolstoy to Japan was Uchida Roan. His most important achievement was a translation of *Resurrection* in 1905. Konishi Matsutarō, who studied in Russia and met Tolstoy, translated *Childhood* and other works.

Tolstoy's literary influence can be seen in the Japanese naturalist writers Shimazaki Tōson, Tayama Katai, CHIKAMATSU SHŪKŌ, and MASAMUNE HAKUCHŌ. Masamune wrote that *The Death of Ivan Ilyich* was one of the works used as models by the naturalist writers. Tolstoy's pacifism influenced the writing of Kinoshita Naoe's *Ryōjin no jihaku,* which used motifs from *Resurrection.* Arishima Takeo and Shiga Naoya of the Shirakaba school were also influenced by Tolstoy. Arishima used *Anna Karenina* as a model in the structure and psychological description of *Aru onna* (1911–13; tr *A Certain Woman,* 1978).

Uchida Roan's translation of Dostoevsky's *Crime and Punishment* in 1892 influenced both Kitamura Tōkoku and Shimazaki Tōson. Tōson discussed this influence in great detail in his *Haru*

(1908). The motif of Tōson's *Hakai* (1906; tr *The Broken Commandment,* 1974) is from Rousseau's *Confessions,* as already noted, but it also owes something to *Crime and Punishment.* In the early years of this century KASAI ZENZŌ, HAYAMA YOSHIKI, and Akutagawa Ryūnosuke were among the writers influenced by Dostoevsky. In the 1930s Kobayashi Hideo published a critical work on Dostoevsky, which deeply influenced many novelists.

Since World War II, Dostoevsky has been studied by SHIINA RINZŌ and HANIYA YUTAKA, and it has recently been discovered that Kawabata Yasunari read widely in Dostoevsky.

Besides the three writers mentioned above, Aleksandr Pushkin, Mikhail Lermontov, Nikolai Gogol, Anton Chekhov and Maxim Gorky have been widely read. Chekhov's influence has been especially great on the modern Japanese theater. Finally, Russian writers have clearly had an impact on proletarian writers in Japan.

German Influences——Whereas English and American literature were introduced and influenced Japanese literature soon after the Meiji Restoration and were soon followed by French and Russian literature, the influence of German literature came relatively late. Friedrich von Schiller's *Wilhelm Tell* was translated by Saitō Tetsutarō and Izumi Masukichi in 1880 as *Suisu dokuritsu jiyū no yuzuru,* but it was read as a popular story and though it had some influence on the Freedom and People's Rights Movement (Jiyū Minken Undō), it did not have any literary influence. Schiller's *Maria Stuart* was translated in 1883 by Fukuchi Gen'ichirō, but it too was received as a popular story. Goethe's work was first translated in 1884, but the selections did not convey the essence of Goethe. The first translation that made an impression in literary circles was Mori Ōgai's translation of "Mignon's Song" in a collection of poems entitled *Omokage* (1889). Of Goethe's novels, *Die Leiden des jungen Werthers* was translated in 1891 by Takayama Chogyū from an English translation and in 1894 by Ryokudō Yashi (also known as Yoda Hajime) from the original German. It was at this time that Kitamura Tōkoku and Shimazaki Tōson began to read many English translations of Goethe. *Faust* was translated in 1904 by Takahashi Gorō (1856–1935) and in 1912 by Machii Masamichi, but the translation that remains unsurpassed even today is Mori Ōgai's 1913 version. Modern works which have been directly influenced by *Faust* include Kitamura Tōkoku's dramatic poem "Hōraikyoku" (1891), the poem "Nōfu" in Shimazaki's *Natsukusa* (1898), and Mori Ōgai's drama *Tamakushige futari Urashima* (1902). In a broader sense, MUSHANOKŌJI SANEATSU's *Ningen banzai* (1922; tr *Three Cheers for Man,* 1963), NAGAYO YOSHIRŌ's *Takezawa sensei to iu hito* (1924–25), and KURATA HYAKUZŌ's play *Chichi no shimpai* (1922) reveal the influence of *Faust.* Mori Ōgai's *Gerhart Hauptmann,* a study of the author and his work, was published in 1906. The naturalist school writer Tayama Katai has written that his "Futon" (1907) was directly influenced by Hauptmann.

Although Friedrich Hölderlin, Wilhelm Müller, Nikolaus Lenau, and Eduard Mörike were all translated and widely read, none was so well received as the poet Heinrich Heine. In 1889 Mori Ōgai introduced and translated several of Heine's poems. TAOKA REIUN and Takayama Chogyū were influenced by Heine. The contemporary novelist NAKANO SHIGEHARU summarized Heine's life and literary contributions in *Heine jinsei dokuhon* (1936). In addition, YANAGITA KUNIO read Heine's prose from the standpoint of a scholar of folklore. Next to Heine, the German poet most widely read in Japan has been Ranier Maria Rilke. Mori Ōgai discussed Rilke's drama in 1909, but it was not until the 1930s that his work came to have a direct influence on the Japanese poets Hori Tatsuo, TACHIHARA MICHIZŌ, and ITŌ SHIZUO. Of the postwar poets, Sasazawa Yoshiaki (b 1898) and MURANO SHIRŌ both claim to have been greatly influenced by Rilke.

Thomas Mann was first mentioned in Japanese in 1904 by KURIYAGAWA HAKUSON, but it was only after World War II that novelists such as Mishima Yukio, KITA MORIO, and TSUJI KUNIO were influenced by his work. In general, German literature has been much studied and translated in Japan, but because of its abstract philosophical tendencies, Japanese writers have not made an effort to fully understand and incorporate it into their own creations. For this reason German literature has not been as influential as English, American, French, and Russian literature.

Other European Influences——Educated Japanese in the early Meiji period were probably familiar with the names of Dante and Boccaccio, but the first lengthy introduction to an Italian writer was the publication of Ueda Bin's study of the former, *Shisei Dante* (1901). Literary works influenced by Dante include Natsume Sōseki's "Shumi no iden" (1906; tr "The Heredity of Taste," 1970),

Masamune Hakuchō's *Meimō* (1922) and *Nihon dasshutsu* (1949), and Akutagawa Ryūnosuke's "Haguruma" (1927; tr "The Cogwheel," 1965). The post–World War II writers Noma Hiroshi and Ōoka Shōhei have included elements of Dante's thought in their works. Among the Christian thinkers influenced by Dante were Uchimura Kanzō, Fujii Takeshi (1888–1930), and Tsukamoto Toraji (1888–1973).

The relationship between the Spanish and Japanese cultures dates back to the 16th century. There has, however, been no significant exchange between the two literatures. A children's version of Miguel de Cervantes' *Don Quixote* was published in 1887 and a complete translation was done by KATAGAMI NOBURU and Shimamura Hōgetsu in 1915. However, both of the translations were from English versions of the novel and a translation from the original Spanish did not appear until after World War II. Young postwar writers studied *Don Quixote* as the original picaresque novel, but there has yet to be a literary work directly influenced by Cervantes.

Of the Scandinavian writers, Hans Christian Andersen was the first to be translated. His children's stories began to appear in 1888. Mori Ōgai's *Sokkyō shijin* was responsible for showing Andersen's work in a perspective other than children's literature. Shimazaki Tōson, Ueda Bin, and HIGUCHI ICHIYŌ all read Andersen as a romantic. However, Andersen's reputation as a writer of children's literature became fixed, and his work influenced such writers as OGAWA MIMEI, Akita Ujaku (1883–1962), and Hamada Hirosuke (1893–1973).

The Norwegian dramatist Henrik Ibsen was introduced to Japan by Tsubouchi Shōyō, Mori Ōgai, and Ueda Bin between 1892 and 1905. With Ibsen's death in 1906, the study of his work began in earnest with Shimamura Hōgetsu as the leader. During this period *A Doll's House*, *Ghosts*, *The Wild Duck*, and *Hedda Gabler* were frequently staged. Tsubouchi Shōyō and Mori Ōgai looked upon Ibsen as a dramatist, and Shimazaki Tōson and Arishima Takeo were interested in him as a theorist. Ibsen's plays as translated by OSANAI KAORU are mentioned in Mori Ōgai's *Seinen* (1910–11) and Tanizaki Jun'ichirō's *Seishun monogatari* (1932–33). Iwano Hōmei's *Honoo no shita* (1906) and MAYAMA SEIKA's *Dai ichininsha* (1907) were influenced by Ibsen's *Ghosts*. In addition Nagata Hideo, Kikuchi Kan, and YAMAMOTO YŪZŌ were also influenced by Ibsen's work.

The Father by Swedish dramatist August Strindberg was translated in 1907 by Ueda Bin and became famous after being staged by Osanai Kaoru in 1911. Strindberg's autobiographical novels were enthusiastically read by Japanese I-novelists (see I-NOVEL), and Yamamoto Yūzō and Mushanokōji Saneatsu were especially influenced by them.

📖 Etō Jun, *Natsume Sōseki* (1965). Fukuda Mitsuharu, ed, *Ōbei sakka to Nihon kindai bungaku*, 5 vols (1974–75). Hasegawa Izumi, *Mori Ōgai ronkō* (1962, 1970). Hasegawa Izumi, ed, *Mishima Yukio jiten* (1976). Itagaki Naoko, *Sōseki bungaku no haikei* (1956). Kamei Shunsuke, *Kindai bungaku ni okeru Hoittoman no ummei* (1969). Kawatake Toshio, *Hikaku engekigaku* (1967). Kimura Ki, *Nichibei bungaku kōryūshi no kenkyū* (1960). Kimura Ki, *Hikaku bungaku shin shikai* (1975). Kobori Keiichirō, *Wakaki hi no Mori Ōgai* (1969). Matsuda Jō, *Hikaku bungaku jiten* (1978). Nakajima Kenzō, ed, *Hikaku bungaku kōza*, 4 vols (Shimizu Kōbundō 1971–74). Nihon Hikaku Bungakukai, ed, *Hikaku bungaku* (1953). Nihon Hikaku Bungakukai, ed, *Hikaku bungaku kenkyū: Sōseki no hikaku bungakuteki kenkyū* (1954). Ōta Saburō, *Kindai sakka to seiō* (1977). Sadoya Shigenobu, *Nihon kindai bungaku no seiritsu* (1978). Sasabuchi Tomoichi, *Bungakukai to sono jidai* (1960). Shimada Kinji, *Kindai hikaku bungaku* (1956). Shimada Kinji, *Nihon ni okeru gaikoku bungaku, hikaku bungaku kenkyū* (1975–76). Takeda Katsuhiko, *Kawabata bungaku to seisho* (1971). Takeda Katsuhiko, ed, *Kawabata Yasunari* (1978). Yanagida Izumi, *Meiji bungaku kenkyū*, 10 vols (1950–65). Yamoto Tadayoshi, *Natsume Sōseki* (1971). Yasuda Yasuo, *Hikaku bungaku ronkō* (1969). Yoshida Seiichi, *Shizen shugi no kenkyū* (1955). Yoshida Seiichi, ed, *Nihon kindai bungaku no hikaku bungakuteki kenkyū* (1971). Yoshitake Yoshinori, *Kindai bungaku no naka no seiō* (1974).

Takeda Katsuhiko

Western literature in Japanese translation

Translated Western literature has played an important role in introducing foreign cultures and literary works to Japan. The first purely literary work to be translated into Japanese was *Aesop's Fables* in the late 16th century (see JESUIT MISSION PRESS). However, Japan's long period of NATIONAL SECLUSION intervened, and it was not until the Meiji period (1868–1912) that translation of Western literature began on a large scale.

19th-Century Translations——With the opening of the country in the 19th century after over 200 years of national seclusion, many books by philosophers and politicians were translated. The foreword to FUKUZAWA YUKICHI's book *Gakumon no susume* (1872–76, tr *An Encouragement of Learning*, 1969) contains his famous expression, "God has not created a man superior to another or inferior to another." This is a paraphrase of the statement in the US Declaration of Independence (1776) that all men are created equal. In 1878 Oda Jun'ichirō (1851–1919) translated *Ernest Maltravers* by Edward Bulwer-Lytton (1831–91) and its sequel *Alice* under the Japanese title *Ōshū kiji karyū shunwa*. This was translated into classical literary Japanese, as opposed to the spoken language. It was widely read and influenced a Japanese genre known as the political novel (SEIJI SHŌSETSU). Subsequently, 12 volumes of Bulwer-Lytton's novels were translated over a decade. Seven novels by Benjamin Disraeli (1804–81) and 25 of Shakespeare's works were also translated. Translations of historical novels by Sir Walter Scott (1771–1832) satisfied the political enthusiasm of the time, as did his *Lady of the Lake*.

The early Meiji-period translations were extremely free and informal in their language, and were thus instrumental in breaking down the traditional Chinese-inspired literary style and in paving the way for literary writing in colloquial Japanese. An important translation in this respect was *Yoru to asa* (Bulwer-Lytton's *Night and Morning*), as translated by Masuda Katsunori in 1889. This fostered public demand for the informal, colloquial writing style, and writers like FUTABATEI SHIMEI and YAMADA BIMYŌ worked actively for the development of such a style (see GEMBUN ITCHI). Futabatei in his *Aibiki* (1888) successfully translated in beautiful colloquial Japanese a chapter from the *Sportsman's Sketches* of Ivan Turgenev (1818–83), and in effect the new Japanese literary style was formed.

INOUE TETSUJIRŌ, YATABE RYŌKICHI, and TOYAMA MASAKAZU translated poetry by Shakespeare, Tennyson, Gray, and Longfellow and published them, along with a number of Yatabe's and Toyama's original poems, in *Shintaishi shō* (1882, Collection of New-Style Poems). This was the first book of Western poetry translated into Japanese and paved the way for many more translations by Japanese poets of Western poetry and nursery rhymes. UEDA BIN's *Kaichōon* (1905) contained translated verses of Dante, Baudelaire, Hugo, Heine, Mallarmé, Browning, and Shakespeare, and MORI ŌGAI published a book of verses entitled *Omokage* (1889) that contained passages translated from Byron. *Kaichōon* and *Omokage* were regarded as models of translated verse and greatly influenced future poets. *Ōbei meika shū* (1894) by Ōwada Takeki (1857–1910) contained poems which were translated into Japanese in the traditional style of alternating five- and seven-syllable metrical units. The poetry of Walt Whitman (1819–92) was first introduced to Japan in 1892 by NATSUME SŌSEKI; however, a complete translation of his *Leaves of Grass* did not appear until the Taishō period (1912–26). Whitman's poetry, with its enthusiasm for democratic ideas, was to become particularly popular during that period. The translation of Whitman's free verse into colloquial Japanese served as a guide for the movement to write poetry in the common language. *Leaves of Grass* not only encouraged the modernization of literary Japanese but also offered many ideas influential in Japan's progress toward modernization.

Yoshitake Yoshinori

20th-Century Translations——The selection of works to be translated and the quality of the translations themselves have both improved remarkably since the beginning of the 20th century, and from about the 1920s three trends became evident: socialist and communist revolutionary literary works suddenly came to be translated; literary works using surrealism, stream-of-consciousness, and similar techniques were translated; and American literary works, beginning with those of Sinclair Lewis (1885–1951), Sherwood Anderson (1876–1941), and such contemporaries as Eugene O'Neill (1888–1953) were introduced.

Expressionist poems, such as those written immediately following the Russian Revolution by Sergei Esenin (1895–1925), and the plays written by the German Ernst Toller (1893–1939) are among translated works falling into the category of socialist or communist works. During the 1920s, there was an outpouring of Marxist literature in translation, especially of the treatises of Marx, Engels, and Lenin. As one would expect, these works greatly influenced the so-called Japanese PROLETARIAN LITERATURE MOVEMENT; translations of various essays by Vladimir Friche (1870–1929) and of *Die Theorie des Romans* and other works by György Lukács (1885–1971) laid the foundation for Japanese proletarian literary theory. Among the novels translated, *And Quiet Flows the Don* by Mikhail Sholokhov (b 1905) gained great popularity. In addition, almost all the works of Maxim Gorky (1868–1936) were translated and published in 20 volumes between 1922 and 1931. With the rise of militarism in Japan during the 1930s, however, this type of literature was strictly censored, and such translations sharply decreased.

Among works using experimental techniques, *Ouvert la Nuit* and *Fermé la Nuit* by Paul Morand (1888–1976) received a great deal of attention. Such works provided the basis for the SHINKANKAKU SCHOOL which included such novelists as KAWABATA YASUNARI and YOKOMITSU RIICHI. In fact Kawabata himself translated short stories by Lord Dunsany (1878–1957) and John Galsworthy (1867–1933). In particular, *Manifeste du surréal* by André Breton (1896–1966), which was translated in 1929, gave young Japanese poets a new direction. *Le Bal du comte d'Orgel* by Raymond Radiguet (1903–23) was translated in 1931 and widely accepted among young readers. Beginning in the mid-1930s, various works by André Gide (1869–1951), Paul Valéry (1871–1945), Marcel Proust (1871–1922), Thomas Mann (1875–1955), Rainer Maria Rilke (1875–1926), and Hans Carossa (1878–1956) were also translated and soon became popular. (Kawabata's *Snow Country* contains an episode in which the protagonist translates essays on the dance by Valéry and Alain.)

In the third trend, contemporary American writers in translation gained a wide readership. The works of Eugene O'Neill (1888–1953) were especially popular. *The Long Voyage Home* and *Ile* were translated in 1924, and two different translations of *Anna Christie* appeared in 1927 and 1928. Two new translations of *Desire under the Elms* came out in 1924. Other translations of American works included *An American Tragedy* by Theodore Dreiser (1871–1945) and *A Farewell to Arms* by Ernest Hemingway (1899–1961) in 1930 and *The 42nd Parallel* by John Dos Passos (1896–1970) and *Main Street* by Sinclair Lewis (1885–1951) in 1931. Although American literature attained great popularity in Japan, as in the case of socialist or revolutionary writings, political events exerted a major influence: before and during World War II American literature fell out of favor, with a corresponding decrease in the number of works translated.

After World War II, however, translated Western literature in Japan attained a degree of popularity unknown since the Meiji Restoration (1868). During the years directly following the surrender a flood of translations that could not be published during the war poured out one after another. From the beginning of the 1950s literature began to be translated in a more systematic fashion, displaying four overall trends: American literature became the mainstream of translated Western literature; translated existentialist works influenced many of Japan's young writers; literary works by Catholics were translated, and the number of Catholic Japanese writers (ENDŌ SHŪSAKU; MIURA SHUMON; and SONO AYAKO, to name a few) increased; and a great number of literary works containing explicit sexual descriptions were translated.

American works began to appear soon after the war. In 1946 the previously translated *Adventures of Tom Sawyer* and *Adventures of Huckleberry Finn* of Mark Twain (1835–1910) were republished, and soon afterward the old translations of "The Gold Bug" and "The Fall of the House of Usher" by Edgar Allan Poe (1809–49) appeared in the bookstores. During the first few years after World War II, essays by Ralph Waldo Emerson (1803–82) and Henry David Thoreau (1817–62) as well as Walt Whitman's *Leaves of Grass* were newly translated. Of the works of William Faulkner (1897–1962) *Sanctuary* was published in 1950, followed by *Intruder in the Dust* in 1951. About this time the works of John Steinbeck (1902–68) also began to receive attention. A translation of *The Moon Is Down* was published in 1951, followed by one of *Tortilla Flat* in 1952; the 1955 translation of *East of Eden* became a best seller. (*The Grapes of Wrath* had been translated previously in 1938.) However, Hemingway attained greater popularity in Japan than either Faulkner or Steinbeck. A translation of *A Farewell to Arms,* published in 1930, and one of *For Whom the Bell Tolls,* published just after war broke out in the Pacific, were read widely; there are currently four different translations of *A Farewell to Arms* and *The Snows of Kilimanjaro* in print. Because some of Hemingway's earliest works were discovered after the 1955 publication of his "complete" works, two subsequent complete works have been published.

Among existentialist works, the first translation was *Inimité* by Jean-Paul Sartre (1905–80), and the complete works of Sartre were published in 15 volumes in 1953. The works of Camus (1913–60) came to be read soon after those of Sartre. A translation of *The Plague* was published in 1950, followed by *The Stranger* in 1951. By 1955 all 15 of Camus' works had been translated. By 1950 two translations of works by Franz Kafka (1883–1924), *Amerika* and *The Castle,* had appeared; a translation of *The Trial* had been published during the war. Two other writers related to existentialism, Sören Kierkegaard (1813–55) and Fyodor Dostoevsky (1821–81), were also widely translated into Japanese. By 1949, 12 volumes of Kierkegaard's selected works were published, and 43 volumes containing the complete works of Dostoevsky were published between 1947 and 1951. Among Japanese writers, ABE KŌBŌ in particular has been influenced by such existentialist works.

Works by Catholic writers were translated before the war as well as after. *On Literature* by T. S. Eliot (1888–1965) was translated in 1946. Published in academic journals, Eliot's essays on literary theory influenced the new generation of literary critics. Many of Eliot's poems, including "The Waste Land," were translated during the 1950s. Translations of books by Graham Greene (b 1904), *The Third Man* and *The Confidential Agent,* were published in 1951.

Translations also played a part in the postwar sexual revolution in Japan. An abridged version of *Lady Chatterley's Lover* by D. H. Lawrence (1885–1930) had been published before the war, but the complete edition of 1950 was banned. In 1952 and 1955 abridged translations were again published. (Translations of Lawrence's *Apocalypse* and *Pornography and Obscenity* had been published in 1933.) The work of Henry Miller (1891–1980)—*Tropic of Cancer, Black Spring,* and *Sexus* were translated in 1952—also created quite a sensation. The following year *The Air-Conditioned Nightmare* and *The Smile at the Foot of the Ladder* were translated; Miller's devoted readers were in agreement with his criticisms of contemporary civilization.

After 1960, beginning with translations of the works of J. D. Salinger (b 1919), urban American Jewish literature became popular in Japan. Black literature began to be translated as well, and in 1962 a 13-volume set of selected works of black literature was published. The "anti-*roman*" works of Alain Robbe-Grillet (b 1922), Michel Butor (b 1926), and others were also translated, as were the works of dramatists such as Samuel Beckett (b 1906), Eugene Ionesco (b 1912), and John Osborne (b 1929). See also WESTERN LITERATURE AND JAPANESE LITERATURE. *Takeda Katsuhiko*

Western-style pictures, early

(*yōga; seiyōga*). Japanese art inspired by the styles of Europe, from the largely Portuguese-influenced NAMBAN ART ("southern barbarian" art) of the late 16th and the early 17th centuries to the Dutch-influenced *kōmōga* ("red-hair" pictures) of the 17th to the 19th centuries.

Japanese Western-style art of the 16th century was basically of two types: that which employed Western techniques of oil painting and engraving to depict largely religious subjects, and that which used traditional Japanese materials and methods of execution to illustrate the Europeans and the exotica they introduced to Japan.

In 1549 the missionary Francis XAVIER arrived and inaugurated the first era of active contact between Japan and the West. For the next 50 years there was comparatively free cultural intercourse. Jesuit priests brought religious art with them and also gave instruction in its production. In 1590 the JESUIT MISSION PRESS was set up in Kyūshū and the fathers there taught the art of engraving to Japanese converts; the earliest extant engraving believed to have been executed in Japan is a portrait of a standing virgin and child produced at the Jesuit seminary at Arie, Kyūshū, in 1597. Several oil paintings of religious subjects survive from around the same time, though much was destroyed in the later anti-Christian persecutions.

While Christian converts were adopting Western techniques for the purpose of imitating European religious paintings and engravings, artists associated with traditional Japanese schools, such as the KANŌ SCHOOL, were incorporating foreign subject matter of a nonreligious nature into their art. Most extant pictures of this type are on folding screens (*byōbu*) and illustrate missionaries and Portuguese traders, great foreign ships, the strange plants, animals, and inventions brought from abroad, and maps and European cityscapes.

With the expulsion of the missionaries in 1614 and the prohibition of Christianity and expulsion of the Portuguese traders in 1639 (see NATIONAL SECLUSION), the chief inspiration for Western-style art became pictures introduced by the Dutch at their single port of call, DEJIMA in Nagasaki. Pictures of foreigners became known as *kōmōga* ("red-hair" pictures), based on the belief that the Dutch, like Japanese demons, had red locks. A school of Western-style painting flourished in Nagasaki (see NAGASAKI SCHOOL), and the metropolitan centers of Kyōto and Edo (now Tōkyō) were quick to follow suit.

By the 18th century, UKIYO-E prints depicting foreigners had become exceedingly popular. Individual woodblock artists of the major cities generally achieved fame in their own right, but designers of Nagasaki woodblock prints tended to remain anonymous while the names of their publishing houses, such as Hariya, Toshimaya, Bunkindō, and Yamatoya, became well known. Woodblock masters of Edo and Kyōto also found a lucrative sideline in pictures that illustrated Western techniques or foreign landscapes. Western linear perspective *(uki-e)* is especially evident in prints by members of the UTAGAWA SCHOOL: UTAGAWA TOYOHARU, Utagawa Kuninaga (fl ca 1806–29), UTAGAWA KUNISADA, and UTAGAWA KUNIYOSHI. The European landscapes of Toyoharu and Kuninaga often display astonishing flights of fancy.

Western art continued to have an influence on Japanese arts and crafts (including LACQUER WARE and CERAMICS) throughout the Edo period (1600–1868), in spite of Japan's official seclusion policy. Even the famous naturalistic artist MARUYAMA ŌKYO got his start by employing Western linear perspective for illustrations of foreign and indigenous scenes. Through the influence of the Western-style artist, biologist, and author, HIRAGA GENNAI, the unlikely region of Akita in northern Japan became a center of Western art under the patronage of the painter and ruling *daimyō*, SATAKE SHOZAN, and his chief retainer, ODANO NAOTAKE (see AKITA SCHOOL).

But the chief pioneer and popularizer of Western-style art in Japan was SHIBA KŌKAN, a Renaissance man who studied all aspects of Western learning, including geography, astronomy, and the natural sciences. He is best remembered as the originator of copperplate etching in Japan and as one of the first to develop the art of oil painting. In the art of engraving he was followed by his contemporary AŌDŌ DENZEN, an artist who was also Kōkan's rival in painting, and Yasuda Raishū (fl mid-19th century).

Painters of the latter part of the Edo period surpassed Kōkan both in technical proficiency and in artistic merit. Araki Jogen (1765–1824) brought the oil painting technique to a remarkably high standard, and KAWAHARA KEIGA created Western-style works of exquisite control and dramatic intensity.

Early Western-style art in Japan was from start to finish an amalgam of styles and techniques. Western-oriented artists never acquired enough knowledge of European techniques to enable them to discard native traditions. Painting in the European manner thus remained derivative and amounted to experimentation with Western style, technique, and subject matter, usually combined with influence from Chinese art. Japanese traditions lay just beneath the surface and often obtruded into the European effect artists sought to achieve. The result was a hybrid not unlike that achieved by artists who practiced Chinese styles: a synthesis of foreign techniques and native traditions. See also YŌGA.

Cal French, *Through Closed Doors: Western Influence on Japanese Art* (1977). Kōbe Shiritsu Namban Bijutsukan, *Kōbe Shiritsu Namban Bijutsukan zuroku*, 5 vols (1968–72). Sakamoto Mitsuru, Sugase Tadashi, and Naruse Fujio, *Namban bijutsu to yōfūga*, vol 25 of *Genshoku Nihon no bijutsu* (1970).　　Cal FRENCH

Weston, Walter (1861–1940)

English missionary and alpinist; the "father of Japanese mountaineering." He came to Japan in 1889 as a missionary of the Church of England. During three periods of residency in Japan, totaling 14 years, he climbed Mt. Fuji (Fujisan) and various peaks in the Chūbu mountain region and made the first ascent of such mountains as HOTAKADAKE. His *Mountaineering and Exploration in the Japanese Alps*, published in London in 1896, spread the fame of the Japanese Alps. In 1905, with his counsel, the Japan Alpine Club was organized. He was awarded the Fourth Class Order of the Sacred Treasure in 1937.　　TAKEDA Fumio

whales

(kujira). In Japanese *kujira* is the general name for mammals of the order Cetacea. Whales of the suborder Mysticeti (baleen, or toothless, whales) are often seen when populations which forage in the Arctic Ocean migrate south for breeding in winter. The following species are most commonly seen in Japan: the *semi kujira* (right whale; *Eubalaena glacialis*), the *zatō kujira* (humpback whale; *Megaptera novaeangliae*), and the *nagasu kujira* (fin whale; *Balaenoptera physalus*). Belonging to the suborder Odontoceti (toothed whales), the male *makkō kujira* (sperm whale; *Physeter catodon*) migrates north in winter, and the female, after giving birth, migrates with her young during July and August. In addition, among the dolphin family, the *mairuka* (common dolphin; *Delphinus delphis*), the *suji iruka* (blue white dolphin; *Stenella caeruleoalba*), and the *kama iruka* (Pacific white side dolphin; *Lagenorhynchus obliquidens*) are commonly seen.

The Japanese have long been interested in whales. The word *kujira* appears in the *Kojiki* (712). The whale has been regarded with awe as a divine messenger among fishermen. Buddhism, which was introduced to Japan in the 6th century, forbade people to eat four-footed beasts, but the whale was considered a fish, and eventually it became an important source of protein for the Japanese. The parts of the whale's body are used in a variety of ways in Japan. See also WHALING.　　IMAIZUMI Yoshiharu and SANEYOSHI Tatsuo

whaling

(hogei). In Japan, whaling legally refers to the hunting of whales with a harpoon gun fired from a power-driven catcher boat. It includes factory-ship whaling, land-based whaling, and small-scale whaling, all of which are designated as fishery operations, and regulated in Japan by the Ministry of Agriculture, Forestry, and Fisheries. It is thus distinguished from dolphin hunting, which is classified as free fishery, subject to licensing by the prefectural government concerned.

History——The early Japanese caught whales that had run aground or wandered into bays, but it was not until 1606 that whaling became an organized industry, at Taiji (now in Wakayama Prefecture). In the early days of the industry, whales were hunted by hand harpooning; after a unique net whaling method was developed in 1675, whaling spread to a number of places along the coasts of western Japan and reached the height of its prosperity from 1810 to 1850. However, while whalers of Western countries took to the ocean in quest of whales, Japanese whalers were confined to nearby coastal waters by the NATIONAL SECLUSION policy of the Tokugawa shogunate (1603–1867). From about 1820, whalers from the United States and other Western countries began to appear in Japanese waters. The numerous Western whalers soon caused a rapid decline in the number of right whales, the main catch of the Japanese whalers, causing the antiquated Japanese whaling industry to languish until the turn of the 20th century. In the 1890s Japanese whalers tried American-style whaling methods but without much success.

At the turn of the century the appearance off the Korean shore of Russian whalers, who employed modern whaling methods, prompted Japanese whalers to modernize their equipment. In 1897 they adopted modern whaling techniques from Norway. From about 1906 onward coastal whaling gathered momentum, and soon the Japanese extended their reach from Taiwan in the south to the Kurils in the north, establishing a number of land stations to process their catches. Beginning in the 1930s, they employed small catcher boats and specialized in the hunting of smaller species in which larger whalers were not interested. In 1934 Japan sent a whaling fleet to Antarctic waters for the first time; this marked the beginning of Japanese factory-ship whaling. In the ensuing years, Japan steadily increased the size of its whaling fleet, some of which was sent to the northern extremes of the Pacific Ocean in 1940 and 1941.

World War II dealt a near fatal blow to the Japanese whaling industry. All six of Japan's factory ships were lost, as well as many of the catcher boats and overseas whaling stations. Following the war's end, coastal whaling was revived immediately in response to the food crisis. In 1946 factory-ship whaling was begun again in the waters surrounding the Bonin (J: Ogasawara) Islands, and another fleet was sent to Antarctic waters. In 1952 factory-ship whaling was resumed in the North Pacific as well. By the end of the first half of the 1960s, seven factory-ship whaling fleets were operating in the Antarctic, and three in the North Pacific. The Japanese whaling industry had surpassed its prewar peak, setting the stage for its three largest whaling companies to make great strides in the ensuing years.

However, beginning in the latter half of the 1960s, whaling regulations were stiffened by the International Whaling Commission, established pursuant to the International Whaling Control Treaty, and Japan's whaling industry came under increasing pressure to reduce its operations. By 1977 the number of its whaling factory ships had been reduced to one and its large-scale whaling stations to four.

Whaling Operations and Whalers——Japanese whalers use the modern Norwegian method of whaling. This method is applied to three different types of whaling: large-scale, small-scale, and factory-ship. In large-scale whaling, sometimes called coastal whaling, the whalers use a land station, operating within a radius of 2,300 nautical miles (4,260 km or 2,645 mi) of the station and periodically landing at the station to dispose of their catch. Large-scale whalers usually caught various baleen whales and sperm whales. Since 1976, however, they have been allowed to catch only Bryde's whales (*Balaenoptera edeni*) and sperm whales. The number of large whalers once reached as many as 12, in 1908. However, by 1977 large whalers had been reduced to 3, due to liquidation and consolidation. The number of whaling stations was reduced from 30 to 4 in the areas of northeastern Honshū (2), Chiba, and Wakayama.

Small-scale whaling is a branch of large-scale whaling. The size of the catcher boats employed in small-scale whaling is restricted to less than 50 tons, as against 400 to 700 tons for large-scale whaling, and the geographic scope of their operations is also limited. The species they are permitted to catch are restricted to mink (or little piked) whales (*B. acutorostrata*) and toothed whales (except sperm whales). The number of small catcher boats increased dramatically after 1945 and reached 70 in 1947, but under the guidance of the government it gradually decreased, becoming 7 in 1976. The main fishing grounds today are the waters off Hokkaidō, northeastern Honshū, and Chiba.

Factory-ship whaling is a deep-sea operation carried out by a whaling fleet, which typically consists of a whaling factory ship, a refrigerator vessel, an oil tanker, catcher boats, scouting boats, and meat carriers. While small whalers must wait for whales to wander into coastal waters, large whaling fleets traverse the oceans in search of prey. Factory-ship whaling requires a great deal of capital, and the "big three" whaling companies (TAIYŌ FISHERY CO, LTD, Nihon Suisan, and KYOKUYŌ CO, LTD) had been engaged in factory-ship whaling since before World War II. After the war, however, they were forced to reduce their operations because of drastic decreases in their catch quota. In 1976 the whaling divisions of the "big three" were consolidated into the Japan Joint Whaling Company, Ltd, to ensure the continuation of the whaling business. Factory-ship whaling is conducted in the North Pacific and the Antarctic Ocean, mostly hunting the same species allowed large-scale whalers. The major catch in the Antarctic Ocean is mink whales.

Whale Products——Primary products of the whale include whale meat, baleen whale oil, sperm whale oil, and meat extract. These primary products are in turn processed into secondary and tertiary products. In Western countries, the primary objective of whaling is the production of whale oil. Whale meat is usually not used as food; instead, it is processed into meal, other forms of feed, or fertilizers. By contrast, whale meat constitutes a significant (though proportionately small) source of animal protein in the Japanese diet, in which animal protein is scarce. As such, it has an important economic value—so much so that there is a saying in Japan that "a whale brings prosperity to seven fishing villages." The whaling industry in Japan is thus supported by the market for whale meat and oil. Because of this, the Japanese whaling industry has managed to survive on a much reduced quota, while whalers of Western countries have disappeared one by one.

Whale meat is shipped to market in frozen, refrigerated, or salted form, and is served raw or cooked. It is also canned or processed into sausages. *Sarashikujira* (tail flukes which are cut thin and slightly scalded with steaming hot water) is a favorite whale dish. Blubber and the meat of the ventral grooves serve as materials for whale bacon, while *matsuurazuke*, made of the whale's nasal cartilage, is considered a delicacy. Organs such as the kidney, the small intestine, and the heart are also edible, as is the salted hide of the baleen whale.

The nonedible part of the whale's body is put into a cooker for oil extraction, and from its waste, liquid food (such as soluble protein and whale meat extract), animal feed (meal), and fertilizers are produced. Baleen whale oil is used for making margarine and other shortenings, while toothed whale oil is used for making lubricants, detergents, pharmaceuticals, and cosmetics. The teeth, the baleen, and the bones are used as materials for various artifacts, and the tendons are used as gut for tennis rackets. Together with the hide, they are also used as materials for gelatin. So useful are whales that a Japanese saying states that "no part of a whale can be discarded."

Supply and Demand of Whale Products——Whale meat production in Japan peaked at 218,000 metric tons (240,000 short tons) in 1962, but because of drastic decreases in the catch quota, it fell to 44,000 metric tons (48,000 short tons) by 1976. At one time, Japan exported whale meat unfit for human consumption as pet food, but since 1972 no such waste meat has been exported. Rather, Japan has long been an importer of whale meat, and as domestic production has decreased, imports have continued to increase despite shrinking worldwide catch quotas. Imports reached an all-time high of 32,000 metric tons (35,000 short tons) in 1976. Japan's demand for whale meat remains very strong. In recent years it has been estimated at about 130,000 metric tons (143,000 short tons) annually, but there is no longer enough whale meat available to meet the demand.

Production of baleen whale oil registered a record 130,000 tons in 1972 but soon thereafter decreased drastically, totaling only 7,000 metric tons (7,700 short tons) in 1976. Even in the peak years domestic demand for baleen whale oil was small (perhaps around 20,000 metric tons [22,000 short tons] a year), and Japan exported the bulk of its production; the whale oil industry thus made a significant contribution to the earning of foreign exchange. Domestic demand fell sharply with decreasing production, and in recent years it has become almost negligible, leaving much of the remaining production for export. Production of sperm whale oil peaked at 47,000 metric tons (52,000 short tons) in 1964 and then tapered off to 17,000 metric tons (19,000 short tons) by 1976. Domestic demand grew to 30,000 metric tons (33,000 short tons) by 1968 but has decreased to 15,000 metric tons (16,500 short tons) in recent years.

Whaling Regulations——The introduction of modern whaling methods around the turn of the century and the resulting growth of Japan's coastal whaling industry brought the question of conserving whale resources to the fore. To deal with the situation and to foster cooperation among the whaling companies, in 1909 the government promulgated a Ministry of Agriculture and Commerce Ordinance on "Whaling Control Regulations" and followed it with several revisions. The revisions of 1934, 1938, and 1949 were designed to bring the nation's whaling controls into line with the Geneva Whaling Control Convention of 1931, the International Whaling Convention of 1937, and the International Convention for the Regulation of Whaling of 1946. Regulations for the Control of Factory-Ship Whaling were promulgated in 1934 and amended in 1936, 1938, and 1949. In prewar years, small-scale whaling operations were unregulated except in the waters off Chiba Prefecture. However, as the number of small whalers increased during the postwar food shortage, the need for regulation arose. In 1947 the government instituted Small-Scale Whaling Control Regulations, making small-scale operations subject to license by the Ministry of Agriculture, as with large-scale and factory-ship whalers. While still under the Allied Occupation, Japan was allowed in 1951 to become a signatory of the 1946 International Convention for the Regulation of Whaling. In the ensuing years, international controls have become increasingly complex and rigorous. The government assigns fishery inspectors to whaling factory-ships and to land-based whaling stations to supervise their operations. In addition, Japan has received international observers from the United States and the Soviet Union into its whaling stations and on its factory ships.

Because it has a limited land area in which to develop a livestock industry, Japan has traditionally sought to procure animal protein resources from the sea and has devoted great efforts to the development of fisheries. The vast ocean surrounding Japan is richly endowed with biological resources. Because of their renewable nature, they offer the possibility of continuous production if they are managed rationally. Since the latter half of the 1960s, sentiment supporting the protection of whales has run high in the world, especially in the United States. This is reflected in the fact that more than half the signatories of the International Convention for the Regulation of Whaling are nonwhaling countries. As a result, the regulation of whaling has intensified to the point where the whaling industry is faced with a serious crisis. Against such a background, the Japanese whaling industry has reduced its scale of operations to a bare minimum, with a view to the promotion of efficient use of the ocean's biological resources. Every effort is being exerted to effect both a recovery of the world's whale population and the continuation of the industry's activities. See also WHALES.

■——N. A. MacKintosh, *The State of Whales* (1965). Maeda Keijirō and Teraoka Yoshio, *Hogei* (1952). W. E. Schevill, ed, *The Whale Problem* (1974). ŌSUMI Seiji

wheat and barley

(*komugi* and *ōmugi*; often collectively referred to as *mugi*). Both of these grains were introduced to Japan at nearly the same time in the 3rd or 4th century AD from China. They were cultivated as winter crops in dry fields and as second crops in paddy fields after the rice harvest. Since farmers were required to pay their land tax with rice throughout the premodern period, they were often obliged to eat wheat and barley as supplementary foods. However, because of the oceanic monsoon climate and the coincidence of the ripening and harvesting periods with the rainy season, Japan is not particularly suitable for the growing of wheat and barley. Cultivation is done on a small scale, and productivity is low. Japanese wheat is mainly winter wheat. The quality of grain is medium to soft and unfit for bread. Its main use is for noodles; it is also used in making soy sauce and *fu* (wheat-gluten bread). Production in 1980 was 583,000 metric tons (641,000 short tons). Two types of barley are grown, husked and naked. Both are polished, pressed or ground, mixed with rice and boiled. Roasted barley is used to make *mugicha* or barley water, a tea-like drink.

Since the end of World War II the habit of eating bread has spread widely among the Japanese. This has increased the demand for wheat, and the growth of livestock breeding has increased the demand for barley for feed. However, the import of large quantities of barley from the United States at less than half the price of the domestic barley has resulted in a drastic decrease in production in Japan since 1962. Total 1980 production was 968,000 metric tons (1,065,000 short tons). The cultivation of two-rowed barley, used for brewing beer, has also decreased sharply because of the recent import of malt at low prices.

Rye (*raimugi*) and oats (*embaku*) were introduced to Japan from Europe during the Meiji period (1868–1912), but these are cultivated principally for livestock feed.   HOSHIKAWA Kiyochika

whitebait

(*shirauo*). *Salangichthys microdon;* a brackish-water fish of the class Osteichthyes, order Salmoniformes, family Salangidae. It swims upstream in the spawning season and grows to 10 cm (4 in) in length during its one-year lifespan. The distribution ranges from Lake Abashiri in Hokkaidō to Okayama Prefecture on the Pacific coast of Japan and from Sakhalin and Vladivostok to the west coast of Kyūshū along the coast of the Sea of Japan. The body of the *shirauo* is colorless and it is often confused with the *shirouo* (*Leucopsarion petersi*) of the family Gobiidae. Both species are eaten.   ABE Tokiharu

For the common people of Edo (now Tōkyō) the arrival of the *shirauo* was a harbinger of spring; they were caught from the river Sumidagawa, which was not polluted then. It was customary to present the first catch of *shirauo* to the shōgun's family. Many works mentioning *shirauo* are found among the *haiku* poems of the Edo period (1600–1868). The frail beauty of the fish is captured in a haiku poem by Matsuo Bashō (1644–94): "Frail fish, *shirauo*/You will splinter into nothingness/ if you run into a rock."   SAITŌ Shōji

white-collar workers

From the beginning of Japanese industrialization, office and supervisory staff have been distinguished from factory personnel. A small nucleus of highly educated, permanent (tenured) employees, which today would be labeled a white-collar elite, was recognized at the outset. With time, the privileges and welfare benefits given this permanently employed group were extended to lower-status clerical employees and then to skilled blue-collar workers. Modern Japanese organizations, beginning in the 19th century, recognized and gave priority to formal education, a key distinguishing asset of any white-collar group. More recently, in the 1960s and 1970s, public education advanced to the point where all but a small minority of young workers possessed high school degrees or better, and clerical and service-sector employment expanded more rapidly than jobs in manufacturing. As a result, a progressive expansion of the white-collar class has occurred. In addition, company personnel systems have tended to treat blue-collar workers in the same manner as office workers throughout the post–World War II era. This trend toward more homogeneous status and benefits has meant that many white-collar jobs are no longer high in prestige. Just as blue-collar

work has been "bureaucratized," white-collar work has also undergone "proletariatization." The relevance of the distinction between white and blue is eroding as a result. The looser Japanese term SARARĪMAN ("salaryman"), although generally implying white-collar worker, is not very precise; it is therefore well suited to the Japanese situation as it stands today.

White-collar workers' attitudes do have distinguishing characteristics despite the fact that blue-collar colleagues are joining them in a common work- and life-style. They prefer to join large, prosperous companies where job security, pay, and benefits are best. Status implications of organizational size are a matter of considerable importance, as is one's rank within the organization. Less tied to neighborhoods than shopkeepers and urban factory workers, white-collar workers depend on workplace affiliations for extracurricular social activities and acquaintances. Education is a major preoccupation at home, as it greatly determines the future status of children, themselves destined for white-collar positions. Income is linked to seniority, and consumption patterns are highly predictable according to age.

The key distinction among white-collar workers is between men and women. Male white-collar workers are organizational careerists, while female office workers almost inevitably leave jobs and career for marriage. Women generally do not aspire to the status of managers, nor do they remain long enough to enjoy the seniority benefits of long service. Since female labor is less expensive and less permanent, most large organizations today seek ways to reduce the number of male white-collar positions while increasing female clerical positions. See also LABOR; LABOR MARKET; EMPLOYMENT, FORMS OF; EMPLOYMENT SYSTEM, MODERN; WOMEN IN THE LABOR FORCE; OCCUPATIONAL STRUCTURE.

——Hayashi Chikio et al, *Nihon no howaito karā* (1964). Thomas P. Rohlen, *For Harmony and Strength: Japanese White-Collar Organization in Anthropological Perspective* (1974). Ezra Vogel, *Japan's New Middle Class* (1963).   Thomas P. ROHLEN

White Paper on the Economy

(*Keizai hakusho*). A report published annually by the ECONOMIC PLANNING AGENCY on the current trends of the Japanese economy. First published by the ECONOMIC STABILIZATION BOARD in July 1947, it is the oldest of the white papers issued by the government. The report analyzes in depth the central issues of each fiscal year.   KATŌ Masashi

White Paper on the National Standard of Living

(*Kokumin seikatsu hakusho*). An annual economic report published by the ECONOMIC PLANNING AGENCY on the living conditions of the general population. The first report was published in June 1956. In addition to analyzing the national standard of living, recent reports have touched on social welfare, income distribution, and other pertinent social issues.   KATŌ Masashi

white papers

(*hakusho*). Reports released periodically by government ministries and agencies to inform the public of facts concerning the areas under their jurisdiction. The first white paper in Japan was the Keizai Jissō Hōkokusho (Report on Actual Economic Conditions) published by the ECONOMIC STABILIZATION BOARD in 1947. Written by the economist Tsuru Shigeto (b 1912), it explained in clear and simple terms the state of Japan's economy and the problems the nation faced immediately after World War II. The report was highly praised, and a *Keizai hakusho* (WHITE PAPER ON THE ECONOMY) has since been issued annually. The *Dokusen hakusho* (White Paper on Monopolies; 1948), *Tsūshō hakusho* (White Paper on International Trade; 1949), and *Rōdō hakusho* (White Paper on Labor; 1950) were other early examples. Today almost all government ministries issue white papers. Although they formerly released them without prior consultation, it has been the practice since 1963 to coordinate positions and predictions with other ministries before publication, so that white papers today may be regarded as expressing the official policy of the government as a whole. See table on following page.   KATŌ Masashi and KOMINE Takao

White papers

Major Annual White Papers of Japan			
Area	Title	Ministry or agency	Year of first publication
Agriculture	Nōgyō hakusho	Ministry of Agriculture, Forestry, and Fisheries	1961
Atomic energy	Genshiryoku hakusho	Atomic Energy Commission	1956
Construction	Kensetsu hakusho	Ministry of Construction	1949
Crime	Hanzai hakusho	Ministry of Justice	1960
Defense	Bōei hakusho	Defense Agency	1970
Disaster prevention	Bōsai hakusho	National Land Agency	1963
Economy	Keizai hakusho	Economic Planning Agency	1947
Education	Kyōiku hakusho	Ministry of Education	1959
Environment	Kankyō hakusho	Environment Agency	1972
Fire defense	Shōbō hakusho	Fire Defense Agency	1960
Fishery	Gyogyō hakusho	Ministry of Agriculture, Forestry, and Fisheries	1964
Foreign policy	Gaikō seisho	Ministry of Foreign Affairs	1957
Forestry	Ringyō hakusho	Ministry of Agriculture, Forestry, and Fisheries	1965
Health and welfare	Kōsei hakusho	Ministry of Health and Welfare	1956
International trade	Tsūshō hakusho	Ministry of International Trade and Industry	1949
Labor	Rōdō hakusho	Ministry of Labor	1950
Living conditions	Kokumin seikatsu hakusho	Economic Planning Agency	1956
Local government finance	Chihō zaisei hakusho	Ministry of Home Affairs	1953
Maritime safety	Kaijō hoan hakusho	Maritime Safety Agency	1956
Monopoly	Dokusen hakusho	Fair Trade Commission	1948
Nuclear safety	Genshiryoku anzen hakusho	Nuclear Safety Commission	1981
Police	Keisatsu hakusho	National Police Agency	1973
Posts and telecommunications	Tsūshin hakusho	Ministry of Posts and Telecommunications	1974
Public employees	Kōmuin hakusho	National Personnel Authority	1978
Science and technology	Kagaku gijutsu hakusho	Science and Technology Agency	1958
Small and medium enterprises	Chūshō kigyō hakusho	Small and Medium Enterprises Agency	1964
Tourism	Kankō hakusho	Prime Minister's Office	1964
Traffic safety	Kōtsū anzen hakusho	Prime Minister's Office	1971
Transport	Un'yu hakusho	Ministry of Transport	1964
Utilization of national land	Kokudo riyō hakusho	National Land Agency	1975
World economy	Sekai keizai hakusho	Economic Planning Agency	1959
Youth	Seishōnen hakusho	Prime Minister's Office	1956

SOURCE: Ōkurashō (Ministry of Finance), Hakusho no hanashi (annual): 1982.

White Russians

(hakkei rojin). Originally, supporters of the tsarist regime who fought the Bolsheviks during the Russian Civil War (1918–20); subsequently, a term applied loosely to stateless Russian émigrés of any number of political persuasions. Of the more than one million Russians who abandoned their homeland in the wake of the October Revolution of 1917, approximately 250,000 entered China via Siberia and Mongolia. About 100,000 settled in Manchuria, principally in Harbin, while most of the remainder gravitated to Shanghai, Tianjin (Tientsin), and Qingdao (Tsingtao). A few joined older Russian communities in Tōkyō, Kōbe, and Hakodate.

Some White Russians were fortunate enough to be able to continue their trades or professions in exile. Lawyers and doctors launched successful practices. Entrepreneurs opened pharmacies, dress shops, and cafés along Shanghai's Nanjing (Nanking) Road or Harbin's Kitaiskaya. Athletic types in Shanghai joined the Russian Regiment of the SHANGHAI INTERNATIONAL SETTLEMENT or the French Concession's Russian Volunteer Detachment. Women found work as governesses, secretaries, or domestic servants. Others, however, failed to secure employment commensurate with their education and social standing. Of these, some eked out a living peddling cheap cloth or acting as doormen. During the 1920s, "Russian girl" became a euphemism for a Caucasian harlot in Shanghai, Harbin, and Kōbe. Regardless of their source of income, nearly all White Russians shared a peculiar vulnerability which derived from their statelessness.

In 1931–32, the Japanese seizure of Manchuria was welcomed by many White Russians as a harbinger of law and order. Within a short time, however, disillusionment had set in, and White Russians were leaving Manchuria by the thousands in favor of Shanghai. Germany's invasion of the USSR in 1941 further strained White Russian–Japanese relations by kindling pro-Soviet patriotism.

White Russians in Harbin hailed the Red Army when it entered the city in August 1945, and thousands of émigrés throughout the Far East responded to Soviet calls for repatriation during the next decade. Today, ethnic Russians have all but disappeared from China, but a few thousand live in Japan and carry Japanese citizenship.

John J. STEPHAN

White Tiger Brigade → Byakkotai

Whitman, Charles Otis (1842–1910)

American biologist who pioneered zoological studies in Japan. Born in Maine. Recommended by biologist Edward Sylvester MORSE, he came to Japan as Morse's successor at Tōkyō University. He taught zoology there from 1879 to 1881. Influenced by his training in Germany, he introduced German-style biological research methods to Japan, including the use of the microscope.

SUZUKI Zenji

Whitney, Courtney (1897–1969)

American lawyer, major general, and close adviser to General Douglas MACARTHUR. Head of the Government Section of SCAP (headquarters of the Allied OCCUPATION of Japan) from 1945 to 1951, he was a dominant figure in the constitutional and legal reform of Japan and in the purge of wartime leaders. He entered the army in 1917 and joined the newly created Air Service in 1920. He received a law degree from National University in Washington in 1923, then in 1927 resigned from the Army Air Corps and went to the Philippines where he practiced law until 1939. Returning to active service in 1940, he was assigned to General MacArthur's staff in 1943 and served throughout the war and most of the Occupation period with MacArthur. When the general was recalled in 1951, Whitney, who later said he "preferred to walk the plank with General MacArthur," returned to the United States and left military service, serving as adviser to and biographer of MacArthur. He wrote *MacArthur, His Rendezvous with History* in 1956.   Richard B. FINN

wild boar

(*inoshishi*). The Japanese wild boar (*Sus scrofa leucomystax*) is a subspecies of the wild boar (*S. scrofa*) found in a wide area of Eurasia. Inhabiting Amami Ōshima, Kyūshū, Shikoku, and Honshū, it is most common in southern Japan, and few are found north of the Kantō area of Honshū. Among wild boars the *inoshishi* is of medium size, with head and body measuring about 140 cm (55 in) in length and weighing approximately 100 kg (220 lb). Body coloring varies greatly, some being almost black and others brown or yellowish. The omnivorous *inoshishi* often inflicts damage on crops grown in mountain valleys. Along with the deer, the *inoshishi* have the highest commercial value of any game in Japan.
          IMAIZUMI Yoshiharu

The *inoshishi* rivals the bear as the most ferocious of Japan's wild animals. Its fierce, direct charge has become a common metaphor for strong action that ignores consequences. Warriors who only attacked and never retreated were once known as *inoshishi musha* (a wild boar *samurai*), and a short, thick neck is described as a "wild boar's neck" (*ikubi*). The domestication and commercial raising of *inoshishi* for their meat first became an important activity in the Meiji period (1868–1912), although it had already been carried out on a small scale in earlier times. The meat of the *inoshishi* is still a highly prized delicacy.   SANEYOSHI Tatsuo

wildcats

(*yamaneko*). In Japanese, *yamaneko* is the common name of the wild species of the family Felidae of a medium or small size. Two species are found in Japan, the Tsushima *yamaneko* (*Prionailurus bengalensis manchurica*; head and body about 45 cm or 18 in long, tail about 20 cm or 8 in long) of the island of Tsushima, Nagasaki Prefecture, and the Iriomote *yamaneko* (*Mayailurus iriomotensis*; head and body about 50 cm or 20 in long, tail about 23 cm or 9 in long) of the island of Iriomotejima, Okinawa Prefecture. The former is a subspecies of the leopard cat (*P. bengalensis*) distributed extensively in Southeast Asia. The body is amber and there are reddish brown vertical stripes on the head. Very few individuals now survive. The latter is endemic to Iriomotejima and was declared a new species in 1967. The body is grayish brown. It is thought to be phylogenetically quite primitive. Its population size was estimated at seventeen, by a 1977 survey. The islands of Iriomotejima and Tsushima have areas of 290 square kilometers (about 112 sq mi) and 682 square kilometers (about 263 square mi) respectively and are the smallest and the second smallest islands in the world inhabited by wildcats; it is feared that the deforestation of both islands and the smallness of the cats' habitats may lead to their eventual extinction. Both species have been designated as protected species.
          IMAIZUMI Yoshiharu

wild ducks

(*kamo*). The general name for small and medium-sized birds of the family Anatidae. Of the 36 species recorded in Japan, 24 are also found in Europe and 20 in North America. Among species not found in Europe and America are the *karugamo* (spotbill duck; *Anas poecilorhyncha*) which breeds throughout Japan and has the same plumage for males and females; the *tomoegamo* (Baikal teal; *A. formosa*), a winter visitor distinguished by yellow and green spots on the head; the *yoshigamo* (falcated teal; *A. falcata*), which breeds in Hokkaidō and has a green and purple crest; the *ryūkyūgamo* (Indian whistling duck; *Dendrocygna javanica*), which breeds in the southern Ryūkyūs; the *akahajiro* (Baer's pochard; *Aythya baeri*), a rare visitor to Japan; and the *oshidori* (mandarin duck). The *kammuri tsukushigamo* (crested shelduck; *Tadorna cristata*) is now extinct; only three preserved specimens remain.   TAKANO Shinji

A duck-hunting expedition by the emperor Ōjin is mentioned in early Japanese mythology recorded in the NIHON SHOKI, and, whether or not this can be accepted as historical fact, it may be surmised on the basis of various mentions in early literature that the elite of the YAMATO COURT crossed Ōsaka Bay to the island of Awajishima to conduct formal hunts. The hunting of wild ducks

continues to this day. The *kamo* became particularly important in the lives of the common people starting in the Edo period (1600–1868) when it was welcomed as a culinary delicacy. In Edo (now Tōkyō) it was sent as a gift during celebrations at the close of the year and savored in rice gruel or in stew during the first days of the New Year.   SAITŌ Shōji

wild geese → geese

Williams, Samuel Wells (1812–1884)

American missionary and sinologist. In 1833 Williams was sent by the American Board of Commissioners for Foreign Missions to Guangzhou (Canton), China, where he took charge of the board's printing shop and became editor of its monthly journal, *The Chinese Repository* (1832–51), which remains an important source of information on mid-19th-century China. In 1837 he sailed to Japan aboard the American ship *Morrison* in an unsuccessful attempt to repatriate Japanese castaways, who taught him their language (see MORRISON INCIDENT). In 1853–54 Williams returned to Japan as the official interpreter for Commodore Matthew C. PERRY in his trade negotiations with the Tokugawa shogunate. On his return to China he became interpreter-secretary in the American legation at Beijing (Peking) and helped conclude the Tianjin (Tientsin) Treaty (1858), which ended the Anglo-French War against China. Among his many works on China are *The Middle Kingdom* (1848; rev ed, 1883) and *A Syllabic Dictionary of the Chinese Language* (1874). Around 1875 he translated the complete texts of Genesis and the Gospel of Matthew into Japanese, but his manuscripts were destroyed in a fire before they could be published. In 1876 Williams returned to the United States and the following year became professor of Chinese language and literature at Yale University.

Willis, William (1837–1894)

British physician. Graduated from Edinburgh University in 1859; joined the British mission to Japan in 1861. During his first years in Japan he treated the British who had been attacked by *samurai* of the Satsuma domain (now Kagoshima Prefecture) in the RICHARDSON AFFAIR and those who were injured in the KAGOSHIMA BOMBARDMENT, the subsequent British retaliatory bombardment of the capital of Satsuma. Willis also aided the Imperial Army's wounded in the BOSHIN CIVIL WAR. After the Meiji Restoration (1868) he was appointed professor and clinical chief of the Igakkō (later Tōkyō University's faculty of medicine). However, when that institution adopted German medical practices as their model in 1870, Willis resigned to accept a position as head of the hospital and medical school in Kagoshima that later became the medical department of Kagoshima University. After a brief trip to England in 1875, Willis returned to Kagoshima the following year. With the outbreak of the SATSUMA REBELLION in 1877, however, he withdrew to Tōkyō, where he remained until his final return to England in 1881.

Willoughby, Charles Augustus (1892–1972)

US Army major general and longtime intelligence chief for General Douglas MACARTHUR. Born in Germany, Willoughby came to the United States as a young man, graduated from Gettysburg College in 1914, and was commissioned as an officer in the army. One of the "Bataan crowd" (senior US Army officers whose association with MacArthur began in the Philippines at the start of World War II), he served with MacArthur from 1941 to 1951. During the OCCUPATION period in Japan he was known for his disagreement with liberal policies advocated by other advisers to MacArthur, especially regarding the economic reform of Japan and the purge of wartime officials. He was the author of several books, including *MacArthur, 1941–1951* (1954) and an account of the activities in Japan of the German spy (for Russia) Richard Sorge (see SORGE INCIDENT), *Shanghai Conspiracy: The Sorge Spy Ring* (1952).
          Richard B. FINN

willows

(*yanagi*). *Salix* spp. Deciduous trees of the family Salicaceae. Various species of willow grow throughout Japan and are widely appreciated for their graceful form. The name *yanagi* is used in Japan to refer to willows in general and, more specifically, to the weeping willow (*S. babylonica*). Also known as *shidareyanagi* or *itoyanagi*, this tree was introduced to Japan from China in early times. It reaches a height of 5–10 meters (16–33 ft). Its supple branches hang down heavy with leaves and sway gracefully in the wind. Its flowers blossom before the leaves enlarge.

The *unryū yanagi* (*S. matsudana* var. *tortuosa*) also originated in China. Its branches are bent and its trunk twisted, giving it a unique appearance. They are often used in flower arrangements. The *kinuyanagi* (*S. kinuyanagi*) is indigenous to northern and central Honshū; the undersides of its leaves are silvery. The *nekoyanagi* (*S. gracilistyla*) is a tree of the pussy willow type, cultivated for the fuzzy catkins which appear on its branches in early spring. The *furisode yanagi* (*S. eucopithecia*) is noted for its luxuriant autumn foliage. The *kuroyanagi* (*S. melanostachys*) has branches covered with blackish flower spikes and which are widely used in Japanese flower arrangements. The *kōriyanagi* (*S. koriyanagi*) is grown for its branches, which are used in making such woven items as trunks and baskets. Since willow wood has a light grain, is soft and pliable and easily cut, it is commonly used as a material for drafting boards, cutting boards, wooden clogs (GETA), and matchsticks.

Matsuda Osamu

wills

(*yuigon; igon*). The legal expression or declaration, made in accordance with a prescribed form, of a person's wishes as to the disposition of his or her property, to take effect after death. In Japanese law, wills can determine the disposition of property or status (such as household headship), or the execution of the will. With respect to property, a will can specify a bequest, an act of endowment, a trust, a disinheritance or revocation of disinheritance, the designation of a share of inheritance and its consignment to a trusteeship, the designation of special beneficiaries, the method and person in charge of dividing the estate, a prohibition against division of the estate, responsibility for bonding the heirs, or the method of reducing bequests. It can also specify the presiding officer for ancestral rites. A will can acknowledge or designate someone as guardian or guardian supervisor. It may also designate an executor or may delegate authority to make such a designation.

Anyone 15 years of age or older who has the mental capacity to make a rational judgment can independently make a valid will, even if a court has judged him incompetent or quasi-incompetent (see PERSON WITHOUT CAPACITY). A will is valid only if made according to the requirements of the CIVIL CODE. A decedent's repeated statements during life or his deathbed words do not have the force of a will. The reason for requiring strict compliance with legal formalities is to minimize family conflicts and false claims. A will can be made only by a single person on a single document.

The Civil Code provides seven procedures for making a will. With a holographic will the testator writes by hand the entire text of the will, the date, and his or her name and affixes his or her seal to the document. Printed documents or voice recordings do not have validity as a written document. A notarial will is composed in the presence of at least two witnesses who hear the testator dictate the will to a notary public, who records it. The will is then signed and sealed by the testator, notary, and witnesses. With a secret will the testator signs and applies his seal to the will, inserts it into an envelope, and uses his seal to close it. A notary public and at least two witnesses then sign and apply their seals to the envelope. Four simplified methods are also recognized under special circumstances. These methods can also be subsumed under the categories of wills made during emergencies and wills made in remote places. These special methods permit an oral recitation to be written as a will by a witness, but such a will must be recognized by a family court. Bequests specified within a will can modify the share of the estate that would otherwise pass to the decedent's successors by law. See also INHERITANCE LAW.

Ono Kōji

wind-bells

(*fūrin*). Small bells of metal, glass, bamboo, or pottery, which are hung under the eaves and tinkle when moved by a breeze. To the Japanese these *fūrin* are a standard feature of summer. To catch the breeze, a feather or a small rectangular piece of poem paper (*tanzaku*) is sometimes attached to the clapper.

Miyamoto Mizuo

winter sports

Winter sports in Japan consisted largely of children's sledding, snowshoeing, and snow games until the 20th century, when Western sports such as skiing, ice skating, ice hockey, bobsledding, and the biathlon were introduced and became popular among adults. Japan's main winter sports areas are found in HOKKAIDŌ, along the coast of the Sea of Japan, and in the central highlands of HONSHŪ, where snow and ice are plentiful. Easily accessible from population centers such as Tōkyō and Ōsaka, these areas have become the sites of many ski and skating resorts.

Skiing was first introduced into Japan in 1911 under the direction of Major Theodor von LERCH, an Austrian military attaché serving in Japan. Under his supervision, soldiers of the Imperial Army practiced skiing in Takada, Niigata Prefecture. In 1913 the first ski club was founded and competitions were held. The Japanese made their Olympic debut at the second Winter Olympics in 1928, and at the 1956 Winter Olympics, IGAYA CHIHARU won a silver medal in the men's slalom event. Igaya's achievement, the highest by a Japanese skier at the time, generated increased enthusiasm for skiing in Japan. The 11th Winter Olympics were held in Sapporo, Hokkaidō, in 1972 (see SAPPORO WINTER OLYMPIC GAMES).

Interest in skiing has continued to grow in recent decades. Approximately 60,000 skiers are currently registered with the Ski Association of Japan, and the total number of skiers probably approaches 10 million. There are approximately 800 ski areas in Japan. In 1973 the Japan Professional Ski Racers' Association was established, and skiing has been gaining popularity as a spectator sport.

Ice skating was first introduced by Americans in Sapporo in 1877, and between 1908 and 1915 Lake SUWA in Nagano Prefecture became a favorite locale for recreational and competitive skating. Japanese have participated in skating events in the Winter Olympics since 1932, and since 1936 in ice hockey events. The National Skating Union of Japan and the Japan Ice Hockey Federation comprise approximately 15,000 skaters, with 473 hockey teams. Japan's first skating rink was built in Tōkyō in 1932, and in the 1960s the number of rinks nationwide increased to 200. Recreational skating has become more popular with widespread construction of skating rinks in the cities, and now over 3 million people regularly enjoy the sport.

Bobsledding, tobogganing, luge, and biathlon groups were formed at the time of the Sapporo Winter Olympics, but few courses exist for these sports and participation remains relatively low. However, enthusiasts are actively working to heighten national interest in these sports and to participate in international competition.

Inoue Keizō

wire-relayed broadcasting

(*yūsen hōsō*). Also known as cable broadcasting. Wire-relayed broadcasts started in Japan in 1932 when the Ministry of Communications (Teishinshō) and NHK (Japan Broadcasting Corporation) built an experimental facility to receive radio transmissions at one place and retransmit them to homes by means of cable. This kind of community reception facility spread to many areas throughout the country during World War II and was used for emergency communications such as air-raid warnings. After the war it spread rapidly in areas where radio reception was poor, e.g., Hokkaidō and southern Kyūshū.

Cable broadcasting also developed in agricultural and mountain villages as an important medium for the announcements of various government agencies and other village information. By attaching a handset to cable broadcasting equipment, subscribers could communicate with each other; in recent years such equipment has also been tied in with the general telephone system.

Today wire-relayed broadcasting is used in urban public address systems and to transmit music, by subscription, to background music systems. CABLE TELEVISION is also being developed.

Hayashi Shigeju

Wirgman, Charles (1832–1891)

English painter, draftsman, and cartoonist. Brother of the painter Theodore Blake Wirgman, Charles left a captaincy in the army to sail for Japan as a correspondent for the *Illustrated London News*. He arrived in Yokohama in 1861 and remained there until his death. Wirgman exercised his humor in the publication of Japan's first magazine, *Japan Punch*, an amusing, often satirical, block-printed periodical illustrated with his sketches, which he published almost monthly between 1862 and the spring of 1887. He displayed his goodwill by teaching the techniques of European painting to many eager Japanese artists of the Meiji period (1868–1912), including the painter and print designer KOBAYASHI KIYOCHIKA and the cartoonist Nozaki Bunzō. In the 1860s he traveled throughout the Japanese countryside with the English diplomat Ernest SATOW, who recorded the delight with which Wirgman's impromptu sketches were received by local maidens and shopkeepers. Two of his watercolors of Japanese subjects were shown in London in the 1870s, and an exhibition of his watercolors, also of Japanese subjects, was held in London in 1921, but his influence was largely personal, and little of his original work seems to have survived.　*Roger* KEYES

wisteria, Japanese

(fuji). *Wisteria floribunda.* Also known as *nodafuji.* A deciduous climbing shrub of the family Leguminosae which grows wild in mountainous areas of Japan and is commonly planted in gardens. The stem grows extemely long, forms numerous branches, and coils around other objects in a clockwise direction. The alternate compound leaves are odd pinnate, each consisting of 13–19 egg-shaped leaflets. The leaves are thin and, when young, both sides are covered with tiny hairs. Around April the plant produces purple, fragrant, butterfly-shaped flowers in large hanging clusters 30–90 centimeters (12–36 in) long. After flowering, it bears flat leguminous seeds. Many varieties have been cultivated as ornamentals, including the *kushakufuji,* with flower clusters reaching 200 centimeters (80 in) long, the white-flowered *shirobanafuji,* the double-flowered *yaefuji,* and the pale red-flowered *akebonofuji.*

A similar species found in Japan is the *yamafuji (W. brachybotrys)* which grows wild in mountainous areas of the southwestern area of the country. Its stem coils counterclockwise, and it has more leaf hairs than the *fuji;* its flower clusters are short, but the flowers are larger. Horticultural varieties of *yamafuji* are also planted in gardens as ornamentals, and a white-flowered type called *shirafuji* is particularly popular.　MATSUDA Osamu

witch hazel

(mansaku). *Hamamelis japonica.* Deciduous tree of the family Hamamelidaceae which grows wild in mountain areas of Japan and is also cultivated. It reaches a height of about 4–6 meters (13–20 ft). The leaves are alternate and oval, and wavy-toothed on the upper part. In early spring, the plant produces clusters of yellow flowers on short branches before the leaves come out. The flower has four sepals and four straplike petals which twist across each other when the flower opens. Varieties found in Japan include the *nishiki mansaku* with purplish red flowers, the *akabana mansaku* and *atetsu mansaku* with reddish flowers, and the *maruba mansaku* with round leaves and red or purplish yellow flowers.　MATSUDA Osamu

witnesses

(shōnin). Persons who appear before a judicial, quasi-judicial, or other investigating body to testify about what they personally experienced. As provided for in the Code of Civil Procedure and the Code of Criminal Procedure, witnesses are used in civil and criminal trials. Any person within the jurisdiction of Japanese law has a duty to serve as a witness before the court. Parties to civil actions and criminal defendants are not called as witnesses in their own cases. In civil cases examination of witnesses is made only on motion by one of the parties, but in criminal cases the court may examine a witness on its own motion. A duly summoned witness who does not appear is punishable and can be taken to the court under arrest. A witness is normally required to take an oath. In civil cases witnesses must be examined first by the party who moved for examination and then cross-examined by the other party. The judge examines thereafter supplementarily. In criminal proceedings such cross-examination is also the rule, although the law specifies that the judge examine witnesses first. A witness can refuse to give testimony that can lead to a criminal prosecution against him or against certain persons having a close relationship with him. Members of certain groups such as physicians, dentists, pharmacists, lawyers, notaries, and clergymen can refuse to testify about facts known through their professional activities. Public officials, cabinet ministers, and members of the Diet can refuse to testify about official secrets unless the court has obtained consent from the supervising agency, the cabinet, or the Diet, respectively. The Code of Criminal Procedure specifi-

cally provides that the agency, the cabinet, or the Diet cannot withhold consent except where the interest of the state would be damaged if it were granted. In civil cases a witness can also refuse to testify when asked about technical or occupational secrets. Witnesses receive a fixed compensation and reimbursement for travel expenses.　*TANIGUCHI Yasuhei*

Witte, Sergei Iul'evich (1849–1915)

Russian diplomat who, as finance minister, worked for the establishment of the Trans-Siberian Railway to foster economic development in Russia's Far Eastern territory. The TRIPARTITE INTERVENTION, which forced Japan to return the Liaodong (Liaotung) Peninsula to China following the Sino-Japanese War of 1894–95, owed much to Witte's diplomatic skills. He was later appointed head of his country's delegation to the peace conference concluding the Russo-Japanese War of 1904–05 and was successful in inducing the Japanese to give up their demands for indemnity (see PORTSMOUTH, TREATY OF). Witte subsequently served as prime minister of Russia (1905–06).

Wo → Wa

wolf, Japanese

(ōkami). *Canis lupus hodophilax,* Temminck. A now extinct subspecies of the common wolf (*Canis lupus lupus,* Linnaeus). In Japanese called *Nippon ōkami* or *hondo ōkami,* and also historically, *ōkami, ōkame,* or *yama inu* ("mountain dog"). Usually the term "Japanese wolf" does not include the very large Hokkaidō or Yezo wolf (*Canis lupus rex,* Pocock or *Canis lupus hattai,* Kishida), which belonged to a different subspecies ranging in the Hokkaidō region until the middle of the Meiji period (1868–1912). The Japanese wolf was confined to Honshū, Shikoku, and Kyūshū, and died out at approximately the same time.

Intact stuffed or skeletal specimens of the Japanese wolf are rare, but a considerable number of osteological materials have been studied. The general conformation of the Japanese wolf is distinguished from that of the continental common wolf by a smaller body size and shorter legs. The average length of the body including the head is 104 centimeters (41 in) and the tail approximately 30 centimeters (12 in). The coat color is generally wolfish gray, with some darker or brownish shades. The skull is rather broad and short, and the stop on the profile line is usually not as clearly developed as in the dog. Distinguishing marks of the cranium of the Japanese wolf are that the tympanic bullae are rather small and flat, and the posterior end of the center line of the hard palate (internal nares) has an indented notch rather than a small projection as seen in other wolf subspecies. This characteristic is found only in the Korean wolf and in a few individuals of other East Asian wolves. The coronoid process of the ascending ramus has a turned-back apex. According to measurements taken from currently available specimens (about 20 individuals), the length of the upper carnassial tooth (P^4: the fourth premolar of the upper jaw) ranges between 20.5 and 23.3 millimeters, averaging 21.78 millimeters; the length of the lower carnassial tooth (M_1: the first molar of the lower jaw) is between 24 and 28.51 millimeters, averaging 25.61 millimeters. The width of the first molar of the upper jaw (M^1) is comparatively narrow. These measurements are significant for distinguishing the skulls of Japanese wolves from those of dogs.

The behavior of the Japanese wolf differs little from that of the continental common wolf; however, it seems to have adapted in ways better suited to the mountainous and heavily forested Japanese environment. It is presumed that a considerable number of Japanese wolves existed on the major islands until quite recently. The reason for their relatively rapid extinction is not well established. The two most plausible explanations are an epidemic of canine distemper in the late 19th century, and rapid ecological changes associated with land development. In this latter case, deforestation with a consequent decrease of the deer population (considered a major prey of the wolf in Japan) and a government ban on the dumping of domestic animal carcasses were probably leading factors. There is also speculation that some of the remaining Japanese wolves were absorbed into the feral dog population, which was always fairly large. The Japanese wolf, however, has no relationship to the origin of the indigenous Japanese dog (see DOG, JAPANESE).

Although there are still occasional reports of an individual or small packs of these wolves in remote areas, none of these has been authenticated. The last true specimen of the Japanese wolf was acquired in Nara Prefecture in 1904 or 1905 and sent to the British Museum. In the Hokkaidō area, because of wolf depredation upon government-sponsored animal husbandry, deliberate efforts to exterminate the wolf by poisoning were made. As a result the Hokkaidō wolf disappeared around 1889.

The paleontological record shows that when the Japanese islands were connected to the Asian continent in the Pleistocene period, a subspecies of large wolf, the same size as the recent Hokkaidō and Siberian wolves, once roamed the area. Their remains have been found sporadically in Upper Pleistocene deposits in Honshū and Shikoku. By the end of the Pleistocene period, however, this large wolf either died out or retreated further north and was gradually replaced by a smaller subspecies, possibly of southern continental origins. At the time the Japanese archipelago separated from the mainland, these smaller wolves were dominant. The wolf bones excavated from Jōmon-period sites are almost all of this smaller type, comparable to those of the recently extant Japanese wolves. There is some evidence that even into historical times a slightly larger wolf (similar to the medium-size modern wolves of China and Korea) may have existed in some parts of Japan. However, since the range of individual variation among wolves is great, the taxonomic status of these few exceptional cases is not certain.

The etymology of the word ōkami is not entirely clear. In ancient times names such as ōkami ("great god"), magami ("true god"), or ōkuchi no magami ("true god with the big mouth") were used to refer to the wolf. Common people used terms such as ōkame (from ōkami), yama no kami ("mountain god"), or o inu sama ("honorable dog"). It is thought that possibly the use of the original name of the animal was tabooed for religious reasons, perhaps motivated by awe or respect, and the eponymous term ōkami ("great god") came into common use.

The animal was worshiped as a god who could protect people from misfortune, disease, and damage to crops by wild animals. Even now shrines sacred to the wolf and related folk rituals are found sporadically in remote regions. The skull of the wolf (or often, in fact, a dog's skull) was used as a charm for the security of the family and was thought to be useful in chasing the demons of mental disease, especially "fox possession" (see FOXES). Such worship of the wolf was once pervasive in mountainous areas in Japan and may have some connection with the wolf cult or totemism as found in northeast Asia.

Throughout history, the Japanese wolf has often been confused with the feral dog and vice versa, being called yama inu, yama no inu, or oinu. In many cases the terms have been used synonymously, for example, in documents or paintings when one or the other is obviously mistakenly identified.

The position of the wolf in legend and superstition has been highly ambivalent. Revered and viewed as a protector on the one hand, the wolf has also been feared and loathed. Fear of the wolf may have been imported with Chinese culture. Certain beliefs held that wolves scavenged human graves or attacked people with poisonous fangs. There is also a legend of wolves gathering in hordes of a thousand (sembiki ōkami). It was thought that a wolf attacked a solitary traveler by jumping over his head, turning, and biting him to death. Consequently, travelers believed that to hold a dagger over their heads was an effective prophylactic charm. Lacking such, it was thought that even long fingernails, or a woman's ornamental hairpin would do.

The legend of the wolf who follows a traveler from a distance (okuri ōkami) is a good example of the ambivalence attached to the wolf. If a traveler suspected he was being followed, he was not to turn around until he reached a village, lest he be attacked. It was also thought that the "following wolf" was a protector on the road. The scientific nomenclature of the Japanese wolf incorporates this legend in the term "hodophylax."

■——Hiraiwa Yonekichi, Inu to ōkami (1942). Imaizumi Yoshinori, Nippon honyū dōbutsu zusetsu (1949). Naora Nobuo, Nipponsan ōkami no kenkyū (1965). Saitō Hirokichi, Nihon no inu to ōkami (1964). Yanagita Kunio, Rōshi Zatsuwa (1932, 1933).

Hiroshi SAKAMOTO

women in Japanese religion

Women's relations with religion have a complex history in Japan, because of both the changing social status of women and the wide variety of religious beliefs. In shamanistic folk religion and Shintō, women have been thought to have special power to communicate with the divine. Throughout the premodern period, itinerant women associated with many different religious groups helped develop and spread oral traditions and the performing arts, which were originally linked with popular religion. But from the 6th century on, certain Buddhist and Confucian tenets supported views of women's inferiority, although some women of the elite actively promoted Buddhism and many more became Buddhist nuns. Certain popular Buddhist sects developing around the 13th century welcomed men and women believers equally, asserting that Buddha's grace and one's faith could transcend gender; Christianity welcomed women believers both in the 16th century and, after the long Tokugawa repression, in modern times. In the 19th and 20th centuries the tradition of women as influential links with the divine reemerged with the founding of several new religions. Furthermore, women have long been largely responsible for religious observances within homes and for the support of established religious sects and movements.

Shamanism and Shintō——Both north Asian and Pacific-Southeast Asian elements are thought to have combined in ancient Japanese folk religion. As in many other cultures, women's procreative power was regarded as sacred, and this led to their major role in agricultural rites, especially rice-planting. But more significantly, unlike the standard practice in north Asian nomadic cultures, SHAMANISM in Japan (as in Korea and the Ryūkyū Islands) became partly the province of women. This factor—as well as woman-centered marriage patterns in which a husband joined his wife's family or lived separately—contributed to women's high status in early Japanese society. The task of women shamans called MIKO was to mediate between humanity and divine forces, usually by entering a trance and communicating a message from the divine, often in a particular manifestation that had possessed them. Some of them used a bow made from wood of the azusa tree to help link them with the kami, so they were sometimes called azusa-miko.

Such attributes seem to have led to actual ruling power for some women. The 3rd-century Chinese chronicle WEI ZHI (Wei chih) refers to the "sorcery" of the woman ruler HIMIKO, and the early 8th century chronicle KOJIKI describes how the empress JINGŪ was possessed by a kami so powerful that it slew her husband, whose place she then took in leading an expedition to Korea.

The tradition of powerful women shamans is clearly linked to the designation of the goddess AMATERASU ŌMIKAMI as the principal deity in the SHINTŌ pantheon. Since she was considered the ancestress of the imperial family, her worship was actively promoted by the YAMATO COURT. Legend has it that ceremonies in her honor were held within the emperor's residence until the (legendary) 10th emperor SUJIN had his daughter Toyosukiirihime establish a separate shrine nearby. YAMATOHIME (daughter of the [legendary] 11th emperor Suinin) was sent to establish a more distant permanent site of worship for the goddess at ISE SHRINE. This began the custom (which lasted until the 14th century) of appointing at the start of each new reign an imperial princess to serve as the high priestess (saigū) at Ise; still another princess (designated the saiin) was sent to preside at the KAMO SHRINES. In the countryside, priestesses were often selected as children to serve for several years at local shrines.

The powerful role of women in both religion and government began to wane from the 6th century on, with the adoption of different beliefs and patterns of rule from mainland Asia. The process of change was gradual and uneven, so that, for example, a miko might summon a spirit which would then be dealt with by a Buddhist priest, and there were attempts to equate the goddess Amaterasu with the "Sun Buddha" DAINICHI (Skt: Mahāvairocana; see RYŌBU SHINTŌ). However, starting at the court and spreading throughout the countryside, women shamans at last became little more than passive vessels for divine possession that would generally be induced and interpreted by men. Yet certain shamanistic practices have continued even up into modern times. Although such customs were officially banned in 1873, since the new government wished to eliminate "superstition" and "purify" Shintō, many women were still surreptitiously called on to summon spirits. In fact, a surprising number of women openly resumed such work with the new religious freedom after World War II.

Some scholars believe that Okinawa's culture preserved certain patterns long lost in Japan proper, and they give as an example the existence in Okinawa of not only women mediums (yuta) but also politically influential priestesses (nuru; in Japanized pronunciation, noro). Until the Japanese annexation of the Ryūkyū Islands in 1879, a female religious hierarchy paralleled and supported the male political hierarchy, and a few surviving village *nuru* continue their ceremonies even today.

Religious ceremonies and the performing arts have been linked in most cultures, but in Japan women more or less associated with religious groups have had an unusually prominent role in developing and spreading various dances, songs, and narratives. Legend has it that the female divinity Amenouzume no Mikoto danced to lure the goddess Amaterasu out from hiding, and this story gave rise to the custom of having four women (called *sarume*) assigned to dance at certain early court ceremonies. More important, there were many women among the various traveling performers who helped spread a wide range of cultural and religious traditions throughout the countryside. While some of these women were associated with Buddhism (see below), others performed in only partly religious dance-plays (SARUGAKU), and still others carried on the ancient practices of shamans and mediums. They often followed a set route each year to offer their services, then returned to their own home-base settlements *(miko-mura)*. The dances of "walking shamans" *(arukimiko)*, combined with Buddhist devotional dances (NEMBUTSU ODORI), contributed in the early 17th century to the performances of OKUNI, the woman credited with the founding of *kabuki* theater. Even today, blind women singers and narrative-reciters (GOZE) and sightless women paid to communicate with the dead *(itako)* continue to make their rounds, generally in northern Honshū.

Buddhism—— The original Buddhist texts show ambivalence on women's salvation: some imply women's equality, while others state that women are inherently impure and must be reincarnated as men before attaining Nirvana. Legend has it that the Buddha was reluctant to allow women to enter monastic orders, but then relented when his own mother (or, in some versions, aunt) wished to become a nun. Other enlightened women also appear as patrons of Buddhism in the sutras. However, sutra passages devaluing women were later emphasized to support patriarchal tenets.

When Korean and Chinese cultural imports, including modified Buddhism, came to be seen as tools for strengthening imperial power in Japan, both men and women of the elite became involved in promoting such beliefs and practices. As early as the 6th century, SOGA NO UMAKO sponsored three women to become Buddhist nuns; one of them, Zenshin Ni (b 566?), even went to the Korean state of Paekche to study Buddhism. In the mid-8th century, the founding of temples for nuns, as well as for monks, was decreed throughout the country (see KOKUBUNJI). The reigning empress KŌKEN and the empresses KŌMYŌ and DANRIN were especially active in promoting Buddhism. During the Heian period (794–1185), elite women commonly attended Buddhist religious ceremonies and went into retreat at Buddhist temples; many—·including members of the imperial family for whom there were no suitable marriage partners—eventually cut their hair and became nuns *(ama* or *bikuni)*, although some of these continued to live with their families. A few women underwent rigorous rituals with ascetic masters (HIJIRI) in order to "purify" themselves, but beliefs about women's general inferiority in spiritual matters still led to barring them from certain sacred places (see NYONIN KINZEI).

From early in the Kamakura period (1185–1333), rapidly spreading popular Buddhist movements, especially the JŌDO SECT and JŌDO SHIN SECT, taught that all people—regardless of social status, sex, or even moral worth—could achieve rebirth in the Pure Land paradise if they called on the mercy of Amida Buddha. SHINRAN, founder of the Jōdo Shin sect, defied tradition by encouraging priests to marry, and he was aided in his evangelism by his wife Eshin Ni (1182–1268?) and their daughter Kakushin Ni (1224–83).

Many laymen became active in forming groups called *kō*, which organized pilgrimages and collected money for the support of temples (and Shintō shrines as well). While many women of the lower classes thus became fervent Buddhist believers, upper-class women also continued to promote the founding of temples and to became nuns. In fact, 15 elite nuns' temples (designated *bikuni go-sho*) were founded or headed by an imperial princess or other high-born woman; there were also five designated Zen temples for nuns (the Amadera Gozan) in both Kamakura and Kyōto. Illustrious nuns included ABUTSU NI, who wrote the travel diary *Izayoi nikki* in the 13th century; Bunchi Ni (or Bunchi Nyoō; 1619–97), first daughter of Emperor GO-MIZUNOO; and Tenshū Ni (1609–45), daughter of TOYOTOMI HIDEYORI, who became one of the abbesses of the temple TŌKEIJI, a refuge for wives seeking divorce (see KAKEKOMIDERA). But there were also nuns from other backgrounds as well: for example, a nun from a *sake*-brewer's family, Jion Ni (1716–78), helped

ISHIDA BAIGAN promote his merchant-oriented ethical system, SHINGAKU.

Itinerant nuns helped spread popular Buddhist beliefs, especially through their explication of "hell scrolls"; some were known as singing nuns *(uta bikuni)*, nuns collecting temple contributions *(kanjin bikuni)*, or nuns associated with the Kumano shrines (Kumano *bikuni)*. Sometimes, especially in the 17th and 18th centuries, women wearing nun's habits engaged in prostitution. With the Meiji Restoration of 1868, women of the imperial family and elite were generally no longer allowed to become nuns, although other women continued to do so. In Japan today, there are still a number of nuns' temples *(amadera)*, and women form around one-third of the total Buddhist clergy.

Christianity—— When Christianity entered Japan in the mid-16th century, it gained women converts among all classes, from the wives and daughters of *daimyō* lords (such as HOSOKAWA GRACIA) to the peasant women who fought and died beside their men in the SHIMABARA UPRISING of 1637–38. Again, when Christianity was officially reintroduced to Japan in the 1870s, women from many different backgrounds were influenced. Hundreds of girls benefited from the comparatively progressive education at MISSION SCHOOLS. Some Christian women became prominent educators themselves, including TSUDA UMEKO, KAWAI MICHI, YASUI TETSU, and HANI MOTOKO.

Social reform efforts, such as the antiprostitution movement, have been much inspired by Christian ideals, and thousands of Japanese women have participated in Christian activist groups. Even before 1900, YAJIMA KAJIKO founded the KYŌFŪKAI (Japan's version of the Woman's Christian Temperance Union), and YAMAMURO KIEKO worked beside her husband to establish the Japanese branch of the SALVATION ARMY. These groups are still active in Japan today, as is the YWCA (Young Women's Christian Association), which was long led by the woman minister UEMURA TAMAKI.

New Religions—— Given the deep-rooted Japanese belief in women's affinity for the divine, it seems hardly surprising that several women were instrumental in founding some of the NEW RELIGIONS in Japan from the mid-19th century on. Among the best known are NAKAYAMA MIKI, founder of TENRIKYŌ, and DEGUCHI NAO, founder of ŌMOTO. Another woman, KOTANI KIMI, founded in 1925 the REIYŪKAI, based on Nichiren Buddhism; a vigorous offshoot of this group, the RISSHŌ KŌSEIKAI, was started in 1938 partly through the inspiration of still another woman, Naganuma Myōkō (1889–1957). After World War II, KITAMURA SAYO—called the Great Goddess (Ōgamisama) by her followers—led the Tenshō Kōtai Jingū Kyō, popularly known as the "dancing religion" *(odoru shūkyō)*. Significantly, all of these "living goddesses" in modern times showed the characteristic shaman's sequence of physical and spiritual hardship, "possession by a god," and great personal charisma.

In Japan today, women, especially older women, are generally the most numerous and dedicated supporters of the new religions, as well as of the long-established Buddhist sects and of the still surviving practices associated with Shintō and folk religion.

OGURI Junko and Nancy ANDREW

women in Japan, history of

Japanese history provides striking examples of changes in the status of women, linked with other broad socioeconomic trends. A woman-centered marriage pattern in ancient times contributed to considerable religious and political influence by women. Then the growing acceptance of Confucian and Buddhist views on women's inferiority from the 6th century onward both reflected and reinforced a shift toward patriarchal family structure. However, upper-class women were often highly literate, and they retained such rights as property inheritance until these were eroded by the transition to a war-oriented feudal economy beginning in the 12th century. The rigid social controls of the Edo period (1600–1868) decreed women's subordination, but women's work was always indispensable not only in agriculture but also in the developing trades of the cities. Women were generally less subject to violence and less isolated from men in Japan than in certain other cultures, and they were never crippled by any such practice as the Chinese foot-binding. Furthermore, their resourcefulness, endurance, and strength of character were often expected to equal or exceed that of any man.

Early High Status—— Modern studies of Japanese women, pioneered by the woman historian TAKAMURE ITSUE, make use of family records, anthropological data, mythology, and early literature to show how Japanese marriages originally centered on women. Until at least the 11th century, it was customary at all social levels for a husband to join the family of his wife (in the marriage pattern called MUKOIRIKON) or to live separately and visit his wife on certain nights (a pattern called *kayoi kekkon*). Furthermore, a daughter of a property-holding family was entitled to the family house and a share of income rights when an inheritance was divided. These practices and a fairly lenient attitude toward sexuality are reflected in the 8th-century poetry collection MAN'YŌSHŪ (which includes many poems by women such as ŌTOMO NO SAKANOUE NO IRATSUME) and the famous 11th-century novel THE TALE OF GENJI by the court lady MURASAKI SHIKIBU.

Marriage between children of the same father was originally tolerated if their mothers were different; in fact, the archaic term *se* could mean either a lover, husband, or brother. But as paternity came to be considered more important, incest was increasingly restricted. A striking example of changing mores can be seen in the two different accounts of the 5th-century imperial princess Sotoori-hime (also known as Karu no Ōiratsume). The early-8th-century record of myth and history, KOJIKI, says that the love between the princess and her brother the crown prince led to his banishment, but she followed him and they reunited to live together. However, in a second version of the same story in the NIHON SHOKI, a history compiled only slightly later but more influenced by Confucianism, the princess alone was banished.

Another hint of the shift toward male dominance appears even in the *Kojiki* legend of the deities IZANAGI AND IZANAMI: the female deity Izanami was blamed for the birth of a deformed offspring. Because she had spoken first in her marriage rite with the male Izanagi, the rite had to be performed again "properly," with the male deity taking the initiative.

It is not clear how long woman-centered families persisted in the countryside, but apparently these were customary among peasants for some centuries after the upper classes, beginning with the warriors, adopted the practice of sending a bride to join her husband's family (a pattern called YOMEIRIKON), with more attention paid to economic or other advantages for both families than to the preferences of the young couple. This type of marriage and related mores eventually spread to all social levels, but vestiges of the older ways seem to have remained in certain rural areas until as late as the 19th century. For example, in some parts of northeastern Japan, the first child of either sex was expected to be the heir; in the case of a daughter, her husband was then adopted into the family. See also KINSHIP; YOBAI; SEX IN JAPANESE FOLK CULTURE.

Besides their early central role in families, Japanese women have traditionally had an unusually prominent role in dealing with the supernatural. As in almost all early cultures, people in prehistoric Japan produced ceramic figures celebrating woman's fertility (see JŌMON FIGURINES). Japan's native religion, SHINTŌ, has been one of the few religions in the world to retain a principal female deity, the goddess AMATERASU ŌMIKAMI, who is thought to have evolved from the concept of a shamaness mediating between humanity and supernatural beings. Her main place of worship, the Inner Shrine of the ISE SHRINE, is said to have been founded by the princess YAMA-TOHIME; the high priestesses *(saigū)* there were members of the imperial family until the 14th century. Also serving at Shintō shrines were two of the major women poets of the *Man'yōshū*: NUKATA NO ŌKIMI and SANO NO CHIGAMI NO OTOME. Even today, the tradition of women's importance in Shintō is continued by shrine-maidens (still called MIKO, the original term for shamaness) and occasionally women serving as priests (*negi* or KANNUSHI).

Furthermore, women's major role in Shintō and SHAMANISM was apparently linked with actual ruling power in early Japan, as evidenced by such semilegendary figures as the priestess-queen HI-MIKO and the warrior-empress JINGŪ. Some scholars, perhaps in an effort to deny a tradition of women rulers, have claimed that the stories of Yamatohime, Himiko, and Jingū refer to just one historical figure rather than many, but there is much evidence to the contrary.

In fact, in the 7th and 8th centuries, it was even acceptable for a woman to reign as "emperor" *(tennō)*, and six women did so: SUIKO (r 593–628), SAIMEI (r 655–661; also r 642–645 under the name Kō-gyoku), JITŌ (r 686–697), Gemmei (r 707–715), Genshō (r 715–724), and KŌKEN (r 749–758; also r 764–770 under the name Shōtoku). But after the court moved to Heiankyō (Kyōto) in 794, women *tennō* did not appear again until the 17th and 18th centuries, when the imperial court had no ruling power; the two at that time were Mei-shō (r 1629–43) and Go-Sakuramachi (r 1762–70).

From the Taika Reform through the Heian Period——There is still much debate over the reasons for the shift to a patriarchal family pattern and women's resultant loss of status. One common explanation is the development of agriculture, but that had taken place in Japan long before this shift, and in any case, a woman-centered agricultural society is not inconceivable. It would also clearly be an oversimplification to say that new attitudes devaluing women were accepted *in toto* from mainland Asia, yet certain concepts found in the imported CONFUCIANISM and BUDDHISM could readily be used to justify such change.

Under the new Confucian-style laws made as part of the TAIKA REFORM in the mid-7th century, women were barred from becoming government officials *(kanri)* and a woman's share of government-distributed land (KUBUNDEN) was set at two-thirds of that for a man. However, Confucian-style patriarchal sex morals took many more centuries to spread, even among the elite. The ideal of an extended patriarchal family, "three generations under one roof," was never institutionalized in Japan, as it was in China. Instead, continuity of the "stem family" (see IE) was most emphasized, and this could be maintained by adoption. In fact, Japanese have often valued fictive kinship ties (such as to a feudal lord or other leader) more than blood ties.

Some sects of Buddhism taught that women were sinful temptresses who must be reborn as men before they could attain enlightenment. Yet many women of the elite actively promoted the spread of Buddhism—notably the empresses KŌMYŌ and DANRIN. Furthermore, beginning with the 6th-century nun Zenshin Ni, it became common for women of high-ranking families to take vows as Buddhist nuns in later life. See also WOMEN IN JAPANESE RELIGION; NYONIN KINZEI.

Also emerging around this time were two customs that would affect many women's lives throughout the rest of Japan's premodern history: one was the practice of sending hostages to cement alliances and the other was the related practice, continued into modern times, of using marriages to establish ties between families (see KEIBATSU). As early as the 6th century, local chieftains sent female relatives as hostages (UNEME) to the YAMATO COURT (ca 4th century–ca mid 7th century). Then, in the following centuries, the imperial court was dominated by so-called marriage politics.

Even before the capital was established at Nara in 710, the FUJI-WARA FAMILY came to control the court largely through the practice of marrying Fujiwara women to emperors whenever possible. To begin with, FUJIWARA NO FUHITO married two of his daughters to two successive emperors: Fujiwara no Miyako (also known as Kyūshi; d 754) was married in 697 to Emperor MOMMU and gave birth to the future emperor SHŌMU, then Shōmu was eventually married to his aunt, Fuhito's younger daughter (later Empress Kō-myō) by his influential wife AGATA NO INUKAI NO TACHIBANA NO MICHIYO.

With such practices continuing, sexual and political problems were often entangled at the imperial court during the Heian period (794–1185; for an example, see KUSUKO INCIDENT). Around the end of the 10th century, to balance factions within the Fujiwara family, Emperor Ichijō was made to keep simultaneously two consorts with the nearly equal ranks of KŌGŌ and CHŪGŪ: they were FUJIWARA NO TEISHI and her cousin Shōshi (JŌTŌ MON'IN).

Centered around the Heian court, often portraying its affairs as well as their own, were the great women writers of the 9th through 12th centuries: ONO NO KOMACHI, Lady ISE, SEI SHŌNAGON, Mura-saki Shikibu, IZUMI SHIKIBU, AKAZOME EMON, and the authors of the poetic diaries KAGERŌ NIKKI, SARASHINA NIKKI, and SANUKI NO SUKE NO NIKKI. While their male relatives struggled to master the more prestigious, imported styles of Chinese poetry and prose, such women developed new literary forms in pure and elegant Japanese. Yet although their works are now recognized among the finest in literature, with a lasting impact on Japan's aesthetics, little is known about these women's individual lives or even their true names; they are called by literary sobriquets or identified only as some man's mother or daughter (as in the case of the 13th-century poet FUJI-WARA NO TOSHINARI NO MUSUME).

The Impact of Warfare——The ever-present danger of warfare in Japan from the 12th through the 16th century made it most practical for only one person (the oldest, or sometimes the ablest, son) to inherit family property, in order to better consolidate lands and defend them against outsiders. Naturally, women's eventual loss of property rights made them dependent on their male relatives. Such altered family patterns, war, and other social changes such as the development of cities led to a growth of prostitution, and brothels were established at major transportation centers.

The harsh and sometimes precarious life of the provincial warrior demanded courage and endurance from women as well as men. Women of the warrior class were expected to strive, and even die, for family honor if necessary; to help defend their homes, they were trained in certain martial arts, especially the use of a blade-headed staff (NAGINATA). If their husbands died, they were expected to take responsibility for raising their children in the warrior tradition. In medieval legend and literature there are vignettes of striking bravery by women, such as TOMOE GOZEN riding to battle, and SHIZUKA GOZEN defiantly dancing before her captors. A few women used their status as relatives of ruling warriors to exercise political power themselves (for example; IKE NO ZENNI, HŌJŌ MASAKO, and HINO TOMIKO).

For many warrior families, the struggle to better their positions often led to "strategic marriages" (seiryaku kekkon) or the outright surrender of female relatives as hostages. TOYOTOMI HIDEYOSHI was especially notorious in this regard: he forced his half-sister Asahi Hime (1543–90) to leave her current husband and marry TOKUGAWA IEYASU in 1586, and then a few months later Hideyoshi sent as an additional hostage his own mother (known as Ōmandokoro or Tenzui In; 1500–1592). Around the same time another famous political pawn, ODANI NO KATA (sister of ODA NOBUNAGA), chose death in a flaming castle rather than the prospect of a third hostage-marriage, but her three daughters were used to promote further alliances. The eldest of them, YODOGIMI, became the mother of Hideyoshi's two sons, but in 1615 she died in the same manner as her mother (see ŌSAKA CASTLE, SIEGES OF).

The unsettled conditions of the 12th through the 16th centuries encouraged the spread of new types of popular Buddhism (the JŌDO SECT and JŌDO SHIN SECT) with their promise of salvation for all believers, including women, in paradise after death. In the 13th century the priest SHINRAN, founder of the Jōdo Shin sect, defied convention by encouraging priests to marry; he was aided in his evangelism by his wife Eshin Ni (1182–1268?) and their daughter Kakushin Ni (1224–83). In the later 16th century Christianity became popular at both high and low social levels, and it was espoused by such women as HOSOKAWA GRACIA.

The era of the greatest women writers was past by the end of the 12th century, but some noteworthy poems were still produced by women, including those of Princess SHIKISHI, composed around 1200; the 13th-century KENREI MON'IN UKYŌ NO DAIBU SHŪ; and the 14th-century works of EIFUKU MON'IN and her circle. Two important medieval women's diaries are that of ABUTSU NI, written as she traveled to Kamakura to appeal a law case, and the TOWAZUGATARI (tr The Confessions of Lady Nijō, 1973).

On the popular level, strong and even domineering women of the lower classes were sometimes depicted in story collections and comic plays (SETSUWA BUNGAKU; KYŌGEN). Female ghosts and demons (hannya) were common figures in literature and folklore, as were the powerful and mysterious "snow woman" (YUKI ONNA) and "mountain woman" (YAMAMBA).

Intinerant singing nuns (uta bikuni) helped spread nationwide an oral tradition of both religious and secular tales. Songs and dances were also spread by women entertainers called SHIRABYŌSHI and kugutsume. Other women entertainers and dancers, originally connected with Shintō shrines, were known as arukimiko; at the beginning of the 17th century, this tradition produced the woman performer OKUNI, who is credited with the founding of KABUKI theater.

The Edo Period

The strictures considered proper for women during the Edo period were outlined in the 18th-century, Confucian-style moralistic work ONNA DAIGAKU. It stressed that a woman should obey her parents until her marriage, then her husband and his family, then her sons in her old age: in short, all individual interests should be secondary to those of the family. This work also said that a wife should be humble, frugal, and hard-working and always remember that she could readily be divorced for disobedience, barrenness, jealousy, ill health, or even for talking too much. In contrast, divorce was legally granted to a wife only if her husband abandoned her or committed a serious crime, or in rare cases if she fled from her home to one of the two official "divorce temples" (KAKEKOMIDERA). Women's adultery could be punished by death, but it was permissible for wealthy men to maintain concubines outside or inside their homes. However, the status of such secondary wives or mistresses (mekake), which had been comparatively high in preceding eras, declined to that of near-servants.

The day-to-day reality of women's domestic lives may not usually have been as harsh as the Onna daigaku and official laws indicate; it seems clear that Japanese women in the Edo period, as they do today, took pride in controlling the management of their homes. In particular, older wives or mothers of the official household head were accorded considerable respect and freedom of action. A woman also had more social leverage if her husband had been "adopted" into her family, in a pattern resembling the former woman-centered marriages (see ADOPTION). Many young girls from the lower classes became servants for a few years in the homes of elite families, then married and introduced to some extent the customs of such homes into their own, in this way continuing women's role as channels for contact between different areas and social levels.

At the higher levels of society, strategic marriages were still the rule. For example, to strengthen ties between the imperial court and the Tokugawa shogunate, TOKUGAWA KAZUKO was sent to be an imperial consort in 1620, and as late as 1862 the imperial princess KAZU was forced to marry the shōgun TOKUGAWA IEMOCHI. The keeping of female hostages was institutionalized in the practice of forcing daimyō lords to leave their wives in Edo (now Tōkyō) whenever they returned to their own domains (see SANKIN KŌTAI). Certain families vied to send their daughters to the shōgun's harem (ŌOKU), since his favorites were supposedly able to promote the careers of their male relatives. At least one woman, KASUGA NO TSUBONE, is said to have influenced the shogunal succession.

Despite the limitations imposed by law and custom, women at other social levels benefited in many ways from the peace of these centuries, which fostered greater stability in the countryside and lively economic and cultural development in the cities. Education also spread, especially through the village schools (TERAKOYA); women's literacy in this period has been estimated at around 15 percent, a relatively high figure for a premodern society.

Life was undeniably hard in farming and fishing villages, where over 80 percent of the population lived. Women's work in agriculture, such as planting rice and tending silkworms, was at least as demanding as men's work. (AMA, women who dive to gather seaweed and shellfish, were even expected to provide most of the support for their families.) But, except for several serious famines, there was a gradually rising standard of living in the countryside, largely due to stabilized population growth. Many rural women were not married until their early twenties, and they tended to limit the number of their children by abortion or infanticide (mabiki) if other methods failed. In many rural areas, girls in their mid-teens entered "girls' groups" (musume-gumi), which often allowed them to live separately from their parents and to have some part in the choice of their marriage partners. (See also WAKAMONO-GUMI.)

The influx to the cities of many men without their families prompted the Tokugawa shogunate, like previous shogunates, to license and supervise brothel districts (yūkaku) as part of its system of rigid social control. (In fact, there were also many unlicensed prostitutes outside such districts.) YOSHIWARA, northeast of Edo's center, became the best known of these "pleasure quarters," with over 2,000 prostitutes. Their lives were restricted and often tragic, since most had been indentured there because of poverty. Yet certain high-ranking courtesans (tayū or oiran) became famous for their wit, artistic skill, and character as well as their beauty, and a few customers even went bankrupt in courting them. Sometimes customers paid large sums to free women permanently from the brothels and then married them. Alongside the complicated classifications of the courtesans, there emerged a more or less separate group of women dancers and musicians, now best known by the name GEISHA.

The courtesans drew attention the way movie stars do in modern times; they were a favorite subject for woodblock print artists (see UKIYO-E), for novelists such as SAIKAKU, and for the creators of BUNRAKU puppet-plays and kabuki performances. In addition, such purveyors of popular culture delighted in the thinly disguised portrayal of scandals in the upper classes, including the shōgun's household (see SEN HIME and EJIMA INCIDENT). They also spread tales of the loves and tragedies of the lower classes: for example, the destructive MEIREKI FIRE of 1657 and the Tenna fire of 1682 in Edo were each dramatized as being caused by a young woman's frustrated passion.

Some women continued to write notable poetry from the 17th through the early 19th centuries; they included Inoue Tsūjo (1660–1738), ARAKIDA REIJO, KAGA NO CHIYO, and ŌTAGAKI RENGETSU. In the 18th century, IKE NO GYOKURAN earned a good reputation as a painter. Also during this period, folk songs were spread and developed by wandering blind women musicians (GOZE).

Finally, women still maintained a major role in Shintō and shamanistic folk religion. One woman, NAKAYAMA MIKI, founded a new religion called TENRIKYŌ shortly before Japan became open to contact with Western nations in the mid-19th century.

See also CLOTHING; COSMETICS; FAMILY; FEMININE LANGUAGE; HAIRSTYLES; MARRIAGE; PROSTITUTION.　　　*Nancy* ANDREW

Women and Modernization

Women and Modernization——The vast social changes sweeping Japan during its modernization from the 1860s to the 1940s affected women's lives with regard to their education, their work, and in general ways. However the 1898 Meiji CIVIL CODE generally reflected traditional family law and ideology. As in the West, women were granted only limited rights to divorce or to own property, and a wife required her husband's consent in certain legal actions. Although the traditional ideal of women as "good wives and wise mothers" (*ryōsai kembo*) remained strong, some Japanese absorbed liberal ideals from the West and campaigned for women's suffrage and other rights until the militarist suppression of the late 1930s. Legal controls and socioeconomic conditions continued to restrict women's activities even more than those of men throughout Japan's modernization, but the groundwork for postwar reforms was laid by prewar movements.

In the Meiji period (1868–1912) some leaders of opinion like MORI ARINORI and FUKUZAWA YUKICHI criticized the traditional Confucian concepts of women, but the government based its educational policy on the principal that girls should be educated as homemakers, at whatever level of schooling. Education for women was generally separate from education for men, and at all levels lagged behind that provided for boys, although the introduction of universal primary education in 1873 meant that increasing numbers of girls were educated at least through the primary grades. In 1899 the Higher Girls' School Order (Kōtō Jogakkō Rei) stipulated that there should be at least one higher school for girls in each prefecture, where girls would be taught primarily domestic science and literature.

The use of women workers contributed to the success and speed of Japan's industrial revolution. The textile industry played an especially significant role in the transformation of the economy, both because of its traditional origins and its importance in foreign trade. It thrived in large part because it hired cheap female labor, housed in dormitories and required to work long hours (as portrayed in the work JOKŌ AISHI). In the 1890s, women factory workers far outnumbered men in similar jobs.

During the early phases of the industrial revolution the tradition became established of employing young unmarried women in the lowest-paid positions on a temporary or part-time basis and of excluding them from management-level positions. This tradition has continued, making it difficult even today for women to take entrance examinations of the sort that channel male college graduates into life-time positions in large corporations (see WOMEN IN THE LABOR FORCE).

In Japan's major cities, more new employment opportunities appeared for women as modernization proceeded; some began to work in the new department stores and telephone exchanges, others in "milk bars," beer halls, and cabarets. A few, such as Ozawa Tomiko, began to advance into such fields as secretarial work and journalism, and growing numbers were employed as teachers. OGINO GINKO and YOSHIOKA YAYOI were pioneer women doctors.

A less publicized feature of Japan's economic development has been the role of women in family businesses, where they have been counted as unpaid family labor, omitted from employment statistics. Especially in small- and medium-size businesses and cottage industries, women have often made major contributions. It is noteworthy that women in small family businesses sometimes function as accountants. In agriculture, as in family businesses, the work of farm wives counts as unpaid family labor, but it has been essential in the maintenance of rural productivity (see WOMEN, RURAL).

Changes in Lifestyle and Attitudes

Changes in Lifestyle and Attitudes——Since even the court of Emperor Meiji adopted Western fashions in the 1870s, these quickly spread among the elite and nouveau riche. Among the lower classes, too, the customs for married women of blackening the teeth and shaving the eyebrows had largely disappeared before 1900. Victorian bustles and later the flapper fashions of the 1920s appeared in Tōkyō and other major cities. The "modern boy" (*mobo*) and "modern girl" (*moga*), wearing straw hats and dancing the Charleston, symbolized the emerging urban culture of the Taishō period (1912–26).

Changes in fashion were naturally supported by the growth of the mass media; both films and stage plays had considerable impact. (MATSUI SUMAKO's portrayal of Nora in Ibsen's *A Doll's House,* first performed in Tōkyō in 1911, caused great controversy.) Even more influential were the new mass circulation magazines for women, beginning with the intellectual JOGAKU ZASSHI in the mid-1880s (see WOMEN'S MAGAZINES).

Women also began to pioneer in new literary forms and styles. Best known are the sensitive stories of HIGUCHI ICHIYŌ and the passionate poetry of YOSANO AKIKO; other prominent women writers of the Meiji and Taishō periods were KOZAI SHIKIN, MIYAKE KAHO, and the translator WAKAMATSU SHIZUKO. Women writers who expressed strong social and feminist concerns included YANAGIHARA BYAKUREN, TAMURA TOSHIKO, SATA INEKO, HIRABAYASHI TAIKO, and MIYAMOTO YURIKO.

Popular journalism made much of scandals involving women who went beyond the bounds of traditional morality. Some incidents were truly sensational, such as the crimes of TAKAHASHI ODEN and Abe Sada's 1936 murder of her lover (basis of the 1976 film *Ai no Korīda*), but often the press would focus on trivialities, making a "scandal" out of the claim that a member of the Seitōsha feminist group had once ordered an exotic foreign cocktail. The lives of unconventional women were sometimes made wretched by adverse publicity.

Modernization led to increasing numbers of nuclear families and greater freedom of association between boys and girls in the cities, but this was, ironically, paralleled by the decline of communal youth houses (see WAKAMONO-GUMI) that had allowed some free contact among young people in the countryside (see MARRIAGE).

Some women had participated actively in the struggles leading to the Meiji Restoration, and women such as KISHIDA TOSHIKO joined the FREEDOM AND PEOPLE'S RIGHTS MOVEMENT of the 1880s. Soon after the turn of the century, other well-known women were such diverse figures as the elite nationalist OKUMURA IOKO, the socialist FUKUDA HIDEKO, the anarchist KANNO SUGA, and a former prostitute who became a social commentator, YAMADA WAKA.

Christian women joined in serious, occasionally militant, efforts for social reform. In 1886, YAJIMA KAJIKO and SASAKI TOYOJU founded the KYŌFŪKAI, Japan's branch of the Woman's Christian Temperance Union; in the early 1900s, Christian activists such as YAMAMURO KIEKO of the Salvation Army and Hayashi Utako (1877–1946) worked to rescue and rehabilitate prostitutes.

Around the start of the Taishō period, stirrings of feminist thought began among a small circle of women intellectuals. The earliest feminist group was the SEITŌSHA (Bluestocking Society), organized by HIRATSUKA RAICHŌ in 1911. Most of the "new women" of Taishō were products of the higher education for women which began at the turn of the century. The primary avenue of activity for these women was intellectual and literary, but the journal of the Seitōsha, called *Seitō,* showed an evolution from literary to social concerns. The courage and initiative of Raichō was matched by other *Seitō* contributors such as its second editor ITŌ NOE, who was later killed for her anarchist activities.

Although the Seitōsha was disbanded in 1916, it prepared the way for the 1920 founding of the SHIN FUJIN KYŌKAI (New Woman's Association), dedicated to achieving political rights for women (see WOMEN'S SUFFRAGE). Leaders of the new group were Hiratsuka Raichō, OKU MUMEO, and ICHIKAWA FUSAE. The Shin Fujin Kyōkai disbanded in 1922 because of internal difficulties and government repression, but it had achieved repeal of the law barring women from political meetings. Women activists gained experience in working together during relief efforts after the Tōkyō Earthquake of 1923. Other feminists active around this time were KAMICHIKA ICHIKO, KUBUSHIRO OCHIMI, KAWASAKI NATSU, and YAMATAKA SHIGERI.

Meanwhile, beginning as early as 1886, labor strikes by women had been on the rise, and in 1919 the women's section of the pioneer labor group YŪAIKAI sponsored a mass rally of textile workers to sanction a resolution to the International Labor Organization about the plight of women workers in Japan. In 1921 women socialists such as YAMAKAWA KIKUE formed the SEKIRANKAI (Red Wave Society) and made efforts to observe May Day and International Women's Day.

After over two-and-a-half years of study in the United States, Ichikawa Fusae returned to Japan in early 1924, when the women's movement was again at a low ebb. Inspired by the feminist activities she had observed abroad, she threw her energies into a new organization soon known as the FUSEN KAKUTOKU DŌMEI (Women's Suffrage League), which became the central organization of the nonsocialist feminist movement. At Diet sessions this group repeatedly lobbied for women's suffrage, but such efforts were weakened by a four-way split among the left-wing political parties, each of which had a women's section. Often leftist women criticized Ichikawa for being concerned only with suffrage rather than with a wider range of women's problems. When women failed to gain the franchise with men in 1925 (see UNIVERSAL MANHOOD SUFFRAGE MOVEMENT), many turned to organizing auxiliary groups in the proletarian parties and labor federations. However, the number of leftist women involved in these auxiliaries at any one time was not more than about a thousand, and their attention was divided between social and political issues.

Lacking the support of the proletarian movement as a whole, the "bourgeois feminists" also faced open hostility as they sought to persuade traditionally oriented women to join the suffrage cause. Few such women could conceive of any role for themselves other than that of "good wife and wise mother."

FAMILY PLANNING was another issue supported by certain Japanese women leaders, inspired by neo-Malthusian ideas entering Japan at the turn of the century. Women's magazines were publishing articles and advertisements on contraceptives by 1918. Ishimoto Shizue was an active advocate of family planning and she continued such activities as a Diet member after World War II under the name KATŌ SHIZUE. In 1922 the government revealed its hostility to the idea of family planning when Margaret SANGER was nearly refused permission to land in Japan. In 1937, as the demand for new soldiers and workers was increased by war in China, the birth control movement was suppressed.

The left-wing women's movement, like the social democratic movement generally, weakened in the face of implacable government hostility against "dangerous thought." Leftist organizations were decimated in 1928–29 by the arrests of thousands, including women labor activists such as TANNO SETSU. Nevertheless, successful women's strikes occasionally occurred even up into the 1930s, such as the one organized largely by Akamatsu Tsuneko (1897–1965) against the Nihon Celluloid Company in 1931. In addition, the national women's meetings of 1930 (Zen Nihon Fusen Taikai; All Japan Women's Suffrage Conference) and 1931 (Dai Nippon Rengō Fujinkai; Greater Japan United Women's Society), with hundreds of delegates, showed widespread support for women's suffrage and other reforms.

After 1930 many women's groups worked together for suffrage, led by the Fūsen Kakutoku Dōmei. Under HAMAGUCHI OSACHI's Minseitō cabinet in 1930, there was some shift in the climate of opinion concerning women, and the government went so far as to push a female civil rights bill through the lower house of the Diet. Before the measure could be steered through the House of Peers (the upper house), however, it encountered formidable opposition from city mayors, who launched a concerted campaign against it. In the face of all these obstacles, even a weakened civil rights bill for women failed to pass the House of Peers. By the early 1930s rightwing sentiment forced the women's movement, along with other protest movements, to modify its demands. The efforts of Ichikawa and others were accordingly diverted from the suffrage issue to other problems affecting the lives of women.

Women in Wartime——Japan's two main national patriotic societies for women were the DAI NIPPON KOKUBŌ FUJINKAI (National Defense Women's Association) and the smaller but older AIKOKU FUJINKAI (Patriotic Women's Association). Although these two groups performed essentially the same functions, the former was more successful because of its broader base and closer community ties. In 1942 the government arranged a merger of these two groups (along with the Dai Nippon Rengō Fujinkai) into the DAI NIPPON FUJINKAI (Great Japan's Women's Society).

More significant was the mobilization of many young women into the work force. However, it remained government policy during the entire war not to draft married women but to keep them at home producing more potential soldiers and citizens. Even at the height of the war effort, three-fourths of the workers in manufacturing and construction were still male.

In late 1943 a national labor registration system was introduced, requiring that unmarried women between the ages of 16 and 25 enroll as potential workers. Previous patriotic labor associations were absorbed into the organization of the Joshi Rōdō Teishintai (Volunteer Labor Corps) in 1944. During this year registration was expanded to unmarried women from 12 to 39, owing to the deterioration of the war effort. Such women were urged by government-organized TONARIGUMI (neighborhood associations) to join the corps and work for a year, later for two years. Finally, in October

1944, women workers in war industries were frozen in their jobs, in the closest approach to compulsory service for women.

The majority of married women during the war years continued to work on farms and in family businesses and shops, in many cases without their husbands. However essential their duties, especially in agriculture, they were still classified as unpaid family labor.

In addition, as members of *tonarigumi*, women organized civil air defense drills, distributed government notices, and distributed rations. Women were exhorted to eschew luxuries and to wear *mompe*, the baggy work pants worn by farm women. Marriage and childbirth were officially encouraged. The government's natalist policy failed, however, to have the desired effect, and in 1944–45 the birthrate dropped, no doubt because so many men were at the front and nutritional levels were inadequate. *Joyce C. LEBRA*

Women in Contemporary Japan——Profound changes in the economic, social, and political status of Japanese women were set in motion during the Allied OCCUPATION after World War II. Constitutional guarantees and other reforms introduced during that period gave women a full legal basis for equality. Over the decades since then, prosperity, urbanization, the spread of educational opportunity, and other factors have supported further improvements in the position of women. However, the nature of family life, informal policies and practices in the employment world, and popular attitudes toward women's roles all contribute to the gap that still exists between legal standards and social reality.

Legal Changes——The new CONSTITUTION of 1947 introduced during the Occupation specifically forbade "discrimination in political, economic or social relations because of race, creed, sex, social status or family origin." The new constitution also made provision in article 24 that "marriage shall be based only on the mutual consent of both sexes" and on the "equal rights of husband and wife," and that "with regard to choice of spouse, property rights, inheritance, choice of domicile, divorce, and other matters pertaining to marriage and the family, laws shall be enacted from the standpoint of individual dignity and the essential equality of the sexes." These provisions make the constitution of 1947 one of the most progressive in the world regarding guarantees for women's equality in society and the family.

The constitution established the basis for women's equal educational opportunities, and, at the same time, new education laws aimed at ending the prewar multitrack system, which had relegated women to an inferior "girls' track," and opened the way for a public school system that has become largely coeducational (see EDUCATION, FUNDAMENTAL LAW OF; SCHOOL EDUCATION LAW OF 1947).

The Labor Standards Law enacted in April 1947 set the basis for fair treatment of women workers. While some of these measures, modeled on the women's labor laws then in force in the United States, fall into the category of protective legislation rather than measures for securing equal work rights, the new law led to vast improvements in conditions for women workers (see LABOR LAWS; WOMEN WORKERS, PROTECTIVE LEGISLATION FOR).

New provisions introduced into the Civil Code further implemented the constitutional guarantee of women's equality in family life. Prewar provisions in the Civil Code on matters relating to MARRIAGE, DIVORCE, and property rights of married women, as well as other matters coming under family law, had consistently favored the husband. In the postwar reform of the Civil Code, husbands and wives were placed on legal parity in the marriage relationship. Today both can terminate marriage on the same grounds, for unchastity, desertion, continued absence, mental illness, or any other serious reason making continuation of the marriage difficult. Family courts were set up to intervene in matters such as child custody and property disputes in which divorce is under consideration (see FAMILY COURT). Women can now negotiate contracts without their spouses' consent. Marriage itself can be entered into on the consent of both parties without parental permission when both have reached legal age (18 for males; 16 for females). Whereas the old code had required that a woman be registered under the name of her own family head or that of her husband, today she may apply for registration in her own name.

Since the democratic system of the United States was the model for the American Occupation, laws regarding women in Japan are generally similar to those for American women. In fact, in some ways—particularly in the specific constitutional guarantee of equality—Japanese women are far ahead of women in many countries, including the United States. Thus women activists now generally campaign not to change laws but to see them enforced. Notable examples involve the laws regulating work. Women have brought to court a number of cases in which they charged that a company's employment policies were in violation of women's constitutional guarantee of equality. Most of the cases disputed the right of companies to force the retirement of women for various reasons not applicable to men, e.g., marriage, childbirth, or a set age earlier than the retirement age of men. More than a dozen cases involving women and labor laws had come to court by 1980, and in the large majority of these, decisions favored the women plaintiffs.

Work —— In 1975 women constituted 37 percent of Japan's total workers, with almost half of all women of working age in the labor force. Over the last few years, the rate of work force participation for both males and females has declined slightly, but this has been due largely to the rising prosperity in postwar Japan, which has enabled more young people to seek higher education, thereby delaying their entry into the work force. There has also been a decrease in the percentage of working women in the 25–29 age range. This is the period in which childbearing tends to be concentrated in Japan, and it appears that the prosperity Japan has experienced since the 1960s has allowed more mothers to stay home with their young children.

As in other advanced industrial societies, one of the most notable features of women's work force participation has been the entry or reentry of married women and women in their forties and fifties. By 1975, 51 percent of all women workers were married, a figure that had more than doubled between 1960 and 1975. The increase of older women workers is also striking.

Yet women workers in Japan, like those in most advanced industrial societies, continue to be found doing mainly nonprofessional and menial jobs. In 1975, 73 percent of all women workers were clerical or service workers or factory operatives, while they made up only 5.2 percent of those in the category of managers and officials. Shorter periods of service, combined with the relatively younger age of women workers, also contribute to the lower wage level for women workers. Women's wages still average only about 60 percent of those for men.

The Labor Standards Law of 1947 includes a number of measures aimed at improving working conditions for women. The law provides for a maternity leave of six weeks before and after delivery and allows mothers to nurse infants on the job. The Working Women's Welfare Law, which went into effect in 1972, strengthens the provisions of the original law. The 1975 Child Care Leave Bill, designed mainly for medical nurses and public school teachers, allows women with children under 12 months of age to take up to one year's unpaid leave with the assurance that they can return to their former posts.

One of the main problems of married working women is child care. According to the 1970 census, over one million married women workers had children under age six. The number of children in day nurseries almost doubled between 1969 and 1976. In 1976 there were 18,934 day nurseries in Japan, of which 11,956 were public and 6,978 were private, accommodating 1.8 million children under age six. However, the number of children on waiting lists is large, and there is much concern among working mothers about improving the quality of facilities and extending the hours of available care. The traditional alternative to day care in Japan has been to rely on grandparents and other relatives—a solution that many working mothers continue to prefer. But in urban areas, parents often cannot be accommodated in the homes of their adult children, so working mothers must seek outside day care. The practice of hiring babysitters or live-in domestic helpers, common in many countries, is rare in Japan (see also WOMEN IN THE LABOR FORCE).

Family —— Three major forces have done much to alter the nature of women's role in Japanese family life. The first was the democratization process set in motion by the Allied Occupation. The second has been urbanization. Women's status in the prewar family was based on an extended-family arrangement. But in the postwar period, young people have increasingly deserted the countryside for the city, where the nuclear family has become the norm. Whereas in the traditional extended family the wife's chief function was to bear sons to preserve family continuity, now increased value is placed on companionship for mutual understanding in the modern urban marriage. A third factor has been prosperity. The acquisition of appliances has greatly simplified housework and relieved it of much of its previous drudgery. Prosperity has also meant more money for leisure activities, and young married couples are far more likely to have money for an occasional family outing or vacation. More families now feel financially able to provide higher education for daughters, one essential aspect of change, since the educational attainment of the wife is closely related to the balance of power and status in the marital relationship. Finally, postwar economic growth through the early 1970s gave rise to labor shortages, which brought new employment opportunities to women and thus provided growing numbers of women with an independent economic base within marriage.

In the prewar period, the extended family exercised control over members by playing the decisive role in choosing the marriage partners in a system of arranged marriages (*miai kekkon;* see MIAI). There were also some "love matches" *(ren'ai kekkon),* in which the partners themselves made an independent decision to marry, but among middle- and upper-class families these were much less common.

In the early postwar period, arranged marriage continued to be the main method of mate selection. A study in the mid-1950s showed that 73 percent of marriages in large cities and 86 percent of those in farming areas were still arranged. But the number of "love" marriages has been increasing rapidly over the last two decades. Meanwhile, the arranged marriage system has itself changed in the postwar period. Today many Japanese see it as little more than a method to introduce young people of carefully matched backgrounds who can then decide for themselves whether they will marry.

In the prosperous 1960s the rate of marriage increased in Japan. The age at marriage is now usually around 25 or younger for women and around 26 or older for men. The divorce rate, though rising, still remains very low compared to that in many advanced industrial societies, for a number of reasons. One is a strong cultural emphasis on maintaining family harmony. Another factor is the problems a divorced woman faces: there is no provision in Japanese civil law for alimony, and the amounts of money awarded for child support tend to be extremely small. Some public assistance is available for divorced women, but again, amounts are minimal.

Within the marriage relationship itself it is difficult to assess how things have changed in the postwar period. The nature of family life is affected by the growing number of nuclear families, the improved educational attainment of women, and the increase in the number of married women who work. The impact of all of these things has been in the direction of greater communication and companionability; however, the basic pattern of marriage continues to be one in which the worlds of the husband and wife are kept separate and distinct: the husband's life centers on his work, the wife's on home and children. The Japanese husband generally tells his wife very little of what goes on at the office and tends to spend a great deal of his leisure time with his male coworkers in a social life which does not include wives. For her part, the wife usually develops her own life centering on the home and neighborhood. Though the pattern has changed in the late 1970s, full-time housewives have been generally less involved in outside activities such as volunteer work or civic groups than women in the United States. Within the home, the wife's authority is undoubtedly great. She generally has full responsibility for managing the family budget and makes most of the decisions relating to her children. Since her role satisfaction depends heavily on how well she manages her sphere, she generally does not ask for or expect help with home chores from her husband. According to a survey in the late 1970s, housewives spent nearly seven hours a day engaged in housework, whereas husbands spent only six minutes on home chores.

The same survey indicated that the average amount of time spent by housewives for social, cultural, and recreational activities is now six hours daily, twice the time spent in the prewar years. An exception to this general pattern is women in agriculture. In 1975 only 13 percent of Japan's total labor force were engaged in agriculture, but of that total, 52 percent were women. In the pattern of agriculture today, 86 percent of farm households have one or more members engaged in industrial or other outside work, with the result that farm wives typically do a large share of the farming and in many cases manage the whole farm enterprise. Farming duties, in combination with household chores and child-rearing, leave many farm wives with little time for leisure activity (see also FAMILY; HOUSEWIVES; WOMEN, RURAL).

Education —— The educational reforms undertaken by the Occupation had a profound impact on the status of women. Reform of educational content meant eliminating the "morals" course of prewar days, which had idealized the traditional family system within which women had an inferior status. The postwar educational curricula have given strong support to the democratization of family life and to the equality of women. Even more significant, reforms aimed at making education available to all on the basis of ability opened the way to dramatic increases in the educational level of women.

Women's enrollment in educational institutions at all levels has increased steadily over the postwar period. In 1955 only 47 percent of female students went beyond the nine years of compulsory education to enter upper secondary schools, whereas 56 percent of the male students continued their schooling. But by 1975 the rate of advancement for girls had outstripped that for boys: 93 percent for girls, as compared to 91 percent for boys. The movement of women into higher education also has been increasing at a phenomenal rate. In 1955, 15 percent of female high school graduates entered higher education, as compared to 21 percent for males, whereas by 1975, the figure, increased to 35 percent, had exceeded that for males (34 percent).

These figures, however, do not mean that educational patterns for men and women are now the same. Though so many women go on to higher education, a high percentage choose two-year JUNIOR COLLEGES rather than four-year institutions. In 1975 women made up 86 percent of the enrollment in junior colleges but only 21 percent of the enrollment in four-year institutions. The percentage of women in the prestigious national universities is even lower, although it is increasing. Many parents—and many daughters themselves—continue to feel that educating daughters has different goals from educating sons and that the goal of preparing women for home life may be compromised if they are educated in the competitive environment of a major university.

A similar explanation may be offered for the fundamental difference in the fields of study selected by men and women. In upper secondary school, the majority of girls take a general education course, whether or not they plan to go on to college. Few prepare for technical jobs that would bring good pay. If they do choose a vocational course, they take home economics to prepare themselves to become wives and mothers, or they enter a commercial course so that they can find clerical jobs after graduation. Boys also take the general education course but with further education in mind, or they enter a special vocational course in order to leave high school with a skill.

In higher education the tendency is even more pronounced for women to elect study options on a pattern different from that of male students and to gravitate to "women's" majors over those which lead more directly to careers. For women the most common major is literature; the number of women in literature combined with those in nursing and home economics constitutes approximately two-thirds of all women students (see also WOMEN'S EDUCATION).

Life Expectancy and Birthrates——The average life expectancy for Japanese women is one of the highest in the world. In 1975 it stood at 76.9 years, as compared to 71.7 for males. At the same time the birthrate has declined and stabilized in the postwar period. The average number of children born to each family was 5.14 in 1940. By 1967, it had dropped dramatically to 1.69, and now has stabilized at around 2.

A number of factors contribute to Japan's success at keeping its population size so well in hand. One is the responsiveness of the Japanese public to changes in government population policy; another is the widespread availability of both contraceptive measures and legal ABORTION. According to a survey on birth control conducted by the Prime Minister's Office in the early 1970s, contraception by condom and rhythm method accounted for 90 percent of preventive efforts, and the IUD for 10 percent; pills for purposes of contraception are not legally available in Japan. In the absence of any particular religious or other traditions in conflict with the practice, abortion is a common method of ending unwanted pregnancies for women of all ages in Japan. A measure has come before the Diet several times to limit the availability of abortion by eliminating "economic reasons" as a legal grounds for attaining one. The proposed revision of the existing law has been widely protested by women's groups, the JAPAN MEDICAL ASSOCIATION, the Family Planning Federation of Japan, and numerous other civic groups, and so far has been defeated each time it has come before the Diet (see also FAMILY PLANNING).

Political Participation and Volunteer Work——In 1945 Japanese women gained full political rights. The Election Law was revised in December 1945 to permit women to vote and run for political office. In the first election of the postwar period, held on 10 April 1946, over 20 million women went to the polls for the first time. The turnout of 67 percent of eligible women voters was much higher than most people had predicted and not far below the 78.5 percent

for men. Since 1946 the gap between the voting rates of women and men has continued to close, and since the election of July 1968 the voting rate for women has exceeded that for men. Japan is today one of the few countries in the world where women outvote men. (It is among the electorate under age 50 that the voting rate for women surpasses that for men. In rural areas and among voters over 50, men continue to outvote women.)

Yet Japanese women, like women in virtually all countries of the world today, are underrepresented in the effective political life of the country. The first postwar election brought 39 women into the Diet, but since then, women have generally held only between 20 and 25 Diet seats at any time, which represents less than 3 percent of the total membership. In other elective bodies they are even further underrepresented. In 1975 there were only 32 women, as contrasted to 2,796 men, in prefectural assemblies, representing only 1.1 percent of the total. In municipal assemblies, they held only 1.8 percent of the seats in the same year. In village assemblies, they had the least representation of all, with only 0.5 percent of all seats.

In the national government, women were appointed to positions mainly in those bureaus and commissions bearing directly on "women's" concerns. For example, in 1975 some 39 percent of all mediation commissioners of the family courts and 35 percent of all public and child welfare commissioners were women. The number of women in managerial posts in the civil service is quite low. A 1973 study conducted by the International Labor Organization (ILO) of women's representation in managerial positions in national administrations in 56 nations ranked Japan next to the bottom, above only Pakistan.

On the other hand, all of the major political parties have women's sections attached to them, and Japan has women's groups that parallel many of the organizations found in the United States, such as the League of Women Voters, the Association of University Women, and the Parent-Teacher Association. About 2.7 million women belong to the National Council of Women's Organizations of Agricultural Cooperatives. There are approximately 25,000 regional women's organizations, with a total membership of 6 million, affiliated with the National Federation of Regional Women's Organizations (CHIFUREN). One of the most active women's groups is the Housewives Association (SHUFUREN), which has branches all over Japan and has campaigned mainly for consumer protection (see also CONSUMER MOVEMENT). Women, especially middle-class urban women, have also played a major role in CITIZENS' MOVEMENTS that arose in Japan in the 1960s and 1970s to protest problems of ENVIRONMENTAL QUALITY and nuclear power plants. Women have also been a major source of support for the PEACE MOVEMENT in the postwar period.

The feminist movement in Japan, made up of groups and organizations committed to improving women's status, has a number of sources of support. The Women's and Young Workers' Bureau of the Ministry of Labor has played an active role in promoting the status of women, as has a special section in the Prime Minister's Office. There are numerous associations made up of professional women in various fields, such as the Women Lawyers' Association and the Federation of Business and Professional Women's Clubs. These groups, along with other organizations such as the Women's Democratic Club, have actively supported many measures aimed at improving the status of Japanese women. In the early 1970s a number of students and young middle-class women took part in informal groups inspired partly by the resurgence of "women's liberation" in Western nations.

——Robert O. Blood, Jr., *Love Match and Arranged Marriage: A Tokyo–Detroit Comparison* (1967). George DeVos and Hiroshi Wagatsuma, "Value Attitudes towards Role Behavior of Women in Two Japanese Villages," *American Anthropologist* 63 (1961). Keiko Higuchi, "The PTA—A Channel for Political Activism," *Japan Interpreter* 10 (Autumn 1975). Sumiko Iwao, "A Full Life for Modern Japanese Women," in Nihonjin Kenkyūkai, ed, *Text of Seminar on Changing Values in Modern Japan* (1977). Japan Ministry of Education, *The Status of Women in Japan* (1968; 1971 [C], 1977). Japan External Trade Organization, "Female Employment in Japan," *Now in Japan* 19 (December 1975). Takashi Koyama, *The Changing Social Position of Women in Japan* (1961). Joyce Lebra, Joy Paulson, and Elizabeth Powers, ed, *Women in Changing Japan* (1976). Susan J. Pharr, "Japan: Historical and Contemporary Perspectives," in Janet Z. Giele and Audrey C. Smock, *Women: Role and Status in Eight Countries* (1977). Susan J. Pharr, "A Radical U.S. Experiment: Women's Rights Laws and the Occupation of Japan," in L. H. Redford, ed, *The Occupation of Japan: Impact of Legal Reform* (1978).

Women in the labor force—— Table 1

Labor Force Participation, by Sex												
Population (millions)		Population aged 15 and older (millions)		Labor force (millions)		Labor force participation rate				Percentage of work force occupied by women	Unemployment rate	
Male	Female	Male	Female	Male	Female	Male		Female			Male	Female
(A)	(B)	(C)	(D)	(E)	(F)	E/A	E/C	F/B	F/D	F/(E + F)		
1955	44.24	45.83	28.57	30.68	24.55	17.40	55.5	85.9	38.0	56.7	41.5	2.6	2.3
1960	46.30	48.00	31.51	33.70	26.73	18.38	57.7	84.8	38.3	54.5	40.7	1.6	1.7
1965	48.69	50.52	35.29	37.58	28.84	19.03	59.2	81.7	37.7	50.6	39.8	1.1	1.3
1970	51.37	53.30	38.25	40.60	31.29	20.24	60.9	81.8	38.0	49.9	39.3	1.2	1.0
1975	55.09	56.85	40.99	43.44	33.36	19.87	60.6	81.4	35.0	45.7	37.3	2.0	1.7
1980	57.59	59.46	43.41	45.91	34.65	21.85	60.2	79.8	36.7	47.6	38.7	2.0	2.0

SOURCE: First two columns: Sōrifu Tōkeikyoku (Prime Minister's Office, Statistics Bureau), *Wagakuni no jinkō* (1982). Remainder: Rōdōshō (Ministry of Labor), *Fujin rōdō no jitsujō* (annual): 1982.

Women in the labor force—— Table 2

Male-Female Wage Differentials by Age Group, 1980

Age	Female wages as a percentage of male wages (contracted earnings)
under 18	89.0
18–19	85.7
20–24	81.4
25–29	72.2
30–34	60.6
35–39	52.1
40–44	47.4
45–49	48.1
50–54	51.6
55–59	57.1
60–64	67.1
65 +	71.7
Average for all age groups	55.9

NOTE: Contracted earnings mean monthly cash earnings, i.e., regular pay plus overtime, not including bonus payments. With bonus payments, the average for all age groups in 1980 was 53.8 percent.
SOURCE: Rōdōshō (Ministry of Labor), *Fujin rōdō no jitsujō* (annual): 1982.

Susan J. Pharr, *Political Women in Japan* (1980). Alexander Szalai, *The Situation of Women in the United Nations* (1973). Taketsugu Tsurutani, *Political Change in Japan* (1977). US Department of Labor and Japan Ministry of Labor, *The Role and Status of Women Workers in the United States and Japan* (1976).   Susan J. PHARR

women in the labor force

From the Meiji Period through World War II—— Women were an important part of Japan's labor force in traditional society—especially in agriculture—before the Meiji Restoration of 1868, but concern with female labor as a separate component of economic life really began with industrialization, the emergence of wage labor, and the employment of many women away from home in the later 19th century. The Meiji period (1868–1912) was characterized by the flow of women workers—some on a "voluntary" basis but most for very low wages—into the textile industry, which became Japan's major source of foreign exchange.

Given the laissez-faire ideology prevalent among entrepreneurs (which was buttressed by a growing sense of nationalism), working conditions deteriorated as the number of women in factories rapidly increased. In the early years of Meiji, much of the work force was supplied by the households of impoverished *samurai* and artisans. Later, labor recruiters came to travel into small agricultural villages and hamlets to "buy" girls for factories, paying their families a lump sum in return for a contract of a year or more. Despite family obligations, many of these girls later attempted to escape from the factories.

Although concentrated in the textile industry, women outnumbered men in the total labor force until about 1930. Their entry into other manufacturing industries was stimulated by the industrialization occurring after the Russo-Japanese War of 1904–05 and during World War I. With improved educational opportunities from the 1920s on, an increasing number of women moved into a variety of other jobs, becoming doctors, teachers, office clerks, and telephone operators. When the worldwide depression of the 1930s fostered protectionist policies to promote Japan's self-reliance and self-sufficiency, the resultant expansion of heavy industry further diversified women's employment opportunities; for example, the chemical industry (rubber and synthetic fibers) became a major employer of women. As an increasing number of men joined the military forces, opportunities in skilled occupations were expanded, and women came to operate precision machinery and lathes side by side with men in factories manufacturing parts for engines and machines.

The poor working environment and overcrowded dormitories for young textile operatives first received wide publicity with the surveys of the Ministry of Agriculture and Commerce, published as SHOKKŌ JIJŌ (1903, The Conditions of Factory Workers), and with YOKOYAMA GENNOSUKE's *Nihon no kasō shakai* (1899, Japan's Lower Classes). The movement for legislation to protect women and minors was begun in the 1890s but stalled during the war with Russia. Numerous factors soon served to revive these efforts, such as the budding labor movement; the growing vociferousness of socialists, anarchists, and other reformers; the rising public recognition of the need for policies to promote the well-being of Japan's workers; and the resolution on women at the First International Conference of the International Labor Law Association in Berne in 1906.

The FACTORY LAW OF 1911, implemented in 1916, limited workdays for women to 12 hours, forbade night work between 10:00 PM and 4:00 AM, required a minimum of two days off per month, and a minimum of one hour off for rest during the workday. It legislated sleeping quarters and bathing facilities for women separate from those for men. Along with various health and safety regulations, it set the following minimum standards for workers' dormitories: one bed per person, floor space equal to 1.5 *tatami* mats per person in sleeping rooms, sheets for beds, and at least two airings of bedding per month. However, the law applied only to places of work with more than 15 employees, so many women were still not legally protected. The poor conditions which continued in the textile plants are recorded in Ishihara Osamu's *Jokō to kekkaku* (1913, Women Workers and Tuberculosis), KAWAKAMI HAJIME's *Bimbō monogatari* (1916, Tale of Poverty), and Hosoi Wakizō's JOKŌ AISHI (1925, The Tragic History of Women Workers). Although certain improvements were realized during the 1920s, the depression and growing militarism in the 1930s stymied further progress.

The post–World War II labor movement initially focused on the need to provide a basic means of living for the work force. Although priority was given to the working conditions of male household heads as primary breadwinners, women continued to supply a large share of Japan's labor. With many women left single by the wartime loss of men, the absence of adequate welfare benefits and the ineffectiveness of minimum-wage legislation, the labor force participation rate of women was necessarily high in the immediate postwar years. Nevertheless, the research of Arisawa Hiromi, Obi Keiichirō, and others clearly shows that the labor force behavior of Japanese women has resembled that of women in other industrialized countries, with a negative correlation between women's labor-force participation rate and the income of the household head.

Ross MOUER

Women Workers Today—— Since the end of World War II, there has been an increase in the average age of working women, in the number of married women workers, and in the level of education. As a result, the situation of Japanese working women is now generally similar to that of their Western counterparts. In both Japan and the West, women make up approximately a third of the total labor force; more than half of working women are married; their age composition is characterized by the so-called M-shaped labor participation curve, with a sharp but temporary drop during childbearing years; and they earn lower wages than men. Yet, in Japan, strong vestiges of male preference from the past still result in comparatively greater discrimination against women in the labor force.

Increasing numbers of women employees. Until about 1950 more than 60 percent of working women were "family workers," mainly in agriculture. With the decline of primary industries and the development of secondary and tertiary industries, the number of women employees has increased. In 1970, 30.9 percent of the female labor force was working in family enterprises as family workers and 54.7 percent in outside enterprises as employees; by 1980, family workers had declined to 23.0 percent and employees had increased to 63.2 percent. (The actual number of female employees increased from 10,960,000 to 13,540,000 during that period.) Since women employees make up more than 90 percent of the total female labor force in the United States, Sweden, and England, the percentage of family workers in Japan is still considerably higher than in other developed countries.

Women's entry into "prestige professions" has been slow in Japan. The percentage of judges, prosecutors, and lawyers who are women doubled between 1960 and 1975 but is still under 3 percent. The percentage of women physicians was 9.6 in 1960, but 15 years later this figure remained the same. The percentage of women civil servants in managerial posts is still less than 1 percent. The greatest gains for women in professional employment have been in such fields as public-school teaching and social work.

Other changes. Before World War II most working Japanese women were young and single, but this is no longer true. The average age of female employees was 23.8 in 1949, 26.3 in 1960, 29.8 in 1970, and 34.9 in 1980. In 1960 the ratio of female employees under 30 to those over 30 was 63:37. Rapid economic growth in the 1960s caused a labor shortage and made it possible for women of middle and advanced age to find employment. Thus, the same ratio dropped to 53:47 in 1970 and to 35:65 in 1980. The number of employed females under the age of 19 has markedly decreased because more girls are entering senior high school. Furthermore, many women previously engaged in agriculture as family workers have now become employees in nonagricultural industries, and many housewives have begun to seek paid employment.

In 1955 the percentage of married women in the total female labor force was 20.9. During the 1960s, as Japan experienced rapid economic growth and many companies began to offer part-time employment, the number of married women employees rose considerably. Several factors made it possible for housewives to become employees: a constant labor shortage and technological development in industry, the increased use of modern conveniences in homes, the declining birth rate, a growing desire for cash income to improve living standards, and the rising educational level and social consciousness of the women themselves. The percentage of married women employees in the total female labor force rose to 41.4 in 1970 and to 57.4 in 1980.

The traditional view that women should devote themselves to their homes after marriage dies hard among employers and employees alike, so the length of uninterrupted employment at the same firm has tended to be short. Yet today, not only do many women employees work until the time of childbirth, many continue to work after childbirth as well. Thus, the average length of uninterrupted employment at the same firm rose from 3.6 years in 1949 to 4.0 years in 1960, 4.5 years in 1970, and 6.3 years in 1980. A number of recent court decisions have tended to rule against forcing women to retire upon marriage or upon having passed the "appropriate" age for marriage (commonly set at 30), but are less clear on systems that retire women at 50 (the normal retirement age for men is 55). Now it has become common for women to take paid jobs for at least a few years after they complete their schooling. In 1949, 75 percent of

women employees had completed primary education and 25 percent, secondary education or above. In 1968, 52 percent of female employees had acquired a secondary or higher level of education, and the figure had risen to 65 percent by 1979. (In 1968, 8 percent of women employees had completed either university or junior college education; this figure was 17 percent in 1979.)

Distribution of women workers. Clerical and related jobs accounted for the largest percentage of all female employees in 1980, excluding self-employed and family workers (32.7 percent), followed by craft and production-process workers (23.2 percent), professional and technical workers (13.0 percent), service workers (12.9 percent), sales workers (11.6 percent), manual laborers (4.0 percent), transport and communications workers (1.0 percent), managers and officials (0.8 percent), and full-time farmers, lumberers, and fishermen (0.7 percent). This order of distribution has not changed for some time, but the numbers of women employees in each occupation have varied. The numbers of women employees have been increasing in professional and technical occupations (the number of women in such occupations in 1975 was 77.6 percent greater than it had been in 1965, and the percentage of all people engaged in such occupations who were women increased from 37.6 percent in 1965 to 44.4 percent in 1975). However, the numbers of women employees in manual labor have declined (by 38.6 percent) as have those in agriculture, forestry, and fishing (by 35.5 percent), and transport and communications (by 22.7 percent).

Wages. Article 4 of Japan's Labor Standards Act of 1947 stipulates the principle of equal pay for equal work. Schoolteachers and women in the bureaucracy receive the pay most nearly equal to that of their male counterparts. Nonetheless, the principle of equal pay for equal work tends to lose meaning because of the strong tendency to channel women into dead-end jobs, to favor men in promotion rounds, and to relabel work given to women.

According to one survey of permanent employees in firms with over 30 employees, the average monthly wage paid to women employees in 1980 was ¥166,397 (US $734), only 53.8 percent of the average monthly wage paid to men. Discriminatory payment is also common in Western Europe and in the United States, but the difference in Japan between men's and women's wages is still the greatest among the developed countries. This seems largely due to Japan's long-established SENIORITY SYSTEM of wages, which presupposes "lifetime" employment of male household heads. The length of uninterrupted employment at the same firm, employee age, and level of education are basic factors, while wages for specific responsibilities and positions, dependency allowances, and housing allowances are secondary factors of the seniority wage system. As noted above, the length of uninterrupted employment, average age, and educational level of women have tended to be considerably lower than those of men. Very few women attain positions of high responsibility in business firms, and few at any level receive allowances for dependents and housing. However, the wage differential between men and women seems to have narrowed some over time. In 1960, wages for women were 42.8 percent of those for men, but the figure rose to 50.9 in 1970 and 53.8 in 1980.

Working time and protective legislation. Article 61 of the Labor Standards Act limits overtime work and prohibits holiday work for women, while article 62 prohibits late-night work by women. In 1980 the average number of monthly working hours for women employees was 164.1 hours (compared to 181.2 for men), and the average number of monthly working days for women employees was 21.8 (22.0 for men).

Article 65 stipulates six weeks' maternity leave both before and after childbirth, as well as the transfer of pregnant women to light work. Article 66 provides for nursing leave, and article 67 allows for leave during menstruation. Articles 9 and 10 of the Welfare Acts for Working Women, proclaimed in 1972, stipulate the employer's obligation to take appropriate measures for the health of pregnant and postpartum women employees. Article 11 provides for nursing leave and other childcare arrangements for working women. In 1975 another law was enacted prescribing nursing leave for women teachers in primary and secondary schools, nurses in hospitals, and female employees in welfare institutions. See also WOMEN WORKERS, PROTECTIVE LEGISLATION FOR.

Local governments, subsidized by the national government, manage Homes for Working Women which provide advice on improving their quality of life, lectures, and facilities for vacation and recreation; there were 141 such homes in 1982. National and local governments, acting on the basis of the CHILD WELFARE LAW, have also been establishing more nurseries for children of women employees; in 1980, 22,036 public and private nurseries were authorized by the Ministry of Health and Welfare and 1,996,000 young children were using those facilities. The national government also provides loans for employers who wish to establish nurseries within their firms.

Future problems and prospects. The proportion of temporary and day laborers among women (nearly 20 percent in 1980) has been higher than that among men (5 percent) throughout the past decade. Therefore, when the overall economy is booming, the employment of women rises, but during economic recessions, such as that which followed the oil crisis of 1973, women are the first to be laid off.

Businesses still generally employ women only in low-level jobs because of the belief that women are less able than men, the long-established view that women should work only until marriage or childbirth, and the fact that women's working conditions are regulated by protective legislation. Thus, it is difficult even for women college graduates to find jobs suited to their skills and to advance within the firm once employed.

The United Nations International Women's Year (1975) stimulated discussions of working conditions for women that gave rise to two contradictory views. One is that, aside from minimum childbirth provisions, special protection for women should be abolished and that women employees should be encouraged to accept overtime and late-night work. The other is that it would be dangerous to abolish the protection that Japanese women now enjoy since labor conditions in Japan remain inferior to those in Western Europe and the United States. With the increase of young married women in the work force who do not wish to interrupt their employment, the shortage and inadequacy of nursery facilities have also come to receive considerable attention.

These are the major problems that Japanese working women currently face. Women's consciousness of their plight has risen; national and local governments, labor unions, and private organizations, as well as individuals, have begun to address these issues. Thus, it would seem that gradual changes will continue to occur in the overall situation of Japanese working women in the future. See also LABOR. ———*Fujii Toshiko*

———Higuchi Jirō, "Fujin rōdōsha no undō ni kansuru bunken," *Rōdō undō* 112 (April 1975). *Josei no shokugyō no subete* (annual). Kaji Etsuko, "The Invisible Proletariat: Working Women in Japan," *Ampo* 18 (Autumn 1973). Kobayashi Takumi, *Fujin rōdōsha no kenkyū* (1976). Kurokawa Toshio et al, ed, *Fujin rōdōsha no chingin to koyō* (1978). Joyce Lebra, Joy Paulson, and Elizabeth Powers, *Women in Changing Japan* (1976). Ōba Ayako and Ujihara Shōjirō, *Fujin rōdō*, vol 2 of *Gendai fujin kōza* (Aki Shobō, 1969). Rōdōshō Fujin Shōnen Kyoku, *Fujin rōdō no jitsujō* (annual, 1952–). *Rōdō undō*, special issue, "Kokusai fujin nen to fujin rōdōsha," 112 (April 1975). Shōda Akira, ed, *Joshi pātotaimā: Rōmu kanri no jittai to hōritsu mondai* (1971). Takahashi Hisako, *Fujin rōdō no hōritsu mondai* (1975). Takahashi Nobuko, "Women's Wages in Japan and the Question of Equal Pay," *International Labor Review* 3.1 (January 1975). Yamamoto Shigemi, *Aa, Nomugi Tōge: Aru seishi kōjo aishi* (rev ed, 1972).

women, rural

In the late 19th and early 20th centuries, Japan was an agrarian society. In the early part of the Meiji period (1868–1912), the agricultural population was 80 percent of the total. This fell to 70 percent in the Taishō period (1912–26) and 60 percent in the late 1920s and the 1930s. In the late 1970s it was 20 percent. Thus in Japan industrialization and urbanization took place in an extremely short period of time, resulting in a rather extraordinary accumulation of contradictions.

Under the Tokugawa shogunate (1603–1867), rural women faced heavy responsibilities as can be seen, for example, in the KEIAN NO OFUREGAKI (1649), a set of detailed instructions issued by the shogunate on how peasants should conduct their daily lives. In a society based on principles of self-sufficiency, rural women, besides engaging in agricultural production, had to prepare clothing, food, and other necessities of life for their families: they spun thread, wove cloth, and sewed clothes. They were also expected to engage in silkworm raising and other farm sidelines. It was only in the mid-Meiji period, when raw cotton began to be imported and cheap clothing became available in the rural areas, that women were released from these extra-agricultural duties. However, the social and economic problems caused by a suddenly emergent capitalism were particularly evident in the rural areas. The most striking example

was the female workers employed at low wages in spinning factories, the forerunners of Japan's modern industry. Most of these were the daughters of poor peasants in backwater areas. The LAND TAX REFORM OF 1873–1881 was advantageous to rich farmers and landlords but disadvantageous to poor farmers. As a commodity economy rapidly developed, impoverished farmers who needed cash often sent their daughters to spinning and other factories for a small sum, just as many in former times who could not deliver the rice tax had indentured their daughters as prostitutes. Cheap wage labor by women was one of the factors that supported the rapid development of Japan's capitalism. When young women became ill from the harsh labor conditions, they were simply returned to their villages with no welfare provisions. See JOKŌ AISHI.

Social scientists began to pay attention to the problems of working women only during the late 1920s, and to the problems of rural women around 1935. In *Nihon nōson fujin mondai* (1937, The Problems of Rural Women in Japan), Maruoka Hideko listed some of the leading causes for the plight of rural women: small family income and recurrent debts caused by the economic structure of rural areas; the panic and shock of crop failures stemming from social causes; the heavy responsibilities of rural women in addition to traditional pressures put on all women under the economically and socially restrictive family system; and the scarcity of public welfare facilities.

Even after the LAND REFORMS OF 1946 and the new constitution, which promised the establishment of a democratic society, the above conditions did not immediately improve, since traditional concepts have been slow to change. The role of women in farming communities has been given greater recognition, especially since the 1960s, when rapid economic growth siphoned away male labor.

The number of employed rural women in 1976 was 19,670,000, of whom 4,650,000 (23.6 percent) were engaged in agriculture. In 1956, 8,200,000 women were engaged in agriculture, 52.7 percent of the total 15,560,000-woman work force. In 20 years, the ratio of farming women was reduced by half, while the number of women in other productive sectors increased correspondingly. In 1976, 2,830,-000 men and 4,650,000 women worked in agriculture, with women accounting for 62.2 percent of the entire farming work force. Women have thus been liberated from the old subordinate status, but the problems of excessively heavy labor, health, and the insecurity of agriculture supported only by old people and women have yet to be solved.

Such changes in rural life can be attributed to the mechanization and the adoption of scientific farming methods as well as the simplification of housework through conveniences such as electricity, appliances, and instant food. When the level of mechanization in 1976 is compared with that of 1954, the number of power-driven rice transplanters is greater by a factor of 2.5, binders by 1.3, and combines by 2. In 1970, 70 percent of rice transplanting was done by machine and the traditional Asian-type intensive labor was becoming a thing of the past. Although the national economic growth rate had dropped from its mid-1960s peak, the speed of changes in the farming system was not affected. The simplification of housework was exemplified in the dissemination of modern conveniences: the utilization rate in the rural areas was 97.7 percent for washing machines, 98.4 percent for refrigerators, 90.5 percent for vacuum cleaners (1977). The rural figures are not much different from those for the cities.

The picture is not wholly positive, however. There has been an increasing need for more cash income because of rising living costs, as well as a dependence on extra-agricultural income and an increase in problems arising from the uncontrolled use of agricultural chemicals. Injuries from agricultural chemicals as well as premature births and miscarriages are increasing each year. According to a Ministry of Health and Welfare survey, between 1957 and 1975 there were 22,290 reported accidents caused by agricultural chemicals, but the actual figure is considered to be much higher. Another problem is the reduction in the number of women willing to marry into farm families. Farmers seek brides for their sons from other farming families, yet they hope that their own daughters will marry salaried workers.

Modern Japanese rural women must deal with a wide variety of problems having to do with the family such as housework, child rearing, and so forth, as well as with the practical running of the farm itself. In a 1977 survey, 60 percent of rural women were found to be incapable of handling basic accounts, and only 17 percent participated in planning decisions concerning the family farm. To deal with such problems in an organized way, women's sections of agricultural cooperative associations have been established. In 1977 there were 3,915 such groups, with 2,699,738 members. The central organization is the National Union of Agricultural Cooperative Women's Guild. Young wives' groups have been especially active. Reports and evaluations of local group activities are given at meetings of the central organization once a year. See also WOMEN IN JAPAN, HISTORY OF; WOMEN IN THE LABOR FORCE.

——Maruoka Hideko, *Nihon nōson fujin mondai* (1937). Maruoka Hideko, ed, *Murazukuri nijūnen* (1969).

MARUOKA Hideko

women's education

A concept and practice weak in early Japanese history, which partially emerged in the Heian period (794–1185), gained strength from the 13th to 16th centuries, varied according to class during the Edo period (1600–1868), and was most highly developed during modern times (1868 to the present).

Early history. In ancient days, when the deities described in the myths, rulers, and other people of importance were male and female, men and women seem to have been similarly "educated" for life. The KOJIKI (712, Records of Ancient Matters) tells us about the legendary JINGŪ, a ruler remembered not only as a veteran warrior who led conquering armies to Korea but also as a folk heroine who taught her people to fish with line and bait. By the Heian period, the rustic tribal leaders of Jingū's time had become an extremely literate, aesthetically sophisticated aristocracy. Since this evolution was abetted by several centuries of massive borrowing from China where separate male and female spheres had long been sharply differentiated, it is not surprising that Heian aristocratic women, though as highly educated as their menfolk, were not educated identically with them. One monopoly of "women's education" during the Heian period was dyeing, cutting, and sewing of fine cloth for the elaborate clothing worn by both sexes. Men studied Chinese (KAMBUN), the official language of court and politics, but women were supposed to read and write only Japanese. Yet the writings of brilliant late 10th-century literary women like MURASAKI SHIKIBU and SEI SHŌNAGON reveal that some women did pursue unladylike Chinese studies, albeit covertly. And the essential calligraphic, musical, and above all poetical skills demanded of all aristocrats formed the backbone of education for both sexes.

Feudal times. After 1185 the Heian courtiers were replaced by a new ruling class of warriors, and between that date and 1600 Japan became a society increasingly dominated by males. Although respect for the culture of women of the declining aristocratic class remained high, Chinese Confucian ideas emphasizing the subordination of women gained ground among the *samurai* elite. Not all warrior men were literate, and even fewer samurai women were taught their letters. Those who were, studied with tutors at home as did the males in their families. Heian literature was still valued and fine female poets appeared, but most copybooks for teaching girls to read and write painted ugly images of "woman" and contained abundant Confucian instruction in absolute obedience to parents and husbands and husbands' relatives. This tendency reached a peak during the Edo period when Confucianism became the state ideology. Samurai boys studied Chinese classics in domainal schools established by their lords, while their sisters stayed home learning to write simple characters from Confucian copybooks or memorizing the 19 injunctions for submissive behavior in the ONNA DAIGAKU (1716, The Great Learning for Women). Most of a samurai girl's education, however, involved mastery of weaving, sewing, and household management. Because substantial numbers of lower class families wanted to educate their children too, commoner schools (TERAKOYA) offered the offspring of merchants, artisans, and peasants a curriculum of basic reading, writing, and arithmetic. Schoolboys outnumbered schoolgirls four to one, but in the towns especially, where a merchant wife was expected to help with the family business, girls as well as boys were sent to these schools and many *terakoya* teachers were women. In addition to Confucian morality, *terakoya* textbooks for girls contained practical information about pregnancy, infant care, and cosmetics. A part of the education of some commoner daughters was preparation to go into service at a lord's mansion or to enter one of the female entertainment professions. Such preparation included calligraphy, music, dance, painting, storytelling, and poetry lessons from specialized teachers.

Modernizing nation. After the Tokugawa shogunate was overthrown in 1867–68, the new government enthusiastically endorsed "modern" education for all classes and both sexes. In 1871 five girls, ranging in age from 6 to 15, were sent to the United States to study.

(Three of them went on to graduate from distinguished American colleges.) The Education Order of 1872 (Gakusei) made parents responsible for seeing that "boys and girls without distinction" attended primary school. Young women as well as men flocked to study Western languages, thought, medicine, and science in the new schools which were springing up in the cities. Educational policy throughout the Meiji period (1868–1912) strove to narrow the gap between school attendance of boys and girls. In 1873 only 18 percent of the female primary school age population was in school compared to 39 percent of primary school age boys. By 1910 primary school attendance of both boys and girls was approximately 98 percent. On the other hand, post-primary educational opportunities for women were soon drastically curtailed. Within a few years many schools for older students stopped taking women, and in 1879 the government banned coeducation above the primary school level. Because a girl was expected to become "a good wife and wise mother" (*ryōsai kembo*), government planners viewed higher education for women as peripheral to the school, college, and university programs they were organizing to recruit and train male talent.

Thus on the secondary school level, girls' high schools (*kōtō jogakkō*) were intended to be terminal finishing schools. Their curriculum was one year shorter and of a lower academic standard than that of the middle schools for males, but many of them did offer a teacher's training course. Since the Meiji government was keen to get female teachers into the primary schools, such courses received official encouragement. In addition the government opened normal schools (*shihan gakkō*) for women, although not as frequently as it established such institutions for men. (In 1882, 11 of the 76 prefectural normal schools were women's normal schools.)

Because public education concentrated on males, for girls and women private schooling, a field in which Christian missionaries were active, played an enormously important role. It answered the heavy demand for female secondary schooling, with institutions fashioned after government models: in 1899 out of the 28 girls' high schools all but 8 were privately operated. At the same time, private educators founded post-secondary institutions for women which offered first-rate academic studies previously available only to men. In 1900 TSUDA UMEKO (1865–1929), the youngest of the girls sent to the United States in 1871, founded Joshi Eigaku Juku (now Tsuda College) to give a rigorous training in English language and literature to women. The same year another pioneer, YOSHIOKA YAYOI (1871–1959) opened Tōkyō Women's Medical School (Tōkyō Joigakkō) with four students. Dr. Yoshioka had received her own medical training before the abolition of coeducational facilities, and she was determined to help other women who wanted to qualify as physicians. The following year NARUSE JINZŌ (1858–1919) established Japan Women's University (Nihon Joshi Daigaku). His goal was to educate his students as human beings, as women, and as Japanese subjects. Out of these innovating efforts came generations of education-hungry, ambitious young women, many of whom became educators, authors, and physicians. These colleges also encouraged other private ventures in women's education. By the end of the 1920s they had been joined by sister institutions—advanced art and music schools, a dental college, pharmaceutical colleges, other medical colleges, and colleges of economics and commerce. Because the periodic increases in the number of government schools for girls was always niggardly, right up until Japan's defeat in World War II in 1945 private schools continued to bear the main responsibility for female education.

Post-World War II. In 1945 a new education system, reorganized along American lines, raised many women's colleges to university status and opened all public educational institutions to those who could pass their entrance examinations regardless of sex. However, traditions of segregated education and differentiated adult sex roles remained strong: although some women did enter previously all-male schools and universities, large numbers of them still entered private girls' schools or colleges or women's universities. Statistics for 1980 reveal that although equal numbers of young men and women went on to post-secondary schooling after high school, the majority of the women went to junior colleges rather than to the (mainly coeducational) universities where less than 23 percent of the students were female.

——R. P. Dore, *Education in Tokugawa Japan* (1965). Ivan Parker Hall, *Mori Arinori* (1973). Inoue Kiyoshi, *Nihon josei shi* (1948; rev ed 1954). Karasawa Tomitarō, *Nihon no joshi gakusei* (1958). Kikuchi Dairoku, *Japanese Education* (1908). Murasaki Shikibu, *The Tale of Genji*, tr Edward G. Seidensticker (1976). Donald L. Philippi, tr, *Kojiki* (1969). Rōdōshō Fujin Shōnen Kyoku, *Fujin rōdō no jitsujō* (annual). Shibukawa Hisako, *Kyōiku*, vol 1 of *Kindai Nihon josei shi* (1970). Shikitei Samba, *Ukiyoburo* (1809). Shimamoto Hisae, *Meiji no joseitachi* (1966).   E. Patricia TSURUMI

women's magazines

According to the 1978 *Shuppan nenkan* (Publishers' Yearbook), there were no fewer than 39 magazines for women in Japan. Of the 57 magazines listed in the 1978 report of the Audit Bureau of Circulation, 13 were for women, with 5,056,000 copies, or one-fourth of the total number of magazines printed that year.

During the middle and latter part of the Meiji period (1868–1912), an array of new magazines appealing to specific audiences appeared. In 1884 the first women's magazine, *Jogaku shinshi*, was published. It was succeeded the next year by JOGAKU ZASSHI. Advocating a Christian and enlightened outlook, *Jogaku zasshi* sought to introduce Western ideas of family life. Other magazines such as *Iratsume, Kijo no tomo, Nihon no jogaku, Jokan,* and *Katei zasshi* also began to be published, but all these had a low circulation or were short-lived, with none of the success of *Jogaku zasshi*. Toward the end of the Meiji period several magazines edited by women, notably SEKAI FUJIN by FUKUDA HIDEKO and *Seitō* by HIRATSUKA RAICHŌ, attracted public attention. Women's magazines published during this time were not, generally speaking, produced by commercial publishers but were put out by nonprofit organizations to spread the views about women held by the publishers, who were also contributors and editors.

The years following the end of the Meiji period to the 1950s saw the consolidation of women's magazines as professional enterprises. Magazines that appeared in the last years of Meiji, such as *Fujin gahō*, FUJIN NO TOMO, and *Fujokai*, rose in circulation. New magazines were FUJIN KŌRON (1916), SHUFU NO TOMO (1917), and *Fujin kurabu* (1920). Although *Fujin kōron* purported to be a serious journal of opinion, most of the magazines of this period were eminently practical. The format set during the Taishō period (1912–26)—apart from certain government restrictions during World War II—was to continue in essentially the same form into the 1940s.

Beginning with *Shūkan josei* in 1957, there was a proliferation of weekly magazines for younger women: *Shūkan myōjō* (1958), *Josei jishin* (1958), *Josei sebun* (1963), and *Yangu redī* (1963, Young Lady). This no doubt reflected Japan's economic recovery in general, and more specifically, technical improvements in mass production and marketing. It also reflected other changes: women were better educated, and the continuing increase in the number of nuclear families, fewer children, and more household appliances, meant more free time. The marriages and divorces of popular entertainers, fiction, comics, advice on romantic love, fashion, and similar topics formed the substance of these magazines. The circulations of these magazines grew rapidly in their early years, but since the 1970s they seem to have reached a plateau. Even so, each of these weeklies continues to have an average circulation of about 500,000.

A new direction—and a new phase—was opened up in the 1970s by magazines with exotic names such as *An-an, Non-no, More (Moa), Kurowassan* (Croissant), and *With (Uizu)*. *An-an* was clearly an imitation of the French magazine *Elle,* and *More,* of the American magazine *Cosmopolitan*. There was a marked trend toward internationalization, which was further evidenced by the publication of Japanese editions of two American women's magazines, *Family Circle* and *Cosmopolitan*.

Each of these new magazines used a large format and paper of good quality, with displays of color photographs, full-page advertisements, and articles in no particular order. Meant to be "looked at" rather than read, these were to lead to the appearance of glossier magazines for older women, such as *Misesu* (Mrs) and *Madamu* (Madame). The focus of these magazines of the late 1970s shifted from the traditional subjects of marriage, childcare, and housekeeping to fashion, travel, and other leisure-time pursuits. A new emphasis on women as individuals rather than as wives and mothers is perhaps a result of the women's liberation movement.

Despite the introduction of these new magazines, traditional magazines continue to be popular; according to the 1978 report by the Audit Bureau of Circulation, magazines with a circulation of more than 500,000 copies during the first half of 1978 included *Josei jishin, Josei sebun, Bishō, Shufu no tomo,* and *Shufu to seikatsu*. *Fujin kurabu* and *Misesu* had circulations of 400,000 each, and *Shūkan josei* and *Fujin kōron,* 300,000 each. In other words, magazines catering to different audiences and originating in different periods of publishing history have flourished together. None of these maga-zines deals in depth with issues related to politics or economics. They are all saturated with advertising, which takes up 20 to 60 percent of the pages.   INOUE Teruko

women's suffrage

Although many Westerners have assumed that women's voting rights were a gift from the Allied Occupation for which the Japanese people were unprepared, in fact, a women's suffrage movement in Japan had existed long before the law granting women this right took effect in December 1945.

Sweeping social changes after the Meiji Restoration of 1868 created new opportunities for women and led ultimately to their demand for political and other social rights. Although only a small percentage of girls attended higher educational institutions in the early years of the Meiji period (1868–1912), those who did, began to sense a discrepancy between the new fervor for self-improvement and the traditional emphasis on woman's role as wife and mother. A few forward-looking Japanese men like FUKUZAWA YUKICHI and MORI ARINORI criticized traditional views on women, but government leaders both ignored these criticisms and overlooked the early demands for women's rights made by a small number of male and female participants in the FREEDOM AND PEOPLE'S RIGHTS MOVEMENT. The men who devised the constitution of 1889 and the Civil Code of 1898 reaffirmed their faith in the traditional family system and refused to recognize women as public persons before the law. The PUBLIC ORDER AND POLICE LAW OF 1900 further guaranteed the exclusion of women from politics by forbidding them even to attend political rallies or to join political associations.

It was not until after World War I and the new interest in TAISHŌ DEMOCRACY that politicians began to take the feminists' demands seriously. Encouraged by widespread discussion of the "woman problem" *(fujin mondai),* the nascent manhood suffrage movement, and women's rights gains in Western nations, women organized the SHIN FUJIN KYŌKAI (New Woman's Association) in early 1920. They were primarily responsible for passage of an amendment to the Public Order and Police Law in 1922 that permitted women to attend political rallies.

Of the numerous women's groups committed to suffrage that were formed in the following years, the FUSEN KAKUTOKU DŌMEI (Women's Suffrage League) was the most influential. Established by ICHIKAWA FUSAE and other prominent activists in December 1924, the league came under bitter attack from socialists, conservatives, and the general public thoughout its 16-year history. The women's suffrage movement was more than just an attempt to get the support of politicians for proposed legislation granting women the right to join political associations or parties, to participate in local politics (referred to as civil rights by suffragists), and to vote and stand as candidates to the House of Representatives on the national level. By demanding rights, the suffragists were making an assault on a social system which did not prescribe rights for women, only duties. In the years after the MANCHURIAN INCIDENT of 1931, when emphasis was increasingly placed on preservation of the status quo and women's important role in the family, it became more difficult for the suffragists to continue talking about rights. Not only did the concept of women's suffrage seem foreign in origin, it was also considered selfish during the militaristic 1930s to think about oneself and ignore society's larger concerns. The women's suffrage movement ended with the dissolution of the Fusen Kakutoku Dōmei in October 1940, in the militarist suppression of all progressive movements in Japan.

Largely a product of cooperation between Japanese feminists and women staff officers in the Allied Occupation, a bill extending rights to women on the national level was promulgated on 17 December 1945. In accordance with the provisions of the POTSDAM DECLARATION, the Japanese government granted women over the age of 20 the right to vote for members of the House of Representatives and permitted those over 25 to become candidates in national elections. Suffragists who had worked for this one goal welcomed the new opportunity and encouraged women to participate actively in politics. Although the number of women seeking elective office in Japan has never been as high as it was during the first postwar election in April 1946 (there were 79 women candidates), women's awareness of politics and social concerns has grown since the war. See also CONSUMER MOVEMENT.

📖——Ichikawa Fusae, *Ichikawa Fusae jiden: Senzenhen* (1974). Ichikawa Fusae, *Watakushi no fujin undō* (1972). Mitsui Reiko, *Gendai fujin undō shi nempyō* (1963). Takamure Itsue, *Takamure*

Itsue zenshū, vol 5 (Rironsha, 1966). Yoneda Sayoko, *Kindai Nihon josei shi*, 2 vols (1972). Yoshimi Kaneko, *Fujin sanseiken*, vol 2 of *Kindai Nihon josei shi* (1971).　　　　Kathleen MOLONY

women workers, protective legislation for

Provided by article 3 and chapter 6 of the Labor Standards Law (Rōdō Kijun Hō), this legislation was drafted in 1947 in accordance with the International Labor Conventions to set minimum standards for women's working conditions. At that time, it was felt that women needed special protection in the workplace, but now, in light of current technological advances, some feminists criticize the Labor Standards Law as discriminating unfairly against women.

Article 4 calls for equal wages irrespective of sex, but so far it has proved ineffective in securing women commensurate pay. Chapter 6 makes special provisions for women and minors. For example, working more than an 8-hour day or a 48-hour week is considered overtime for women and minors; under the law, they may work only an extra 2 hours per day and are limited to 6 extra hours per week and a total of 150 extra hours per year. They are also prohibited from working between 10:00 PM and 5:00 AM, with a few exceptions for such positions as stewardesses and nurses. Women are specifically barred from jobs that are considered dangerous, such as those involving exposure to heavy machinery, poisonous substances, high voltage, or extreme temperatures. They are also prohibited from working underground. Women are entitled to childbirth leave six weeks prior to expected delivery and may not work during the six weeks following. New mothers are also entitled to two nursing periods of 30 minutes each, but this provision is impractical without nearby day-care facilities for infants. One unusual provision allows women in certain strenuous jobs the right to take a day or so of paid leave during their menstrual periods.

These provisions have been cited by businesses as reasons why women cannot be promoted to executive positions or jobs in media that require much overtime and night work. Professional women would like to have these restrictions relaxed, but blue-collar women feel this legislation is still necessary to protect them from exploitation. See also LABOR LAWS; EQUALITY OF THE SEXES UNDER THE LAW; WOMEN IN THE LABOR FORCE.　　　　Eileen HARGADINE

woodblock prints → ukiyo-e; modern prints

wooden clogs → geta

wooden tablets → mokkan

woodenware

(mokkōhin). Wood has traditionally been an important building material in Japan. The 8th-century chronicle NIHON SHOKI mentions the use of Japanese cypress *(hinoki)* for palace construction, Japanese cedar *(sugi)* and camphor *(kusu)* for boats, and *maki* (a kind of yellow wood) for coffins. From ancient times "first-grade oak" *(ichiigashi)* was generally used for bows, red oak *(akagashi)* for farm implements, and Japanese boxwood *(tsuge)* for combs. The grain, as well as the color of the wood, is considered an important aesthetic element, and even today wooden articles are still made from traditionally esteemed varieties of wood.

The oldest known wooden articles in Japan, including some lacquer ware, were made with stone tools and date from the second millennium BC. In the period around 200 BC, iron tools and lathes were used to make wooden farm implements. By around 100 BC, the main wooden products were household utensils. A sophisticated knowledge of lumbering, sawing, processing, cutting, lathing, and drilling was achieved. The many 4th- and 5th-century tools that have been unearthed, including handled planes, saws, chisels, and adzes, indicate a high standard of workmanship.

With the introduction of Buddhism to Japan in the 6th century, new building needs arose, and the arrival of woodworkers from the continent resulted in rapid advancements in techniques. One of the most impressive achievements of this time is the Tamamushi Shrine in the temple HŌRYŪJI in Nara. In the 8th century a woodworkers' bureau was set up by the government to meet increasing demands.

Woodcraft techniques reached a high point in the Nara period (710–794), and among the treasures of the 8th-century SHŌSŌIN art

repository are numerous articles made of imported wood, such as *shitan* (rosewood) and *byakudan* (sandalwood), decorated with MOTHER-OF-PEARL INLAY, tortoiseshell (see TORTOISESHELL WARE), and ivory.

In the Heian period (794–1185), as LACQUER WARE and MAKI-E became popular, the role of woodcraft makers was reduced to supplying material to lacquer and *maki-e* artists. However, in the 16th century, the art was revived when tea masters, who appreciated the simple beauty of woodenware, began to adopt such ware for their ceremonies. With the flourishing of the merchant class in the Edo period (1600–1868), demand for woodenware increased and production centers sprang up in various parts of the country. Some of the outstanding examples of woodenware produced today are the bamboo ware of Shizuoka Prefecture, the poplar ware of Akita Prefecture, and the paulownia chests of Niigata Prefecture. See also FOLK CRAFTS.　　　　NAKASATO Toshikatsu

woodpeckers

(kitsutsuki). Birds of the family Picidae, noted for their sharply pointed bills with which they chip tree trunks for insects. They lay their white eggs in cavities chiseled deep into tree trunks or branches. Eleven species are found in Japan. Most of these are also found in Europe, but four are unique to Asia or Japan: the large red, white, and black *kitataki* (white-bellied black woodpecker; *Dryocopus javensis),* formerly found on the island of Tsushima and now believed to be extinct; the greenish yellow *aogera* (Japanese green woodpecker; *Picus awokera),* found from Honshū southward; the dark red *noguchigera* (Pryer's woodpecker; *Sapheopipo noguchii),* found on Okinawa; and the white and brown striped *kogera* (Japanese pygmy woodpecker; *Dendrocopos kizuki*), the smallest of Japanese woodpeckers.　　　　TAKANO Shinji

word games

(kotoba asobi). With its relatively simple phonetic structure and abundance of homophones, the Japanese language lends itself to puns and other word games. The KAKEKOTOBA (pivot words) in WAKA poetry, the intricate system of capping verses through puns and word association in RENGA AND HAIKAI linked verse, and the humor based on word play in ZAPPAI AND SENRYŪ comic verses are all evidence of the importance of word games in the Japanese literary tradition. Although there is much less emphasis on the use of puns and word play in modern literature, word games are still enjoyed by both adults and children. Apart from puns, the most popular forms are *nazo nazo* (RIDDLES), capping of verses and one liners, tongue twisters, and palindromes (see also PROVERBS).

Shiritori, or capping, was a favorite pastime of Heian period (794–1185) courtiers. Typically, two or more persons would hold a competition in which each took turns capping a series of verses. As one person read a *waka* poem of 31 syllables, the next person would take the last word or syllable from it and start a new verse. In this way, a chain of verses was created. However, since the capping was done only on the basis of the last word or syllable, unlike the later *renga* linked verse, in which the poems are linked both verbally and thematically, these early *shiritori* verses could go on indefinitely without much regard for meaning or thematic continuity. In later times, namely the Edo period (1600–1868), *shiritori* was also played by townsmen at parties and gatherings. By then, as might be expected of exuberant townsmen, capping was extended to jokes, single words, and phrases. Today it is exclusively a children's game in which single words are linked according to the last syllable. For example: *ringo* (apple), *gorira* (gorilla), *rajio* (radio), *okane* (money), *nezumi* (mouse), and so on.

Tongue twisters, or *hayakuchi,* have also long been popular. GAGAKU court musicians of the Heian period included among their repertoire the singing of songs at a very fast tempo. In the Kamakura period (1185–1333) the tradition was further developed into humorous *sōga,* or "fast songs," performed at banquets to entertain the new warrior aristocrats. In time these "fast songs" were taken up by the common people. In later periods, *hayakuchi* became less musically oriented and more recitative.

In the Edo period the most accomplished master of the tongue twister was the *kabuki* actor Ichikawa Danjūrō II. In the title role as a medicine vendor in the play *Uirōuri* (1718), he held forth with a humorous *hayakuchi* monologue lasting several minutes. The play later became one of the specialties of the Ichikawa family of kabuki actors. Today, as with other forms of word game, tongue twisters are played mostly by children. Some well-known examples are: *Namamugi namagome namatamago* (uncooked wheat, uncooked rice, and uncooked eggs); *Tonari no kyaku wa yoku kaki kuu kyaku da* (The guest next door is a guest who likes to eat a lot of persimmons); *Tōkyō Tokkyo Kyoka Kyoku* (The Tōkyō Patent Office).

Kaibun are palindromes. Composing palindromic poetry was a popular pastime of Chinese poets from early on, and Japanese *waka* poets also took to composing such verses as a poetic exercise and as a diversion from serious poetry. In the Edo period *renga* and *haikai* poets further popularized this practice and competed with one another. Today *kaibun* are less intricate and are usually made up of single words and expressions as in *taue uta* (*ta u e u ta*, or "rice planting song") and *tsukue e kutsu* (*tsu ku e e ku tsu*, "shoes on the desk").

workers' compensation

(*rōdōsha saigai hoshō*). Compensation given to a worker or surviving family members in the event of injury or death resulting from on-the-job accidents. There were instances in the Edo period (1600–1868) of compensation given to mine workers on the occasion of work-related accidents in the form of mutual aid provided by the Tomoko Dōmei (Friend's League). During the Meiji period (1868–1912), laws that provided government compensation for workers in government enterprises and compensation for workers in the mining industry were instituted. The FACTORY LAW OF 1911 (Kōjō Hō) prescribed compensation by employers in the case of accidents that were not due to serious fault on the part of the employee; it obligated employers to provide medical expenses, sick pay, disability benefits, aid to surviving family members, and funeral expenses. In 1922 the Health Insurance Law (Kenkō Hoken Hō) was enacted, and measures were taken to ensure compliance by employers in providing aid. With the enactment of the 1947 Labor Standards Law (Rōdō Kijun Hō; see LABOR LAWS) and Workers' Compensation Law (Rōdōsha Saigai Hoshō Hō) after World War II, workers' accident compensation was set up under a unified system and freed from the dependence on charity that had characterized such aid in prewar years. Its special features included such items as no-fault liability of the employer, reparation for on-the-job accidents, compensation to workers or surviving family members which enabled maintenance of a standard of living equal to that before the accident, and enforcement of compensation under the jurisdiction of government control. See MEDICAL AND HEALTH INSURANCE.

KURITA Ken

Worker–Farmer Party → Rōdōsha Nōmintō

work hours

Prior to World War II, work hours in Japan were long and set unilaterally by employers. The FACTORY LAW OF 1911, which went into effect in 1916, was aimed substantially at abuses of child and female labor, but its provisions were very narrowly constructed, and the hours of labor remained uncontrolled. As part of the general postwar reform program, the Labor Standards Law, passed in 1947, mandated 8 work hours per day and 48 work hours per week, thus bringing Japanese work hours closer to international standards. Special provisions were included to protect children under 18 and women. However, it still remains common for employees to work long hours to fulfill the reciprocal expectations of the Japanese employment system, and average work hours are thus longer than the legislated limits. Overtime work is permitted under special circumstances by the Labor Standards Law: during an emergency, for official government business, or by written agreement with a body representing a majority of workers. Permission from an inspection office is required, except for government business. Most overtime hours are worked by agreement with a workers' association. Overtime compensation of 125 percent of normal pay (150 percent at night) is compulsory by law.

Shift duty is declining on the whole, except among large manufacturers, where it is increasing. In such industries as steel or chemicals, three shifts are common and two shifts are found in transportation equipment assembly and textiles finishing plants.

As a result of decreased work hours in the 1960s, Japanese work hours now approach Western standards. The traditional workweek is still at least five-and-a-half days, however, and the five-day week is not yet widespread. At most, an employee might work a five-day week every other week or once a month. There is variety in the length of work hours depending on the size of the enterprise, with large enterprises leading the way toward shorter hours. See also LABOR LAWS; LABOR; EMPLOYMENT SYSTEM, MODERN.

KURITA Ken

work regulations

(*shūgyō kisoku*). Rules governing the terms and conditions of employment. Work regulations may be set unilaterally or collectively by trade unions and by employers of work groups. In Japan they are usually set by employers, who take into consideration the union's opinion and seek its consent. The Labor Standards Law (Rōdō Kijun Hō) of 1947 (see LABOR LAWS) provides that an employer with more than 10 regularly employed workers must establish work regulations and stipulate working conditions. He must ask the opinion of the majority unions within his establishment or else representatives of a majority of his employees. He must also submit his regulations to the LABOR STANDARDS INSPECTION OFFICES and display or post them for employee examination. The supervision offices are authorized to order changes in regulations that contradict laws, ordinances, or collective agreements. Individual EMPLOYMENT CONTRACTS contradicting legitimate regulations are similarly regarded as null and void. The purpose of the Labor Standards Law is to ensure at least a minimum standard of working conditions and to recognize the legal priority of work regulations set by collective agreement over those unilaterally set by employers. *HANAMI Tadashi*

World War I

Declaration of War —— On 1 August 1914 Germany, a member of the Triple Alliance with Austria and Italy, declared war on Russia, a member of the Triple Entente with Britain and France. The day after Germany declared war against France on 3 August, Britain declared war against Germany. On the Shandong (Shantung) Peninsula in China the German concession at Qingdao (Tsingtao; see JIAOZHOU [KIAOCHOW] CONCESSION) and the British concession at Weihaiwei were both fortified. A conflict between British and German troops in Shandong might have easily involved the British base at Hong Kong and German bases in the Mariana, Caroline, and Marshall islands. The ANGLO-JAPANESE ALLIANCE, as revised in 1911, would have required Japanese participation on the British side.

On 4 August Japan announced neutrality but promised to support Britain if requested to repel a German attack on Hong Kong or Weihaiwei. On 7 August Japan received a British request to destroy armed German merchant cruisers in Chinese waters. On 8 August Japan decided to enter the war on Britain's side. When Japan also announced its intention of eliminating German power from Shandong, Britain tried to ensure that such action would "not extend to the Pacific Ocean beyond the China seas." But Japan refused to accept any limits on its operations and declared war on 23 August, one week after sending to Berlin an ultimatum that had gone unanswered.

Military Operations —— Japan moved swiftly against German possessions in Shandong and the Pacific islands. On 26 August a combined Japanese and British fleet blockaded Qingdao, but the German Far Eastern fleet had already left the area. On 2 September Japanese troops arrived in Shandong, British troops a few weeks later. On 7 November about 3,000 Germans surrendered to a combined force of about 29,000 Japanese and 1,000 British troops. During October the Japanese had eliminated German power from the Mariana, Caroline, and Marshall islands. By the end of 1914 the Japanese had suffered about 2,000 casualties and taken about 5,000 German prisoners. German possessions in Shandong and the Pacific islands north of the equator were under Japanese control.

Twenty-One Demands —— Almost immediately after these victories, Japan presented the so-called TWENTY-ONE DEMANDS to China's President YUAN SHIKAI (Yüan Shih-k'ai) on 18 January 1915. When Yuan leaked to the foreign press these demands for recognition of much greater Japanese influence and privileges in China, Britain and the United States issued protests to Japan. Agreeing to drop some of the demands, Japan forced Yuan to accept the remainder in treaties and agreements signed on 25 May 1915.

Political Relations with the Allies —— Throughout 1915 and 1916 German efforts to make a separate peace with Japan and Russia proved unsuccessful. In 1916 Russia offered Japan a sector of the Russian-controlled CHINESE EASTERN RAILWAY in Manchuria in return for munitions. On 3 July Japan and Russia signed an agreement not to make a separate peace and to consult each other on what common action might be required if the territorial rights or interests of either party were menaced by a third power in Asia (see RUSSO-JAPANESE AGREEMENTS OF 1907–1916). The term, "third power," could refer to Germany, Britain, or the United States.

In 1917 Japan attempted to consolidate its recent gains in China and the Pacific by improving relations with Britain and the United States. In January Britain requested Japan to send destroyers to the Mediterranean. Japan agreed, in return for British recognition of Japan's right to German possessions in Shandong and the Pacific islands north of the equator. Japan agreed to recognize British rights to the German islands south of the equator. Shortly after this secret agreement, Japan received similar recognition of its claims from France, Italy, and Russia.

When the United States entered the war on 6 April, Americans and Japanese found themselves as allies despite their competition for influence in China, naval rivalry in the Pacific, and racial discrimination against persons of Japanese origin legally residing in the United States. The LANSING–ISHII AGREEMENT of 2 November 1917 indicated a degree of compromise, however ambiguous: the United States recognized Japan's "special interests" in China, and both sides affirmed the independence and territorial integrity of China, the principle of the Open Door, and equal opportunity for commerce and industry in China.

During 1918 Japan continued to extend its influence and privileges in China. The estimated total value of all Japanese loans to China during 1917 and 1918, including the NISHIHARA LOANS, was between ¥150,000,000 and ¥200,000,000. In return for the loans, Premier DUAN QIRUI (Tuan Ch'i-jui) guaranteed the privileges granted to Japan in the 1915 treaties and ceded additional railway and mining rights. Duan also agreed to closer military, economic, and political cooperation with Japan.

The Bolshevik Revolution of 1917, Russia's separate peace with Germany, and its civil war in areas close to territory under Japanese control increased Allied apprehensions about the chaotic situation in Russia. On 8 July 1918 the United States invited Japan to join an American intervention in Siberia, each side contributing about 7,000 troops. The alleged objective of this intervention was to assure the swift arrival of Czech soldiers traveling along the Trans-Siberian Railway to Vladivostok to join the Allies in Western Europe by way of the Pacific Ocean. Japan accepted the American invitation; however, it sent 12,000 troops instead of 7,000 and soon increased its forces in Siberia to about 70,000. See also SIBERIAN INTERVENTION.

Military Expansion and Economic Growth——Japanese military and economic power grew rapidly during the war. The naval budget had grown from ¥83,260,000 in 1914 to ¥215,903,000 in 1918 and ¥316,419,000 in 1919. At the beginning of 1914 there were Japanese troops in Taiwan (taken from China in 1895 following the SINO-JAPANESE WAR OF 1894–1895), parts of Mainland China (increases allowed by the BOXER REBELLION Protocol in 1901), parts of South Manchuria and the southern half of Sakhalin (taken from Russia in 1905 following the RUSSO-JAPANESE WAR), and Korea (annexed in 1910). By the end of 1918, Japanese troops also held former German territory in Shandong and the Pacific islands north of the equator, additional parts of China proper, part of northern Manchuria, and part of eastern Siberia. During the war Japan profited from the inability of former suppliers to meet continuing demand in Asian markets. Orders for munitions poured in from the Allies, and foreign demand for Japanese shipping increased. The value of Japanese exports rose about threefold between 1913 and 1918; their volume rose by about 50 percent.

Japan's industrial boom and the influx of capital during the war led to rampant inflation, and the steep rise in prices for such daily necessities as rice easily outstripped the rise in wages for Japan's growing urban population. One result was the participation of more than a million people in the RICE RIOTS OF 1918, which broke out in some 300 locations throughout the country. But on the whole, the spectacular growth of the economy, industry, armed forces, and empire during World War I was a source of pride to many Japanese; and it was with great confidence that Japan approached the Paris Peace Conference in 1919. See VERSAILLES, TREATY OF.

■——Russell H. Fifield, *Woodrow Wilson and the Far East: The Diplomacy of the Shantung Question* (1952). Gaimushō Hyakunenshi Hensan Iinkai, ed, *Gaimushō no hyakunen*, vol 1 (1969). A. Whitney Griswold, *The Far Eastern Policy of the United States* (1938). Akira Iriye, *Across the Pacific* (1967). Arthur S. Link, *Wilson: The Struggle for Neutrality, 1914–1915* (1960). Ernest R. May and James C. Thomson, ed, *American–East Asian Relations: A Sur-*

vey (1972), especially the article by Roger Dingman on 1917–1922. James W. Morley, ed, *Japan's Foreign Policy, 1868–1941: A Research Guide* (1974). Nagaoka Shinjirō, *Daiichiji taisen to Nihon* (1965). Ian Nish, *Alliance in Decline: A Study in Anglo-Japanese Relations, 1908–1923* (1972). Ian Nish, *Japanese Foreign Policy, 1869–1942* (1977). Usui Katsumi, *Nihon to Chūgoku: Taishō jidai*, in *Kindai Nihon gaikō shi sōsho*, vol 7 (Hara Shobō, 1972).

Frederick F. CZUPRYNA

World War II

World War II was a vast turbulence of separate but interrelated wars. Japan's war with China beginning in 1937 played an important part in propelling Japan toward war with the United States, Great Britain, and their allies in 1941. With Japan's attack on Pearl Harbor on 7 December 1941, war became global except in one respect: the Soviet Union and Japan remained at peace until 9 August 1945, when the Soviets attacked.

Historians agree now, no less than in the 1940s, that militarist expansionism was the principal cause of Japan's involvement in World War II, though they now perceive this expansionism as more complex and less preconceived than they did at the time of the war. Historians also now believe that the United States, though essentially defensive, contributed to the coming of the war, and they recognize how world conflicts and tension in the decade before Pearl Harbor contributed to Japan's difficulties and accelerated its expansion.

Japanese Expansionism——Throughout the world, and especially in Japan, the 1930s was a decade of fear in contrast to the relative optimism of the 1920s. Fear arose mainly from the world economic crisis that began with the American stock market crash of 1929 and led to the collapse of international trade and to economic autarky, that is, closed, self-reliant national economies. In Japan, which was heavily dependent on foreign trade, there was increased pressure from many quarters to take control of sources of vital raw materials and markets, and this encouraged the militarists bent on imperial expansion.

The world economic crisis also had adverse political effects by weakening moderate, centrist parliamentary parties in Japan and spurring totalitarian forces on the left and right. Japan was vulnerable to the authoritarianism, chauvinism, and militarism of the 1930s. Liberal party government had not taken firm root, and nationalism was an especially powerful force. Japanese perceived their essential values threatened by modern, Western forms of political, social, and economic development. RIGHT WING groups such as the AMUR RIVER SOCIETY proliferated, and the most radical of these dedicated themselves to elimination of the emperor's moderate-minded advisers. Thus the period 1930–36 was a time of political assassination, and plotting by radical groups, both military and civilian, profoundly intimidated Japan's moderate, Western-oriented leadership. This internal crisis paved the way for the army to assume a decisive role in both domestic and foreign policy.

The IMPERIAL JAPANESE ARMY was dangerously volatile in the early 1930s. Imbued with the *samurai* spirit, self-appointed guardian of essential Japanese virtues, and embittered by years of lean arms budgets, its radical fringe engineered the MANCHURIAN INCIDENT of 1931 and demanded that the nation confront its enemies and prepare for total war. At the same time it was riddled with clique rivalries and disputes over the requisite arms and skills for modern war. The tendency in Japan for junior officers to intimidate their seniors and the passing away of the original leaders of the MEIJI RESTORATION added to the climate of insubordination and violence. Young army officers influenced by ultranationalism joined in plots and assassinations. Hoping to end domestic violence, the civilian leadership submitted to army demands. After the FEBRUARY 26TH INCIDENT, the army finally restored discipline in its ranks. By then it was firmly in control of the Japanese government. Only the IMPERIAL JAPANESE NAVY, with its alternative objectives of southern expansion (see SOUTHERN EXPANSION DOCTRINE), offered competition.

The Japan that emerged from this turmoil of the early and mid-1930s was bent on conflict. Preparing for what it regarded as the total war inevitable as a result of its China involvement, the military encouraged the development of heavy industry, built up the armed forces, and mobilized the population. The role of the Diet and political parties diminished as government became increasingly authoritarian and totalitarian. Links binding Japan to the interwar treaty order—the League of Nations and the Washington Treaty system—snapped one by one (see LEAGUE OF NATIONS AND JAPAN; WASHINGTON CONFERENCE; WASHINGTON NAVAL TREATY OF 1922). Japan's Western-oriented statesmen and bureaucrats bowed to new PAN-ASIANISM, occasionally exercising restraint, but focusing on tactics, not objectives. National self-sufficiency and Asiatic hegemony became the guiding assumptions of the Foreign Ministry and the military.

Japanese policy tended to be ambiguous and haphazard, however. No rational scheme for achieving the above aims existed. Japan steadily widened its sphere in Northeast Asia by moving beyond Manchuria into Inner Mongolia and North China, but it expected war with the Soviet Union, not China. Access to the natural resources of Southeast Asia was regarded as essential and justifying large navy increases, but confrontation with the Western colonial powers that controlled the region remained hypothetical. Implicit in Japan's quest for hegemony was a scale of conflict altogether beyond its means.

When hostilities broke out in North China in July 1937 with the MARCO POLO BRIDGE INCIDENT, the Japanese army expected that quick, massive deployments of troops would snuff out Chinese resistance. Instead the Chinese retreated to the interior and refused to submit. Facing strong Soviet forces in the north, which defeated the powerful Japanese GUANDONG (KWANTUNG) ARMY in unpublicized border encounters and incidents in 1940, Japan was unable to concentrate on achieving victory in China. The war became a quagmire, sucking in Japan's resources and straining relations with the United States and other nations involved in China. See SINO-JAPANESE WAR OF 1937–1945; UNITED STATES AND JAPAN.

Effects of the European War —— Japan's war in China dragged on against a background of mounting tension in Europe and finally, in September 1939, of war between Germany and the Western democracies. In April and May of 1940 the full force of the German army and air force smashed Denmark, Norway, Holland, Belgium, and France. Hitler stood at the Channel, and England was besieged.

Crisis in the Western world tended to aggravate the East Asian crisis. Germany presented Japan with tempting but dangerous opportunities. The two nations had common enemies, immediate and prospective. Chief among these was the Soviet Union. The Japanese feared the Red Army and communist influence in East Asia. Cooperation with Germany would neutralize these threats. Another common enemy was Britain, the leading imperial power in East Asia, together with its colonial partners France and the Netherlands. Antipathetical to both Germany and Japan and possessing prodigious latent power, but remote and passive, was the United States.

Cooperation between Germany, Italy, and Japan began in 1936 with the ANTI-COMINTERN PACT, which provided an ideological base for closer links. Germany's victory in the West in 1940 jeopardized the possessions of European colonial powers, making them tempting prizes for the Japanese not only because of their resources, but now as bases for encircling and subduing China. And Japanese leaders feared that unless Japan joined Germany in the division of territorial spoils, Germany would preempt them. Japan joined the Axis alliance with the TRIPARTITE PACT in September 1940, thereby locking itself into the widening world conflagration.

It was a fragile partnership. Japan by 1940, like Germany, was an authoritarian police state, but it was not fascist. The Nazi myth of Aryan superiority was an implicit insult to the Japanese. The Axis alliance pledged each nation to join the others in war if the others were attacked, but Japan reserved the right to determine what was an attack. Germany and Japan had common enemies but no common strategy. The German-Soviet Pact of 1939, which permitted Germany to concentrate on the Western Front, confounded Japan and led to the fall of the HIRANUMA KIICHIRŌ cabinet. Japan was deaf to German entreaties that Japan join in war on the Soviet Union in June 1941, having composed a neutrality pact with Moscow, and instead turned southward. For Japan the object of the Axis alliance was to paralyze the United States, to neutralize and perhaps temporarily resolve conflicts with the Soviets, and to exploit the colonies of prostrate European powers. The alliance fulfilled virtually none of these expectations. Again Japan had expanded its commitments to enhance its security, only to find that it had deepened its predicament.

Japanese-American Confrontation —— Deep-seated, long-standing antagonism existed in the Japanese-American relationship. Japan's emergence as a great power following its victories over China and Russia at the turn of the century posed a threat to American interests in the western Pacific. Since that time, each navy had regarded the other as its most likely enemy in the event of war. To Americans, Japan appeared as a trade rival in China and a menace to

the sovereignty and integrity of that nation for which they had come to feel a special affection and responsibility. The Japanese on their part bitterly resented American racial discrimination and immigration restrictions aimed particularly at Asians. They regarded as hypocrisy American preaching about self-determination and equality of nations in Asia when the United States maintained a sphere of influence of its own in the Western Hemisphere.

In spite of this antagonism, however, the two nations had maintained a mutually profitable trade and investment relationship. Americans strongly opposed bold adventures in distant lands during the interwar period and especially during the isolationistic 1930s. Furthermore, with a navy below treaty limits and a minuscule army, the United States lacked the strength to challenge Japan in East Asia.

Throughout the 1930s the United States never risked war with Japan. On behalf of China it invoked the principles of the League of Nations, the NINE-POWER TREATY, and the KELLOG-BRIAND PACT, all violated by Japan in China. It resumed the development of naval armament and repeatedly and consistently protested Japan's violation of treaties and injury to American citizens, property, and interests in China. But equally consistently, it sought to avoid provoking Japan, and only at the very end of the decade turned toward economic coercion. At the same time the United States avoided any step that might condone or encourage what most Americans regarded as Japan's predatory and lawless conduct. Thus, while no event of the 1930s pointed directly toward Pearl Harbor, the accumulation of grievances and hostility made resolution of conflict increasingly difficult.

The two nations came to a decisive confrontation as a result of the European war. President Franklin D. ROOSEVELT determined that America's vital interest lay in supporting the Western democracies against Hitler and that therefore, because of military stringency, the United States must adopt a defensive posture in the Pacific. But the world of 1940–41 could not be so neatly divided. The war in Europe had profound ramifications elsewhere. German victory in the West tempted Japan to advance into Southeast Asia, which in turn prompted American countermeasures partly to protect Britain's resources and communications and sustain Britain at home and in the Middle East. Then the Axis alliance firmly identified Japan in the American mind with its fascist European partners. Later, American officials feared Japan would join Hitler against Russia if given any respite or assurance in China or the Pacific. And China needed help and encouragement to remain in the war fighting Japanese armies.

Above all, Roosevelt hoped to create a grand coalition against the Axis and to prove American determination and reliability as a partner and ally after years of isolationism. He needed to rally the American public to a responsible American role in international affairs. To do so he had to uphold the values of international conduct that Japan had consistently flouted.

The deterrence of further Japanese expansion became the object of American policy. In July 1939 the United States gave notice abrogating the Japanese-American commercial treaty, thereby permitting embargo of American exports to Japan (see NONRECOGNITION POLICY). In May 1940 the president ordered the fleet to remain at Pearl Harbor as a first step in plans for war with Japan. Then when Japan moved into northern Indochina in September 1940, the United States began embargoing exports, extending the list product by product, month by month. The critical hardening of the American position occurred in the summer of 1941 when Japan moved into southern Indochina. The government froze Japanese assets in the United States, capped its list of embargoed goods by denying the most critical item, oil, dispatched heavy bombers and reinforcements to the Philippines, and extended Lend-Lease to China. A coordinated embargo by the Dutch, the British Commonwealth, and the United States cut off all of Japan's access to foreign oil, on which it almost entirely depended. Extension of Lend-Lease to the Soviet Union and joint command and defense arrangements for the Southwest Pacific–Southeast Asia region completed the encirclement of Japan.

American leaders profoundly misread the impact of their moves on Japan. They intended to force Japan to a standstill; instead they boxed Japan into a corner and forced it to move, for Japan's leaders were certain they must do something. The nation's capacity for war and defense, indeed its self-respect and standing, would shrivel as its oil reserves dwindled. One alternative was to strike the United States soon, before its defenses were complete and before the vast naval armada laid down in 1940 took to sea. The other alternative was to negotiate in the hope that Japan could make concessions and withdrawals but still retain control of territory it considered vital in

North China and Manchuria, secure an honorable end to the China war, and gain access to essential oil supplies. Through the late summer and fall of 1941 Japan pursued both alternatives and at the same time prepared for attack.

The negotiations were tortuous, bewildering, at times bumbling, and immensely fatiguing. But peace did not fail through poor communication, for months of exchanges made the position of each side clear to the other. The government of General TŌJŌ HIDEKI was prepared to make major concessions to the United States. It would practically negate the Axis alliance by assuring the United States that in the event of a German-American war Japan would not feel bound to come to Germany's assistance. Japan would also agree to withdraw from Indochina and large parts of China, but only on the condition that the United States exert pressure on China to negotiate an end to the war, and it insisted on retaining garrisons in North China for an extended period. The Americans were not prepared to accept these China demands. No matter how hard the diplomats tried, their solutions inevitably involved the United States and threatened Chinese integrity and sovereignty. Roosevelt was not willing to assume such a role, since it would negate the very values through which he was seeking to rally public support and build an anti-Axis coalition. Worsening chances of agreement was a suspicion of Japanese intentions recently confirmed by the decoding of Japanese messages indicating preparations for attack. But it was a fundamental conflict of interest that eventually brought Japan and the United States into collision.

Japan's decision for war was a desperate gamble. The nation's leaders calculated that Japan's security depended on maintaining its preponderance in East Asia, which in turn required access to the resources of Southeast Asia, especially the oil of Sumatra and Borneo. Only by force could access be assured, they reasoned, and that meant war with the Netherlands and the British Commonwealth; such a war would automatically involve Britain's partner, the United States. Admiral YAMAMOTO ISOROKU, Commander of the Combined Fleet, advised that, given this threat from the American quarter, a preemptive strike should be launched against Pearl Harbor to neutralize the American fleet before attacks southward. Malaya and the East Indies would provide oil and rubber, but to protect them Japan's fleets and armies would advance to the borders of India, the northern coast of Australia, and through sequences of island chains to the mid-Pacific. China surrounded would finally succumb. Behind this far-flung perimeter with its network of air and naval bases the imperial fleet would lie in wait. Japan's leaders knew that America's industrial capacity was vastly greater than theirs. They hoped, nevertheless, that the United States would find the penetration of these barriers too painful and costly and compromise or simply desist. They risked being wrong in their estimate of American will, but that risk was preferable to bowing to American demands. To Japan's military leadership, such humiliation would be intolerable.

Japan Attacks —— After months of negotiations in Washington, Secretary of State Cordell HULL concluded that further negotiation was hopeless, in spite of the American military's desire for delay, and presented the Japanese with a comprehensive restatement of the American position on 26 November 1941. This the Japanese construed as an ultimatum, though it was not intended as such. Already their military movements were under way. A strike force built around six large aircraft carriers steamed silently across the northern Pacific to a launching position just north of Oahu, subject to recall until the last hours of its voyage. At dawn on 7 December Japanese bombers and torpedo planes dealt devastating blows to the American fleet in Pearl Harbor and to surrounding airfields. (See PEARL HARBOR, ATTACK ON.)

The attack was a success in the short term, for it damaged or destroyed every battleship in the harbor. In the long term, the attack failed because no American aircraft carriers happened to be in harbor and the repair and supply facilities of the base survived virtually intact. Most important, the attack so angered Americans as to overcome the indifference and isolationism on which Japan's leaders had counted.

Two strongholds, the Philippines and Malaya, lay in the path of the Japanese advance on the Indies. Neither proved an impediment. Hours after Pearl Harbor, Japanese aircraft caught General Douglas MACARTHUR's planes on the ground at Clark Field, north of Manila in the Philippines, and destroyed most of them. Coordinated land, sea, and air attacks cleared Luzon of American sea and air power and bottled up the American-Filipino army on the Bataan Peninsula. These forces held out until 6 May 1942, longer than the Japanese expected, but, isolated as they were, they failed to stem the campaign southward. The conquest of Malaya was stunning. Troops entering northern Malaya pressed southward so vigorously that British-Indian-Australian forces never had a chance to regroup and stand. Demoralized and poorly led, they retreated to Singapore, with the Japanese hard on their heels. This bastion of British strength in the East surrendered on 15 February 1942. Meanwhile, Japanese forces converged on the Dutch East Indies, leaping from Borneo and Celebes to Sumatra and in March to Java. By the time resistance ceased in the Philippines, British forces were in full retreat in Burma, and Japan controlled the northern coast of New Guinea, the Bismarcks, the northern Solomons, the Gilberts, and Guam and Wake islands in the Central Pacific.

The Japanese campaigns of December 1941 through early 1942 amounted to some of the most stunning feats in military history. With the bulk of the Japanese army tied down in China and in Manchuria, only 11 divisions were available for the southward advance. By careful planning, bold action, and close interservice coordination, Japan used its limited forces against successive targets, defeating its enemies piecemeal. The carrier force that struck Pearl Harbor attacked the British fleet at Ceylon (now Sri Lanka) in April. The Japanese capturing Singapore were outnumbered more than two to one. These smashing triumphs the Japanese portrayed as a boost for Asian freedom from Western imperialism and white supremacy, and indeed the prestige of the West in Asia and the rule of the West in Southeast Asia never fully recovered.

The Greater East Asia Coprosperity Sphere —— Japan designated its new realm the GREATER EAST ASIA COPROSPERITY SPHERE, a term suggestive of equality and mutual benefit. The Tōjō government recognized the importance of Asian nationalism. Encouragement of nationalistic aspirations in areas of marginal economic importance might foster cooperation and lessen the burden of rule. More significant, Asian nationalism was a prime propaganda weapon to lure the government of CHIANG KAI-SHEK in Chongqing (Chungking) to peace, belabor the British in India, and divide the British from the anticolonialist Americans. Thus Japan surrendered to the puppet Nanjing (Nanking) regime of WANG JINGWEI (Wang Ching-wei) its unequal treaty privileges in China and promised to withdraw its troops from China when general peace was restored. Japan also promised eventual independence to Burma and the Philippines, and, as the Allies closed in, fulfilled these pledges through subservient regimes. Formally, at least, Japan respected the independence of Siam (now Thailand). On 5 and 6 November 1943 the Greater East Asia Conference convened in Tōkyō with representatives from MANCHUKUO (Manchuria), China, Siam, Burma, the Philippines, and India. It called for mutual respect of independence and cooperation among the nations of East Asia.

In reality the Greater East Asia Coprosperity Sphere was a sham. The sphere revolved around Japan as leader and guardian. Japan's convenience dictated continued Vichy French colonial rule in Indochina. Japan's prosecution of the war required the exploitation of local labor services and raw materials, especially oil, rubber, and tin. In the long term Japan expected to maintain colonial rule in the East Indies, Malaya, and in strategic bases along its extended defense perimeter. To this end, Japan's dreaded military police, the *kempeitai*, and the army brutally mistreated inhabitants of the coprosperity sphere nations. Trade was lopsided; since Japan's industries produced mostly for war, the satellites received little for their raw material exports, and even less as American submarines increasingly played havoc with Japanese shipping. Economic dislocation, inflation, military devastation, malnutrition, and political suppression were the facts of life in Greater East Asia.

Deadlock in the Pacific —— Initial success encouraged Japan's war leaders to extend their defense perimeter in the Central and Southwest Pacific. Seizure of Port Moresby in New Guinea, facing Australia, was the first step in a plan to cut communications between the United States and Australia. However, the Americans were ready, thanks to advance warning from "Magic," a system of decoding secret Japanese messages. "Magic" might have alerted the Americans to the Pearl Harbor attack had they heeded it, but thereafter it proved a crucial weapon in the Pacific War. On 6–8 May 1942, Japanese and American naval forces battled in the Coral Sea, south of New Guinea. The Americans suffered greater loss, but the Japanese withdrew their Port Moresby invasion force. It was the first time the Japanese were stopped in the Pacific.

Japan's Central Pacific thrust met a decisive rebuff. One object was to secure bases for defense of the home islands from air attacks such as the raid on Tōkyō of 18 April 1942 by army bombers launched from an American carrier. More important to Admiral

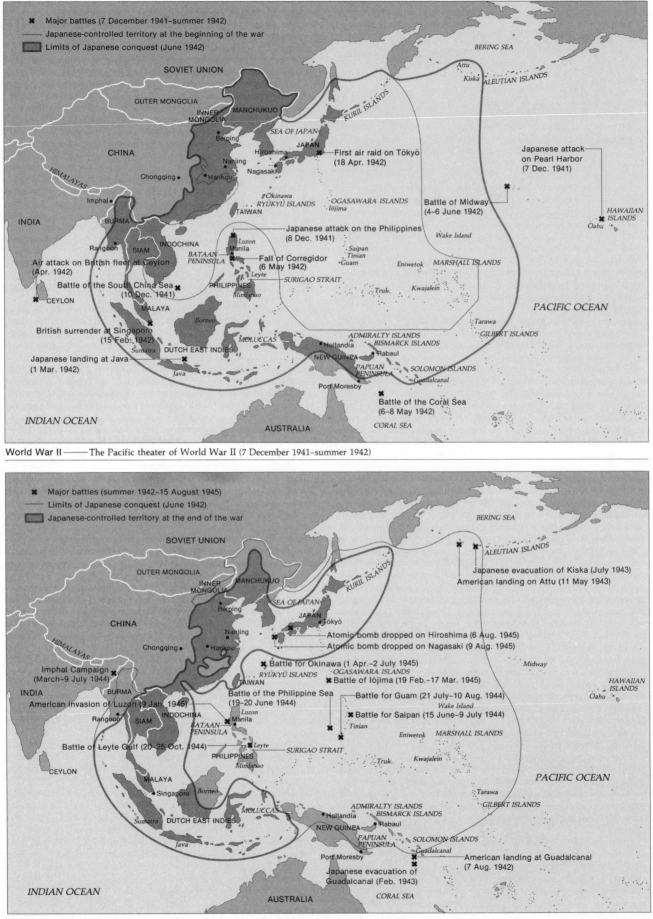

Major battles (7 December 1941–summer 1942)
Japanese-controlled territory at the beginning of the war
Limits of Japanese conquest (June 1942)

BERING SEA

SOVIET UNION

OUTER MONGOLIA

INNER MONGOLIA

MANCHUKUO

Attu
Kiska
ALEUTIAN ISLANDS

CHINA

Beiping

SEA OF JAPAN

KURIL ISLANDS

JAPAN

Chongqing
Hankou
Nanjing
Hiroshima
Nagasaki

First air raid on Tōkyō
(18 Apr. 1942)

Japanese attack on Pearl Harbor
(7 Dec. 1941)

HIMALAYAS

Imphal

INDIA

BURMA

Okinawa
RYUKYU ISLANDS
Iōjima

OGASAWARA ISLANDS

Battle of Midway
(4–6 June 1942)

HAWAIIAN ISLANDS
Oahu

Rangoon
SIAM
INDOCHINA

Luzon
Manila
BATAAN PENINSULA

Japanese attack on the Philippines
(8 Dec. 1941)

Fall of Corregidor
(6 May 1942)

Wake Island

Saipan
Tinian
Guam

Air attack on British fleet at Ceylon
(Apr. 1942)

Battle of the South China Sea
(10 Dec. 1941)

CEYLON

PHILIPPINES
Leyte
Mindanao

SURIGAO STRAIT

Eniwetok

MARSHALL ISLANDS

Kwajalein

Truk

PACIFIC OCEAN

MALAYA
Borneo

British surrender at Singapore
(15 Feb. 1942)

Japanese landing at Java
(1 Mar. 1942)

Sumatra

DUTCH EAST INDIES

Java

MOLUCCAS

Hollandia

NEW GUINEA

PAPUAN PENINSULA

Port Moresby

ADMIRALTY ISLANDS
BISMARCK ISLANDS
Rabaul

SOLOMON ISLANDS
Guadalcanal

Tarawa
GILBERT ISLANDS

INDIAN OCEAN

AUSTRALIA

CORAL SEA

Battle of the Coral Sea
(6–8 May 1942)

World War II——The Pacific theater of World War II (7 December 1941–summer 1942)

Major battles (summer 1942–15 August 1945)
Limits of Japanese conquest (June 1942)
Japanese-controlled territory at the end of the war

BERING SEA

SOVIET UNION

OUTER MONGOLIA

INNER MONGOLIA

MANCHUKUO

KURIL ISLANDS

ALEUTIAN ISLANDS

Japanese evacuation of Kiska (July 1943)
American landing on Attu (11 May 1943)

CHINA

Beiping

SEA OF JAPAN

JAPAN
Tōkyō

Chongqing
Hankou
Nanjing

Atomic bomb dropped on Hiroshima (6 Aug. 1945)
Atomic bomb dropped on Nagasaki (9 Aug. 1945)

HIMALAYAS

INDIA

Imphal Campaign
(March–9 July 1944)

BURMA

American invasion of Luzon (9 Jan. 1945)

RYUKYU ISLANDS

OGASAWARA ISLANDS

Battle for Okinawa (1 Apr.–2 July 1945)

Battle of Iōjima (19 Feb.–17 Mar. 1945)

Midway

HAWAIIAN ISLANDS
Oahu

TAIWAN

Battle of the Philippine Sea
(19–20 June 1944)

Battle for Guam (21 July–10 Aug. 1944)

Wake Island

Rangoon
SIAM
INDOCHINA

Luzon
Manila
BATAAN PENINSULA

Battle for Saipan (15 June–9 July 1944)

Tinian

Eniwetok

MARSHALL ISLANDS

CEYLON

Battle of Leyte Gulf (20–25 Oct. 1944)

Leyte

SURIGAO STRAIT

PHILIPPINES
Mindanao

Truk

Kwajalein

PACIFIC OCEAN

MALAYA
Singapore
Borneo

Sumatra

DUTCH EAST INDIES

Java

MOLUCCAS

Hollandia

NEW GUINEA

PAPUAN PENINSULA

Port Moresby

ADMIRALTY ISLANDS
BISMARCK ISLANDS
Rabaul

SOLOMON ISLANDS
Guadalcanal

Tarawa
GILBERT ISLANDS

American landing at Guadalcanal
(7 Aug. 1942)

Japanese evacuation of Guadalcanal (Feb. 1943)

INDIAN OCEAN

AUSTRALIA

CORAL SEA

World War II——The Pacific theater of World War II (summer 1942–15 August 1945)

Yamamoto, the seizure of Midway Island and the western Aleutians would challenge the American fleet to a decisive engagement while Japanese superiority lasted. Late in May 1942 the Japanese navy deployed eastward across the Pacific in scattered groups that would combine for the kill. Forewarned, Admiral Chester Nimitz, commander of the Pacific Fleet, reinforced Midway and gathered three carriers northeast of the island. The Japanese air strike on Midway on 4–6 June brought a fierce counterattack from the undetected American fleet, which destroyed four Japanese carriers, the heart of Japan's offensive naval power, at the expense of one American carrier. Yamamoto withdrew. After the Battle of MIDWAY the Japanese navy went on the defensive.

During the rest of 1942 the main action of the Pacific War shifted back to the Southwest Pacific. Here the Allies went on the offensive to prevent the Japanese from securing control of the northern rim of the Coral Sea. In spite of heavy engagements elsewhere, they supplied the precious troops, planes, and ships to recapture New Guinea's Papuan Peninsula and to secure a foothold in the Solomons at GUADALCANAL. The Japanese resisted tenaciously and skillfully, inflicting and suffering severe casualties. Ground fighting in this fetid, malarial climate was as grueling as anywhere in the war. In the Solomons, Japanese and American naval vessels of every type—even battleships—traded savage blows. In successive battles the Japanese sank or heavily damaged 14 American and Australian cruisers.

Slowly, painfully, Australian and American troops hemmed the Japanese into a pocket on the north coast of Papua and eliminated it by 21 January 1943. On Guadalcanal the American marines barely held their own with a trickle of supplies and reinforcements until American sea and air power prevailed and Japanese reinforcement became too costly. Early in February 1943 the Japanese evacuated Guadalcanal.

In spite of these reverses Japan had no reason to despair in the spring of 1943. Chiang Kai-shek, receiving aid in driblets across the Himalayas, and more preoccupied with his communist foes than the Japanese, posed no threat. The British were too weak to recapture Burma. Japan's sprawling resource basin in Southeast Asia remained intact. The enemy's Southwest Pacific campaigns, at their current pace and cost, posed only a distant threat. Still unscathed were Japan's main bases in the Bismarcks and the Pacific Mandates.

Even so, the outlook was ominous. Hitler had been defeated at Stalingrad, and Anglo-American offensives were gaining in North Africa, opening the Mediterranean and jeopardizing Italy. The Americans steadily became more powerful. From precarious reliance on one or two carriers in the Pacific, the US Navy was beginning to fill out toward the dozens of carriers, small and large, it deployed in 1944 and 1945. American submarines increasingly tore away at Japan's merchant marine, straining the vital inner sea links of the empire. On 18 April 1943 American aviators, alerted by "Magic," intercepted Admiral Yamamoto's plane in the Solomons and shot it down, killing the brilliant fleet commander.

Mounting Allied Offensives —— Allied progress in the Pacific in 1943 was plodding. More significant was the development of strategy and method. The Americans came to realize that air power was the key to victory, but only in the closest combination with land and sea power, and they strove to gain air bases ever closer to Japan's vital communications and the homeland. The surest way was step by step, not island to island so much as combat radius to combat radius. Nimitz in the Central Pacific and MacArthur in the Southwest Pacific selected targets within reach of existing bases and suitable for runways or fleet anchorages, often bypassing key Japanese defense points like Rabaul and Truk. For each invasion, they prepared the way with heavy air attacks, especially from roving fast carrier forces that blocked Japanese reinforcement of any threatened point. After beating down local Japanese air power, the Americans bombarded the invasion site. Troop landings followed, with amphibious techniques, vehicles, and armament improving with each campaign. Close behind came construction battalions to build a new base. Eventually, the long arm of air power reached out to Tōkyō.

In May 1943 the Anglo-American leadership opened a second front in the Pacific. MacArthur would continue along the New Guinea coast while Nimitz attacked through the Central Pacific islands. During 1943, fighting in the Southwest Pacific was the old-fashioned scouring type: clearing the Solomons island by island and the New Guinea coast mile by mile, leaving no Japanese in the rear. Early in 1944 MacArthur's campaign accelerated, leapfrogging existing fronts and strong points to secure the Bismarck and Admiralty island groups and seize Hollandia, 500 miles westward on New Guinea. Beyond were the Moluccas and then the long-sought Phil-

ippines. Meanwhile, Nimitz attacked the Gilbert Islands where, on Tarawa, the issue for a time was in doubt. Central Pacific forces then bypassed Japanese bases to assault Kwajalein and Eniwetok in the Marshalls. By June 1944 Nimitz was poised for a thousand-mile leap to the Marianas.

Turning Point in the Marianas —— The battle for the Marianas began with landings on Saipan on 15 June 1944. Admiral Toyoda Soemu (1885–1957), Combined Fleet commander, at first deployed southward, believing that MacArthur's drive posed the main threat, and then redirected his entire strength at Saipan. He believed that Japan's island- and carrier-based air forces could deal to the American fleet the knock-out blow Japan had longed for since Midway. But American air strikes up and down the island defense chain eliminated Toyoda's land-based air support and enabled Admiral Raymond Spruance to concentrate on Japanese carrier attacks. In the greatest naval air battle of the war the Japanese lost all but 35 of their 430 planes. The Combined Fleet withdrew and Spruance, sagely guarding his beachheads, declined pursuit. After bitter fighting Saipan was secured on 9 July 1944.

The Marianas was a decisive defeat for Japan; the defense screen had been breached; the Philippines and the inner communications of the Japanese empire lay open to attack; the striking power of the Japanese fleet had been gutted. Persistent defeat and retreat caused increasing restiveness in the Japanese government and tension between the armed services. The JŪSHIN (former prime ministers) and the emperor himself spoke of the need for a compromise peace. Having suffered a resounding defeat instead of delivering the promised victory, Prime Minister Tōjō resigned on 18 July 1944. Aware of the need still to appease the army, the senior statesmen settled on General KOISO KUNIAKI as his successor, with a member of the peace faction, Admiral YONAI MITSUMASA, as his deputy.

Japan's growing inclination toward peace had distinct limitations. The government required an honorable peace that would satisfy the army, but the Allies demanded unconditional surrender. Tragically, the government believed that the road to peace lay through Moscow and that in return for Japanese concessions the Soviets might throw their weight behind a compromise. But Premier Joseph Stalin had already promised at Tehran in 1943 to join the Allies against Japan after the defeat of Germany, and nothing Japan could offer would be as attractive as what the Soviet Union could seize by itself, with Allied blessing. Sustained by the illusion of Soviet mediation, the Koiso cabinet determined to fight on.

The Marianas victory was no less significant to the victors. As Allied leaders surveyed the war fronts against Japan it became much clearer that the Pacific provided the most direct and promising routes to the Japanese home islands. The prospects of the China front dimmed dramatically in 1944 when Japan's one successful late-war offensive, south from Hankou (Hankow), overran American airbases in southwest China before running out of steam. Chiang Kai-shek was more recalcitrant, ineffective, and demanding than ever. Now American long-range B-29 bombers could strike Tōkyō more easily from Saipan than from China. In Burma, after the collapse of a Japanese offensive on the Indian frontier in the spring of 1944, the initiative finally passed to the Allies. The British planned a major offensive at the end of 1944, after the monsoons, but its objective, Rangoon, was about as far from Tōkyō as any place in the Greater East Asia Sphere.

Only in the Pacific had Allied drives achieved momentum and power; only the Pacific offered dramatic progress. This realization, together with expectation of an early end to the European war and Soviet assistance against Japan led to a radical shift in American objectives and timetables. Now MacArthur was to skip Mindanao and join with Central Pacific forces for a massive assault on Leyte in the central Philippines, to be followed by campaigns on the main island of Luzon. Taiwan and the coast of China were excluded from the planning, and American eyes turned toward the Bonin and Ryūkyū (Okinawa) islands as a base from which to isolate the Japanese home islands, assault them from the air, and, if necessary, invade them.

The Last Assaults —— The final phase of the Pacific War began on 20 October 1944 when the US Sixth Army landed on the island of Leyte in the Philippines. The Japanese reacted strongly. In a cleverly planned series of concentric attacks on 25 October the Japanese navy hurled its remaining might at the beachhead. The southern Japanese force coming through Surigao Strait met a formidable array of American battleships, cruisers, and destroyers, which performed the classic naval maneuver of crossing the *T* and virtually destroyed it. The northern Japanese forces, however, came near to stunning success. Admiral Ozawa Jisaburō's (1886–1966) near-empty carriers succeeded in decoying Admiral William Halsey's fast carrier groups away from the scene while Admiral Kurita Takeo's powerful fleet of battleships and cruisers slipped through San Bernardino Strait undetected. But for extremely aggressive action by American escort carriers and destroyers and his own caution and confusion, Kurita might have entered Leyte Gulf and caused havoc. Instead, he retired, and with him went Japan's last hope for a dramatic sea victory. (See LEYTE GULF, BATTLE OF.)

MacArthur invaded Luzon on 9 January 1945. Heavy fighting continued until the fall of Manila in March, but by then the Philippines, like the rest of southeast Asia and the southwest Pacific, was already a strategic backwater. On 19 February 1945 US marines landed on IŌJIMA (Iwojima), an island in the Bonin group halfway between Saipan and Honshū and therefore considered vital in the forthcoming air assault on Japan.

Japan began and ended the Pacific War in desperation, but it was calculating desperation. By 1944 Japanese leaders knew they could neither win nor keep much if any of the empire. They believed they might at least preserve the nation's honor and existence by giving ground only at prohibitive cost to the enemy. The enemy might then, estimating its casualties in an invasion of the home islands, settle for something short of unconditional surrender. Japan chose two methods of exacting such a toll. The first was a new defense of its remaining outlying islands. The island commander would concede the beaches and retreat to hills through which ran a maze of underground emplacements and tunnels. Here he and his men would die, but the enemy, advancing foot by foot, would pay dearly. Thus at Iōjima American marines suffered 60 to 75 percent battle casualties. The second method was the KAMIKAZE SPECIAL ATTACK FORCE, a corps of young pilots prepared to undertake one-way missions against enemy ships, guiding their planes and bombs to deck and death. Such suicidal acts had occurred earlier in the war but not in organized fashion until the Philippines campaign.

The war ended in a crescendo of violence, as exemplified in the battle for Okinawa. This central island in the Ryūkyū chain would have provided airfields and anchorages for the assaults on Japan itself. Fifty thousand American combat troops landed on the first day of invasion, 1 April 1945, and eventually increased to 172,000. In almost three months of fighting virtually the entire Japanese defending force of 110,000 perished, together with 150,000 Japanese civilians. The Americans suffered some 50,000 killed and wounded on land and sea, and thousands more nonbattle casualties. The Kamikaze corps together with piloted rocket bombs delivered about 1,900 attacks and conventional Japanese planes perhaps twice as many more. They destroyed 30 ships and craft and damaged another 368. A favorite target was American destroyers, at least 50 of which were sunk or damaged. The scale of fighting for Okinawa was small compared to plans for the invasion of the home islands, which was planned to begin with an attack on Kyūshū in November by 750,000 troops.

Japan's greatest devastation came from the air. On 10 March 1945, American B-29 Superfortress bombers from Saipan and Tinian began massive incendiary raids on Japan's major cities. The bombers—three, four, or five hundred to a raid—would fly in low over a selected portion of the defenseless city and cover it with clusters of napalm sticks. Jellied gasoline quickly ignited wooden housing. Perhaps as many as 100,000 died in the first fire-bombing raid on Tōkyō. Successive raids destroyed half the city, including government buildings, and damaged the Imperial Palace. By the end of May, most of Yokohama, Nagoya, Ōsaka, and Kōbe had been incinerated. At least 13 million Japanese were homeless.

On 6 August 1945 an American B-29 bomber dropped an ATOMIC BOMB on Hiroshima. It exploded in the air above the city, obliterating it. Some Japanese experts estimate that 100,000 people died that day and another 100,000 later from injuries and effects of radiation (there are lower estimates; see ATOMIC BOMB RELATED DISEASE). On 9 August the United States dropped a second atomic bomb that destroyed Nagasaki.

Japan's Surrender——Though Japan was encircled and devastated, its surrender was obtained by only the slenderest of margins. The invasion of Okinawa led to the resignation of the ineffectual Koiso cabinet, as the loss of Saipan had precipitated the fall of Tōjō. Marquis KIDO KŌICHI, lord keeper of the privy seal and the emperor's chief instrument in maneuvering for peace, now gained *jūshin* approval for selection of the aged Admiral SUZUKI KANTARŌ as prime minister. Suzuki had the requisite military background but, more important, the emperor knew his former grand chamberlain well and implicitly trusted him to seize any opportunity for peace

that circumstances permitted. With Suzuki as premier, Yonai as navy minister, and TŌGŌ SHIGENORI as foreign minister, peace advocates now formed a significant force, yet they were still severely handicapped. In the first place, the military services, especially the army, remained determined to fight rather than sue for peace and dishonor their dead. Given the army's record of coup and assassination, this adamant posture was truly intimidating. Second, Japan's leaders persisted in the delusion that the Soviet Union would mediate peace. Finally, Allied terms offered the peace faction no encouragement.

The rise of peace sentiment did not go unnoticed in Washington. A number of officials recognized that unconditional surrender meant no surrender, for the Japanese would never buy peace at the price of abandoning the emperor system, the very essence of their national existence. These officials saw the importance of the emperor in effecting surrender and maintaining stability during the occupation. They were appalled at the human cost of ending the war and now feared the promised Russian intervention. They therefore framed a proclamation that warned of untold destruction if Japan continued the war, but also promised that when the vestiges of militarism had been removed, the Japanese people, if they so wished, could retain the emperor.

President Harry S. TRUMAN preferred to await the test of an atomic device in July before deciding. When the test succeeded, assurances to the Japanese seemed less pressing. Advisers warned him that the American people would not approve less severe peace terms; former Secretary of State Cordell Hull believed they would regard assurances on the emperor as appeasement. Accordingly, the POTSDAM DECLARATION of 26 July 1945 counterbalanced a dire warning only with the promise that Japan would continue to exist as a nation; it was silent on the emperor. The Suzuki cabinet could not accept it but hoped to avoid provocation by not rejecting it outright, and therefore announced that Japan would ignore it. Unfortunately the word for ignore, *mokusatsu*, has the connotation of "treat with contempt" and was received in that sense by Washington. Truman saw no reason to rescind authorization to use the atomic weapons when they were ready, and they were used.

An additional, but by no means crucial, motivation may have been Truman's desire to demonstrate America's awesome new strength to the Russians. The primary and sufficient reason, however, was his determination to use every available means to end the war promptly. Neither he nor most American officials found a moral difference between the atomic weapon and mass incendiary raids.

After Hiroshima and just before Nagasaki, on 9 August, the Soviet Union declared war on Japan, attacking Manchuria from east and west. In the face of these triple shocks and with all hope of a negotiated peace gone, the peace proponents were now determined to secure the best terms available. Even now, however, the military was adamant, and Kido turned to the desperate and unprecedented expedient of arranging the intervention of the emperor in the decision process. At an imperial conference that night, Emperor Hirohito spoke sadly of the sufferings of his people, the sacrifices of his soldiers and sailors, and the unbearable thought of his fighting men disarmed and his loyal servants punished. But the time had come to "bear the unbearable," and he sanctioned acceptance of the Potsdam Declaration with Tōgō's proviso that the lawful status of the emperor be recognized. The cabinet complied.

The American reply conceded a little and that was just barely enough. At least it specifically mentioned the emperor, whose authority to rule would be subject to the supreme commander of the Occupation forces. The ultimate form of government in Japan would be established by the "freely expressed will of the Japanese people." As the emperor pointed out, if the people did not want the institution it would be useless to insist on keeping it. Again the service chiefs and war minister resisted, and again the emperor intervened, ordering his ministers to accept the American terms. Bowing to the emperor's will, they signed.

Even then the outcome was in doubt. Young army officers who had unsuccessfully sought support for a coup managed to gain control of the division guarding the Imperial Palace. They sealed off the palace and searched for the recording of the emperor's message to the people proclaiming the end of the war but failed to find it. Superior officers quelled the revolt the next day, and the imperial rescript was broadcast as planned on 15 August. With Allied acceptance of Japan's surrender, war ended.

Japan had been continuously at war from the start of hostilities with China in 1937 to its surrender in 1945, longer than any nation involved in World War II except China. Three million Japanese died in those eight years, fewer deaths than the Soviet Union, Germany, or China suffered, but a high loss in relation to total population. Foreign armies did not wage battle on the soil of the main Japanese islands as they did with enormous destructiveness in the Soviet Union, Germany, and Italy, but the American air raids of 1945 rivaled the most devastating bombardments of German cities, and Japan alone sustained nuclear attack. Defeat deprived Japan not only of the fruits of conquest since 1931, but of all the territories, economic interests, and rights it had gained by war and diplomacy since the late 19th century. The Japan of 1945 was reduced to the proportions of the Japan that had reluctantly opened its door to the West in 1854. World War II was the greatest disaster in Japanese history; yet the Japanese polity survived, revived, and achieved unprecedented affluence, stability, and peace. See also WORLD WAR II, JAPANESE SOCIETY DURING; HISTORY OF JAPAN: postwar history; OCCUPATION.

■■ ——Dorothy Borg, *The United States and the Far Eastern Crisis of 1933–1938: From the Manchurian Incident through the Initial Stage of the Undeclared Sino-Japanese War* (1964). Dorothy Borg and Shumpei Okamoto, ed, *Pearl Harbor as History: Japanese-American Relations, 1931–1941* (1973). John Hunter Boyle, *China and Japan at War, 1937–1945* (1972). J. R. M. Butler, ed, *History of the Second World War: United Kingdom Military Series* (1954–64). Robert J. C. Butow, *Japan's Decision to Surrender* (1954). Robert J. C. Butow, *Tojo and the Coming of the War* (1961). Basil Collier, *The War in the Far East, 1941–1945* (1969). James B. Crowley, *Japan's Quest for Autonomy: National Security and Foreign Policy, 1930–1938* (1966). Herbert Feis, *The Road to Pearl Harbor: The Coming of the War between the United States and Japan* (1950). Hattori Takushirō, *Dai Tōa sensō zenshi*, 8 vols (1953–56). Hosoya Chihiro, Saitō Makoto, Imai Seiichi, and Rōyama Michio, ed, *Nichi-bei kankei shi: kaisen ni itaru jūnen, 1931–1941*, 4 vols (1971–72). Akira Iriye, *Across the Pacific: An Inner History of American-East Asian Relations* (1967). F. C. Jones, *Japan's New Order in East Asia: Its Rise and Fall, 1937–1945* (1954). William L. Langer and S. Everett Gleason, *The Challenge to Isolation* (1953). William L. Langer and S. Everett Gleason, *The Undeclared War, 1940–1941* (1953). David J. Lu, *From Marco Polo Bridge to Pearl Harbor: Japan's Entry into World War II* (1961). Nihon Kokusai Seiji Gakkai Taiheiyō Sensō Gen'in Kenkyūbu, ed, *Taiheiyō sensō e no michi*, 7 vols (1962–63). Stephen E. Pelz, *The Race to Pearl Harbor: The Failure of the Second London Naval Conference and the Onset of World War II* (1974). Paul W. Schroeder, *The Axis Alliance and Japanese-American Relations, 1941* (1958). Christopher Thorne, *Allies of a Kind: The United States, Britain, and the War Against Japan, 1941–1945* (1978). John Toland, *The Rising Sun: The Decline and Fall of the Japanese Empire* (1970). — Waldo HEINRICHS

World War II, Japanese society during

World War II for the Japanese was a total national effort affecting every citizen. The wartime period brought enormous changes to civilian life, yet not even the shock of complete defeat in August 1945 upset the underlying stability of the Japanese social system. Some of the adjustments in daily living forced by the war were temporary inconveniences, but many other shifts caused permanent changes in people's habits, attitudes, and behavior. A strong family system helped society adapt to both the wartime emergency and the transformed cultural milieu of defeat.

The internal history of Japan during the war years is divided into four phases: early mobilization, from July 1937 to September 1940; consolidation and regimentation, from September 1940 to May 1942; full-scale general participation, from mid-1942 to late 1944; and destruction and defeat, from late 1944 to August 1945. Mobilization required the use of both ideology and strong organization to involve all citizens in the war effort. Once that was accomplished, important changes took place in the routines of working, eating, playing, and growing up. The social dislocation in the last months of the war was enormous: people fled to the countryside to escape enemy bombers, they suffered from hunger, diseases, and fatigue, and they died in air raids.

Preparation for War —— When shooting broke out near Beiping (Peiping, now Beijing or Peking) in July 1937, the Japanese government at first gave more attention to rallying civilian morale than to preparing the economy for a sustained war. In October 1937 Prime Minister KONOE FUMIMARO began a three-year NATIONAL SPIRITUAL MOBILIZATION MOVEMENT to prepare people for sacrifices. The state sponsored parades and public ceremonies to make citizens

more conscious of the war in China, and the authorities encouraged symbolic economies like simplified dress and hairstyle and the "rising-sun box lunch" *(hinomaru bentō)*, a pickled red plum on a bed of white rice (reproducing the pattern of the national flag or Hinomaru). Censorship, propaganda, and the state-controlled school system helped spread the spiritual mobilization to every village in the country.

During the first three years of the war, the government complemented its ideological campaign with a program to organize people into units to aid the national buildup. Households were obliged to form Neighborhood Associations (TONARIGUMI) for civil defense, street sweeping, fire watching, sanitation, and public health—crucial local activities in a time of emergency. By 1940 nearly every village and block in Japan had set up neighborhood associations, and most of them had begun to function effectively. Many were dominated by old local elites, and it is not clear to what extent the central government was able to manipulate the associations. Factory laborers, housewives, and young persons not attending school were forced to join large-scale organizations as a part of the early wartime preparedness.

Economic planning, however, went forward very deliberately in the first years of the fighting. One reason for the delay in changing to a wartime economy was that the Japanese at first expected the war to be brief, making all-out mobilization unnecessary. Another was that politicians, industrialists, bureaucrats, and military officials had great trouble agreeing on a coordinated program. A third reason was the haphazard nature of labor and consumer policies, since the state was reluctant to upset traditional employer-worker or male-female relationships. By July 1940, when Prince Konoe returned as prime minister, the Japanese people were psychologically inured to the morale-boosting campaigns and economically unprepared for a war of general mobilization.

Konoe's "New Order" —— Konoe remained in power until mid-October 1941, long enough to preside over the series of decisions that led to war between Japan and the United States. Konoe announced his NEW ORDER MOVEMENT in September 1940 to organize domestic society more tightly on two levels. All political parties were absorbed into the new IMPERIAL RULE ASSISTANCE ASSOCIATION, a huge amalgam of civilian organizations. At the local level, the New Order Movement completed the drive to build neighborhood associations throughout the country.

The Imperial Rule Assistance Association soon proved to be clumsy and overcentralized in its organization, but it helped to muzzle the state's political opponents. So did the Cabinet Information Bureau, the main agency for media censorship and propaganda. Formal resistance to the war scarcely existed at any point before the surrender, partly because the state had enough organizational control over groups and communications to block collective opposition. Another reason was that the army and police had a monopoly on arms. A third was that the most likely resistance leaders had long since been jailed; the threat of prison and torture—not underlying agreement with the cabinet's nationalistic ideology—cowed potential dissenters into silence.

On the local level the effects of the "new structure" movement were less clear. Although every residential district was now enmeshed in the web of neighborhood associations, the worsening war situation forced the local units to take on more and more duties formerly carried out by the central government. The most important of these was the distribution of food and clothing rations, starting in October 1942. Although they were nominally creatures of the state, the neighborhood associations in the end showed signs of substantial local autonomy.

Full-Scale Participation —— It was only after Japan plunged into all-out war in December 1941 that the cabinet finally began a systematic program to put more people to work in farming and in arms plants. At its peak, the adult civilian labor force approached 33 million in late 1942, after which it dipped slightly because of the military draft. In 1944 the total civilian work force jumped to 33.5 million, including 1.8 million students who were now mobilized for full-time labor. Nearly all employees were on the job by inducement rather than coercion. Only 8 percent of male workers were recruited through the NATIONAL SERVICE DRAFT ORDINANCE, and even when the factories were critically short-handed, the government never legally required married women to take jobs, since it did not wish to go against long-standing social attitudes about appropriate female roles.

In both city and country, most workers earned progressively less because inflation rose faster than earnings. Taxes, forced savings, and crop donations cut family incomes further. As consumer goods disappeared from stores, housewives were driven to the black market, where commodity prices rose to many times their official levels. Yet most employees had no alternative to staying on the job because of strong social pressure to keep on working and because their families needed the wages more than ever in stringent times.

The economy of scarcity induced the government to begin food rationing in December 1940, and within a year every citizen was receiving a basic allotment of 330 grams of rice per day—an amount that remained unchanged until the last months of the war when it was further decreased to 300. Clothing was allocated by a ticket system that granted city people 100 points each year but farmers only 80. Citizens were told to "make do" with substitutes for nearly all daily items. Homes and cities soon took on a shabby look. Thanks to victory gardens, the black market, and resourceful farmers, food was reasonably adequate until the last year of the conflict. Then the American naval blockade, heavy aerial bombardments, and ruinously cold weather during the 1945 spring planting halved the amount of food available.

In spite of declining food intake, the public remained surprisingly healthy during the war years. The national emergency prompted the government to establish medical insurance and new public health centers. After Pearl Harbor, physicians, facilities, and medicines grew scarce just as nutrition was growing worse, but no major epidemics took place. Tuberculosis, always a health menace, became even more rampant. The TB death rate rose from 203 per 100,000 in 1937 to 225 in 1943, as a result of urban crowding, long work hours, inadequate food, sunlight, and ventilation, and substandard sanitation. Venereal and mental diseases both declined, contrary to the experience of most other countries in the war. Because of inferior diets young people were demonstrably shorter and lighter in 1946 than their counterparts a decade earlier.

Children who grew up in wartime invariably attended at least six years of school and performed farm or factory labor services on the side. After early 1944 formal lessons were reduced to an hour or two per day so that older children could work full time. A majority of children were reared at least temporarily in fatherless homes because of conscription, but juvenile crime did not increase significantly.

For all citizens, full-scale participation in the war effort meant fewer leisure-time diversions. The authorities banned most foreign films and music, closed down luxury entertainments, and sent *geisha* and prostitutes to work in the war plants. Even more decisive than the official puritanism were the stringencies of a shrinking war economy. As food and drink grew scarce and professional entertainers were drafted, Japan's thriving amusement industry contracted to a handful of "people's bars," serving low-grade *sake*. By late 1944 the marketplace offered ordinary citizens little refreshment and even less cheer.

The Ravages of Wartime—— During the last eight months of the war, more than 10 million Japanese fled the cities to escape the American bombings, which eventually destroyed a quarter of the country's houses and claimed a half-million civilian lives. Already the government had forcibly resettled 350,000 urban schoolchildren in village temples, shrines, and resort hotels, despite the psychic toll of being separated from their families. Once the B-29s began their unceasing raids, the great majority of city residents voluntarily took refuge with relatives or acquaintances in the countryside. The population of rural Japan rose from 42 million in February 1944 to 52.5 million in November 1945 (two-thirds of the refugees were females). The burden on schools, housing, food supplies, and patience in the villages was gigantic. Yet nearly all the families managed to take in their urban cousins during the crisis.

Those who stayed on in the cities suffered even more gravely. In eight months the American planes dropped 160,000 tons of explosives and incendiaries on 66 Japanese cities. (The Allies unloaded 1,360,000 over Germany during 1942–45.) Because housing was very dense and flammable, the air raids destroyed nearly a quarter of all Japanese dwellings, in addition to 42 percent of the urban industrial zones. The greatest of the fire bombings turned eastern Tōkyō into an enormous pyre on 10 March 1945, killing 100,000 civilians and burning an area as large as Manhattan from the Battery to Central Park. Only the agony at Hiroshima on 6 August exceeded the disaster in Tōkyō. By persistence and determination the victims somehow endured the unbearable.

War and Society—— In mobilizing for World War II, the Japanese government bent certain organizational needs to the demands of ideology. The state deferred to popular conventions about community solidarity, women's roles, and the low status of Korean residents in Japan, even at the cost of a more rational labor plan. The emperor was important as a symbol of the wartime nation, but the political, military, and economic institutions he legitimized in time became their own raisons d'être. At the very end, however, neither the dogmas nor the organizations were so crucial for preserving order as the basic integrity of the social body.

The state's main policies between 1937 and 1945 were centralizing, regimenting, and intended to slow social trends that had been developing for decades. Labor conscription, media controls, altered school curricula, commodity rations, and campaigns to lift the birth rate were based on a conservative social vision predating the mass consumer economy.

But total war exerted an even more powerful pull in the opposite direction. The simple need to fight for national survival accelerated many prewar changes caused by urbanization: crowding, the steady depopulation of the countryside in spite of temporary evacuation from the cities, the nuclearization of families, and the decline of patriarchy. Despite the government's reluctance to mobilize their labor fully, women were forced by the economy of scarcity to take jobs in unprecedented numbers—and their share of the work force remained permanently higher after the surrender.

The war affected large-scale social organizations much more than small ones. The state itself was the largest and most altered of all, first swelling to gigantic proportions during the fighting and then undergoing considerable reforms after 1945. The great manufacturing and trading companies substantially increased their wealth and oligopolistic powers during 1937–45. After the surrender they survived OCCUPATION efforts to trim their influence and now rank among the world's most powerful corporations. Intermediate-level organizations, such as school, youth, farm, and women's groups and religious bodies, were much affected while the fighting continued but were generally free to resume their normal activities after 1945—albeit with altered curricula, as in the case of the education system. The smallest institution, the family, was the firmest source of social continuity. War made surprisingly little difference to Japan's long-term patterns of marriage, divorce, fertility, or juvenile crime, and it was the family that provided refuge under the extreme conditions of mass aerial bombardment and utter defeat.

Altogether, World War II claimed 3 million Japanese lives and destroyed $26 billion worth of national wealth. It obliterated the Japanese empire, reduced the influence of the military in Japanese society, trimmed the power of large landlords through forced rice-delivery schemes, and cleared the track for the dazzling economic expansion of the 1950s and 1960s, when the country was no longer hobbled by a large defense budget.

Fierce and brutalizing though it was, the war scarcely touched the deep underlying structures of Japanese society—particularly the family pattern of small groups. Core values like teamwork, harmony, loyalty, and competence were not threatened by even the shock of total war. The greatest change was the permanent transformation of Japanese culture that took place because of the war. Inasmuch as nearly every Japanese had participated in the war in some fashion, people's outlooks on themselves and their country were fundamentally changed. War and peace became the dominant cultural motifs shaping their perception of the past and the present, leading to the revolutionary internationalization of Japanese fashions, taste, arts, and letters in the years after 1945.

■—— Akimoto Ritsuo, *Sensō to minshū* (1974). Jerome B. Cohen, *Japan's Economy in War and Reconstruction* (1949). Robert Guillain, *Le peuple japonais et la guerre* (1947). T. R. H. Havens, *Valley of Darkness: The Japanese People and World War Two* (1978). Ienaga Saburō, *Taiheiyō sensō* (1968; tr *The Pacific War*, 1978). Masuo Kato, *The Lost War* (1946). Kurashi no Techō Sha, ed, *Sensōchū no kurashi no kiroku* (1969). Rekishigaku Kenkyūkai, ed, *Taiheiyō sensō shi*, 6 vols (1971–73). Gwen Terasaki, *Bridge to the Sun* (1957).   T. R. H. HAVENS

World War II, nonrepatriated Japanese soldiers from

(kyū nihonhei mondai). There have been many problems relating to the finding and rescuing of Japanese soldiers who remained in foreign theaters of operations after the end of World War II. In many instances these soldiers remained behind because they did not know that the war had ended or because they had been indoctrinated with the idea that they should never surrender. By 1975, 22 had been

rescued from Southeast Asia and the South Pacific. Of these, the cases of Yokoi Shōichi (b 1915), who returned from Guam in 1972, and Onoda Hiroo (b 1922), who returned from Lubang Island in the Philippines in 1974, are well known. These problems are handled by the War Victims' Relief Bureau of the Ministry of Health and Welfare. ———— *Kondō Shinji*

wrestling

Amateur Western-style wrestling was introduced to Japan in 1931 with the founding of a wrestling club at Waseda University. In the following year the Japan Amateur Wrestling Federation was established, and in 1934 the first national wrestling tournament was held. Even before the sport was introduced to Japan, a Japanese had participated in an Olympic wrestling competition. This was Naitō Katsutoshi, who in 1924, while a student in the United States, won a silver medal in the featherweight class of freestyle wrestling at the Paris Olympics. By the late 1970s, 16 Japanese had won Olympic gold medals in the sport. In 1979 about 5,600 amateur wrestlers were registered with the Japan Wrestling Association.

Professional Western-style wrestling was introduced to Japan from the United States in 1951. Its popularity increased when Rikidōzan, a famous SUMŌ wrestler, turned to professional Western-style wrestling. At the peak of his popularity he drew audiences of one million a year. Currently there are three professional wrestling associations for men and one for women. ———— *Watanabe Tōru*

Wright, Frank Lloyd (1867–1959)

American architect. Wright first visited Japan in 1905 and traveled widely. He became a knowledgeable collector of woodblock prints and published a short appreciation of the print in 1912. Although he denied any direct Japanese influence upon his work, his Prairie Houses share many characteristics with traditional Japanese architecture. He designed the old IMPERIAL HOTEL in Tōkyō, completed in 1922; the front lobby was disassembled and moved to the open-air museum, MEIJI MURA, in 1976 before the hotel was demolished. Some of Wright's other designs in Japan include the Odawara Hotel (1917), a Ginza movie theater (1918), the Yamamura House (1924), and the school Jiyū Gakuen (1927), designed with his pupil Endō Arata. ———— *Watanabe Hiroshi*

written vernacular Japanese, development of → gembun itchi

Wu Peifu (Wu P'ei-fu) (1874–1939)

(J: Go Haifu). An important warlord in North China during the "warlord period" (1916–28)—a chaotic period of military struggles among regional interests in the absence of an effective central government—who was sought by the Japanese military in the 1930s to head a puppet government in China. Wu became the leader of the Zhili (Chihli) clique, a Chinese warlord faction, after the Anhui (Anhwei) Zhili War (1920) and in 1922 became the dominant figure in North China. Although he lost control of the Beijing (Peking) government in 1924, Wu continued to rule the areas of Henan (Honan), Hubei (Hupeh), and Hunan until the summer of 1927, when he was defeated by the forces of the Guomindang (Kuomintang; Nationalist Party). In his struggles with other northern militarists in the 1920s, Wu justified his attacks on the grounds that they had engaged in secret dealings with Japan (see DUAN QIRUI [Tuan Ch'i-jui]; ZHANG ZUOLIN [Chang Tso-lin]). Wu had first become known to the Japanese military in 1903 when he was assigned to a Japanese army intelligence unit in Chefoo (now Yantai or Yen-t'ai) in Shandong (Shantung). He had later been decorated by the Japanese government for reconnaissance missions made in Korea and Manchuria during the RUSSO-JAPANESE WAR (1904–05). In 1935, when the Japanese GUANDONG (KWANTUNG) ARMY stationed in Manchuria wanted to establish a separate, Japanese-controlled state in North China, Colonel DOIHARA KENJI tried to persuade Wu to head its government. He refused, but when the Chinese communists and the Guomindang agreed to cooperate against Japanese invasion after the XI'AN (SIAN) INCIDENT (December 1936), Wu, who feared growing communist influence in China, looked more favorably on cooperation with Japan. He was again approached by Doihara in 1938, this time to head a new government which would replace the PROVISIONAL GOVERNMENT OF THE REPUBLIC OF CHINA in Beiping (Peiping) and the REFORM GOVERNMENT OF THE REPUBLIC OF CHINA in Nanjing (Nanking). Wu's demands for Chinese control of the proposed regime went beyond what the Japanese were willing to meet. It was only after Wu's death that the Japanese agreed on WANG JINGWEI (Wang Ching-wei) to head the REORGANIZED NATIONAL GOVERNMENT OF THE REPUBLIC OF CHINA.

📖——Wu Peifu, *Wu Peifu xiansheng ji* (*Wu P'ei-fu hsien-sheng chi*; 1960). Okano Masujirō, *Go Haifu* (1939).

X

Xavier, Francis (1506–1552)

Anglicized form of the Spanish name Francisco de Javier. He introduced Christianity to Japan and set up the first Christian mission in the country. Born in northern (Basque) Spain in 1506, he studied at the University of Paris and was one of the founder members of the Society of Jesus. Appointed apostolic delegate for Asia, he left Europe in 1541 and labored in India and Malacca. In the latter place, in 1547, he met a Japanese fugitive named Anjirō, whose glowing account of his native country fired Xavier with enthusiasm to evangelize Japan. Xavier reached Kagoshima with two Jesuit companions on 15 August 1549, and with Anjirō as his less than adequate interpreter, he preached Christianity and compiled a simple catechism, with the result that about 100 people accepted baptism. A year after his arrival Xavier visited Hirado and Yamaguchi, but wishing to obtain permission to preach throughout the whole country, he made his way to Kyōto in the depth of winter in an unsuccessful bid to meet Emperor Go-Nara. He left Japan at the end of 1551 to attend to business in India but with the ultimate purpose of evangelizing the Chinese, who, as he had observed, were held in high esteem by the Japanese. He died en route to China on 3 December 1552 on the small island of Shangchuandao (Shang-ch'uan-tao; also spelled Sancian) in the estuary of the Pearl River.

A charismatic and zealous apostle, Xavier highly regarded the Japanese ("the best race yet discovered") and commented on their sense of honor and courtesy. Owing to Xavier's brief stay in the country and his inability to speak the language well, the work of organizing and consolidating the newly founded mission fell to his Jesuit successors (see JESUITS). Xavier's life and work have been meticulously recorded in Georg Schurhammer's monumental four-volume biography, *Franz Xaver: Sein Leben und Seiner Zeit* (1953–73), translated into English as *Francis Xavier: His Life and Times*, 4 vols (1973–82).   Michael COOPER

Xi'an (Sian) Incident

(Seian Jiken). The arrest of CHIANG KAI-SHEK by one of his army commanders in December 1936, resulting in a united Chinese resistance to Japanese aggression. Chiang believed that his domestic communist opposition had to be suppressed before China could actively resist Japanese encroachment. The largest contingent in the forces sent to eradicate the communists' base area in Yan'an (Yenan) in northwest China was the Manchurian army under ZHANG XUELIANG (Chang Hsüeh-liang). Having been driven from Manchuria by the Japanese in 1931, this army was sympathetic to communist proposals to end the civil war and unite against Japan.

On 3 December 1936 Chiang Kai-shek flew to Zhang's headquarters in Xi'an to urge more active fighting against the communists. Early in the morning of 12 December he was arrested by Zhang, who presented him with eight demands, including termination of the civil war and the release of political prisoners. On 14 December Zhang and the communist armies announced the formation of a united anti-Japanese command. On 15 December a communist delegation led by ZHOU ENLAI (Chou En-lai) arrived in Xi'an, and Zhou helped to arrange a compromise settlement. Chiang apparently accepted Zhang's demands in principle while refusing to put his agreement on paper. On 25 December Chiang was released and flew back to Nanjing (Nanking) with Zhang, who had surrendered to him for punishment.

Chiang emerged from the incident with his reputation intact. The new policy of resistance led to the formation of the United Front in September 1937, two months after war with Japan had begun.
📖 ——James M. Bertram, *First Act in China* (1938). Edgar Snow, *Red Star over China* (1938). Lyman Van Slyke, *Enemies and Friends: The United Front in Chinese Communist History* (1967).
                    Robert ENTENMANN

Xinmin Hui (Hsin-min Hui)

(Japanese pronunciation Shimminkai; New People's Society). An organization launched by the Japanese army occupying North China in December 1937. It acted as the propaganda arm of the Japanese-sponsored PROVISIONAL GOVERNMENT OF THE REPUBLIC OF CHINA and sought to spread Japanese ideas to the Chinese through the school system, radio, newspapers, libraries, the cinema, and other media.   John H. BOYLE

Y

Yabakei

Gorge on the upper and middle reaches of the river YAMAKUNI-GAWA, northwestern Ōita Prefecture, Kyūshū. Noted for strangely shaped rocks and peaks, narrow ravines, dense forests, and blue meandering streams. Part of Yaba–Hita–Hikosan Quasi-National Park. AONODŌMON, a tunnel through a large rock, the temple Rakanji, and hot springs such as Morizane and Shigira are also located nearby.

Yabe Hisakatsu (1878–1969)

Geologist and paleontologist noted for his studies on the geological formation of the Japanese islands. He showed that the Japanese islands were separated from the Asian mainland during the Pleistocene epoch about one million years ago. Born in Tōkyō, he graduated from Tōkyō University and taught at Tōhoku University from 1911 to 1939. He received the Order of Culture in 1953.

yabukōji

Ardisia japonica. An evergreen shrub of the family Myrsinaceae which grows thickly on hills and in woods throughout Japan. Appreciated for its beauty, it is often used as a ground cover in gardens. It propagates itself by means of a subterranean stem which produces a stalk 10–20 centimeters (4–8 in) high. The leaves are alternate and grow in one or two whorls at the end of the stalk. They are thick and glossy, oblong in shape, and have pointed tips and fine serrations along the edges. In the summer, flower stalks appear from the leaf axils and bear two to five small white hanging blossoms. *Yabukōji* is prized for its evergreen foliage and bright red berries and has customarily been used as a decoration at New Year's and at wedding festivities as a symbol of celebration. It has been cultivated since ancient times, giving rise to the development of many new varieties, and has long been cherished as a BONSAI plant. Its berries are also used in traditional folk medicine as a detoxicant and diuretic. Similar species, such as *karatachibana (A. crispa)* and *manryō (A. crenata),* are also very popular. ——MATSUDA Osamu

yabusame

(mounted archery). Although it has the appearance of a martial art, *yabusame* is actually a warrior's form of prayer or religious exercise, being performed in shrine precincts by mounted archers who shoot at three stationary targets while riding at a full gallop. It is said that it was first practiced by order of Emperor Kimmei (509–571; r 531 or 539 to 571) at the Usa Hachiman Shrine, Kyūshū, to pray for peace and abundant harvests, although the first recorded instance is the *yabusame* performed in 1096 in the presence of the retired emperor SHIRAKAWA.

There are four parts to a *yabusame* ceremony. First, the group leader, mounted on his horse, points a drawn bow and arrow at the sky and at the ground for eternal peace between heaven and earth. Next, all riders take turns shooting at three 60-centimeter (2 ft) square targets with five rings of different colors, mounted about 46 meters (50 yd) apart in a straight line 2 meters (6.5 ft) from the track along which the horses gallop. A rider starts about 27 meters (30 yd) before the first target with one arrow nocked and three more in a quick-draw quiver. To draw, nock, and loose the next two arrows at the gallop, let alone hit the targets, requires a high degree of horsemanship and archery. Riders who hit all three targets are allowed to perform the next ceremony, shooting at three clay bull's-eyes about 9 centimeters (3.5 in) in diameter. Finally, targets are presented to the leader for inspection.

The excitement and spectacle of *yabusame* are heightened by the riders' elegant raiment. In recent times, *yabusame* has been per-formed annually at the TSURUGAOKA HACHIMAN SHRINE in Kamakura on 16 September and at Meiji Shrine in Tōkyō as part of the Culture Day program on 3 November.

Originally, an archer who missed a target was obliged to commit suicide. MINAMOTO NO YORITOMO, the founder of the Kamakura shogunate (1192–1333), insured against needless loss of skilled warriors by enlarging the targets and framing them with garlands of flowers, which, if touched, counted as a hit. Under Yoritomo *yabusame* was annually observed at the Hachiman Shrine in Kamakura. The Ashikaga shōguns (1338–1573) had little interest in *yabusame,* and it fell into disuse under their regime. It was revived by the eighth Tokugawa shōgun, TOKUGAWA YOSHIMUNE, and was performed by his command on 15 March 1728 before the Hachiman Shrine of Takada no Baba in Edo (now Tōkyō) to pray for the health of the shogunal heir, Ieshige, who was sick with smallpox.

Since its beginning there have been only three families entrusted with the "correct practice" of *yabusame:* the Miura, the Ogasawara and the Takeda, the most important of which are the latter two. The Ogasawara dropped *yabusame* from their family "etiquette" (see OGASAWARA SCHOOL OF ETIQUETTE) in 1882. Today, they specialize in archery, calligraphy, tea, and other arts, and perform a rather slow-motion *yabusame* at the Hachiman shrine in Kamakura, more as a sort of medieval pageant than as a prayer. The Takeda family etiquette of ancient practice is preserved intact by the Kaneko family of Kamakura, whose head, Kaneko Yūrin, was officially named 35th head of the Takeda school in 1933. It is the Takeda group that performs *yabusame* religiously, in every sense of the word, at the Kamakura and Meiji shrines and at Samukawa, the oldest shrine in the Sagami area of Kanagawa Prefecture. ——*John E.* THAYER *III*

Yabuta Teijirō (1888–1977)

Chemist. Born in Shiga Prefecture. Graduate of and professor at Tōkyō University. In 1938 he succeeded in isolating a crystalline substance, gibberellin, from cultured *Gibberella fujikuroi,* a rice blight fungus of the class Ascomycetes. This gibberellin, which accelerates the growth rate of young rice plants, was later proven to be a plant hormone. Yabuta also determined the chemical structure of kojic acid, which is a metabolic product of *Aspergillus oryzae,* the fermenting agent in malted rice. A member of the Japan Academy, Yabuta received the academy prize in 1943 and was awarded the Order of Culture in 1964. ——AIDA Kō

Yachiyo

City in northwestern Chiba Prefecture, central Honshū. The construction of many large housing complexes since World War II has made it a residential suburb of Tōkyō. Manufacturers of machinery and metal products are located here. Pop: 134,479.

Yaeyama Islands

(Yaeyama Shotō). Group of islands southwest of the Miyako Islands, southwestern Okinawa Prefecture. Forming the western half of the Sakishima Islands, the Yaeyama Islands include the two main islands of ISHIGAKIJIMA and IRIOMOTEJIMA, and TAKETOMIJIMA, Kobamajima, Kuroshima, Haterumajima, and YONAGUNIJIMA. The islands have a hilly terrain and a warm climate, with high temperatures and humidity; subtropical plants and mangroves flourish here. The principal agricultural products are pineapples and sugarcane. The islands are noted for the production of traditional textiles (see OKINAWAN TEXTILES). Area: 584 sq km (225 sq mi).

Yagi Hidetsugu (1886–1976)

Electrical engineer. Noted for his pioneering research in shortwave and microwave signal propagation with Uda Shintarō, a junior colleague. Their efforts led to the development of the Yagi–Uda antenna, the basic antenna configuration used in the majority of today's outdoor television and radio antennas. Born in Kyōto, he graduated from Tōkyō University in 1909. In 1919, after studying in Europe and the United States, he became professor at Tōhoku University and there began his work with signal propagation systems. He also served as president of Ōsaka University and Tōkyō Institute of Technology and received the Order of Culture in 1956.

Yagi Jūkichi (1898–1927)

Poet. Born in Tōkyō. Graduate of Tōkyō Higher Normal School (later Tōkyō University of Education). He published his first collection of poems, *Aki no hitomi*, in 1925 while teaching at a middle school. Although he was a Nonchurch Christian (see MUKYŌKAI), his verse is rich in religious sentiment and is considered the best example of Christian poetry in Japan. He wrote poems in a simple, quiet style, independent of any particular poetry group. His principal collections of poems are *Mazushiki shinto* (1928) and *Yagi Jūkichi shishū* (1942), both published posthumously.

yagō

(house name; also *iena* or *kadona*). Identifying name, other than the family name, which is applied to a family residence or family line. In the former case, *yagō* belonged to the house itself and was usually assumed by new inhabitants when the house changed hands, but in the latter case, the name was retained by the family line even after moving. The *yagō* sometimes became almost a trademark and was more closely identified with the house or family than the actual family name. Although it is not known when the custom first developed, mention of *yagō* appears in Muromachi-period (1333–1568) chronicles. *Yagō* were often used in villages where many people who had the same family name wanted to distinguish lineages with higher status. Some *yagō* were derived from the locations of houses, for example, Hara ("meadow") and Sakamoto ("foot of the hill"), or when applied to a family line, from the relationship of main and junior lines (see HONKE AND BUNKE). Others were derived from family occupations, standing in the community, or the provinces from which families originated, as in Mikawaya ("Mikawa house") or Surugaya ("Suruga house"). During the Edo period (1600–1868), it became customary for KABUKI families to assume *yagō*; the renowned actor ICHIKAWA DANJŪRŌ, for example, was known as Naritaya. Today *yagō* frequently serve as names for Japanese businesses, especially retail stores. 　*INAGAKI Shisei*

Yagyū

District in the northeastern part of the city of Nara, northern Nara Prefecture, central Honshū. On the Yamato highland (Yamato Kōgen). Principal farm products are rice and tea. To alleviate Nara's water shortage, a reservoir has been constructed in Yagyū. It is the home of the Yagyū family which founded the Yagyū school of fencing.

Yagyū Munenori (1571–1646)

Master swordsman active early in the Edo period (1600–1868). Born in Yagyūnoshō (now part of the city of Nara), he learned fencing from his father, Yagyū Muneyoshi (1527–1606), who founded the Yagyū or Shinkage school of swordsmanship. Munenori entered the service of TOKUGAWA IEYASU, and, having distinguished himself in the Battle of SEKIGAHARA (1600) and the sieges of Ōsaka Castle (1614 and 1615; see ŌSAKA CASTLE, SIEGES OF), he won the confidence of the Tokugawa family and was designated fencing instructor to the shōguns TOKUGAWA HIDETADA and TOKUGAWA IEMITSU. In 1632 he was appointed inspector general (ŌMETSUKE) and charged with surveillance of *daimyō*. By the end of his career he held land assessed at 12,500 *koku* (see KOKUDAKA). His descendants served as fencing instructors to the shogunal family throughout the Edo period. Together with a contemporary swordsman, MIYAMOTO MUSASHI, Yagyū has been celebrated in popular literature.

Yahagigawa

River in central Aichi Prefecture, central Honshū, originating in the mountains on the border of Nagano, Gifu, and Aichi prefectures, and flowing through Okazaki Plain to empty into Mikawa Bay at the city of Nishio. The multipurpose Yahagi Dam is located on the upper reaches. The water is utilized for irrigation, industry, and drinking. Length: 117 km (73 mi); area of drainage basin: 1,830 sq km (706 sq mi).

Yahata → Yawata

Yahikoyama

Also called Yahikosan. Mountain in central Niigata Prefecture, central Honshū, near the Sea of Japan coast. In its eastern foothills is Yahiko Shrine and a flourishing shrine town. The summit commands a panoramic view of the Sea of Japan, Sado Island, and the Niigata Plain. Yahikoyama is part of Sado–Yahiko Quasi-National Park. Height: 638 m (2,093 ft).

Yaita

City in northern Tochigi Prefecture, central Honshū. Formerly a farming and lumbering city, it has become industrialized with the construction of industrial complexes and the opening of an expressway in the early 1960s. Manufactures include electrical appliances, textiles, steel, and toys. Pop: 32,747.

Yaizu

City in central Shizuoka Prefecture, central Honshū. On Suruga Bay, it has long been an important fishing port. Catches include tuna and bonito. There is also a thriving seafood processing industry. Of historical interest is the Yaizu Shrine, dedicated to the legendary hero, Prince YAMATOTAKERU. Pop: 104,362.

Yajima Kajiko (1833–1925)

Educator and Christian activist. Born in Higo Province (now Kumamoto Prefecture). Leaving her violent and alcoholic husband after 10 years of marriage, she went in 1872 to Tōkyō, where she studied at the Kyōin Denshūjo, a school for teachers. At age 41 she secretly bore an illegitimate child, which she sent away but later adopted; her nephew, the writer TOKUTOMI ROKA, revealed the truth of this daughter's parentage shortly before Kajiko's death.

In 1878 she was appointed principal of the Christian girls' school Shinsakae Jogakkō; then in 1880 she became principal of the similar Sakurai Jogakkō. From 1889 to 1914 she served as head of the Joshi Gakuin (Women's Academy, still a respected secondary school), which resulted from a merger of the two schools.

Baptized in 1880 and influenced by American women who had come to Japan, such as the missionary M. T. True and the touring Woman's Christian Temperance Union speaker Mary Leavitt, Kajiko founded in 1886 the KYŌFŪKAI (Japan's version of the Woman's Christian Temperance Union). As its director for almost 35 years, she campaigned for women's rights, the abolition of licensed prostitution, and the temperance movement. After the age of 70, she traveled abroad four times to represent this group.

Yakai Incident

(Yakai Jiken). Murder case that led to one of the most protracted and controversial court cases in Japanese history; it involved, specifically, the legality of relying solely on the confession of one suspect, and the possible use of police coercion. On 24 January 1951 an aged couple living in the Yakai district of the village of Ogō (now the town of Tabuse), Yamaguchi Prefecture, were robbed and murdered in their home. The police apprehended Yoshioka Akira, and as a result of his confession four other men were charged as his accomplices. Yoshioka was sentenced to life imprisonment at the second trial, but the four alleged accomplices continued to appeal for 17 years and 8 months. Finally, in October 1968, the four were declared innocent by the Supreme Court. The case was much discussed in the popular press during the trials and became the subject of Imai Tadashi's film MAHIRU NO ANKOKU (1956, Darkness at Noon).

Yakedake

Active volcano on the border of Nagano Prefecture and Gifu Prefecture, central Honshū; the only active volcano in the Hida Mountains.

Yakushiji

The East Pagoda (right), West Pagoda (center), and main hall (left) of Yakushiji. The temple was built on its present site during the 720s. Only the East Pagoda, which has been designated a National Treasure, survives from the 8th century. Nishinokyō, Nara.

Lava from an eruption sometime in the past changed the course of the river Azusagawa from the Gifu side to the Nagano side and created the valley called KAMIKŌCHI. An eruption in 1915 dammed the Azusagawa, creating Taishō Pond. The volcano erupted again in 1962. It is part of the Chūbu Sangaku National Park. Height: 2,455 m (8,052 ft).

yakko

1. Before the Nara period (710–794), the term *yakko* referred to slaves, particularly male slaves. Under the RITSURYŌ SYSTEM, established in the 7th century, *yakko* became the lowest social stratum, public and private slaves (NUHI). The status of *nuhi* was officially abolished in the early 10th century, but in succeeding centuries the term *yakko* or *nuhi* continued to be used in reference to the bond servants of wealthy families.

2. During the Edo period (1600–1868), servants attached to *daimyō* or *hatamoto* (direct shogunal vassal) houses were often called *yakko*. They formed bands (*kumi*), swaggered about as dandies in the gay quarters, and were feared by townsmen as rowdies. In imitation of these HATAMOTO YAKKO, the town rowdies without feudal affiliation referred to themselves as MACHI YAKKO. With his large twisted moustache, the *yakko* was a favorite figure in daimyō processions, in which he served as a forerunner or rearguard, carrying an ornamental spear.

3. In the Edo period the term *yakko* was also used to refer to women forced into slavery as a form of punishment. The punishment was imposed on women who illegally bypassed barriers (SEKI-SHO) on the highways and on the wives and daughters of men condemned to exile or death.   *Yoshiyuki* NAKAI

yakubyōgami

Also called *ekibyōgami*, *ekijin*, and *eyami no kami*. Type of god believed to cause epidemics and plagues. Since the Heian period (794–1185), observances called *goryōe* were conducted to enshrine and thereby pacify vengeful spirits (GORYŌ) who were thought responsible for plagues and other disasters. During the medieval period (13th–16th centuries), the god of plagues was frequently personified, appearing as a white-haired old man in red robes, or as an old woman with a monstrous visage. To keep this god away, protective talismans (GOFU) or dolls with frightening faces were placed at the entrance of houses. On the other hand, in some regions the *yakubyōgami* is placated by being invited at New Year's to lodge for a night in the household.   *Ōtō Tokihiko*

yakudoshi

(danger years). According to Japanese folk belief, critical or unlucky years—those ages when an individual is most likely to experience calamities or misfortunes. Although there are local and historical variations, according to the OMMYŌDŌ school of divination ages 25 and 42 for men, and 19 and 33 for women, are deemed critical years. Of these, age 42 for men and 33 for women are considered espe-

cially critical. (The designation of these particular ages as *yakudoshi* may stem from the inauspicious homonyms that pronunciation of their digits yield in Japanese: 42, for example, yields *shini*, homophonous with the word for death.) It is customary in these critical years to invite relatives and acquaintances to a banquet and to visit temples and shrines. The 61st and 70th years of life are also deemed *yakudoshi* for both men and women, but their observance is accompanied by celebration of longevity as well. See also SHICHIGOSAN; LIFE CYCLE.   *Inokuchi Shōji*

Yakumo mishō

Treatise on Japanese classical (WAKA) poetry by Emperor JUNTOKU (1197–1242, r 1210–21), who was exiled to the island of Sado after the Jōkyū Disturbance (1221). The work was begun toward the end of his reign and completed sometime during his exile. It is the first systematic study of *waka* history and *waka* techniques as they had developed up to the end of the Heian period (794–1185), and it included such topics as poetic style, rhetorical devices, subject matter, and vocabulary.

yakusa no kabane

A status system under which eight (*yakusa*) honorary cognomens (*kabane*) were granted to certain families; instituted by the emperor TEMMU in 684 to strengthen imperial authority in the wake of the JINSHIN DISTURBANCE (672), it replaced an older system of honorary titles. The cognomens were appended to the family names, as in Kibi no Ason Makibi. The cognomens were *mahito, ason (asomi), sukune, imiki, michinoshi, omi, muraji,* and *inagi* (or *inaki*). *Mahito* and *ason* were granted to close relatives of the imperial family and *sukune* and *imiki* to members of other illustrious lineages. The last four ranks were generally given to lesser government officials. See UJI-KABANE SYSTEM.   *Kitamura Bunji*

Yakushidake

Mountain in the Hida Mountains, southeastern Toyama Prefecture, central Honshū. The summit, composed of quartz porphyry, forms a plateau. On its eastern slope is a cirque group designated as a natural monument. The mountain has been a center of worship since ancient days; on the summit is the temple Yakushidō. The mountain is rich in alpine flora. Height: 2,926 m (9,597 ft).

Yakushiji

One of the three head temples of the HOSSŌ SECT of Buddhism located in Nishinokyō, a western suburb of the city of Nara. Yakushiji is a monastery-temple which was first built in the Asuka district on a site that is today located within the city limits of Kashihara in Nara Prefecture. When the capital was established at Nara, Yakushiji was rebuilt on its present site mostly during the 720s. Owing to a number of fires, earthquakes, and typhoons, the Nara buildings perished but were rebuilt in later centuries. Only a three-storied pagoda remains as a reminder that Yakushiji was a splendid architectural achievement of the Nara period (710–794). The temple was dedicated to the Buddha Yakushi (Skt: Bhaiṣayaguru; the Buddha of healing), whose famous image with flanking attendants remains the main icon (*honzon*) of the temple.

The construction of Yakushiji derives from a vow of Emperor TEMMU (r 672–686) in 680 to make an image of Yakushi to bring about the recovery of his ailing consort; however, work did not actually begin until 687. This pious vow was believed to have cured the empress's illness within a short time. After the death of the emperor in 686 his wife, who succeeded him on the throne as Empress JITŌ (r 686–697), carried out the work on the temple and the image, the latter being completed in 697, when the "eye-opening" or consecration ceremony for the image was held. The temple was ready to receive priests who were appointed to it the following year by Emperor MOMMU (r 697–707). (In recent years, on the basis of stylistic evidence, many art historians date the sculptures to the period 719–729, rather than 697 as recorded in the NIHON SHOKI.)

Since Yakushiji was an imperially sponsored temple, it was conceived on a magnificent scale. The architects chose a plan that focused on the *kondō* (main hall), the hall in which the image of Yakushi was to be displayed. Although most early temple layouts in Japan emphasized the pagoda—e.g., SHITENNŌJI, where the pagoda is located directly in front of the *kondō,* or HŌRYŪJI, where the pagoda shares the central position with the *kondō*—the architects opted for a Korean plan, which drew attention to the *kondō* by moving it into the center of the courtyard. They minimized the importance of the pagoda by duplicating it, placing one each toward the southwest and southeast corners of the compound. The plan was epoch-making in Nara, where twin pagodas consequently became typical. The original Yakushiji in the Asuka district, now designated Moto Yakushiji, remained standing until the Heian period (794–1185). Unlike other great temples that were moved from the Asuka district to the new capital and were enlarged and embellished in the process, Yakushiji alone retained its original layout. The West Pagoda was destroyed during the civil war of 1528–31 leaving only the foundation stones (it was rebuilt in 1981). Other buildings were restored and rebuilt in styles ranging from those of the Kamakura period (1185–1333) to those of the Edo period (1600–1868). Only the East Pagoda, completed in Nara in 730, escaped the calamities that struck the temple over the years. Though similar in height to the five-storied pagoda of Hōryūji, the Yakushiji pagoda is a three-storied structure. Each story is supplied with a subsidiary roof *(mokoshi)* slightly smaller than its main roof. This unusual feature of larger and smaller roofs lends the pagoda an undulating, rhythmical appearance with musical overtones unlike that of Hōryūji, which is more architectonic. The pagoda finial *(sōrin)* also is unique, one of its components being a gilt-bronze "water flame" ornament *(suien)* in which celestials descend by means of fluttering scarves, playing musical instruments and bringing offerings. Cast in openwork, they face the pagoda as though they were protecting deities.

All the original buildings within the main compound had subsidiary roofs. The Buddhist scholar Ōe no Chikamichi (d 1151) on a pilgrimage to Nara admired the *kondō,* which he described as a two-storied edifice with subsidiary roofs that made it appear as though it had four stories. The *kondō* was severely damaged several times before it perished in a fire caused by civil war in 1528. It was rebuilt in 1600 but only one story high.

Inside the *kondō* on a white marble platform is installed the Buddha Yakushi seated on a pedestal. He is flanked by standing figures of Nikkō (Skt: Sūryaprabha) and Gakkō (Skt: Candraprabha), the bodhisattvas of the sun and the moon respectively. Each image, about 2.7 meters (over 9 ft high), expresses serenely the exalted state of enlightenment. Classical in proportion and bearing, the ample, naturalistic bodies, originally gilded, now shine in black, lustrous tones. Yakushi's hands and feet are engraved with such symbols as the wheel *(hōrin;* Skt: *dharma-cakra),* and the swastika that are among the 32 physical marks of a Buddha. The pedestal is rectangular, more like those of the Asuka region than those of Nara, where the lotus pedestal was the norm. Yakushi's seat is richly decorated with exotic motifs found in China during the contemporary Tang (T'ang) dynasty (618–907), such as grapevines, jewel patterns, and grotesque figures. Beneath them are the four directional animals of Chinese derivation. Another Yakushi triad, similar in size but inferior in execution, stands in the *kōdō* (lecture hall), dating from 1805.

Southeast of the main compound is the Tōindō (East Hall), originally built in the early 720s. The present structure, dating from 1285, is in the native *wayō* style of architecture. Outstanding among the images it preserves is the stately Shō Kannon (Skt: Ārya Avalokiteśvara), the main deity worshiped at the Tōindō, now contained in a black tabernacle. It is a masterpiece, cast in bronze, somewhat earlier than the Yakushi triad of the *kondō.* Annual services at the Tōindō include the Jion'e, performed yearly on 13 November, in memory of Cien Dashi (Tz'u-en Ta-shih, 632–682), the first patriarch of the Hossō (Ch: Faxiang or Fa-hsiang) sect, who is known to the Japanese as Jion Daishi. He was a disciple of Xuanzang (Hsüantsang, 685–762), famous for his travels in Central Asia and India, and for his translations of Buddhist scriptures from Sanskrit into Chinese, many of which Faxiang annotated. An extant portrait of Fa Xiang, painted possibly for the first service held at the Tōindō in 1061, was hung for the occasion and worshiped.

Other important Buddhist ceremonies continue to be conducted at Yakushiji to this day. Notable is the Saishōe, an annual three-day ritual initially conducted beginning on 3 March in the year 830. It was performed by monks who presided over the prestigious Gosaie and Yuimae ceremonies held at the Imperial Palace and KŌFUKUJI respectively. At the Saishōe these monks lectured on a popular sutra called the *Konkōmyō saishōō kyō* (Skt: *Suvarṇa prabhāsottama-rāja-sūtra)* and offered prayers for the tranquility of the state and a rich harvest. This sutra was also chanted at the annual Kichijō Kekae ceremony held in January, when Kichijōten (Skt: Śrīmahādevī; see TEMBU), the goddess of wealth, beauty, and fecundity is worshiped. A small portrait of the beautiful Kichijōten holding a magical jewel *(nyoihōshu;* Skt: *cintā-maṇi)* was painted around 772 when the ceremony was first held at Yakushiji. The ritual involves repentence for transgressions and prayers for a fertile harvest. Another ritual performed at Yakushiji had its origins with the earliest Buddhist lay communities in India who worshiped symbols associated with the Buddha, such as the stupa, his footprints, the bodhi tree, or an umbrella, long before the emergence of images the Buddha. The BUSSOKUSEKI, a stone monument carved in 753, depicting the Buddha's footprints, is preserved at Yakushiji. It is inscribed around the sides in Chinese with information concerning its origin. Behind it stands a stele with 21 verses in praise of the footprints. Written in *man'yōgana,* the Japanese script employed during the Nara period (see the section on the *Man'yō* writing system in the article on the MAN'YŌSHŪ), the verses were chanted while the worshiper circumambulated the footprints.

When Shintō gods came to be viewed as protectors of Buddhist temples, the monk Eishō had a shrine dedicated to HACHIMAN built between the years 889 and 897 on the grounds of the Yakushiji. The present shrine dating from the Edo period contains statues of Hachiman dressed as a Buddhist monk, the goddess Nakatsuhime, and Empress JINGŪ. They were each carved from a single block of wood late in the 9th century and are among the finest examples of Shintō sculpture extant.   *Lucie R.* WEINSTEIN

Yakushima

Island 60 km (37 mi) south of the Ōsumi Peninsula, Kagoshima Prefecture, southern Kyūshū. It is a mountainous island; MIYANOURADAKE (1,935 m; 6,347 ft), the highest peak in the Kyūshū region, is located in the central part of the island. Yakushima has the heaviest precipitation in Japan, with the annual rainfall amounting to 4,000 mm (158 in) in the coastal regions and 10,000 mm (394 in) on the mountaintops. The climate is warm and the average year-round temperature in the coastal regions is 19.3° C (66.7° F). Forestry is an important industry, and the Japanese cedar *(yakusugi)* grown here is known for its quality. Agricultural products are sugarcane, sweet potatoes, *ponkan* oranges *(Citrus reticulata),* and livestock. The chief marine product is flying fish. Part of the Kirishima–Yaku National Park, the island has numerous hot springs and great natural beauty. Area: 500 sq km (193 sq mi).

yakuza

("gangster, gambler, good-for-nothing"). Like their criminal counterparts around the world, Japanese gangsters are social parasites who exploit human weakness for profit while dignifying their trade with elaborate codes of honor and behavior. In Japan, these codes are a pastiche of the Neo-Confucian-based Tokugawa ethics (see GIRI AND NINJŌ; JINGI) and the *samurai* or warrior code (see BUSHIDŌ). The enforced stability and ensuing ennui of the law-and-order Tokugawa shogunate (1603–1867) created an urban environment of wealth and leisure, ideal for the growth of gambling, organized vice, extortion, and blackmail. The word *yakuza* is taken from a gambling game called "three-card" *(sammai karuta)* which became popular in this period. Similar to twenty-one or blackjack, the object of three-card was to come as close to a total of 19 as possible without exceeding it. Thus if you drew 8 *(ya),* 9 *(ku),* and 3 *(sa* or *za)* you got 20 which, though close to 19, was useless, good-for-nothing, *yakuza.* For status-seeking gangsters to adopt such a seemingly derogatory name is strange only in a Western context. In Japan it expressed the townsman's bravado in the face of authority and conformed to the practice of ritualized self-belittlement in polite conversation ("My house is a filthy place, but please enter"). It also carried an implied threat that could be used to create confusion and fear among hard-working, law-abiding citizens to whom a man who could make a living "doing nothing" must be a criminal. According to a National Police Agency survey made in late 1978, there are about 110,000 *yakuza* in 2,500 gangs in Japan.   *John E.* THAYER III

Yalta Conference

Conference of the leaders of the Allied powers, held at Yalta in the Crimea on 4–11 February 1945, attended by Prime Minister Winston Churchill of the United Kingdom, President Franklin Roosevelt of the United States, and Premier Joseph Stalin of the Soviet Union.

The major objective of the conference was to deal with the issues of the surrender and occupation of Germany and postwar European security. The summit was also important in determining Allied policy in the war against Japan, particularly plans for the Soviet entrance into the Pacific War after the defeat of Germany, and the political future of Japan's Asian empire after the war.

During the conference, Roosevelt revealed his conception of the future security relationships in Asia. He considered China to be the key to peace in the region. The United States, in his view, would dominate China and Japan and share control over Korea with the Soviet Union. The power of the former "imperialist" nations of the United Kingdom and France would be offset by the presence of the Soviet Union in Asia.

Soviet entry into the Pacific War was negotiated almost entirely between the United States and the Soviet Union. The British were excluded from the discussions, and Churchill merely signed the agreement which called for the Soviets to enter the war within three months of the German surrender. Under pressure from the United States and the United Kingdom, the Soviet Union had earlier made verbal promises to enter the battle against the Japanese. At Yalta, these promises were cemented into an agreement.

In exchange for this agreement, the Soviets demanded the return of Japan's acquisitions in the RUSSO-JAPANESE WAR of 1904–05: southern Sakhalin, and two ports on the Liaodong (Liaotung) Peninsula, Port Arthur (Ch: Lüshun) and Dalian (Ta-lien; J: Dairen). Stalin also demanded control over the railway network across Manchuria (the Chinese-Eastern and South-Manchuria railways) that linked the Soviet Union to strategic warm-water ports. When Roosevelt suggested modifying these demands, the Soviets inserted morally justifying language into the agreement, including references to the "restoration" of Soviet "rights" violated by the "treacherous attack of Japan."

The political dickering over the Soviet demands held importance for Roosevelt's postwar political scheme. The United States agreed immediately to the return of the Kurils and southern Sakhalin (and the adjacent islands), which were considered important by the Soviets in the security of the region north of Vladivostok. However, Roosevelt did not agree to Soviet leases of Port Arthur and Dalian but insisted that they be free ports; the United States and the Soviet Union compromised by agreeing to a Soviet lease of Port Arthur and the internationalization of Dalian. Roosevelt explained to Stalin that he needed leverage to force the British to make Hong Kong a free port. Stalin accepted a proposal to operate the Manchurian railroads through a joint company with the Chinese. It was also agreed that the status quo in the Mongolian People's Republic would be maintained.

In the absence of Churchill, Roosevelt unveiled his postwar vision to Stalin on 8 February. He proposed to exclude Britain from a trusteeship over Korea, putting it under the control of the United States, the Soviet Union, and China. He proposed to force the French out of Indochina and to place that region under a similar trusteeship. Roosevelt further suggested that the Soviet Union participate in the elimination of European power by competing with the United Kingdom in shipping, adding that the United States would sell them the ships. Stalin went along with this design, disavowing interest in Manchuria and professing to recognize Chinese sovereignty over it. Roosevelt proposed an expanded Chinese government, which would include the Chinese communist opposition—a proposal similar to the plan for a reorganized government for Poland in the Soviet sphere agreed to during the same conference.

📖 ——Diane Shaver Clemens, *Yalta* (1970). Herbert Feis, *Churchill, Roosevelt, Stalin: The War They Waged and the Peace They Sought* (1957). US Department of State, *Foreign Relations of the United States, Diplomatic Papers: The Conferences at Malta and Yalta, 1945* (1955).   Diane Shaver CLEMENS

Yalu River, Naval Battle of

Known in Japan as the Battle of the Yellow Sea (Kōkai Kaisen). Naval battle of the SINO-JAPANESE WAR OF 1894–1895. On 17 September 1894, in the Yellow Sea off the mouth of the Yalu River 12 warships of the Imperial Japanese Navy, under the command of Vice-Admiral Itō Sukeyuki, engaged and defeated a Chinese fleet of 14 warships under Admiral Ding Ruchang (Ting Ju-ch'ang). Three ships of the Chinese fleet were sunk and two ran aground. Some Japanese ships were heavily damaged but none were sunk. After this battle Japan controlled the Yellow Sea.   ICHIKI Toshio

Yamabe no Akahito (?–ca 736)

Poet; court official. One of the most important poets of the MAN'-YŌSHŪ (ca 759, Collection for Ten Thousand Generations or Collection of Ten Thousand Leaves), Japan's first great anthology of vernacular poetry, which contains 37 *tanka* and 13 *chōka* ("long poems") by him. An official of low rank, he was one of the last of the "poets laureate"—semiprofessional poets and musicians of the 7th and early 8th centuries who composed verse commemorating imperial births, deaths, and so forth, and celebrating excursions of the sovereign and his courtiers to the provinces. All of his surviving poems appear to have been written during the reign of Emperor SHŌMU (701–756; r 724–749), whom he accompanied to such places as the royal pleasance in the beautiful mountains of Yoshino, southwest of the capital Nara. He also evidently made several long journeys on his own, composing poems on Mt. Fuji and other famous sites. Although most of his *chōka* seem derivative and formalistic, among his *tanka* are some of the loveliest in the *Man'yōshū*. At his best he combines beauty of imagery in description with quiet lyricism in carefully wrought formal structures.

Akahito came to be known to later ages as the great nature poet of the *Man'yōshū*. His status was enhanced by a famous statement of KI NO TSURAYUKI (872?–945), who in his Japanese preface to the KOKINSHŪ (ca 905, Collection of Ancient and Modern Times), the first imperial anthology of classical Japanese poetry, singles out Akahito with KAKINOMOTO NO HITOMARO (fl ca 685–705) as the two great poets of the early literary period. In addition to his poems in the *Man'yōshū*, some 50 others by or attributed to him are found in various imperial anthologies. Of these a large number are duplications of *Man'yō* poems or slightly altered variants; others are listed in different works as by other poets or by unknown authors. His personal collection, *Yamabe no Akahito shū*, was compiled many years after his death. Its 322 *tanka* and 2 *chōka* include many false attributions, and the collection is in general a very unreliable source.

📖 ——Robert H. Brower and Earl Miner, *Japanese Court Poetry* (1961). Ian Levy, *The Ten Thousand Leaves* (1981–). Nippon Gakujutsu Shinkōkai, *The Man'yōshū: One Thousand Poems* (1940, repr 1965).   Robert H. BROWER

yamabiraki

(literally, "mountain opening"). Ceremonies held annually at local mountains on the first day of the climbing season. The ritual was traditionally conducted by mountain ascetics (YAMABUSHI) so that the general public could "enter" the sacred mountains. In the case of especially sacred mountains such as FUJISAN and Kiso Ontake (see ONTAKESAN), the several pilgrim groups (KŌ) dedicated to each mountain would climb on its opening day. The term has in recent years been used simply to designate the beginning of the mountain climbing season. There is a similar rite at rivers (see KAWABIRAKI).   INOKUCHI Shōji

yamabōshi

Cornus kousa. A deciduous tree of the dogwood family (Cornaceae) which grows wild in hilly areas of Honshū, Shikoku, and Kyūshū. Its trunk grows straight and reaches about 3–8 meters (10–26 ft) in height. Its leaves are alternate, oval, wavy at the edges, and pointed at the tip. In summer flower stalks grow from the branch tips and produce a cluster of flowers surrounded by four large white bracts which strongly resemble petals. The clusters are composed of numerous florets, each of which has four petals, four stamens, and one pistil. After the flowers have blossomed, globular berries develop; when they ripen to a red color, they are edible. *Yamabōshi* flowers are popular as alcove decorations for the tea ceremony.

A flowering dogwood species similar to *yamabōshi*, the *Amerika yamabōshi* (*C. florida*), also known as *hanamizuki*, is often planted in public parks and private gardens. It was first introduced to Japan from the United States in 1909 in gratitude for the cherry trees sent from Tōkyō to Washington, DC. The flower clusters of the *mizuki* (*C. controversa*), a tree which reaches more than 10 meters (40 ft) high, are also pretty, though without the showy bracts.   MATSUDA Osamu

yamabuki

Kerria japonica. A deciduous shrub of the rose family (Rosaceae) found in mountainous areas throughout Japan and also widely cultivated in gardens. It reaches a height of about 2 meters (6–7 ft) and has a delicate stem with green bark and well-developed pith. The leaves are alternate, ovate in shape, and have irregular serrations along the edges. In spring a single five-petaled yellow blossom appears on the tip of each growing branch. Horticultural varieties include the double-flowered *yaeyamabuki* ("Japanese rose"; *K. japonica* f. *pleniflora*), the most commonly cultivated variety in Japan; a six to eight-petalled type called *kikuzaki yamabuki* (*K. japonica* var. *stellata*); and the *shirobana yamabuki* (*K. japonica* var. *albescens*), which has white blossoms with a yellow tint. Another commonly cultivated plant of the rose family called *shiroyamabuki* (*Rhodotypos scandens*) has white blossoms similar to those of the *yamabuki* but is not actually related; it can be distinguished from the *yamabuki* by its four-petaled, four-sepaled blossoms and opposite leaves. Since the *yamabuki* is common in mountains and fields of Japan, the stem pith is often used for making toys by children living in the countryside. The plant has long been well known abroad; it is considered as one of the finest Japanese shrubs in America and Europe. MATSUDA Osamu

yamabukisō

Hylomecon japonicum. A perennial herb, akin to the celandine, of the poppy family (Papaveraceae) which grows mainly under trees in mountainous sections of Honshū and is known as one of the most beautiful wild plants of spring. It reaches a height of about 30 centimeters (12 in) and its stem and leaves contain a yellow juice. The pinnate compound leaves grow from the base of the stem on long stalks. They have five to seven leaflets of a round or diamond shape that sometimes divide into three or five lobes and have serrations along the edges. During April or May four-petaled blossoms of a vivid yellow color similar to those of the YAMABUKI appear in the leaf axils. MATSUDA Osamu

yamabushi

(literally, "one who lies in the mountains"). The name given during the Heian period (794–1185) to ascetics, usually men, who practiced austerities in mountains in order to attain holy or magic powers. Later applied to the members of the SHUGENDŌ order.

The traditional costume of the *yamabushi* comprises 16 items which are of practical use during an ascetic sojourn in the mountains and also embody transforming symbolism designed to carry the disciple from a profane to a sacred state. They are thus comparable with the magic clothes of the shaman. The items include a small black cap (*tokin*), a tunic with baggy trousers (*suzukake*), a collar with six colored tufts (*kesa*), a Buddhist rosary (*nenju*), a conch-shell trumpet (*hora*; see HORAGAI), a staff with rings (*shakujō*), and a fur rug hanging down from the waist in the back (*hishiki*). The *yamabushi*'s hair, unlike that of a Buddhist priest, was allowed to grow.

Although the principal tasks of the *yamabushi* are healing and exorcism, they are also celebrated for such spectacular feats as firewalking and climbing up ladders of swords. During the Edo period (1600–1868) they tended to settle in villages as resident exorcists, often marrying a MIKO, with the aid of whose mediumistic powers they performed their cures of sickness and possession.

There are many references to *yamabushi* in literature, among the most famous being the *kabuki* play *Kanjinchō* and the chapter "Yūgao" in the TALE OF GENJI. Carmen BLACKER

yamachawan

(literally, "mountain teabowl"). Simple unglazed stoneware food bowls produced in many parts of Japan during the mid-12th through the 13th centuries. More refined bowls, often ash-glazed, were made at such centers as SANAGE in what is now Aichi Prefecture during the 11th and early 12th centuries, and the continuity of form clearly shows that *yamachawan* were derived from these (see CERAMICS: ash-glazed wares).

Despite being wheel-thrown, *yamachawan* are generally rather misshapen. The clay used was seldom refined and many examples show rather large pieces of quartz in the fabric body. In many respects these humble bowls may be considered the final representatives of the SUE WARE tradition. A feature that links them to the *sue* tradition is the foot rim, which, when present, was attached to the otherwise finished vessel and not "turned" or trimmed from the base of the bowl. *Yamachawan* were fired in kilns with a reducing atmosphere and hence are gray in tone. The pieces seldom exceed 17

Yamabushi

A *yamabushi* of the Shugendō order in traditional costume blowing on a conch-shell trumpet (*horagai*).

centimeters (about 7 in) in diameter and 5 centimeters (about 2 in) in depth. At Sanage several hundred kiln sites dating to the late 12th century have been discovered. *Yamachawan* were made for local needs and it appears that they ceased to be produced when simple lacquer bowls became readily available. Brian HICKMAN

Yamada

City in central Fukuoka Prefecture, Kyūshū. The development of the CHIKUHŌ COALFIELD in the Meiji period (1868–1912) led to rapid growth, but in the late 1950s, due to reduced demand, many mines were closed. Efforts are being made to attract new industries. Pop: 14,858.

Yamada Bimyō (1868–1910)

Novelist; poet. Real name Yamada Taketarō; other pen name Bimyōsai. Born in Tōkyō, Bimyō studied at Daigaku Yobimon (a preparatory school for what is now Tōkyō University), where he founded the literary magazine *Garakuta bunko* in 1885 with OZAKI KŌYŌ and other members of the KEN'YŪSHA group. Failing to enter Tōkyō University, he turned to professional writing in 1887, establishing himself with a collection of short stories titled *Natsukodachi* (1888), of which the most famous is "Musashino" (first published 1887). These stories were the first in Japanese literary history to be written exclusively in the spoken language (see GEMBUN ITCHI). Bimyō is remembered primarily for this contribution to the development of modern Japanese literature, although he was not very successful as a novelist. He was also an early advocate of the new-style poem (*shintaishi*) which was introduced in 1882. His principal works include the novels *Chōkai shōsetsu tengu* (1886–87) and *Kochō* (1889), and an essay on the new colloquial style, *Gembun itchiron gairyaku* (1888).

Yamadadera remains

The vestiges of the Buddhist temple Yamadadera, located at Yamada, the city of Sakurai, Nara Prefecture. Construction of the temple is said to have begun in 641 at the behest of Soga no Ishikawamaro (d 649), a member of the powerful SOGA FAMILY, and been completed in 676. From the remaining stone and earthen foundations, it was long believed that the plan of the temple followed the so-called SHITENNŌJI style—a rectangular compound with the pagoda, main hall, and lecture hall arranged in a straight line. Excavations in 1976 and 1978, however, revealed that the main hall and pagoda were surrounded by a corridor and formed a separate interior compound. Among the excavated artifacts were ROOF TILES and BUDDHA TILES. Portions of the eastern corridor were uncovered in excavations in 1982. An image of Yakushi Nyorai (Skt: Bhaiṣaya-guru; the healing Buddha), originally enshrined in the main hall, is now preserved in the temple KŌFUKUJI. See also BUDDHIST ARCHI-TECTURE. KITAMURA Bunji

Yamada Isuzu (1917-   )

Actress. Real name Yamada Mitsu. Born in Ōsaka, she joined Nik-katsu Productions (see NIKKATSU CORPORATION) in 1930 and ap-peared in ITAMI MANSAKU's masterpiece, Kokushi musō (1932, Peerless Patriot). She transferred to Daiichi Productions in 1934 and won recognition for her performances in MIZOGUCHI KENJI's Na-niwa erejii (1936, Ōsaka Elegy) and Gion no shimai (1936, Sisters of the Gion). Later she moved to Tōhō (see TŌHŌ CO, LTD) to costar with HASEGAWA KAZUO in Tsuruhachi Tsurujirō (1938). She starred in KINUGASA TEINOSUKE's Hebi Hime sama (1940, Snake Princess) and MAKINO MASAHIRO's Onnakeizu (1943, Lineage of Women). She reached the peak of her popularity in the late 1930s and the 1940s. Since 1950 she has also performed on stage, joining the Ge-kidan Mingei from 1950 to 1952, and forming her own group, the Gendai Haiyū Kyōkai in 1954. Although not a beauty, she brings an earthy vitality to her performances. She was awarded the Geijutsu-sai Taishō (National Art Festival Grand Prize) for her distinguished performance in the film Tanuki (1974, Badger). ITASAKA Tsuyoshi

Yamada Kōsaku (1886-1965)

Composer and conductor. Born in Tōkyō; after early musical studies at Tōkyō Music School, he studied composition in Berlin with Max Bruch and K. L. Wolf in the period 1908-14. In 1914, under the patronage of the entrepreneur IWASAKI KOYATA (1879-1945), he formed a symphony orchestra, which led to the creation of the Tō-kyō Philharmonic Orchestra in the following year. He also became active in composition (particularly of songs), and in spreading Dal-croze eurhythmics in Japan. In the period 1917-19 he was in the United States, where he had collections of his work published and conducted the New York Philharmonic Orchestra at Carnegie Hall. In 1920 he formed the Japan Opera Association, and gave the first Japanese performances of works by Wagner and Debussy. His own vocal music shows the influence of Richard Strauss and Scriabin. In the 1930s he made several visits to Europe and the Soviet Union. His works, amounting to over 750 items in 15 volumes, include Ochitaru tennyo (1912) and Tsurukame (1934). David B. WATERHOUSE

Yamada Moritarō (1897-1980)

Marxist economist. Born in Aichi Prefecture. A graduate of Tōkyō University, Yamada became an assistant professor there but re-signed in 1930 during a crackdown on communist sympathizers. During World War II he studied Chinese agriculture at the Tōa Kenkyūjo (East Asia Research Institute). He became a professor at Tōkyō University after the war, and taught there until his retirement in 1957. He was also active in the Nōchi Kaikaku Kiroku Iinkai (Agrarian Reform Recording Committee) and the Tochi Seido Shi Gakkai (Land System History Association). Yamada turned from theoretical study of Marxist economics to empirical research on Japanese capitalism. Together with NORO EITARŌ, Ōtsuka Kinno-suke, and HIRANO YOSHITARŌ, Yamada edited the massive Nihon shihon shugi hattatsu shi kōza (1932-33, Lectures on the History of the Development of Japanese Capitalism). Nihon shihon shugi bun-seki (1934, Analysis of Japanese Capitalism), a collection of the arti-cles he wrote for this series, became a theoretical mainstay of the KŌZAHA faction of Marxist economists, which, along with the rival RŌNŌHA, was one of the two major schools of Marxist thought in prewar Japan. Among Yamada's major postwar works is Nihon nō-gyō seisanryoku kōzō (1960), a study of agricultural productivity in Japan. SUGIHARA Shirō

Yamada Nagamasa (?-1630)

Adventurer active in Siam (now Thailand) in the early 17th century. Born in Suruga Province (now part of Shizuoka Prefecture). After serving a local lord as palanquin bearer, in 1611 he traveled to Siam on a ship licensed by the shogunate to trade overseas (see VERMIL-

ION SEAL SHIP TRADE). He settled in the Siamese capital, Ayuthia (now Ayutthaya; north of modern Bangkok), and became the leader of its Japanese community (NIHOMMACHI), furthering diplomatic re-lations between Japan and Siam and engaging in trade. Having led a Japanese force in battle for King Songtham, he was awarded the prestigious official title oya senaphimok. When the king's death was followed by a succession dispute in 1628, Nagamasa led some 800 Japanese and 20,000 Siamese to secure the throne for the king's son. Soon afterward, however, with 300 other Japanese he was banished to Ligor, a remote southern region, by an ambitious member of a rival branch of the royal family. There Nagamasa was wounded in a battle with invaders from neighboring Pattani and died from poison administered to his wounds by his Siamese servant. His son there-upon burned the city of Ligor and escaped to Cambodia, where he joined that country's army and died in battle against Siam. The Japanese settlement in Ayuthia was burned in October 1630, but the survivors were allowed to return in about 1633.
■——Miki Sakae, Yamada Nagamasa (1936).

Yamada Saburō (1869-1965)

Scholar of international law. Born in Nara Prefecture. An 1896 graduate of Tōkyō University, he became a professor there in 1900 and lectured on private international law until his retirement in 1930. One of his best-known scholarly essays was a defense of article 2 of the CIVIL CODE, which granted foreigners equal rights under Japa-nese law. Apart from his research, Yamada served as chairman of the Faculty of Law at Tōkyō University, as president of Keijō Uni-versity (now Seoul National University) in Korea (then a Japanese colony), as president of the JAPAN ACADEMY, and as director-in-chief of the Japanese Association of International Law (Kokusai Hō-gakukai). His publications include Kokusai shihō (2 vols, 1932-34, Private International Law). SAWAKI Takao

Yamada Tomohiko (1936-   )

Novelist. Born in Yokohama. Graduate of Waseda University. Em-ployed by a bank and also active as a writer. His works deal mainly with parent-child relationships or white-collar office workers. Col-lections include Chichi no shanikusai (1968, Father's Carnival) and Jikken shitsu (1972, The Laboratory).

Yamada Waka (1879-1956)

Social commentator and reformer. Born in Kanagawa Prefecture; maiden name Asaba. Seeking employment abroad to restore her family's fortunes, she fell into the hands of a procuress, who forced her to work as a prostitute in Seattle, Washington, from around 1897 to 1903. She escaped to a Presbyterian-sponsored refuge in San Francisco, where she was baptized. She soon married Yamada Kaki-chi (1865-1934), who had worked at odd jobs in the United States for almost 20 years while educating himself, especially in sociology but also in several languages. The two returned in 1906 to Tōkyō, where Kakichi opened a small language school. He educated his wife and encouraged her to produce numerous translations and es-says, which she began to publish in Seitō (Bluestocking), the maga-zine of the feminist group SEITŌSHA, in 1913. During this time she became friendly with young women leaders such as HIRATSUKA RAICHŌ and ICHIKAWA FUSAE; in fact, these two first met at her home.
Yamada Waka later contributed to many publications such as SHUFU NO TOMO, but she became most widely known for her an-swers to letters from troubled women published in the newspaper Tōkyō asahi shimbun (now ASAHI SHIMBUN) beginning in 1931. She served as president of the Bosei Hogo Remmei (Motherhood Protection League) from its founding in 1934 until 1937, when the Diet agreed on a bill for financial aid to poverty-stricken mothers of small children. She also established a refuge for mothers and chil-dren in Hatagaya, Tōkyō. In 1937 she returned to the United States on a survey and lecture tour, meeting with Eleanor Roosevelt in the White House. She spent the years from the end of World War II in 1945 until her death managing a retraining center for former prosti-tutes. Nancy ANDREW

Yamada Yōji (1931-   )

Film director. Graduated from Tōkyō University in 1954 and joined SHŌCHIKU CO, LTD, in the same group with director ŌSHIMA NA-

GISA. Yamada served as an assistant director and scriptwriter for several years until his first directing opportunity in 1963. He is creator of the popular "Tora san" series, known as *Otoko wa tsurai yo* (It's Tough Being a Man), and the first of these comedies, made in 1969, vaulted him to prominence. Since then he has turned out two Tora san episodes each year in addition to several other films, among them *Kazoku* (1970, Family; shown abroad as *Where Spring Comes Late*) and *Shiawase no kiiroi hankachi* (1977, Yellow Handkerchief of Happiness). His films dominated the Japanese film world of the 1970s, winning two Kinema Jumpō awards and numerous other awards in addition to being financially successful. He is the only Japanese director producing films on a regular basis with both a high level of artistic achievement and popular, commercial appeal. Yamada's films are noted for promoting the virtues of small-town or rural family life. He has been adept at depicting the difficulties ordinary people face in coping with the expansion of technology and urbanization. All of his characters are somehow at odds with progress and yet they try, often unsuccessfully, to accommodate themselves to the currents of their times.   *David* OWENS

Yamada Yoshio (1873–1958)

Philologist and grammarian. Born in Toyama Prefecture, Yamada in his early years taught at several junior high and high schools in various parts of Japan and participated in the work of the Kokugo Chōsa Iinkai (Commission to Investigate the National Language). He served on the faculty of Tōhoku University from 1924 through 1933.

Yamada's most substantial contribution to Japanese language studies was a long series of grammatical works based on both Japanese and European traditional grammar. *Nihon bumpōron* (Japanese Grammar; part 1, 1902, part 2, 1908) was either extended or revised in *Nihon bumpō kōgi* (1922, Lectures on Japanese Grammar), *Nihon bumpō yōron* (1931, Essentials of Japanese Grammar), and *Nihon bumpōgaku gairon* (1936, Outline of Japanese Grammar).

The books deal primarily with the Japanese literary language as generally used in the early part of this century. Yamada's other works include studies of colloquial Japanese like *Nihon kōgohō kōgi* (1922, Lectures on Colloquial Japanese Grammar), studies of the historical development of Japanese grammar like *Naracho bumpō shi* (1913, History of Nara Period Grammar) and *Heianchō bumpō shi* (1913, History of Heian Period Grammar), and studies of the history of linguistics in Japan like *Kokugogaku shi* (1943, History of Japanese Language Studies).   *George* BEDELL

Yamaga

City in northern Kumamoto Prefecture, Kyūshū. Yamaga is known primarily for its hot springs. Rice, melons, and tobacco are grown. *Sake* breweries and silk reeling and electrical appliance plants are located here. The lantern festival of Yamaga Shrine attracts visitors in August. A number of ornamented tombs (see KOFUN) are in the area. Pop: 32,837.

Yamaga Sokō (1622–1685)

One of the leading scholars of the Edo period (1600–1868), known for his contributions in three separate fields: Confucian studies, military science, and Japanese history. Born in Aizu (now part of Fukushima Prefecture) and raised in Edo (now Tōkyō). Sokō's education began when he enrolled at the age of seven in the school of HAYASHI RAZAN, the outstanding Confucian scholar of the time. Later, he became proficient in military science and also explored the inner meanings of Shintō, in all cases studying under well-known master teachers.

At the age of 30, already a recognized scholar, Sokō accepted employment for the first time, as military instructor for the domain of Akō, near modern Kōbe. Eight years later, he resigned in order to open his own school of classical and military studies in Edo. There, Sokō soon began to teach an original interpretation of Confucianism, rejecting the orthodoxy of the Zhu Xi (Chu Hsi) school, which was supported by the shogunate and presided over by the Hayashi family. At the same time he was developing a philosophical foundation for the *samurai* ethic, later to be called BUSHIDŌ. His unusual ideas attracted interest, and the school grew until his students numbered over 2,000, including even a number of feudal lords (*daimyō*).

In 1665 Sokō took the bold step of publishing a short book, the SEIKYŌ YŌROKU (Essentials of the Sacred Teachings), which openly questioned the validity of accepted interpretations of Confucian

thought. As an innovative military instructor with a wide and influential following, he had already aroused some suspicion and enmity in the feudal society of the time. The book, which amounted to an attack on the ideological foundation of the shogunate, was too threatening to be tolerated. It was banned by the authorities, and Sokō was exiled from Edo and placed in the custody of the lord of Akō.

Although he was restored by his lord to his former position, Sokō now devoted himself increasingly to the study of Japanese history, which was to become his final and most absorbing intellectual interest. Pardoned in 1675, he returned to Edo to spend the last 10 years of his life unostentatiously, engaged primarily in research and writing.

Certain aspects of Yamaga Sokō's thought were more highly regarded in later periods. First, he is credited with initiating the return to the original teachings of Confucius which came to be designated as KOGAKU (Ancient Learning). Yet each of the Kogaku scholars was an independent thinker, and the later contributions of others in this field were eventually given more attention than Sokō's earlier ideas.

In military science, Sokō successfully integrated European firearms and artillery with traditional Chinese tactics and strategy, his approach being one of the first examples of the "Eastern spirit and Western technology" concept, which in one form or another was to be so widely supported at a later date in both China and Japan. Under Sokō's collateral descendants, his "Yamaga school" of military training continued to flourish and to provide instructors for various domainal schools, so that here Sokō's precepts were valued up to the very end of the Edo period.

However, it was in connection with his *bushidō* thought and patriotic view of Japanese history that Sokō's influence became even more significant, continuing through the Meiji Restoration of 1868 and well into the 20th century. It was he who in 1656 wrote what is now considered the earliest work on *bushidō*, the *Bukyō yōroku*, and he later expanded on the subject. He argued that the samurai, living on a comfortable stipend in a time of peace, must have some function. This, as he saw it, was to serve the nation as a living example of dedication to duty, the second Confucian virtue. Material possessions and comfort should be sacrificed to duty, and in the final analysis, honor must be considered more important than life. This stern concentration on duty and honor distinguished Sokō's concept of *bushidō* from Confucianism in general and had an indelible effect on the Japanese character when *bushidō* principles later became the ideal for the whole nation.

In his treatment of Japanese history, Sokō wrote primarily to enhance national pride and patriotism, at a time when other scholars were completely engrossed in the study of China. The best known of his historical works, the CHŪCHŌ JIJITSU (True Facts of the Central Realm), written in 1669, ridiculed the China-worshipers of his day and demonstrated the many ways in which Japan excelled all other nations. Among these points were: the special influence of Japanese water and soil, creating a particular Japanese spirit; the beauties of pure Shintō and the consequent necessity to eradicate Buddhism; the unique characteristic of the Japanese state arising from the unbroken imperial line; and the divine authority of the emperor as ruler and educator of his people. It is for such ideas, with their close relation to significant trends of thought from the 1870s to the 1940s, that Yamaga Sokō is still remembered.

——Hirose Yutaka, ed, *Yamaga Sokō zenshū* (Iwanami Shoten, 1942). *Yamaga Sokō bunshū* (Yūhōdō Shoten, 1926). Hori Isao, *Yamaga Sokō* (1959). Inoue Tetsujirō, *Nippon kogakuha no tetsugaku* (4th ed, 1907).   *David M.* EARL

Yamagata

Capital of Yamagata Prefecture. During the Edo period (1600–1868) Yamagata prospered as a castle town, a POST-STATION TOWN at the junction of several highways, and a distribution center for *benibana* (safflower), wax, and raw silk. Today principal products are rice, *sake*, canned fruits, foodstuffs, sewing machines, and cast iron goods. Yamagata University is located here, as are a prefectural museum and library. The nearby mountain range ZAŌZAN, which is a popular ski area, the Hanagasa Festival in August, and the temple RISSHAKUJI, said to have been founded in the 9th century, are of interest. Pop: 236,984.

Yamagata Aritomo (1838–1922)

Political leader of the Meiji (1868–1912) and Taishō (1912–26) periods. Architect of the modern Japanese army, he also played a major role in building the political institutions of Meiji Japan. As one of the early political leaders from the Chōshū domain (now Yamaguchi Prefecture), he served in a variety of official posts, including chief of the army, minister of war, minister of home affairs, minister of justice, prime minister, privy councillor, and "elder statesman" (genrō). He was a political revolutionary in the early phase of his career but emerged later as one of the principal conservative leaders of Japan in the late Meiji era.

Like most of the Meiji oligarchs, Yamagata rose from modest beginnings. He was born in Hagi, a castle town of Chōshū, into a family of low-ranking samurai. Also in common with the other future leaders of the nation, he emerged first as a member of that band of restive, young, activist samurai of western Japan whose militant spirit had been stimulated by the crisis caused by the OPENING OF JAPAN and by the inspiring teaching of such men as YOSHIDA SHŌIN. For 10 years Yamagata devoted his energies to the radical, loyalist SONNŌ JŌI (Revere the Emperor, Expel the Barbarians) movement, participating in actions against foreigners and in the intradomain and national struggles to destroy the Tokugawa shogunate (1603–1867) and restore the emperor to power. He rose to prominence through his qualities of leadership in the semimodern militia of Chōshū, the KIHEITAI, which contributed to the larger triumph of Chōshū's effort in the MEIJI RESTORATION of 1868. It was his reputation as an able commander that earned him a position of importance in the new Meiji government.

The second phase of Yamagata's career began with his appointment in 1870 as assistant vice-minister of military affairs following a year abroad to study European military systems. It is notable for his contributions to the building of military and then civil institutions in the development of a centralized, stable Meiji state. He advanced rapidly within the new military establishment and can be credited with three major achievements: the enactment of the CONSCRIPTION ORDINANCE OF 1873, the defeat of the SATSUMA REBELLION led by SAIGŌ TAKAMORI in 1877, and the 1878 reorganization of the army along Prussian lines with the adoption of an independent general-staff system. The introduction of universal conscription requiring three years of active service was a far-reaching reform that not only provided a base for constructing a Western-style army but shattered the traditional class distinction between samurai and commoners. The conscript soldiers proved to be disciplined, resourceful fighters in their defeat of the former samurai forces under Saigō. The army reorganization following Saigō's defeat grew out of Yamagata's favorable impression of Prussian military organization and from his perception of the growing threat of liberalism to monarchical authority in Europe. Thus, the establishment of a separate general staff with command functions independent of both the army minister and the cabinet was intended to improve military organization and to prevent civil interference in military decisions. The chief of the General Staff was accorded direct access to the emperor, and to emphasize the importance of this new post, Yamagata resigned as army minister in December 1878 and became its first occupant. His determination to improve the armed forces as well as his fear of political influence adverse to the discipline and morale of soldiers and sailors also led him to issue a series of regulations culminating in the IMPERIAL RESCRIPT TO SOLDIERS AND SAILORS of 1882. These codes of conduct defined the guiding ideals for servicemen, emphasizing absolute loyalty to the emperor and enjoining soldiers to eschew politics. Thus, by stressing a code of loyalty for servicemen, by making the army and navy responsible solely to the emperor as supreme commander, by insulating the high command from civil influence, and by passing a law (1900) that permitted only generals and admirals on active duty to serve as service ministers in the cabinet (see GUMBU DAIJIN GEN'EKI BUKAN SEI), Yamagata set a pattern of military life free from outside interference.

In 1882 Yamagata resigned as chief of the General Staff to become president of the Board of Legislation (Sanjiin). His shift into the civil bureaucracy, without any loss of influence among the military, coincided with a new phase in Meiji history, one in which major attention was given to constructing a new political framework for the promised constitutional government. As head for 16 months of the Legislative Board and then for over seven years as home minister, he did much to shape the major features of the civil bureaucracy. First, he reorganized the Home Ministry (Naimushō), selecting as bureau heads men to his liking who in due course formed the nucleus of a trusted personal clique in the civil bureaucracy. Second, he reformed the police system, modernizing the force through establishment of a training school for officers and centralizing authority through a metropolitan police board supervised by the

home minister. Third, he was responsible for the enactment in 1888–90 of a new local government system. His ideas about local self-government developed from his conviction that the primary objective of a constitutional system was to promote harmony and unity between rulers and ruled. Yamagata disliked political parties and had utter contempt for politicians, who, he was convinced, divided the nation for narrow, selfish motives. His response as home minister to the FREEDOM AND PEOPLE'S RIGHTS MOVEMENT, therefore, was to devise laws restricting political party activities and controlling excessive agitation (see PEACE PRESERVATION LAW OF 1887). But he also felt that simple repression was not the final answer to the unrest that nourished popular parties. Discontent, he believed, could be dispelled by laws encouraging greater participation of responsible citizens in local government. While in their final form the local government laws of 1888 and 1890 contained fewer features of local autonomy than Yamagata had envisioned, they did combine a limited jurisdiction of local officials, from the prefectural down through the district, city, town, and village levels and some popular participation of the local citizenry, with an integration of local administration into the national polity.

Yamagata entered a new stage in his political career during the 1890s. He was named to his first term as prime minister (December 1889–May 1891), in the same year he was promoted to the rank of full general, and he was a field marshal when he led his second cabinet from November 1898 to October 1900. Although he deprecated his political ability, saying that he was "merely a soldier," he was an adroit politician. With the authority he had acquired in the military and civil bureaucracies, he was well placed to lead the country through the early uncertainties of constitutional government. The salient features of his two ministries reflected his conservative view that the government, as an instrument for maintaining imperial authority to further national interests, should act as a responsible servant of the emperor, not of the people, and that political parties should be prevented from infiltrating the bureaucracy, forming cabinets, or holding executive power. Neither of his cabinets lasted long, but both passed measures to strengthen the political and spiritual authority of the state. During his first ministry, he was the moving force behind the 1890 IMPERIAL RESCRIPT ON EDUCATION; his second ministry was characterized by policies to shore up the authority of the bureaucracy in the face of ITŌ HIROBUMI's growing interest in party government and the encroachment of parties on the executive power represented by the short-lived Ōkuma Shigenobu–Itagaki Taisuke cabinet of 1898 (see ŌKUMA CABINET). For example, in 1899 civil service laws were issued that denied key posts in the bureaucracy to political party members; in 1900 his cabinet passed the PUBLIC ORDER AND POLICE LAW to suppress labor and peasant agitation; and in the same year all possibility of civil control of the military was foreclosed by the ordinance stipulating that only officers of the two highest ranks on active duty could be appointed army and navy ministers. These measures were accomplished at the price of some compromises with opposition parties in the Diet. Yamagata skillfully formed a temporary alliance with the KENSEITŌ party and in 1900 agreed to a modest extension of the franchise in return for votes to pass his budget, which included a tax increase to meet enlarged, primarily military, expenditures.

Yamagata's greatest satisfaction came from directing the military's crucial role in Japan's achievement of a new place in the international order. A month after the outbreak of the SINO-JAPANESE WAR OF 1894–1895, he was appointed commander of the First Army. His field service was cut short by serious illness and he returned home to become army minister, a post that drew on his organizational talent but denied him the opportunity to enhance his reputation as a commander of troops. In 1896 he led a diplomatic mission to Moscow that produced the YAMAGATA–LOBANOV AGREEMENT, giving Russia and Japan equal rights and privileges in Korea. In 1902 he supported the ANGLO-JAPANESE ALLIANCE, concluded by his protégé, Prime Minister KATSURA TARŌ, and during the RUSSO-JAPANESE WAR (1904–05) he served as chief of the general staff.

For his services to the nation he was named prince (kōshaku) in 1907. During the last 20 years of his life Yamagata was the most honored and influential member of the group of elder statesmen known as the GENRŌ, particularly after the death of Itō in 1909. Although throughout these years he occupied formal, if largely honorary, government positions, such as president of the PRIVY COUNCIL from 1903 to 1922 and member of the Board of Field Marshals and Fleet Admirals, he preferred to exert his great influence informally through his loyal followers. From behind the scenes he played an important advisory role in foreign affairs, spoke on domestic issues through his disciples in the cabinet, and virtually dictated the selection of prime ministers until his death.

——Roger F. Hackett, *Yamagata Aritomo in the Rise of Modern Japan* (1971). Oka Yoshitake, *Yamagata Aritomo: Meiji Nihon no shōchō* (1958). Roger F. HACKETT

Yamagata Bantō (1748–1821)

Ōsaka rice merchant and scholar. Real name Hasegawa Yūkyū; also known as Masuya Kouemon. Bantō is his scholarly name (*gō*). Born in the village of Kazume in Harima Province (now part of Hyōgo Prefecture), he went to Ōsaka when he was 13 and was adopted by his uncle, Masuya Kyūbei, manager in a rice and financial business owned by the Yamagata family. He entered the service of Yamagata Shigekata, the second head of the family business. With his financial expertise, Bantō succeeded in restoring the fortunes of the then-ailing Yamagata family business, as well as those of the Sendai domain, for which the Yamagata were financiers. For these and other achievements, in 1805 he was accorded virtual membership in the Yamagata family. He then changed his name to Yamagata Yoshihide.

With Yamagata Shigekata's help, Bantō was allowed to study at the KAITOKUDŌ, a school founded by Ōsaka merchants for the education of commoners. He became the pupil of the brothers Nakai Chikuzan and NAKAI RIKEN, as well as of the physician and astronomer, ASADA GŌRYŪ, a close associate of the institution. Bantō also had access to the Aijitsu Bunko, the large book collection of the fourth family head, Yamagata Shigeyoshi, whom Bantō tutored from childhood.

Bantō's approach to his studies reflected his own personality as well as the general spirit of the Kaitokudō school as it had been from the time of MIYAKE SEKIAN, its first head. Those at the school who particularly influenced Bantō included Goi Ranshū (1697–1762), who was known for his theories of "true knowledge" and "corroboration through actual experience," and Nakai Riken, who was favorably impressed by Western science and medicine. From the Aijitsu Bunko and the many imported scientific instruments purchased with Yamagata family funds, Bantō attained a firm grounding in Rangaku, as the study of Western science was then called (see WESTERN LEARNING). He attempted a synthesis of the traditional Chinese Confucian idea of *li* (ultimate principle; J: *ri*) and Western concepts regarding material force. In his preference for "materialist" philosophical ideas, he arrived at a system of thought far in advance of his teachers.

In 1802 Bantō completed the six-volume work *Saiga no tsugunoi* (What Cai Wo [Tsai Wo] Wrote instead of Napping), an early version of his magnum opus, *Yume no shiro*. Another important work was a statement directed to the shogunate and the domain concerning rice-pricing practices. In this he drew upon his wide experience as a rice merchant and emphasized the importance of farmers as rice producers, while playing down the role of traders and craftsmen. He advised the government to accumulate surplus rice to sell during shortages. If this was not possible, then the government should not forbid rice hoarding by merchants during a bad year, since such restrictions would make the merchants' acquisition of rice from the countryside impossible. Only if the merchants seemed to be making inordinate profits did he advise government restrictions against hoarding. He said that government price manipulation was actually harmful and that such matters should be left to merchants.

In 1820 Bantō finally completed *Yume no shiro* (Instead of Dreams). In the introduction to this work, which consists of 12 sections and draws upon 380 separate references (according to his count), Bantō states: "I have studied new theories and the nature of new discoveries and hereby made a correction of the popular notions concerning them." Since the work consists of talks that Bantō gave to his own children and to shopkeepers after closing hours, there is much repetition. Nevertheless, the book is outstanding in its attempt to overcome superstitious beliefs.

In an effort to comprehend the essential nature of all phenomena, Bantō always made it a point to "doubt all doubtful matters and argue all things which can be argued." He would not discuss the implications of historical documents before determining whether they were accurate. With this insistence upon concrete proofs, he critically evaluated a variety of phenomena in nature and human affairs.

In his studies of astronomy Bantō tended to believe that the earth moved, although he conducted no investigations to prove this. He also theorized that there was life on other planets. In other writings he pointed to the European colonization of Asia to demonstrate the threat foreigners posed to Japan. Bantō also sought a way to lighten the burden of memorizing thousands of Chinese characters by simplifying the writing system. He carefully studied all new medical publications, displayed an understanding of physiological experiments on the kidneys, and defended the Caesarean section surgical technique.

Despising all superstition, Bantō considered religious leaders, especially Buddhists and their followers, as his enemies and criticized their inaccurate interpretation of phenomena to support their claims. He also refused to recognize the importance of rites for the dead and absolutely denied the existence of the soul after death. He developed a "materialistic" view of life and death and tried to use this rationalistic approach in his daily life. Writing about the value of the 8th-century chronicle NIHON SHOKI in understanding ancient Japan, he maintained that all records in the work prior to Emperor ŌJIN were completely unreliable. This attitude prefigured modern research on early Japanese history. Bantō's convincing and far-reaching theories regarding human affairs and natural phenomena drew the attention of many thinkers. In matters of daily life, however, he approved of the feudal system, revering TOKUGAWA IEYASU as a god who had brought an age of peace to the nation.

During the transitional Tempō era (1830–44) and the years following, Bantō's ideas spread to government, financial, and educational circles. The Meiji period (1868–1912) finally saw publication of his treatise "Mukihen," a part of *Yume no shiro*, which denied the existence of the soul. There developed a movement aimed at introducing and propagating Bantō's special system of thought. During the Taishō period (1912–26), scholars unearthed facts about his life, and research was undertaken to place his works in economic and business history. There followed studies, in the period prior to World War II, on his materialism. In the post–World War II years, studies in several areas have deepened understanding of Bantō's thought, leading to an increased appreciation of Bantō as a thinker of universal stature, comparable to contemporary thinkers in France, China, Korea, and the United States.

——Arisaka Takamichi and Mizuta Norihisa, ed, *Tominaga Nakamoto; Yamagata Bantō*, in *Nihon shisō taikei*, vol 43 (Iwanami Shoten, 1973). Suenaka Tetsuo, *Yamagata Bantō no kenkyū: Yume no shiro hen*, 2 vols (1971). Albert Craig, "Science and Confucianism in Tokugawa Japan," in M. B. Jansen, ed, *Changing Japanese Attitudes toward Modernization* (1965). SUENAKA Tetsuo

Yamagata Basin

(Yamagata Bonchi). In central Yamagata Prefecture, northern Honshū. Flanked by the Ōu and Asahi mountains, it consists of an alluvial fan below the fault scarp of the Ōu Mountains and the flood plain of the river Mogamigawa's upper reaches. The area produces rice, apples, cherries, and grapes and also has numerous mulberry fields. The major city is Yamagata. Length: 40 km (24.8 mi); width: 10 km (6.2 mi).

Yamagata Daini (1725–1767)

Radical Confucian teacher who advocated rebellion against the Tokugawa shogunate (1603–1867) and was executed for treason in what is known as the MEIWA INCIDENT; also known as Yamagata Ryūsō. Yamagata was born in Kai Province (now Yamanashi Prefecture) and was adopted into the Murase family, a *samurai* family whose head was a constable in the post-station town of Kōfu. After serving as a police guard for five years, he returned to his native area, took the family name Yamagata, and studied medicine. In 1752 Yamagata journeyed to Edo (now Tōkyō), where he practiced medicine among the poor and also gained employment as a private physician for a high-ranking official, the junior councillor (*wakadoshiyori*) Ōoka Tadamitsu (1709–60). Through Ōoka's patronage he gained appointment as an intendant (*daikan*) with a regular stipend. He severed ties with the shogunate around 1759 and taught at his Edo residence. More than a thousand students, including the political economist HONDA TOSHIAKI and the imperial-loyalist Fujii Umon (1720–67), are said to have studied with him.

While still in shogunate employ, Yamagata wrote his famous treatise *Ryūshi shinron* (1759), advocating military overthrow of the very government he served. Describing the system as corrupt and cruel to the peasantry, Yamagata sought to explain through the use of Confucian ideas why this was so, and what strategies were appropriate to deal with it.

From Neo-Confucian thought, and from the school of YAMAZAKI ANSAI in particular, Yamagata drew the idea of "rectification of names." Governments belonged to a universal category of things which possessed unifying definitions that were constant and transcended arbitrary human intentions. One of these constant principles of government was that in times of peace society ought to be managed by the principle of culture (bun), not by military authority (bu). The Tokugawa shogunate, however, governed in precisely the opposite manner, relying on military power as though society were still in an emergency situation of general warfare. The result was injustice throughout the land, the maintenance of a superfluous warrior aristocracy, the oppression of the peasantry, and, most important, the continuation of an ambiguous hierarchy in which the symbol of culture, the emperor, was kept concealed in virtual exile so that the shogunate might rule through military means.

From OGYŪ SORAI and his student DAZAI SHUNDAI, Yamagata Daini took the idea that political structures were not sacrosanct, that they were artificial constructs devised and revised over time according to changing conditions. For these men, the purpose of government was ethical, to provide peace and well-being for society as a whole. The test of whether this purpose was being carried out was the direct and empirical observation of how political structures solved specific social and economic crises. In Yamagata's time peasant uprisings (HYAKUSHŌ IKKI) were common, and everywhere it was apparent that the shogunate was corrupt and incapable of fulfilling its proper function.

It was also from Dazai Shundai that Yamagata borrowed his strategy of revolt. The source of injustice was not a particular individual but the structural basis of authoritative law, in short the Tokugawa shogunate as a whole. The correction of injustice, therefore, must be strategically persuasive, such as by directly confronting the shogunate in Edo, or fortifying a regional domain and mobilizing warriors and peasants alike.

Through samurai associates of the domain of Obata (now Gumma Prefecture), Yamagata plotted just such a "regional" strategy. He drew on the support of TAKENOUCHI SHIKIBU, a loyalist ideologue close to members of the imperial court in Kyōto. He also chose as his aide Fujii Umon, the son of one of the participants in the famous FORTY-SEVEN RŌNIN INCIDENT of 1703. The shogunate learned of the plot, however, and arrested Yamagata and his colleagues for treason on 21 December 1766. Before his execution on 22 August 1767 he wrote a short verse in which he likened himself (and others of similar mind) to the moon on a cloudy night that must wait, without malice, for clear skies.

The significance of Yamagata Daini is suggested in that final poetic vision. The mode of political criticism and the strategy of revolt he shaped would be repeated by men who shared his view and would gain importance as a basis of action in the final overthrow of the Tokugawa shogunate in the 1860s. In these years, his writings, especially his Ryūshi shinron, were circulated widely among samurai seeking ways to justify the use of violence against a regime in which they no longer believed.

■ ——Bitō Masahide, Nihon hōken shisō shi kenkyū (1961). Maruyama Masao, Nihon seiji shisō shi kenkyū (1952), tr Mikiso Hane as Studies in the Intellectual History of Tokugawa Japan (1974). Tetsuo Najita, "Restorationism in the Political Thought of Yamagata Daini, 1725–1767," Journal of Asian Studies 31.1 (1971). Tetsuo Najita, "Political Economism in the Thought of Dazai Shundai, 1680–1747," Journal of Asian Studies 31.4 (1972).

Tetsuo NAJITA

Yamagata–Lobanov Agreement

Pact concerning Japanese and Russian interests in Korea; signed by Army Minister YAMAGATA ARITOMO and Russian Foreign Minister Aleksei Lobanov-Rostovski (1824–96) in St. Petersburg (now Leningrad) on 9 June 1896. Japan's victory in the SINO-JAPANESE WAR OF 1894–1895 had eliminated Chinese sovereignty over Korea and left the Korean government under Japanese control, but Russia was determined to establish its influence in the peninsula. Japan pressed modernizing reforms on Korea, but its high-handed tactics incurred the animosity of the Korean ruling class, which aligned itself with the Russians. In October 1895 Queen MIN, the central figure in a conservative, anti-Japanese political clique, was murdered by Japanese troops and some Japanese adventurers with the connivance of MIURA GORŌ, the Japanese minister in Seoul. This act resulted in popular uprisings and riots, and the Korean king, KOJONG (1852–1919), fled for safety to the Russian legation, where he was to remain for a year. Thus Russia had gained a great advantage, and Japan was forced to negotiate to save what remained of its ambitions in the region. The two nations reached a temporary understanding in the Komura–Weber Agreement of May 1896, but Yamagata decided to take advantage of his invitation to the coronation of Tsar Nicholas II to work out a more formal accord. The Yamagata–Lobanov Agreement provided for joint Russian-Japanese aid to Korea to reform its army and government finances, continued Japanese administration of the Pusan–Seoul telegraph line, the right of Russia to build a telegraph line from its border to Seoul, and the delimitation of parts of Korea to which the two countries might send troops. The agreement contained large concessions on the part of Japan. Japan was able to exact more favorable terms, however, in the NISHI–ROSEN AGREEMENT of April 1898.

Yamagata Masao (1898–)

Naval architect whose basic research in naval architecture, particularly in hull design, laid the foundation for the rapid development of Japan's modern shipbuilding industry. Born in Tōkyō, he graduated from Tōkyō University in 1921. After serving in the Ships Bureau of the Ministry of Transport, he taught at Tōkyō University from 1947 to 1958, and was dean of engineering from 1956 to 1958. He received the Order of Culture in 1967.

Yamagata Prefecture

(Yamagata Ken). Located in northeastern Honshū and bordered to the north by Akita Prefecture, to the east by Miyagi and Fukushima prefectures, to the south by Fukushima and Niigata prefectures, and to the west by the Sea of Japan. The terrain is predominantly mountainous, with the ŌU MOUNTAINS running north and south along the eastern edge of the prefecture, and the Dewa and Asahi mountain ranges rising along the coast on the west. Between these mountain chains the river Mogamigawa flows northward and then westward, emptying into the Sea of Japan at Sakata. The estuary of the Mogamigawa forms Shōnai Plain, and most of the prefecture's level areas are located along this river. The climate is characterized by warm summers and snowy winters.

The Yamagata area was still occupied by EZO tribesmen during the formative years of the Japanese nation. The central government gradually extended its control, and in 712 the area became part of the newly established province of Dewa. During the latter part of the Heian period (794–1185), it came under the domination of the ŌSHŪ FUJIWARA FAMILY, who in turn yielded to a succession of warlords. For most of the feudal period it was divided into several smaller domains. The present name and borders were established in 1876 after the Meiji Restoration.

A predominantly rural prefecture, it is one of Japan's major rice-producing areas. There are also numerous orchards. Forestry is another major component of the economy. Manufacturing, concentrated around the cities of Sakata and Yamagata, centers on food processing, textiles, machinery, woodworking, and chemicals.

Attractions include Bandai–Asahi National Park and Zaō, Chōkai, and Kurikoma quasi-national parks. ZAŌZAN is also one of Honshū's principal ski areas. The hot spring resorts of Zaō, Kaminoyama, Higashine, Ginzan, and Akakura are well known. Area: 9,326 sq km (3,600 sq mi); pop: 1,251,878; capital: Yamagata. Other major cities include Yonezawa, Tsuruoka, Sakata, and Tendō. See map on following page.

Yamagishikai

Utopian movement initiated in 1953 by Yamagishi Miyozō (1901–61) and others, with headquarters in the city of Yokkaichi, Mie Prefecture. The movement's goal is peaceful achievement of the "Z Revolution" (Zetto Kakumei), whereby government policy would be determined by unanimous agreement of the people, use of money abolished, unemployment alleviated by planned production, and a society based on mutual trust and absence of all physical and spiritual illness. Each month the movement sponsors two sessions that stress the cultivation of emotional equanimity and a positive attitude toward work. Members join one of 30 farm communes, to which they donate all their wealth. Within the communes, decisions are reached by group consensus and there are no permanent leaders; responsibility for the chief functions of the commune changes hands every six months. Married couples live together, but children attending school live in dormitories and visit their parents only on weekends. The farm communes are the economic base of the move-

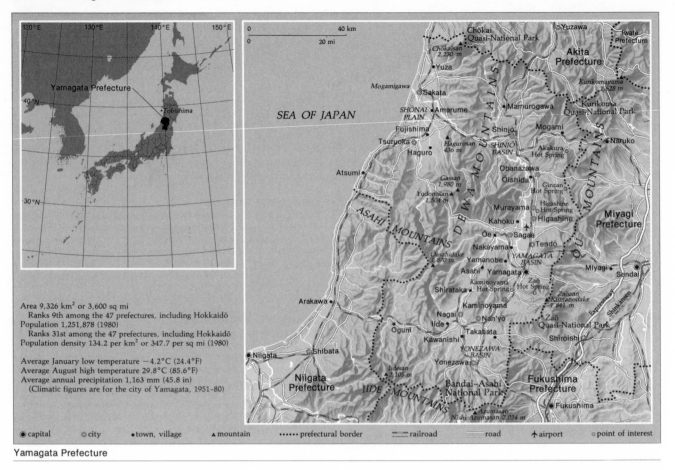

Area 9,326 km² or 3,600 sq mi
   Ranks 9th among the 47 prefectures, including Hokkaidō
Population 1,251,878 (1980)
   Ranks 31st among the 47 prefectures, including Hokkaidō
Population density 134.2 per km² or 347.7 per sq mi (1980)

Average January low temperature −4.2°C (24.4°F)
Average August high temperature 29.8°C (85.6°F)
Average annual precipitation 1,163 mm (45.8 in)
   (Climatic figures are for the city of Yamagata, 1951-80)

◉ capital   ◎ city   ● town, village   ▲ mountain   ••••• prefectural border   ══ railroad   ═══ road   ✈ airport   ○ point of interest

Yamagata Prefecture

ment, their produce being sold through a nationwide network of 1,700 consumer cooperatives.

Yamagiwa Katsusaburō (1863–1930)

Pathologist. Born in Shinano Province (now Nagano Prefecture). Graduate and professor of Tōkyō University. In 1915, by continuous painting and rubbing of tar on the ears of rabbits, Yamagiwa and Ichikawa Kōichi (1888–1948) for the first time succeeded in inducing chemical carcinogenesis. For this achievement Yamagiwa received the Japan Academy Prize and a German award. See also BIOLOGY; MEDICINE: medical research.   ACHIWA Gorō

Yamaguchi

Capital of Yamaguchi Prefecture, western Honshū. Yamaguchi was a flourishing castle town and port under the rule of the ŌUCHI FAMILY in the 14th to 16th centuries. Francis XAVIER visited here in 1550 to propagate the Christian religion. However, when the MŌRI FAMILY, which replaced the Ōuchi in 1555, transferred its base to Hagi, the town began to decline. The principal agricultural product is rice. There are no modern industries apart from some milk and beverage factories. Of interest are the St. Francis Xavier Memorial Cathedral, built in 1950 to commemorate his missionary work, the garden of the Jōeiji temple, the Yamaguchi Gion Festival held at Yasaka Shrine in July, and the Yuda Hot Spring located to the southwest. Yamaguchi is also the base for tours to the plateau AKIYOSHIDAI. Pop: 114,744.

Yamaguchi Basin

(Yamaguchi Bonchi). In central Yamaguchi Prefecture, western Honshū. Extending along a fault line running from northeast to southwest, it consists of small alluvial fans along the river Fushinogawa's upper reaches and of its flood plain. Rice is the principal product of the area. Numerous Yayoi-period graves and relics have been discovered there. The major city is Yamaguchi, west of which lies the Yuda Hot Spring. Area: approximately 40 sq km (15 sq mi).

Yamaguchi Hitomi (1926–   )

Novelist; essayist. Born in Tōkyō. Graduate of Kokugakuin University. While working as an advertising copywriter, he won the Naoki Prize in 1962 for his novel *Eburimanshi no yūga na seikatsu*, which captures with humor and pathos the life of an average white-collar worker (*Eburimanshi* means Mr. Everyman). He continued to write similar novels, one of which is *Majime ningen* (1965, A Serious Person). Reflecting the modest circumstances of the prewar Tokyoites among whom he grew up and the bitter experiences of his generation during World War II, his writings mock affluent Japanese urban society of the 1960s. Other works include a series of essays that he began publishing in 1963 under the general title *Danseijishin*.

Yamaguchi Kaoru (1907–1968)

Western-style painter. Born in Gumma Prefecture. He studied Western-style painting (YŌGA) at the Tōkyō Bijutsu Gakkō (now Tōkyō University of Fine Arts and Music) and while still a student began to participate in various exhibitions, including the Nikaten and the Teiten in Tōkyō, and the Kokugakaiten in Kyōto. He graduated in 1930 and spent three years in Europe, where he was strongly influenced by the styles of the Paris school. On his return to Japan, he participated in the founding of the Shinjidai (New Age) group in 1934 and the Jiyū Bijutsuka Kyōkai (Free Artists Association) in 1937. In 1950 he helped to organize the Modern Art Association. A recipient of several major awards, Yamaguchi had many students. He began teaching at the Tōkyō University of Fine Arts and Music in 1953, and was appointed professor in 1964.

Yamaguchi no Atai Ōguchi (fl 7th century)

Buddhist sculptor. According to the NIHON SHOKI (720), one of Japan's first historical chronicles, Yamaguchi no Atai Ōguchi carved 1,000 images of Buddha (SENTAI BUTSU) by order of Emperor Kōtoku in 650. His name also appears in the inscription on the halo (*kōhai*) of the image of Kōmokuten, one of the Four Heavenly Kings (Shitennō) in the *kondō* (main hall) of the Nara temple HŌRYŪJI.

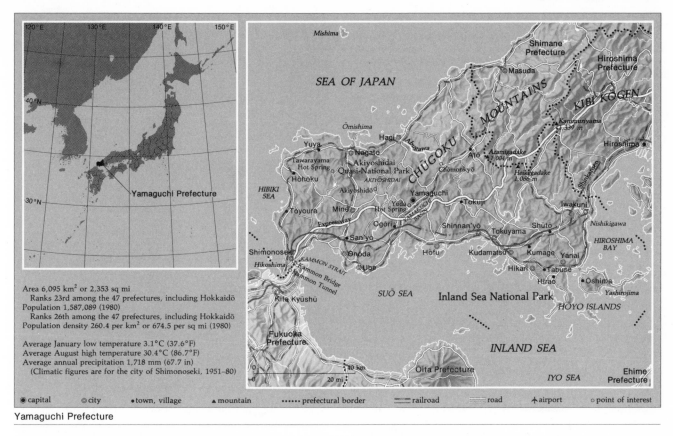

| ◉ capital | ◎ city | ●town, village | ▲ mountain | ••••• prefectural border | ═══ railroad | ▭▭ road | ✈ airport | ○ point of interest |

Yamaguchi Prefecture

Yamaguchi Prefecture

(Yamaguchi Ken). Located at the western tip of Honshū and bordered by the Sea of Japan to the north, Shimane and Hiroshima prefectures to the east, the Inland Sea to the south, and the Hibiki Sea to the west. The city of Shimonoseki is connected to Kyūshū by both a tunnel and a bridge. The prefecture is divided into an industrial area along the Inland Sea coast to the south and a rural area along the Sea of Japan coast to the north. The terrain consists mostly of low mountains and plateaus, and the coastline is rocky and heavily indented. The climate is generally mild, especially along the seacoast. Typhoons are relatively frequent.

Its proximity to the Korean peninsula and its stragetic location between western Honshū and Kyūshū led to its early development. After the TAIKA REFORM of 645 it was divided into the two provinces of Suō and Nagato. These provinces flourished under the rule of the ŌUCHI FAMILY and later the MŌRI FAMILY during the feudal period, and came to be known together as Chōshū. Samurai from Chōshū, such as ITŌ HIROBUMI, INOUE KAORU, and KIDO TAKAYOSHI, played a leading role in the overthrow of the Tokugawa shogunate in the closing years of the Edo period (1600–1868). The present prefectural name and boundaries were established in 1871.

Rice is the major crop in Yamaguchi; citrus and other fruits are also grown. The Inland Sea coast area has rapidly developed as a center for numerous heavy and chemical industries.

Tourist attractions include its coastline, both on the Inland Sea and the Sea of Japan. Yamaguchi and Hagi retain traces of their past as castle towns. Akiyoshidai Quasi-National Park is noted for its karst (limestone) topography (see AKIYOSHIDAI). Hot spring resorts include Yuda and Yumoto. Area: 6,095 sq km (2,353 sq mi); pop: 1,587,089; capital: Yamaguchi. Other major cities include Shimonoseki, Ube, Tokuyama, Iwakuni, Hōfu, and Hagi.

Yamaguchi Seishi (1901–)

Haiku poet. Real name Yamaguchi Chikahiko. Born in Kyōto. Graduate of Tōkyō University. He became a contributor to HOTO-TOGISU, a major modern haiku magazine founded in 1897, and quickly rose to prominence. However, opposed to the objective description of nature advocated by *Hototogisu* coterie leader TAKA-HAMA KYOSHI, he left the group in 1935 to join *Ashibi*, a coterie founded by another dissenter, MIZUHARA SHŪŌSHI. In his poems Yamaguchi attempted to make haiku more relevant and personal by incorporating motifs from daily life. His principal collections are *Tōkō* (1932) and *Wafuku* (1955).

Yamaguchi Sodō (1642–1716)

HAIKU poet of the early Edo period. Real name Yamaguchi Nobu-aki. Born in Kai Province (now Yamanashi Prefecture), he was a close friend of the noted haiku poet BASHŌ, whose early stylistic development he is believed to have influenced. He went to Edo (now Tōkyō) when he was in his twenties, became a student of the Confucian scholar HAYASHI GAHŌ, and subsequently earned a minor post in the Tokugawa shogunate. He retired early, however, and went to live in Katsushika on the outskirts of Edo to devote himself to poetry, calligraphy, and the tea ceremony. It was in the early 1680s, when Bashō was attempting to transcend the intrinsic limitations of the DANRIN SCHOOL of *haikai* by turning to Chinese poetry, that Sodō, with his other-worldly attitude and knowledge of Chinese literature, wielded the greatest influence over Bashō's poetic development. This influence is apparent in the new directions taken by Bashō in his anthology, *Minashiguri* (1683), with its professed spiritual affinity to Li Bo (Li Po), Du Fu (Tu Fu), and the mystic-poet Hanshan. Sodō's own verses have the quality of refinement and loftiness seen in Japan as characteristic of Chinese poetry, and which Sodō's disciples would later call the Katsushika style after his place of retirement. A collection of his haiku is found in *Tokutoku no kuawase*.

Yamaguchi Yoshiko (1920–)

Film actress. Born in Fushun, Manchuria. She made her motion picture debut under the Japanized Chinese name Ri Kōran (Ch: Li Xianglan or Li Hsiang–lan). She played leading roles in films such as Watanabe Kunio's *Byakuran no uta* (1938; Song of the White Orchid), *Nessa no chikai* (1940; Promise in the Hot Sand), and Fushimizu Shu's *Shina no yoru* (1940; China Nights). After World War II she made a new start as Yamaguchi Yoshiko, but was never able to recapture her prewar popularity. In 1951 she married Japanese American sculptor Isamu NOGUCHI. Divorced, she later married Ōtaka Hiroshi, a diplomat. In 1974 she was elected to the upper house of the Diet. ITASAKA TSUYOSHI

Yamaha Motor Co, Ltd

(Yamaha Hatsudōki). Yamaha Motor's principal product is motorcycles, but it also produces motorboats, sailboats, fishing vessels, Japanese-style ships, outboard motors, diesel engines, snowmobiles, golf carts, multipurpose engines, and generators. The brand name Yamaha is well known internationally. The firm was established in 1955 after becoming independent of NIPPON GAKKI CO, LTD. Ever since its motorcycles won prizes in the 1958 Catalina Race, the company has been active in world Grand Prix races. Yamaha began exporting motorcycles early on; now an average of 70 percent of total production is exported. Four overseas branch offices have been established in the United States, Canada, the Netherlands, and Brazil. It has also joint ventures in Iran, Pakistan, Malaysia, Indonesia, Mexico, Colombia, and technical tie-ups with companies in 20 countries around the world. Sales for the fiscal year ending April 1982 totaled ￥515.8 billion (US $2.1 billion), of which motorcycles accounted for 70.7 percent, outboard motors 6.3 percent, boats 3.9 percent, snowmobiles 2.4 percent, and parts and other products 16.7 percent. In the same year the firm was capitalized at ￥6.2 billion (US $25.3 million). The head office is in Iwata, Shizuoka Prefecture.

Yamaichi Securities Co, Ltd

(Yamaichi Shōken). One of the four largest securities companies in Japan. Yamaichi Securities' principal lines of business are the purchase and sale of stocks and the underwriting of public and corporate bonds. It was established in 1897. In 1951 the company advanced into the investment trust field and expanded its operations. In 1965, however, as a result of the recession and the drastic fall in the value of stocks, cancellations of investment trusts began pouring in; only after obtaining special funds from the Bank of Japan was the company able to recover its financial status. The company has overseas subsidiaries in Hong Kong, London, Amsterdam, Frankfurt, Zürich, Montreal, and New York. Sales for the fiscal year ending September 1981 totaled ￥132.9 billion (US $577.8 million), and capitalization stood at ￥38.9 billion (US $169.1 million) in the same year. The head office is located in Tōkyō.

Yamaji Aizan (1864–1917)

Journalist. Original name Yamaji Yakichi. Born in Edo (now Tōkyō) into the family of a shogunate retainer, Yamaji became a Christian soon after his graduation from Tōkyō Eiwa Gakkō (now Aoyama Gakuin University) and was briefly an editor for the Methodist magazine *Gokyō* (Defending the Faith). In 1892 he joined the Min'yūsha, the publishing house founded by TOKUTOMI SOHŌ; his articles for its journal, *Kokumin no tomo* (The Nation's Friend), in particular, his polemical exchanges with TAKAYAMA CHOGYŪ on ancient Japanese history, attracted much interest. His writings, however, were distinguished more for their originality than for their analytical rigor. Yamaji later worked for the newspaper *Shinano mainichi shimbun* and lectured in the provinces, but in 1903 he founded his own magazine, *Dokuritsu hyōron* (Independent Review). As tension between Russia and Japan increased on the eve of the RUSSO-JAPANESE WAR (1904–05), he editorialized in favor of war; his nationalism was characterized by a blend of Confucianism and historical materialism. In 1905, with the journalist Shiba Teikichi (1869–1939), Yamaji founded the Kokka Shakaitō (National Socialist Party) to oppose what he perceived as the rising tide of Marxism in Japan. Besides contributing to such leading journals as CHŪŌ KŌRON and *Taiyō*, Yamaji wrote many books, including the biography *Ogyū Sorai* (1893), *Kirisutokyō hyōron* (1906, A Critique of Christianity), *Shakai shugi kanken* (1906, A Personal View of Socialism), *Gendai kinken shi* (1907, The Power of Money in Recent History), and *Ashikaga Takauji* (1909).

Yamakawa Hitoshi (1880–1958)

Marxist writer and theoretician, whose life spanned much of Japanese socialist history. Born in Kurashiki, Okayama Prefecture. Like many other Japanese socialists of the decade 1900–1910, Yamakawa first became interested in social reform when he came into contact with Christianity. He studied at Dōshisha (see DŌSHISHA UNIVERSITY) in Kyōto from 1895 to 1897.

After leading a protest against the school's administration, Yamakawa left Dōshisha and went to Tōkyō to study but soon abandoned his studies. With two other young men in 1900 he began a small monthly paper for young people. Because of articles criticizing the arranged marriage of the crown prince, the three were arrested for lese majesty, and Yamakawa was imprisoned for almost four years. In prison Yamakawa turned seriously to socialism, reading various works in English on economics. After his release he returned to Kurashiki, where he read Marx's *Das Kapital* and articles on socialism in the *Encyclopaedia Britannica*. He subscribed to the socialist weekly, the HEIMIN SHIMBUN (Commoner's News) and mailed his membership application to the newly founded JAPAN SOCIALIST PARTY (Nihon Shakaitō) in February 1906. (The party was dissolved the next year.)

The following January he went to Tōkyō to join the fledgling socialist movement, just as the mainstream, under the influence of KŌTOKU SHŪSUI, was turning from Christian socialism to anarcho-syndicalism. Yamakawa became an assistant editor of the *Heimin shimbun*, contributing articles on anarchism and the "general strike." To a successor paper in 1908 he contributed a long, serialized article on *Das Kapital*, the first exposition on Marxian economics to appear in Japanese. Arrested for parading with banners inscribed with socialist slogans (RED FLAG INCIDENT OF 1908), he was imprisoned from 1908 to 1910 and thereby escaped being implicated in the HIGH TREASON INCIDENT OF 1910, in which the government executed or imprisoned most of the socialist movement's leaders for allegedly plotting to assassinate the emperor.

Yamakawa rejoined the reviving socialist movement in 1916 and soon became its intellectual leader, achieving national fame for his articles attacking the growing democratic (MIMPON SHUGI) movement of the period. During the years 1916 to 1937 he wrote prodigiously, mainly on Marxism, contemporary Japan, and socialist political strategy, contributing to intellectual magazines or to socialist journals he helped found and edit. In 1916 he married Aoyama Kikue (YAMAKAWA KIKUE), a fellow socialist.

In 1922 in his famous article "A Change of Direction for the Proletarian Movement" ("Musan kaikyū undō no hōkō tenkan"), which appeared in the July–August issue of *Zen'ei* (Vanguard), Yamakawa acknowledged the failure of anarcho-syndicalism to attract workers and advocated a proletarian political movement. In his shift toward political action, he was greatly influenced by the Bolsheviks' success in Russia. From 1918 to 1921 he was the foremost writer in Japan on Lenin and the Bolsheviks and participated in founding the JAPAN COMMUNIST PARTY (JCP) in 1922. He also favored its dissolution in 1924 and refused to join in reestablishing this illegal party, believing that one broadly based legal proletarian party was appropriate for Japan, a country he considered quite different from 1917 Russia. He also disagreed with the Comintern-directed JCP concerning the historical stage of Japan's development and the revolutionary tactics appropriate for this stage. Yamakawa considered Japan an advanced capitalist, even imperialist society, dominated by the bourgeois middle class, the workers' primary enemy. In contrast, the JCP saw Japan as still dominated by semifeudal remnants, with the main enemies being the monarchy and the landlord class. This difference in interpretation was the origin of the NIHON SHIHON SHUGI RONSŌ (Controversy on Capitalism in Japan), which took place in the 1930s and in the postwar era.

With universal manhood suffrage enacted in 1925, Yamakawa and his followers, who came to be known as the RŌNŌHA (Labor-Farmer Faction) after their magazine *Rōnō*, worked to unite the Left in a single broadly based proletarian political party. This failed because of ideological clashes among socialist activists. During the 1930s the socialist Left was also split by the question of whether to support Japanese militarism at home and expansion abroad. The Rōnōha opposed this militarist drift. Yamakawa, whose health was never good, retired in 1927 from active leadership to devote himself to writing. Nevertheless, he and many of his followers were arrested in 1937 and 1938 along with other leftists in the so-called POPULAR FRONT INCIDENT (Jimmin Sensen Jiken).

After World War II Yamakawa called for the formation of a "democratic united front" to include Marxist socialists and the JCP, but he refused to join the JCP and helped found the Japan Socialist Party. He was critical of the right-wing socialist cabinet of KATAYAMA TETSU of 1947 and 1948, considering it not a truly socialist government. He encouraged the split of the Socialist Party in 1951. The new Left-wing Socialist Party (Saha Shakaitō) was led by Rōnōha people like SUZUKI MOSABURŌ and had SAKISAKA ITSURŌ as its chief theoretician. Although the move was opposed by Yamakawa, the Socialist Party reunited in 1955 but came under Rōnōha leadership as its left wing did increasingly well in elections. Since Yamakawa's death in 1958 the Rōnōha has split, largely over the question of the extent to which socialists should cooperate with popular democratic governments. See also MODERN PHILOSOPHY.

━━━Works by Yamakawa: Yamakawa Kikue and Yamakawa Shinsaku, ed, *Yamakawa Hitoshi zenshū*, vols 2–8, 19 (Keisō Shobō, 1966–79). Yamakawa Kikue and Sakisaka Itsurō, ed, *Yamakawa Hitoshi jiden* (1961). Works about Yamakawa: Koyama Hirotake et al, *Nihon no hi-Kyōsantō Marukusu shugisha: Yamakawa Hitoshi no shōgai to shisō* (1962). Thomas D. Swift, "Yamakawa Hitoshi and the Dawn of Japanese Socialism," PhD dissertation, University of California (1970).   *Thomas D. SWIFT*

Yamakawa Kikue (1890–1980)

Socialist and feminist. Born in Tōkyō into a family of *samurai* background; maiden name Aoyama. She graduated from Joshi Eigaku Juku (now Tsuda College) and soon after began to publish essays in such magazines as the feminist *Seitō* (see SEITŌSHA) and the socialist *Shinshakai* (New Society). In 1916 she married the socialist YAMAKAWA HITOSHI and, despite hardships, continued her writings and translations of works on socialism and feminism. In 1921 she helped found the SEKIRANKAI (Red Wave Society), the first women's socialist organization in Japan. She also helped her husband edit socialist journals, including *Rōnō* (Labor-Farmer), and she reported on such topics as women factory workers for general intellectual magazines like *Kaizō* (Reconstruction). In *Musansha undō to fujin no mondai* (1928, The Proletarian Movement and Problems of Women), she tried to integrate into the socialist movement's program such demands as equal pay for equal work and maternity rights.

After World War II she joined the newly organized Japan Socialist Party and served as the first director of the new Women's and Minors' Bureau in the Ministry of Labor from 1947 to 1951. Her autobiography has been published under the title *Onna nidai no ki* (1956, A Story of Mother and Daughter).

━━━Yamakawa Kikue, *Yamakawa Kikue shū*, 11 vols (Iwanami Shoten, 1981–82).

Yamakunigawa

River in northern Ōita Prefecture, Kyūshū, originating in the mountain Hikosan and flowing through the Nakatsu Plain into the Suō Sea. The gorge called YABAKEI is located on the upper and middle reaches. Length: 89 km (55 mi); area of drainage basin: 540 sq km (208 sq mi).

yamamba

Sometimes called *yamauba*. A female demon believed to live in the mountains. The *yamamba* is thought to have originally been a mountain deity (YAMA NO KAMI) or a mountain deity's female servant. While most commonly described as a female demon who devours humans, the *yamamba* sometimes appears in legends and folklore as a humorous, stupid old hag.   *INOKUCHI Shōji*

Yamamoto Baiitsu (1783–1856)

A third generation BUNJINGA painter who specialized in decorative BIRD-AND-FLOWER PAINTING *(kachōga)* as well as landscapes in the Chinese style. Real name Yamamoto Shinryō. Born in Nagoya, in his youth Baiitsu studied with practitioners of a variety of painting schools, including the NAGASAKI SCHOOL, KANŌ SCHOOL, and MARUYAMA-SHIJŌ SCHOOL. As a teenager he became the protégé of a rich Nagoya businessman and collector of Chinese paintings named Kamiya Ten'yū. At the home of his patron he befriended the slightly older *bunjinga* painter NAKABAYASHI CHIKUTŌ (1776–1853). In 1802, following Ten'yū's death, the two artists departed for Kyōto to study Ming (1368–1644) and Qing (Ch'ing, 1644–1912) dynasty paintings in the circle of literati headed by RAI SAN'YŌ (1781–1832). Baiitsu was subsequently active in both Kyōto and Edo (now Tōkyō) and formed a painting society with TANI BUNCHŌ (1763–1840). It seems that his bird-and-flower compositions were so successful that he aroused the professional jealousy of his colleagues and his reputation was deliberately discredited.

His best work is characterized by a genuine sensitivity to natural forms combined with unsurpassed technical mastery of brushwork on silk. In his bird-and-flower paintings he uses seductively soft and mellifluous color harmonies. The broad surfaces of leaves are enlivened with vibrant shading imparted through a wet-on-wet technique called *tarashikomi*. Thin and precisely controlled outlines are bled

into adjoining areas of wash. The rich density of overlapping forms and the complexity of strokes creates a more convincingly naturalistic image than is typical of *bunjinga* painting. The style of this bird-and-flower genre has been linked with late Ming court artists such as Zhou Zhimian (Chou Chih-mien, active ca 1580–1610). Baiitsu's quiet landscape paintings are light and luminous with soft, feathery strokes using split- and dry-brush techniques.

Julia MEECH-PEKARIK

Yamamoto Fujiko (1931–   )

Film actress. Born in Ōsaka. She made her debut in Mori Issei's *Hana no Kōdōkan* (1953, The Glorious Kōdōkan). Until 1962 she was a leading star for Daiei Productions, appearing in such films as KINUGASA TEINOSUKE's *Yushima no shiraume* (1955, White Plum of Yushima), YOSHIMURA KŌZABURŌ's *Yoru no kawa* (1956, Night River), and Masumura Yasuzō's *Hyōheki* (1958, Ice Precipice). She is particularly noted for her classic beauty. In 1963 her request to be released from her exclusive contract with Daiei Productions was denied, and when she took a public stand against this restrictive agreement made by leading movie companies, she found herself blacklisted. Even after Daiei's bankruptcy in 1971, she refused to return to acting.   *ITASAKA Tsuyoshi*

Yamamoto Gombei → Yamamoto Gonnohyōe

Yamamoto Gonnohyōe (1852–1933)

Admiral and political leader of the Meiji (1868–1912) and Taishō (1912–26) periods and twice prime minister (1913–14, 1923–24); also known as Yamamoto Gombei. The third son of a *samurai* family in the Satsuma domain (now Kagoshima Prefecture). During the upheavals that led to the MEIJI RESTORATION of 1868, Yamamoto served in the Eighth Satsuma Rifle Corps. He participated in the final battles of the BOSHIN CIVIL WAR against supporters of the Tokugawa shogunate. Following the Restoration, Yamamoto enrolled in the Naval Training Academy and, upon graduation in 1874, was assigned to a German warship for additional study in navigation. Yamamoto spent the years between 1878 and 1888 at sea. He then became chief secretary to the minister of the navy. He was one of the most influential figures in planning naval strategy during the SINO-JAPANESE WAR OF 1894–1895 and in the administration of the Navy Ministry. Promoted to rear admiral in 1895, he became navy minister in the second YAMAGATA ARITOMO cabinet of 1898, a post he held in successive cabinets for six years.

In 1913, during the TAISHŌ POLITICAL CRISIS, Yamamoto was appointed prime minister to form a cabinet to replace the faltering KATSURA TARŌ cabinet. In alliance with the Rikken Seiyūkai party, headed by SAIONJI KIMMOCHI and HARA TAKASHI, Yamamoto's cabinet carried out important reforms, in particular, abolishing the administrative rule that allowed only officers on active duty to serve as army and navy ministers (see GUMBU DAIJIN GEN'EKI BUKAN SEI). The SIEMENS INCIDENT of 1914, a scandal that involved naval officers, forced Yamamoto's resignation. He also retired from the navy. In 1923, however, Yamamoto was again summoned to form a cabinet; it was during his tenure that the recovery from the great TŌKYŌ EARTHQUAKE was begun. Assuming responsibility for the TORANOMON INCIDENT, in which an assassination attempt was made on the prince regent by a left-wing radical, Yamamoto resigned on 7 January 1924 and withdrew from politics completely.

A figure of enormous prestige in the navy, Yamamoto was called "Mr. Minister" even when he was not actually in that position. From within the Navy Ministry, Yamamoto maintained unity among leaders from Satsuma. While the army was often called "the army of Chōshū" (now Yamaguchi Prefecture), the navy was identified with Satsuma, largely because of Yamamoto's personal domination (see HAMBATSU; GUMBATSU). His identification with the navy, however, also tarnished his political image and he was often criticized harshly by the press. Yamamoto was recognized for his achievements with numerous imperial awards, including the Grand Order of the Chrysanthemum.

━━━Ko Hakushaku Yamamoto Kaigun Taishō Denki Hensankai, ed, *Yamamoto Gonnohyōe den* (1938).   *Tetsuo NAJITA*

Yamamoto Hokuzan (1752–1812)

Confucian scholar of the Edo period (1600–1868). Born in Edo (now Tōkyō). Hokuzan was largely self-taught and established his reputation with *Kōkyō shūsetsu* (Lectures on the Xiao jing [Hsiao ching]), written when he was only 21. Influenced by Inoue Kinga (1732–84), a scholar associated with the so-called SETCHŪGAKUHA, a syncretic school of Confucianism, he vigorously opposed the Tokugawa shogunate's policy (known as the Kansei Igaku no Kin) of employing only adherents of the Zhu Xi (Chu Hsi) school of Neo-Confucianism. He eschewed all official posts, preferring to teach at his home, where he had an extensive library. Hokuzan was also a poet of note and wrote a book on poetic theory in which he introduced the theories of the Chinese Ming poet Yuan Hongdao (Yüan Hung-tao).

Yamamoto Hōsui (1850–1906)

Western-style painter. Real name Yamamoto Tamenosuke. Born in Mino (now part of Gifu Prefecture), he started out by studying Japanese literati painting (BUNJINGA) in Kyōto. He soon became interested in Western art and studied oil painting first with Goseda Hōryū (1827–92) and Charles WIRGMAN in Yokohama, and then with Antonio FONTANESI at the Kōbu Bijutsu Gakkō, the first national art school in Japan (then part of Kōbu Daigakkō, a predecessor of Tōkyō Institute of Technology). From 1878 to 1887 he studied in Paris at the Ecole des Beaux Arts under Jean Léon Gérôme. At this time he became a friend of KURODA SEIKI. Upon his return to Japan, he taught Western-style painting and opened his own private school, the Seikōkan. He helped to found two artist groups, Meiji Bijutsukai (1889) and the HAKUBAKAI (1896). His last years were spent as a stage designer. He is remembered for his oils in the academic Barbizon-school style of 19th-century France.

Yamamoto Isoroku (1884–1943)

Naval officer and commander in chief of the Combined Fleet during World War II. Born in Nagaoka, Niigata Prefecture, the sixth son of Takano Teikichi, a school principal and former retainer of the Nagaoka domain, he later was adopted by the Yamamoto family. Upon graduating from the Naval Academy he served in the RUSSO-JAPANESE WAR of 1904–05 and was wounded in the Battle of TSUSHIMA in May 1905.

After the war Yamamoto saw several assignments at sea as a gunnery officer. He graduated from the Naval War College in 1916. Three years later he was ordered to study abroad; he spent his first year at Harvard University and his second at the Japanese embassy in Washington. He served again in Washington from 1926 to 1928 as naval attaché. These experiences not only deepened his understanding of the United States as a country and naval power but also convinced him that Japan and the United States should not go to war.

Yamamoto was particularly interested in the future prospects of naval aviation; earlier as a captain serving in an air unit and later as commander of an aircraft carrier, he had promoted the development of the long-range bomber. As vice minister of the navy from 1936, he strongly opposed the proposed TRIPARTITE PACT among Japan, Germany, and Italy on the grounds that this would invite a war between the United States and Japan. The pact was eventually signed in 1940, and Navy Minister YONAI MITSUMASA, who was worried about the possible assassination of Yamamoto by extremist groups, named him commander of the Combined Fleet.

Although Yamamoto was pessimistic about the long-term prospects of war with the United States, seeing that war was inevitable, he proposed a surprise attack on Pearl Harbor, the American naval base in Hawaii (see PEARL HARBOR, ATTACK ON). The operation on 7 December 1941 (8 December Japanese time) devastated the US Pacific Fleet. In the first six months of the Pacific War, the Japanese navy won one victory after another, but the June 1942 invasion of Midway Island planned by Yamamoto ended in a great defeat. The Battle of MIDWAY marked the turning of the tide; American forces began their counteroffensive in the Solomon Islands in August 1942. On 18 April 1943, while on his way to inspect front-line units, Yamamoto was killed when his plane was shot down by American fighter planes (the Japanese military code had been broken). He was given the posthumous title of fleet admiral.

——Agawa Hiroyuki, *Yamamoto Isoroku* (1964–65), tr John Bester as *The Reluctant Admiral: Yamamoto and the Imperial Navy* (1980). HATA Ikuhiko

Yamamoto Jōtarō (1867–1936)

Businessman and politician. Born in what is now Fukui Prefecture. After finishing elementary school he joined the MITSUI company as an apprentice in 1881. After a long period of service in its Shanghai branch, he was named managing director in 1909. He was obliged to resign in 1914 after becoming implicated in the SIEMENS INCIDENT, a bribery case involving a German firm, naval officers, and Mitsui. In 1920 he was elected to the Diet as a leading member of the RIKKEN SEIYŪKAI party and was reelected five times. As president of the SOUTH MANCHURIA RAILWAY from 1927 to 1929, he worked to promote Japanese economic expansion in northeast China. He also played a prominent part in the TŌHŌ KAIGI (1927), a government conference to formulate Japan's China policy.

Yamamoto Kajirō (1902–1973)

Film director. Began in comedies, later initiated a new documentary style in *Uma* (1940, Horse). Following World War II he returned to making comedies.

Yamamoto was a jack-of-all-trades during the early part of his career at NIKKATSU CORPORATION; he acted in comedies and wrote scenarios while serving as an assistant director to MURATA MINORU. Upon becoming a director himself he specialized in comic films. His reputation was built on his wartime films. He made *Uma* after several years of planning and preparation. Although a fiction film about a girl and her horse, *Uma* included much documentary footage of horses. Yamamoto's nearly unprecedented attempt at verisimilitude had a lasting effect on the film industry and subsequently influenced a documentary movement.

Yamamoto worked actively in making "national policy films" (*sen'i kōyō eiga*) during the war. His 1942 *Hawai-Marē oki kaisen* was the most elaborate of these, involving extensive and sophisticated miniature work and costing about ten times more than the average picture of the time. For the rest of his career Yamamoto made mostly comedies of a variety derived from the Japanese music hall tradition. *David* OWENS

Yamamoto Kansai (1944–)

Fashion designer. Born in Kanagawa Prefecture. Attended Nihon University. His designs are avant-garde, colorful, and marked by freedom in silhouette. He was the first Japanese designer to hold a fashion show in London (1971). HAYASHI Kunio

Yamamoto Kenkichi (1907–)

Literary critic. Real name Ishibashi Teikichi. Born in Nagasaki Prefecture, he was the son of Meiji novelist ISHIBASHI NINGETSU. He graduated from Keiō Gijuku (now Keiō University) and worked as an editor before helping to found *Hihyō*, a coterie magazine of a group of critics, in 1939. His reputation as a critic was established with *Shishōsetsu sakka ron* (1943), a collection of essays on modern writers and the I-NOVEL. Well-acquainted with traditional forms of art such as *haiku* and *waka*, he developed a literary theory based on his concept of aesthetic archetypes, which he believed transcended individual authors. In 1966 he received the Japan Art Academy Prize, and in 1969 he became a member of that academy. His principal critical works are a study on haiku, *Junsui haiku* (1952); comparative studies of classic and modern literature, *Koten to gendai bungaku* (1955); and *Kakinomoto no Hitomaro* (1958–61), a critical work on the late-7th-century poet Kakinomoto no Hitomaro.

Yamamoto Kiyoshi (1892–1963)

Agronomist and leader of the Japanese immigrant community in Brazil. Born in Tōkyō and graduated from Tōkyō University, Yamamoto went to Brazil in 1926 and became general manager of Casa Tozan, a subsidiary of the MITSUBISHI CORPORATION. A highly respected man of culture, he played a guiding role among Japanese immigrants, especially in the period of confusion following World War II. He was the founder and first president of the Japanese Culture Society of Brazil (Sociedade Brasileira de Cultura Japonesa) and the Brazilian-Japanese Cultural Association (Aliança Cultural Brasil-Japão). SAITŌ Hiroshi

Yamamoto Sanehiko (1885–1952)

Publisher and politician. Born in Kagoshima Prefecture, he founded the publishing company Kaizōsha in 1919 and began the magazine KAIZŌ, which played an important role in disseminating democratic and socialist ideas during the Taishō (1912–26) and early part of the

Shōwa (1926–) periods. Yamamoto was known for his progressive editorial policies. In the late 1920s, he published the *Gendai Nippon bungaku zenshū* series, the first inexpensive editions of modern Japanese literature (see EMPON). In 1930 Yamamoto was elected to the House of Representatives. Kaizōsha was dissolved in 1944 because of military pressure, but Yamamoto revived the company after the war. He returned to politics but was purged by the American Occupation authorities for his activities during the war. The purge was lifted in 1951 and he once again became the president of Kaizōsha.

ARASE Yutaka

Yamamoto Satsuo (1910–   )

Film director. Known for his treatment of timely social and political themes. One hallmark of his style is length; most of his films run longer than two and a half hours as their complicated plots unravel toward stirring, though usually predictable, conclusions.

He began with SHŌCHIKU CO, LTD, in 1933 and served for a time as assistant to NARUSE MIKIO, later moving with Naruse to TŌHŌ CO, LTD. At Tōhō after the war he became embroiled in labor disputes as a union leader and the company eventually expelled him.

Social and political "message films," frequently based on actual incidents and tinged with left-wing political rhetoric, have always been Yamamoto's forte. His *Shinkū chitai* (1952, Vacuum Zone) is regarded as one of the most powerfully effective antiwar films to come out of Japan. *Shiroi kyotō* (1966, The Ivory Tower), about corruption at the highest levels of the medical profession, won a Kinema Jumpō Award in 1967. It was in the 1970s, however, that his broadsides against corruption in high places found their most appreciative audience. *Kareinaru ichizoku* (1974, The Family), about abuses of the banking industry, *Kinkanshoku* (1975, Solar Eclipse), about election fraud, and *Fumō chitai* (1976, Barren Zone), an account of the LOCKHEED SCANDAL, all met with great popular success.

David OWENS

Yamamoto Senji (1889–1929)

Biologist, social activist, and politician. Born in Kyōto, Yamamoto went to Canada as a youth to work and study. After his return to Japan in 1911, he took a degree in zoology at Tōkyō University and became a lecturer at Kyōto and Dōshisha universities. Influenced by Margaret SANGER, the American advocate of family planning who visited Japan in 1922, he became active in the birth control movement. Late in 1925 he was ousted from his teaching positions in the wake of the so-called Kyōto University Gakuren Incident, in which several dozen leftist students were arrested under the new PEACE PRESERVATION LAW OF 1925. Thereafter he was gradually drawn to socialism and later headed a small school for workers in Kyōto. In 1928 he was elected to the Diet as a member of the RŌDŌ NŌMINTŌ (Labor-Farmer Party). Remaining in the Diet even after the dissolution of the party, he opposed the revision of the Peace Preservation Law to establish capital punishment for subversive activities and also spoke out against the government's China policy. On the very day the revision passed the Diet, Yamamoto was stabbed to death by a right-wing terrorist.

Yamamoto Shūgorō (1903–1967)

Novelist and short-story writer known chiefly for his stories of the common people. His works enshrine the popular virtues of traditional Japan and are marked by sympathy for the underdog, dislike of authority, humor, and delicacy of description. Born Shimizu Satomu in the village of Hatsukari in Yamanashi Prefecture, he came of a family that lived by rearing silkworms, horse dealing, and small-scale retailing. These comparatively humble origins, together with his youthful experiences in the working districts of Yokohama and Tōkyō and his experience of various natural disasters would seem to have left their mark on his literature.

When he was four he lost his grandparents and an aunt and uncle in a landslide. Following this, his mother took him to join his father, who was working at Ōji in Tōkyō, where he entered primary school. The family subsequently moved to Yokohama, where he finished primary school. It was during this period that, with the encouragement of a teacher, he conceived the desire to become a writer. On leaving school, he went to Tōkyō to serve as an apprentice in a pawnshop run by a man called Yamamoto Shūgorō, whose name he was later to take. The latter encouraged him in his studies, sent him to school to study English and bookkeeping, and generally gave him support until he was able to stand on his own feet. When the shop was destroyed in the TŌKYŌ EARTHQUAKE OF 1923, he went to the Kansai district, where he found work as a journalist, but returned to Tōkyō the next year and took a job with a magazine. In 1926 he made his literary debut with the story "Sumadera fukin" and in the same year published a three-act drama, *Hōrinji iki*. Leaving the magazine in 1928, he devoted himself thenceforth to literature.

His early work was written mainly for children, but in 1932 he wrote "Dadara Dambei," his first popular story for adults. He continued to produce mainly stories for juveniles and detective stories until around 1945, but a series of short stories on contemporary themes published in *Asahi gurafu* from 1933 to 1936 are noteworthy, since four of them formed the basis of his later, well-known *Aobeka monogatari* (1960). The years from around 1940 to 1945 yielded a number of short stories on *samurai* themes, mostly set in the Edo period (1600–1868), which show at its most typical his preoccupation with the popular Japanese virtues. Another successful work of the same period was a series of stories for women entitled *Nihon fudōki* (1942–45).

Losing his first wife in 1945 he remarried in 1946, but became more and more of a literary recluse in the succeeding years. Notable products of the years from 1945 to 1950 include stories showing, often with a typical compassionate humor, the lives of ordinary people or low-ranking samurai in Edo (now Tōkyō). Two examples are *Otafuku monogatari* (1949) and *Uso'a tsukanee* (1950). *Yamahiko otome* (1951) showed a rare nostalgia for his home district of Kōshū.

During the 1950s his work was varied, including *Momi no ki wa nokotta* (1954–56), a long political-historical novel about Harada Kai, an Edo-period retainer of the DATE FAMILY, and, especially, a wide range of short stories dealing with political and historical themes, the lives of ordinary people in pre-Meiji and modern Japan, life in the gay quarters, and so on. His *Nagai saka* (1964–66) is largely autobiographical. A central theme of his work is unrewarded devotion to a person or cause; from the 1959 *Chikushō-dani*, a religious tendency becomes more pronounced and is carried on in works such as *Sabu* (1963) and *Ogosoka na kawaki* (1967). His works are collected in *Yamamoto Shūgorō zenshu* (Shinchōsha, 1967–70).

John BESTER

Yamamoto Tamesaburō (1893–1966)

Businessman. Born in Ōsaka Prefecture. Taking over his family's bottle-making business, Yamamoto established Nippon Bottle Manufacturing in 1918. He later served as managing director of Nippon Brewery and Mineral Water and executive director of Dai Nippon Breweries. Yamamoto became president of ASAHI BREWERIES, LTD, in 1949 when Dai Nippon Breweries split into two separate firms. He also operated hotels, played an active role in the business-industrial community, and served as a patron of the arts.

MAEDA Kazutoshi

Yamamoto Yasue (1906–   )

Actress. Born in Kanda, Tōkyō. In September 1921 she entered the Gendaigeki Joyū Yōseijo (School of Modern Theater Training for Actresses), headed by Ichikawa Sadanji II (1880–1940). She made her debut at the Teikoku Gekijō (Imperial Theater) in OSANAI KAORU's play *Daiichi no sekai* (1921; tr *The First World*, 1959). She became a founding member of his famous Tsukiji Shōgekijō (Tsukiji Little Theater) in June 1924, playing leading roles in 67 productions. After Osanai's death in 1928 she joined Hijikata Yoshi (1898–1959) in founding the Shin Tsukiji Gekidan (New Tsukiji Theater Company), where she played in a series of leftist-proletarian dramas until the police proscribed the company in 1940. Until the end of the war she worked in radio broadcasting, a field in which she later distinguished herself by winning the Hōsō Bunka Shō (Broadcasting Prize) in 1952. In 1947 she joined the Budō no Kai (The Grape Society), founded by KINOSHITA JUNJI and Okakura Shirō (1909–59). In 1951 she was honored by the Ministry of Education for her role as Tsū in Kinoshita's internationally acclaimed play *Yūzuru* (1949; tr *Twilight Crane*, 1956), of which she has since given 700 performances. In 1966 she founded the Yamamoto Yasue no Kai (Yamamoto Yasue Society), dedicated to research in folklore and traditional theatrical forms. Yamamoto Yasue has a unique stage presence and a polished sense of diction. Throughout her long career she has consistently worked to perpetuate the artistic spirit of old theater within the context of new drama.

A. C. SCOTT

Yamamoto Yūzō (1887–1974)

Playwright; novelist. Born in Tochigi Prefecture. Yamamoto studied German literature at Tōkyō University, where together with AKUTA-GAWA RYŪNOSUKE and KIKUCHI KAN he published the third series of the literary magazine known as *Shinshichō*. Interested in Western theater, Yamamoto translated several Strindberg plays. Three of his own best plays are *Eijigoroshi* (1920; tr *A Case of Child Murder*, 1930), *Sakazaki Dewa no Kami* (1921; tr *Lord Dewa*, 1935), and *Dōshi no hitobito* (1923), which were all part of the SHINGEKI (new theater) movement. In 1928 he began publishing serial novels. *Nami* (1928), *Onna no isshō* (1932–33), and *Robō no ishi* (1937) are notable for their idealistic protagonists, who care nothing for personal or national glory but only for the good of society. Following World War II he was involved in efforts to reform and simplify the Japanese language and was elected to the House of Councillors. He was awarded the Order of Culture in 1965.

Yamamura Bochō (1884–1924)

Poet; novelist. Born in Gumma Prefecture. Real name Tsuchida Hakkujū. His *Sei sanryō hari* (1915, Sacred Prism), remains unique in modern Japanese poetry. Consisting of poems juxtaposing apparently unrelated images, this book shocked the Japanese literary world. Since then it has been described as imagist, cubist, symbolist, futurist, and surrealist. The most frequently anthologized poem from it is "Fūkei" (Landscape), which skillfully uses the visual effect of typography. Among his other books of poems, *Kaze wa kusaki ni sasayaita* (1918, The Wind Whispered to the Grass and Trees) and *Kozue no su nite* (1921, In the Tree-Top Nest) differ from *Sei sanryō hari* in their religious tone and straightforward approach. The posthumously published *Kumo* (1924, Clouds) is notable for the kind of simplicity often termed "oriental." One of his several novels, *Jūjika* (1922, The Cross), describes a Christian proselytizer's illicit affair with his convert.   *Hiroaki* SATŌ

Yamamura Saisuke (1770–1807)

Geographer in the latter part of the Edo period (1600–1868). Also called Yamamura Masanaga. Born in Hitachi Province (now part of Ibaraki Prefecture), Yamamura studied world geography with ŌTSUKI GENTAKU, the well-known scholar of Dutch Learning. His *Teisei zōyaku sairan igen* (1802), a revision of *Sairan igen* (a geographical treatise by ARAI HAKUSEKI), is representative of the type of geographical work published during the years of National Seclusion.

Yamamuro Gumpei (1872–1940)

A founder and important leader of the Japanese branch of the SALVATION ARMY. Born in Okayama Prefecture, in his youth he worked as a typesetter in a printing factory in Tōkyō. He became a Christian in 1887 and, influenced by NIIJIMA JŌ, entered Dōshisha University but left without graduating. When members of the English Salvation Army came to Japan in 1895, he helped organize its Japanese branch and the next year became its first Japanese officer, eventually rising to the rank of commander. With his wife, YAMAMURO KIEKO, he strove to abolish public prostitution and to establish various social welfare programs. He worked to evangelize the poor and the laboring class. The best known of his many writings was the book *Heimin no fukuin* (1899, The People's Gospel), which was repeatedly reissued before being banned in 1940.

TANAKA Akira

Yamamuro Kieko (1874–1916)

Pioneer in Japan's SALVATION ARMY (Kyūseigun) who worked with her husband, YAMAMURO GUMPEI, for Christian social reform. Born in Iwate Prefecture. She graduated in 1895 from Meiji Girls' School and began campaigning with the KYŌFŪKAI (Japan's version of the Woman's Christian Temperance Union). In 1899 she married and became a "soldier" in the branch of the Salvation Army founded by her husband. From about 1900 Kieko and Gumpei were especially active in rehabilitating prostitutes. Their daughter Yamamuro Tamiko (1900–1981) was also active in Salvation Army work, especially after World War II.

Yamana family

Warrior family of the Muromachi period (1333–1568); descended from Nitta Yoshinori (a grandson of NITTA YOSHISADA) of the Seiwa Genji branch of the MINAMOTO FAMILY, from whose domain in Kōzuke Province (now Gumma Prefecture) they took their name. After helping ASHIKAGA TAKAUJI in his rise to power, they were granted large estates in Hōki Province (now part of Tottori Prefecture) and by 1363 were military governors (SHUGO) of five provinces in western Honshū. The Yamana became one of the four families (*shishiki*) who rotated as heads of the Board of Retainers (SAMURAI-DOKORO) of the Muromachi shogunate, and they briefly extended their power over 11 provinces, though not with shogunal consent. (As Japan then had 66 provinces in all, the Yamana were called "Lords of a Sixth.") Several members of the family rose up against the shōgun ASHIKAGA YOSHIMITSU in the MEITOKU REBELLION (1391), and the Yamana lost all but two provinces. But in 1441 YAMANA SŌZEN participated in the defeat of the forces of AKAMATSU MITSUSUKE, who had assassinated the shōgun ASHIKAGA YOSHINORI, and the family temporarily regained its former holdings. The rivalry between Sōzen and the shogunal deputy (*kanrei*) HOSOKAWA KATSUMOTO was one of the principal causes of the ŌNIN WAR (1467–77), a struggle that effectively ruined both families, though the Yamana survived as minor lords. Their descendants served the Tokugawa shogunate (1603–1867) as bannermen (*hatamoto*).

Yamanaka

Town in southern Ishikawa Prefecture, central Honshū. It is noted for its hot spring, said to have been discovered in the 8th century by the priest Gyōki. A local lacquer ware, *yamanaka-nuri*, is well known, as is KUTANI WARE, produced in Kutani to the south. Pop: 12,055.

Yamanaka, Lake

(Yamanakako). Lake in southeastern Yamanashi Prefecture, central Honshū. One of the FUJI FIVE LAKES located on the northeastern slope of Mt. Fuji (Fujisan), it was created by lava flows from Fujisan. Common carp, crucian carp, and pond smelt inhabit the lake. The *fujimarimo (Fuji aegagropilae),* a kind of water plant that grows here, is designated a natural monument. The lake is popular for its fine views of Fujisan. There are excellent camping grounds and, in season, swimming, skating, and angling. Many villas and recreational facilities are located on the banks of the lake. Area: 6.4 sq km (2.5 sq mi); circumference: 14 km (9 mi); depth: 13.3 m (43.6 ft); altitude: 981 m (3,218 ft).

Yamanaka Sadao (1909–1938)

Film director. Noted for innovative handling of period films. His directorial career spanned only six years, but he gave a new direction to the period film by shifting the emphasis from a romantic to a more realistic treatment of the warrior culture. Rather than portray heroic deeds and derring-do, Yamanaka concentrated on the lives of ordinary townspeople of the Edo period (1600–1868). When members of the *samurai* class were included, they were often RŌNIN (masterless samurai) in the throes of destitution. This approach was daring in the 1930s, an era when Japan's military leaders were trying to glorify the warrior spirit of BUSHIDŌ which had customarily been celebrated in the standard period film.

Yamanaka's influence, though brief, carried over to the next generation of filmmakers. This is reflected in the work of such directors as KOBAYASHI MASAKI, whose period films reflect a concern for character and for ordinary lives. Yamanaka's greatest masterpiece was *Ninjō kamifūsen* (1937, Humanity and Paper Balloons), which he completed just before being drafted into the Imperial Japanese Army. Yamanaka was sent as a foot soldier to China, where he died in 1938.   *David* OWENS

Yamanaka Shikanosuke (1545–1578)

Also known as Yamanaka Yukimori. A warrior of the Sengoku period (1467–1568) famed for his loyalty and persistence in the cause of his dispossessed lords, the AMAKO FAMILY of Izumo Province (now part of Shimane Prefecture). In 1566 the Amako were conquered by the rising MŌRI FAMILY, *daimyō* of Aki (now part of

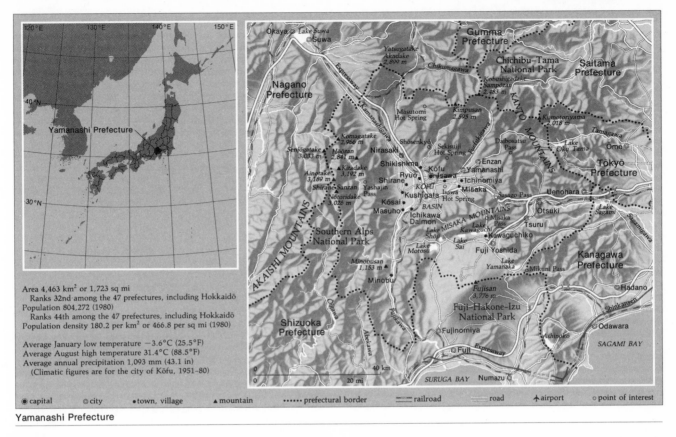

| ◉ capital | ◎ city | • town, village | ▲ mountain | ••••• prefectural border | ▭▭▭ railroad | ▭▭▭ road | ✈ airport | ◦ point of interest |

Yamanashi Prefecture

Hiroshima Prefecture), and Shikanosuke became a RŌNIN (masterless *samurai*). Having persuaded Amako Katsuhisa (1553–78) to renounce the priesthood and assume the family headship, Shikanosuke strove to help him recover his ancestral domains. In 1569, with the Mōri engaged in an invasion of Kyūshū, Katsuhisa and Shikanosuke succeeded in reoccupying much of Izumo and maintained a hold there for two years but were frustrated by the defection of old Amako vassals to the Mōri side; Shikanosuke himself was captured but escaped. In 1573–74 Katsuhisa and Shikanosuke attacked the Mōri flank in Inaba (now part of Tottori Prefecture), probably with the covert support of the hegemon ODA NOBUNAGA, but were again defeated. In 1576 open conflict erupted between Nobunaga and the Mōri; late in the next year, Nobunaga sent TOYOTOMI HIDEYOSHI on a campaign against the Mōri, and Katsuhisa and Shikanosuke were entrusted by him with the important front-line fortress of Kōzuki in Harima (now Kōzuki Chō, Hyōgo Prefecture). This position was strategically suited for yet another advance into the old Amako territories, but in the summer of 1578 it fell to a siege, Amako Katsuhisa committed suicide, and Yamanaka Shikanosuke, again a captive of the Mōri, was killed.
George ELISON

Yamanashi

City in central Yamanashi Prefecture, central Honshū. Its major industry is agriculture, mainly the growing of grapes and peaches. Numerous wineries are located in the city. Sericulture also flourishes. In recent years, electrical appliance and machine plants have been established. Pop: 30,494.

Yamanashi Prefecture

(Yamanashi Ken). Located in central Honshū and bordered by Tōkyō, Kanagawa, Shizuoka, Nagano, and Saitama prefectures. The terrain is mostly mountainous, and principal ranges include Kantō, Misaka, and Akaishi. Mt. Fuji (Fujisan), the highest peak in Japan, lies on the border with Shizuoka Prefecture. The principal level areas are the KŌFU BASIN in the center of the prefecture and the Gunnai region to the south near Fujisan. The contrast between summer and winter weather is strong, and precipitation is less than average for Japan.

The area was known after the TAIKA REFORM of 645 as Kai Province. It came under the control of a succession of military families, including the Kai Minamoto, Takeda, and Asano, after the

Heian period (794–1185). For most of the Edo period (1600–1868) it was directly controlled by the Tokugawa shogunate. It was given its present name and borders in 1871 following the Meiji Restoration.

Agriculture is the major activity; crops include rice, fruits, and vegetables. Its grapes are particularly well known, and the prefecture is the center of the country's wine production. Industry is largely limited to light manufacturing such as textiles and crystal processing. Since World War II new industries producing electrical goods, machinery, and precision instruments have been developed.

Proximity to the Tōkyō area and a wealth of lakes and mountains make Yamanashi a popular tourist area, with the greatest attraction being Fujisan and the string of five lakes at its base (see FUJI FIVE LAKES). The three national parks, Fuji–Hakone–Izu, Chichibu-Tama, and the Southern Alps, span part of the prefecture. Hot springs include Masutomi, Sekisuiji, and Isawa. MINOBUSAN is the head temple of the NICHIREN SECT of Buddhism and attracts a large number of pilgrims and tourists. Area: 4,463 sq km (1,723 sq mi); pop: 804,272; capital: Kōfu. Other major cities include ŌTSUKI, TSURU, and FUJI YOSHIDA.

Yamana Sōzen (1404–1473)

Military leader of the Muromachi period (1333–1568). Born into a family that traditionally held high offices in the Muromachi shogunate, in 1432 he became military governor *(shugo)* of several provinces in western Honshū. In 1441 he played a major role in the defeat of AKAMATSU MITSUSUKE, who had assassinated the shōgun ASHIKAGA YOSHINORI. In recognition of his services, his family was granted three provinces in western Honshū formerly held by Mitsusuke. In 1450 he devolved the family leadership to his son and became a monk, changing his name from Yamana Mochitoyo to Sōzen. His religious vows were a mere formality, since he retained all of his political power. Sōzen was actively involved in the shogunal succession dispute of 1465, opposing the leader of the powerful Hosokawa family, HOSOKAWA KATSUMOTO. Sōzen supported Ashikaga Yoshihisa, son of the shōgun ASHIKAGA YOSHIMASA and HINO TOMIKO, as shogunal heir, while Hosokawa supported Yoshimasa's younger brother Ashikaga Yoshimi. The succession dispute was one of the principal causes of the ŌNIN WAR (1467–77), in which Sōzen was chief commander of troops deployed in the western half of Kyōto, battling with Hosokawa's troops in the eastern half. Both men died of illness in 1473 while the war was still in progress.

yamane → dormouse, Japanese

yama no kami

(god of the mountain). There are various types of deities called *yama no kami,* each associated with a different occupational group. Farming folk venerate a mountain deity that is identical with the TA NO KAMI (god of the paddies): the *yama no kami* descends from the mountains in early spring to become the *ta no kami* and, after the harvest, returns to his abode in the mountains. This particular type of *yama no kami* also embodies the spirits of the people's ancestors (see ANCESTOR WORSHIP). Mountain folk such as hunters, woodcutters, and charcoal makers venerate either a male or a female *yama no kami,* whereas lathe workers (KIJIYA, who live in the woods and tend to be itinerant) believe the *yama no kami* to be a married couple. As deities worshiped in Shintō, *yama no kami* are identified as the god Ōyamatsumi no Kami or the goddess Konohana no Sakuyahime.

In general these *yama no kami* are fearsome and terrifying, in some places being equated in popular belief with TENGU, malevolent creatures said to inhabit mountain recesses. They are frequently depicted as having only one eye and one leg. They are also said to bear 12 children each year or to be particularly averse to that number. In northeastern Japan, the *yama no kami* is often identified with the god of childbirth; as the event draws near, the supplicant goes to the mountains to solicit his visitation. *Yama no kami* can be placated with their favorite foods—rice cakes *(mochi),* the hearts of game animals, or morsels of *okoze* (stonefish). Festivals honoring *yama no kami* are generally held on the 7th, 9th, 12th, or 17th day of particular months. It is forbidden to go into the mountains on such days, since that is when the deity is believed to take an inventory of his or her trees, and the aroused *yama no kami* would be sensitive to any intrusion into the forest. *Ōtō Tokihiko*

Yamanote

District of urban Tōkyō, roughly consisting of Bunkyō and Minato wards and wards between and to the west of them, an area bounded on the east by the eastern half of the Japanese National Railways urban loop, the Yamanote Line. The name, which means hill or bluff, designates the district as the hilly part of Tōkyō as opposed to the level district to the east, which is known as SHITAMACHI. The Yamanote district contains many middle-class and upper-middle-class residential areas, with important shopping centers around stations of the western half of the Yamanote loop such as Shinjuku, Shibuya, and Ikebukuro. Modern Standard Japanese is based on the language of educated speakers of the Yamanote district.

Yamanouchi Kazutoyo (1545–1605)

General of the Azuchi–Momoyama period (1568–1600); the founding father of the Tosa domain (now Kōchi Prefecture), one of the more important *daimyō* domains of the Edo period (1600–1868). The son of a petty baron *(dogō)* of Owari Province (now part of Aichi Prefecture), Kazutoyo in 1573 entered the service of TOYOTOMI HIDEYOSHI, the future national unifier. He distinguished himself in Hideyoshi's Battle of SHIZUGATAKE in 1583 and KOMAKI NAGAKUTE CAMPAIGN in 1584 and attained daimyō status in 1585. That year he was first granted a domain assessed at 19,800 *koku* (see KOKUDAKA) at Takahama in Wakasa Province (now Takahama Chō, Fukui Prefecture), and then was assigned as a counselor to Hideyoshi's adopted son TOYOTOMI HIDETSUGU and transferred to a 20,000-*koku* domain at Nagahama in Ōmi Province (now Shiga Prefecture). After participating in the ODAWARA CAMPAIGN of 1590, Kazutoyo was granted a 59,000-*koku* fief at Kakegawa in Tōtōmi Province (now part of Shizuoka Prefecture) and made the intendant (DAIKAN) of Hideyoshi's immediate holdings *(kurairichi)* in that province. In the great conflict which led to the Battle of SEKIGAHARA (1600), Kazutoyo adhered to the future shōgun TOKUGAWA IEYASU and after Ieyasu's victory was rewarded with the 202,600-*koku* domain of Tosa in Shikoku. His takeover of that province, where he encountered resistance from partisans of the defeated former daimyō, Chōsokabe Morichika (1575–1615), was marked by ruthless measures. Kazutoyo's consort Kenshōin (1557–1617) is the subject of many anecdotes that portray her as the provident and perspicacious model of a samurai wife. *George ELISON*

Yamanouchi Pharmaceutical Co, Ltd

(Yamanouchi Seiyaku). A company engaged in the manufacture and sale of pharmaceuticals; it was established in 1923. Its principal products are antibiotics, supplied to doctors and hospitals. Aside from importing technologies from major overseas companies, Yamanouchi also licenses its own technologies to foreign pharmaceutical firms. It has an overseas office in New York. Sales for the fiscal year ending December 1981 totaled ¥85.4 billion (US $390.1 million), and the company was capitalized at ¥5.4 billion (US $24.7 million) in the same year. The head office is in Tōkyō.

Yamanouchi Sugao (1902–1970)

Archaeologist. Born in Tōkyō. After graduating from Tōkyō University in anthropology, he taught at Tōhoku University and Tōkyō University before becoming a professor at Seijō University in Tōkyō. Yamanouchi established the first comprehensive typology and chronology for JŌMON POTTERY. His chronology was at variance with that established by radiocarbon dating, a technique that he did not accept. He is also remembered for his studies on the methods, such as cord-twisting, used for making the designs on Jōmon vessels. Many of his works are collected in *Yamanouchi Sugao senshi kōkogaku rombun shū,* 5 vols (1969–72). *ABE Gihei*

Yamanouchi Toyoshige (1827–1872)

Also known as Yamanouchi Yōdō. *Daimyō* of the Tosa domain (now Kōchi Prefecture) and a major figure in the events leading to the MEIJI RESTORATION of 1868. He became daimyō in 1848 and carried out modernizing reforms with the help of YOSHIDA TŌYŌ. After the arrival in 1853 of Commodore Matthew PERRY, Toyoshige worked with such daimyō as MATSUDAIRA YOSHINAGA and TOKUGAWA NARIAKI in urging the shogunate to carry out political and military reforms to strengthen the nation. He also joined them in supporting TOKUGAWA YOSHINOBU in the 1858 shogunal succession dispute and in opposing the signing of the ANSEI COMMERCIAL TREATIES. Both issues were settled when II NAOSUKE became great elder *(tairō),* and Toyoshige, like most of Ii's opponents, was forced to resign as daimyō (1859) and placed in domiciliary confinement.

After Ii's assassination in 1860, Toyoshige returned to national politics, although he remained active in his domain as well, suppressing extremist antishogunate officials such as TAKECHI ZUIZAN. He and Matsudaira Yoshinaga advised the shōgun TOKUGAWA IEMOCHI and worked diligently for a reconciliation between the imperial court and the shogunate (see MOVEMENT FOR UNION OF COURT AND SHOGUNATE). When he realized that the military overthrow of the Tokugawa shogunate was inevitable, he followed the advice of his retainers GOTŌ SHŌJIRŌ and SAKAMOTO RYŌMA and convinced the new shōgun, TOKUGAWA YOSHINOBU, to return his governing mandate to the emperor (see TAISEI HŌKAN) in November 1867. Even this concession failed to satisfy the antishogunate forces, and in the end Toyoshige allowed Tosa to join in the military coup d'etat that abolished the shogunate and restored imperial rule. A Tokugawa loyalist to the end, Toyoshige then attempted unsuccessfully to have Yoshinobu appointed to the new government. He himself served briefly as a councillor *(gijō).*

Yamanoue no Okura (660–ca 733)

Government official; major poet of the early 8th century. His surname is usually pronounced Yamanoe.

Of somewhat obscure origins (one theory holds that he was a naturalized Korean), Okura became a minor bureaucrat, and in 702 was given a clerical post in a mission of government representatives and students sent to the court of Tang (T'ang) China. His studies abroad enhanced his reputation as a scholar of Chinese. In 721, at the age of 61, he was appointed tutor to the crown prince, the future emperor SHŌMU (701–756; r 724–749), and in 726, he was made governor of the province of Chikuzen in northern Kyūshū. Despite his advanced age, he remained in this remote post for some six years, returning to the Nara capital in 731 or 732. By this time he had only risen to the relatively low junior fifth court rank, and there is no further record of his official life until his death in 733 or thereabouts.

Poetry——Okura is one of the most outstanding poets of the Nara period (710–794), and one of the best represented in the MAN'YŌSHŪ (ca 759, Collection for Ten Thousand Generations or Collection of Ten Thousand Leaves), the first great anthology of vernacular Japanese poetry. His distinctive manner combines narrative, lyrical, and philosophical elements with a marked strain of Confucian-inspired didacticism and social consciousness, and sets him apart from the other great poets of the age. The moral and social concern of his poetry, particularly of some of his most famous *chōka* ("long poems") was lost upon later generations of court poets, who prized the aesthetic qualities and personal lyricism of native poetry above all other considerations. His works preserved in the *Man'yōshū* number 10 to 12 *chōka*, one *sedōka* ("head-turning poem"), and from 47 to 63 *tanka*, depending upon how certain headnotes and other evidence are interpreted. An additional group of 10 *tanka* attributed to some fisherfolk of Chikuzen are also in all likelihood his. Apart from his poetry in Japanese, the *Man'yōshū* contains two poems and a short prose essay in Chinese by him. His poetic output and the variety and quality of his verse appear to have burgeoned in his mid-60s after his arrival in Chikuzen to serve as governor. A partial explanation may be that he was stimulated by the congenial literary friendship he formed with ŌTOMO NO TABITO (665–731), then serving as viceroy of the military headquarters at DAZAIFU. During Tabito's term there, Dazaifu became a center of literary activity frequented by many government officials and local notables, with poetry parties, banquets, and the like hosted by him.

Nearly all of Okura's *chōka* are among the foremost in the *Man'yōshū*. They cover a wide range of subjects and modes: elegies on the deaths of his wife and son, laments on his own old age and worries about his surviving children, moral exhortations, farewell verses addressed to ambassadors and officials, and lines written on behalf of others. Unlike the case of most other important contemporary poets, verses on love and nature constitute only a small fraction of Okura's surviving works, but a broader warmth and compassion infuse his poems of social concern. These qualities are seen particularly in his famous "Dialogue on Poverty" ("Hinkyū mondō"), an imaginary exchange between a poor man and an even poorer one on the miseries of their lives. Typically, in the concluding envoy Okura calls not for action or reform but offers instead a Buddhist-inspired counsel of resignation and acceptance. Less apparent than his styles and choice of subject matter, but also unique and important, were his experiments with prosody, especially the creation of a stanzaic effect in some of his *chōka* by emphasizing divisions of thought and structure with unusual combinations of long or short lines. Apart from his own verse, Okura also compiled an anthology of vernacular poetry entitled *Ruijū karin* (Classified Forest of Verse). Though not extant, it is believed to have been an important source for the compilers of the *Man'yōshū*.

■——Robert H. Brower and Earl Miner, *Japanese Court Poetry* (1961). Ian Levy, *The Ten Thousand Leaves* (1981–). Nippon Gakujutsu Shinkōkai, *The Man'yōshū: One Thousand Poems* (1940, repr 1965).

Robert H. BROWER

Yamaoka Sōhachi (1907–1978)

Novelist. Real name Fujino Shōzō. Born in Niigata Prefecture. An editor of a popular literary magazine in the 1930s, he turned to professional writing when his story "Yakusoku" won a prize from a weekly magazine in 1938. During World War II, he wrote propaganda stories, and afterwards was forbidden to publish under the OCCUPATION PURGE. Yamaoka made a comeback as a novelist with his period novel, *Tokugawa Ieyasu* (1950–67), about the founder of the Tokugawa shogunate (1603–1867). During Japan's rapid economic growth in the 1960s, this novel was widely read by businessmen looking for management guidelines from Ieyasu's administrative expertise. Other historical novels include *Oda Nobunaga* (1954–60) and *Haru no sakamichi* (1971).

Yamaoka Tesshū (1836–1888)

Also known as Yamaoka Tetsutarō. Swordsman and retainer of the Tokugawa shogunate; active at the time of the MEIJI RESTORATION (1868). Born in Edo (now Tōkyō). Yamaoka, who had studied with the master swordsman Chiba Shūsaku (1793–1855), held a minor post in the shogunate's military academy, the Kōbusho. In 1862, under shogunate orders, he and Takahashi Deishū (1835–1903) organized a police force of highly skilled swordsmen to monitor antishogunate activities. When imperial forces marched on Edo (now

Tōkyō) in the spring of 1868 to anticipate resistance to the new imperial regime, KATSU KAISHŪ, the commander of the Tokugawa forces, commissioned Yamaoka to conduct preliminary negotiations with SAIGŌ TAKAMORI, leader of the imperial army. A meeting subsequently took place between Katsu and Saigō in Shizuoka, and Edo Castle, the Tokugawa headquarters, was peacefully surrendered. After the restoration Yamaoka served in several prefectural gubernatorial posts and as an aide to Emperor MEIJI.

Yamasa Shōyu Co, Ltd

Manufacturer of soy sauce, flavor enhancers, and biochemicals related to nucleic acids. Established in 1645. Yamasa is its brand name. The second largest Japanese soy sauce manufacturer and the founder of the nucleotide industry. Products are exported mainly to the United States, but also to numerous countries in Europe and Asia. Sales totaled ¥34 billion (US $155.3 million) in 1981, and the company was capitalized at ¥375 million (US $1.7 million) in the same year. The head office is in Chōshi, Chiba Prefecture.

Yamashiro no Kuni Ikki

A league (IKKI) formed for mutual assistance by KOKUJIN (local *samurai* proprietors) and JIZAMURAI (yeoman warriors) of southern Yamashiro Province (now part of Kyōto Prefecture) in January 1486 (Bummei 17.12), at a time when that part of the province had been transformed into a battleground by 20 years of strife between Hatakeyama Yoshinari (d 1490) and his adopted brother Hatakeyama Masanaga (d 1493), a conflict that had been the immediate cause of the ŌNIN WAR (1467–77). Meeting in council, the rural notables demanded the withdrawal of both Hatakeyama armies from their area, the restoration of manorial rights to their proprietors or *honke,* (court aristocrats and religious institutions), and an end to the construction of toll barriers (SEKISHO). Within a week, the Hatakeyama forces had withdrawn; and within two months after that, the league had adopted a set of regulations (*okitehō*) and designated a group of 36 leaders to administer the affairs of the region in a monthly rotation of three. This body of self-government claimed half-rights (HANZEI) over the land rents of many of the area's estates (SHŌEN), asserted the right to administer criminal justice (KENDAN) and refused to acknowledge the authority of the SHUGO (military governor) of Yamashiro appointed by the shogunate in the summer of 1486, Ise Sadamichi, denying him and his agents entry into their sphere of influence. The league's organization is sometimes described as encompassing the entire province, and indeed it came close to doing so, extending over the Uji, Kuze, Tsuzuki, and Sagara districts of Yamashiro; another, similar league was formed in 1487 in the Otokuni district. The *kokujin* league of southern Yamashiro dissolved in 1493, having served its purpose. The *ikki* was in no sense a popular uprising. On the contrary, the confederation's samurai and quasi-samurai leaders used it to buttress their own interests; even the demand for the return of *shōen* proprietors' rights may have been nothing more than a device to ensure that those rights would slip into the hands of local landholders. Some historians interpret the Yamashiro no Kuni Ikki as a conclusive sign that the "popular energy" manifested in the activities of peasant leagues (TSUCHI IKKI) before the Ōnin War had faded, with the initiative passing to petty provincial notables, the *jizamurai* and *kokujin*. See also KUNI IKKI.

George ELISON

Yamashiro no Ōe, Prince (?–643)

Eldest son of the regent Prince SHŌTOKU; his mother was a daughter of the powerful court official SOGA NO UMAKO. After his father's death, Yamashiro no Ōe occupied an important position in political affairs as the head of the most illustrious princely family. Following the death of the reigning empress SUIKO in 628, he claimed the succession but was thwarted by Prince Tamura (593–641), who had the support of Umako's son Soga no Emishi (d 645) and ascended the throne as Emperor Jomei (r 629–641). The prince's subsequent career is obscure. In 643 forces under SOGA NO IRUKA, Emishi's son, attacked his residence, and he and all his family were forced to commit suicide. The NIHON SHOKI and the JŌGŪ SHŌTOKU HŌŌTEI SETSU describe the prince as a tragic hero. *KITAMURA Bunji*

Yamashiro Province

(Yamashiro no Kuni). One of the five home or central (KINAI) provinces; established under the KOKUGUN SYSTEM in 646, it comprised what is now central and southern Kyōto Prefecture. The region was

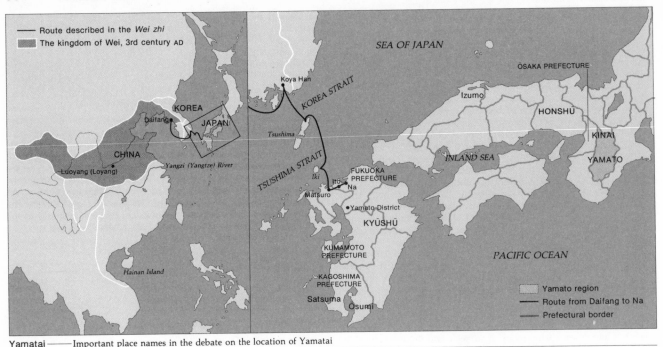

Yamatai————Important place names in the debate on the location of Yamatai

settled in the 5th century by the HATA FAMILY and other naturalized Koreans (KIKAJIN). From 741 to 744, Emperor SHŌMU maintained his official residence at KUNI NO MIYA in the southernmost part of the province, and Yamashiro again became the site of an imperial capital in 784 with the founding of NAGAOKAKYŌ. Ten years later the capital was moved to another location in Yamashiro: HEIANKYŌ (now the city of Kyōto) was to remain the seat of Japan's imperial government for 1,075 years.

Kyōto lost much of its political significance to Kamakura when MINAMOTO NO YORITOMO chose that eastern city as the headquarters of the military government he founded in 1192; but the Kamakura shogunate stationed in Kyōto a military governor (Kyōto shugo), replaced after the JŌKYŪ DISTURBANCE of 1221 by the so-called Rokuhara deputies (ROKUHARA TANDAI), to keep watch over the imperial court. Kyōto and the province that surrounded it again became the political heartland of the country in the Muromachi period (1333–1568), when the Muromachi shogunate was located in the city. For a time in the 14th century, the shogunate's Board of Retainers (SAMURAI-DOKORO) was given the added duty of overseeing Yamashiro, and after 1385 military governors (SHUGO) from various vassal families of the ruling Ashikaga line were appointed to control the increasingly unruly province.

With the decline of the Muromachi shogunate's power in the 15th century, Kyōto and southern Yamashiro were scourged repeatedly by peasant uprisings (TSUCHI IKKI) and other disturbances; the ŌNIN WAR (1467–77) devastated the area. Toward the end of the century southern Yamashiro became the center of a league of local proprietors, the YAMASHIRO NO KUNI IKKI, and that part of the province was ruled by a council of 36 local warrior-proprietors (KOKUJIN) from 1486 to 1493. For much of the 16th century, Yamashiro was the center of contention among rival warlords who sought to dominate Kyōto; in 1582 it was the first province surveyed under TOYOTOMI HIDEYOSHI's great nationwide cadastral survey (Taikō kenchi; see KENCHI). The Azuchi-Momoyama period (1568–1600) is named after the site of the palatial castle that Hideyoshi built in Fushimi, another town in Yamashiro.

During the Edo period (1600–1868) the Tokugawa shogunate exercised strict control over Yamashiro through its Kyōto deputies (KYŌTO SHOSHIDAI). After the MEIJI RESTORATION of 1868, the imperial capital was moved to Tōkyō, and Yamashiro was for a time divided into two prefectures, Kyōto and Yodo, but these were consolidated into Kyōto Prefecture on 22 November 1871.

KITAMURA Bunji

Yamashiro Tomoe (1912–   )

Novelist, especially concerned with the sufferings of rural women. Born into a farm family in Hiroshima Prefecture; maiden name To-

kumo. She studied Western painting briefly in Tōkyō and then turned to the problems of working people. In 1935 she married the communist Yamashiro Yoshimune (1900–1945). Both were imprisoned in 1940, and her husband died in jail. Her works include Fuki no tō (1948, A Stalk of Butterbur), Niguruma no uta (1955, Handcart Songs), and Toraware no onnatachi (1980, Imprisoned Women, 10 vols).

Yamashiroya Incident

(Yamashiroya Jiken). Scandal of the early 1870s involving Yamashiroya Wasuke (1836–72), a merchant from Yamaguchi Prefecture who did extensive business with the Army Ministry as an official purveyor (GOYŌ SHŌNIN). Taking advantage of his ties with Army Minister YAMAGATA ARITOMO, also from Yamaguchi, Yamashiroya was able to borrow large sums of money from the ministry, some ¥650,000 in all. He lost most of it speculating in the raw-silk market, and with the remaining cash he went to Paris, where his extravagance aroused the suspicions of Japanese consular officials and led to an investigation of his financial affairs. Upon returning to Japan, Yamashiroya was asked by Yamagata to return the money. Unable to do so, he committed suicide at the Army Ministry office.

Yamashita–Shinnihon Steamship Co, Ltd

(Yamashita–Shinnihon Kisen). A tramp operator, established in 1964 by the merger of the Yamashita Steamship Co and the Shinnihon Steamship Co. The company operates ships for the exclusive transport of iron ore, coal, lumber, and mineral oil, in addition to container ships, bulk carriers, and tankers. It has subsidiaries incorporated overseas in London, New York, and Hong Kong. As of March 1981 the company operated 152 ships totaling 8,530 deadweight tons. Sales in the fiscal year ending March 1981 totaled ¥212.4 billion (US $936.5 million), and the company was capitalized at ¥18.3 billion (US $80.2 million) in the same year. The head office is in Tōkyō.

Yamashita Tarō (1889–1967)

Businessman and pioneer in Japan's overseas oil development efforts. Born in Akita Prefecture, he graduated from Sapporo Agricultural College (now Hokkaidō University) and then went to Manchuria, where he was successful in business. He served in executive capacities in many companies, including the presidencies of both Korean Chemical and Tōhoku Mining. In 1956 Yamashita established Japan Oil Export (now ARABIAN OIL CO, LTD) with the support of ISHIZAKA TAIZŌ, KOBAYASHI ATARU, and other business leaders to develop oil resources in the Persian Gulf.

TANAKA Yōnosuke

Yamashita Tomoyuki (1885–1946)

Also known as Yamashita Hōbun. Army general. Born in Kōchi Prefecture; graduate of the Army Academy (1905) and the Army War College (1916). He rose rapidly in the army, holding various assignments in the Army General Staff Office and abroad, but fell from grace temporarily for openly sympathizing with the mutineers in the FEBRUARY 26TH INCIDENT of 1936. With the outbreak of the Pacific War in 1941, Yamashita was appointed commander of the 25th Army and sent to Malaya. He became famous for his capture of the British naval base at Singapore (see MALAYAN CAMPAIGN) on 15 February 1942. In 1944 he was sent to the Philippines to defend the Japanese-occupied islands against the Allied counteroffensive. After the war he was tried by a military commission in Manila for atrocities committed by soldiers under his command. Although the defense established that Yamashita had no direct knowledge of the crimes, he was pronounced guilty and hanged (see WAR CRIMES TRIALS).

Mutsu Gorō

Yamatai

Also called Yamataikoku. Name of a country in the Japanese islands, visited by Chinese envoys in AD 240 and the years immediately following and described in the Chinese book *Sanguo zhi* (*Sankuo chih;* History of the Three Kingdoms), written by Chen Shou (Ch'en Shou; 233–297) toward the end of the 3rd century. There are a few earlier and fragmentary references to Japan in the Chinese histories, but this is the oldest extensive description of Japan in any language, and its rich lode of information on the 3rd-century Wa people, as the Chinese called the Japanese, and their fascinating queen, HIMIKO, is fundamental to any understanding of early Japanese history. If this famous account is illuminating, so is it puzzling, largely because of the frustrating obscurity of its data on the location of Yamatai, Himiko's capital. During the 3rd century the Wa people of Yamatai and its subordinate communities had achieved a major stage in the development of the Japanese nation, yet the inability of historians to solve the problem of its location hampers our understanding of the historical process.

Chen Shou and the Wei zhi—— Chen Shou himself probably had no direct knowledge of Japan. He apparently depended on archival records and earlier historical treatments of the short-lived Wei dynasty (220–265), the northernmost of the three kingdoms into which China was divided for much of the 3rd century. One important earlier compilation, now known only in fragments, was the *Wei lüe* (*Wei lüeh;* J: *Giryaku*) of Yu Huan (Yü Huan), dating from around 250 and known to have had a section on Japan. Chen's history of Wei, or WEI ZHI (*Wei chih;* J: *Gishi*), was the first and largest part of the *Sanguo zhi.* The last volume of the *Wei zhi,* devoted to "accounts of the eastern barbarians" and covering the peoples of Manchuria, Korea, and Japan, has a section on the Japanese Wa people, or Woren (Wojen; J: *Wajin*). Among Japanese scholars this account is conventionally referred to as the *Gishi wajinden* (the Wei Zhi Account of the Wa People), although strictly speaking this is not a correct form of citation.

Chen's account begins with an itinerary describing the journey from the Chinese commandery of Daifang (Tai-fang; near modern Haeju in South Hwanghae Province, northern Korea) to the towns on the northwest Kyūshū coast, and from there on to Yamatai. The crucial last part of this itinerary was probably based on hearsay, given its abundant contradictions and the fact that concrete observations on the flora, fauna, and climate, prominent in the earlier itinerary, are lacking. The itinerary includes important information on the population and official titles in the key communities. Following the itinerary is an extensive statement on the manners and customs of the land of the Wa, and a brief section on administrative and social structure. Next there is a substantial statement on Queen Himiko, the character of her rule, and her close diplomatic relations with Wei from 239 until her death a short time after 247. The account then concludes with some details of the succession struggle that followed her burial.

The Land of the Wa and Queen Himiko—— The interesting ethnographic description of the Wa shows a sharply stratified society, with social and regional distinctions indicated by tattoo markings. Although living quarters were segregated according to age and sex, the mixing of the sexes in public activity appeared noteworthy to the Chinese observers. There was an intense concern with pollution and purification. Many of the customs struck the Chinese as similar to those of the tropical south, and they cited Hainan Island as a com-

parison. These observers believed that the land of the Wa extended far to the south, and that its capital, Yamatai, was about equal in latitude to the mouth of the Yangzi (Yangtze) River.

There appears to have been considerable commerce, both between communities and with towns in Korean and Chinese territory on the peninsula. The sea routes between Kyūshū and Korea were busy, with most of the population of Tsushima and Iki (two large island communities in the Korea Strait that still have the same names today) engaged in this commerce. There was a revenue office for the collection of various levies in grain and other products. Each community had markets, which were under the supervision of a senior official based at Ito (ITOKOKU) in northwestern Kyūshū and appointed by Queen Himiko in Yamatai. This person had great power, and the Chinese were impressed by the strict searches of boats involved in foreign trade or diplomatic relations.

Queen Himiko was a personage of considerable mystery. According to the Chinese observers, the Wa had once been ruled by a king, but at some time during the 160s and 170s there had been a civil war that ended with the accession of Himiko. She devoted herself completely to religious affairs (unfortunately not further described) and was able to "delude the crowd." By 240, she had attained great age; assuming she was between 10 and 15 at her accession, she might have been in her nineties when she died in the late 240s. She had no husband but was assisted by her younger brother, who exercised power for her. Of a thousand personal servants and slaves, only one was a man. She lived in a towered palace behind forbidding walls and was guarded constantly. Very few ever saw her.

In 239 Himiko sent envoys to the Wei Chinese commandery at Daifang, and the authorities there conducted them and their tribute, including patterned cloths and 10 human beings, to the Wei capital at Luoyang (Loyang). The following year Wei sent a return embassy, which presented the queen with a golden seal with purple tassel and the title of "Monarch of the Wa, Friendly to Wei." Among the many rich presents were 100 bronze mirrors. The Wei edict stated that the queen should use these treasures to impress upon her people that Wei had concern for her. In 247, after further diplomatic exchanges in 243 and 245, Himiko again addressed the Wei court, reporting a war between herself and the kingdom of Kunu (or Kona), said to be south of Yamatai, and Wei sent back envoys with statements of support.

Sometime after the 247 embassy, Himiko died. A huge burial mound, 100 paces in diameter, was raised for her, and over 100 servants were killed and interred with her. She was at first succeeded by a king, but the country would not accept him and a civil war erupted. Ultimately a 13-year-old girl, Iyo (emended by some to Toyo), was made queen, whereupon the strife ceased. Wei responded with an embassy of recognition and support. Unfortunately, at this point the account comes to an end. A later Chinese work, the *Jin shu* (*Chin shu*), records an envoy from the Wa queen in 266, but after that date there is in Chinese books a total silence on Wa affairs that lasts for more than 150 years. And when once again the Wa are noticed, the queen and her country have disappeared and a completely different kind of situation obtains in Japan.

The Location of Yamatai—— The *Wei zhi*'s itinerary from Korea to Kyūshū had the envoys proceeding 7,000 *li* from Daifang to Koya Han (modern Kimhae, South Kyŏngsang Province, southern Korea), from there crossing the sea 1,000 *li* to Tsushima, thence 1,000 *li* southward to Iki, thence another 1,000 *li* to Matsuro, identified with the Matsuura Peninsula on Kyūshū. (Because the *Wei zhi* was a Chinese text written by Chinese, its proper names and Japanese words should ideally be interpreted in the light of the northern Chinese pronunciation of the 3rd century. Although such treatment is possible to an extent, it would introduce prohibitive complexity; therefore, with some misgivings, the modern Japanese forms conventional in the literature have been used here.) The distances are greatly exaggerated. Values proposed for the length of the Wei *li* vary from scholar to scholar, but at most the trip across the Korea Strait would have been a journey of 300, not 3,000, *li*. It is speculated that the travelers found it difficult to estimate distances at sea, but in fact the *Wei zhi*'s land distances are also considerably exaggerated.

Once on Kyūshū, the way lay reportedly 500 *li southeast* from Matsuro to Ito, the administrative center where the envoys were received, thence *southeast* 100 *li* to Na (NAKOKU), thence *east* 100 *li* to Fumi. Matsuro, Ito, and Na evoke historically known names of communities near the northwest Kyūshū coast, and there is no disagreement among scholars on their identification. However, the three communities are actually in a *northeast* line starting from Matsuro, and it is at this point that the itinerary becomes problematic. On the location of Fumi there is less agreement. Wherever it was, one proceeded from there *south* for 20 days by sea to Toma, and thence *south* 10 days by sea and one month by land to the queen's capital at Yamatai. *South* of Yamatai at an unspecified distance was the hostile country of Kunu. *North* of it were some 20 named communities for which distances were omitted.

If one takes the directions as given, it is clear that Yamatai lay to the south, not in central Japan to the east. Wherever on Kyūshū Fumi was, a journey south by sea for a month and by land for another month seems most improbable. Most readers have assumed that the distances were overstated (with considerable speculation on the motives) and that both Toma, a town said to have comprised over 50,000 households, and Yamatai, with its reported 70,000 households, must have been somewhere in the central or southern part of Kyūshū.

It is important to emphasize at this point that the oldest Japanese historical works, the *Kojiki* (712) and the *Nihon shoki* (720), contain nothing about Yamatai and Queen Himiko. Moreover, the *Wei zhi* would have presented some difficulty to the compilers of these works, for whom it was dogma that Japan's rulers had always ruled from Yamato, in the Nara Plain in central Japan and far from Kyūshū. There is some evidence that the compilers faced this problem, since for the period 200–269, the *Nihon shoki* has the female "regent" Empress JINGŪ ruling in Yamato. The facts that the span of this regency safely includes the years in which Wei had contact with the Wa queen and that other parts of the coverage for this period show indubitable evidence of chronological manipulation by the compilers suggest that Empress Jingū was inserted into the Yamato ruling line to account for the *Wei zhi*'s information while at the same time implicitly rejecting it. In addition, there are three references to the *Wei zhi* account, presenting salient facts of the diplomatic exchange but mentioning neither "Yamatai" nor "Himiko," inserted into the Jingū chronicle as notes. The impression left by this treatment is that, if there had been any diplomatic contact with Wei—and the *Nihon shoki* is not saying there had been—it would have involved the legitimate female ruler in Yamato. In effect, readers with access to both Chinese and Japanese accounts were asked implicitly to take Himiko as Empress Jingū and Yamatai as Yamato.

In fact, this was the interpretation of the very few medieval and early modern scholars who commented on the *Wei zhi*. ARAI HAKUSEKI, for instance, gave the Chinese text a moderately critical treatment in his *Koshitsū* (1716, Treatise on Ancient History) and even attempted to identify many of the place names, but he passed over in silence the geographical contradictions involved in the location of Yamatai. He simply said that Yamatai was Yamato.

The Kyūshū Theory——The first scholar to depart from this view was MOTOORI NORINAGA. In his *Gyojū gaigen* (1778, An Outline on the Subduing of Foreigners), an anti-Chinese polemic on Japan's historical foreign relations, he took the *Wei zhi* directions literally, emended "one month" to "one day," and concluded that Yamatai was in Kyūshū and not to be identified with Yamato. He believed that the Wei observers were mistaken in thinking that the queen herself was in Yamatai. Possibly they had heard of Japan's queen (Jingū), but any diplomatic representation from her must have been bogus, since in Motoori's deep belief no Japanese ruler would ever have sent tribute to China. By dissociating the queen from Yamatai he was able to locate the latter in Kyūshū, as the *Wei zhi* seemed to require, without dishonoring the sacred Yamato tradition. Many scholars of the 19th century adopted Motoori's view. Some came to think that the Wa were really the KUMASO people of the *Nihon shoki*, that Yamatai was therefore located in the Satsuma area of southern Kyūshū, and that the woman named Himiko had usurped the authority of the real queen in Yamato. Because of the great distances indicated by the *Wei zhi*, most of the early Kyūshū theorists located Yamatai as far south as possible, in the Satsuma and Ōsumi areas (now Kagoshima Prefecture).

But this created geopolitical problems. It was hard to imagine that a regime so far removed from the major areas of Kyūshū life could have dominated those areas, which, as history, tradition, and (later) archaeology showed, were in the northwest. Moreover, the *Wei zhi* located Kunu south of Yamatai, but there was nothing south of Satsuma. In 1910 SHIRATORI KURAKICHI decided to reject entirely the long trip indicated by the *Wei zhi* and accept only its statement that the total distance from Daifang to Yamatai was 12,000 *li*. Since 10,700 *li* had already been accounted for in getting to Fumi, only 1,300 *li* (a short distance, thought Shiratori) remained for the

leg from Fumi to Yamatai. Shiratori therefore decided that Yamatai was in the Kumamoto area. South of that, in Satsuma, was the queen's enemy Kunu. According to Shiratori, neither Yamatai nor Kunu was within the sphere of the main Yamato state in the KINAI (Kyōto–Ōsaka–Nara) area until their supposed conquest by Yamato some time during the 4th century.

The Yamato Theory Reborn——Shiratori's treatment put the Kyūshū theory on much firmer philological and historical foundations than the earlier proponents had achieved and attracted the support of many later scholars. Yet, just at the time of his epochal article in 1910, there appeared another by NAITŌ KONAN that revived the traditional Yamato, or Kinai, theory. The many localization problems of the Kyūshū theory, together with a residual belief in the basic Yamato tradition, encouraged Naitō to reexamine the *Wei zhi* text. Citing a number of instances of confusion between south and east in Chinese historical writing, he emended "south" to "east" and thus turned the itinerary toward the Kinai area. This theory had the advantage of not having to reject, as had Shiratori, the *Wei zhi*'s great distances, with which Naitō could easily reconcile a long voyage through the Inland Sea. In bringing Yamatai back to Yamato, he could also draw on other material in the *Nihon shoki* to clarify the *Wei zhi* text. Thus he postulated that Himiko (or Himeko, in the spelling of some) could be identified with Yamato Hime no Mikoto (see YAMATOHIME, PRINCESS), whose brother reigned as Emperor KEIKŌ and who herself was the high priestess of Ise, an identification that seemed to offer both phonetic and circumstantial congruence. Naitō also made many other identifications involving titles and place names.

Among the supporters of the reinvigorated Kinai theory were many archaeologists, chief among them TAKAHASHI KENJI and later UMEHARA SUEJI and Kobayashi Yukio (b 1911), all of Kyōto University. To them the Yamatai problem was more than a textual issue; without archaeological support no theory could be established. According to them, the archaeological data showed the preeminence of the Kinai area over Kyūshū and the steady extension of Kinai culture into the eastern and western parts of Japan. Almost all archaeologically known Late Han and Wei mirrors had been unearthed in the Kinai area, including one dated 239 (and thus linked with Himiko) that had been found in Ōsaka Prefecture. (Kyūshū theorists retorted that these mirrors would have been passed on as treasures for generations and only later brought to the Kinai area and buried; Kobayashi argued vigorously against this claim.) Moreover, the archaeologists argued that none of the Kyūshū sites identified with Yamatai, either in Kagoshima, Kumamoto, or Fukuoka prefectures, yielded any evidence that supported the existence of a major political center of 70,000 households in the 3rd century. Such a center, they insisted, could only be found in the Kinai. There were archaeologists who argued the Kyūshū case, but as a group archaeologists have tended toward the Kinai theory.

The Kinai–Kyūshū Standoff——From the appearance of the articles by Shiratori and Naitō in 1910, no fundamentally new theory arose, only new arguments for the old theories. Chief among the later Kyūshū supporters have been Hashimoto Masukichi (1880–1956), Enoki Kazuo (b 1913), and Furuta Takehiko (b 1926). Hashimoto, in many books and articles, argued every aspect of the question at great length and in detail, refining the localization and historical arguments. Developing the views of some earlier Kyūshū theorists, he argued for the location of Yamatai in the Yamato District in southwestern Fukuoka Prefecture. Enoki, in 1947, introduced his "radial" theory to explain the Kyūshū distances. He believed it was an error to regard the *Wei zhi* itinerary as a sequential statement, leading from place to place to place. Rather, Ito, where the envoys were officially received, would have served as the focal point from which all the other distances radiated. Thus Na was 100 *li* southeast of Ito, Fumi 100 *li* east of it, and Toma and Yamatai both south of it. This had the advantage of not making Kyūshū seem improbably long, and making Yamatai closer to Ito than Toma was, and thus more centrally located. Enoki's theory was warmly welcomed by Kyūshū supporters for its apparent solution of many of the most difficult geographical problems. Furuta, author of *Yamatai wa nakatta* (1972, There Was No Yamatai), pointed out that the reading "Yamatai" depends on an emendation in the text, which has "Yamaichi," or, in his reading, "Yama(w)i" (the graphic emendation of *-ichi* to *-tai* had long been made by both Chinese and Japanese scholars on the basis of a well-established variant in other Chinese texts). What was to be found, said Furuta, was a place called Yamai. He found such a place and thus separated himself from the many Kyūshū theorists who, because of the presumed linguistic identity of

Yamatai and Yamato, looked for Kyūshū sites named Yamato. This, he thought, freed the problem from many historical complications.

There have also been many refinements in the Kinai theory. One is the postulation of the eastward voyage not through the Inland Sea but by way of the northern shore of Honshū (via the Sea of Japan), first proposed by Kasai Shin'ya (1884–1956) and reinforced by Suematsu Yasukazu (b 1904). This theory identified the major center of Toma (with 50,000 households) with Izumo (Idumo), a known major center of early Japan, and clarified the sea and land legs of the Yamatai trip. Another refinement improved the rationale for emending "south" to "east" in the first place; the seeming arbitrariness of this change by Naitō had long been a target of Kyūshū theorists. Mishina Shōei (1902–71) and Miyai Yoshio (b 1910) argued for emending not only south to east but all directions 90° to the left. Miyai pointed out that the axis of communication in ancient Japan was east and west, with north and south perceived in a sideways orientation, a thesis for which he offered interesting linguistic support. To a Japanese, "front" and "left" would have meant "east" and "north" respectively; to Chinese, with their well-known southward orientation, these would have meant "south" and "east" respectively. Presumably, these contrasting perceptions would have led to confusion when Japanese explained the itinerary to Chinese. This emendation, a structural one with an objective rationale, seemed to permit an integral rationalization of the location of all the *Wei zhi* place names, not just Yamatai. (It will be recalled that the towns Matsuro, Ito, and Na, which the *Wei zhi* presents on a *southeast* axis, actually lie on a northeast axis.) This put Kunu to the east, not in the south, and in fact the Chinese *Hou Han shu* variant of the *Wei zhi* text states east in this context.

The Significance of the Yamatai Debate —— By the 1960s, most minds had been made up and few would change. Kinai and Kyūshū theorists often seemed to be speaking only to their respective partisans. The basic arguments for each theory were set, and the opposition between them became endemic. But the debate proliferated. Moreover, the mass media became attracted to the issue, and as Sunday magazine reporters and filmmakers took up the Yamatai theme it often became romanticized and trivialized. Mishina Shōei, who wrote an extremely useful history of the debate, observed that this new era saw the "merchandising of Yamatai" *(Yamatai no shōhinka)*.

But the localization of Yamatai is not a mere game, as it has sometimes seemed. If the growth and formation of the Japanese state is to be understood, it is of fundamental importance to know where Yamatai was. The Chinese description of Queen Himiko's land, which is earlier, fresher, and more concrete than any Japanese account of the 3rd century, and completely free of the ideological considerations and "imperial historiography" *(kōkoku shikan)* bound up with the *Nihon shoki,* has to be one of the principal starting points in any investigation of Japanese history. Was Kyūshū a relatively backward area brought within the Yamato state by conquest from the east (Kinai theory)? Or was it a culturally and politically advanced area that provided the base for an eastward conquest and the true establishment of Yamato (Kyūshū theory)? Was Yamato a development of a Yamatai in the Kinai, or did it come into being quite independently of a Yamatai far off in Kyūshū? How would Yamatai's contrasting locations affect the importance of continental influences? If Yamatai was in Kyūshū, continental influence was closer and more important in development; if it was in the Kinai, continental influence was farther away and of less importance in development. What significance would the localization argument have for the theory of Egami Namio (b 1906) and others that the definitive Japanese state was established by invaders from the continent during the 4th century (see HORSE-RIDER THEORY)? What would these people have conquered, and where, and in what sequence?

No explanation of Japan's formative process can avoid the Yamatai issue. Yamatai's localization is a primary task of Japanese historiography. And yet, given the great differences in the two principal theories, and the determination and zeal with which they are advocated by very serious scholars, it is difficult to imagine that there will be an early solution.

🔖 ——Mishina Shōei, *Yamatai koku kenkyū sōran* (1970). Saeki Arikiyo, *Kenkyūshi: Yamatai koku* (1971). Saeki Arikiyo, *Kenkyūshi: Sengo no Yamatai koku* (1972). Ryusaku Tsunoda and L. C. Goodrich, *Japan in the Chinese Dynastic Histories* (1951). John Young, *The Location of Yamatai: A Case Study in Japanese Historiography* (1957).   Gari LEDYARD

Yamataka Shigeri (1899–1977)

Feminist and social reformer. Also known by her married name, Kaneko Shigeri, until her divorce in 1939. Born in Mie Prefecture, she attended Tōkyō Women's Higher Normal School (now Ochanomizu University); she first worked as a reporter in 1920 for the newspaper *Kokumin shimbun* and then for the women's magazine SHUFU NO TOMO. She helped ICHIKAWA FUSAE found the FUSEN KAKUTOKU DŌMEI to campaign for women's suffrage during the 1920s. Faced with growing government suppression, she turned her attention to the welfare of mothers and widows and in 1934 joined with YAMADA WAKA and others to form the organization that in 1935 became the Bosei Hogo Remmei, or Motherhood Protection League. She continued working with Ichikawa both during and after World War II, especially in the cause of promoting new rights for women. She also helped organize war widows to improve their lot. In 1952 she founded the women's social reform league CHIFUREN and long served as its president (see also CONSUMER MOVEMENT). With its backing she was elected in 1962 and 1965 to the House of Councillors, where she served until 1971.

Yamatake–Honeywell Co, Ltd

Electric company producing process-control devices, air conditioning control devices, as well as other control and electronic equipment. The largest domestic producer of air conditioning and fuel control devices, Yamatake–Honeywell is also the second largest producer of industrial measuring instruments. Yamatake was established in 1906 by Yamaguchi Takehiko and in 1920 concluded an exclusive sales agreement with Brown Instruments of the United States, which was acquired by Honeywell in 1934. In 1952 Yamatake Honeywell concluded a licensing and joint-venture agreement with Honeywell. The technological level is high, and the company's various products are exported and sold through Honeywell's worldwide sales network. The firm has a joint venture manufacturing company in Taiwan. Sales totaled ¥67.4 billion (US $305 million) in the fiscal year ending September 1981. In the same year the export ratio was 22 percent and the company was capitalized at ¥4.2 billion (US $19 million). The head office is in Tōkyō.

Yamatane Museum of Art

(Yamatane Bijutsukan). Located in Tōkyō. A collection of about 700 Japanese-style paintings from the Meiji period (1868–1912) to the present, most of them bought by Yamazaki Taneji (b 1893), president of the Yamatane Security Co, Ltd. The museum opened in 1966 and emphasizes works of the recent past. The gallery and the installation—the work of TANIGUCHI YOSHIRŌ—is a fine example of contemporary Japanese museum design.   *Laurance* ROBERTS

Yamata no Orochi

Name of a mythological, eight-headed, eight-tailed snakelike monster slain by SUSANOO NO MIKOTO. Susanoo, younger brother of the sun goddess AMATERASU ŌMIKAMI, had been banished from the High Celestial Plain (TAKAMAGAHARA) for his bad conduct (see TSUMI). Descending to earth in what is now part of the district of Izumo, he found an old couple weeping, saying that this monster, having eaten seven of their daughters, now demanded the last. After offering it rice wine, Susanoo killed it during its inebriated sleep and found in its tail the sword Murakumo no Tsurugi. The Murakumo sword became one of the three IMPERIAL REGALIA granted by Amaterasu to Ninigi no Mikoto, and it reappeared in subsequent mythological and historical accounts, in which it is renamed Kusanagi no Tsurugi. It is said to be kept at the ATSUTA SHRINE in Nagoya. Attempting to provide interpretations of this myth, scholars have proposed that the monster was actually a river or certain communities that were pacified, but no single convincing argument has emerged.   *Allan G.* GRAPARD

Yamate Kiichirō (1899–   )

Novelist. Real name Iguchi Chōji. Born in Tochigi Prefecture. After graduating from middle school, he worked as a magazine editor while writing historical short stories. He became a professional writer in 1940 with the publication of his first collection of stories, *Uguisu-zamurai* (1940), and its sequel, *Momotarō-zamurai* (1940). His postwar novels like *Yumesuke senryō miyage* (1947), filled with optimism and human warmth, held great emotional appeal for the war-stricken Japanese.

Yamato

City in central Kanagawa Prefecture, central Honshū. Formerly a tiny hamlet cultivating mulberry trees, it became a military base during World War II. It now has automobile, audio equipment, and foodstuff industries. Pop: 167,934.

Yamato

A name that refers in its broadest sense to the country of Japan or to things Japanese, especially in contrast to things Chinese, as in *yamato-e* (Japanese painting) or *yamato-gokoro* (the spirit of Japan).

Specifically, Yamato or Yamato Province (Yamato no Kuni) is the ancient name of Nara Prefecture. The name is generally thought to have derived from *yama* (mountain) and *to* (place), appropriate for a region surrounded by mountains; but scholars believe that Yamato is related to YAMATAI, the name of a legendary Japanese queendom mentioned in the 3rd-century Chinese chronicle WEI ZHI *(Wei chih)*. Between the 4th and 8th centuries, Yamato, especially the mountain basin located in the northwest corner of the province, was the center of early Japanese culture and politics. Historians generally divide the span of Yamato eminence into two periods. The protohistoric Yamato period from ca 300 to 710 witnessed the rise of the first unified state in Japan, while the ensuing Nara period (710–794) saw the adoption of a centralized bureaucracy on the Chinese model and the rise of a civilization based on Buddhist ideology.

The Yamato period is also commonly known by its archaeological name, the KOFUN PERIOD, derived from the thousands of mounded burial tombs (KOFUN) built by the ruling strata during that time. Traditional archaeological interpretation regards the appearance of mounded tomb building and the spread of a standardized ritual set of HAJI WARE in the late 3rd or early 4th century as indicating the unification of western Japan under a centralized Yamato state. Historians have recently challenged this view, claiming that unification of the area was probably not accomplished until well into the 6th or even the 7th century.

Before construction of the monumentally spacious capitals FUJIWARAKYŌ and HEIJŌKYŌ, political activity in the Nara period centered on palaces erected by each successive ruler in a location to his liking. Although few archaeological remains of these residences are known, some approximate locations exist in place names and references in the early chronicles *Kojiki* (712) and *Nihon shoki* (720). Scholars have designated these successive political foci collectively as the YAMATO COURT (ca 4th century–ca mid-7th century).

Gina Lee BARNES

Yamato

Battleship of the Imperial Japanese Navy; the largest battleship ever built. Along with the battleship *Musashi*, the *Yamato* was constructed as part of the naval buildup following the abrogation of the London Naval Treaty in 1936 (see LONDON NAVAL CONFERENCES). Construction was begun at Kure Naval Shipyard in 1937 and completed in December 1941 in great secrecy. The *Yamato*'s main features were a displacement of 64,000 tons; a main battery of nine 46-centimeter (18-in) guns; a secondary battery of twelve 15.5-centimeter (6.1-in) guns and a supplementary armament of twelve 12.7-centimeter (5-in), high-angle guns; six aircraft; a speed of 27 knots; a cruising range of 7,200 nautical miles; a length of 250 meters (820 ft); a beam of 39 meters (128 ft); and a crew of about 2,500. It was considered impregnable.

The *Yamato* participated in the battles of MIDWAY, the PHILIPPINE SEA, and LEYTE GULF. On 7 April 1945, with enough fuel only for a one-way voyage, the *Yamato* sailed for Okinawa as part of a Special Surface Attack Force. It was escorted by one cruiser and eight destroyers, practically the only remaining surface strength of the navy. Attacked by some 390 Allied planes, it was sunk off Bōnomisaki, southwest of Kyūshū. More than 4,000 men were killed on the *Yamato* and the escorting ships. The disaster marked the end of the Imperial Japanese Navy. *ICHIKI Toshio*

Yamato Bunkakan

A museum located near Nara. It has a superb collection of approximately 2,000 items of East Asian art comprising paintings, sculpture, calligraphy, ceramics, lacquer, prints, and textiles. The Japanese paintings include scrolls of the Heian period (794–1185), sutras, and rare Buddhist iconographic items; mandala of the Kamakura period (1185–1333); 15th- and 16th-century *suibokuga* (ink paintings);

Momoyama screens; and RIMPA-style works of the Edo period (1600–1868). Chinese items include paintings and calligraphy of the Song (Sung; 960–1279) dynasty, while ceramics are represented by tomb figures from the Han (206 BC–AD 220) through the Tang (T'ang; 618–907) dynasties, and vases, bowls, and ewers of the Song dynasty. The publications of the museum include a seven-volume catalog of the collection. There is a comprehensive program of loan exhibitions and special shows of the museum's own material. Lectures and research form an important part of the museum's activities. See also MUSEUMS. *Laurance ROBERTS*

Yamato court

(Yamato *chōtei*). Center of the archaic Japanese polity (ca 4th–ca mid-7th centuries), situated in YAMATO (now Nara Prefecture); the term is used in distinction to the centralized bureaucratic state that came into being with the TAIKA REFORM of 645. It is difficult to say when the Yamato polity emerged. If one accepts the theory that the country of YAMATAI, mentioned in the 3rd-century Chinese history WEI ZHI *(Wei chih)*, is identical to the Yamato court, and if one further accepts the theory that locates it in northern Kyūshū, then one may fix the beginnings of Yamato rule early in the 4th century. If, on the other hand, one locates Yamatai on the Nara Plain, one may fix it as early as the first half of the 3rd century. In any case, archaeological evidence, Chinese histories, and the myth-shrouded accounts in the KOJIKI (712) and NIHON SHOKI (720) all seem to indicate that sometime in the 3rd or 4th century a local chieftain based in Yamato subdued neighboring chieftains and achieved a measure of political unity in central Honshū.

The Yamato ruler was not in any sense a sovereign; he was rather a primus inter pares acting as mediator for a loose confederation of similar chieftains whose support was essential for the maintenance of his own succession. Through war, diplomacy, and marriage alliances, he extended his control, and it is clear that by the 5th century he had achieved a political hegemony that reached as far as northern Kyūshū in the southwest and the Kantō plain in the northeast. He did not rule a "state" in the modern sense.

The members of the ruling elite built imposing tumuli, or burial mounds (KOFUN). The artifacts found in them, such as iron swords and armor, *magatama* beads (see BEADS, ANCIENT), and pottery vessels, show a strong continental influence. Indeed the resemblance is such that some scholars have claimed that these tumuli were the work of certain horse-riding conquerors who came from Korea in the 4th century (see HORSE-RIDER THEORY). Be that as it may, the tombs indicate a warring aristocratic society capable of organizing human resources on a large scale.

By the 6th century a single kingly line (the ancestors of the later imperial family) seems to have emerged, the head of which began to assert his prerogatives as a ruler. He devised a system of ranks and titles. Chieftains of important kin-groups (UJI) such as the Ki (see KI FAMILY), Kose, and Katsuragi were designated *omi* (see KABANE). The Ōtomo (see ŌTOMO FAMILY), Mononobe (see MONONOBE FAMILY), and Nakatomi *uji*, who performed hereditary functions (such as defense and worship) for the court, were designated *muraji* (see UJI–KABANE SYSTEM). Lesser chieftains were called TOMO NO MIYATSUKO; they supervised specialized service groups called BE, who supplied labor and craft goods to the ruling house and the nobility. The Yamato ruler also appropriated rice lands *(miyake)* for his use, while the local chieftains derived their support from lands called TADOKORO.

As for regional control, according to the Chinese history SUI SHU (History of the Sui Dynasty [589–618]), the country was already divided into *kuni* (provinces), which were subdivided into *agata*. These territorial units were governed by KUNI NO MIYATSUKO and AGATANUSHI, who were responsible for collecting tribute. Rather than true appointment, however, the granting of these offices seems to have been a confirmation of de facto local power.

The immigrant groups (KIKAJIN) that came from Korea during the 5th and 6th centuries also contributed to the growing prestige of the Yamato court. Because of their knowledge of writing and advanced techniques of agriculture, ironworking, pottery, and weaving, families like the AYA FAMILY and HATA FAMILY gained prominence in political and military affairs. According to the *Kudaraki* (Records of Paekche), fragments of which survive in the *Nihon shoki*, the Yamato rulers initiated diplomatic relations with the Korean kingdom of PAEKCHE in 366. The FIVE KINGS OF WA, mentioned in the *Song shu* (Sung shu, History of the Liu–Song Dynasty [420–479]) as having sent tribute to Chinese emperors several times between 413 and 478, apparently hoped to strengthen Japanese influence in Korea with Chinese help. They are believed by some Japanese scholars to have gained a foothold in KAYA, at the tip of the Korean peninsula, and availed themselves of iron ore, but to have lost their enclave in 562. In 668, when the state of SILLA unified the peninsula, the Japanese withdrew altogether.

Perhaps one of the most significant events in the history of the Yamato court was the introduction of BUDDHISM. Although 538 is given as the official date, the Japanese must have been acquainted with Buddhist teachings much earlier through Korean immigrants. In any case, the question of whether or not to embrace this new religion precipitated a conflict among the major court families. The pro-Buddhist faction led by the SOGA FAMILY triumphed in 587. Official acceptance of Buddhism signaled the beginning of a wholehearted emulation of Chinese culture.

The victorious Soga now dominated court affairs. SOGA NO UMAKO installed his niece on the throne (SUIKO, the first of the Yamato rulers to take the title *tennō*, or "emperor"). The Soga were at first restrained by Prince SHŌTOKU, who, inspired by the Chinese political system, made every effort to enhance the prestige of the ruling house. After his death in 622, however, they made no attempt to hide their own imperial ambitions. They were eventually overthrown in 645 by Prince Naka no Ōe (later Emperor TENJI) and FUJIWARA NO KAMATARI. With the help of such advisers as TAKAMUKO NO KUROMARO and the priest SŌMIN, these two leaders carried on the work of Shōtoku, establishing a centralized bureaucracy on the Chinese model and reasserting the sovereign's authority over the people and land in the Taika Reform. By the time of the formulation of the TAIHŌ CODE (701) and the building of a new capital, Heijōkyō, at what is now Nara (710), the Yamato court had come to preside over an integrated state.

yamato-damashii

(Japanese spirit). A phrase used until the end of World War II to describe spiritual qualities supposedly unique to the Japanese people. These range from physical and moral fortitude and courage, sincerity and devotion, to what the Germans called *Volksgeist*. During the militaristic period, from the early 1930s to the end of World War II, *yamato-damashii* was equated with unquestioning loyalty to emperor and nation.

Over time, the definition of *yamato-damashii* has changed, as reflected in literary works. Originally, in the Heian period (794–1185), *yamato-damashii* was used to distinguish native ideas and patterns of behavior from those of China, a nation much admired and emulated at the time. The first use of the term *yamato-damashii* appears in the 11th-century *Genji monogatari* (TALE OF GENJI). As Prince Genji is about to send his son Yūgiri to the imperial college after the coming-of-age ceremony, he gives his thoughts on education: "Even a man of noble birth is liable to ridicule if he lacks learning. Only when he has mastered Chinese learning will his *yamato-damashii* be manifested and esteemed in society." In this case, *yamato-damashii* is seen as the matrix and Chinese learning as a cultural accretion.

Another reference is found in the *Ōkagami* (ca 12th century). Fujiwara no Tokihira (871–909), the courtier responsible for SUGAWARA NO MICHIZANE's exile and generally vilified, is described by the author as being capable, talented, and endowed with a good measure of *yamato-damashii*. In a story in the KONJAKU MONOGATARI (ca 1120), *yamato-damashii* is equated with maturity and good sense. One Kiyohara no Yoshizumi, a man of high learning, is killed by a thief for stupid behavior—that is, for want of *yamato-damashii*. *Yamato-damashii* is seen as a requisite for professional advancement in *Chūgaishō*, the memoirs of the regent Fujiwara no Tadazane (1078–1162). Tadazane quotes the scholar ŌE NO MASAFUSA as saying that it was not absolutely necessary to have Chinese learning in order to be chancellor or regent, *yamato-damashii* alone being quite sufficient to rule the nation. In contrast, JIEN, the author of GUKANSHŌ (ca 1220), criticizes Fujiwara no Kimizane (1043–1107) for aspiring to the chancellorship when he is so clearly lacking in *yamato-damashii*, in other words, the mental qualifications indispensable to the holder of so important an office. Finally, in *Eihyakuryō waka*, a poetry anthology of the period of Northern and Southern Courts (1336–92), there is a poem that suggests that to understand the Chinese classics truly even a learned scholar must have *yamato-damashii*.

After this period there is no evidence of the use of the word until the latter part of the Edo period (1600–1868), when it was rediscovered by KOKUGAKU (National Learning) scholars. Once again, the term took on different meanings: MOTOORI NORINAGA (1730–1801) equated *yamato-damashii* with the feminine spirit *(onnagokoro)* that was the essence of the courtly literature of the Heian period and held that it should counter the sycophantic attitude of pro-Chinese Japanese Confucianists. His follower HIRATA ATSUTANE and others, however, reflecting the conditions of the time, made *yamato-damashii* synonymous with the militant idea of SONNŌ JŌI (Revere the Emperor, Expel the Barbarians). And it was in this sense that it was taken up enthusiastically by militarists and ultranationalists in the modern era and made the ideological cornerstone of public education.

SAITŌ Shōji

yamato-e

A term denoting Japanese-style painting. The word Yamato originally referred to the heartland of Japan, the region around Nara, the first permanent capital; the suffix *e* means pictures or paintings. It seems to have come into use in the mid-9th century when Japanese artists were beginning to produce works that differed at first in subject matter and, later, in style and format as well, from the paintings that had been produced under Chinese influence. Hence the term *yamato-e* came to be used in opposition to *kara-e* ("Chinese-style painting").

Though no examples of early *yamato-e* remain today, from the literature of the 9th, 10th, and 11th centuries we know that favorite themes centered on the passage of the seasons and the activities of the people in and around Heiankyō (now Kyōto), the capital from 794. The major categories into which this subject matter was divided are *shiki-e*, or paintings of the four seasons, *tsukinami-e*, or activities of the 12 months, and *meisho-e*, or pictures of famous places. *Meisho-e* seem to have been very similar to *shiki-e* in that the famous places depicted were those that were considered to be particularly beautiful at a certain time of the year: the Tatsuta River (Tatsutagawa) carrying the orange maple leaves of autumn on its blue waters, Mt. Yoshino (Yoshinoyama) covered by the pale pink blossoms of flowering cherry trees, and so on.

There was also a strong link between *yamato-e* and Japanese-style poetry, the 31-syllable WAKA, which became popular at about the same time. Often at the request of the imperial family or members of the nobility an artist would be asked to translate the content of a favorite poem into visual images to be painted on folding screens or sliding doors (see SCREEN AND WALL PAINTING). Poets also were frequently invited to compose a poem on the subject of a screen painting and add it as an inscription on the surface of the screen. Many of the themes of *meisho-e* were derived not from direct observation of the landscape, but rather from well-known poems.

Today the term *yamato-e* has taken on a much broader meaning and encompasses not only Japanese themes but also formats and styles of painting that are considered to be distinctively Japanese. The narrative EMAKIMONO (handscroll) is now treated as a prime example of *yamato-e*, as are the various styles of painting associated with it: the *tsukuri-e* or "made-up picture" style (in which colors are laid on thickly) of the GENJI MONOGATARI EMAKI, and the freer, more calligraphic manner of the SHIGISAN ENGI EMAKI. The term has even been applied to such works as the *Maple Leaf* sliding doors by HASEGAWA TŌHAKU in the Chishakuin in Kyōto and the screens painted by SŌTATSU.

The term *yamato-e* has been the subject of some controversy because, in its broadest sense, it should properly include every Japanese painting that is not a direct copy of a Chinese or Korean work, or in its most narrow meaning, only those works that show no influence from foreign sources. However, when used in a moderately limited fashion to denote paintings depicting typical Japanese themes such as the passage of the seasons or narratives derived from Japanese literature, *yamato-e* connotes those aspects of developed indigenous art that represent the core of Japanese aesthetic preferences, the heart of Japanese taste.

📖——Ienaga Saburō, *Painting in the Yamato Style*, tr John M. Shields (1973). Okudaira Hideo, *Narrative Picture Scrolls*, tr Elizabeth ten Grotenhuis, in vol 5 of *Arts of Japan* (1973).

Penelope E. MASON

Yamatogawa

River in Nara and Ōsaka prefectures, central Honshū, originating in the mountain Kaigahirayama and joined by numerous lesser streams in the Nara Basin, flowing into the Ōsaka Plain to empty into Ōsaka Bay at the border of the cities of Sakai and Ōsaka. The water is utilized for irrigation, as well as for drinking and industry by Sakai. Length: 71 km (44 mi).

Yamatohime, Princess

(Yamatohime no Mikoto). Daughter of the legendary emperor Suinin and aunt of the legendary prince YAMATOTAKERU. According to the traditional account of the founding of the ISE SHRINE, she was commanded by the sun goddess, AMATERASU ŌMIKAMI, to go to the river Isuzugawa in Ise (now part of Mie Prefecture), build a shrine, and dedicate herself to the worship of the goddess. The chronicle KOJIKI (712) relates that Prince Yamatotakeru, before embarking on his eastern expedition to subdue the EZO people, stopped at the shrine to pay his respects and received from his aunt a sacred sword that was later designated one of the three IMPERIAL REGALIA, the traditional symbols of imperial legitimacy. It is important to note that, in both of these legends, Princess Yamatohime is described in the context of her relationship to the ruling dynasty of the YAMATO COURT and its mythical progenetrix, Amaterasu Ōmikami. In modern times, some scholars have identified Yamatohime with the 3rd-century female ruler HIMIKO, mentioned in the late-3rd-century Chinese history WEI ZHI (Wei chih). KITAMURA Bunji

Yamato Kōriyama

City in northern Nara Prefecture, central Honshū. Toyotomi Hidenaga, the brother of the hegemon TOYOTOMI HIDEYOSHI, built a castle here in 1585. It came under the rule of the Yanagizawa family during the Edo period (1600–1868). It is a major center of goldfish breeding. There is an emerging electrical appliance industry. Attractions include the cherry blossoms at Kōriyama Castle, the garden at Jikōin, and the temple Kongōsenji. Pop: 81,262.

Yamato monogatari

(Tales of Yamato). One of the *uta monogatari* (poem tales; see MONOGATARI BUNGAKU), a genre that flourished during the Heian period (794–1185). In most printed editions of this work, there are 173 episodes of varying lengths and two long appended sections. A general characteristic of the poem tale is that it consists of a collection of anecdotes, each of which centers on one or more WAKA poems. These anecdotes are in some cases united by a central hero, but there is no such unity in *Yamato monogatari*.

The Yamato of the title probably refers to both the name of an ancient Japanese province and to Japan itself. The compiler-editor of the original text was in all probability a Heian courtier who took an interest in anecdotes about people at the court and the poems they composed; he was also familiar with old legends. It is fairly certain that the original text was revised shortly after 996, and that the work known today as *Yamato monogatari* is not the product of a single writer. A careful study of the official titles of the historical characters appearing in the first half of the work leads one to believe that the original text was completed sometime in 951 or 952 and that additions were made in subsequent years.

The original text of *Yamato monogatari* may be considered a product of the period halfway between the compilation of the *waka* anthology KOKINSHŪ (905) and the writing of the TALE OF GENJI (ca 1000). In the first half of the work, the episodes consist mainly of anecdotes about men and women who moved in court circles describing the circumstances under which they composed certain poems. The poems are the central elements of these anecdotes, which are generally very brief, the prose passages often no more than introductory notes to the poems. The prose passages in the latter half of the work are somewhat longer and far more interesting. A number of the episodes are based on ancient legends, and the writer is at greater pains to describe the emotions of the characters. There is a heavier emphasis on the story, with the poems playing a secondary role. One may venture to say that *Yamato monogatari* suggests the development of Japanese literature from a series of poems, accompanied by headnotes, to the great narrative works in Japanese prose with only occasional poems embellishing the text. This classic provides us with a picture of Heian society in the early 10th century; furthermore, it has been a source for a number of later works, ranging from Nō plays to works of the modern period. See also HEICHŪ MONOGATARI. *Mildred TAHARA*

Yamato sanzan

The Three Hills of Yamato viewed from a rise overlooking the Nara Basin. Unebiyama, celebrated for its graceful shape, is visible at center left, with Miminashiyama and Amanokaguyama to its left and right, respectively. The hills figure in the poetry of ancient Japan, most notably in a poem from the first book of the *Man'yōshū*.

Yamato period

The name of the period from ca 300 to 710. The period saw the consolidation of sovereign rule by the YAMATO COURT; the introduction of Buddhism from Korea; the regency of Prince SHŌTOKU and the beginning of conscious emulation of Chinese political institutions; and the TAIKA REFORM of 645. It was preceded by the Yayoi period (ca 300 BC–ca AD 300) and followed by the Nara Period (710–794). The Yamato period is also known among archaeologists as the KOFUN PERIOD, after the large KOFUN or mounded tombs that were built during this time.

yama torikabuto

Aconitum japonicum. Also called *torikabuto*. A perennial herb of the family Ranunculaceae, found in the wooded mountain areas of central northern Honshū and Hokkaidō. The plant has underground tubers and an erect stem which reaches a height of about 100 centimeters (39 in), with the upper part slightly bent. The leaves are alternate, have long petioles, are deeply split into 3–5 lobes, and have a glossy surface. In late autumn, numerous helmet-shaped bluish-purple flowers blossom in clusters that appear from the leaf axils. The tuber of the *yama torikabuto* contains a potent poison said to have been used by the AINU people to poison the tips of arrows for their bear-baiting festivals. Another species found growing wild in Japan is the *reijinsō (A. roczyanum),* similar in appearance to the *yama torikabuto* but with more slender stems. It reaches a height of about 50–100 centimeters (20–39 in) and has light purple blossoms which give the plant its name, since their shape resembles that of the headgear used by performers called *reijin* in traditional dances. The *hana torikabuto (A. chinense),* which originated in China, is cultivated in Japan and used as a cut flower because of its attractive bluish purple blossoms. *MATSUDA Osamu*

Yamato Sanzan

(The Three Hills of Yamato). Three hills in the city of Kashihara, Nara Prefecture, central Honshū: Unebiyama (199 m; 653 ft), Amanokaguyama (152 m; 499 ft), and Miminashiyama (140 m; 459 ft). The hills rise abruptly from the alluvial soil of the Nara Basin to form a triangle, each point approximately 3 km (2 mi) from the other; they are formed from igneous rocks. The three hills are mentioned in the MAN'YŌSHŪ, an 8th-century poetry anthology, and other ancient literature.

Yamato Takada

City in northwestern Nara Prefecture, central Honshū. A POST-STATION TOWN during the Edo period (1600–1868), it is now a producer of textiles, knitted goods, stockings, rubber, plastics, and foodstuffs. Pop: 61,713.

Yamatotakeru no Mikoto → Yamatotakeru, Prince

Yamatotakeru, Prince

(Yamatotakeru no Mikoto). Legendary hero of ancient Japan. Supposedly the son of the legendary 12th emperor KEIKŌ, Prince Yamatotakeru is said to have been responsible for extending the territory controlled by the YAMATO COURT through his subjugation of the aboriginal KUMASO in Kyūshū and the EZO people of northeastern Honshū. He is not thought to be a historical figure but rather the embodiment of the heroic acts of numerous warriors who fought for the Yamato court over the many years of its consolidation of power.

The story of Prince Yamatotakeru appears in the chronicles KOJIKI (completed in 712) and NIHON SHOKI (completed in 720). His original name was Ousu no Mikoto and he was also known as Yamato Oguna. (Some scholars believe that the name Ousu no Mikoto is connected with the *usu*, or hand mill, used to grind new grain during agricultural harvest rites such as the NIINAMESAI. The name Yamato Oguna is thought to mean "mysterious youth of Yamato.") In the account given in the *Nihon shoki*, he traveled at the age of 16 upon the order of the emperor Keikō to southern Kyūshū on a campaign to subdue the Kumaso and returned a conquering hero to the Yamato court. He also led campaigns against the Ezo in the Kantō area and is reported to have died from illness at the age of 30 in Nobono in what is now northwestern Mie Prefecture. (The *Kojiki* does not record these ages. It does, however, mention that his hair was braided at his temples, the traditional hair style for a youth of 15 or 16, when he went to subdue the Kumaso.) The name Yamatotakeru was bestowed on him by the defeated, dying chief of the Kumaso in honor of the heroism and military prowess of this man from Yamato.

There are considerable differences between the accounts in the *Kojiki* and *Nihon shoki* concerning Yamatotakeru, and these shed some light on the way this heroic tale developed, probably between the 5th and 7th centuries.

Subjugation of the Kumaso. In the *Kojiki* account Emperor Keikō is concerned about the violent behavior of his son and sends him off on a campaign against the Kumaso. The *Nihon shoki*, on the other hand, reports Emperor Keikō himself as having previously led an army to Kyūshū to suppress the Kumaso. In this account the Kumaso rise up again, and it is then that Yamatotakeru is sent to resubjugate them.

According to the *Kojiki*, when Yamatotakeru is about to leave on his subjugation campaign he receives women's clothing and a sword from his aunt YAMATOHIME, the custodial priestess at the ISE SHRINE. This section is not found in the *Nihon shoki*, although the latter does list the names of 54 of his followers, none of which are given in the *Kojiki*. The object of the campaign also differs in the two accounts. In the *Kojiki* Yamatotakeru subdues the brothers Kumasotakeru, while in the *Nihon shoki* Emperor Keikō had already suppressed the Kumasotakeru, and Yamatotakeru is sent to subjugate a leader called Kawakamitakeru.

There are also discrepancies in the scenes surrounding Yamatotakeru's triumphal return. In the *Kojiki* he suppresses an uprising by Izumotakeru in Izumo (modern Shimane Prefecture) on his way back. The *Nihon shoki* contains a suppression mission similar to this one but places it in the time of the earlier legendary emperor, SUJIN; in its account Yamatotakeru does not enter Izumo but rather returns to Yamato via Kibi (modern Okayama Prefecture) and Naniwa (present-day Ōsaka).

Subjugation of the Ezo. The *Kojiki* and the *Nihon shoki* also differ in their narratives of the Ezo subjugation. In the *Kojiki* Yamatotakeru, ordered on a mission to subdue the Ezo by his father Emperor Keikō, meets again with his aunt, Yamatohime, and expresses to her the fear that his father wishes him an early death. Yamatohime encourages him to proceed and gives him a sword and a bag containing a piece of flint. Nothing like this is found in the *Nihon shoki* account. Instead it tells us that his older brother, Ōusu no Mikoto (not to be confused with Ouso no Mikoto), was the one ordered to go on the mission and Yamatotakeru bravely sets out on the campaign when his brother shirks his duty. In the *Kojiki* account Yamatotakeru is sent off with a halberd made from the holly tree (a sacred tree reputed to drive away evil), whereas the *Nihon shoki* records the gifts as a hand ax and a broadax (both signs of a general).

The course and area of subjugation also differ considerably in the two chronicles. This area is given as the southern Kantō region in the *Kojiki*, while the *Nihon shoki* has Yamatotakeru advancing as far north as the southern Tōhoku region. The *Nihon shoki* thus shows the sovereignty of the Yamato court as extending over a larger area, thereby emphasizing the spread of its control more than the *Kojiki* does.

Other differences. There are also a number of differences between the two accounts in their telling of several traditional tales regarding Yamatotakeru. In the *Kojiki* the story of Yamatotakeru being beset by bandits on an open plain and threatened with death in a prairie fire is placed in Sagami (modern Kanagawa Prefecture). The victim of a surprise attack, he uses the sword from his aunt to cut down the grass around him and then uses the flint to set his own fire to drive off his attackers. The *Nihon shoki* sets this episode in Suruga (present-day Shizuoka Prefecture); although he still drives away the bandits by setting a fire, the *Nihon shoki* does not say that the flint was a gift from his aunt.

Similarly, the *Kojiki* and *Nihon shoki* give different settings for the episode in which Yamatotakeru cries out *"Azuma haya"* (Oh, my wife!) as he remembers his spouse Ototachibanahime, who had sacrificed herself by jumping into the sea (making herself an offering to the sea god) during a storm in Hashirimizu no Umi (the present-day Uraga Channel). The *Kojiki* records this utterance as taking place at Ashigara no Saka (the Ashigara Pass in the southwestern section of the present Kanagawa Prefecture), whereas the *Nihon shoki* places it at Usuhi no Saka (the Usui Pass along the border between Gumma and Nagano prefectures). As another example, the mountain god of Ibukiyama (a mountain along the border between Shiga and Gifu prefectures) takes the form of a boar in the *Kojiki* but that of a snake in the *Nihon shoki*.

Yamatotakeru's death. Thinking of his homeland, Yamato, Yamatotakeru dies from illness in Nobono. The manner in which this final scene takes place also differs in the two accounts. In the *Kojiki* Yamatotakeru composes four poems as he awaits his death, and he is known and loved by the Japanese as the author of a poem describing the beauty of Yamato, "the greatest of all nations, a truly beautiful land surrounded by mountains as though by a great green wall." The *Nihon shoki*, however, records this poem as having been composed by Emperor Keikō at the time of his campaign against the Kumaso.

Upon his death, Yamatotakeru's soul takes the form of a swan and flies away. But once again the course of that flight differs in the two legendary accounts.

Historical significance. The story of Yamatotakeru presents us with an archetypal hero figure, probably developed between the 5th and 7th centuries. The *Kojiki* account gives a fuller depiction of this ancient noble hero, whereas the *Nihon shoki* emphasizes the growing power of the Yamato state. The latter contains Confucian elements as well as the ideology of an absolute monarchy. Some theories hold that the tales about Yamatotakeru developed in connection with the Takerube (see BE), a military group established by the Yamato court.

The Yamatotakeru narrative is also worthy of attention as a work of literature, with the *Kojiki* having perhaps the greater literary value. Related legends can be found in works such as the FUDOKI, local histories written during the Nara period (710–794). See also HERO WORSHIP.

■——Ivan Morris, *The Nobility of Failure: Tragic Heroes in the History of Japan* (1975). Tōma Seita, *Yamatotakeru* (1958). Ueda Masaaki, *Yamatotakeru* (1960). Yoshii Iwao, *Yamatotakeru* (1978).

UEDA Masaaki

Yamawaki Tōyō (1704–1762)

Edo-period (1600–1868) physician of the classicist school of medicine (*koihō*) whose "trial and experimentation" doctrine played a substantial role in advancing premodern Japanese medicine. Native of Kyōto; original family name Shimizu. Adopted by Yamawaki Genshū, a court physician, to whose post he later succeeded.

On 30 March 1754 Yamawaki, following a suggestion of his former teacher GOTŌ KONZAN, performed Japan's first officially approved dissection of the human body at Rokkaku prison on the outskirts of Kyōto. Five years later, a record of the dissection containing four anatomical illustrations was published under the title *Zōshi*. This dissection took place 17 years earlier than the famous one prompting SUGITA GEMPAKU and his colleagues to translate a Dutch anatomy book. Yamawaki also reprinted a Chinese medical work of the Tang (T'ang) dynasty (618–907), the *Waitai mi yaofang*

(*Wai-t'ai mi yao-fang*, 24 vols) in 1746. His other writings include *Yōjuin isoku* (1751), *Saisei yogen*, and *Yōjuin hōkan*.

YAMADA Terutane

Yamazaki

District in the town of Ōyamazaki, southern Kyōto Prefecture, central Honshū. Since ancient times, the Yamazaki district has been a center of river and land transportation. In 1582 it was the site of an important battle between Toyotomi Hideyoshi and Akechi Mitsuhide. Now the district is a commuters' community for the cities of Kyōto, Ōsaka, and Kōbe. It is also a center for rail and land transportation.

Yamazaki Ansai (1619–1682)

Prominent Neo-Confucian scholar and philosopher of the early part of the Edo period (1600–1868), and the founder of Suiga Shintō (or SUIKA SHINTŌ), a syncretic combination of Ise Shintō (or WATARAI SHINTŌ) and YOSHIDA SHINTŌ theories with SHUSHIGAKU, the Neo-Confucian philosophy of Zhu Xi (Chu Hsi). Through his scholarship and teaching he exerted an immense influence, both direct and indirect, upon his contemporaries and thinkers of later periods.

Ansai's father was a *samurai* who had left the service of the lord of Himeji, moved to Kyōto, where Ansai was born, and barely supported his family by practicing acupuncture. As a child, Ansai showed great intelligence, and when he was about 10 years old his father sent him to the temple ENRYAKUJI on Mt. Hiei (Hieizan), the headquarters of the Tendai sect, to become a Buddhist priest. The following year he moved to MYŌSHINJI of the Rinzai Zen sect in Kyōto. Subsequently, at the age of 17, he went to a temple in Tosa Province (now Kōchi Prefecture). Since the latter part of the Muromachi period (1333–1568), Tosa had been a center of the Neo-Confucian studies known as NANGAKUHA ("Southern Learning"), and upon his arrival Ansai was immediately exposed to Neo-Confucianism. Ansai studied Confucian writings avidly with TANI JICHŪ, a leader of the Nangakuha school, and NONAKA KENZEN, the chief retainer of the Tosa domain, and began to question Buddhism.

According to Ansai's autobiography, the turning point of his career came at the age of 23 when he attended a lecture on the Confucian classic *The Doctrine of the Mean* (Ch: *Zhongyong* or *Chungyung*) given by Tani, which led him to abandon Buddhism and turn to the Neo-Confucian philosophy of Zhu Xi. This action displeased the lord of Tosa, and Ansai had to return to Kyōto. In 1646 he returned to secular life, and the following year he published the *Hekii* (Refutation of Heresies), in which he proclaimed his total acceptance of Zhu Xi's philosophy and denounced Buddhism. To Ansai, Zhu Xi was the true transmitter of Confucian philosophy, and for the rest of his life he dedicated himself to the propagation of the philosophy of the Zhu Xi school through teaching and publication of various texts with his commentaries. In 1655 he began to lecture on Shushigaku in Kyōto. His school, called Kimon, flourished in both Kyōto and Edo (now Tōkyō) and was said to have attracted 6,000 students during his lifetime, including ASAMI KEISAI, SATŌ NAOKATA, and MIYAKE SHŌSAI. He also won the favor of the senior shogunal adviser HOSHINA MASAYUKI, through whom he exerted some influence on the shogunate. Ansai was not an original Neo-Confucian thinker. His understanding of Zhu Xi's philosophy took the form of a rigorous moralism, with strong emphasis on the concept of TSUTSUSHIMI or self-restraint and the virtue of loyalty to one's lord. However, his *Bunkai hitsuroku* (Reading Notes) is probably one of the best introductions to the philosophy of the Zhu Xi school as it developed not only in China but also in Korea. Ansai especially esteemed and acknowledged his indebtedness to a Korean Neo-Confucian, Yi T'oegye (1501–70).

Soon after he left the Buddhist priesthood, Ansai engaged himself in the study of Shintō. Just as he regarded Zhu Xi's philosophy as the true way of China, Shintō to him was the way of Japan. He advocated, therefore, simultaneous study of Shintō and Confucianism *(shinju kengaku)*. Compared to his Neo-Confucian studies, regarding Shintō Ansai was more a systematic theorist and mystic. His Suiga Shintō, while synthesizing Ise and Yoshida Shintō theories, added a new dimension and philosophical depth by incorporating Neo-Confucian concepts. Its doctrines are highly esoteric. This combination of Neo-Confucian rationalism and Shintō nonrationalism caused a bitter controversy among his disciples, and some criticized him severely and left his school. In Suiga Shintō Ansai expressed strong nationalistic sentiments which he claimed to have learned from Zhu Xi. The impact of Ansai's Suiga Shintō on the

Meiji Restoration of 1868 should not be ignored; along with Fukko Shintō (RESTORATION SHINTŌ) of the National Learning (Kokugaku) school, it provided important ideological support for the leaders of the Restoration Movement.

■——Seki Giichirō, ed, *Yamazaki Ansai zenshū*, 2 vols (1937). Seki Giichirō, ed, *Zoku Yamazaki Ansai zenshū*, 3 vols (1937). Abe Yoshio, *Nihon Shushigaku to Chōsen* (1965). Okada Takehiko, "Yamazaki Ansai: Practical Learning as Personal Experience of Truth," tr Miyaji Hiroshi, in Wm. T. de Bary and I. Bloom, ed, *Principle and Practicality* (1979). Miyaji Hiroshi, "Yamazaki Ansai and the Formulation of Suiga Shintō," in *Actes du 29e Congrès Internationale des orientalistes*, Japon, vol 1 (1976). Taira Shigemichi, *Kinsei Nihon shisōshi kenkyū* (1969). Hiroshi MIYAJI

Yamazaki Baking Co, Ltd

(Yamazaki Seipan). Company engaged in the baking and selling of bread, as well as Japanese- and Western-style confectioneries. Established in 1948, it has bakeries and sales outlets throughout the country, through which a dominant 22 percent of the domestic market is maintained. Yamazaki is the country's largest bread-baking firm. Immediately after World War II, when there was a serious food shortage in Japan, it installed modern equipment in its bakeries and reduced costs through mass production. Supplying customers with fresh bread and utilizing a huge sales network totaling 22,900 retail stores, the firm grew rapidly. With overseas offices in New York, Paris, and Taipei, Yamazaki is affiliated with the National Biscuit Co of the United States, whose products it sells domestically. An affiliated firm, Kansai Yamazaki Co, Ltd, is the second largest company in the field in sales proceeds. Yamazaki has expanded in recent years into the soft drink and convenience store business. Sales totaled ¥172.6 billion (US $788.3 million) in 1981, of which 55 percent came from bread, 34 percent each from Japanese- and Western-style confectioneries, and 11 percent from other sources. The company was capitalized at ¥7 billion (US $32 million) in the same year. The head office is in Tōkyō.

Yamazaki, Battle of

(Yamazaki no Tatakai). Also known as the Battle of Tennōzan. Battle fought on 2 July 1582 (Tenshō 10.6.13) between the forces of TOYOTOMI HIDEYOSHI and AKECHI MITSUHIDE in the Yamazaki district near the town of Ōyamazaki on the border between Settsu and Yamashiro provinces (now parts of Ōsaka and Kyōto prefectures). Mitsuhide had assassinated the hegemon ODA NOBUNAGA in the HONNŌJI INCIDENT 11 days earlier while Hideyoshi was on a campaign against the powerful MŌRI FAMILY in Bitchū Province (now part of Okayama Prefecture). Hideyoshi, however, was able to disengage and march his troops with remarkable speed to the Ōsaka area, where he secured the support of Nobunaga's son Oda Nobutaka (1558–83) and *daimyō* such as Ikeda Tsuneoki (1536–84), Korezumi Gorozaemon (Niwa Nagahide; 1535–85), Nakagawa Kiyohide (d 1583), and TAKAYAMA UKON. In contrast, Mitsuhide's hoped-for allies HOSOKAWA YŪSAI and TSUTSUI JUNKEI failed to heed his call for assistance. Unprepared for a major encounter, Mitsuhide was also badly informed: when he finally moved to occupy the crucial high ground of Tennōzan on 1 July, he found it in the hands of Nakagawa's troops and withdrew to Shōryūji Castle (now the city of Nagaokakyō, Kyōto Prefecture); when he sallied forth again the next afternoon and drew up his 16,000 men along the Emmyōji River, he found himself threatened with encirclement by the three-pronged advance of Hideyoshi's 40,000-man army, spearheaded by Nakagawa and Takayama. Mitsuhide retreated to Shōryūji and fled the fort when it was surrounded, but was killed by marauding peasants; on 3 July, Shōryūji fell and Hideyoshi's victory was complete. The Battle of Yamazaki was the great unifier's first step to national hegemony.

George ELISON

Yamazaki Masakazu (1934–   )

One of the major playwrights of literary and philosophic importance writing in Japan in the post–World War II period. Brought up in Manchuria during World War II and educated in philosophy at Kyōto University, Yamazaki has maintained an interest in contemporary philosophical modes of thought that reveals itself in much of his work for the theater. His first important play, *Zeami* (1963), a recreation in modern psychological and poetic terms of the life of ZEAMI, the founder of the medieval Nō theater, was widely appreci-

Yanagawa

A group of tourists enjoys one of Yanagawa's popular attractions, boating along the creeks which thread the city.

ated in Japan and has since been produced in English and Italian versions. The subject matter of his plays ranges from contemporary Japan to incidents in Western history (his 1972 *Ō, Eroīzu!* is a dramatization of the relationship between the famous 12th-century French cleric Abélard and his student and lover Héloise) and Japanese history as well, notably in his 1973 *Sanetomo shuppan* (Sanetomo Sets Sail), which has also been produced in English. In addition to his dramas, Yamazaki is well known for his writings on aesthetics, history, and such literary figures as MORI ŌGAI.

J. T. RIMER

Yamazaki Naomasa (1870–1929)

Geographer. Born in Kōchi Prefecture. After graduating from Tōkyō University, he went to Germany and Austria to study modern geography. He founded departments of geography at Tōkyō University and Tōkyō Bunrika University (later Tōkyō University of Education; now Tsukuba University). Yamazaki was particularly interested in geological formations and proposed theories concerning the former existence of glaciers in Japan and the fault structure of the Japanese archipelago. With Satō Denzō he edited the 10-volume *Dai Nihon chishi* (1903–15).

Yamazaki Sōkan (1465?–1553?)

Renga (linked verse; see RENGA AND HAIKAI) and HAIKU poet of the Muromachi period (1333–1568). Popularly called the father of haiku for having compiled the earliest haiku anthology, *Inu tsukubashū* (1540s?), whose title, "Doggerel Tsukubashū," parodied those of the *renga* anthologies TSUKUBASHŪ and SHINSEN TSUKUBASHŪ. The title also gave indication of the comic and even licentious quality of its verses in contrast to serious, orthodox *renga*. This anthology signaled the contemporary reaction against the complicated rules and belletristic vocabulary of *renga*, and was to influence the radical DANRIN SCHOOL of haiku. Of Sōkan himself little is known. He is said to have been a *samurai* in the service of the shōgun Ashikaga Yoshihisa, upon whose death he became a monk and retired to Yamazaki in Kyōto, whence his name.

Yame

City in southern Fukuoka Prefecture, Kyūshū. Primarily a farming area, it produces rice, tea, mandarin oranges, grapes, and pears; stock raising and dairy farming are active. There are also cottage industries producing handmade Japanese paper *(washi)*, Buddhist altars, paper lanterns, carp streamers *(koinobori)*, and stone lanterns. The Iwatoyama tomb, one of the Yame tomb cluster, which dates from the Kofun period (ca 300–710), is located here. Pop: 39,408.

Yame tomb cluster

Cluster of mounded tombs (KOFUN) near the city of Yame, Fukuoka Prefecture; located on a low plateau extending 2 to 3 kilometers (1.2 to 1.9 mi) from east to west. The cluster comprises 11 keyhole-shaped and some 60 round tombs that are believed to have been built in the late 5th and early 6th centuries for Tsukushi no Kuni no

Miyatsuko Iwai, a local chieftain who rebelled against the YAMATO COURT (ca 4th century–mid-7th century) in 527 (see IWAI, REBELLION OF), and his kinsmen. Several tombs are adorned with stone figures, and many of the burial chambers in the tombs are decorated with paintings or carvings.

—— Mutō Naoji and Kagamiyama Takeshi, "Chikugo Ichijō Sekijin'yama kofun," *Fukuoka Ken shiseki meishō tennen kinembutsu chōsa hōkokusho* 12 (1935).

ABE Gihei

Yamizo Mountains

(Yamizo Sanchi). Mountain range running north to south in northwestern Ibaraki Prefecture, central Honshū. The highest peak is Yamizosan (1,022 m; 3,352 ft) in the north. The northern part of the mountains, known for hot spring spas and beautiful gorges, is part of Oku Kuji Prefectural Natural Park. Tsukubasan, which marks the southern end of the Yamizo Mountains, is an important tourist attraction in Ibaraki and part of Suigō-Tsukuba Quasi-National Park.

Yanagawa

City in southwestern Fukuoka Prefecture, Kyūshū; at the mouth of the river Chikugogawa. It first developed as a castle town. An extensive network of creeks draws water from the river to irrigate farmland. Rice and rushes are grown. There is an active farm machinery industry. The poet KITAHARA HAKUSHŪ was born here. Pop: 45,587.

Yanagawa Seigan (1789–1858)

Confucianist and poet of the latter part of the Edo period (1600–1868); known for his brilliant composition of *kanshi* (poems in Chinese; see POETRY AND PROSE IN CHINESE). Real name Yamagawa Mōi. Born in the province of Mino (now part of Gifu Prefecture), Seigan went to Edo (now Tōkyō) in 1807 where he studied with the Confucian scholar YAMAMOTO HOKUZAN. A habitual wanderer in his early life, he spent much time traveling around the country, all the while composing poetry. Becoming renowned for his verse in the elevated Tang (T'ang) style, in 1832 he finally settled in Edo and opened a school called the Gyokuchi Ginsha, which attracted a considerable number of pupils. Drawn to the Wang Yangming school (see YŌMEIGAKU) of Confucianism, which stressed theory translated into action, he was closely associated in Edo and later in Kyōto, where he moved in 1846, with loyalists of the proimperial movement, a number of whom, like the noted philosopher SAKUMA SHŌZAN, studied *kanshi* under him. His wife, with whom he had an especially happy marriage and who was his constant traveling companion, was also known as an accomplished *kanshi* poet; she wrote under the pen name Kōran. Two pupils of his who achieved a measure of distinction as *kanshi* poets were Mori Shuntō (1818–88) and ŌNUMA CHINZAN. Seigan's chief collection of poetry was his *Seiganshū* (1831–37).

Yanagawa Shunsan (1832–1870)

Late-Edo-period journalist and scholar of WESTERN LEARNING (Yōgaku). Born in Nagoya, he studied Dutch science and English and earned a high reputation in Edo (now Tōkyō) for his writings on Western Learning. He entered the field of journalism in 1863 when he was ordered by shogunate officials to submit summaries of articles concerned with Japan in English-language newspapers. In 1867 he began publishing the magazine *Seiyō zasshi*, which introduced Western things to Japan. The *Chūgai shimbun*, which he established in 1868, was the most complete newspaper of the time and became the prototype for later newspapers.

ARIYAMA Teruo

yanagi → willows

Yanagida Izumi (1894–1969)

Scholar of Japanese and English literature. Born in Aomori Prefecture. Graduate of Waseda University in English literature. As an editor for a publishing firm, he translated many works of Western writers, including Whitman, Thoreau, and Carlyle. He helped found the Society for the Study of Meiji Civilization (Meiji Bunka Kenkyūkai) in 1924 and edited the 24-volume *Meiji bunka zenshū* (1927–30), the first important collection of materials for the study of the culture of the Meiji period (1868–1912). One of the first to insist on a systematic research methodology based on primary sources in the study of the Meiji period, he exerted a profound influence on the next generation of scholars. His principal works include *Seiji shōsetsu kenkyū* (3 vols, 1935–39), a study of early Meiji political novels; *Tayama Katai no bungaku* (2 vols, 1957–58), a critical biography of novelist TAYAMA KATAI; and *Meiji shoki no bungaku shisō* (2 vols, 1965), a study of literary trends early in the Meiji period.

Yanagihara Byakuren (1885–1967)

Waka poet and social activist. Born in Tōkyō, the daughter of a count; real name Yanagihara Akiko. She began her study of traditional poetry with SASAKI NOBUTSUNA. After divorcing her first husband because of his declining health, she married Itō Den'emon (1860–1947), a Kyūshū mining magnate. In 1921 she left him to marry a young social reformer, Miyazaki Ryūsuke (1892–1971), the son of MIYAZAKI TŌTEN, and joined her new husband in the labor movement. She attracted notice for the passionate style of her poetry in the anthologies *Fumie* (1915, Trodden Images) and *Kichō no kage* (1919, Screen Shadows) and for her autobiographical novel, *Ibara no mi* (1928, The Fruit of Thorns). Having lost her son in World War II, she became active in postwar peace movements.

Yanagi Muneyoshi (1889–1961)

Also known as Yanagi Sōetsu. Art historian and leader of the Japanese folk-craft movement *(mingei undō)*. He studied at Gakushūin (Peers' School) and was a member of the so-called SHIRAKABA SCHOOL. While still a student he joined SHIGA NAOYA and others in starting the magazine *Shirakaba,* in which Yanagi published a number of his articles on European painting and sculpture. He graduated from Tōkyō University in 1913. Having learned of the work of William Blake from the British ceramist Bernard LEACH, at age 25 he published a study on Blake's mysticism and artistic achievements.

In 1916 he made his first trip to Korea and was deeply impressed by its artistic tradition. In the field of politics, he took a stand in support of Korean independence from Japanese colonial rule. In 1923 he published *Kami ni tsuite* (On Godhood), reflections about his search for a religious consciousness transcending the modern sense of self. In 1924 Yanagi founded the Museum of Korean Art in Seoul.

While studying the decorative arts of Korea and Japan he became aware of a beauty, heretofore ignored, inherent in implements used in daily life; he subsequently developed a strong interest in the creative capacities of the common people. As a means of categorizing this quality of beauty he adopted a new term, *mingei* (folk crafts). In 1926 Yanagi, TOMIMOTO KENKICHI, HAMADA SHŌJI, and KAWAI KANJIRŌ published *Nihon mingei bijutsukan setsuritsu shuisho* (Prospectus to Establish a Japan Folk-Craft Museum). This led to the collection of folk-craft objects and the development of a movement for the appreciation of the decorative arts deriving from folk tradition. In 1929 he delivered a series of lectures on oriental art at Harvard University and sponsored an exhibition of ŌTSU-E, a type of folk painting of the Edo period (1600–1868), in Boston. He founded the journal *Kōgei* (Decorative Arts) in 1931.

Yanagi publicized his discoveries of works of folk art collected throughout Japan and fostered the development of a group of artists who became known as the folk-craft school *(mingeiha)*. In 1936, with the aid of Ōhara Magosaburō and others, he established the JAPAN FOLKCRAFT MUSEUM at Komaba in Tōkyō. Three years later he became deeply involved in movements working to maintain the integrity of regional and minority cultures, and he became critical of government policy concerning the natives of Hokkaidō (see AINU). He also advocated preserving the dialect of Okinawa in the face of efforts by prefectural officials to encourage the adoption of standard Japanese. After World War II Yanagi returned to religious studies and the subject of Buddhist art. His major writings are collected in *Yanagi Muneyoshi senshū,* 10 vols (Shunjūsha, 1954–55).

📖 ——Kumakura Isao, *Mingei no hakken* (1978). Mizuo Hiroshi, *Yanagi Muneyoshi* (1978). Tsurumi Shunsuke, *Yanagi Muneyoshi* (1976). KUMAKURA Isao

Yanagisawa Kien (1704–1758)

Also known as Ryū Rikyō. Pioneer of literati (BUNJINGA) painting. Born in the Kōriyama domain in the province of Yamato (now Nara Prefecture), the second son of a high-ranking *samurai* who served the Yanagisawa family. Kien studied not only painting but also calligraphy, poetry, philosophy, medicine, Buddhism, and the tea ceremony. In brushwork he was at first a pupil of a KANŌ SCHOOL master, but at age 12 he decided to follow the great Chinese *bunjinga* masters.

In his choice Kien was doubtless influenced by OGYŪ SORAI, the great Confucian scholar, who served the Yanagisawa family. Also, through his domainal lord, who was a patron of the ŌBAKU SECT of Buddhism, Kien developed ties with Ōbaku Zen monks, who probably introduced him to Chinese paintings, books, and wood-block prints. He often followed the style of the Chinese academic bird-and-flower painter SHEN NANPIN (Shen Nan-p'in), who had come to Nagasaki in 1731 and transmitted his decorative and semirealistic methods to Japanese pupils. As a result, many of Kien's paintings are carefully detailed and strongly colored flower studies, not at all literati in spirit.

Kien was especially skilled in painting bamboo; his *Finger-Painted Bamboo* is noted for its freedom of composition and technique. His calligraphy is also Chinese in style, showing the influence of Dong Qichang (Tung Ch'i-ch'ang) in running script and other late-Ming calligraphers in clerical script. As teacher and adviser to such *bunjinga* artists as IKE NO TAIGA and his wife IKE NO GYOKURAN, Kien helped foster an interest in Chinese brushwork that was to affect the painting of the Edo period (1600–1868) profoundly.
Stephen ADDISS

Yanagisawa Yoshiyasu (1658–1714)

Statesman of the Edo period (1600–1868). The son of a minor retainer in the service of TOKUGAWA TSUNAYOSHI when the latter was *daimyō* of the Tatebayashi domain (now part of Gumma Prefecture). Yoshiyasu began his career as a page in attendance on his father's lord. With Tsunayoshi's succession as shōgun in 1680, Yoshiyasu's fortunes began to rise. In 1688 he was made a daimyō, receiving a stipend of 10,000 *koku* (see KOKUDAKA) and appointed chamberlain (SOBAYŌNIN) to the shōgun, a post created by Tsunayoshi to bypass the established channels of shogunate power and extend the personal authority of the shōgun. As Tsunayoshi's favorite and trusted adviser, Yoshiyasu's power and influence steadily increased. By 1694 his stipend had been increased to 70,000 *koku,* and he was made the daimyō of Kawagoe domain (now part of Saitama Prefecture) and given an official status equal to members of the senior council (RŌJŪ). In 1701 he was granted the use of the surname Matsudaira, the original surname of the Tokugawa, and in 1704 was granted 150,000 *koku* in the domain of Kōfu (now part of Yamanashi Prefecture), thitherto held only by members of the main line of the Tokugawa family. However, Yoshiyasu's influence was totally dependent upon his personal connection to Tsunayoshi and was not translatable into a bureaucratic power base. Upon the death of Tsunayoshi in 1709, Yoshiyasu retired from official shogunate service and lived in seclusion until his death five years later.

Yanagisawa Yoshiyasu was the first and most remarkable of a series of shogunal retainers who rose from obscurity to positions of power as shogunal favorites. His career established the pattern of an alliance between shōgun and personal attendants against the entrenched interests of the shogunate bureaucracy and the high-ranking hereditary vassals of the shogunate. After Tsunayoshi's death, Yoshiyasu was often charged with responsibility for encouraging the shōgun in extravagant outlays on buildings, processions, and eccentricities such as the notorious "edicts on compassion to living things" (SHŌRUI AWAREMI NO REI), which required the people to go to extraordinary lengths in showing respect for animals. In popular gossip he was painted as an evil and corrupt man who enticed the shōgun to indulge in sensual pleasures and who schemed to have his wife sleep with the shōgun with the intent of foisting his own son upon the shōgun as the latter's heir. Though without historic credence, this image of Yoshiyasu reflected the general dissatisfaction with Tsunayoshi's eccentric dictatorship, of which the inordinate favor shown to Yoshiyasu was a part.

The real figure of Yanagisawa Yoshiyasu, modern scholarship suggests, was far from the ambitious villain of popular lore—a timid person who carried out faithfully the wishes of Tsunayoshi and his mother, Keishō In. Obeying Tsunayoshi's desire to promote Confucianism as well as Buddhism, Yoshiyasu took into his service and used as advisers the Confucian scholars OGYŪ SORAI and HOSOI KŌTAKU, thus contributing to the conversion of the shogunate's policy from the early military rule to the mid-Edo period emphasis on civil government.
Kate NAKAI

Yanagita Kunio

Yanagita Kunio in front of his home in April 1957.

Yanagita Kunio (1875–1962)

Founder of Japanese FOLKLORE STUDIES *(minzokugaku)*. A scholar and poet who also worked as a journalist and government bureaucrat, Yanagita's extensive research and writing established the framework for other folklore research in Japan. Born in Hyōgo Prefecture, he was the sixth son of Matsuoka Misao, a scholar, teacher, and Shintō priest. Following his graduation in law at Tōkyō University in 1900, he married into the influential family of Yanagita Naohei and took on the Yanagita name. He worked as a government bureaucrat from 1900–1919, first in the Ministry of Agriculture and Commerce and later in the Legislative Bureau and the Imperial Household Ministry. He worked as a journalist for the *Asahi shimbun* from 1919 to 1930. An avid traveler and prolific writer (over 100 books and 1,000 articles), he contributed many articles to journals of the latter part of the Meiji period (1868–1912). His classic *Tōno monogatari* was published in 1910.

Yanagita gave full attention to developing the discipline of folklore from around 1930. If there is a unifying theme to his work, it is the search for the elements of tradition that explain Japan's distinctive national character. Yanagita did not focus on any one person, village, or region; his unit of analysis was Japan. His attempt to collect and systematize the vast amount of information available on the popular tradition has given his work an impersonal, abstract quality. In Yanagita's work an emphasis on shared customs and habits replaced the historical specificity and structural analysis found in the writings of historians and sociologists. Yanagita's selected works are contained in the 36-volume *Teihon Yanagita Kunio shū*.

Yanagita's folklore methodology combined many approaches. His reading of history and his interest in the nativistic KOKUGAKU (National Learning) tradition guided his study of Japanese folk religion. Foreign folklore research, especially British folklore studies, supplied the framework for his own research. Extensive travel and field work contributed to the vast body of information that has become the cornerstone of later folklore studies.

The central problem in Japanese folklore studies since 1960 has been how to differentiate academic folklore research from the personality and style of its founder. Yanagita was learned but no theoretician. He was schooled in the ways of literary elegance and was never comfortable with the purely academic style that was demanded for the establishment of folklore as a scientific discipline. His terminology remained vague and his research projects were often left incomplete.

In the two decades since his death, Yanagita has become a legend. His folklore disciples look to him as their mentor and the

systematizer of Japanese folklore. Conservative nationalists speak with praise of his devotion to the study of folk religion. Progressives, attracted to Yanagita's love for the common man, portray him as a rebel and anarchist. Writers and poets find his literary style an inspiration to their own creativity. The average person faced with social and environmental disruption is inspired by Yanagita's views on nature and the family.

——Kamishima Jirō, *Yanagita Kunio kenkyū* (1973). Ronald A. Morse, *Kindaika e no chōsen: Yanagita Kunio no isan* (1977). Nakamura Akira, *Yanagita Kunio no shisō* (1977).   Ronald A. MORSE

Yanai

City in southeastern Yamaguchi Prefecture, western Honshū. Long known for the production of soy sauce and the fabric *yanaijima,* it has been rapidly industrialized since 1960 with the construction of factories by Hitachi, Ltd. The Chausuyama tomb, dating from the Kofun period (ca 300–710), is located here. Pop: 38,234.

Yanaihara Tadao (1893–1961)

Economist and educator. Born in Ehime Prefecture. A disciple of UCHIMURA KANZŌ, founder of the Nonchurch (MUKYŌKAI) Christian movement, he was well known for his courageous stand against Japanese militarism during the period 1931–45 (from the MANCHURIAN INCIDENT until Japan's unconditional surrender).

Yanaihara was the son of a doctor and studied at the most prestigious institutions in Japan, namely Daiichi Kōtō Gakkō (First Higher School) and Tōkyō University. After a brief career in a private firm, he was recalled to his alma mater and was soon sent to Europe for further study. Upon his return, he occupied the chair of Colonial Policy in the Faculty of Economics at Tōkyō University. He was very productive as a scholar and published such substantial books as *Shokumin oyobi shokumin seisaku* (1927, Colonization and Colonial Policy). He insisted on making scientific, objective studies of the Japanese colonies (see COLONIALISM), and he refused to make colonial studies a handmaiden to colonial administration. His academic detachment and his keen sense of justice based on his faith made him increasingly critical of Japan's official policies from the Manchurian Incident on; he gradually became a target of attack from right-wing scholars backed by militarists. He was pressured into resigning from Tōkyō University in December 1937, a few months after the outbreak of war with China. After his resignation he lived as a prophetlike figure throughout the war years, teaching the Bible to a group of Nonchurch Christians and doggedly publishing his one-man magazine *Kashin* (Good News) despite official interference. He served as the president of Tōkyō University from 1951 to 1957 and was widely acknowledged as a major intellectual and spiritual leader. See also PACIFISM.

——Yanaihara Tadao, *Yanaihara Tadao zenshū* (Iwanami Shoten, 1963–65). Fujita Wakao, *Yanaihara Tadao* (1967). Nishimura Hideo, *Yanaihara Tadao* (1975). Yūzō Ōta, "Yanaihara Tadao, 1893–1961: The Man as a Pacifist," *Kyōyō gakka kiyō* 6 (March 1974).   Yūzō ŌTA

Yan'an (Yenan) Government

The Chinese communist government from the mid-1930s to 1949, the period of resistance against Japan and the ensuing period of civil war with the Chinese Guomindang (Kuomintang; Nationalist Party).

Forced out of their Jiangxi (Kiangsi) base by the Guomindang in late 1934, the Chinese communists arrived in northern Shaanxi (Shensi) in October 1935 after the epic Long March. At the end of 1936, Yan'an, a town in northern Shaanxi, was declared the capital of the Chinese Soviet Republic, with jurisdiction over a remote, infertile, and undeveloped area covering contiguous sections of Shaanxi, Gansu (Kansu), and Ningxia (Ningsia) provinces.

The Chinese communists claimed that their choice of the Shaanxi–Gansu–Ningxia border region as a base was predicated on their determination to confront Japanese aggression in North China. As the Guomindang retreated before the invading Japanese after the outbreak of the SINO-JAPANESE WAR OF 1937–1945, communist forces moved into the countryside and organized guerrilla resistance against Japan, expanding into North and Central China. From April 1940 until the end of the war NOSAKA SANZŌ, exiled leader of the Japan Communist Party, was in Yan'an, indoctrinating captured Japanese soldiers and engaging in other anti-Japanese activities.

The success of the Chinese communists in rousing the peasants to a guerrilla war against Japan and the implementation of an agrarian policy benefiting the peasants contributed to a shift in Chinese popular perception of political legitimacy: the communists and not the Guomindang were now seen as the defenders of China. The Chinese communists defeated the Guomindang in the civil war that followed Japan's surrender, and on 1 October 1949 the People's Republic of China was proclaimed at the new capital, Beijing (Peking). ■——Chalmers A. Johnson, *Peasant Nationalism and Communist Power: The Emergence of Revolutionary China, 1937–1945* (1962). Mark Selden, *The Yenan Way in Revolutionary China* (1971). Edgar Snow, *Red Star Over China* (rev ed, 1968).

Yanmar Diesel Engine Co, Ltd

Machinery maker which produces engines for agricultural machines and for ships. It also produces construction equipment and small-sized electric generators. The company is the largest producer of small-sized diesel engines in Japan. Established in 1912 by Yamaoka Magokichi, it was the first company in the world to develop and commercialize the small-sized diesel engine. The engine was widely used on agricultural machines and fishing boats. After World War II the company expanded its operations to include the production of small-sized tractors, tilling and planting machines for rice fields, and also maritime leisure equipment. Joint venture subsidiary firms in Brazil, Malaysia, Indonesia, the Philippines, and Thailand manufacture and sell the company's products. The company has been managed by the Yamaoka family since its inception. Sales for the fiscal year ending March 1982 totaled ¥189.5 billion (US $787 million), and capitalization stood at ¥1.2 billion (US $4.9 million) in the same year. The head office is in Ōsaka.

Yano Fumio → Yano Ryūkei

Yano Ryūkei (1850–1931)

Writer and politician. Real name Yano Fumio. Born in what is now Ōita Prefecture; graduate of Keiō University. After working briefly for the newspaper YŪBIN HŌCHI SHIMBUN, in 1878 he joined the government along with ŌKUMA SHIGENOBU, the liberal politician who was his patron. When Ōkuma was ousted in the POLITICAL CRISIS OF 1881, Yano left his post also. In 1882 he returned to the *Yūbin hōchi shimbun* as its president and made the paper the organ of the RIKKEN KAISHINTŌ (Constitutional Reform Party), which Ōkuma founded in opposition to the government in power. In 1883–84, with the intention of enlightening the public on the virtues of the proposed constitutional government, he published the political novel, *Keikoku bidan* (A Noble Tale of Statesmanship; see SEIJI SHŌSETSU). A romanticized version of the struggle of ancient Thebes to throw off Spartan domination, it inspired many young readers with notions of freedom and independence. Many of them, it was said, memorized the speeches of Epaminondas, the hero. In his later years Yano turned his attention to social problems and wrote for the newspaper *Ōsaka mainichi shimbun*. His works include the novels *Ukishiro monogatari* (1890, The Floating Fortress) and *Shin shakai* (1902, The New Society).

Yano Tsuneta (1865–1951)

Businessman. Born in Okayama Prefecture. Yano attended Tōkyō University but left in 1889 before completing his studies. He served in the Ministry of Agriculture and Commerce in 1898 and drafted the Insurance Business Law (Hokengyō Hō) in 1900. Yano left the ministry in 1902, established Daiichi Seimei, the first mutual insurance firm in Japan (see DAI-ICHI MUTUAL LIFE INSURANCE CO), and guided the company to success. All other life insurance companies followed Daiichi Seimei's lead and became mutual insurance corporations after World War II.   YUI Tsunehiko

Yao

City in central Ōsaka Prefecture, central Honshū; a satellite city of Ōsaka. Traditional products are toothbrushes and thread. Several medieval temples, including Jōkōji, as well as Yayoi period (ca 300 BC–ca AD 300) tumuli *(kofun)* are located here. Pop: 272,706.

Yarigatake

Mountain on the border of Nagano and Gifu prefectures, central Honshū. It is the second highest peak in the Hida Mountains and the fourth highest mountain in Japan. The summit is crowned by a spear-shaped rocky peak, and on the slopes near the top are ice-scoured areas. The trails linking it with TSUBAKURODAKE and HOTAKADAKE are popular with climbers. Height: 3,180 m (10,430 ft).

Yasaka Shrine

(Yasaka Jinja). A Shintō shrine in Higashiyama Ward, Kyōto; also called Gionsha and Gion Tenjin; dedicated to the deity SUSANOO NO MIKOTO, his consort, and eight of their children. Although conflicting traditions exist regarding its origin, there is general agreement that the shrine was originally sacred to Gozu Tennō, a deity who protected Gion Shōja (Skt: Jetavana-vihāra), a monastery in India in which the Buddha frequently resided. By the 10th century, Gionsha had become one of the most popular shrines in Kyōto and was believed to be particularly efficacious in pacifying vengeful spirits (GORYŌ), protecting warriors, bringing prosperity, and averting illness. According to the prevailing notions of Buddhist-Shintō syncretism, the Buddhist deity Gozu was identified with the native Japanese deity Susanoo no Mikoto. The shrine's vicinity gradually developed into a commercial area and brothel district during the medieval and premodern periods. The main sanctuary of the shrine, known for its Gion-style architecture (see SHINTŌ ARCHITECTURE), dates from 1654. The official name of the shrine was changed to the present non-Buddhist designation in 1871. It has many offshoot shrines throughout the country. A major festival of Kyōto, the GION FESTIVAL, is held at the shrine for approximately a month in July. See also HONJI SUIJAKU.   *Stanley WEINSTEIN*

Yasakayahama

Rocky coastal area between the towns of Kainan and Mugi, southeastern Tokushima Prefecture, Shikoku. Located on the Pacific Ocean, it is included in Muroto–Anan Coast Quasi-National Park. It was a difficult stretch on the highway Tosa Kaidō in former days, but today a Japanese National Railways line and a state highway run along the coast. Length: 10 km (6 mi).

Yasato

Town in central Ibaraki Prefecture, central Honshū; on the eastern slopes of the mountain Tsukubasan. The principal activity is farming, mainly vegetables and fruits. The Magnetic Observatory of the Meteorological Agency is located here. Pop: 28,316.

Yashajin Pass

(Yashajin Tōge). Located in western Yamanashi Prefecture, central Honshū, at the northern end of the Akaishi Mountains. The pass is celebrated for its spectacular natural scenery and panoramic views of SHIRANE SANZAN and other mountains of the Southern Alps National Park. Altitude: 1,770 m (5,806 ft).

Yashica Co, Ltd

A manufacturer of medium-priced cameras, the Yashica Co was established in 1949. With its successful mass production and sales of double-lens reflex cameras, the company was a pioneer in the popularization of the camera. In 1983 it merged with Kyō Ceramic Co, Ltd, a manufacturer of ceramic products for the electronics industry. Yashica has manufacturing subsidiaries in Hong Kong and Brazil and nine overseas sales companies including ones in the United States, West Germany, and Canada. Sales for the fiscal year ending March 1982 totaled ¥22.6 billion (US $93.9 million), with the export ratio at 66.4 percent. The company was capitalized at ¥1.2 billion (US $5 million) in the same year. The head office is in Tōkyō.

Yashima

Formerly an island, now connected to the mainland, jutting into the Inland Sea, northeast of the city of Takamatsu, Kagawa Prefecture, Shikoku. It is a mesa-type plateau covered with pine trees. A historic and scenic spot, it was the site of many battles during the war between the Minamoto and the Taira families in 1185. Its summit commands a magnificent view of the Inland Sea. It is part of the Inland Sea National Park. Elevation: 292 m (958 ft).

Yashio

City in southeastern Saitama Prefecture, central Honshū. Formerly a farming area, it is now a residential suburb of Tōkyō, with textile, machine, and metal industries. Pop: 62,734.

Yashiro Hirokata (1758–1841)

KOKUGAKU (National Learning) scholar of the latter part of the Edo period (1600–1868). Born in Edo (now Tōkyō), the son of a direct shogunate vassal or "houseman" (gokenin). He assisted his teacher, the renowned scholar HANAWA HOKIICHI, in compiling a collection of historical and literary documents known as the GUNSHO RUIJŪ. Famous for his calligraphy, he was promoted to the position of scribe (yūhitsu) in the service of the shogunate. In 1817 he began compiling the Shokoku fūzoku toijō kotae (Answers to Questionnaires on Customs in All Areas). With the aid of Ishihara Masaakira (d 1821) and other scholars, he sent out questionnaires to scholars in various feudal domains. These forms solicited information concerning customs related to weddings, funerals, house-raising celebrations, various types of performers, and similar topics. It is not known exactly to whom the questionnaires were distributed or how many replies were received. The 20 or so surviving replies, fragmentary and irregular in content, suggest that the survey was not very successful, yet it still provides valuable information on Edo-period customs. His other main works include the Kokon yōrankō (1842), an encyclopedic work on Japan and China of nearly 600 sections (maki), incomplete at the time of his death. He was also known for his private collection of around 50,000 volumes of Japanese and Chinese classics which, unfortunately, were destroyed during World War II.　　　　　　　　　　　　　　　Ōtō Tokihiko

Yashiro Seiichi (1927–　　)

Playwright. Born in Tōkyō; graduated from Waseda University with a major in French literature. In 1949 he joined the Bungakuza (Literary Theater), a theater company organized by KISHIDA KUNIO. He won critical acclaim for his Kiiro to momoiro no yūgata (1959), a serious play about young people and conflict in postwar Japan. Recurring themes in his work are the problems of love, individual ego, and faith. In 1968 Yashiro published a play titled Yoake ni kieta (1968, They Vanished at Dawn), an open testament of his conversion to Catholicism. Among his best recent work is a series of three entertaining plays about famous UKIYO-E artists, including Sharaku kō (1972, Sharaku), for which he won the 1972 Yomiuri Literary Prize, and Hokusai manga (1973; tr Hokusai Sketchbook, 1979).

Yaskawa Electric Mfg Co, Ltd

(Yasukawa Denki Seisakusho). Company engaged in the manufacture and sales of electric machinery and equipment. Established in 1915, it is well known for the production of electric motors. Some 93 percent of the blast furnaces of Japan's steel industry use the company's control systems. It has technical tie-ups with a Swiss company, a French company, an English company, and two American firms, overseas incorporated firms in the United States, Brazil, and West Germany, and several offices abroad. The export ratio for its products was 20.9 percent in 1981. Future plans call for the further development of its multipurpose and heavy electric machinery products and electricity conservation equipment. Sales for the fiscal year ending March 1982 totaled ¥92.8 billion (US $385.5 million), and it was capitalized at ¥9 billion (US $37.4 million). The head office is located in Kita Kyūshū, Fukuoka Prefecture.

Yasuda

Business enterprise founded in 1880, when YASUDA ZENJIRŌ opened the Yasuda Bank; major financial combine (ZAIBATSU) of the pre-World War II era, whose holding company was dissolved in 1945 by the OCCUPATION authorities; enterprise grouping (KEIRETSU) of the postwar period (now known as the Fuyō Group). Unlike the MITSUI, MITSUBISHI, and SUMITOMO zaibatsu, the Yasuda zaibatsu's activities were centered predominantly in finance, branching out only

marginally into light industry, warehousing, real estate, and heavy industry.

From his beginnings in the 1860s as a streetcorner money changer in Edo (now Tōkyō), Yasuda Zenjirō rapidly built a financial empire on the basis of his bank. In 1887 he set up the Yasuda Hozensha as a holding company to protect his family's wealth and, with a loan from the Yasuda Bank, increased its capital to ¥1,000,-000. In 1893 he converted the Yasuda Bank into a limited partnership and in 1894 reorganized the Yasuda Hozensha along lines prescribed by the new COMMERCIAL CODE. In 1899 he set up Yasuda Shōji, Ltd, a trading company capitalized at ¥1,000,000, which absorbed sulphur mines, nail factories, warehouses, and other concerns that had previously been under his personal management. The following year he made Yasuda Bank a limited liability corporation, increasing its capital to ¥2,000,000. In 1905 he revised the bylaws of the Hozensha and placed it in control of both the bank and the trading company. Both became joint-stock companies in 1919, the bank with capital of ¥10,000,000 and the trading company with ¥1,000,000. The Hozensha, its capital now at ¥10,000,000, became their principal stockholder. At this time Yasuda subsidiaries numbered 17 banks and 16 companies, with Yasuda Hozensha acting as their holding company.

Despite its lack of direct subsidiaries in industry, the Yasuda Hozensha had considerable investments in the industrial Asano zaibatsu. Yasuda Zenjirō made these loans almost unconditionally, because of his friendship with ASANO SŌICHIRŌ, the founder of the combine. The Yasuda zaibatsu also maintained close ties with the group of companies and industries built up by MORI NOBUTERU.

After Zenjirō's death in 1921, YŪKI TOYOTARŌ was brought in from the Bank of Japan to manage the holding company. In 1923 he effected the merger of 11 banks into the Yasuda Bank, raising its capital to ¥150,000,000 and its deposits to ¥542,000,000, more than any other Japanese bank. In 1929 leadership of the zaibatsu passed to Mori Kōzō (1873–1944), who saw the bank safely through the financial and political crises of the 1930s. Mori retired in 1941 and was succeeded by Rear Admiral Takei Daisuke (1887–1972), who headed the Yasuda Bank and served as a director of the Yasuda Hozensha during World War II.

In October 1945, when the Occupation authorities called for ZAIBATSU DISSOLUTION, Yasuda-affiliated banks and companies included such famous concerns as MARUBENI CORPORATION. Numbering 30 in all, they had total assets of ¥480,000,000. If two groups closely allied to the Yasuda zaibatsu, Oki Electric and Oki Electric Stock, are added to the list, the number of its subsidiaries rises to 59 and their total assets to ¥517,800,000.

Since the 1950s former Yasuda subsidiaries have been loosely affiliated as an enterprise group; its most notable members include FUJI BANK, LTD; YASUDA TRUST & BANKING CO, LTD; and YASUDA FIRE & MARINE INSURANCE CO, LTD.

■——Johannes Hirschmeier and Tsunehiko Yui, The Development of Japanese Business, 1600–1973 (1975). Mochikabu Kaisha Seiri Iinkai, Nihon zaibatsu to sono kaitai: Shiryō (1950), has a comprehensive bibliography. William W. Lockwood, The Economic Development of Japan (1954). Mission on Japanese Combines, Report to the Department of State and the War Department, pt 1 (1946).
Eleanor M. HADLEY

Yasuda Fire & Marine Insurance Co, Ltd

(Yasuda Kasai Kaijō Hoken). One of Japan's leading firms in the sale of types of insurance other than life insurance. The forerunner of the firm was a fire insurance company established in 1888, the first of its kind in Japan. In 1893 it became a company within the former Yasuda zaibatsu, and took its current name after a merger with two other firms in 1944. Yasuda Fire & Marine Insurance belongs to the Fuyō group (former Yasuda zaibatsu). The company deals chiefly in automobile insurance. It does not issue life insurance. With 23 overseas offices, 7 subsidiary firms, and approximately 350 claim agents, the company plans to expand its international operations in the future. In the fiscal year ending March 1982 net insurance premiums totaled ¥375.7 billion (US $1.6 billion), of which optional automobile insurance accounted for 38.8 percent, fire insurance 18.2 percent, compulsory automobile liability insurance 14.5 percent, marine and transportation insurance 8.6 percent, and other types of insurance 19.9 percent. Total assets amounted to ¥945.1 billion (US $3.9 billion) and the company was capitalized at ¥30 billion (US $124.6 million). The head office is located in Tōkyō.

Yasuda Trust & Banking Co, Ltd

(Yasuda Shintaku Ginkō). Yasuda Trust & Banking Co was established in 1925 as one of the enterprises of the former Yasuda *zaibatsu* and ranks highly in the trust-banking field in Japan. The company engages in ordinary banking, but specializes as a trust bank in long- and middle-term financing, annuity trusts, real estate, and securities. It belongs to the Fuyō group, successor to the Yasuda *zaibatsu*. It has three overseas branches and two firms incorporated overseas. In the fiscal year ending March 1982 total available funds amounted to ¥6.2 trillion (US $25.8 billion), and the company was capitalized at ¥30 billion (US $124.6 million) in the same year. The head office is in Tōkyō.

Yasuda Yojūrō (1910–1981)

Literary critic. Born in Nara Prefecture. Graduate of Tōkyō University. While still a student, he helped publish *Kogito* in 1932, a coterie magazine of German-influenced romantic poets that emerged to replace the declining so-called proletarian literary movement. He organized a new coterie, the NIHON RŌMANHA, in 1935 and became the leading literary critic to advocate the reawakening of the Japanese national spirit and the traditional appreciation of beauty, thus contributing directly to the rise of ultranationalism in the late 1930s and 1940s. His principal works include the critical essays *Nippon no hashi* (1936), *Kindai no shūen* (1941), *Bi no yōgo* (1941), and *Go-Toba In* (1942).

Yasuda Yukihiko (1884–1978)

Japanese-style painter; well known for his elegant but simple treatment of Japanese historical themes in the YAMATO-E style. Real name Yasuda Shinzaburō. Born in Tōkyō, he began at age 15 to study the traditional TOSA SCHOOL style under Kobori Tomone (1864–1931) at the Tōkyō Bijutsu Gakkō (now Tōkyō University of Fine Arts and Music). The influential art scholar and critic OKAKURA KAKUZŌ recognized Yasuda's ability and sent him to Nara to study classical Japanese art. Yasuda contracted tuberculosis in his twenties, but this did not prevent him from participating in the reorganized JAPAN FINE ARTS ACADEMY from 1914. He taught at his alma mater from 1944 to 1951. In 1948 he received the Order of Culture and became a member of the JAPAN ART ACADEMY (Nihon Geijutsuin). In addition to his paintings on historical themes, he is noted for his portraits and bird-and-flower paintings. He has collected Chinese antique pottery and done research on the Edo-period Zen poet-priest RYŌKAN. Yasuda's concern with composition, his strong but subtle lines, and the total effect of refinement and purity in his paintings have set him apart from his contemporaries.

Yasuda Zenjirō (1838–1921)

Financier and founder of the YASUDA financial and industrial combine. Born in what is now Toyama Prefecture, as a youth he went to Edo (now Tōkyō), where he worked as apprentice to a wholesale toy merchant and later to a retailer of dried fish. He then became a money changer and within a few years had established a small but lucrative business. Cunning and industrious, Yasuda took advantage of the political and social disorders following the Meiji Restoration of 1868 and reaped huge profits by buying up the shaky paper currency (DAJŌKAN SATSU) of the time at a discount and selling it back to the government for full value. He soon acquired a virtual monopoly over money changing in Tōkyō, thanks to special privileges granted by the government, which relied heavily on rich merchant houses to finance much of its early economic activity (see SEISHŌ). Beginning with the Third National Bank (Daisan Kokuritsu Ginkō) in 1876, Yasuda founded a series of banks, most notably the Yasuda Bank (see FUJI BANK, LTD), and subsequently diversified into railways, insurance, and other enterprises. He came to control dozens of companies, including the YASUDA FIRE & MARINE INSURANCE CO, LTD, which together formed one of Japan's largest ZAIBATSU. Famous for his parsimony, Yasuda nonetheless contributed to the construction of a public hall in Hibiya Park in Tōkyō and donated the Yasuda Lecture Hall at Tōkyō University. He was assassinated in 1921 by an ultranationalist when he refused a request for a donation.

Yasugawa

River in Shiga Prefecture, central Honshū, originating in the Suzuka Mountains and emptying into Lake Biwa. Deltas are well developed along the lower reaches and yield large rice crops; the Yasugawa Dam for irrigation is located on the upper reaches. Length: 41 km (25 mi).

Yasugi

City in eastern Shimane Prefecture, western Honshū. During the 16th century Yasugi flourished as a port for shipping iron made from ore mined from the nearby Chūgoku Mountains. It later became a post-station town on the San'indō highway. The construction of a steel mill in 1899 led to the establishment of numerous subcontracting plants. Farm products include pears and bamboo shoots. Attractions are Zuikōsan Kiyomizudera, a medieval temple set in a grove of ancient trees, and Saginoyu Hot Spring. Pop: 32,661.

Yasuhara Teishitsu (1610–1673)

Haikai (see HAIKU) poet. Real name Yasuhara Masaakira. A paper merchant from Kyōto, he was a disciple of MATSUNAGA TEITOKU, the founder of the Teimon school of *haikai*. He became Teitoku's official successor at the age of 41. Though unquestionably devoted to the tradition of Teitoku, he created friction among his fellow disciples through his somewhat overbearing criticism of their works. He is best remembered as the compiler of the comprehensive Teimon anthology *Gyokukaishū* (1656), and as the author of a pioneering study on dialects, *Katakoto* (1650).

Yasui Sokken (1799–1876)

Confucian scholar of the Edo period (1600–1868). Born in the Obi domain (now part of Miyazaki Prefecture). Sokken studied in Ōsaka with the Confucian scholar Shinozaki Shōchiku (1781–1851) and at the SHŌHEIKŌ, the shogunate academy of Confucian studies in Edo (now Tōkyō). He taught at the Obi domain school and later at the Shōheikō. His interests included astronomy, calendar making, and the West. When Commodore Matthew PERRY's expedition threatened Japan's self-imposed seclusion in 1853, Sokken urged military preparedness in a work entitled *Kaibō shigi* (1852, A Discussion of Coastal Defense). After the overthrow of the Tokugawa shogunate in 1867, he devoted himself to writing. Although he lectured on the official Zhu Xi (Chu Hsi) doctrine (SHUSHIGAKU) as a professor at the Shōheikō, Sokken leaned toward the earlier interpretation of the classics before Shushigaku. His works include *Rongo shūsetsu* (1872), a commentary on the Confucian *Analects*.

Yasui Sōtarō (1888–1955)

Western-style painter. Born in Kyōto, Yasui studied painting at the Kansai Bijutsuin (Kansai Art School) under ASAI CHŪ. From 1907 to 1914 he studied in Paris and was taught by Jean-Paul Laurens at the Académie Julian. During this period he was strongly influenced by Pissarro and Cézanne. On his return to Japan, he became a member of Nikakai, a major Western-style painting (YŌGA) organization. After a hiatus of several years because of illness, he established himself as one of the most successful Western-style painters of his generation. His style reflected contemporary European trends, and he painted mainly still lifes, landscapes, and portraits. He became a member of the Imperial Fine Arts Academy (Teikoku Bijutsuin) in 1935 and helped to found the artist group Issuikai in 1936. Yasui taught at the Tōkyō Bijutsu Gakkō (now Tōkyō University of Fine Arts and Music) from 1944 to 1952 and was awarded the Order of Culture on his retirement.

Yasui Takuma (1909–)

Economist. Born in Ōsaka Prefecture. After graduating from Tōkyō University in 1931, Yasui taught at his alma mater and became an associate professor in 1939. In 1944 he became a professor at Tōhoku University. He moved to Ōsaka University in 1965 and became head of the university's Social and Economic Research Institute. He later became professor at the International Christian University. He also served as chairman of the Theoretical Economics and Econometrics Association, succeeding NAKAYAMA ICHIRŌ. In 1971 Yasui was the first economist to receive the Order of Cul-

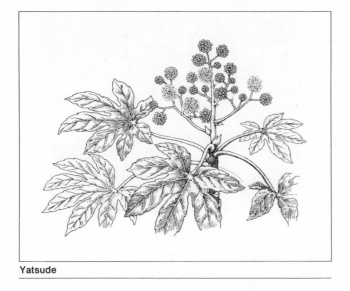

Yatsude

ating all those who had died in the campaigns to reestablish imperial rule. To emphasize the importance of the new shrine, an imperial prince was appointed chief priest. In 1879 the Shōkonsha was renamed Yasukuni Jinja (Shrine for Establishing Peace in the Empire). The shrine became the symbolic head shrine for prefectural *shōkonsha* (these were redesignated *gokoku jinja* in 1939). Services are held on 22 April and 18 October. Ties between the imperial family and the shrine have been exceptionally close, as can be seen by the emperor's periodic visits to the shrine. For the spring and autumn memorial services and on the occasion of certain special rites such as those of new group enshrinements *(gōshi)* of war dead, the emperor dispatches an emissary *(chokushi)* as his personal representative.

Before the end of World War II the shrine was used by the military to promote patriotic and nationalistic sentiments. After Japan's defeat in 1945 the government was compelled, first by the Occupation authorities and after 1947 by the new constitution, to terminate all support for Yasukuni Shrine, which was converted into a private religious organization. In the mid-1950s the Liberal Democratic Party, the Bereaved Families Association (Nihon Izokukai), and other conservative groups launched a movement to provide government support for Yasukuni. Since 1969 such a bill has been submitted almost yearly to the Diet but has not passed because of intense opposition from the Socialist and Communist parties, powerful Buddhist organizations, Christian groups, and prominent intellectuals, who see any state support for Yasukuni as a threat to religious freedom. The Yasukuni controversy flared up again in 1979, when Prime Minister Ōhira, accompanied by several members of his cabinet, paid a "private visit" to the shrine during the spring memorial services even though it had just been learned that General TŌJŌ HIDEKI (1884–1948) and six other wartime leaders who had been hanged by the Allied Powers as "war criminals" had been collectively enshrined there several months earlier. See also STATE SHINTŌ.   *Stanley* WEINSTEIN

ture. Yasui contributed greatly toward the mathematical elaboration of Léon Walras's general equilibrium analysis and its amplification into dynamic stabilization theory. Yasui's works on economics include *Kinkō bunseki no kihon mondai* (1955, Basic Problems of Equilibrium Analysis) and *Yasui Takuma chosakushū*, 3 vols (1970–71, Collected Works of Yasui Takuma).   *Yamada Katsumi*

Yasui Tetsu (1870–1945)

Educator; Japan's first woman college president. Born in Tōkyō into a former *samurai* family. Graduating in 1890 from the Women's Higher Normal School (now Ochanomizu University), she began her teaching career there. In 1897 she went to England for three years of study and was baptized a Christian soon after her return to Japan. From 1904 to 1907 she worked in Bangkok, Thailand, where she helped to start the Queen's School. She took up teaching again in Japan at such government-sponsored institutions as the Peers' School. In 1918 she took the post of dean at the newly founded mission-sponsored TŌKYŌ WOMEN'S CHRISTIAN UNIVERSITY and subsequently served as its president from 1924 until 1940. Yasui emphasized the development of character and individual responsibility among the students, even when the university was severely criticized because a few of its students joined leftist organizations during the 1930s.

Yasukawa Daigorō (1886–1976)

Business executive. Son of Yasukawa Keiichirō, a well-known coal mine developer. Born in Fukuoka Prefecture; graduated from Tōkyō University. Yasukawa established YASKAWA ELECTRIC MFG CO, LTD (Yasukawa Denki Seisakusho), in 1915 with his father and elder brother, and started to manufacture motors. He became company president in 1936. He also served for a time as director of the Coal Agency after World War II, became the first director of Japan's ATOMIC ENERGY RESEARCH INSTITUTE in 1956, and devoted himself to the development of atomic energy in Japan. Yasukawa was chairman of the organizing committee of the Tōkyō Olympic Games in 1964.   *Kobayakawa Yōichi*

Yasukuni Shrine

(Yasukuni Jinja). Shintō shrine in the Kudan district of Chiyoda Ward, Tōkyō, dedicated to the spirits of the approximately 2,400,000 persons who died in Japan's various wars since 1853, both civil and foreign. The origins of the shrine go back to 1868, when Prince Arisugawa Taruhito (ARISUGAWA NO MIYA TARUHITO) conducted a memorial service *(shōkonsai)* in Edo Castle for those who fell in the imperial cause during the expedition that he led from Kyōto. A similar ceremony was held shortly thereafter at the Katō Parade Grounds in Kyōto to commemorate those who had died in the struggle against the Tokugawa shogunate (1603–1867). In accordance with the wishes of Emperor Meiji (r 1867–1912), a shrine designated Shōkonsha (Shrine for Inviting the Spirits) was established in 1869 at the top of Kudan slope in present-day Chiyoda Ward, Tōkyō, vener-

Yasumi Toshio (1903–   )

Screenwriter. Born in Ōsaka. Known for two outstanding films that depict manners and customs in Ōsaka: *Meoto zenzai* (1955, Marital Relations), and *Neko to Shōzō to futari no onna* (1956, A Cat, Shōzō, and Two Women), both directed by TOYODA SHIRŌ. Yasumi became a screenwriter after first working as a municipal employee, a magazine staff member, and a translator. During World War II he wrote screenplays to heighten war morale: *Kessen no ōzora e* (1943, Toward a Decisive Battle in the Sky), directed by Watanabe Kunio; *Asagiri gunka* (1943, War Song of the Morning Mist), directed by Ishida Tamizō; and *Ato ni tsuzuku o shinzu* (1945, They Will Follow), also directed by Watanabe. After the war, however, Yasumi made a complete turnabout and wrote screenplays such as *Minshū no teki* (1946, Enemy of the People), directed by IMAI TADASHI, a film that exposed the illicit activities of business combines (ZAIBATSU) during World War II, and *Sensō to heiwa* (1947, War and Peace), a full-scale antiwar picture directed by YAMAMOTO SATSUO and Kamei Fumio. At the same time, Yasumi continued to write screenplays affirming the war, like *Senkan Yamato* (1953, Battleship Yamato), directed by Abe Yutaka. Other screenplays he wrote are *Banka* (1957, Dirge; directed by GOSHO HEINOSUKE) and *Yoshino no tōzoku* (1955, Yoshino Bandits; directed by Ōsone Tatsuyasu), an historical film based on Schiller's *The Robbers* and set in Japan's Muromachi period (1333–1568).   *Itasaka Tsuyoshi*

Yasuoka Shōtarō (1920–   )

Novelist. Born in Kōchi Prefecture. Studied at Keiō University. Emerging as a writer in the post-World War II literary wave, he won the 1953 Akutagawa Prize for his two short stories "Inki na tanoshimi" and "Warui nakama" (both 1953). In 1959 his novelette of the same year *Umibe no kōkei* received the Noma Prize. He wrote in the autobiographical style of the *watakushi shōsetsu* or I-NOVEL and is known for his somewhat self-deprecating tone. With a sharp sense of irony, he also criticizes others and society in general. Other works include the novels *Maku ga orite kara* (1967), *Tsuki wa higashi ni* (1970–71), and an account of his travels in the United States, *Amerika kanjō ryokō* (1962).

Yatabe Ryōkichi (1851–1899)

Botanist. Son of a doctor in Nirayama (now in Shizuoka Prefecture). He studied botany at Cornell University. Upon returning to Japan, he contributed to the establishment of modern botany in Japan as director of the Tōkyō Education Museum (now the National Science Museum), as a professor at Tōkyō University, and as director of the KOISHIKAWA BOTANIC GARDEN. He founded the Tōkyō Biological Society in cooperation with the American zoologist E. S. MORSE and also participated in the founding of the Tōkyō Botanical Society. He was an advocate of the use of the Roman alphabet for writing Japanese and a poet in the "new style" verse *(shintaishi)* of the Meiji period. SUZUKI Zenji

Yatomi

Town in southwestern Aichi Prefecture, central Honshū. The predominantly agricultural area is fast becoming a residential town for commuters to nearby Nagoya. Goldfish and Java sparrows *(shiro bunchō)* are bred here. Pop: 30,801.

yatsude

Fatsia japonica. An evergreen shrub of the ginseng family (Araliaceae), indigenous to coastal woods in Shikoku, Kyūshū, and central and western Honshū. It is also widely cultivated as a garden plant. The stems, which reach a height of 2–3 meters (7–10 ft), grow in clusters and have a thick pith. Alternate leaves 20–40 centimeters (8–16 in) in diameter grow from the tops of the stems and are a shiny dark green. The name *yatsude* literally means "eight-handed" and is derived from the leaves' eight-lobed palmate shape, although some leaves have seven or nine lobes instead of eight. Each lobe is serrated, and pointed at the tip. The genus name, *Fatsia,* has its origin in the native Japanese name. The young leaves emerge in late autumn or early spring and are covered with light brown hairs. The blossoms, which appear in large terminal clusters in late autumn, have white petals with a slight yellow tint. The fruit is round and ripens to black or dark blue.

Because *yatsude* serves as a shade plant, it is commonly found in Japanese gardens and exported to China, Europe, and America. Several ornamental varieties having white or yellow mottled foliage have been developed. Tea made of the dried leaves, which are rich in a kind of saponin, is used to help clear the throat of mucus. The recently popular horticultural species *Fatshedera lizei* is an intergeneric hybrid of *yatsude* and *Hedera helix* (English ivy). See photo on preceding page. MATSUDA Osamu

Yatsugatake

Group of volcanoes on the border of Nagano and Yamanashi prefectures, central Honshū. Composed of pyroxene andesite and conglomerate rock, the group consists of eight peaks. The highest is Akadake (2,899 m; 9,509 ft). The foothills, less than 1,500 m (4,920 ft) in height, form vast plateaus where farms and resort areas have developed. The area, known for its large variety of alpine flora, comprises one of the sight-seeing centers of Yatsugatake-Chūshin Kōgen Quasi-National Park.

Yatsushiro

City in central Kumamoto Prefecture, Kyūshū. It developed in the Edo period (1600–1868) as a castle town. Cement, paper, pulp, and *sake* industries are active. *Igusa* (rushes) for making the outer covering for floor mats *(tatami)* are grown locally. The sea near Yatsushiro is known for what the Japanese call *shiranui,* an eerie glow created by bioluminescent fish. Hinagu Hot Spring also attracts visitors. Pop: 108,194.

Yatsushiro Sea

(Yatsushiro Kai). Also known as the Shiranui Sea. Formerly called Yatsushiro Bay (Yatsushiro Wan). Inlet of the East China Sea between the Amakusa Islands and the southwestern coast of Kumamoto Prefecture, Kyūshū. Land reclamation has long been extensively practiced in the northern part. Principal activities are shellfish and laver *(nori)* culture and fishing for sardines and prawns. Area: approximately 650 sq km (251 sq mi); deepest point: approximately 50 m (164 ft).

Yawata

City in southern Kyōto Prefecture, central Honshū; on the river Yodogawa. It first developed as a shrine town around the IWASHIMIZU HACHIMAN SHRINE. The principal activity is farming, the main

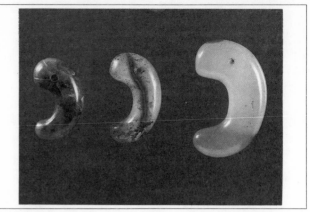

Yayoi culture

Magatama from a 4th-century mounded tomb. Jadeite (left) and agate. Length of right bead 4.9 cm. Kumano Shrine, Saitama Prefecture.

Yayoi culture

Three burial jars *(kamekan)* excavated from the Uryūdō site in Ōsaka Prefecture. Thought to have been used for the bodies of children, these were capped with stones or smaller vessels and collectively deposited in an unmarked pit. Earthenware. Heights (left to right) 43.5 cm, 76.0 cm, 56.0 cm. Middle Yayoi period. Kyōiku Iin Kai, Higashi Ōsaka.

products being vegetables, tea, and fruit. Rapid urbanization has led to a significant decline in the farming population. Pop: 64,882.

Yawatahama

City in western Ehime Prefecture, Shikoku. Situated on the Uwa Sea, it is a base for trawler fishing. Seafood processing and textiles are its main industries. Mandarin oranges are grown on the slopes of nearby mountains. Pop: 43,825.

Yawata Iron and Steel Works

(Yawata Seitetsujo). Japan's largest steel mill; established, with a budget of ¥4,090,000, by the government in Yawata Mura (now part of the city of Kita Kyūshū), Fukuoka Prefecture, in 1896, as part of the country's program to strengthen itself militarily and industrially (FUKOKU KYŌHEI). The project was placed under the jurisdiction of the Ministry of Agriculture and Commerce (Nōshōmushō), which invited German engineers to help build the mill with the Western technology of the day. Construction expenses were mainly covered by public bonds and by the indemnity paid by China after the SINO-JAPANESE WAR OF 1894–1895. When the mill began operations in 1901, it employed 2,283 workers and 1,691 miners; projected annual production was set at 60,000 metric tons (about 66,000 short tons), but by 1934 the mill produced 1,400,000 metric tons (about 1,540,000 short tons) of pig iron and 1,680,000 metric tons (about 1,850,000 short tons) of steel ingots. In 1940 it produced

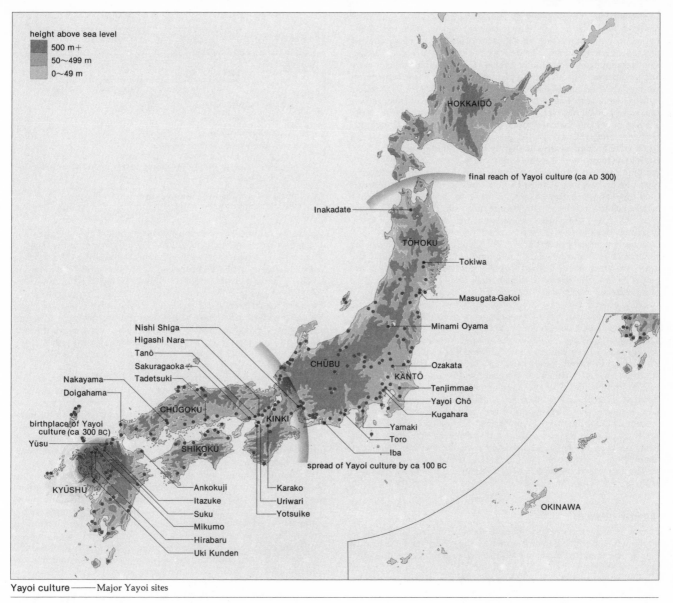

height above sea level
500 m+
50~499 m
0~49 m

HOKKAIDŌ

final reach of Yayoi culture (ca AD 300)

Inakadate

TŌHOKU

Tokiwa

Masugata-Gakoi

Minami Oyama

Nishi Shiga
Higashi Nara
Tanō
Sakuragaoka
Tadetsuki
Nakayama
Doigahama

CHŪBU

Ozakata
KANTŌ
Tenjimmae
Yayoi Chō
Kugahara

CHŪGOKU

KINKI

Yamaki
Toro
Iba

birthplace of Yayoi
culture (ca 300 BC)
Yūsu

SHIKOKU

spread of Yayoi culture by ca 100 BC

Ankokuji
Itazuke
Suku
Mikumo
Hirabaru
Uki Kunden

Karako
Uriwari
Yotsuike

KYŪSHŪ

OKINAWA

Yayoi culture —— Major Yayoi sites

1,682,000 metric tons (about 1,854,000 short tons) of pig iron, 2,382,-000 metric tons (about 2,625,000 short tons) of steel ingots, and 1,927,000 metric tons (about 2,124,000 short tons) of rolled steel. Iron ore was imported mainly from the Daye (Ta-yeh) mines in Hubei (Hupeh) Province, China, and the Unyul mines in Korea. The mill concentrated on producing armaments and railway equipment and thus played a major role in meeting Japan's expanding military needs. In 1934 the mill merged with five private companies to form the Nippon Seitetsu (Nippon Steel Co). After World War II the company was separated into the Yawata Seitetsu and Fuji Seitetsu companies by the OCCUPATION authorities. In 1970 the two merged to form the NIPPON STEEL CORPORATION.

Yayoi culture

The culture of the Yayoi period (ca 300 BC–ca AD 300); it is distinguished from the preceding JŌMON CULTURE by irrigated rice cultivation and the use of bronze and iron artifacts. There was considerable contact with China and Korea during this period, and it is supposed that these technological innovations, which spread northward from Kyūshū, were made under continental stimuli. Social stratification developed among the populace, which lived in small communities, and by the Late Yayoi period (ca 100–ca 300) Japan was divided into a number of small political units (kuni) centering on regional chieftains.

Technological Advances —— Some chipped stone tools—arrowheads, axes, and small knife-like blades (see STONE TOOLS)—of the

Jōmon culture continued to be used by the Yayoi people. Stone axes and adzes of the Yayoi period, however, were mostly polished and very large; in addition to chopping and cutting, some were used to till the soil. A polished blade (ishibōchō) was developed for reaping rice. Other new polished-stone tools included columnar chisels and flat plane blades; these were used for making wooden objects such as hoes and spades, weaving implements, containers, and utensils (see TORO SITE). Some wooden bowls from the KARAKO SITE are known to have been turned on a lathe (rokuro). YAYOI POTTERY consisted mainly of long-necked jars, wide-mouthed pots, deep basins, and pedestaled bowls. These utilitarian vessels bore simple geometric designs and were probably produced by regional specialists. In contrast to the Jōmon people, the Yayoi people knew how to smelt iron and forge simple implements; containers, weapons, and farming and craft tools have been found in abundance alongside stone and wooden utensils. Some items, particularly BRONZE MIRRORS, were obtained from the continent, but by the Late Yayoi, the Japanese themselves were making bronze mirrors, bronze bells (DŌTAKU), and BRONZE WEAPONS. Sandstone molds for casting these objects have been found in both northern Kyūshū and the Kinai (Kyōto-Ōsaka-Nara) region. Techniques were also developed for producing jasper and jade magatama (see BEADS, ANCIENT); molds for pouring glass magatama and round beads have also been found.

Food, Clothing, and Housing —— Cloth woven from flax and paper-mulberry fibers was the basic clothing material. Men wrapped lengths of cloth around their bodies, while women cut slits in the cloths and slipped them over their heads. Both men and women wore *magatama* beads strung into necklaces and bracelets and rings made of shells or bronze. Great changes of diet occurred in the transition from a hunting and gathering society to one primarily dependent on rice. Paddy fields were enclosed by dikes and irrigation techniques were gradually refined. Crops such as millet, beans, and gourds were grown to supplement the diet. Most settlements were established on coastal terraces and plains or along large rivers. Villages were surrounded by ditches for protection or drainage (see IBA SITE). Dwellings (see PIT HOUSES) were simple structures, with earthen floors and thatched roofs, built closely together. Communal granaries and wells completed the village facilities, and the paddy fields were located nearby in slightly lower, moister areas.

Belief Systems —— It is fair to assume that the beliefs of the agricultural Yayoi society differed greatly from those of the Jōmon society. The archaeological record offers evidence of religious festivals honoring various deities. Again, unlike on the continent, where they filled a utilitarian purpose, the bronze bells, spearheads, and daggers seem to have been used exclusively for ceremonial purposes. Bronze mirrors were also used as ritual objects. Divination was carried out by searing deer bones. The Yayoi people developed the practice of secondary burial. Some time after the initial burial, the bones were exhumed, washed, possibly painted with red ocher, and placed in jars; the jars were then buried, often collectively, in large pits, some of which were surrounded by moats. The custom of burying objects with the dead also developed during this period; mirrors, beads, and bronze weapons have been discovered in dolmen burials (see PREHISTORIC BURIALS).

Late Yayoi Society —— Much of our information on Late Yayoi society comes from contemporary Chinese histories such as the WEI ZHI (*Wei chih;* covering the period 220–265). They describe a highly stratified society in which wealthy landholders ruled the multitudes of common people. The *Wei zhi* mentions a kingdom called YAMATAI that controlled some 30 other "countries," each ruled by a chieftain; it relates that markets flourished, taxes were collected, and a system of punishments was prescribed for malefactors. Thus we know that the society was fairly complex and well organized. Moreover, political, economic, and military specialization was vigorously developing—a change that would seem to presage the society of the succeeding KOFUN PERIOD. See the section on the Yayoi period in HISTORY OF JAPAN: prehistory.
                                                                SAITŌ Tadashi

Yayoi period

(Yayoi *jidai*). A prehistoric period, dated from about 300 BC to about AD 300, during which wet-rice agriculture and the use of bronze and iron first appeared in Japan; so called because of certain characteristic pottery discovered in the Yayoi section of Bunkyō Ward, Tōkyō, in 1884. It was preceded by the JŌMON PERIOD (ca 10,000 BC–ca 300 BC), which was distinguished by a hunting and gathering way of life, and was followed by the KOFUN PERIOD (ca 300–710), which was distinguished by the construction of large tumuli or grave mounds (KOFUN) and the formation of an incipient state. See the section on the Yayoi period in HISTORY OF JAPAN: prehistory; YAYOI CULTURE.
                                                                Gina Lee BARNES

Yayoi pottery

The unglazed earthenware of the Yayoi period (ca 300 BC–ca AD 300). Yayoi pottery evolved in northern Kyūshū from the mixing of a local tradition of JŌMON POTTERY with the newly imported pottery of immigrant rice cultivators, probably in the 3rd century BC (see YAYOI CULTURE). In the Early Yayoi period, both Yayoi pottery and wet-rice technology were spread throughout western Japan by a migration of people from northern Kyūshū. In western Japan Yayoi pottery replaced the pottery of the earlier Jōmon period (ca 10,000 BC–ca 300 BC), but in eastern Japan it mingled with the local Jōmon traditions, taking on many of the latter's decorative techniques. Thus, the Yayoi styles of eastern and western Japan are very different, and Yayoi pottery was recognized as distinct from Jōmon pottery only after the excavation of the MUKŌGAOKA SHELL MOUND in the Yayoi section of Tōkyō in 1884.

During the 1936–37 excavation of the KARAKO SITE in Nara Prefecture, five different styles of Yayoi pottery were identified for western Japan. Each of these styles was thought to represent one phase of the Yayoi period, and now these styles are acknowledged to extend throughout western Japan. Although Yayoi IV style ceramics occurred contemporaneously in Kyūshū and the Kansai region (Ōsaka-Kyōto-Nara), they are assigned to the Late Yayoi in Kyūshū

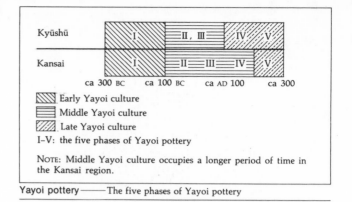

Yayoi pottery —— The five phases of Yayoi pottery

NOTE: Middle Yayoi culture occupies a longer period of time in the Kansai region.

and to the Middle Yayoi in the Kansai region. This is because the distinction between Middle and Late Yayoi is made on the basis of other cultural aspects such as the disappearance of the stone reaping knife. A slightly artificial chronological division of the Yayoi period results. (The divisions I through V should be regarded as true chronological phases, and the Early, Middle and Late groupings as artificial units for archaeological analysis.) Yayoi wares of eastern Japan are assigned type-site names rather than style names, as in Western Japan; thus the distribution of eastern Yayoi pottery types through space and time resembles that of the preceding Jōmon types.

Each Yayoi style or type contains a characteristic array of shapes—jars, cooking pots, bowls, pedestaled bowls, and jar stands—having common attributes of manufacture. Exterior surface finishing techniques included surface burnishing, paddling, shaving, scraping with a piece of wood (leaving a characteristic scratched surface), and smoothing with a wet cloth. Interior finishing techniques included scraping, shaving, and smoothing. Vessels were coil- or ring-built and not made on a potter's wheel, although a turntable was probably employed for the application of decorations, such as parallel combing, and for the finishing of rims.

Within each Yayoi style several decorative techniques were employed, some of them limited to vessels of certain shapes and others used on several shapes in common. Late Yayoi pottery, however, was relatively undecorated. Geometric incised-line patterns, comb patterns, raised-band appliqués, and punctates were common in western Japan, where painted or slipped surfaces were rare. In eastern Japan, zoned cord-marking was continued from the Jōmon tradition, and patterned paddling, incised-line geometrics, and appliqués were popular. In Late Yayoi, many drawings on Kansai-region vessels closely match, in execution and content, the pictures of deer, people, and houses depicted on bronze bells (DŌTAKU) from the same area.

Few Yayoi kilns are known, and it is thought that the earthenware was usually fired in open stacks, but it is certain that simple pit-kilns with ventilation facilities were used in some regions of Kyūshū. Kyūshū is also known for its Middle Yayoi PREHISTORIC BURIALS, in which very large, wide-mouthed jars were used as coffins. During the Late Yayoi, in the Inland Sea area, Yayoi pottery was again associated with funerary rites, eventually giving birth to the HANIWA tradition of funerary sculptures. The HAJI WARE of the succeeding Kofun period (ca 300–710) was a direct continuation of the Yayoi tradition. See also CERAMICS.

■ ——Kobayashi Yukio and Sugihara Sōsuke, ed, *Yayoishiki doki shūsei*, 4 vols (1958–68). Sahara Makoto, *Yayoi doki*, no. 125 of *Nihon no bijutsu* (October 1976). Kuraku Yoshimichi, *Yayoi doki*, in *Nihon no genshi bijutsu*, vol 3 (Kōdansha, 1979).
                                                                Gina Lee BARNES

year-end fair

(*toshi no ichi*). Also called *sekki ichi*. A fair traditionally held in the latter part of December at shrines, temples, or in local neighborhoods, where decorations and sundry goods are sold in preparation for the NEW YEAR holidays. *Toshi no ichi* are often held on special festival days (ENNICHI) of shrines and temples. Originally these year-end fairs provided opportunities for farmers, fisherfolk, and mountain dwellers to exchange their respective goods and to buy clothes and other necessities for the coming year. The *toshi no ichi* held traditionally on 17–18 December at the Asakusa Kannon tem-

Yayoi pottery

Ceremonial jar unearthed in Nagoya, Aichi Prefecture. Assigned to the Middle Yayoi period, this vessel shows the geometric incised-line patterns typical of much Yayoi pottery. A turntable was probably used for the application of decoration. Unglazed earthenware painted with red ocher after firing. Height 24.3 cm. Tōkyō National Museum.

ple in Tōkyō is one of the oldest and most famous. *Toshi no ichi* can still be seen throughout rural Japan, and modified versions have become an integral part of year-end sales at urban department stores.

INOKUCHI Shōji

"yellow peril"

A phrase used throughout the Western world to describe the threat of an alleged Asian, usually Chinese, invasion. The phrase has almost always involved the fear of military conquest but has also occasionally been used to describe the danger of being overrun by prolific Asian immigrants. Only in the first half of the 20th century was the term generally used to describe a presumed Japanese threat, and such use was largely restricted to the United States, Canada, Australia, and New Zealand. The term seems to be a direct translation of Kaiser Wilhelm II's vaporings about a *gelbe Gefahr* threatening Eastern Europe and eventually all Christendom. The kaiser was speaking of an imaginary Chinese threat, and the phrase he coined was used in the United States as early as 1895. The fear of an Asian invasion of North America, however, antedates the term by more than a quarter century, having originated from the fears of Californians and others on the West Coast of a Chinese invasion that arose about the time of the anti-Chinese movement of the late 1860s. The most influential work warning of the yellow peril was Homer Lea's *The Valor of Ignorance* (1909; 2nd ed, 1942), an apocalyptic tale that described a successful Japanese military invasion and conquest of the Pacific coast of North America. The notion of a yellow peril, which evidently filled some psychic need in occidentals, quickly became part of their general cultural baggage. It was popularized by individuals representing the entire ideological spectrum, from the rightist newspaper magnate William Randolph Hearst, perhaps the most influential American Japanophobe, to the English Fabian novelist H. G. Wells. Yellow-peril notions are now more than a century old, and over the years their focus has changed twice. In the second half of the 19th century China was the bugaboo; from about 1905 to 1945 it was Japan; and since the rise of the People's Republic, China again represents the threat. The degree to which yellow-peril notions of various kinds contributed to the outbreak of the Pacific War of 1941–45 cannot, of course, be calculated, but by the 1920s, jingoes in the United States, the British Commonwealth, and Japan wrote as if a future American-Japanese or Anglo-American-Japanese war

were inevitable. Yellow-peril notions since the 1970s have nowhere been more prevalent than in the Soviet Union.

📖 ——Roger Daniels, "The Yellow Peril," in *The Politics of Prejudice: The Anti-Japanese Movement in California and the Struggle for Japanese Exclusion* (1962; 2nd ed 1978). Heinz Gollwitzer, *Die gelbe Gefahr*, (Göttingen, 1962). Richard Austin Thompson, *The Yellow Peril* (1979). *Roger DANIELS*

Yellow Sea, Battle of → Yalu River, Naval Battle of

yellowtail

(buri). *Seriola quinqueradiata*, a migratory fish of the class Osteichthyes, order Perciformes, family Carangidae. It grows to a length of more than 1 meter (39 in). It is distributed along the entire coast of Japan, the east and the south coasts of the Korean peninsula and the East China Sea, moving north in spring and summer and south in autumn and winter. The fry drift with floating algae and are caught for culturing. The cultured fish is called *hamachi*. The cultivation of the yellowtail started in the Ōsaka region and is still carried on more actively in western Japan than in eastern Japan. *Buri* dishes include *sashimi* (sliced raw fish) and *teriyaki* (broiled with soy sauce).

ABE Tokiharu

Buri was a favorite fish among the common people during the Edo period (1600–1868). Salted *buri* is a traditional New Year's dish in the Kansai (Kyōto-Ōsaka) area, in contrast with the salted salmon of the Kantō (Tōkyō) area. The name *buri* does not appear in early court records. The names *hamachi* and *buri* are recorded in the *Kagakushū* (completed in 1444), which leads to speculation that *buri* fishing may have been started in the Muromachi period (1333–1568), with the catch increasing as fishing techniques improved.

SAITŌ Shōji

yen

(en in modern standard Japanese). The yen was established as the unit of monetary account in Japan by the enactment of the Shinka Jōrei (New Currency Regulation) of 1871. The newly established Meiji government introduced a decimal system of currency (one-hundredth of a yen was called a *sen,* and one-tenth of a *sen* was called a *rin*) to replace the complex system of currency of the Edo period (1600–1868; see MONEY, PREMODERN). The new money was named yen (*en,* meaning "round") because the coin was minted in a round shape, whereas the Edo-period coins had been oval and oblong.

The new currency regulation adopted a gold standard, which pegged the yen to a parity of 1.5 grams (0.05 oz) of gold, the equivalent of one Mexican dollar (the standard unit for East Asian trade at the time). In actual practice, the yen was equal to 374 grams (13.2 oz) of silver, and the system functioned as a silver standard. From the beginning of the Meiji period (1868–1912), various kinds of inconvertible paper currency were also issued, particularly at the time of the SATSUMA REBELLION of 1877. The BANK OF JAPAN was established in 1882 with the objective, among others, of disposing of this inconvertible currency and replacing it with notes convertible to silver.

The value of silver, however, began to depreciate against gold as a result of an increase in silver supplies, owing to the discovery of new mines and mining technology, and the adoption of a gold standard by several industrialized countries. This led to the depreciation of the yen against the currencies of Europe and the United States and to considerable inflation in Japan.

Japan returned to the gold standard through enactment of a new currency law in 1897, after the Chinese government paid the equivalent of 230 million taels of gold in British money in reparations for the SINO-JAPANESE WAR OF 1894–1895. The value of the yen was set at 0.75 grams (0.03 oz) of gold (equivalent to US \$0.50), and the Bank of Japan notes were made convertible to gold.

In response to a similar decision made by the United States, Japan dropped the gold standard and prohibited the export of gold in September 1917. After World War I, the United States returned to the gold standard, but the Japanese government was unable to do so because of a series of economic crises. It was not until January 1930 that Japan finally reintroduced the gold standard. However, the timing of this action was unfortunate, since it coincided with the onset of the worldwide depression, and the restoration of the prewar parity only served to aggravate the depression in Japan. The everyday life of the Japanese people was severely affected by unemployment and a reduction in the standard of living; in December 1931 Japan abandoned the gold standard. In February 1942 a new Bank of Japan law was enacted, authorizing the government to determine the maximum number of bank notes to be issued irrespective of the amount of gold held in reserve by the bank.

After World War II, the Japanese economy was beset by serious inflation, which the government attempted to control through emergency monetary measures, including a currency reform. All old yen notes were taken out of circulation and replaced gradually with new yen notes. In April 1949 a unified exchange rate of 360 yen to one US dollar was adopted. This exchange rate was officially recognized by the executive board of the International Monetary Fund (IMF) in May 1953, when it established the yen's parity at about 2.5 milligrams of gold.

The gradual liberalization of foreign trade and the internationalization of the yen began around this time. Japan signed the General Agreement on Tariffs and Trade (GATT) in 1955 and joined the United Nations in 1956. In 1960, yen accounts held by nonresidents on current transactions were made freely convertible to foreign exchange, opening the door to convertibility of the yen. In 1964, Japan agreed to Article 8 of the IMF charter, obliging the country to lift all restrictions on foreign exchange transactions. In the same year, Japan joined the Organization for Economic Cooperation and Development (OECD).

During the 1960s, the Japanese BALANCE OF PAYMENTS turned positive, and FOREIGN CURRENCY RESERVES increased substantially. As a result of the economic policy adopted by the United States in 1971 (see NIXON SHOCKS), Japan was forced to abandon the established parity of 1949; the Smithsonian Agreement of December 1971 established a new exchange rate of 308 yen to one US dollar. In February 1973, the US dollar was again devalued against gold, and the yen and other major currencies moved to a floating exchange rate system.

The major problems of the yen in the future relate to its internationalization. Although the US dollar continues to be used as a major international currency for foreign trade, the Japanese yen, together with the Deutsche mark, will have to share some of the responsibility. If the yen is to play this role, necessary interventions in the foreign exchange market to smooth the functioning of the floating exchange rate system may cause unintended changes in the money supply. Since monetary policy will become more important in coping with inflation, these monetary shocks will not be welcomed by policymakers.

Another problem debated in recent years is redenomination, i.e., the adoption of a "new yen" equal to 100 or 1,000 current yen. This proposal, which aims at simplifying calculations and record-keeping, is likely to be discussed further in the future. See also MONETARY POLICY; YEN, REDENOMINATION OF.

—— T. F. M. Adams and Iwao Hoshii, *A Financial History of Japan* (1972). Mikami Ryūzō, *En no tanjō—kindai kahei seido no seiritsu* (1975). Takagaki Torajirō, *Kindai Nippon kin'yūshi* (1955). Yoshino Toshihiko, *En no rekishi* (1955). *NAKAGAWA Kōji*

Yenan government → Yan'an (Yenan) Government

yen credit

(en shakkan). A long-term loan extended by authorized Japanese government agencies to foreign governments. The granting of these loans is based on official agreements between the government of Japan and the government of the borrowing country. Yen credit was initially extended by the EXPORT-IMPORT BANK OF JAPAN in cooperation with various commercial banks. Since the late 1960s, the OVERSEAS ECONOMIC COOPERATION FUND has played the primary role in the granting of yen credit.

The first yen credit was extended to India in February 1958 in the amount of ¥18 billion (US $50 million). Through the early 1960s, the few loans extended each year were mostly given to Southeast Asian countries. Since the late 1960s, both the number and amounts of yen credits have been increased, and the borrowing countries now include developing countries in Latin America and Africa. In 1977 the total credit extended amounted to ¥1.4 trillion (US $5.4 billion). In recent years the terms of the loans have been eased in response to the increased accumulation of debts by the developing countries. The grace period, for example, is 10 years, and the payment period

Yen

Conversion Rates Used in the Encyclopedia of Japan
(in yen per US dollar)

1949–1970	360
1971–1972	308
1973	271.22
1974	291.51
1975	296.80
1976	296.55
1977	268.51
1978	210.44
1979	219.14
1980	226.74
1981	220.53
1982	249.04

NOTE: From 1949 to 1970, the fixed rate of exchange was ¥360 per US dollar. This basic rate was determined by the Minister of Finance, with the approval of the cabinet, under the Foreign Exchange and Foreign Trade Control Law of 1949.

This encyclopedia adopts the convention of using the revalued exchange rate of ¥308 per US dollar for the years 1971 and 1972; though, in fact, the rate was a result of the Smithsonian Agreement of December 1971 and was in effect from December 1971 to February 1973.

The exchange rates given here for 1973 and after are yearly averages of daily interbank spot rates at which the largest turnovers were recorded on the Foreign Exchange Market in Tōkyō, according to figures supplied by the Bank of Japan to the International Monetary Fund.

SOURCE: Nippon Ginkō (Bank of Japan), *Gaikoku keizai tōkei nempō* (annual): 1983.

is 30 years. Japan's total foreign aid in 1977 amounted to approximately ¥1.5 trillion (US $5.58 billion). This was equal to 0.81 percent of the nation's gross national product (GNP). This figure falls short of the international goal of 1 percent of GNP and is also substantially below the average for industrialized countries of 1.02 percent. The Japanese government has committed itself to increasing foreign aid, and yen credit is expected to increase rapidly. See also FOREIGN AID POLICY. *SUZUKI Kōichi*

yen, redenomination of

The act of redenominating the unit of currency is referred to in Japan as "denomination" (J: *denomi*). The need for this arises when inflation results in an increase by several digits, leading prices and other numerical indicators to become unwieldy in size. Prior to World War II the standard unit in Japan was the yen, as it is today, but the price of a typical meal was a fraction of a yen, and could be expressed as the next smallest unit, or *sen,* equivalent to one-hundredth of a yen. Owing to hyperinflation immediately following World War II and gradual inflation thereafter, a typical noon meal cost about ¥500 (about US $2) or more in the late 1970s. To eliminate inconveniences resulting from the use of such large numbers, a proposal for carrying out a "denomination" was made in the early 1970s. This would involve dividing all prices and other monetary expressions by a convenient unit such as 100 or 1,000 and possibly reintroducing the *sen.* See also WEIGHTS AND MEASURES: monetary units; MONEY, PREMODERN. *C. Tait RATCLIFFE*

Yi dynasty

(J: Richō). Korea's last kingdom, founded in 1392 by YI SŎNG-GYE and ended in 1910 by the Japanese annexation. The kingdom is properly called Chosŏn (J: Chōsen), but it is commonly known as the Yi dynasty. Its span of 518 years was marked by many cultural and technological innovations, but its remarkable longevity was made possible by the durability of its Confucian institutions. Despite Japanese marauders (WAKŌ) in the 14th and 15th centuries and the Japanese INVASIONS OF KOREA IN 1592 AND 1597, the Yi dynasty remained important to Japan as a channel for trade and cultural exchange.

The Yi dynasty may be divided into three major periods: Early Yi (1392–1592), from dynasty founding and consolidation to maturity; Middle Yi (1592–1800), from the Japanese and Manchu invasions to the end of the 18th-century renaissance under the kings Yŏngcho and Chŏngcho; and Late Yi (1800–1910), from dynastic decline and reforms to the Japanese occupation.

As a Confucian state with a political system modeled on that of China, its government was monarchical, bureaucratic, and centralized, political power being balanced between the throne and the bureaucracy drawn from the landholding *yangban* aristocracy. Upon the founding of the new dynasty, General Yi Sŏng-gye (known posthumously as T'aejo), a statesman of unusual ability, established his royal legitimacy with imperial sanction from the ruler of the Ming dynasty (1368–1644) of China. In 1401 the Yi dynasty was formally acknowledged as a tributary of China and remained so until the late 19th century. The state consisted of eight provinces with its capital at Seoul. The important organs of the central government included the State Council, the Royal Secretariat, the Six Ministries, and the Censorate. Unlike Japan, Korea under the Yi dynasty maintained a centralized bureaucratic system and so did not experience the development of feudalism.

There were three major classes in Yi society. The *yangban* were the political and social elite who monopolized power and prestige. Although the Yi codes did not stipulate that *yangban* status was hereditary, a majority of *yangban* were members of old and prominent lineages known as *ssijok* (J: *shizoku*), which enjoyed an aristocratic and scholarly way of life. *Sangin* (J: *jōjin*) were the commoners, consisting of farmers, fishermen, craftsmen, and merchants, who bore the major burdens of state tax and corvée labor. *Ch'ŏnmin* (J: *semmin*), the lowborn, were at the bottom of the social scale and included public and private slaves, female entertainers (*kisaeng*), and butchers. Between *yangban* and commoners was a small group called *chungin* (J: *chūnin*), or "middle people," who performed specialized tasks in foreign languages, medicine, mathematics, and astronomy. The status of *chungin* and *ch'ŏnmin* was essentially hereditary, and a rigid line separated them from *yangban* and commoners throughout much of the dynasty. The distinction between *yangban* and commoners, on the other hand, was more social and political than legal and economic. Although a few commoners attained official status, the *yangban* were a social elite mostly descended from generations of officials. The path to political success lay in obtaining a Confucian education and passing the civil service examinations. However, both education and examinations were used as tools by the *yangban* to perpetuate the political power of their own class.

The early Yi dynasty was characterized by cultural creativity and technological innovations. Improved movable-type printing, invented in Korea two centuries before Gutenberg, enabled large-scale publication in the fields of literature, philosophy, religion, medicine, history, geography, and music. The first printed map of Japan appeared in mid-15th-century Korea in the *Haedong chegukki* (J: *Kaitō shokokki*), edited by Sin Suk-chu (1417–75). A purely phonetic alphabet (HAN'GŬL) was invented in 1443 and promulgated by King Sejong in 1446; around the same time the rain gauge and sundial were invented. Ceramic art continued to develop: celadon, called *punch'ŏng* (known in Japan as *mishimade*), and white porcelain were produced in large quantities. However, the invaders under Hideyoshi not only destroyed Korean potteries and kilns but also carried off many potters to Japan, where they did much to develop the Japanese porcelain industry. Among Yi painters, who excelled not only in painting but also in calligraphy and poetry, was Kang Hŭi-an (1419–64), who influenced the Japanese SESSHŪ TŌYŌ. Korean scholars such as YI HWANG and Yi I (1536–84) made original contributions to Neo-Confucian philosophy. Korean Confucianism, with its emphasis on ethical-ritual formality and status considerations, influenced Japanese Confucian scholars in the Edo period (1600–1868), from YAMAZAKI ANSAI and OGYŪ SORAI to MOTODA NAGAZANE.

In the early Yi period, Korea was primarily concerned with its coastal security against Japanese marauders and with the establishment of formal relations with Japan, then ruled by the Muromachi shogunate (1338–1573). As peaceful contacts increased, commercial and cultural exchange followed. From 1404 to the mid-16th century, Japan sent more than 60 missions to Korea, while Korea sent 5 to Japan. During this time Japan, which viewed Korea as being more in the mainstream of Buddhist culture, acquired the Korean edition of the Buddhist scriptures (Skt: Tripitaka) and technological aid for temple construction. Recognizing the complexity of internal politics

in Japan in that period, Korea, unlike China, officially granted trade rights to certain *daimyō* and merchants. As the number of Japanese traders increased, however, Korea in 1426 tried to confine such trade to its three southern ports of Naeip'o (now Chep'o), Pusanp'o (now Pusan), and Yŏmp'o (near modern Ulsan; see SAMP'O INCIDENT). Japanese ships brought to Korea spices from Southeast Asia and from Japanese minerals such as copper, tin, and lead and fine swords and screens. For these Korea exchanged furs, medicines, and books, but its major export commodity into the early 18th century was cotton cloth, which Japan prized greatly. With the decline of the Muromachi shogunate, the island of TSUSHIMA in the Korea Straits became the point of official contact between Japan and Korea. In 1592 and 1597, Toyotomi Hideyoshi, who had recently unified Japan and was determined to conquer Ming China through Korea, invaded Korea with massive forces and caused much destruction.

In a treaty signed in 1609, peace was restored with Japan, now ruled by the Tokugawa shogunate (1603–1867). Between 1607 and 1811 Korea sent 12 embassies (CHŌSEN TSŪSHINSHI) to Edo (now Tōkyō). Korea accommodated Japanese envoys in a special walled compound (WAEGWAN) near Pusan but because of its policy of seclusion did not allow them to go to Seoul. Tokugawa Japan, itself isolated from the rest of the world under a NATIONAL SECLUSION policy, was still able through Korea to maintain contact with the culture and technology of China. Soon after the Meiji Restoration of 1868, the new Japanese government demanded that the Yi dynasty open the country to foreign trade, and in 1876 Korea was forced to conclude the unequal Treaty of KANGHWA. See also KOREA AND JAPAN: premodern relations.

📖——Nakamura Hidetaka, *Nissen kankei shi no kenkyū* (1965–69). Nakamura Hidetaka, *Chōsen: Fūdo, minzoku, dentō* (1971). Ri Kihaku (Yi Ki-baek), *Kankoku shi shinron* (1979).
Fujiya KAWASHIMA

Yi Hoe-sŏng → Lee Hwe-song

Yi Hwang (1501–1570)

(J: Ri Kō). The most prominent Confucian scholar of Korea during the YI DYNASTY (1392–1910); commonly known by his pen name Yi T'oegye (Ri Taikei). Born into a prominent family in the Chinbo Yi clan, he passed the preliminary civil service examination (*chinsa*) in 1528 and the higher civil service examination (*munkwa*) in 1534. During his distinguished career as a civil official he was also a prolific author of commentaries on Neo-Confucianism, especially the thought of the Song (Sung) Chinese philosopher Zhu Xi (Chu Hsi). Many of his writings reached Japan at the time of the INVASIONS OF KOREA IN 1592 AND 1597 and thus contributed to Neo-Confucian studies in Japan (see SHUSHIGAKU). *C. Kenneth* QUINONES

yin and yang → ommyōdō

Yin Rugeng (Yin Ju-keng) (1889–1947)

(J: In Jokō). A pro-Japanese Chinese politician active in the 1930s. Studied at Waseda University in Tōkyō. Yin participated in the Chinese Revolution of 1911 and joined the Guomindang (Kuomintang; Nationalist Party). Following the Northern Expedition mounted by CHIANG KAI-SHEK to crush the warlords in North China, he parted company with Chiang and began to develop close ties with agents of the Japanese GUANDONG (KWANTUNG) ARMY from whom he was said to have received financial aid in return for assisting in the smuggling of Japanese goods into North China. He reached the pinnacle of his career—and from the standpoint of the Guomindang, the pinnacle of notoriety—in November 1935 when he became chairman of the EAST HEBEI (HOPEH) ANTICOMMUNIST AUTONOMOUS GOVERNMENT. This puppet organization represented the spearhead of the Guandong Army's drive to make North China an autonomous region subject to Japanese control. After the East Hebei regime was absorbed into the larger collaborationist PROVISIONAL GOVERNMENT OF THE REPUBLIC OF CHINA in February 1938, Yin Rugeng's star declined. After the war he was captured by the Guomindang government in Nanjing (Nanking) and executed on 1 December 1947. *John H.* BOYLE

Yi Sam-p'yong → Ri Sampei

Yi Sŏng-gye (1335–1408)

(J: Ri Seikei). The founder of Korea's YI DYNASTY (1392–1910); reigned as King T'aejo (J: Taiso) from 1392 to 1398. As a military official of the preceding KORYŎ dynasty (935–1392), Yi led punitive expeditions against Japanese pirates (WAKŌ) based on offshore islands. In 1388 he was ordered to expel Ming Chinese forces from Korea's northern border; he considered the effort hopeless, rebelled against the Koryŏ government, and subsequently established his own dynasty. Locating his capital at Seoul, he initiated a reform program that ultimately sinicized Korea's bureaucracy, legal codes, intellectual tradition, and social mores. *C. Kenneth QUINONES*

Yi Sun-sin (1545–1598)

(J: Ri Shunshin). One of the greatest military heroes in Korean history; admiral of the YI DYNASTY's (1392–1910) navy during the Japanese INVASIONS OF KOREA IN 1592 AND 1597. Commanding a fleet of "turtle ships" (iron-clad vessels resembling turtles, he repeatedly cut Japanese supply lines between Tsushima and the Korean peninsula in 1593, forcing the Japanese to shift to defensive tactics. Jealous Korean officials had him briefly imprisoned in 1597, but he was restored to command in October 1597, only to be killed in a final battle with retreating Japanese soldiers in 1598. Admiral Yi is revered throughout Korea as a paragon of military virtue and devotion to country. *C. Kenneth QUINONES*

Yi Wan-yong (1858–1926)

(J: Ri Kan'yō). Pen name Iltang. Signed Korea's Treaty of Annexation with Japan in 1910. The adopted son of the prominent Ubong Yi clansman and official, Yi Ho-jun, Yi Wan-yong passed the higher civil service examination (*munkwa*) in 1882, studied English at the Civil Service Academy (Yug'yŏng Kongwŏn) in Seoul, and spent one year (1887) at the Korean legation in the United States. He was a persistent advocate of Westernization and cooperated with the various foreign powers that dominated Korea between 1890 and annexation in 1910. He was among the five cabinet ministers who were considered national traitors for signing the KOREAN-JAPANESE CONVENTION OF 1905. Yi was promoted to prime minister of the Korean government by ITŌ HIROBUMI, resident general of Korea from 1906 to 1909, and in August 1910 signed the treaty that incorporated Korea into the Japanese empire. Ennobled with a Japanese peerage title, he has since been viewed by Koreans as the man who sold their nation to Japan. See also KOREA AND JAPAN: early modern relations. *C. Kenneth QUINONES*

YMCA

The first Young Men's Christian Association in Japan opened in Tōkyō in 1880. The Young Men's Christian Association Union of Japan (now the National Council of the YMCAs of Japan) was formed in 1903 and immediately joined the World Alliance of YMCAs, which held its fourth world conference in Japan in 1965. The YMCA promotes sports and physical education, outdoor recreation, and cultural and citizenship programs for youth. It encourages cultural exchange among the youth of Asia through sports and other activities and sponsors Japanese language instruction in many Asian countries. In 1978 Japan had 28 city YMCAs, 51 high school YMCAs, and 71 college YMCAs with a total membership of about 70,000. *SHIBANUMA Susumu*

yobai

Nocturnal tryst, usually a man visiting a woman for sexual purposes before or even after their formal marriage. This was a natural consequence of an early Japanese pattern of marriage, in which the wife often continued to live with her parents (see MUKOIRIKON). The term evolved from the verb *yobu* ("to visit"), although later it came to be written with the characters for "night" and "crawl." These visits are frequently mentioned in such early literary masterpieces as the MAN'YŌSHŪ and the TALE OF GENJI, and the custom itself may have persisted in some rural areas until modern times. But as the virilocal marriage pattern became more firmly established in the countryside from the 17th century onward, *yobai* became more a subject of folktales and gossip than a widespread practice. It also came to be considered immoral, and a man on a *yobai* visit was supposed to cover his face with a towel so that he could remain officially anonymous if he were discovered or rejected by the woman. Certain folk songs refer to *yobai* visits made by women as well. See also MARRIAGE; SEX IN JAPANESE FOLK CULTURE.

David W. PLATH

yobikō → cram schools

Yoda Yoshikata (1909–)

Screenwriter. Known for his close collaboration with the director MIZOGUCHI KENJI. Born in Kyōto. After losing his job with the Sumitomo Bank because of leftist activities, Yoda began his career as a screenwriter at Nikkatsu Productions (see NIKKATSU CORPORATION). His first movie was Murata Minoru's *Shiroi ane* (1931). As screenwriter for Mizoguchi Kenji's *Naniwa erejii* (1936, Ōsaka Elegy) and *Gion no shimai* (1936, Sisters of the Gion), Yoda concentrated on reproducing natural-sounding dialogues, a noteworthy attempt in the early period of talking pictures. Yoda wrote the majority of Mizoguchi's screenplays, including such classics as *Saikaku ichidai onna* (1952, The Life of Oharu), *Ugetsu monogatari* (1953, Ugetsu), *Sanshō-Dayū* (1954, Sanshō the Bailiff), and *Chikamatsu monogatari* (1954, A Story from Chikamatsu or Crucified Lovers). In his book *Mizoguchi Kenji no hito to geijutsu* (1964, Mizoguchi, the Man and His Art), Yoda recollected how relentlessly demanding Mizoguchi had been of his staff while filming these movies. Yoda also wrote a number of novels, poems, and essays, including a well-known collection of essays entitled *Kyō no onna* (1971, The Women of Kyōto). *ITASAKA Tsuyoshi*

Yodogawa

River in the Kinki region, central Honshū, originating in Lake Biwa, Shiga Prefecture and emptying into Ōsaka Bay. It changes its name three times: the upper reaches are called SETAGAWA, then it is called UJIGAWA when it enters Kyōto Prefecture, and from the town of Ōyamazaki it is called Yodogawa. It was used for river transportation during the medieval period (13th–16th centuries) and earlier, being connected with the transportational network of the Inland Sea and Lake Biwa. It flourished as a transportation route between Fushimi, Kyōto's outer port, and Ōsaka in premodern days. Numerous electric power plants are located on the river. The water is used for irrigation as well as for drinking by the city of Ōsaka, Ōsaka Prefecture, and Hyōgo Prefecture. The river also provides water to the HANSHIN INDUSTRIAL ZONE and the neighboring industrial regions. Length: 75 km (47 mi); area of drainage basin: 8,240 sq km (3,181 sq mi).

Yodogawa Steel Works, Ltd

(Yodogawa Seikōsho). A company engaged in the manufacture, processing, and sale of steel plates, construction material, rolls, and steel ingots, Yodogawa Steel Works was established in 1935. Its galvanized sheet iron, sold under the brand name Cherry, is well-known overseas. In Japan, the company is a leading manufacturer of prepainted galvanized sheet iron. It exports various types of steel sheets and rolls for steel and paper making. The company also provides plant engineering and operations guidance to foreign countries. Future plans call for the development of high-quality, surface-treated steel sheets and the expanded production and sale of household metal products. Sales totaled ¥121 billion (US $502.7 million), with a high export ratio of 23 percent, in the fiscal year ending March 1982; the company was capitalized at ¥5.5 billion (US $22.8 million) in the same year. The head office is in Ōsaka.

Yodogimi (1567?–1615)

(more properly, Yodo no Nyōbō, "the Lady of Yodo"). Concubine of the national unifier TOYOTOMI HIDEYOSHI. This name refers to her residence in Yodo Castle on the southwestern outskirts of Kyōto, built in 1589; her personal name was Chacha. The daughter of the hegemon ODA NOBUNAGA's sister ODANI NO KATA and the *daimyō* ASAI NAGAMASA, Yodogimi as a child experienced the inordinate stresses of survival in a country divided by war: her father was destroyed, and her younger brother hunted down and executed by her uncle in 1573; her mother's second husband, SHIBATA KATSUIE, was destroyed by Hideyoshi in 1583, and Odani no Kata joined him in suicide; Chacha herself and her two sisters were thrown on the mercy of the victor. It is uncertain when she was taken into Hideyoshi's household, but she became his favorite as the mother of his only two children, Tsurumatsu (1589–91) and Hideyori (see TOYOTOMI HIDEYORI). Early in 1599, five months after Hideyoshi's death, Hideyori and his entourage took up residence at Ōsaka Castle, and Yodogimi began to make her influence felt as a leader of the party in Ōsaka that was determined to preserve the primacy of Hideyori and the Toyotomi family vis-à-vis TOKUGAWA IEYASU. After Ieyasu attained the rank of shōgun in 1603 and his son TOKUGAWA HIDETADA succeeded to it in 1605, that intransigent policy became more and more illusory, especially since the Tokugawa were equally determined to eliminate the vestigial Toyotomi threat. The conflict was resolved in the Ōsaka Campaigns of 1614–15 (see ŌSAKA CASTLE, SIEGES OF); Hideyori and Yodogimi committed suicide on 4 June 1615 (Keichō 20.5.8) as Ōsaka Castle fell to the Tokugawa assault.

George ELISON

Yodoya Tatsugorō

The name of successive heads of an Ōsaka merchant family of the Edo period (1600–1868); occasionally used to refer specifically to the fifth-generation head. Their real name was Okamoto; their ancestor Tsuneyasu moved to Ōsaka sometime around 1619 and opened a lumber business under the trade name Yodoya. Gaining the confidence of the TOKUGAWA FAMILY, the Yodoya amassed enormous wealth as dealers in the government-controlled raw silk trade with China (ITOWAPPU) and as agents (*kuramoto;* see KURAYASHIKI) for *daimyō* in the Ōsaka rice market. In 1705 the fourth (some say fifth) head of the family was censured by the shogunate for his extravagant style of living, which was considered unbecoming for a merchant; the family fortune was confiscated and its members banished from Ōsaka. The incident became the subject of many literary works, among them CHIKAMATSU MONZAEMON's play *Yodo no koi shusse no taki nobori* (1708, The Carp of Yodo Climbs the Ladder of Success).

yōeki

A general term for the corvée labor levied on the populace by the government during the 7th and 8th centuries. Initially called *edachi* or *kuwayoboro* and involving forced labor for large projects, it was formalized as an official tax to be levied nationwide after the TAIKA REFORM of 645. Under the RITSURYŌ SYSTEM of government that developed in the late 7th century, corvée labor was divided into *saieki* (annual service) and *zōyō* (miscellaneous service), and detailed regulations appeared in the TAIHŌ CODE of 701. *Saieki* was levied by the central government and as a rule called for 10 days of labor per year in the capital; it could be commuted to payment of 26 *shaku* (7.9 m or 8.6 yd) of cloth. In the event that the capital were moved or a temple reconstructed, 30 to 50 days of labor (called *koeki*) could be requisitioned. *Zōyō* was levied by the provincial governors (KOKUSHI) for such local projects as repairing government buildings and riverbanks. It ranged from 15 to 60 days annually (60 for male adults, 30 for those between 61 and 65, and 15 for youths from 17 to 20; these ages are in premodern Japanese reckoning, in modern reckoning they would be one year less); this too could be commuted to payment in silk cloth or such other commodities as hemp, cotton, salt, and iron products. Within the privately held estates (SHŌEN) that grew up in the Heian period (794–1185), corvée labor came to be known as BUYAKU.

KITAMURA Bunji

yōga

(Western-style painting). Although Western art had been known in Japan since the 16th century, serious interest in it remained circumscribed during the Edo period (1600–1868). However, toward the end of the Edo period and early in the Meiji period (1868–1912), a knowledge of Western art was perceived to be indispensable for drawing plans of fortifications, armaments, naval vessels, and industrial machinery. (For pre-Meiji Western-style art, see NAMBAN ART; WESTERN-STYLE PICTURES, EARLY.)

In 1857 KAWAKAMI TŌGAI, a scholar of WESTERN LEARNING with training in Japanese painting, was directed by the shogunate school of Western studies (BANSHO SHIRABESHO) to make a systematic study of Western techniques of drawing and painting. Three

years later he began to teach these methods to a group of *samurai,* scholars, and KANŌ SCHOOL artists, which included TAKAHASHI YUICHI. Yuichi and a few other ambitious artists also sought additional training from an English correspondent of the *Illustrated London News* then living in Yokohama, Charles WIRGMAN.

After the Meiji Restoration in 1868, the new government embarked upon an extensive program of modernization, including the introduction of Western art. Pencil drawing was one of the Western subjects incorporated into the curriculum of a nationwide system of elementary schools established in 1871, and a department of Western art was set up at the Tōkyō Higher Normal School (Tōkyō Kōtō Shihan Gakkō) to train the requisite teachers. Tōgai and Yuichi also opened private schools where they could pursue with their pupils the artistic, rather than the technical, aspects of Western art.

New industries were started and buildings were imported *in toto,* since Japanese architecture offered no precedents for factories, railroad stations, and the like. Western architecture was also adopted for schools, post offices, banks, and government and public buildings. Architecture was added to the curriculum of the College of Technology (Kōbu Daigakkō) in Tōkyō, and an Englishman, Josiah CONDER, was engaged in 1877 to train the first generation of Japanese architects. The affiliated Technological Art School (Kōbu Bijutsu Gakkō) was established at the college the previous year, and an Italian painter of the Barbizon school, Antonio FONTANESI, and two other Italian artists were invited to come to Japan to teach there. The ablest graduates were sent abroad for additional training, and by 1887 were competent enough to erect a new Imperial Palace in Tōkyō with Western-style audience chambers. By the end of the Meiji period, they had produced the AKASAKA DETACHED PALACE, a structure as grandiose as its Western prototypes, which currently serves as the official guest house for foreign dignitaries.

The Kōbu Bijutsu Gakkō also attracted many who wished to become painters and were eager to study under foreign teachers and use materials otherwise unobtainable. Since the government had need of portraits and other oil paintings to decorate official buildings, HARADA NAOJIRŌ, YAMAMOTO HŌSUI, and other promising young artists were sent abroad for further study, and they soon gained recognition in foreign exhibitions. Koyama Shōtarō (1857–1916), ASAI CHŪ, and other members of the Jūichijikai (Eleven Character Society) remained in Japan and were influential as teachers at the Tōkyō Normal School and other major institutions. These artists also established private schools that were active throughout the Meiji period.

Despite their accomplishments and growing popularity, the Western-style painters felt threatened in 1882 when opponents of Western art thwarted plans for a permanent art school that would include *yōga* and sought to debar its proponents from official exhibitions. The traditional artists had found staunch allies among certain government officials: those who since 1867 had been in charge of Japan's participation in international expositions and had been impressed by the enthusiastic foreign response to traditional Japanese arts. These officials formed an organization in 1879 called the Ryūchikai Society ("Dragon Pond" Society) to stimulate broader interest in the traditional arts and to encourage NIHONGA, or Japanese-style painting, in order to furnish new designs and products that could earn some of the foreign currency sorely needed to finance Japan's industrialization. Thus Western-style artists were excluded from numerous exhibitions they sponsored and from the Domestic Competitive Painting Exhibitions (Naikoku Kaiga Kyōshinkai) held in 1882 and 1884. This was a serious setback for *yōga* artists, who had as yet found little private patronage.

The Western-style artists' most implacable foe was a conservative faction in the Ministry of Education led by Kuki Ryūichi (1852–1931), who had been a delegate to the Paris Exposition of 1878. Kuki enlisted the support of Ernest FENOLLOSA who, in a well-known speech to the Ryūchikai in 1882, decried the study of Western art and urged the Japanese to recognize the superiority of their native arts. That same year Fenollosa's pupil and Kuki's protégé, OKAKURA KAKUZŌ, publicly debated with Koyama Shōtarō on the merits of CALLIGRAPHY as an art form; they differed again in 1884 over art education when they served as members of the Pictorial Research Committee (Zuga Chōsakai) of the Ministry of Education that decided to replace pencil drawing with traditional brush and ink painting in the elementary schools. In 1889 the Tōkyō Bijutsu Gakkō (now Tōkyō University of Fine Arts and Music) was established; only courses in the traditional arts were offered. In 1888 Kuki became director of the Imperial Museum (now the TŌKYŌ NA-

TIONAL MUSEUM), which had been recently reorganized and was devoted exclusively to oriental art. To the further detriment of Western-style art, this appointment also entitled Kuki to serve as vice-president of all government expositions.

Western-style artists responded by banding together in 1889 to form the Meiji Fine Arts Society (Meiji Bijutsukai) and named the president of Tōkyō University as head of the organization. The board of directors included such influential political figures as HARA TAKASHI. Their first exhibition in the fall of 1889 was attended by the empress and members of the court. With this backing, yōga artists were enabled to take part in the third Domestic Industrial Exposition (Naikoku Kangyō Hakurankai) held in Tōkyō in the spring of 1890. But Asai Chū, Koyama Shōtarō, and other major artists refrained from exhibiting their work, thus sowing dissension in the ranks of the Meiji Fine Arts Society. The curiously eclectic painting of *Kannon Riding on a Dragon* exhibited by Harada Naojirō, in no way comparable to his insightful and sensitively rendered picture of *The Shoemaker* painted four years earlier in Europe, reflected the plaintive attempts of some yōga artists to seek acceptance by resorting to traditional and historical themes. Such evidence suggests that the major problem confronting Western-style painters was not mastery of the new oil-painting techniques, at which they in fact quickly became highly skilled, but a social and cultural estrangement that made it difficult to transform Western techniques into creative and valid artistic expressions. The exhibitions had the unfortunate effect of formalizing the growing dichotomy between Japanese-style and Western-style painting, and this was to inhibit the development of modern Japanese painting for more than a half a century.

The success of KURODA SEIKI signaled a decisive turning point in the development of yōga. The scion of an aristocratic and politically prominent family, he was sent to Paris in 1884 to study law but decided that he could just as well distinguish himself and bring credit to his country as a painter. He studied for six years with a popular salon figure, Raphael Collin, who taught him to paint in the *plein air* manner, a style that was more likely to win widespread approval than impressionism or other avant-garde movements. In 1893, just prior to his return to Japan, Kuroda won official recognition for his painting *Morning Toilette*, exhibited at the Société Nationale des Beaux Arts in Paris.

The casual subjects and bright colors of the paintings that he exhibited at the Meiji Fine Arts Society in 1894 had a startling effect upon artists schooled in the more realistic rendering and somber palette of an older generation of European teachers. Such promising pupils as WADA EISAKU and OKADA SABURŌSUKE transferred to the private school that Kuroda opened together with his friend, Kume Keiichirō (1866–1934). Overcoming Kuki's objections concerning the propriety of publicly exhibiting a painting of a nude, Kuroda entered *Morning Toilette* at the fourth National Industrial Exposition held in Kyōto in 1895. The following year Okakura invited him to teach a course on yōga at the Tōkyō Bijutsu Gakkō. Kuroda was also a founder of HAKUBAKAI (White Horse Society), a group of younger yōga artists who banded together in competition with the Meiji Fine Arts Society.

In 1898 Kuroda persuaded Francophile officials involved in preparations for the Paris Exposition of 1900 to oust Okakura from the directorship of the Tōkyō Bijutsu Gakkō and Kuki from his government-appointed positions. Kuroda was soon the dominant figure in Japanese art circles, and he shifted the emphasis of the Tōkyō Bijutsu Gakkō from *nihonga* to yōga, attracting such promising artists as AOKI SHIGERU, SAKAMOTO HANJIRŌ, Nakamura Tsune (1887–1924), and KISHIDA RYŪSEI. Other influential yōga groups were the Pacific Painting Society (Taiheiyō Gakai), led by younger members of the Meiji Fine Arts Society, and the Kansai Art School (Kansai Bijutsuin), led by Asai Chū, perhaps the ablest artist of that era and the teacher of a leading figure of the succeeding era, UMEHARA RYŪZABURŌ. The numerous officials and artists who attended the Paris Exposition of 1900 succeeded in establishing in 1907 a Japanese version of the French Salon, the Ministry of Education's annual exhibit, BUNTEN, which assured all the major factions of *nihonga* and yōga representation.

Yōga had evolved as an adjunct of Western technology and architecture, and both painters and patrons belonged to the Westernized, university-educated, and professional segments of society. But in general their knowledge of Western art was limited and largely secondhand, and they had difficulty absorbing the succession of new styles brought back by younger artists who studied abroad. Yōga artists became increasingly estranged from Japanese culture,

and the format of Western-style paintings did not lend itself to the decorative requirements of Japanese architecture. Hence, yōga artists were highly dependent upon official and public commissions. Despite the increased recognition accorded them, yōga artists continued to occupy an economically precarious position throughout the Meiji period.

▪ ——Minoru Harada, *Meiji Western Painting*, tr Akiko Murakata, adapted by Bonnie F. Abiko, *Arts of Japan*, vol 6 (1974).

Ellen P. CONANT

Yōgaku → Western Learning

yojō

An aesthetic ideal fostered by WAKA poets. Written with Chinese characters that literally mean "excess feeling," but usually translated as "overtones," it refers to the meanings a poem obliquely implies in addition to its overtly stated message. The term, pronounced *yosei* in premodern times, was most frequently used in *waka* criticism from the 11th to the 13th century. At times its connotations overlapped those of YŪGEN.

Yojō was originally a Chinese word; the germ of the concept first surfaced in Japan when KI NO TSURAYUKI (872?–945), in his preface to the KOKINSHŪ (ca 905, A Collection of Ancient and Modern Times), criticized the poetry of ARIWARA NO NARIHIRA (825–880) for failing to give adequate expression to his overabundant feelings. However, other poets like MIBU NO TADAMINE (fl ca 910) and Minamoto no Michinari (d 1019) equated *yojō* with suggestiveness and affiliated it with one of the 10 exemplary styles of *waka*. Following this line of interpretation, FUJIWARA NO KINTŌ (966–1041) considered *yojō* one of the two main ingredients needed for the highest type of *waka*. With such poets as FUJIWARA NO TOSHINARI (1114–1204), his son FUJIWARA NO SADAIE (1162–1241), and KAMO NO CHŌMEI (1156?–1216), *yojō* became part of a complex literary aesthetic that valued poetry of rich symbolism, featuring subtle allusions, exquisite imagery, and cryptic diction. Chōmei's statements that an autumn mountain is more beautiful when seen through a mist and that a young woman looks lovelier when in silent grief are attempts to convey the essence of *yūgen* under which he specifically subsumes *yojō*.

The concept of *yojō* can be observed outside *waka* criticism, too. For instance, KOMPARU ZENCHIKU (1405–70?), in discussing the art of the Nō drama, insisted that an actor's performance should "have an aura of unstated sentiment." The concept is also latent in the aesthetics of the painter Tosa Mitsuoki (1617–91), who observed that "blank space is also part of a painting," and in the poetics of the *haiku* master BASHŌ (1644–94). Though somewhat overshadowed by *yūgen* in later centuries, the term remains one of the most pervasive concepts in Japanese literature and art.

▪ ——Robert H. Brower and Earl Miner, *Japanese Court Poetry* (1961). Yasuda Ayao, *Nihon no geijutsu ron* (1965, 1972).

Makoto UEDA

Yojōhan fusuma no shitabari trial

Obscenity trial concerning the publication of the short story "Yojōhan fusuma no shitabari" (Paper Lining of the Sliding Doors of a Four-and-a-Half-Mat Room). The short story, allegedly written by the early-20th-century author NAGAI KAFŪ, was published by NOSAKA AKIYUKI in the July 1972 issue of the magazine *Omoshiro hambun*, of which he was the editor. In February of the following year, he and the publisher of the magazine, Satō Yoshinao, were indicted on charges of disseminating obscene matter. Although a number of well-known authors appeared in court in their defense, the Tōkyō District Court in 1976 found them guilty, stating that, "Even in comparison with generally accepted ideas concerning obscenity in today's society, 'Yojōhan fusuma . . .' is still obscene literature." Both were fined. The defendants and their lawyer appealed their case, but in March 1979 the Tōkyō High Court upheld the lower court's decision. In November 1980 a further appeal to the Supreme Court was also rejected. See also OBSCENITY.

Yōjōkun

(Precepts for Health). Manual on health by the Neo-Confucian scholar KAIBARA EKIKEN; written in 1713, when the author was 83. Drawing on his readings and his own experience, Ekiken gives specific advice on topics ranging from diet, sexual activity, and bathing

Yokkaichi

An aerial view of Yokkaichi. Ise Bay can be seen at the top right.

Yokohama

Yokohama harbor with Yamashita Park and the Marine Tower (lower center).

to medicinal herbs and acupuncture. The book reflects the author's belief that cultivation of the body and spirit go hand in hand. Its simple style made it enormously popular with the common people of his time.

Yōkaichi

City in central Shiga Prefecture, central Honshū. A flourishing market town from as early as the 13th century (a market was held here on the 8th day of each month), it is still a commercial center, with numerous machinery, chemical, and textile plants. Tea and tobacco are cultivated in the surrounding areas. Pop: 37,777.

Yōkaichiba

City in northeastern Chiba Prefecture, central Honshū. It developed in the Edo period (1600–1868) as a market town on the highway Chōshi Kaidō. Today the principal activities are commerce and agriculture. Rice production and vegetable farming flourish. Pop: 31,341.

Yokaren

(Junior Pilot Training Corps). Abbreviation for Kaigun Hikō Yoka Renshūsei (Aviation Cadets of the Imperial Japanese Navy). The cadets, ranging in age from 14 to 23, took a three-to-four-year course at a school, established in 1930, at Kasumigaura, Ibaraki Prefecture. They played an active role in the Sino-Japanese War of 1937–45 and the Pacific War.   Hata Ikuhiko

Yokkaichi

City in northern Mie Prefecture, central Honshū, on Ise Bay. The largest industrial and commercial city in the prefecture, it developed originally as a market center and one of the post-station towns along the highway Tōkaidō during the Edo period (1600–1868). Its textile industry dates from the Meiji period (1868–1912). The construction of a great petrochemical industrial complex after World War II has led to serious air pollution. Plate glass, textiles, and foodstuffs are also produced. Agricultural products include vegetables and tea. Pop: 255,442.

yokoana

("horizontal caverns"). A tunnel tomb or burial cavern used from the late 5th to 8th centuries. These developed simultaneously with the family, corridor-style stone chamber (see KOFUN) in the latter part of the Kofun period (ca 300–710). The stone chambers and *yokoana* existed in clusters and were used over long periods for multiple family interments. Two kinds of tunnel tombs are found: those dug directly into the exposed walls of cliffs or hillsides, and those dug underground with an L-shaped tunnel as an entrance. The latter were prevalent in southern Kyūshū. Tunnel tombs from the Kofun period often resemble the layout of corridor-style stone chambers, with a passage leading to a main burial room. The chambers may contain platforms to receive a corpse or a variety of coffins. These included clay capsules with small trap doors, and lidded clay containers supported by numerous legs. Grave articles were similar to those in the tomb mounds *(kofun)*: SUE WARE, horse trappings (see HORSE TRAPPINGS, ANCIENT), BRONZE MIRRORS, beads (see BEADS, ANCIENT), weapons and armor. Later tunnel tombs, called *yagura,* date from the early part of the Kamakura period (1185–1333) through the middle of the Muromachi period (1333–1568). These are found mainly around the city of Kamakura in Kanagawa Prefecture and contain cinerary urns, Buddhist JIZŌ statues, and GORINTŌ or other stone monuments.

——Sakazume Shūichi et al, "Tokushū ōketsubo kenkyū no genjō," *Kōkogaku jānaru* 110 (1975). Satō Kōji, "Kofun jidai kōki ni okeru ōketsubo no yōsō," *Sundai shigaku* 16 (1965). Yamamoto Kiyoshi, "Yokoana no keishiki to jiki ni tsuite," *Shimane daigaku ronshū (Jimbun kagaku)* 11 (1962).   Gina Lee BARNES

Yokohama

Capital of Kanagawa Prefecture, central Honshū, on Tōkyō Bay. It is the country's largest port. A small fishing port up to the end of the Edo period (1600–1868), with the signing of the HARRIS TREATY between Japan and the United States in 1858, Yokohama was opened to foreign trade. The first railway line in Japan was constructed between Yokohama and Shimbashi in Tōkyō in 1872. Industrialization started with the reclamation of land at the mouth of the river Tsurumigawa in 1913. The city was heavily damaged during the Tōkyō Earthquake of 1923 and by Allied bombings in World War II, but it has recovered completely. Today, together with the neighboring city of Kawasaki, Yokohama is the center of the KEIHIN INDUSTRIAL ZONE. Huge steelmaking, shipbuilding, automobile, chemical, oil refining, electrical appliance, and food-processing factories are located here. The port of Yokohama handles the export of ships, automobiles, cameras, and television sets and the import of oil, soy beans, and machinery. The city is served by major railways and expressways. Municipal government offices are located in the Kannai district, while the shopping and theater districts are in Motomachi and Isezakichō. Tourist attractions include Yamashita Park, the garden SANKEIEN, the library KANAZAWA BUNKO, and the temple Sōjiji of the Sōtō sect of Zen. Area: 421.46 sq km (162.68 sq mi); pop: 2,773,822.

Yokohama Archives of History

(Yokohama Kaikō Shiryōkan). Collection of Japanese and foreign materials principally concerning the opening of Japan and the port of Yokohama during the late 19th century. Established by the city of Yokohama in 1981. It is housed in the former British Consulate and situated on the site in Yokohama where the KANAGAWA TREATY of 1854 was concluded. The archive's main activity is the collection, preservation, and display of historical materials; it also sponsors historical lectures and courses. Its collection of administrative materials, provincial documents, drawings and illustrations, photographs, books, and audio-visual materials totaled some 90,000 items in 1981. Included are the Paul C. Blum (1898–1981) collection (about 6,000 items) of Japanese and foreign books on Yokohama and materials (about 100 items) concerning James C. HEPBURN.

yokohama-e

(literally, "Yokohama pictures"). UKIYO-E–style woodblock prints inspired by the arrival of foreigners in the early and mid-1860s at the newly opened port of Yokohama. Yokohama-e were designed in great numbers, mostly by artists of the UTAGAWA SCHOOL, and published in Edo (now Tōkyō).

In 1858 a treaty was concluded between five foreign nations and Japan opening several ports to foreign trade. One of the designated ports was the fishing village of Yokohama, south of Edo. The first printed views of Yokohama were published in Edo late that year. As the first foreign merchants and their families began to arrive, the Japanese became fascinated by their strange manners, costumes, attitudes, and occupations. Yokohama was some distance from Edo, and neither Japanese nor foreigners were allowed to travel freely, so to help satisfy public curiosity, Edo print publishers sent artists to Yokohama to sketch the foreigners and hired writers to supply the information, or rather misinformation, that was often included above the pictures when they were published as woodblock prints. The most observant and interesting of these artists was Utagawa Sadahide (1807–ca 1873), while others included Yoshiiku, Yoshikazu, and Yoshitora; most of them were pupils of UTAGAWA KUNIYOSHI.

Prints were commonly issued in sets of five, including separate pictures of Americans, French, Dutch, English, and Russians, representing each of the Five Treaty Nations; or six, with an additional picture of Chinese, who, although not party to the treaty, had also been allowed entrance to the port. The other common format was the triptych, showing panoramic views of buildings, ships, parades, and domestic scenes. Hundreds of these prints were published between 1860 and 1862, after which their popularity quickly waned. The Japanese artists' struggle to depict the unfamiliar foreigners led to odd pictorial conventions and compromises, which lent the Yokohama prints a warmth and humorous charm that endeared them to the foreigners they portrayed. *Roger* KEYES

Yokohama Incident

(Yokohama Jiken). A series of repressive actions taken by the SPECIAL HIGHER POLICE in Yokohama against journalists during World War II. Beginning with the arrest of HOSOKAWA KAROKU for writing an allegedly procommunist article for the magazine KAIZŌ, more than 30 journalists, most of them associated with *Kaizō*, CHŪŌ KŌRON, and the IWANAMI SHOTEN PUBLISHERS, were arrested and jailed between 1942 and 1945 under the 1941 revision of the PEACE PRESERVATION LAW OF 1925 (Chian Iji Hō). In July 1944 *Kaizō* and *Chūō kōron* were ordered to cease publication. The charges against the journalists were patently unfounded, and by the end of the war not one of them had been brought to trial, although three had died from harsh treatment in prison. The rest were released shortly after the war. The affair is also known as the Tomari Incident, after Hosokawa's hometown in Toyama Prefecture, where he and fellow journalists had met, allegedly to revive the Communist Party. The novel *Kaze ni soyogu ashi* (1949–51, Like a Reed Shaken in the Wind) by ISHIKAWA TATSUZŌ is based on this incident.

Yokohama mainichi shimbun

Japan's first modern Japanese-language daily newspaper. It was started in 1871 by Iseki Moriyoshi, the governor of Kanagawa Prefecture. In time it evolved into the political news organ of the FREEDOM AND PEOPLE'S RIGHTS MOVEMENT (Jiyū Minken Undō). In 1879 it was bought by the liberal journalist NUMA MORIKAZU, who moved the paper to Tōkyō, where it became known as the *Tōkyō-Yokohama mainichi shimbun*. It earned a reputation for calling public attention to shady government deals in Hokkaidō (see HOKKAIDŌ COLONIZATION OFFICE SCANDAL OF 1881). In the mid-1880s the paper took on a more general news format but continued to be active in liberal campaigns, especially under SHIMADA SABURŌ, who took over management of the paper in 1894. It editorialized against prostitution, was critical of the government handling of the ASHIO COPPER MINE INCIDENT, and came out against going to war with Russia on the eve of the Russo-Japanese War (1904–05). The banner was changed to *Mainichi shimbun* in 1886 and then to *Tōkyō mainichi shimbun* in 1906. It continued publishing until 1940 when it was absorbed by the *Teito nichinichi shimbun*.

Yokohama Rubber Co, Ltd

(Yokohama Gomu). The second largest manufacturer of automobile tires in Japan after BRIDGESTONE TIRE CO, LTD, Yokohama Rubber also produces industrial products and aircraft components. Affiliated with the Furukawa group, the company was established in 1917 with capital furnished on an equal basis by FURUKAWA ELECTRIC CO, LTD, and B.F. Goodrich Co of the United States. The company originally manufactured car and bicycle tires and tubes, but after World War II started to diversify by producing synthetic rubber, plastics, and various industrial rubber products, including belts, hoses, and cushions. The development of radial tires increased sales, and tires are now exported. Sales companies are incorporated in the United States and Australia; the company is affiliated with a tire-manufacturing company in Ethiopia financed by that nation's government. Sales for the fiscal year ending December 1981 totaled ¥208.7 billion (US $953.2 million) and the export ratio was 28 percent. The company was capitalized at ¥9.6 billion (US $43.8 million). The head office is in Tōkyō.

Yokohama Specie Bank

(Yokohama Shōkin Ginkō). Established in 1880 under government auspices as a commercial bank with the twin objectives of increasing the supply of silver specie in Japan and serving the financial needs of export industries and Japanese trading companies, it was given special status in 1887. Receiving generous assistance from the government and the Bank of Japan, it played an important role in the promotion of Japanese external trade and the acquisition of foreign exchange. After the Russo-Japanese War of 1904–05, it functioned as a colonial bank for Japanese interests in Manchuria and in the years 1909–18 represented Japan in international banking consortiums organized to provide loans to China. By 1919 the bank had increased its capital from ¥3 million to ¥100 million and expanded its branch network to cover all the major cities of the world. Early in the Shōwa period (1926–), it served as an organ of government financial policy, helping to support the international value of the yen. In 1947, by order of the OCCUPATION authorities, it was reorganized as a commercial bank and renamed the BANK OF TŌKYŌ, LTD.

Yokoi Kinkoku (1761–1832)

Painter of the NANGA school. Real name Yokoi Myōdō. Kinkoku was born in Ōmi Province (now Shiga Prefecture), not far from the town of Ōtsu long known for its folk paintings called *ōtsu-e*. At the age of nine he was sent to a strict Buddhist temple school. There he displayed a rebellious attitude; his escapades included stealing fruit and candy, running away, and seducing a girl from the town. He finally escaped and made his way to Edo (now Tōkyō), where he lived in a temple and studied both Buddhism and Confucianism. After attempting to seduce a nun, he was expelled and began the life of a wanderer. In the following years he learned fencing and archery, composed *haiku* poems, climbed mountains, was married and soon divorced, worked in a bun shop, made a pilgrimage to Ise, and sold spurious charms to other travelers.

He settled for a few years as the only monk of a small temple on Mt. Kinkoku, from which he took his art name. Although he served at Buddhist ceremonies, became the town scribe, toured the countryside as a flute-playing mendicant (*komusō*) and reciter of ballads (*jōruri*), he seems to have most enjoyed flying kites with the village children.

Eventually Kinkoku married again and settled in Nagoya, where he joined a circle of haiku poets and began painting in earnest. His earliest works had been handscrolls illustrating the life of the monk HŌNEN, executed in the brightly colored style of the TOSA SCHOOL of painting. Kinkoku soon changed to rendering landscapes in soft washes, a style more closely associated with the MARUYAMA-SHIJŌ SCHOOL. In his final 25 years, Kinkoku turned to the works of the *nanga* poet-painter Yosa BUSON for inspiration. Even when Kinkoku directly copied Buson paintings, however, the results were different. Where Buson had depicted landscapes with a subtle and delicate touch, Kinkoku preferred rough, quick, and energetic brushwork. He was especially effective in rendering rocks and mountains, perhaps because of his mountain-climbing experiences.

He also brushed many haiku paintings *(haiga)*, usually of figure subjects, with a relaxed and spontaneous charm. Kinkoku's paintings, long ignored, have become well known in the past decade.

■——Cal French, *The Poet-Painters* (1974).　　*Stephen* ADDISS

Yokoi Shōnan (1809–1869)

Scholar; reformer. Rose to national prominence during the final decade of the Edo period (1600–1868). A teacher and political adviser, a determined seeker of solutions to 19th-century Japan's crises in finance and morale, and a leading counselor at the topmost decision-making level of the Tokugawa shogunate during the crisis surrounding the signing of the ANSEI COMMERCIAL TREATIES, he was a dynamic and influential figure until the final collapse of the Tokugawa shogunate in 1867–1868.

Shōnan was born Yokoi Heishirō, the second son in a middle-ranking *samurai* family of the Kumamoto domain in Higo Province (now Kumamoto Prefecture). Facts on Shōnan's early schooling are missing, but in 1833 he was admitted to Jishūkan, a domainal school that had a reputation for academic excellence. Three years later he was appointed graduate-assistant; in his memoirs one of his students, MOTODA NAGAZANE, praised him for his lucid mind and forthright set of values.

In 1839 Shōnan was sent by the domainal government to study at Edo (now Tōkyō) for three years. His meeting with FUJITA TŌKO of the Mito domain (now part of Ibaraki Prefecture) was decisive in spurring both on to a practical reformist course. However, after only 10 months Shōnan was recalled to Kumamoto on complaint by a domain official in Edo that he was unable to hold his liquor and that his impulsively outspoken nature might jeopardize the domain's standing with the shogunal government. He was placed on parole in the change of his elder brother. This was the first of a series of difficulties Shōnan was to face with his domainal elders throughout his career.

During his years of semiconfinement Shōnan expanded his studies of the Chinese philosophers. In time he came to question the teachings of Neo-Confucianism (SHUSHIGAKU), the school officially prescribed by the Tokugawa shogunate, which declared that in the natural order the ruler rules and the subjects obey. With other like-minded samurai, he formed the Jitsugakutō (Practical Party) and stressed the need for practical reforms.

At about this time Shōnan opened a school, named Shōnandō after the pseudonym of the 14th-century imperial loyalist Kusunoki Masatsura. Soon Yokoi himself came to be called "Shōnan." He also worked on a manuscript on Emperor GO-DAIGO and corresponded with Fujita Tōko.

In 1851 Shōnan, now 42, was allowed to travel. His students financed a six-month tour to Edo and elsewhere in Japan. During Shōnan's 1851 tour nowhere was he more enthusiastically received than at the Fukui domain in Echizen Province (now Fukui Prefecture). Here he met HASHIMOTO SANAI, the brilliant young political activist. In the years that followed, his advice was to be sought by Echizen officials, especially the younger samurai, on problems ranging from education to domainal business enterprises and foreign relations. Shōnan invariably stressed the need to integrate dignity and morality with practical application of policies. In 1857 the Echizen *daimyō* MATSUDAIRA YOSHINAGA invited him to teach at the domainal academy. Shōnan was honored as he had never been at Kumamoto. During the next four years Shōnan advised Yoshinaga on national as well as domainal matters, accompanying him to Edo on one occasion.

In the summer of 1862 Yoshinaga, who was known for his moderation, was suddenly elevated to acting head of the shogunal government *(seiji sōsai)* in a move by the shogunate to gain imperial approval of the Ansei commercial treaties (1858), which it had been forced to sign by foreign powers. Shōnan was called to Edo, where he advised Yoshinaga on reform within the shogunate and closer cooperation with the imperial court (see MOVEMENT FOR UNION OF COURT AND SHOGUNATE). He also called for the opening of Japan to foreign trade, a thorough reform of domainal finances to strengthen Japan's military position, and a larger voice for the more powerful domains in shogunal affairs.

Shōnan returned to Kumamoto in 1863. Because of his dangerous ideas, however, he was stripped of his samurai status and placed under house arrest. At the time of the MEIJI RESTORATION (1868) the new government honored him with the post of counselor *(san'yo),* but the following year he was struck down by samurai assassins who suspected him of being a Christian and of harboring republican sentiments.

■——Works by Yokoi Shōnan: *Yokoi Shōnan ikō hen,* ed Yamazaki Masatada (1938). D. Y. Miyauchi, ed and tr, "*Kokuze sanron* (The Three Major Problems of State Policy)," *Monumenta Nipponica* 23.1–2 (1968). Studies: Harold Bolitho, *Treasures among Men: The Fudai Daimyo in Tokugawa Japan* (1974). D. Y. Miyauchi, "Yokoi Shōnan (1809–1869): A National Political Adviser from Kumamoto Han in Late Tokugawa Japan," *Journal of Asian History* 3.1 (1969). D. Y. Miyauchi, "Yokoi Shōnan's Response to the Foreign Intervention in Late Tokugawa Japan, 1853–1862," *Modern Asian Studies* 4.3 (1970). Conrad Totman, *Politics in the Tokugawa Bakufu, 1600–1843* (1967).　　*Dixon Y.* MIYAUCHI

Yokoi Tokiyoshi (1860–1927)

Agriculturist and agricultural economist of the late Meiji (1868–1912) and early Taishō (1912–26) periods. Born in Higo Province (now Kumamoto Prefecture). Graduate of Komaba Agricultural School (now part of Tōkyō University). After teaching in Fukuoka Prefecture and then serving as a technician in the Ministry of Agriculture and Commerce, he taught agricultural science at Tōkyō University from 1890 to 1922. Yokoi was concurrently from 1911 the first president of Tōkyō University of Agriculture, a private institution. Following his master Max FESCA, he was a devoted teacher of agricultural science; many of his pupils went on to become influential officials and teachers in the field. He wrote *Shōnō ni kansuru kenkyū* (1927), a study of peasantry, and other books.

KATŌ Shunjirō

Yokoi Yayū (1702–1783)

Real name of Yokoi Tokitsura, *haibun* essayist and *haiku* poet. Yayū was born in Nagoya, the son of a high-ranking official of the Owari domain (now Aichi Prefecture), and received the traditional literary and martial education of one of his station. After some years in an official position in the Owari domain, he was appointed in 1741 as chief of the *ōbangashira,* the security organization charged with policing the three castles of the Tokugawa shōgun, in Edo (now Tōkyō), Ōsaka, and Kyōto. Yayū was apparently a conscientious official, but his real interests lay in literature, and especially in the random essay genre known as *haibun.* From the time of his retirement from official life in his 53rd year until his death three decades later, he devoted himself to study and writing. This was the most productive period of his life as a *haibun* writer.

The thematic scope of Yayū's *haibun* is broad, extending from the profundities of love, death, and old age to such everyday ephemera as rice cakes, wooden sandals, and the joys of smoking. The best of Yayū's *haibun* are an impressionistic mosaic of erudite allusion, daily commonplace, and gentle humor presented in a rich classical style, with a skillful display of *engo* (associative words), suggestion, and the other devices of the haiku poet. His most important work, and one of the best known of the *haibun* collections, is *Uzuragoromo* (Quail Cloak), published between 1788 and 1823.

■——Iwata Kurō, ed, *Kampon uzuragoromo shinkō* (1958). Lawrence Rogers, "Rags and Tatters: The *Uzuragoromo* of Yokoi Yayū," *Monumenta Nipponica* 34.3 (1979).　　*Lawrence W.* ROGERS

Yokomitsu Riichi (1898–1947)

Novelist. One of the most important Japanese writers of the two decades ending in 1945. Yokomitsu was a tireless innovator and modernist whose imagination was often stimulated by new developments in European art and literature, and yet his personal orientation remained essentially nationalistic. His efforts at creating new forms and styles in Japanese fiction and his own commercial success as a writer made him a dominant figure in the Japanese literary scene, particularly of the 1930s.

Yokomitsu was born in a hot spring resort in Fukushima Prefecture, near where his father, a contractor specializing in the construction of railroads and tunnels, was temporarily working. His early years were spent in a succession of different places, either traveling with his father or staying with relatives at his mother's hometown, the village of Tsuge in Mie Prefecture. The family's unsettled life continued throughout Yokomitsu's school years; he attended a total of six schools in Tsuge, the city of Ōtsu in Shiga Prefecture, and the town of Ueno in Mie Prefecture, most of the time living with relatives or other families, once being boarded at a Buddhist temple.

These places and experiences later provided the setting for much of his early fiction. In 1916 he enrolled in Waseda University in Tōkyō, but most of his time was taken up by literary coterie activities, and he was dropped for nonattendance the following year. He reenrolled in 1918, but was eventually dropped for good in 1921.

Early Works —— From his public school days Yokomitsu had begun to develop an idiosyncratic, consciously literary prose style. The first seven years after his arrival in Tōkyō, including his nominal college years, were spent writing fiction and occasionally publishing it in coterie or other small magazines. He met and obtained the encouragement of the influential writer KIKUCHI KAN. He had a troubled, jealousy-stricken love affair with the younger sister of a friend, and they eventually began to live together as husband and wife. By 1920 or 1921 he had written one of his finest works, the novelette *Kanashimi no daika* (The Price in Sadness), a psychological portrait of a young writer whose creative imagination tells him that his wife and one of his friends are attracted to each other; to prove his suspicions, he sets up a trap that succeeds only in actually bringing them together. This is the first appearance of a frequent Yokomitsu character type, the over-self-conscious, overimaginative character who causes unhappiness to himself and others. *Kanashimi no daika* was not published in full until 1955, eight years after Yokomitsu's death (he published an altered short-story version under a different title in 1924).

Another fine work of this period is the historical novelette *Nichirin* (The Sun), the subject of which is Himiko, the female ruler mentioned in a Chinese account of 3rd-century Japan (see YAMATAI). In *Nichirin* the male rulers of a number of neighboring states destroy each other over desire for the beautiful Himiko, and she is thus able to create a unified kingdom under her own rule. The tale and its characters are caricatures. What distinguishes *Nichirin* is its pictorial quality, its highly polished, rhythmical style, and its effective use of symbolism. Yokomitsu is said to have begun *Nichirin* after reading the Japanese translation of Flaubert's *Salammbo* and to have labored over the writing for two years; certainly the novelette is reminiscent of *Salammbo* in its combination of barbarous theme and beauty of language. When Kikuchi Kan founded the important magazine *Bungei shunjū* in 1923, Yokomitsu became a staff member. The publication in May that year of both *Nichirin* and the short story "Hae" (The Fly)—the latter in *Bungei shunjū*—brought Yokomitsu wide recognition for the first time. From this point on, his life was that of an increasingly well-known professional writer.

The School of New Sensibilities —— In 1924 Yokomitsu and a number of other young writers formed the literary group known as the SHINKANKAKU SCHOOL (School of New Sensibilities). One of the group was KAWABATA YASUNARI, who was to remain a close friend of Yokomitsu's throughout the latter's life. Yokomitsu was the group's chief ideological spokesman, and it was his own writing style of this period that became known as the Shinkankaku style. The ideology was one of artistic modernism, with an appeal to such European avant-garde movements as futurism, dadaism, and expressionism. It stood in conscious opposition to the Marxist ideology of the currently fashionable PROLETARIAN LITERATURE MOVEMENT. It also called for a new form of artistic fiction to supplant the unimaginative, thinly fictionalized autobiographical novel (the so-called I-NOVEL) that was the dominant modern Japanese genre in "pure" (as opposed to popular) literature. The Shinkankaku prose style was the one Yokomitsu had already developed in such works as *Nichirin*, with its rhythmic and other sound effects and its symbolism, but now heightened by the introduction of even more startling imagery and the use of visual effects that resembled those of the European expressionist film.

Many of Yokomitsu's own early works—and some of his best stories of the middle 1920s—were in fact autobiographical, but these became increasingly fictionalized and embellished with artistic patterning as he proceeded into the decade, and completely fictional works, often with remote settings and extreme situations, came to predominate. Of the stories with an autobiographical basis, the best are a series based on the illness and death (in 1926) of Yokomitsu's first wife. In these the attempts of a young writer or artist to comfort his dying wife are complicated by remembered jealousies; these and his thoughts and hallucinations before and after her death are expressed in extravagant language and imagery. The best known of the series is "Haru wa basha ni notte" (1926, Spring, Riding in a Carriage); others are "Furueru bara" (1925, Trembling Rose), "Ga wa doko ni de mo iru" (1926, There Are Moths Everywhere), and "Hanazono no shisō" (1927, Thoughts in the Flower Garden).

Though small in scale, these stories include some of the masterpieces of modern Japanese literature.

Many of the purely fictional stories of this period are satirical attacks on the Marxist idea of economic determinism. (*Nichirin*, with its sexual-determinist theme, is also partly in this category.) Two examples are "Shizuka naru raretsu" (1925, Silent Ranks), in which the fates of two city-states are seen as determined by geological changes in the river valleys in which they are situated, and "Naporeon to tamushi" (1926, Napoleon's Ringworm), in which Napoleon Bonaparte is seen as driven to his wars of conquest by the itchings of a huge patch of ringworm on his belly.

Shanghai —— Yokomitsu remarried early in 1927. Later that year the Shinkankaku school's magazine, *Bungei jidai*, ceased publication, and the group drifted apart. Yokomitsu himself continued to write in the Shinkankaku style for a few more years, most notably in his one full-length novel of the period, *Shanhai* (1928–31, Shanghai). In 1928 Yokomitsu went to Shanghai to visit a Japanese friend, and many of the descriptions in the novel are based on the impressions he stored up during his one month's stay there, but the novel itself is set a few years earlier, during the May 30th Incident of 1925, a violent encounter between protesting Chinese workers and foreign settlement police. *Shanhai* is a nightmare montage of scenes in the streets, the Japanese factories, the Turkish baths, and the taxi-dance halls, within which foreigners of various nationalities, many of them spokesmen for differing ideologies, pursue their points of view. The ideologies are shown to be irrelevant to the actual situation: the city and all the characters of the novel are being controlled by remote and invisible forces, which, as the novel proceeds, draw them increasingly into a whirlpool of danger and violence. (In this respect *Shanhai* bears comparison with André Malraux's later novel of Shanghai in the year 1927, *La Condition Humaine* [1933].)

Shanhai also shows traces of the nationalism that was to become more evident in Yokomitsu's works as Japan moved toward World War II. The Japanese man who is the novel's central intelligence becomes involved with (among other women) a female leader of the striking Chinese workers. He is able to understand her protests against all foreign (including Japanese) exploitation of the Chinese, and he is evidently not fully convinced by the counterargument he mouths that Japan would save its fellow Asians from Western colonialism; nevertheless, his moody conclusion is that he cannot help being Japanese and supporting his country's colonialist interests. Such reservations aside, *Shanhai* is among all of Yokomitsu's longer fiction the most completely successful as a work of art.

The Psychological Monologues —— After *Shanhai* Yokomitsu abandoned the Shinkankaku style, and even before that novel's completion he had begun to experiment with a radically different style—that of the short stories "Kikai" (1930, Machine) and "Jikan" (1931, Time). In both of these stories the interrelationships of a group of people placed in an extreme situation are presented through the consciousness of a first-person narrator who is one of the group. The style is one of extremely long and convoluted sentences, relieved by little paragraphing, which follow the meandering thoughts of the narrator. It has been described as Yokomitsu's attempt at stream-of-consciousness (the works of James Joyce were being introduced to Japan at about this time); however, it more nearly resembles the psychological monologues of some of Dostoevsky's characters.

In "Kikai," the more celebrated of the two stories, the narrator tells of jealousy and outbreaks of violence among the workers of a small metal nameplate factory. The narrator, who has been invited to participate in the chemical process of the master of the shop, becomes something of an inventor himself. He discovers invisible mechanisms at work among the chemicals and concludes that he and the other warring workers are being manipulated by some invisible machine. When one of the workers is poisoned, apparently by accident, the narrator suspects that he himself may have been led to cause the accident; however, he is no longer able to judge his own actions. Both the inventor as a character and the theme of an inexplicable mechanism controlling human beings were to appear frequently in Yokomitsu's fiction.

Shin'en and Monshō —— The psychological monologue of "Kikai" and "Jikan" attracted much attention at the time, and they are among the most widely known and discussed of Yokomitsu's works; however, they are hardly typical, and in fact he wrote only a few other stories in this style, all in 1930 and 1931. He had already begun *Shin'en* (1930–32, The Imperial Mausoleum), the first of his novels for a wider audience (the first part of it was serialized in a newspaper), and most of his fiction from this point on was written in a plainer, more "normal" style of Japanese prose. (He himself said that his earlier works reflected a period of struggle against the Japanese language and his later ones an attitude of submission to it.) *Shin'en* is a story of complex love relationships among a group of wealthy, sophisticated Japanese men and women (the type of fiction that is referred to by Japanese critics as the "salon novel"). One of the women shoots her husband while on a hunting expedition— accidentally, but under ambiguous psychological circumstances.

The much longer novel *Monshō* (Family Crest), which was published in 1934 followed by a continuation in 1940, has as one of its main characters an inventor who engages in a series of attempts to derive products such as alcoholic beverages and soy sauce from such unlikely (and inexpensive) raw materials as banana skins and the residues from fish-processing factories. Even when he comes closest to success, he is constantly defeated by factors beyond his control such as sudden changes in economic conditions; nevertheless, he always tries again. The other main character is the overly self-conscious intellectual of so many of Yokomitsu's works, who is contrasted with the inventor, and with whose wife the inventor has had a relationship in the past. The inventor's indefeatability and optimism (said to derive from the old family stock of which he came) were qualities that Yokomitsu identified with the "true Japanese spirit," and such characters appear frequently in his later, more nationalistic fiction.

In 1935 Yokomitsu published an essay entitled "Junsui shōsetsu ron" (Theory of the Pure Novel), in which he maintained that if the "pure novel" were to be produced in Japan and for the Japanese people it would have to be at the same time both pure and popular literature. This statement would hardly have surprised a Western audience, long accustomed to the idea that great literature can be at the same time popular, but it, and other sentiments in the essay, created a great controversy in the Japanese literary world, where a rigid distinction between "pure" and "popular" literature had been maintained. The novel *Kazoku kaigi* (Family Conference), which was serialized in newspapers in 1935, is usually seen as Yokomitsu's effort to put his theories into practice. However, he had already been trying to reach a wider audience, and it is equally likely that the essay was a statement of what he had been attempting in works such as *Shin'en* and *Monshō*. He continued to produce novels aimed at a general audience (often serialized in newspapers or women's magazines), and in some years thereafter he was serializing two full-length works simultaneously.

Ryoshū——In 1936 Yokomitsu went to Europe as a correspondent for two Japanese newspapers, partly to cover the Berlin Olympics. The record of his six months' travels was published as *Ōshū kikō* (1936, A European Travel Diary), but a more important result of the trip is the long, unfinished novel (2 volumes in most editions) that was to occupy the final 10 years of his life: *Ryoshū* (1937–46, A Traveler's Sadness). Yokomitsu was visiting for the first time the Europe from which he had derived so many influences in his youth, and in his increasingly nationalistic mood of the 1930s he was apparently very uneasy with what he found there, an uneasiness that is reflected in the prolixity and diffuseness of the novel. The characters of *Ryoshū* are a group of Japanese intellectuals brought together by chance in Europe, and many of the novel's pages are devoted to their observations while traveling and to their conversations, in which they attempt to come to grips with the problem of Eastern (meaning Japanese) civilization versus Western. Some of the characters are spokesmen for a pro-European internationalist point of view, but the main male character, particularly, is obsessed with what he sees as the incompatibility of East and West.

What there is of novelistic plot in *Ryoshū* concerns the relationship between this male character and a woman member of the group. They fall in love, but he is unable to bring himself to decide to marry her. His indecision continues after their return to Japan. He is too conscious of the fact that she is a Catholic and that 16th-century followers of this foreign religion defeated his own ancestors in Kyūshū. He takes refuge in mystical speculations about the superiority of the supposed thought of ancient Shintō over Western science and mathematics. By the end of World War II Yokomitsu had brought his characters up to the eve of Japan's invasion of China in 1937, and an engagement between the couple had finally been announced.

After the war Yokomitsu brought out a new edition of *Ryoshū*, with some of the more nationalistic passages deleted, and he evidently intended to bring his characters forward into the peacetime era. However, he died of a stomach ulcer complicated by pleurisy before this plan could be realized. In the last analysis this most ambitious work of his, although it contains many pages of fine writing, must be counted a failure as a novel.

In the two years of his life that remained after World War II, Yokomitsu managed to complete two fine works, one *Yoru no kutsu* (1947, Shoes in the Night), a diary of the experience of defeat, and the other the posthumous short story "Bishō" (1948, The Smile), which tells of an encounter, in the last days of the war, between a middle-aged writer and a young inventor (of the irrepressible Japanese type) who claims to have discovered a new, powerful weapon that will ensure Japan's victory.

Most of Yokomitsu's longer works and many of his collections were brought back into print immediately after the war, a reflection of his prewar stature. Before long, however, he had fallen into relative obscurity. He had been denounced by some of his peers as a collaborator with the militarist regime for his "literary home front" activities during the war, and younger readers perhaps regarded his works as experimental and dated. In the late 1970s only *Ryoshū* and a volume of short stories were widely available in paperback reprints, and his collected works had been long out of print. However, a growing number of scholars and critics had begun to reassess his work. In 1982 a new, definitive collected works was in progress, and in December of that year there was a well-attended exhibition of manuscripts, photographs, and memorabilia in a Tōkyō department store. His final place in the history of modern Japanese literature was, however, yet to be determined.

📖——Works by Yokomitsu: *Yokomitsu Riichi zenshū*, 12 vols (Kawade Shobō, 1955–56); definitive edition: *Teihon Yokomitsu Riichi zenshū*, 13 vols (Kawade Shobō Shinsha, 1981–). Translations: Dennis Keene, tr, *Love and Other Stories of Yokomitsu Riichi* (1974). "Hae," tr John Nathan as "The Fly," *Japan Quarterly* 12.1 (1965). "Haru wa basha ni notte," tr John Nathan as "Spring in a Surrey," *Japan Quarterly* 12.1 (1965). "Jikan," tr Donald Keene as "Time," in Donald Keene, ed, *Modern Japanese Literature* (1957). "Kikai," tr Edward Seidensticker as "Machine," in Ivan Morris, ed, *Modern Japanese Stories* (1961). "Shizuka naru raretsu," tr John Bester as "Silent Ranks," in Yokomitsu Riichi, *Time, and Others* (1965).

Works about Yokomitsu: Hoshō Masao, *Yokomitsu Riichi* (1966). Inoue Ken, *Yokomitsu Riichi* (1974). Inoue Ken, *Hyōden Yokomitsu Riichi* (1975). Dennis Keene, *Yokomitsu Riichi: Modernist* (1980). Kuritsubo Yoshiki, *Yokomitsu Riichi* (1981).

Alan CAMPBELL

Yokomizo Seishi (1902–1981)

Novelist. Born in Hyōgo Prefecture. Graduate of Ōsaka Pharmaceutical College. An avid reader of mystery stories from youth, Yokomizo began writing while managing a pharmaceutical business. He joined the publishing house Hakubunkan in 1926, but left in 1932 to devote himself full-time to writing. Novels of this period include *Onibi* (1935) and *Ningyō Sashichi torimonochō* (1938–39). Immediately after the war, he established his name as a leading mystery writer with *Honjin satsujin jiken* and *Chōchō satsujin jiken* (both 1946). His fiction, based on the orthodox Western detective story format, has served as the model for postwar mystery writing in Japan. Other works include *Akuma ga kitarite fue o fuku* (1951–53).

Yokoo Tadanori (1936–   )

Artist, known for collage posters. Born in Hyōgo Prefecture. From childhood, he showed intense interest in the colors and designs in his family's clothing store. After working briefly for a newspaper in Kōbe, he joined the Nippon Design Center, Inc, in 1961, and was almost at once recognized with awards from the Art Directors Club of Tōkyō. His work, influenced by the pop art and psychedelic movements, incorporates photos and bits from traditional Japanese, Western, and even Buddhist art, often all in the same poster. He has received a long series of awards and recognitions both in Japan and abroad, including a one-man show in 1970 at the Museum of Modern Art in New York. He is also known for his numerous essays on art and life.

Yokose Yau (1878–1934)

Poet. Real name Yokose Torahisa, other pen name Tonemaru. Born in Ibaraki Prefecture. Crippled by rickets in childhood, he stayed home after completing grade school, devoting all his time to reading and writing poems, which he submitted to a children's literary magazine, *Bunko.* After achieving some recognition in the magazine, he published his first collection of poems, *Yūzuki,* in 1899, but it was with his second collection, *Hanamori* (1905), that he established his name as a poet. His poems, melancholy and lyrical in tone, are written in the simple rhythms of local folk song. Other collections include *Nijūhasshuku* (1907).

Yokosuka

City in southeastern Kanagawa Prefecture, central Honshū. Situated at the mouth of Tōkyō Bay, Yokosuka is favored with a natural harbor. During the Edo period (1600–1868), the Uraga magistrate's office was located here to check ships approaching the shogunal capital of Edo (now Tōkyō). It was also the site of a shogunate shipyard. From 1884 the city developed as Japan's first naval base. Since World War II, it has served as a naval base of the US Navy and the Japanese Maritime Self Defense Force. Its principal industries are automobile manufacturing and shipbuilding. A monument to the Englishman William ADAMS, who arrived in Japan in 1600 and was granted an estate in the area, is in Tsukayama Park in the Hemi district. Pop: 421,112.

Yokosuka Shipyards

(Yokosuka Zōsenjo). Predecessor of the Yokosuka Naval Arsenal (Kaigun Kōshō). It was originally the Yokosuka Seitetsusho, a foundry and shipyard built by the Tokugawa shogunate in 1866 under the direction of the French naval engineer François VERNY (1837–1908) at Yokosuka, Kanagawa Prefecture. The shipyard was taken over by the new government immediately after the Meiji Restoration of 1868, and the following year it was placed under the Navy Ministry. In 1871 it was renamed the Yokosuka Zōsenjo. In 1876 it produced its first naval vessel, the wooden-hulled *Seiki* with a displacement of 897 tons, under the guidance of French engineers. Four years later an all-Japanese team was able to build another wooden-hulled warship, the *Iwaki.* The shipyard was renamed the Kaigun Kōshō in 1903 and was counted among the four largest arsenals in Japan until the end of World War II. (The other three were at Tōkyō, Kure, and Sasebo.)

Yokota Kisaburō (1896–   )

Scholar of international law and third chief justice of the Supreme Court. Born in Aichi Prefecture, he graduated from Tōkyō University in 1922 and became a research associate. After studies in France and Germany from 1926 to 1928, he was named a professor at Tōkyō University in 1930 and taught public international law there until his retirement in 1957. In the same year he became a member of the United Nations Committee on International Law. He served as chief justice of the Supreme Court from 1960 to 1966. Influenced by Hans Kelsen (1881–1973) and other advocates of the "pure theory" of law, Yokota considered international law as a single, self-contained body of law completely independent of social or cultural values. After World War II Yokota called for the removal of the emperor because of his responsibility for the war. He also took article 9 of the 1947 constitution (see RENUNCIATION OF WAR) to require complete abolition of any military capability; but as the international situation changed, he asserted that, in accord with the right of self-defense, it was permissible for Japan to take measures to ensure its national security. At the same time, he urged the judiciary to exercise great restraint in ruling on the constitutionality of laws (see JUDICIAL REVIEW). His writings include *Kokusaihō* (2 vols, 1933, International Law), *Jieiken* (1951, The Right of Self-Defense), and *Kokusaihōgaku* (1955, The Study of International Law).

SATŌ Kōji

Yokote

City in the Yokote Basin, southeastern Akita Prefecture, northern Honshū. Yokote began as a CASTLE TOWN under the rule of the Onodera family during the Kamakura period (1185–1333). Local products include apples and Yokote *momen,* a traditional cotton fabric. Yokote is known for its annual winter festival, in which snow huts called *kamakura* are built for children. Pop: 43,773.

Yokoyama Taikan

Detail of an imaginary portrait of the ancient Chinese poet and court official Qu Yuan (Ch'ü Yüan; J: Kutsugen) in a heroic pose. Completed in 1898, the work shows Taikan's interest in the atmospheric use of lights and darks. Ink and colors on paper. Entire work 132.7 × 289.7 cm. Itsukushima Shrine, Hiroshima Prefecture.

Yokote Basin

(Yokote Bonchi). A graben basin in southeastern Akita Prefecture, northern Honshū. Bounded by the Ōu and Dewa mountain ranges, it consists of piedmont alluvial fans below the fault scarps of the Ōu Mountains and the flood plain of the river Omonogawa's upper reaches. Paddy fields, irrigated with water from Lake Tazawa, are found around the fans and on the lowlands. Apples and grapes are also cultivated. The major cities are Yokote, Ōmagari, and Yuzawa. Length: approximately 60 km (37 mi); maximum width: 15 km (9.3 mi).

Yokoyama Gennosuke (1871–1915)

Writer about social problems of the latter part of the Meiji period (1868–1912). Born in Toyama Prefecture; studied at Igirisu Hōritsu Gakkō (now Chūō University). Under the influence of the writer FUTABATEI SHIMEI, Yokoyama became interested in life at the lower levels of Japanese society. In 1894 he joined the newspaper *Mainichi shimbun* and traveled throughout the country to investigate living conditions among the poor, including urban slum dwellers, textile workers, and rural tenant farmers. He later gathered information on factory workers for the Ministry of Agriculture and Commerce. Yokoyama's best-known work, *Nihon no kasō shakai* (1899, Japan's Lower Classes), a summary of his observations, called public attention to the plight of the working poor at a time of rapid industrialization and is still highly regarded for its accuracy and insights.

Yokoyama Taikan (1868–1958)

A prominent painter in the movement led by OKAKURA KAKUZŌ to develop a new style of Japanese painting respectful of, but not enslaved to, the nation's past traditions.

Taikan was born Sakai Hidemaro in Ibaraki Prefecture to an old *samurai* family. Taikan was later adopted into his mother's family and took the name Yokoyama. He attended the Tōkyō School of English in preparation for a government career. Upon graduation, however, he chose instead to pursue an interest in painting and enrolled in the Tōkyō Bijutsu Gakkō (now Tōkyō University of Fine Arts and Music), which had just opened under Okakura's directorship. There he first studied under the Kanō-style painter HASHIMOTO GAHŌ but was particularly inspired by Okakura's nationalist ideals and became his most devoted disciple.

In 1895 he spent a year teaching at the Kyōto Municipal School of Fine Arts and Crafts, returning to the Tōkyō Bijutsu Gakkō as an assistant professor of painting in 1896. Taikan left this post the following year when Okakura was forced to resign as the result of an institutional dispute. Later, Taikan, with SHIMOMURA KANZAN and HISHIDA SHUNSŌ, helped Okakura organize the JAPAN FINE ARTS ACADEMY (Nihon Bijutsuin). Besieged by numerous setbacks, the academy eventually closed, but Taikan was among those to reestablish it in 1914. In the interim he traveled to India (1903), to Europe and the United States (1904–05), and to China (1910). In 1930 he was sent to Italy as an art ambassador.

One of Taikan's early attempts to revolutionize Japanese-style painting involved the emphasizing of light and the deemphasis of line, which resulted in softly blurred contours of figures and objects. Public and critical response was negative, however, and he later abandoned the style. But the break with the past had been effected by this departure from the norm and the way was cleared for the ensuing innovations and experiments of modern painters. Taikan later turned to monochrome ink painting, attracted by the unlimited tonal potential of black, which he began to explore as enthusiastically as he had previously explored the color spectrum. An early masterpiece in this medium is his famous *Wheel of Life* scroll of 1923.

Inspired by his energy and dedication, a number of young artists joined him when the Japan Fine Arts Academy was reopened, but he remained more an honored elder than a teacher and took no disciples. In 1931 he was appointed a member of the Imperial Fine Arts Academy; he received the Order of Culture in 1937. After World War II, during which he strongly supported Japan's policies, both his art and popularity entered a gradual decline.   *Margo* STIPE

Yōmei Bunko

(Yōmei Library). A private library, located in the Utano district of Kyōto, based on the collection of the KONOE FAMILY, who were also known by the name Yōmei because they lived near the Yōmei Gate of the Imperial Palace in Kyōto. The collection contains some 10,000 manuscripts, National Treasures, and rare art objects as well as more than 10,000 books and other printed records. As one of the GO-SEKKE, the five branches of the Fujiwara family whose heads served for centuries as imperial regents, the Konoe built up a priceless repository, which includes such unique items as the original manuscript of MIDŌ KAMPAKU KI, the diary of FUJIWARA NO MICHINAGA. The modern statesman KONOE FUMIMARO reassembled the collection and established the library as a private foundation in 1938. It is open to the public.   *Theodore F.* WELCH

Yōmeigaku

(Wang Yangming school). A system of thought expounded by the Ming dynasty (1368–1644) Chinese philosopher Wang Yangming (1472–1529; J: Ō Yōmei, hence Yōmeigaku, *gaku* meaning studies). Wang Yangming emphasized the "good knowing" (Ch: *liangzhi* or *liang-chih;* J: *ryōchi*) innate in all men and argued that awakening to this good knowing was a process by which *li* (J: *ri*), the ultimate universal principle, was "realized." He also emphasized the union of thought and action, placing stress on practice (and thus putting trust in individual effort toward betterment) rather than on theory or on scholarly investigation of things in pursuit of an objective or substantive *li*. This antischolastic conception of *li* contrasted with the more intellectualist, rationalist approach of the Zhu Xi (Chu Hsi) school of Confucianism (see SHUSHIGAKU), which had the support of the Tokugawa shogunate in Japan.

During the Edo period (1600–1868), supporters of the Zhu Xi school were numerous in Japan, and the school played a pivotal role in the development of ideas. There were also important followers of the Wang Yangming school in Japan, but they tended to be isolated from each other. Moreover, most of them drew not only upon the teachings of the Wang Yangming school but also on those of other schools in formulating and articulating their systems of thought.

The first patriarch of the Wang Yangming school (Yōmeigaku) in Japan was NAKAE TŌJU (1608–48). In his youth, Tōju studied the teachings of the Zhu Xi school, but around the time he gave up his position as a member of the *samurai* class, he assumed a critical stance toward Zhu Xi's views. Tōju was drawn to the Chinese Five Classics, with their religious orientation, rather than to the more philosophically oriented Four Books, which were the classics for the Zhu Xi school. (The Four Books: *Daxue* or *Ta-hsüeh,* The Great Learning; *Zhongyong* or *Chung-yung,* the Doctrine of the Mean; *Lun yu* or *Lun yü,* the Confucian Analects; *Mengzi* or *Meng-tzu,* the Mencius. The Five Classics: *Yi jing* or *I ching,* The Book of Changes; *Shu jing* or *Shu ching,* The Book of Documents; *Shi jing* or *Shih ching,* The Book of Odes; *Li ji* or *Li chi,* The Book of Rites; *Chun qiu* or *Ch'un ch'iu,* The Spring and Autumn Annals.) Tōju was also greatly inspired by the *Xiao jing* (*Hsiao ching;* The Book of Filial Piety), with its emphasis on the virtue of filial piety (which embraced not only duties toward one's parents and ancestors but also devotion

to Heaven). It was at about this time that Tōju came to know Wang Yangming's thought and read a collection of the sayings of Wang Longxi (Wang Lung-hsi, 1498–1583), a disciple of Wang Yangming. Tōju embraced the idea that the universe sprang from the "Great Emptiness" (Ch: Taixu; T'ai-hsü; J: Taikyo), over which the "Supreme Lord" rules. He maintained that "good knowing" is the human being's sharing in the mind of the Supreme Lord. Tōju also conceived a deep reverence for the supreme deity of Japan, AMA-TERASU ŌMIKAMI.

Later, Tōju read the works of Wang Yangming in their entirety, and was at the same time influenced considerably by other late Ming-dynasty doctrines which insisted on unity among the three traditions of Confucianism, Buddhism, and Taoism. He preached that the entire world is as one under the rule of the Supreme Lord of the Great Emptiness and that all people are children of the Supreme Lord.

Tōju emphasized that in our actual dealings in the everyday world, there are appropriate times, places, and social positions suitable for particular actions. Among the Classics, he placed particular weight on *The Book of Filial Piety,* as well as on *The Great Learning,* books considered in Japan to be the fundamental documents of the Wang Yangming school. *The Great Learning* mentioned here is the original version of that classic, the *Daxue guben* (*Ta-hsüe ku-pen*), which Wang Yangming had exalted.

KUMAZAWA BANZAN (1619–91) studied in his youth with Nakae Tōju and was particularly attracted to Tōju's thinking about appropriate "time, place, and social position," to the extent that he made this a basic tenet in his own philosophy. Banzan put great emphasis on the practical character of Wang Yangming's teachings. Thus, he taught that wide knowledge did not guarantee successful conduct of the affairs of state; it was also necessary to understand humanity and actual social conditions. While he followed Tōju's concept of the Great Emptiness and expressed a reverence for Shintō, he interpreted its teachings within a Confucian framework and was more critical of Buddhism than was Tōju.

MIWA SHISSAI (1669–1744), the son of a Shintō priest, predictably demonstrated a strong affiliation with Shintō. He is said to have revitalized Yōmeigaku after the deaths of Tōju and Banzan. He first studied under SATŌ NAOKATA of the YAMAZAKI ANSAI faction of the Zhu Xi school and later converted to Yōmeigaku. He held that the Four Books and Five Classics were but an expression of the innate "good knowing" and that the essence of these documents was thus found in our own hearts. His great contribution was the first annotation, in China or Japan, of the *Chuanxilu* (*Ch'uan-hsi-lu;* J: *Denshūroku;* Instructions for Practical Living), a collection of Wang Yangming's sayings and writings. The publication of this work was chiefly responsible for the increased popularity of Yōmeigaku. Shissai's lectures on the *Chuanxilu* were also published.

SATŌ ISSAI (1772–1859) was a Confucian scholar in the service of the shogunate school, the SHŌHEIKŌ. He lectured in public on the Zhu Xi school but was a private admirer of Wang Yangming. His *Denshūroku rangaisho* is a study of the composition and various editions of the *Chuanxilu.* Another of his works is the *Genshi shiroku,* which exerted considerable influence in the final years of the shogunate. Issai's position represents a synthesis between the schools of Zhu Xi and Wang Yangming.

The last important figure in Yōmeigaku was ŌSHIO HEIHACHIRŌ (1793–1837). He was a local officer of the law in Ōsaka as well as a scholar. Ōshio regretted the discontinuation of studies on "good knowing" after Shissai's death and preached, following Tōju and Banzan, that the "good knowing" in a person's heart was at one with the universal Great Emptiness. After death, according to Ōshio, we return to the Great Emptiness to live forever.

Ōshio is notable for his exceptional bravery in transforming his "good knowing" into moral action. Ōshio was sympathetic to the rather radical line within the Chinese Wang Yangming school represented by Wang Longxi. Furthermore, Ōshio was in favor of promoting national defense, a position upheld in the writings of Wang Yangming. (At the time, Japan was in a state of national crisis because of pressure from Western countries.) Ōshio led an uprising in protest of the suffering endured by the people during the great famine of the Tempō era (1830–44; see TEMPŌ FAMINE). When the uprising failed, he committed suicide. This revolt is related to his individual interpretation of Wang Yangming's doctrines. Also noteworthy are Ōshio's wide reading in Chinese philosophical writings, especially from the Ming period, which is reflected in his works, and the logical clarity exhibited in his critical commentaries.

YAMASHITA Ryūji

yomeirikon

Patrilocal marriage, whereby the husband and wife take up residence in or near the house of the husband's parents. The wedding reception is sponsored by the husband's family. *Yomeirikon* developed together with the evolution of the warrior class in the latter part of the Heian period (794–1185). It represented a significant shift from the earlier prevalent practice of matrilocal marriage (MUKOIRI-KON), and from marriages requiring relocation or even dual residences. *Yomeirikon* became more widespread during the Edo period (1600–1868). This was in part due to the dominance of government-supported Neo-Confucian philosophy whereby primary emphasis was placed on the loyalty of the *samurai* to his lord and, similarly, of the wife to her husband. Samurai families were required by social convention to marry into families of the same rank. Thus, with a go-between's (NAKŌDO) assistance family patriarchs took great care in arranging marriages and frequently sought prospective candidates in distant locales. The wife's filial duties to her old home decreased and she became isolated in her new home through commitments to her husband and his family. The practice of *yomeirikon* became increasingly customary among commoners during and after the Edo period. Today a growing member of couples live apart from their parents and the word *yomeiri* has in general come to mean marriage. NOGUCHI Takenori

yomena

Aster, or *Kalimeris, yomena.* A perennial herb of the chrysanthemum family (Compositae), which grows wild in the hills, fields, and wetlands of Honshū , Shikoku, and Kyūshū. The young leaves are edible. It grows 30–100 centimeters (12–39 in) high. Its alternate leaves are oval to lanceolate and coarsely serrated. From summer to autumn the top of the stem branches out and bears flowers about 2.5 centimeters (1 in) wide. Each flower head has yellow tubulous (disk) flowers surrounded by faint purple ray flowers.

Similar species include the *nokongiku* (*Aster ageratoides* var. *ovatus*), which resembles the *yomena* but has longer hair (pappus) on the fruit; and the *kongiku* (*A. ageratoides* var. *ovatus* f. *hortensis*), which bears deeper purple flowers. MATSUDA Osamu

yomihon

(literally, "reading books," as opposed to popular illustrated works appreciated more for their pictures than for their stories). A genre of late-18th- and early-19th-century narrative prose fiction (see GESAKU), characterized by historical settings, didactic and moralistic story lines blended with the supernatural and by heavy reliance on Chinese prose models. *Yomihon* are the immediate forerunners of the modern popular romance, but the genre included collections of short stories, full-length historical romances, and even prose discourses with a minimal imaginative framework. The format was modeled after that of the UKIYO-ZŌSHI, an earlier form of prose fiction, and popular Chinese works of the Ming (1368–1644) and Qing (Ch'ing; 1644–1912) dynasties.

Yomihon were typically composed of sets of several thin volumes, usually five in number, each having a separate title slip pasted on the front and at least a pair of illustrations, mostly by artists of the UKIYO-E school. The first volume often carried a series of frontispieces with captions or inscriptions describing the contents, and the text was hand-printed from individually carved woodblocks. Each volume consisted of 15 to 20 double leaves bound in heavy, variously colored paper covers, sometimes decorated with an embossed or printed design; for display purposes, the sets were wrapped in attractively designed paper envelopes.

The origin of the *yomihon* genre can be traced to early 18th-century interest in Chinese colloquial fiction, which was stimulated by the Chinese study group organized by OGYŪ SORAI (1666–1728) and Okajima Kanzan (1674–1728). The historical romance, *Shuihu-zhuan* or *Shui-hu-chuan* (Water Margin; tr *All Men Are Brothers*, 1933), was especially attractive as a model for Japanese works. The narrative technique of master *yomihon* writer Takizawa BAKIN (1767–1848), for example, was especially indebted to this and other Chinese models. In addition to this adventure novel, ghostly themes taken from both classical Chinese and Japanese literature as well as contemporary Chinese vernacular works served as vehicles for the moralistic, often didactic, *yomihon* romances. Many *yomihon* were direct adaptations of Chinese fiction and retained much of the original linguistic style; usually the prefaces were written in Chinese and the text in a modified form of classical Japanese with a heavy sprinkling of Chinese constructions. Early works were marred by a stiffness of style caused by this transposition, but later *yomihon* attained a high level of stylistic excellence.

The early *yomihon*, typically collections of short stories, were published in the Kyōto and Ōsaka area. The first *yomihon* recognized by Japanese scholars was a set of nine short stories, *Hanabusa sōshi* (1749, A Garland of Tales), mostly adapted from three popular Chinese collections, written by an Ōsaka physician, Tsuga Teishō (1718–94?). Later, in the 19th century, *yomihon* were issued in Edo (now Tōkyō) and developed into full-length historical novels. The most successful of all *yomihon* date from this period: the ghostly *Ugetsu monogatari* (1776; tr *Tales of Moonlight and Rain*, 1974) written by UEDA AKINARI (1734–1809), and the adventuresome NANSŌ SATOMI HAKKENDEN (1814–42, Satomi and the Eight "Dogs") by Bakin, represent the culmination of the traditional art of storytelling. Other notable authors of this period include TAKEBE AYATARI (1719–74) and SANTŌ KYŌDEN (1761–1816).

Yomihon were designed to enlighten readers as well as entertain them. The authors tried to express their views of life in elegant prose with a neoclassical flavor and to reach a wide audience, thereby creating new interest in classical learning, public affairs, and foreign as well as native literature. *Yomihon* writers usually paid close attention to plot construction and matters of technique, which had great influence on the pioneers of modern Japanese literature and gave impetus to the contemporary Japanese historical novel, still a popular literary form. Although later authors, such as TSUBOUCHI SHŌYŌ (1859–1935), criticized the *yomihon* for lack of realism and character development, they themselves often wrote in a style reminiscent of Akinari and Bakin, implicitly accepting the moral standards and *samurai* values of their predecessors. See also LITERATURE: Edo literature.

Asō Isoji, *Edo bungaku to Shina bungaku* (1946). Donald Keene, *World Within Walls* (1976). Nakamura Yukihiko, Takeda Mamoru, and Nakamura Hiroyasu, ed, *Hanabusa-zōshi, Nishiyama monogatari, Ugetsu monogatari, Harusame monogatari* (1973). Nakamura Yukihiko, *Kinsei bungei shichō kō* (1975). Leon Zolbrod, *Takizawa Bakin* (1967). Leon Zolbrod, tr, *Ugetsu monogatari* (1974). Leon M. ZOLBROD

Yomi no Kuni → afterlife

Yomitan

Village on the western coast of Okinawa, Okinawa Prefecture. Its economy depends largely on the American military forces, which take up some 80 percent of the area. The principal farm product is sugar cane; there is also hog raising. Pop: 26,517.

Yomiuri shimbun

One of Japan's largest national daily newspapers. The *Yomiuri* was launched in 1874 by the Nisshūsha newspaper company as a small daily aimed at ordinary readers and quickly gained in popularity. During the 1880s and 1890s the paper made a name for itself as a literary arts publication by having writers like OZAKI KŌYŌ as regular contributors. In 1917 the name of the news company was changed to Yomiuri Shimbun Sha to match the name of the paper. From the early 1920s most newspapers began putting out evening editions as part of a package system for subscribers. The *Yomiuri*, however, continued to publish only a morning paper and came close to bankruptcy. In 1924 SHŌRIKI MATSUTARŌ took over management of the company. His innovations included sensational news coverage, a full-page radio program guide, sponsorship of an invitation to American professional baseball teams to visit Japan, and establishment of Japan's first professional baseball team (now known as the Yomiuri Giants), all of which contributed to a dramatic increase of its circulation. The *Yomiuri* later began putting out an evening edition. Emphasis was shifted to broad news coverage aimed at readers in the local Tōkyō area. By 1941 it had the largest circulation of any daily newspaper in the Tōkyō area. In 1942, under wartime conditions, it merged with the HŌCHI SHIMBUN and became known as the *Yomiuri-Hōchi*. Following the end of the war in 1945 there was an internal struggle for democratization of management, and for a time the company union had control over editorial policy. In 1946 management officials plotted a rollback with the support of the American Occupation authorities, which touched off a second dispute over control of the paper, and in the end the company union was defeated in its bid for control. That same year the *Yomiuri* reverted to its original name. In 1952 it began publishing in Ōsaka and then went nationwide. It has three main offices located in Tōkyō, Ōsaka, and Kita Kyūshū, and regional offices in Sapporo and Takaoka as well as some 20 overseas news bureaus. It has special affiliations with the Associated Press (AP), Agence France Presse (AFP), and Tass wire services and with the *Washington Post* and *Daily Mail.* Each of its three main offices is an independent financial concern. In addition to its large daily, the Yomiuri Shimbun Sha publishes an English-language paper *(Daily Yomiuri),* a weekly magazine, and other regular publications as well as books. The *Yomiuri shimbun* is listed in the 1981 *Guinness Book of World Records* as the world's largest circulating newspaper. Circulation: 8.68 million in 1981.

Yomiuri Telecasting Corporation

(Yomiuri Terebi). An Ōsaka-based commercial television broadcasting company serving the Kinki (Kyōto–Ōsaka) area. It was established in 1958 with funds from the YOMIURI SHIMBUN, one of Japan's largest national daily newspapers, and other sources. An affiliate of the Nippon News Network (NNN), its weekly programming includes dramas, documentaries, animated films, and a wide variety of multifaceted company-produced specials which are circulated among other network stations. The company began operation as an auxiliary educational television station but has now become a general programming station.   SUDŌ Haruo

Yonago

City in western Tottori Prefecture, western Honshū. Situated on the Sea of Japan, Yonago developed as a castle town in the beginning of the 17th century and then prospered as a distribution center for iron and cotton goods. Pulp and textile mills as well as steel, food-processing, and woodwork manufacturing plants are located in its coastal districts. The city is a base for trips to Daisen, a mountain that attracts many tourists. Kaike Hot Spring is located here. Pop: 127,375.

Yonagunijima

Island 70 km (43 mi) northwest of the island of Iriomotejima, Okinawa Prefecture. One of the YAEYAMA ISLANDS. It is the westernmost point of Japan at longitude 122° 55′ east. It is a tableland, with its highest point at 231 m (758 ft). The coast is made up of raised coral reefs. The island has numerous hot springs and rice fields. Area: 28.5 sq km (11 sq mi).

Yonai Mitsumasa (1880–1948)

Admiral and prime minister (1940). Born in Iwate Prefecture. A graduate of the Naval Academy, he served in numerous important navy posts, becoming commander-in-chief of the Combined Fleet in 1936 and full admiral the following year. As navy minister in the HAYASHI SENJŪRŌ, the first KONOE FUMIMARO, and the HIRANUMA KIICHIRŌ cabinets, he took a pro-American, pro-British stance and firmly opposed the army's proposal for an alliance with the Axis powers. He became prime minister in January 1940 and tried to steer a moderate course despite growing pro-Axis, nationalist pressure from the army. In July, however, Yonai was forced to step down when the army refused to replace Army Minister Hata Shunroku (1879–1962), who had resigned at Yonai's behest. He served again as navy minister in several cabinets during and immediately after World War II and presided over the dissolution of the Japanese navy.

yonaoshi rebellions

(yonaoshi ikki; literally, "world renewal" rebellions). Peasant rebellions that occurred mainly during the years 1866–69. For the most part they arose in the territories directly administered by the Tokugawa shogunate (TENRYŌ) and in the proshogunate domains of eastern Japan. Characteristically, *yonaoshi* revolts resembled intra-peasant civil wars in which many of the poor or smallholding farmers, tenants, and agricultural day laborers rose against the rich of their villages. In the largest of these rebellions, such as the Bushū uprising in the Musashi Plain (now Tōkyō and Saitama prefectures)

and the Shindatsu uprising in Fukushima, both occurring in June of 1866, tens of thousands of peasants and day laborers were organized according to village into units of up to 1,000 men. They marched from village to village, threatening the destruction of individuals or villages that did not accede to their demands for alms or rice. Also demanding the free return of pawned goods and mortgaged land, the rebels most often aimed their attacks at usurers, pawnbrokers, and merchants associated with the sale of silk or cotton. After periods of up to a week, during which considerable property damage but relatively few deaths and casualties occurred, domainal or shogunate forces suppressed the revolts, frequently with the aid of village-recruited peasant troops. They arrested suspected leaders and reprimanded local village authorities for allowing local conditions to deteriorate into anarchy.

Peasants and rural wage laborers who participated in these rebellions often came from the most commercially advanced rural districts in eastern Japan, particularly from silk-producing areas involved in trade with Yokohama. Since the opening of Japanese ports to Western trade in 1858, many of these men had prospered as either wage earners or small producers of raw silk and silk cocoons for foreign export. The immediate occasion of the *yonaoshi* revolts was a precipitous rise in rice prices in 1866, caused by the shogunate's requisitioning of supplies for the second of its CHŌSHŪ EXPEDITIONS, combined with an unstable silk market that worsened the effect on silk producers of continuously rising commodity prices. All *yonaoshi* revolts reflected the effects of a growing commercialization of the countryside, in which economic organization conditioned all social relationships within the village and changing market conditions keenly affected the life of the wage earner and small-scale producer.

Commercial relations had increasingly affected rural society since the 18th century, and poorer peasants had carried out "property smashing" (UCHIKOWASHI) against usurers and the well-off in villages since that time. But *yonaoshi* rebellions marked a major change in the stated objectives and language of peasant protest. In earlier rebellions (HYAKUSHŌ IKKI), peasants had sought their lord's aid, requesting his grace and benevolence and acknowledging his authority. But now peasants claimed that they were the "lords" of *yonaoshi* who would "save other poor people" *(kyūmin tasukeai)* and work "for all the people" *(bammin no tame).* They described their leaders as "gods of equality" *(yonarashi no kami)* and "divine rectifiers of world renewal" *(yonaoshi daimyōjin).* When they received aid from the rich, they described the act of charity as worthy of the age of Maitreya (MIROKU), a millennium when rice and food would be plentiful. Throughout the Edo period (1600–1868) the chiliastic doctrines of Maitreya had been embraced by many villagers as expressions of their wish for the regeneration of this world and their hopes for a fine harvest. In religious associations such as Fujikō (see KŌ), *yonaoshi* had also been associated with the doctrines concerning Maitreya. Members of the elite who had carried out programs of relief for the poor, such as MATSUDAIRA SADANOBU in the 1780s, or who had led rebellions in protest against the corruption of the shogunate, such as ŌSHIO HEIHACHIRŌ in the 1830s, had also been called *yonaoshi daimyōjin.* But only with the *yonaoshi* rebellions did these doctrines become identified with the peasants' attempt to create a world in which social relations would become radically egalitarian and identified with the coming of the age of Maitreya. Though short-lived, the *yonaoshi* rebellions demonstrated how divided the village was and pointed to the continuing potential for strife in local agrarian society. See also EEJANAIKA; OKAGE MAIRI.

——Haga Noboru, *Yonaoshi no shisō* (1973). Sasaki Junnosuke, "Yonaoshi no jōkyō," in Nihonshi Kenkyūkai, ed, *Kōza Nihonshi,* vol 5 (1970). Irwin Scheiner, "Benevolent Lords and Honorable Peasants: Rebellion and Peasant Consciousness in Tokugawa Japan," in Tetsuo Najita and Irwin Scheiner, ed, *Japanese Thought in the Tokugawa Period: Methods and Metaphors* (1978). Irwin Scheiner, "The Mindful Peasant: Sketches for a Study of Rebellion," *Journal of Asian Studies* 32.4 (1973). Shōji Kichinosuke, *Yonaoshi ikki no kenkyū* (1970). Patricia Sippel, "Popular Protest in Early Modern Japan: The Bushū Outburst," *Harvard Journal of Asiatic Studies* 32.2 (1977). Yasumaru Yoshio, *Nihon no kindaika to minshū shisō* (1974).   Irwin SCHEINER

Yoneshirogawa

River in northern Akita Prefecture, northern Honshū, originating in the Ōu Mountains, in the northwestern part of Iwate Prefecture, and flowing west through Hanawa, Ōdate, and Takanosu basins as well as through the Noshiro Plain, to empty into the Sea of Japan at the city of Noshiro. Large mineral deposits are located along the river; Akita cedar forests cover the regions through which it flows. The city of Noshiro, at the river's mouth, is a flourishing collection and shipping center for lumber. Length: 136 km (84 mi); area of drainage basin: 4,100 sq km (1,583 sq mi).

Yonezawa

City in southern Yamagata Prefecture, northern Honshū. In the Edo period (1600–1868), it was a flourishing castle town belonging to the UESUGI FAMILY. It is now the most important city in the Yonezawa Basin. Long known for its *yonezawa-ori* and other silk fabrics, in recent years synthetic fiber cloth and wool fabrics have become predominant. Products include rice and apples. Electric appliances and machinery are also manufactured. There are numerous hot springs, including Goshiki, Azuma, and Shirabu. It is the base camp for climbing the mountain Azumasan; other surrounding mountains provide excellent skiing. Pop: 92,824.

Yonezawa Basin

(Yonezawa Bonchi). A fault basin in southern Yamagata Prefecture, northern Honshū. Bounded by the Ōu and Iide mountain ranges, it consists of alluvial fans below the fault scarp and of the flood plains of the river Mogamigawa's upper reaches. Grapes, pears, persimmons, and apples are cultivated, and mulberry fields abound. Rice is grown in the low-lying regions. The major city is Yonezawa. Length: approximately 25 km (16 mi); width: approximately 20 km (12 mi).

Yon'ichiroku Jiken → April 16th Incident

yōnin

(literally, "distant appointment"; also known as *yōju*). A practice whereby an appointed official, particularly a provincial governor (KOKUSHI), received the title and stipend belonging to an office but remained in the capital without taking up his assigned provincial post. In the Nara period (710–794) *yōnin* was permitted only in cases when appointees, often high-ranking courtiers, held concurrent positions in the capital. A deputy *(mokudai)* was delegated to the provincial office to oversee administration and ensure that revenues were forwarded to the absentee governor. From late in the Heian period (794–1185) the practice became commonplace even among those who held no appointments at court, and the term *yōnin kokushi* was used in contrast with the term ZURYŌ, or those officials who actually went to their provincial assignments. The practice is considered to have been a major factor in the decline of the Chinese-style RITSURYŌ SYSTEM of government.

Yono

City in southeastern Saitama Prefecture, central Honshū. Formerly a market town on the highway Kamakura Kaidō, it now has textile, precision instrument, and automobile plants. Pop: 72,326.

yoriai

1. Group meetings to decide matters of joint concern; especially village meetings to discuss cooperative labor, festivals, tax allotments, and local regulations. Such meetings gained importance as cultivators began to form self-governing groups *(sō)* in the 14th century. They were dominated by the more prominent landholders (MYŌSHU and later MURA YAKUNIN), but in the Edo period (1600–1868) many villages allowed even the lowliest tenant farmers to participate. These meetings allowed for some degree of local autonomy and provided a link between the villages and outside officials. Even today, village meetings are called *yoriai*.

2. In the Kamakura shogunate (1192–1333), an informal, secret council of about 10 of the most important officials of the regent HŌJŌ FAMILY; also known as the Yoriaishū, it usurped the power of the shogunate's official Council of State (HYŌJŌSHŪ) from the time of HŌJŌ TOKIMUNE in the late 13th century.

3. In the Tokugawa shogunate (1603–1867), direct shogunal vassals (HATAMOTO) with incomes over 3,000 *koku* (see KOKUDAKA)

but no official posts were known as *yoriai*. They were responsible for miscellaneous tasks such as guard duty outside Edo Castle.

4. In poetry linked-verse (see RENGA AND HAIKAI), *yoriai* is a type of linking based on free association with a word in the preceding verse, sometimes through mediation of a poem from the classics.

yoriki and dōshin

Yoriki (literally, "strength that is offered") is a term whose meaning changed over time, but it generally referred to a warrior who assisted another warrior superior in rank. Thus in the Muromachi period (1333–1568) a *yoriki* was a *samurai* who served *daimyō* or high-ranking samurai commanders; during the 16th century the term identified a mounted samurai who commanded other samurai or ASHIGARU (footsoldiers). During the Edo period (1600–1868) the Tokugawa shogunate used the term *yoriki* to identify low-level samurai commanders roughly analogous to modern noncommissioned officers. They headed patrol and guard units whose members were designated *dōshin* (literally, "like-minded" or "shared hearts"). Both *yoriki* and *dōshin* were of the broader GOKENIN category of Tokugawa vassals, and the significant distinction between the two was not that the former nominally were mounted samurai and the latter unmounted but rather that the former were of higher hereditary status, drew larger hereditary family stipends, and were entrusted with more important military duties. The hundreds of *dōshin* made up the basic police force of most city commissioners' (MACHI BUGYŌ) offices and with the help of MEAKASHI, detectives in their private employ, they apprehended criminals.

Conrad TOTMAN

yorioya and yoriko

(literally, "foster parent and foster child"). A social bond between superior and inferior in premodern times modeled on the parent-child relationship. It is said to have originated in the Kamakura period (1185–1333), when the *sōryō* (leaders of the BUSHIDAN or local warrior bands) enlisted warriors from outside their kin groups and expressed their ties as lord and vassal in terms of parent-child roles. In the early part of the Muromachi period (1333–1568) this relationship was often employed by warlords to control their expanding bodies of retainers. By the Sengoku (Warring States) period (1467–1568) it had become a common basis for organizing the retainers of the great DAIMYŌ houses. The lesser proprietary lords (RYŌSHU) allied with the daimyō usually became *yoriko*, and his more powerful retainers became *yorioya* charged with their supervision. The *yorioya-yoriko* relationship did not function only in times of war but was a permanent part of the social hierarchy. The *yorioya* were empowered to discipline the *yoriko* under them, to bring *yoriko* legal claims before the daimyō, and to investigate and mediate *yoriko* land disputes. Because the *yoriko* received confirmation (ANDO) of their landholdings from the daimyō, however, they enjoyed the status of direct retainers and could not be treated as vassals by the *yorioya*.

Not limited to the warrior class, the *yorioya-yoriko* relationship appeared also in the villages, both in labor-service organization and in patron-client ties between landlords and farmers. In the cities, similar bonds were widely established between artisans or merchants and their apprentices *(hōkōnin)* by the Edo period (1600–1868). There were also at that time groups of *yoriko* who provided temporary labor and services. Among these were the *buke yoriko*, warriors hired to escort daimyō on journeys between their domains and Edo (see SANKIN KŌTAI), and the *machikata yoriko*, urban laborers employed by manufacturers. Each of these groups had a foreman or gang boss (*oyabun*; formally called *hitoireya*, or agent) who found employment for them and acted as a guarantor. See also OYABUN-KOBUN.

Ueda Nobuhiro

Yōrō

Town in southwestern Gifu Prefecture, central Honshū. Situated on the river Ibigawa, the entire town is encircled by embankments of the WAJŪ type to prevent flooding. Farming is the principal occupation. Yōrō Falls, associated with a well-known legend about a filial son, is a part of Gifu-Yōrō Prefectural Park. Pop: 31,372.

Yōrō Code

(Yōrō Ritsuryō). Fundamental legal code of ancient Japan. A revision of the TAIHŌ CODE of 701, the Yōrō Code was drafted and presented to the court by FUJIWARA NO FUHITO in 718 (Yōrō 2). It was put into effect in 757—37 years after Fuhito's death—by his grandson FUJIWARA NO NAKAMARO, who exercised great power within the court at that time. By continuing his grandfather's work, Nakamaro doubtless hoped to glorify his family name and to legitimize his own position. The *ryō*, regulations for administrative, fiscal, and other aspects of government, filled 10 chapters *(kan)*; they survive almost complete in an official commentary, RYŌ NO GIGE, and in a commentary by private scholars, RYŌ NO SHŪGE, both written in the 9th century. The *ritsu*, or penal regulations, also in 10 chapters, survive only in fragments. The Yōrō Code served as the basis of government until the early 10th century. The bureaucratic structure and names of posts designated in the code remained in use at the imperial court throughout the period of WARRIOR GOVERNMENT until the introduction of the modern cabinet system in 1885. See also RITSURYŌ SYSTEM   *Kitamura Bunji*

Yōrōgawa

River in central Chiba Prefecture, central Honshū, originating in Kiyosumiyama, a small mountain near the town of Amatsu Kominato, and flowing north through the Bōsō Hills to empty into Tōkyō Bay. The upper reaches are noted for their beautiful gorges. Large-scale land reclamation projects have been implemented at the river's mouth, with the reclaimed land a part of the Keiyō Industrial Region. Length: 68 km (42 mi); area of drainage basin: 258 sq km (100 sq mi).

Yoronjima

Island 20 km (12 mi) northeast of the main island of Okinawa. It is one of the AMAMI ISLANDS and is under the jurisdiction of Kagoshima Prefecture. The island is composed of raised coral reefs; the highest point is 97.2 m (319 ft). Agricultural products are sugarcane, squash, and bananas. The special product of the island is Ōshima *tsumugi* (pongee). Tourism is one of its main industries today. Area: 20.8 sq km (8.03 sq mi).

Yōrō Ritsuryō → Yōrō Code

Yorozu chōhō

A newspaper popular in the latter part of the Meiji period (1868–1912); founded in 1892 by KUROIWA RUIKŌ. It quickly gained popularity through its probing coverage of current social problems, sensational exposés, and serialization of Kuroiwa's translations of Western novels. In the years before the Russo-Japanese War (1904–05), its editorial staff included UCHIMURA KANZŌ, KŌTOKU SHŪSUI, and SAKAI TOSHIHIKO, all of whom campaigned against the war but resigned when Kuroiwa took a prowar stance. The *Yorozu* also voiced its opposition to the domain cliques (HAMBATSU) who held many offices in government, but from the Taishō period (1912–26) on it gradually lost influence. In 1940 it merged with the *Tōkyō maiyū shimbun*.

Yorozuya Kinnosuke (1932–)

Movie actor known for his roles in numerous period films *(jidaigeki)*, including the very popular series *Daibosatsu Tōge* (1957–59) and *Miyamoto Musashi* (1961–65). He was born in Tōkyō. A former KABUKI actor, Yorozuya switched to motion-picture acting and made his film debut under the name Nakamura Kinnosuke in 1954 in *Hiyodori zōshi*. He signed an exclusive contract with the Tōei motion picture company (see TŌEI CO, LTD) and appeared in two popular Tōei period-film series: *Fuefuki dōji* (1954) and *Benikujaku* (1955), which boosted him to stardom. In the movie series *Isshin Tasuke* (1958–63), directed by Sawashima Tadashi, Yorozuya injected a speedy tempo into period films to create a "new wave." He changed his name to Yorozuya Kinnosuke in 1972.
                    Shirai Yoshio

Yoru no nezame

(Nights of Fitful Waking). Also known as *Yowa no nezame, Nezame monogatari, Nezame.* One of three tales *(monogatari)* from the mid-11th century attributed to the daughter of Sugawara no Takasue (SUGAWARA NO TAKASUE NO MUSUME; b 1008). Extant texts all show evidence of several missing chapters. Though written in a court style reminiscent of the TALE OF GENJI (ca 1000 AD), this work differs remarkably in its treatment of characterization and narrative development. In contrast to the broad scope of time and place in the *Tale of Genji,* characters in *Yoru no nezame* live within their thoughts with barely a passing glance at the seasons or the world around them. Narrative development is confined largely to interior monologues. Characterization centers upon the processes of maturity in a single female character, the Lady Nezame.

Yoru no nezame is a work devoted to examining the dual burdens of sacrifice and survival. Its theme is of survival through the process of maturation from young girl to responsible mother who provides for her children without the security of a stable spouse or household. The steady strengthening of resolve in a woman bred to passivity must surely have stirred the hearts of Heian-period (794–1185) readers. Lady Nezame's eventual triumph concludes with her sacrifice of the role of mother-provider for the integral way of living to be found in the cloistered yet earthbound world of her own thoughts. Though she marries an older man, who dies soon thereafter, and is pursued by many suitors, including the emperor, Lady Nezame's affinities remain bound to the gentleman meant for her elder sister and with whom she will never live. Though her three children by this man are the chains that bind her to this life and prevent her from becoming a Buddhist nun, their eventual successes provide a means of transcending the difficulties of her predicament. The fateful though steadfast attachment of Lady Nezame to her great love provides moments of balanced joy and sadness. Fragments of an illustrated handscroll of *Yoru no nezame* survive; they are among the finest achievements of Heian art.
                    Kenneth L. Richard

Yoru no tsuzumi

(Night Drum). A 1958 film directed by IMAI TADASHI and starring ARIMA INEKO, MIKUNI RENTARŌ, and MORI MASAYUKI, which attacked Japan's feudal social traditions. The screenplay, by HASHIMOTO SHINOBU and SHINDŌ KANETO, was based on an original play by the 18th-century dramatist CHIKAMATSU MONZAEMON.

In the film, the lonely wife of a provincial lord is seduced by an itinerant music teacher while the husband she loves is away fulfilling government duties. Tokugawa social code demanded that the wife kill herself for her transgressions in order to spare her husband shame. Although her devoted spouse forgives her, he must carry out his obligation to the code and kill his wife when she cannot bring herself to commit suicide. To fulfill the rest of his obligation he then hunts down and kills the teacher only to realize that he has not acted according to his own moral convictions, but by society's abstract rules and in so doing he has destroyed his integrity and human worth.

To create a powerful sense of the inevitable cruelty of the social system, Imai does not film his tale in a straightforward narrative style. Rather, he begins after the seduction has occurred and pieces the story together with a series of sharp flashback fragments. The film is shot largely in close-up, giving it an emotional intensity rarely matched in Japanese films.
                    David Owens

yoryūdo

(literally, "dependent people"; also pronounced *yoriudo* or *yoribito*).
1. Scribes; bureaucratic staff members or clerks in the ministries of the imperial government of the Heian period (794–1185) and later in the Kamakura (1192–1333) and Muromachi (1338–1573) shogunates. They were scholars and legal experts hired to process various kinds of ministerial paperwork. In the Heian government they dealt with such diverse matters as estate (SHŌEN) management in the Records Office (KIROKU SHŌEN KENKEIJO) and poetic anthologies in the Office of Poetry (Waka-dokoro). Under the Kamakura and Muromachi shogunates they staffed the Board of Retainers (SAMURAIDOKORO), the Administrative Board (MANDOKORO), and the Board of Inquiry (MONCHŪJO).
2. From the late 10th through 13th centuries, the term was also applied to farmers and laborers who lent their services to estates other than those to which they officially belonged. The estates that employed *yoryūdo* were usually those of court nobles and religious institutions that did not have their own labor force. In return for their labor, the *yoryūdo* apparently enjoyed exemption from various corvée duties levied by the government and their original proprietors. As the structure of the estate system tightened, almost all

cultivators as well as other workers came more firmly under estate control.

Yosa Buson → Buson

Yōsai → Eisai

Yosano Akiko (1878–1942)

Noted poet and feminist writer. Maiden name Hō Shō. Daughter of a confectionary shop owner, she was born in the city of Sakai in Ōsaka Prefecture. An avid reader from early youth, she graduated from the Sakai Girls' School in 1895 and contributed her earliest known poems to the journal of the local poetry group in 1899.

When YOSANO TEKKAN began publishing a monthly, MYŌJŌ (Bright Star), Akiko was one of its first contributors. The two met in 1900 and the following year they were married, although Tekkan remained actively involved with both his former wife Takino and with another woman poet, Yamakawa Tomiko (1879–1909), a friend of Akiko. Also in 1901, soon after moving in with Tekkan, Akiko produced her first volume of poems, *Midaregami* (tr *Tangled Hair*, 1935; 1971). It contained nearly 400 poems of passion and sensuality. Both *Midaregami* and Akiko's love affair created a sensation in the literary world, but, after the initial harsh criticism, *Midaregami* was enthusiastically accepted. A following of young poets kept alive for a decade *Myōjō*, which Akiko coedited. Poems in *Midaregami* helped break the spell of traditional constraints on TANKA, and Akiko began publishing her new, modern verses that deemphasized syllable count and limitations on subject matter. One example of her style follows:

> Like this black hair
> These thousand strands of hair
> This hair in tangles,
> Now all tangled lie my thoughts
> My thoughts are a tangled skein.
>
> (tr E. A. Cranston)

During the remainder of her career, Akiko published over 20 more volumes of poetry and much social commentary, including criticism of Japan's foreign aggression. However, by 1908 the new poetry movement was in decline and *Myōjō* was discontinued. Tekkan and Akiko traveled extensively in Europe in 1911, meeting such leading artists and writers as Emile Verhaaren and Auguste Rodin. Some of the couple's poems were translated and published in Paris.

Akiko also published many commentaries on classic and modern literature, and her translations of the TALE OF GENJI into modern Japanese (1912 and 1939) set the standard for later, similar works. She wrote and gave public lectures on various social issues, including education and women's suffrage. In 1921 she became dean and lecturer of the newly established free coeducational school Bunka Gakuin, which she had founded with Tekkan and others.

In spite of the arduous school duties and care of her family of 11 children with its endless financial struggle, Akiko kept her house open to new poets and writers and helped many of them gain their start in the literary world. Although she did not publish much poetry in her last years, she wrote continuously for magazines and newspapers. Akiko's last major contribution was the *Shin man'yō-shū* (New Man'yōshū, 1937–39), which she compiled with 9 other leading poets. Containing 26,783 poems by 6,675 contributors dating back 60 years, it is a valuable source for *waka* written since the early Meiji period.

Akiko died from a stroke in 1942 at the age of 63. Her death in the midst of the war went virtually unnoticed, and following the war's end, her works were routinely ignored by literary historians, critics, and the general public. Literary fashions, however, come and go in cycles. Though short-lived, Akiko's new poetry movement was significant in the history of Japanese poetry; she and other romantic poets infused classic poetry with new spirit and soul in fresh and novel expression, and today she is again highly regarded.

Amy T. MATSUMOTO

Yosano Tekkan (1873–1935)

Poet. Real name Yosano Hiroshi. Born in Kyōto Prefecture. Actively involved in the movement of the 1890s to modernize traditional WAKA poetry. Yosano was a romantic and a patriot, and flamboyant masculinity is an important theme in his early poems. He established his own poetry group, Shinshisha, in 1899 with its own journal, MYŌJŌ, and his romantic poetry soon developed to full maturity. During the first decade of the 20th century Yosano's coterie supported many talented poets, among them Hō Akiko, whom he later married (see YOSANO AKIKO). His works include *Bōkoku no on* (1894), a collection of criticism, and *Tōzai namboku* (1896), a collection of his poems.

yose

Indigenous form of vaudeville. The principal origins of *yose* go back to itinerant storytellers, particularly *kōshaku* performers, who were active as early as the 12th century. Roadside *kōshaku* (later called KŌDAN) artists began to establish a stable base for their work early in the 18th century by performing together in semipermanent huts which became forerunners of *yose* theaters.

Yose theaters also evolved from the practice of RAKUGO performers of renting space in restaurants during off hours and charging low admission. Through such enterprising activities these humorous storytellers expanded their audiences far beyond the elite few who could afford the expensive restaurants and brothels where *rakugo* was usually performed. By 1800, *rakugo* artists, following the lead of *kōshaku*, were appearing in makeshift *yose* theaters that held 50 to 90 persons.

Most *yose* theaters operate on a traditional *iromonoseki* (mixed-bill) policy in which a variety of acts complement star storyteller performers. Although *rakugo* is the traditional foundation on which *yose* bills are built, the two-comedian MANZAI act has become the center of 20th-century programs.

Yose embraces other oral arts. NANIWA–BUSHI (alternatively known as *rōkyoku*) moved into *yose* theaters in the 1880s. *Mandan* (a single stand-up comedian with a routine based on topical material) has its beginnings in the mid-1920s. Many *yose* programs feature a *konto* act which is a burlesque sketch with three to six actors. Occasionally the *konto* is a musical parody. Singers, musicians, and novelty acts round out the four-to-five-hour performance of 12 to 15 acts. Programs change three times a month at the typical 200-seat *yose* theater.

The most frequently seen musical acts in *yose* are singers of pop music and of Japanese folk songs. There are also jazz, rock, and novelty bands along with solo instrument virtuosi. Other acts—often a mixture of Japanese and Western traditions—include magicians, jugglers, top and dish spinners, acrobats, and ventriloquists.

Among the traditional acts still appearing are *kowairo* (impressions of the voices and mannerisms of the famous, principally actors); *monomane* (imitations of animal and natural sounds); *hyakumensō* ("100-faces," facial contortions for comic and imitative effect); *kamikiri* (rapid cutting of pictures from paper); and *shigin kembu* (sword dances accompanied by the recitation of poetry).

Throughout the history of *yose*, certain theaters have specialized in all-*kōdan* performances. In the late 19th century, there were similarly exclusive theaters reserved for *gidayū* (see GIDAYŪ–BUSHI). The Ōsaka area has a tradition of specialized *manzai* theaters.

Yose flourished in the 19th century as inexpensive professional entertainment. In 1850 there were 220 *kōdan* and 172 mixed-bill theaters in Edo (now Tōkyō) with over 300 *yose* theaters elsewhere. Fifty years later, Tōkyō had 42 *kōdan* and 36 mixed-bill *yose* houses. *Kōdan, rakugo, manzai,* and *naniwa-bushi* became staples on radio during the 1920s, while many *yose* theaters closed due to the rapid rise in the popularity of movies. Since 1961, an average of one *kōdan* and four regular *yose* theaters are open in Tōkyō. Apart from the few surviving theaters, *yose* lives on in television and radio performances and in special live concerts. *Manzai* more than holds its own as the principal comedy form on television.

■——Geinōshi Kenkyūkai, ed, *Yose* (1971). Sekine Mokuan, *Kōdan rakugo konjaku dan* (1924). Tsurumi Shunsuke, *Nihon no taishū geijutsu* (1962).

J. L. ANDERSON

yōshi → adoption

Yoshida–Acheson exchange of notes

Exchange of notes constituting an agreement between the United States and Japan relating to assistance to be given by Japan in support of United Nations actions. Signed on 8 September 1951 by US

Secretary of State Dean Acheson and Japanese Prime Minister YO-SHIDA SHIGERU, the documents expressed the desire of the United States, and the willingness of Japan, to permit and facilitate the support, in and about Japan, of forces engaged in United Nations actions. The exchange was a direct result of the outbreak of the Korean War earlier in July, and it provoked a strong reaction from the Japanese public, who resented the fact that American military bases in Japan could be used to engage in international conflicts in which Japan was not directly involved. The notes were followed by the Agreement concerning the Status of United Nations Forces in Japan, which became effective on 11 June 1954. On 19 January 1960, when the United States–Japan Security Treaty was renewed (see UNITED STATES–JAPAN SECURITY TREATIES), notes were exchanged declaring the continued effectiveness of the Yoshida–Acheson exchange of notes as long as the Agreement concerning the Status of United Nations Forces remained in force.

Yoshida Hideo (1903–1963)

Fourth president of the advertising agency DENTSŪ, INC. Born in Fukuoka Prefecture, he graduated from Tōkyō University and joined Dentsū in 1928. In 1947 he was elected company president, following efforts after World War II to bring younger men into the company's executive ranks. He was energetic in his efforts to modernize the advertising business and established Dentsū as one of the world's major advertising agencies. He was also a driving force in early commercial radio and television broadcasting in Japan.

KAWAKAMI Hiroshi

Yoshida Hiroshi (1876–1950)

Western-style painter and woodblock print artist. His original family name was Ueda. Born in Kurume, Fukuoka Prefecture. Yoshida first studied oil painting with Yoshida Kasaburō, who later adopted him, and then with Koyama Shōtarō (1857–1916). In 1902 he established the Pacific Painting Society (Taiheiyō Gakai) with other artists. He made several trips to Europe and the United States and won prizes at the Paris (1900) and St. Louis (1904) world expositions. A meeting in 1920 with Watanabe Shōzaburō, a printer of UKIYO-E, awakened an interest in woodblock printing. He made numerous landscape prints, although he left the actual cutting and printing to craftsmen.

Yoshida Isoya (1894–1974)

Architect. Born in Tōkyō. One of the creators of the modern sukiya-style (see SUKIYA-ZUKURI), Yoshida graduated in 1923 from what is now Tōkyō University of Fine Arts and Music. After a trip to Europe and America in 1925–26, he turned to the task of reinterpreting traditional Japanese architecture. Among the many innovative features he introduced into the sukiya-style is the ōkabe construction method, which hides columns within walls and frees spaces from the rigors of traditional proportion. His representative buildings include Kineya House (1936), the GOTŌ ART MUSEUM (1960), the Yamato Bunkakan (1960), the Gyokudō Art Museum (1961), and the temple Chūgūji (1968). WATANABE Hiroshi

Yoshida Issui (1898–1973)

Poet. Real name Yoshida Yoshio. Born in Hokkaidō; studied at Waseda University. He made his appearance in the poetry world after being recognized by the poet KITAHARA HAKUSHŪ, and aimed for a pure and lucid lyricism in his poetry. His collected poems include Umi no seibo (1926), Koen no sho (1930), and Miraisha (1948); one of his works of poetry criticism is Kodai ryokuchi (1958).

ASAI Kiyoshi

Yoshida Kanetomo (1435–1511)

Shintō priest. His family was the Yoshida (originally Urabe) line that served the court first in the capacity of divinator in the Heian period (794–1185) and later as priest of the Yoshida Shrine in Kyōto (hence the surname Yoshida, assumed in 1387), and whose members were known as scholars of classical and Shintō studies. (YOSHIDA KENKŌ, author of the Tsurezuregusa, was from this family.) Kanetomo himself was ambitious to centralize Shintō under his family's authority. In 1484 he built at the Yoshida Shrine an altar that he claimed would be central for all the nation's shrines and at which

they would be honored. He further alleged, in 1489, that the divinity embodied in the regalia of the Ise Shrine had transferred itself to this altar. He elaborated the form of worship, drawing on rituals of ESOTERIC BUDDHISM and thus emphasizing the ritualistic aspect of Shintō.

Kanetomo is considered to be the author of two books, which were basic for his Gempon Sōgen Shintō (popularly known as YO-SHIDA SHINTŌ or Yuiitsu Shintō) and which synthesized medieval Shintō doctrines: the Shintō taii, a summary of Yoshida Shintō doctrine, and the Yuiitsu shintō myōbō yōshū, a compendious work asserting that Shintō gods were the supreme rulers of the universe and of humankind and that Shintō, especially as maintained by the Yoshida family, was superior to all the Buddhist or Confucian traditions. With his wide knowledge and diplomatic skill, Kanetomo gained favor with the court and the shogunate and paved the way for Yoshida Shintō's hegemony in the Shintō world during the Edo period (1600–1868).

——Miyachi Naokazu, Shintō shi, vol 3 (1963). Ōsumi Kazuo, ed, Chūsei shintō ron, vol 19 in Nihon shisō taikei (Iwanami Shoten, 1977). TSUCHIDA Tomoaki

Yoshida Kenkō (ca 1283–ca 1352)

Also known as Urabe Kenkō. Author best known for his Tsurezuregusa, (ca 1330; tr Essays in Idleness, 1967), a philosophical miscellany which is one of the best loved and most admired examples of classical Japanese prose and is ranked with SEI SHŌNAGON's Makura no sōshi as one of the masterpieces of the ZUIHITSU genre. Kenkō's precise dates are uncertain, and it has been suggested that his death occurred as late as 1362. His given name was originally Kaneyoshi; that of Kenkō, from another reading of the same Chinese characters, was adopted when he entered religious life. Some authorities assert that Urabe is the only historically correct form of his surname. The Urabe were hereditary Shintō diviners. Kenkō's father served the emperor Go-Uda (r 1274–87) in this capacity, and one of Kenkō's brothers held similar posts. Another brother was a learned Tendai Buddhist monk. Kenkō himself, as a young man, was steward to the family of Horikawa Tomomori, whose father was the maternal grandfather of the emperor Go-Nijō (r 1301–08). In 1301 he obtained a position at court as kurōdo, which he held for six years; this was followed by the post of sahyōe no suke. At some time before 1313, he became a monk. He was not attached to any temple or master, however, and in his book he writes of monks—whether with admiration, amusement, or scorn—as an outsider. His reasons for taking the tonsure are not known; conventionally they have been thought to be the death of a patron, but the immediate cause may well have been simply inner conviction. It is probable that he first lived in seclusion near the Shūgakuin Detached Palace. In his late thirties he resided at Yokawa. At some time either in his late forties or shortly before his death he had a hermitage at a place called Narabi no Oka, near the temple Ninnaji. All of these residences were in or near Kyōto. He journeyed, however, to the Kantō region in eastern Japan on several occasions (the first probably while still a layman) and late in life visited Ise. There are many entries in Tsurezuregusa on such subjects as what qualities are to be wished for in a friend or how a man should best comport himself in society; and while the conception, popular in the Edo period (1600–1868), of the Narabi no Oka priest as a gentleman-hermit undoubtedly contains much that is exaggerated and sentimentalized, it is clear that he did not by any means sever his ties with the imperial court.

As a poet Kenkō was an adherent of the Nijō school, which was patronized by the Daikakuji faction of the imperial house; following the accession in 1318 of the Daikakuji prince who became the emperor GO-DAIGO (r 1318–39), he became especially active in poetic circles within the capital. The Nijō school was ultraconservative in its poetic practice; perceiving the age as one of general decay, its members felt that the highest duty of the poet was to preserve unchanged the precious heritage of the past. Toward the end of his career he drew closer to the rival, innovative Reizei school, but the rapprochement is generally thought to have been personal rather than artistic. Kenkō seems to have sympathized with Go-Daigo during that emperor's struggle against the Hōjō, but he was essentially only an onlooker in the political arena, and after the emperor's flight into exile he accepted with equanimity the patronage of the shōgun ASHIKAGA TAKAUJI (1305–58) and his brother Tadayoshi (1306–52); in this he did not differ from the Nijō school generally and many others (e.g., the Zen monk KOKAN SHIREN; 1278–1346) who had close connections with the court. Legend has it that in old age he was a tutor of etiquette to the Ashikaga general Kō no Moronao (d 1351); such stories provided material for Edo dramatists, but their historicity is doubtful.

Writings —— Kenkō was praised as one of the "four deva kings" of the poetry of the Nijō school. Over 280 WAKA appear in the anthology of his poems which he himself selected, and poems by him appear in imperial anthologies. It may well be that his poetry deserves more attention than recent critics have generally accorded it. His reputation, however, rests on his prose.

Tsurezuregusa consists of 243 brief entries ranging in length from a single sentence to a few pages. The order is not random, although it may seem so to the casual reader; the arrangement invokes principles of association similar to those used in some SE-TSUWA BUNGAKU collections and in poetry anthologies. There is no firm evidence as to when it was composed; the most generally accepted date is 1330–31, but an alternative theory which has found some acceptance is that the first 30 entries were written as early as 1319. The hypothesis that the work as a whole came into being in stages would account for some inconsistencies in it. It might be remarked, however, that some measure of inconsistency, at least on a superficial level, is inherent in a work of this sort and is likely to be accounted one of its charms. Moreover, one may doubt whether some of the supposed contradictions really exist. One of the examples often cited of Kenkō's inconsistency is his attitude toward women; but when in one section he condemns marriage and in another he says that there is something lacking in the young man who entirely avoids romantic entanglements, he is not talking about the same thing. He is not even talking about quite the same world, for one statement refers to experiences with which he is familiar and disillusioned (or would like to convince himself he is), while the other refers to an idealized image that derives its emotional power for him through its association with fiction and the past. Kenkō himself says that his book is the product of "jotting down at random whatever nonsensical thoughts have entered my head." This description of his own book must, however, be taken with caution. It arises from the same considered unpretentiousness that he recommends to every well-bred man—the refusal to make a show, whether of riches, or of sorrow, of love affairs, erudition, or holiness. Japanese critics increasingly, and with justice, take Kenkō seriously as one of the great thinkers of his age.

The individual sections take varied shapes: reminiscences, anecdotes and strings of anecdotes (often of a monitory nature), meditations, judgments, notes and queries on factual matters, dreamlike fragments of narrative, descriptions, outbursts. Some are gnomic in their brevity, number 229 reading in its entirety: "They say that a good carver uses a slightly dull knife. Myōkan's knife cut very poorly." A very few of the anecdotes are told for sheer entertainment; others, which seem to be told for entertainment, in fact illustrate one of Kenkō's themes, the undesirability of eccentricity. Many of the anecdotes relate instances of the mastery of some art by the member of a past generation or deal with someone's knowledge of a vanished or soon-to-vanish court custom.

Kenkō is obsessed with time. That aspect of his thought to which Japanese critics point as both most profound and most typical is his *mujōkan,* his sense of the transience of worldly things, whether of the glories of past ages, or of the beauties of the seasons, or of youth and vigor, or of life itself. In this he is not alone; impermanence had been a major theme in Japanese literature almost from its beginnings. But few other writers express it so poignantly, and none deals so variously with its implications. Again and again he reminds his reader of the imminence of death. Each moment of life is a gift of incalculable worth; the wise man is he who values it to the full. As did the Heian poets, he finds nature most beautiful precisely in its changeability; it is beginnings and endings, he says, that are most interesting, not fulfillment. A famous passage begins, "Are we to look at cherry blossoms only in full bloom, the moon only when it is cloudless? To long for the moon while looking on the rain, to lower the blinds and be unaware of the passing of the spring—these are even more deeply moving." Kenkō's attitude toward transience is by no means the wholehearted acceptance it is sometimes assumed to be. Rather, he has found a way of making it bearable by transforming it into emotion: the sensitive individual experiences not transience itself, but a quality abstracted from it. Similarly, Kenkō searches the past for verities which, though they can be forgotten, are in essence changeless; this is why each scrap of ancient usage he can record is precious to him. He repeatedly decries modern language and modern fashions; modern poetry, especially, he finds lacking in feeling. "Why is it?" he exclaims, "that even the most

careless utterance of men of former days should sound so splendid?" Along with the prizing of what is past and perishable goes the valuing of what is old and worn, or incomplete. Too much polish, in furnishing a house, for example, is repellent and stifling; room must be left for the imagination, and in everything simplicity and quietness are the best.

Although Kenkō is often compared with the author of *Makura no sōshi,* a more apt comparison might be with KAMO NO CHŌMEI, author of the *Hōjōki.* Each chose a life of seclusion; each found in it a remedy for the ills of life in a difficult age. Chōmei's solution was conventional; even the small lapses into worldliness he allows himself are provided for by time-honored religious and poetic traditions for the conduct of the hermit. For Kenkō, a more complex individual, the remedy was incomplete; the tension between his deepest desires and the realities of life and of the age could allow no resolution. In praising changeability itself and at the same time seeking out the past, Kenkō lives with this irresolution, and it is this quality that gives his work much of its vital interest for modern readers. 🔖 ——Kanda Hideo, Nagazumi Yasuaki, and Yasuraoka Kōsaku, ed, *Hōjōki, Tsurezuregusa, Shōbōgenzō zuimonki, Tannishō:* vol 27 of *Nihon koten bungaku zenshū* (Shōgakukan, 1971). Donald Keene, ed and tr, *Essays in Idleness* (1967). Tomikura Tokujirō, *Urabe Kenkō* (1964). *Marian* URY

Yoshida Kōgyō

The leader of a group of companies engaged in the manufacture of zippers, materials for zipper production, manufacturing machinery, and aluminum construction material. Yoshida Kōgyō was founded in 1934 by YOSHIDA TADAO (b 1908) to process and sell zippers, and it took its current name in 1945. It is the world's largest manufacturer of zippers, and its sales of aluminum materials are the highest in Japan. Its brand name, YKK, is well known both in Japan and abroad. The company uses an integrated process for the manufacture of its products from raw materials to the finished product, and the principal manufacturing equipment used in both domestic and foreign plants has been developed and produced by the company itself. Some 15,000 units of machinery are manufactured annually with technology developed by the company. In the management sphere, the company adheres to the principle of "three-way distribution of the fruits of the company," sharing profits with clients, sales agencies, and affiliates. To enable employees to share in management, the company has adopted a system by which they are allocated company stock, and a large number of employees are allowed to attend the monthly meetings of the board of directors.

Overseas operations were begun at an early date, and the company exports its products to 125 countries. It has established 38 plants in 37 countries and opened 99 business offices throughout the world. Sales of Yoshida Kōgyō and its affiliates were ¥453.8 billion (US $1.9 billion) in the fiscal year ending March 1982, of which zippers constituted ¥204.3 billion (US $848.7 million) and aluminum construction material ¥249.5 billion (US $988 million). Overseas sales of zippers amounted to ¥117.3 billion (US $487.3 million) in the same year. The company is planning to enter overseas markets for aluminum construction material in the future as part of an overall plan to increase the ratio of overseas operations. Sales of the parent company alone totaled ¥201.1 billion (US $835.4 million) and capitalization stood at ¥5.6 billion (US $23.3 million). The head office is in Tōkyō.

Yoshida Mitsuyoshi (1598–1672)

Mathematician of the Edo period (1600–1868). Born in Kyōto, he studied traditional Japanese mathematics (WASAN) under Mōri Shigeyoshi and later with Suminokura Soan (1571–1632), a merchant-scholar to whom he was related. Mitsuyoshi translated the Chinese work *Suanfa tongzong* (Suan-fa t'ung-tsung; 1593, Systematic Treatise on Arithmetic) into Japanese. In 1627, using that work as a model, he wrote *Jinkōki* (Numbers Large and Small), a textbook explaining the use of the abacus and its application to practical problems such as changing money, computing taxes and interest, and calculating surface area and volume. Including simple mathematical games and illustrated with color prints, the book went through at least 10 printings in the author's lifetime and was widely pirated and imitated. *Jinkōki* was extremely important in spreading knowledge of mathematics throughout Japanese society.

Yoshida Shigeru

Yoshida at his home in Ōiso, Kanagawa Prefecture, in December 1961.

Yoshida Seiichi (1908–)

Scholar of Japanese literature. Born in Tōkyō; graduate of Tōkyō University. Yoshida has taught at many universities, including Tōkyō University. His scientific approach to modern literary studies emphasized a close study of original texts. In 1958 he received the Japan Art Academy Award for *Shizen shugi no kenkyū,* a two-volume historical study of the Japanese naturalist literature of the early 20th century. Other principal works include *Akutagawa Ryūnosuke* (1942), a critical biography of the novelist Akutagawa, and *Kindai bungaku hyōron shi: Meijihen* (1974), a collection of critical essays.

Yoshida Shigeru (1878–1967)

Yoshida Shigeru had the rare pleasure of carving a niche in history long after it appeared that history had passed him by. A career diplomat who retired from his last post in 1938, he emerged from relative obscurity after World War II to become the most famous politician of postwar Japan, serving as prime minister for a total of 86 months between May 1946 and December 1954. Yoshida's first cabinet (May 1946–May 1947) bore great, albeit grudging, responsibility for enacting many of the reforms demanded by Allied OCCUPATION authorities. The second through fifth Yoshida cabinets (October 1948–December 1954) oversaw Japan's transition from alien control to restoration of sovereignty (formally attained in April 1952)—and from "reform" to "reconstruction." Popularly known as the Yoshida Era, this latter period witnessed the consolidation of two strong legacies to subsequent decades: the hegemony of big business, bureaucracy, and conservative party politics within Japan; and Japan's tight military and economic alliance with the United States.

Yoshida was 67 years old when he became prime minister for the first time, and 76 when his last cabinet collapsed. His prior association with party politics was negligible. His modus operandi was bureaucratic and autocratic, as conveyed by his famous nickname of "One Man" (Wamman), and his political proclivities were proudly conservative. He was an empassioned patriot and loyalist; a defender, even in the bleakest days of war and defeat, of the great legacy of the Meiji (1868–1912) and Taishō (1912–26) periods; and a vigilant Red-baiter and guardian against "dangerous thoughts." Although known from prewar years as a friend and supporter of the Anglo–American powers as well as an "old liberal," Yoshida was critical of almost all of the basic early policies of the Allied Occupation, including the extensive purge, constitutional revision, land reform, ZAIBATSU DISSOLUTION and economic deconcentration,

decentralization of the police and educational systems, and promotion of local autonomy. The conjunction of the conservative Yoshida Era on the one hand and, on the other hand, the popular images of the Occupation "revolution" and the "new Japan" which purportedly emerged from this is thus jarring and suggestive. Among other things, Yoshida's career helps illuminate continuities between imperial Japan and post-1945 Japan.

Yoshida was born in Yokohama on 22 September 1878 and was soon adopted by Yoshida Kenzō and his wife Kotoko. His real father was Yoshida Kenzō's close friend TAKENOUCHI TSUNA, a former *samurai* from Tosa (now Kōchi Prefecture) who supported the victorious imperial cause in the Meiji Restoration (1868) and went on to enjoy a successful career as a politician and entrepreneur. The name of Yoshida's real mother is not recorded; she was Takenouchi's mistress, apparently a *geisha.* In the Yoshida household, the young Shigeru was exposed to a variety of influences. His adoptive father was a former samurai from Fukui who had studied WESTERN LEARNING in Nagasaki before the Restoration, later spent several years in England, and served for a time as a manager for Jardine Matheson and Company in Yokohama before establishing his own trading company. Yoshida Kenzō died in 1887, leaving his adopted son a large inheritance and a lonely adolescence. The young heir grew up as the only child of Yoshida Kotoko, a correct and disciplined woman who was the granddaughter of a famous Confucian scholar, Satō Issai.

In his mid-teens, Yoshida concluded he was not cut out to follow in the commercial footsteps of his adoptive father, and in 1897 he entered the higher-school course of the elite Gakushūin, or Peers' School. Under its headmaster, KONOE ATSUMARO, the Gakushūin was developing a new school for diplomats, and Yoshida continued on in this program. When Konoe died in 1904, however, the program was terminated, and Yoshida transferred to the law department of Tōkyō University in 1905. He graduated in 1906 and passed the foreign service examinations the same year, ranking seventh out of 11 successful candidates. In 1909 Yoshida married Makino Yukiko, the eldest daughter of MAKINO NOBUAKI, son of the Meiji oligarch, ŌKUBO TOSHIMICHI. Makino held a succession of prominent official positions from the 1920s; he was one of the emperor's closest advisers, and through him Yoshida gained entrée to the higher court circles.

Although Yoshida became identified with the so-called pro-Anglo-American clique within the Foreign Ministry, his diplomatic career and concerns were oriented primarily toward the extension of Japanese influence in Asia. He regarded cooperation with the Western powers as essential to this goal, and the ANGLO-JAPANESE ALLIANCE (1902–23), under which Japan expanded during the first 15 years of Yoshida's career, always remained an exemplary model of "diplomatic sense" in his mind—a model he would have occasion to evoke in the post-1945 period, when he led Japan into the bilateral military alliance with the United States. At the same time, however, Yoshida's prewar career as a manager of the empire imbued him with the conviction that Japan could not prosper without close ties with China as well as with the West; in the postwar period this led to tensions within the United States–Japan alliance when the Yoshida government was forced to adhere to the American policy of containment of China. In general, in both the prewar and postwar periods Yoshida tended to regard the Far Eastern policy of the United States as unenlightened in comparison with that of Great Britain.

Yoshida's diplomatic career was only moderately successful. After serving in Mukden (1907–08), London (1908–09), and Rome (1909–12), he was appointed consul in the strategic port of Andong (Antung), on the border between Manchuria and Korea. Early in 1913, he assumed the concurrent position of secretary to the governor-general of Korea, a post then filled by General TERAUCHI MASATAKE, who later became prime minister. In December 1916 Yoshida was assigned to the Washington embassy, but the appointment was withdrawn when it was learned that in 1915 he had initiated a small protest movement among Japanese officials in Manchuria against the heavy-handed TWENTY-ONE DEMANDS presented to China by the government of ŌKUMA SHIGENOBU. After several insignificant assignments in Tōkyō and a brief term as consul in Jinan (Tsinan) in 1918, Yoshida accompanied the Japanese delegation to the Paris Peace Conference in 1919, serving as a rather menial aide to Makino. From 1920 to 1922 he was first secretary in the London embassy.

In the 1920s Yoshida emerged as a critic of the international system based on agreements reached at the WASHINGTON CONFERENCE of 1922 and one of the most outspoken Japanese advocates of an assertive "positive" policy toward China. As consul general in Tianjin (Tientsin) in 1922–25 and Mukden (Ch: Shenyang) in 1925–28, he responded harshly to the rise of Chinese nationalism. He admonished his more conciliatory colleagues to keep in mind that "the past history of Japan has always been that we punish those who behave impolitely to us," and evoked the example of the Western colonial or neocolonial powers in defending his own "realistic" and unsentimental proposals for strengthening Japan's position on the continent. In advocating cooperation with the West at this time, Yoshida most frequently had in mind joint action against China. Such proposals not only placed him at odds with the mainstream within the Foreign Ministry, led by SHIDEHARA KIJŪRŌ, but were also criticized as being too militant by some of Japan's top military officers. In 1928 Yoshida successfully solicited the post of vice-foreign minister in the TANAKA GIICHI cabinet. He remained in this post under the succeeding cabinet of HAMAGUCHI OSACHI until early 1931, when he was appointed ambassador to Italy.

In the 1930s Yoshida played the awkward role of opposing Japan's quest for autarky while at the same time soliciting Western acquiescence in Japanese aggression. He was recalled from Italy at his own request in late 1932 and, after rather enigmatically declining the ambassadorship in Washington, held no significant position until his formal retirement from the foreign service in November 1935. In the wake of the FEBRUARY 26TH INCIDENT of 1936, Yoshida helped organize the first slate of proposed ministers for the HIROTA KŌKI cabinet, five members of which were vetoed by the military. Yoshida, listed as foreign minister, was one of the five rejected nominees, whereupon Hirota appointed him ambassador to Great Britain. Yoshida's endeavor to effect a comprehensive solution to both the China impasse and the global economic crisis by reviving cooperation among the imperialist powers vis-à-vis China was aborted by the MARCO POLO BRIDGE INCIDENT of July 1937, and he was recalled from London in late 1938. Yoshida opposed both the ANTI-COMINTERN PACT of 1936 and the TRIPARTITE PACT of 1940. Throughout the 1930s he maintained close contact with his Anglo-American acquaintances, especially US Ambassador Joseph C. GREW, and in November 1941 he helped draft Proposal B, Japan's final offer in the Hull–Nomura talks, which preceded the outbreak of war between Japan and the United States. Between 1942 and 1945 Yoshida was involved in desultory proposals to replace the TŌJŌ HIDEKI government and effect an advantageous surrender. These proposals, premised upon the belief that the war situation posed the threat of communist revolution and destruction of the national polity (kokutai) in Japan, culminated in the famous Konoe Memorial (Konoe Jōsōbun), a proposal submitted to the emperor by former prime minister KONOE FUMIMARO in February 1945. Largely because of his role in helping draft the Konoe Memorial, Yoshida was arrested by the military police in April 1945 and held for over two months before being released.

In September 1945 Yoshida replaced SHIGEMITSU MAMORU as foreign minister in the HIGASHIKUNI NARUHIKO cabinet, and he continued in this post under the succeeding SHIDEHARA KIJŪRŌ cabinet (October 1945–May 1946). This position established him as a key contact between the Japanese government and Occupation authorities, and he quickly emerged as a leading defender of the old civilian elites and a blunt critic of proposals for serious constitutional revision or structural renovation in Japan. Yoshida helped arrange the symbolically significant meeting between the emperor and General Douglas MACARTHUR on 27 September 1945, after which MacArthur openly supported both the Japanese throne and its current occupant, Emperor HIROHITO. In early 1946 Yoshida also set up an important research group within the Foreign Ministry charged with planning for Japan's future sovereignty and security.

When HATOYAMA ICHIRŌ, president of the JIYŪTŌ (Liberal Party), was abruptly purged after the general election of April 1946, he persuaded Yoshida to succeed him as party president and, ipso facto, the next prime minister of Japan. Prior to its resignation in May 1947 the first Yoshida cabinet was forced to assume responsibility for extension of the purge and such reformist legislation as the constitutional revision, land reform, and several basic labor laws. It introduced the economic policy of "priority production" (keisha seisan) at the end of 1946 but failed to curb the mounting inflation that ravaged Japan in the early postwar years. Yoshida, however, did savor several conservative victories during this period. In addition to seeing the throne preserved in the new constitution, he was successful in soliciting MacArthur's intervention against the general strike planned for 1 February (see GENERAL STRIKE OF 1947). And, as one

of its last acts, his government sponsored a revision of the election law that weakened the leftist parties and minority groups at the polls.

In October 1948, when the cabinet of ASHIDA HITOSHI resigned following disclosure of the SHŌWA DENKŌ SCANDAL, Yoshida was returned to the premiership although his party did not hold a majority in the lower house. In January 1949 he called a general election and won a stunning majority victory that laid the parliamentary base for the ensuing "Yoshida Era." Both Yoshida's party (at this time called the Democratic Liberal Party) and his own personal position were strengthened by recruitment of a number of skilled former bureaucrats, some of whom became key figures in the so-called Yoshida School (Yoshida Gakkō), the premier's inner circle of key lieutenants; the later prime ministers IKEDA HAYATO and SATŌ EISAKU emerged as Yoshida's protégés at this time. The powerful third Yoshida cabinet (February 1949–October 1952) was able to capitalize upon both the reverse course in US Occupation policy, which had begun in 1947–48, and the immense economic stimulation of the Korean War. During the tenure of this government, the shift in economic priorities from deconcentration and democratization to stabilization and reconstruction was accelerated; the labor movement was subjected to increasing restraints; the OCCUPATION PURGE of militarists and ultranationalists was gradually rescinded, while a RED PURGE involving over 20,000 individuals was carried out in both the public and private sectors in 1950; new domestic peace-preservation legislation was introduced; and Japan attained sovereignty under the terms of the SAN FRANCISCO PEACE TREATY, the controversial "separate peace" signed in September 1951.

Until the end of the Occupation in 1952 Yoshida held the position of foreign minister concurrently with the premiership. He regarded the San Francisco settlement as his greatest accomplishment, although it was obtained at the price of considerable tension both domestically and internationally. As quid pro quo for a nonrestrictive peace treaty, Yoshida agreed to a bilateral security treaty with the United States (see UNITED STATES–JAPAN SECURITY TREATIES) under which Japan committed itself to the continued presence of American military bases in sovereign Japan and to Japan's own rearmament. The prime minister himself had broached the possibility of post-treaty bases as early as May 1950, but prior to the outbreak of the Korean War (25 June 1950) he had resisted United States pressures for rearmament.

Although rearmament was subsequently carried out under the Yoshida government—beginning with establishment of the NATIONAL POLICE RESERVE in July 1950, and accelerating with the creation of the NATIONAL SAFETY FORCES in October 1952 and the SELF DEFENSE FORCES in June 1954—Yoshida to the end resisted American pressures for a considerably more rapid and massive expansion of personnel strength. The US target figure at this time was 325,000–350,000 Japanese troops by 1954–55; at the end of the Yoshida Era, designated personnel strength was approximately 180,000, including a small navy and air force. From 1946 to 1950 Yoshida had advanced the most literal and unqualified interpretation of article 9, the RENUNCIATION OF WAR clause of the new constitution as prohibiting armament even for self-defense. After the establishment of the National Police Reserve, he and his spokesmen engaged in convoluted semantics to defend the legality of the new military, eventually adopting the explanation that article 9 did not prohibit maintenance of a "military without war potential." The implication of the Yoshida government's position on rearmament was that creation of a bona fide military, institution of a military draft, or dispatch of Japanese troops overseas would require constitutional revision—but that such a course was neither necessary nor feasible at that time. In March 1954 Yoshida created a Committee to Investigate the Constitution within his party (which had reverted to its original name of Japan Liberal Party), but this reflected a response to conservative pressures rather than a commitment to revision on his own part.

Yoshida was less strenuous and less successful in opposing another American demand which became clearer in the wake of the San Francisco Peace Conference: Japanese participation in the containment of China. To ensure US Senate ratification of the peace treaty, in the famous "Yoshida Letter" of December 1951 the prime minister agreed to establish diplomatic ties with the routed Guomindang (Kuomintang) regime of CHIANG KAI-SHEK. Although Yoshida and his aides were openly critical of American China policy, beginning in 1951 they in practice adhered to the blueprint for a capitalist bloc that—under the rubric "United States–Japan economic cooperation"—integrated the economies of Japan, the United States, and the anticommunist regimes of Southeast Asia.

These policies were vulnerable to criticism from conservatives as well as progressives, and from 1952 Yoshida faced a mounting challenge from former purgees (centering on Hatoyama) and accused war criminals (notably Shigemitsu and KISHI NOBUSUKE) who reentered the political arena. As this political influence began to wane, Yoshida's personal gestures became more flamboyant. In September 1952, he threw water from a glass at a photographer, and was captured in the act in a well-publicized photograph. In November 1952, he concluded a formal presentation to the emperor by referring to himself as "Your Loyal Servant Shigeru" (Shin Shigeru), a shocking gesture to many Japanese in that it denied the concept of public servant and evoked the obsequiousness of the feudal period and mindless emperor worship of the era of imperial Japan. During hearings in the Diet in February 1953, the prime minister enhanced his notoriety by calling a socialist questioner a stupid fool (baka yarō); the incident led to a vote of no-confidence, which in turn led to Yoshida's dissolution of the Diet and calling of the general election that preceded the fifth Yoshida cabinet. In 1954 he somewhat tarnished his reputation for personal probity by intervening in the investigation of the massive SHIPBUILDING SCANDAL to protect some of his political henchmen. Such incidents became well-remembered vignettes in the political lore of postwar Japan, often overshadowing the more substantial developments of the closing years of the Yoshida Era.

The fourth and fifth Yoshida cabinets (formed in October 1952 and May 1953) continued the campaign to "rectify the excesses" of the early postwar period and succeeded in revising some of the Occupation reforms pertaining to education, police decentralization, local autonomy, and antimonopoly policy. The Mutual Security Agreement (see UNITED STATES–JAPAN MUTUAL DEFENSE ASSISTANCE AGREEMENT) signed in March 1954 further defined and regulated the intricately meshed military, economic, and technological relationship between Japan and the United States, but the Yoshida government remained pessimistic concerning the future of Japan's "shallow economy" and endeavored to encourage a broader and more purely economic "Marshall Plan for Asia" on the part of the United States. Yoshida personally carried this appeal to the United States in the autumn of 1954, but his mission was a failure in all respects. Washington was unreceptive, and Yoshida's conservative enemies at home took advantage of his absence to mobilize a final successful assault against him. He was ousted as president of the Liberal Party shortly after his return to Japan in November and forced to dissolve his fifth and final cabinet in early December. He was replaced as prime minister by Hatoyama.

Although Yoshida departed from the premiership in an atmosphere of rancor at home and uncertainty concerning Japan's future internationally, he lived for another 13 years—long enough to see the emergence of Japan as an economic power and to enjoy the mellow status of a venerable elder statesman. He published his memoirs in four volumes in 1957–58 and wrote a variety of articles and essays. His estate in Ōiso attracted a procession of conservative party bosses, fledgling diplomats, and visiting dignitaries, and in 1964 he was decorated with the Supreme Order of the Chrysanthemum (Daikun'i Kikka Shō).

📖——Yoshida Shigeru, Kaisō jūnen, 4 vols (1957–58), tr in abridged form by Ken'ichi Yoshida as The Yoshida Memoirs (1962). John W. Dower, Empire and Aftermath: Yoshida Shigeru and the Japanese Experience, 1878–1954 (1979). Inoki Masamichi, Hyōden Yoshida Shigeru, 3 vols (1978; 1980; 1981). Kōsaka Masataka, Saishō Yoshida Shigeru (1968). Yoshida Naikaku Kankō Kai, ed, Yoshida naikaku (1954), the massive official history of the Yoshida cabinets. John W. Dower

Yoshida Shintō

A school of Shintō transmitted within the Yoshida family (before 1378 known as Urabe), who were the hereditary priests of the Yoshida Shrine and Hirano Shrine in Kyōto. The beginnings of Yoshida Shintō—also called Urabe Shintō or Yuiitsu Shintō ("The only Shintō")—go back to Urabe Kanekata, a 13th century scholar who compiled the Shaku nihongi, a major commentary on the Nihongi or NIHON SHOKI (720, Chronicle of Japan), and his son, Kanefumi, who wrote the earliest surviving commentary on the KOJIKI (712, Records of Ancient Matters). The greatest thinker of the school was YOSHIDA KANETOMO (1435–1511), who systematized its doctrines in

two important treatises, Shintō taii (The Gist of Shintō) and Yuiitsu shintō myōbō yōshū (An Anthology of the Doctrines of the Only Shintō), in which he sought to establish his family as the arbiters of Shintō orthodoxy in opposition to the Shirakawa family, who were the hereditary heads (haku) of the Office of Shintō Worship (Jingikan) in the government.

Kanetomo recognized three types of Shintō: (1) Honjaku Engi Shintō or the rituals and legends associated with the various regional shrines; (2) RYŌBU SHINTŌ, the belief that the Inner and Outer Shrines of Ise corresponded to the two mandalas of SHINGON SECT Buddhism; and (3) "Shintō of the Original Source" (Gempon Sōgen Shintō), the formal name for Yoshida Shintō, which was so designated because of its belief in a supreme primordial deity who preceded heaven and earth, transcended the creative forces of in (Ch: yin) and yō (Ch: yang), was the source of the myriad deities of Shintō and was also immanent in all living creatures. Kanetomo designated this sublime deity Daigen Sonshin ("The Venerable Deity of the Great Origin") and equated him with the Shintō deity Kuninotokotachi no Kami mentioned in the Kojiki and Nihongi.

Under the apparent influence of Buddhism, Kanetomo divided Yoshida Shintō into (1) an exoteric teaching revealed in the three Shintō classics, the Sendai kuji hongi (9th century?, Annals of Ancient Matters of Preceding Reigns), the Kojiki, and the Nihongi, and (2) an esoteric teaching spoken by the deity Amenokoyane no Mikoto and subsequently transcribed in Chinese by the Taoist god of the Pole Star. This esoteric teaching, supposedly transmitted secretly within the Yoshida family, involves a number of rituals such as the goma (the kindling of a sacred fire to burn away defilements) and the kanjō (anointing the head with holy water), which are borrowed from Shingon Buddhism. Despite its claim to represent a pure, if hitherto unrevealed, transmission, Yoshida Shintō is in fact a highly eclectic school that draws upon Confucianism, Taoism, the doctrines of yin-yang and the five forces (or elements; see OMMYŌDŌ), and especially the elaborate rituals of Shingon Buddhism.

In 1484 Kanetomo erected within the precincts of the Yoshida Shrine in Kyōto a sanctuary called the Daigengū dedicated to the supreme deity of Yoshida Shintō as well as to all the deities mentioned in the Engi Shiki (927, Procedures of the Engi Era) and the Shintō pantheon at large, in the hope of eventually bringing all shrines in Japan under its jurisdiction. While his plan was not completely successful, by the Edo period (1600–1868), many Shintō priests sought certification from the Yoshida family. With the emergence of STATE SHINTŌ after the Meiji Restoration in 1868, Yoshida Shintō lost its special standing with the Shintō clergy.

Stanley WEINSTEIN

Yoshida Shōin (1830–1859)

Scholar, teacher, writer, expert in the military arts, and ideologue of the SONNŌ JŌI (Revere the Emperor, Expel the Barbarians) movement of the late Edo period (1600–1868). Shōin was born in the village of Matsumoto on the outskirts of Hagi, the castle town of the Mōri daimyō of Chōshū (now Yamaguchi Prefecture). His father, who was a low-ranking samurai, supplemented his meager finances by farming. Shōin's personal name was Norikata, and his common name was Torajirō. He used a variety of literary names, of which Shōin ("pine shadow") and Nijūikkai Mōshi ("21 times audacious samurai") were the most common.

Shōin was adopted by his uncle, Yoshida Daisuke, an instructor in the Hagi Yamaga school of military science with whose founder, YAMAGA SOKŌ (1622–85), the Yoshida family had traditional links. Shōin was to be deeply influenced by Yamaga's teachings on both the military sciences and loyalty to the emperor. The following year (1836), on the death of his uncle, Shōin became the heir apparent to the Yamaga school, to which end his education was directed under the supervision of another uncle, Tamaki Bunnoshin (1810–76). Early in 1838 he was registered at the Meirinkan, the official Chōshū domain school for the sons of samurai, where his rapid progress in both military science and the Chinese classics drew favorable attention from his daimyō. Ten years later he was appointed instructor in the Meirinkan as an expert in military strategy, ethics, government, and Chinese history.

In 1850 Shōin made a brief fact-finding tour of western Kyūshū, his first journey outside Chōshū. In 1851 he accompanied his daimyō on a visit to Edo (now Tōkyō), where he met young activists from other domains and came under the influence of the political thinker SAKUMA SHŌZAN, whose school he joined briefly. During his stay in Edo, Shōin made a journey to northeasthern Honshū; he visited the Mito domain (now part of Ibaraki Prefecture) and came under the influence of its proimperial scholars (see MITO SCHOOL). He incurred official disfavor, however, for traveling without proper documentation, and when he returned to Hagi, he was deprived of both samurai status and income. However, the daimyō, who had been one of his pupils in military science, soon permitted further journeys throughout Japan. In 1854, at the instigation of Sakuma Shōzan, Shōin defied the NATIONAL SECLUSION edicts and with a friend, Kaneko Jūsuke (1831–55), attempted to stow away on Commodore Matthew PERRY's flagship, USS *Powhatan*, at anchorage in Shimoda, on the southern tip of the Izu Peninsula. His avowed purpose was to acquaint himself with conditions in the West in order to strengthen Japan.

This escapade, which resulted first in his imprisonment and subsequently in house arrest (1855), consolidated his thinking on *sonnō jōi* and national politics and opened up a fruitful field for writing and teaching. In the Shōka Sonjuku, a private school that he established in his house, Shōin gathered together a group of young samurai who later played key roles in overthrowing the shogunate and carrying out the Meiji Restoration. This group included such brilliant men as TAKASUGI SHINSAKU, KUSAKA GENZUI, ITŌ HIROBUMI, and YAMAGATA ARITOMO. His immense patriotism led him to involvement in an unsuccessful plot to assassinate the high shogunal official MANABE AKIKATSU. He was arrested once more, sent to Edo for a trial, and executed at Temmachō prison in the penultimate of the ANSEI PURGE (1859). His spirit is honored at shrines in Hagi and at Setagaya, a ward of modern Tōkyō.

Shōin's writings include books on national defense, government, manners and customs of foreign countries, travel diaries, commentaries on the Chinese classics, many poems, and collections of letters, of which 867 were written in the last 10 years of his life. Some of the more famous works are *Kōkokushi* (1858, Aspirations of a Hero); *Kaikoroku* (1855, Record of the Past); and *Ryūkonroku* (1858, Record of an Everlasting Spirit).

■ ——Yamaguchi Ken Kyōikukai, ed, *Yoshida Shōin zenshū*, 2nd ed, 12 vols (Iwanami Shoten, 1938–40). W. G. Beasley, *The Meiji Restoration* (1972). H. Dumoulin, "Yoshida Shōin (1830–59)," *Monumenta Nipponica* 1 (1938). H. J. J. M. Van Straelen, *Yoshida Shōin, Forerunner of the Meiji Restoration* (1952).

Maida S. COALDRAKE

Yoshida Tadao (1908–)

Businessman. Founder of the company YOSHIDA KŌGYŌ, known for its YKK-brand products. Born in Toyama Prefecture. With only an elementary-school education, Yoshida started work at a trading company. He began a fastener production venture in 1934 and established Yoshida Kōgyō in 1945. Yoshida succeeded in making YKK-brand products widely known throughout the world by using a highly mechanized production system, from raw materials to finished products. He has advocated a workers' stockholding system, and so does not list his company's stocks on the market.

MAEDA Kazutoshi

Yoshida Tōgo (1864–1918)

Historian and geographer. Born in Echigo (now Niigata Prefecture), he was mainly self-taught. While teaching at an elementary school he contributed articles on history to TAGUCHI UKICHI's journal *Shikai* (1891–96) and to the newspaper *Yomiuri shimbun*. Yoshida's *Dai Nihon chimei jisho* (1900–1907), a study of place names in Japan, established his reputation as a scholar and earned him a position on the faculty of Waseda University. Interested also in NŌ drama, he argued in his *Zeami jūrokubushū* (1909) that ZEAMI and KAN'AMI wrote both the music and the texts of certain Nō plays.

Yoshida Tomizō (1903–1973)

Pathologist known for producing "Yoshida sarcoma." Born in Fukushima Prefecture; graduate of Tōkyō University. With his teacher SASAKI TAKAOKI, Yoshida succeeded in inducing an artificial liver cancer in rats with an azo dye. He engaged in cancer research in Germany from 1935 to 1938. In 1943, at Nagasaki Medical College, he produced an ascites tumor in rats for the first time, naming it Yoshida sarcoma. Transplantable into other rats, this was a great contribution to the study of malignancies. Besides teaching at Nagasaki Medical College, Yoshida held posts at Tōhoku University and

Tōkyō University and served as director of the Cancer Institute, director of the Japanese Foundation for Cancer Research, and president of the Nippon Medical Association. Yoshida received the Japan Academy Prize twice (1936 and 1953), as well as the Order of Culture in 1959.

NAGATOYA Yōji

Yoshida Tōyō (1816–1862)

Reformer of the Tosa domain (now Kōchi Prefecture) at the end of the Edo period (1600–1868); also known as Yoshida Masaaki. Yoshida, brought to a position of power by the *daimyō* YAMANOUCHI TOYOSHIGE in 1853, planned a series of reforms in the domainal administration, but conservative opposition soon resulted in his removal from office. In 1857 conditions forced the domainal authorities to recall him to lead a reform program. Yoshida planned to create a domain monopoly in certain agricultural products, to adopt Western techniques of shipbuilding and casting artillery, and to establish ability, rather than birth, as the basis for promotion. His proposals were opposed both by conservatives and by radical anti-Western, proimperial (SONNŌ JŌI) activists in Tosa; he was assassinated by a *samurai* of the latter faction.

Yoshihara Oil Mill, Ltd

(Yoshihara Seiyu). Company producing cooking oil and oil cake. Established in 1855, it was engaged in making cottonseed oil but has switched to soya oil in recent years. In 1966 the company established the Japan Soya Products Co jointly with HOHNEN OIL CO, LTD, to expand into the production of soybean protein. Production is centered on cooking oil for commercial purposes but efforts are being made to develop the household market. The firm is affiliated with the SUMITOMO CORPORATION. Sales totaled ¥53.9 billion (US $246.2 million) in 1981, and the company was capitalized at ¥1.1 billion (US $5 million) in the same year. The head office is in Ōsaka.

Yoshiharu Shikimoku

Domainal law code (BUNKOKUHŌ) enacted in 1567 by the ROKKAKU FAMILY, *daimyō* of Ōmi Province (now Shiga Prefecture); known also as Rokkakushi Shikimoku. After the warlord Rokkaku Yoshiharu (1545–1612) killed one of his retainers, internal strife weakened his domain militarily and led to an invasion by the neighboring lord ASAI NAGAMASA. Yoshiharu's chief vassals therefore drafted a code and forced him to accept it in order to reconsolidate the domain. It sets forth detailed administrative regulations and carefully defines the rights and obligations of rulers and subjects alike; it is known especially for its elaborate monetary regulations.

Yoshiigawa

River in eastern Okayama Prefecture, western Honshū, originating in the Chūgoku Mountains and flowing south through the Tsuyama Basin and Okayama Plain to empty into the Inland Sea. The water in the upper reaches is utilized for electric power; that of the lower reaches is used for irrigation. Tourist attractions include the Okutsukyō, a gorge on the upper reaches, and Okutsu Hot Spring. Length: 133 km (83 mi); area of drainage basin: 2,060 sq km (795 sq mi).

Yoshii Isamu (1886–1960)

TANKA poet; playwright. Born in Tōkyō, Yoshii enrolled in Waseda University in 1905 but attended only a short while. That same year he joined the New Poetry Society (Shinshisha), founded by the poet YOSANO TEKKAN in 1899, and began contributing *tanka* to its magazine MYŌJŌ, one of the most influential literary journals of the period and a central vehicle of the romantic school. As a member of the *Myōjō* coterie he became closely associated with such leading men of letters of his day as MORI ŌGAI, UEDA BIN, KINOSHITA MOKUTARŌ, and KITAHARA HAKUSHŪ. He subsequently left the New Poetry Society and joined the PAN NO KAI, a group of writers and painters that had been formed in 1908 by Mokutarō, Hakushū, and others who shared a similar attraction for romanticism and aestheticism. In 1909 he became an editor of the poetry magazine *Subaru*, which succeeded *Myōjō*. Yoshii early gained a reputation as a decadent poet and is perhaps best remembered for his love poetry. His first representative collection of *tanka*, *Sakahogai* (1910), records the joys and sorrows of a young poet overly given to wine and sexual desire. In his later years he developed a more subdued poetic style, as found in the collections *Ningenkyō* (1934) and *Keieishō* (1956). He is also known for his modern symbolist plays in the style of the Belgian dramatist Maurice Maeterlinck. *Gogo sanji* (1911) is an early collection of 11 one-act plays. Yoshii's career spans many years and genres.

Yoshikawa Eiji (1892–1962)

Novelist. Real name Yoshikawa Hidetsugu. In his hands Japanese POPULAR FICTION, hitherto written primarily for entertainment, was elevated to something approaching a true people's literature *(kokumin bungaku)*.

Yoshikawa was born into an ex-*samurai* family in Kanagawa Prefecture, but his father's drinking and extravagant habits brought the family to financial ruin. The love and devotion that his mother gave her children under these dire circumstances made a lasting impression on the future author. When he was 11 he left school for a succession of jobs, working as shop boy, peddler, and construction worker, but managed to continue his education in night school.

Yoshikawa's literary instincts were inherited from his mother, who was very fond of reading. In childhood his imagination was fed by children's books that he managed to borrow from the local booklender. Through his study of *senryū* poetry (see ZAPPAI AND SENRYŪ) he acquired skill in the observation of human behavior (he wrote *senryū* under the pen name Kijirō). These influences converged in his first published work, *Enoshima monogatari* (1914), an account of the miracle-working goddess Benzaiten (Skt: Sarasvati). In 1921, he joined the staff of the newspaper *Maiyū shimbun*, but it failed in the general chaos following the great Tōkyō Earthquake of 1923. Without a job, Yoshikawa decided that it was futile to fight against fate, and turned to writing full time.

The year 1925 saw the magazine serialization of Yoshikawa's *Kennan jonan*, a novel centering on the vendetta and love affairs of a handsome swordsman of the Edo period (1600–1868). The series proved immensely popular, and was followed closely by a succession of adventure novels: *Naruto hichō* (1926–27), *Edo sangokushi* (1927–29), and *Moeru Fuji* (1932–33). About this time he also wrote his autobiographical *Kankan mushi wa utau* (1930–31) and his humorous story *Arupusu taishō* (1933–34).

Having grown tired of fantastic adventure stories, Yoshikawa turned to *Miyamoto Musashi* (1935–39; tr *Musashi*, 1981), an account of the 17th-century master swordsman MIYAMOTO MUSASHI, in which he stressed that the true way of the sword lies in doing battle with the self, and that only by conquering all selfish desire does one arrive at that spiritual realm wherein the way of the sword and the way of Zen are one. The awareness of one's limits and the seeking of personal fulfillment within those limits constituted a revival of the traditional view of life that was welcomed by many readers. Other works belonging to this period include *Shinsho taikōki* (1939–45) and *Bairi sensei gyōjōki* (1941).

Following the trauma of Japan's defeat in 1945, Yoshikawa decided to look at history anew through the eyes of the ordinary man. The product of this reassessment was what proved to be his lifework, *Shin Heike monogatari* (1950–57, New Tales of the Heike; tr *The Heike Story*, 1956), in which the tumultuous power struggles of the late 12th century are seen through the eyes of a groundkeeper in the Imperial Palace. In depicting the arrogance of power and the indomitability of the common people, Yoshikawa, who saw history as ultimately a pile of bleached bones, meant to cast judgment on the present—postwar Japanese society.

The hallmark of Yoshikawa's writing (especially in his later works) was his basic conservatism. He believed that popular literature should aim for moral edification as well as diversion and that the realities of the present should always be seen in the light of past history, and these convictions accounted for his enormous popularity. He became the first writer of popular fiction to receive the Order of Culture in 1960.

📖——Collected Works: *Yoshikawa Eiji zenshū*, 48 vols (Kōdansha, 1966–70). Ozaki Hotsuki, *Denki Yoshikawa Eiji* (1970). Yoshikawa Eiji, *Shin Heike monogatari*, tr Fuki Wooyenaka Uramatsu as *The Heike Story* (1956). Yoshikawa Eimei, *Chichi Yoshikawa Eiji* (1974). ASAI Kiyoshi

Yoshikawa Kōjirō (1904–1981)

Scholar of Chinese literature. Born in Hyōgo Prefecture, Yoshikawa was a graduate of Kyōto University, where he studied with Kanō

Naoki (1868–1947), a China specialist, and was heavily influenced by the Qing (Ch'ing, 1644–1912) academic tradition emphasizing philology. After studying in China for several years, Yoshikawa taught at Kyōto University from 1931 to 1967. He also translated into Japanese and annotated numerous Chinese works, among which are *Gen zatsugeki kenkyū* (1948), on Yuan (Yüan) dynasty drama, and *Toho shiki* (1949), on the poet Du Fu (Tu Fu). His collection of translations of Tang (T'ang) dynasty (618–907) poems, *Tōshisen* (1954), on which he collaborated with the poet MIYOSHI TATSUJI, is widely read.

📖——*Yoshikawa Kōjirō zenshū*, 24 vols (Chikuma Shobō, 1973–76).

Yoshikawa Koretari (1616–1694)

Also known as Yoshikawa Koretaru or Kikkawa Koretari. Shintō thinker and founder of Yoshikawa Shintō. Born in Nihombashi in Edo (now Tōkyō). His father died when he was an infant, and he was adopted by a merchant family. Finding himself ill-suited for business, in 1651 he retired to Kamakura to devote himself to the study of Shintō. He went to Kyōto in 1653 and entered the service of Hagiwara Kaneyori (1588–1660), then head of the Yoshida family, and was initiated into the teachings of YOSHIDA SHINTŌ. He lectured on Shintō in Edo and earned the confidence of members of the Tokugawa family and various *daimyō*. In 1682, during the rule of shōgun TOKUGAWA TSUNAYOSHI, he was appointed *shintōkata* (director of Shintō affairs); this office thereafter became a hereditary office of the Yoshikawa family until the end of the Edo period (1600–1868). His theology was based mainly on Yoshida Shintō, with elements from Song (Sung) dynasty (960–1279) Confucianism. He held Shintō to be the fountainhead of all things, including other religions. He emphasized TSUTSUSHIMI (seriousness of mind) as the way of mankind and stressed the importance of the rite of *oharai* (purification). As the teacher of YAMAZAKI ANSAI Yoshikawa greatly influenced Yamazaki's attempts to synthesize Shintō and Neo-Confucianism.

yoshikiri → reed warblers

Yoshimasu Tōdō (1702–1773)

Physician of the classicist school *(koihō)* who contributed greatly to the Japanization of Chinese medicine. Real name Tamenori. Also known as Yoshimasu Shūsuke. A native of Aki (now part of Hiroshima Prefecture), Yoshimasu studied *koihō* in Kyōto and opened a practice with the help of YAMAWAKI TŌYŌ. He rejected the *yin-yang* and five elements theories (OMMYŌDŌ) of the body held by the *goseihō* ("latter day school" of medicine; see MEDICINE: history of medicine) as meaningless speculations, and said that medical treatment should be based on the observation of actual symptoms. He experimentally confirmed the effectiveness of treatments described in the Chinese medical classics, the *Shang han lun* and the *Jingui yaolüe (Chin-kuei yao-lüeh)*, and published the methods in a book entitled *Ruijuhō (1764)*. He believed that all disease originated in the abdomen and asserted that abdominal palpation was more important in diagnosis than examination of the pulse, long regarded as the most effective diagnostic method. He devised a new technique for palpating the abdomen and greatly simplified traditional Chinese medical methods. Yoshimasu was also an advocate of the theory that all diseases were caused by one poison *(mambyō ichidoku)* and proposed aggressive treatment with powerful drugs, which effected a cure by "blinding" *(menken)*, a specific vital reaction occurring when chronic diseases take a rapid turn for the better. He said in *Idan* (1759) that physicians cured sickness but death was decided by Heaven. This statement aroused much controversy among physicians at the time. He trained many eminent physicians and his treatment system was widely used throughout the country.

YAMADA Terutane

Yoshimi "hundred-cave" tunnel tombs

(Yoshimi *hyakketsu*). A cluster of some 230 tunnel tombs (see YOKOANA) dug into the tuff cliffs along the river Ichinokawa in Yoshimichō, Saitama Prefecture; generally dated to the 6th and 7th centuries. They were first investigated in 1887 by the anthropologist TSUBOI SHŌGORŌ, who thought they were cave dwellings. Each cavern is divided into an entrance corridor and an inner chamber; the latter is equipped with a platform to receive the coffins of one generation of one family. Burial goods include cylindrical and curved beads, HANIWA sculptures, iron arrowheads, and SUE WARE; some skeletal remains have also been recovered. *ABE Gihei*

Yoshimoto Ryūmei → Yoshimoto Takaaki

Yoshimoto Takaaki (1924–)

Literary critic; poet. Commonly known as Yoshimoto Ryūmei. Graduate of Tōkyō Institute of Technology. With the publication of two poetry collections, *Koyūji to no taiwa* (1952) and *Ten'i no tame no juppen* (1953), he became known as a radical poet. Turning to criticism, he wrote about such issues as the validity of the proletarian literary theory (see PROLETARIAN LITERATURE MOVEMENT) and the responsibility of writers for World War II. His independent radical stance, which rejected all established institutions, especially the Communist Party, exerted significant influence on the New Left Movement of the 1960s. A prolific critic, he has written on a wide range of subjects, including religion, folklore, linguistics, and psychology. His principal works of literary criticism include *Geijutsuteki teikō to zasetsu* (1959), *Jojō no ronri* (1959), *Gisei no shūen* (1962), *Mosha to kagami* (1964), *Gengo ni totte bi to wa nanika* (1965), and *Kyōdō gensō ron* (1968).

Yoshimura Junzō (1908–)

Architect. Born in Tōkyō. While a student at the Tōkyō School of Fine Arts (now Tōkyō National University of Fine Arts and Music), Yoshimura began working for the American architect Antonin RAYMOND. He started his own firm in 1943. In 1945 he joined the faculty of the Tōkyō School of Fine Arts, where he subsequently taught for 25 years. He is especially well known as an innovative designer of houses, showing sensitivity to wood as a building material. His works include the traditional style Japan House (1954) at the Museum of Modern Art in New York, the Aichi Prefectural University of Arts (1971), and the Nara National Museum (1973), for which he won the Japan Art Academy Prize in 1974.

WATANABE Hiroshi

Yoshimura Kōzaburō (1911–)

Film director. Trained at SHŌCHIKU CO, LTD, as an assistant to SHIMAZU YASUJIRŌ. His early career was marked by repeated failure until he made *Anjōke no butōkai* (1947, A Ball at the Anjō House), which won the coveted Kinema Jumpō Award. Since then he has directed some 40 films, both period pieces and contemporary dramas, mostly for DAIEI CO, LTD.

Although he developed a bad name with company management at Shōchiku early in his career (he was notorious for wasting precious film stock, among other things), Yoshimura turned out what is now considered one of the best Japanese war films, *Nishizumi senshachō den* (1940, The Story of Tank Commander Nishizumi). Immediately following the war he wrote and directed one of the first of many films to focus on the problems of postwar Japanese society, *Anjōke no butōkai*, which he has said is based on his own experiences. Yoshimura joined Daiei in 1951 and worked almost exclusively for that company until its collapse in 1971. He has made films in almost every genre imaginable, but he has repeatedly returned to themes related to the struggles of women. For this he came to be regarded as a successor to the great director MIZOGUCHI KENJI.

David OWENS

Yoshinogawa

River in Kōchi and Tokushima prefectures, Shikoku, originating in the Shikoku Mountains and flowing east into the Kii Channel at the city of Tokushima. It is the largest river in Shikoku. The middle reaches cut through the Shikoku Mountains, forming transverse valleys, and creating the Ōboke and Koboke gorges which are tourist attractions. The lower reaches form a farming area that once produced *ai* (indigo plant) but that now principally produces rice, vegetables, and flowers. Electric power projects have resulted in the construction of dams on the upper reaches. Length: 194 km (120 mi); area of drainage basin: 3,650 sq km (1,409 sq mi).

Yoshino Hideo (1902–1967)

TANKA poet. Born in Gumma Prefecture. Yoshino enrolled at Keiō University but left shortly after because of illness. He studied *tanka* composition with AIZU YAICHI. His best work came after World War II in collections like *Kansenshū* (1947, Cold Cicada). He was an admirer of the 19th-century poet-priest RYŌKAN and, like him, was influenced by the MAN'YŌSHŪ, an 8th-century anthology of Japanese verse. *Ryōkan Oshō no hito to uta* (1957) is the title of his well-known biography of Ryōkan. He was noted for his tight, succinct style of *tanka,* and in 1958 he was awarded the Yomiuri Literary Prize for his collected poems, *Yoshino Hideo kashū* (1958).

Yoshino–Kumano National Park

(Yoshino–Kumano Kokuritsu Kōen). Situated in central Honshū on the KII PENINSULA in Wakayama, Nara, and Mie prefectures. This park comprises the districts of Yoshino and Kumano, as well as a section of the peninsula's southeast coastline. The northern Yoshino district is characterized by mountains famed for temples of the mountain ascetic sect (SHUGENDŌ), such as Kimbusenji on YOSHINOYAMA, whose cherry blossoms are a major tourist attraction each spring. To its south are ŌMINESAN (also known as Sanjōgatake; height: 1,719 m or 5,638 ft) and Shakagatake (1,800 m; 5,904 ft). Ōminesan is another center for religious exercises of Shugendō Sect. To the east is ŌDAIGAHARASAN (1,695 m; 5,560 ft), one of the wettest areas in Japan, where moss thrives amid maples, firs, and Japanese birch trees. The southern Kumano district is typified by low mountains covered with evergreens and, to the east, long coastline stretching to the cape SHIONOMISAKI, the southernmost point of Honshū. The rivers KUMANOGAWA and TOTSUKAWA wind through dramatic scenery, for example, at the gorge DOROKYŌ on the Kitayamagawa, a tributary of the Kumanogawa. NACHI FALLS (133 m; 436 ft), to the south, is Japan's highest waterfall. Nearby is the famous Kumano Nachi Shrine, a center of the mountain ascetic sect. Area: 560.2 sq km (216.2 sq mi).

Yoshino Sakuzō (1878–1933)

Scholar and principal spokesman for liberal democratic ideas and reform during the Taishō period (1912–26). He was known for his journalistic writing, especially that published in CHŪŌ KŌRON, a leading monthly aimed at the educated middle class. Yoshino was the eldest son of a shopkeeper in the town of Furukawa, a market town in Miyagi Prefecture. After graduating from a local primary school in 1892, he continued his education in Sendai at middle school (1892–97) and then at the prestigious Second Higher School (1897–1900). A bright and able student, he was invariably at the top of his class. In 1898, while attending a Bible class run by an American Baptist missionary, he became a convert to Christianity. As a student in the Law Faculty at Tōkyō University between 1900 and 1904, he was an active member of the Hongō Church.

After two years of postgraduate study, Yoshino went to China in 1906 as a tutor to Yuan Keming (Yüan K'o-ming), eldest son of YUAN SHIKAI (Yüan Shih-k'ai). On his return to Japan in 1909 he was appointed assistant professor in the Law Faculty at Tōkyō University. Except for a study trip to Europe (1910–13), and a brief stint on the editorial staff of the newspaper *Ōsaka asahi shimbun* (1924), Yoshino served on the university faculty until his death.

The most important influences on his intellectual development were philosophical idealism, which made him distrustful of positivist or materialistic explanations of sociopolitical phenomena; liberal Protestantism, which imparted a strong sense of social concern and a lifelong belief in the spiritual equality of mankind; and liberal constitutionalism, which shaped his views on political practice. Departing from the traditional interests of Law Faculty professors, he stressed the importance of discussing practical political problems and policies rather than debating the location or character of state sovereignty. He enlivened his lectures on political history with comments on contemporary national and international events.

His principal fame came with the publication in 1916 of an article entitled "Kensei no hongi o toite sono yūshū no bi o nasu no michi o ronzu" (On the Meaning of Constitutional Government and the Methods to Perfect It). He argued that, although formal sovereignty was lodged in the imperial institution, responsible representative government was still possible under the Meiji CONSTITUTION. He argued that the "spirit of constitutional government" lay in *mimpon shugi* (literally, "people-as-the-base-ism"), a translation of "democracy" that he differentiated from *minshu shugi* ("popular sover-

Yoshinoyama

The famous cherry trees of Yoshinoyama. The main hall of the temple Kimbusenji is visible at the top of the hill in the distance.

eignty"), the usual translation. *Mimpon shugi* meant that the government should act on behalf of the popular welfare and that the people, through the mechanisms of elections and responsible cabinets, should be the ultimate judge of whether it did so. He was attacked from the right by those who said that representative government was incompatible with the KOKUTAI (the state structure or polity unique to Japan as embodied in the imperial institution) and from the Left by those who said that he was an apologist for bourgeois domination.

In subsequent writings Yoshino shifted from the theoretical justification of representative democracy to issues of practical reform. He was an early advocate of universal manhood suffrage, and despite a distrust of the existing political parties, he urged an end to GENRŌ (elder statesmen) interference in politics, institutionalization of cabinet responsibility to the Diet, and curbing the powers of extraparliamentary forces such as the HOUSE OF PEERS, the PRIVY COUNCIL, and the military high command. He also supported a policy of greater self-rule for colonial areas such as Korea, and he advocated a peaceful and cooperative foreign policy in China.

He was not outspoken about his views on social problems, but he favored active social welfare policies, legal recognition of labor unions, and legislation to regulate labor-employer relations. He was critical of radical elements in the labor movement and left-wing socialists, whose atheism, materialism, and conflict tactics he deplored, but in 1925 he lent his support to the organization of the moderate SHAKAI MINSHŪTŌ (Socialist People's Party; founded in December 1926).

During his final years Yoshino's interest turned to the study of recent Japanese history, especially the early part of the Meiji period (1868–1912). He apparently hoped to demonstrate that there were historic roots in Japan for the establishment of liberal democratic politics. His most enduring contribution, however, was the compilation of the 24-volume *Meiji bunka zenshū* (1927–30), a collection of rare Meiji historical materials. He died at the age of 55 after suffering many years from tuberculosis.

■——Peter Duus, "Yoshino Sakuzō: The Christian as Political Critic," *Journal of Japanese Studies* 4.2 (1978). Tetsuo Najita, "Some Reflections on Idealism in the Political Thought of Yoshino Sakuzō," in Bernard S. Silberman and H. D. Harootunian, ed, *Japan in Crisis* (1974). Tanaka Sōgorō, *Yoshino Sakuzō* (1958). Peter DUUS

Yoshinoyama

Hills in the town of Yoshino, central Nara Prefecture, central Honshū, extending about 8 km (5 mi), from the river Yoshinogawa to the mountain called ŌMINESAN. The area is known for its cherry blossoms and numerous historical sites such as the remains of Yoshino Palace, the mausoleum of Emperor GO-DAIGO, and the temple KIMBUSENJI. Yoshinoyama is also known as a place where MINAMOTO NO YOSHITSUNE sought refuge. It forms the northern part of Yoshino-Kumano National Park. Height: 300–700 m (984–2,296 ft).

Yoshioka Yayoi (1871–1959)

Physician, educator, public official, and founder of Japan's first medical college for women. Born in Shizuoka Prefecture, the daughter of Washiyama Yōsai, the doctor who introduced Western medicine to that area. Like her two older brothers, she went to Tōkyō to attend Saisei Gakusha Medical College; after receiving her license in 1892, she opened her own practice in Tōkyō in 1895. That same year she married Yoshioka Arata (1868–1922), a former medical student who had been teaching her German at his own small private school. Aided by her husband, she opened the Tōkyō Joigakkō (Tōkyō Women's Medical School), starting out with four students in 1900. For one of their lessons, she allowed her students to witness the birth of her own son. Expanding rapidly to an enrollment of several hundred, the school became in 1912 the Tōkyō Joshi Igaku Semmon Gakkō (Tōkyō Women's Medical Professional School). As its first president, Yayoi fought for its full accreditation, which meant that its graduates would become licensed doctors automatically; this status was granted in 1920. She also operated a hospital (the Tōkyō Shisei Byōin) and was an active member of various government and public organizations. She was purged after World War II by US Occupation authorities for her government service, but when the purge was lifted in 1951, she again became president of the school she had founded, which was renamed Tōkyō Joshi Ika Daigaku (Tōkyō Women's Medical College). In 1955 she received Japan's highest award for women, the Fujin Bunka Shō.

Yoshishige no Yasutane (ca 931–1002)

A man of letters who later entered the Buddhist priesthood, adopting the name Jakushin. His works include *Nihon ōjō gokuraku ki* (984), a collection of tales in Chinese (KAMBUN) about Japanese personages who had attained rebirth in Amida's Western Paradise; and *Chiteiki* (982), a description, also written in Chinese, of the deterioration of the Kyōto capital that is said to have influenced KAMO NO CHŌMEI's *Hōjōki*. *Douglas E. MILLS*

Yoshiwara

(abbreviation of Shin Yoshiwara). Old name for what is now part of the Senzoku district, Taitō Ward, Tōkyō. From the early years of the Edo period (1600–1868) until 1958, Yoshiwara was the location of the most famous of the government-regulated centers for PROSTITUTION in Japan. The generic term for these licensed quarters was *yūkaku* ("play quarter"), *kuruwa* ("quarter"), or *iromachi* ("love town"). The idea of setting aside certain areas of the cities where prostitution could be practiced and controlled was part of the policy of the Tokugawa shogunate (1603–1867) to create a highly regulated society. Yoshiwara was founded in Edo (now Tōkyō) in 1617 when the shogunate granted a license to Shōji Jin'emon (1576–1644).

Since Edo, Kyōto, and Ōsaka were the three main cities during the Edo period, it is not surprising that the respective licensed quarters of those cities were the largest and most famous (Yoshiwara in Edo, Shimabara in Kyōto, and Shimmachi in Ōsaka), although almost every city had its own small version of Yoshiwara. The total number of Yoshiwara prostitutes generally varied between 2,000 and 3,000, with numerous other resident employees, in as many as 200 separate establishments. As long as it was contained within these licensed areas, prostitution was legal in Japan through 1957, when promulgation of the PROSTITUTION PREVENTION LAW (passed the year before) abolished the licensed quarters. Yoshiwara thus had a history of almost three-and-a-half centuries.

It would be a mistake to think of Yoshiwara as a simple collection of brothels; rather, it was a highly stratified and complex world in itself that provided the means for a very sophisticated level of entertainment. New genres of music, art, and literature developed around it, so that it played a large role in the cultural history of Edo-period Japan.

Many scholars have pointed out that in the strictly stratified society of the time, quarters like Yoshiwara provided the one institutionalized escape from social repression and control. That is, the social ranks of warrior, farmer, artisan, and merchant (SHI-NŌ-KŌ-SHŌ), which dictated how a person lived, married, worked, and dressed, were of secondary importance to the main key for enjoying oneself in Yoshiwara—namely, money. These quarters were open to all who could afford them, so a wealthy farmer or merchant had one area at least where he was the equal of the *samurai*. In fact, the townsmen (*chōnin*) came to dominate these quarters as they became richer and samurai became poorer from the early 18th century on.

The Setting —— The first location designated for the establishment of the licensed quarter in Edo was a piece of swampy land that had to be filled in before building could commence. Because of the reeds (*yoshi*) growing there, it was named Yoshiwara, or "reed plain," although afterward the first of the two Chinese characters with which the word was written was changed to one meaning "auspicious." After the quarter was destroyed by the MEIREKI FIRE in 1657, it moved to another location and was named Shin (new) Yoshiwara. The original place came to be called Moto (original) Yoshiwara (it is now part of the Nihombashi business district of Tōkyō). The new Yoshiwara included approximately 7.9 hectares (19.5 acres) of land, and the streets were laid out in a grid. Willow trees were planted by the gate and on the streets within—a symbol of prostitution taken from China. Cherry trees also lined the main streets, and the women of Yoshiwara were often compared to the pale blossoms blooming at night.

Like almost all of the licensed quarters, Edo's Yoshiwara was physically enclosed, surrounded by a moat and walls, and access was by means of one entry called the *ōmon*, or great gate. The reasons for this were twofold: to keep customers from sneaking away without paying and to keep the prostitutes from escaping. Within these walls were the various houses where the women lived and different types of teahouses where customers arranged for liaisons.

The system for arranging these meetings underwent several historical changes, involving different types of establishments. First there were the *ageya* ("houses of assignation"), where guests would request that a certain prostitute be called. The *ageya* made all the arrangements for calling the woman from her residence. By 1760, however, the *ageya* had disappeared, and its functions were taken over by teahouses called *hikite-jaya*. Customers had to go through these teahouses in order to engage a prostitute, and these houses were in a sense the pivot around which business revolved in Yoshiwara.

The guest paid the teahouse for all services, and the money for the prostitute was then passed on to the brothel owner. The customer might have already picked out a woman by strolling along and looking at the prostitutes sitting in rooms separated from the streets by vertical wooden bars, or in more modern times he might have leafed through a selection of photographs (*shashin mitate chō*) in the teahouse for his choice. The higher-class brothels did not exhibit their women in barred rooms (*harimise*) in front, since their fame and beauty were supposed to be matters of common knowledge. When the customer made his choice, a servant from the teahouse accompanied him to the brothel where the woman resided. Entertainers called GEISHA (or *hōkan*, if they were male) could also be called by the customer, and these arrangements again were made by the teahouses. The *hikite-jaya* made their profits by commissions on the fees paid to the prostitutes and geisha and by percentages levied on the food and drink consumed by the customers. They also received tips (*chadai*) for their service. In addition to the teahouses, there was a great variety of brothels (*jorōya*) of differing rank, depending on the quality of the women within them. Fees, called *agedai*, varied accordingly.

The Women —— There was a bewildering variety of names, both general and specific, for the different levels of prostitutes. They can be most broadly categorized as licensed (*kōshō*) or unlicensed (*shishō*). All the prostitutes within quarters like Yoshiwara were *kōshō*, although the *shishō* flourished around the fringes of the licensed quarters and in other unauthorized quarters (*okabasho*) such as Shinagawa and Shinjuku. Common general terms for prostitutes have been *jorō*, *shōfu*, or *baishunfu*, and there were other names as well, such as *shōgi* or *yūjo* (literally, "play women") for licensed prostitutes; the terms *keisei* and *oiran* generally referred to higher-ranking courtesans. For the unlicensed, there were slang terms such as *yotaka* ("night hawks") or *funamanjū* ("boat dumplings"). Periodically the government would round up the unlicensed women in Edo and place them in Yoshiwara. In 1668 *shishō* called "hell women" (*jigoku*) and unlicensed prostitutes operating out of bathhouses (women called *yuna*) were transported en masse to Yoshiwara.

The earliest classification of prostitutes, before the Yoshiwara proper was founded, consisted of two classes: *tayū* and *hashi jorō*. *Tayū* were the highest class, and thus the term "courtesan" is probably a more appropriate translation than "prostitute." After the founding of the Edo Yoshiwara, three more classes of women were added: *koshi jorō*, *tsubone jorō*, and *kirimise jorō*. When the entire quarters were moved in 1657, the *hashi jorō* and *tsubone jorō* classes went out of existence and the *sancha jorō* and *umecha jorō* classes were created. By the 1870s the classification had again changed, and the types of prostitute were, in order of rank: *yobidashi*, *chūsan*, *tsukemawashi*, *zashiki mochi*, *heya mochi*, *kirimise*, *kendon*, and *teppō*. Still other terms were used in other parts of Japan.

The higher the rank of the woman, the more money was charged, and the women at the top of the hierarchy had a considerable amount of discretion as to whom they would meet. The *tayū* or *yobidashi* had to be courted by the customers and generally money alone was no guarantee of receiving their favors. A certain degree of style, flair, and culture was necessary to win them.

The *yobidashi* and *chūsan* walked freely about the quarters on their distinctive high clogs (GETA), whereas the other grades of women sat in the barred rooms for exhibition. Often the higher-class women were famous for both their beauty and skill in the arts, and they were the subjects of many contemporary woodblock prints (UKIYO-E) and literary works. The names of certain courtesans (such as Takao) became so prestigious that they were adopted by several women in succession. One of the grand spectacles of Yoshiwara was the *oiran dōchū*, a parade of the high-class courtesans, which moved in stately splendor through the main street of the quarter. Ordinary townsmen and visitors from the countryside flocked to Yoshiwara to view the spectacle. Accompanying the courtesans as maids were little girls called *kamuro* (or *kaburo*), styled after the young female pages who attended the court nobles in an earlier age. The number of *kamuro* attending a courtesan was a good indication of her rank. *Kamuro* who showed promise of beauty or cleverness could themselves become high-class courtesans, and were trained to this end by the owners of the brothels where they lived.

Although some prostitutes were born into the profession as daughters of prostitutes, it was very common for the brothel owners to pay for girls from impoverished families. Professional procurers called *zegen* were employed for this purpose. Since the shogunate had officially banned the outright sale of persons, girls were indentured with contracts for fixed periods, commonly 10 years, but often such periods were extended and many died before the contract expired. Parents who handed over their daughters were given a sum called *minoshirokin* ("money for the body"), and the girl became almost a slave to the brothel owner. If the parents, or perhaps a patron later on, could come up with the money to buy her out of bondage, she could leave the quarters; this was known as *miuke*, or "redemption." Theoretically it was possible for a prostitute to work her own way out of debt slowly, but in practice most of them only fell into deeper debt through the skillful machinations of the brothel, such as extravagant charges for clothes and bedding. There are stories of desperate women with no chance of escape who would have so welcomed any chance to commit suicide that they had to be watched closely at all times.

In 1792 *zegen* were outlawed because of charges of kidnapping young girls, but this decree served more as a check on than an actual abolishment of the practice. In 1872, however, when Japan was becoming increasingly sensitive to foreign opinion, a law ordered the cancellation of all prostitutes' indenture contracts. However, debts deemed reasonable were not cancelled, and many of the women had no choice but to reapply for permission to continue their trade. At this point, brothels were renamed *kashizashiki* ("rooms for rent"), but business went on as usual.

Besides the prostitutes themselves, other kinds of people catering to the customer in Yoshiwara were the *yarite*, an older female manager (often a former prostitute), who would oversee the women of a particular brothel and initially greet and make arrangements with customers; *wakaimono*, male servants who acted as overseers, watchmen, and caretakers; men who provided horses, boats, or (from the 1870s) RICKSHAWS; and *hōkan* and geisha, male and female entertainers who played music and offered humorous skits for the customers' enjoyment.

Daily Routine —— From the time that Yoshiwara was licensed there were regulations about prices and times of business. In its early history prostitutes could only be engaged in the afternoon.

(The appeal of unlicensed prostitutes was that they could undercut the Yoshiwara prices and conduct business at any hour.) Later, Yoshiwara came to be open at night as well, although the government periodically revoked night business. Ultimately, the nights became the busiest times, earning Yoshiwara the sobriquet of "the nightless city" *(fuyajō)*.

It is said that the women of Yoshiwara made no distinction between night and day—it was always business. From 8:00 to 10:00 in the morning they bade farewell to their previous evening's customers (a time called *kinuginu*), and from 10:00 until noon they napped and prepared for the afternoon's business *(hirumise)*, which lasted from 2:00 until 4:00. Later, with the change to primarily evening engagements, Yoshiwara was very quiet in the afternoons and the women had then their only free time of the day. Vendors sold their wares during this time, and the government doctor made his inspections from noon until 2:00. The evening business *(yomise)* began at 6:00 and technically ended at 10:00; the closing time was called *hike*. Although the main gate was closed, a small side door called the *kugurido* was left open for certain guests until midnight. Some houses even delayed closing time until 1:00 or 2:00 in the morning.

In relations with the higher class courtesans, sexual consummation generally did not take place until the third meeting. A customer's initial visit was called *shokai* ("first meeting"); the second, *ura* ("behind the scenes"); and finally, *najimi* ("intimacy"). Sometimes "instant *najimi*" could be established by paying the fees for all three meetings at once. Relations with lower-class prostitutes did not need this elaborate procedure.

A ceremony was performed between guest and courtesan symbolizing a marriage of sorts: as in the wedding ritual, the couple drank three times from each of three cups of *sake* (the ceremony called *sansan kudo*). The woman did not usually remain with one customer the whole night but had several in different rooms whom she visited in turn (a practice called *mawashi*). In the morning, the woman came to bid each guest farewell and request that he return soon.

The residents of Yoshiwara spoke an argot called *kuruwa kotoba* (language of the gay quarters), or more popularly, *arinsu kotoba*—*arinsu* being this dialect's variation of the standard word *arimasu* (to be). This argot was heavily flavored with speech mannerisms from Kyōto, and there were many special slang phrases in use only in the quarters. Linguists propose that the reason for the development of the special dialect was that women could hide their regional backgrounds with this way of speaking, and also it would later serve to "mark" them should they try to escape. The ceremony conducted when meeting a customer was performed using ritual phrases in this special dialect, supposedly mimicking the language of the nobles in court.

The End of the Yoshiwara—The real splendor of Yoshiwara had long passed by the time such quarters were abolished. Even early in the 19th century, the geisha of various districts such as Fukagawa were said to excel the women of the licensed quarters in beauty and sophistication. By the 20th century, other forms of female entertainers, some with Western influence, were attaining great popularity at the expense of the by this time rather "quaint" Yoshiwara. In 1916 the practice of exhibiting women behind bars was ended. Many in Japan were protesting the existence of licensed prostitution as a "feudalistic practice"; from the early 1900s on, Christian-influenced and liberal Japanese also campaigned to abolish licensed prostitution, along with calling for other social reform. Quieted during the war, this movement again attained strength during the Allied OCCUPATION and finally culminated in the abolition of licensed prostitution and quarters like Yoshiwara.

■——J. E. DeBecker, *Yoshiwara: The Nightless City* (1905). Nakano Eizō, *Kuruwa no seikatsu* (1965). Uemura Yukiaki, *Nihon no yūri shi* (1929). *Liza* CRIHFIELD

Yoshiya Nobuko (1896–1973)

Novelist. Born in Niigata Prefecture, the daughter of a government official. Yoshiya's stories began to be published while she was still in her teens, and her early work *Hana monogatari* (serialized 1916–24, The Tale of Flowers) became especially popular among female students. Such works as *Chi no hate made* (To the Ends of the Earth), which won the *Ōsaka asahi shimbun* prize in 1920, reflect the Christian influences she received while studying in Tōkyō. Her novels, as part of the growing wave of mass culture, were widely read by women; these focus on women's ideals, problems, and rela-

tions with other women. (She herself lived and traveled with her lifelong woman companion Momma Chiyo.) In addition to biographies of modern women writers, her principal works include *Onna no yūjō* (1933–34, Women's Friendship), *Otto no teisō* (1936–37, A Husband's Chastity), *Onibi* (1951, Demon Fire), *Atakake no hitobito* (1951–52; tr *The Ataka Family*, 1964–65), and *Tokugawa no fujintachi* (1966, Tokugawa Ladies).

■——*Yoshiya Nobuko zenshū*, 12 vols (Asahi Shimbunsha, 1975–76).

Yoshiyuki Junnosuke (1924–   )

Novelist and short-story writer. Yoshiyuki employs sex as a medium to examine the nature of human existence. In his many stories and novels, Yoshiyuki's pursuit of this theme is relentless, but it is counterbalanced by a refined prose style and sparkling wit, which together produce a tragicomic effect. Yoshiyuki stands in the tradition of Edo period (1600–1868) popular fiction (GESAKU) in his partiality to themes connected with pleasure quarters and in his craftsmanship. Though grouped with the writers of the confessional I-NOVEL *(watakushi shōsetsu)*, his coolness and objectivity set him apart.

Born in the city of Okayama, Yoshiyuki moved to Tōkyō with his family at the age of three. His father, Yoshiyuki Eisuke (1906–40), had a brief but flamboyant career as a popular avant-garde writer before becoming an unsuccessful stockbroker and throwing out all his books but three he had written himself; after this he lived off the earnings of his wife, whom he had set up in the new profession of Western-style beauty salon operator.

Yoshiyuki began to write while still in high school. There he found the invasion of militarism into the classroom unbearable, and obtaining a medical release, took a leave of absence from school. As a result he did not accompany several of his classmates who went on to medical school in Nagasaki and thus escaped death from the atomic bomb. A short while later, after only four days as an army draftee, Yoshiyuki was discharged for an asthmatic condition which has troubled him ever since.

Near the end of the war he studied English literature at Tōkyō University. Although he did not graduate, he did help publish a small literary magazine, *Ashi* (Reed), in which his wartime writing, with its attitude of resistance to conformity, appeared. In 1947, Yoshiyuki, troubled by asthma and poverty, took a job writing for a scandal magazine called *Modan Nihon* (Modern Japan), and for six years was bound up with its declining fortunes. Here, in place of reading and literary conversation, he received an education in the darker side of society that reinforced his antipathy to conformity and his sympathy for social outcasts. Afterwards, he was often to depict the world of prostitutes as an expression of this sympathy.

In 1954, while recovering from a bout of tuberculosis, Yoshiyuki received the highly prestigious Akutagawa Prize for "Shūu" (tr "Sudden Shower," 1972), and at this time he decided to devote himself to writing full time. In "Shūu" a young man's purpose in visiting a prostitute to avoid becoming entangled in a love relationship is subverted when he finds himself emotionally attached to her. Others of his best short stories, like "Shōfu no heya" (1958, A Prostitute's Room; tr "In Akiko's Room," 1977), are also set in the Tōkyō brothel quarters, the world of prostitutes and their clients.

Among his outstanding novels are *Honoo no naka* (1956, In the Flames), an autobiographical account of his life and loves in wartime Tōkyō, and *Suna no ue no shokubutsugun* (1963, Vegetable Kingdom on the Sand), which became a best seller. *Anshitsu* (1969; tr *The Dark Room*, 1975), one of Yoshiyuki's several prize-winning novels, best exemplifies the main elements of his writing: the protagonist, a writer of modest reputation with a comfortable income, has struggled through the war, overcome poverty, and survived illness, but he is unable to keep from thinking that his life is in vain. There are women in his life, but he has no wish for marriage or children. He wants only noncommittal relationships based purely on sex. Among his women friends he finds his sexual ideal—a woman who is infertile. Despite his feeling that with the absence of the generative function there is only death, at the end of the novel he is returning again to the woman's dark room. *Shimetta sora, kawaita sora* (1971, Moist Sky, Dry Sky) is the odyssey of a relationship between the author himself and his girlfriend, juxtaposed with an unusual account of their journey together in the United States and Europe. In 1978 Yoshiyuki won the Noma Literary Prize for the story "Yūgure made" (Until Dusk); this is considered his second most important work after *Anshitsu.*

Yoshiyuki has not confined himself to "pure literature" *(jumbungaku)* but has also produced popular fiction for a clearly conceived mass audience. In his serious writing, however, he has sought and achieved clarity of expression, crispness of style, and the objectivity of an original and independent mind.

📖——Yoshiyuki Junnosuke, *Yoshiyuki Junnosuke zenshū,* 8 vols (Kōdansha, 1971–72). Yoshiyuki Junnosuke, *Anshitsu* (1969), tr John Bester as *The Dark Room* (1975).　　　　　Miyoko DOCHERTY

Yoshizawa Kenkichi (1874–1965)

Diplomat. Born in Niigata Prefecture; graduate of Tōkyō University. While minister to China from 1923 to 1929, he met with Soviet Minister Lev M. KARAKHAN in Beijing (Peking). These "Yoshizawa–Karakhan Talks" opened the way for resumption, in 1925, of formal relations between Japan and Russia for the first time since the Russian Revolution. Later ambassador to France and representative to the League of Nations, Yoshizawa became foreign minister in the cabinet of INUKAI TSUYOSHI in 1932. From 1941 to 1944 he served as ambassador to French Indochina. Purged by OCCUPATION authorities after World War II, he was appointed ambassador to Nationalist China in 1952. Even after his retirement, Yoshizawa continued to work in support of the Republic of China in Taiwan.

Yōteizan

Also called Ezo Fuji. Stratovolcano in the Nasu Volcanic Zone, on Oshima Peninsula, southwestern Hokkaidō. Ōgama, a crater on the summit with a diameter of 700 m (2,296 ft), changes into a crater lake when the snow melts. The summit commands an excellent view of the countryside. Extending radially from the peak to the foot of the mountain are numerous deep valleys. Yōteizan has many parasitic volcanoes and abundant alpine flora. In the foothills, asparagus and potatoes are cultivated. Yōteizan is part of Shikotsu–Tōya National Park. Height: 1,893 m (6,209 ft).

youth

Unlike many countries where the LIFE CYCLE is socially defined as progressing directly from childhood to adulthood, Japan, at least since the Muromachi period (1333–1568), has treated youth as a distinct stage in the life-cycle. Although the definition might differ depending on the locality and time period in Japan, "youth" refers to roughly the ages 14 to 24; youth are considered *seinen* (literally, "green years") or *wakamono* (young people) as distinct from *kodomo* or *shōnen* (children) and *otona* (adults).

Traditional Youth Groups——While *wakamono* and *seinen* can refer to both sexes, traditionally greater attention was devoted to the transitional problems of males. This may have been a result of the primogeniture system, which became the general pattern for family inheritance in Japan in the Muromachi period or earlier. Under this system, first sons face the prospect of waiting for many of their physiologically adult years before taking over the family inheritance, for it is only as the household head ages that he can be replaced, while younger sons face uncertainty in seeking their adult role. Males are constrained to overcome these difficulties before they marry and establish their own families, so their uncertainty also influences the situation of young women. The troubled transitional state of primogeniture-based societies does not always generate an institutional response, but in Japan the solution was to socially define youth as a distinct stage and to create youth groups *(seinen-gumi)* and other institutions to ease youth through this stage.

In the Edo period (1600–1868), *seinen-gumi* were more often known as *wakamono-gumi* or *wakamono renjū* and consisted of lodges *(wakamono yado)* established by local communities where young people could gather to talk, play games, train in martial arts, and take up special studies. On festival days they would demonstrate their skills before the village by competing in contests of strength and agility or by carrying a portable shrine *(mikoshi)* on their shoulders. In some communities young women participated along with men, but usually they participated in parallel institutions.

Male *samurai* youth, who mainly lived in urban areas, were educated in schools established from above by fief lords, in contrast to the *wakamono-gumi* established from below. By the end of the Edo period, the vast majority of male youth participated in one or the other of these institutions. To commemorate the end of the youth stage, local communities would hold a special ceremony (GEMPUKU). Even today, on 15 January the coming of age of all youth who have reached the age of 20 in the past year is celebrated in special ceremonies *(seijinshiki)* organized by their local communities.

The Beginning of the Modern Period——When Japan moved into the Meiji period (1868–1912), government reforms abolished the distinction between samurai and commoners and insisted that all, other than the nobility, should compete on the basis of merit for social positions. One result was that a large number of commoner youth moved to the cities to seek jobs in the expanding commercial and industrial sectors. Prestigious employers in both the public and private sectors came to place increasing emphasis on educational credentials as the key criteria for selecting personnel, and passing entrance examinations for the limited number of places available, particularly at the better-known schools, became the focus of extraordinary effort on the part of ambitious youth. Youth who became involved in post-primary-level educational competition had little time for participation in the *wakamono-gumi.* A sentiment also developed that participation in these groups was old-fashioned when contrasted to visits to the urban entertainment centers or participation in political groups, labor unions, and peasant movements. However, in the eyes of many political leaders, youth's "modern" behavior was increasingly decadent, and it gradually led to efforts on the part of the government to control and direct the actions of youth. Along with the expansion of formal education, the government in 1915 formed a National Youth Association to promote and coordinate the activities of local youth associations *(seinendan).* The establishment of youth training centers *(seinen kunrenjo)* in 1926 and of youth schools (SEINEN GAKKŌ) for elementary school graduates in 1935 further expanded government involvement in youth activities. By the late 1930s the government was requiring that all civilian youth attend one of these institutions for a certain number of hours each week. At the same time, youth participation in suspect political groups was strongly discouraged.

Youth Since World War II——Following Japan's defeat, the educational system was thoroughly reformed, and the central offices for coordinating youth associations as well as the youth training institutes were dismantled. Ultimately, schools, local governments, and the central government came to share power; compared with the wartime period, the central government's capacity to influence the youth stage was sharply curtailed.

In the immediate postwar period youth flirted with the new values of democracy. Labor and political protest movements rapidly accelerated, the loyalty of young workers weakened, so-called love marriages—as opposed to arranged marriages—became popular, and juvenile delinquency increased. Government leaders worried that youth were practicing distorted democracy, emphasizing rights but neglecting responsibilities.

Japanese youth mounted major social protests from 1959 to 1960 and from 1965 into the early 1970s that had a profound impact on society (see STUDENT MOVEMENT). In the first period, the main target was the United States–Japan Security Treaty, and as a result of this protest the Kishi government, which favored a strengthened revision of the treaty, was toppled. The protests starting in the late 1960s were aimed at the Vietnam War, the inequalities of the capitalist system, and especially at the state of higher education (see UNIVERSITY UPHEAVALS OF 1968–1969). At one point during this period, over one third of Japan's four-year institutions of higher education were closed due to student unrest.

In retrospect, Japanese youth's concern with education is not surprising. By the mid-1960s, the postwar baby-boom cohort was beginning to compete for admission to institutions of higher education, resulting in an extraordinary intensification of the "examination hell." At the time, places in institutions of higher education were available for less than one third of the cohort. At the most prestigious institutions, at least 10 applications were submitted for each available place. Campuses were overcrowded, teachers underpaid and often derelict in their teaching duties, and administration was inefficient and often arrogant. Student protest resulted in some reforms, particularly in the university curriculum. In the 1970s, youth political activity shifted to environmental issues. At the same time, in contrast with the immediate postwar period, a surprisingly large proportion of youth expressed a sense of apathy vis à vis politics.

Given the democratic framework of postwar society, the government has necessarily exercised restraint with respect to the political activities of youth. However, it has taken an active role in facilitating the employment of youth by distributing information on employment opportunities and aiding independent employment agencies. The happy result is that, since the mid-1950s, nearly 90 percent of all youth, regardless of school level, have been able to obtain jobs within three months of finishing their education. In recent years, the government has also stepped up its program for creating low-cost recreational facilities for youth.

Most Japanese youth move directly from school into some form of work, and most large workplaces have established special programs to receive new recruits. Programs generally begin with a two-week to two-month session intended to acquaint youth with the goals of the work place and the meaning of work. This is followed by on-the-job training under the guidance of more experienced workers who are expected also to serve as big brothers and sisters (sempai) of the recruits. In the early years of work, most employees find time for leisure activities, but gradually their activities become workplace bound.

Japanese youth have become thoroughly Westernized in their appearance and recreational interests. Avidly copied Western fashions are often mixed with the uniforms many students and company workers wear. They tend to read few books; instead thick volumes of comics (MANGA) are big sellers. Attitudes toward sex appear to be very relaxed. Watching television is probably the most popular leisure activity, followed by comic books, sports, and going to discotheques. College students tend to spend a fair amount of time chatting or reading in coffeehouses (kissaten).

Deviance —— Over the course of modernization Japanese society has come to provide an increasing variety of choices for youth, but few second choices. Once a child heads on a particular educational course, it is difficult to shift to a new direction. Young workers who quit their first workplace experience difficulty in obtaining a good second job. The pressure to succeed in school appears to have intensified over the postwar period. The various difficulties inherent in this transitional stage are often cited to explain the exceptionally high rate of SUICIDE among youth in Japan. The rate for 15- to 24-year-olds was particularly high in the period of the late 1940s through the mid-1950s, but after that it leveled off to a rate approximately double that for youth in Western societies.

Japan's rate of JUVENILE CRIME has always been comparatively low, but in the early 1970s it began to increase, leading to speculation that Japan was conforming to the standard pattern of industrialized societies. Aside from traffic violations, the major juvenile crime in 1978 in number of cases was shoplifting. This was followed by motorcycle and bicycle theft. Since 1970, there has been a modest rise in drug and sex offenses.

The Psychology of Youth —— It is interesting to reflect on the causes of this distinctive pattern of deviance—the relatively high incidence of suicide and the low incidence of delinquency. Also, why have these rates, after an initial postwar increase, declined? One factor must surely be the extent to which society keeps youth busy and involved. Japanese youth are either in school or at work; there is virtually no youth unemployment. Also, most youth maintain close personal ties with their families and friends. These social ties seem to discourage frustrated individuals from carrying out crimes against other people, but they do not always prevent them from crime against themselves.

Another approach toward an explanation is to consider the psychology of youth. With the postwar democratizing reforms and the more liberal ideological ethos, youth have been taught to seek greater equality, participation, and opportunities to express their individuality. Initially they were confused, torn between the more traditional heierarchical values and the new democratic ethos. Moreover, adult institutions, while paying lip service to the new values, did not always practice them. Conflicts were rampant and certainly were responsible for the upturn in deviance. However, since the mid-1960s youth have become more confident in their new values. One of the striking illustrations of this change comes from the survey of the national character conducted by the Tōkei Sūri Kenkyūjo (Institute of Statistical Mathematics) every five years since 1953. One of the questions asked requires the respondents to choose one out of six possible "life purposes":

1. work hard and get rich
2. study earnestly and make a name for yourself
3. live a life that suits your own taste
4. live each day as it comes
5. live a pure and just life
6. give everything in service of society

The first two are considered "ambitious" answers, the latter two as

"serious" socially responsible answers, and the middle two and especially number three as individual answers. In 1953, only 34 percent of the respondents aged 20 to 24 selected the third answer. By 1973 the percentage aged 20 to 24 selecting this response was 53 percent. There was a similar increase in the proportion selecting the fourth answer while the proportion for the remaining answers declined. This survey indicated similar shifts in a number of other items that reflect egalitarian and participatory values.

Thus over the postwar period the values of youth have undergone major changes, which were resisted by Japan's adult institutions until well into the 1960s. However, gradually they have come to respect and accommodate the new values of youth by introducing changes in education, work, and other institutions. Following a period of exceptional strain, it appears that a new integration is being developed between the youth and adult stages.

—— William K. Cummings, *Education and Equality in Japan* (1980). Nobutaka Ike, "Economic Growth and Intergenerational Change in Japan," *American Political Science Review* 67 (December 1973). Robert J. Lifton, "Youth and History: Individual Change in Postwar Japan," *Daedalus* 91 (Winter 1962). Sōrifu Seishōnen Taisaku Hombu, *Seishōnen hakusho* (annual). Jean Stoetzel, *Without the Chrysanthemum and the Sword* (1955). Tōkei Sūri Kenkyūjo, *Dai 3 Nihonjin no kokuminsei* (1975). Yoshida Noboru et al, *Gendai seinen no ishiki to kōdō* (1978).   William K. CUMMINGS

youth clubs

(seinendan). Associations for young men and women, usually between the ages of 15 and 25, and primarily found in rural communities. These groups developed out of the traditional youth associations (wakamono-gumi for men and musume-gumi for women) of the Edo period (1600–1868). The seinendan gained momentum during the Meiji period (1868–1912) and developed into vocational and study group centers as a spontaneous popular response to the trends of "modernization and enlightenment" pervasive throughout Japanese society at the time. In 1893 the government established legislation to encourage and regulate these centers. In 1906 the seinendan fell under the guidance of the Home Ministry and the Ministry of Education. From that time these associations became heavily influenced by the government's efforts to stir up nationalistic sentiments among the Japanese populace, and they grew increasingly militaristic. As government-backed organizations, the seinendan helped mobilize village youth for military service in addition to their traditional services of fire fighting, policing, and festival preparations. Before and during World War II, all seinendan were organized under a series of governmental umbrella organizations that included the Federation of Youth Groups of Imperial Japan (Dai Nippon Rengō Seinendan, organized in 1925), the Youth Groups of Imperial Japan (Dai Nippon Seinendan, organized in 1934), and the Youth and Boys Groups of Imperial Japan (Dai Nippon Seishōnendan, organized in 1941). Toward the war's close the government replaced such quasi-military organizations with student military corps (gakutotai). Since the Occupation period (1945–52), seinendan have been voluntary youth associations for study and social activities. The movement of youth from rural communities has tended to decrease even further the role of the seinendan, and many young men and women now seek alternate activities in university and extracurricular-study settings. See also YOUTH; WAKAMONO-GUMI.

NOGUCHI Takenori

Yoyogi National Gymnasia

Representative work of 20th-century Japanese architecture. Designed by architect TANGE KENZŌ and structural engineer Tsuboi Yoshikatsu (b 1907), the dynamically paired gymnasia were specially constructed for the 1964 Tōkyō Olympics. The larger gymnasium houses a swimming pool and the smaller, a basketball court. The structure consists of a high-tensile cable and steel-suspension roof over a reinforced-concrete base. Originally the center of debate over the reconciling of modern and traditional architecture, this sports facility is now considered a monument to modern international architecture.   WATANABE Hiroshi

YS-11

A transport aircraft with two turbo-propeller engines developed in Japan after World War II and manufactured by Nihon Aeroplane Manufacturing Co, Ltd, as the first postwar Japanese transport aircraft. It is suitable for local airport operations because it requires a short runway of only 1,200 meters (about 3,900 ft) for safe takeoffs and landings, and yet has a seating capacity of 60 to 64 passengers. The world aircraft market had been completely closed to the Japanese aircraft industry for some time after World War II, but the features outlined above contributed to the export of 76 YS-11 aircraft to countries in North and South America, Europe, and Asia. Imported equipment includes the engines, propellers, and some of the accessories from the United Kingdom and some components from the United States. See also AVIATION.   KIMURA Hidemasa

Yūaikai

(Friendship Association). A labor group organized by the pioneering labor leader SUZUKI BUNJI and 14 others in August 1912. Japan's first workers' organization, it played an important role in the growth of the Japanese labor movement. The principles established at the time of its inception were mutual aid through friendship and cooperation; the improvement of character, furthering of knowledge, and development of skills; and the improvement of the status of workers through unity. The organization started publishing the newspaper *Yūai shimpō* in 1912 and succeeded in attracting members from large businesses. Membership reached 2,451 in 1914, 10,000 in 1916, and 30,000 in 1918. At first, the Yūaikai was opposed to socialism and emphasized cooperation between labor and management. Among its advisers were Kuwata Kumazō (1868–1932), a scholar of social policies, and Ogawa Shigejirō (1864–1925), a social worker. The Yūaikai was also supported by capitalists such as SHIBUSAWA EIICHI. During the development of Japan's capitalism at the time of World War I, the Yūaikai was involved in labor disputes, and NOSAKA SANZŌ, who was later a member of the Japan Communist Party, and Hisatome Kōzō became members. In 1917 the Yūaikai was engaged in a total of 70 labor disputes and gradually took on the characteristics of a labor union, playing a central role in the labor movement. The attitude of the government and business changed abruptly at this transformation, and many local chapters of the Yūaikai were forced to dissolve. However, after World War I, with the advent of brilliant leaders such as Asō Hisashi (1891–1940) and Tanahashi Kotora (1889–1973), the Yūaikai began to be politically active again. It changed its name to Dai Nippon Rōdō Sōdōmei Yūaikai in August 1919 and switched from an executive system to a representative council system of organization. It also included in its platform the freedom to organize labor unions and an eight-hour work day. In 1921 its name was changed to Nihon Rōdō Sōdōmei (see SŌDŌMEI).

Yuan Shikai (Yüan Shih-k'ai) (1859–1916)

(J: En Seigai). Official of the Qing (Ch'ing) dynasty (1644–1912) and president of the Republic of China during its first years, Yuan rose to prominence while contesting Japanese initiatives in Korea in the early 1880s. He spent the next decade representing Qing interests in Seoul. The ensuing SINO-JAPANESE WAR OF 1894–1895 displaced Chinese influence in Korea, but the Japanese remembered Yuan's skillful maneuver against their Korean aspirations.

At home Yuan subsequently rose to the highest offices in the Chinese empire. Among his efforts in foreign affairs was an unsuccessful plan to entice the United States into counterbalancing and blocking Japan in Manchuria. As prime minister during the Chinese Revolution of 1911, Yuan negotiated with the revolutionaries the abdication of the Qing emperor. He emerged from the revolution as president of the new republic.

At first the Japanese government accepted Britain's lead in supporting Yuan's presidency. When Chinese civil conflict broke out in the summer of 1913, however, the Japanese military clandestinely assisted the anti-Yuan revolutionaries, who nonetheless failed. In May 1915 Yuan capitulated to a Japanese ultimatum in the negotiations over the TWENTY-ONE DEMANDS. But the Japanese triumph was sullied by the unfavorable light Yuan's government managed to cast on Japanese behavior.

In the latter part of 1915, Yuan guided a movement to end the republic and enthrone himself. A rebellion in defense of the republic attracted official Japanese support. Although Yuan abandoned his monarchical hopes in March 1916, Japanese financial and political support for his numerous Chinese enemies continued. Still president but preparing for exile, Yuan died in Beijing (Peking) on 6 June 1916.

🕮 ——Jerome Ch'en, *Yüan Shih-k'ai* (1972). Li Zongyi, *Yuan Shikai zhuan* (1980). Stephen Robert MacKinnon, *Power and Politics in Late Imperial China: Yuan Shi-kai in Beijing and Tianjin, 1901–1908* (1980). Ernest P. Young, *The Presidency of Yüan Shih-k'ai: Liberalism and Dictatorship in Early Republican China* (1977).
                                                        Ernest P. YOUNG

Yuasa Hachirō (1890–1981)

Christian educator, entomologist, twice president of DŌSHISHA UNIVERSITY in Kyōto (before and after World War II) and first president of INTERNATIONAL CHRISTIAN UNIVERSITY in Mitaka, Tōkyō. His father, Jirō, of Annaka, Gumma Prefecture, was an early convert of NIIJIMA JŌ and treasurer of the Dōshisha; his mother, Hatsuko, was a sister of the brothers TOKUTOMI SOHŌ and TOKUTOMI ROKA. Graduating from Dōshisha Academy in 1908, young Yuasa left for the United States and after three years as a ranch hand in Livingston, California, entered Kansas Agricultural College. He received a doctorate in entomology at the University of Illinois. Appointed to one of the first chairs of the Agriculture Faculty of Kyōto University in 1923, he was given the opportunity to travel and study in Europe.

Dōshisha called him to be its 10th president in 1935. He resigned within two years over a matter of principle in an altercation with the instructor of military training. Soon after, he attended a conference of the World Council of Churches in Madras, and continued on to America, where he chose to stay during World War II as a "Christian witness," although an enemy alien. Cared for by American friends, he toured the Japanese relocation camps offering encouragement. Returning to Kyōto in 1946, he again served as president of Dōshisha until 1950, when he became first president of International Christian University, a post he held until 1962. Well known as a collector and a supporter of the folk craft (*mingei*) movement, he was a surpassing speaker in both English and Japanese and was active in YMCA and UNESCO affairs. He earned a doctorate from Tōkyō University in 1931 and received honorary degrees from Rutgers University and Dōshisha.

🕮 ——Center for American Studies, Dōshisha University, ed, *Aru riberarisuto no kaisō—Yuasa Hachirō no Nihon to Amerika* (1977).
                                                        Otis CARY

Yuasa Jōzan (1708–1781)

Confucian scholar of the Edo period (1600–1868). Born in Bizen Province (now part of Okayama Prefecture), he went to Edo (now Tōkyō) to study with HATTORI NANKAKU and DAZAI SHUNDAI, both scholars associated with the KOBUNJIGAKU, a school of Confucianism begun by OGYŪ SORAI in criticism of Neo-Confucianism. Returning to Bizen, he attained high posts in the domain administration but was rebuked for expressing his candid opinions. He devoted the remainder of his life to writing. His *Jōzan kidan* (1739), a collection of anecdotes about famous warriors from the Sengoku (1467–1568) to the early Edo period was widely read and admired for its simple prose and lively descriptions.

Yūbari

City in central Hokkaidō. Located in the heart of the ISHIKARI COALFIELD; its coal industry has gradually declined. Efforts are being made to introduce new industries. Pop: 41,715.

Yūbaridake

Mountain in the Yūbari mountain range, central Hokkaidō. A rugged mountain composed of Cretaceous-period sandstone, argillite, and hornfels. Alpine flora such as Yūbari gentian (Yūbari *rindō*) grow on the summit. Yūbaridake is part of a prefectural natural park. Height: 1,668 m (5,471 ft).

Yūbari Mountains

(Yūbari Sanchi). Mountain range running north to south in central Hokkaidō. The principal peaks are YŪBARIDAKE (1,668 m; 5,471 ft) and ASHIBETSUDAKE (1,727 m; 5,665 ft). The mountains drop steeply to the Furano Basin in the east. The ISHIKARI COALFIELD is located along the western foothills.

Yūbin hōchi shimbun

A newspaper founded in 1872 by MAEJIMA HISOKA and others, the *Yubin hōchi shimbun* was a prominent voice for the FREEDOM AND PEOPLE'S RIGHTS MOVEMENT (Jiyū Minken Undō) in the 1870s and early 1880s. Led by KURIMOTO JOUN, YANO RYŪKEI, INUKAI TSUYOSHI, and OZAKI YUKIO, it became a political tabloid for the RIKKEN KAISHINTŌ (Constitutional Reform Party). In 1886, however, the paper went commercial, concentrating on human interest stories, scandal items, police news, and employment opportunities. It halted publication in 1894 and was reorganized as the HŌCHI SHIMBUN.

Yu Dafu (Yü Ta-fu) (1896–1945)

(J: Iku Tatsufu). An important Chinese writer in the 1920s. Educated in Japan and conscripted as an interpreter by the Japanese military police in Sumatra during World War II. He went to Japan as a young man and studied economics at Tōkyō University. In Tōkyō, Yu met other young Chinese writers, among them GUO MORUO (Kuo Mo-jo) and ZHANG ZIPING (Chang Tzu-p'ing), with whom he founded in 1921 the Creation Society (Chuangzao She or Ch'uang-tsao She), a group advocating romantic literature.

In 1922 Yu returned to China, where he was a leading figure in the Creation Society until 1927. Yu's early writings, largely autobiographical treatments of his experiences in Japan, had been decadent in tone, but later, influenced by his friendship with LU XUN (Lu Hsün) and after a bout with tuberculosis, he became increasingly concerned with morality and the social context of the individual's inner life.

Yu renewed his friendship with Guo Moruo on a trip to Japan in 1936, and after the outbreak of war between China and Japan in 1937, he joined Guo in anti-Japanese propaganda work in Hangzhou (Hangchow), Zhejiang (Chekiang). From 1938 Yu worked in anti-Japanese organizations among Chinese in Singapore. When Singapore fell to Japan soon after the outbreak of World War II, Yu fled incognito to Sumatra, where he was forced to serve as an interpreter for the Japanese military police. He reportedly used his position to protect patriotic Chinese. Shortly after Japan's surrender in 1945, Yu was arrested and presumably killed by the Japanese military police. ▨——Yu Dafu, *Dafu quanji* (*Ta-fu ch'üan-chi*; rev ed, 1947, 1966).

Yudanaka Hot Spring

(Yudanaka Onsen). Located in the town of Yamanouchi, northeastern Nagano Prefecture, central Honshū. Simple saline and sulfur spring; water temperature 49–97°C (120–207°F). Part of the Yamanouchi Hot Springs, it is a departure point for visitors to the highlands SHIGA KŌGEN and Kusatsu and Manza hot springs.

Yudonosan

Also known as Yudonoyama. Mountain in central Yamagata Prefecture, northern Honshū. Yudonosan is one of the three holy mountains of Dewa, along with GASSAN and HAGUROSAN. Yudonosan Shrine is on its summit. Height: 1,504 m (4,933 ft).

Yufuin

Town in central Ōita Prefecture, Kyūshū. With many hot springs, Yufuin is known primarily as a health resort. Rice production, lumbering, and stock farming are carried on here. Pop: 11,904.

Yugashima Hot Spring

(Yugashima Onsen). Located in the town of Amagi Yugashima, central Izu Peninsula, eastern Shizuoka Prefecture, central Honshū. An earthy carbonated spring; water temperature averages 50°C (122°F). Located on the upper reaches of the river Kanogawa, it is famous for such scenic spots as the Jōren Falls and the Seko Falls. Yugashima is mentioned in numerous literary works including Kawabata Yasunari's (1899–1972) "Izu no odoriko" (1926; tr "The Izu Dancer," 1955).

Yugawara

Town in southwestern Kanagawa Prefecture, central Honshū. It has long been known as a hot spring resort, being mentioned in the *Man'yōshū*, the 8th-century poetry anthology. Pop: 25,456.

yūgen

An aesthetic ideal cultivated by poets and dramatists from the 12th through the 15th centuries. A comprehensive term, *yūgen* broadly designated an ambiance of mystery, darkness, depth, elegance, ambiguity, calm, transience, and sadness. As the relative proportion of these components differed among different theorists, the meaning of *yūgen* varied considerably within the general range of its connotations.

The word *yūgen* originated in China (Ch: *you xuan* or *yu hsüan*), where it described an object lying too deep to see or comprehend. It often appeared in a Buddhist context, referring to ultimate truth that could not be grasped through intellect. The term entered Japanese literary criticism in the early 10th century, when Ki no Yoshimochi, the author of the Chinese preface to the KOKINSHŪ employed it in connection with the ways in which poetry had been written in ancient times. Later critics applied the term to descriptions of certain WAKA poems, meaning "profound" or "mysterious," or both. In such early usages, however, *yūgen* was still merely a descriptive term and not an aesthetic concept.

Yūgen developed into a poetic principle in the 12th century, when it was integrated with the concept of YOJŌ, or "overtones." Underlying this was the aesthetic notion that *waka* should embody emotion so delicate or subtle that it could only be suggested obliquely through overtones. The poet KAMO NO CHŌMEI (1156?–1216) explained *yūgen* as "a sentiment unexpressed in word, a vision invisible in form" and went on to liken it to the sight of a lovely woman silently grieving in the gathering dusk. Fujiwara no Shunzei (FUJIWARA NO TOSHINARI; 1114–1204), the foremost exponent of *yūgen* in his day, commented that "A fine poem often evokes associations not overtly expressed in word or form." An example he cited was a poem on the autumn moon that made the reader hear a deer's cry not described therein. Shunzei used *yūgen* as one of his main criteria of judgment at poetry contests he refereed.

In the 13th and 14th centuries *yūgen* came to imply a more elegant, ethereal beauty, although connotations of "overtones" persisted. This shift in emphasis was due largely to the influence of Shunzei's son, Fujiwara no Teika (FUJIWARA NO SADAIE; 1162–1241), who was much attracted to an ambiance known as *en* (ethereal charm). Although Teika offered no detailed explanation of *yugen* in his writings, according to legend, he once explained *yūgen* by telling a story of an ancient Chinese emperor who had a brief romance with a heavenly goddess. The beautiful goddess, before her final return to heaven, told the grief-stricken emperor to watch the morning clouds hanging over a certain high mountain whenever he longed for her. Teika felt the beauty of *yūgen* was manifest in the image of this emperor gazing at the clouds. While the authenticity of this legend cannot be ascertained, it remains one of the best expositions of *yūgen* in this new phase.

The three major artists who propagated this type of *yūgen* were the *waka* poet SHŌTETSU (1381–1459), the *renga* poet and theoretician NIJŌ YOSHIMOTO (1320–88), and the Nō playwright ZEAMI (1363–1443). Zeami, in particular, was an ardent exponent of *yūgen*, so much so that he argued that all styles of Nō acting had to have it latently. He had an apt metaphor for *yūgen*: a white bird with a flower in its bill. That *yūgen* permeated Zeami's theory of acting indicates its pervasive effect on medieval arts. For many artists in the 13th and 14th centuries, *yūgen* epitomized the glory of Heian culture that had long been lost. It was elegant beauty observed from a distance, with a sense of both yearning and futility.

In the 15th century, calm resignation came into greater prominence among the components of *yūgen*. Prolonged social unrest and the influence of Zen Buddhism may have contributed to this change in emphasis. Two main exponents of *yūgen* in this last phase were SHINKEI (1406–75), Shōtetsu's student and an expert *renga* poet, and KOMPARU ZENCHIKU (1405–70?), Zeami's son-in-law and a Nō theoretician. Shinkei felt that *yūgen* lay not in visible shape or color but in the beholder's attitude, and he encouraged poets to perceive supreme beauty in such monochromatic subjects as pampas grass on a withered moor or a wan moon in the dawning sky. Zenchiku went even further and claimed that the sun, the moon, the constellations, the mountains, the seas, trees, and grass all displayed *yūgen*. He thought that when an attitude of calm acceptance was manifested in art it took the form of *yūgen* and exuded tranquil beauty.

As the central concept in medieval aesthetics, *yūgen* exerted considerable influence on artists of the succeeding centuries, especially on men of letters who looked to medieval culture for their creative inspiration. WABI, a central principle of the TEA CEREMONY, and SABI, a dominant aesthetic in *haikai,* were both greatly indebted to *yūgen,* particularly the *yūgen* of the Shinkei–Zenchiku variety. When Western-type realism began to dominate the literary scene in the 20th century, *yūgen* provided the core of an aesthetic to which more traditionally minded artists could resort. Free-verse poets like KITAHARA HAKUSHŪ (1885–1942) and HAGIWARA SAKUTARŌ (1886–1942) and novelists like IZUMI KYŌKA (1873–1939) and TANIZAKI JUN'ICHIRŌ (1886–1965) all expressed a predilection for the traditional beauty of which *yūgen* was an important component. Even such writers as NATSUME SŌSEKI (1867–1916) and MISHIMA YUKIO (1925–70), while outwardly leaning toward the clarity and intellectualism of Western civilization, seem to have been inwardly attracted to *yūgen,* as suggested in *Kusa makura* (1906; tr *The Three-Cornered World,* 1965) and *Tennin gosui* (1970–71; tr *The Decay of the Angel,* 1974), respectively. *Yūgen* is diametrically opposed to the Hellenistic tradition in its emphasis on mystery and ambiguity, and in that respect constitutes an essential part of the identity of traditional Japanese culture.

📖 ——Hisamatsu Sen'ichi, *The Vocabulary of Japanese Aesthetics* (1963). Nose Asaji, *Yūgen ron* (1944). Ōnishi Yoshinori, *Yūgen to aware* (1939). Taniyama Shigeru, *Yūgen no kenkyū* (1943). Makoto Ueda, *Literary and Art Theories in Japan* (1968). Makoto UEDA

Yugyōji

Formal name Shōjōkōji. Head temple of the JI SECT of Pure Land Buddhism, located in the city of Fujisawa, Kanagawa Prefecture. Yugyōji was established in 1325 by the fourth head of the sect, Donkai (1265–1327). Among the patrons of the temple were the shōgun ASHIKAGA TAKAUJI (1305–58), Emperor Go-Komatsu (1382–1412), and the Tokugawa family. Yugyōji suffered ruin many times. It was extensively damaged in a fire in 1911 and again in the Tōkyō Earthquake of 1923, losing many of its treasures. The buildings, however, have since been restored. Stanley WEINSTEIN

yūhitsu

(secretaries). Clerks whose duty was to draft and write final copies of documents for their masters; the documents were then validated by the master's signature or monogram (KAŌ). Under the Kamakura (1192–1333) and Muromachi (1338–1573) shogunates, the post of *yūhitsu* became an official one attached to the High Court (HIKITSUKE), although court nobles and military houses continued to employ *yūhitsu* in a private capacity. Under the Tokugawa shogunate (1603–1867) *yūhitsu* were attached to the senior councillors (RŌJŪ) and to the junior councillors (WAKADOSHIYORI). There were two ranks: *oku yūhitsu,* some 20 to 40 clerks who dealt with personal and confidential documents, and *omote yūhitsu,* some 30 to 80 who handled ordinary government records.

yui

(literally, "tying"). A form of traditional cooperative labor. *Yui* is a mutual exchange of labor in which, for example, one repays a day of labor from someone by working one day for that person. In actual practice, *yui* principally occurs in farm villages during rice planting and harvesting when a large amount of labor is necessary. In many cases, a number of farm households form a *yui* association, pledging to help each other when additional labor is needed. The repayment of *yui* may occur after some time has elapsed, as in the case of helping at funerals or rethatching roofs. NOGUCHI Takenori

Yui Shōsetsu (1605–1651)

Teacher of military science in the early part of the Edo period (1600–1868). Born in Suruga Province (now part of Shizuoka Prefecture). After studying military arts with Kusunoki Fuden, Shōsetsu opened a school in Edo (now Tōkyō). His fame gradually spread, and he counted among his students several *daimyō* and *hatamoto* (senior Tokugawa vassals). Shortly after the death of the third shōgun, TOKUGAWA IEMITSU, in 1651 (Keian 4), he organized *rōnin* (*samurai* who became masterless because their daimyō had been deprived of their domains) and, with MARUBASHI CHŪYA and others, plotted the overthrow of the Tokugawa shogunate (see KEIAN INCIDENT). The conspiracy was discovered, and Shōsetsu, who was at Kunōzan in Suruga plotting to overtake Sumpu Castle, committed suicide. According to a note he left behind, Shōsetsu had no inten-

Yukawa Hideki

Yukawa Hideki in his study in November 1975.

tion of overthrowing the shogunate but merely wanted to bring the plight of the *rōnin* to the attention of the authorities. In fact, after this incident, fewer daimyō were dispossessed of their domains.

Yukar → Ainu language

Yukawa Hideki (1907–1981)

Theoretical physicist. Renowned for his numerous pioneering works in particle physics, including the meson theory and the theory of nonlocal fields. Born in Tōkyō, he graduated from Kyōto University in 1929. He became an instructor at the newly established physics department at Ōsaka University in 1933 and began his inquiry into the nature of elementary particles. He introduced the meson theory a year later, and, working with some of the most brilliant Japanese physicists of the day, including SAKATA SHŌICHI, continued to unravel the mysteries of the atomic nucleus in the following years. In 1939 he joined the faculty of Kyōto University and in 1943 he received the Order of Culture. In 1948, a year after he introduced the theory of nonlocal fields, he was invited by J. Robert Oppenheimer to become visiting professor at the Institute for Advanced Study in Princeton, New Jersey. A year later he became a professor at Columbia University; in that same year he became the first Japanese to receive the Nobel Prize. Returning to Japan in 1953, he served in many high-level governmental and educational posts, including that of director of the Kyōto University Research Institute for Fundamental Physics. Along with Sakata and TOMONAGA SHIN'ICHIRŌ, another Nobel laureate, he was a most vocal spokesman for the cause of peace and the peaceful use of atomic energy. His publications include *Ryōshi rikigaku josetsu* (1947, Introduction to Quantum Mechanics) and *Yukawa Hideki jisenshū* (1971), a collection of his essays in five volumes.

Yuki

Town in western Hiroshima Prefecture, western Honshū. Some 90 percent of the town's area is forested. Principal activities are dairy farming, cultivation of *shiitake* (a species of mushroom), and sericulture. The Yuki and Yunoyama hot springs are located here. Pop: 4,241.

Yūki

City in western Ibaraki Prefecture, central Honshū; on the river Kinugawa. Yūki developed as a castle town under the rule of the Mizuno family and became known for its handwoven Yūki *tsumugi* silk. *Geta* (clogs) and *tansu* (chests) are also produced locally. More modern manufactures include electrical appliances and textiles. Pop: 49,259.

Yūki family

Warrior family (later *daimyō*) from the Kamakura period (1185–1333) through the Edo period (1600–1868); descended from FUJI-

WARA NO HIDESATO (fl early 10th century). His 10th-generation descendant Oyama Tomomitsu (1168–1254) served MINAMOTO NO YORITOMO from 1180 and was enfeoffed at Yūki in Shimōsa Province (now part of Ibaraki Prefecture), whence the family took its name. In 1289 Tomomitsu's grandson Sukehiro moved to Shirakawa in southern Mutsu Province (now Fukushima Prefecture) and founded a branch of the family there. During the period of schism between the NORTHERN AND SOUTHERN COURTS (1336–92) Tomosuke of the Shimōsa branch of the Yūki served under ASHIKAGA TAKAUJI on behalf of the Northern Court, while the Shirakawa Yūki, led by Munehiro (d 1338) and his son Chikatomo (d 1347), supported the Southern Court. In consequence, the Shimōsa branch flourished during the Muromachi period (1333–1568), while the Shirakawa branch declined (it was finally destroyed by TOYOTOMI HIDEYOSHI in 1589). Yūki Ujitomo (1402–41) sided with Ashikaga Mochiuji (1398–1439), Kamakura kubō, (governor-general of the Kantō region; see KUBŌ), in his rebellion against the Muromachi shogunate; after his death in battle the family was briefly eclipsed, but it rose again under Ujitomo's son Shigetomo, who established regional hegemony as a SENGOKU DAIMYŌ in the Yūki area. His great-grandson Masakatsu (1504–59) drew up the well-known domainal code YŪKIKE HATTO. His heirless son Harutomo (1534–1614) in 1590 adopted TOKUGAWA IEYASU's son Hideyasu (1574–1607). The Yūki fought under Ieyasu in the Battle of SEKIGAHARA (1600) and were enfeoffed in the rich domain of Echizen (now part of Fukui Prefecture). In 1626, as a further honor, they were granted the shogunal surname Matsudaira.

Yūkike Hatto

Also known as Yūkishi Shin Hatto, New Laws of the Yūki Family. A domainal law code (BUNKOKUHŌ) of the Sengoku period (1467–1568), enacted by Yūki Masakatsu (1504–59), the lord of a regional domain in Shimōsa Province (now Ibaraki Prefecture), on 26 December 1556 (Kōji 2.11.25). The code consists of a preamble, 104 articles, and a 2-article supplement; another supplementary article is subscribed by Masakatsu's successor, Harutomo (d 1614). Not surprisingly, in view of the YŪKI FAMILY's history of decline in the 15th century and tenuous recovery in the 16th, the lawgiver was preoccupied with the security of his house and the loyalty of his retainers. Accordingly, the code warns "anyone who would be disloyal" that "his family shall be extirpated, its holdings expropriated, and its very name eradicated" (art. 22); samurai are reminded that they must perform or be punished, no matter how distinguished their forefathers' service (art. 28); they are cautioned against making baseless denunciations but urged at the same time to report any suspicion of a plot against the Yūki, "even if there is no proof" (art. 13). Extensive segments of the code (e.g., arts. 66–71) deal with military preparedness, but the vassals are repeatedly enjoined not to take action except on the daimyō's orders. The daimyō's supremacy in his domain is to be unchallenged; accordingly, factionalism and partisanship in quarrels are severely proscribed (arts. 3–6). A personal, sometimes effusive (e.g., arts. 62, 94) tone predominates in this code, and some of its articles (such as art. 65, which dictates the proper topics of conversation in the daimyō's castle) appear almost trivial. Overall, Yūki Masakatsu gives the impression that his 16th century samurai were a drunken and disorderly lot who needed disciplining. *George ELISON*

yuki onna

(snow woman). Also called yuki jorō. An apparition of a woman dressed in white, believed to appear on snowy nights. Pale and cold like the snow, she is often blamed for mysterious happenings. She is associated with children and is sometimes thought to be a woman who died in childbirth, frequently appearing with a baby in her arms. At times the spirit itself is described as a child with one eye and one leg. Depending on the locale, the yuki onna is thought to appear at the New Year or 15 January (koshōgatsu), or on nights of the full moon. The yuki onna is thought to be a form of a deity of the New Year (TOSHIGAMI) who is said to visit people at the end or beginning of each year. See also GHOSTS. *INOKUCHI Shōji*

Yūki Shōji (1927–)

Novelist. Real name Tamura Yukio. Born in Tōkyō; graduate of Waseda University. He took up writing detective stories after working in a district prosecutor's office. He gained recognition for such works as Gomesu no na wa Gomesu (1962), a spy novel, and Yoru no owaru toki (1963), a detective novel about corrupt law enforcement officers. Known for his hard-boiled style, he received the 63rd Naoki Prize for his novel Gunki hatameku moto ni (1969–70) in 1970, which dealt with the crimes and injustices committed by Japanese military officers during World War II. This novel was made into a motion picture directed by SHINDŌ KANETO in 1972.

Yūki Toyotarō (1877–1951)

Financier. Born in Yamagata Prefecture. After graduating from Tōkyō University, Yūki joined the Bank of Japan in 1903. He served as chief of various branch offices, and eventually became a director. In 1921 he joined the YASUDA zaibatsu (financial combine), which he served as an active leader. He became president of the INDUSTRIAL BANK OF JAPAN, LTD, in 1930, finance minister in 1937, and governor of the Bank of Japan from 1937 through 1944. During World War II he worked to expand the munitions industry and to formulate and promote wartime financial and monetary policies. *ASAJIMA Shōichi*

yukiwarisō

Anemone hepatica var. japonica, or Hepatica acuta. Also known as misumisō. A wild perennial herb of the family Ranunculaceae which grows to a height of 5 to 10 centimeters (2–4 in) on tree-shaded hills in Honshū. The leaves grow in clusters from the plant's base on long petioles and are split into three-pointed lobes. By mid-February several flower stalks produce white blossoms. A variety of yukiwarisō, called suhamasō (A. hepatica var. japonica f. nipponica, or Hepatica triloba) has leaves with less pointed lobes. The flowers, which bloom in mid-February, are usually white but sometimes red or purple. The name yukiwarisō, which literally means "a plant which breaks through the snow," was originally applied to the species Primula modesta of the family Primulaceae (see PRIMROSES), which grows wild from central Honshū northward to Hokkaidō. Nowadays it also refers to the misumisō and suhamasō, since they are often grown in hothouses for use as New Year's flowers. *MATSUDA Osamu*

Yukuhashi

City in northeastern Fukuoka Prefecture, Kyūshū; on Suō Sea. Formerly a market and POST-STATION TOWN, its principal products are rice, vegetables, fruit, and dairy products. Nori (a kind of seaweed) is cultivated on the coast. Pop: 61,838.

Yumigahama

Also known as Yomigahama or Kyūhin. Sandspit located in western Tottori Prefecture, western Honshū, near the cities of Sakaiminato and Yonago. Separates the Miho Bay from the Nakaumi Sea. Farming was the principal activity before and immediately after World War II. It is being developed under the Nakaumi New Industrial City Development Plan. Length: 18 km (11 mi) north to south; width: 1–2 km (0.6–1.2 mi) east to west.

Yunoyama Hot Spring

(Yunoyama Onsen). Located on the eastern slope of Gozaishoyama at an altitude of 460 m (1,509 ft), northern Mie Prefecture, central Honshū. A radium spring; water temperature 26°C (79°F). Located within Suzuka Quasi-National Park, it is said to have been discovered 1,200 years ago. This spring is a popular tourist spot with many visitors from Nagoya and Ōsaka. A ropeway leads to the summit of Gozaishoyama.

Yun Pong-gil (1908–1932)

(J: In Hōkichi). A member of KIM GU's Korean Patriotic League, Yun threw a bomb at Japanese dignitaries during the 29 April 1932 celebration of the Japanese emperor's birthday in Shanghai. General Shirakawa Yoshinori, commander of Japanese forces in Shanghai, and Kawabata Teiji, chairman of the Japanese Residents Association, were killed. The injured included SHIGEMITSU MAMORU, Japan's minister to China; Murai Kuramatsu, consul-general in Shanghai; Major General Ueda Kenkichi, and Admiral NOMURA KICHISA-

BURŌ. Yun was captured by Japanese authorities after mass arrests of Koreans in the city, tried in Ōsaka, and executed. The incident increased Chinese support for Kim Gu's anti-Japanese activities. See also KOREA AND JAPAN: Japanese colonial control of Korea.

C. Kenneth QUINONES

Yuragawa

River in northern Kyōto Prefecture, central Honshū, originating in the Tamba Mountains and flowing west through the Fukuchiyama Basin, where it changes to a northeastern course, to empty into Wakasa Bay. The multipurpose Ōno Dam is located on the upper reaches. Length: 146 km (91 mi); area of drainage basin: 1,880 sq km (726 sq mi).

yuri → lilies

Yuri Kimimasa (1829–1909)

Government official of the Meiji period (1868–1912). Born in the Fukui domain (now part of Fukui Prefecture). He studied under the Confucian scholar YOKOI SHŌNAN and, together with HASHIMOTO SANAI, worked for administrative reform in his domain. He joined the national government after the MEIJI RESTORATION (1868) and bore the chief responsibility for drafting the CHARTER OATH, the first official statement of the guiding principles of the new government. Made responsible for managing the government's financial affairs and meeting the budgetary requirements for military expenses, Yuri initiated the issuance of Japan's first paper currency (DAJŌKAN SATSU) in 1868. He left the government the following year as a result of disagreements over financial policy. He accompanied the IWAKURA MISSION to Europe in 1871. On returning he joined ITAGAKI TAISUKE and others in petitioning for a representative assembly and in 1875 was appointed to the GENRŌIN (Chamber of Elders), the protosenatorial body.

Yuriwaka legend

Folk legend, originating in the coastal regions south of Yamaguchi Prefecture. The nobleman Yuriwaka goes on an expedition to conquer demons and returns after many years of ordeals, but no one recognizes him until he subdues a horse of his lord that no one else but he can handle. He then marries the daughter of the lord. Some variants of the story describe him as drawing an iron bow. Because of its resemblance to the story of Ulysses, some scholars believe the legend to be of foreign origin. Others, however, contend that the themes of testing a hero and recognition by tokens are universal.

SUCHI Tokuhei

Yūseishō → Ministry of Posts and Telecommunications

yūsoku kojitsu

A term referring to the ceremonies, manners, and customs of the ancient imperial court and the medieval warrior houses or to the study of these as precedents. In the Heian period (794–1185) the term (from yūsoku, "learned or cultured man," and kojitsu, "ancient customs") was used in reference only to the customs of the imperial family and those related to the court. However, in the Kamakura (1185–1333) and Muromachi (1333–1568) periods, the term came to include the practices of the warrior class, and later it also came to mean the study of cultural and ceremonial precedents set by the court aristocracy and warrior class. In its meaning as a field of study, yūsoku kojitsu includes subjects such as court ceremonies, religious rituals, the ranking system, clothing, etiquette in serving food, entertainment, arts, and in the case of warriors, arms and armor. The focus was placed on the Engi (901–923) and Tenryaku (947–957) eras, the highpoint of court culture (see ENGI TENRYAKU NO CHI) and the diaries of emperors and court nobles were used as source materials. There were many schools of yūsoku kojitsu, including some that transmitted their scholarship orally. Early works on court practices and usage include GŌKE SHIDAI (1111), SHŪGAISHŌ (mid-Kamakura period), KIMPISHŌ (1213 or 1221), SHOKUGENSHŌ (1340), and KUJI KONGEN (ca 1422). In the Edo period (1600–1868), when the shogunate tried to imitate the Kyōto aristocracy, it used these works as references. Warrior families like the Kira, Hatakeyama,

Yūzen

Long-sleeved silk kimono with hand-drawn yūzen dyeing. The pattern, on a red ground, is of the streamers (noshi) traditionally used in wrapping gifts. Decorated with gold foil and embroidery. Length 156.5 cm. 17th century. Yūzenshi Kai, Kyōto.

Takeda, Ōsawa, and Ōtomo, which were well versed in traditional court customs (see KŌKE), took charge of protocol for the shogunate. Customs and ceremonies such as YABUSAME, KASAGAKE, INUO-UMONO, and jarai (a form of archery) were established. Works describing such customs of warrior culture include Buke myōmoku shō (1821) and Teijō zakki (1843). The tradition of yūsoku kojitsu is still preserved today at the imperial court, as witnessed in the ceremony of the enthronement of the emperor and in the DAIJŌSAI (a special thanksgiving ceremony held only when a new emperor is enthroned).

YAMANOBE Tomoyuki

Yu Sŏng-nyong (1542–1607)

(J: Ryū Seiryū). Pen name Sŏae (Seigai); a leading scholar-official of the YI DYNASTY (1392–1910) during the Japanese INVASIONS OF KOREA IN 1592 AND 1597. A P'ungsan Yu clansman, he entered officialdom after passing the higher civil service examination (munkwa) in 1566 and rose to the highest post in the central government. Yu worked with Admiral YI SUN-SIN to rally resistance to Toyotomi Hideyoshi's invasion and served as liaison between Korea's royal court and Ming Chinese armies sent to aid Korea. He is also revered in Confucian academies for his contributions to Korean Confucian scholarship.

C. Kenneth QUINONES

Yü Ta-fu → Yu Dafu (Yü Ta-fu)

Yuzawa

City in southeastern Akita Prefecture, northern Honshū. Yuzawa flourished as a castle town from the early part of the Edo period (1600–1868). The city has long been known for its fine rice wine (sake). The lumber and furniture industry also flourished. Pop: 37,797.

Yuzawa

Town in southern Niigata Prefecture, central Honshū. A POST-STATION TOWN during the Edo period (1600–1868), with the opening of the Shimizu Tunnel in 1931, it became a resort area for residents of the Tōkyō and Yokohama areas. Attractions include skiing at nearby Tanigawadake and Naebasan, and several hot springs. Pop: 9,514.

yūzen

Abbreviation of *yūzen-zome*. Textile dyeing method similar in principle to *rōkechi-zome* (see WAX-RESIST DYEING). Originated by Miyazaki Yūzen, a late-17th-century fan painter from Kyōto, the technique was perfected by around 1720 and used throughout the Edo period (1600–1868). The method allowed for the first time detailed and painterly dyed patterns on textiles.

The orthodox, hand-drawn process *(tegaki yūzen)* involves drawing a fine outline design on cloth with tracing fluid made from the *tsuyukusa (Commelina communis)* plant; this outline is covered with glutenous rice paste. The resulting lines, called *itome*, appear as thin white outlines after the dyeing procedure. The entire cloth is then covered with soybean milk to prevent blurring during the dyeing process. When the soybean milk dries, a brush is used to paint in the designs with various colored dyes. The colored portions of the design are then covered with rice paste-resist after which the cloth is brushed with dye to color the background. The dye is then fixed through steaming and the cloth is rinsed thoroughly in running water to remove the rice paste and tracing fluid. When it is dry, additional work such as embroidery can be added.

Since this technique can be applied not only on linen but also on CHIRIMEN or cotton, *yūzen* was eagerly welcomed by the dyeing industry from around the Genroku era (1688–1704), when sumptuary laws restricted the textiles allowed the dyers in their work and prohibited the merchant classes from wearing silk.

Hand-drawn *yūzen* results in a very clear design but the technique is extremely time consuming and therefore costly. A more economical method was developed using stencils called *kata yūzen*. In this method, a design is cut into treated paper *(katagami)*, which is then attached to the cloth and brushed over with dyes of various colors. The result lacks the clarity of line found in the hand-dyeing method, but its strength was that large quantities could be produced. Even everyday wear of muslin for children was made in this fashion. See also KATAZOME.

Since the paste is washed off in Kyōto in the water of the river Kamogawa, *yūzen* dyeing is also called *kamogawa-zome* or sometimes Kyō *yūzen*. The art is designated an Important Cultural Property and it is still carried on by a few known masters, primarily in Kyōto. The techniques were also popular in Kanazawa, another area known for its handicrafts.　　　　　　　　　　*William G. MORTON*

Yūzonsha

(Survivors' Society). Political society organized in 1919 by KITA IKKI, ŌKAWA SHŪMEI, Mitsukawa Kametarō (1888–1936), and other rightists. The previous year, Mitsukawa and Ōkawa had founded the Rōsōkai (Society of the Old and the Young) to discuss social problems, and in 1919 they decided to form a small propagandist group from among its right-wing elements. The Yūzonsha called for a reorganization of Japan as outlined in Kita's secretly printed book *Nihon kaizō hōan taikō* (1919, Basic Plan for a National Reorganization). It also called for a revival of patriotic spirit and the liberation of the peoples of Asia. The membership included NISHIDA MITSUGI, Kanokogi Kazunobu (1884–1949), and Yasuoka Masahiro (b 1898), all later associated with the ultranationalist movements of the 1930s. The Yūzonsha disbanded in 1923 when Kita and Ōkawa, who were temperamentally incompatible and disagreed on tactical issues, parted over Kita's insistence on publicly opposing the forthcoming visit of the Soviet representative Adolf IOFFE to normalize relations between Japan and the Soviet Union. Although it accomplished little in practical terms, the Yūzonsha was the parent body of several other patriotic societies, such as the Kōchisha, formed by Ōkawa and Mitsukawa in 1925, and the Kinkei Gakuin, formed by Yasuoka in 1927.

Yuzuki no Kimi (fl late 4th century?)

Semilegendary ancestor of the HATA FAMILY. According to the chronicle *Nihon shoki* (720), Yuzuki came to Japan from the Korean state of Paekche around AD 400 during the reign of Emperor ŌJIN (late 4th to early 5th century) and successfully petitioned to have admitted to Japan a large number of fellow immigrants (KIKAJIN), who arrived from southern Korea two and a half years later after having been detained by the Korean state of SILLA. It is said that the newcomers brought gifts of gold, silver, precious stones, and silk cloth, and that the emperor granted them land in Yamato Province (now Nara Prefecture). The genealogical record SHINSEN SHŌJI-ROKU and the chronicle *Sandai jitsuroku* claim that Yuzuki was a "prince" (J: *ō;* Ch: *wang*) and that his father, "Prince Gongman" (Kung-man), who came to Japan during the reign of the legendary emperor Chūai, was an 11th generation descendant of the first emperor of the Qin (Ch'in) dynasty (221 BC–206 BC) of China.
　　　　　　　　　　William R. CARTER

Yūzū Nembutsu sect

Japanese Buddhist sect founded upon the Pure Land teachings of RYŌNIN. Its distinctive doctrine holds that by practicing the NEMBUTSU (chanting of the Buddha AMIDA'S name) one joins with or interfuses *(yūzū)* with other practitioners and that leads to one's birth in the Pure Land of Amida. Other outstanding figures in the history of the sect include the sixth patriarch, Ryōchin (1147–1251), the supposed author of the *Yūzū nembutsu engi*, a pictorial history of the sect; the seventh patriarch, Ryōson (1279–1349), who revived the sect in the early 13th century after it had been dormant for over 100 years; and the 46th patriarch, Yūkan (1649–1716), who wrote the *Yūzū emmonshō*, the first systematic exposition of *yūzū nembutsu*.
　　　　　　　　　　Robert RHODES

yuzurijō

(deed of property transfer). In the history of Japanese law, a document prepared by the transferor and given to the transferee at the time of a transfer of land or other property. Used from the Heian (794–1185) through the early part of the Muromachi (1333–1568) periods, they were also called *yuzuribumi* or *shobunjō*. In the examples that survive from the mid-Heian period, the transferee was usually a wife, child, or other relative. Although they varied in format, no *yuzurijō* was valid that did not include all the following items: a description of the land or property to be transferred; an expression of intent to transfer, addressed to the transferee; the date of the transfer; and the name and monogram (KAŌ) of the transferor. In addition, many *yuzurijō* contained accounts of how the transferor had acquired the property and why he chose to transfer it, as well as admonitions to the transferee. *Yuzurijō* were submitted for official approval in the jurisdiction to which the transferor belonged. For example, in the Kamakura period (1185–1333) it was common for shogunal vassals to obtain the shōgun's confirmation (ANDO) for such documents. If more than one *yuzurijō* were drawn up for the same property, the one with the later date was recognized. The use of *yuzurijō* was widespread from the 13th through the 14th century but declined abruptly thereafter.　　　　*UEDA Nobuhiro*

YWCA

The Japan Young Women's Christian Association was established in 1905 and joined the World YWCA in 1906. Since World War II, it has supported the spirit of the Japanese constitution in a way consistent with Christianity and with the aim of protecting fundamental human rights and ensuring world peace. In 1954 it sent a resolution appealing for the abolishment of nuclear weapons to the World YWCA and to YWCAs in every nation. In 1956 it held a conference of Asian women to honor the 50th anniversary of its foundation. There are 23 city-based YWCAs in Japan and 30 school-affiliated YWCAs in participating middle and high schools. The Japan YWCA has about 15,000 members.　　　*SHIBANUMA Susumu*

YX project

(YX *keikaku*). Project for the development of a transport aircraft to which the Japanese aircraft industry has devoted its total energy as a successor to the YS-11. In 1971 the Japanese Civil Transport Aircraft Development Corporation and Boeing Aircraft entered into a joint research and development agreement and have conducted joint studies on the YX project ever since. Based on this plan Boeing Aircraft set to work, in the fall of 1978, on the development of the Boeing 767 transport aircraft with two jet engines. The Japanese aircraft industry is sharing 15 percent of the developmental workload for this aircraft. The Boeing 767 is a medium-size, semi-wide-bodied aircraft, with a seating capacity for 220 passengers and two aisles. It is expected to enter service in 1986. See also AVIATION.
　　　　　　　　　　KIMURA Hidemasa

Z

za

Trade or craft organizations of merchants, artisans, or service personnel; originating in the 11th century, they were most active during the Muromachi period (1333–1568). *Za* were organized to restrict entry and competition within specific product or service markets and to ensure the economic advantage of their members. Each *za* was protected by a patron, who, in exchange for fees and services, guaranteed official recognition of the *za* and protected it from competition from outsiders within his sphere of influence. Early *za* were patronized by Buddhist temples or Shintō shrines, but as the Kyōto aristocracy and the imperial house gradually lost the revenues from their landed estates (SHŌEN), they too turned to *za* patronage as a source of income. During the Muromachi period the shogunate derived some of its income from *za*, and many of the regional *daimyō* also sponsored *za* to control commerce and handicraft production and obtain additional cash income.

Among the best known *za* were the Ōyamazaki oil *za* patronized by the IWASHIMIZU HACHIMAN SHRINE and the cotton *za* under the YASAKA SHRINE, both in Kyōto. The Gion cotton *za* conducted business from specific locations in Kyōto where *za* members lived and worked, while the Ōyamazaki oil *za* included numerous itinerant merchant-priests who purchased sesame seeds and sold lamp oil over an extensive area from the Kyōto region to as far away as the Kantō plain.

Za membership varied considerably. The Kyōto Kayochō rice merchants' *za* included 120 members in 1438, and the Kyōto branch of the Ōyamazaki oil *za* included 64 members in the 14th century. Most *za* were much smaller and included around 10 members. The number of *za* controlled by single patrons varied. The Kōfukuji temple in Nara controlled about 80 *za* of various types; they included *za* for food products, daily necessities, artisans, and entertainers. Most patrons sponsored fewer *za*, and aristocratic patrons only one or two. For example, the noble SAIONJI FAMILY in Kyōto derived their income from the fish merchants' *za*. Regional *za* existed in temple towns and port towns. As commercial agriculture increased, rural *za* emerged to compete with the urban and market *za*.

A major purpose of *za* was to obtain exemptions from business taxes, market fees, road and river barrier tolls, and other levies. This privilege increased in importance in the 14th and 15th centuries as transport taxes and toll barriers spread throughout the Kinai region. Another *za* function was to establish a monopoly in a location or for a specific type of service. Various builders' *za* held monopoly rights to construction in temple or shrine precincts. Peddlers, retailers, wholesalers, or shopkeepers enjoyed monopoly rights in specific areas. Other *za* held monopolies over production technology. Still others enjoyed monopsony rights to purchase specific products from a specified area. As rural trade expanded, these rights were difficult to enforce, and conflicts between independent merchants and *za* merchants increased. When this occurred, *za* patrons attempted to expand their organizations or create rural *za* to absorb the competition.

As rural trade increased, *za* used their influence to disrupt the competition. They confiscated goods, destroyed production facilities, and urged their patrons and political authorities to fine and punish their opponents. Yet, as local authority was decentralized following the ŌNIN WAR (1467–77), the *za* began to decline. Some of the *za* were supported by local daimyō, who used them to collect business taxes, but others were displaced by official merchants.

From the mid-16th century daimyō began to abolish *za*, toll barriers (SEKISHO), and other restrictions, which were seen to impede the expansion of trade and handicraft production. As the daimyō consolidated their authority in castle towns, they required increased quantities of goods and services, and abolition of the *za* and the toll barriers reduced prices for many goods. *Za* survived into the Edo period (1600–1868), but only for a few products such as silver, gold, and red seal ink. By and large, they were replaced by new forms of commercial organization like KABUNAKAMA. See also RAKUICHI AND RAKUZA.

■ ——Sasaki Gin'ya, *Chūsei no shōgyō* (1961). Toyoda Takeshi, "The Growth of Commerce and the Trades," in John W. Hall and Toyoda Takeshi, ed, *Japan in the Muromachi Age* (1977). Toyoda Takeshi, *A History of Pre-Meiji Commerce in Japan* (1969). Toyoda Takeshi, "Za to dosō," in *Iwanami kōza: Nihon rekishi*, vol 6 (Iwanami Shoten, 1963). Kozo Yamamura, "The Development of Za in Medieval Japan," *Business History Review* 47.4 (1973).

William B. HAUSER

zaibatsu

Industrial and financial combines of a conglomerate type that grew to great size and attained a dominant position in the Japanese economy between the Meiji period (1868–1912) and World War II. Although the holding companies of those combines were officially dissolved during the post-World War II Occupation period, the new corporate groupings (KEIRETSU) that appeared after the war are often regarded as their direct successors and have become the subject of lively controversy.

The term *zaibatsu* lacks precision for a number of reasons. Composed of two elements respectively meaning wealth *(zai)* and group, clique, or estate (BATSU), it was originally a political term meaning "the estate of wealth" or "wealthy clique," but since about the time of World War I it has commonly been applied to the business combines that constituted the principal source of this wealth.

There is also a historical dimension to this vagueness. Although Westerners speak of some *zaibatsu* as developing from the early years of the Meiji period, the Japanese do not speak of an "estate of wealth" until the World War I period. In other words, in the Japanese view, it took many years before those who built these combines accumulated fortunes of such magnitude as to constitute a separate group, and hence it was many years before the term came to be applied to the combines themselves.

Additional ambiguities arise in the corporate usage of the term. Were all large combines *zaibatsu*, or only those combines controlled by the families that had founded them? During the post-World War II OCCUPATION, the agency of the Japanese government in charge of *zaibatsu* holding-company dissolution argued that only family-dominated combines were *zaibatsu*, yet it placed in the same category one combine where there was no family domination. Ambiguity is compounded by references to postwar business groupings as constituting a *zaibatsu* revival, even though these groupings differ from the prewar combines in several important ways.

Commentators agree in describing the so-called Big Four combines (MITSUI, MITSUBISHI, SUMITOMO, and YASUDA) as *zaibatsu*. These four were set on the path to exceptional position by governmental favors starting early in the Meiji period. Beyond the Big Four, consensus is lacking as to which families and groupings should be included. Under the Occupation six additional combines were designated: Nissan, Asano, FURUKAWA, Ōkura, Nakajima, and Nomura. Other groups such as Shibusawa, Matsushita, Riken, and Nitchitsu (Chisso) could also have been considered *zaibatsu*, depending upon the criteria chosen.

Combine Defined —— A combine is a complex of companies resting on a common ownership base and operated as a unit. Unified direction of the member companies, the subsidiaries and subsubsidiaries, is achieved through controls exercised through a top holding company, the command center of the grouping. The top HOLDING COMPANIES of the leading combines either did nothing but control, as in the case of Mitsui, or controlled with some operating functions as well, as in the case of Sumitomo, whose holding company included a department that served as the group's trading company.

While ownership control was generally exercised through the top holding companies, owning families supplemented or supplanted this in some cases by direct holdings in the subsidiary firms. In addition there was a moderate amount of intersubsidiary ownership.

By the time of World War II the combines had grown to extraordinary size. There were no reliable statistics on the number of companies making up the several combines—every submission to the Occupation authorities differed—but the Mitsui combine comprised some 300 corporations and the Mitsubishi some 250. With such size it is evident that careful organization was required in order to integrate the combine's activities.

Those subsidiaries most important to the combine—typically those establishing its product breadth—were termed "designated" (chokkei in the case of Mitsui and Sumitomo, bunkei in the case of Mitsui) subsidiaries and were tightly controlled. These designated subsidiaries served in turn as holding companies for an array of subsidiaries beneath them, and where their subsidiary networks were especially large, they were themselves referred to as "second-level" holding companies. In addition to the designated subsidiaries, there were "ordinary" (bōkei) subsidiaries. Typically, but not always, the level of ownership by the top holding company was highest among the designated subsidiaries.

Ownership: The Key Control Device—— Not only did the families retain exclusive ownership of the shares of the top holding companies in the older combines until shortly before the outbreak of World War II, but until the late 1920s and early 1930s they did not permit public participation in the shareholding of their designated subsidiaries. With the enormous increase in investment occasioned by Japanese expansion on the Asian mainland in the 1930s and the outbreak of the Pacific War in 1941, outside ownership was imperative and became substantial. When the public was permitted to hold some stock in MITSUBISHI HEAVY INDUSTRIES, LTD, in 1934, the shares offered were oversubscribed by a factor of 27. Whether family control was diminished was, however, another matter. When in 1943 the MITSUI BANK, LTD, and Shibusawa's Daiichi Bank (see DAI-ICHI KANGYŌ BANK, LTD) were pressured by the government into merging and shareholding was divided evenly between them, the terms of agreement contained a revealing stipulation: "The Mitsui zaibatsu shall make no objection to resolutions passed by the Board of Directors."

Family control of the combines was determined according to house (ie) law. The most elaborate and formal structure in this regard was that of the House of Mitsui, which was composed of 11 houses. The relative rank and proportionate income of the 11 houses were determined in the 1722 will of MITSUI TAKATOSHI, as drafted by his son Takahira, and were revised in 1900. Only the heads of the 11 houses were permitted to hold shares of the top holding company.

Officer Appointments and Interlocks—— While ownership was the key control device, appointment of officers for the top holding companies and appointment or approval of officers for the designated subsidiaries were further critical means of family control. To be approved for appointment as an officer in the top holding company required demonstration not only of exceptional business talent but of fealty to the controlling family.

In addition to family members who might serve in an interlocking capacity on the boards of the holding company and key subsidiaries, there were extensive interlocks among key executive officers. For example, in the Mitsubishi combine in 1945, two managing directors of the holding company each held positions on the boards of nine subsidiaries, and one of the standing directors of the top holding company held 10 other positions. In the Sumitomo combine, the managing director of the top holding company in 1945 was chairman of the board of 10 key subsidiaries and a board member of 4 additional subsidiaries.

Another aspect of personnel control was the use of contracts. In the Sumitomo combine, "representative directors" (daihyō torishimariyaku) with the power to commit the subsidiary were obliged to sign a contract with the top holding company wherein they pledged to refer virtually every topic that might come up in board meetings to the top holding company for guidance before a vote was taken by their board. In a document that the Sumitomo top holding company submitted to Occupation authorities, it was explained that "according to law, an officer of the board is supposed to possess certain rights within certain limits, but in the case of the Sumitomo zaibatsu structure this is not so (i.e., among designated subsidiaries), because the board is placed under the strict orders of the holding company."

In the 1930s there were new additions to the established zaibatsu circle, including such groupings as Nissan. These shinkō (new) zaibatsu were frequently described as "democratic," because shareholding was fully open to the public and no family fealty was involved in officer appointments.

Control through Credit—— Credit was the third major control device of the combines. Any business is obliged to rely on credit for financing. In the prewar period this was largely for commercial purposes, unlike the postwar situation, where it has significantly been used for investment. By obliging subsidiaries to rely primarily on the financial institutions of the combine, the top holding company gained additional means of control. Under the zaibatsu system there was very little, if any, intercombine lending or borrowing when the combines had their own financial institutions. Mitsui Bank did not lend to a Mitsubishi subsidiary, nor the MITSUBISHI BANK, LTD, to a Mitsui subsidiary. However, if financial needs were in excess of what the combine could provide, it was possible—with holding company approval—to borrow from domestic banks that were not within a combine network, or from abroad.

The significance of having a commerical bank within the combine, and thus the assurance of preferred access to credit, can be seen in the fact that each of the Big Four had a commercial bank, while only one of the six other combines designated under the Occupation had a commercial bank. Without such access to credit, the member companies of the Other Six were unable to expand as rapidly as the members of combines in which credit was more easily obtained. In the Mitsubishi combine, the bank was for several decades a department of the top holding company. It was not separately incorporated until 1919 and public participation in its stock was not permitted until 1929. It was frankly described as an "organ" (kikan) bank.

Centralized Buying and Selling—— Centralized buying and selling through their own trading companies was the fourth major control device of the combines. Subsidiaries of the combine were obliged to sign "sole agency agreements" with the trading company pledging that they would do their buying and selling through the trading company. In this way the weight of the entire combine could be brought into each commercial negotiation; in this way also the families could monitor events.

Discriminatory business practices were common under the zaibatsu system. Prices charged in transactions within the combine were often far lower than those charged outsiders. For example, Mitsui took over the insignificant Takasago Life Insurance Company and built it into one of Japan's largest by offering special terms to Mitsui combine employees. Similarly, Mitsui was able to succeed in the volatile Malayan rubber trade, where British and other businessmen failed, because Mitsui Trading could secure more favorable prices from Mitsui Shipping than those extended to outsiders. Mitsui Trading also secured advantageous rates from its casualty company, TAISHŌ MARINE & FIRE INSURANCE CO, LTD, and, of course, it had its far-flung commercial intelligence network.

The discriminatory practices of the trading companies went beyond price discrimination. Until World War II, they were able to determine how much foreign competition a rival Japanese producer would be obliged to face. If, for example, a combine wished to bend an independent rival to its will in an area where it lacked production of its own, its trading company could subject the rival to competition from abroad by bringing in cheaper foreign goods.

The trading companies were also the major vehicle for the importation of technology before 1945. Since their loyalty was to their combine grouping, the imported foreign technology was licensed to subsidiaries within the combines. Only if combine subsidiaries were not interested did it go beyond.

"Cordial Oligopoly"—— Under the zaibatsu system, an unusual feature of Japan's big business sector was that concentration took a conglomerate path, unlike the Western pattern in which concentration took the path of monopoly. Japanese combines embraced activities as diverse as banking, insurance, trading, mining, shipbuilding, and manufacturing of electrical machinery, trucks, aircraft, and chemicals, with the same group of oligopolists competing in market after market. However, no combine was consistently in a first-place position. In certain markets Mitsui was first, in others, Mitsubishi, and so forth. This situation tended to lead to a condition of "cordial oligopoly," in which Mitsui was not likely to challenge Mitsubishi in markets of its strength because it was subject to Mitsubishi retaliation in markets where Mitsubishi was stronger.

Public Distrust—— The cumulating power of capital, together with close political ties (cemented by cash payments from zaibatsu top holding companies to parties and politicians) and the absence of any laws against discriminatory business practices, resulted in few new faces in Japan's big business sector until the 1930s, when the industrial buildup for expansion on the Asian mainland began and the *shinkō zaibatsu* came into prominence. The major political parties of the period, the RIKKEN SEIYŪKAI and the RIKKEN MINSEITŌ, were widely regarded as little more than pawns of the Mitsui and Mitsubishi interests respectively. Thus, when debate developed early in the 1930s between political parties and the military over the size of the military budget, it was not difficult to turn the issue into an anti-*zaibatsu* campaign and to have it appear that those who endorsed increased military budgets were the only true supporters of the emperor. So emotionally charged did matters become that in 1932 three top leaders were assassinated in as many months—a finance minister, the chairman of the board of the Mitsui holding company, and a prime minister (see MAY 15TH INCIDENT; LEAGUE OF BLOOD INCIDENT).

Older and Newer Zaibatsu —— It has often been asserted, both in Japan and in the West, that the older combines were overwhelmingly oriented toward peaceful commercial activities, while the newer *zaibatsu* eagerly joined in Japan's program of military expansion. In fact the older *zaibatsu* were far bigger suppliers of the military. It is true that the newer *zaibatsu* devoted a larger proportion of their activity to the military than the older *zaibatsu*, the older *zaibatsu* having preempted other options, and this may have given rise to the misconception. However, military-related activities by the older *zaibatsu* were almost always more important in absolute terms. Domestically, the position of the Big Four went from 12 percent of Japan's total paid-up capital in 1941 to 24.5 percent in 1945. There was an even sharper change in their position overseas, but "greatly benefiting" from the military program is not the same as "instigating" or "helping to conceive."

The basic problem of the *zaibatsu* lay not so much in their complicity in militaristic policies as in their antidemocratic character. In order to be viable, the system required a hierarchy of exceptional proportions. That membership in labor unions mushroomed after 1945, when Occupation authorities lifted restrictions against unionization, bespeaks the latent forces that *zaibatsu* authoritarianism had suppressed. By 1949 there were some 7 million union members in a total work force of 15 million. Before unions were destroyed in the 1930s, their peak membership had been less than half a million. The *zaibatsu* system represented private powers of such magnitude as to find democratic values intolerable. It could accommodate the military, with its hierarchical values, but not unions.

After Japan's defeat in World War II, American Occupation authorities made ZAIBATSU DISSOLUTION one of the key elements in their program of preventing a recurrence of Japanese militarism and democratizing Japan's economy. Among the measures taken by the Japanese government during the Occupation under American direction were the dissolution of the holding companies of the Big Four *zaibatsu*, sale to the public of the stockholdings of *zaibatsu* family members, an economic purge, and enactment of an ANTIMONOPOLY LAW and other legislation prohibiting excessive economic concentration.

A Zaibatsu Revival? —— The period following the revisions of the Antimonopoly Law in 1949 and 1953, the rescinding of the economic purge (see OCCUPATION PURGE) in 1951, and the end of the Occupation in 1952 saw a tendency for the former *zaibatsu* subsidiaries to form themselves again into groups informally centered on banks and coordinated by periodic meetings of the presidents of the member companies. In popular articles and learned studies, writers often describe these corporate groupings as revived *zaibatsu*. If one judges by common usage, the term *zaibatsu* is now taken to refer to the former groups and to any corporation bearing the name of the former subsidiaries, although they are now corporations in their own right.

However, this phenomenon does not necessarily constitute a *zaibatsu* revival, even though the Big Four and other business groupings having a historical *zaibatsu* base and sharing, for the most part, the same names as the former *zaibatsu* are major facts of Japanese economic life. Holding companies remain outlawed under the Antimonopoly Law. There is no family domination of the complexes. Ownership is fragmented, in contrast to the prewar *zaibatsu* pattern. The banks of the groupings typically hold the highest shares, but when the 1977 amendments to the Antimonopoly Law become fully effective, their shares will be limited to a maximum of 5 percent. There is no central direction to personnel appointments; each corporation makes its own decisions. Buying, selling, and credit activities

extend across group lines, and the means by which the trading companies built themselves such extraordinary power, the "sole agency contract," remains outlawed under the Antimonopoly Law. While it may therefore be concluded that there is not a *zaibatsu* revival in Japan, concentration is increasing in the economy as major companies and their subsidiaries hold a rising share of corporate ownership.

■ —— G. C. Allen, "The Concentration of Economic Control," in E. B. Schumpeter, ed, *Japan and Manchukuo* (1940). G. C. Allen, *Japan's Economic Expansion* (1965). T. A. Bisson, *Zaibatsu Dissolution in Japan* (1954). Corwin D. Edwards, *Trade Regulations Overseas* (1966). Edna E. Ehrlich, "The Role of Banking in Japan's Economic Development," unpublished PhD dissertation, New School (1960). Eleanor M. Hadley, "Concentrated Business Power in Japan," unpublished PhD dissertation, Radcliffe College (1949). Eleanor M. Hadley, *Antitrust in Japan* (1970). Johannes Hirschmeier and Tsunehiko Yui, *The Development of Japanese Business, 1600–1973* (1975). W. W. Lockwood, *The Economic Development of Japan* (1954). Mitsubishi Economic Research Institute, *Mitsui, Mitsubishi, Sumitomo* (1955). Mitsui Gomei Kaisha, *The House of Mitsui* (1933). Mochikabu Kaisha Seiri Iinkai, *Nihon zaibatsu to sono kaitai*, textual volume, 1951; data volume, 1950. The data volume contains a bibliography on the *zaibatsu* of over 1,600 titles, most of them in Japanese but also including foreign publications. Oland Russell, *The House of Mitsui* (1939). State-War Mission on Japanese Combines, *Report* (1946). Kozo Yamamura, *Economic Policy in Postwar Japan* (1967). M. Yoshino, *Japan's Managerial System* (1968). Eleanor M. HADLEY

zaibatsu dissolution

A series of actions taken after World War II by the Occupation authorities through the instrumentality of the Japanese government to break up the giant family-dominated financial and industrial combines known as ZAIBATSU, which had largely controlled the Japanese economy.

The Dissolution Program —— The question of formulating a *zaibatsu* dissolution program first emerged in wartime conferences in Washington as civilian and military officials began to plan American postwar policy regarding Japan. It was generally agreed that American security interests would best be served by initiating a comprehensive program of social, political, and economic change which would lead to the creation of a new Japan, both peaceful and democratic.

The *zaibatsu* had rapidly increased their share of Japan's total paid-up capital during the war years, and by the war's end in 1945 the so-called Big Four combines—MITSUI, MITSUBISHI, SUMITOMO, and YASUDA—controlled one-fourth of the paid-up capital of the Japanese economy (see Table 1). Unlike the pattern of concentration in the West, which took the path of monopoly, the *zaibatsu* took a conglomerate path. Thus, each *zaibatsu* was spread across a wide range of markets. In the case of the two largest, Mitsui and Mitsubishi, their operations ranged across the entire breadth of the industrial, commercial, and financial sectors of the economy. It was this high level of economic concentration that convinced American planners that *zaibatsu* dissolution was crucial to the economic democratization process in Japan.

Within the US Department of State, which together with the War and Navy departments had responsibility for drafting American postwar policy toward Japan, there were sharp differences of view as to what policy should be taken concerning the *zaibatsu*. The economists in the newly created International Business Practices Branch of the State Department's Commodities Division argued that economic concentration was concentration, whether achieved through monopoly in one market or conglomerately by strong positions across a wide range of markets, and that since concentrated economic power was antithetical to democracy, the *zaibatsu* should be dissolved. Political officers with long experience in Japan opposed this argument, claiming that the *zaibatsu* had historically been supporters of parliamentary government, that they had stoutly opposed the military and had been dragged into the war against their best efforts to prevent it. The economists ultimately won out, and the State Department's recommended policy of dissolving Japan's giant business combines, adopted by the State-War-Navy Coordinating Committee, followed United States policy toward concentrated business in Germany.

To take something apart one needs to know how it has been put together. American knowledge of how the *zaibatsu* created their business organizations was woefully inadequate, but as it subsequently developed, so too was Japanese knowledge, as the *zaibatsu* had always been secretive concerning their own operations. Hence it is not surprising that the dissolution program was neither smooth nor consistent in its development.

The *zaibatsu* dissolution program consisted of a number of actions taken in the name of the program as well as actions which were taken for other purposes but which had a very real impact on the outcome. The heart of the program was an enormous operation to dispose of the securities held by the *zaibatsu* holding companies and those held outside the holding companies by the *zaibatsu* family members. It also included enactment of an antitrust statute, the dissolution of the Mitsui and Mitsubishi trading companies, and passage of the Law for the Elimination of Excessive Concentrations of Economic Power and the Law for the Termination of Zaibatsu Family Control. The actions which were technically outside the program but which had a bearing on its outcome were the Capital Levy Law, the economic purge, the Financial Institutions Reconstruction and Reorganization Law, and the Enterprise Reconstruction and Reorganization Law. A reparations program resting on removal of existing plant and equipment along the lines originally contemplated would also have had a very real effect, but as US reparation proposals were progressively scaled down, the impact was minor. A number of countries did not sign the 1951 peace treaty because it did not make provisions for reparations. The reparations that Japan subsequently paid these countries were out of current production, a quite different matter.

Among the Japanese, *zaibatsu* dissolution was variously interpreted as an expression of American monopoly capitalism seeking to enhance business opportunities for itself, or as dedicated to democratizing the Japanese economy and establishing a "right of enterprises." Given the prevalence of the Marxian viewpoint among Japanese intellectuals, it was easy to interpret the program as a means of enhancing future business opportunities for American corporations. In point of fact, however, such thinking was totally absent from the minds of those who pushed through a deconcentration program for Japan.

The Yasuda Plan —— The starting point of the action was an initiative taken by the Big Four *zaibatsu*. With public knowledge in Japan that General Douglas MACARTHUR, supreme commander for the Allied powers (SCAP), would call for dissolution of the *zaibatsu*, Yasuda put forward a plan in the fall of 1945 to dissolve its holding company; it was joined by the three other combines.

Under the Yasuda plan, the securities of the four top holding companies were to be turned over to a public body for sale to the public, and "directors and auditors" of the to-be-dissolved holding companies promised to "resign all offices held by them in such holding companies immediately after the transfer of securities . . . and cease forthwith to exercise any influence . . . in the management or policies." *Zaibatsu* family members offered to "resign all offices held by them in any financial, commercial, noncommercial or industrial enterprises," thus not limiting their resignations to the top holding company alone. But with respect to "exerting influence," the promise was only to exert no influence over the management of policies of the to-be-dissolved holding companies.

After review by the Japanese government, the plan was submitted to MacArthur on 4 November 1945. On 6 November MacArthur accepted it, but pointed out that "full freedom of action is retained by the Supreme Commander for the Allied Powers to elaborate or modify the proposed plan at any time and to supervise and review its execution."

MacArthur's instructions from the Joint Chiefs of Staff were to dissolve "large Japanese industrial and banking combines or other large concentrations of private business control." However, there is a considerable difference between dissolving "holding companies" and "combines." The top holding companies represented the "nerve" or "command" center of the combines, but not all controls for coordinating the corporations making up the combine were found in the holding company. There were combine controls exercised through the trading company and commercial banks in each grouping, and, in certain instances, there was strong intersubsidiary shareholding. In addition, the *zaibatsu* families had very large direct investments outside their holding companies. All of these areas were outside the proposed action.

Among the measures taken at SCAP's behest to remedy the inadequacies of the original Yasuda plan was the disposal of shares held outside the holding companies by *zaibatsu* family members. To accomplish this, 56 "*zaibatsu* persons" were designated, apparently only those family members who held shares in the top holding

---

Zaibatsu dissolution —— Table 1

Zaibatsu Share of the Japanese Economy, 1945
(in percentages)

Industry	Big four[1] zaibatsu	Six lesser[2] zaibatsu	All other companies
Banking and insurance	49.7	3.3	47.0
Mining	28.3	22.2	49.5
Metal working	26.4	15.4	58.2
Machinery and equipment	46.2	21.7	32.1
Shipbuilding	5.0	7.5	87.5
Chemicals	31.4	7.1	61.5
Textiles	17.4	1.4	81.2
Farm and marine products, foodstuffs	2.7	7.7	89.6
Electricity and gas	0.5	—	99.5
Land transport	4.9	0.7	94.4
Shipping	60.8	0.6	38.6
Foreign and domestic trade	13.6	6.7	79.7
Total[3]	24.5	10.7	64.8

[1] Mitsui, Mitsubishi, Sumitomo, and Yasuda.
[2] Nissan, Asano, Furukawa, Ōkura, Nakajima, and Nomura.
[3] Includes other industries not listed here.
NOTE: Percentages are calculated on the basis of paid-up capital per industry.
SOURCE: Noda Kazuo, *Zaibatsu* (1967).

---

companies. Because under the Mitsui House rules only the heads of the 11 families making up the House of Mitsui were permitted to hold shares in the top holding company, only 11 Mitsui persons were designated. In the two-family pattern of the Iwasaki, who controlled the Mitsubishi combine, 11 persons were designated, as the Iwasaki were less restrictive concerning which family members could own shares in the top holding company. Furthermore, the number of designated holding companies whose stocks were to be sold off was increased to 83. This did not in any sense indicate that there were 83 *zaibatsu*. Rather, a number of key subsidiaries such as MITSUI MINING CO, LTD, and the MITSUBISHI HEAVY INDUSTRIES, LTD, which constituted "second-level" holding companies, were included to eliminate the additional intragroup holdings which existed below the top holding company level.

Sale of Zaibatsu Securities —— Administration of the securities disposal portion of the *zaibatsu* dissolution program was in the hands of the Holding Company Liquidation Commission, a body specifically created for this purpose. A SCAP representative attended all meetings. Although MacArthur accepted the Yasuda plan and its proposal for such a commission in November 1945, the commission did not come into operation until August 1946.

Compensation to *zaibatsu* family members was to be in the form of their proportionate share of the proceeds of the sales minus administrative expenses in 10-year, nonnegotiable government bonds. Non-*zaibatsu* persons holding shares in companies to be dissolved received their compensation in liquid form. While American authorities were outraged at any suggestion of confiscating property, the virulence of the ensuing inflation did in fact make compensation to *zaibatsu* family members close to confiscatory.

An Antitrust Statute —— In accepting the Yasuda plan in November 1945, MacArthur called upon the Japanese government to submit a draft antitrust statute for the purpose of keeping the Japanese economy deconcentrated. An antitrust proposal acceptable to SCAP headquarters was finally developed and was enacted in April 1947 as the Law concerning the Prohibition of Private Monopoly and Methods of Preserving Fair Trade.

Among the provisions of this legislation were the prohibition of holding companies, the core organ of the *zaibatsu* structures; the prohibition of sole agency contracts, the device by which the combines had obliged member companies to make all purchases and sales through the trading companies of the grouping; and the prohibition of cartels. In addition, there were restrictions on bank shareholding in nonfinancial companies and also on interlocking directorates in all circumstances where the effect would be to reduce competition. A Fair Trade Commission (Kōsei Torihiki Iinkai) was established to enforce these measures. Originally far tougher than comparable American legislation, the statute was modified in 1949 and, following resumption of Japanese sovereignty, major amendments were made in 1953. Many foresaw even further weakening, but this did not come about, and in 1977 the statute was strengthened (see also ANTIMONOPOLY LAW).

Dissolution of Two Giant Trading Companies ——— In July 1947 MacArthur suddenly ordered the dissolution of Mitsui Trading and Mitsubishi Trading, Japan's two largest trading companies, the first and only case of SCAP ordering the dissolution of operating companies. Fascinatingly enough, while MacArthur was coming under increasingly strong attack in the United States for the vigor of his *zaibatsu* dissolution program, not a whisper of criticism was made against this order, which was clearly the most "radical" action of the entire program.

The Deconcentration Law ——— In December 1947, MacArthur succeeded in getting through the Japanese Diet an exceptionally controversial piece of legislation, the Law for the Elimination of Excessive Concentrations of Economic Power, or the Deconcentration Law, for short. Modeled on legislation already enacted by American Occupation officials in Germany, it was directed at those operating companies of such size as to pose serious barriers to market entry. Where operating companies were of such size, the law called for splits.

Part of the problem of this legislation was its timing, though there was also insufficient explanation of its rationale. Confusingly, it followed enactment of the permanent antitrust legislation. Because the Yasuda plan concerned only holding companies, and because the scale of giant operating companies was seen as being realistically beyond the scope of the newly created Fair Trade Commission, which was to administer the Antimonopoly Law, MacArthur sought to make these changes in the structure of operating companies, and assumed that the Fair Trade Commission would then be able to maintain deconcentrated markets. When the number of preliminary designations of companies deemed possibly to have excessive concentrations of economic power was announced for the first two of the four categories designated under the program, the situation was further aggravated, as many individuals came to believe that SCAP was trying to create atomistic competition.

A significant portion of the furor over this legislation can be explained by two additional factors: American businessmen were permitted in postwar Japan for the first time in August 1947, and it was only then that they gained firsthand knowledge of the deconcentration measures. What they found they did not like, possibly because they feared that a strong antitrust policy in Japan presaged a more active antitrust approach in the United States.

Furthermore, Senator William Knowland (R–Calif) in December 1947 acquired an unauthorized copy of FEC 230, the *zaibatsu* dissolution recommendations of the State–War Mission on Japanese Combines (headed by Corwin D. Edwards), which had been submitted to the State and War departments in 1946 and, following adoption by the US government, submitted to the Far Eastern Commission, the ostensible top policy-making body for the Occupation. Senator Knowland was outraged by what he read. However, this was only a policy paper, considerably more extreme than anything that had been or would be enacted into law.

Such a hue and cry went up over the Deconcentration Law that MacArthur proposed the creation of a Deconcentration Review Board made up of prominent American businessmen selected by the Department of the Army to review whether the proposed splits would have a retarding influence on Japan's economic recovery. Members of the review board arrived in Japan in May 1948. They proceeded to ignore totally the conditions for their presence, and at once set about to reverse the deconcentration policy in Japan. As a result of their efforts, only 11 of the 325 preliminary designations in categories 1 (industrial firms) and 2 (service and distributive firms) resulted in corporate reorganizations, and no designations were made in categories 3 (insurance firms) and 4 (banks).

Law for the Termination of Zaibatsu Family Control ——— This legislation was enacted 7 January 1948, one year after the economic purge (see next section). It was designed to deal with *zaibatsu* use of personal ties to bind their complexes of companies together, and was administered by the Holding Company Liquidation Commission. It covered 1,682 subsidiaries of the 10 designated *zaibatsu*, and ostensibly 3,668 corporate officers (both dead and living) became subject

to removal from their positions under its provisions. However, this was a pyrrhic victory, as the reform phase of the Occupation had already passed, and only 40 removals were eventually made.

Financial Institutions Reconstruction and Reorganization Law and Enterprise Reconstruction and Reorganization Law ——— In consequence of the SCAP-directed government cancellation of war indemnity payments to businesses enacted 18 October 1946, virtually all major Japanese corporations faced bankruptcy in the absence of other actions. Also on 18 October 1946 the Diet passed the Financial Institutions Reconstruction and Reorganization Law and the Enterprise Reconstruction and Reorganization Law, bringing these companies within the provisions of legislation passed two months earlier to deal with bankruptcy problems arising from general economic dislocation. This earlier legislation, the Law concerning Emergency Measures for the Accounts of Companies, created "special accounting companies," which were to draw up plans for submission to the appropriate cabinet minister for the financial reorganization of their companies. A 1950 SCAP report states that 4,762 companies had submitted plans under the Enterprise Reconstruction and Reorganization Law.

Under the accounting provisions of the law, many companies were split into two or more successor companies, and most deconcentration of operating companies was ultimately accomplished in this manner. Furthermore, the establishment of new companies called for new boards of directors. The successor companies established under this legislation proved to be considerably more important than the economic purge in putting new blood into Japanese corporate leadership.

Capital Levy Tax ——— In order to meet the problems of rising inflation and imbalanced budgets as well as to effect a more equal distribution of wealth, SCAP called for a capital levy tax in the fall of 1946. The Capital Levy Law enacted on 17 November 1946 provided for a tax on personal net assets of ¥100,000 and above, with rates beginning at 25 percent and progressing by incremental margins to 90 percent on assets of ¥15 million and above. Of all the *zaibatsu* family members, only one (Sumitomo Kichizaemon VIII) was able to go through this and various other measures and some years later be among the highest taxpayers in the nation.

Economic Purge ——— The economic purge that MacArthur was ordered to carry out by the Joint Chiefs of Staff came about by extension of the political purge. The political purge occurred in January 1946; the economic purge, after a year of argument within SCAP headquarters, in January 1947. MacArthur's instructions were as follows:

> You will prohibit the retention in or selection for positions of important responsibility or influence in industry, finance, commerce, or agriculture of all persons who have been active exponents of militant nationalism and aggression, of those who have participated in such organizations as the Imperial Rule Assistance Association, and of any who do not direct future Japanese effort solely towards peaceful ends. (In the absence of evidence, satisfactory to you, you will assume that any persons who have held key positions of high responsibility since 1937, in industry, finance, commerce, or agriculture have been active exponents of militant nationalism or aggression.)

Described this way, all top *zaibatsu* and other business leaders were automatically made into "active exponents of militant nationalism and aggression."

Companies coming under the purge were selected under various criteria, the most important of which was "conspicuously monopolistic," even though, as has been noted, monopoly in the sense of high market position was exceedingly rare in Japan. The corporate officers purged under this category numbered 405, out of a total of 626 for all categories. They represented 160 companies within Japan and 85 companies which had operated abroad (Korea, China, Manchuria, Formosa, and elsewhere). However, a number of businessmen, seeing that they would be purged, had resigned in anticipation. When these resignations were added to those directly purged, the total number of business executives affected by the purge under all criteria numbered 1,535.

The purge was not intended to deny Japan the talent of its top executives. While the "purgees" could not realistically remain within their corporations (technically, such an option was open, since only specified positions were denied them), they were free to take positions in corporations outside their business grouping. One result of this measure was a weakening of the ties by which the complexes of *zaibatsu* companies were bound together, but the structure proved so clumsy and awkward that the Law for the Termination of Zaibatsu Family Control discussed above was enacted a year after the purge. In 1951 the purge was rescinded and purged individuals were freed from all restrictions.

Summary and Assessment——The actions taken to deconcentrate the Japanese economy under Occupation measures—the sale of securities, the purge, and under the Deconcentration Law—may be summarized in Table 2.

As the foregoing account makes clear, the economic deconcentration program did not move smoothly and consistently toward its objectives. And in 1948, with the communist victory in China imminent and a heightening of the cold war, the United States increasingly lost interest in reforming Japan. It sought an ally, and for this purpose it wanted Japan at maximum strength. Thus the deconcentration effort was aborted.

However, for all its shortcomings and inconsistencies, the *zaibatsu* dissolution program accomplished a great deal. By making the former combine subsidiaries their own masters through the dissolution of the holding companies, the program vastly increased market competition. This increased market rivalry was a major factor in Japan's remarkable postwar economic growth. Under the combine system, the key subsidiaries were not free to develop their own market strategies. All actions were conceived from the viewpoint of the combine as a whole. By dissolving the top holding companies, market strategy was transformed. Companies made decisions on the basis of what was to their own advantage rather than on the basis of an overall combine strategy. Intense rivalry broke out, and the faster the economy grew, the more intense it became.

While the economic deconcentration program originally received an enormous amount of criticism from the Japanese business community, UEMURA KŌGORŌ (1894–1978), the president of Japan's most influential business organization, KEIDANREN, observed over two decades later that "The *zaibatsu* dissolution was a major factor in Japan's high postwar growth."

━━━━━T. A. Bisson, *Zaibatsu Dissolution in Japan* (1954). Corwin D. Edwards, "The Dissolution of the Japanese Combines," *Pacific Affairs* (September 1946). Corwin D. Edwards, *Trade Regulation Overseas* (1966). Eleanor M. Hadley, *Antitrust in Japan* (1970). Eleanor M. Hadley, "Trust Busting in Japan," *Harvard Business Review* (July 1948). Eleanor M. Hadley, "Japan: Competition or Private Collectivism?" *Far Eastern Survey* (14 December 1949). Eleanor M. Hadley, "From Deconcentration to Reverse Course," in Smithsonian Institution, *Americans as Proconsuls: U.S. Military Government in Germany and Japan, 1944–52* (forthcoming). Holding Company Liquidation Commission, *Laws, Rules and Regulations Concerning the Reconstruction and Democratization of Japanese Economy* (1949), includes the original form of the Antimonopoly Law. Hiroshi Iyori, *Antimonopoly Legislation in Japan* (1969). Kazuo Kawai, *Japan's American Interlude* (1960). Edwin M. Martin, *The Allied Occupation of Japan* (1948). Mochikabu Kaisha Seiri Iinkai, *Nihon zaibatsu to sono kaitai*, 2 vols (1950–51). State–War Mission on Japanese Combines, *Report* (1956; the recommendations of the report were classified and not part of the published version. For the text of the declassified recommendations, see Hadley, *Antitrust in Japan*).

Eleanor M. HADLEY

zaigō shōnin

(rural merchants). Also known as *zaikata shōnin*. Merchants who were based in the rural hinterlands of large cities late in the Edo period (1600–1868). Such merchants had been active in the farming villages since the late 1600s, but it was only with the increased production of cash crops in the early 18th century that they became a force in the market economy. By the early 19th century, *zaigō shōnin* were a nationwide phenomenon. Within the distribution system *zaigō shōnin* dealt in items like raw and ginned cotton, cotton goods, rapeseed, cottonseed, oil, vegetables, indigo, and safflower dye as well as rice and other grains. Some of them were of wealthy farmer background, while others came from relatively poor circumstances. At first they were powerless against the urban merchants' associations (KABUNAKAMA), which under official patronage enjoyed monopolistic rights on the sale and distribution of goods; but with the support of the rural producers they were gradually able to bypass these guilds and form their own distribution networks. The banding together (see KOKUSO) in 1823 of more than 1,000 villages in the cotton-growing area of Settsu Province (now part of Ōsaka Prefecture) to protest *kabunakama* privileges greatly strengthened the

Zaibatsu dissolution——Table 2

Dissolution Programs	
Action taken against designated holding companies	Number of companies affected
Outright dissolution	16
Dissolution followed by reorganization	26
Reorganization without dissolution	11
None	30
Total	83
Stock disposal program	Value of stocks disposed
Antitrust	
Holding Company Liquidation Commission	¥8.3 billion (proceeds from sale)
Fair Trade Commission	¥1.3 billion (paid-up value)
Other	
Finance Ministry (capital tax levy)	¥1.7 billion (proceeds from sale)
Closed Institutions Liquidation Commission	¥3.1 billion (proceeds from sale)
Total	¥14.4 billion
Personnel program	Number of persons affected
Law for the Termination of Zaibatsu Family Control	40
Economic purge	1,535
Total	1,575
Reorganization under the Deconcentration Law	Number of companies affected
Companies split	11
Companies directed to make minor changes	8
Total	19

SOURCE: Eleanor M. Hadley, *Antitrust in Japan* (1970). Reprinted by permission of Princeton University Press. Copyright © 1970.

zaigō shōnin and was one factor leading to the shogunate's abolition of *kabunakama* in 1841. When the shogunate later revived the *kabunakama* system in 1851, it sought to combine both urban and rural merchants in a single body. Now part of a privileged group, the *zaigō shōnin* began to identify less with the rural producers; this in turn led to the formation of new groups of village-based merchants. Some rural merchants became wholesalers and worked through a contract system, offering advance payment; others became owner-managers of enterprises such as *sake* breweries. Because they helped to organize rural production and to integrate it into the commercial economy, they are considered by some Japanese historians, who consider the Meiji Restoration to have been a "bourgeois" revolution, as representing what Marxists term the substructure of Japanese society that contributed to the overthrow of the Tokugawa shogunate.

TSUDA Hideo

zaikai

(financial circles). A term generally used by the media to refer to leading businessmen who speak on behalf of the business community as a whole. To intellectuals opposed to the power of big business, the *zaikai* represents big capital in general. To participants in leading organizations of business people, the *zaikai* as popularly conceived does not exist, for to use the term as an analogue to *seikai* (political circles) and *kankai* (bureaucratic circles) implies more unity in the business community than actually exists. Representatives of the media commonly refer to the chairman of the KEIDANREN (Federation of Economic Organizations) as the "prime minister of the business community," but business leaders deny that he has such power.

The public image of the business community originated in the Meiji period (1868–1912) when prominent business leaders began working closely with government leaders to develop the nation's

Zaōzan

A winter scene on Zaōzan, which is known for its ice-covered trees.

basic industries. From then until the present day, the dominant figures of the business community have generally been from basic industries given priority by the government for national development. In the 1950s and 1960s when earmarked industries played an important role in Japan's period of most rapid growth, government priorities for land allocation, capital allocation from the development banks, special tax incentives, special research funds, and protection from imports played a key role in economic development. Prominent business leaders met frequently to discuss these issues, and a sense of community developed to deal with general issues of common concern. To ensure good channels of communication with politicians, funds have been collected by the largest business associations and given to political parties on behalf of business as a whole. This has helped to ensure that the dominant political parties would consider the views of leaders who spoke on behalf of business as a whole.

Four business associations are ordinarily considered the main pillars of zaikai strength. These are the Keidanren, the JAPAN CHAMBER OF COMMERCE AND INDUSTRY (Nihon Shōkō Kaigisho), the JAPAN COMMITTEE FOR ECONOMIC DEVELOPMENT (Keizai Dōyū Kai), and the Japan Federation of Employers' Associations (NIKKEIREN). Keidanren, founded in 1946, is an association of major business corporations, numbering over 700 by the late 1970s. It is in turn divided into a number of functional subcommittees concerned with major issues confronting the nation and into a number of other committees organized along industrial sector lines. Since the mid-1950s it has been the most powerful of the business associations, and it is the main financial contributor to the LIBERAL DEMOCRATIC PARTY, both directly and indirectly. It facilitates frequent meetings of major businessmen who are in constant contact with each other at its headquarters in Tōkyō.

Since the latter part of the Meiji period each business establishment has been required by law to belong to a chamber of commerce, which thereby serves as a registration agency. Since most of the businesses belonging to chambers of commerce are small businesses, they tend to represent the interests of small business. In small- and middle-sized communities throughout Japan, chambers of commerce tend to represent local business interests.

The Japan Committee for Economic Development was formed shortly after World War II by enterprising young businessmen interested in reforming and modernizing Japanese management practices. Because members are individuals rather than companies, it tends to represent ideals, goals, and new conceptions rather than more immediate economic concerns.

The Japan Federation of Employers' Associations was formed in 1948 to represent Japanese employers vis-à-vis labor groups. In the late 1940s and early 1950s when labor strife was widespread, it was a powerful organization and occupied much of the time of business leaders. Since the mid-1950s, when labor problems have centered on basic wage increases, it has become a more routinized organization concerned with economic analysis of wage differentials and with related educational tasks. It continues to represent management interests in dealing with wages and working conditions.

Keidanren is not only a national organization but also doubles as the Tōkyō-area organization of leaders of large businesses. In the eight other major regions of the country, there are comparable business organizations representing the interests of the larger industrialists. The strongest of the other regional organizations is Kankeiren (Kansai Keizai Rengōkai), which is located in the Ōsaka–Kyōto–Kōbe area.

Among the best-known zaikai leaders since World War II are ISHIZAKA TAIZŌ (1886–1975), president of Keidanren from 1956 to 1968; KOBAYASHI ATARU (1899–1981), a close adviser of Prime Minister YOSHIDA SHIGERU and the first head of the JAPAN DEVELOPMENT BANK, established in 1951; DOKŌ TOSHIO (b 1896), former president of ISHIKAWAJIMA–HARIMA HEAVY INDUSTRIES CO, LTD, and of the TŌSHIBA CORPORATION, who served as president of Keidanren from 1974 to 1980; and INAYAMA YOSHIHIRO (b 1904), chairman of NIPPON STEEL CORPORATION, who became Keidanren president in 1980. *Ezra F. VOGEL*

zaike

1. (literally, "at home"). Buddhist laymen who lived at home. The term was used in contrast to *shukke,* monks and nuns who took formal holy orders and normally lived in monasteries and temples. *Zaike* of the JŌDO SHIN SECT performed various priestly functions. Males were called UBASOKU or *konji;* females were called *ubai* or *konjinyo.*

2. Under the SHŌEN system of landholding in the 10th to 16th centuries, *zaike* referred to peasants who were attached to estate proprietors (RYŌSHU) and cultivated their fields. They were originally considered chattels, but in time, especially in the Kyōto–Nara–Ōsaka region, they were able to claim rights over the plots they farmed and came to resemble the MYŌSHU, or independent small freeholders.

zaisei tōyūshi

(fiscal investment and loan program). A large governmental loan program, utilizing surplus funds from Japan's National Treasury. The funds originate with government-run savings, pension, and life insurance programs and are pooled into a special account at the Ministry of Finance.

Investments and loans are made to contribute to social welfare through housing and highway construction, to improve the environment, or to add to social capital. Funds are extended to governmental financial institutions, including the HOUSING LOAN CORPORATION, PEOPLE'S FINANCE CORPORATION, SMALL BUSINESS FINANCE CORPORATION, and JAPAN DEVELOPMENT BANK; to public corporations, including the JAPANESE NATIONAL RAILWAYS, NIPPON TELEGRAPH AND TELEPHONE PUBLIC CORPORATION, Japan Housing Corporation, and JAPAN HIGHWAY PUBLIC CORPORATION; and to local governments. The funds are extended through loans, investments, and the underwriting of bonds.

The scale of this program's operation, a total outlay of ¥16.8 trillion (US $76.6 billion) in 1979, stood at 43.6 percent of the general account budget of the national government, justifying the often-used designation of the program as the "second budget." The program also plays an important role in the government's efforts at economic stabilization, since its funds can be invested with great discretion and flexibility, while government expenditures require the deliberation and approval of the Diet. *UDAGAWA Akihito*

Zama

City in central Kanagawa Prefecture, central Honshū. It was the site of the Army Academy from 1937 to the end of World War II and of an American Occupation camp after the war. Automobile and machinery plants are located here. Recently the city has become a dormitory suburb of Tōkyō and Yokohama. Pop: 93,501.

Zambōritsu → Libel Law of 1875

Zaō Hot Spring

(Zaō Onsen). Located in the southeastern part of the city of Yamagata, southeastern Yamagata Prefecture, northern Honshū. An alum and vitriol spring; water temperature 41–55°C (106–131°F). Located in the ZAŌZAN volcano group at an altitude of 880 m (2,886 ft), it is a base camp for excursions into the Zaō district, which is noted for its skiing.

Zaōzan

Group of volcanoes, in the Nasu Volcanic Zone, on the border of Miyagi and Yamagata prefectures, northern Honshū. The group is bisected by the Katta Pass. Kita Zaō, to the north, is a double volcano with Kumanodake and Kattadake forming its crater rims and Goshikidake (1,679 m; 5,507 ft) forming a central cone. Minami Zaō to the south includes Byōbudake (1,817 m; 5,960 ft), Ushiro Eboshidake, and Fubōzan. Snowfall is heavy. The area is known for its skiing and autumn foliage. Hot springs include the Gaga and Zaō hot springs. Zaōzan has been designated as Zaō Quasi-National Park. The highest peak is Kumanodake (1,841 m; 6,038 ft). See photo on preceding page.

zappai and senryū

Zappai is a general term covering a number of forms of comic poetry that evolved from *haikai* (see RENGA AND HAIKAI) verse during the Edo period (1600–1868). It established itself as an independent poetic genre directed toward popular taste during the Genroku era (1688–1704), when *haikai* drifted away from its original identity as a comic verse form and took on a more serious character. Most *zappai* forms are based on the 5-7-5 syllabic structure of the *hokku* (see HAIKU). *Senryū* is one of the best-known types of *zappai* and expresses the feelings and insights of people in everyday situations.

Types of Zappai——Some *zappai* forms such as *maekuzuke* and *kasazuke* follow the principles of linked verse, in which the poet adds a capping verse *(tsukeku)* to a previously given verse *(maeku)*. Zappai also includes independent, unlinked forms which developed from the *hokku,* such as *kiriku* and *oriku. Senryū* was a relatively late unlinked form which developed from the *tsukeku* portion of *maekuzuke* verses.

Maekuzuke was a traditional form of literary amusement in which a given short verse of 14 syllables was capped by a long verse of 17 syllables to arrive at the 31-syllable length of the traditional *tanka* form; alternately, a long verse could be capped by a short one. *Maekuzuke* represents the original form of Japanese linked verse, and even after it was superseded by the longer and more sophisticated linked verse forms of *renga* and *haikai,* it survived both as a comic entertainment and a practice form by which poets could study and improve their linking technique. In the early Genroku era *maekuzuke* achieved great popularity among the urban population, and *maekuzuke* competitions in which *tsukeku* on a given *maeku* were selected and graded by professional poetry masters drew large numbers of participants. Winning verses were printed and distributed, and prizes were awarded.

Unlike *haikai* poetry, in which the *maeku* and the *tsukeku* were considered equally important, *maekuzuke* composition emphasized the interest of the *tsukeku* alone. For this reason, the 14-syllable short verse was fixed as the *maeku,* and its content became simple to the point of being perfunctory. Ultimately it lost all poetic meaning and served merely to introduce the theme of the 17-syllable long verse, which simultaneously gained great freedom in both content and expression. With the surge in popularity of *maekuzuke* in the Genroku era, many professional poetry masters began to follow the public trend of viewing *maekuzuke* composition as an end in itself rather than as a mere practice technique, and some devoted themselves exclusively to the judging of *maekuzuke.* Among the most notable of these masters were Tachiba Fukaku (1662–1753), Shūgetsu (fl early 18th century), and KARAI SENRYŪ (1718–90).

In *kasazuke,* the major linked-verse form of *zappai,* a 5-syllable *maeku* is capped by a 12-syllable *tsukeku.* The completed poem is thus 17 syllables long, like a *hokku,* although unlike a *hokku* it does not require a season word. This break from the conventional number of syllables in each verse gave rise to numerous other metrical variations.

Kiriku and *oriku,* both of which were nonlinked forms, also did away with the principle of establishing a seasonal theme. This feature greatly simplified verse composition and won favor with amateur poets daunted by the complexities of using season words. Unlike the linked-verse forms, *kiriku* and *oriku* were meant to be composed and appreciated as complete poems, rather than as parts of a continuing series. In *kiriku,* as in *kasazuke,* a verse of 12 syllables was added to a given verse of 5 syllables to create a complete poem of 17 syllables. Although originally less attention may have been paid to linking technique in *kiriku* than in *kasazuke,* the two forms were sufficiently similar to be considered later as a single type, commonly referred to as *kammurizuke.*

Oriku was an acrostic form in which either 2 given syllables were used respectively as the starting syllables for 2 lines of 7 syllables each, or 3 given syllables were used to start 3 lines of a verse in a 5-7-5 syllable pattern. While there were precedents for this type of poetic amusement in the earlier *waka* tradition, it reached the height of its popularity in the mid-18th century, especially in the Ōsaka area.

Senryū——As the *tsukeku* portions of *maekuzuke* verses came to be read and appreciated by themselves, they were called *kyōku* to distinguish them from *hokku,* with which they shared the same 17-syllable structure. The style of *tsukeku* selected and published by the *maekuzuke* judge Karai Senryū swept the entire nation starting in the Meiwa era (1764–72), and came to be known as Senryū-style *kyōku. Senryū* is a modern abbreviation of this term.

Starting with *Mutamagawa* (1750), a number of collections of superior *tsukeku* from *maekuzuke* competitions had been published without their *maeku.* These collections were widely read in the city of Edo (now Tōkyō), and led to the publication in 1765 of the first *Yanagidaru,* a collection of *tsukeku* selected by the immensely popular standards of Karai Senryū. Favorably received by Edo readers, it was followed by 22 more *Yanagidaru* collections issued by Senryū himself and, after his death, by 144 more issued by his successors. The early editions showed Senryū's marked preference for a style similar to that of contemporary *haikai* poetry, but in treating the verses as independent entities and completely ignoring their origin as *tsukeku* they went a step beyond *Mutamagawa.*

The popularity of the *Yanagidaru* series led to an increased emphasis on the independence of the *tsukeku* in Senryū's *maekuzuke* competitions, and in his last years the competitions abandoned the *maeku* entirely and were limited to 17-syllable *kyōku.* At the same time, the light, witty, realistic sketches of everyday life in the *haikai* vein that had been predominant in the early *Yanagidaru* collections were gradually replaced by verses with an emphasis on humor, often quite bawdy, and novelty. This tendency was intensified by the practice of using set topics *(kudai)* for verse composition in place of the *maeku,* and ultimately led to both the production of large numbers of nearly identical verses and a tendency to overindulge in obscenity and stilted wordplay in an effort to achieve new comic effects. After the Meiji Restoration of 1868, however, a reform movement worked to curb excesses in *senryū* and revive it as a satirical poetic genre. It survives to this day as a form of poetic amusement, composed primarily by amateurs.

Literary Characteristics of Senryū——*Senryū* verse deals primarily with everyday people in everyday situations. One need not be a specialist to compose it. In fact, one notable characteristic of the *Yanagidaru* collections was that the poets remained anonymous; the tastes shown by the selector gave the collection its only touch of personal identity. In presenting historical legends it gives them a popular twist, and it tends to treat nature and living things from a distinctly human perspective. The qualities that give literary value to *senryū* are the light, witty realism of its expression and its penetrating, intuitive observation of human foibles and events generally overlooked by poets in other genres. At its best, the keen insights of *senryū* into social mores and daily life make for superior satire, but its inclination toward sharpness sometimes causes it to take an irresponsibly negative view of mankind and society, falling to the level of mere sarcasm and scandal-mongering.

■■——R. H. Blyth, *Senryū* (1949). Miyata Masanobu, *Zappaishi no kenkyū* (1972). Okada Hajime, ed, *Yanagidaru zenshū* (Sanseidō, 1976–79). Suzuki Masatada et al, ed, *Kibyōshi, Senryū, Kyōka,* vol 46 of *Nihon koten bungaku zenshū,* (Shōgakukan, 1971).

SHIRAISHI Teizō

zashiki warashi

A kind of household tutelary god traditionally believed to live in the homes of old and well-to-do families in the northern part of Honshū, particularly in Iwate Prefecture. Said to appear in the form of a young boy with long hair and a red face and to bring riches to the family, it could also be mischievous, bearing down on the chests of sleeping persons during the night. INOKUCHI Shōji

Zasso Ketsudansho

(Court of Miscellaneous Claims). Extrastatutory board for adjudication of miscellaneous claims; established in 1333 by Emperor GO-DAIGO to impose some order on the legal chaos created by his KEMMU RESTORATION (1333–36). Like the High Court (HIKITSUKE)

set up by the fallen Kamakura shogunate (1192–1333), it dealt chiefly with land claims. Its staff was made up largely of former officials of the Hikitsuke, but warriors and courtiers also participated. The establishment of the Zasso Ketsudansho showed Go-Daigo's recognition of the need to maintain the feudal law system that had developed over the previous 150 years.

zatō

1. Heads of guilds (ZA) of entertainers or merchants in the Muromachi period (1333–1568).

2. Lowest of four ranks (kengyō, bettō, kōtō, and zatō) given to members of a guild of blind male entertainers (tōdōza) formed early in the Muromachi period. It later became a general term for blind men, usually members of the tōdōza, who shaved their heads and wore the vestments of a Buddhist priest, earning their living as musicians, singers, and storytellers, or as practitioners of ACUPUNCTURE or massage (see BIWA HŌSHI; AMMA). During the Edo period (1600–1868) they were protected by the shogunate and permitted to demand payment for their services from samurai and townsmen. The guild prospered, and members used their earnings (zatōgane) to make high interest loans. Zatō are distinguished from GOZE, blind female entertainers.   INAGAKI Shisei

zatsumu sata

(literally, "miscellaneous proceedings"). A legal term used under the Kamakura shogunate (1192–1333) in reference to litigation over money, serfs and servants, and movable property and employed also in cases involving private or public loans (SUIKO), taxes, commercial transactions, or the forcible return of cultivators who had absconded. In contrast, the term KENDAN (or kendan sata) referred to police proceedings in criminal matters, and shomu sata meant litigation over landholdings. Both zatsumu sata and shomu sata cases were generally adjudicated by the shogunate's Board of Inquiry (MONCHŪJO) or, within the city of Kamakura, by the Administrative Board (MANDOKORO).

zazen → Zen

Zeami (1363–1443)

Also known as Seami, or Kanze Motokiyo. The brilliant actor, playwright, and critic who established NŌ (sarugaku) as a classic theatrical art.

Life—— Zeami's father, KAN'AMI, headed a SARUGAKU troupe in the province of Yamato (now Nara Prefecture). In 1374 the shōgun, the young ASHIKAGA YOSHIMITSU, saw the two perform in Kyōto, and he was so smitten by Zeami's boyish genius and grace that he made Zeami his protégé and admitted him to his highly artistic court. At Kan'ami's death Zeami took over the troupe, but it was not until 1402 that he adopted the artistic name by which he has since been known.

In 1422, Zeami became a Sōtō Zen monk and was succeeded by KANZE MOTOMASA, his gifted elder son. However in 1429, ASHIKAGA YOSHINORI, a new shōgun who favored On'ami (Zeami's nephew), barred Zeami and Motomasa from his palace. In 1430 Zeami's younger son, Motoyoshi, also gave up Nō to become a monk. Then in 1432 Motomasa died. Zeami was grief-stricken. Henceforth it was On'ami who reigned in the world of Nō. In 1434, Zeami was exiled to the island of Sado, having perhaps provoked this trial by refusing to impart his secret teachings to On'ami. Zeami returned to Kyōto only a few years before his death. His only direct successor was his son-in-law KOMPARU ZENCHIKU.

Works—— Plays. Zeami urged the actor to write his own plays, and he himself is generally credited with about 90—although the strictest standards of attribution allow him only 21. Moreover Zeami revised so completely the other plays he used that no Nō text survives intact from before his time. Masterpieces definitely by Zeami include Takasago, Tadanori, Izutsu, and Kinuta.

Critical writings. These consist of 21 treatises, some of disputed authenticity, which together with the items below were rediscovered only in the early 1900s. The best known is Fūshi kaden (The Transmission of the Flower of Acting Style) in seven parts dated from 1400 to 1418, which purports to transmit Kan'ami's teachings. Others are Shikadōsho (1420, Essay on the Way to the Flower), Kakyō (1424, The Mirror of the Flower), and Kyūi shidai (undated, The

Order of the Nine Grades). Essential too is Sarugaku dangi (Conversations on Sarugaku), Zeami's comments on his art recorded by Motoyoshi in 1430.

Other works. Museki isshi (1433, A Page on the Ruin of a Dream) is a lament for Motomasa; Kintōsho (1436, The Book of the Golden Isle) is a poetic account of Zeami's exile. A few letters also survive.

Artistic Ideals—— Zeami wrote often of hana (flower) and of yūgen (subtle beauty). The former distinguishes the fine actor, the latter the fine performance or play. "Flower" refers to freshness and aptness. An actor who gives his audience the feeling that they are seeing for the first time, with keen emotion, an otherwise familiar role, has the "flower." Indeed, Zeami said of the old master who is no longer agile but whose art is supreme that his performance is like flowers blossoming on a gnarled old bough. Yūgen, on the other hand, ranges in meaning from "grace" or "elegance" to something like "ineffable mystery." The final scene of the play Obasute may serve to illustrate yūgen: an ancient woman, left to die in the wilds, dances in white on a mountaintop under the full moon and sings of the loveliness of paradise.

Like other medieval artists, Zeami understood art as a "way" toward human perfection. His ideal actor achieved flawless responsiveness and expressive freedom. Thus Zeami wrote that Kan'ami could suit his style in any role to any audience so as to touch that audience most deeply. Moreover he taught that the master actor, having once achieved the highest "flower," may descend again to disport himself in those roles which any beginner may take, thus closing the circle of his "way" and displaying a naturalness beyond rank or judgment.

📖——René Sieffert, Zeami: La tradition secrète du nō (1960). Kawase Kazuma, Tōchū Zeami nijūsanbu shū (1945). Kobayashi Shizuo, Zeami (1958). Nishi Isshō, Zeami kenkyū (1976), with complete bibliography.   Royall TYLER

Zekkai Chūshin (1336–1405)

Zen monk of the RINZAI SECT; poet; a disciple of MUSŌ SOSEKI who became leader of his lineage after GIDŌ SHŪSHIN's death. Together with Gidō, he has been called one of the "two jewels" of GOZAN LITERATURE (Chinese learning as cultivated in the medieval Japanese Zen monasteries). Born in Tosa Province (now Kōchi Prefecture) the son of a samurai family, Zekkai visited China between 1368 and 1378 and studied under masters of the lineage of Dahui Zongyao (Tahui Tsung-yao). Among the events of his trip was an interview with the Ming emperor Taizu (T'ai-tsu), who questioned him about Japan and to whom he presented verses. Zekkai was one of the most accomplished technically of all Gozan poets; he is said to have been one of the few who could think in Chinese. The trend toward secularization of subject matter in Gozan literature is especially noticeable in his poetry. His patrons included the shōguns ASHIKAGA YOSHIMITSU and Ashikaga Yoshimochi, who employed him to write state documents because of his facility with parallel prose. His poems are collected in the anthology Shōkenkō.   Marian URY

zelkova

(keyaki). Zelkova serrata. A deciduous tree of the elm family (Ulmaceae) which grows wild on plains and slopes in Honshū, Shikoku, and Kyūshū and is also widely cultivated. Its trunk is erect and tall, sometimes attaining a height of 30 meters (98 ft) and a diameter of 2 meters (7 ft). It grows numerous thin branches. The leaves are oblong lanceolate in shape with pointed tips, fine veins, and serrate edges. It develops tiny light yellowish green flowers which bloom in clusters.

An indigenous Japanese tree, the zelkova was formerly known as tsuki or tsukinoki. Favored for its shape and for both its spring and autumn foliage, it is planted along roadsides, in parks, in the precincts of shrines and temples, and around farmhouses. Zelkova wood is strong, glossy, fine-grained, durable, warp-resistant, and easily worked; it is used as material for buildings, bridges, ships, and miscellaneous furniture and utensils. Zelkova ash is used in making ceramic wares.   MATSUDA Osamu

Zempa

(Zen school). A group of sculptors of Buddhist images active in the Nara area in the early and middle part of the Kamakura period

(1185–1333). When the prominent KEI SCHOOL sculpture workshop (BUSSHO) moved from Nara to Kyōto, sculptors remaining in the Nara area later became known as the Zen school, since many of them, such as Zen'en and Zenkei, had the character *zen* in their names. Their artistic antecedents are unclear and their individual styles, despite a common preference for small images with finely detailed work, retain a strong personal character. The group had close ties with EIZON, the abbot of the temple Saidaiji. The images they created at the time of the temple's restoration may still be seen.

Zen

Zen is perhaps best defined as the meditation school of East Asian Buddhism. The content of its teachings stems from the so-called Mahāyāna Buddhist tradition, although the form of its practice owes much to pre-Buddhist yoga. The Zen (Ch: Chan or Ch'an, from Skt: *dhyāna*, meditation) school arose in China out of the encounter between Buddhism and indigenous Taoist thought; it survived the persecution of Buddhism in 845 and was held in high regard for several centuries. Zen blossomed again after being brought to Japan, where DŌGEN (1200–1253) developed Mahāyānist metaphysics in an original and profound way. *Zazen* (meditation; Ch: *zuochan* or *tso-ch'an*) and the study of KŌAN (Ch: *gongan* or *kung-an*), the two practices that characterize Zen, prepare the way to enlightenment *(satori)*. Whereas the SŌTŌ SECT (Ch: Caodong or Ts'ao-tung) primarily cultivates *zazen* (meditation in the lotus posture, from *za* "sitting" and *zen* "meditation"), the other main Zen school in Japan, the RINZAI SECT, emphasizes *kōan* practice. This sect traces its origins back to the Chinese master Linji (Lin-chi; J: Rinzai, d 867). Originally, in China, *kōan* were official documents to be used as a basis for judgments, whereas among Zen monks, the word came to mean pithy statements for novices to exhaust their thinking on and thereby progress in meditation. Rinzai Zen exercised a profound influence on many segments of Japanese culture.

History——*Chan in China.* The history in China of Chan (Zen) gives us some idea of what the pioneer Japanese monks brought back from the land where this school was first developed. By the time the Japanese became interested in it, Chinese Zen had reached a certain plateau in its development. Although its heyday was over, and it had split into various lineages in the course of propagation, Chan monasteries and temples were esteemed throughout the country, especially as a result of their artistic achievements and their exchange of ideas with Confucianists. Zen meditation had taken on a definitive form and was practiced seriously and successfully, although not with the fervor of earlier times. The picture of Zen history we have from Chinese Buddhist accounts of that time is not entirely reliable but is to this day regarded as authentic by Zen schools. The main features of this picture include the following:

1. The founder of Chan was said to be the Indian monk Bodhidharma (d ca 532), who came to China. There are many legends of his *kōan*-like exchanges with Emperor Wudi (Wu-ti; r 502–549) of the Liang dynasty; of his nine-year meditation facing a wall; of his first disciple, Huike (Hui-k'o; 487–593), who is said to have cut off an arm to demonstrate his zeal; of his final dialogue with his disciples; of his testing their understanding; and of the particular form of meditation ascribed to him, namely, meditation in the lotus posture culminating in sudden realization.

2. The Chan movement of the Tang (T'ang) dynasty (618–907) is said to have been started by the sixth patriarch, Huineng (638–713), who may be regarded as the actual establisher of Zen in China in spite of the many spurious elements in his history. The Platform Sutra ascribed to him clarified the essential traits of the Chan Way. The weight of his authority supported the Chan masters of the Tang period. The "Chan forests" where their monasteries were located were said to emit a "thunderous roar" and possess a "mystical density" that attracted "seekers of the Way" from all parts of China.

3. The "five houses" of the Chan tradition were established toward the end of the Tang dynasty and during the period of the Five Dynasties (907–960). Two of these schools, the Linji and Caodong, endured and were transplanted to Japan.

4. The practice of *kōan*, a Chinese device, was begun by the Linji school. It acquired an eloquent literary form in the *kōan* collections, especially the *Biyanlu* (*Pi-yen-lü*, 1125; J: *Hekiganroku*, tr *Blue Cliff Record*, 1961, 1977) and the *Wumenguan* (*Wu-men kuan*; J: *Mumonkan*, tr 1966, 1977). Other Chan literature of China, particularly sayings of the masters such as the 10th-century *Linjilu* (J: *Rinzairoku*) were brought to Japan by Japanese monks.

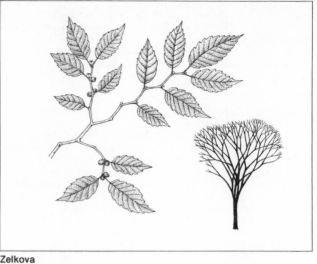

Zelkova

Zen in Japan. The introduction of the Chan school into Japan is one of the most important events in Japanese religious history. Together with the proclamation of faith in the Buddha AMIDA and the rise of the NICHIREN SECT, it marks the renewal of Buddhism during the Kamakura period (1185–1333). To be sure, there had been meditation practices in Japanese Buddhism since its beginnings, as there were in all forms of Buddhism, and monks such as DŌSHŌ (629–700) of the HOSSŌ SECT and Gyōhō (8th century) knew of Zen and had taught its precepts. But even though Chinese Zen masters came to Japan and endeavored to propagate this tradition, Zen did not gain a firm footing quickly. It did not develop into a major branch of Japanese Buddhism until the time of EISAI (1141–1215) and Dōgen, who took advantage of the increasing exchange between Chinese and Japanese Buddhism. Eisai and Dōgen seriously studied the way of Zen in China and then diligently propagated its tenets in Japan. Many Japanese Buddhist monks began to journey to China with the express intention of studying Zen there. Zen became established in Japan, however, only by resisting the attack of the powerful TENDAI SECT and SHINGON SECT of Buddhism.

The Zen movement, introduced into Japan through the two main channels of Rinzai and Sōtō, quickly found a place there. The achievements of the Rinzai school were conspicuous in the nation's imperial and shogunal capitals, Kyōto and Kamakura respectively, which saw the rise of the Five Great Temples (GOZAN) modeled after the Chinese Five Temples. These became active cultural centers as well as sites of religious practice. The central sites were these five temples—at first a total of five temple-monasteries divided between the two cities and later five monasteries each in Kyōto and Kamakura, some of which eventually had compounds for nuns as well as for monks. The monks' monasteries were headed by outstanding abbots who were often granted the title "national teacher" *(kokushi)* by the imperial court in recognition of their accomplishments. Eisai, after founding Japan's first Rinzai temple, Shōfukuji, in the city of Hakata (now in Fukuoka Prefecture) in 1191, became the first abbot of Jufukuji in Kamakura and then of KENNINJI (founded in 1202), located in Kyōto, both of which were to become part of the Five Temple system. He exhorted people to practice Zen in a treatise entitled, "The Propagation of Zen for the Protection of the Country" (KŌZEN GOKOKU RON). Although Eisai was the first Japanese Rinzai monk, he does not count among the great religious figures of his time; he left behind no significant successor, and soon after his death Kenninji began to show signs of decline.

The most outstanding Japanese figure in Rinzai Zen during this early period was ENNI Ben'en (also known as Shōichi Kokushi; 1202–80), who returned from a six-year stay in China with the seal of enlightenment from the Yangqi (Yang-ch'i) lineage of the Linji (Rinzai) school. He served as head of the Kyōto temple TŌFUKUJI and at the same time undertook reform measures at Kenninji. There is still extant a striking portrait of this master by the celebrated painter MINCHŌ.

The "national teacher" NAMPO JŌMYŌ (Entsū Daiō Kokushi; 1235–1308) also belongs to this early period. He received his first Zen training in Kamakura, spent several years in China studying the sources of the tradition, and returned first to Kamakura, then moved

Zen——Bodhidharma and Huike

Detail of a painting by Sesshū Tōyō (1420–1506) of the Zen patriarch and his disciple. Colors on paper. 1496. Sainenji, Aichi Prefecture.

on to head Zen temples in Kyūshū for about 30 years. He finally became the abbot of Manjuji in Kyōto and KENCHŌJI in Kamakura, two of the most important Zen monasteries. His name is also remembered because of his disciple SŌHŌ MYŌCHŌ (Daitō Kokushi; 1282–1337), the renowned founder and abbot of DAITOKUJI in Kyōto. In Kamakura, the shogunal capital of that era, Chinese masters, such as RANKEI DŌRYŪ and Mugaku Sogen were at work, founding the temples Kenchōji (1253) and ENGAKUJI (1282), respectively. It is characteristic of this first phase of Rinzai Zen in Japan that both Chinese and Japanese masters were active (see also ISSAN ICHINEI). Many other Rinzai temples made significant contributions to the Zen movement of medieval Japan. In addition to Daitokuji, both NANZENJI and TENRYŪJI in Kyōto became influential centers of Japanese culture.

The history of the Sōtō school, the second main current of Zen brought from China to Japan, seems more straightforward. Dōgen, considered the founder of the school in Japan, outshone all the masters of his time in the depth of his religious experience and the power of his creative thinking. He is numbered among the five or six great religious minds of Japan. It was in China that he attained enlightenment and the seal of approval to succeed his master Rujing (Ju-ching; 1163–1228) in the Sōtō lineage. Dōgen did not intend to introduce a new Zen sect to Japan. A determined foe of any sectarianism, he earnestly wished only to lead his disciples to the Buddha's original enlightenment, which he himself had experienced as a result of the strict guidance of his master Rujing. Today his true followers still prefer to speak of "Dōgen Zen" rather than the Zen of the Sōtō sect.

After his sojourn in China, Dōgen was first active in small temples near Kyōto. He built the first completely independent Zen temple and meditation hall, Kōshō Hōrinji (also called Kōshōji), which attracted a number of excellent disciples, in 1233. Later, distraught by the hostility and political intrigues of the capital, he withdrew to a temple that a lay disciple had built for him in the district of Echizen (now Fukui Prefecture). This monastery, called EIHEIJI (Temple of Eternal Peace), became the center of the Sōtō school. Far removed from the boisterous capital, the school was able to spread into the countryside. SŌJIJI, a temple founded by Keizan (1268–1325), was another important Sōtō temple.

During the Muromachi period (1333–1568) Chinese cultural influence on Japan reached its highest level. Important trade relations with the Asiatic mainland, carried on chiefly by Buddhist monks, began to develop. In contrast to other Buddhist schools, which exhibited serious marks of decay at that time, Zen displayed extraordinary vitality and spread broadly.

The temple MYŌSHINJI, established in 1337, became a model for the strict discipline espoused by its first abbot Kanzan Egen (1277–1360). The most famous monk of the time was MUSŌ SOSEKI (Musō Kokushi; 1275–1351). Together with those of GEN'E (1279–1350), GIDŌ SHŪSHIN (1325–88), and his highly gifted disciple ZEKKAI CHŪSHIN (1336–1405), his works are representative of the literature of the Five Temples (GOZAN LITERATURE) devoted to the study of the Chinese classics of the Song (Sung) period (960–1278) and the Neo-Confucian philosophy of Zhu Xi (Chu Hsi; see SHUSHIGAKU). Though no inner affinity between the two ways of thought is discernible, Japanese Zen disciples were most receptive to Neo-Confucian metaphysics, which they characteristically interpreted in a naturalistic sense. Through their efforts Chinese philosophy became highly and widely appreciated in Japan.

Musō induced the shōgun ASHIKAGA TAKAUJI to issue a general decree in 1338 to build Zen temples in 66 localities—these were called "temples to pacify the country" (ankokuji). Although this plan was only partly realized, it was actually a continuation of the old system of provincial temples (KOKUBUNJI), which during the Nara period (710–794) assured the spread of Buddhism throughout Japan. It was by means of these provincial temples and by the use of Japanese-style sermons (kana hōgo) that Zen achieved its great influence over the general populace. During this period, Zen exerted a formative influence on the arts of INK PAINTING (sumi-e), NŌ drama, TEA CEREMONY, FLOWER ARRANGEMENT, and landscaping (see GARDENS). The aesthetics nurtured in these arts was to remain a definitive force in Japanese culture.

As Zen became established under shogunal patronage, however, criticism arose from within. IKKYŪ was perhaps the most notable monk in this regard. His iconoclastic directness in criticizing smug Buddhists, along with his eccentric behavior, made him a popular figure long remembered in Japanese Zen.

The Edo period (1600–1868) afforded peace and an environment beneficial for the popularization of Zen. Ideas based on Zen found their way into the education of the common people, and, in particular, into BUSHIDŌ (the samurai ethic). As part of the religious policy of the Tokugawa government, temples and members of all Buddhist sects were officially registered for the first time. The Rinzai school, divided into numerous sects named after the head temple of each, did not claim as large a membership as the Sōtō school with its two main temples, Eiheiji and Sōjiji. Not all Zen temples had meditation halls. Until the end of the Edo period, the temple was a center of community life, but with the advent of modernization and secularization in the 20th century, the spiritual significance of temples, those of the Zen school included, declined sharply.

Outstanding among Rinzai monks at the beginning of the Edo period were TAKUAN SŌHŌ (1573–1645) and BANKEI YŌTAKU (1622–93), both remarkable as meditation masters and as men close to the common people. Takuan taught the affinity between Zen and swordsmanship; Bankei was responsible for making Zen accessible to the simplest of the unlettered. HAKUIN (1686–1769), one of the greatest of Japanese Rinzai monks, was renowned as an artist of exceptional achievement and as a powerful religious leader. He was active at the small temple Shōinji in the village of Hara near Mt. Fuji, and in his lifetime this site became famous throughout Japan, attracting hundreds of followers. Hakuin gave kōan practice a definitive form. His life represents a pinnacle in the history of Zen mysticism, and no other Zen master is thought to have articulated such a wealth of inner experience.

Also preserved from the Edo period are the names of many outstanding Sōtō masters. Moreover, a third branch of Zen was introduced during this period, the ŌBAKU SECT, which bore the name of the famous master Huangbo (Huang-po; J: Ōbaku, d 855?), though it was not actually a continuation of his lineage. The Chinese master Yinyuan (Yin-yüan; J: INGEN; 1592–1673) brought this form of Zen, which was steeped in sutra study, to Japan. This practice, developed during the Ming dynasty (1368–1644), is a combination of Zen and NEMBUTSU, the invocation of the name of the Amida Buddha. The membership in this branch remained small, but the Chinese architecture and ornamentation of its central temple MAMPUKUJI in Uji, southeast of Kyōto, attracted much interest. The sutras are chanted in Chinese and to this day all the activities of the Ōbaku school exhibit the cultural atmosphere of China's Ming period.

The Meiji government was highly favorable toward the indigenous SHINTŌ religion and ordered that all syncretistic associations with Buddhism be dissolved. Though adversely affected by this decree, Buddhism was already deeply rooted in Japan and soon regained a position of importance. The most prominent Rinzai figure of this period was Imakita Kōsen (1816–92), who became the abbot of ENGAKUJI in Kamakura in 1875 and went on to head the Meiji government's Bureau for Religion and Education. His successor, Shaku Sōen (1859–1919), is known as the teacher of D. T. SUZUKI (1870–1966), Zen's principal exponent in the West.

The Intellectual Background of Zen——D. T. Suzuki continually made the point that Zen is not a philosophy, not metaphysics, not even a religion; it is neither pantheistic nor monotheistic. For Suzuki, Zen cannot be subsumed under any category; at best we can grasp it through the symbol of "a cloud floating in the sky." And yet the careful study of its intellectual history can certainly serve to clarify the Way of Zen. A few perspectives follow.

Prajñā (wisdom) and śūnyatā (emptiness): wisdom sees the emptiness of all things. All phases in the development of Zen Buddhism are shaped and permeated by the philosophy of the Mahāyāna, as represented by the *Prajñāpāramitā* (Perfection of Wisdom) sutras and the school of thought known as the Middle Way (Mādhyamika), exemplified by the great Indian Mahāyāna thinker Nāgārjuna (ca 150–250). There is controversy as to the interpretation of the central notion, emptiness (Skt: *śūnyatā*; J: *kū*); in Zen literature this notion becomes *mu*, or nothingness. The unmasking of the phenomenal world as nothingness so radically achieved by the school of the Middle Way is accepted by Zen, but Zen does not take this view in a nihilistic sense. Rather, Zen masters employ negation to push the disciple to extremes of experience in order to reach true reality. In order for the eye of wisdom to be opened, the temporary and apparent nature of all things must be comprehended.

The *Prajñāpāramitā* sutras call emptiness "the wisdom which has gone beyond" *(prajñā-pāramitā),* a notion which figures importantly in Zen Buddhism. The Heart Sutra, which is the most condensed text of this group of sutras, is recited daily in Zen monasteries. The word for emptiness *(kū-kū-kū . . .)* resounds throughout the temple halls and, like the *mu-mu-mu* recited by the practitioner during meditation, expresses the radical negation achieved by ridding the mind of all conceptual thinking. *Prajñā* (wisdom) is activated in Zen meditation and leads to a higher dimension of consciousness. The eye of *prajñā* (J: *hannya*) sees "true emptiness" as a union with "wondrous being" *(shinkū, myōu).* "Wondrous" in this twofold expression indicates the attainment of transcendence, a concept echoed in the term *pāramitā* ("has gone beyond"). The *Prajñāpāramitā* sutras give expression to the very essence of the Zen way of enlightenment.

Yogācāra: idealism and consciousness. The second main direction of Mahāyāna philosophy, the Yogācāra or Vijñānavāda school, emphasizes psychological aspects, and Zen owes much to this source as well. Although not advocating the Yogācāra's idealism, in which the phenomenal world was only a construct of the perceiver's mind, Zen Buddhism undeniably leans toward an idealistic understanding of the world. Although Zen does not consider the world to be entirely illusory, that is, to be *māyā,* as in much of Indian thinking, neither does it take it to be fully real. Zen does not answer the philosophical problems inherent in idealism but rather remains uncommitted. In one *kōan* the sixth patriarch encounters two monks disputing over whether a flag was moving or the wind was moving; the patriarch retorts, "It is not the wind that is moving; it is not the flag that is moving; it is your mind that is moving." The practitioner of Zen cannot attach a philosophical judgment to the sixth patriarch's words, but the reference to the mind or consciousness does point to the Yogācāra teaching that all things are projections of the mind.

The psychological direction of Yogācāra is an extension of ancient Indian teachings on consciousness. Zen pays particular attention to the aspect of consciousness that Yogācāra calls *ālaya* (storehouse). This storehouse is the repository of all potential ideas in thought, a meditative state which Zen sees as preliminary to final realization. The *Laṅkāvatāra-sūtra,* belonging to the Yogācāra school and much esteemed in Zen Buddhism, also provides correlations with Zen, in particular with regard to the gestures, grimaces, and other methods used in stimulating a breakthrough, and in the interpretation of the experience as a sudden turning back *(parāvritti)* to the roots of the mind.

Avataṃsaka: cosmotheism. The *Avataṃsaka* sutras do not correspond to any particular sect in India, but, following their relatively late (418–420) translation into Chinese, they inspired a distinct new school. The teachings of this Huayan (Hua-yen; J: Kegon) school included elements from both the Middle Way and the Yogācāra idealism of mind-only, the two basic philosophical currents of Ma-

Zen——Zazen

Monks meditating at the temple Eiheiji in Fukui Prefecture. Another monk holds a stick to strike those whose minds wander.

hāyāna. It reached the highest stage of its development in China and incorporated the essential traits of the Chinese mind to an extent that no other school achieved. The golden age of Huayan coincided with the rise of the Zen schools in China, whose masters evinced a fondness for the *Avataṃsaka* sutras, traditionally said to be preached by Śākyamuni immediately after his great awakening.

Zen's cosmotheistic world view stems from the *Avataṃsaka* sutras. The unity and totality of the universe, elucidated in striking metaphors in these sutras, form a central point of the Zen Buddhist experience; the enlightened practitioner experiences himself as one with the whole universe. This experience has a religious flavor deriving from these sutras and from the practice of meditation as well; reality is experienced as holy. Such a religious world view is clearly evident in the cultural expressions of the Zen way. The fusion with nature uniquely depicted in Zen art has its roots in Avataṃsaka philosophy.

The Taoist contribution. It is difficult to assess the extent and significance of Taoism in the formation of Zen in China, if only because the Mahāyāna Buddhism transplanted there displayed a remarkable similarity with the ideas of indigenous Chinese religions, especially Taoism. Taoist elements are unmistakable in Chan, but the identification of such elements as distinct from similar ones from the Mahāyāna sutras is difficult.

This is also true of the central idea of the Dao (Tao), the Way. The Buddhist sutras speak of the Buddha Way or the Buddha Path, and of setting out on the Path, a notion which includes inner realization. The significance which the Dao (now identified with enlightenment) acquires for Zen Buddhism reaches further. Examples of this are literally countless. Many *kōan* express the simple fact that one has had a sudden breakthrough with the words: "And he attained the Way (the Dao)."

Certain Buddhist hymns show Taoist influences in their praise of emptiness and exhortation to act in accord with nature. Zen literature continually admonishes one to avoid discrimination and duality in a typically Taoist manner. The two characteristics we have pointed out, namely a fondness for negation and for a cosmic worldview, are shared by the Zen way and the Taoist wisdom of Laozi (Lao-tzu) and Chuangzi (Ch'uang-tzu).

The accomplishment of the Zen masters. Influenced by this intellectual and religious background and the perspectives which Zen assumed, the Zen movement developed and grew through the experience and thinking of its masters. The different schools and proponents articulated and interpreted nearly identical tenets differently, showing that the masters were not merely passive recipients but creative individuals.

Though the historical picture we have of him is not entirely reliable, Huineng, the sixth patriarch, seems to have been the founder of Zen as we know it. His understanding of realization is that of the "middle way," according to which "seeing" is "not seeing," "thinking" is "not thinking," "form" is "no-form," and "mind" is "no-mind." This identity extends to "self-nature" and to Buddha. In the light of negative theology, enlightenment can be seen as an experience of Being open to transcendences (as in the writings of D. T. Suzuki and Thomas Merton, among others). In all Zen stemming from Huineng, suddenness is the essential feature of the Zen experience; there is an activating of one's nature which is subject to no causal nexus.

Linji (Rinzai) is the most significant figure in the Chinese lineage of Huineng. His blunt, powerful method of teaching, using shouts (Ch: *he* or *ho*; J: *katsu*) and blows with a stick, is celebrated; less well known are his outstanding achievements as a thinker. The dialectic of his "four formulas" is a study in transcendence of all opposites, and he impresses upon us that the "true man of no rank" is not different from the concrete person but lights the way to the transcendent reality of Buddha-nature.

Buddha-nature forms the center of the Japanese Zen master Dōgen's thinking. All being, as he expounds, is Buddha-nature; yet Buddha-nature is not only being and non-being, but is also becoming. The "becoming of Buddha-nature" serves as Dōgen's point of departure for his theory of time, often compared to Heidegger's thought, according to which being is time and time is being. Dōgen's thought combines various streams of the Mahāyāna, and continues today to influence the Kyōto school of philosophy begun by NISHIDA KITARŌ (1870–1945).

Practice and Enlightenment——Zen practice consists of meditation in the lotus posture (*zazen*) and *kōan* study. Practice is directed toward enlightenment (*satori*), yet the two are not linked in a necessarily causal relationship. The enlightenment experience can occur without a specific practice of Zen. On the other hand, practice is not to be regarded as futile even if years of effort do not culminate in the enlightenment experience. Practice is worthwhile in itself.

Meditation in the lotus posture (zazen). Zazen is not entirely of Zen origin. The basic form of *zazen* is taken from the Indian tradition of yoga, which covers a wide range of meditation practices. Zen meditation uses, with some modifications, the first links of Patañjali's classic *Yoga* sutra. Among the numerous postures (*āsana*) of yoga, Zen chose the lotus posture, regarded as the most perfect one in yoga as well. The practitioner sits with his legs crossed and drawn in, and his back perfectly upright. Zen does not teach complicated breathing techniques but rather recommends breathing in a natural, rhythmical way with a prolonged exhalation. Beginners practice counting the in-breaths and out-breaths, whereas more advanced students let their breathing take its natural course. The remaining links (*anga*) in the yogic scheme are implied in Zen meditation but not taken up separately. By shutting out all sense impressions and conscious thinking, the Zen practitioner seeks to attain the highest possible state of mental concentration. What is desired is an objectless meditation devoid of conceptual thought that can only be described in negative terms. Any means or devices utilized are also of a negative form, epitomized by the constant repetition of the sound *mu*, which literally means "not" or "nothingness" and alludes to the first *kōan* in the *Wumenguan (Mumonkan)* collection, that concerning the Buddha-nature of a dog.

Meditation in the lotus posture should be viewed first of all as a concentration exercise, calming body and mind, that is, the whole person, and thus supplying the requisite conditions for higher states of consciousness. Prolonged sitting may further be connected with a higher awareness, i.e., a tranquil unification of mental capacities not brought about by an explosive breakthrough and different from the genuine experience of enlightenment in Zen.

Zazen can also be said to represent the enlightened state of mind itself. This conception is found particularly in the teachings of Dōgen and his school. The lotus posture is the external sign of enlightenment, just as Śākyamuni and all Buddhas sitting in this posture reveal the enlightened Buddha-nature. The Zen disciple possesses Buddha-nature, or rather is the Buddha-nature, which is manifested through sitting.

Dōgen and his school did not believe that their view endowed *zazen* with excessive significance. The Rinzai school also acknowledges the value of sitting in the lotus posture but makes the point that perfect realization is also possible without any practice. Rinzai points out several dangers in the Sōtō understanding, such as becoming attached to sitting or promoting a quietistic asceticism that goes only halfway, refining the mind but not attaining a dynamic breakthrough. During the Song dynasty in China there was much dispute between the Rinzai and Sōtō schools, and this disagreement is now a chapter in the history of Zen. On the other hand, Rinzai disciples also practice *zazen*, and the number of Sōtō students intensely striving for experiences is not small. The difference between the two schools is in their emphasis.

Kōan study. Kōan practice began in China, though we can only partially determine the date of origin. The grotesque events, bizarre scenes, exchanges (*mondō*) between disciples and master, paradoxical expressions and words of wisdom, which make up the content of the *kōan*, stem from the early period of Chinese Zen. But a *kōan* does not consist of only these elements. We can distinguish three phases in the formation of the *kōan*: first, the recognition that certain events or expressions could assist in awakening an experience and are appropriate for practice; next, the evolving of a method out of the formulated *kōan* questions, which were collected and handed down for practice; finally, the differentiation and arrangement into a system.

Reports in the chronicles concerning the prolific golden age of Zen in the Tang period give the impression that *kōan*-like episodes were practically a daily occurrence. Masters with a fiery spirit would ignite a spark in their disciples by these exchanges. Gradually, the functional character of the interchanges became increasingly important. The significance of stories and expressions as a method to lead one to awakening was recognized by the 10th century, when *kōan* were inserted into collections of the Rinzai school. The pinnacle of this literary genre came with the *Biyanlu (Hekiganroku)* and the *Wumenguan (Mumonkan)*. These *kōan* collections hand down not only the episodes and verbal exchanges but also the commentaries of such experienced masters as Yuanwu Keqin (Yuan-wu K'o-ch'in; 1063–1135) and Wumen Huikai (Wu-men Hui-k'ai; 1183–1260), who vigorously drilled the point of each case into the student's mind. Verses concerning enlightenment add literary embellishment and psychological weight.

A *kōan* cannot be solved rationally. The practitioner is obliged to "hold" the *kōan* constantly in mind, day and night. Concentration increases until the tension causes rational thinking to give way under the pressure and a breakthrough occurs. This is the "turn back to the roots of consciousness" that opens the mind to a new way of seeing. Concentration, confrontation with an inescapable situation, and a breakthrough comprise the psychological progression in this practice. Because this practice can be traumatic and requires careful monitoring to advance, *kōan* practice cannot be undertaken without the personal guidance of the master in private interviews (*dokusan*). The content in *kōan* has some influence on the interpretation of the experience.

The *kōan* are intricately ordered according to such things as kind, content, and function. It was the Japanese master Hakuin who perfected the *kōan* system. He added to approximately 1,700 *kōan* the famous "sound of one hand clapping," which uniquely displays the paradoxical character of the enlightenment experience: "When you clap your hands together a sound arises. Listen to the sound of one hand."

Enlightenment (satori). The enlightenment of Zen Buddhism, similar to any mystical experience, is ineffable. The inner experience can only be described and interpreted. Certain characteristics are clearly evident in such descriptions. The suddenness of the experience has been set down as one mark of Zen enlightenment. It is the result of a long search and of frequent disputes with other Buddhist schools which teach a gradual ascent to the highest level of experience. A repudiation of levels and degrees is characteristic of Zen, which advocates a direct collision with reality in order to attain the Supreme Way. It is true that the practitioner may be aware of signs of an impending psychic change that are recognized by the master. Yet the practitioner may also be totally deluded in judging his own condition and mistake illusions (called *makyō*, literally, "demon's realm") for enlightenment. Such psychic phenomena, not altogether harmless, may immediately precede a genuine enlightenment experience.

Many accounts of this experience describe it as a merging or becoming one with the whole universe. A cosmic flavor can be detected in Zen literature, in its hymns and verses, and also in many *kōan*. This feature is especially prevalent among the Japanese who feel an intimate association with nature. The enlightened person is absorbed into the universe. One would not be far afield in finding in Zen enlightenment a proximity to the so-called "cosmic consciousness" which psychologists of religion discover in intuitive experiences.

Feelings of ecstasy accompany the experience of total unity or oneness. A surging joy—what Buddhists call "Dharma rapture"—overcomes the enlightened person and, completely forgetting himself, he feels at one with everything. The subjective certainty of such experiences is indubitable. When the master acknowledges that the experience is genuine, an immediate awareness of reality has most likely taken place. One who experiences enlightenment is thought to go beyond the trivial self of his usual consciousness. In Zen Buddhism, this act of transcending is expressed by way of negation. What is experienced is different in kind from the things surrounding the person; it is not anything he "knows" and is in fact everything the person does not know.

The Cultural and Artistic Dimension of Zen——All the Zen arts breathe the spirit of Zen and are called "ways" (*dō*; Ch: *dao*), whether painting, landscaping, tea ceremony, calligraphy, and poetics fostered in the temples, or the military skills of archery, swordsmanship, and martial arts practiced in the wider sphere of the temples' influence. The intensive practice of one of these "ways" can also lead to a genuine Zen experience. Simplicity, naturalness, harmony, precision—in short, the essentials of action and achievement—are the hallmarks of the spirit of Zen.

The sources of Japanese Zen culture and art lie in its monasteries, above all the important temples built in the Kamakura and the Muromachi periods when Zen first blossomed in Japan. The temple complex of Tōfukuji, one of the earliest sites of genuine Zen practice in Japan, fostered cultural activities together with an ardent religious training under the direction of Shōichi Kokushi (Enni Ben'en). A high point in the history of painting was reached with the artist-monk Minchō (1352–1431), whose magnificent portraits and brush paintings served as models for succeeding generations. SHŌKOKUJI, one of the Five Temples (Gozan) of Kyōto, was also a center of Chinese brush painting.

The leading artist in Zen at the beginning of the Muromachi period was Musō Soseki, the founder and abbot of Tenryūji and creator of some of Kyōto's most beautiful gardens. He is also famous for his calligraphy. For two years (1334–36) Musō Soseki also served as abbot of Nanzenji, which enjoyed the privileged favor of the court and was accorded a special position above the Five Temples. The Nanzenji complex eventually comprised many buildings, gardens, and works of art.

The most significant of all temple-monasteries was the expansive estate of Daitokuji. From the time of its founding by the celebrated Sōhō Myōchō (Daitō Kokushi), it was a center of spiritual inspiration for the responsive higher echelons of society in the capital. The second great figure connected with this temple was the abbot Ikkyū, a patron of the arts and an original artist himself. His lay disciple Murata Jukō (1422–1502) was the founder of the tea ceremony (*sadō*) in Japan; SEN NO RIKYŪ (1522–91), the most famous Japanese tea master, is of this lineage. He too had a tea hut and garden on the grounds of Daitokuji, the site of numerous works of art, including architecture, gardens, and paintings. The history of this temple through the generations is an indication of the increasing secularization of Rinzai Zen in the capital city.

The Zen Movement Today——The pioneer of Zen in the West is D. T. Suzuki, whose numerous writings and lectures in America and Europe introduced Zen Buddhism to the public and awakened much interest and appreciation for it. He initiated the scholarly study of Zen Buddhism, which was to have important consequences; he gave Westerners access to the wisdom of the East as preserved in Zen; and introduced its meditation practice. Today scholars in a variety of disciplines carry on the research he began, and the wisdom he radiated lives on in the circle of his disciples. His influence is felt most strongly in the meditation movement of our day.

There are various schools and lineages within Zen Buddhism, and consequently, a wide variation in practices. Hybrid forms developed between schools, and methods were also mixed with those of other branches of Buddhism. Different forms of Zen Buddhist meditation found their way to the West just as different schools of yoga did. Zen centers arose in America and in European countries, especially in England, France, and Germany.

Zen meditation for Christians. Two questions can be raised with respect to this topic. Can the Zen method of meditation be separated, as a technique, from its Buddhist underpinnings without losing its substance as Zen? Can the Zen method be used in Christian meditation without harm to the substance of Christianity? Buddhists and Christians give different answers to these two questions; and the answer can vary within Buddhism or Christianity as well. Father H. M. Enomiya-Lassalle was the first to attempt to make use of the Zen method in Christian meditation. In his Zen Meditation for Christians, as he calls it, he adheres strictly to the practice that he learned in Zen Buddhist temples. Other Christian meditation masters are endeavoring to adapt Zen to the Christian faith. These efforts are related to the dialogue between Buddhism and Christianity, which

Zenga——Circle, Triangle, and Square

One of the best-known works of the Zen monk Sengai Gibon (1750–1837). Ink on paper. 28.3 × 48.2 cm. Idemitsu Art Gallery, Tōkyō.

has made good progress and already borne fruit. The final result of Christian attempts with Zen meditation cannot yet be foreseen.

Zen is often seen as a bridge between the two hemispheres. Nourished within the great Asiatic cultures of India and China and reaching maturity in Japan, it has found a deep resonance in the West. In a time in which technology threatens to dominate the world, Zen awakens a demand among many for spiritual values necessary for human life.

——H. Benoit, *The Supreme Doctrine: Psychological Studies in Zen Thought* (1955). Heinrich Dumoulin, *A History of Zen Buddhism* (1963 and 1969). Heinrich Dumoulin, *Zen Enlightenment: Its Origins and Meaning* (1979). H.M. Enomiya-Lassalle, *Zen Meditation for Christians* (1974). H.M. Enomiya-Lassalle, *Zen-Way to Enlightenment* (1966). Eugen Herrigel, *Zen in the Art of Archery* (1957). T. Hirai, *The Psychophysiology of Zen* (1974). Philip Kapleau, *The Three Pillars of Zen: Teaching, Practice, Enlightenment* (1965). Miura Isshū and Ruth Fuller Sasaki, *Zen Dust: The History of The Koan Study in Rinzai (Lin-chi) Zen* (1966). Shibayama Zenkei, *Zen Comments on the Mumonkan* (1974). D.T. Suzuki, *Essays in Zen Buddhism*, 3 vols (1970). D.T. Suzuki, *Zen and Japanese Culture* (1959). P.B. Yampolsky, tr, *The Platform Sutra of the Sixth Patriarch* (1971). P.B. Yampolsky, tr, *The Zen Master Hakuin: Selected Writings* (1971). Heinrich DUMOULIN

zenga

A term that literally means "Zen painting," but is usually used more specifically to refer to the painting and calligraphy of the great monks of the Edo period (1600–1868) in Japan. Almost all these monks were Zen masters of the RINZAI SECT, SŌTŌ SECT, or ŌBAKU SECT, but the brushwork of a few monks of non-Zen sects is also considered *zenga*.

By the end of the Muromachi period (1333–1568), Zen painting traditions were being practiced primarily by professional painters. Some of these artists were monks attached to Zen temples, but their primary duties consisted in executing paintings. Their principal subject was landscape, but they also rendered figure studies and bird-and-flower themes, usually in ink on paper. Although they followed the traditions of the great Song (Sung) dynasty (960–1279) Chinese artists such as Muqi (Mu-ch'i; J: MOKKEI) and Liang Kai (Liang K'ai), Japanese professional painters tended to substitute technical skill for depth of feeling.

The Azuchi–Momoyama (1568–1600) and early Edo periods were a time of artistic as well as political and economic change in Japan. After the long civil wars, a newly stable government and economic well-being brought new vigor to the arts. The sumptuous golden screens of the Azuchi–Momoyama period, with bold designs in rich colors, replaced the more subtle and traditional ink paintings of the Zen tradition. However, many artists of the period such as KAIHŌ YŪSHŌ were equally adept at decorative screens and powerful ink paintings (*suibokuga*). Zen-inspired works continued to be produced, but they displayed a new boldness of design and vigor of brushwork.

In the early Edo period, traditional Zen themes were treated by professional artists of the KANŌ SCHOOL, but there was little true vitality to be seen in the ink paintings of the Kanō masters. Instead, true *zenga* was born from the spontaneous expression of the great monks of the age.

Much of the revival of true Zen brushwork must be associated with calligraphy. Although Zen monks were seldom trained in painting as such, they had usually studied calligraphy for decades before they started to execute paintings in the late years of their lives. Therefore their spontaneous ink works were largely free from excessive reliance upon painting traditions and were at the same time disciplined by mastery of brush and ink. Most *zenga* masters became equally known for calligraphy and painting; in many cases, calligraphy was their primary vehicle of expression.

Other factors helped to spark the revival of Zen-monk painting. One of these was the importance of the TEA CEREMONY, at which an appropriate scroll would be hung in the *tokonoma*. Masterpieces from the past were treasured, and the calligraphy of contemporary monks, especially of the abbots of the great Kyōto Zen temple DAI-TOKUJI, was also prized for this purpose. The blunt and powerful brushwork of such notable abbots as TAKUAN SŌHŌ and Kōgetsu Sōgan (1570–1643) was considered ideal for viewing during the tea ceremony.

The revival of Zen painting was also spurred by the emigration of much of the Chinese Huangbo (Huang-po; J: Ōbaku) sect in the middle of the 17th century. Led by the abbot Yinyuan (Yin-yüan; J: INGEN) and his great pupil Muan (J: Mokuan; 1611–84), the Ōbaku sect was granted special permission to build the temple MAMPUKUJI in Uji, not far from Kyōto. Although their Zen was more syncretic and less pure than the native Rinzai and Sōtō traditions, the Ōbaku monks greatly influenced and enriched Japanese cultural life. Many Ōbaku monks were poets, seal carvers, painters, and calligraphers. The latter art was particularly admired by cultured Japanese; the broad and fluent calligraphy of Ingen and Mokuan was so prized that even today many examples are to be seen in Japanese museums, temples, and private collections.

The chief factor in the rise of *zenga*, however, was the interest of the greatest Japanese monks in communicating directly through brush and ink. One of the finest monk-painters in the early Edo period was FŪGAI EKUN (also known as Ana Fūgai as he lived much of his life in an *ana* or cave). His paintings, almost all of which depict the first Zen patriarch Bodhidharma (J: Daruma) or the eccentric monk Hotei (see SEVEN DEITIES OF GOOD FORTUNE), have a direct intensity that is lacking in the work of professional painters. Having experienced the rigors of a life much like that of Bodhidharma, Fūgai expressed the insight and concentration that he learned through his intense meditation.

The greatest Zen monk of the Edo period was also the greatest Zen painter, HAKUIN. Like many other monks, he did not begin to express himself through brushwork until late in his life. His "early" works, executed while he was in his sixties, show a great charm and grace. His later works, brushed before his death at age 84, have a unique monumentality.

The most original and delightful of later *zenga* artists was SENGAI GIBON. The humor that can be seen in much *zenga* is especially characteristic of Sengai, who must have viewed the world with a wry smile.

Zenga continues to be brushed and, as before, primarily by monks of advanced age. At its best, *zenga* is at once a personal statement of Zen enlightenment and an art form that can be appreciated in purely artistic terms. Whether a portrait of a Zen master, freely brushed calligraphy, or a simple circle (representing the moon, the all, the void), *zenga* is now understood as an artistic expression at once simple and profound. See also BUDDHIST ART; INK PAINTING; CALLIGRAPHY.

📖——Stephen Addiss, *Zenga and Nanga* (1976). Stephen Addiss, *Obaku: Zen Painting and Calligraphy* (1978). Yasuichi Awakawa, *Zen Painting* (1970). *Stephen* ADDISS

Zengakuren

(Zen Nihon Gakusei Jichikai Sōrengō, or All-Japan Federation of Student Self-Governing Associations). The national organization of the Japanese left-wing student movement; founded on 18 September 1948. Despite a continued history of factionalism and schism that by the late 1960s had created several rival "Zengakuren," the name Zengakuren has become established both in Japan and abroad as a virtual synonym for the powerful left-wing student movement in post-World War II Japan.

The Zengakuren is not a voluntary political group, but rather, as the name indicates, a national federation of separate *jichikai* ("self-governing associations"), or student governments, which are typically organized within each faculty of a university. All students in a given faculty are automatically members of the *jichikai* and compulsory dues are collected with tuition. It is this guaranteed source of revenue and the ability to claim huge membership (in the range of hundreds of thousands) that has made control of *jichikai* such a logical technique of organization for the student left. The Zengakuren has consistently controlled a majority of all university *jichikai* in Japan, although the actual number of politically active students in any given *jichikai* is apt to be a small minority.

The Zengakuren was founded by student members of the JAPAN COMMUNIST PARTY (JCP) and for a decade thereafter was an integral part of JCP politics. A crucial split in the Zengakuren occurred in 1958 when the mainstream leadership was assumed by the Communist League (Kyōsan Shugisha Dōmei, nicknamed the "Bunto" from the English word "bund"), a group opposed to the JCP. The Bunto continued to control the Zengakuren by a slight majority during the United States–Japan Security Treaty crisis of 1960.

After 1960 the Zengakuren split up into several rival federations. In July 1960 the pro-JCP elements organized a new Zengakuren, which since 1964 has been known as the MINSEI Zengakuren. The anti-JCP New Left forces have for the most part been divided between the fiercely independent Kakumaru Faction and a shifting alliance of other factions that first took shape as the "Sampa" (Three Faction) Zengakuren in December 1966. The alliance broke up in July 1968, and there have since been four or five rival Zengakuren groupings, with the pro-JCP Minsei consistently controlling more *jichikai* than all other groups combined. See also STUDENT MOVEMENT.

📖——Stuart Dowsey, ed, *Zengakuren: Japan's Revolutionary Students* (1970). Kurata Keisei, *Ampo Zengakuren* (1971). *Henry D.* SMITH II

Zenitaka Corporation

(Zenitaka-Gumi). Comprehensive construction company engaged in the construction of buildings and public works. Owned by the Zenitaka family. Established in Ōsaka in 1887, the corporation specialized in the construction of bridges and caisson projects. Before World War II, orders from the military accounted for a large portion of the company's sales, but after the war, orders were evenly divided between the government and the private sector for the construction of industrial facilities and installations. The firm has subsidiaries in the United States and Brazil. Sales for the fiscal year ending October 1981 totaled ¥182.4 billion (US $788.3 million), and the company was capitalized at ¥3.7 billion (US $16 million). The head office is in Ōsaka.

Zeniya Gohei (1773–1852)

Wealthy merchant-trader of the Edo period (1600–1868); born in Kaga Province (now Ishikawa Prefecture), where his family had for several generations maintained a moneychanging business, hence the name Zeniya ("money shop"). Gohei established a lucrative business transporting goods on the newly developed sea routes connecting Hokkaidō (then called Ezo) and Aizu (now Fukushima Prefecture) with the major ports of Japan. In about 1830 he received a license to act as trade agent for the Kaga domain, and, working closely with Okumura Hidezane and other high Kaga officials, he reaped huge profits in the trade of domain products. At his peak Gohei is said to have owned 20 ships with a capacity of 1,000 *koku* (1 *koku*=about 0.28 cu m or 10 cu ft) or more, as well as numerous smaller vessels. Through his association with Okumura and his loans to the impoverished Kaga domain government and its indigent officials, Gohei gained great wealth and power. In his later years Gohei fell from grace, having failed in a project to reclaim the Kahoku marshes; his entire assets were confiscated, and he was thrown into prison, where he died.

zeniza → kinza, ginza, and zeniza

Zenkōji

Buddhist temple in the city of Nagano, Nagano Prefecture, affiliated with both the TENDAI SECT and JŌDO SECT of Buddhism. According to the temple's own tradition its principal object of worship, known as the Ikkō Sanzon, which is an image of Amida Buddha flanked by two bodhisattvas backed by a common nimbus, was the first Buddhist image to arrive in Japan, i.e., it was identified with the image that reportedly was sent in 552 by the king of the Korean state of Paekche to Emperor Kimmei (r 531 or 539 to 571). The image was traditionally believed to be of Indian origin, although no art historian would now accept that view. When the Buddhist religion was suppressed in Japan in 585 because of opposition from the MONONOBE FAMILY, the image was thrown into the sea. It was reputedly retrieved by one Honda Yoshimitsu (another reading of Yoshimitsu is Zenkō, hence the temple's name), who in 602 brought it to his home in Nagano. Zenkōji was supposedly built in 642 to house this image.

The actual origins of Zenkōji, however, are not known, the name Honda Yoshimitsu appearing for the first time in the thirteenth century, although the temple itself seems to have existed by the time of Emperor Heizei (r 806–809). The temple suffered serious damage by fire numerous times but was rebuilt after each disaster under royal or shogunate patronage. The great popularity of the Zenkōji statue of Amida, which was widely believed to have miraculous powers, led to its being moved and temporarily installed in various other temples. In 1568 the famous general TAKEDA SHINGEN built in his home province of Kai (now Yamanashi Prefecture) the temple Shinzenkōji (New Zenkōji), in which he enshrined the famous image. In 1582 the great hegemon ODA NOBUNAGA brought the image to his stronghold in Gifu. It was moved two more times before 1597, when Nobunaga's successor as military dictator, TOYOTOMI HIDEYOSHI, installed the image in Hōkōji, a temple in Kyōto. The following year he permitted its return to Zenkōji in Nagano.

The main hall (kondō) of Zenkōji has been designated a National Treasure and dates from the reconstruction of 1707. The Daikanjin, a subtemple within the Zenkōji precincts in which the abbot lives, is formally affiliated with the Tendai sect. Another subtemple within the Zenkōji precincts, the Daihongan, is a convent that has belonged to the Jōdo sect since 1878. There are now 62 temples named Zenkōji and many more copies of the main images scattered throughout Japan—evidence of the enormous popularity of the Zenkōji cult.

Stanley WEINSTEIN

Zenkunen no Eki → Earlier Nine Years' War

Zen Nihon Bukkyō Kai

(Japan Buddhist Federation). Formed in 1954 through the unification of the Nihon Bukkyō Rengōkai (Japan Buddhist League), Sekai Bukkyōto Nihon Remmei (World Fellowship of Buddhists, Japan Center), and prefectural Buddhist associations, for the purpose of coordinating Japanese Buddhist activities. Ōtani Kōchō (b 1903) served as its first president. To advance the aims of supporting Buddhist activities in Japan and promoting international cultural contacts through Buddhism, the federation holds an annual national convention and participates in the biennial congress of the World Fellowship of Buddhists.

Robert RHODES

Zen no kenkyū

(A Study of Good). The first major work of NISHIDA KITARŌ (1870–1945), the most prominent modern Japanese philosopher. Published in 1911, the book was composed of four essays, "Pure Experience," "Reality," "Good," and "Religion," which had previously appeared in various philosophical journals. Nishida developed his ideas for the work while teaching at the Fourth Higher School in Kanazawa and while conducting, on a personal level, a rigorous discipline of Zen meditation. Although the title of the work would indicate that Nishida's main concern is with ethics, actually the first of the four parts of the work, "Pure Experience," constitutes the kernel of Nishida's thought. He sought in "pure experience" that which was prior to the separation or opposition of subject and object, mind and body, and spirit and matter. In so doing, he strove to comprehend these oppositions. From this "pure experience" as the basis, he attempted to deduce the principles underlying epistemology, ethics, and religion. Although Nishida was influenced by the prevailing ideas of William James and other Western philosophers, the basic ideas of this work are derived from oriental religious concepts which stress the concreteness and immediacy of reality. This work was highly admired by Japanese philosophers

Zenkōji

The main hall (hondō) of Zenkōji in Nagano, Nagano Prefecture. Dating from 1707, when Zenkōji was reconstructed under shogunate patronage, it houses the celebrated Ikkō Sanzon, a triad in gilt bronze of the Buddha Amida with attendants. 24 × 54 m. National Treasure.

and hailed as the first truly original philosophical work by a Japanese in the modern period.

📖——Nishida Kitarō, *Zen no kenkyū* (1911), tr Valdo H. Viglielmo as *A Study of Good* (1960). David Dilworth, "The Range of Nishida's Early Religious Thought: *Zen no kenkyū*," *Philosophy East and West* 19.4 (1969).

Valdo H. VIGLIELMO

Zenrinkoku hōki

(Precious Record of Friendly Relations with Neighboring Countries). Three-volume collection of documents concerning Japanese diplomatic and religious contacts with China and Korea during the Muromachi period (1333–1568). Compiled in 1470 with commentaries by Zuikei Shūhō (1391–1473), a Zen priest of the temple Shōkokuji in Kyōto, it is the earliest systematic account of Japanese foreign relations. Zuikei was an adviser to the eighth Muromachi shōgun, ASHIKAGA YOSHIMASA (r 1443–74), for whom he drafted diplomatic communications. The first volume of *Zenrinkoku hōki* covers Japan's foreign relations from earliest times to 1392; it relies heavily on the GENKŌ SHAKUSHO, a history of Buddhism written in 1322. The second and third volumes contain the correspondence of Japanese military rulers and Buddhist monks with their Chinese and Korean counterparts from 1398 to 1486 (some material having been added after Zuikei's death). The author is remembered for his criticism of the shōgun ASHIKAGA YOSHIMITSU (r 1368–94) for having accepted the suzerainty of the Ming dynasty (1368–1644) of China, although recent research has indicated that this view of Yoshimitsu was fairly prevalent in high government circles.

Zensen

(abbreviation of Zensen Dōmei; Japan Federation of Textile Industry Workers Unions). Formed in 1946 as a federation of unions of workers in the textile industry. Recently it has expanded to include unions in the distribution, retail, and consumer product manufacturing sectors, reflecting the diversification within the textile companies themselves. Zensen is the largest member organization of DŌMEI (Japanese Confederation of Labor), with 455,000 members in 1978. It has been a leader of the right-wing sector of Japanese labor since the end of World War II. Zensen was a member of SŌHYŌ (General Council of Trade Unions of Japan) from 1950 to 1953. Since 1964, however, it has been affiliated with Dōmei. A member of the International Confederation of Free Trade Unions by virtue of its affiliation with Dōmei, Zensen is also affiliated with the International Textile, Garment, and Leather Workers Federation. With its policy of placing emphasis on labor-management cooperation, the federation has held regular meetings with organizations of managers in each industry. Lately Zensen Dōmei has been active in organizing workers in smaller textile enterprises and supermarkets.

Kurita KEN

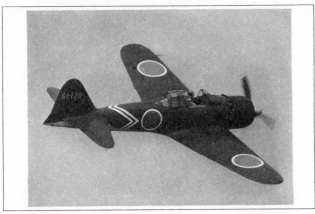

Zero Fighter

A Zero Fighter with wartime markings.

imperial army division from 1896 through World War II is now occupied by the Japanese Ground Self Defense Force. Pop: 38,081.

Zentsūji

Head temple of the Zentsūji branch of the SHINGON SECT of Buddhism, located in the city of Zentsūji, Kagawa Prefecture. Zentsūji, which is the oldest Shingon temple, is said to have been built in 806 by KŪKAI, the founder of the Shingon sect, at his birthplace on land donated by his father Saeki Zentsū (hence the name of the temple). Zentsūji suffered destruction by fire several times; the present *kondō* (main hall), housing a statue of Yakushi Nyorai (Skt: Bhaiṣayaguru; the Buddha of healing), and the *mieidō* (portrait hall), which enshrines Kūkai's portrait, date from the 17th century. In 1931 Zentsūji became the head temple of the independent Ono branch of Shingon, from that time called the Zentsūji branch. As the birthplace of Kūkai, the temple is one of the three sacred places of the Shingon tradition, along with Mt. Kōya (KŌYASAN) and the temple TŌJI, and an important stop for pilgrims visiting the 88 temples associated with Kūkai in Shikoku (see PILGRIMAGES). The Zentsūji branch claimed about 289,000 followers in 1979.

Stanley WEINSTEIN

Zero Fighter

(Zerosen). The principal fighter plane of the Imperial Japanese Navy in World War II. In 1937 Mitsubishi Heavy Industries was entrusted with the development of a fighter plane that could be used on aircraft carriers. The plane was officially adopted in July 1940 and designated the Zeroshiki Kanjō Sentōki, or Zerosen, for short. The following month Zero fighters were used in aerial attacks on Chongqing (Chungking) in the Chinese interior, where the Chiang Kaishek government had retreated. Its maximum range of 420 nautical miles was extraordinary for that era. A modified version was used at the beginning of the Pacific War; the power of its 20-millimeter (.79 in) machine guns and its long cruising range initially brought great strategic advantages, but from 1942 onward, it was overtaken by such American fighters as the P-38, F4U, F6F, and P-51. Toward the end of the war the Zerosen was used to carry out dive-bombing attacks and suicide missions (see KAMIKAZE SPECIAL ATTACK FORCE). Nearly 10,400 were produced during the war.

——Okumiya Masataka and Horikoshi Jirō, *Zerosen* (1953). Okumiya Masataka and Horikoshi Jirō, *Zero! The Story of the Japanese Navy Air Force, 1937–1945* (1957). *ICHIKI Toshio*

Zhang Xueliang (Chang Hsüeh-liang) (1898–)

(J: Chō Gakuryō). Often called the Young Marshal. The eldest son of ZHANG ZUOLIN (Chang Tso-lin), the Chinese warlord based in Manchuria, he held high military commands during the frequent civil wars in North China between 1920 and 1928. With the acquiescence of other Manchurian commanders and Japanese government officials, Zhang succeeded to the leadership of Manchuria after his father's assassination in 1928. Despite Japanese warnings not to subordinate Manchuria to the newly established Nationalist government at Nanjing (Nanking), Zhang pledged allegiance to that government and cooperated with CHIANG KAI-SHEK in attempts to weaken the Japanese position in Manchuria. His actions were one cause of the MANCHURIAN INCIDENT of 1931.

In 1935 Nanjing assigned Zhang to command operations against the communists in northwest China. Zhang gradually became convinced that the anticommunist struggle was not in China's interest and that all Chinese should unite to resist Japan. In December 1936 he and his associates seized Chiang Kai-shek and forced him to discuss China's future with representatives of the Chinese Communist Party. Out of this affair—known as the XI'AN (SIAN) INCIDENT—came the agreement to form the United Front against Japan. Although he agreed to end his nonresistance policy, Chiang Kaishek imprisoned Zhang. When the Nationalist government fled to Taiwan in 1949, they took Zhang with them, still a prisoner. Although formally freed in 1961, he continued to live in relative seclusion on Taiwan. *James E.* SHERIDAN

Zenshinza

A KABUKI company, left-wing in ideological stance. Founded in May 1931, by kabuki and SHINGEKI actors, many of whom had some connection with the proletarian arts movement. The kabuki actors in particular were profoundly dissatisfied with the hierarchical and highly commercialized organization of the kabuki theater. The principles of equality enunciated at the founding meeting of Zenshinza were high-minded and sincere, but it soon proved impossible to sustain them in the theatrical world of the early 1930s. Zenshinza's attitude of no compromise with commercial kabuki could not be put before the survival of the company, and in 1932 *Chūshingura* (The Tale of the Forty-Seven Rōnin), anathema to the Left in general, was performed with great success at a major kabuki theater. The platforms and slogans adopted by Zenshinza continued to be left-wing, but financial stability was being assured by stage productions (and later film versions) of classical kabuki plays, many of which received high critical praise. Zenshinza's activities during the rest of the 1930s may be divided into four parts: kabuki, *shingeki* (mainly historical plays), *taishūgeki* (popular drama), and films. In 1937 the company fulfilled a long-standing ambition to establish community life by constructing a study center which included rehearsal rooms and living accommodations. Here at least equality could be practiced and a corporate identity fostered. In 1938 most of the *shingeki* actors left the company in protest at continuing productions of plays which they thought inappropriate in the political circumstances of the later 1930s. Zenshinza managed to continue performing, mainly on tour, during the war, and in the difficult postwar years promoted its very successful Youth Theater Movement (Seinen Gekijō Undō), under which performances of Shakespeare in translation were given to audiences of schoolchildren all over Japan. In March 1949 in a protracted general meeting, the Zenshinza members decided that they would all join the Japan Communist Party. Subsequent performances on tour were often linked with appearances at political demonstrations, and this occasioned a number of difficulties with the police authorities in the 1950s. During the 1960s and 1970s Zenshinza concentrated on productions of classical kabuki, still placing most emphasis on touring but also frequently playing in the large theaters of Tōkyō and the Kyōto–Ōsaka area. It initiated several new projects (including "study" productions of CHIKAMATSU MONZAEMON dramas) and appeared often on television. Zenshinza was fortunate from the start in having actors of great ability (such as Kawarasaki Chōjūrō, Kawarasaki Kunitarō, and Nakamura Kan'emon), but it is in the ensemble acting of its productions of classics that its major contribution to modern kabuki lies.

——Brian F. Powell, "Communist Kabuki: A Contradiction in Terms?" in James Redmond, ed, *Drama and Society* (1979). Sakamoto Tokumatsu, *Zenshinza* (1953). *Brian* POWELL

Zentsūji

City in Kagawa Prefecture, Shikoku. The birthplace of KŪKAI, the founder of the Shingon sect of Buddhism, it developed as a temple town of Zentsūji, an important temple of the sect. The site of an

Zhang Ziping (Chang Tzu-p'ing) (1895–?)

(J: Chō Shihei). Chinese writer of modern, popular romantic fiction who, during the SINO-JAPANESE WAR OF 1937–1945, served in the Japanese-sponsored, collaborationist government of WANG JINGWEI

(Wang Ching-wei). In 1912 Zhang went to Japan and received a degree in geology from Tōkyō University in 1922. During his first years in Tōkyō, Zhang met GUO MORUO (Kuo Mo-jo) and YU DAFU (Yü Ta-fu), who shared an interest in modern, vernacular fiction, and in 1921 he joined with Guo and Yu in founding the Creation Society (Ch: Chuangzao She or Ch'uang-tsao She) to promote romantic literature in China. After his return to China he continued to write and to work with the Creation Society in Shanghai. He later taught geology and literature and engaged in business ventures. Following Japan's defeat in World War II, in 1947 Zhang was arrested and tried by the Guomindang (Kuomintang; Nationalist Party) government for his cooperation with Wang's collaborationist reorganized government (1940–45; see REORGANIZED NATIONAL GOVERNMENT OF THE REPUBLIC OF CHINA). The outcome of his trial is unknown. Among his works are Qunxing luanfei (1931; Ch'ün-hsing luan-fei), a fiction, and Ziping zizhuan (1934; Tzu-p'ing tzu-chuan), an autobiography.

Zhang Zuolin (Chang Tso-lin) (1873–1928)

(J: Chō Sakurin). Known as the Old Marshal in distinction to his son ZHANG XUELIANG (Chang Hsüeh-liang), the Young Marshal. A Chinese warlord who ruled Manchuria more or less as an independent satrapy from about 1920 until his assassination by Japanese militarists in June 1928. From the end of 1926 until the spring of 1928 Zhang also controlled portions of North China, including the weak and discredited national government in Beijing (Peking).

Zhang's relations with Japan were close and complex. In the years after 1920, the Japanese government provided continuing aid to Zhang to help him preserve order and promote Japanese interests in Manchuria. Zhang generally fulfilled those expectations, but he was not a passive Japanese puppet. He tried to limit Japanese economic and political activities, although with little success. At the same time, Japanese military and political leaders were inconsistent in their policies toward Zhang. While they warned him against involvement in Beijing political struggles, for fear of adverse effects on Manchurian stability, they provided large sums of money and other assistance to help Zhang defeat the Zhili (Chihli) clique of warlords in 1924. Japan also intervened to assure the defeat of an attempt by GUO SONGLING (Kuo Sung-ling) to overthrow Zhang in 1925. In 1927 and early 1928, however, Japanese officials urged Zhang to abandon North China's politico-military conflicts and to concentrate on maintaining order and stability in Manchuria.

When later in 1928 CHIANG KAI-SHEK's Nationalist armies were pushing north to drive Zhang from power in Beijing and perhaps Manchuria, Japanese officials in Manchuria, both military and political, as well as leaders of the TANAKA GIICHI government in Tōkyō sharply disagreed among themselves over how best to protect and strengthen Japanese interests in Manchuria. Some wanted to negotiate additional concessions from Zhang as the cost of continued support. Others favored direct action to expand Japanese military power in Manchuria.

In late May 1928 Prime Minister Tanaka ruled against military intervention. That decision so incensed some extremist military officers in Manchuria that they decided to assassinate Zhang and exploit the subsequent turmoil to Japan's advantage. Colonel Kōmoto Daisaku, a staff officer in the GUANDONG (KWANTUNG) ARMY, organized a plot whereby Zhang's train was blown up as it was returning to Mukden in the early hours of 4 June. Zhang died a few days later, but the plotters did not realize their other goals. More moderate leaders maintained control in both the government and the army, agreeing to have Zhang Xueliang succeed to his father's position. Tōkyō authorities proved unable to impose any meaningful punishment on the guilty officers, and the Tanaka government fell. The incident foreshadowed the MANCHURIAN INCIDENT of 1931, when similarly unilateral military action in Manchuria successfully defied civil authority in Tōkyō.   James E. SHERIDAN

Zheng Chenggong (Cheng Ch'eng-kung) (1624–1662)

(J: Tei Seikō). Chinese warlord who supported the Ming dynasty (1368–1644) of China during the dynasty's last days. Known to Westerns as Coxinga or Koxinga. As a military commander he resisted the Qing (Ch'ing) dynasty (1644–1912) after the fall of the Ming and played an influential role in the attempted movement to restore the Ming dynasty. His father was a Chinese maritime warlord named Zheng Zhilong (Cheng Chih-lung), who was later given

a military position by the Ming, and his mother was a Japanese woman, the daughter of Tagawa Shichizaemon, a native of Hirado, an island in what is now Nagasaki Prefecture. Zheng was born on Hirado, but was eventually summoned by his father to China, where he was educated. Even after his father surrendered to the Qing, Zheng continued to resist the new dynasty and made an unsuccessful attempt to capture Nanjing (Nanking) in 1658–59. He succeeded in establishing a base on Taiwan in 1661 and used it to mount attacks on mainland China. He died of an illness the following year. Zheng is better known to Japanese as Kokusen'ya (Ch: Guo Xingye or Kuo Hsing-yeh, a title granted to him by the Ming royal family). He is the hero of CHIKAMATSU MONZAEMON's play Kokusen'ya kassen (1715; tr The Battles of Coxinga, 1951).

Zheng Xiaoxu (Cheng Hsiao-hsü) (1860–1938)

(J: Tei Kōsho). Chinese official with intense loyalty to the Manchu Qing (Ch'ing) dynasty (1644–1912), who from 1932 to 1935 served as premier in the restoration of the last Qing emperor, PUYI (P'u-i), in the puppet state of MANCHUKUO.

From 1891 to 1894 Zheng served in Qing-dynasty consulates at Tōkyō, Kōbe, and Ōsaka. In 1923 he joined Puyi, who had been deposed in 1912, and helped arrange his flight from warlord-dominated Beijing (Peking) to the Japanese settlement in Tianjin (Tientsin). As the Guomindang (Kuomintang; Nationalist Party) unified China in its Northern Expedition (1926–28), Zheng concluded that Puyi and the cause of a Qing restoration would be better served by Japan than by internal Chinese forces. In August 1928 Zheng went to Japan to broach the question of a Qing restoration; but the Japanese indicated active interest only in mid-1931, when they were becoming increasingly dissatisfied with ZHANG XUE-LIANG's (Chang Hsüeh-liang) control of Manchuria. After the Mukden Incident of September 1931, DOIHARA KENJI, head of special intelligence for the Japanese GUANDONG (KWANTUNG) ARMY stationed in Manchuria, began negotiations with Puyi and his advisers for the establishment of an independent Manchu state. While pressing the Japanese to make the new state a monarchy instead of a republic, Zheng persuaded Puyi's other advisers that they should take advantage of Japan's terms, using them as a first step toward the long-range goal of restoring the dynasty at Beijing.

In November 1931 Zheng went secretly with Puyi to Port Arthur (Ch: Lüshun; now part of Lüda) in Japanese-controlled Guandong. Puyi became chief executive eight days after the puppet state of Manchukuo was established on 1 March 1932. Two years later, largely through Zheng's efforts, Puyi was given the title of emperor. Zheng's interpretation of Confucianism contributed to the formulation of the core of the Manchukuo ideology of wang dao (wang tao; J: ōdō; "kingly way" or rule by benevolent example). During his tenure as premier, Zheng often disagreed with the Japanese. Final decisions in the Manchukuo government were always controlled by the Japanese, and Zheng resigned in May 1935, a disappointed man.

Zhong Gui (Chung Kuei) → Shō Ki

Zhou Enlai (Chou En-lai) (1898–1976)

(J: Shū Onrai). Chinese communist leader and premier of the People's Republic of China. A native of Shaoxing (Shao-hsing), Zhejiang (Chekiang) Province, Zhou was born into a gentry family. After his father's death he lived with relatives in Jiangsu (Kiangsu) Province and in Mukden (Ch: Shenyang). He studied at the prestigious Nankai (Nan-k'ai) Middle School in Tianjin (Tientsin) from 1912 to 1917. Upon his graduation Zhou went to study in Japan with financial support from his uncle. At Waseda University he enrolled as an extra-mural student. Later, at Kyōto University, he attended lectures given by KAWAKAMI HAJIME, an eminent economist influenced by Marx and other European Socialists. He also took part in Chinese student politics in Japan. After the nationalist demonstrations against Japan in the MAY FOURTH MOVEMENT of 1919, Zhou returned to China.

He enrolled in Nankai University in Tianjin and became involved in political activities. In the winter of 1919–20 he joined a Marxist discussion group at Beijing (Peking) University led by Chen Duxiu (Ch'en Tu-hsiu) and Li Dazhao (Li Ta-chao), later two of the founders of the Chinese Communist Party. MAO ZEDONG (Mao Tse-tung) was also a member of the group. In 1920 Zhou was imprisoned for several months for his part in an anti-Japanese demonstration. Upon his release he left for France with a group of students on a work-study program. He devoted himself to political work among Chinese in both France and Germany and helped to organize the European headquarters of the Chinese Communist Party, which had been founded in Shanghai in 1921. In 1924 Zhou returned to China.

The communists were at that time working closely with SUN YAT-SEN and the Guomindang (Kuomintang; KMT; Nationalist Party). Zhou was appointed deputy political director of the Huangpu (Whampoa) Military Academy, which CHIANG KAI-SHEK directed. During the Northern Expedition of 1926–27 Zhou organized labor in Shanghai and directed the general strike of April 1927, which allowed KMT armies to take the city.

After Chiang's attack on the communists in April, Zhou went underground, emerging among the top leadership of the Jiangxi (Kiangsi) Soviet in the early 1930s. In 1934–35 Zhou took part in the Long March to Yan'an (Yenan). In 1937 he helped to forge a new alliance with the KMT, and served as the principal communist liaison to the wartime nationalist capital of Chongqing (Chungking) during the war against Japan. After the war he represented the communists in unsuccessful negotiations with the KMT.

After the communist victory in 1949, Zhou served as premier of the People's Republic of China until his death. He served concurrently as foreign minister until 1958.

▰——Howard L. Boorman and Richard C. Howard, ed, *Biographical Dictionary of Republican China* (1967). Hsu Kai-yu, *Chou En-lai: China's Grey Eminence* (1968). Donald W. Klein and Anne B. Clark, ed, *Biographical Dictionary of Chinese Communism* (1971). Robert ENTENMANN

Zhou Hongqing (Chou Hung-ch'ing) Incident

(J: Shū Kōkei Jiken). Diplomatic crisis between Japan and the Republic of China (Taiwan) that began in October 1963 when Zhou Hongqing, an interpreter for a delegation of Chinese industrial officials touring Japan, attempted to seek asylum in the Soviet embassy in Tōkyō. He was handed over to Japanese authorities, to whom he expressed a desire to go to Taiwan. He then changed his mind, first seeking to stay in Japan and later asking to be sent back to the People's Republic of China. The Japanese government finally returned him to Mainland China in January 1964 despite a strong protest by the Taiwan government that Japan had acted against Zhou's will. This incident resulted in a diplomatic crisis, with Taiwan temporarily recalling all staff officers from its embassy in Tōkyō and canceling its governmental procurement contracts in Japan. See also CHINA AND JAPAN: China and Japan after 1912.

Zhou Zuoren (Chou Tso-jen) (1885–1966)

(J: Shū Sakujin). Modern Chinese essayist, scholar, and translator. Zhou Zuoren joined his brother LU XUN (Lu Hsün) in literary activities in Japan and China and, during the SINO-JAPANESE WAR OF 1937–1945, held educational posts under the Japanese puppet governments in North China.

In 1906 Zhou Zuoren went to Japan, where he studied Western and Japanese literature at Rikkyō University and, with Lu Xun and others, studied under the Chinese scholar-revolutionary Zhang Binglin (Chang Ping-lin; 1868–1936). In their journal *Xin sheng* (*Hsin sheng*; New Life), founded in 1907, Zhou Zuojen and Lu Xun translated the East European authors who exemplified a spirit of resistance that the brothers hoped to instill in China.

In 1911 Zhou returned to China with his Japanese wife, Habuto Nobuko, whom he had married in 1909. He taught at various universities as an expert on foreign and Chinese literature, continuing his translations, which included modern Japanese fiction, and advocating social realism and humanism. He also produced several essays dealing with Japan's utopian Atarashiki Mura (New Village), which he visited after meeting its founder, MUSHANOKŌJI SANEATSU, during a 1919 trip to Japan. Discouraged by political and social developments and by the increasingly rigid politicization of literary factions, Zhou withdrew from literary circles after 1927.

Zhou remained in North China after its fall to Japan in the Sino-Japanese War, becoming chancellor at Beijing (Peking) University in 1939 and, in the next year, minister of education in the collaborationist government of WANG JINGWEI (Wang Ching-wei). After his trial on a charge of treason following Japan's defeat in 1945, Zhou's death sentence was commuted to imprisonment, and in 1949 he was given a pardon and released.

▰——David E. Pollard, "Chou Tso-jen: A Scholar Who Withdrew," in Charlotte Furth, ed, *The Limits of Change: Essays on Conservative Alternatives in Republican China* (1976). Ernst Wolff, *Chou Tso-jen* (1971).

Zhu Xi (Chu Hsi) school → Shushigaku

Zōjōji

High ranking temple of the JŌDO SECT of Buddhism, located in Minato Ward, Tōkyō. Zōjōji, originally known as Kōmyōji, is said to have been first established by Shūei (809–884), who had been a disciple of KŪKAI (774–835), the founder of the Shingon sect. In 1393 Shōsō (1366–1440), a convert to Jōdo from Shingon, on becoming abbot, switched the affiliation of Zōjōji to the Jōdo sect. In 1590 TOKUGAWA IEYASU, who was soon to establish the Tokugawa shogunate, designated Zōjōji as his family temple and burial ground. Throughout the Edo period (1600–1868) Zōjōji enjoyed great prestige from its association with the shogunate. The temple declined after the Meiji Restoration in 1868 and suffered extensive damage during the air raids in 1945. The reconstruction of the Zōjōji on a smaller scale was completed in 1974. Stanley WEINSTEIN

zoological gardens

(*dōbutsuen*). As of 1980, there were 68 zoological gardens in Japan. However, there were only about 30 major zoological gardens with 100 or more kinds of animal. The biggest Japanese zoological garden is the UENO ZOOLOGICAL GARDEN in Tōkyō, with about 900 species of animals, followed by the Higashiyama Zoological Gardens in the city of Nagoya, with more than 300 kinds. A special type of zoological garden is the Japan Monkey Center located in Inuyama in Aichi Prefecture. Here monkeys and apes are gathered from all over the world for use in research as well as for educational purposes.

The first zoological garden in Japan was the Ueno Zoological Garden, opened in 1882; it was followed by those in Kyōto (1903) and Ōsaka (1915). The Ueno Zoological Garden was created as one part of a museum within the jurisdiction of the Ministry of Agriculture and Commerce. At first primarily a research facility, it later grew in importance as a recreation area.

The increasing importance of zoological gardens as recreational facilities is evident from the so-called safari parks where animals live in a more-or-less natural environment and through which visitors can ride in cars or buses. Such zoological gardens, keeping animals mainly from Africa, were first opened in Miyazaki Prefecture in 1971, followed by others in Ōita and Yamaguchi prefectures. These were established by private enterprises with an eye to profit rather than as educational facilities. A forerunner of the natural habitat zoological gardens was the Tama Zoological Park in the suburbs of Tōkyō, built by the Tōkyō metropolitan government in 1958. Though much smaller in scale than the safari parks, it was the first lion farm in Japan.

▰——Sasaki Tokio, *Dōbutsuen no rekishi: Nihonhen* (1975). SUZUKI Zenji

zōri

A kind of thonged footwear. Zōri can be made of any material on hand; straw, rush, etc. Zōri have been used widely for at least a millenium. The small, short kind called *ashinaka zōri* ("half-foot zōri"), being easy to run in, were an important item for *samurai*. Today the kind of traditional zōri worn with KIMONO are almost exclusively for women; they consist of a wedge covered with leather, cloth, vinyl, or finely woven straw and thongs made of cloth or leather. See also FOOTGEAR, TRADITIONAL. MIYAMOTO Mizuo

Zōsen Gigoku → Shipbuilding Scandal of 1954

zōshiki

1. General term for low-ranking hereditary occupational groups under the RITSURYŌ SYSTEM of administration that was instituted in the late 7th century; attached to government offices, these groups engaged in manufacturing and menial work. In a narrower sense, *zōshiki* referred to the *tomobe* (servants of the imperial family) and

the *zakko* (or *zōko;* skilled craftsmen). These were considered the lowest stratum of the free commoners (RYŌMIN), partly because some of the *tomobe* and most of the *zakko* were descended from Chinese and Korean immigrants but also because they were not engaged in agriculture, which was considered the most important kind of productive labor. With the breakdown of the *ritsuryō* system, most *zōshiki* were absorbed into private landed estates (SHŌEN), although some remained in the service of the imperial house (see also SEMMIN).

2. Under the Kamakura (1192–1333) and Muromachi (1338–1573) shogunates the lowest class of *banshū* (swordsmen) were called *zōshiki;* they were essentially servants and performed such tasks as cleaning and guard duty.

3. From the end of the Muromachi period through the Edo period (1600–1868) the term *zōshiki* was applied to a semiofficial organization that assisted the shōgun's Kyōto deputy (KYŌTO SHOSHIDAI) with the administration, police duties, and judicial matters of Kyōto.

Zou Taofen (Tsou T'ao-fen) (1895–1944)

(J: Sū Tōfun). Chinese journalist, best known for his editorship (1926–33) of the *Shenghuo zhoukan* (*Sheng-huo chou-k'an;* Life Weekly) in Shanghai, his advocacy of civil liberties, and his leadership in the NATIONAL SALVATION ASSOCIATION for a unified Chinese resistance to Japanese aggression in China. Through the *Shenghuo zhoukan,* Zou urged opposition to Japan after the MANCHURIAN INCIDENT in 1931, criticizing the conciliatory policy of the Guomindang (Kuomintang; Nationalist Party) government under CHIANG KAI-SHEK and raising contributions through his magazine to aid those fighting the Japanese in Manchuria. The Guomindang closed Zou's *Shenghuo zhoukan* in 1933, and for the remaining 10 years of his life Zou continued to call for a united front against Japan's invasion of China, founding journals that were successively banned by the Guomindang.

In 1935 Chinese opposition mounted against Japanese agitation for the separation of North China. Zou was a leading figure in the formation of the Shanghai National Salvation Association (January 1936), and the All China Federation of National Salvation Associations (May 1936). With six other movement leaders he was arrested by the Guomindang on 23 November 1936 and held until the war with Japan began in July 1937, after which the official Guomindang policy also became one of resistance to Japan.

Zou moved with the Guomindang government to Chongqing (Chungking). His journals spurred popular enthusiasm for the war effort until increasing Guomindang press censorship forced him to flee in 1941. Zou went first to Hong Kong, and when Hong Kong fell to Japan, he went to communist-held Jiangsu (Kiangsu), where he continued to advocate united resistance to Japan and the establishment of a democratic government in China.

━━━Zou Taofen, *Jingli* (*Ching-li;* 1937). Zou Taofen, *Taofen wenchi* (*T'ao-fen wen-chi;* 1959).

zuihitsu

(random jottings; literally, "following the brush"). A Japanese literary genre, consisting typically of a random essay or loose collection of jottings, with no clear structure other than association of ideas and written on the spur of the moment to express the author's thoughts on such subjects as people, nature, and art. Personal in nature, the *zuihitsu* discloses the unembellished, individual character of its author. Compared to the Western essay genre, the *zuihitsu* is less formal and more fragmentary, exhibiting the natural bent of the Japanese people towards intuition rather than towards logical thinking. The *zuihitsu,* along with NIKKI BUNGAKU, or diary literature, occupies an important position in Japanese literary history.

The first collection of *zuihitsu* to be recognized as a work of literature was the *Makura no sōshi* (Pillow Book) of the late 10th century court lady SEI SHŌNAGON (tr *The Pillow Book of Sei Shōnagon,* 1967). A collection of observations on the beauty of nature and the world of human affairs, it is permeated with her keen wit and intelligence. The *Makura no sōshi* is the epitome of the *zuihitsu* collection, both in style and content and is considered one of the three masterworks in the genre together with the *Hōjōki* (1212; tr *The Ten-foot Square Hut,* 1928) by KAMO NO CHŌMEI (1156?–1216)

and the *Tsurezuregusa* (ca 1330; tr *Essays in Idleness,* 1967) by YOSHIDA KENKŌ (ca 1283–ca 1352).

Although the *Hōjōki* is thus classified as a *zuihitsu,* it is a longer, more carefully structured work than most. It takes the form of a Buddhist philosophical treatise, with balancing parts that are matched by parallel sentence structure in the language. Nevertheless, the passages in which the author reflects on the simple pleasures of the Buddhist recluse in contrast to the vanities of city life are in the spirit of the *zuihitsu.*

The *Tsurezuregusa* is more typical of the genre. It, too, is based on the Buddhist view of the transiency of life and records the random thoughts of the author, who had given up his aristrocratic life to become a recluse. Strongly literary in nature, it displays a deep insight into human beings and their actions. With these three works as models, the *zuihitsu* emerged as a strong force in Japanese literature.

In the Edo period (1600–1868) it became customary for scholars of the Chinese or Japanese classics and for *haiku* poets to write *zuihitsu;* their commentaries on *haiku* and *waka* and other literary works were largely written in this form. Philosophical essays were also written in the *zuihitsu* style. Representative *zuihitsu* of this period include *Sundai zatsuwa* (1732) by the Confucian scholar MURO KYŪSŌ (1658–1734), *Kagetsu sōshi* (1796–1803) by the political reformer MATSUDAIRA SADANOBU (1758–1829), *Uzuragoromo* (1788–1823) by the poet YOKOI YAYŪ (1702–83), and *Tamakatsuma* (1793–1801) by the literary scholar MOTOORI NORINAGA (1730–1801).

Even in modern times, the traditional conception of the *zuihitsu* as chiefly an appreciation of nature persisted. Eventually, however, the development of a more modern consciousness led to the use of *zuihitsu* as a vehicle for social criticism. Not only men and women of letters, but also scientists, journalists, and other public figures found it convenient to express themselves in the flexible, intellectually undemanding form of the *zuihitsu.*

Zuisenji

Temple in the city of Kamakura, Kanagawa Prefecture, belonging to the ENGAKUJI branch of the RINZAI SECT of ZEN Buddhism. Regarded as one of the 10 major Rinzai monasteries in eastern Japan, Zuisenji was founded in 1327 by MUSŌ SOSEKI, a distinguished Zen monk, and was richly patronized by the Ashikaga family, beginning with the military leader Ashikaga Motouji (1340–67). The temple is noted for its superb garden, which is said to have been designed by Musō Soseki. Among its many treasures is a statue of its founder carved from a single block of wood.   *Stanley* WEINSTEIN

zuryō

Resident provincial administrators or deputy governors in the latter half of the Heian period (794–1185) who carried out administrative duties while the titular governors (*yōnin kokushi;* see KOKUSHI) remained in the capital. The term *zuryō,* originally meaning to "receive" a predecessor's document of release from his term of appointment, by the 9th century came to refer to governors who went to their provinces and "received" the administration. As the RITSURYŌ SYSTEM of government broke down and members of the FUJIWARA FAMILY monopolized the higher posts, lower-ranking nobles competed for appointment as *zuryō.* They were able to enrich themselves through harsh taxation, and the term *zuryō* (often translated as "tax manager") acquired strong connotations of avarice and greed. Some *zuryō* purchased renewal of their appointments (*chōnin*) or returned to the capital wealthy; others remained as provincial magnates, often becoming the leaders of warrior bands (BUSHIDAN). The latter came into conflict with the Fujiwara and provided financial and military support for retired emperors who challenged Fujiwara dominance (see INSEI). With the appointment to the provinces of SHUGO ("constables," later military governors) by the Kamakura shogunate (1192–1333), the *zuryō* were shorn of their power.   *G. Cameron* HURST III

Zushi

City in southeastern Kanagawa Prefecture, central Honshū. On the western coast of scenic Miura Peninsula and convenient to Tōkyō, Zushi has long been a favored residential and resort town. It provided the setting for several works by TOKUTOMI ROKA. Pop: 58,481.

Zushoryō

(Bureau of Books and Charts). Also known as Toshoryō. Archival library created under the TAIHŌ CODE of 701; the earliest known official archive in Japan. The Zushoryō preserved the records of the eight ministries of the imperial government and was nominally responsible for compiling the official histories of Japan (see RIKKOKUSHI). It served also as a general secretariat—a selecting, compiling, and copying agency—for the Ministry of Central Imperial Affairs (Nakatsukasashō), to which it was attached. The director (kami) of the Zushoryō was an important official with a large staff that included copyists, ink and brush makers, and clerical assistants; he also supervised the Kamiyain or Kan'yain, which manufactured paper for all government ministries.

The functions of the Zushoryō were greatly reduced during the period of warrior rule (1192–1868), but the bureau was revived in 1884 under the restored Imperial Household Ministry (Kunaishō). The famous novelist MORI ŌGAI served as its director from 1917 to 1922. After World War II the Zushoryō was merged with the Bureau of Imperial Mausolea (Shoryōryō) to form the ARCHIVES AND MAUSOLEA DEPARTMENT, IMPERIAL HOUSEHOLD AGENCY.

Theodore F. WELCH